# HOLLYWOOD'S GREAT LOVE TEAMS

## BY JAMES ROBERT PARISH

As author

THE FOX GIRLS
THE PARAMOUNT PRETTIES
THE SLAPSTICK QUEENS
GOOD DAMES

As co-author

THE EMMY AWARDS: A PICTORIAL HISTORY
THE CINEMA OF EDWARD G. ROBINSON
THE MGM STOCK COMPANY: THE GOLDEN ERA
THE GREAT SPY PICTURES
THE GEORGE RAFT FILE
THE RKO GALS
VINCENT PRICE UNMASKED
FILM DIRECTOR'S GUIDE: THE U.S.

As editor

THE GREAT MOVIE SERIES
ACTORS' TELEVISION CREDITS: 1950-1972

As associate editor

THE AMERICAN MOVIES REFERENCE BOOK
TV MOVIES

# HOLLYWOOD'S GREAT LOVE TEAMS

## JAMES ROBERT PARISH

Editor

T. Allan Taylor

Research Associates

John Robert Cocchi                    Florence Solomon

Rainbow Books

CARLSTADT, NEW JERSEY

First Rainbow Printing March 1977

ISBN 0–89508–004–4 (previously ISBN 0–87000–245–7)

# Dedicated To

A.L.Z.E.

with deep appreciation

# KEY TO THE FILM STUDIOS

AA       Allied Artists Picture Corporation
AVCO/  Avco Embassy Pictures Corporation
  EMB
CIN      Cinerama Releasing Corporation
COL      Columbia Pictures Industries, Inc.
EMB     Embassy Pictures Corporation
FN        First National Pictures, Inc. (later part of Warner Bros.)
FOX      Fox Film Corporation
LIP       Lippert Pictures, Inc.
MGM    Metro-Goldwyn-Mayer, Inc.
MON     Monogram Pictures Corporation
PAR      Paramount Pictures Corporation
RKO      RKO Radio Pictures, Inc.
REP      Republic Pictures Corporation
20th      Twentieth Century-Fox Film Corporation
UA        United Artists Corporation
UNIV     Universal Pictures, Inc.
WB       Warner Bros. Inc.

# Acknowledgments

RESEARCH CONSULTANT:
Doug McClelland
Richard Braff
Alan Brock
Mrs. Loraine Burdick
Lois Cole
*Classic Film Collector* (Samuel K. Rubin)
Morris Everett, Jr.
Olivier Eyquem
*Filmfacts* (Ernest Parmentier)
*Film Fan Monthly* (Leonard Maltin)
*Films and Filming*
*Films in Review*
Robert W. Friess
Pierre Guinle
Mrs. R. F. Hastings
Richard M. Hudson
Ken D. Jones
René Jordan
Miles Kreuger

David McGillivray
Albert B. Manski
Alvin H. Marill
Jim Meyer
Mrs. Earl Meisinger
Peter Miglierini
Don Miller
Norman Miller
*Monthly Film Bulletin*
Christopher Moor
*Movie Poster Service* (Bob Smith)
*Movie Star News* (Paula Klaw)
Jeanne Passalacqua
Michael R. Pitts
*Screen Facts* (Alan G. Barbour)
Charles Smith
Mrs. Peter Smith
Don Stanke
Roz Starr Service
Charles K. Stumpf
Lou Valentino
Jerry Vermilye

*And special thanks to Paul Myers, curator of the Theatre Collection at the Lincoln Center Library for the Performing Arts, and his staff: Monty Arnold, Rod Bladel, Donald Fowle, Steve Ross, Maxwell Silverman, Dorothy Swerdlove, Betty Wharton; page Juan Hodelin, and Donald Madison, Photographic Services.*

# Table of Contents

CHAPTER      PAGE

1. Ronald Colman—Vilma Banky .............................................. 23
2. John Gilbert—Greta Garbo ................................................... 41
3. Charles Farrell—Janet Gaynor ............................................. 61
4. Clark Gable—Joan Crawford ............................................... 97
5. Clark Gable—Jean Harlow ................................................. 123
6. Dick Powell—Ruby Keeler .................................................. 147
7. George Brent—Kay Francis ................................................ 175
8. William Powell—Myrna Loy ............................................... 199
9. Leslie Howard—Bette Davis ............................................... 249
10. Fred MacMurray—Claudette Colbert .................................. 269
11. Nelson Eddy—Jeanette MacDonald ................................... 295
12. Errol Flynn—Olivia de Havilland ....................................... 331
13. James Stewart—Margaret Sullavan .................................... 369
14. Tyrone Power—Loretta Young ........................................... 389
15. Mickey Rooney—Judy Garland .......................................... 411
16. James Cagney—Ann Sheridan ........................................... 455
17. Walter Pidgeon—Greer Garson .......................................... 475
18. Clark Gable—Lana Turner ................................................ 513
19. Spencer Tracy—Katharine Hepburn .................................... 533
20. Alan Ladd—Veronica Lake ............................................... 569
21. Jon Hall—Maria Montez ................................................... 597
22. Van Johnson—June Allyson .............................................. 623
23. Humphrey Bogart—Lauren Bacall ...................................... 647
24. Tony Curtis—Janet Leigh .................................................. 671
25. David Niven—Deborah Kerr .............................................. 693
26. Paul Newman—Joanne Woodward ..................................... 715
27. Rock Hudson—Doris Day .................................................. 743
28. Richard Burton—Elizabeth Taylor ...................................... 759

Index ................................................................................... 801

# Introduction

From the very beginning of motion picture production in Hollywood in the early part of this century, profit-anxious producers have searched for and latched onto any available gimmick in order to "insure" their particular property a hefty boxoffice receipt. Such guarantee factors might be some technique innovation such as a *first* in the industry, e.g. the first full length feature, or all-talking film, or color movie, or 3-D or widescreen picture, etc. Likewise, the film's backers might try to sell their product as the first motion picture to deal with a hotly topical event (the Japanese attack on Pearl Harbor), a formerly taboo subject (abortion), or a new social craze (rock 'n' roll dancing).

On the other hand, it took many years for film industry executives to realize or take full advantage of the possible combination of two distinct trends in the motion picture business. One: almost as soon as motion pictures outgrew their infancy pangs, it became clear that filmgoers were extremely eager to see particular players, such as Florence Lawrence ("the Biograph Girl"), featured over and over again in new movies. By the 1910s, the medium's money men faced up to the inevitable. The expensive star system, long an accepted aspect of the theatre world, could no longer be avoided in the new medium. Two: just as dear to the hearts of moviegoers as comedy shorts, newsreels, outdoor dramas, or action-packed serials, or more so, once the first novelty of films wore off, was their desire to witness celluloid tales of passionate romance, as daring and elaborate as the mores of the time would allow.

The Vitagraph Company was one of the first outfits to fully understand these new cravings of the moviegoing audiences. From its stock company it drew two physically contrasting British players, stocky John Bunny and spindly Flora Finch, to join their talents as a screen team, mostly in short comedies but sometimes in the studio's multi-reel presentations. These two players were exceedingly popular right up to Bunny's death in 1915, and they paved the way for such other silent comedy teams as Charlie Chaplin and Edna Purviance, and Harold Lloyd and Bebe Daniels. By the time Universal Pictures had established Grace Cunard and Francis Ford as potent co-stars of such cliffhanging serials as *Lucille Love, Girl of Mystery* (1914), Essanay had garnered a tremendous following for its recent pairing of matinee idol Francis X. Bushman with lovely Beverly Bayne in such romantic society dramas as *Under Royal Patronage* (1914).

Unlike the earlier film personalities of Mr. and Mrs. Sidney Drew, who were imported from the stage to join a movie firm's stock company, Bushman and Bayne could be regarded as the American movies' first authentic red-hot love team. Had not filmgoers been horrified to later discover that the stars were wed in real life, Bushman and Bayne might have continued as a potent screen pair well into the 1920s. Meanwhile, a new silver screen combination had arisen in the pairing of Harold Lockwood and May Allison, who together spanned fourteen productions from *The Secretary of Frivolous Affairs* (1915) to *The Hidden Children* (1917).

Ironically, Hollywood, fully entrenched in the studio star system, did not see fit to pull out all the stops again in promoting a new love team until the middle of the Roaring Twenties. Then it was astute cinema pioneer Samuel Goldwyn who teamed dashing Ronald Colman with the screen's most beautiful blonde, Vilma Banky, in *The Dark Angel* (1925). As soon as the positive boxoffice returns became clear, Goldwyn rushed to rematch his two contract lead players, and other movie producers took the hint. Warner Bros., under the prompting of John Barrymore, signed Dolores Costello as his leading lady for *The Sea Beast* (1926), and it seemed the terrific screen chemistry provided by these screen lovers would pave the way for further celluloid reunions. Although Barrymore and Costello wed (1928) offcamera, they were never to be re-paired oncamera.

Just as the age of the silent cinema was waning in the face of technical progress, two new screen teams emerged as movie duos who were to become more legendary than the successful Colman-Banky combination or the insufficiently heralded matching of Richard Barthelmess and Dorothy Gish. Metro-Goldwyn-Mayer linked John Gilbert with Greta

Garbo in *Flesh and the Devil* (1927) and Fox aligned Janet Gaynor with Charles Farrell in *Seventh Heaven* (1927). The Garbo-Gilbert romancing smoldered oncamera and off, and even though none of their four additional joint screen appearances matched the lavish amorous excesses of *Flesh and the Devil*, their names to this day are jointly synonymous with exotic love. On the other hand, the tandem first screen appearance of Gaynor and Farrell, symbolizing the best of simple youth earnestly in love, would carry over for another seven years of filmmaking as their studio milked the sentimental romantic combination to its fullest boxoffice return. More so than the Garbo-Gilbert star pairing, Gaynor and Farrell set a pattern for other future screen teams to duplicate, leading Fox to hope for equal success by matching James Dunn with Sally Eilers in *Bad Girl* (1931), or later inspiring Samuel Goldwyn to pair Farley Granger with Cathy O'Donnell in *They Live by Night* (1948).

With the success of Paramount's *Abie's Irish Rose* (1928), Nancy Carroll and Charles "Buddy" Rogers seemed to be everyone's ideal of the "nice kids" screen lovers and they were seen together in four later studio pictures. By 1929 talkies were here to stay and while Gaynor and Farrell, and the others, were continuing to retain their joint marquee allure, offscreen husband and wife Mary Pickford and Douglas Fairbanks appeared together in *The Taming of the Shrew* for their United Artists company. Although the moviegoing public was now sophisticated enough to accept a real life man and wife making love oncamera, Shakespeare's comedy was not that successful a screen venture to warrant further joint celluloid excursions by Mr. and Mrs. Fairbanks. Two years later, Alfred Lunt and Lynn Fontanne, the stage's leading husband-and-wife dramatic team, would make a united foray into the cinema with Metro's elaborate version of *The Guardsman* (1931), but the couple quickly decided to return to the more artistically rewarding confines of the legitimate stage.

It was in 1931 that moviedom went hog-wild publicizing the romantic virtues of this or that new screen team, and Metro, where there were more stars than there were in the heavens, led the way in creating new silver screen love pairs. Although he was just consolidating his position as a new movie lead, Clark Gable proved to be the king of screen team material,° just as later he would be pronounced the King of the Movies. In *Dance, Fools, Dance* (1931) he was first matched with Joan Crawford. Later, he and elite Norma Shearer shared footage in *A Free Soul* (1931), and in *The Secret Six* (1931) Gable and brassy Jean Harlow traded celluloid looks and dialog. These three professional alliances, which would

---

°An interesting study could be made concerning the dynamic charisma of stars like Barbara Stanwyck, Edward G. Robinson, Paul Muni, Marilyn Monroe, and Marlon Brando, who are so strongly arresting, in solo, oncamera, that throughout their careers they never were capable of "being" just part of a screen team.

span the 1930s, demonstrated the virtues of a studio system in which it was feasible to pair and re-pair contract leads in picture after picture, molding the productions to the chemistry generated by the co-stars.

In 1932 Metro set the trend for another gambit in screen teaming when it cast Johnny Weissmuller in *Tarzan, The Ape Man* with Maureen O'Sullivan as Jane (Parker). As the follow-up, *Tarzan and His Mate* (1934), and the subsequent four co-starring features demonstrated, love teaming and the series genre were quite compatible. MGM would further test this theory with the "perfect" husband-and-wife love team of William Powell and Myrna Loy, who parlayed *The Thin Man* (1934) into a six-entry mystery series, while co-starring for a total of fourteen features. Later this same studio would have Laraine Day (as nurse Mary Lamont) join Lew Ayres in *Calling Dr. Kildare* (1939) and remain with the young screen doctor for six additional medical-oriented installments. The champ in this field was, of course, Columbia's *Blondie* series which cast Arthur Lake and Penny Singleton together for twenty-eight domestic comedy features between 1938 and 1950. Proving again (as had Marie Dressler-Wallace Beery, Charles Ruggles-Mary Boland, and Slim Summerville-ZaSu Pitts years before) that "love" teams did not always have to be beautiful youngsters, Marjorie Main and Percy Kilbride clicked so solidly in *The Egg and I* (1947) that Universal quickly prepared the *Ma and Pa Kettle* series to headline these rambunctious middle-agers.

On the other hand the ability to play incomparable love scenes was not always the gimmick that brought two co-stars together. Crooner Dick Powell and tap dancer Ruby Keeler appealed to musical movie patrons in Warner Bros.' *42nd Street* (1933) and continued their particular brand of screen entertainment together for six other movies. That same year, RKO featured Fred Astaire and Ginger Rogers in *Flying Down to Rio,* a picture which actually starred Dolores Del Rio and Gene Raymond. The public, however, was quick to proclaim Astaire and Rogers as that musical's hit ingredients and the elegant pair dueted through nine subsequent movies. Metro hit paydirt in a revived operetta cycle with those lilting personalities, Jeanette MacDonald and Nelson Eddy, in *Naughty Marietta* (1935). By the end of the decade that same studio had discovered that Mickey Rooney, famed adolescent star of the *Andy Hardy* series (in which he made puppy dog romantic advances to Ann Rutherford), was the perfect screen song-and-dance partner for ultra-talented Judy Garland. If musical love teams diminished in importance during the World War II years with the less excellent Donald O'Connor-Peggy Ryan, June Preisser-Freddy Stewart, Robert Paige-Jane Frazee mini-musicals, Twentieth Century-Fox revived the species in fine fashion with the teaming of blonde pin-up queen Betty Grable and hoofer Dan Dailey in *Mother Wore Tights* (1947). Warner Bros. took the clue and matched Doris Day with Gordon MacRae in *Tea for Two* (1950).

While heart-throbbing romance was usually the key ingredient in the oncamera activities of a screen team, there were many boxoffice combinations that gained their special niche with the moviegoing public for other acting proclivities. Kay Francis and George Brent personified sartorial elegance at Warner Bros., and it was that same studio that revived the dying swashbuckling cycle and, with the benefit of dashing cardboard hero Errol Flynn and paper-thin heroine Olivia de Havilland, created *Captain Blood* (1935) and many other pulsating adventure epics to follow. Paramount's *The Gilded Lily* (1935) offered moviegoers the combination of Claudette Colbert and Fred MacMurray who spent more time cavorting in tongue-in-cheek comedy than in courting. In like manner, this comic ambiance was displayed by Irene Dunne and Cary Grant in *The Awful Truth* (1937) and similar films thereafter.

In the 1930s when the studio star system was running full reign and filmmaking was at a productive peak, players would often be paired in several features, but never really emerge as a solid "love team." For example, James Cagney and Joan Blondell were both in *Sinners' Holiday* (1930), their first feature film, and in six additional pictures, but Cagney proved to be far more memorably aligned when teamed with the "Oomph Girl" Ann Sheridan in three movies, including *Angels with Dirty Faces* (1938). Sometimes two lead players were recast together more for the reason of sharing screen time in a very good picture rather than for their oncamera interplay, an example being Leslie Howard and Bette Davis in *Of Human Bondage* (1934) and *The Petrified Forest* (1936). (By the time of *It's Love I'm After* (1937) they were playing to one another, rather than at the audience.) There may be some cinephiles who would insist that the screen linkage of Margaret Sullavan and James Stewart in four features does not rate as an example of love teaming since these stars were too distinctive as individual personalities. However, this author is of the opinion that the sophisticated, weepy Sullavan and the lanky, gawky Stewart offered a marvelous give and take oncamera that completely warrants their inclusion in the category of a love team.

Because of the lack of significant financial resources, it was far rarer for the smaller and/or poverty row studios to sustain love team combinations on their rosters. If they could at all afford to maintain a selection of contract players, they were hardly able to afford to properly publicize an acting pair to the extent that the public would become aware of this pairing and would go see a particular film because of the actor and actress teamed. A rare example to the contrary was Cecilia Parker (later a MGM player and best known as the sister in the Andy Hardy series) and Eric Linden, who had been paired first at MGM in *Ah, Wilderness!* (1935) and *Old Hutch* (1936) and then moved over to Grand National for *In His Steps* (1936), *Girl Loves Boy* (1937) and *Sweetheart of the Navy* (1937).

If vapid prettiness had been the key ingredient of such teams as Tyrone

Power and Loretta Young in the late 1930s, the 1940s brought a new kind of screen pairing. There were still examples of the "gosh-gee" or American wholesome school of love pairing as with freckle-faced June Allyson and Van Johnson, or the exotic escapist fare as displayed by Maria Montez and Jon Hall, or even still sagebrush love adventure film fare as personified by Roy Rogers and Dale Evans. However, there was a new resiliency to the screen personalities of many love teams. There were now more mature film unions, such as benevolent Greer Garson and magnanimous Walter Pidgeon, and as contrast, the flinty Spencer Tracy and women's libber Katharine Hepburn, both couples from the MGM film factory. The World War II years also spawned the teaming of tough souls such as Alan Ladd and Veronica Lake at Paramount, and Warner Bros.' subsequent matching of Humphrey Bogart and Lauren Bacall. Rita Hayworth (once teamed with Charles Quigley in 1930s programmers) and Glenn Ford, first seen together in Columbia's *The Lady in Question* (1940), brought a new dimension of erotic explicitness to screen love in the solid, if tawdry ambiance of *Gilda* (1946) and *Affair in Trinidad* (1952). The latter were a long way from the gushy cuteness of Warner Bros.' Joyce Reynolds and Robert Hutton of *Janie* (1944), *Always Together* (1947), etc.

By the 1940s, television, the altered post-war financial structure, and the changing public taste had taken their toll of the Hollywood system, necessitating sharp cutbacks everywhere along the line. With the actor rosters cut way down in accordance with the diminished production schedule, producing executives were far more concerned with manufacturing a particular film rather than building two players within a film in order to act as a joint team in future assignments. Now there generally had to be some special impetus to lead to any such new screen union. Off-camera romances between players, mogul and star, director and starlet always had played a key role in casting decisions, but in the 1950s such real-life romance took on a new prominence in the waning phenomenon of love teams. With the major exceptions of Frankie Avalon and Annette Funicello in American International Pictures' beach blanket musicals, Rock Hudson-Doris Day in their modern comedy stand, nebulous blondes Troy Donahue-Connie Stevens at Warner Bros., and the David Niven-Deborah Kerr mature screen liaisons, *marriage* soon became the motivating gimmick behind new love teams. An excellent illustration of this emphasis is demonstrated by the celluloid pairing of that wholesome twosome, Tony Curtis and Janet Leigh, who had wed in 1951 and had been quickly adopted by fan magazine readers as the nicest young marrieds around. In 1953 they starred in *Houdini* and made five other joint features before the end of the decade. Likewise, Paul Newman and Joanne Woodward, while romantically unattached to one another when they began making *The Long, Hot Summer* (1958), wed before that year was out. They continued oncamera and off as a husband-and-wife team, later demonstrating a new slant to their professional union when he directed her in *Rachel, Rachel* (1968). These two sets of marrieds were the outstanding successes of the decade as men and wives who worked in front of the camera together. Other such couples included Rex Harrison and Lilli Palmer, Bette Davis and Gary Merrill, Dick Powell and June Allyson, Marge and Gower Champion, Jose Ferrer and Rosemary Clooney, Audrey Hepburn and Mel Ferrer, Natalie Wood and Robert Wagner, Hope Lang and Don Murray, and, of course, Lucille Ball and Desi Arnaz.

Proving how quickly times and more change, the permissive 1960s turned not to marriage but to the failure thereof in its search for the necessary impetus in creating what became the most lucrative screen union in movie history. During the long, long course of producing *Cleopatra* (1963), Elizabeth Taylor and Richard Burton enjoyed a grand passion which was detailed *ad nauseum* in the news media to a seemingly insatiable public. They defied convention with their scandal. Then, after *The V.I.P.s* (1963) they decided to wed, and in the course of the next hectic decade before their marriage collapsed, revived and then died, made nine additional films together. None of these films, with the exception of *Who's Afraid of Virginia Woolf?* (1966) were of much artistic value, but some of them were big money earners. Now that the defunct Taylor-Burton union is a reality, the only successors to that couple's tarnished twin-throne seem to be the far less exciting married pair, Charles Bronson and Jill Ireland (she is the ex-Mrs. David McCallum), who quietly continue to make such lucrative movies together as *Rider on the Rain* (1970), *Someone Behind the Door* (1971), *The Mechanic* (1972), and *The Valachi Papers* (1972), as well as the forthcoming *Ten-Second Jailbreak* (1975) and *Dynamite Man* (1975). According to trade sources, the Bronson-Ireland pact with Italian producer Dino De Laurentiis (now based in New York City) has catapulted them right up into the old Taylor-Burton million dollar league. *Mama mia!!*

Today "love teams" seem an antiquated leftover from the glorious days of the golden age of motion pictures. Sadly but realistically it must be realized that this essentially gimmicky concept of film production is a thing of the past and one that we are not likely to witness again.

❈ ❈ ❈ ❈

A brief word about the selection of star teams for this volume is necessary. Never before in preparing a book has this author experienced so many conflicting opinions among associates and movie devotees concerning the choice of entries. There were those who jocularly insisted that Donald O'Connor and Francis the Talking Mule should be included in the discussion, just as there were those who felt the camaraderie displayed by that triumvirate of funsters, The Three Stooges, qualified them for consideration.

Two obvious love teams (Ginger Rogers-Fred Astaire and Charles "Buddy" Rogers-Nancy Carroll) are not included in the author's compilation. Quite frankly, he did not feel anything further could be said about these two star teams that had not already been expertly covered by Arlene Croce in *The Fred Astaire and Ginger Rogers Book* (1972), *Starring Fred Astaire* (1973) by Stanley Green and Burt Goldblatt, and by Paul L. Nemcek in *The Films of Nancy Carroll* (1969). Making the final selection of the twenty-eight teams included was obviously this author's attempt to present a representative panorama of the specific Hollywood phenomena of love teams. Had space permitted, an examination of the special chemistry created by the likes of Marlene Dietrich-Gary Cooper, John Garfield-Priscilla Lane, Irene Dunne-Cary Grant, Bing Crosby-Bob Hope-Dorothy Lamour, James Stewart-June Allyson, Rita Hayworth-Glenn Ford, and innumerable others would have been this author's greatest pleasure.

JAMES ROBERT PARISH
New York City

*January 18, 1974*

# HOLLYWOOD'S GREAT LOVE TEAMS

In **The Magic Flame** (UA, 1927)

# Chapter 1

# Ronald Colman & Vilma Banky

## RONALD COLMAN

**5′ 11″**
**153 pounds**
**Brown hair**
**Brown eyes**
**Aquarius**

*Real name: same. Born February 9, 1891, Richmond, Surrey, England. Married Thelma Raye (1919); divorced 1934. Married Benita Hume (1938), child: Juliet. Died May 19, 1958.*

FEATURE FILMS:

*The Toilers* (Neville Bruce, 1919)
*Sheba* (Hepworth, 1919)
*Snow in the Desert* (Broadwest, 1919)
*A Daughter of Eve* (Walturdaw, 1919)
*A Son of David* (Broadwest, 1919)
*Anna the Adventuress* (Hepworth, 1920)
*The Black Spider* (British and Colonial, 1920)
*Handcuffs or Kisses* (Selznick, 1921)
*The Eternal City* (Associated FN, 1923)
*The White Sister* (Metro-Goldwyn, 1923)
*Romola* (Metro-Goldwyn, 1924)
*$20 a Week* (Selznick, 1924)
*Tarnish* (Associated FN, 1924)
*Her Night of Romance* (FN, 1924)
*A Thief in Paradise* (FN, 1925)
*His Supreme Moment* (FN, 1925)
*The Sporting Venus* (Metro-Goldwyn, 1925)
*Her Sister from Paris* (FN, 1925)
*The Dark Angel* (FN, 1925)
*Stella Dallas* (UA, 1925)
*Lady Windemere's Fan* (WB, 1925)
*Kiki* (FN, 1926)
*Beau Geste* (Par., 1926)
*The Winning of Barbara Worth* (UA, 1926)

*The Night of Love* (UA, 1927)
*The Magic Flame* (UA, 1927)
*Two Lovers* (UA, 1928)
*The Rescue* (UA, 1929)
*Bulldog Drummond* (UA, 1929)
*Condemned* (UA, 1929)
*Raffles* (UA, 1930)
*The Devil to Pay* (UA, 1930)
*The Unholy Garden* (UA, 1931)
*Arrowsmith* (UA, 1931)
*Cynara* (UA, 1932)
*The Masquerader* (UA, 1933)
*Bulldog Drummond Strikes Back* (UA, 1934)
*Clive of India* (UA, 1935)
*The Man Who Broke the Bank at Monte Carlo* (Fox, 1935)

*A Tale of Two Cities* (MGM, 1935)
*Under Two Flags* (20th, 1936)
*Lost Horizon* (Col., 1937)
*The Prisoner of Zenda* (UA, 1937)
*If I Were King* (Par., 1938)
*The Light That Failed* (Par., 1939)
*Lucky Partners* (RKO, 1940)
*My Life with Caroline* (RKO, 1941)
*The Talk of the Town* (Col., 1942)
*Random Harvest* (MGM, 1942)
*Kismet* (MGM, 1944)
*The Late George Apley* (20th, 1947)
*A Double Life* (Univ., 1948)
*Champagne for Caesar* (UA, 1950)
*Around the World in 80 Days* (UA, 1956)
*The Story of Mankind* (WB, 1957)

# VILMA BANKY

5′ 6″
125 pounds
Blonde hair
Blue-gray eyes
Capricorn

*Real name: Vilma Lonchit. Born January 9, 1903, Budapest, Hungary. Married Rod La Rocque (1927); widowed 1970.*

**FEATURE FILMS:**

*Im Letzten Augenblick* (Hungarian, 1920)
*Galathea* (Hungarian, 1921)
*Tavaszi Szerelem* (Hungarian, 1921)
*Veszélyben a Pokol* (Hungarian, 1921)
*Kauft Mariett-Aktien* (German, 1922)
*Das Auge des Toten* (German, 1922)
*Schattenkinder des Glücks* (German, 1922)
*Die Letzte Stinde (Hotel Potemkin)* (Austrian, 1924)

*Das Verbotene Land (Die Lebe Des Dalai Lama)* (Austrian, 1924)
*Clown aus Liebe (Der Zirkuskönig)* (Austrian, 1924)
*Das Schone Abenteuer (The Lady From Paris)* (German, 1924)
*Das Bildnis (L'Image)* (Austrian, 1925)
*Sollman Heiraten (Intermezzo Einer Ehe in Sieben Tagen* (German, 1925)
*The Dark Angel* (FN, 1925)
*The Eagle* (UA, 1925)

24

*The Son of the Sheik* (UA, 1926)
*The Winning of Barbara Worth* (UA, 1926)
*The Night of Love* (UA, 1927)
*The Magic Flame* (UA, 1927)
*Two Lovers* (UA, 1928)

*The Awakening* (UA, 1928)
*This Is Heaven* (UA, 1929)
*A Lady to Love* (MGM, 1930)
*Die Sehnsucht Jeder Frau* (MGM, 1930)
*The Rebel* (Deutche-Universal, 1933)

In **Two Lovers** (UA, 1928)

In **The Dark Angel** (FN, 1925)

With pilot Joe Kelly (left) and president Hanshue, of Western
Air Express, at time of **The Winning of Barbara Worth**

In **The Winning of Barbara Worth** (UA, 1926)

In **The Night of Love** (UA, 1927)

# THE DARK ANGEL
*(First National, 1925) 7,341'*

Presenter, Samuel Goldwyn; director, George Fitzmaurice; based on the play by H. B. Trevelyan; screenplay, Frances Marion; camera, George Barnes.

Ronald Colman (Captain Alan Trent); Vilma Banky (Kitty Vane); Wyndham Standing (Captain Gerald Shannon); Frank Elliott (Lord Beaumont); Charles Lane (Sir Hubert Vane); Helen Jerome Eddy (Miss Bottles); Florence Turner (Roma).

New York Premiere: Mark Strand Theatre—October 11, 1925
No New York Television Showing

## Synopsis

Because he has been unexpectedly ordered back to the front, Captain Alan Trent is unable to obtain the requisite marriage license and he and his fiancée, Kitty Vane, spend the night in an English inn. Later in battle, Alan is blinded and taken prisoner by the Germans. When he is reported to be dead, his friend Captain Gerald Shannon attempts to assuage Kitty's grief with his own gentle courtship. After the war, Gerald locates Alan in a far distant corner of England where the veteran is now writing children's stories for a meagre living. More loyal to his former war buddy than to his own abiding love for Kitty, he tells her of Alan's reappearance. She goes to him. Although Alan conceals his blindness and pretends he no longer loves her, she sees through his noble deception. They are reunited in happiness.

◆◆◆

Shrewd, colorful American producer Samuel Goldwyn (né Goldfish) was as determined a global movie talent scout as he was the coiner of flavorful aphorisms. In 1924 he signed a film agreement with thirty-three-year-old Britisher Ronald Colman, who had gained audience favor in two Lillian Gish features, *The White Sister* (1923) and *Romola* (1924). During the next decade Colman starred in eighteen Goldwyn productions, from *Tarnish* (1924) to *The Masquerader* (1933). Also in 1924, during one of Goldwyn's frequent European tours, he visited Budapest where he happened to see a photograph of twenty-one-year-old Vilma Banky in a shop window. She had been in motion pictures since 1920, her debut being the Hungarian feature *Im Letzten Augenblick*. Persistent Goldwyn was convinced that the blonde beauty had the right qualities to become a fabulous Hollywood star, but he had great difficulties in arranging a meeting with her. Not until the very night he was to leave Budapest could he set up a conference. Once he explained to the naive young lady what Hollywood was about and why he wanted her to come to California, she readily signed a five-year contract.

By the time Banky sailed for America in March 1925, she had made at least thirteen Continental feature films. Although the movie medium was still silent she was very anxious to learn English in order to better adapt to her new surroundings. She promised the press who greeted her in New York at Goldwyn's prodding, that she would "Spik-speak Eeen-gleesh like as an Angerican in a year." And that yes, "I learn many beau-utifool things in English, yes. . . . Hot Dickety-dog."

Goldwyn had also seen a performance of H. B. Trevelyan's romantic drama, *The Dark Angel,* during his trans-Atlantic sojourn, and was determined to make this the first co-starring vehicle of willowy Banky and dashing, dark-haired Colman. Contract scenarist Frances Marion was set to work adapting the drama to suit the particular stars and the conventions of the silent cinema.

By the time *The Dark Angel* premiered at Manhattan's Mark Strand Theatre on October 11, 1925, the industry and the public had been well brainwashed into thinking that a major event was in store for them. Goldwyn, always perspicaciously lavish with his publicity budget, had informed viewers-to-be that in *The Dark Angel* there were "Heart beats mingling with the drum beat of war—society pageant of amazing surprises—fantasy—colorful love scenes—all here to thrill and inspire in one of the year's finest films." Respected director George Fitzmaurice, who helmed this Samuel Goldwyn production, assured the press that Colman had never been better and that Banky "combines that indefinable something which apparently is the birthright of an European actress—that instinctive grace and gift of self-repression which stamps indelibly the born artiste—with the less subtle but more effective method of expression which marks the interpretation of the American player. The combination is irresistible."

*The Dark Angel* was filled with romanticism, renunciation, and nobility, ingredients dear to the hearts of 1920s moviegoers, allowing each of the lead players to excel in their pantomime work of unbridled emotions. If one considered it just a bit shocking that Colman and Banky, without benefit of clergy, spend a night together in that idyllic English inn, it was made very clear that Colman's Alan Trent was a captain in the British Army, it was wartime, and he was going off to battle the very next day. And the couple had had all the good, proper intentions of being wed, if only *fate* had not intervened.

Fate weaves its brooding spell throughout *The Dark Angel:* Colman being blinded in action, his being listed as dead, Wyndham Standing's chance discovery of his comrade-in-arms, etc. The inspired displays of self-sacrifice are naturally saved for the film's final reels. Standing, although deeply in love with Banky, is sparked to selflessness and informs her that Colman is very much alive. He knows she will go to him, but he has to speak the truth. Thus, on the very day she is to wed Standing she finds that her loved one, for whom she had pined, is very much of this world. Can she be so cruel and unfair to loyal Standing? Will he understand that her heart demands she go to Colman? With a sigh and a gulp he releases her, and she changes her bridal attire for a tailored suit and rushes forth to find the man she waited for, for so many years. The sightless Colman is prepared for her arrival. He will not be a burden to her, and masks his undimmed passion beneath indifference. Having memorized each single detail of his room, he pretends to be as sharp-sighted as the next person. But Banky, initially hurt by his coolness, penetrates his disguise and quickly comprehends that his love for her is still intact. They can embrace in true love and devotion, prepared for their own eternity of joint happiness.

The *New York Times'* Mordaunt Hall praised this tearjerker because "There is no repetition of action, the narrative being unfolded with admirable skill." (*Variety* did suggest that perhaps the direction lagged in spots and that the intrusive comedy relief was overdone in spots.) Colman received his share of reviewers' approbation ("gives a bang-up performance," said *Variety*), but it was wonderously featured Banky who received the bulk of critical comment. Her delicate flaxen-hair beauty was perfectly set off in tandem to the darkly etched features of 5' 11" Colman. *Variety* rhapsodized, ". . . a blonde, she has hair which is not bobbed but light, and soft eyes that are expressive and a set of good looks such as one rarely views. In other words, the girl is there all around and her acting here is as such and as professional as if she had been used to American studios for years." Mordaunt Hall (*New York Times*) substantiated, ". . . [she] is a young person of rare beauty, a girl who might be American or English, with soft, fair hair, a slightly retrousse nose and lovely blue eyes which have the suggestion of a slant. Her acting is sincere and earnest and her tears seem very real. She is so exquisite that one is not in the least surprised that she is never forgotten by Hilary [sic] Trent when, as a blinded war hero, he settles down to dictating boys' stories."

Obviously, Goldwyn was overjoyed that his faith in his Hungarian import had been supported by critics and public alike, that in this 5' 6" beauty he had what seemed to be the perfect vis-a-vis for his prize contractee, Colman.

*The Dark Angel* would be remade by Goldwyn, with less noteworthy success, in 1935 with Fredric March, Merle Oberon, and Herbert Marshall as co-stars. Some twenty-five years thereafter, producer Ross Hunter announced he would prepare an even lusher remake of the evergreen script, with perhaps Lana Turner starring. The project never came to fruition.

## THE WINNING OF BARBARA WORTH
### *(United Artists, 1926) 8,757'*

Producer, Samuel Goldwyn; director, Henry King; based on the novel by Harold Bell Wright; screenplay, Frances Marion; art director, Carl Oscar Borg; titler, Rupert Hughes; music score, Ted Henkel; camera, George Barnes, Gregg Toland; editor, Viola Lawrence.

Ronald Colman (Willard Holmes); Vilma Banky (Barbara Worth); Charles Lane (Jefferson Worth); Paul McAllister (The Seer); E. J. Ratcliffe (James Greenfield); Gary Cooper (Abe Lee); Clyde Cooke (Tex); Erwin Connelly (Pat Mooney); Sam Blum (Horace Blanton); Edwin Brady (Cowboy); Fred Esmelton (George Cartwright); William Patton (Little Rosebud).

New York Premiere: Mark Strand Theatre—November 28, 1926
No New York Television Showing

### Synopsis

Eastern engineer Willard Holmes is called back to the Colorado River territory to assist in the mammoth irrigation project instigated by his unscrupulous stepfather, James Greenfield, banker Jefferson Worth, and a group of New York financiers. Once there, Willard meets Barbara, Worth's lovely adopted daughter. Because Greenfield plans to doublecross his partners, he tries to break up this budding romance. When Willard learns from a fellow engineer, Abe Lee, that the dam construction is faulty, he moves away to form another desert reclamation city. Greenfield does his best to ruin Willard's rival settlement, but Willard and Abe fight all odds and obtain refinancing. Meanwhile, Greenfield's dam overflows and floods his town. Abe, Barbara's other suitor, proves valiantly courageous in warning Willard of the catastrophe, but dies for his efforts leaving the path clear for Willard to claim Barbara for his wife.

◆◆◆

In the year since their last teaming, both Ronald Colman and Vilma Banky had gained enormous popularity in their separate cinema work. Colman had displayed marked versatility in such vehicles as *Stella Dallas* (1925), *Kiki* (1926), and in the French Foreign Legion screen classic, *Beau Geste* (1926). Similarly, Banky, known as "The Hungarian Rhapsody" and "the most lovely woman on the screen," had solidified her boxoffice standing by appearing as Rudolph Valentino's leading lady in two features, *The Eagle* (1925) and *The Son of the Sheik* (1926), the latter released after the matinee idol's untimely death.

To reunite his remarkable screen lovers, Samuel Goldwyn, now releasing his product through United Artists, chose Harold Bell Wright's 1911 novel which had sold over one million copies. (It had also been adapted into a drama by Edwin Royle in 1914 with Edith Lyle starring in the Broadway version.) The Goldwyn picturization of *The Winning of Barbara Worth* is said to have cost over $780,000 with most of the lensing done on location in the Black Rock Desert area between Gerlach and Winnemucca, Nevada, near the Idaho border. A small town was constructed at the 6,000-foot elevation site for use in this Henry King-directed feature.

According to scenarist Frances Marion, neither Colman nor Banky were very happy with their screen assignments. Although each had appeared in desert dramas before, neither felt at ease with the assigned role,

31

he as a virile cowboy type, she as the desert blossom. The critics agreed, "Miss Banky is essentially a hothouse flower and not the type one would expect to see living in a desert shack. In this picture her beauty, however, is a delight to gaze upon, and she gives a competent performance" [Mordaunt Hall (*New York Times*)]. "The role of Willard Holmes offers Colman very little chance for emotional work, although he characterizes the Eastern engineer with typical virility" (Hall of the *Times*). The *New York Herald-Tribune* found both stars completely "out of their element."

But clever Goldwyn knew the public's tastes were more easily satisfied than those of the fourth estate. *The Winning of Barbara Worth* proved to be an outstanding hit of 1926. As that supreme arbiter of the masses, Louella Parsons, enunciated: "It is the type of entertainment that any exhibitor who wishes to fill his theatres will book without a moment's hesitation." They did.

What elements lured the filmgoers into the theatres to see *The Winning of Barbara Worth*? Within its capricious story, there is the desert ambiance magnificently captured by cinematographers George Barnes and Gregg Toland, accompanied by the specially contrived blowing sandstorms and the climactic raging flood as the Colorado River whips through the Imperial Valley and sweeps into the settlement of Kingston. For many the visual wonder of this aquatic special effect rivaled that of the parting of the Red Sea in Cecil B. DeMille's *The Ten Commandments* (1923).

Most of all this film presented an intriguing, if subsidiary, situation for Colman and Banky to rekindle their oncamera sparking. Banky had never before appeared so beautiful on screen ["a perfect tribute to perfect photography" (*Photoplay* magazine)] as she wavers between suitors Colman and Gary Cooper (an extra in previous films, but now in his sensational feature movie acting debut). Whether Banky will choose the more aristocratic Colman or the more basic but equally ardent Cooper is the strong undercurrent of suspense which crosses through *The Winning of Barbara Worth*, although at most times this theme is overshadowed by the grander nature of the epic story of the vast Southwest.

## THE NIGHT OF LOVE
### *(United Artists, 1927) 7,600'*

Producer, Samuel Goldwyn; director, George Fitzmaurice; based on the play by Pedro Calderon de la Barca; adaptation-screenplay, Lenore J. Coffee; art director, Carl Oscar Borg; camera, George Barnes, Thomas Brannigan.

Ronald Colman (Montero); Vilma Banky (Princess Marie); Montagu Love (Duke de la Garda); Natalie Kingston (Donna Beatriz); John George (Jester); Bynunsky Hyman, Gibson Gowland (Bandits); Laska Winter (Gypsy Bride); Sally Rand (Gypsy Dancer).

New York Premiere: Mark Strand Theatre—January 24, 1927
No New York Television Showing

## Synopsis

In medieval Spain, Montero, son of the gypsy leader, is about to wed according to custom, when the Duke de la Garda demands his right as a feudal lord to take the virgin bride to his castle for a night. Rather than acquiesce in the Duke's order, the girl commits suicide and Montero, swearing revenge, turns outlaw. When the Duke later takes Princess Marie, the king's niece, for his bride, Montero and his bandit group kidnap her and the Duke after the wedding feast, taking them to a deserted castle stronghold near the sea. The Duke is then branded and returned to his people, while Princess Marie, in spite of her initial feelings, finds herself falling in love with Montero. She later returns to the Duke, who, disguised as a priest, hears her confession of love, and imprisons her. Montero is captured by the Duke and sentenced to the stake. But the swashbuckling hero inspires the onlooking mob to riot, and in the rebellion the Duke is killed.

◆——◆——◆

With the profitable boxoffice returns from *The Winning of Barbara Worth,* there was no questioning the magic of the Ronald Colman-Vilma Banky screen teaming, and Samuel Goldwyn hastily assigned them to *The Night of Love.* The Latin American screen hero popularized by Rudolph Valentino, Antonio Moreno, and others was still very much in vogue, and it was decided to have Britisher Colman follow suit, reasoning a swashbuckling gypsy could be just as romantic as a sheik. After all in the silent cinema, anything was possible.

*Droit du seigneur,* a concept which would supply the basis for Charlton Heston's *The War Lord* (1965), was a feudal reality. However, as depicted in *The Night of Love,* it became merely a plot contrivance used to bring the Colman-Banky love team together, apart, and together again, all for the vicarious delectation of the entranced filmgoer. "Where there is nothing startlingly novel, so far as screen stories are concerned, in having a romance between a handsome gypsy chieftain and a lovely, flaxen-haired Princess, the idea is embellished when these characters are impersonated by Ronald Colman and Vilma Banky" [Mordaunt Hall (*New York Times*)]. As *Photoplay* magazine appropriately sized up the situation, "What a combination, those two."

Carl Oscar Borg, who had created the sets for *The Winning of Barbara Worth* was on hand to provide the contrasting locales—gypsy camp, seventeenth-century Spanish castle, etc.—for *The Night of Love.* Such scenes lent great atmosphere to the romantic maneuverings of Colman who, heartbroken at the death of his beloved gypsy bride, turns to banditry and lives a Robin Hood-like existence. The visual highlight of the film, of course, was the lavish wedding feast ordered by the Duke (Montagu

Love) for his young bride (Banky). Encased in a fifty-pound bridal gown made of peach-colored chiffon velvet (according to press releases) with fox and pearl trim, she was truly an exquisite vision of loveliness, the finest adornment midst the bountiful celebration. (Later when Banky has been abducted to the gypsy camp, the sight of her traipsing about the campfire site in her elaborate finery would cause many viewers to snicker.)

Director George Fitzmaurice was well aware that the public expected large doses of stylized love making between Colman and Banky. From his experience of helming *The Dark Angel,* he knew just how to accomplish this feat, while still maintaining discretion within the mores of the time. If the filmgoing public was wondering whether this exercise in screen romancing would be the same tempestuous event as in past Colman-Banky features, co-star Colman had a ready, if not comprehensible, explanation for the press and the fans. "We [Banky and Colman] have learned that there is always something new about love making and that no two people in love ever behaved precisely the same."

The profits from *The Night of Love* were sufficiently huge to convince one and all that the carping of the critics meant little where the team of Colman and Banky were concerned. The usually generous *Variety* was wont to complain, "Film is highly theatric. Smacks very much of the studio and doesn't get off the screen to convince at any point. Yet no one will deny the production effort and picturesqueness."

## THE MAGIC FLAME
### (United Artists, 1927) 8,308'

Producer, Samuel Goldwyn; director, Henry King; based on the play *König Harlekin* by Rudolph Lothar; adaptation, Bess Meredyth; continuity, June Mathis; titlers, George Marion, Jr., Nellie Revell; art director, Carl Oscar Borg; assistant director, Robert Florey; theme song, Sigmund Spaeth; technical adviser, Captain Marco Elter; camera, George Barnes.

Ronald Colman (Tito the Clown/The Count); Vilma Banky (Bianca, the Aerial Artist); Agostino Borgato (The Ringmaster); Gustav von Seyffertitz (The Chancellor); Harvey Clark (The Aide); Shirley Palmer (The Wife); Cosmo Kyrle Bellew (The Husband); George Davis (The Utility Man); André Cheron (The Manager); Vadim Uraneff (The Visitor); Meunier-Surcouf (Sword Swallower); Paoli (Weight Thrower).

New York Premiere: Rialto Theatre—September 18, 1927
No New York Television Showing

# Synopsis

Bianca, the premiere aerial star of Baretti's traveling circus, deeply loves Tito the clown, and rejects the amorous advances of the Crown Prince of Illyria, who poses as Count Cassati. The Prince displays his unprincipled courtship techniques when he pursues the wife of a neighboring squire and kills her husband when he finds the couple together. Thereafter, the Prince lures Bianca to his hotel by means of a forged letter, but she escapes in time by using her acrobatic skills to exit through a window. Meanwhile Tito has come to her rescue and kills the Prince in a skirmish. Because he bears a strong resemblance to the late Prince, Tito assumes his identity and is able to escape prosecution. Bianca, believing that Tito has been killed, seeks revenge. During the fake prince's coronation, she attempts to assassinate him, but he reveals his true identity. Together they escape and rejoin the circus.

◆——◆——◆

Predating by a decade his Ruritanian escapades in the dual roles of *The Prisoner of Zenda* (1937), Ronald Colman was teamed for a second time in 1927 with Vilma Banky. The combination of the subject matter (based on Rudolph Lothar's 1904 German play) and the direction of Henry King, who had supervised *The Winning of Barbara Worth*, did much to make this the best of the Colman-Banky screen releases, filled as it was with lyric love, hissable villains and sigh-producing romances. "Here is nearly everything—melodrama, comedy, romance, pathos, beautifully produced and directed" (*Photoplay* magazine). ". . . a graceful story that fit them trimly" (*Variety*).

Aside from the technical problems, oncamera dual roles always place the performer in question in a very rough spot, forcing the player to sufficiently split the characteristics of his/her screen personae so that viewers could, and would, accept him/her as two distinct individuals. Relying on a minimum of contrasting makeup, Colman acquitted himself well in his double assignment. His Prince was a swaggering soul who would be repugnant to the likes of virginal Banky, while his Tito was not the typical circus clown who hides a sad soul beneath his makeup smile. Colman's Tito was a virile soul, full of romance and compassion, who braves most any obstacle for his lady fair. *Photoplay* magazine ranked Colman's performance as "superb."

In an interesting change of pace, the liltingly beautiful Banky was provided with a true proletarian characterization, no longer a Princess or a well-bred young British or American woman, but a professional entertainer who uses her gymnastic proficiency to earn her keep. That is not to say that she appeared overly rambunctious or indelicate of movement in *The Magic Flame*. As *Photoplay* magazine confirmed, the "new" Banky was still graceful and beautiful, "[she] surpasses all her previous work as Bianca. She is extraordinarily lovely."

*Variety* quickly summed up the reasons for *The Magic Flame* succeeding at the boxoffice. "Romantic novelty splendidly produced and capitally acted by those two highly satisfactory screen players. . . ."

## TWO LOVERS
### *(United Artists, 1928) 8,817'*

Producer, Samuel Goldwyn; director, Fred Niblo; based on the novel, *Leatherface: A Tale of Old Flanders* by Emmuska Orczy; adaptation, Alice D. G. Miller; titler, John Colton; assistant director, H. B. Humberstone; music, Hugo Riesenfeld; songs, Wayland Axtell; Abner Silver; camera, George Barnes; editor, Viola Lawrence.

Ronald Colman (Mark Van Rycke); Vilma Banky (Donna Leonora de Vargas); Noah Beery (The Duke of Azar); Nigel De Brulier (The Prince of Orange); Virginia Bradford (Grete); Helen Jerome Eddy (Inez); Eugenie Besserer (Madame Van Rycke); Paul Lukas (Don Ramon de Linea); Fred Esmelton (Meinherr Van Rycke, the Bailiff of Ghent); Harry Allen (Jean); Marcella Daly (Marda); Scotty Mattraw (Dandermonde Innkeeper); Lydia Yeamans Titus (Innkeeper's Wife).

New York Premiere: Embassy Theatre—March 22, 1928
No New York Television Showing

### Synopsis

The Duke of Azar forces his niece, Donna Leonora de Vargas, of the Spanish nobility, to wed Mark Van Rycke, the son of the Burgomaster of Ghent. The marriage is rumored to be a political alliance, solidifying the relationships of the victors and the vanquished. However, the Duke is really hoping to uncover the diplomatic secrets of William of Orange, the tacit leader of the Flemish rebels who are attempting to cast off Spanish rule. Through her uncle's persuasion, Donna Leonora puts aside her love for Don Ramon de Linea, chief of the Spanish forces in Ghent, and turns to spying activities for the Duke. Her hatred of the Flemings increases when Don Ramon is murdered by Leatherface (really Mark) the chief bodyguard and advisor to William of Orange. Slowly she comes to realize that the Flemish cause is just, which leads her to make a daring ride to Ghent in order to help save the lives of a band of conspirators. After assisting the Flemish in their capture of a fortress guarding Ghent, she is reunited with her estranged husband Mark, and they are free to find happiness together.

◆——◆——◆

Nineteen hundred and twenty-seven had been a portentous year for the Ronald Colman-Vilma Banky love team. They had enjoyed two enormous boxoffice successes, which were only topped in publicity and lavishness by Banky's dreamlike wedding to actor Rod La Rocque. The marriage celebration was reputed to be the most resplendent that Hollywood had ever experienced. If the public had been vaguely aware that Colman had been wed to Thelma Raye since 1919 (they would divorce in 1934), it had not spoiled the illusion that perhaps the two great screen lovers matched their ardor offscreen as well as in front of the camera. But Banky's meticulously documented nuptials ended that audience fantasy.

Even more crucial to the boxoffice well-being of the cinema's leading romantic couple were the ascendency of two other major Hollywood love teams, concocted by rival studios. MGM teamed Greta Garbo with John Gilbert in *Flesh and the Devil* (1927) and Fox answered the challenge with the pairing of Janet Gaynor and Charles Farrell in *Seventh Heaven* (1927), both duos destined for even greater popularity with their subsequent movie vehicles. Profit-conscious Goldwyn decided that now was the time to take his two high-powered romantic stars and make one final feature with them together before launching them to a hopeful greater glory in separate pictures.

*Two Lovers*, very loosely based on the Baroness Orczy's 1916 novel *Leatherface: A Tale of Old Flanders*, was selected as the swashbuckling vehicle to "celebrate" the final oncamera teaming of Colman and Banky. As a concession to the growing demand for talking films, Goldwyn provided a budget for a synchronized musical score and sound effects to be employed in this feature. In order to earn back the huge production costs on the project as quickly as possible, *Two Lovers* debuted at the Embassy Theatre on March 22, 1928 as a two-showings-a-day special attraction with a $1.65 ticket top admission.

*Two Lovers*—the title really had little to do with the story—is a typical variation of Baroness Orczy's *The Scarlet Pimpernel* theme, filled with the heroics of a dashing rescuer of the oppressed who is equally gallant to noble ladies no matter how undeserving they initially seem to be. Colman played Mark Van Rycke in his best Douglas Fairbanks, Sr. manner, capering about on horseback and dueling with all the athletic agility of his esteemed prototype. While Colman was complimented for being "vigorous," Banky seemed stifled by her assignment as a not very gracious heroine, who first betrays her husband (Colman) and then her country. "Miss Banky is charming," reported Mordaunt Hall (*New York Times*) "but here she appears to have been told to look as lovely as she possibly can. And she does."

In the course of *Two Lovers*, which certainly would have made an excellent film vehicle for the next decade's Errol Flynn and Olivia de Havilland, Colman undergoes floggings, beatings, and assorted torments, but persists in his dual quest: to free the Flemish and to win the love of his cold bride. If the wild melees of the battle scenes or the persuasive villainy of Noah Beery did not snare the viewer's attention, such a person might well recall the sequence in *Two Lovers* in which Colman and his bride of a few hours are riding in their elegantly appointed carriage. He attempts to embrace his unwilling bride, only to have her rejections matched by the inclement weather (rain and lightning) and a road accident (a carriage wheel becomes loose). Dashing Colman refuses to be stymied by acts of humans, gods, or the script. He quickly has Banky mount one of the horses. He jumps on behind her, and they ride off to the inn in Dendermonde, where he solicitously sees to the comforts of his drenched, but still beautifully coiffured bride.

Only the more pragmatic moviegoer could fail to be entranced by this latest hymn to romantic love.

## THE YEARS AFTER

After *Two Lovers*, Vilma Banky's film career dragged badly. She was cast with Ronald Colman's own supposed discovery, Walter Byron, in *The Awakening* (1928), but the screen chemistry was missing, as it was in *This Is Heaven* (1929) with James Hall. By this time, sound moviemaking was in Hollywood to stay and Banky, whether from indifference or inability, just could not master a comprehensible English. Reportedly Samuel Goldwyn settled her film contract for one million dollars. In 1930 she traveled to MGM where she was cast, appropriately enough, as an immigrant mail-order bride opposite Edward G. Robinson in a rendition of Sidney Howard's play *They Knew What They Wanted*, re-entitled *A Lady to Love*. She and Robinson also appeared in the German-language version of the film, *Die Sehnsucht Jeder Frau* (1930). Thereafter, Banky toured with her husband in the stage vehicle *Cherries Are Ripe*, and soon drifted into semi-retirement, content to reside in domesticity, broken occasionally by a stage appearance or a trip to Europe for brief filmmaking. She remained wed to Rod La Rocque until his death in 1970.

Colman was far more fortunate in his post-Banky period. After a disappointing teaming with Goldwyn's latest discovery, Lili Damita in *The Rescue* (1929), he made his talking picture debut that year in *Bulldog Drummond*. Cinema historian Richard Griffith wrote: "Striking good looks were perhaps the basis of his Silent fame, but from the moment he spoke it was apparent that here was an actor who not only understood his craft but was far ahead of his time." He was Oscar-nominated for *Bulldog Drummond*, but lost to George Arliss of *Disraeli*. After breaking with Goldwyn in 1933, Colman signed with Darryl F. Zanuck's Twentieth Century Productions, starring in several elaborate swashbuckling yarns including *Clive of India* (1935) for which he shaved his famed mustache. His most noteworthy role was as the idealist in Frank Capra's *Lost Horizons* (1937). Five years later he played in another James Hilton story, *Random Harvest*, with regal Greer Garson as his flinty co-star. In 1948, thirty-one years after entering films, he finally won an Oscar for his performance as the crazed actor in *A Double Life*. Thereafter, he appeared in only three more films, mostly cameo bits. In 1949 he and his second wife, Benita Hume, premiered a sophisticated domestic comedy series on radio. "The Halls of Ivy" was a hit in that medium and later enjoyed lesser popularity as a television series with the two players repeating their original roles. To the end of his life (1958), Colman deeply regretted that advancing age had robbed him of the opportunity to play the type of movie swashbuckling roles he enjoyed so much.

In the course of the film *Sunset Boulevard* (1950), William Holden peers into Gloria Swanson's swimming pool and muses, "Vilma Banky and Rod La Rocque must have swum there a thousand midnights ago." And indeed to post-1930s generations who had never seen Banky oncamera, she seemed a primitive but enduring myth from the earlier, carefree days of Hollywood and America's twentieth century. Word-of-mouth and published reminiscences perpetuated the legend of her fabulous Church of Good Shepherd wedding with the reception for six hundred guests at the Beverly Hills Hotel, but far fewer people recalled or discussed the charisma of the Colman-Banky screen teaming. For a brief period in the Roaring Twenties the duo made moviegoers' hearts beat faster as audiences vicariously experienced the Colman and Banky version of cinema romance. When Colman and Banky indulged in blatantly rapturous embraces oncamera, it was an emotional experience to behold, a feat not duplicated by the more heralded 1920s teaming of Greta Garbo and John Gilbert or Janet Gaynor and Charles Farrell. The five Colman-Banky pictures offer up a canon of celluloid sensuality not equalled since, although the Errol Flynn-Olivia de Havilland combination tried to match the courtly aura of brandished love. Gone are the styles and opinions of the 1920s, and with it, the magic of Colman and Banky.

In **A Woman of Affairs** (MGM, 1929)

# Chapter 2

# John Gilbert
# &
# Greta Garbo

## JOHN GILBERT

5′ 11″
135 pounds
Brown hair
Brown eyes
Cancer

*Real name: John Pringle. Born July 10, 1897, Logan, Utah. Married Olivia Burwell (1917); divorced 1922. Married Leatrice Joy (1923), daughter: Leatrice; divorced 1924. Married Ina Claire (1929); divorced 1932. Married Virginia Bruce (1932), daughter, Susan; divorced, 1934. Died January 9, 1936.*

FEATURE FILMS:

*Hell's Hinges* (Triangle, 1916)
*Bullets and Brown Eyes* (Triangle, 1916)
*The Apostle of Vengeance* (Ince-Triangle, 1916)
*The Phantom* (Ince-Triangle, 1916)
*Eye of the Night* (Ince-Triangle, 1916)
*Shell '43'* (Ince-Triangle, 1916)
*Princess of the Dark* (Ince-Triangle, 1917)
*Happiness* (Triangle, 1917)
*The Millionaire Vagrant* (Triangle, 1917)
*Hater of Men* (Triangle, 1917)
*Golden Rule Kate* (Triangle, 1917)
*The Devil Dodger* (Triangle, 1918)
*Nancy Comes Home* (Triangle, 1918)
*More Trouble* (Pathé, 1918)
*Shackled* (W. W. Hodkinson, 1918)
*Three X Gordon* (W. W. Hodkinson, 1918)
*Wedlock* (W. W. Hodkinson, 1918)

*The Mask* (Triangle, 1918)
*The Dawn of Understanding* (Vitagraph, 1918)
*White Heather* (Hiller and Wilk, 1919)
*The Busher* (Par., 1919)
*Heart O' the Hills* (FN, 1919)
*The Red Viper* (Tyrad, 1919)
*Should a Woman Tell?* (Metro, 1919)
*Widow by Proxy* (Par., 1919)
*The Servant in the House* (FBO, 1920)
*The Great Redeemer* (Metro, 1920)
*The White Circle* (Par., 1920)
*Deep Waters* (Par., 1921)
*Shame* (Fox, 1921)
*Ladies Must Live* (Par., 1921)
*Gleam O'Dawn* (Fox, 1922)
*Arabian Love* (Fox, 1922)
*The Yellow Stain* (Fox, 1922)
*Honor First* (Fox, 1922)
*The Count of Monte Cristo* (Fox, 1922)
*Calvert's Valley* (Fox, 1922)
*The Love Gambler* (Fox, 1922)
*A California Romance* (Fox, 1922)
*While Paris Sleeps* (W. W. Hodkinson, 1923)
*Truxton King* (Fox, 1922)
*Madness of Youth* (Fox, 1923)
*St. Elmo* (Fox, 1923)
*The Exiles* (Fox, 1923)
*Cameo Kirby* (Fox, 1923)
*The Wolf Man* (Fox, 1924)
*Just Off Broadway* (Fox, 1924)
*A Man's Mate* (Fox, 1924)
*Romance Ranch* (Fox, 1924)
*The Lone Chance* (Fox, 1924)
*His Hour* (Metro-Goldwyn, 1924)

*Married Flirts* (Metro-Goldwyn, 1924)°
*He Who Gets Slapped* (Metro-Goldwyn, 1924)
*The Snob* (Metro-Goldwyn, 1924)
*The Wife of the Centaur* (Metro-Goldwyn, 1925)
*The Merry Widow* (Metro-Goldwyn, 1925)
*The Big Parade* (MGM, 1925)
*La Boheme* (MGM, 1926)
*Bardelys the Magnificent* (MGM, 1926)
*Flesh and the Devil* (MGM, 1927)
*The Show* (MGM, 1927)
*Twelve Miles Out* (MGM, 1927)
*Love* (MGM, 1927)
*Man, Woman and Sin* (MGM, 1927)
*The Cossacks* (MGM, 1928)
*Four Walls* (MGM, 1928)
*Masks of the Devil* (MGM, 1928)
*Show People* (MGM, 1928)°
*A Woman of Affairs* (MGM, 1929)
*Desert Nights* (MGM, 1929)
*A Man's Man* (MGM, 1929)°
*The Hollywood Revue of 1929* (MGM, 1929)
*His Glorious Night* (MGM, 1929)
*Redemption* (MGM, 1930)
*Way for a Sailor* (MGM, 1930)
*Gentleman's Fate* (MGM, 1931)
*Chiri Bibi* or *The Phantom of Paris* (MGM, 1931)
*West of Broadway* (MGM, 1932)
*Downstairs* (MGM, 1932)
*Fast Workers* (MGM, 1933)
*Queen Christina* (MGM, 1933)
*The Captain Hates the Sea* (Col., 1934)

°Guest Appearance

# GRETA GARBO

**5′ 6″**
**125 pounds**
**Golden hair**
**Blue eyes**
**Virgo**

*Real name: Greta Lovisa Gustafsson. Born September 18, 1905, Stockholm, Sweden.*

**FEATURE FILMS:**

*Peter the Tramp* (Erik A. Petschler, 1922)
*The Story of Gösta Berling* (Svensk Filmindustri, 1924)
*The Street of Sorrow* (Sofar-Film, 1925)
*The Torrent* (MGM, 1926)
*The Temptress* (MGM, 1926)
*Flesh and the Devil* (MGM, 1927)
*Love* (MGM, 1927)
*The Divine Woman* (MGM, 1928)
*The Mysterious Lady* (MGM, 1928)
*A Woman of Affairs* (MGM, 1929)
*Wild Orchids* (MGM, 1929)
*The Single Standard* (MGM, 1929)
*A Man's Man* (MGM, 1929)°
*The Kiss* (MGM, 1929)

*Anna Christie* (MGM, 1930)
*Romance* (MGM, 1930)
*Inspiration* (MGM, 1931)
*Susan Lenox: Her Fall and Rise* (MGM, 1931)
*Mata Hari* (MGM, 1932)
*Grand Hotel* (MGM, 1932)
*As You Desire Me* (MGM, 1932)
*Queen Christina* (MGM, 1933)
*The Painted Veil* (MGM, 1934)
*Anna Karenina* (MGM, 1935)
*Camille* (MGM, 1936)
*Conquest* (MGM, 1937)
*Ninotchka* (MGM, 1939)
*Two-Faced Woman* (MGM, 1941)

°Guest Appearance

In **Queen Christina** (MGM, 1933)

In **Flesh and the Devil** (MGM, 1927)

In **Love** (MGM, 1927)

# FLESH AND THE DEVIL
## *(MGM, 1927) 8,759'*

Director, Clarence Brown; based on the novel *Es War* by Hermann Sudermann; screenplay, Benjamin F. Glazer; titler, Marian Ainslee; assistant director, Charles Dorian; wardrobe, André-ani; sets, Cedric Gibbons, Frederic Hope; camera, William Daniels; editor, Lloyd Nosler.

John Gilbert (Leo von Sellenthin); Greta Garbo (Felicitas von Kletzingk); Lars Hanson (Ulrich von Kletzingk); Barbara Kent (Hertha Prochvitz); William Orlamond (Uncle Kutowski); George Fawcett (Pastor Brenckenburg); Eugenie Besserer (Leo's Mother); Marc MacDermott (Count von Rhaden); Marcelle Corday (Minna).

New York Premiere: Capitol Theatre—January 9, 1927
New York Television Debut: Channel 13—August 28, 1973.

## Synopsis

Austrians Leo von Sellenthin and Ulrich von Kletzingk, two youths who grow up together, swear lasting friendship through a blood oath. Together they attend military school and meet at home on annual holidays. Leo encounters the fascinating Felicitas von Kletzingk at the railroad station and later at a lavish ball. When the two are later discovered in an affair by her husband Count von Rhaden, he and Leo engage in a duel, and the former is killed. Leo is forced into the foreign service and departs for the American west, while Ulrich, unaware of her affair with Leo, eventually weds Felicitas. Three years later, learning that he has been pardoned by the Emperor and will not be punished because of the duel, Leo returns home. Unsuccessfully he attempts to avoid renewing his romance with Felicitas. When Ulrich finds out, Felicitas insists that it was Leo who tempted her. Ulrich and Leo arrange for a duel, but each is unable to fire the fatal shot. Meanwhile, Felicitas hopes to save Leo and hastens across an ice-packed river to prevent the duel, but falls through the ice and drowns. Leo and Ulrich become friends again, with Leo now taking an avid interest in eighteen-year-old Hertha Prochvitz.

◆━━◆━━◆

Having starred in *The Big Parade* (1925) and *La Boheme* (1926), twenty-nine-year-old John Gilbert was approaching the zenith of his screen career as the ultimate romantic silent movie lead when he was first teamed with the twenty-one-year-old Swedish import, Greta Garbo, in *Flesh and the Devil*. She had already intrigued American filmgoers with her impressively sensitive performances in MGM's *The Torrent* (1926) opposite Ricardo Cortez, and in *The Temptress* (1927) opposite Antonio Moreno. Having professionally auditioned with two of its best matinee idols, MGM thought it good boxoffice to now pair her with Gilbert, who, since the death of Rudolph Valentino, was reputed to be the supreme oncamera lover. Metro selected Hermann Sudermann's 1893 novel *Es War (The Undying Past)* as the vehicle for these two performers' oncamera union. It was a fitting literary work, with its story of grand emotions—honor, love, loyalty—to be told in the elaborate manner that was becoming MGM's firm trademark: plush solid settings, meticulous camerawork, expert matte shots, and above all, resourceful direction that would emphasize the erotic nature of the triangular romance.

Although Garbo's mentor,* Swedish film director Mauritz Stiller, informed his Hollywood acquaintances that "Those fools at Metro will ruin her" with such pictures as *Flesh and the Devil,* on the contrary, the film solidified her growing reputation as one of the elite of the love goddesses, whose uncanny mysticism would always be one of her most alluring qualities.

In weaving this glossy tale of two comrades-in-arms torn apart by their love for a temptress, director Clarence Brown infused the expansive film with a strong sense for the environment. He showed how this environment had enveloped the characters and that none of them could help being the type of person he or she was. Brown's approach made the actors' performances all the more credible, even though it was a filmmaking procedure more frequently employed in European films—especially those of Sweden—than in America.

The major theme of *Flesh and the Devil* is enunciated by Pastor Brenckenburg (George Fawcett), who informs a troubled Gilbert, in the course of the story, that when the devil cannot reach man through his spirit, then he sends a woman to get him through the flesh. In essence, this premise is a very moralistic concept and the evil-must-suffer finale substantiates this pious approach. However, Metro was well attuned to the fact that audiences wanted titillating diversion while being preached at, and *Flesh and the Devil* is full of entertaining emotional high spots. There are scenes of a grand ball, the dashing duelists, an engulfing illness, a desperate chase across a frozen lake, and even a reel of gratuitous comedy in the opening barrack sequences. More important to the film's boxoffice success were the picture's torrid love scenes—often played in heady close ups—that elicited terrific comments from impressed film viewers. Garbo personified the exotic object waiting to be cherished, with Gilbert (and Lars Hanson, too) overeager to share rapturous kisses with this beguiling lady, unmindful that her aura of erotic passion was leading them into dangerous waters.

From the first moment that Garbo and Gilbert meet oncamera in this film, electricity sparks between them. He is returning home on holiday from military life, and at the railroad station encounters an aloof, mysteri-

---

*Stiller had been replaced as director on both Garbo's *The Torrent* and *The Temptress.*

ous lady. She drops her bouquet of flowers, he gallantly rushes to retrieve it, but before returning them to her, he picks off a flower to keep as a memento of this galvanic meeting. Later they meet at the ball, and soon they have left the others to converse in the shadows of the deserted garden. As he lights a cigarette, she coyly blows out the match, leading her ardent admirer to confess, "You know—when you blow out that match—it's an invitation to kiss you." Almost immediately the couple launch into a passionate kissing scene, all the more exciting because it transpires in semi-darkness. Still later the two share a hearthside tryst, with Garbo radiant in her striking long evening dress, and Gilbert her romantic servant, bundled in a full-length fur coat. In the tradition of all good femme fatales, it is Garbo, rather than Gilbert, who initiates the passionate embracing at this juncture, and the camera captures their amour to the fullest degree in what is described as one of the fullest and best horizontal love scenes in the American cinema. Thereafter, proving once again that love and hate are closely allied emotions, it is Gilbert, having returned from exile in America who discovers that temptress Garbo wants to renew their romance at the expense of his best friend Hanson, the man she has recently wed. It is too much for the honorable soul and he almost strangles her, but Hanson enters the bedroom and soon the two men find themselves forced by honor and tradition to submit to a duel on the morrow.

Without a doubt, the voluptuous byplay and interplay of Garbo and Gilbert as two people hopelessly and violently in love stunned the imagination of moviegoers and critics alike. "Frankly," wrote the *New York Herald-Tribune's* critic, "never in our screen career have we seen seduction so perfecting done." In analyzing the film's success on this point, the same paper observed, "Never before has John Gilbert been so intense in his portrayal of a man in love. . . . Never before has a woman so alluring, with a seductive grace that is far more potent than mere beauty, appeared on the screen. Greta Garbo is the epitome of pulchritude, the personification of passion."

*Variety* was even more enthusiastic about *Flesh and the Devil* and Garbo who had been known before as "The Norma Shearer of Sweden." "Here is a picture that is the pay off when it comes to filming love scenes. There are 3 in the picture that will make anyone fidget in their seats and their hair to rise on end—and that ain't all. . . .

"The film is a battle between John Gilbert starred, and Greta Garbo featured, for honors and if they don't star this girl after this picture Metro-Goldwyn doesn't know what is missing. Miss Garbo properly billed and given the right material, will be as great a money asset as Theda Bara was to Fox in years past. This girl has everything."

While undoubtedly a good deal of the romantic aura to *Flesh and the Devil* was due to director Clarence Brown, an equal portion of the ardor recorded on film was the result of the burgeoning romance between Garbo and Gilbert. "It was love at first sight and it lasted through many years," said director Brown sometime later. It soon became known to the industry and then to the eager public that the shy, seclusion-seeking Garbo and the reckless, frollicking, temperamental Gilbert were "that way" about one another. While the reticent Garbo would hardly speak of her offcamera relationship with Jacky (pronounced by the star as "Yacky"), he was soon extolling the many virtues of his "Flicka," launching into zealous tirades of her magical qualities, "The most alluring creature you have ever seen. Capricious as the devil, whimsical, temperamental and fascinating . . . what magnetism when she gets in front of the camera! What appeal! What a woman! One day she is childlike, naive, ingenuous, a girl of ten. The next day she is a mysterious woman a thousand years old, knowing everything, baffled deep. Garbo has more sides to her personality than anyone I have ever met."

As a result of her personal triumph in *Flesh and the Devil*, Garbo struck the studio, and was quickly able to renegotiate her MGM contract with Louis B. Mayer on far more favorable terms. She had become a true daughter of Hollywood!

## LOVE
### *(MGM, 1927) 7,365'*

Producer-director, Edmund Goulding; based on the novel *Anna Karenina* by Leo Tolstoy; adaptation, Lorna Moon; continuity, Frances Marion; titlers, Marian Ainslee, Ruth Cummings; set design, Cedric Gibbons, Alexander Toluboff; music score, Ernst Luz; song, Howard Dietz and Walter Donaldson; wardrobe, Gilbert Clark; camera, William Daniels; editor, Hugh Wynn.

Greta Garbo (Anna Karenina); John Gilbert (Vronsky); George Fawcett (Grand Duke); Emily Fitzroy (Grand Duchess); Brandon Hurst (Karenin); Philippe De Lacy (Serezha the Child).

New York Premiere: Embassy Theatre—November 29, 1927
New York Television Debut: Channel 13—September 10, 1973

### Synopsis

Anna Karenina, wed to wealthy Karenin in czarist Russia, meets a young officer named Vronsky and promptly falls in love with him. When her husband refuses to give her a divorce, she leaves him and her child, Serezha, to become Vronsky's mistress. But it is not long before Vronsky wishes to resume his career as a professional soldier. Realizing her tragic fate and that she has nothing in her future once Vronsky goes back to his comrades-in-arms, she commits suicide by throwing herself in front of a train at the railroad station.

Alternate ending: After her husband's timely death, Anna and Vronsky are happily reunited, when on the same day he and Anna happen to visit Serezha at his military school.

———◆———◆———◆———

With the rising importance of the "Swedish Sphinx," MGM decided to cast Garbo in a modern dress rendition of Leo Tolstoy's famed novel, *Anna Karenina* (1875-77). Experienced scenarist Frances Marion struggled long and hard with the continuity of the screenplay, trying to telescope Tolstoy's giant-sized novel into workable cinema terms. Marion later recalled that at one point in her arduous task, her studio supervisor informed her, "Needs a lot of changes. Too sophisticated. Highbrow stuff won't go over, . . . Need hotter love scenes. Also build up the climax by putting more suspense into it. Otherwise, it's a pretty good job."

Once having overcome the scripting obstacle, MGM put the film into production, but soon ran into difficulty. Director Dmitri Buchowetsky was unable to make the production jell, and filming was halted. Ricardo Cortez and Lionel Barrymore were dropped from the cast and John Gilbert and Brandon Hurst set to replace them, with Edmund Goulding now directing the film. Although Goulding was a very diplomatic soul, he had great problems with his tempestuous stars. They would be warm and friendly to each other one day, and the next hardly speak to one another. More to the point, Goulding had difficulty restraining the irritating egocentricities of Gilbert who was now insistent on "directing" much of the film himself, interfering with Goulding's progress, all in a vain effort to impress the aloof Garbo.

Eventually the film was completed and the studio geniuses took great pride in the revised title tag which enabled them to publicize the picture as "John Gilbert and Greta Garbo in *Love*. . . . What more could be said about a picture—see it." (The release title was certainly an improvement over an earlier suggestion that the picture be called *Heat*.)

*Love*, which opened on a two-a-day schedule at the Embassy Theatre in New York on November 29, 1927, provided ample opportunity for the star team to embrace in romantic clinches. Right from the opening scene in which Garbo's elaborate sled bogs down in a snow storm, leading to her meeting with Gilbert, he is instantly infatuated with her, and they promptly embrace, which later causes him to apologize, particularly when he realizes she is a married woman. The couple meet again several times at the horse races and they decide to run away together. But their sweet infatuation soon turns sour as Gilbert misses his army friends and the excitement of the military life. The finale° finds Gilbert pardoned by the Grand Duke (George Fawcett) with Garbo left alone on a railroad station

°In the alternate ending, used in general release and seen in today's television print, Anna does not commit suicide. Instead, three years pass from the time she and Vronsky separate. On one of her many visits to Serezha at his military academy, she encounters Vronsky, he having just learned that her husband is now dead. They embrace and plan to resume their romance. This tacked-on finale, dreamed up by Metro to appease patrons who wanted their silver screen love team to "live happily ever after," was entirely out of keeping with what had transpired before in the film.

platform, the outline of her face shrouded by a veil. The headlights of a train engine are seen approaching and then a shadow leaps in front of the onrushing train.

Garbo's most effective scene in *Love*, as in the remake *Anna Karenina* (1935) in which she co-starred with Fredric March, occurs at that moment when, after an absence from her husband (Brandon Hurst), she sneaks into their home for a glimpse of their little son. She steals upstairs and moves quietly into the child's bedroom. The boy awakens and because he has been told that his mother is dead, he thinks he is now dreaming. Then he realizes he is awake, and joy spreads over both their faces as he and Garbo embrace in a happy reunion.

While the boxoffice returns on *Love* were very good indeed, the critical reception was mixed. Most agreed with Mordaunt Hall (*New York Times*), "Greta Garbo, the Swedish actress, outshines any other performance she has given on the screen. . . . Miss Garbo is elusive. Her heavy-lidded eyes, the cold whiteness of her face and her svelte figure compel interest in her actions. Sometimes she reminds one of a blonde Mona Lisa and on other occasions she is gentle and lovely. . . ." But there was disapproval of Gilbert's very mannered, strutting performance as the Russian officer. "Mr. Gilbert's part in this picture is cleverly done, but it might have been even better if he had controlled his stare and his smile" (Hall of the *Times*).

That even such fan magazines as *Motion Picture* were disturbed by the quality of *Love* raises some doubts about the legend that has grown up around the Garbo-Gilbert screen encounters. That publication's reviewer wrote, "Lovers of Tolstoy will be disappointed. Those who like to study the Gilbert-Garbo embraces will be disappointed. In fact the only people who won't be disappointed, like myself, are those who have always thought of Greta Garbo merely as the only woman in pictures who dresses worse than Alice Terry. Because Greta is surprising, and her grace and beauty and fine acting make a cheap, melodramatic picture into something at least interesting, if not good. I recommend it solely that you may see what she was able to do with little help from the script, the director, or John Gilbert."

The trade journal *Variety* had its own flavorful prognostication of Garbo's future in the cinema as the result of *Love*. ". . . [she] isn't now as big as she should be or will be, always remembering it's the stories that count. Neither has she been in enough pictures of late. But if handled, and she will allow herself to be handled, she's the biggest skirt prospect now in pictures."

## A WOMAN OF AFFAIRS
### *(MGM, 1929) 8,319'*

Director, Clarence Brown; based on the novel *The Green Hat* by

Michael Arlen; continuity, Bess Meredyth; titlers, Marian Ainslee, Ruth Cummings; art director, Cedric Gibbons; assistant director, Charles Dorian; gowns, Adrian; song, William Axt and David Mendoza; camera, William Daniels; editor, Hugh Wynn.

Greta Garbo (Diana Merrick); John Gilbert (Neville Holderness); Lewis Stone (Hugh); John Mack Brown (David); Douglas Fairbanks, Jr. (Geoffrey Merrick); Hobart Bosworth (Sir Morton); Dorothy Sebastian (Constance).

New York Premiere: Capitol Theatre—January 20, 1929
New York Television Debut: Channel 13—September 10, 1973

## Synopsis

An elegant English girl, Diana Merrick, loves Neville Holdering. However, his father disapproves of her family's way of life and he forbids Neville and Diana to wed. Actually, Diana's brother Geoffrey is a wastrel, and her own conduct is not always laudable. Having been rejected she throws herself into a reckless way of existence, finally marrying Geoffrey's friend, David, unaware that he is a thief. On their honeymoon in France, David learns the police are on his trail and he commits suicide. Diana now sets out to repay the victims of David's past crimes. Meanwhile Neville has wed another woman, Constance, but still loves Diana. He returns to Diana when she reappears in England a few years later. Realizing that their love is strong but will ruin them, Diana sends Neville away telling him to return to his wife who is pregnant. Having already lost her brother who died of alcoholism, Diana now can find no further reason to live. She crashes her car into the tree beneath which she and Neville first discovered that they were in love, and dies.

◆━━◆━━◆

Greta Garbo had already starred in *The Divine Woman* (1928) as a Parisian temptress and played a Russian spy in *The Mysterious Lady* (1928), when MGM deemed it wise to adhere to public demands to reunite their popular love team, Garbo and John Gilbert, in yet another movie vehicle. Clarence Brown, who had helmed *Flesh and the Devil*, was assigned to direct the new film, with Garbo's favorite cinematographer, William Daniels, behind the cameras. The chosen property was Michael Arlen's inordinately popular novel, *The Green Hat* (1924). Because of its risque qualities the novel had to undergo extreme plot alterations as well as title and character name changes before Will Hay's industry censor board would allow the film to be made. Although the feature would masquerade under a tantalizing alias, the studio insured that all possible viewers would definitely link *A Woman of Affairs* with the (in)famous *The Green Hat*. The film's publicity stated the picture was based on "The famous story by Michael Arlen." There were few wise people who missed the connection. A synchronized sound effect and music score were added to the essentially silent *A Woman of Affairs* so that this prestige film could claim to be keeping abreast of the fast-encroaching talkie picture revolution. (Sheet music of the film's theme song, "Love's First Kiss," was sold in theatre lobbies showing the picture.)

In Michael Arlen's original story, John Mack Brown's character had suffered from syphilis, which made the book plot line more daring and certainly more logical. However, to assuage the more sensitive tastes of filmgoers, the ailment was changed to the crime of thievery in the photoplay. Therefore, the young man now dies for "decency," not "purity." Other such unsubtle dilutions of the original material took a great deal of punch out of the tale, allowing *Photoplay* magazine to advise its readers, ". . . the beauty of the love story lifts the picture to exalted heights and purges it of any possible tinge of sordidness."

Garbo, who had three inches of her hair shorn off for *A Woman of Affairs,* sported a new sleek, smoothed-down coiffure, thus completing her transformation into the Hollywood-styled contemporary love goddess. Although the studio publicized the film as "The world-famous pair of screen lovers in the perfect performance of their romantic careers" there was no zest to the film. As *Variety* described it, ". . . the kick is out of the material, and worse yet, John Gilbert, idol of the flappers, has an utterly blah role. Most of the footage he just stands around, rather sheepishly, in fact, while others shape the events. . . . Miss Garbo saves an unfortunate situation throughout by a subtle something in her playing that suggests just the exotic note that is essential to the whole theme and story. Without her eloquent acting the picture would go to pieces."

There is one scene in *A Woman of Affairs* which harkens back to the golden moments of earlier Garbo-Gilbert films. Garbo's character has informed Gilbert regarding her emerald ring, "I would only take it off for the man I love." Later, during a couch love scene, the camera slowly pans down to her hand just as the special ring is slipped off.

In 1934, MGM would remake *The Green Hat* as *Outcast Lady* with Constance Bennett and Herbert Marshall co-starred. This talkie rendition had even less impact than its more famous predecessor.

## A MAN'S MAN
### *(MGM, 1929) 6,683′*

Director, James Cruze; based on the play by Patrick Kearney; screenplay, Forrest Halsey; titler, Joe Farnham; art director, Cedric Gibbons; song, Al Bryan and Monte Wilhitt; wardrobe, David Cox; camera, Merritt B. Gerstad; editor, George Hively.

William Haines (Mel); Josephine Dunn (Peggy); Sam Hardy (Charlie);

Mae Busch (Violet); John Gilbert (Himself); Greta Garbo (Herself); and Gloria Davenport.

New York Premiere: Capitol Theatre—June 2, 1929
No New York Television Showing

## Synopsis

Peggy follows the great American dream and heads for Hollywood, hoping to be one of the fortunate few who crash the movies and find stardom. While struggling to gain an entree, she meets Mel, a pleasant but easily-duped soda jerk whom she eventually weds. Later Mel purchases some worthless oil stock from Charlie, an assistant director with a bad reputation, who is making a pass for Peggy. Charlie persuades the hopeful girl that he can make her a movie star, if she is cooperative. Both Peggy and Mel eventually realize Charlie's true character, and in a climactic fight, Mel beats up Charlie.

◆◆◆

*Merton of the Movies* (1924) and *Show People* (1928) were certainly more illustrious examples of behind-the-scenes Hollywood movie-making than *A Man's Man,* while the MGM starring team of William Haines and Josephine Dunn had been far more engaging in their previous *Excess Baggage* (1928). There was little to recommend this picture to its audiences and it was judged as "an example of much ado about nothing" [Mordaunt Hall (*New York Times*)].

Within the story, movie star hopeful Peggy (Josephine Dunn) wants to be another Greta Garbo, and therefore, it is imperative within the scenario for her (and the audience) to catch a glimpse of the famous star. Dunn and the viewer have their chance to spot the screen idol entering Grauman's Theatre with John Gilbert for the premiere of MGM's *White Shadows of the South Seas* (1928). Since by the time *A Man's Man* was released the Garbo-Gilbert romance was a thing of the past—he wed actress Ina Claire in 1929—the guest appearance was an obviously dated inclusion and hardly the bonus the producers intended.

## QUEEN CHRISTINA
### *(MGM, 1933) 100M.*

Producer, Walter Wanger; director, Rouben Mamoulian; story, Salka Viertel, Margaret P. Levine; screenplay, Viertel, Harwood; dialog, S. N. Behrman; art directors, Alexander Toluboff, Edwin B. Willis; music, Herbert Stothart; costumes, Adrian; sound, Douglas Shearer; camera, William Daniels; editor, Blanche Sewell.

Greta Garbo (Christina); John Gilbert (Don Antonio); Ian Keith (Magnus); Lewis Stone (Oxenstierna); Elizabeth Young (Ebba); Sir C. Aubrey Smith (Aage); Reginald Owen (Prince Charles); George Renaevent (French Ambassador); Gustav von Seyffertitz (General); David Torrence (Archbishop); Ferdinand Munier (Innkeeper); Akim Tamiroff (Pedro); Cora Sue Collins (Christina as a Child); Edward Norris (Count Jacob), Lawrence Grant, Barbara Barondess (Bits); Paul Hurst (Swedish Soldier); Ed Gargan (Fellow Drinker); Wade Boteler (Rabble Rouser); Fred Kohler (Member of the Court); Dick Alexander (Peasant in Crowd); Major Sam Harris (Nobleman).

New York Premiere: Astor Theatre—December 26, 1933
New York Television Debut: CBS—June 30, 1960

## Synopsis

It is announced that Queen Christina, ruler of Sweden, is to wed Prince Charles, renowned hero of the armies. Her former lover, Magnus, wants the marriage arranged, knowing that Christina does not love Charles. Christina, however, rebuffs her chancellors' suggestion, claiming she is not yet ready for a husband. One day while riding in the snow, she encounters Don Antonio, the Ambassador from Spain, and later meets him again at an inn. He does not realize that beneath her boy's clothes she is a woman. Because the tavern is overcrowded they are forced to share a room. During the next few days he discovers her sex but not her identity, and they fall in love. When they meet yet again at the court he informs her that he has been sent to arrange a marriage between her and the King of Spain. Nevertheless the couple meet often, causing Magnus to rouse the people against this interloper. Christina sends Don Antonio away and then abdicates. When she arrives at the place where she is to meet him, she finds him mortally wounded in a duel, killed by Magnus. She leaves for Spain with his body, never to return.

In *Anna Christie* (1930) Greta Garbo talked. In that picturization of the Eugene O'Neill play she solidified her reputation as a sound film star. Although most of her subsequent vehicles in the early 1930s ranged from insipid [*Inspiration* (1931)] to quixotic [*Susan Lenox: Her Fall and Rise* (1931)] to exotic [*Mata Hari* (1932)], she achieved her biggest success in the all-star *Grand Hotel* (1932)* in which she played the fading ballerina.

After *As You Desire Me*, released in early 1932, Garbo was off the screen for nearly eighteen months, spending a good deal of the time on holiday in Sweden. Before she went abroad, her good friend Salka Viertel persuaded the star to read some of the new biographies of the fascinating Queen Christina (1626-1689), including Margaret Goldsmith's *Christina of*

*At one point in the pre-production work on *Grand Hotel*, John Gilbert had been slated to play opposite Garbo, but the studio substituted John Barrymore as the Baron von Gaigern in place of the fading Gilbert.

*Sweden* and Faith Compton MacKenzie's *The Sybil of the North*. Viertel and Margaret P. Levine thereafter collaborated on a screenplay built around the colorful monarch and sent the scenario to Garbo who was then in Stockholm. Garbo read it, liked it, and wired MGM that she would sign a new two-pictures-a-year contract, providing for $250,000 per film, if *Queen Christina* were to be among the first vehicles. The studio agreed, and Garbo, via freighter, returned to Hollywood in late April, 1933.

Since the conclusion of his "stormy, historic and once-glorious romance" with Garbo, John Gilbert had suffered assorted reversals. His first full talking film, *His Glorious Night* (1929), met with sharp critical pans, leading the fickle public to promptly disown their once dashing screen lover whose screen voice was unromantic, higher pitched than expected. While MGM was seemingly doing its best to sabotage the remnants of Gilbert's fast-deteriorating film career, he and Ina Claire divorced in 1932. The same year he wed the twenty-two-year-old MGM contractee, Virginia Bruce, with whom he had played in *Downstairs* (1932). Bruce would give birth to a daughter, named Susan, and in 1934 the couple would divorce.

While it was considered a generous, nostalgic gesture on Garbo's part to hire Gilbert as her screen vis-a-vis for *Queen Christina,* he certainly was not the first choice of the studio, nor even her first choice. Leslie Howard had rejected the role, not wanting to be overshadowed by Garbo. Other contenders tested for the part included Franchot Tone, Nils Asther, and Bruce Cabot. Laurence Olivier had signed a contract for the film and even had rehearsed love scenes with the actress. However, she decided that the Britisher would not do in the part, and hence Metro resurrected contractee Gilbert for the assignment.

In reality, Queen Christina of Sweden was a short, ugly, mannish monarch who enjoyed smutty stories and slept with her lady-in-waiting. Legend had it that the Queen abdicated her throne rather than have to undergo the ignominy of a wedding. Whatever the actuality of this unique ruler, the Hays production code office certainly would not permit the delineation of *such* a royal figure on the screen at this time. Therefore the only remaining overt perversion left in the idealized film character is the Queen's penchant for wearing leather trousers. The more knowing viewer could figure out why the Queen had a valet (C. Aubrey Smith) rather than a chambermaid, one of the odd facts about the striding on-screen Queen who washed her face in the snow, read Voltaire, who said she expected to die "not an old maid, but a bachelor," and who had taken oaths of allegiance to her country as the new *king*.

If one takes into consideration the prologue sequences in *Queen Christina* in which Cora Sue Collins parades as Christina the child, and the later riding scenes and crowd sequences which use a double for the title role, Garbo is not oncamera that much of the one hundred minutes of running time. Nevertheless when she is oncamera she dominates each frame, being forceful as the queen and charming as a woman. At the time of release, everyone commented that Garbo's performance revealed that the twenty-eight-year-old star had gained a "new gravity and maturity." It was a posture to become closely associated with the legendary Garbo of years to come.

But there was much more than seriousness to Garbo's *Queen Christina* performance. Arriving at the inn after helping Don Antonio (Gilbert) free his coach from the muddy road, she becomes involved with the tavern guests who are arguing over the number of lovers their Queen has had. Garbo, still dressed in her boyish clothes, jumps on the dining table and fires a pistol into the air. Then in a jocular, confiding tone, she says, "Well, gentlemen, I have the painful duty of telling you that you are both wrong— the sixes and the nines. The truth is the Queen has had twelve lovers this past year. A round dozen. . . . And now if you will permit me I shall stand a round of drinks for all of you. Landlord, the punch!" This is not the Garbo of old who was noted for being just a lady of tears, woes, and mystery.

Just as Garbo's revelation to Gilbert that "In my home I am very constrained" is a very telling statement of her complex screen personae, so is the famed idyll scene in which she and Gilbert are ensconced in an upper room of the inn for over two days. Noted critic C. A. Lejeune has said that this ". . . bedroom scene . . . would have stripped any other actress spiritually naked. But Garbo is still her own mistress at the end of it." It was a very difficult cinematic interlude to carry through successfully since the audience from the start, unlike Gilbert's ambassador, knows that this bold young man is really a woman and a Queen at that. Before the couple, who have become lovers, leave the now-sacred chambers, Garbo has a wonderful scene in which she drifts about the room, touching and studying each item, including the fruit on the table. When the mesmerized Gilbert asks what she is doing, she replies in her caressing, throaty voice, "I have been memorizing this room. In the future, in my memory, I shall live a great deal in this room."

The other notable sequence of the picture is the finale, as the Queen stands at the bow of the ship carrying her and her dead lover (Gilbert) to Spain. For years after its release, audiences repeatedly asked what could Garbo have been thinking about in this wonderously, devastating fragment of captured grandeur as the final closeup holds in frame her elegantly chiseled face. Director Rouben Mamoulian later explained that he had told Garbo, "I want your face to be a blank sheet of paper. I want the writing to be done by every member of the audience. I'd like it if you could avoid blinking your eyes, so that you're nothing but a beautiful mask."

When *Queen Christina* premiered at the Astor Theatre on December 26, 1933, with a two-dollar ticket tops, a hugh electric sign over the marquee proudly—and simply—announced "Garbo." It was just one indication that *Queen Christina* was her picture and hers alone. The reviewers were in accord that she had never been finer onscreen. In contrast, Gilbert was scarcely noted by the reviewers. As Thornton Delehanty (*New York Post*) stated about the picture: "Every effort is made to gear up the attachment of the Queen for the Latin emissary to an incandescent level and all that results is a series of desultory flourishes, none of which could possibly be construed as feverish." As soon as Gilbert appeared oncamera, it was immediately obvious that his past years of humiliation in the film colony had taken their toll. The thirty-six-year-old actor, overly made up for his beplumed part, was far too restrained in mannerism, as he was also noticeably nervous in his role as Garbo's consort-lover. Mordaunt Hall (*New York Times*) kindly noted "he acts very well," while Walter Ramsey (*Modern Screen* magazine) cited the picture as a "come-back" for the once great matinee idol. How times had changed!

Forty years after the release of *Queen Christina*, Warner Bros. filmed *The Abdication* with Peter Finch and co-starring Liv Ullmann as the seventeeth-century Swedish ex-monarch who journeys to Rome to convert to Catholicism. According to the new film's publicists, the crown worn by Garbo in *Queen Christina* was acquired for use by Miss Ullmann in the new venture.

## THE YEARS AFTER

It has been perhaps justifiably stated that Hollywood killed John Gilbert. The ignominy of the ludicrous *His Glorious Night* (1929) and the humiliation of being billed second below the title in *Way for a Sailor* (1930) robbed the former star of his magnificent professional confidence. With his characteristic lack of restraint, he floundered nobly in his declining Hollywood years. After Columbia's dismal *The Captain Hates the Sea* (1934), in which he was far better than the production warranted, he was professionally at liberty and took to drinking to fill his rash of vacant hours. He died of an alleged heart attack on January 9, 1936, destined to become the prime example (and laughing stock) of how talkies so easily destroyed a once lustrous career. Perhaps the detailed biography of Gilbert being written by his daughter, Leatrice Joy Gilbert, will shed new light on this Hollywood tragedy.

Meanwhile, fate and Greta Garbo would decree that she only make six additional features after *Queen Christina*. She was Oscar-nominated for *Camille* (1936) but lost to Luise Rainer of *The Good Earth*, as she lost again in 1939 when her comedy performance in *Ninotchka* was overshadowed by Vivien Leigh's emoting in *Gone with the Wind*. The ill-fated *Two-Faced Woman* (1941) drove Garbo into temporary professional exile which eventually became permanent. MGM was seemingly not very upset by the loss, for World War II had cut off the bulk of their European release market, the biggest area for Garbo's expensive but arty productions. In 1954, Hollywood belatedly recognized the greatness that is Garbo by presenting her in absentia with a special Oscar "for her unforgettable screen performances." She has remained to this day a mysterious figure, cloaked in self-styled ambiguities that shroud her personal life and the ramifications of her past, illustrious film career.

In **The First Year** (Fox, 1932)

# Chapter 3

# Charles Farrell
# &
# Janet Gaynor

## CHARLES FARRELL

6' 2"
182 pounds
Brown hair
Brown eyes
Leo

*Real name: same. Born August 9, 1902, Onset Bay, Massachusetts. Married Virginia Valli (1931). Widowed 1971.*

### FEATURE FILMS:

*The Cheat* (Par., 1923)
*Rosita* (UA, 1923)
*Wings of Youth* (Fox, 1925)
*The Love Hour* (Vitagraph, 1925)
*Clash of the Wolves* (WB, 1925)
*Sandy* (Fox, 1926)
*A Trip to Chinatown* (Fox, 1926)
*Old Ironsides* (Par., 1926)
*The Rough Riders* (Par., 1927)
*Seventh Heaven* (Fox, 1927)
*Street Angel* (Fox, 1928)
*Fazil* (Fox, 1928)
*The Red Dance* (Fox, 1928)

*The River* (Fox, 1928)
*Lucky Stars* (Fox, 1929)
*Sunny Side Up* (Fox, 1929)
*Happy Days* (Fox, 1930)
*City Girl* (Fox, 1930)
*High Society Blues* (Fox, 1930)
*Liliom* (Fox, 1930)
*The Princess and the Plumber* (Fox, 1930)
*The Man Who Came Back* (Fox, 1931)
*Body and Soul* (Fox, 1931)
*Merely Mary Ann* (Fox, 1931)
*Delicious* (Fox, 1931)

After Tomorrow (Fox, 1932)
The First Year (Fox, 1932)
Wild Girl (Fox, 1932)
Tess of the Storm Country (Fox, 1932)
Aggie Appleby, Maker of Men (RKO, 1933)
Girl Without a Room (Par., 1933)
The Big Shakedown (FN, 1934)
Change of Heart (Fox, 1934)

Fighting Youth (Univ., 1935)
Forbidden Heaven (Rep., 1936)
Falling in Love (Times, 1936)
Moonlight Sonata (British, 1937)
The Flying Doctor (Australian, 1937)
Just Around the Corner (20th, 1938)
Flight to Fame (Col., 1938)
Tail Spin (20th, 1939)
The Deadly Game (Mon., 1941)

# JANET GAYNOR

**5'**
**96 pounds**
**Auburn hair**
**Brown eyes**
**Libra**

Real name: Laura Gainor. Born October 6, 1906, Philadelphia, Pennsylvania. Married Lydell Peck (1929); divorced 1933. Married Gilbert Adrian (1939), child: Robin; widowed 1959. Married Paul Gregory (1964).

**FEATURE FILMS:**

The Johnstown Flood (Fox, 1926)
The Shamrock Handicap (Fox, 1926)
The Midnight Kiss (Fox, 1926)
The Blue Eagle (Fox, 1926)
The Return of Peter Grimm (Fox, 1926)
Seventh Heaven (Fox, 1927)
Sunrise (Fox, 1927)
Two Girls Wanted (Fox, 1927)
Street Angel (Fox, 1928)
Four Devils (Fox, 1929)
Christina (Fox, 1929)
Lucky Star (Fox, 1929)
Sunny Side Up (Fox, 1929)
Happy Days (Fox, 1930)
High Society Blues (Fox, 1930)
The Man Who Came Back (Fox, 1931)
Daddy Long Legs (Fox, 1931)
Merely Mary Ann (Fox, 1931)
Delicious (Fox, 1931)

The First Year (Fox, 1932)
Tess of the Storm Country (Fox, 1932)
State Fair (Fox, 1933)
Adorable (Fox, 1933)
Paddy, The Next Best Thing (Fox, 1933)
Carolina (Fox, 1934)
Ciudad de Carton (Cardboard City) (Fox, 1934)*
Change of Heart (Fox, 1934)
Servants' Entrance (Fox, 1934)
One More Spring (Fox, 1935)
The Farmer Takes a Wife (Fox, 1935)
Small Town Girl (MGM, 1936)
Ladies in Love (20th, 1936)
A Star Is Born (UA, 1937)
Three Loves Has Nancy (MGM, 1938)
The Young In Heart (UA, 1938)
Bernardine (20th, 1957)

*Guest Appearance

Janet Gaynor and Charles Farrell: (top) in 1929
and (bottom) 1951.

In **Seventh Heaven** (Fox, 1927)

In **Street Angel** (Fox, 1928)

In **Lucky Star** (Fox, 1929)

Sharon Lynn, Frank Richardson, El Brendel, Marjorie White; (seated) Charles Farrell, Janet Gaynor in **Sunny Side Up** (Fox, 1929)

Song sheet from **Happy Days** (Fox 1929)

In **Delicious** (Fox, 1931)

Advertisement for **The Man Who Came Back** (Fox, 1931)

In **The Man Who Came Back**

Song Sheet from **Merely Mary Ann** (Fox, 1931)

In **Merely Mary Ann**

In **Tess of the Storm Country** (Fox, 1932)

James Dunn, Janet Gaynor, and Charles Farrell in **Change of Heart** (Fox, 1934)

# SEVENTH HEAVEN
## *(Fox, 1927) 8,500'*

Presenter, William Fox; director, Frank Borzage; based on the play by
Austin Strong; screenplay, Benjamin Glazer; titlers, Katherine Hilliker,
H. H. Caldwell; song, Erno Rapee and Lew Pollack; sets, Harry Oliver;
assistant director, Lew Borzage; camera, Ernest Palmer; editors, Hilliker,
Caldwell.

Janet Gaynor (Diane); Charles Farrell (Chico); Ben Bard (Colonel
Brissac); David Butler (Gobin); Marie Mosquini (Madame Gobin); Albert
Gran (Boul); Gladys Brockwell (Nana); Emile Chautard (Pere Chevillon);
George E. Stone (Sewer Rat); Jessie Haslett (Aunt Valentine); Brandon
Hurst (Uncle George); Lillian West (Arlette).

New York Premiere: Sam H. Harris Theatre—May 25, 1927
No New York Television Showing

## Synopsis

Chico, an energetic Paris sewer worker, hoping to be promoted to the
rank of street cleaner, burns prayer candles with the belief that God will
give him the desired opportunity. He becomes angered when his prayer
for a blonde wife creates no response. Later he rescues waifish Diane,
who has been maltreated by her cruel sister, Nana. When Diane is de-
nounced to the police, Chico claims that she is his wife. He takes her to his
walk-up flat, his seventh heaven, and soon they are blissfully in love. But
then World War I breaks out and he is called into service interrupting
their marriage plans. Diane braves the war as a munitions worker. Following the Armistice she receives word that Chico is dead. However, he
returns, blinded, but still able to restore Diane's faith and love.

◆━━◆

On October 30, 1922, John Golden's production of Austin Strong's very
romantic drama, *Seventh Heaven*, opened at New York's Booth Theatre.
Both the play and its stars, Helen Menken and George Gaul, were pronounced hits, and the show ran for a mighty 704 performances. Meanwhile, Fox film mogul William Fox, anxious to improve the quality of his
studio's production output, purchased the screen rights to *Seventh Heaven*
and assigned the project to contract director Frank Borzage. To star in this
vehicle, Winfield R. Sheehan, Fox vice-president in charge of production,
selected two young, but not inexperienced, players. His protégée, twenty-
one-year-old Janet Gaynor, had already had sizeable screen parts in six
feature films, including the Friedrich W. Murnau *Sunrise* (1927), made
before but not released until after *Seventh Heaven*. Her film directors,
including Irving Cummings and John Ford, were impressed with her

striking, winsome, Irish-like charm, and *Variety* had labeled her a real find for the movies. Many people were already hinting that Gaynor might be the cinema's new Lillian Gish or Lois Moran. Twenty-five-year-old Charles Farrell had been in films since 1923's *The Cheat* and *Rosita*, and more recently had made a very favorable impression in Paramount's historical sea drama, *Old Ironsides* (1926). The well-proportioned six-foot-two-inch Farrell seemed the right physical type to enact the role of "that remarkable fellow" in tandem with the waifish, vulnerable-appearing five-foot-tall Gaynor.

By 1970s standards, *Seventh Heaven* may seem to many filmgoers an example of mawkish slop, laughable in its contrived plotline which anxiously baits the susceptible viewer into crying buckets of tears. However, the story was geared for audiences of another time, when silent films were *the* medium and most anything handled with intelligence could impress and sway the masses, because, as in the good fairy tales of childhood, if one believed enough, anything was possible. And unlike today's more cynical, knowing moviegoing public, filmgoers of the roaring 1920s wanted to make each visit to the cinema palace a rewarding sojourn into fantasyland. In that simpler era, vicarious enjoyment of the range of human emotion was an ordinary experience to be unabashedly enjoyed by the spectrum of society. For such an audience, *Seventh Heaven* was tender, poetic, tragic, and filled with grandly human qualities.

Even today Paris as a city holds quixotic appeal for movie audiences, a place where romance is supposed to abound and the improbable is said to be more likely possible. Thus the film's setting was a perfect backdrop for the highly emotional attachment between Farrell's robust sewer cleaner, Chico, and Gaynor's abused, tattered Diane. With no pun intended, Farrell's character was clearly an easy-going man of the street, full of ordinary desires and aspirations, a braggart soon to be elevated to the ranks of romantic hero by his encounter with Gaynor. She, in turn, was a girl struggling to survive in the helter skelter days of pre-World War I France when the poor were poorer and the mistreated more mistreated.

Thus, when Farrell rescues Gaynor from the abuses of her absinthe-crazed harridan of a sister (Gladys Brockwell) and later saves her from police arrest by gallantly insisting that the defenseless lass is his wife, he takes on new dimensions as does Gaynor. For many of those viewers who have enjoyed *Seventh Heaven*, either on initial release, national reissue, or art house showings, the most precious moment within the film occurs when clumsy Farrell volunteers to take the susceptible Gaynor back to his flat, not for amorous byplay but just for shelter (a fact quickly accepted by 1920s filmgoers in an era when moral standards were far more severe and unflexible). Their surrealistic climb up the flights of stairs, floor by floor, might seem an exhausting journey for the practical-minded, but for the romantically inclined it represented a trip into heavenly fantasy, as the couple slowly climb away from the cares of the world into their own special retreat, their own patch of Paris within a sight of the Eiffel Tower. At first, Farrell pities his guest, but then, as her appreciation grows to devotion and develops into love, he becomes annoyed and depressed by the responsibility, intuitively realizing it will severely limit his impromptu way of life. However, love then asserts itself within his soul and he too shares the bliss that has sustained Gaynor since they first met. The couple's romantic fervor is echoed in the synchronized sound track theme song used for this essentially silent film.

Joe Franklin and William K. Everson in *Classics of the Silent Screen* (1959) say of *Seventh Heaven*, "Its story is maudlin, lugubrious and dishonestly sentimental. Every trick in the book is tried, rearranged, and tried again, to squeeze the last tear out of the spectator . . . . [It] is something of a rosy-hued *Broken Blossoms*—with a happy ending, of course, despite all signs to the contrary." This evaluation may be gratuitous regarding the first portion of *Seventh Heaven* but it certainly holds true about the film's final reels. Just as the couple are about to marry, he is called off to war. She pines for four years on the homefront, working in a defense factory, of course, while he braves the dangers of the front lines (the distracting battle front scenes destroy much of the story's previous intimacy). Gaynor's Diane receives word that her Chico is dead. Suddenly her little seventh heaven holds no more meaning. Her dreams are shattered and her faith in God is broken. But then, as if by a miracle, her loved one returns. To make the reunion more heart rending, he is blind (but the viewer knows Farrell's Chico carries a mental picture of Gaynor in his mind's eye for eternity). Now she will have to care for him as he once did for her. And so these storybook lovers lived happily ever after . . . . or so the viewer was led to believe by the film.

To state it mildly, *Seventh Heaven* was a commercial (and artistic) sensation. *Photoplay* magazine acknowledged, "It is permeated with the spirit of youth, of young love, of whimsy." As for the film's two leads, *Photoplay* enthused, "They are twin joys, those kids, their work entirely unmarred by studied technique. And this picture should plant them firmly near the top of the picture world." *The New York Times* was less effusive but equally enthusiastic, with Mordaunt Hall complimenting Gaynor for being "true and natural throughout. Never once does she falter in her difficult task of reflecting the emotions of the character she portrays. . . . She is winsome from the moment one beholds her countenance. She can cry and smile simultaneously and she impresses one by her depiction of faith." As for Farrell's screen work, Hall added, "Sometimes he may seem to be a little too swaggering, but what of it? The actions suit the young man's agreeable bombast." Alfred B. Kuttner in the *National Board of Review* magazine perhaps best summed up the critical opinion: "Janet Gaynor as Diane and Charles Farrell as Chico played directly in terms of the screen. They made the shameless, frank appeal of youth and beauty which dissolves the strictures of the old in warm memories and evokes the helpless rapture of the young. They were graceful with the grace of beautiful animals. This Chico was shy as a young man might be shy, and Diane's shyness was a trembling sweet thing to see. Neither of them acted shyness."

In the first annual Academy Awards, *Seventh Heaven* was well represented. While the film lost out as Best Picture of the year *(Wings* won), Gaynor, on the basis of her performances in *Seventh Heaven, Sunrise,* and *Street Angel* (also with Farrell) was named Best Actress. Borzage was voted the Best Director, and Benjamin Glazer won an Oscar for the Best Screen Adaptation.

Over the years the legend surrounding the wondrousness of *Seventh Heaven* would grow, with the film always referred to as a landmark of cinema romanticism. Fox tried to duplicate the success of the 1927 film by remaking the story in 1937 with James Stewart and Simon Simone in the Farrell-Gaynor roles. But times and tastes had vastly changed, and the new rendition was quickly forgotten as was an unpopular 1950s Broadway musical rendition of the story.

## STREET ANGEL
### *(Fox, 1928) 9,221'*

Presenter, William Fox; director, Frank Borzage; based on the novel *Cristilinda* by Monckton Hoffe; adaptation, Philip Klein, Henry Roberts Symonds; screenplay, Marion Orth; titlers, Katherine Hilliker, H. H. Caldwell; assistant director, Lew Borzage; camera, Ernest Palmer; editor, Barney Wolf.

Janet Gaynor (Angela); Charles Farrell (Gino); Alberto Rabagliati, Gino Conti (Policemen); Guido Trento (Neri the Police Sergeant); Henry Armetta (Mascetto); Louis Liggett (Beppo); Milton Dickinson (Bimbo); Helena Herman (Andrea); Natalie Kingston (Lisetta); David Kashner (The Strong Man); Jennie Bruno (Landlady).

New York Premiere: Globe Theatre—April 9, 1928
No New York Television Showing

### Synopsis

A poor Neapolitan girl, Angela, desperate to purchase medication needed for her sick mother, becomes a girl of the street. However, after coming into conflict with the local police, she flees and takes refuge with a traveling circus. She meets Gino, a struggling painter, who asks her to pose for a Madonna portrait. But the authorities find her and she is forced to serve a jail term, while Gino, who has grown to love her, becomes despondent and fast loses interest in his art work. Released from prison,

Angela notices her portrait in a church and later, she encounters Gino. She manages to convince him that despite her unsavory past, she is still worthy of having posed as the Madonna, and the couple are reunited.

◆ ◆ ◆

With the resounding boxoffice receipts on *Seventh Heaven*, it was natural that Fox would renegotiate contracts with the two leads of that film and star them in another project, also directed by Frank Borzage. The advertisements for the new film happily proclaimed, "Let *Street Angel* Transport You to the Seventh Heaven of Delight."

Using Monckton Hoffe's 1926 novel *Cristilinda* as a basis for *Street Angel*, the screen's new love team (who for many had surpassed the more rarefied cinema pairing of Greta Garbo and John Gilbert or the Ruritanian escapading of Ronald Colman and Vilma Banky) had a dramatic situation contrasting with their first film. For here, it is Charles Farrell's Gino who is the more idealistic, vulnerable soul, the budding painter who is inspired to great art work by his love for the radiant, resilient Janet Gaynor, cast as Angela. He is unaware of her seamy past, nor is he cognizant that she has sacrificed her purity to save her mother's life, or that she had escaped being sent to a workhouse by running away. He is only aware of his love for her and the seeming fact that she adores him. She looks so like a Madonna to Farrell's Gino that he insists he must paint her for all the world to see and cherish.

Once again, Farrell's screen character is a simple man, a bit more cultured in this outing, but still clumsy and certainly not a businessman. This fine specimen of manhood basks in the simple joys of life and exudes his own brand of gallantry. Having sold his treasured painting of Gaynor, not caring that the buyer plans to transform the work of art into an "Old Master" for resale, Farrell's Gino is overjoyed when he is next hired to prepare the mural decorations for a stately church. With the money advanced on the project he purchases baskets of food, wine, and fruit, and in a state of ecstasy, returns to the lodgings where he and Gaynor have separate sleeping quarters. Once again, as in *Seventh Heaven*, fate has decided to separate them. The police have trailed Gaynor and she is to be taken away to jail. She convinces the law to allow her one last hour with Farrell. She is distraught. How can she destroy his illusions about her purity? He misinterprets her tears of sadness as tears of joy for his good fortune. Then she announces she must depart. He whistles a few bars of "O Sole Mio" (this film gave token nod to the new trend of talking pictures by using a musical score, sound effects, and a few talking sequences). As she is being led away to the workhouse, she nervously whistles the same tune.

One of the outstanding assets of *Street Angel* was the carefully composed cinematography of Ernest Palmer, who had worked on *Seventh Heaven*. *The New York Times'* Mordaunt Hall acknowledged, "Never has the camera been used quite so effectively and artistically as it is in this subject, for in the background of the sombre side of Naples there are the compelling shadows, the inspired old arches, the slender iron railings over the footworn steps and, in many of the scenes, there hangs a soft mist through which the characters sometimes fade gradually from view."

In the easygoing days of the silent cinema it was possible for movie players to be all things to many people. Thus Gaynor and Farrell, who were basically as American as apple pie, could be convincingly Gallic in *Seventh Heaven* and seemingly very Italian in *Street Angel*. Once again the team clicked at the boxoffice. "These two kids strike a fresh, new note on the screen" stated *Photoplay* magazine which referred to the players as "those babes in the wood." "The charm of Janet Gaynor lingers like the fragrance of a rose" *(New York American)*. "When all is said and done Charles Farrell is a very remarkable fellow" *(Los Angeles Herald)*.


## LUCKY STAR
### *(Fox, 1929) 8,784′*

Presenter, William Fox; director, Frank Borzage; based on the story *Three Episodes in the Life of Timothy Osborn* by Tristram Tupper; screenplay, Sonya Levien; dialog, John Hunter Booth; titlers, Katherine Hilliker, H. H. Caldwell; assistant director, Lew Borzage; art director, Harry Oliver; sound, Joseph Aiken; camera, Chester Lyons, William Cooper Smith; editor, Hilliker, Caldwell.

Janet Gaynor (Mary Tucker); Charles Farrell (Timothy Osborn); Guinn Williams (Martin Wrenn); Paul Fix (Joe); Hedwiga Reicher (Mrs. Tucker); Gloria Grey (Milly); Hector V. Sarno (Pop Fry).

New York Premiere: Roxy Theatre—July 21, 1929
No New York Television Showing

### Synopsis

Mary Tucker leads a luckless existence as a drudge on the rundown farm of her impoverished mother, a widow who wants her children to enjoy a better life than hers. When the local village men return after the Armistice, Mrs. Tucker intends that Mary should wed Martin Wrenn, an ex-sergeant who has returned to his pre-war job as a power linesman. However, Mary's heart belongs to Timothy Osborn, a former linesman who now must do menial jobs because he was crippled in the war. Just as Mrs. Tucker is about to give Mary to Wrenn in marriage, Timothy somehow regains his strength, thrashes Wrenn, and claims Mary for his bride.

◆—◆—◆

The studio was experiencing a winning streak with the triumvirate of Janet Gaynor, Charles Farrell, and director Frank Borzage. Therefore, it propelled them into a new project, *Lucky Star*, based on a 1927 *Saturday Evening Post* story. As *The New York Times'* Mordaunt Hall reported, "Once more they have begun with an ordinary story and by good acting and exceptional direction have brought from it an unusual picture."

The big novelty of *Lucky Star* for Gaynor-Farrell fans was that their screen idols had full talking sequences within this film. At last the idealized lovers of *Seventh Heaven* were speaking onscreen to their public! Fortunately for this movie star pair, their natural speaking voices were in accord with the type of cinema yarns that had become their exclusive province: proletarian romance. Hall, of the *Times*, was neither thrilled nor offended by the players' particular vocal equipment, "Mr. Farrell's voice has a twang to it; Miss Gaynor's seems that of a very young girl." While this was no real endorsement, conversely it was no slap. Since most moviegoers of that day were still unaware of what good diction and modulation on the screen should be, Gaynor and Farrell could pass muster in their public speaking test. (Those moviegoers living in the smaller towns where local theatres were not yet wired for sound would have to wait for a later date to hear the stars actually talk oncamera.)

Of the Gaynor-Farrell films to date, *Lucky Star* had the most preposterous storyline. The scenario asked viewers to accept the adage that love can conquer all, and that this love would give paralyzed Farrell the strength to crawl over the hill to Gaynor's farm and then the energy to lick the equally big-framed Guinn Williams. What gave *Lucky Star* its charm, above and beyond the established screen chemistry of the unsophisticated screen lovers, was the bucolic flavor of the tale, ranging from the rundown farm of Mrs. Tucker (Hedwiga Reicher) to Farrell's simple abode, and including the gossipy townsfolk who twitter with mixed excitement-disapproval that Williams has returned from the war "still wearing his uniform." Above and beyond Farrell's climactic physical regeneration scene, *Lucky Star* craftily engineers the viewer's sympathy by presenting Gaynor as the most infectiously delightful of rural slaveys. She does the farm chores for her shrewish but loving mother, while daydreaming of that unspecified happiness that must lie ahead for her somewhere. She intuitively knows there must be something better ahead for a girl who has never known real love or happiness.

Thus, the plot situation of *Lucky Star* convinces the viewer that the Gaynor-Farrell romance must be made in heaven and just has to be. So she is drawn to renewing her acquaintance with war veteran Farrell, who is now pictured as a pathetic cripple who spends his immobilized days mending items in order to eke out a meagre living. One day she comes to his lonely and desolate house, determined to speak to him again (they had quarreled the day he left for overseas). She picks up a stone and hurls it through the window, and soon they are picking up the threads of their relationship, which grows from friendship to love.

Interestingly enough, there are no ghastly villains in this piece. Reicher's Mrs. Tucker has led a tough life and her hard experiences apparently have drained all compassion from her soul. Nevertheless, in her own inarticulate way, she deeply cares for her family and thinks that she is doing right by Gaynor in pushing her into a marriage with the bragging but able-bodied and well-employed Williams. And Williams is certainly not the moustache-twirling culprit of the old melodramas. He is, rather, a swaggering, blustering, simple soul who rejoices in his own good health and fortune, without caring that others are less fortunate. He simply wants what he wants.

In the early portions of *Lucky Star* there are several scenes on the power line poles in which Farrell and Williams, rivals in both work and love, clash in their manly way in a very similar manner to the George Raft-Edward G. Robinson conflict in the later *Manpower* (1941).

## SUNNY SIDE UP
### *(Fox, 1929) 80M.*

Presenter, William Fox; director, David Butler; story-dialog, Buddy DeSylva, Ray Henderson, Lew Brown; adaptation, Butler; songs, DeSylva, Brown, and Henderson; choreography, Seymour Felix; costumes, Sophie Wachner; assistant director, Ad Schaumer; music directors, Howard Jackson, Arthur Kay; art director, Harry Oliver; sound, Joseph Aiken; camera, Ernest Palmer, John Schmitz; editor, Irene Morra.

Janet Gaynor (Molly Carr); Charles Farrell (Jack Cromwell); El Brendel (Eric Swenson); Marjorie White (Bee Nichols); Frank Richardson (Eddie Rafferty); Sharon Lynn (Jane Worth); Mary Forbes (Mrs. Cromwell); Joe Brown (Joe Vitto); Alan Paull (Raoul); Peter Gawthorne (Lake); Jackie Cooper (Tenement Boy).

New York Premiere: Gaiety Theatre—October 3, 1929
No New York Television Showing

### Synopsis

Young society man Jack Cromwell is spending his summer at the fashionable Long Island resort of Southampton, while, in contrast, department store worker Molly Carr lives in an Lower East Side tenement. Each is content, until one day Jack meets Mary, and she is provided with the opportunity to sample the rich life. Mrs. Cromwell disapproves of Mary, even though the girl has done her best to disguise her improverished background by having her pals Bee Nichols, Eddie Rafferty, and Eric Swenson act as maid, chauffeur, and valet to her. For a time it seems that Jack is so agog over his mercenary upper-crust flapper girl friend, Jane Worth, that there is no hope for Mary. But eventually, after the Cromwell's big charity show, Jack comes to his senses and is reunited with the forgiving Mary.

77

With the trend of movie musicals fully established, it was only natural to star Janet Gaynor and Charles Farrell in an all-talking, all-singing, and some-dancing cinema outing. To concoct the vehicle, Fox used its ace writing-composing Tin Pan Alley trio of Buddy DeSylva, Ray Henderson, and Lew Brown [who would be subjects of their own musical movie biography, *The Best Things in Life Are Free* (1956)]. In contrast to the previous Gaynor-Farrell pictures, *Sunny Side Up* was a very contemporary story set in the thriving metropolis of New York, with Farrell cast in a new cinema guise as a scion of the Four Hundred. *Photoplay* magazine prosaically summed up the film by saying, "Something new for Janet and Charles, after their royal line of sobby little love stories. But they came through like good troupers, and you'll care for the results."

While the Gaynor-Farrell silent films had showcased the two stars to equal advantage, Gaynor would fare much better in talking movies, being more adaptable to the requirements of more realistic emotion and better capable of verbalizing her visual image. In *Sunny Side Up*, Gaynor's Molly Carr is one of those delightful working girls, much in the manner of the more vivacious Marion Davies. Gaynor's shopgirl may live in a dreary walk-up flat, suffocate in the summer's heat, and find her greatest diversion in sitting on the building stoop and chatting with her neighbors and pals, but she is a spunky lass who has enough energy at the end of her department store workday to be a lively companion to her friends, Marjorie White, El Brendel, and Frank Richardson.

Soon Gaynor is launched into her first production number, performed for the neighborhood during the Fourth of July block party. Gaynor has prepared a soft shoe-song number entitled, unsurprisingly, "Sunny Side Up," the title referring to cheerfulness in spite of the Depression and not any style of fried eggs. With a borrowed top hat and cane, Gaynor presents a fine figure of a trim Irish colleen. Her voice is deep, but light, in quality and a bit nasal. Her time stepping is inexpert; however, she has vivacity and bounce with a glitter of happiness in her eyes.

In contrast, Farrell's Jack Cromwell is the stereotype of the racquet-swinging, ukulele-strumming blue blood who devotes his days to the swimming pool, his evenings to the veranda cocktail hour, and his nights to escorting in his shiny new roadster vapid young society girls to the local country club dance. While it was a limp one-dimensional, gutless characterization to have to play, Farrell's weak interpretation of the part displayed more energy than conviction.

In the course of *Sunny Side Up* each star has his/her particular theme song, Gaynor refraining "I'm a Dreamer, Aren't We All" on several occasions, and Farrell having his vocal moments with "If I Had A Talking Picture of You." During one rendering of this song, Farrell is seated at a piano with Gaynor's radiant face superimposed on the sheet music. The musical highlight of *Sunny Side Up* occurs during the midst of the inevitable encounter between the unswerving ritzy set and the accommodating *hoi polloi*. Gaynor's Molly, decked out in a becoming wardrobe and supported by her pals as bogus domestics, is ill at ease in the swank surroundings of a Long Island estate where the lowliest butler has more breeding and a bigger bank accout than she. But during the charity show, she comes to life, for performing for the public is something she can handle, even if her personal life has fallen to tatters (Farrell is being very inattentive since he is being swayed by his society friends to stick to his own class). There occurs one of the cinema's most grotesque but crudely captivating production numbers, staged by Seymour Felix in the best pre-Busby Berkeley tradition. "Turn on the Heat" would be considered high camp today, but in its time the number was received by a willing public as imaginative entertainment. The stage for this outdoor extravaganza number is separated from the oncamera audience by the swimming pool moat, giving the production gymnastics its own isolated, special, unreal look. Within the elaborate routine, the society chorines emerge from igloos, the fake snow soon melts, and, in its place, tropical plants and palm trees shoot up, during which time the girls undulate to the changing native beat. The song closes with tongues of flames darting up on the "island" and the chorus plunging into the pool.

Among the rash of 1929 movie musicals, *Sunny Side Up* fared well. The august publication *Cinema* stated, "*Sunny Side Up* and *The Love Parade* [with Maurice Chevalier and Jeanette MacDonald], each in its special way, are among the year's leaders in finding out how sound and action can combine on the screen in a special form of its own." It should be noted that director David Butler chose to emphasize the plot of this Fox musical, sacrificing the potential romantic mood for a semblance of pace, Within the genre's artifices, this balance worked sufficiently well, but it is still interesting to conjecture how Frank Borzage of *Seventh Heaven*, etc. would have handled the film and the cinema team.

The full range of vocal display by Gaynor and Farrell in *Sunny Side Up* led Mordaunt Hall in *The New York Times* to offer a complete account of his reaction to the event. "Miss Gaynor's voice may not be especially clear, but the sincerity with which she renders at least two of her songs is most appealing. Her performance is as fine as anything she has done on the screen. So far as her singing is concerned, she is not supposed to be any prima donna. . . . Mr. Farrell's singing is possibly just what one might expect from the average young man taking a chance on singing a song at a private entertainment. His presence is, however, ingratiating and his acting and talking are natural. He may not strike one as an experienced stage actor, but his speeches and even his singing suits the part."

## HAPPY DAYS
### (Fox, 1929) 80M.

Presenter, William Fox; director, Benjamin Stoloff; stager, Walter Catlett; dialog, Edwin Burke; story, Sidney Lanfield; art director, Jack Schulze; songs, Con Conrad, Sidney Mitchell, Archie Gottler; L. Wolfe Gilbert and Abel Baer; James Hanley and James Brockman; Joseph McCarthy and James Hanley; Harry Stoddard and Marcy Klauber; choreography, Earl Lindsay; assistant director, Ad Schaumer, Michael Farley, Lou Breslow; costumes, Sophie Wachner; camera, Lucien Androit, John Schmitz; Grandeur camera, J. O. Taylor; editor, Clyde Carruth.

Charles E. Evans (Colonel Billy Batcher); Marjorie White (Margie); Richard Keene (Dick); Stuart Erwin (Jig); Martha Lee Sparks (Nancy Lee); Clifford Dempsey (Sheriff Benton); James J. Corbett, George MacFarlane (Interlocutors); Janet Gaynor, Charles Farrell, Victor McLaglen, El Brendel, William Collier, Sr., Tom Patricola, George Jessel, Dixie Lee, Nick Stuart, Rex Bell, Frank Albertson, Sharon Lynn, Whispering Jack Smith, Lew Brice, J. Farrell MacDonald, Will Rogers, Edmund Lowe, Walter Catlett, Frank Richardson, Ann Pennington, David Rollins, Warner Baxter, J. Harold Murray, Paul Page, The Slate Brothers, Flo Bert, George Olsen and Orchestra (Principals); Helen Mann, Mary Lansing, Beverly Royed, Joan Navarro, Catherine Navarro, John Christensen, Dorothy McNames, Vee Maule, Hazel Sperling, Bo Peep Karlin, Georgia Pembleton, Marbeth Wright, Miriam Hellman, Margaret La Marr, Consuelo De Los Angeles, Lee Auburn, Betty Halsey, Joyce Lorme, Myra Mason, Eileen Bannon, Theresa Allen, Pear La Velle, Barbara La Velle, Gertrude Friedly, Dorothy Krister, Doris Baker, Melissa Ten Eyck, Kay Gordon, Betty Gordon, Jean De Parva, Joan Gaylord, Charlotte Hamill, Alice Goodsell, Gwen Keate, Virginia Joyce, LaVerne Leonard, Betty Grable, Marjorie Levoe, Pat Hanne, Estella Essex (Chorus Women); Jack Frost, John Westerfelt, Douglas Steade, Peter Custulovich, John Lockhart, Randall Reynolds, Carter Sexton, Leo Hanley, George Scheller, Kenneth Nordyke, Marius Langan, Ralph Demaree, Glen Alden, Frank McKee, Bob McKee, Joe Holland, Ed Rockwell, Clarence Brown, Jr., Roy Rockwood, Enrico Cuccinelli, Harry Lauder, Ted Waters, Thomas Vartian, J. Harold Reeves, Phil Kolar, Frank Heller, William Hargraves, Ted Smith (Chorus Men).

New York Premiere: Roxy Theatre—February 13, 1930
No New York Television Showing

## Synopsis

Margie, a soubrette on Colonel Billy Batcher's Mississippi riverboat, longs for the bright lights of New York City. She is even willing to forego the love of Dick, the Colonel's handsome grandson. When the showboat is in imminent danger of bankruptcy, Margie puts her personal ambitions aside, and goes to the city to request various star troupers, who had all served their apprentice years under the Colonel, to come to his rescue. The stars agree to stage a benefit in Memphis. The show is a big success and Margie is reunited with Dick.

Fox Films had already entered the big musical revue talking film sweepstakes with its *Fox Movietone Follies of 1929* and *Fox Movietone Follies of 1930*. To insure that its new musical revue would spark the public's interest in the already waning genre, the studio filmed the picture in its new wide screen process. Such Grandeur required a forty-two by twenty foot screen for proper viewing. (Grandeur foreshadowed the studio's "innovating" CinemaScope process, adopted some twenty-three years later.) The stunt worked. "*Happy Days* may not be exciting, but through the medium of its presentation it affords a really good and impressive entertainment" [Mordaunt Hall *(New York Times)*].

Admittedly the plot to *Happy Days* was slight, and, although vivacious Marjorie White was the ingenue lead, the film was so over-loaded with guest appearances by studio stars that she was nearly lost in the soft shoe shuffle. Because the "big show" within the movie took place in a Memphis riverboat setting, it was natural to use a minstrel show foundation, with no less than James J. Corbett and George MacFarlane as the interlocutors. The name acts included George Jessel, ex-Ziegfeld Follies stars Will Rogers and Ann Pennington, the Slate Brothers, and those *What Price Glory* co-stars, Edmund Lowe and Victor McLaglen, the latter in a talk song recitation.

What of Fox's highly exploitable love team, Janet Gaynor and Charles Farrell? They were briefly, but adequately, featured in a cutesey song interlude. Dressed as babies they chanted the melody to the James Hanley-James Brockman tune, "We'll Build a Little World of Our Own," while they constructed their own minature abode.

## HIGH SOCIETY BLUES
### *(Fox, 1930) 102M.*

Presenter, William Fox; associate producer, Al Rockett; director, David Butler; based on the story *Those High Society Blues* by Dana Burnett; adaptation-dialog, Howard J. Green; assistant director, Ad Schaumer; costumes, Sophie Wachner; songs, Joseph McCarthy and James Hanley; sound Joseph E. Aiken; camera, Charles Van Enger; editor, Irene Morra.

Janet Gaynor (Eleanor Divine); Charles Farrell (Eddie Granger); William Collier, Sr. (Horace Divine); Hedda Hopper (Mrs. Divine); Joyce Compton (Pearl Granger); Lucien Littlefield (Eli Granger); Louise Fazenda (Mrs. Granger); Brandon Hurst (Jowles); Gregory Gaye (Count Prunier).

New York Premiere: Roxy Theatre—April 18, 1930
No New York Television Showing

## Synopsis

When Eli Granger sells his thriving Iowa business to Horace Divine, he moves his family to the wealthy suburb of Scarsdale, New York. He happens to purchase a home just across the street from the Divines. Although the Divines snub their *nouveaux riche* neighbors, the two children, Eleanor and Eddie become good friends, and he teaches her to play the ukelele. Mrs. Divine has already planned that Eleanor should wed Count Prunier, but the daughter has fallen in love with Eddie. Meanwhile Mr. Divine and Mr. Granger have embarked on conflicting business manipulations on Wall Street, adding business rivalry to their already established social enmity. However, when Eleanor and Eddie elope, their union sets the stage for the two families to become reconciled.

◆◆◆

According to the Fox publicity department, "Janet Gaynor and Charles Farrell have a surprise for even their most faithful admirers in this tender musical romance bubbling with carefree youth, fun, and melody, and seasoned with the matchless wit of William Collier, Sr., king of high comedy." However, there was little real novelty to this entry, based on a 1925 *Saturday Evening Post* story, which bore too striking a resemblance to that stage-film winner, *Abie's Irish Rose*, which, in turn, owed a good deal of its structural premise to William Shakespeare's *Romeo and Juliet*. In fact, reported Mordaunt Hall *(New York Times)*, "High Society Blues is scarcely an intelligent affair, The lines and actions allotted to Miss Gaynor and Mr. Farrell seem often suited to persons about half their age." As for the stars' performances, the *Times* proclaimed Gaynor "a clever little actress, whose singing might be better. Mr. Farrell is bolder in his speech than in previous films. His singing is much like Miss Gaynor's, amateurish, and perhaps suited to the character he acts." On the other hand, *Variety*, always more prone to favor its advertisers' products, was more generous in its appraisal, "The elfin Janet Gaynor is at her best in young romance, playing here with a faint suggestion of wistfulness that is inexpressibly telling. Young Farrell [he was then twenty-eight years old] achieves a capital effect as a rather awkward swain with a sensitive funny bone. Two charming young figures here in a picture that will add something to their gallery of screen portraits."

In *High Society Blues*, also directed by David Butler, it was decided that for a change Gaynor should be the rich one, and Farrell, the proletarian American. Neither was particularly at ease in his/her new pose, leaving most of the amusing interplay for the likes of Collier, Sr. and elegantly snobbish Hedda Hopper in tandem with the hick charm of those delightful rubes, Louise Fazenda and Lucien Littlefield. The humor, as such, was rather basic, and geared to demonstrate that, while the social classes may not mix, love eventually conquers all.

One scene has Farrell and his family, newly arrived in the East and just settled into their new abode, deciding to be neighborly and paying a call on Gaynor's aristocratic family. So, the quartet (including Joyce Compton as Farrell's sister) saunter into Gaynor's mansion, unmindful that they are interrupting a swank evening bridge party. They proceed to make themselves at home in the best rural tradition, much to the dismay of their unwilling hosts. Later, when Farrell is in rivalry with snooty Gregory Gaye for Gaynor's hand in marriage, Farrell resorts to some good old-fashioned American inventiveness in order to rid himself of the foreigner. In the midst of giving the Count a ukulele lesson (everyone was learning the charms of this musical instrument in *High Society Blues*), Farrell sees to it that the Frenchman's thirst is quenched with a hearty dose of liquor, sufficient to make him drunk and unable to attend his own wedding, thus paving the way for Farrell to elope with Gaynor. (Just to make sure that everything ends happily ever after for everyone, Gaye later takes a solid interest in Compton.)

Because *High Society Blues* was deemed a "musical," there just had to be interpolated song interludes. Thus, there were "I'm in the Market for You" and "Just Like in a Storybook," with Gaynor and Farrell accompanying themselves on the ukulele.

Gaynor herself would be so dissatisfied with *High Society Blues*, she being the more prestigious and vocal of the acting team, that she not only refused to do further screen musicals, but packed up and went to Hawaii for a long vacation with her mother. While Gaynor was away pouting, Fox offered her the co-starring lead with Farrell in *Liliom* (1930), but she refused and Rose Hobart was substituted. That same year Farrell would also co-star with Maureen O'Sullivan in *The Princess and the Plumber*.

### THE MAN WHO CAME BACK
#### (Fox, 1931) 74M.

Presenter, William Fox; director, Raoul Walsh; based on the story and novel by John Fleming Wilson and the play by Jules Eckert Goodman; screenplay, Edwin J. Burke; scenic designer, Joseph Urban; sound, George Leverett; camera, Arthur Edeson; editor, Harold Schuster.

Janet Gaynor (Angie); Charles Farrell (Stephen Randolph); Kenneth MacKenna (Captain Trevelyan); William Holden (Thomas Randolph); Mary Forbes (Mrs. Gaynes); Ulrich Haupt (Charles Reialing); William Worthington (Captain Gallon); Peter Gawthorne (Griggs); Leslie Fenton (Baron le Duc).

New York Premiere: Roxy Theatre—January 2, 1931
No New York Television Showing

#### Synopsis

Stephen Randolph, of a very wealthy New York family, leads a wild and reckless life. His father, Thomas Randolph, orders him to go to California to find work and make good in life. But instead, Stephen squanders his money and spends most of his time in San Francisco drinking. He does encounter a young entertainer, Angie, with whom he falls in love as she does with him. Later, however, his father has the wastrel waylaid and shipped to Shanghai. Once there and on his own, he happens to wander into an opium den where he is aghast to discover Angie, now a drug-addicted floozy. She explains that when he had disappeared so suddenly she thought he had deserted her, and thereafter she no longer cared what happened to her. He relates the true facts and the couple decide to wed, determined to shed their vices. They move to Honolulu where they establish themselves in a hard-working way of life. After a successful year, Stephen returns to the States to visit his father and make amends. At the end of his six month visit he is anxious to return to Angie. Mr. Randolph speaks of Angie in a depreciatory manner which causes great resentment in Stephen. But he soon discovers that his father was jesting and had already brought her to the Randolph home, thus happily reuniting the couple.

◆━◆━◆

After the relatively unsuccessful *High Society Blues* and Gaynor's revolt, the studio decided to star the love team (her fifth film in a row with Charles Farrell) in a more solid, dramatic screen vehicle. The property was Jules Eckhert Goodman's 1916 play version of John Fleming Wilson's earlier story and novel, *The Man Who Came Back*. The drama, starring Mary Nash and Henry Hull had enjoyed a 480-performance run on Broadway, and was later transferred into a 1924 Fox film starring George O'Brien and Dorothy Mackaill. Thus, the tale was a proven commodity.

From the tenor of the film's publicity, the viewer knew he was in for a hardy dose of melodrama. "Step by step, shoulder to shoulder, they fought their way back from the very gutter of civilization to the highroad of society and decency." But the average filmgoer could have predicted what such a stern drama starring the known quantities as Gaynor and Farrell would become in the end result. The studio and the stars had tried for a lyric effect but had missed such an effect with this overwrought drama directed by Raoul Walsh. "Sophisticates will give it one big horse laugh. At moments it touches *7th Heaven's* romance, but only at moments" *(Photoplay* magazine).

Even by 1931 standards *The Man Who Came Back* was unmitigated rot, more incredible than tolerable. The Depression had caused filmgoers to be sounder in their choice of escapist entertainment, and the overabundance of coincidence and allegedly soul–tearing drama was too much for any sensible moviegoer to endure as satisfactory filmfare. The photoplay was as variant in its switching of moods as it was in altering its locales which changed from New York to San Francisco to Shanghai to Honolulu and then back to New York. To make matters worse, for a good deal of the picture Farrell's so-called hero was not very admirable, being a well-bred souse who passes bad checks and flirts with the girls, only to lose his chance at happiness with cafe performer Gaynor when he is shanghaied to China.

Filmgoers still nostalgically recalled the beauty of the Gaynor-Farrell oncamera romancing in *Seventh Heaven* and *Street Angel*. In *The Man Who Came Back* the scenario all but obliterated these fond memories. Viewers had to endure the outrageous sight of unshaven drunk Farrell stumbling into a Shanghai den of iniquity and encountering bleary–eyed, dope addicted Gaynor. Talk of contra-typecasting!

One of the other damaging elements of the film was its contrived torrents of cruel fate. For example, once the couple are in Hawaii, who should appear on the scene but none other than a friend of Farrell's father, Captain Trevelyan (Kenneth MacKenna), who feigns friendship but really has designs on Gaynor. He is the dastardly soul who informs the regenerated woman that her spouse is again drinking heavily, which leads her to tell Farrell a lie that she has returned to drugs, hoping it will push him back into rehabilitation. Overwrought soap opera rears its head yet again when Farrell thereafter learns his father is desperately ill and that he is needed back in New York. The young man is forced to "choose" between family and wife. What torment! What drama! What rubbish!

## MERELY MARY ANN
### *(Fox, 1931) 72M.*

Director, Henry King; based on the play by Israel Zangwill; screenplay, Jules Furthman; incidental song, James F. Hanley; cameras, John Seitz, Arthur Arling; editor, Frank Hull.

Janet Gaynor (Mary Ann); Charles Farrell (John Lonsdale); Beryl Mercer (Mrs. Leadbatter); J. M. Kerrigan, Tom Whitely (Draymen); Lorna Balfour (Rosie Leadbatter); Arnold Lucy (Vicar Smedge); G. P. Huntley, Jr. (Peter Brooke); and Harry Rosenthal.

New York Premiere: September 13, 1931
No New York Television Showing

### Synopsis

Chargirl Mary Ann is enraptured by the musical talents of John Lonsdale, a composer who lives in the rooming house where she works. Although she loves him, he is rather rude to her, since he is unaccustomed to seeing ladies with bare hands, let alone with such hands as the raw, red ones that hard–working Mary Ann has. In time, however, John begins to take an interest in her. His unwillingness to compose popular tunes makes it difficult to earn enough to pay for his rent and other living expenses. Finally he is summoned by a great publisher. Meanwhile, Mary Ann suddenly inherits a great fortune. Now John is reluctant to wed her, because he does not want it to seem that he is marrying her for her riches. They part. One of his compositions, written for Mary Ann, is produced in London and proves a great success. Mary Ann, now very much a lady, is present at the first performance. Although he is successful, he is unhappy and goes back to the old inn where he used to meet Mary Ann. While playing at the piano and reflecting on the past and happier times Mary Ann enters the room quietly, smiling, He is overjoyed for he knows she has come to see him.

◆——◆——◆

At the height of their boxoffice power in the late 1920s, film fans speculated whether Janet Gaynor and Charles Farrell might not duplicate their oncamera romancing with an offscreen marriage. But then in 1929 Gaynor wed industry publicist Lydell Peck. While this nuptial union was not particularly touted to the press for obvious reasons, there was no holding back the news when, in 1931, Farrell wed actress Virginia Valli. This union was just another reminder to moviegoers that the celluloid passion of the two lovebirds was as synthetic as their vehicles.

With the reality of their personal lives and the diminishing returns of their recent films catching up with them, Fox deemed it wise to harness Gaynor and Farrell once more to the type of quaint, idyllic vehicle that had once won them legions of admirers. Thus *Merely Mary Ann* was dredged up and prepared for a new outing. Back in 1903 Israel Zangwill's play original had enjoyed a 148-performance Broadway run with Edwin Ardin and Eleanor Robson in the lead parts. Later it became a 1916 Fox feature about the same time a Continental rendition was directed by Hungarian Michael Curtiz.

Considering the plotline of *Merely Mary Ann, The New York Times'* Mordaunt Hall was rather benevolent when he applauded the movie for its "laudable note of restraint." If a present-day viewer can manage to ignore the plot fabrications (impecunious musician Farrell possessing such a luxurious wardrobe, the sudden million-dollar windfall to Gaynor, etc.) then he/she may find some adroit moments provided by the stars. In particular, viewers in 1931 enjoyed the sequence in which struggling artist Farrell (who comes from a well-bred background) carefully explains to attentive cleaning girl Gaynor (who survives on fifteen shillings a month) that *his* mother and sister *always* wore gloves when in the company of a man. So the next time Gaynor comes to his room to perform her daily cleaning chores, she carefully covers her scrub girl's hands with white gloves, making sure that her beloved notes her demonstration of gentility. Another good sequence occurs when draymen J. M. Kerrigan and Tom Whitely arrive to remove Farrell's piano because he is too far behind in his payments. Before fulfilling the onerous threat which has left Farrell bewildered and Gaynor in tears, Kerrigan sits down at the piano and plays a little ditty. Among the other supporting players adding whimsy, if not charm, to the movie were Beryl Mercer as a flavorful, vacillating landlady, and Arnold Lucy as a rather overblown musical comedy-style clergyman.

## DELICIOUS
### (Fox, 1931) 96M.

Director, David Butler; based on the story by Guy Bolton; screenplay, Bolton, Sonya Levien; songs, Ira and George Gershwin; camera, Ernest Palmer; editor, Irene Morra.

Janet Gaynor (Heather Gordon); Charles Farrell (Larry Beaumont); El Brendel (Jansen); Manya Roberti (Olga); Virginia Cherrill (Diana Van Bergh); Olive Tell (Mrs. Van Bergh); Lawrence O'Sullivan (Detective O'Flynn); Raul Roulien (Sascha).

New York Premiere: Roxy Theatre—December 25, 1931
No New York Television Showing

### Synopsis

Heather Gordon, a lively Scottish lass, is bound for the United States to live with her uncle. During the ocean voyage she becomes friendly with a group of Russian entertainers. One of them, Sascha, falls in love with her and composes a song for her. They both sneak up to the first-class deck to find a piano. They are discovered and are about to be ousted when Larry Beaumont, a wealthy polo-playing American, insists that they are his guests. This displeases Larry's fiancée, Diane Van Bergh. Soon Larry and Heather fall in love. When the ship docks, Heather is shocked to learn that her uncle refuses to have her live with him and as a result she must go back to Scotland. Sascha begs her to wed him so she might remain in the country, but she refuses. Instead, she escapes from the immigration authorities by hiding in the stall where Larry's horse is kept. This brings her to his home, where she is discovered by his valet Jansen, who had befriended her on the transatlantic trip. He hides Heather in the guest house, where she is later found by Larry. He is pleased to see her. Since she does not want to become a burden to him, she departs and joins her Russian friends, becoming an entertainer with their troupe. All the while she is pursued by the customs men. Finally she becomes so frantic that she agrees to wed Sascha. On the day of her marriage she learns that Larry has been injured. She rushes to his home, whereupon Diane telephones the authorities to pick up Heather. She escapes again, but eventually gives herself up and is put aboard a boat heading back to Scotland. However, Larry, having recovered, learns of her imminent departure and rushes to

87

the ship. He joins her onboard, telling her the voyage will be their honey-moon.

◆━◆━◆

After the downgrading *High Society Blues* and *The Man Who Came Back*, Fox teamed Janet Gaynor with Oscar-winning Warner Baxter in *Daddy Long Legs* (1931), and then persuaded Gaynor to try another musical with Charles Farrell. To insure that the film reached the public before any possible unfavorable reviews, the picture was rushed into 162 theatres around the country for the holiday season and then played off in deep saturation bookings at a larger number of second-run theatres.

Theatre programs for *Delicious* described the fim venture as "a screen poem, presenting a lyrical setting to the lilting refrains of George Gershwin's music." The critics did not quite agree. "Mr. Gershwin's music is eccentric and aggressive, and the film is, in its conventional sentimentality, its precise antithesis" *(London Times)*.

Marion Davies may have been *Marianne* (1929) and *The Floradora Girl* (1930), but Gaynor was equally as appealing as the ebullient Heather Gordon in this whimsical Guy Bolton story structured for the screen in partnership with Sonya Levien. The film's highlight occurs early in the story when Gaynor, in the company of her Scottish terrier, Tammy, day-dreams about her welcome to America. In her imagination, she pictures herself as "Someone from Somewhere" with Mr. Ellis and his little island greeting her. The reception committee would consist of policemen, photographers, marines, and other dignitaries waving a cheery hello, topped off by officials hanging a big key to Gotham about her neck.

With this delightful episode as evidence of her whimsical nature, Gaynor proceeds further to charm the viewer as she politely accedes to the romantic overtures of Russian Raul Roulien, joining him in a furtive trip from steerage to first class so that they may hear the song ("Delish-ious") that he has composed on the ocean voyage just for her. Later Gaynor meets Larry Beaumont (Charles Farrell). Because he has been slumming in the cargo hold in order to visit his pet pony, Pancho, she mistakes him for a groom, not realizing he is the rich and famous polo player. Thereafter *Delicious* bogs down in conventionality, distilled by the pedestrian tale of her love for upper class Farrell. Since he is engulfed by his global sports reputation and is so overwhelmed by the attentions of attractive but unworthy upper cruster Virginia Cherrill, it takes seemingly forever for Farrell to awaken to Gaynor's real worth.

Wisely, much of the focus in *Delicious* remains on Gaynor, who, later, decked out in peasant costume with painted red cheeks, joins her friends' cabaret act to perform the song number "Katinkitschka." For comic relief there is valet El Brendel who performs the novelty number, "Bla-Bla-Bla." Farrell, whose boxoffice value was diminishing, particularly now that Fox had several new leading men, such as song-and-dance lead James Dunn, found himself saddled with an especially bland role filled with trivial dialog. As the exasperatingly passive young man, it is not until near the film's final frames that he finally informs Cherrill that he never wants to see her again. Upon re-encountering the about-to-depart Gaynor, he tells her, "Night after night, I've stayed awake worrying about you. There's something terribly important I've wanted to ask you." Then, at long last, he proposes. For the sake of the film, which was a very lengthy 96 minutes, he might have said it all a lot earlier!

The New York critics were restrained in their reaction to *Delicious* and to the co-stars. "Miss Gaynor gives an appealing performance. Mr. Farrell's diction is still wanting in tonal quality" [Mordaunt Hall *(The New York Times)*]. However, the *London Times* was distressed by Gaynor's abiding oncamera mannerisms, which after so many films were overly familar to any conscientious filmgoer. ". . . her affectations are increasing at such an alarming rate that there is a real danger that in her next film she will relapse into baby-talk once and for all."

## THE FIRST YEAR
### *(Fox, 1932) 80M.*

Director, William K. Howard; based on the play by Frank Craven; screenplay, Lynn Starling; sound, Albert Protzman; camera, Hal Mohr; editor, Jack Murray.

Janet Gaynor (Grace Livingston); Charles Farrell (Tommy Tucker); Minna Gombell (Mrs. Barstow); Leila Bennett (Hattie); Dudley Digges (Dr. Anderson); Robert McWade (Fred Livingston); George Meeker (Dick Loring); Maude Eburne (Emily Livingston); Henry Kolker (Pete Barstow); Elda Vokel (Helen).

New York Premiere: Roxy Theatre—August 21, 1932
No New York Television Showing

### Synopsis

Tommy Tucker and Grace Livingston wed and move to a small country town. During the first year of marriage, Grace, who is far more ambitious than the easygoing, bashful Tommy, becomes discontented and is susceptible to the advances of her former beau, Dick Loring. Meanwhile, Tommy, who had invested their small savings in property, engineers a sale to the railroad, and to cement the deal, invites two of the principals involved, Mr. and Mrs. Barstow, home for dinner. The occasion is a social disaster. Grace leaves for her parents' home, but while she is gone, Tommy closes the deal and comes to get Grace. They are reconciled and she tells him that she is to have a baby.

◆ ◆ ◆

In studying the joint films of Janet Gaynor and Charles Farrell it

89

might appear that the star team by this point had long since diluted their drawing power, but not so. The 1932 Quigley Publication first annual poll of circuit and independent exhibitors in the United States tried to determine the leading money-making stars. This poll revealed that Gaynor placed number two and Farrell number four. It demonstrated that the veteran celluloid love pair was still more appealing to the masses, especially in rural areas, than the newer, swankier love team competition, MGM's Joan Crawford and Clark Gable (who placed number three and nine respectively in the same survey).

Fox dug deep into its old script barrel for this Gaynor-Farrell vehicle, based on Frank Craven's Broadway success of 1920 that had been a Fox film in 1926, featuring Matt Moore and Kathryn Perry. For a change the project was suitable to the stars, offering them a chance to perform gentle comedy in the country setting (the entire town was constructed on studio soundstages) that always accentuated the better qualities of the team's bucolic personalities. The critics were quick to approve. "Not since their days of silent pictures have Miss Gaynor and Mr. Farrell appeared to such advantage on the screen as they do in their current study. They have both improved greatly in their diction and they are well suited to the roles" [Mordaunt Hall *(New York Times)*]. Some viewers might have wished for more gusto in the funny scenes, but there was enough zest to the film to compensate for the draggy episodes.

*The First Year*, like Paramount's *Up Pops the Devil* (1931), has its share of romantic complications concerning the necessary adjustments a husband and wife must make during the initial years of marriage. The best moment of *The First Year* is provided by director William K. Howard midway through the film in a marvelous dining room scene that would be improved upon only in George Stevens' *Alice Adams* (1935). It is the night of the dinner party being given for very important guests (Minna Gombell and Henry Kolker) whose signature on a real estate sale holds the key to Gaynor-Farrell's financial future. Farrell is annoyed that he has to wear dress clothes, and is more upset when he discovers there is no (bootleg) gin for his guests. Gaynor's mom (Maude Eburne) is orginally scheduled to serve the elaborate dinner to the fancy guests, but when she is unable to accommodate, black girl Leila Bennett is hired to substitute, forcing pressured hostess Gaynor to take time to teach the bewildered domestic proper decorum. (All to no avail, one might add, although Bennett does come up with a bottle of synthetic gin.) At the dinner table chaos reigns. One of the cantaloupes is not fit to serve so Gaynor must pretend she is on a diet. Bennett is clumsy and soon drops the vegetable dish. Gaynor then makes a casual remark which irritates her guests. It is one of those awkward occasions which is amusing to watch if the viewer withholds any empathy for the principals.

In *The First Year*, Dudley Digges, who had so often played screen skunks, was cast as the good-natured uncle (Dr. Anderson) who brings Gaynor and Farrell together again at the finale. It was George Meeker who was cast as the scoundrel, Gaynor's past sweetheart, who drops in during the big dinner, and stays to make small talk with Gaynor and to annoy Farrell. The latter gives Meeker a sound thrashing before the final fadeout.

## TESS OF THE STORM COUNTRY
### *(Fox, 1932) 80M.*

Director, Alfred Santell; based on the novel by Grace Miller White and the drama by Rupert Hughes; screenplay, S. N. Behrman, Sonya Levien, Hughes; sound, W. D. Flick; camera, Hal Mohr.

Janet Gaynor (Tess Howland); Charles Farrell (Frederick Garfield Jr.); Dudley Digges (Captain Howland); June Clyde (Teola Garfield); George Meeker (Dan Taylor); Edward Pawley (Ben Letts); Claude Gillingwater (Frederick Garfield, Sr.); Matty Kemp (Dillon); DeWitt Jennings (Game Warden).

New York Premiere: Roxy Theatre—November 18, 1932
No New York Television Showing

### Synopsis

Wealthy Frederick Garfield, Sr. of Rock Bayou has no use for the squatters who live in the area below his fine house on the hill. Among those who suffer at his hands are motherless Tess Howland and her New England seafaring father, Captain Howland, who find their humble dwelling burned. Later Captain Howland is carted off to prison for a crime actually committed by Ben Letts. Tess, who has come to love Garfield's son, Frederick Jr., loses him when he finds her with a child he believes to be her illegitimate offspring. In actuality she is caring for the out-of-wedlock child of Frederick's sister Teola. Finally, at the church where the baby is to be baptized, Teola admits the truth, leaving the way for young Frederick and Tess to be reunited, with one another and with the repentant Mr. Garfield.

◆—◆—◆

Grace Miller White's 1909 melodramatic novel, which was later made into a play, had enjoyed popularity as a 1922 Mary Pickford-Lloyd Hughes photoplay. Although it seemed to be stretching good fortune to rehash the creaking property a decade later, Fox surprised the more urban-minded industry set by coming up with a winner in its new *Tess of the Storm Country*. ". . . the team of Gaynor and Farrell being what it is, *Tess* being what she is, and the sentimental old plot being what it is, it will make its mark in the small and a good many of the large towns [John S. Cohen, Jr. *(New York Sun)*].
*Tess of the Storm Country* did offer Janet Gaynor one of her most

boisterous screen roles as the overly optimistic, effervescent soul who can reef a sail and weather a sou'wester with the best of them. She is an admirable companion for her salty seafaring father (Dudley Digges), and equally at ease cavorting with the household's little pet monkey, Peggy, who is remarkably bright. Gaynor's Tess endures a series of emotional setbacks in the course of the eighty-minute story, enough to unhinge most any other girl. Her house is destroyed, her father jailed, and the boy whom she has saved from drowning (Farrell) disavows her when he believes she is an unwed mother. Nevertheless, she still goes on, buoyed by her resiliency and spurred on by her desire to prove to mean old Claude Gillingwater and stubborn Farrell that virtue is its own reward. At one point, the athletic miss vents her anger at unperceptive Farrell by tossing bric-a-brac at him. Mostly, however, she sets her own straight and true course, knowing with all her heart that goodness just has to triumph.

It was to the credit of all the performers in *Tess of the Storm Country* that to a great extent they overcame this tearjerker's incredible trite dialog. Fortunately for the most part, pathos was avoided and the saccharine coating was not made too unbearable. Once again, Gaynor, who had a much larger part than Farrell, was criticized for not shedding her overly familiar mannerisms. But her flock of fans were an amazingly indulgent bunch, ever faithful to this pert lass, no matter how she might let them down with her cinema emoting.

Never one to let a venerable property die a natural death, Twentieth Century-Fox resurrected *Tess of the Storm Country* again in 1961, this time updating the tale as a modest vehicle for contract player Diane Baker.

## CHANGE OF HEART
### (Fox, 1934) 74M.

Director, John G. Blystone; based on the novel *Manhattan Love Song* by Kathleen Norris; screenplay, Sonya Levien, James Gleason, Samuel Hoffenstein; song, Harry Akst; camera, Joseph Aiken; editor, Margaret Clancy.

Janet Gaynor (Catherine Furness); Charles Farrell (Chris Thring); James Dunn (Mac McGowan); Ginger Rogers (Madge Rountree); Beryl Mercer (Harriet Hawkins); Gustav Von Seyffertitz (Dr. Kreutzmann); Shirley Temple (Shirley); Irene Franklin (Greta Hailstrom).

New York Premiere: Radio City Music Hall—May 10, 1934
No New York Television Showing

### Synopsis

When Catherine Furness, Chris Thring, Mac McGowan, and Madge Rountree graduate from college, they decide to embark for New York to make their way in life. Each has his or her heart set on a different career: Catherine as a newspaper girl, Chris as a lawyer, Mac as a radio crooner, and Madge as a stage star. Chris loves Madge, and Catherine loves Mac. However, Madge is flighty and cannot make up her mind. Only at times does she think she loves Mac. Mac really cares for Catherine and begs her to wed him, but she refuses. Eventually they all obtain jobs in New York, with Madge deciding to try her luck in California as the companion of a wealthy stage producer. This change of events causes Chris' illness, and it is Catherine who nurses him back to health. He then realizes he loves Catherine and they marry. Things are going well until Madge returns East and decided she wants Chris back. But Chris has long since become disenchanted with her, and tells Madge that now Catherine is the only girl for him. They are both delighted when Chris' office offers him a junior partnership. Later Madge decides she really does care for Mac.

◆━━◆━━◆

In the two years that had elapsed since *Tess of the Storm Country* Janet Gaynor had not only divorced but had resolidified her boxoffice standing by joining with Will Rogers in the very popular *State Fair* (1933) and the more-than-acceptable *Carolina* (1934) a rendering of Paul Green's *The House of Connelly*, with Lionel Barrymore and Robert Young as her solid co-stars. On the other hand, Farrell's marquee allure had so dimmed that he was relegated to playing in three minor features away from Fox, including the programmer *The Big Shakedown* (1934), with Bette Davis. Then he was recalled to Fox for *Change of Heart* which proved to be his last term contract feature.

*Change of Heart* found the picture's other co-stars, James Dunn and Ginger Rogers, handling the juicier roles; he playing a character full of infectious blarney and she as a snappy gold digger. Even Gaynor was allowed a new celluloid guise, as a small-town girl who adjusts to big city life and people. Farrell, as in many past cases, proved to be the weakest link. Director John G. Blystone allowed him to accentuate the shallow immaturity of his characterization by overplaying the hickish nature of Chris Thring who is forever referring to himself as "a businessman." The critics had no fear of enraging readers when they wrote of the twelfth screen reunion of Gaynor and Farrell, "*Change of Heart* puts both these players back where they started from, which isn't so much a tragedy in Farrell's case, since he has never managed to get anywhere else" [Thornton Delehanty (*New York Post*)].

Because Kathleen Norris was noted for her sentimental studies of domesticity, it was no major surprise that a screenplay from one of her works should be judged ". . .an innocuous little romance which steadfastly refrains from indulging in any suggestion of subtlety" [Mordaunt Hall (*New York Times*)]. If one is overcome by the sugary cuteness of the scenes involving Beryl Mercer's welfare center for babies where Gaynor works, and by Farrell's amateurish attempts at mawkish sympathy in his fever scene, there is one screen moment when the team does come alive with some of their cinema chemistry of old. Farrell is recuperating in his boarding house room and his constant attendant-nurse Gaynor decides it is high time her young man has his sprouting whiskers removed. So in the best Charlie Chaplin tradition she shaves him herself.

Considering that *Change of Heart* would end the seven-year teaming of the Gaynor-Farrell screen partnership, it is rather prophetic to recall Marguerite Tazelaar's review of the picture in the *New York Herald-Tribune:* "A tribute to their beautiful teamwork lies in the fact that the memory of *Seventh Heaven* lingers on in the minds of those who enjoyed the fine artistry of Janet Gaynor and Charles Farrell in this old picture. Nor has a series of subsequent poor parts for both of them dimmed altogether recognition of the particular talent of each. But enough bad stories will in time nick the edge of even skilled craftsmen, and therefore it is with regret we report that *Change of Heart* does not help either Miss Gaynor or Mr. Farrell."

## THE YEARS AFTER

From 1935 onward, Charles Farrell's movie career dipped as quickly as it had risen back in 1927. A series of lead roles in minor features here and abroad and pairing with Milli Monti in a Broadway rendition of *Seventh Heaven* (1939) did nothing to reestablish public interest in him. His show business life came to a halt with the 1941 Monogram feature, *The Deadly Game*. Much more successful was his persistent avocation of tennis playing which led to the formation of the Palm Springs Racquet Club by himself and movie colony pal Ralph Bellamy. Ths venture developed into a thriving business enterprise.

Meanwhile, Janet Gaynor continued with her film career, which seemed to have been short-circuited by Darryl F. Zanuck, the new head of Twentieth Century-Fox who expressed his total disinterest in her professional future. After *Ladies in Love* (1936), in which she was but one of four female co-stars, she took the hint and left the lot. David O. Selznick promptly signed her for the lead in his Technicolor *A Star Is Born* (1937) and she was Oscar-nominated, but lost the Best Actress Award to Luise Rainer of *The Good Earth*. Following the completion of Selznick's *The Young in Heart* (1938), Gaynor announced her screen retirement to become the wife of costume designer Gilbert Adrian, by whom she later had a son named Robin.

It was not until 1951 that Gaynor and Farrell were professionally reunited. As part of the twenty-fifth anniversary celebration for *Seventh Heaven*, the stars recreated their roles on "Lux Radio Theatre" on March 26, 1951. Once back in harness Farrell turned to television and "My Little Margie" which proved to be a smash hit video series, providing both himself and co-star Gale Storm with a 128-episode run. The duo also was heard in a radio edition of the show. In 1956 Farrell starred in a short-lived summer replacement show called "The Charlie Farrell Show" in which he played himself, the manager of the Racquet Club at Palm Springs. Thereafter he confined his activities to managing this lucrative operation.

Gaynor was lured back to acting with television guest assignments, and then, in 1957, when her old industry nemesis Darryl F. Zanuck was away from Twentieth Century-Fox, she returned to the studio to join with Pat Boone in his first motion picture, *Bernardine.* Just before she was scheduled to appear on Broadway in *The Midnight Sun,* her husband died (September 13, 1959). Nevertheless, Gaynor went on with the show, which failed. In 1964 she wed producer Paul Gregory and there were trade rumors that she would star in a television series, but plans never materialized.

Today,\* nearly fifty years after Gaynor and Farrell first teamed on-camera, the former screen pair hold an exalted position in the realm of contemporary American folklore. It is established legend that *Seventh Heaven* and its leading players represent all that is best of the naively simple aspects of silent screen romancing: pure, unrefined, earnest, optimistic, inspirational. Neither the stars' subsequent eleven co-features (mostly talkies) nor the passing of mores-shattering decades have altered the initial thinking that Gaynor and Farrell personify the noblest, most romantic facets of rural-bred America.

\*In late 1973, Gaynor and Farrell hosted a charity showing of *Seventh Heaven* in Palm Springs, suggesting that a national tour of the presentation might well be in order.

In **Dancing Lady** (MGM, 1933)

# Chapter 4

# Clark Gable
## &
# Joan Crawford

## CLARK GABLE

6' 1"
190 pounds
Brown hair
Gray eyes
Aquarius

*Real name: William Clark Gable. Born February 1, 1901, Cadiz, Ohio. Married Josephine Dillon (1924); divorced 1930. Married Rhea Langham (1931); divorced 1939. Married Carole Lombard (1939); widowed 1942. Married Sylvia Hawkes (1949); divorced 1952. Married Kay Spreckels (1955), child: John. Died November 16, 1960.*

### FEATURE FILMS:

*Forbidden Paradise* (Par., 1924)
*The Merry Widow* (MGM, 1925)
*The Plastic Age* (FBO, 1925)
*North Star* (Associated Exhibitors, 1926)
*The Painted Desert* (Pathé, 1931)
*The Easiest Way* (MGM, 1931)
*Dance, Fools, Dance* (MGM, 1931)
*The Secret Six* (MGM, 1931)
*The Finger Points* (FN, 1931)
*Laughing Sinners* (MGM, 1931)
*A Free Soul* (MGM, 1931)
*Night Nurse* (WB, 1931)
*Sporting Blood* (MGM, 1931)
*Susan Lennox—Her Fall and Rise* (MGM, 1931)
*Possessed* (MGM, 1931)
*Hell Divers* (MGM, 1931)
*Polly of the Circus* (MGM, 1932)
*Strange Interlude* (MGM, 1932)
*Red Dust* (MGM, 1932)

*No Man of Her Own* (Par., 1932)
*The White Sister* (MGM, 1933)
*Hold Your Man* (MGM, 1933)
*Night Flight* (MGM, 1933)
*Dancing Lady* (MGM, 1933)
*It Happened One Night* (Col., 1934)
*Men in White* (MGM, 1934)
*Manhattan Melodrama* (MGM, 1934)
*Chained* (MGM, 1934)
*Forsaking All Others* (MGM, 1934)
*After Office Hours* (MGM, 1935)
*Call of the Wild* (UA, 1935)
*China Seas* (MGM, 1935)
*Mutiny on the Bounty* (MGM, 1935)
*Wife Versus Secretary* (MGM, 1936)
*San Francisco* (MGM, 1936)
*Cain and Mabel* (WB, 1936)
*Love on the Run* (MGM, 1936)
*Parnell* (MGM, 1937)
*Saratoga* (MGM, 1937)
*Test Pilot* (MGM, 1938)
*Too Hot to Handle* (MGM, 1938)
*Idiot's Delight* (MGM, 1939)
*Gone with the Wind* (MGM, 1939)
*Strange Cargo* (MGM, 1940)
*Boom Town* (MGM, 1940)

*Comrade X* (MGM, 1940)
*They Met in Bombay* (MGM, 1941)
*Honky Tonk* (MGM, 1941)
*Somewhere I'll Find You* (MGM, 1942)
*Adventure* (MGM, 1945)
*The Hucksters* (MGM, 1947)
*Homecoming* (MGM, 1948)
*Command Decision* (MGM, 1948)
*Any Number Can Play* (MGM, 1949)
*Key to the City* (MGM, 1950)
*To Please a Lady* (MGM, 1950)
*Across the Wide Missouri* (MGM, 1951)
*Callaway Went Thataway* (MGM, 1951)
*Lone Star* (MGM, 1952)
*Never Let Me Go* (MGM, 1953)
*Mogambo* (MGM, 1953)
*Betrayed* (MGM, 1954)
*Soldier of Fortune* (20th, 1955)
*The Tall Men* (20th, 1955)
*The King and Four Queens* (UA, 1956)
*Band of Angels* (WB, 1957)
*Run Silent, Run Deep* (UA, 1958)
*Teacher's Pet* (Par., 1958)
*But Not For Me* (Par., 1959)
*It Started in Naples* (Par., 1960)
*The Misfits* (UA, 1961)

# JOAN CRAWFORD

**5′ 4″**
**130 pounds**
**Brown hair**
**Blue eyes**
**Aries**

*Real name: Lucille Le Sueur. Born March 23, 1904, San Antonio, Texas. Married Douglas Fairbanks, Jr. (1929); divorced 1933. Married Franchot Tone (1935); divorced 1939. Married Phillip Terry (1942); divorced 1946. Married Alfred Steele (1956); widowed 1959. Children adopted while Miss Crawford was unmarried: Christina, Cathy, Christopher, Cindy.*

## FEATURE FILMS:

*Lady of the Night* (Metro-Goldwyn, 1925)

*Proud Flesh* (Metro-Goldwyn, 1925)

*Pretty Ladies* (Metro-Goldwyn, 1925)

*Old Clothes* (Metro-Goldwyn, 1925)

*The Only Thing* (MGM, 1925)

*Sally, Irene and Mary* (MGM, 1925)

*The Circle* (Metro-Goldwyn, 1925)

*The Boob* (MGM, 1926)

*Tramp, Tramp, Tramp* (FN, 1926)

*Paris* (MGM, 1926)

*The Taxi Dancer* (MGM, 1927)

*Winners of the Wilderness* (MGM, 1927)

*The Understanding Heart* (MGM, 1927)

*The Unknown* (MGM, 1927)

*Twelve Miles Out* (MGM, 1927)

*Spring Fever* (MGM, 1927)

*West Point* (MGM, 1928)

*Rose Marie* (MGM, 1928)

*Across to Singapore* (MGM, 1928)

*The Law of the Range* (MGM, 1928)

*Four Walls* (MGM, 1928)

*Our Dancing Daughters* (MGM, 1928)

*Dream of Love* (MGM, 1928)

*The Duke Steps Out* (MGM, 1929)

*Hollywood Revue of 1929* (MGM, 1929)

*Our Modern Maidens* (MGM, 1929)

*Untamed* (MGM, 1929)

*Montana Moon* (MGM, 1930)

*Our Blushing Brides* (MGM, 1930)

*Paid* (MGM, 1930)

*Dance, Fools, Dance* (MGM, 1931)

*Laughing Sinners* (MGM, 1931)

*This Modern Age* (MGM, 1931)

*Possessed* (MGM, 1931)

*Grand Hotel* (MGM, 1932)

*Letty Lynton* (MGM, 1932)

*Rain* (UA, 1932)

*Today We Live* (MGM, 1933)

*Dancing Lady* (MGM, 1933)

*Sadie McKee* (MGM, 1934)

*Chained* (MGM, 1934)

*Forsaking All Others* (MGM, 1934)

*No More Ladies* (MGM, 1935)

*I Live My Life* (MGM, 1935)

*The Gorgeous Hussy* (MGM, 1936)

*Love On the Run* (MGM, 1936)

*The Last of Mrs. Cheyney* (MGM, 1937)

*The Bride Wore Red* (MGM, 1937)

*Mannequin* (MGM, 1938)

*The Shining Hour* (MGM, 1938)

*Ice Follies of 1939* (MGM, 1939)

*The Women* (MGM, 1939)

*Strange Cargo* (MGM, 1940)

*A Woman's Face* (MGM, 1941)

*When Ladies Meet* (MGM, 1941)

*They All Kissed the Bride* (Col., 1942)

*Reunion in France* (MGM, 1942)

*Above Suspicion* (MGM, 1943)

*Hollywood Canteen* (WB, 1944)

*Mildred Pierce* (WB, 1945)

*Humoresque* (WB, 1946)

*Possessed* (WB, 1947)

*Daisy Kenyon* (20th, 1947)

*Flamingo Road* (WB, 1949)

*It's a Great Feeling* (WB, 1949)

*The Damned Don't Cry* (WB, 1950)

*Harriet Craig* (Col., 1950)

*Goodbye, My Fancy* (WB, 1951)

*This Woman Is Dangerous* (WB, 1952)

*Sudden Fear* (RKO, 1952)

*Torch Song* (MGM, 1953)

*Johnny Guitar* (Rep., 1954)

*Female on the Beach* (Univ., 1955)

*Queen Bee* (Col., 1955)

*Autumn Leaves* (Col., 1956)

*The Story of Esther Costello* (Col., 1957)

*The Best of Everything* (20th, 1959)

*What Ever Happened to Baby Jane?* (WB, 1962)

*The Caretakers* (UA, 1963)

*Strait-Jacket* (Col., 1964)

*I Saw What You Did* (Univ., 1965)

*Berserk!* (Col., 1967)

*Trog* (WB, 1970)

In **Laughing Sinners** (MGM, 1931)

Earle Foxe, Joan Crawford, and Clark Gable
in **Dance, Fools, Dance** (MGM, 1931)

In **Possessed** (MGM, 1931)

In **Chained** (MGM, 1934)

In **Forsaking All Others** (MGM, 1934)

In **Love on the Run** (MGM, 1936)

In **Strange Cargo** (MGM, 1940)

# DANCE, FOOLS, DANCE
## *(MGM, 1931) 81M.*

Director, Harry Beaumont; story, Aurania Rouverol; continuity, Richard Schayer; dialog, Rouverol; songs, Frank Crumit and Lou Klein; Dale Winbrow and L. Cornell; Roy Turk and Fred Ahlert; Dorothy Fields and Jimmy McHugh; camera, Charles Rosher; editor, George Hively.

Joan Crawford (Bonnie Jordan); Lester Vail (Bob Townsend); Cliff Edwards (Bert Scranton); William Bakewell (Rodney Jordan); William Holden (Stanley Jordan); Clark Gable (Jake Luva); Earle Foxe (Wally Baxter); Purnell B. Pratt (Parker); Hale Hamilton (Selby); Natalie Moorhead (Della); Joan Marsh (Sylvia); Russell Hopton (Whitey); James Donlan (Police Reporter); Mortimer Snow, Sherry Hall (Reporters); Tommy Shugrue (Photographer); Robert Livingston (Jack, a Hood); Harry Semels (Dance Extra).

New York Premiere: Capitol Theatre—March 20, 1931
No New York Television Showing

## Synopsis

When their wealthy father Stanley Jordan dies after the stock market crash, spoiled Bonnie and Rodney Jordan are left to fend for themselves. Bob Townsend, with whom Bonnie has been conducting an affair, asks her to wed him, but she refuses. Rodney accepts a job with bootlegger Jake Luva, informing Bonnie, who has obtained a newspaper post, that he is selling stocks. After Luva engineers a gangland killing of seven men, the newspapers are convinced he did it, but lack conclusive proof. When Bonnie's reporter friend Bert Scranton discovers telltale evidence about Luva, the hoodlum forces Rodney to kill him. Thereafter Bonnie is detailed to gain the confidence of Luva and unearth the truth. She poses as an entertainer and wins a job in his club. Soon she is his favorite and eventually learns the stark truth about her brother. When Luva learns Bonnie's identity he decides to take her for a one way ride. But Rodney interferes and he and the gangster wipe each other out. Bonnie manages to escape and reports the headline story. Now she agrees to wed Bob Townsend.

◆◆◆

"More thrilling than *Paid*—More exotic than *Our Modern Maiden*—the star you love." So ran the advertisement for *Dance, Fools, Dance*, the first of Joan Crawford's four 1931 MGM releases. There was no doubt that Crawford, the perfect flapper of the silent cinema, was also one of the most popular of Hollywood's younger movie stars, and, in fact, growing in international popularity with each new Metro release. She was still undergoing her vital young heroine career stage, proving here, as she would years later in other screen guises, that there were few others on the movie scene who could put such energy into a characterization.

It was purely by chance that Crawford's *Dance, Fools, Dance* featured relative screen newcomer Clark Gable in a supporting role, for he had joined the Metro stock company only a short time before and had yet to find his place in films or in the studio. Before the year was over he would co-star with Crawford in two additional studio pictures—which was no accident—for the public was discovering what Crawford had been quick to sense. "There is probably only one other man of our time whose personality incorporated the same blend of toughness and tenderness, the same ability to be a woman's man and a man's man—Ernest Hemingway."

*Dance, Fools, Dance* is one of those improbable melodramas loosely hinged on such well-known real life events as the murder of Chicago reporter Jake Lingle and the notorious St. Valentine's Day Massacre in that city. As Andre Sennwald *(New York Times)* observed, ". . . a metaphysician might exhaust his learning trying to reconcile it with the melodrama of newspapers and gangdom . . . [but] the picture is a brisk and lively entertainment of its sort."

Crawford was given full opportunity to do a bit of everything in *Dance, Fools, Dance.* As the wealthy socialite she can defy conventions by joining her yachtmates in an evening swim clothed only in her underwear. Later, as an earnest reporter, she vamps her way into the good graces of hoodlum Jake Luva (Gable), has the chance to perform a song number, wears shimmering gowns, and acts as seemingly tough as that admirable screen broad Natalie Moorhead, here portraying a character named Della. No matter what it may seem, there is no doubt that Crawford's Bonnie Jordan is a virtuous girl, only doing her best to woo her brother (William Bakewell) back onto the right path, and to prove to her upper crust beau (Lester Vail) that she is not just an empty-headed, speakeasy-loving playgirl.

In *Night Nurse* (1931) Gable smacks star Barbara Stanwyck across the face; this shocking physical act of disrespect would be repeated by Gable later in the year in *A Free Soul* where he roughs up tantalizing, ritzy society girl, Norma Shearer. In *Dance, Fools, Dance,* Crawford "enjoyed" a similar brutal encounter. As the actress later recalled, "In the one scene where he (Gable) grabbed me and threatened the life of my brother, his nearness had such impact my knees buckled. If he hadn't held me by both shoulders I'd have dropped." In short, although Crawford was at the time wed to Douglas Fairbanks, Jr. and Gable was in the midst of divorcing Josephine Dillon and marrying Rhea Langham, there was more than just acting between *she* and *he* in their joint scenes.

With its made-to-order plot, *Dance, Fools, Dance* reached no artistic peaks, and it was Gable who received sturdier reviews than Crawford. "Clark Gable's characterization of the gang chieftain is a vivid and authentic bit of acting . . . Miss Crawford's acting is still self-conscious but her admirers will find her performance well up to her standard" *(Variety).*

# LAUGHING SINNERS
## *(MGM, 1931) 71M.*

Director, Harry Beaumont; based on the play *Torch Song* by Kenyon Nicholson; continuity, Bess Meredyth; dialog, Martin Flavin; additional dialog, Edith Fitzgerald; song, Martin Broones and Arthur Freed; sound, Charles E. Wallace; camera, Charles Rosher; editor, George Hively.

Joan Crawford (Ivy Stevens); Neil Hamilton (Howard Palmer); Clark Gable (Carl Loomis); Marjorie Rambeau (Ruby); Guy Kibbee (Cass Wheeler); Cliff Edwards (Mike); Roscoe Karns (Fred Geer); Gertrude Short (Edna); George Cooper (Joe); George F. Marion (Humpty); Bert Woodruff (Tink); Henry Armetta (Tony the Chef); Lee Phelps (Salesman).

New York Premier: Capitol Theatre—July 3, 1931
No New York Television Showing

## Synopsis

When entertainer Ivy Stevens is brushed off by traveling salesman Howard Palmer, life loses its meaning and she attempts suicide by planning to jump from a bridge into the river. However, she is saved at the last moment by Carl, a Salvation Army worker. He inspires within her a faith in God and she joins the mission group in its streetside crusading. But later, through bad luck, she reencounters Howard at a hotel and they recommence their old affair, even though he is now wed to the sluttish Edna. In the morning Ivy repents of her misdeed, and becomes hysterical. Carl breaks into the room, hears her tale of woes, and insists that she must still maintain faith in her ideals and that everything will right itself once again. She realizes that life with Howard would only be a downward trail, and that Carl, who now admits he loves her, has the answers for their joint happiness ahead.

◆◆◆

Joan Crawford had already completed filming *Laughing Sinners* on the Culver City soundstages, when it was decided to scuttle the footage with Johnny Mack Brown and reshoot those scenes with Clark Gable, whom audiences had liked so much as Crawford's partner in *Dance, Fools, Dance.* Since Gable was still playing onscreen underworld figures more often than not, the role of a crusading Salvation Army worker was a bit of a surprising and ludicrous change of pace for the thirty-year-old actor.

Crawford, with her hair more blonde than ever, acquitted herself best in the early cabaret scenes of *Laughing Sinners*, where she danced and performed the torch song, "What Can I Do—I Love That Man." Her performance as a rejuvenated bad girl was a weak foreshadowing of her intense Sadie Thompson in *Rain* (1932) and was so overstuffed with platitudinous posturing that even the most devoted Crawford fans found the celluloid going far too sticky. More than one critic of the day suggested that Gable might have done much better had Metro cast him in the showier role of the dirty dog of a salesman, a part which gave Neil Hamilton the upper edge in the limelight sweepstakes.

By the time *Laughing Sinners*, based on a seventy-performance 1930 Broadway drama, was released, Crawford and Gable were rumored to be "that way" about one another on and off the set, and their mutual attraction was very evident and obvious in the picture. Perhaps the team's best moment onscreen in this joint effort occurred when they walk through the park together, hand in hand, with noble thoughts in their minds, as in the background one hears a soft rendition of an evangelical hymn.

Guy Kibbee, who had appeared in the Broadway stage original of the story, repeated his role as the funeral supplies salesman and had several good moments in the film, such as the instance when the inebriated man wanders into Crawford's hotel room by error.

If *Laughing Sinners* had been made in today's film market (which of course it would not have been) in which an actor sinks or swims on each of his few yearly screen exposures, Crawford and Gable might have experienced great professional problems. Even the more generous reviews were devastating in their fashion. "New leading man Clark Gable is rather unconvincing as the saviour of fallen Joan Crawford, who is better than usual in a film that is less than average in its overall scheme. It doesn't live up to its publicity" [Andre Sennwald *(New York Times)*].

## POSSESSED
### *(MGM, 1931) 72M.*

Director, Clarence Brown; based on the play *The Mirage* by Edgar Selwyn; adaptation, Lenore Coffee; song, Max Leif and Joseph Meyer; camera, Oliver T. Marsh.

Joan Crawford (Marian Martin); Clark Gable (Mark Whitney); Wallace Ford (Al Mannings); Skeets Gallagher (Wally); Frank Conroy (Travers); Marjorie White (Vernice); John Miljan (John); Clara Blandick (Mother).

New York Premiere: Capitol Theatre—November 27, 1931.
No New York Television Showing

### Synopsis

Marian Martin, an employee in a box factory, is determined to make a finer life for herself, which is the reason she refuses to marry Al Manning, a cement worker in the same factory. When a train is delayed at the town's station, Marian happens to meet one of its passengers, a New Yorker named Wally, who increases her discontent with her present existence by telling her enticing stories of life in the big city. He flippantly tells her to look him up if she should come to Manhattan. This is all Marian needs; she leaves her small town and journeys to New York. Wally hardly remembers her, but he does introduce her to attorney Mark Whitney, a rich and influential figure about town. Because he is already married and dares not risk a divorce scandal which could damage his political ambitions, Mark sets Marian up as his mistress. Three years pass, and now, as "Mrs. Moreland," a wealthy divorcee, Marian can pose as a cultured lady. Meanwhile, Al Manning, who has become a modestly successful businessman, appears in New York, seeking Mark's assistance to put through a road construction project. Although she still cares for Al no more than she did when they were both small town dwellers, Marian seriously considers wedding him, or at least pretending that she will, in order to make Mark believe that he has no obligation to her and may pursue his political goals without fear. However, at a large rally, hecklers ask about Marian. She, being in the audience, stands up to inform everyone that she is no longer part of his life and that he is now a man of the people. She leaves the auditorium hastily, but Mark catches up to her and explains that no matter what happens from now on, they belong together.

Depicting working girl nobility was definitely Joan Crawford's stock-in-trade at this strategic stage in her professional career, and *Possessed*, based on a 1920 play, was a gaudy display of this rags-to-sanctity genre at its best or most meretricious, depending on where the viewer's standards and movie star loyalties lay.

Can a factory worker (Crawford), who tries to better herself by accepting a rich city lover, find happiness with a well-bred gentleman (Clark Gable), with whom she has shared a bed but not a marriage license? According to *Possessed*, yes, *if* she has suffered enough. With the double standard of morality still in force, Crawford's Marian Martin was considered by moviegoers of the day to be just another innocent victim of an unfair social system in which the man always had his sexual way, while the woman received the stigma of "tramp" for bestowing her favors. Of course, no one had forced the heroine to step out of her small town milieu and to embark on a dangerous urban life in which hurt and humiliation were common penalties. But the tenor of the picture begs the viewer to forget that subtle point while vicariously experiencing the pains of maturation that Crawford's unsophisticated heroine must endure in the process of becoming a lady of the world.

Each step along the way of this Horatio Alger story provides Crawford with ample opportunity to do what she did better than most any other contemporary on the Hollywood scene, that is, posture with style. Whether daydreaming in the box factory, suffering her first masculine rebuff in the big city, discovering that her new beau (Gable) is so much above her socially, or later becoming the refined lady (who can rebuke the butler for not serving Chambertin Burgundy at room temperature), Crawford "pretended" oncamera with a self-determination that was fascinating in its own ambiance of conviction. That her assorted attitudinizing, as in the protracted auditorium speech scene, lacked the ring of authenticity, bothered very few. Nevertheless, there are those critics who agree with cinema historian René Jordan that "there is an inherent hypocrisy that infects the women she played, and it works against the sincerity he (Gable) was so good at."

But at this point, some forty years later, it is academic to quibble with the successful, if even then shopworn, formula that did so much for Crawford's movie career and the studio's coffers. As the blue collar worker turned *demi-monde*, she had the opportunity in *Possessed* to wear exquisite clothes and jewelry, exude charm and dramatics, and even sing "How Long Can It Last" in three different languages. These items in themselves were sufficient to satisfy the boxoffice customers. But *Possessed* had more. It continued the successful oncamera relationship of Crawford and Gable as they glided through seventy-two minutes of footage, displaying few awkward moments in traveling over the course set out by the bumpy screenplay. Could any viewer feel anything but sympathy for a girl who was such a forgiving soul that no matter what her lover did (he even slapped her and called her a "little tramp"), she was ready to come back at his beck and call? Moreover, the Lenore Coffee scenario managed with great ingenuity to retain Crawford's sanctified halo as an essentially good girl, while Gable, moving away again from his standard gangster characterizations, was still the tough, aggressive soul. Though more refined here, he is still a he-man who thinks of himself first, that is, until he almost loses the girl of his life near the finale.

Amidst the myriad contemporary reviews of *Possessed*, one critical essay stands out with more than passing interest. The *London Times* printed an intriguing query for Miss Crawford: "Why must she keep on experimenting with her appearance? Taken all in all, she is, I think, one of the most beautiful young women on the screen. Why isn't she content to remain so, without continually painting her eyebrows at a new and stranger angle, rioting with her lipstick and positively running amok with her clothes?"


## DANCING LADY
### (MGM, 1933) 94M.

Executive producer, David O. Selznick; associate producer, John W. Considine, Jr.; director, Robert Z. Leonard; based on the novel by James Warner Bellah; screenplay, Allen Rivkin, P. J. Wolfson; music, Lou Silvers; songs, Jimmy McHugh and Dorothy Fields; Burton Lane and Harold

Adamson; Richard Rodgers and Lorenz Hart; choreography, Sammy Lee, Edward Prinz; costumes, Adrian; camera, Oliver T. Marsh; editor, Margaret Booth.

Joan Crawford (Janie Barlow); Clark Gable (Patch Gallagher); Franchot Tone (Tod Newton); Fred Astaire (Himself); Nelson Eddy (Himself); May Robson (Dolly Todhunter); Winnie Lightner (Rosette Henrietta La Rue); Robert Benchley (Ward King); Ted Healy (Steve); Moe Howard, Jerry Howard, Larry Fine (Three Stooges); Gloria Foy (Vivian Warner); Art Jarrett (Art); Grant Mitchell (Jasper Bradley, Sr.); Maynard Holmes (Jasper Bradley, Jr.); Sterling Holloway (Pinky the Author); Florine McKinney (Grace Newton); Bonita Barker, Dalie Dean, Shirley Aranson, Katharine Barnes, Lynn Bari (Chorus Girls); Jack Baxley (Barker); Frank Hagney (Cop); Pat Somerset (Tod's Friend); Charlie Williams (Man Arrested in Burlesque House); Ferdinand Gottschalk (Judge); Eve Arden (Marcia the "Southern" Actress); Matt McHugh (Marcia's Agent); Charlie Sullivan (Cabby); Harry C. Bradley, John Sheehan (Author's Pals); Stanley Blystone (Traffic Cop); Charles C. Wilson (Club Manager); Bill Elliott (Cafe Extra); Larry Steers, C. Montague Shaw (First Nighters).

New York Premiere: November 30, 1933
New York Television Debut: CBS—August 5, 1957

### Synopsis

Bad luck and the need for daily bread force stage performer Janie Barlow to accept work in a cheap downtown New York burlesque house. Wealthy Tod Newton leads a party of friends on a slumming expedition to the burlesque house where he is immediately attracted by Janie's refreshing young beauty. When the show is raided by the police and the cast taken into court on an indecency charge, Tod pays Janie's $50 fine. Later he attempts to seduce her, but she insists she will repay every penny she borrowed and that crashing Broadway is the most important goal in her life at present. She does accept Tod's assistance to meet Patch Gallagher, director of Jasper Bradley's musical shows. Patch does not approve of Janie's backhanded way of joining the cast, but he agrees to give her a chance in the chorus. Janie soon wins his friendship by her hard work and he later decides to feature her in the revue. Meanwhile, Tod has persuaded Janie to say she will wed him if the show folds. So Tod buys Bradley out and closes the production. When Janie learns this she gives Tod the heave-ho, and she and Patch manage to scrape together the necessary funds to open the show, which is a success. Patch and Janie realize now that they are in love.

◆━━━◆

With Warner Bros.' fabulously successful *42nd Street* setting the pace, new MGM executive producer David O. Selznick determined to outdo that film with *Dancing Lady*. Joan Crawford, who had not had a real hit since *Grand Hotel* (1932), needed to reestablish her boxoffice image after her loanout to United Artists for *Rain* (1932) and the misfire of *Today We Live* (1933) on the home lot. Not only was she given established screen favorite Clark Gable as a lead* (she held up production until he was available, and substituted for signed Lee Tracy), but the well-mounted production utilized the excellent services of two screen newcomers, Fred Astaire and Nelson Eddy, in brief roles, as well as a cast of hundreds performing to the choreographed steps of Sammy Lee. For comedy relief there was Robert Benchley, Winnie Lightner, Ted Healy, and the Three Stooges. For romantic contrast there was Franchot Tone, and for good measure a stunning Adrian wardrobe for Crawford.

Having loaded the deck so carefully, it was pretty difficult for *Dancing Lady* to be anything but a hit, even in a year crowded with entries in the lastest screen musical cycle. "Saying it's a backstage show is hardly enough. There have been plenty of those, and the mere presentation of one more probably would not stir the paying public. But *Dancing Lady* is so basically different that it belongs in another category. Everything is built upon a fundamental story. What happens is only the result of working to its logical conclusion" *(Variety)*.

It was strange that even at this point in his meteoric movie career, Gable was being mishandled by Metro, who cast him inappropriately as the Warner Baxter–style hard driving stage director in *Dancing Lady*. He seemed very awkward and ill at ease in his actually subordinate role, mouthing such clichéd lines as, "Hey, that kid has talent" . . . "Go out there and show them you're a star" . . . and "Okay, now you're in the top spot where you've got twice as far to fall."

On the other hand, Crawford was asked to exercise her assorted bag of well-established tricks, which she did very well. Once more she played the poor but honest working girl who retains her virtue until the right man comes along with a legitimate proposal. Within *Dancing Lady*, she had full occasion to display her modest dancing ability, and, if she was not another Ginger Rogers, she at least acquitted herself with fine style, whether tenuously joining with the burlesque chorus in "Hey, Young Fella," trying to audition to Ted Healy's singing of "Ida," or engaging in her big production numbers. In her performance as Janie Barlow, Crawford outdid herself in projecting that surefire ingredient which always wooed the patrons to her side, i.e. demonstrating an inexhaustible determination which made the more susceptible viewer admit to himself, "Gee, if she is working that hard, she must be good." Just observing Crawford maneu-

---

*Crawford had fretted when Gable was not cast in her *Letty Lynton* (1932). In 1933 she and Gable were to star in Josef von Sternberg's production of *The Prize Fighter and the Lady*, while the following year, both stars were announced for *The Hollywood Revue* which was produced without their presence. In 1937, Crawford was thought of for *Parnell* with Gable but Myrna Loy did the part; and in the *Gone with the Wind* (1939) sweepstakes, press agents once publicized that Crawford and Gable would be the "ideal" team.

vering this gimmick throughout the "My Dancing Lady" play-within-the-movie rehearsal sessions, proves this point. For many, *Dancing Lady* seemed the apogee of Crawford's early 1930s film career, for here she sings, tap dances, frowns, cajoles, swallows hard, and makes glittering lights shine from her oh so expressive eyes.

While offcamera it was a pretty well known fact that Crawford and MGM player Franchot Tone were contemplating marriage, oncamera she could not decide in *Dancing Lady* between Gable or Tone. For plot balance, she had her "moments" with each of them, a swimming scene with Tone at his plush home, capped by the two players kissing underwater. With Gable, who suffered an appendectomy in the course of production, she indulged in romantic byplay while heaving a medicine ball back and forth, which concludes with both Crawford's ideals and hand being bruised by the no-nonsense Gable. While it took Crawford nearly ninety–four minutes to make the momentous decision of which beau was right for her, audiences could have predicted the outcome from the start. A weak-willed playboy (Tone) is certainly no match for a tough-as-nails, creative he-man (Gable).

After the big build-up of rehearsal watching, viewers of *Dancing Lady* might have hoped for more imagination in the two big production numbers which conclude the picture. The formal ensemble of "Hey Ho, The Gang's All Here," with Crawford and Astaire leading into a magic carpet interlude which transports them into the "Let's Go Bavarian" routine, was pleasant but hardly outstanding, even with the actress garbed in a fancy peasant's outfit and a braided blonde wig. "That's the Rhythm of the Day" was the elaborate but static costumed moving tableau number which provided Eddy with a chance to be the audience's historical tour guide.

## CHAINED
### (MGM, 1934) 74M.

Producer, Hunt Stromberg; director, Clarence Brown; story, Edgar Selwyn; screenplay, John Lee Mahin; costumes, Adrian; art directors, Cedric Gibbons, Alexander Toluboff, Edwin B. Willis; music, Herbert Stothart; camera, George Folsey; editor, Robert J. Kern.

Joan Crawford (Diane Lovering); Clark Gable (Mike Bradley); Otto Kruger (Richard Field); Stuart Erwin (Johnny); Una O'Connor (Amy); Marjorie Gateson (Mrs. Field); Hooper Atchley, Phillips Smalley, Edward Le Saint, Gordon De Main (S. S. Officials); Theresa Maxwell Conover (Secretary); Adrian Rosley (Chef); Louis Natheaux (Steward); Lee Phelps (Bartender); Ward Bond (Sailor); Ernie Alexander (Deck Steward); Grace Hayle, Nora Cecil (Spinsters); Auguste Tollaire (Chess Player); Mickey Rooney (Boy Swimmer); Paul Porcasi (Hotel Manager); Akim Tamiroff

(Ranch Chef); Chris Pin Martin (Peon); George Humbert (Cafe Manager); Gino Corrado (Waiter); Sam Flint (Clerk); Nick Copeland (Chauffeur); Tom Mahoney (Doorman); Colin Chase (Photographer); Frank Parker (Reporter); Franklin Parker (Third Mate); William Stack (Butler); Kendall McComas (Boy); Wade Boteler (Mechanic); Keenan Wynn (Double for Joan Crawford in Speedboat Sequence).

New York Premiere: Capitol Theatre—August 31, 1934
New York Television Debut: CBS—June 29, 1958

### Synopsis

Middle-aged, married business man Richard Field has made his former secretary, Diane Lovering, his mistress. Field has asked his wife for a divorce, but she refuses. Distressed by the unpleasantness, he suggests that Diane take a cruise to Buenos Aires until things can be settled. Aboard ship she encounters wealthy Argentine rancher Mike Bradley. Although she feels herself falling deeply in love with Mike, her loyalty to Field, for whom she feels affection but not passion, prevents her from declaring her full emotions to Mike. When Diane returns to New York she learns that Field's wife has now consented to the divorce and that he is already making wedding plans for Diane. Diane writes Mike a terse note, hoping it will make him forget her. However, on a business trip to New York, Mike does meet Diane, and she is soon confessing that she really loves him but cannot be disloyal to her husband. Mike persists in his love for Diane, and follows the couple to their Lake Placid lodge where he tells Field all. The older man proves to be a considerate realist, comprehending that youth must have its day. He steps aside, leaving Diane free to find happiness with Mike.

◆ ◆ ◆

The ads proclaimed, "When Clark takes lovely Joan in his arms . . . it's the grandest thrill the screen can give! Because you've asked for an encore to *Dancing Lady*, . . . the screen's perfect lovers are together again." But this was really just another regulation MGM sex drama, with no tense scenes or hot conflicts to balance the tepid and purified story geared to appease the industry's production code. "To say that it is banal, obvious, and down to the lowest standards of cinema mush is to understate the case" [Thornton Delehanty *(New York Post)*].

Because of *Chained*'s very improbable nature, in which the handsome lead characters drift about in the tinsel world of MGM fabrication, no one really expected Joan Crawford and Clark Gable to emote in a serious manner. "The two stars, who certainly know their business, wisely decide to pass their time tossing charm and personality all over the place, which is obviously what the film requires for audience appeal" [Richard Watts, Jr. *(New York Herald-Tribune)* ].

There were moments in *Chained* when Gable rightly seemed bored with his stock characterization, but Crawford was still giving her complete oncamera effort to a mawkish tale in which she may have besmirched her reputation but not her soul. Within this film, she magnetically transforms the shipboard scenes into a travel agent's delight, first forcing herself to be a good sport in accepting the expensive trip underwritten by the understanding Richard Field (Otto Kruger), and then, between her many sherry-flip drinking bouts at the bar, accepting and enjoying the camaraderie of Gable and his dumb but nice buddy (Stuart Erwin). Such scenes as the sojourns to the indoor swimming pool, moonlight strolls about the sparkling deck, and carefree dinners add up to convert Crawford into a woman truly in love, but also a person, whom the audience knows full well, who must remain true to her benefactor (Kruger). This loyalty is the weakest element in the plotline, and it takes a good deal of script cheating for scenarist John Lee Mahin [who had done such a fine job with the Gable-Jean Harlow *Red Dust* (1932)] to have determined Gable end up with his lady fair, no matter how awkwardly Kruger must be shoved out of the stars' way.

For *Chained*, Crawford received her best press notices for the extravagant Adrian wardrobe and her varied coiffure changes.

## FORSAKING ALL OTHERS
### *(MGM, 1934) 84M*

Producer, Bernard H. Hyman; director, W. S. Van Dyke II; based on the play by Edward Barry Roberts, Frank Morgan Cavett; screenplay, Joseph L. Mankiewicz; music, Dr. William Axt; art director, Cedric Gibbons, Edwin B. Willis; gowns, Adrian; song, Gus Kahn and Walter Donaldson; camera, Gregg Toland, George Folsey; editor, Tom Held.

Joan Crawford (Mary Clay); Clark Gable (Jeff Williams); Robert Montgomery (Dill Todd); Charles Butterworth (Shep); Billie Burke (Paula); Frances Drake (Connie); Rosalind Russell (Eleanor); Tom Ricketts (Wiffens); Arthur Treacher (Johnson); Greta Meyer (Bella).

New York Premiere: Capitol Theatre—December 20, 1934
New York Television Debut: CBS—January 13, 1960

### Synopsis

Jeff Williams returns from Spain just in time to be best man at the marriage of his childhood friends, Mary Clay and Dill Todd. However, Dill leaves Mary at the altar to wed his mistress, Connie. Jeff, who has always loved Mary, but could never surmount her preference for Dill, tries to console her. Thereafter, Dill, who is bridling under the yoke of marriage to Connie, makes a fresh play for Mary. She still loves him and forgives his past indiscretions. Once again Mary and Dill plan to wed, and Jeff is forced to take a back seat to the proceedings. But before the ceremony occurs, Mary realizes that it was Jeff who did all the thoughtful things which she had credited to Dill, and she decides it is Jeff whom she must wed. She and Jeff depart for Europe.

◆━◆

Transforming the 1933 Broadway play which had starred Tallulah Bankhead into a Joan Crawford-Clark Gable screen vehicle took some crafty doing, but thanks to a witty script by Joseph L. Mankiewicz and fast pacing direction by W. S. Van Dyke II, *Forsaking All Others* emerged as an engaging picture in which " . . . the film's sledge-hammer whimsies are not only bearable but intermittently diverting" [Andre Sennwald *(New York Times)*]. Best of all, this film avoided that tongue-in-cheek moralizing of the typical Crawford films to that date. Because Gable would win an Oscar that year, for *It Happened One Night*, critics, historians, and fans tend to overlook the general excellence of the production which united him oncamera with Crawford for the sixth time.

The focus for this chic divertisement was the depiction of the chic Park Avenue set who glitter with their material values and scintillating urbane humor, but have the sketchiest of moral standards. Robert Montgomery was cast as the third spoke on the romantic wheel, and he was at his caddish, clownish best as the man who toys so cavalierly with Crawford's honest affection. In direct contrast, Gable was offered as the understanding (and most sympathetic) big brother chap who maintained a jaunty smile on his lips even while his heart was pining for capricious Crawford. It surely must have amazed Gable's ever-growing legion of fans to witness their screen idol standing around as a good-natured faithful soul, smothering his feelings for the heroine, and being such a thoughtful chap as to send her blue cornflowers for her wedding to another man. At least, the script was kind enough to allow Gable the final victory, as Crawford raced aboard his transatlantic ship before it departed New York, in time to admit she loved him truly and that she was ready to take the thrashing he has always promised her.

With Charles Butterworth and Billie Burke on hand for feather-brained humor interludes, and Rosalind Russell displaying a bit of her brash, forthright personality, it would hardly seem necessary for the film to indulge in Mack Sennett–style slapstick, but that it did. In the course of *Forsaking All Others,* with its soundstage Adirondacks outdoor sets, Montgomery and Crawford, both attired in white and she riding on the handlebars of his bicycle, are catapulted over a fence into a pig sty. Later, when drenched in a storm and drying off in a conveniently available cabin, Montgomery is found warming himself by the fire and quickly gets a very hot seat. Crawford had her share of visual antics in falling off a masseuse's table, doing a slide in the mud, and surviving a slapdash car accident. For the sake of his screen dignity, Gable's character remained aloof from these oncamera shenanigans.

Eileen Creelman (*New York Sun*) summed it all up: "Mr. Gable, steadily improving is charming and gay as the patient suitor. Miss Crawford, handsome in spite of those Adrian costumes, is just Miss Crawford."

## LOVE ON THE RUN
### *(MGM, 1936) 81M.*

Producer, Joseph L. Mankiewicz; director, W. S. Van Dyke II; based on the story *Beauty and the Beast* by Alan Green, Julian Brodie; screenplay, John Lee Mahin, Manuel Seff, Gladys Hurlbut; costumes, Adrian; sound, Douglas Shearer; camera, Oliver T. Marsh; editor, Frank Sullivan.

Joan Crawford (Sally Parker); Clark Gable (Michael Anthony); Franchot Tone (Barnabas Pells); Reginald Owen (Baron Spandermann); Mona Maris (Baroness); Ivan Lebedeff (Prince Igor); Charles Judels (Lieutenant of Police); William Demarest (Editor); Dewey Robinson (Italian Father); Bobby (Bobs) Watson (Italian Boy); Betty Jane Graham (Italian Girl); Charles Trowbridge (Express Company Manager); George Davis (Sergeant of Police); Donald Meek (Caretaker); Harry Allen (Chauffeur); James B. Carson (French Waiter); Billy Gilbert (Cafe Manager); Reynolds Denniston (Inspector McCaskill); Egon Brecher (Dr. Gorsay); Richard Lancaster (English News Photographer); Donald Kerr, Charles Irwin (Movie Cameramen); Otto H. Fries (Mechanic); Elsa Buchanan, Viola Moore, Iris Moore (English Department Store Girls); Nanette Lafayette (French Maid); Lilyan Irene (Bit); Norman Ainsley (Newspaper Reporter); Jimmie Aubrey (Airplane Mechanic); Bob Cory (Assistant to Inspector McCaskill); Gunnis Davis (Hotel Elevator Man); Douglas Gordon (Cockney Comic Chauffeur); Frank Du Frane (Assistant to Editor); H. L. Fisher-Smith (Reporter); John Power (English Major Domo); Montague Shaw (Hotel Manager); Yorke Sherwood (London Bobbie); Tom Herbert (Comic Taxi Driver); Adi Kuznetzoff (Rudolph, Baron's Servant); Phillips Smalley, Richard Powell, Margaret Marquis, Eleanor Stewart, Leonard Kinsky, Jack Dewees (Bits); Alice Ardell (French Maid); Joe Mack (Hack Driver); Duke York (Paul, Baron's Chauffeur); Agostino Borgat (French Comptroller); Fred Cavens, Fred W. Malatesta (French Waiters); Gennaro Curci (French Train Announcer); Alphonse Martel (French Spy); Frank Mayo (Traveling Man); Frank Puglia (Waiter); Genaro Spagnoli (French Taxi Driver); Jacques Vanair (French Telegraph Operator); Viola Moore (Cockney Telephone Girl); Robert du Couedic (French Clerk); Bobby Watson (Assistant Manager); George Andre Berenger (Comedy Reactionary).

New York Premiere: Capitol Theatre—November 27, 1936
New York Television Debut: CBS—August 2, 1959

## Synopsis

At the last moment, American heiress Sally Parker, who lives abroad, cannot go through with her wedding to Prince Igor of Taluska. She leaves him at the altar and takes refuge in her hotel suite. Meanwhile, Michael Anthony and Barnabas Pells, correspondents for rival newspapers, are assigned to get the scoop on stratosphere flier Baron Spandermann. Sally and Michael meet, and she, not knowing he is a newsman, enlists his help in escaping from her ticklish social predicament. Before long, Michael is Sally's escort in a daring ruse, for they have discovered that the Baron and his wife are actually spies out to grab British fortification secrets. Having stolen the Baron's plane, Michael and Sally make an amateurish but safe landing in the French countryside, and, disguised as peasants, head for Paris. After cabling the story to his paper, Michael joins Sally in spending the night at an old palace where he confesses he loves her. But the next morning when Sally sees the newspaper headlines she realizes Michael's true occupation and, believing he is just capitalizing on their adventure, she quarrels with him. To get even with Michael, Sally takes off with Barney who has been dogging the couple's trail. On the Nice–bound train, the Baron captures Sally, while Barney is thrown off the train. Michael comes to Sally's timely rescue, and after the spies are rounded up, he and Sally take off in the Baron's plane, leaving Barney holding the bag once again.

◆—◆—◆

Since Clark Gable's Oscar-winning *It Happened One Night* (1934), MGM had been seeking its own runaway heiress cinema tale in which to star its boxoffice king. *Love on the Run* was deemed just that vehicle. To play the very wealthy heroine of the piece, a girl who abhors vulgar publicity, the studio selected Joan Crawford. While she was no Claudette Colbert-style comedienne, Crawford gave the role a balance of glamour and charm, no mean feat in themselves. Franchot Tone, Crawford's real-life husband, was selected for the standard "other man" role in the celluloid proceedings. (One can only wonder how such studio casting affected the Crawford–Tone marriage.)

John T. McManus (*New York Times*) ranked *Love on the Run* "A slightly daffy cinematic item of absolutely no importance." It had a bit of everything with proficient director W. S. Van Dyke II blending together the styles of Frank Capra and Rene Clair into an amalgam full of his own breezy way, and creating a flowing concoction of nonsense episodes. Any film that insisted that the canceled London wedding of heiress Sally Parker (Crawford) would knock the brewing European war off the front page headlines could not be taken seriously, and *Love on the Run* was one among many such madcap movie entries that existed in its own private fantasyland. For diversion, the film offered monocled Reginald Owen and svelte Mona Marris as dastardly Axis spies, Ivan Lebedeff as a cavalier fortune-hunting Price, and Donald Meek as a most daffy palace caretaker.

*It Happened One Night* had its famous bus ride, so *Love on the Run* tried to follow suit by having Gable and Crawford tear across Europe, first in a borrowed plane, then in an ox cart, and later proceeding by train. Crawford had proven in the poorly received *The Gorgeous Hussy* (1936) that historical characterizations were not her celluloid forte, but in *Love on the Run* she demonstrated that MGM's onscreen arbiter of sobby, soggy dramas could, when pushed, manage to shed her pedestaled glamour to emote on a more carefree humane level. Granted she was still very much the lady of the wide eyes and flowing hair, but here she projected a casualness that was most commendable. For example, there was the scene when she and Gable spend an evening at the palace of Fontainbleau where they stop in Mme. de Maintenon's chambre, dress in Louis XV costumes, and perform a minuet which ends in a hula dance.

The pivotal plot question of *Love on the Run* hinged on Crawford's reactions when she learns that Gable is really one of those nasty, hounding newsmen she so despises. Nevertheless, this being a movie comedy, the action soon moves onto other adventures as she is kidnapped by the spies and later rescued by resilient Gable.

Because forced infectiousness was too often substituted for artful spontaneity, *Love on the Run* did not become a boxoffice winner. Critics such as Howard Barnes (*New York Herald-Tribune*) complimented Crawford on "her surprising volatile and amusing performance," while chiding Gable for being "less artful in holding to a key of bright insouciance."

## STRANGE CARGO
### *(MGM, 1940) 113M.*

Producer, Joseph L. Mankiewicz; director, Frank Borzage; based on the novel *Not Too Narrow, Not Too Deep* by Richard Sale; screenplay, Lawrence Hazard; art director, Cedric Gibbons; music, Franz Waxman; camera, Robert Planck; editor, Robert J. Kern.

Joan Crawford (Julie); Clark Gable (Andre Verne); Ian Hunter (Cambreau); Peter Lorre (Cochon); Paul Lukas (Hessler); Albert Dekker (Moll); J. Edward Bromberg (Flaubert); Eduardo Ciannelli (Telez); Victor Varconi (Fisherman); John Arledge (Dufond); Frederic Worlock (Grideau); Paul Fix (Benet); Bernard Nedell (Marfeu); Francis McDonald (Moussenq); Betty Compson (Suzanne); Charles Judels (Renard); Jack Mulhall (Dunning); Dewey Robinson (Georges); Harry Cording, Richard Alexander, Bud Fine, James Pierce, Hal Wynants, Christian J. Frank, Mitchell Lewis, Stanley Andrews, Dick Cramer, Ray Teal, Jack Adair (Guards); Gene Coogan, Eddie Foster, Frank Lackteen, Harry Semels (Convicts); Art Dupuis (Orderly); Stanley Andrews (Constable); William Edmunds (Watchman).

New York Premiere: Capitol Theatre—April 25, 1940
New York Television Debut: CBS—February 7, 1957

## Synopsis

Julie is a shady cafe performer in a shabby town near a French penal colony in New Guinea. One night she encounters prisoner Andre Verne who is on wharf duty. Later Moll and other criminals, including Cambreau, Telez, Hessler, Dufond, Flaubert, and Cochon, escape from the compound and strike out through the jungle to the seacoast where a boat awaits them. Along the way they encounter Andre who has escaped and taken the now out-of-work Julie with him. In the course of the group's trek, most of them die, with each being comforted by the Christ-like, gentle, mysterious Cambreau. Finally the only survivors are Julie, Andre, and Cambreau. Cynical but decent, Andre refuses to be softened by the philosophy of Cambreau, but after pushing Cambreau overboard and then rescuing him, Andre has a change of heart. With his rediscovered faith in God, Andre tells Julie he loves her, and asks her to wait for him while he returns to the penal colony to serve out his sentence. She readily agrees.

◆—◆—◆

For Joan Crawford to eschew glamour for dramatic authenticity was a strong indication that she realized her glorious MGM days were passing behind her and that she must create a new personality if she wished to survive in the Hollywood professional jungle. "At last," wrote Lee Mortimer (*New York Daily Mirror*) of *Strange Cargo*, "Joan Crawford has been given a role that approaches her own horizon, in which she can convince the most skeptical that her range is far beyond a spitfire adventuress or an animated fashion-form." That the script and direction did its best to obscure the tarnished nature of Crawford's Julie (the girl was a prostitute!) was not the star's fault and she did her best to suggest by implication the sordid background of the "heroine."

Too bad that Crawford's superior emoting in *Strange Cargo* should occur in a movie so plagued by censorship and boxoffice problems. It was one of the first major Hollywood pictures to receive a roasting from the Legion of Decency, which abhored the film *in toto*. The Legion declared, "This picture, in which religion is the prominent issue, presents a naturalistic concept of religion contrary to the teachings of Christ, irreverent use of Scripture and lustful complications in dialogue and situations." The censorship group gave *Strange Cargo* a C (condemned) rating. Even after the studio made the demanded changes in the completed picture and it was rerated by the Legion to Class A, section 2 (unobjectionable for adults), many cities still refused to book the picture and it suffered from this underexposed release.

Above and beyond its sensitive subject matter, *Strange Cargo* had major internal artistic problems. The allegory presentation was considered too slim a gambit upon which to expand the basic "I-escaped–from-Devil's Island" theme. Moreover, because of the star system philosophy, director Frank Borzage was not able to focus as intensely as he should have on the Christ-like figure of Cambreau (Ian Hunter), but had to subvert screen time to the relationship between Crawford and Gable (he being at the peak of his popularity with the prior year's *Gone with the Wind*).

Adding to these problems, Metro had initially hard-sold the picture as a sensual screen study. "But alas for the sensation seekers. Though Clark does everything masculine except lower his wings like an amorous rooster and Joan is the toughest female this side of a lady wrestler, that's not the trouble. They do nothing off color" [Archer Winsten *(New York Post)* ].

How has *Strange Cargo* been rated in the annals of screen history? Ivan Butler in *Religion in the Cinema* (1969) appropriately categorizes the movie as "A minor film, but not without a certain atmosphere." Of the stars' performances, Howard Barnes *(New York Herald-Tribune)* was quite typical of his fellow journalists when he wrote, "Clark Gable contributes an acceptable portrait of a convict on the lam . . . Joan Crawford is as good as you could expect any actress to be in the preposterous role of the drab [cabaret entertainer] . . ."

For the record, Crawford, for the first time since *Paid* (1930), scarcely wore any face makeup oncamera in *Strange Cargo* and her three–dress readywear wardrobe cost under forty dollars.

## THE YEARS AFTER

After *Strange Cargo*, Joan Crawford would only make four additional films on the home lot before her MGM studio contract was terminated. The George Cukor-directed *A Woman's Face* (1941) provided her with a solid dramatic vehicle, but the remake of *When Ladies Meet* (1941) and the World War II Resistance dramas, *Reunion in France* (1942) and *Above Suspicion* (1943), were empty shells of entertainment. On loanout, Crawford replaced the late Carole Lombard in Columbia's comedy *They All Kissed the Bride* (1942), but Crawford proved to be no Lombard. A much subdued Crawford signed on at Warner Bros., but Bette Davis was the queen bee at that studio and save for a brief guest appearance in *Hollywood Canteen* (1944) Crawford remained professionally idle for nearly two years. Then came Michael Curtiz' *Mildred Pierce* (1945), which brought Crawford an Oscar and a renewed stretch as a leading lady, first as a liberated, taut society dame in *Humoresque* (1946) and *Harriet Craig* (1950), and then as the tough moll in *Flamingo Road* (1949), *The Damned Don't Cry* (1950), and *This Woman Is Dangerous* (1952). Along the way Crawford performed in the much underrated *Possessed* (1947) as the schizoid involved with Raymond Massey and Van Heflin, and *Goodbye,*

*My Fancy* (1951), in which she vibrated proper waves as the career woman who finds herself falling in love with love and sugary ideals.

The 1950s were a transitional decade for Crawford, who returned to the Dore Schary-controlled MGM for *Torch Song* (1953), then found herself forced to accept a Western at lower echelon Republic. Ironically, this film, *Johnny Guitar* (1954), directed by Nicholas Ray, has gained a sterling reputation among Europeans. A six picture deal at Columbia led to such quivering soap operas as *Autumn Leaves* (1956) and the would-be exploitative *The Story of Esther Costello* (1957). In 1956 Crawford married Alfred Steele, vice-president of the Pepsi Cola Company, and the marriage launched the star on a whole new career as a good will ambassadress for the company, a post which has continued long after Steele's death in 1959. Joining with Bette Davis, another veteran star, in the grand guignol *What Ever Happened to Baby Jane?* (1962), Crawford proved she was not washed up in Hollywood. Crawford's most recent films have been shoddy mock horror entries, including the dismal *Trog* (1970). She has appeared in several television episodes ranging from "The Lucy Show" to "Route 66" to substituting for daughter Christina on the daytime soap opera "The Secret Storm." Today, Crawford, still very much the active living legend, devotes her energies to retaining her amazing celebrity status, making an occasional video commercial or talk show appearance, and authoring such books as *My Way of Life* (1971).

Clark Gable would continue on for another twenty years of moviemaking after *Strange Cargo*, finding a luscious post-Crawford co-star in Metro's Lana Turner. After Gable's untimely death in 1960, it would be Crawford (the supreme self-publicist and Gable-booster) who would best sum up the legend that was Gable:

"Clark Gable was the King of an empire called Hollywood. The empire is not what it once was—but the King has not been dethroned, even after death. . . . [he] was the most exciting costar I ever had. I never got over the tremendous magic of that man. It was like a magical thrill that never diminished. . . . He was a fine man and a natural actor . . . a pro from the word go. To this day, Clark Gable has remained my favorite costar."

In **Hold Your Man** (MGM, 1933)

# Chapter 5

# Clark Gable
# &
# Jean Harlow

## CLARK GABLE

*For biographical and career data, see Chapter 4, Clark Gable-Joan Crawford.*

## JEAN HARLOW

**5′ 3½″**
**109 pounds**
**Blonde hair**
**Gray-blue eyes**
**Pisces**

*Real name: Harlean Carpentier. Born March 3, 1911, Kansas City, Kansas. Married Charles McGrew (1927); divorced 1931. Married Paul Bern (1932); widowed 1932. Married Hal Rosson (1933); divorced 1935. Died June 7, 1937.*

### FEATURE FILMS

*Moran of the Marines* (Par., 1928)
*Fugitives* (Fox, 1929)
*Close Harmony* (Par., 1929)

*Love Parade* (Par., 1929)
*The Saturday Night Kid* (Par., 1929)
*New York Nights* (UA, 1929)

Hell's Angels (UA, 1930)
City Lights (UA, 1931)
The Secret Six (MGM, 1931)
Iron Man (Univ., 1931)
Public Enemy (WB, 1931)
Goldie (Fox, 1931)
Platinum Blonde (Col., 1931)
Three Wise Girls (Col., 1932)
The Beast of the City (MGM, 1932)
Red-Headed Woman (MGM, 1932)
Red Dust (MGM, 1932)
Dinner at Eight (MGM, 1933)

Hold Your Man (MGM, 1933)
Bombshell (MGM, 1933)
The Girl From Missouri (MGM, 1934)
Reckless (MGM, 1935)
China Seas (MGM, 1935)
Riffraff (MGM, 1935)
Wife Versus Secretary (MGM, 1936)
Suzy (MGM, 1936)
Libeled Lady (MGM, 1936)
Personal Property (MGM, 1937)
Saratoga (MGM, 1937)

Lionel Barrymore, Clark Gable, and Jean Harlow in **Saratoga** (MGM, 1937)

Jean Harlow, John Mack Brown, and Clark Gable
in **The Secret Six** (MGM, 1931)

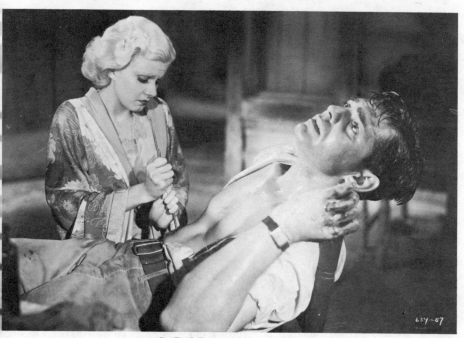

In **Red Dust** (MGM, 1932)

On the set of **Hold Your Man** (MGM, 1933)

Wallace Beery, Clark Gable, and Jean Harlow in **China Seas** (MGM, 1935)

Advertisement for **Wife Versus Secretary** (MGM, 1936)

Jean Harlow, Clark Gable, and Myrna Loy in **Wife Versus Secretary.**

# THE SECRET SIX
## *(MGM, 1931) 83M.*

Director, George Hill; story-screenplay, Frances Marion; sound, Robert Shirley; wardrobe, Rene Hubert; camera, Harold Wenstrom; editor, Blanche Sewell.

Wallace Beery (Louis Scorpio); Lewis Stone (Richard Newton); John Mack Brown (Hank Rogers); Jean Harlow (Anne Courtland); Marjorie Rambeau (Peaches); Paul Hurst (Nick Mizoski the Gouger); Clark Gable (Carl Luckner); Ralph Bellamy (Johnny Franks); John Miljan (Smiling Joe Colimo); DeWitt Jennings (Chief Donlin); Murray Kinnell (Dummy Metz); Fletcher Norton (Jimmy Delano); Louis Natheaux (Eddie); Frank McGlynn (Judge); Theodore Von Eltz (District Attorney); Tom London (Hood).

New York Premiere: Capitol Theatre—May 1, 1931
New York Television Debut: CBS—July 3, 1961

## Synopsis

In Central during Prohibition, Louis Scorpio, known as Slaughterhouse for his past job in the stockyards, joins with Nick Mizoski and Johnny Franks in the bootleg liquor business. They are guided in their illegal activities by an experienced, but drunkard attorney, Richard Newton. When their successful business spreads to the big city, a rival gangster leader, Smiling Joe Colimo, becomes anxious over the competition. Franks and some henchmen pay a call on Colimo's brother at one of his hangout clubs. Franks kills Colimo's brother and later pushes the blame onto Scorpio, hoping that Colimo's men will eliminate his troublesome cohort. However, Scorpio is only wounded and, learning of his partner's doublecross, kills Franks. Hank Rogers and Carl Luckner, two crime reporters, set out to investigate this rash of gangland killings. When fast-rising kingpin Scorpio notes the newsmen hanging around his cafe, he pays club hatcheck girl Anne Courtland a bonus to keep the reporters busy and diverted from their professional goal. Meanwhile, six leading businessmen in town, who are known only as the masked "Secret Six," hire Hank to get evidence against Scorpio's gang. He locates the gun used by Scorpio for his killings, but is spotted in his investigations and is killed on a subway train. Angered by the murder, Anne agrees to cooperate with the law in bringing Scorpio to trial. Carl, who is now working for the "Secret Six," keeps track of Scorpio, who has been acquitted by the bought jury, and trails the gang when they kidnap Anne. Later he himself is captured, but when the police raid the hideout, Carl is able to set Anne free. Scorpio and Newton attempt to flee but in an argument over the divisions of the cash stakes, Scorpio shoots Newton who, before he expires, guns down Scorpio.

In a year loaded with the release of such top flight gangster melodramas as *Little Caesar, Public Enemy,* and *Quick Millions, The Secret Six* still stands out as an extraordinary feature. "The picture is unusually well directed and it moves with a pulsating speed" [Thornton Delehanty *(New York Post)*]. Director George Hill, obviously influenced by the stark effectiveness of the German cinema, loaded his production with intriguing tracking shots. He was very successful in creating an ominous atmosphere which rose about the continual gunplay, and, for good measure added the silent-serial-like masked vigilante group known as "The Secret Six." (The latter element is the one aspect of the film which, upon rescreening today, evokes audience laughter.) At the time of its initial release, *The Secret Six* created such a furor of notoriety that some states (New Jersey, among others), banned the film entirely, while other jurisdictions had their censor boards stringently cut the running continuity, unsuccessfully removing some of the nonstop violence and gore.

The focal point of *The Secret Six* was unequivocally Wallace Beery. In fact, scenarist Frances Marion, having provided Beery with a meaty role in *The Big House* (1930), had been ordered by MGM studio executive Irving Thalberg to create a new vehicle for gruff star Beery. She modeled her screenplay on an Al Capone-type character, who becomes in the film the thug Louis Scorpio, who drinks milk and peddles beer. Next in importance to Beery in this film was contract player Lewis Stone, cast as the shady lawyer Richard Newton whose three favorite items in life were money, liquor, and his walking stick. His shifty-eyed, cerebral performance was far removed from his later benign screen series characterization as the judge in the *Andy Hardy* pictures.

Within *The Secret Six*, neither ash-blonde Jean Harlow nor moustacheless Clark Gable have big roles, but each created substantial stirs within the moviegoing audience. Harlow had survived her Hal Roach comedy short days and had made an effective splash with Howard Hughes' *Hell's Angels* (1930). This was her first Metro feature, and although she was billed above veteran player Marjorie Rambeau, the latter actress had more solid oncamera time in *The Secret Six* in her role as Peaches, a rough and tumble moll who never forgives Beery for plugging her John, Ralph Bellamy. On the other hand, Gable, who would have twelve 1931 releases, had made his initial screen mark with fans earlier that year as the bootlegger in Joan Crawford's *Dance, Fools, Dance.* As René Jordan carefully delineates in his book, *Clark Gable* (1973), *The Secret Six* found Gable playing the first of his many onscreen reporter roles. However, the distinction between his characterization as a newsman or a racketeer was very thin indeed, leading many viewers to mistake Gable as a close ally of the underworld. And small wonder, for throughout the movie Gable's Carl Luckner pals around with the hoodlums and accepts their bribes. Only later is it revealed that he is an undercover agent for the black-masked "The Secret Six."

Others in the compelling cast of *The Secret Six* included John Mack

Brown, whose star on the studio lot was fast waning. He was billed above Gable, playing a rival reporter (of the *Tribune*) who also makes a play for Harlow while he and Gable are ostensibly tracking down evidence on the hoodlum ring. When Gable and Brown are tipped off to Harlow's overt charms by her devious boss (Beery), Gable flippantly greets the cigarette counter girl, "Hi, baby. How's business?" Sizing her up pretty quickly, he suggests, "Listen, if you're goin' fall for anybody, make it me. I'm dependable." Just to prove his heart, if not his mind, is on the proper track, he adds, "I even could take you around to meet my Aunt Emma." (This last little bit becomes a running gag in the picture.)

Gable informs Brown, "She is bad. Believe me there's one scoop you're not going to get without a little competition." But because Gable is soon too busy chasing after headline news ("I'm gonna make a big story outta this," he tells Beery who has just climbed up another underworld rung via murder), it proves to be restrained, genteel Brown who becomes the focal point of Harlow's attention, with the two of them kissing in the cloakroom, and later Harlow admitting she is truly falling for Brown because he is on the level. Thereafter in *The Secret Six*, Gable and Harlow encounter each other only fleetingly, until near the climax when he attempts to rescue her and is himself tied up and beaten by Beery who wants information on the vigilantes' identities.

Interestingly enough, while Gable (he of the multi-intoned "yeah") remains constant in his performance level, despite his ambiguously written characterization, it is Harlow who shows more histrionic improvement within the course of the celluloid story. She is not much more than a flashily dressed floozy, baby fat and all, in the movie's opening scenes, as she swaggers in and out of scenes and later postures in her finery purchased by protector Beery. Her delivery is initially slow and insecure, but later in the plot when she rushes onto the subway train to warn Brown that the gang is after him, she has developed a certain finesse, making her hysterics credible. Still later, dressed in a black outfit for Brown's funeral, she demonstates a previously unseen poise as Gable leads her out of the church. Harlow offers her screen best in the courtroom scenes where she admits that she has a $20,000 flat at 118 Park Drive, a limousine, and a eight-carat square-cut diamond, all courtesy of Beery. But when interrogated whether she loves this man, she spits out her answer with remarkable impact: "No! I loathe and despise him!"

*The New York Times'* Mordaunt Hall rated Gable's acting here as "forceful," with Bland Johaneson *(New York Daily Mirror)* commending Harlow for her "plausible character."

## RED DUST
*(MGM, 1932) 83M.*

Producer-director, Victor Fleming; based on the play by Wilson Collison; screenplay, John Mahin; camera, Harold G. Rosson; editor, Blanche Sewell.

Clark Gable (Dennis Carson); Jean Harlow (Vantine); Gene Raymond (Gary Willis); Mary Astor (Barbara Willis); Donald Crisp (Guidon); Tully Marshall (McQuarg); Forrester Harvey (Limey); Willie Fung (Hoy).

New York Premiere: Capitol Theatre—November 4, 1932
New York Television Debut: CBS—March 16, 1958

### Synopsis

In remote, steaming Indo-China, Dennis Carson is in charge of a sprawling rubber plantation, aided in overseeing the native workers by his two assistants, McQuarg and Guidon. On his return from Saigon Guidon travels on the same boat as Vantine, a prostitute one step ahead of the police. She comes to stay at the plantation, Dennis agreeing that she can wait there for the next boat arrival. He is at first indifferent to her, but soon realizes that beneath her tough exterior she is kind and sensitive. In the process he tumbles for her charms, and even asks her to accept a money stake. Later, engineer Gary Willis and his bride Barbara arrive. Soon after, Willis is stricken with fever, and Dennis nurses him back to health. Vantine next reappears on the scene, because the boat has broken down. Because Dennis is falling in love with Barbara he pays scant attention to Vantine. Meanwhile Willis recovers and Dennis sends him, along with McQuarg and Guidon, to supervise the construction of a jungle bridge. While they are away, Dennis and Barbara become more closely involved. When Willis returns, Dennis becomes ashamed of his behavior because Willis admires him so openly. Because he understands that Barbara could not adapt to plantation life, Dennis resumes his affair with Vantine. Barbara becomes furious and wounds Dennis with a gunshot. When Willis rushes in, Vantine covers up by saying Barbara was only protecting herself from Dennis' advances. Willis quits his post and leaves with Barbara. In the end Dennis realizes that, after all, Vantine is the woman for him.

◆━━◆━━◆

Wilson Collison's banal play *Red Dust*, heralded as a "volcanic drama of primitive passions," lasted only eight performances when it opened on Broadway in January, 1928. It fared much better onscreen, reuniting Clark Gable and Harlow in a teeming jungle drama that proved two combustible stars could generate very lucrative heat waves for entertainment-hungry viewers. Given *Red Dust*'s brazen moral values (it became a landmark of 1930s cinema as a high powered sex drama), Gable and Harlow have a chance for full play of their curiously similar sort of good-natured toughness. The best lines go to Harlow and she emerges the more interesting character. She bathes hilariously in a rain barrel, reads Gable a bed-

131

time story about a chipmunk and a rabbit, and carries on in unrestrained fashion. Her effortless vulgarity, humor, and *dishabillé* make a noteworthy characterization, as good in this type of genre as the late Jeanne Eagels' Sadie Thompson was onstage.

Seemingly having exhausted the soundstage boudoirs of New York and Hollywood for story locales, MGM wisely turned to an offbeat setting for *Red Dust*'s usual theme of infidelity. But if the locale was unique, the lead players were more unique in revealing their primitive aspects. Gable and Harlow were matched and contrasted against the more conventional Gene Raymond and duplistic Mary Astor. Gable's Dennis Carson is a rough-and-tumble hard-working man, a carryover from the British empire days when the white man's burden allowed him to play fast and loose with immoral women like Vantine (Harlow), yet still to aspire to wedded bliss with the likes of Astor's seemingly proper Barbara Willis. In this manner a character dichotomy is created that provides sufficiently abrasive storyline conflicts to push *Red Dust* through to a satisfactory conclusion. Under the old double standard, as depicted in the film, men like Gable could make women like Harlow become tarts. However, when asked to acknowledge these women's right to a fair existence, they merely dismiss them as the scum of the earth, that is, until Gable, like the viewer, realizes that this restless platinum blonde tramp is far from the average shady lady who always pops up in cinema representations of the Far East. She has a sense of humor (when cleaning out the parrot cage, she quips, "What you've been eating? Cement?"), a flaunted sensuality (always bra-less, and casually taking a bath in the compound's drinking water barrel), a quick mind beneath her brassy exterior (protecting Gable from Raymond's potential wrath), and a sensitive soul (still able to love a biased character like Gable after all the he-men in her sordid past).

What *Red Dust* boils down to, midst the tropical foliage, rain deluges, sand storms, and the superfluous subplots, is a battle royale between Gable's virility and Harlow's sensuality. It is a tie at the end, which quietly pleases both adversaries involved and the audience as well. *Red Dust* did much to make Gable and Harlow " . . . two of the screen's surest-fire box office bets of the moment" [Martin Dicksten *(Brooklyn Daily Eagle)*].

Perhaps the most important point proved by *Red Dust* was Harlow's natural abilities as a funny broad, in her way just as tart and amusing as the cinema's newest find, Mae West. Analyzing this aspect of the Harlow screen charm, Richard Watts, Jr. *(New York Herald-Tribune)* reported that Harlow " . . . is called upon to go in for the playing of amiably sardonic comedy and, by managing it with a shrewd and engagingly humorous skill, she proves herself a really deft comedienne." This broadening of Harlow's screen talent is all the more amazing when one considers that during production of *Red Dust*, twenty-one-year-old Harlow became a widow, for her producer husband Paul Bern committed suicide under the most peculiar of circumstances.

*Red Dust* would reappear as the basis of the series programmer *Congo Maisie* (1940) starring Ann Sothern. In 1953, *Red Dust* would be remade as *Mogambo,* with Gable repeating his original role, this time cast opposite Ava Gardner and Grace Kelly.

## HOLD YOUR MAN
### *(MGM, 1933) 88M.*

Producer-director, Sam Wood; story, Anita Loos; screenplay, Loos, Howard Emmett Rogers; title song, Arthur Freed and Nacio Herb Brown; art directors, Cedric Gibbons, Merrill Pye; set decorator, Edwin B. Willis; gowns, Adrian; camera, Harold G. Rosson; editor, Frank Sullivan.

Jean Harlow (Ruby Adams); Clark Gable [E. Huntington Hall (Eddie)]; Stuart Erwin (Al Simpson); Dorothy Burgess (Gypsy); Muriel Kirkland (Bertha Dillon); Garry Owen (Slim); Barbara Barondess (Sadie Kline); Paul Hurst (Aubrey Mitchell); Elizabeth Patterson (Miss Tuttle); Theresa Harris (Lily Mae Crippen); Inez Courtney (Maizie); Blanche Frederici (Mrs. Wagner); Helen Freeman (Miss Davis); George Reed (Reverend Crippen); Louise Beavers (Maid); Jack Cheatham, Frank Hagney (Cops); Jack Randall (Dance Extra); G. Pat Collins (Phil Dunn); Harry Semels (Neighbor); Nora Cecil (Miss Campbell the Sewing Instructress); Eva McKenzie (Cooking Teacher).

New York Premiere: Capitol Theatre—June 30, 1933
No New York Television Showing

### Synopsis

In an effort to escape from the police, who are chasing him for having defrauded a man of forty dollars, Eddie Hall rushes into the apartment of tough, young Ruby Adams and she agrees to hide him. They become friends and soon lovers, Ruby dropping her honest boyfriend, Al Simpson. Realizing that her hold over the elusive Eddie is not very strong, Ruby makes him jealous by stating that laundry owner Aubrey Mitchell has big things in store for her. This arouses Eddie's ire and he agrees to go along with his pal Slim in plotting a confidence scheme to bilk Mitchell of his money. Eddie is to walk in on Ruby while she is entertaining Mitchell and, pretending to be her brother, demand some shakedown money. When the appointed time comes, Eddie becomes so enraged with Mitchell's presence that he becomes rough, and when Mitchell in turn becomes pugnacious, Eddie slams him to the ground. When it is learned that Mitchell is dead, Eddie takes it on the lam, leaving Ruby to face the rap. She is sentenced to three years at a state reformatory. She is miserable there for more than the obvious reasons: one, she misses Eddie, and two, she is going to have a baby. Ruby's cellmate, Gypsy, who is Eddie's former mistress as well, is freed. She promptly tells Eddie about Ruby's condition.

When he in turn reveals how kind Ruby has been in making provisions for her on the outside, Gypsy wants to return the favor. She takes Eddie to the prison on visiting day and hides him in the church. With the help of some of the other prisoners they bring the heroine to the church and a black preacher, who had been visiting his daughter, marries them. Meanwhile the matron, having become suspicious of the goings-on, calls the police, who break into the church just as the ceremony is finished. Eddie is arrested and sentenced to prison. Upon his release he joins Ruby and their young son, intending to go straight.

◆——◆——◆

"Together Again in Another Man and Female Drama" proclaimed the MGM publicity releases. The studio was merely capitalizing on what the public already knew, "The popularity of the Jean Harlow-Clark Gable combination cannot be questioned" [Frank S. Nugent *(The New York Times)*].

If Harlow (top billed) and Gable were permitted a great deal of on-camera promiscuity in *Red Dust*, the onslaught of the industry production code bridled them with unconvincing conventionality through much of *Hold Your Man*, the least engaging of their six joint screen ventures.

Harlow's Ruby Adams is a tough Brooklyn hooker who thinks nothing of allowing an unknown, but handsome petty crook like Eddie to pop into her apartment one day while she is taking her bubble bath. Easy come, easy go, she figures, but the slangy dame has not counted on Gable's emotional effect on her. No sooner have the pursuing cops left (he fools them by jumping into the vacated bathtub, lathering his face with soap suds, and pretending to be her husband), than Gable is out to fleece Harlow, stealing back the money he gave her for her trouble. After a brief but tantalizing sally in the living room of her cheap abode, he skips out on her. But sexually agressive Harlow wants her innings and tracks Gable to his favorite cafe. He is playing hard to get, but after a sex-charged slow dance with her, their romance is off and running.

Gable: "Wait till you see how I'll grow on ya."
Harlow: "Yeah . . . like a carbuncle."

Later when they adjourn to his apartment, the little baggage continues her pursuit, but masks it in a fake authoritarian casualness, snidely remarking when she leaves, "I got what I came for." Gable, smirking with his cynical lopsided smile, and eyebrows arched, replies, "Are you sure?"

This is the stuff of good rousing sex drama, but then the movie goes all to pieces, suffocated by a superimposed morality of a regeneration melodrama that ill suits the two liberated screen stars. Gable and Harlow decide to marry (what for?), but instead she finds herself sentenced to a reformatory for his criminal offense. This cloistered institution is completely unlike those dreary repositories of wrongdoers inhabited by Barbara Stanwyck or Sylvia Sidney in their oncamera prison forays. In *Hold Your Man* there are long scenes of Harlow and the girls nobly working at sewing tables, in the kitchen, and in the thoughtfully provided recreation rooms. One of the few good bits in this interminable interlude occurs when the "girls" are herded off to Sunday chapel and in dissonant voices they attempt a bedraggled version of "Onward Christian Soldiers."

Even at this point, this crooks drama-turned-soap opera had yet to hit its high bathos mark, for soon the viewer observes Gable sneaking into the reformatory to see his girl. He decides that a conveniently stashed black preacher in the chapel must marry them now. "Give my kid a chance" Gable ludicrously begs the kindly reverend, and then the story lapses into a minor cliffhanger. Will the basically decent (ha!) couple complete the marriage ceremonies before the police break into the chapel? The answer, of course, is yes, with Gable emerging from his own prison term three years later to the waiting arms of Harlow and their little son. [A similar movie finale was handled far more sassily by Bob Hope and Jane Russell in the comedy Son of Paleface (1952).]

The critics were quick to carp at what MGM had done to the very popular Harlow-Gable team. "Miss Harlow is good in the beginning, excelling as she does in these hardboiled types, althogh we regretted to scent a touch of the Mae West technique in her acting, but later in the subdued, poor caught creature exhibit she seemed miscast. Mr. Gable, giving another of his easy, careless, sex-appealing portrayals, is virtually left out of the picture later. One missed him" [Marguerite Tazellar (New York Herald-Tribune)].

Hold Your Man was the third of four Harlow films in a row that Harold G. Rosson would photograph. Rosson and Harlow would wed in 1933 but by 1935 they would be divorced. At that time, in a rare act of diplomacy MGM substituted Ray June as Harlow's more frequent cameraman.

## CHINA SEAS
### (MGM, 1935) 89M.

Producer, Albert Lewin; director, Tay Garnett; based on the novel by Crosbie Garstin; screenplay, Jules Furthman, James Kevin McGuinness; song, Arthur Freed and Nacio Herb Brown; costumes, Adrian; art director, Cedric Gibbons; camera, Ray June; editor, William Levanway.

Clark Gable (Captain Alan Gaskell); Jean Harlow [China Doll (Dolly Portland)]; Wallace Beery (Jamesy MacArdle); Lewis Stone (Tom Davids); Rosalind Russell (Sybil Barclay); Dudley Digges (Dawson); C. Aubrey Smith (Sir Guy Wilmerding); Robert Benchley (Charlie McCaleb); William Henry (Rockwell); Live Demaigret (Mrs. Volberg); Lilian Bond (Mrs. Timmons); Edward Brophy (Wilbur Timmons); Soo Yong (Yu-Lan); Carol Ann Beery (Carol Ann); Akim Tamiroff (Romanoff); Ivan Lebedeff (Ngah); Hattie McDaniel (Isabel McCarthy); Donald Meek (Chess Player);

Emily Fitzroy (Lady); Pat Flaherty (Second Officer Kingston); Forrester Harvey (Steward); Tom Gubbins (Ship's Officer); Charles Irwin (Bertie the Purser); Willie Fung (Cabin Boy); Ferdinand Munier (Police Superintendent); Chester Gan (Rickshaw Boy); John Ince (Pilot).

New York Premiere: Capitol Theatre—August 9, 1935
New York Television Debut: CBS—March 15, 1959

## Synopsis

Captain Alan Gaskell, skipper of the "Kin Lung" on its way to Hong Kong with a valuable cargo aboard, is angered to find his mistress, China Doll, on board. To complicate matters, Alan's classy British fiancée, Sybil Barclay, has booked passage on the vessel. To console herself for Sybil's presence, China Doll involves herself in a drinking bout with Jamesy MacArdle, a scoundrelly China Seas trader. She manages to drink him under the table after winning a good deal of money from him. A torn fragment of a hundred pound note is among the bills and China Doll suspects that the Oriental writing on it could be important. Meanwhile, Alan has maneuvered the vessel through a typhoon and when he returns to his cabin he finds the China Doll there. He misinterprets her presence, not giving her a chance to warn him about MacArdle's plot to steal the gold aboard. She becomes incensed and decides to join MacArdle. She filches the key to the ship's armory for him and he thus can provide his Malay confederates with arms. After the ensuing battle, MacArdle signals a Malay pirate ship which draws up, and its men board the "Kin Lung." Although Alan is tortured, he refuses to tell the whereabouts of the gold. In the meantime, third officer Tom Davids, who is suffering under the stigma of cowardice, proves his bravery by stealing several bombs from Alan's cabin, putting them on his person and then tossing himself on to the pirate junk, as a human arsenal. The pirate's vessel is almost totally demolished, the Malays aboard the "Kin Lung" are taken prisoner, and MacArdle commits suicide. Alan now realizes that China Doll is the girl for him. He bids farewell to the amazed Sybil.

◆◆◆

For his second project in his new capacity as an independent producer at MGM, Irving Thalberg chose *China Seas*, reasoning, "To hell with art this time. I'm going to produce a picture that will make money." The million-dollar production, with its outstandingly agile cinematography by Ray June, did just that.

*China Seas* was based on the 1931 novel by the late Crosbie Garstin and required more than three years to whip up into proper shape, while reuniting° four players from *The Secret Six:* Clark Gable, Jean Harlow,

°In late 1933 MGM had abandoned preparation to match Gable and Harlow in a picturization of Robert Sherwood's ribald play, *Road to Rome*. George Cukor was to have directed the venture.

Wallace Beery, and Lewis Stone, each in the type of role he played best. Thalberg, who took a very active, concerned interest in this Tay Garnett-directed vehicle, insured the picture's success by converting it into an ocean-going *Grand Hotel* story. The film was quickly rated a "lusty and tempestuous record of romance and bloodshed in tropic waters; . . ." *(New York Post)*. It was a surefire hit at the boxoffice.

In *China Seas*, the viewer is quickly introduced to the cast, as the "Kin Lung" is about to push off from Hong Kong. The assorted passengers and crew are seen boarding the vessel, promising a most diverting eighty-nine minutes ahead. There is hard-working, hard-drinking Captain Alan Gaskell (Gable); third officer Tom Davids (Stone), once a sea captain before he cracked under the pressure; and Sir Guy Wilmerding (C. Aubrey Smith), the upstanding shipline owner. The assorted passengers include a steerage full of coolies. Above deck there is the perpetually soused novelist Charlie McCaleb (Robert Benchley); Scottish merchant and game hunter Jamesy MacArdle (Beery) who has a rascally air; imperious English widow Sybil Barclay (Rosalind Russell) with whom Gable has had an affair and now may wed; and China Doll (Harlow), Gable's very opinionated mistress. These diverse characters are kept within the film's focus by the simple plot premise: the "Kin Lung" must pass through dangerous pirate waters and Gable has a most valuable cargo aboard (250,000 pounds' worth of gold hidden in a steamroller).

If Harlow's Dolly Portland, alias the China Doll, bears striking similarities to Marlene Dietrich's Shanghai Lily in *Shanghai Express* (1932), there is good reason, since scripter Jules Furthman was involved with both films. But Harlow's trollop is much more in the "swell-gal" tradition (she is a faithful mistress, labeling Gable her "number one sweetheart in the archipelago"), and far less a lady of mystery than Dietrich's on-camera high-priced whore. As was Harlow's usual screen custom, she revels in her unbridled (braless) ways, but for the sake of audience sympathy, her character craves the respectability and attention men inevitably offer to refined, silky blue bloods like Russell's Englishwoman. When feisty Harlow learns she may lose Gable to this creature, she warns him, "You can't quit me any more than I can quit you, and you can kiss a stack of cookbooks on that!" In her own temperamental, rowdy way, Harlow proves to be a minor temptress in her slinky Adrian-designed outfits, tampering with Beery's brutish affections and later indulging in a lusty drinking game, "Admiral Puff Puff," with him, all to serve her own jealousy-streaked purposes. That Harlow's China Doll is an unique woman full of many disparate charms is substantiated at the finale when the defeated Beery admits to her, "Lovin' you is the only decent thing I ever did in my life, and even that was a mistake." Within *China Seas*, director Garnett did not forget Harlow's effectiveness with a tart comedy scene. She proved especially effective in her bit of mock politeness as she visits Gable's cabin to warn him of the take-over plot, or in the sequence in the salon where she offers her high-toned English rival (Russell) a well-deserved lesson in deportment.

Oscar-winning [*It Happened One Night* (1934)] Gable, who would appear in two other rugged outdoor dramas in 1935, *Call of the Wild* and *Mutiny on the Bounty*, was well cast as the romantically unrealistic dynamo of a ship's captain, salty yet genteel, rough yet gentle, crude yet refined. Even with a three day's hangover he is perspicacious enough to spot stowaways hiding amidst the Chinese women in steerage. When a typhoon threatens to scuttle the ship he not only steers the vessel onto a safe course, but prevents a young passenger (Beery's real-life adopted daughter, Carol Ann) from being crushed by a careening piano in the salon. On deck, after several coolies have been flattened by the untethered steamroller, Gable is the one man who can secure it in position. Later after the Oriental pirates have boarded the ship and Gable is in the custody of Ngah (Ivan Lebedeff) and his men, Gable bravely undergoes assorted tortures that make James Bond's pain endurance threshold look like kindergarten games. Even after the iron boot is applied to Gable and he has fainted twice, he still refuses to talk. Beery is forced to admit, "There can't be any gold, or he would've talked. Nobody can be that tough!" Having undergone this grueling punishment, Gable's comic-strip-like hero still has enough strength to later point the cannon at the pirate junk and complete the job that Stone's exploded grenades began.

The voyage now over and the gold saved, Gable can once more turn to the ever-present Harlow. He dismisses the Russell affair by telling the loyal blonde, "Yes, I loved her, but not the way I do you." As the film ends he makes it clear he will stand by Harlow at the pending maritime trial.

Once again Gable and Harlow received better notices than the picture itself. "Since the Metro-Goldwyn magnates grimly refuse to permit Miss Harlow, the screen's most talented comedienne, an opportunity to display her brilliant gift for hilarity, it is at least pleasant to find her in so lively and colorful a melodrama as *China Seas*. . . . Mr. Gable's new role wisely permits him to be reasonably rowdy, rather than extravagantly noble, and the result is a highly effective performance" [Richard Watts, Jr. *(New York Herald-Tribune)*].

Gable and Harlow made their second joint appearance on radio's "Hollywood Hotel," this time on August 6, 1935, to present dramatic scenes from *China Seas*.

## WIFE VERSUS SECRETARY
### *(MGM, 1936) 85M.*

Producer, Hunt Stromberg; director, Clarence Brown; based on the story by Faith Baldwin; screenplay, Norman Krasna, Alice Duer Miller, John Lee Mahin; costumes, Adrian; art director, Cedric Gibbons; music,

Herbert Stothart and Edward Ward; camera, Ray June; editor, Frank E. Hull.

Clark Gable (Van Stanhope); Jean Harlow (Helen "Whitey" Wilson); Myrna Loy (Linda Stanhope); May Robson (Mimi); Hobart Cavanaugh (Joe); James Stewart (Dave); George Barbier (Underwood); Gilbert Emery (Simpson); Margaret Irving (Edna Wilson); William Newell (Tom Wilson); Marjorie Gateson (Eve Merritt); Leonard Carey (Taggart); Charles Trowbridge (Hal Harrington); John M. Qualen (Mr. Jenkins); Hilda Howe (Mary Conners); Mary MacGregor (Ellen); Gloria Holden (Joan Carstairs); Tommy Dugan (Finney); Jack Mulhall (Howard); Frank Elliott (Mr. Barker); Greta Meyer (German Cook); Aileen Pringle (Mrs. Barker); Frank Puglia (Hotel Clerk); Myra Marsh (Miss Clark); Holmes Herbert (Frawley); Frederick Burton (Trent); Harold Minjir (Williams); Maurice Cass (Bakewell); Tom Herbert (Business Man); Guy D'Ennery (Cuban Waiter); Niles Welch (Tom Axel); Richard Hemingway (Bridegroom); Paul Ellis (Raoul); Tom Rowan (Battleship); Edward Le Saint, Helen Shipman (Bits); Clay Clement (Herbert); Tom Mahoney (Policeman); Nena Quartaro (Telephone Operator); Charles Irwin (Information Clerk); Andre Cheron (Frenchman); Eugene Borden (Ship's Officer); Hooper Atchley (Postal Clerk); Lucille Ward (Scrub Woman); Clifford Jones (Elevator Boy).

New York Premiere: Capitol Theatre—February 28, 1936
New York Television Debut: CBS—August 5, 1958

### Synopsis

Van Stanhope, a prosperous young publisher, and his attractive wife Linda have been happily wed for three years. Linda finds the idea of being jealous of his pretty secretary, Whitey Wilson, silly, particularly since Whitey is almost engaged to a young man named Dave. Eventually the insinuations of other people begin to have their effect on Linda and she wonders why Van allows Whitey to remain his private secretary when he could easily have advanced her to a better job in the firm. Meanwhile, Van becomes involved in a bid to combine one of his company's magazines with a lower priced weekly and flies to Havana to close the important deal. After he has left, Whitey, the only person knowing of the pending deals, learns some new facts which Van must know immediately. She telephones him and he orders her to come down there at once. Arriving there, she and Van work all night and the next day to complete the negotiation papers. The deal is concluded and he and Whitey celebrate that night. When he fails to telephone Linda as he promised, she calls him. Whitey answers the phone, and Linda is now sure that her husband and Whitey are having an affair. Linda decides on a separation and books passage on a European-bound ship. Whitey goes to the ship

139

and tells Linda that she is a fool to give up Van, since if she leaves she will lose him forever. Whitey returns to the office and is about to comply with Van's order that she buy some new clothes for a forthcoming Bermuda trip, but Linda appears on the scene, and the couple are reconciled. Whitey goes out and finds Dave waiting for her.

◆◆◆

MGM and producer Hunt Stromberg played it safe by loading this grade A soap opera with three top stars and relying on a story by the inestimable Faith Baldwin. With such a combination, *Wife Versus Secretary* was bound to draw in the fans, especially movie stalwarts like wives and secretaries. "It is a slicked-up story, designed for the lowest common denominator trade, and to insure its popular appeal the producers have been careful to give it the full measure of its essential vulgarity" [Thornton Delehanty *(New York Post)*].

Whatever one may think of the film's specious storyline, the cast had admirable production values to back up the wobbly interplay. The shimmering white sets by Cedric Gibbons (effectively captured by cinematographer Ray June) were enhanced by the range of smashing costumes, including Myrna Loy's sublime outfits, Jean Harlow's "practical" workday wardrobe and Clark Gable's carefully tailored, natty suits.

The key to the mundane plot premise of *Wife Versus Secretary* is muttered by Gable at one point in the proceedings, "If you want to keep a man honest, never call him a liar." It is Gable's oncamera mother, that impish, at times imperious, always all-knowing (the wrong things) May Robson who delights in filling Loy's ears with distorted tidbits about Gable's relationship to his too attractive secretary. At first, Loy refuses to heed Robson's gossip, because she firmly believes in marriage, "I try to make his life smooth and pleasant. The opposite of all that back there— worry and action and achievement. I want to be the refuge from that, to laugh or just be quiet with him." But soon Robson's remarks have their effect and the once ideal marriage between Loy and Gable is breaking apart. This situation leads the poorly conceived scenario into making a major blunder, for it forces Loy, known in filmdom as the "perfect wife" oncamera to turn into what Richard Watts, Jr. *(New York Herald-Tribune)* described as "a whining, querulous and suspicious wife who is always being nobly tragic, in a sort of casual Ann Harding fashion." This immediately makes Harlow's Whitey Wilson seemingly a far more appealing character, but even this sympathy reversal has its limits, because Harlow is cast in such an unrealistic haloed light. After all it is hard to believe that our gal Harlow could not only be a very bright secretary (she almost maneuvers the merger deal herself) but is so thoughtful of others' feelings to avoid falling in love with her boss whom she admires with tremendous platonic affection. Thus Harlow ". . . has no chance to be hoydenish and as a result solidifies into something a little too unemotional to carry weight" *(Brooklyn Daily Eagle)*.

As for Gable, usually the virile, self-possessed soul, he is here so agog in his love for conservative Loy that he hardly (!) notices Harlow is a very attractive woman, that is until Loy goads him into re-examining the girl's overall assets, and he comes up with startling figures. Perhaps the apex of the star's atypical performance occurs in the Havana hotel room sequence, where, having celebrated the victory too much, both Gable and Harlow are a bit tipsy. It is a warm, langorous night. They are pleasantly filled with good food and booze, and flushed with success, and for a moment it looks as if they might give in to one another's repressed sexual appeal. But no. All Harlow does is to remove Gable's shoes, ease him onto the bed, and after their coffee and sandwiches are finished, call it quits. Such a scene is most uncharacteristic of the usual Gable and Harlow torrid screen inter-action, but the screenplay insists upon presenting Gable as conventional, dull, and straight-laced.

The one good confrontation scene in *Wife Versus Secretary* occurs aboard the ocean liner with the gentle Harlow informing the righteous Loy that she is crazy to walk out on Gable, for Harlow intends to be right there to grab this wonderful man on the rebound. In these serious intense moments, Harlow is amazingly even-keeled and effective.

## SARATOGA
### *(MGM, 1937) 94M.*

Producer, Bernard H. Hyman; associate producer, John Emerson; director, Jack Conway; story-screenplay, Anita Loos, Robert Hopkins; art director, Cedric Gibbons; music, Edward Ward; songs, Walter Donaldson, Bob Wright, and Chet Forrest; camera, Ray June; editor, Elmo Vernon.

Clark Gable (Duke Bradley); Jean Harlow (Carol Clayton)*; Lionel Barrymore (Grandpa Clayton); Walter Pidgeon (Hartley Madison); Frank Morgan (Jesse Kiffmeyer); Una Merkel (Fritzi O'Malley); Cliff Edwards (Tip O'Brien); George Zucco (Dr. Beard); Jonathan Hale (Frank Clayton); Hattie McDaniel (Rosetta); Frankie Darro (Dixie Gordon); Carl Stockdale (Boswell); Henry Stone (Hard Riding Hurley); Ruth Gillette (Mrs. Hurley); Charley Foy (Valet); Robert Emmett Keane (Auctioneer); Edgar Dearing (Medbury the Trainer); Frank McGlynn, Sr. (Kenyon); Margaret Hamilton (Maizie); Lionel Pape, Pat West, John Hyams (Horse Owners); Sam Flint (Judge); Harrison Greene (Clipper); Irene Franklin, Bill Carey, Ernie Stanton, Franklyn Ardell, John "Skins" Miller, Hank Mann, Nick Copeland, Bert Roach (Passengers on Train); Forbes Murray (Pullman Steward); George Reed, Billy McLain (Butlers); Si Jenks (Gardener); George Chandler, Drew Demorest (Cameraman); Mel Ruick (Tout); Patsy O'Conner (Hurley's Kid); Charles R. Moore, Herbert Ashley (Barten-

*After Harlow's death, Mary Dees was substituted for long shots and back view camera shots so that the film could be completed.

141

ders); Fred Snowflake Toones (Train Porter); Hooper Atchley, Dennis O'Keefe (Bidders); Gertude Simpson (Bit); Joseph E. Bernard (Attendant).

New York Premiere: Capitol Theatre—July 22, 1937
New York Television Debut: CBS—March 31, 1957

## Synopsis

Frank Clayton owns the finest breeding farm in Saratoga, but suffers financial reverses and dies before he can recoup his losses. Clayton was deep in debt to bookmaker Duke Bradley, and the latter had lost a big sum of money to New York stockbroker Hartley Madison, who happens to be engaged to Clayton's daughter, Carol. Duke wants to bet Madison on further races, but Carol refuses to let her fiancée bet on the horses anymore, much to Duke's disgust. Meanwhile, Duke has incurred the wrath of Jesse Kiffmeyer, whose wife Fritzi is an old pal of Duke's. She turns to Duke to find a jockey to ride her new race horse in the big Saratoga Race. Duke hopes to win some big money on Madison in this event, for Madison's prize horse is also entered. Carol suddenly realizes she is falling in love with Duke and is in the midst of writing a letter to Madison to break off their engagement when Duke appears on the scene. Duke loves her, but understands that her late father wanted her to be financially secure and removed from all this race track business. So Duke pretends he cares nothing for her. Carol is furious, tears up her letter, and determines that Madison shall beat Duke at Saratoga. Carol urges Kiffmeyer to sell his jockey's contract to her, and then invites Duke to her home, egging him into betting a large sum with Madison. Fritzi, meanwhile, hires another jockey to ride her horse, who does win. At this point Carol realizes that Duke and his way of life are best for her, and she traipses off with him to the next racing event.

◆ ◆ ◆

Whatever intrinsic merits *Saratoga* may have had were lost on 1937 filmgoers who attended the hastily released MGM feature out of curiosity, for in its way the picture was a visual obituary to a talented actress, Jean Harlow, who died during production on June 7, 1937. Ironically, *Saratoga* proved to be a top moneymaker of the year.

At one point (June 12, 1937), MGM considered scrapping the film on which an estimated $500,000 had already been spent, but then the studio reconsidered. First it was decided to allow newcomer Rita Johnson to be substituted in the lead role, reshooting all of Harlow's scenes in the picture. Then a more practical solution was found. Mary Dees, a fifty-five-dollar-a-week dancer at Warner Bros. and Harlow's screen double, was contracted to finish the quickly rewritten film (mostly plot-bridging middle scenes), with the "stand-in" being masked by big drooping hats or photographed discreetly from the back. The speaking voice of Paula Winslow was utilized to approximate that of Harlow's. Metro dropped the notion of

142

having film player Lionel Barrymore speak an explanation to be interpolated into the movie, of the Harlow-Dees situation.

Just as the gravely ill Spencer Tracy would have portentous dialog to
recite in his last film, *Guess Who's Coming to Dinner* (1967), released
after his death, so Harlow as vibrant Carol Clayton has prophetic character
lines in *Saratoga*. At one point she is kneeling beside her dying oncamera
father, with tears in her eyes. At another spot she says onscreen, "I'm
perfectly well. There's nothing wrong with me." But telltale signs of illness were evident throughout Harlow's *Saratoga* footage. "Looking ill
much of the time and striving gallantly to inject into her performance
characteristic vigor and vibrancy, the result, in face of subsequent events,
is grievous" [Marguerite Tazelaar (*New York Herald-Tribune*)]. The *London Observer* paid tribute to Harlow when reviewing this film, "Jean
Harlow was thoroughly at home in this bright, well-dressed atmosphere.
She was not a great actress, but she was an extremely competent one.
She was that very rare combination of extreme sophistication allied to a
kind of wide-eyed innocence that enabled her both to believe in the part
she was playing and yet stand a little outside it and see how comic everything was."

In this film, which tragically concluded the maturing Gable-Harlow
screen partnership, Gable was back in fine form after the dismal *Parnell*
(1937). Dressed in loud checked suits, his rougish nature was at its ebullient best, whether clashing with that "double crossing Newport termite"
(Walter Pidgeon) or crashing head onward into conflict with Harlow, the
girl he really loves. He even displayed a kindly side to his screen personality when talking with Barrymore or mingling with the four-legged fillies.
Gable and Harlow shared one particularly amusing sequence in *Saratoga*
when he ducked under her bed to escape the detection of her visiting fiancé (Pidgeon). All of which led John T. McManus (*New York Times*) to
accord this "the most likable Gable effort of recent seasons."

## THE YEARS AFTER

By the early 1960s, new generations of enthusiasts had become intrigued with the Jean Harlow personality through television showings of
her feature films. Her bright legend seemed intact until 1964 when an
exceedingly specious biography of the star was published. Because it focused so heavily on her alleged sexual over-adventures, it became an instant bestseller. The growing confusion of myths and "facts" concerning
Harlow reached even more staggering proportions when a year later two
feature films, one starring Carroll Baker, the other spotlighting Carol Lynley, appeared. Both films were blatantly sensational in their misguided
approach. Along the way, the important issue—Harlow's screen talent—
seemed to have been obscured. But by the 1970s, when "that" book and
"those" two movies had fallen into semi-obscurity, the Harlow image

stabilized again into a more rational form, with most interested individuals now more concerned with an appreciation of her nonconformist cinema nature rather than her alleged private life sexual peccadillos.

As with Clark Gable's screen teaming with Joan Crawford and Norma Shearer, his Metro features with Harlow span his professional maturation in the cinema. In their give-and-take acting relationship, with all its healthy animalistic sexual-romantic facets, Gable and Harlow emerged as more dimensional performers, learning to accentuate the qualities of their screen personalities that intrigued moviegoers most. In store for Gable in the post-Harlow years, were his marriage to blonde actress Carole Lombard, his Oscar-nomination for *Gone With the Wind* (1939), and MGM's *Honky Tonk* (1941), the first of his four co-starring pictures with the studio's 1940s blonde bombshell, Miss Lana Turner. At the time of *Saratoga*, it was still another twenty-four years before *The Misfits* which would prove to be Gable's screen and life swan song.

In Dames (WB, 1934)

# Chapter 6

# Dick Powell
# &
# Ruby Keeler

## DICK POWELL

6′
172 pounds
Red hair
Blue eyes
Scorpio

*Real name: Richard E. Powell. Born November 14, 1904, Mountain View, Arkansas. Married Mildred Maund (1925); divorced 1932. Married Joan Blondell (1936), children: Norman, Ellen; divorced 1945. Married June Allyson (1945), children: Pamela, Richard. Died January 3, 1963.*

FEATURE FILMS:

*Blessed Event* (WB, 1932)
*Too Busy to Work* (Fox, 1932)
*The King's Vacation* (WB, 1933)
*42nd Street* (WB, 1933)
*Gold Diggers of 1933* (WB, 1933)
*Footlight Parade* (WB, 1933)
*College Coach* (WB, 1933)
*Convention City* (FN, 1933)
*Dames* (WB, 1934)
*Wonder Bar* (FN, 1934)

*Twenty Million Sweethearts* (FN, 1934)
*Happiness Ahead* (FN, 1934)
*Flirtation Walk* (FN, 1934)
*Gold Diggers of 1935* (FN, 1935)
*Page Miss Glory* (WB, 1935)
*Broadway Gondolier* (WB, 1935)
*A Midsummer Night's Dream* (WB, 1935)
*Shipmates Forever* (FN, 1935)
*Thanks a Million* (Fox, 1935)

Colleen (WB, 1936)
Hearts Divided (FN, 1936)
Stage Struck (FN, 1936)
Gold Diggers of 1937 (FN, 1936)
On the Avenue (20th, 1937)
The Singing Marine (WB, 1937)
Varsity Show (WB, 1937)
Hollywood Hotel (WB, 1937)
Cowboy from Brooklyn (WB, 1938)
Hard to Get (WB, 1938)
Going Places (WB, 1938)
Naughty but Nice (WB, 1939)
Christmas in July (Par., 1940)
I Want a Divorce (Par., 1940)
Model Wife (Univ., 1941)
In the Navy (Univ., 1941)
Star Spangled Rhythm (Par., 1942)
Happy Go Lucky (Par., 1942)
True to Life (Par., 1943)
Riding High (Par., 1943)
It Happened Tomorrow (UA, 1944)

Meet the People (MGM, 1944)
Murder, My Sweet (RKO, 1944)
Cornered (RKO, 1945)
Johnny O'Clock (Col., 1947)
To the Ends of the Earth (Col., 1948)
Pitfall (UA, 1948)
Station West (RKO, 1948)
Rogue's Regiment (Univ., 1948)
Mrs. Mike (UA, 1949)
The Reformer and the Redhead (MGM, 1950)
Right Cross (MGM, 1950)
Callaway Went Thataway (MGM, 1951)
Cry Danger (RKO, 1951)
The Tall Target (MGM, 1951)
You Never Can Tell (Univ., 1951)
The Bad and the Beautiful (MGM, 1952)
Susan Slept Here (RKO, 1954)

# RUBY KEELER

**5′ 4″**
**105 pounds**
**Brown hair**
**Blue eyes**
**Virgo**

*Real name: same. Born August 25, 1909, Halifax, Nova Scotia, Canada. Married Al Jolson (1928), child: Al, Jr.; divorced 1940. Married John Lowe (1941), children: Kathleen, Christine, Theresa, John. Widowed 1969.*

**FEATURE FILMS:**

Show Girl in Hollywood (FN, 1930)°
42nd Street (WB, 1933)
Gold Diggers of 1933 (WB, 1933)
Footlight Parade (WB, 1933)
Dames (WB, 1934)
Flirtation Walk (FN, 1934)
°Guest Appearance

Go into Your Dance (FN, 1935)
Shipmates Forever (FN, 1935)
Colleen (WB, 1936)
Ready, Willing and Able (WB, 1937)
Mother Carey's Chickens (RKO, 1938)
Sweetheart of the Campus (Col., 1941)
The Phynx (WB, 1970)

In **Gold Diggers of 1933** (WB, 1933)

Warner Baxter, Ruby Keeler, Bebe Daniels, Dick Powell in **42nd Street** (WB, 1933)

Ruby Keeler, James Cagney, Joan Blondell, Frank McHugh, and Dick Powell in **Footlight Parade** (WB, 1933)

Dick Powell, Ross Alexander, and Ruby Keeler in **Flirtation Walk** (FN, 1934)

On the set of **Shipmates Forever** (FN, 1935)

In **Shipmates Forever**

Joan Barclay, Paul Draper, Ruby Keeler, Antonio Filauri, and Dick Powell in **Colleen** (WB, 1936)

# 42ND STREET
## (Warner Bros., 1933) 98M.

Producer, Darryl F. Zanuck; director, Lloyd Bacon; based on the novel by Bradford Ropes; adaptation-dialog, James Seymour, Rian James; art director, Jack Okey; assistant director, Gordon Hollingshead; costumes, Orry-Kelly; songs, Al Dubin and Harry Warren; music director, Leo F. Forbstein; dances staged by Busby Berkeley; camera, Sol Polito; editor, Thomas Pratt.

Warner Baxter (Julian Marsh); Bebe Daniels (Dorothy Brock); George Brent (Pat Denning); Una Merkel (Lorraine Fleming); Ruby Keeler (Peggy Sawyer); Guy Kibbee (Abner Dillon); Dick Powell (Billy Lawler); Ginger Rogers [Ann Lowell (Anytime Annie)]; George E. Stone (Andy Lee); Robert McWade (Al Jones); Ned Sparks (Thomas Barry); Eddie Nugent (Terry Neil); Allen Jenkins (MacElroy); Harry Akst (Jerry); Clarence Nordstrom (Groom in "Shuffle Off to Buffalo" Number); Henry B. Walthall (The Actor); Al Dubin, Harry Warren (Songwriters); Toby Wing ("Young and Healthy" Girl); Pat Wing, Gertrude Keeler, Helen Keeler, Joan Barclay, Ann Hovey, Renee Whitney, Dorothy Coonan, Barbara Rogers, June Glory, Jayne Shadduck, Adele Lacy, Loretta Andrews, Margaret La Marr, Mary Jane Halsey, Ruth Eddings, Edna Callaghan, Patsy Farnum, Maxine Cantway, Lynn Browning, Donna Mae Roberts, Lorena Layson, Alice Jans (Chorus Girls); Tom Kennedy (Slim Murphy); Wallis Clark (Dr. Chadwick); Jack La Rue (A Mug); Louise Beavers (Pansy); Dave O'Brien (Chorus Boy); Patricia Ellis (Secretary); George Irving (House Doctor); Charles Lane (An Author); Milton Kibbee (News Spreader); Rolfe Sedan (Stage Aide); Lyle Talbot (Geoffrey Waring).

New York Premiere: Strand Theatre—March 9, 1933
New York Television Debut: Channel 5—February 3, 1957

## Synopsis

Wealthy manufacturer Abner Dillon is infatuated with established stage star Dorothy Brock and agrees to back a new Broadway show in which she is to star. Veteran director Julian Marsh is summoned to supervise the production. He is determined to make this show a success so that he can retire and restore his failing health. Dorothy is really in love with impoverished actor Pat Denning, her one-time vaudeville partner. He is forced to stay away from her during the rehearsals of *Pretty Lady,* so as not to arouse Dillon's suspicions. Peggy Sawyer, a new chorus girl in the show, becomes friendly with Pat. The night before the Philadelphia tryout opening, Dorothy becomes intoxicated and throws Dillon out of her hotel room. She then telephones for Pat to come up to her room. Just as he is about to enter her room the producer spots him. Peggy has observed this interplay and rushes to Dorothy's room to warn her. Dorothy becomes jealous of the well-meaning Peggy and in her attempt to get at Peggy she trips and breaks her ankle. Everyone concerned is heartbroken as Dorothy's accident means that the show cannot open. Dillon, however, by this time has formed an attachment for chorine Ann Lowell and demands that she be given the lead. But Ann realizes she is not good enough for the part and tells the producers that Peggy would fit the role just perfectly. With just a few hours to showtime, Peggy is coached by Julian until they are both exhausted. With tears in his eyes he tells her that everything depends on her. Just before she is to go on stage Dorothy comes to see her and apologizes, wishing her all the luck in the world. She tells Peggy that she is going to wed Pat. Peggy is a hit onstage and the show is saved. She is united with Billy Lawler, a member of the cast. Julian's victory, however, is hollow, for he is a worn-out man.

◆—◆—◆

Today *42nd Street* is regarded by most moviegoers as the highest of high camp, the epitome of the screen musical cliché, with its overabundance of hackneyed situations, well-memorized tag lines, and the repeated intercutting of the outlandish Busby Berkeley kaleidoscopic production routines.

But in its day, *42nd Street* was not a *Dames at Sea* spoof subject, but a legitimate smash hit, playing for more than seven weeks at a Broadway first-run house, grossing over $2.25 million, and creating a new cycle of movie musicals. "The singing cinema comes into its own once again . . . we're offered a comprehensive study of theatrical life, replete with the vernacular of the stage world; the customers, the cues, the lingo, the laughs, the songs, the sorrows; action every minute, packed into a full picture at a breath-taking pace" [Irene Thirer (*New York Daily News*)]. In short, *42nd Street* almost single-handedly revitalized a screen genre pronounced moribund since film producers had unjudiciously jumped onto *The Broadway Melody* (1929) bandwagon and surfeited the public with an unending string of all-talking, all-singing, and all-dancing cinema entertainments.

Within its ninety-eight minutes, *42nd Street* promises much and delivers even more in its parading of theatre types: snappy backstagers Una Merkel and Ginger Rogers (as the monocled, snooty "Anytime Annie"), the Helen Morgan-like Bebe Daniels as the singing toast of Broadway who prefers to wed ham vaudeville actor George Brent, the potbellied sugar daddy of Guy Kibbee, and, most of all, the unrelenting director-taskmaster Julian Marsh (Warner Baxter) who pushes himself and his on-camera cast to new peaks of endurance and productivity.

With such diverting onscreen competition, it is to the credit of both Ruby Keeler and Dick Powell that they strike a memorable chord as the young lovers of *42nd Street*. They were regarded in 1933 not as objects of mirth, but as a catchy new song and dance celluloid team. Twenty-four-year-old Keeler had been on the Broadway show club circuit, making her biggest public impact by wedding beloved stage-film performer Al Jolson in 1928. She had made a movie short and a feature film guest appearance before her real screen debut in *42nd Street* at the same studio where her professionally powerful husband held sway as a contract star. She was already noted as a top tap dancer in the business. Thirty-year-old Powell, a former band vocalist and instrumentalist, had only made his film debut a year before—as a crooner in *Blessed Event*—but the tenor was soon destined to nearly rival Bing Crosby in fan adulation.

If there is any single ingredient which explains the "rightness" of Keeler and Powell as a movie team, it is their freshness as individuals. She is the perpetually naive soul, who, for example, in *42nd Street*, enters the theatre to audition for *Pretty Lady* and innocently walks into the men's room where she encounters Powell in his undershorts preparing for rehearsal. Her slightly nasal soprano voice, floppy hairdo, and air-batting gestures become a blur when she comes alive to tap dance, although, like most distaff practitioners of the art, she looks rather heavy-footed and overly clumsy in her tap shoe pounding exercises. In contrast, Powell, with his perpetually baby fat face and his smart aleck way of smiling and sassily answering anyone's remark, is the perpetual optimist, always sure his big breaks (and those of his pals) lie just beyond the next opening night. His screen characters are always conceited in tone but then he makes his performances (singing-dancing-romancing) seem so casual that they are a joy to behold.

Within the course of *42nd Street,* Keeler's Peggy Sawyer is hired for the *Pretty Lady* chorus only as a favor to Merkel by assistant production manager Andy Lee (George E. Stone). Quickly thereafter, Keeler is eliminated from the lineup by the very demanding Baxter, but then recalled when an extra girl is needed to fill out the set routines. Thereafter, Keeler ambles in and out of the chorus line rehearsals, furthers her acquaintance with slick Powell—the perennial stage juvenile—and succumbs to the friendly charms of Brent, who is nursing a wounded love for Daniels. Keeler and Brent have an amusing scene together when he allows her to sleep at his apartment, making it quite clear to the alarmed miss that he has no intention of seducing her. Later Keeler has her big chance when the accident forces Daniels out of the show. Baxter embarks on a marathon coaching session, determined that Keeler learn each and every one of Daniels' routines to perfection. He orders the frightened young performer, "You're going out a youngster, but you've got to come back a star." And Keeler does just that.

Musically, *42nd Street* is a mixed bag. There are a number of obnoxiously antiquated stage production numbers, all encompassed within the deliberately lumbering "It Must Be June." The torch song, "You're Getting to Be a Habit with Me," sung at rehearsal by Daniels, leads to a wish that she had more to do in the film. The lively rendition of "Young and Healthy" crooned by bouncy Powell to the mannequin-like blonde,

Toby Wing, and a horde of Berkeley chorus girls, benefits from its imaginative staging which utilizes a series of three rotating platforms to showcase the living dolls. Best of all is the story-song, "Shuffle Off to Buffalo," with Keeler and Clarence Nordstrom as the honeymoon couple on their timid way to Niagara Falls aboard an overnight train.

When the critical judgments on producer Darryl F. Zanuck's *42nd Street* were completed, Keeler was judged a new movie star. "She scores something of a minor triumph. There is nothing sensational about her work, either dramatically or musically, but she is so demurely engaging and so amiably effective in her calm, rather artless playing that I should say at the moment, she was rather more valuable as a cinema player than her celebrated husband, Mr. Jolson" [Richard Watts, Jr. *(New York Herald-Tribune)*]. For Powell, *42nd Street* was but the second of six 1933 releases, and he would have to wait a bit more before his winning ways would single him out as the male musical arbiter of the Warner Bros. lot.

For the record, the Gertrude and Helen Keeler in the film's chorus were Ruby's real-life sisters.

---

## GOLD DIGGERS OF 1933
### *(Warner Bros., 1933) 96M.*

Producer, Darryl F. Zanuck; director, Mervyn LeRoy; based on the play *The Gold Diggers* by Avery Hopwood; screenplay, Erwin Gelsey, James Seymour; dialog, David Boehm, Ben Markson; art director, Anton Grot; gowns, Orry-Kelly; dances staged by Busby Berkeley; music director, Leo F. Forbstein; songs, Harry Warren and Al Dubin; camera, Sol Polito; editor, George Amy.

Warren William (J. Lawrence Bradford); Joan Blondell (Carol King); Aline MacMahon (Trixie Lorraine); Ruby Keeler (Polly Parker); Dick Powell [Brad Roberts (Robert Treat Bradford)]; Guy Kibbee (Faneuil Hall Peabody); Ned Sparks (Barney Hopkins); Ginger Rogers (Fay Fortune); Clarence Nordstrom (Don Gordon); Robert Agnew (Dance Director); Tammany Young (Gigolo Eddie); Sterling Holloway (Messenger Boy); Ferdinand Gottschalk (Clubman); Loretta Andrews, Adrien Brier, Lynn Browning, Monica Bannister, Maxine Cantway, Bonnie Bannon, Margaret Carthew, Kitty Cunningham, Gloria Faythe, Muriel Gordon, June Glory, Ebba Hally, Amo Ingraham, Lorena Layson, Alice Jans, Jayne Shadduck, Bee Stevens, Anita Thompson, Pat Wing, Renee Whitney, Ann Hovey, Dorothy Coonan (Gold Diggers); Charles C. Wilson (Deputy); Wallace MacDonald (Wally the Stage Manager); Joan Barclay (Chorus Girl); Eddie Foster (Zipky's Kentucky Hill Billies—Second Man); Billy Barty ("Pettin' in the Park" Baby); Snowflake, Theresa Harris ("Pettin' in the Park"

Black Couple); Wilbur Mack, Grace Hayle, Charles Lane, Sam Godfrey (Society Reporters); Dennis O'Keefe (Extra during Intermission); Jay Eaton (Diner); Hobart Cavanaugh (Dog Salesman); Bill Elliott (Dance Extra); Busby Berkeley (Call Boy); Fred Kelsey ("Detective Jones" Actor); Frank Mills ("Forgotten Man" with Butt); Billy West (Medal of Honor Winner); Etta Moten ("Forgotten Man" Black Singer).

New York Premiere: Strand Theatre—June 6, 1933
New York Television Debut: Channel 5—December 19, 1971

### Synopsis

Carol King, Trixie Lorraine, and Polly Parker are three showgirls out of work. Their spirits are revived when Barney Hopkins tells them he is ready to start a new show, but they are dejected when they learn he has no money. Brad Roberts, a songwriter living in the apartment across the courtyard from the girls, is in love with Polly. He offers to advance the money for *Forgotten Melody* and the showgirls think he is teasing them. But the next morning he arrives at Hopkins' office with a $15,000 check and the show is put into rehearsal. Brad is soon forced to accept a part in the production and sing his own songs. The girls warn Polly that Brad may be a crook, but she has faith in him. They soon find out who he really is when his staid, Back Bay, Boston brother, J. Lawrence Bradford, arrives with a lawyer, Faneuil Hall Peabody, in tow. It seems that Brad belongs to a wealthy society family and Bradford is furious to find him sullying the family name by acting in a show. He also warns Brad not to marry Polly. Thinking he can buy the chorine off, he and Peabody go to the girls' apartment. Carol poses as Polly, and she and Trixie go to lunch with the two men. Bradford finds himself falling in love with Carol. They go out to dinner and he becomes intoxicated. Carol takes him to her apartment and he quickly passes out. Trixie comes home and they decide to teach Bradford a lesson. They undress him and put him into Carol's bed. When he awakens in the morning he is horrified at his supposed conduct and rushes away, leaving a $10,000 check for Carol, which she frames. He then learns that Brad has just married Polly and now realizes that Carol is not the girl in question. When Carol threatens to break off her romance with him unless he forgives Brad and Polly, Bradford complies. Everyone is happy, for Trixie has also found contentment and security, with Peabody as her easy target.

◆━━◆━━◆

After the enormous success of *42nd Street*, Warner Bros. and producer Darryl F. Zanuck quickly put *Gold Diggers of 1933* into production, using as a story foundation Avery Hopwood's play *The Gold Diggers*. This play had earlier served as a basis for a 1923 studio feature with Hope Hampton, Louise Fazenda, and Gertrude Short, and the later *Gold Diggers of*

*Broadway* (1929) with Nancy Welford, Winnie Lightner, Ann Pennington, and Lilyan Tashman. A great deal of the technical (especially dance stager Busby Berkeley and song composers Al Dubin and Harry Warren) and cast talent from *42nd Street* were on hand for the new movie musical and *Gold Diggers of 1933* proved to be a "very satisfactory film revue" [Lucius Beebe *(New York Herald-Tribune)*].

Once again, while the increasingly popular Ruby Keeler-Dick Powell team were an essential element of the film's success, they were far from being the whole show. Keeler's two oncamera showgirl roommates were no slouches in the scene stealing department, as their work in *Gold Diggers of 1933* proved. Aline MacMahon as Trixie Lorraine is self-proclaimed as "the most hard-boiled dame on the dirty white way." She has more tricks than a magician, and has set her cap for a certain type of man, one with "lots of money and no resistance." Pompous but gentle Faneuil Hall Peabody (Guy Kibbee) proves to be her target and with him she will enjoy her own special brand of lush security. Joan Blondell, one of Hollywood's most expert comediennes, has the most sympathetic role in *Gold Diggers of 1933* as Carol King, the hard-working, sincere chorus girl, who refuses to follow the example of morally loose show girl Fay Fortune (Ginger Rogers). Blondell finds herself loving conservative, stuffy J. Lawrence Bradford (Warren William), a "Back Bay codfish" who is really a good guy despite his blue blood and big bankroll. Just to round out the proceedings, there is cigar-chomping Barney Hopkins (Ned Sparks), who provides his own style of hyperactive comedy as the financially off-the-cuff producer who knows how to slap together a good show, but can never find enough willing suckers to back his Broadway ventures.

In the never-never world of movie musicals, Keeler and Powell enjoy a rather idyllic romance in this film. He is the happy-go-lucky pianist-song composer living in the apartment across the courtyard from the trio of girls. He instantly falls in love with Keeler and is forever blowing her kisses from his living room window. Keeler's Polly Parker is a pleasant mixture of reality and fantasy. She is sophisticated enough to wear long false eye lashes and a heavy dose of eye mascara (even when she tumbles off to sleep), but she prudishly paddles around the apartment in a dark, drab, unrevealing bathrobe, and is the wholesome type who drinks milk for breakfast (that is, when she can steal a bottle from a neighbor's ledge). Once again, in this movie, Keeler's character is a blissfully trusting soul, obviously untarnished by her years as a chorine. She is hardly the usual self-sufficient, pushy Broadway type, but rather a sweet young thing who is always relying on the jaunty Powell as she continually implores, "Oh, Brad. What are we going to do?"

Musically, *Gold Diggers of 1933* is an elaborate improvement over *42nd Street*. This time Warren and Dubin provided a more pertinent cheeky musical score. The film opens with a rehearsal of Rogers and the girl chorus performing "We're in the Money," a tribute to America's repression of the Depression. Later there is the intricate "Pettin' in the Park" number in which Powell is the singing narrator of the changing season story-dance. This sequence incorporates a montage of girls roller-skating in the park, blends into their snowball fights, fades into a rain scene with the girls scampering behind venetian-shaded dividers to change into dry clothes, and finally has the femmes emerging in metallic outfits, which, under the prompting of midget Billy Barty, the chorus boys pry open with can openers. Powell and Keeler have joint oncamera activity in the more formal, but equally precision-rhythmed, "Shadow Waltz," in which Keeler capers about in a blonde wig and a Southern belle gown along with fifty other chorus girls. She is at her most physically attractive in this number, which has the dolls "playing" fluorescent-outlined violins. The movie's finale is devoted to the expansive "Remember My Forgotten Man," a paean to World War I veterans who end up on the breadlines. Blondell talk-sings (with dubbing by Marian Anderson) this rousing closer to a sensational movie outing.

## FOOTLIGHT PARADE
### (Warner Bros., 1933) 102M.

Producer, Darryl F. Zanuck; director, Lloyd Bacon; screenplay, Manuel Seff, James Seymour; dances staged by Busby Berkeley; songs, Harry Warren and Al Dubin; music director, Leo F. Forbstein; dialog director, William Keighley; art director, Anton Grot; costumes, Milo Anderson; makeup, Perc Westmore; camera, George Barnes; editor, George Amy.

James Cagney (Chester Kent); Joan Blondell (Nan Prescott); Ruby Keeler (Bea Thorn); Dick Powell (Scotty Blair); Guy Kibbee (Silas Gould); Ruth Donnelly (Harriet Bowers Gould); Claire Dodd (Vivian Rich); Hugh Herbert (Charlie Bowers); Frank McHugh (Francis); Arthur Hohl (Al Frazer); Gordon Westcott (Harry Thompson); Renee Whitney (Cynthia Kent); Philip Faversham (Joe Farrington); Juliet Ware (Miss Smythe); Herman Bing (Fralick the Music Director); Paul Porcasi (George Appolinaris); William Granger (Doorman); Charles C. Wilson (Cop); Barbara Rogers (Gracie); Billy Taft (Specialty Dancer); Marjean Rogers, Pat Wing, Donna La Barr, Marlo Dwyer, Donna Mae Roberts (Chorus Girls); Dave O'Brien (Chorus Boy); George Chandler (Drugstore Attendant); Hobart Cavanaugh (Title-Thinker Upper); William V. Mong (Auditor); Lee Moran (Mac the Dance Director); Billy Barty (Mouse in "Sittin' on a Backyard Fence" Number/Little Boy in "Honeymoon Hotel" Number); Harry Seymour (Desk Clerk in "Honeymoon Hotel" Number); Sam McDaniel (Porter); Fred Kelsey (House Detective); Jimmy Conlin (Uncle); Roger Gray (Sailor-Pal in "Shanghai Lil" Number); John Garfield (Sailor behind Table in "Shanghai Lil" Number); Duke York (Sailor on Table in "Shanghai Lil" Number); Harry Seymour (Joe the Assistant Director).

159

New York Premiere: Strand Theatre—October 5, 1933
New York Television Debut: Channel 5—June 21, 1958

## Synopsis

Chester Kent, the energetic stager of special live prologues for New York movie theatres, works for Silas Gould and Al Fraser, always trying to beat the competition to the punch with novel concepts in miniature stage revues. However, his best ideas are always stolen from under him by people whom his rivals hire or spies they plant in his stage crew. Scotty Blair, who has been introduced into the Gould-Fraser organization by Gould's sister Harriet, is given a chance to direct Chester's chorus line, replacing the overworked Francis. Scotty soon drops Harriet, she turning her attention to a more attentive gigolo. Meanwhile Scotty encounters the rather prim production secretary Bea Thorn, who, it develops, is quite a tap dancer and not a bad looker. Their relationship grows during the arduous rehearsal days, while Nan Prescott, who has been nursing an unrequited love for Chester, sits by and watches Chester being vamped by blonde Vivian Rich. In order to protect his latest production numbers, Chester orders a complete veil of secrecy drawn around the rehearsals, commandeering the rehearsal hall as dormitory-commissary for the chorus, who are not permitted to leave the theatre. On the night of the big try-out of the three new numbers, Joe Farrington becomes drunk and Chester must go on in his place. The routines are a big success, winning Gould and Fraser new bookings. Just as Bea and Scotty have found love, so have Chester and Nan.

◆—◆—◆

"*Footlight Parade* is elaborate, fantastically extravagant in its chorus numbers, slightly less tuneful and considerably more disrobed than its predecessors, well acted and pretty certain to be a smashing economic success" [Richard Watts, Jr. (*New York Herald-Tribune*)]. "Most of the mass-maneuvers in *Footlight Parade* only remotely resemble dances but they are sufficiently bizarre—in many cases, pretty—to be worth watching. They also provide suspense for Warner Brothers' next cinemusicomedy because it is hard to imagine what tricks Director Busby Berkeley can do with his performers next, unless he chops them into pieces" (*Time* magazine).

Above and beyond the fact that *Footlight Parade* offers the most logically structured of all the Busby Berkeley Warners' musicals, providing a very legitimate setting for the elaborate production numbers, the big surprise and treat of the film is that it permitted Broadway hoofer James Cagney to ditch his tough guy cinema roles for a while and perform as a song-and-dance man oncamera. His vital, engaging appearance in *Footlight Parade* did much to make the 102-minute production such a big success in a film market growing crowded with *42nd Street* imitations.

Originally Renee Whitney, cast as Cynthia Kent, was scheduled to be the "Shanghai Lil" girl in *Footlight Parade,* but she was put back into her subordinate role in favor of very popular Ruby Keeler* who added that number to her other chores within the movie. When the picture had first gone into production, Dick Powell was suffering from a throat problem and film singer Stanley Smith was hired to fill the breach, but Powell sufficiently recovered in time for the scenes to be reshot with him, thus reuniting him and Keeler for the third time onscreen.

In *Footlight Parade,* Powell is his nonchalant, cocky self, a gigolo in fact. However, as a slight change of movie personae, Keeler is here cast as an efficient, prim office worker (black-rimmed glasses, close-cropped hairdo, severe black dress) who has little regard for the morally loose Powell. But when she suddenly sheds her spectacles and recombs her hair, she is a new woman, complete with a liberated personality.

When Powell sees the "new" Keeler, he is stunned: "No."

Keeler: "Yes! I got sick of looking like a school teacher."

She informs him that she wants to audition for Cagney's prologue show chorus. Dancer supervisor Powell is bewildered but figures if she can pull such a rapid cosmetic change, perhaps she has a few dance tricks to display. "Let's see what you can do," he says.

In a whiz, Keeler demurely hoists her skirt with one hand, pushes back her flopping front lock of hair, and whips into a tap dance audition. Both Cagney and Blondell, watching this test, nod a hasty approval. In a flash Keeler has resigned from the office staff and has moved on to a stage career. This amazing, rapid-fire, improbable set of events is equalled by some other sequences during the course of *Footlight Parade.* For example, Cagney, lacking any new ideas for his prologues, one day leaves the theatre in disgust. He finds himself riding in a taxi in crowded mid-Manhattan and happens to spot some black children cavorting under the spray of an open water hydrant. "That's what the prologue needs!" Cagney yells out. "A waterfall splashing on beautiful white bodies!" (The racial slight was lost on most filmgoers of 1933.) He rushes back to the theatre, having found his inspiration for a great show-stopping number. Then comes the fantastic montages of the chorus folk forced to take residence at the theatre, with row upon row of chorines bunking down on long lines of cots, or, later, rising for a mass production breakfast in the hastily converted dining room.

While the comedy relief of *Footlight Parade,* supplied to a great extent by girl-hungry, stammering Charlie Bowers (Hugh Herbert), is as important as the underlying plot which includes gold digging Vivian Rich (Claire Dodd), the focal point of the script is, after all, the musical numbers staged by Berkeley. For tuneful warmups there are Powell, Frank

*On August 15, 1933, Ruby Keeler arrived in New York, having departed the shooting of *Footlight Parade,* then in production on the Burbank lot. She did announce that she would soon return to the studio to complete her work in that project.

McHugh and the chorus rehearsing "Ah, the Moon Is Here," and a full-scale dress run-through of "Sittin' on a Backyard Fence," in which Keeler and the girls are garbed in cat outfits, complete with tails attached to their tights, and feline ear hats tied around their heads. Later, on the big night of Cagney's routine tryout, there are three lavish production numbers, following one upon another, almost nonstop.

"Honeymoon Hotel" finds newlyweds Keeler and Powell arriving at the resort spot. They have an instant marriage conducted by the on-premises justice of the peace, but then find great difficulty shaking their well-meaning relatives so that they can enjoy their nuptial night. Midget Billy Barty (the mouse in "Sittin' on a Backyard Fence" routine) is the troublesome little boy in this song-story, remaining behind at the hotel to naughtily peak at the blissful couple long after the other family members have left. The routine ends with Barty in bed with Powell! Then there is the gorgeous "By a Waterfall," with Powell and Keeler on a countryside outing, he in a business suit, she wearing a formal, long summer gown. While he falls asleep, she sneaks behind a rock and changes into a bathing suit, which leads to a succession of cascading girls joining in geometric, acrobatic maneuvers as they dive into a large pool, swimming above and below the surface, but always in seemingly perfect precision with their teammates. The ending has Keeler splashing water on the dreaming Powell.

The final number, "Shanghai Lil," pairs Keeler (as a not very convincing Oriental whore) with American gob Cagney. He is searching a crowded, smoky bar for his lady love, while she proves to be the talk of Shanghai. Much of this number, in which Keeler is dressed in a white silk pants suit complete with black wig styled with two tightly wound side buns, is reminiscent of "Remember My Forgotten Man" with the close order drill marching of the sailors and marching band, proceeding back and forth within the confines of a stage-bound set. Not only does Cagney out-tap-dance Keeler, but his singing, unlike hers, is on tune and enunciated with precision and power.

## DAMES
### (Warner Bros., 1934) 90M.

Producer, Darryl F. Zanuck; director, Ray Enright; story, Robert Lord, Delmer Daves; adaptation-screenplay, Delmer Daves; dances staged by Busby Berkeley; art directors, Robert Haas, Willy Pogany; songs; Harry Warren and Al Dubin; music director, Leo F. Forbstein; costumes, Orry-Kelly; camera, Sid Hickox, George Barnes; editor, Harold McLernon.

Joan Blondell (Mabel Anderson); Dick Powell (Jimmy Higgens); Ruby Keeler (Barbara Hemingway); ZaSu Pitts (Mathilda Hemingway); Guy Kibbee (Horace P. Hemingway); Hugh Herbert (Ezra Ounce); Arthur

Vinton (Bulger); Sammy Fain (Buttercup Baumer); Phil Regan (Johnny Harris); Arthur Aylesworth (Conductor); Leila Bennett (Laura the Maid); Berton Churchill (H. Elsworthy Todd); Patricia Harper, Ruth Eddings, De Don Blunier, Gloria Faythe, Diane Douglas (Chorus Girls); Lester Dorr (Elevator Starter); Eddy Chandler (Guard); Johnny Arthur (Billings the Secretary); Snowflake (Porter); Frank Darien, Eddy Chandler (Druggists); Harry Holman (Spanish War Veteran); Charlie Williams (Dance Director); Phil Tead (Reporter); Eddie Kane (Harry the Stage Manager).

New York Premiere: Strand Theatre—August 16, 1934
New York Television Debut: Channel 5—June 21, 1958

## Synopsis

Eccentric millionaire Ezra Ounce, a die-hard reformer, tells his cousin Horace P. Hemingway, that, since he has proven to be a very moral man, he is going to receive $10,000,000. However, as a proviso, Hemingway must assist Ounce in forming a new society, to be known as the "Ounce Society for the Elevation of American Morals." He warns Hemingway to keep Jimmy Higgens, a distant relative, out of his house because Jimmy has become associated with the theatre. Hemingway starts for home with Ounce as his guest. On the train he is shocked to find stranded chorus girl Mabel Anderson in his compartment, and to keep her quiet he leaves her some money, along with a note requesting her not say anything of the incident. In New York, Mabel meets Jimmy and he tells her about the new play he has prepared, but complains he needs money to produce the show. Mabel hits upon the idea of obtaining the money from Hemingway by a threat of exposing his railroad caper. The scheme works. Meanwhile, Barbara, Hemingway's daughter, who is in love with Jimmy, is jealous of his friendship with Mabel and breaks her engagement with him. The play is put into rehearsal and Barbara is given a role in it. Hemingway is later forced to accompany Ounce to the theatre to close this shocking show, planning to have some hired hoodlums wreck the theatre if quiet persuasion fails. Because the older men have drunk some alcohol-laden medicine, they are tipsy and signal the hoodlums by error. The latter throw eggs, tomatoes, and other foodstuff to break up the show. Ounce, Hemingway, and the entire cast are put in jail. Ounce finds the chorus girls pleasant company and decides to spend his time having fun rather than reforming people. Jimmy and Barbara are reconciled and everyone, except Hemingway's wife Mathilda, is happy.

◆◆◆

This film was obviously a diminution of the old *42nd Street* format. "The plot is trite, the jokes are rather stale, and the coherence of the story is often far from clear. The songs, however, are gay and lilting" [Marguerite Tazelaar *(New York Herald-Tribune)*].

163

By this juncture in the Dick Powell-Ruby Keeler screen alliance, Powell was the more established, versatile member of the set, mostly by virtue of his tremendous cinematic output. Therefore, he was billed higher than Keeler, but still below top-featured Joan Blondell, who would become his real-life wife in 1936.

Within *Dames*, flip-talking gold digger Blondell as Mabel Anderson has her comedy and vocal moments as the high-powered dame. ("I've got seventeen cents and the clothes I stand in, but there's life in the old gal yet.") She is supported in the movie by yammering Hugh Herbert, blustery Guy Kibbee, and fluttery ZaSu Pitts, a trio of diverse laugh-provokers. But it is Powell and Keeler as the two "young" players who tie the film together. They are first seen in a Central Park setting, and he is acting more chivalrous than his usual cinema self.

Keeler: "Jimmy Higgens—why all this love and affection? . . . Do you have a job?" When Powell repeats that his life's desire is still to be a song-writer, Keeler reassures him, "You'll get there yet. You just keep trying." (That is the good old anti-Depression spirit!) Then in a bit of very coy interplay, she adds, "It doesn't seem right our loving each other and being related." (Everyone could relax his sudden fears that the film would thereafter deal with incest, for it develops Powell and Keeler are just *thirteenth* cousins.)

In a later scene, Keeler and Powell are on the Staten Island ferry and he treats her to a rendition of "I Only Have Eyes for You." The beguiled Keeler admits, "Gee, that's swell, Jimmy." Thereafter Powell and Keeler re-encounter Blondell at a stage production office, and once again Keeler is made to demonstrate her screen character's Pollyanna-style naiveté. While Powell and Blondell are closeted in an inner office discussing the possible financing of Powell's stage show, *Sweet and Hot,* Keeler asks a nearby secretarial type, "What are they doing in there?"

Secretary: "Maybe they're planning a double suicide." Poor confused Keeler does a hardy double take.

When Keeler is later auditioning for Powell's upcoming Broadway show, the Delmer Daves scenario takes no chance that any filmgoers might seriously question Keeler's dancing abilities. (After all, by this point in 1934, Ginger Rogers, in tandem with Fred Astaire in RKO movies, was fast being considered the more distinctive example of distaff screen dancer.) Keeler runs through her try-out routine, while Blondell tells Powell, "Jimmy, that girl can dance." Immediately thereafter the on-camera stage manager remarks, "Say, that kid's got plenty of stuff!" So Keeler, using the alias of Joan Grey to fool her prudish relatives, embarks on a show career, later telling her stuffy father (Kibbee), "I'm free, white, and twenty-one, and intend to work."

The two big production numbers in the play-within-the-movie are more intimate showpieces than past Busby Berkeley-staged cinema routines. "The Girl at the Ironing Board" effectively features Blondell in a laundry shop setting, erotically wishing the pajamas she is pressing belonged to a man she could love. Thereafter, a full-scale rendition of the previously heard "I Only Have Eyes for You" opens with Powell and Keeler on a Manhattan subway train riding to the end of the line at 215th Street and concludes with a splendid camera back pan of a railroad yard with the two players stepping across the tracks. In the course of this intricate "I Only Have Eyes for You," Keeler is given an extensive physical dissection by the camera which pans over and on her from assorted angles, and includes a huge jigsaw puzzle kaleidoscope effect of her face.

For a change in their joint screen outings, Keeler is the romantic aggressor in *Dames*. During a backstage break in their performing, she asks Powell, "Do you like me, Jimmy? . . . Well, do you love me, Jimmy?"

Powell: "Meet me after the show."

Keeler (with accented meaning): "You think I won't?" Finally in the film's climactic jail cell sequence, with the horde of gabbing chorus girls surrounding the bemused but happy Herbert, Powell and Keeler are seen off to one corner. She is whispering sweet and suggestive somethings into his attentive ears.


### FLIRTATION WALK
*(First National-Warner Bros., 1934) 97M.*

Producer, Robert Lord; director, Frank Borzage; screenplay, Delmer Daves, Lou Edelman; art director, Jack Okey; choreography, Bobby Connolly; music director, Leo F. Forbstein; songs, Mort Dixon and Allie Wrubel; costumes, Orry-Kelly; camera, Sol Polito, George Barnes; editor, William Holmes.

Dick Powell (Dick "Canary" Dorcy); Ruby Keeler (Kit Fitts); Pat O'Brien (Sgt. Scrapper Thornhill); Ross Alexander (Oskie); John Arledge (Spike); John Eldredge (Lt. Robert Biddle); Henry O'Neill (General Jack Fitts); Guinn Williams (Sleepy); Frederick Burton (General Paul Landacre); John Darrow (Chase); Glen Boles (Eight Ball); University of Southern California and Army Polo Teams (Polo Players); Lt. Joe Cummins (Cadet); Gertrude Keeler (Dancer); Col. Tim Lonergan (General); Tyrone Power (Cadet).

New York Premiere: Strand Theatre—November 28, 1934
New York Television Debut: Channel 9—April 6, 1964

#### Synopsis

Dick Dorcy, an army private stationed in Hawaii, and Kit Fitts, the General's daughter, fall in love with each other after a romantic drive in the moonlight. Kit's fiance, Lt. Robert Biddle, finds them embracing and orders Dick to his quarters. Dick, wishing to avoid a scandal, decides to desert. In order to save him from such disgrace, Kit pretends that she does not love him and tells him to forget her, that their evening together meant nothing to her. Piqued by her attitude, Dick is determined now to become an officer and a gentleman and enrolls in West Point, much to the joy of his army buddy, Sgt. Scrapper Thornhill. Dick becomes a fine student at the Point. Just before graduation time, Kit arrives with her father, who has been made Point superintendent. Dick is cold to her at first, but he cannot resist her charms very long, particularly as she has been made the leading lady of the annual Hundredth Night play. Dick's military career, however, is almost ruined when he is found in Kit's quarters, but he is later forgiven. He graduates from the Point with honors and he and Kit decide to wed.

◆◆◆

Frank Borzage, who had performed such wonders with the past screen team of Janet Gaynor and Charles Farrell at Fox, was now at First National-Warner Bros. and was assigned to this latest effort starring Dick Powell and Ruby Keeler. As a silver screen pair their fame had zoomed ever upward and was now at its peak. As Andre Sennwald of the *New York Times* stated, ". . . the vast popularity of the lyric team of Miss Keeler and Mr. Powell . . . is certainly one of the major phenomena of the current screen."

*Flirtation Walk* boasted the longest location filming trip in the production history of First National Pictures, with lensing in Hawaii and then two weeks of extensive shooting at West Point on the Hudson River in New York. For obvious reasons, the picture was dedicated to the United States Military Academy, "an institution of which our entire nation is justly proud." The finished product was judged by many as "one of the brightest and cleanest pictures of the present fall season."

Much more so than their previous co-starring movie efforts and more effectively than their subsequent vehicles, *Flirtation Walk* contains all the choicest elements of the assorted ingredients which made Powell and Keeler so acceptable to filmgoers of the day—their oncamera capering, verbal sparring, romancing, fighting, making up, and indulging in musical interludes. Thanks to a tight Delmer Daves-Lou Edelman screenplay, *Flirtation Walk* contains the snappiest Powell-Keeler interchanges recorded on film. This picture marks the team's first entry in which the choreography is not handled by Busby Berkeley. Bobby Connolly is their new dance helmer.

Within *Flirtation Walk*, Powell's character is established by contrasting his Dick "Canary" Dorcy with the personality of Sergeant Scrapper Thornhill (Pat O'Brien). O'Brien's military man is a hard-working dedicated soul, a professional soldier through and through. (In this film O'Brien plays one of the more bizarre of 1930s screen conventions, the

166

male duenna, who clucks and coos in the background as his good buddy, Powell, makes professional and romantic strides. Fortunately, O'Brien laces this sticky assignment with his typical, rapid-fire delivery and salty tough guy air.) Powell, on the other hand, is the sort of lackadaisical enlisted man who, on duty at Schofield Barracks in Honolulu, cleans the general's cottage bathroom by sitting in the tub and singing! Powell has been in O'Brien's gunnery crew for two years and still has yet to show signs of adhering to discipline or having any military ambition. O'Brien is forced to admit that perhaps Powell's only real army goal is to be "the Rudy Vallee of the regiment."

When Kit Fitts (Keeler) arrives in Hawaii with her father's military tour party and meets Powell who has been assigned as her personal chauffeur, he promptly drops her little overnight bag, spilling out its contents. She calls him "butterfingers," and their romance is off to a bumpy start. Later at the cottage she observes, "whoever dusted the room must have had housemaid's knees." This censure does not bother breezy Powell.

Keeler (kittenishly): "I won't get to see much of it [the island] in two days."

Powell: "No."

Keeler: "It seems a pity."

Then she dismisses him, being at her most effective when adopting an imperious manner, as he is most engaging when displaying mock obedience.

Keeler: "I think I can manage the bath part alone."

Powell: "I hope so, ma'm."

Keeler: "I'm not a ma'm. I'm a miss."

Later when she orders him to escort her about the island rather than drive her directly to the unpromising reception, he trips down the steps, leading her to exclaim (with excellent timing), "You aren't very light on your feet, are you?" Once in the car, they pass the army camp main gate and she orders, "Drive on, MacDuff." They reach a scenic spot and she has him stop the car. "I thought you are taking orders from me," says Keeler. "Take off your hat . . . call me Kit."

The couple proceed down the hillside to a Hawaiian luau on the beach and watch an elaborate native dance, one which is almost as pulsating and dramatic as the "Totem Tom Tom" routine in MGM's *Rose Marie* (1935). Thereafter Keeler orders Powell to live up to his reputation as the singing bird of the island, demanding, "Sing, mister, or I'll have you thrown in the guardhouse for flagrant disrespect of orders."

Powell naturally complies and after crooning his mild love song, she utters one of the cinema's most precious lines of dialog. "I've seen a luau, and heard you sing. I guess life has practically nothing more to offer me." (Keeler speaks these immortal words with true seriousness.) Later complications force Keeler to *lie* to Powell, "Tonight was just a crazy mistake on my part. You mean nothing to me." Then she disappears from the story action for the time being, for there is a long interlude of audience watching as smart-aleck Powell enrolls at West Point and discovers how tough a plebe's existence can be.

But then Keeler reappears on the West Point sets, with the film picking up its romantic interplay. Keeler and Powell undergo their usual ration of misunderstandings. She is cast in the Academy's annual Hundredth Night Show, a production written, produced by, and starring Powell. She is the first girl to be cast in the traditional revue, but on the first day of rehearsal she arrives late, missing his words of advice to the assembled cast. "The more seriously you read the comedy lines," Powell tells them, "the funnier it is." (He is so right!) He then explains to latecomer Keeler, "The play is a comedy."

Keeler: "That's the rumor I heard. I hope it lives up to your expectations."

Within the course of the school show, Keeler and Powell perform "Flirtation Walk" and "Mr. and Mrs. Is the Name" which coyly recaps their oncamera trials and tribulations at the Point. The Connolly staging for these numbers in which Keeler does not do any real tap dancing is far more conventional than anything Berkeley was wont to use, but it was, on the other hand, more appropriate for the storyline. It is rather obvious in these song numbers that Keeler's soundtrack voice has been dubbed.

The finale of the film has Lieutenant Robert Biddle (John Eldredge) relinquishing his engagement claims on Keeler, allowing Powell to officially become her man. Then, O'Brien, on leave from assignment in Shanghai, joins Keeler in the reviewing stands to watch the processional of cadets, including Powell, on the marching field. For some unexplainable reason, it is not Keeler, who looks rather bewildered, but O'Brien, who has tears of pride flowing forth.

The *New York American*'s Regina Crewe complimented Keeler for being as "sweet as can be" in *Flirtation Walk*, while the *New York Sun's* entertainment scribe acknowledged that Powell ". . . plays the young soldier with as little of the master of ceremonies manner as he can manage. He goes pretty cute at times; but he warbles nicely and looks properly handsome in a uniform."

## SHIPMATES FOREVER
### (First National-Warner Bros., 1935) 109M.

Director, Frank Borzage; story-screenplay, Delmer Daves; songs, Harry Warren and Al Dubin; technical adviser, Com. M. S. Tisdale, U.S.N., Lt. W. J. Beecher, U.S.N., Edward L. Adams, former cadet; music director, Leo F. Forbstein; choreography, Bobby Connolly; gowns, Orry-Kelly; camera, Sol Polito; editor, William Holmes.

Dick Powell (Richard John Melville III); Ruby Keeler (June Blackburn); Lewis Stone (Admiral Richard Melville); Ross Alexander (Sparks); Eddie Acuff (Cowboy); Dick Foran (Gifford); John Arledge (Coxswain Johnny Lawrence); Robert Light (Ted Sterling); Joseph King (Commander Douglas); Frederick Burton (Admiral Fred Graves); Henry Kolker (The Doctor); Joseph Crehan (Spike); Mary Treen (Cowboy's Girl); Martha Merrill (Sparks' Girl); Carlyle Moore, Jr. (Second Classman); Harry Seymour (Harry); Ernie Alexander, Victor Potel (Radio Fans); Emmett Vogan (Officer); James Flavin (Instructor); Guy Usher (Captain); Frank Marlowe (Seaman); Peter Potter (Upper Classman); Ed Keane (Doctor); Dennis O'Keefe (Trainee); Meglin Kiddies (Children).

New York Premiere: Strand Theatre—October 17, 1935
No New York Television Showing

### Synopsis

New York club crooner Richard John Melville III, son of U.S.N. Admiral Richard Melville, is shamed into entering the Naval Academy at Annapolis. He is disliked by his schoolmates because of his refusal to mix with them. His only friend is June Blackburn, a girl descended from a long line of Navy men, who teaches dancing school for the local children. She promises to wed Richard when he graduates from the Academy. Despite the rigors of his four years at Annapolis, he fails to gain the true Navy spirit and plans to reject his commission after graduation. During a subsequent training cruise, the oil in the engine room catches fire and he risks his life to save Coxswain Johnny Lawrence. When Richard is later dismissed from the post hospital, he is a changed man. The midshipmen greet him as a hero. He makes both his father and his fiancée, June, happy when he tells them he will continue in the Navy.

◆◆◆

With the pleasing boxoffice results from *Flirtation Walk* it did not require much imagination to guess that Warner Bros. would reunite director Borzage, scripter Delmer Daves, stars Dick Powell and Ruby Keeler, and lead supporting players Ross Alexander and John Arledge in another musical service tale, this time doing for the navy what had been done for the army. An interesting sidelight is that while Keeler had been co-starring with husband Al Jolson in Warners' *Go into Your Dance* (1935), Powell, among other diverse screen assignments, had played opposite the studio's newly-arrived MGM refugee Marion Davies in *Page Miss Glory* (1935). It was quickly rumored in Hollywood that Powell had become Davies' most popular on and off the set leading man, and that it was no professional coincidence that her Cosmopolitan Productions produced Powell's *Shipmates Forever* for First National-Warner Bros. release.

Location lensing for *Shipmates Forever* was naturally focused at Annapolis in Maryland and later aboard the *U.S.S. Pennsylvania* then berthed off San Pedro, California. *Variety* had to admit, "Powell's singing and Miss Keeler's dancing don't precisely fit into a saga of Annapolis." However, the public did not seem to mind too much. As for the stars' emoting, Marguerite Tazelaar *(New York Herald-Tribune)* reported, "Mr. Powell has had a hard time restraining his buoyant spirits when called upon to be deliberately unpopular, and only in the outbursts of his few song numbers does he appear to be really at ease. Miss Keeler seems to enjoy being June—her tap numbers animate the scenes considerably."

The formula for this film was much the same as in *Flirtation Walk*. Powell once again has an "aw nuts" attitude and must undergo a great deal of harassment and discipline before he becomes a true Navy man, all the time spurred on to his potential officer's life by his Navy father (Lewis Stone) and his locally situated sweetheart, Keeler. At the Annapolis interlude, we have one thousand midshipmen marching across the famous parade ground, and later 1,100 officers and men of the battleship *Pennsylvania* (the flag ship of the Pacific fleet) putting their huge craft through its elaborate paces.

*Shipmates Forever* did offer a few bonuses, particularly for those viewers who had come to appreciate the easy-flowing smart talk between Powell and Keeler. In one of the film's introductory scenes, Powell, a hip crooner in a New York club, encounters Keeler at a quiet outdoor spot on Manhattan's upper Riverside Drive. Their banter is as delightful as the give-and-take conversation they had in *Flirtation Walk*.

He: "My name is Melville—Richard Melville Third—or second or fourth or something. I never did get it quite straight."

She: "I was a Navy girl, yes. My name is June Blackburn. My father was Captain Blackburn—went down with his ship in the war. My brother Jim was a lieutenant . . . Naval air service. He was on the *Akron* when. . . ."

He: "I'm sorry." (The *Akron* was a Navy dirigible which had crashed in 1933.)

As in *Flirtation Walk*, there is no Busby Berkeley to concoct special choreography for the proceedings and the resultant musical interludes are a letdown. Keeler does tap dance, with her young pupils (the Meglin Kiddies) to the tune, "I'd Rather Take Orders from You," while Powell is at his croonerish, smiley best in "I'd Rather Listen to Your Eyes."

That the boxoffice magic of the Powell-Keeler teaming was already wearing noticeably thin is evidenced by contemporary reviewers' reports. John Reddington *(New York American)* wrote, "Miss Keeler is again required to portray sweetness and innocence; and, rather remarkably, succeeds once again, though the attractions of her personality are now suffering from overexposure." It was the beginning of the end for the movie pair as a dual screen entity.

# COLLEEN
## (Warner Bros., 1936) 89M.

Director, Alfred E. Green; story, Robert Lord; screenplay, Peter Milne, Hugh Herbert, Sig Herzig; production numbers staged by Bobby Connolly; art director, Max Parker; music director, Leo F. Forbstein; songs, Harry Warren and Al Dubin; gowns, Orry-Kelly; camera, George Barnes; editor, Byron Haskin.

Dick Powell (Donald Ames); Ruby Keeler (Colleen Riley); Jack Oakie (Joe Cork); Joan Blondell (Minnie Mawkins); Hugh Herbert (Cedric Ames); Louise Fazenda (Alicia Ames); Paul Draper (Paul); Luis Alberni (Carlo); Marie Wilson (Mabel); Mary Treen (Miss Hively); Hobart Cavanaugh (Noggin); Berton Churchill (Logan); J. M. Kerrigan (Pop Riley); Spencer Charters (Dr. Frothingham); Addison Richards (Schuyler); Charler Coleman (Butler); Colleen Colman (Lois); Herbert Evans (Footman); Viola Lowry (Receptionist); Emmett Vogan (Official); Cyril Ring (Client); Harry Depp (Assistant); Shirley Lloyd (Girl); Bob Murphy, Ward Bond (Cops); Alma Lloyd (Nurse); Sarah Edwards, Laura Pierpont (Society Women); John Albright (Page Boy); Alphonse Martel (Head Waiter); Andre Cheron (Waiter); Iris March (Miss Graham); Edward Keane (Edwards); George Andre Beranger (Jeweler); Pauline Caron (Maid); Antonio Filauri (Bartender); Charles E. Delaney (Ship's Radio Operator); Joan Barclay (Cafe Guest).

New York Premiere: Strand Theatre—March 8, 1936
No New York Television Showing

### Synopsis

Cedric Ames falls prey to the charms of an attractive girl, Minnie Mawkins, who works in a candy factory. Minnie, realizing his infatuation, plays up to him, and she is soon taken out of the factory and put in charge of an expensive dress shop which Ames buys for her. Working in cahoots with Minnie to fleece Ames is her boyfriend, Joe Cork. He promises to wed her as soon as she gets Ames to adopt her as his daughter. Donald, Ames' nephew, arrives on the scene and convinces his bewildered uncle that the duo is crooked, and that despite the careful supervision of Colleen Riley, really in charge of the millinery operations, the shop should be closed. Ames buys off Minnie and Cork by paying each of them $25,000. But he goes even further without telling Donald. He sends a lawyer to Colleen, who is now in love with Donald, to offer her $10,000 to release Donald from any matrimonial promises. She accepts the proposition out of spite, using the funds to open a dress shop on a transatlantic vessel, not realizing

Donald and Ames have booked passage on the same ship. In the course of the voyage, all the romantic problems are straightened out.

◆◆◆

The studio publicized this film with the tag, "On your toes everybody, for Warner Bros.' first big Musical in a Year!" But that really was not the case with the resultant *Colleen*. "It is greatly to be feared, however, that the reliable formula is beginning to creak at the joints just a trifle. Although Miss Blondell rolls her eyes and Mr. Herbert giggles fatuously and Jack Oakie rushes blandly to their assistance and every one works with loyal determination, the effect doesn't appear to be as happy as it used to be. Whatever freshness there was to the antics of the familiar story has long since disappeared" [Richard Watts, Jr. *(New York Herald-Tribune)*].

By the time of *Colleen*, Ruby Keeler's movie popularity was waning along with that of Al Jolson, while Dick Powell's star was still riding high at the studio. This picture was a rather hastily contrived project, having a great deal of story similarity to the play-movie *Roberta*, but being far less felicitous than that 1935 RKO picture with Irene Dunne, Fred Astaire, and Ginger Rogers. Actually it was not until well after Jack Oakie and newcomer Paul Draper were hired for *Colleen* and Joan Blondell assigned to gold dig in the proceedings, that Powell's schedule was found to be free (he was then very busy with his popular radio show "Hollywood Hotel"). He was then quickly worked into the storyline, joining Keeler for the seventh and last time in a feature film.

In *Colleen*, the leading subordinate players clearly outshone the romantic team of Powell and Keeler. Blondell was her still infectious self, joining with Oakie in a lively satiric talk-song-mock-ballroom number, "A Boulevardier from the Bronx," while Hugh Herbert as the philandering "unkie punkie" and Louise Fazenda as his long suffering wife, supplied the basic comedy relief. Draper (born in Florence, Italy) made his screen debut as Keeler's dance partner in "You've Gotta Know How to Dance" proving that he was more graceful on his feet than Powell, but was lacking in the requisite charm.

Powell and Keeler maneuvered their usual plotline bickering and romancing, but their antics stirred little joy among filmgoers, leading most critics to agree that as a team they had seen brighter days. (The two came briefly alive during the fashion show number, "I Don't Have to Dream Again," geared as a sentimental fox trot to pace the Modiste shop display, with Powell singing the lyrics and Keeler joining in for stanzas of line recitative.) Frank S. Nugent *(New York Times)* perhaps best summed up the *Colleen* impact. ". . . we prefer one ballroom dance by Ginger Rogers and Fred Astaire to a whole program by Miss Keeler and Mr. Powell."

## THE YEARS AFTER

The undynamic *Ready, Willing and Able* (1937) with Lee Dixon proved to be Ruby Keeler's final Warner Bros. film, for when Al Jolson had a major disagreement with the studio and walked out, he took Keeler with him. Although she had admitted that year that "This film business isn't my whole life," she soon signed a contract with RKO. She did not co-star in a movie with Fred Astaire as anticipated at that studio, but instead was sadly wasted in the drama *Mother Carey's Chickens* (1938), a film previously rejected by Katharine Hepburn and Ginger Rogers. That studio allowed her contract to quietly elapse. After divorcing Jolson, she made a B musical at Columbia entitled *Sweetheart of the Campus* (1941) with Ozzie Nelson. That same year she was remarried, to a real estate investor, and virtually retired from show business. There were a few guest appearances on television in the 1950s, including a 1954 reunion with Dick Powell on the "Ed Sullivan Show." In 1966-67 she toured with Busby Berkeley in several film festivals here and abroad which honored his screen work. There was a brief summer stock stint with *Bell, Book and Candle* in 1968, and, after the death of her husband the following year, she agreed to play the feminine "lead" in the Broadway revival of *No, No, Nanette* (1970), ostensibly a musical supervised by Berkeley and actually featuring Keeler's long-standing stage pal, Patsy Kelly. The show, including Keeler's two dances, "I Want to be Happy" and "Take a Little One Step," proved to be an enormous hit. After a two-year run she returned to California and retirement but in late 1973 she agreed to tour the stock circuit with a new edition of *No, No, Nanette*.

Powell, who, like Keeler, had felt their co-starring roles were limiting them professionally, remained at Warner Bros. through *Naughty But Nice* (1939) with Ann Sheridan. He then moved to Paramount where he was promised more substantial, non-singing assignments. His first, Preston Sturges' *Christmas in July* (1940), was a fine comedy, and his next co-starred him with his wife Joan Blondell in *I Want a Divorce* (1940) as did Universal's *Model Wife* (1941). By the time of the lumbering Dorothy Lamour musical, *Riding High* (1943), Powell had had enough and left Paramount. It was RKO's *Murder, My Sweet* (1944) which finally altered the tenor's screen image, for he portrayed in sterling fashion Raymond Chandler's tough, unshaven private eye, Philip Marlowe. Later, there were two MGM films with June Allyson, the third Mrs. Powell, but by the time of *The Bad and the Beautiful* (1952), he was washed up in movies. Undaunted, Powell joined with David Niven and Charles Boyer in forming a producing company whose "Four Star Playhouse" on television became a great success, leading to his rosy future in the video medium as producer, director (he had helmed the theatrical feature *Split Second* in 1952, and several thereafter), and star-host ["Zane Grey Theatre" (1956), "Dick Powell Theatre" (1961)]. He died of cancer in 1963, leaving a million-dollar-plus estate, and a reputation as a screen actor and vocalist (through reissue LP albums) that continues to grow in strength.

In **The Keyhole** (WB, 1933)

# Chapter 7

# George Brent
# &
# Kay Francis

## GEORGE BRENT

6′ 1″
170 pounds
Black hair
Hazel eyes
Pisces

*Real name: George B. Nolan. Born March 3, 1904, Galway, Ireland. Married Helen Lewis (1926); divorced 1926. Married Ruth Chatterton (1932); divorced 1934. Married Constance Worth (1937); divorced 1937. Married Ann Sheridan (1942); divorced 1943. Married Janet Micheal (1947), children: Suzanne, Barry.*

**FEATURE FILMS:**

*Under Suspicion* (Fox, 1930)
*Fair Warning* (Fox, 1931)
*The Lightning Warrior* (Serial: Mascot, 1931)
*Once A Sinner* (Fox, 1931)
*Charlie Chan Carries On* (Fox, 1931)
*Homicide Squad* (Univ., 1931)
*Ex-Bad Boy* (Univ., 1931)
*The Rich Are Always with Us* (FN, 1932)
*So Big* (WB, 1932)
*Weekend Marriage* (FN, 1932)

*Miss Pinkerton* (FN, 1932)
*The Purchase Price* (WB, 1932)
*The Crash* (FN, 1932)
*They Call It Sin* (FN, 1932)
*42nd Street* (WB, 1933)
*Luxury Liner* (Par., 1933)
*The Keyhole* (WB, 1933)
*Lilly Turner* (FN, 1933)
*Private Detective 62* (WB, 1933)°

°Unbilled Appearance

175

*Baby Face* (WB, 1933)
*Female* (FN, 1933)
*From Headquarters* (WB, 1933)
*Stamboul Quest* (MGM, 1934)
*Housewife* (WB, 1934)
*Desirable* (WB, 1934)
*The Painted Veil* (MGM, 1934)
*The Right to Live* (WB, 1935)
*Living on Velvet* (FN, 1935)
*Stranded* (WB, 1935)
*Front Page Woman* (WB, 1935)
*The Goose and the Gander* (WB, 1935)
*Special Agent* (WB, 1935)
*In Person* (RKO, 1935)
*Snowed Under* (FN, 1936)
*The Golden Arrow* (FN, 1936)
*The Case Against Mrs. Ames* (Par., 1936)
*Give Me Your Heart* (WB, 1936)
*More Than a Secretary* (Col., 1936)
*God's Country and the Woman* (WB, 1936)
*The Go Getter* (WB, 1937)
*Mountain Justice* (WB, 1937)
*Submarine D-1* (WB, 1937)
*Gold Is Where You Find It* (WB, 1938)
*Jezebel* (WB, 1938)
*Racket Busters* (WB, 1938)
*Secrets of an Actress* (WB, 1938)
*Wings of the Navy* (WB, 1939)
*Dark Victory* (WB, 1939)
*The Old Maid* (WB, 1939)
*The Rains Came* (20th, 1939)
*The Fighting 69th* (WB, 1940)
*Adventure in Diamonds* (Par., 1940)
*'Til We Meet Again* (WB, 1940)
*The Man Who Talked Too Much* (WB, 1940)

*South of Suez* (WB, 1940)
*Honeymoon for Three* (WB, 1941)
*The Great Lie* (WB, 1941)
*They Dare Not Love* (Col., 1941)
*International Lady* (UA, 1941)
*Silver Queen* (UA, 1942)
*In This Our Life* (WB, 1942)
*Twin Beds* (UA, 1942)
*You Can't Escape Forever* (WB, 1942)
*The Gay Sisters* (WB, 1942)
*Experiment Perilous* (RKO, 1944)
*The Affairs of Susan* (Par., 1945)
*The Spiral Staircase* (RKO, 1946)
*Tomorrow Is Forever* (RKO, 1946)
*My Reputation* (WB, 1946)
*Lover Come Back* (Univ., 1946)
*Temptation* (Univ., 1946)
*The Corpse Came C.O.D.* (Col., 1947)
*Out of the Blue* (Eagle-Lion, 1947)
*Christmas Eve (Sinner's Holiday)* (UA, 1947)
*Slave Girl* (Univ., 1947)
*Luxury Liner* (MGM, 1948)
*Angel on the Amazon* (Rep., 1948)
*Red Canyon* (Univ., 1949)
*Illegal Entry* (Univ., 1949)
*The Kid From Cleveland* (Rep., 1949)
*Bride for Sale* (RKO, 1949)
*FBI Girl* (Lip., 1951)
*Man Bait* (Lip., 1952)
*Montana Belle* (RKO, 1952)
*Tangier Incident* (AA, 1953)
*Mexican Manhunt* (AA, 1953)
*Death of a Scoundrel* (RKO, 1956)°

°Unbilled Appearance

# KAY FRANCIS

**5′ 5″**
**112 pounds**
**Brown hair**
**Brown eyes**
**Capricorn**

*Real name: Katherine Edwina Gibbs. Born January 13, 1899, Oklahoma City, Oklahoma. Married James Francis (1922); divorced 1925. Married William Gaston (1926); divorced 1928. Married Kenneth MacKenna (1931); divorced 1933. Died August 26, 1968.*

**FEATURE FILMS:**

Gentlemen of the Press (Par., 1929)
The Cocoanuts (Par., 1929)
Dangerous Curves (Par., 1929)
Illusion (Par., 1929)
The Marriage Playground (Par., 1929)
Behind the Makeup (Par., 1930)
The Street of Chance (Par., 1930)
Paramount on Parade (Par., 1930)
A Notorious Affair (WB, 1930)
Raffles (UA, 1930)
For The Defense (Par., 1930)
Let's Go Native (Par., 1930)
The Virtuous Sin (Par., 1930)
Passion Flower (MGM, 1930)
Scandal Sheet (Par., 1931)
Ladies' Man (Par., 1931)
The Vice Squad (Par., 1931)
Transgression (RKO, 1931)
Guilty Hands (MGM, 1931)
24 Hours (Par., 1931)
Girls About Town (Par., 1931)
The False Madonna (Par., 1931)
Strangers in Love (Par., 1932)
Man Wanted (WB, 1932)
Street of Women (WB, 1932)
Jewel Robbery (WB, 1932)
One Way Passage (WB, 1932)
Trouble in Paradise (Par., 1932)
Cynara (UA, 1932)
The Keyhole (WB, 1933)

Storm at Daybreak (MGM, 1933)
Mary Stevens, M.D. (WB, 1933)
I Loved a Woman (WB, 1933)
House on 56th Street (WB, 1933)
Mandalay (FN, 1934)
Wonder Bar (FN, 1934)
Doctor Monica (WB, 1934)
British Agent (FN, 1934)
Living on Velvet (FN, 1935)
Stranded (WB, 1935)
The Goose and the Gander (WB, 1935)
I Found Stella Parish (FN, 1935)
The White Angel (FN, 1936)
Give Me Your Heart (WB, 1936)
Stolen Holiday (WB, 1937)
Confession (WB, 1937)
Another Dawn (WB, 1937)
First Lady (WB, 1937)
Women Are Like That (WB, 1938)
My Bill (WB, 1938)
Secrets of an Actress (WB, 1938)
Comet Over Broadway (WB, 1938)
King of the Underworld (WB, 1939)
Women in the Wind (WB, 1939)
In Name Only (RKO, 1939)
It's a Date (Univ., 1940)
Little Men (RKO, 1940)
When the Daltons Rode (Univ., 1940)
Play Girl (RKO, 1940)
The Man Who Lost Himself (Univ., 1941)

*Charley's Aunt* (20th, 1941)
*The Feminine Touch* (MGM, 1941)
*Always in My Heart* (WB, 1942)
*Between Us Girls* (Univ., 1942)

*Four Jills in a Jeep* (20th, 1944)
*Divorce* (Mon., 1945)
*Allotment Wives* (Mon., 1945)
*Wife Wanted* (Mon., 1946)

In **Living on Velvet** (FN, 1935)

In **Stranded** (WB, 1935)

Genevieve Tobin, Guy Usher, Edward McWade, George Brent, Davison Clark, Kay
Francis, and Eddy Chandler in **The Goose and the Gander** (WB, 1935)

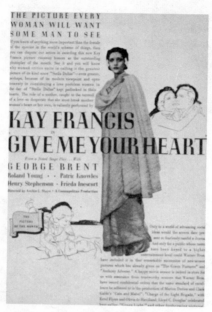

Advertisement for **Give Me Your Heart**

Kay Francis, Roland Young, Helen Flint, Patric Knowles, Frieda Inescort, George Brent, and Mitchell Ingraham in **Give Me Your Heart** (WB, 1936)

Advertisement for **Secrets of an Actress** (WB, 1938)

Isabel Jeans, Ian Hunter, Gloria Dickson, Kay Francis, and George Brent in **Secrets of an Actress**

# THE KEYHOLE
## *(Warner Bros., 1933) 69M.*

Director, Michael Curtiz; based on the story *Adventuress* by Alice D. G. Miller; screenplay, Robert Presnell; dialog director, Arthur Greville Collins; art director, Anton Grot; gowns, Orry-Kelly; music director, Leo F. Forbstein; camera, Barney McGill; editor, Ray Curtis.

Kay Francis (Anne Brooks); George Brent (Neil Davis); Glenda Farrell (Dot); Allen Jenkins (Hank Wales); Monroe Owsley (Maurice Le Brun); Helen Ware (Portia Brooks); Henry Kolker (Schuyler Brooks); Ferdinand Gottshalk (Brooks' Lawyer); Irving Bacon (Grover the Chauffeur); Clarence Wilson (Weems, the Head of the Detective Agency); George Chandler (Joe the Desk Clerk); Heinie Conklin (Departing Guest); Renee Whitney (Cheating Wife); John Sheehan (Bartender); Bill Elliott (Dancing Extra); George Humbert, Gino Corrado (Waiters); Maurice Black (Salesman); Leo White (Porter).

New York Premiere: Radio City Music Hall—March 30, 1933
No New York Television Showing

## Synopsis

Anne Brooks, wed to millionaire Schuyler Brooks, is distraught to learn that her former husband, Maurice Le Brun, had never obtained the divorce he had promised to institute, and now he is demanding $50,000 in hush money. On the verge of a nervous breakdown, she confesses her plight to her sister-in-law, Portia, who advises her to leave the country and procure a divorce from Le Brun. Anne embarks for Havana, but Brooks, who is suspicious of her activities of late, engages Neil Davis to trail her, not informing Neil that Anne is his wife. En route, Anne and Neil become acquainted and spend most of the trip together. Just as Anne had hoped, Le Brun follows her to Cuba, and, because he is not an American citizen, Anne is relying on Portia to arrange matters so that Le Brun will be denied re-entry into the United States. When Portia learns that her brother has had so little faith in Anne, she tells him the whole story. Ashamed of his suspicions, Brooks rushes by plane to join his wife, and sends Neil a cable advising him of his arrival. In the meantime, Anne tells Neil of her troubled past. He, in turn, confesses what he has been doing, but swears that he loves her. Just when Neil is expecting Brooks to arrive at Anne's room, Le Brun shows up on the scene. Neil succeeds in threatening Le Brun, the latter becoming so agitated that, in his attempt to escape by way of the balcony, he falls to his death. When Brooks arrives, Anne tells him that they are not legally wed and that, moreover, she is through with him. She decides to remain with the man she loves, Neil.

In 1931, super talent agent Myron Selznick engineered a talent coup whereby Ruth Chatterton, Kay Francis and William Powell transferred their acting services from Paramount to Warner Bros. At the Burbank studio, Francis continued her screen teaming with suave Powell in their two finest joint pictures, the swank tearjerker *One Way Passage,* and the sophisticated froufrou, *Jewel Robbery,* both done in 1932. Thereafter, while Francis' studio position and popularity continued to gain in stature by veritable leaps and bounds, she enjoyed two of her best movie roles, in *Trouble in Paradise* and *Cynara,* both 1932 releases made on loan to other studios. When she returned to the home lot, Warners put sultry Francis into a series of specious movie assignments which highlighted her abilities to model chic Orry-Kelly wardrobes but ignored her abilities as a steely on-camera comedienne. These soap opera productions were efficiently assembled but indistinctive and empty in content. It should have been a warning to the lustrous actress, but she was too occupied collecting and spending her weekly paycheck to mind properly. In *The Keyhole* the thirty-four-year-old Francis inherited as her leading man twenty-nine-year-old Irish-born George Brent, then wed to Ruth Chatterton whose cinema star was declining while her rival's (Francis) was still ascending.

*The Keyhole* proved quite typical of the Francis-Brent movies to come: slick, turgid, vapid, but *always* an entertaining, well-outfitted enterprise. If one could ignore the banal storyline and the reckless posturing of the two stars (she slurred her "R's" and eschewed most any emotional subtlety, while he tended to mix too much good grooming with monotonous stodginess), their allied oncamera jaunts provided a certain amount of relaxed diversion from the grimness of the Depression. The make-believe world of Francis and Brent rotated about two impeccably mannered personalities, and was filled with tasteful settings, sartorially perfect mannequins, and the most elegant of rarified domestic crises.

*The Keyhole* enjoyed a rather unique advertising campaign:

"Warning to Prudes! Moralists! Hypocrites!

"Tomorrow this theatre will show the only picture this year that keeps abreast of 1933's changing moral standards!

"Don't Come if you're afraid to see what's on the other side of *The Keyhole!*"

Unfortunately the sixty-nine-minute feature (highbrows might call the Michael Curtiz-directed film a classy programmer) did not live up to the advertised expectations as the story ". . . sways from the sublime to the mundane" [Mordaunt Hall (*New York Times*)], an apt critique leading many to wonder how it had been selected as a Radio City Music Hall attraction.

The London *Times* admitted, "There is much to be said for choosing a story which suits the chief actors in a film. But Miss Kay Francis is not only accommodated, as a rule, with plots of one particular kind; the very scenery, down to the smallest details, seems to be arranged as a background without which she never appears." *The Keyhole* was no exception to this London newspaper's general description. Here Francis' Anne Brooks is a respected member of New York's upper crust, a woman traveling in swank surroundings who prefers to forget that her first marriage was to a foreign bounder (Monroe Owsley) or that her second wedding involved a man (Henry Kolker) much older than she whom she tolerates but can never deeply love. However, this film was a typical Hollywoodian depiction of the "Four Hundred" set, with its scenario showing the elite "heroine" as a person of rather ungenerous thoughts. If she dressed exquisitely, displayed a proper regard for high decorum, the film seemed to say, no one had any right to demand anything further of her. That is, until she meets a man she truly loves.

The weakest link of *The Keyhole* was saddling poor Brent with a very unsympathetic oncamera occupation as a professional stool pigeon and wife-framer. This Achilles' heel within the screenplay (along with the gratuitously violent demise of Owsley at the finale) counteracted so strongly against the romantic ambiance of the Francis-Brent team that even indulgent *Variety* had to admit, "As a screen team, they'd be easy to like in a story that could give both a break. This yarn treats neither well."

A further distraction from the refined love making of Francis and Brent was the insertion of celluloid comedy relief anywhere and everywhere in the story. It was a customary ploy in films of those day, but still a particularly obnoxious stumbling block in this entry. *The Keyhole* had the antics of two brash Warner Bros. contract cookies, Allen Jenkins and Glenda Farrell. He appeared as Brent's wise-cracking Brooklynese assistant and she played a smart-mouthed roving gold digger. Each of the salty duo was in the process of enjoying his/her latest posturing at the expense of the gullible souls about them. Jenkins posed as a Park Avenue blade and she pretended to be a member of the international *haut-monde*. Their vivid dialog interchanges did much to distract the viewer's attention from the main subject at hand—the relationship between Francis and Brent.

Within *The Keyhole* Francis glided through her shallow part, changing from blonde to dark-haired coiffure, affecting her most gracious and serene manner, always smartly gowned and continually fascinating with her deep-voiced, gilt-edged personality. Nevertheless the film's faults were well indicated when Richard Watts, Jr. *(New York Herald-Tribune)* bemoaned, "Poor Miss Kay Francis is beset by unworthy males—and, it might be added, by an unworthy story—in the new picture. . . . Of all the unpleasant gentlemen who surround the unhappy heroine this lover is probably the least alluring. He is, you see, a private detective who has been hired to test her virtue—the idea being that, since he is portrayed by George Brent, if any woman can resist him she must be beyond suspicion. Miss Francis resists for quite a while."

## LIVING ON VELVET
*(First National-Warner Bros., 1935) 77M.*

Director, Frank Borzage; story-screenplay, Jerry Wald, Julius Epstein;

art director, Robert Haas; gowns, Orry-Kelly; music director, Leo F. Forbstein; camera, Sid Hickox; editor, William Holmes.

Kay Francis (Amy Prentiss); Warren William (Walter Pritcham); George Brent (Terry Parker); Helen Lowell (Aunt Martha); Henry O'Neill (Thornton); Samuel S. Hinds (Mr. Parker); Russell Hicks (Major); Maude Turner Gordon (Mrs. Parker); Martha Merrill (Cynthia Parker); Edgar Kennedy (Counterman); Sam Hayes (Announcer); Lee Shumway, Emmett Vogan, Selmer Jackson (Officers); Walter Miller (Leader); Stanley King (Soldier); Niles Welch (Major's Aide); May Beatty, Mrs. Wilfred North (Dowagers); Harry Bradley, Jay Eaton, Lloyd Whitlock (Men); Olaf Hytten (Travis); Harry Holman (Bartender); Wade Boteler (Sergeant); Eric Wilton (Lawton); Harold Nelson (Sexton); Frank Dodd (Minister); William Norton Bailey (Drew); David Newell (Smalley); John Cooper (Messenger Boy); Jack Richardson (Taxi Driver); Eddy Chandler (Policeman); Paul Fix (Interne); Frank Fanning (Doorman); Bud Geary (Chauffeur).

New York Premiere: Strand Theatre—March 7, 1935
No New York City Television Showing

### Synopsis

When Terry Parker's parents and sister are killed in an airplane accident in which he was piloting the craft and came out unharmed, he becomes embittered with people and life. He leads a reckless life, defying death, squandering his fortune, and later returns to America broke. His good friend Walter Pritcham takes Terry to a party to meet Amy Prentiss whom Walter hopes to wed. When Amy and Terry meet it is love at first sight. Despite family objections they marry and live in a small Long Island house loaned to them by Walter. Amy desperately attempts to help Terry change his pessimistic views, but she fails. When Terry receives a windfall of $8,000 from some family stock, Amy is pleased because they will now be able to purchase—on their own—what they need for their simple life style. But Terry uses the money to purchase a second-hand airplane for a short-haul passenger service, incurring an additional $2,000 debt. Amy is miserable. Her patience is exhausted and she leaves him, hoping that the separation will bring him to his senses. But when he is later injured in an automobile accident she rushes to his side. When he recovers from this second brush with death, he is a new man in his outlook, paving the way for a happy reconciliation with Amy.

This Kay Francis vehicle, one of four she made for 1935 release, was not initially conceived as a project for reteaming her and George Brent, for in the original Jerry Wald screenplay it was decreed that second-billed Warren William would wind up the lucky man who wins the actress' heart. However, by the time production got underway, William was already finishing his studio contract and the executives felt no necessity

185

to provide him with any new oncamera showcasing. Thus the doctored script found Brent recovering from his story-devised automobile accident and being sufficiently regenerated in his personality to recapture Francis' deep love.

The contrived ending was not the only scripting problem *Living on Velvet* had to overcome, for the seventy-seven-minute story opened on a tragic note (Brent's plane runs out of gas, crashes, and kills his parents and sister), and it required a good deal of scripting ingenuity to lift the subsequent proceedings to a happier note.

For a welcome change, Brent's characterization both on paper and oncamera contained some dimension. His Terry Parker believes that "I'm on the wrong side of the road, outside looking in." On the surface he is carefree, pleasant, restless, slightly bored, and unconcerned with material things (which makes him irresistible to Francis), while underneath he is bearing a grudge against life which has allowed him to live while his loved ones needlessly died. Once again, Francis is cast as an ultra-sophisticated New Yorker, a young woman who quickly discerns that reckless Brent is far more intriguing than her reliable, congenial suitor of long standing. The latter actually proves to be one of the best sports in the annals of the game of love and lives up to his nickname of "Gibraltar," for he is strong as a rock in his devotion to Francis and her every whim. Not only does he offer his former fiancée and his best friend (Brent) his full blessings when they impulsively decide to wed, but he grants them the loan of his Long Island cottage for their honeymoon home.

The first half of *Living on Velvet* provides Francis and Brent with some of their finest oncamera moments. His Terry Parker has been acting like a crude cad before he meets Amy, and she has been a perfect but distracted hostess before he arrives at her swell party. Then they are formally introduced and are immediately attracted to one another, aimlessly bantering as they confirm their initial impression that it is love at first sight. Soon she is deserting her own party to flee into the night with her newly discovered love. A short time later they are wed and enjoying the confines of the cozy little house at Patchogue, Long Island. Francis has a rare cinema opportunity to display traits of domesticity as she and Brent enjoy the novelty of their new marital status. But then the script lets the stars down, forcing Francis to become unsympathetic as the petulant wife who cannot and will not appreciate her husband's need to seek some meaning in his life. (He has a madcap scheme—rather ingenious in its day—to inaugurate an air shuttle service for Long Island to Manhattan commuters). She rigidly refuses to adapt herself to the role of a middle class housewife and everything in turn goes awry. Brent, meanwhile, is urged by the scenario to become more restless, unreliable, and death-defying. Ironically the more proficient Francis and Brent get in displaying the unpleasant aspects of their movie characters, the less the viewer cares for the leads or the film itself.

At least the finer points of the stars' acting styles did not go unnoticed. "Mr. Brent's performance is excellent, and Miss Francis displays not merely a new collection of gowns (which had the female members of the audience cooing) but a somewhat surprising talent for comedy in the earlier sequences" [Frank S. Nugent (*New York Times*)].

## STRANDED
### *(Warner Bros., 1935) 73M.*

Director, Frank Borzage, based on the story *Lady with a Badge* by Frank Wead, Ferdinand Reyher; screenplay, Delmer Daves; additional dialog, Carl Erickson; art directors, Anton Grot, Hugh Reticker; gowns, Orry-Kelly; music director, Leo F. Forbstein; camera, Sid Hickox; editor, William Holmes.

Kay Francis (Lynn Palmer); George Brent (Mack Hale); Patricia Ellis (Velma Tuthill); Donald Woods (John Wesley); Barton MacLane (Sharkey); Robert Barrat (Stan Januaschek); June Travis (Jennie Holden); Shirley Grey (Marvel Young); Henry O'Neill (Mr. Tuthill); Ann Shoemaker (Mrs. Tuthill); Frankie Darro (Jimmy Rivers); William Harrigan (Updike); Joseph Crehan (Johnny Quinn); John Wray (Mike Gibbons); Edward McWade (Tim Powers); Gavin Gordan (Jack); Mary Forbes (Grace Dean); Florence Fair (Miss Walsh); Burr Carruth (Old Man); Emmett Vogan (Officer); Harry C. Bradley (Conductor); Samuel R. McDaniel (Porter); Eily Malyon (Old Maid); John Kelly (Sailor); Joan Gay (Dane); Mae Busch (Lizzie); Edwin Mordant (Surgeon); Harrison Greene (Blustery Man); Eleanor Wesselhoeft (Mrs. Young); Wally Wales (Peterson); Wilfred Lucas (Man Worker); Glen Cavender (Kolchak); Joe King (Dan Archer); Frank Sheridan (Boone); Emma Young (Chinese Girl); Mia Liu (Japanese Girl); Rita Rozelle (Polish Girl); Louise Seidel (Danish Girl); Frank LaRue (Immigration Officer); Lillian Harmer (Desk Attendant); Zeffie Tilbury (Old Hag); Lillian Worth (Blonde); Georgia Cooper (Floor Nurse); Adrian Rosley (Headwaiter); Spencer Charters (Boatman); Junior Coghlan (Page); Jack Richardson, Stan Cavanagh (Taxi Drivers); Edwin Stanley (Police Surgeon); Edward Keane (Doctor); Niles Welch (Safety Engineer); Walter Clyde (Assistant); Milton Kibbee (Timekeeper); Marbeth Wright (Operator); Donald Downen (Clerk); Claudia Coleman (Madame); Patrick Moriarity (Steve Brodie); Sarah Padden (Workman's Wife); Dick French (Clerk); Jessie Arnold (Scrubwoman); Henry Otho (Worker); Vesey O'Davoren (Butler).

New York Premiere: Strand Theatre—June 19, 1935
No New York Television Showing

## Synopsis

Twenty-five-year-old Lynn Palmer, a member of the Traveler's Aid Society, which has its headquarters at the San Francisco train terminal, leads a hectic workday existence catering to the varied needs of the assorted people who apply to her office for assistance of one sort or another. She is more than amazed when construction engineer Mack Hale turns up at her welfare station desk requesting help for one of his steel workers. It develops that nine years prior, Lynn had lived in the same town as Mack and she had had a crush on him. Now he is in charge of the building of the Golden Gate Bridge, and it is his turn to fall in love with her. However, because each have such demanding, time-consuming jobs, they hardly have an opportunity to pursue their romance. When he is not preoccupied in combatting labor problems on the job, she is engulfed with sorting out the confusions of bewildered passengers at the terminal. But their courtship progresses to the point where Lynn throws caution to the wind and rushes to a bridge workers' strike meeting where she convinces the dissatisfied men that Mack and his company are giving the men a fair deal and that they have an obligation to return to their job. At this point Mack reenters the scene with the beaten culprit-troublemaker, Sharkey, in submissive tow. Lynn and Mack decide to wed.

◆◆◆

When outspoken star Kay Francis was on her elegant way to Europe after completing *Stranded,* she indulgently informed the eager press, "I liked it very much. I had the none too usual experience of being satisfied with my work in it. And I hope that the public will agree with me."

Moviegoers might have, and Frank S. Nugent *(New York Times)* did acknowledge "The Francis-Brent team . . . seems to be a happy combination. Mr. Brent's engaging comedy is an excellant antidote to Miss Francis's penchant for heavy tragedy and keeps her from taking her art too seriously."

But once again, the film had scripting problems which scenarist Delmar Daves could not lick. (The picture was originally titled *Lady with a Badge* but studio executives feared the public would think the film a police story, so the more alluring title tag of *Stranded* was created.) What starts out in *Stranded* as an interesting delineation of the workings of the Traveler's Aid Society takes on overtones of social protest, complete with a socialistic versus capitalistic theme, all of which detract from the predictable but essential story contrivance, the career versus marriage struggle-courtship between Francis and Brent. It must have been a novel gimmick in 1935 to incorporate newsreel footage of the building of the San Francisco-Oakland Golden Gate Bridge into the movie, but the repeated insertion of the construction progress quickly became tedious.

As viewers expected and hoped, Francis managed to appear glamourous even in her relatively staid, but very well tailored and becoming

Traveler's Aid outfits. It was in her on-the-job moments that *Stranded* came thankfully to life, as she tended to her various duties: kissing a baby traveling alone on a train, finding a job for a waif after learning that the youth's father has been jailed, locating a young woman reported missing by her distressed relatives and making sure that the girl receives hospital attention. Perhaps the film's most engaging scene occurs when Brent arrives at her office one evening to escort her to dinner and finds that he has become the object of mirth to four Oriental immigrant girls who have misplaced their waiting bridegrooms.

As indicated before, interwoven into the Traveler's Aid section of *Stranded* are several sequences concerned with labor union problems on the bridge construction site. These scenes of labor trouble are heightened when Mike Gibbons (John Wray), on order from troublemaker Sharkey (Barton MacLane), gets some of the men drunk on the job, leading to a quarrel between workers hundreds of feet above the ground in which one of them falls to his death. Despite Brent's honest efforts to solve the racketeer-inspired job dissension, matters grow worse. Thereafter, Francis, smartly groomed as always, enters a rough and tumble labor meeting, and delivers an impassioned plea that might have won Franklin D. Roosevelt's endorsement, but not that of the audience, who were rightly aghast at viewing the star expounding to the proletarian assemblage in a manner more becoming to a Sunday school teacher. Her harangue urged the blue collar workers to "never lose your arrogance" but nobly return to their honorable, honest toil.

"The svelte Kay Francis and the handsome George Brent" did their best with the slipshod *Stranded* as each remains over-dedicated to his/her career until the very final reel, but being "glamourous" and "upstanding" respectively could not fully compensate for what *Variety* termed "lack of heart interest." Among the supporting cast, Patricia Ellis was particularly effective as the socialite who dabbles in Traveler's Aid Work and shows herself to be just a catty young blonde.

## THE GOOSE AND THE GANDER
### *(Warner Bros., 1935) 65M.*

Director, Alfred E. Green; story-screenplay, Charles Kenyon; art director, Robert M. Haas; gowns, Orry-Kelly; music director, Leo F. Forbstein; camera, Sid Hickox; editor, Howard Leonard.

Kay Francis (Georgiana); George Brent (Bob McNear); Genevieve Tobin (Betty Summers); John Eldredge (Lawrence); Claire Dodd (Connie Thurston); Helen Lowell (Aunt Julia); Ralph Forbes (Ralph Summers); William Austin (Arthur Summers); Spencer Charters (Winklesteinbergher); Eddie Shubert (Sweeney); John Sheehan (Murphy); Charles Coleman

(Jones); Wade Boteler, Davidson Clark, Nick Copeland, Cliff Saum, Glen Cavender (Detectives); Al Woods (Bellboy); Milton Kibbee (Garageman); Jack Richardson (Baggage Man); David Newell (Hotel Clerk); Eddy Chandler (Policeman); Guy Usher (Sergeant); Edward McWade (Justice of Peace); Helen Woods (Violet); Gordon (Bill) Elliott (Teddy); Jane Buckingham (Mrs. Burns); Caryle Blackwell, Jr. (Barkley); Olive Jones (Miss Brent).

New York Premiere: Strand Theatre—September 11, 1935
No New York Television Showing

### Synopsis

Georgiana overhears Betty Summers telling Bob McNear that her husband will be out of town and so they can spend the night together at her mountain lodge. When Georgiana learns that Betty is wed to Ralph Summers, her former husband, she seeks revenge for this humiliating situation. Georgiana arranges matters so that the rendezvousing couple cannot reach the lodge, compelling them to spend the night in her home. Matters become further complicated when two jewel thieves, Connie Thurston and Lawrence, posing as wife and husband, and using Ralph's name, are forced to stay at Georgiana's house as well. Georgiana's intention had been to prove to Ralph, whom she had also invited to her home, that Betty was unfaithful. However, she finds she cannot go through with the plan because she has fallen in love with Bob. Thereafter, Georgiana and her aunt Julia take the jewels from the thieves, who leave without knowing it. Ralph, when he finally arrives, instead of finding an unfaithful wife, is a witness to a marriage between Georgiana and Bob.

◆　◆　◆

Based on the bromide, "What's sauce for the goose is sauce for the gander," this elaborate bedroom farce of the smart southern California set mixes elements of such plays as *The Comedy of Errors* and *The Dover Road* in a tale that initially is slow moving, but steps up its rapid pace as the participants intermingle in the mountain lodge setting, almost turning into an American variation of *Hotel Paradiso.*

Although this was ostensibly a starring vehicle for Kay Francis, the queen of the Warner Bros. lot, the script and director Alfred E. Green gave almost equal screen time to Genevieve Tobin as the would-be adultress and Claire Dodd as the snappy wrongdoer. Francis' role as the jealous manipulator of the adult games was not exactly sympathetic, leading the *London Times* to chide, ". . . a film which can drive Miss Francis to coyness stands condemned for that alone."

In a relatively short running time (sixty-five minutes), a great deal happens in *The Goose and the Gander,* between the moment polished Francis composes her scheme at the swank Santa Barbara hotel to the finale which finds she and George Brent having to prove they are *not* jewel thieves to a very bewildered policeman (Spencer Charters). One may wonder why, within the story, alluring Francis would have wed Ralph Summers (Ralph Forbes) in the first place, or in the second place have bothered trying to make a fool of the grasping Tobin. But given this somewhat illogical basis, the star, aided by her acid-tongued aunt (Helen Lowell), energetically sets a trap to capture Tobin and fun-loving Brent *flagrante delicto*. One has to admit, and this was the gimmick of most Francis movie excursions, the situations involved were not the ordinary, run-of-the-mill events which transpired in the average person'd daily life.

Brent, always the celluloid debonair soul in the best Herbert Marshall tradition, played much more of a straight man than usual in *The Goose and the Gander*. *Variety* opined that he appeared a good line feeder (he always was), although the review noted that he was aping—perhaps too much—the quirky style of Edward Everett Horton. In this entry he had one especially effective scene at the mountain cabin where, assigned to share Tobin's bedroom, he nobly spends most of his time camping out on the adjacent roof.

## GIVE ME YOUR HEART
### *(Warner Bros., 1936) 87M.*

Director, Archie Mayo; based on the play *Sweet Aloes* by Jay Mallory; screenplay, Casey Robinson; art director, Max Parker, C. M. Novi; gowns, Orry-Kelly; music director, Leo F. Forbstein; camera, Sid Hickox; editor, James Gibbons.

Kay Francis (Belinda Warren); George Brent (Jim Baker); Roland Young (Tubbs Barrow); Patric Knowles (Robert Melford); Henry Stephenson (Edward, Lord Farrington); Frieda Inescort (Rosamond Melford); Helen Flint (Dr. Florence Cudahy); Zeffie Tilbury (Miss Esther Warren); Elspeth Dudgeon (Miss Dodd); Halliwell Hobbes (Oliver Warren); Russ Powell (Cab Driver); Edgar Norton (Servant); Dick French, Ethel Sykes (Guests); Bruce Warren (Young Man); Elsa Peterson (Young Woman); Louise Bates (Hostess); Ed Mortimer (Host); Carlyle Moore, Jr. (Elevator Man); Phyllis Godfrey (Maid); Eric Wilton (Johnson the Butler); Demetruis Emanuel (Waiter); Mitchell Ingraham (Bartender); Alphonse Martel (Dining Room Captain); Tockie Trigg (Baby Edward); Helena Grant (Nurse); Wayne and Toske (Dance Teams).

New York Premiere: New Criterion Theatre—September 16, 1936
New York Television Debut: Channel 13—May 7, 1959

### Synopsis

Belinda Warren has just returned home to England after spending years in Italy with her father. Soon she and her neighbor, Robert Melford, son of a British lord, are carrying on a secret romance. He is wed to Rosamond, a semi-invalid. Knowing this, Tubbs Barrow, a novelist and playwright, and a friend to all the parties involved, tries to intervene. When he finds out that Belinda loves Robert despite her knowing he loves Rosamond, he can see no way out. She goes to Italy to consult her father, but does not have an opportunity to discuss her problem with him before he succumbs to a heart attack. Belinda returns to England nearly penniless and is forced to live on the bounty of her stiff, unfriendly aunt, Esther Warren. When she informs the understanding Tubbs that she is expecting a child, he later arranges for her to give up the infant boy to Rosamond and Robert who long for a baby of their own. Thereafter Belinda departs for America. Aboard the transatlantic vessel she meets Jim Baker, a noted attorney-businessman. They wed on her terms, for she cannot promise to love him, nor will she reveal the story of her past. As time goes by, her nerves become unsettled and a madcap social life seems to be her only refuge. Then one day Tubbs arrives in New York, and he arranges a meeting between she and Jim, and Robert and Rosamond. When Rosamond, who has recovered from her crippling ailment, notes Belinda's resemblance to the child, she realizes the whole story. So she informs Belinda that at first she thought it would only be possible to hate Robert's ex-flame, but now she finds a kinship to her. Rosamond allows Belinda to see the child again and when she realizes how happy the boy is with Robert and Rosamond, Belinda is finally freed of her guilt pangs. She can now begin her marriage afresh with the patient Jim.

◆━━◆━━◆

"If you've ever been in love, if you've ever been lonely and worried and heartsick, you'll understand and thrill to the story of Linda Warren. It's something you'll never forget." So read the advertisement to *Give Me Your Heart*. While never a forerunner in the tearjerker sweepstakes, Warner Bros. had a first class arbiter of the genre in Kay Francis, the heroine of such past screen operas as *One Way Passage* (1932), *I Love a Woman* (1933), *House on 56th Street* (1933), and more recently *I Found Stella Parish* (1935). After the misfire of allowing Francis to go very "dramatic" in the antiseptic biography of Florence Nightingale, *The White Angel* (1936) the studio was anxious to return their prime star to vehicles which the public knew and expected of Francis. Thus came *Give Me Your Heart* which posed the shattering question "How can I let my own flesh and blood call another woman 'mother'?"

This film was based on *Sweet Aloes*, the play by Jay Mallory (pseudonym of Joyce Cary) which had enjoyed better success on the London stage with Diana Wynyard than in its brief Broadway run in 1935 in which Evelyn Laye starred.

High-level critics had become increasingly annoyed with Francis' repetition of stereotyped screen roles, ignoring the fact that it was the studio rather than the star who had caused the pigeon-hole casting situation.

These critics vented their displeasure by attacking her performance in *Give Me Your Heart*. "The best-dressed woman in the cinema capital is a well-groomed and handsome decoration to the proceedings but no ornament to its histrionics" [Howard Barnes *(New York Herald-Tribune)*]. In fairness, the Casey Robinson screenplay did demand more persuasive emoting than Francis seemed willing to offer, but it is dubious that even a Ruth Chatterton or a Bette Davis could have instilled credibility into the tenuous, precious role of Belinda Warren.

The heroine of *Give Me Your Heart* is a very well-bred young woman who nevertheless allows romantic passion to overcome her sense of propriety and therefore must pay the price of suffering. As she is reprimanded after the fact, her offense has been an "offense against a code, against certain decencies upon which marriage and civilization depend." The distraught woman gives up the nearest and dearest thing to her heart, her child, and in personal disgrace, a la *Madame X,* leaves the scene of her tremendous indiscretion. She embarks for America, having been instructed that "the time comes when every human being must face reality and face it alone."

Once in the United States, she is fortunate enough to wed an affable, understanding man—who else at 1930s Warner Bros. but George Brent? (Frank S. Nugent of the *New York Times* complimented the usually critically bypassed Brent for giving the role of Belinda's baffled husband ". . . a blunt, masculine incomprehension of his wife's turmoil, which is precisely what the part required.") Brent's Jim Baker is unaware of Francis' increased longing for the child she dare not admit exists. She wants that "part of myself" that she has not seen (and perhaps, the viewer wonders, also hankers after Patric Knowles' Robert Medford as well). At this strategic point, *Give Me Your Heart* evolves into a dramatized version of psychotherapy as Francis' Belinda must learn that those verging on mental illness should and *must* fearlessly face up to their past. And this is exactly what Tubbs Barrow (Roland Young) and Dr. Florence Cudahy (Helen Flint) accomplish by bringing Francis into contact once again with her child and his parents.

The wise viewer had been waiting throughout the well-manicured production for the inevitable confrontation between Francis and Rosamond Melford (Frieda Inescort). In the course of the two women's heart to heart chat, Inescort, in a very telling portrayal, confesses that she had held rancor in her heart toward Francis for creating such domestic chaos. "I told myself that I was a civilized woman and it didn't matter. But you only say these things with your mind—not with your feelings."

After the resultant sequence of high bathos when Francis finally has the opportunity to see her beloved (sleeping) child once again, the film skips off to its obligatory happy ending, with Francis and Brent, as in their past joint pictures, facing the future, together and happy.

Was this "The picture every woman will want some man to see"? View it and judge for yourself.

# SECRETS OF AN ACTRESS
*(Warner Bros., 1938) 70M.*

Associate producer, David Lewis; director, William Keighley; based on the story *Lovely Lady* and the adaptation thereof by Milton Krims, Rowland Leigh, Julius J. Epstein; art director, Anton Grot; assistant director, Chuck Hansen; gowns, Orry-Kelly; sound, Charles Lang; camera, Sid Hickox; editor, Owen Marks.

Kay Francis (Fay Carter); George Brent (Dick Orr); Ian Hunter (Peter Snowden); Gloria Dickson (Carla Orr); Isabel Jeans (Marian Plantagenet); Penny Singleton (Miss Reid); Dennie Moore (Miss Blackstone); Selmer Jackson (Thompson); Herbert Rawlinson (Harrison); Emmet Vogan (Spencer); James B. Carson (Carstairs).

New York Premiere: Strand Theatre—October 7, 1938
No New York Television Showing

## Synopsis

Fay Carter, an aspiring Broadway actress waiting for her big chance, becomes acquainted with Peter Snowden, a wealthy architect. He is so impressed with her beauty and talent that he is determined to finance a play with her as the star. His partner, Dick Orr, is very much against the idea, but Peter refuses to listen to him. Once Dick meets Fay, he quickly changes his mind and even falls in love with her, as she does with him. But Dick does not tell her that he is wed, because he wants to ask Carla, from whom he has been separated for two years, to divorce him before he broaches the subject to Fay. In the meantime Fay learns of Dick's marital status and, in despair, turns to Peter and promises to wed him. But Peter realizes that she really loves Dick and, by a ruse, induces Carla to grant Dick a divorce. Fay and Dick then are happily united.

◆━━◆━━◆

After Warner Bros. reneged on granting Kay Francis the promised lead role in *Tovarich* (1937), the $227,000-a-year star threatened a whopping law suit and announced that she and the studio (who had become disenchanted with her anyway) would come to a parting of the way once her present agreement had expired. Thus, Warner Bros., wanting to take full advantage of the remaining months in her contract, dumped Francis into six lifeless, mechanical programmers, mostly fit for the double bill film market. Not content to just treating Francis this way, Warners made their intentions and actions clearly known to the exhibitors and even to the public who were forced to sit on the sidelines as Francis' film career was fed down the proverbial drain. Meanwhile, George Brent, who certainly enjoyed one of the most placid, stable careers in Hollywood's annals, continued to churn out his three to four annual efforts for Warner Bros., forever playing the congenial leading man, and rarely bothering to confront the studio's front office executives with demands for more challenging screen assignments.

At the very best, *Secrets of an Actress* is an "innocuous blend of whimsy and romance" *(New York World Telegram)*, not even sufficient fare for the usual bridge table clientele who thrived on screen studies of ornamental women. Even in her movie days of stooging for the Marx Brothers in *The Cocoanuts* (1929) Francis was always noted more for her chic poise and sartorial splendor than for her acting. Therefore it was (reckless) folly to cast her as an actress, one who supposedly had made her footlights debut at the age of two and boasted a talent which had already attained professional recognition on the road but not yet in New York. Fortunately the screenplay avoids focusing very much on the play-within-the-play device, concentrating rather on the triangular romance between Francis and her two swains, Brent and Ian Hunter. Unfortunately, in *Secrets of an Actress* the leading men are shown as dreary, conventional types: Hunter as a dreamy architect who has always wanted to design stage sets, and Brent as the flippant married man who ultimately relies on his pal (Hunter) to pave the way for his divorce and his subsequent marriage to Francis.

The dialog of *Secrets of an Actress* does sparkle with random wit, as when Brent informs his wife Carla Orr (Gloria Dickson), "You can have a divorce . . . Reno . . . a staggering settlement . . . and custody of your mother" but more often it wallows mundanely in suffocating cliches.

Brent (Kissing Francis): "And I thought I hated you."

Francis: "It's ridiculous. This is so sudden."

Brent: "Lightning never struck faster."

Or Francis informing Brent: "Don't talk. I want to think about us."

Perhaps the biggest ignominy suffered by Hunter, who next to Ralph Bellamy and Robert Young probably lost more screen heroines in 1930s movies than any other actor, was to have to listen to Francis speak those fateful words, "I love you, Peter, but I'm not in love with you." (Thirty-four years later, Doris Day would be uttering those exact words on an episode of "The Doris Day Show.")

One of the few redeeming elements of this inept feature was Isabel Jeans as Francis' drunken actress-roommate, Marian Plantagenet. She becomes drunk at the bar one day and socks Hunter, which leads to the meeting between Francis and Hunter, and paves the way for the subsequent cross-hatched relationships that develop.

As *Variety* judged *Secrets of an Actress*, it "involved no secret other than why it was made," adding, "it's no use hitching race horses [like Francis] to milk wagons."

## THE YEARS AFTER

Because ravishing Kay Francis so frequently glided oncamera through the lofty realms of a chic life, displaying little deep emotion, too many viewers assumed that the loss of her Warner Bros. studio contract did not affect her. However it did affect her tremendously. She was terribly bitter about this career reversal right up to her death. Her pal Carole Lombard maneuvered Francis into a meaty role in RKO's *In Name Only* (1939), but thereafter it was professionally downhill and fast for Francis. Walter Huston, with whom she had starred on stage in the 1920s and later in her first film, *Gentlemen of the Press* (1929), requested her for his co-lead in *Always in My Heart* (1942) and Warner Bros. acquiesced. On "Lux Radio Theatre" in 1943, she and George Brent reunited to perform in *The Lady Is Willing*. In 1944-46 she co-produced and starred in a trilogy of low-budgeted Monogram features which effectively ended her once glamourous screen stardom. She then replaced Ruth Hussey on Broadway in 1946 in *State of the Union*, and, after recuperating from an overdose of pills during a road tour in Ohio, she continued to appear in summer stock productions (*Theatre* in 1952 was her last), and also occasionally on television. When she died of cancer in August of 1968, she left a large estate—worth nearly two million dollars—mostly for the raising and training of guide dogs for the blind.

George Brent remained at Warner Bros. until the early 1940s, his most frequent co-star being Bette Davis, with whom he played in such later features as *Jezebel* (1938), *Dark Victory* (1939), *The Old Maid* (1939), *The Great Lie* (1941) and *In This Our Life* (1942). He made one feature, *Honeymoon for Three* (1941) with witty Ann Sheridan, whom he married the next year, but divorced in 1943. He was a frequent co-star of lesser vehicles in post-World War II Hollywood, the nadir being *Angel on the Amazon* (1948) with Vera Ralston and Constance Bennett. *Mexican Manhunt* (1953) with Hillary Brooke concluded his movie career, for he became ill during production of *Death of a Scoundrel* (1956) and was replaced by John Hoyt. With scarcely a twitch of an eye, he moved over into television displaying the same quiet gentlemanly ways that had insured his lengthy big screen tenure. In 1956 he joined with Mercedes McCambridge and Dane Clark in the adventure television series "Wire Service" which lasted but one season. By 1960 he was nearly retired, only reappearing professionally later in the decade to perform an occasional commercial. Today he and his family live quietly on their ranch in northern California. Hollywood, his career, and all the years in the industry, are very much a thing of the past for him.

Just as the more chic screen team of Norma Shearer and Robert Montgomery and the more talented stage duo of Lynn Fontanne and Alfred Lunt are of an age gone by, so the particular charms of elegant Kay Francis and suave George Brent seem very out of keeping with today's new tenets. But in their day Francis-Brent were Warner Bros.' melodrama equivalent of MGM's droll Myrna Loy and William Powell, and were regarded by the bulk of steady filmgoers as the height of refined, upper class romantics.

William Powell and Myrna Loy in a pose from **Another Thin Man** (MGM, 1939)

# Chapter 8

# William Powell
# &
# Myrna Loy

## WILLIAM POWELL

6′
168 pounds
Brown hair
Brown eyes
Leo

*Real name: William Horatio Powell. Born July 29, 1892, Pittsburgh, Pennsylvania. Married Eileen Wilson, child: William; divorced 1931. Married Carole Lombard (1931); divorced 1933. Married Diana Lewis (1940).*

FEATURE FILMS:

*Sherlock Holmes* (Goldwyn, 1922)
*When Knighthood Was in Flower* (Par., 1922)
*Outcast* (Par., 1922)
*The Bright Shawl* (Inspiration, 1923)
*Under the Red Robe* (Cosmopolitan, 1924)
*Romola* (Inspiration, 1924)
*Dangerous Money* (Par., 1924)
*Too Many Kisses* (Par., 1925)
*Faint Perfume* (B. P. Schulberg, 1925)

*My Lady's Lips* (B. P. Schulberg, 1925)
*The Beautiful City* (Inspiration, 1925)
*White Mice* (Par., 1926)
*Sea Horses* (Par., 1926)
*Desert Gold* (Par., 1926)
*The Runaway* (Par., 1926)
*Aloma of the South Seas* (Par., 1926)
*Beau Geste* (Par., 1926)
*Tin Gods* (Par., 1926)
*The Great Gatsby* (Par., 1926)
*New York* (Par., 1927)

*Love's Greatest Mistake* (Par., 1927)
*Special Delivery* (Par., 1927)
*Senorita* (Par., 1927)
*Paid to Love* (Fox, 1927)
*Time for Love* (Par., 1927)
*Nevada* (Par., 1927)
*She's a Sheik* (Par., 1927)
*Beau Sabreur* (Par., 1928)
*Feel My Pulse* (Par., 1928)
*Partners in Crime* (Par., 1928)
*The Last Command* (Par., 1928)
*The Dragnet* (Par., 1928)
*The Vanishing Pioneer* (Par., 1928)
*Forgotten Faces* (Par., 1928)
*Interference* (Par., 1929)
*The Canary Murder Case* (Par., 1929)
*The Greene Murder Case* (Par., 1929)
*Charming Sinners* (Par., 1929)
*Four Feathers* (Par., 1929)
*Pointed Heels* (Par., 1929)
*The Benson Murder Case* (Par., 1930)
*Paramount on Parade* (Par., 1930)
*Shadow of the Law* (Par., 1930)
*Behind the Makeup* (Par., 1930)
*Street of Chance* (Par., 1930)
*For the Defense* (Par., 1930)
*Man of the World* (Par., 1931)
*Ladies' Man* (Par., 1931)
*The Road to Singapore* (WB, 1931)
*High Pressure* (WB, 1932)
*Jewel Robbery* (WB, 1932)
*One Way Passage* (WB, 1932)
*Lawyer Man* (WB, 1932)
*Double Harness* (RKO, 1933)
*Private Detective 62* (WB, 1933)
*The Kennel Murder Case* (WB, 1933)
*Fashions of 1934* (WB, 1934)
*The Key* (WB, 1934)
*Manhattan Melodrama* (MGM, 1934)
*The Thin Man* (MGM, 1934)
*Evelyn Prentice* (MGM, 1934)
*Reckless* (MGM, 1935)

*Star of Midnight* (RKO, 1935)
*Escapade* (MGM, 1935)
*Rendezvous* (MGM, 1935)
*The Great Ziegfeld* (MGM, 1936)
*The Ex-Mrs. Bradford* (RKO, 1936)
*My Man Godfrey* (Univ., 1936)
*Libeled Lady* (MGM, 1936)
*After the Thin Man* (MGM, 1936)
*The Last of Mrs. Cheyney* (MGM, 1937)
*The Emperor's Candlesticks* (MGM, 1937)
*Double Wedding* (MGM, 1937)
*The Baroness and The Butler* (20th, 1938)
*Another Thin Man* (MGM, 1939)
*I Love You Again* (MGM, 1940)
*Love Crazy* (MGM, 1941)
*Shadow of the Thin Man* (MGM, 1941)
*Crossroads* (MGM, 1942)
*The Youngest Profession* (MGM, 1943)
*The Heavenly Body* (MGM, 1944)
*The Thin Man Goes Home* (MGM, 1944)
*Ziegfeld Follies* (MGM, 1946)
*The Hoodlum Saint* (MGM, 1946)
*Song of the Thin Man* (MGM, 1947)
*Life with Father* (WB, 1947)
*The Senator was Indiscreet* (Univ., 1947)
*Mr. Peabody and the Mermaid* (Univ., 1948)
*Take One False Step* (Univ., 1949)
*Dancing in the Dark* (20th, 1949)
*The Treasure of Lost Canyon* (Univ., 1951)
*It's a Big Country* (MGM, 1951)
*The Girl Who Had Everything* (MGM, 1953)
*How to Marry a Millionaire* (20th, 1953)
*Mister Roberts* (WB, 1955)

# MYRNA LOY

**5' 6"**
**110 pounds**
**Titian hair**
**Green eyes**
**Leo**

*Real name: Myrna Williams. Born August 2, 1905, Raidersburg, Montana. Married Arthur Hornblow, Jr. (1936); divorced 1942. Married John Hertz, Jr. (1942); divorced 1944. Married Gene Markey (1946); divorced 1950. Married Howland Sargeant (1951); divorced 1960.*

**FEATURE FILMS:**

*Pretty Ladies* (MGM, 1925)
*Ben Hur* (MGM, 1926)
*The Cave Man* (WB, 1926)
*The Gilded Highway* (WB, 1926)
*Across the Pacific* (WB, 1926)
*Why Girls Go Back Home* (WB, 1926)
*Don Juan* (WB, 1926)
*The Exquisite Sinner* (MGM, 1926)
*So This Is Paris?* (WB, 1926)
*Finger Prints* (WB, 1927)
*When a Man Loves* (WB, 1927)
*Ham and Eggs at the Front* (WB, 1927)
*Bitter Apples* (WB, 1927)
*The Heart of Maryland* (WB, 1927)
*The Jazz Singer* (WB, 1927)
*If I Were Single* (WB, 1927)
*The Climbers* (WB, 1927)
*Simple Sis* (WB, 1927)
*A Sailor's Sweetheart* (WB, 1927)
*The Girl from Chicago* (WB, 1927)
*What Price Beauty* (Pathé, 1928)
*Beware of Married Men* (WB, 1928)
*Turn Back the Hours* (Gotham, 1928)
*Crimson City* (WB, 1928)
*Pay As You Enter* (WB, 1928)
*State Street Sadie* (WB, 1928)
*Midnight Taxi* (WB, 1928)
*Noah's Ark* (WB, 1929)
*Fancy Baggage* (WB, 1929)
*The Desert Song* (WB, 1929)
*Black Watch* (Fox, 1929)

*The Squall* (FN, 1929)
*Hardboiled Rose* (WB, 1929)
*Evidence* (WB, 1929)
*The Show of Shows* (WB, 1929)
*The Great Divide* (FN, 1930)
*Cameo Kirby* (Fox, 1930)
*Isle of Escape* (WB, 1930)
*Under a Texas Moon* (WB, 1930)
*Cock O' the Walk* (Sono Art-World Wide, 1930)
*Bride of the Regiment* (FN, 1930)
*Last of the Duanes* (Fox, 1930)
*The Truth About Youth* (FN, 1930)
*Renegades* (Fox, 1930)
*Rogue of the Rio Grande* (Sono Art-World Wide, 1930)
*The Devil to Pay* (UA, 1930)
*Naughty Flirt* (FN, 1931)
*Body and Soul* (Fox, 1931)
*A Connecticut Yankee* (Fox, 1931)
*Hush Money* (Fox, 1931)
*Transatlantic* (Fox, 1931)
*Rebound* (RKO-Pathé, 1931)
*Skyline* (Fox, 1931)
*Consolation Marriage* (RKO, 1931)
*Arrowsmith* (UA, 1931)
*Emma* (MGM, 1932)
*The Wet Parade* (MGM, 1932)
*Vanity Fair* (Hollywood Exchange, 1932)
*The Woman in Room 13* (Fox, 1932)
*New Morals for Old* (MGM, 1932)

*Love Me Tonight* (Par., 1932)
*Thirteen Women* (RKO, 1932)
*The Mask of Fu Manchu* (MGM, 1932)
*The Animal Kingdom* (RKO, 1932)
*Topaze* (RKO, 1933)
*The Barbarian* (MGM, 1933)
*The Prizefighter and the Lady* (MGM, 1933)
*When Ladies Meet* (MGM, 1933)
*Penthouse* (MGM, 1933)
*Night Flight* (MGM, 1933)
*Men in White* (MGM, 1934)
*Manhattan Melodrama* (MGM, 1934)
*The Thin Man* (MGM, 1934)
*Stamboul Quest* (MGM, 1934)
*Evelyn Prentice* (MGM, 1934)
*Broadway Bill* (Col., 1934)
*Wings in the Dark* (Par., 1935)
*Whipsaw* (MGM, 1935)
*Wife Versus Secretary* (MGM, 1936)
*Petticoat Fever* (MGM, 1936)
*The Great Ziegfeld* (MGM, 1936)
*To Mary-With Love* (20th, 1936)
*Libeled Lady* (MGM, 1936)
*After the Thin Man* (MGM, 1936)
*Parnell* (MGM, 1937)
*Double Wedding* (MGM, 1937)
*Man-Proof* (MGM, 1938)
*Test Pilot* (MGM, 1938)
*Too Hot to Handle* (MGM, 1938)

*Lucky Night* (MGM, 1939)
*The Rains Came* (20th, 1939)
*Another Thin Man* (MGM, 1939)
*I Love You Again* (MGM, 1940)
*Third Finger, Left Hand* (MGM, 1940)
*Love Crazy* (MGM, 1941)
*Shadow of the Thin Man* (MGM, 1941)
*The Thin Man Goes Home* (MGM, 1944)
*So Goes My Love* (Univ., 1946)
*The Best Years of Our Lives* (RKO, 1946)
*The Bachelor and the Bobby Soxer* (RKO, 1947)
*Song of the Thin Man* (MGM, 1947)
*The Senator was Indiscreet* (Univ., 1947)°
*Mr. Blandings Builds His Dream House* (Selznick, 1948)
*The Red Pony* (Rep., 1949)
*Cheaper By the Dozen* (20th, 1950)
*If This Be Sin* (UA, 1950)
*Belles on Their Toes* (20th, 1952)
*The Ambassador's Daughter* (UA, 1956)
*Lonelyhearts* (UA, 1958)
*From the Terrace* (20th, 1960)
*Midnight Lace* (Univ., 1960)
*The April Fools* (National General, 1969)
*Airport '75* (Univ., 1974)

° Unbilled Appearance

William Powell, Myrna Loy, and Asta in **The Thin Man** (MGM, 1934)

Clark Gable, Myrna Loy, and William Powell in **Manhattan Melodrama** (MGM, 1934)

In **The Great Ziegfeld** (MGM, 1936)

William Powell, Cora Sue Collins, and Myrna Loy in **Evelyn Prentice** (MGM, 1934)

Myrna Loy, William Powell, Spencer Tracy, and Jean Harlow in a publicity pose for **Libeled Lady** (MGM, 1936)

Director W. S. Van Dyke II, William Powell, and Myrna Loy rehearsing for **The Thin Man** broadcast of "Lux Radio Theatre" (June, 1936)

William Powell, Sam Levene, Myrna Loy, Elissa Landi, Edgar Dearing, and Dick Rush in **After the Thin Man** (MGM, 1936)

John Beal, William Powell, Myrna Loy, and Florence Rice in **Double Wedding** (MGM, 1937)

Advertisement for **Love Crazy** (MGM, 1941)

In **Shadow of the Thin Man** (MGM, 1941)

Advertisement for **The Thin Man Goes Home** (MGM, 1944)

Asta, Myrna Loy, and William Powell in **The Thin Man Goes Home**

William Powell, Myrna Loy, Keenan Wynn, and Clinton Sundberg in **Song of the Thin Man** (MGM, 1947)

William Powell, Myrna Loy, Keenan Wynn, Asta, and Dean Stockwell in a publicity pose for **Song of the Thin Man**

# MANHATTAN MELODRAMA
## *(MGM, 1934) 93M.*

Producer, David O. Selznick; director, W. S. Van Dyke II; story, Arthur Caesar; screenplay, Oliver T. Marsh, H. P. Garrett, Joseph L. Mankiewicz; song, Richard Rodgers and Lorenz Hart; art directors, Joseph Wright, Edwin B. Willis; wardrobe, Dolly Tree; special effects, Slavko Vorkapich; camera, James Wong Howe; editor, Ben Lewis.

Clark Gable (Blackie Gallagher); William Powell (Jim Wade); Myrna Loy (Eleanor); Leo Carrillo (Father Pat); Nat Pendleton (Spud); George Sidney (Poppa Rosen); Isabel Jewell (Anabelle); Muriel Evans (May); Claudelle Kaye (Miss Adams); Frank Conroy (Blackie's Attorney); Jimmy Butler (Jim as a Boy); Mickey Rooney (Blackie as a Boy); Landers Stevens (Inspector of Police); Harry Seymour (Piano Player); William N. Bailey, King Mojave, W. R. Walsh (Croupiers); Charles R. Moore (Black Boy in Speakeasy); Thomas Jackson (Snow); John Marston (Coates); Lew Harvey (Crap Dealer); Billy Arnold (Black Jack Dealer); Jim James (Chemin De Fer Dealer); Stanley Taylor (Police Interne); James Curtis (Party Leader); Herman Bing (German Proprietor); Edward Van Sloan (Yacht Skipper); Jay Eaton (Drunk); Harrison Greene (Eleanor's Dance Partner); Leslie Preston (Jim's Dance Partner); William Stack (Judge); Emmett Vogan, Sherry Hall (Assistant District Attorneys); Lee Phelps (Bailiff); Charles Dunbar (Panhandler); John M. Bleifer (Chauffeur); Allen Thompson (Spectator on Street); G. Pat Collins (Miller in Prison); Wade Boteler (Guard in Prison); Sam McDaniel (Black Man in Prison); James C. Eagles (Boy in Prison); Samuel S. Hinds (Warden); Don Brodie, Ralph McCullough, Eddie Hart (Reporters); George Irving (Campaign Manager); Garry Owen (Campaign Manager); Bert Russell (Blind Beggar); Lee Shumway, Carl Stockdale, Jack Kenny (Policemen); Curtis Benton (Announcer); Dixie Lonton (Irish Woman); Pepi Sinoff (Jewish Woman); Donald Haynes (Stud); Bert Sprotte, William Irving (German Note Holders); Alexender Melesh (Master of Ceremonies); Vernon Dent (Old German Man); Henry Roquemore (Band Leader); Jack Lipson (Uncle Angus); William Augustin, Stanley Blystone (Detectives); Oscar Pafel (Assembly Speaker); Leo Lance (Trotsky), Leonid Kinsky (Trotsky Aide), Shirley Ross (Black Singer).

New York Premiere: Capitol Theatre—May 4, 1934
New York Television Debut: CBS—August 24, 1958

## Synopsis

Two East Side kids, Jim Wade and Blackie Gallagher, are orphaned in a maritime disaster. Jim grows up to become an assistant district attorney while Blackie becomes the owner of a large gaming house frequented by the underworld and the fun-loving society elite. Blackie's mistress Eleanor pleads with Blackie to drop the rackets, but he is more than content, reasoning that honesty is for the likes of his pal Jim or fore Father Pat. Later, a chance encounter between Jim and Eleanor cause them to fall in love and Eleanor leaves the disheartened Blackie. Jim is elected D.A., and when he fires his corrupt assistant, Snow, the latter sets out to smear Jim's name and ruin his chances for the gubernatorial sweepstakes. Eleanor learns of the situation and begs Blackie to help. Blackie shoots Snow, but is caught. Jim is forced to prosecute his boyhood pal, thereby cementing his bid for the governor's post. Eleanor eventually tells him that it was for his sake that Blackie committed the murder. Jim hastens to the prison, planning to commute the sentence, but Blackie refuses to have his friend fall down on his principles. Blackie walks bravely to his death with Father Pat at his side. Eleanor and Jim, who have been having domestic problems, decide to try again on a new basis.

◆—◆—◆

In its day, this well-appointed feature was considered a "keen, adult, exciting melodrama" [William Boehnel (*New York World Telegram*)] employing to good advantage a gimmick that would subsequently become *de rigeur* for such outings: two boyhood pals growing up on opposite sides of the law. At the time, Clark Gable was well established as a somewhat versatile star who could play crooks and heroes with equal adeptness. In fact for his prior foray into comedy, *It Happened One Night* (1934), made on loan to Columbia, he would win the Best Actor Oscar of the year. Since her first appearance onscreen in MGM's *Pretty Ladies* (1925), Myrna Loy had suffered a typecasting which limited her to vamp or Oriental villainess roles. Not until such RKO pictures as *The Animal Kingdom* (1932) and *Topaze* (1933) did she shake that stereotype, proving she was at ease in drawing room drama and comedy as well. William Powell had been filmmaking since 1922, enjoying the first real upsurge in his career when sound arrived and his dapper persona could be heard as well as seen, particularly in a series of Paramount *Philo Vance* films and in society dramas with glamorous Kay Francis. After a two-year stay at Warner Bros. where he continued to display his affinity for portraying debonair screen gents, he found his career stagnating and moved over to MGM for his second-billed role in *Manhattan Melodrama*, his first picture under a new Metro contract.

After the film's introductory segment, including the S. S. Slocum riverboat disaster in 1904, which presents the two lead male characters as young East Side mugs, *Manhattan Melodrama* swings into rapid gear, detailing how each youth grows up to realize different ambitions. Gable's Blackie Gallagher is a fast-stepping gambler-racketeer who takes chances with his life as easily as he does with a deck of cards. His mistress is

Eleanor (Loy). She is not the ordinary underworld moll. She is refined, charming, and witty, bantering as easily with the corrupt police officers as with her lover (Gable), the Beau Brummel of the underworld. "You'll win somebody's mother some night," she tells Gable who has just picked up a plush yacht in a gaming interlude. Gable nonchalantly replies, "Sure. Everyone can be paid off with chips." This flip statement and sensitive Loy's reaction to it set the tone for the couple's imminent breakup. Loy is tired of their way of life. "It isn't tonight. It's every night. Worrying about you. Hating what you do. Hating who you meet."

The stage is thus set for the scene where Jim Wade (Powell), a graduate of Columbia Law School, wins the election as the new New York City prosecutor. Gable as usual is too busy with his underhanded business manipulations to keep his promise to attend the victory celebration, so he sends a reluctant Loy in his stead. She catches up with spruce Powell as he steps into a waiting taxi. She jumps in after him, murmuring, "Pardon me if I intrude." After she explains the circumstances behind this peculiar meeting ("Blackie sent me") the duo settle down to a frisky camaraderie that will foreshadow all their joint screen efforts over the next several decades. Loy wryly informs her new-found escort, "Nothing like a district attorney to keep a girl in shape. We must have a good wrestle some day." To match her lighthearted, witty poise, Powell smoothly launches into a recitation of his life story, related in his standard elegant banter. "I was born at home because I wanted to be near mother . . . "

Although Loy is sufficiently impressed by her evening on the town with chipper Powell (who does not even try to kiss her goodnight!) to actually leave the devil-may-care Gable, it is some time before she again meets Powell. This time she insures that their romance carries through to a proper marriage. She adjusts to "being" the spouse of an up-and-coming, honest law enforcer-politician as easily as she had adapted to being part of a gangster's world, gauging her wardrobe and behavior to suit her new role in life. After all, she is batting in a different league with the suave Powell, of whom Gable has often said, "Class. Class. It's written all over him."

In its rather lengthy, leisurely exposition, the film tends to sink into overheated melodrama, especially with the terse sequences in which Gable shoots Snow (Thomas Jackson) in the men's room of Madison Square Garden, and the subsequent sentencing of Gable to the electric chair during which time Loy and Powell almost come to a parting of the ways. With his chipper attitude as death approaches ("If I can't live the way I want, let me die when I want"), Gable grabs the limelight in the picture's closing reel, and remains a haunting image for the viewer as he walks calmly—even jauntily—to his end on death house row. The anticlimactic finale which follows seems excessively lame by comparison. Powell has humbly admitted his (innocent) complicity in the Gable murder case to the state senate, and then, having resigned his civil post, saunters outside to find Loy awaiting him.

Loy: "What are you going to do," she sympathetically inquires.

Powell: "I don't know. Try again from the start. Something else."

Loy: "Let me try with you."

As Thornton Delehanty (*New York Post*) aptly observed of *Manhattan Melodrama* and the performance of the male stars, "Both these actors are helped by the charm and persuasive dignity which Myrna Loy brings to the role of the girl. Her performance confirms the conviction of this department that she is one of the screen's most intelligent and personable players." The *New York Times*, after lauding Gable's emoting, reported, "Miss Loy is charming and competent and Mr. Powell is as easygoing as ever."

Loy and Powell would later recreate their *Manhattan Melodrama* roles on "Lux Radio Theatre" on September 9, 1940.

The film won an Oscar in the Best Original Story category.

## THE THIN MAN
### *(MGM, 1934) 91M.*

Producer, Hunt Stromberg; director, W. S. Van Dyke II; based on the novel by Dashiell Hammett; screenplay, Albert Hackett, Frances Goodrich; assistant director, Les Selander; art directors, Cedric Gibbons, David Townsend, Edwin B. Willis; costumes, Dolly Tree; sound, Douglas Shearer; music director, Dr. William Axt; camera, James Wong Howe; editor, Robert J. Kern.

William Powell (Nick Charles); Myrna Loy (Nora Charles); Maureen O'Sullivan (Dorothy Wynant); Nat Pendleton (Lt. John Guild); Minna Gombell (Mimi Wynant); Porter Hall (McCauley); Henry Wadsworth (Tommy); William Henry (Gilbert Wynant); Harold Huber (Nunheim); Cesar Romero (Chris Jorgenson); Natalie Moorhead (Julia Wolf); Edward Brophy (Joe Morelli); Thomas Jackson, Creighton Hale, Phil Tead, Nick Copeland, Dink Templeton (Reporters); Ruth Channing (Mrs. Jorgenson); Edward Ellis (Clyde Wynant); Gertrude Short (Marion); Clay Clement (Quinn); Cyril Thornton (Tanner); Robert E. Homans (Bill the Detective); Raymond Brown (Dr. Walton); Douglas Fowley, Sherry Hall (Taxi Drivers); Polly Bailey, Dixie Laughton (Janitresses); Arthur Belasco, Ed Hearn, Garry Owen (Detectives); Fred Malatesta (Head Waiter); Rolfe Sedan, Leo White (Waiters); Walter Long (Stutsy Burke); Kenneth Gibson (Apartment Clerk); Tui Lorraine (Stenographer); Bert Roach (Foster); Huey White (Tefler); Ben Taggart (Police Captain); Charles Williams (Fight Manager); John Larkin (Porter); Harry Tenbrook (Guest); Pat Flaherty (Cop/Fighter).

New York Premiere: Capitol Theatre—June 29, 1934
New York Television Debut: CBS—January 10, 1957

## Synopsis

Distressed Dorothy Wynant pleads with Nick Charles to help her find her inventor father, Clyde Wynant, who has been missing for some three months. Nick Charles, seconded by his wealthy, attractive wife Nora, insists that he is through with detective work, but a peculiar chain of circumstances force him to take the case. First the inventor's secretary, Julia Wolf, is found murdered. Evidence points to the inventor as the murderer, particularly since he was divorced from his wife and had been the victim's lover. But Nick is not convinced that the inventor is the killer, even after a gunman who has valuable data on the caper is killed. Nick, accompanied by his wire-haired terrier, Asta, visits the inventor's shop and finds a body there. Although the corpse is unrecognizable, X-rays indicate that the body is that of the inventor. But Nick does not release this information to anyone. He orders the police to collect all the suspects in the case and have them attend a dinner party he and Nora will give. Through a series of questions and accusations Nick uncovers the fact that the inventor's lawyer is the murderer. It seems the attorney, together with the unfaithful secretary, were robbing the inventor. When the inventor learned these facts, the lawyer killed him, hid the body, and later killed the secretary because she knew too much. He then killed the gunman, because that person had seen him murder the secretary. Dorothy, although unhappy that her father is dead, is glad to at least have had his name cleared. She weds, and leaves her neurotic mother, Mimi Wynant. Nick and Nora proceed to California, glad that the adventure is over.

◆——◆——◆

Dashiell Hammett's reputation as a successful detective novelist was exceedingly high when MGM acquired the screen rights to his *The Thin Man* (1932) which studio director "One Take" W. S. Van Dyke II was convinced could be made into an offbeat screen entertainment that could be far more captivating that Warner Bros. picturization (1931) of Hammett's *The Maltese Falcon*, a novel published in 1930. As is well documented elsewhere, Metro's chief, Louis B. Mayer, was initially opposed to Van Dyke's insistence that essentially romantic leads William Powell and Myrna Loy could be effectively teamed as the story's chic spouses who solve capers between drink-laden nights on the town and domestic squabbling at the fireside. Van Dyke pointed out that Powell had been most effective in his Philo Vance character earlier in his film career, and that Powell and Loy had performed admirably together in Van Dyke's *Manhattan Melodrama*. After agreeing to lens the film on a particularly tight production schedule (twelve days), the director obtained a studio okay. As is common knowledge, Van Dyke turned out a genre masterpiece which earned Metro a million dollars and won Powell an Academy Award nomination for Best Actor (he lost to Clark Gable who won for *It Happened One Night*).

Advertisements for *The Thin Man* promised, "It's on the screen. Loaded with laughs". Such come-ons might have seemed strange to any potential filmgoer, wondering how a murder mystery teaming with corpses and skittery suspects could be a chuckle provoker. "Yet so skillfully is the amalgamation of two moods managed, so ably is the adaptation arranged and so engaging is the acting and directing that the new photoplay becomes a shrewdly and completely entertaining work. Vigorous, resourceful and nervously moving, it combines brashness with excitement and emerges as a triumph of cinema mystery narration" [Richard Watts, Jr. (*New York Herald-Tribune*)].

The same ads for *The Thin Man* also requested the would-be viewer, "do not divulge the solution to your friends." What was the mystery all about? First of all, and many a casual film fan tends to forget this fine point, Powell's Nick Charles was not the Thin Man. That tag belonged to lanky Clyde Wynant (Edward Ellis), the confusing head of the peculiar Wynant family, who would not appear in any further installments of the series. Second, and most important of all, the protagonists were offbeat characters. They were a new breed celluloid husband-and-wife team. As William K. Everson described in *The Detective in Film* (1972) " . . . their devotion to each other was obvious, and they had *fun*. They also satisfied a kind of wish fulfillment from audiences in those rather grim days in that they solved the depression by completely ignoring it rather than by offering patronizing platitudes or artificial solutions."

Loy's Nora and Powell's Nick were no antiseptic heroine and hero. One might be initially miffed by Powell's character who so cavalierly rests on his wife's financial laurels, but he never fails to tease her about her affluent status, taking the sting out of the situation.

Loy: "I think it's a dirty trick to bring me all the way to New York just to make a widow out of me."

Powell: "You wouldn't be a widow long."

Loy: "You bet I wouldn't."

Powell: "Not with all your money."

The couple so unpretentiously enjoy leading the good life, and managing in their own way to do good for others, that their formula for happiness can be accepted by the less fortunate viewer. It was a delightful change for filmgoers of the time—and still is even today—to witness a married couple bantering words and exchanging love taps while they retain their dignity as fun-loving upper classers and share great respect for one another. To insure that this novel husband and wife silver screen pair, in which the wife was no second-class member of the team, would be greeted with open arms by the masses, the Albert Hackett-Frances Goodrich script emphasizes the point that Powell and Loy are great drinkers, relying on the theory that the common man much more readily accepts a stranger who imbibes a touch of liquor now and then. In fact, whole scenes in *The Thin Man* are devoted to this subject.

Loy: "Is that my drink over there?"

Powell: "What are you drinking?"

Loy: "Rye."

Powell (Gulping down the contents of the glass): "Yes, yes. It's yours."

Besides, scripters in their adaptation of Hammett's novel reasoned that movie watchers could hardly resist a married couple who share their good times and adventures with a scene-stealing white wire-haired terrier named Asta.

With its sterling cast, which included pert ingenue Maureen O'Sullivan, deliberately bland William Henry, waspish Minna Gombell, tough Natalie Moorhead, dim-witted police lieutenant Nat Pendleton, and such Damon Runyonesque gangster types as Edward Brophy, *The Thin Man* became a winning combination of many parts. The critics, like the public, were in agreement about the deft playing of the two stars, "William Powell, who by now is a past master in the art of sleuthing, is thoroughly in his element as Nick Charles. . . . Myrna Loy as Nora, Charles's wife, aids considerably in making this film an enjoyable entertainment. She speaks her lines effectively, frowns charmingly, and is constantly wondering what her husband's next move will be" [Mordaunt Hall (*New York Times*)].

The boxoffice results of *The Thin Man* not only clinched the fact that MGM should make more follow-ups to the entry instead of just disguised spin-offs (the studio did both), but it demonstrated conclusively that as a team Powell and Loy were unbeatable in offering the public a mixture of sophistication, charm, comedy, and warmth, more so than such other contemporary Metro celluloid teams (Gable and Joan Crawford, Gable and Norma Shearer, Gable and Jean Harlow, Gable and Loy). Powell and Loy would be a strong mainstay of studio production throughout the years to come, as much an asset as such later Culver City screen pairs as Jeanette MacDonald and Nelson Eddy, Mickey Rooney and Judy Garland, or Greer Garson and Walter Pidgeon.

Powell and Loy repeated their *The Thin Man* characterizations on "Lux Radio Theatre" on June 8, 1936.

A video series "based" on *The Thin Man* debuted on NBC-TV in September, 1957 for a two year run. Peter Lawford and Phyllis Kirk were the stars of that skein. In 1974 MGM prepared a *The Thin Man* video pilot, this time featuring Robert Wagner.

## EVELYN PRENTICE
### (MGM, 1934) 80M.

Producer, John W. Considine, Jr.; director, William K. Howard; based on the novel by W. E. Woodward; screenplay, Lenore Coffee; music, Oscar Raclin; art directors, Cedric Gibbons, Arnold Gillespie, Edwin B. Willis; wardrobe, Dolly Tree; camera, Charles G. Clarke; editor, Frank Hull.

Myrna Loy (Evelyn Prentice); William Powell (John Prentice); Una Merkel (Amy Drexel); Harvey Stephens (Lawrence Kennard); Isabel Jewell (Judith Wilson); Rosalind Russell (Nancy Harrison); Henry Wadsworth (Chester Wylie); Edward Brophy (Eddie Delaney); Cora Sue Collins (Dorothy Prentice); Jessie Ralph (Mrs. Blake); Perry Ivins (Dr. Gillette); Sam Flint (Dr. Lyons); Pat O'Malley (Detective Pat Thompson); J. P. McGowen (Detective Mack Clark); Jack Mulhall (Gregory); Clarence Hummel Wilson (Public Defender); Mariska Aldrich (Matron); Herman Bing (Klein the Antique Dealer); Wilbur Mack, Garry Owen, Phil Tead (Reporters); Francis McDonald (Charles the Chauffeur); James Mack (Albert the Butler); Milton Owen (Waiter); Samuel S. Hinds (Newton); Georgia Caine (Mrs. Newton); John Hyams (Mr. Humphreys); Howard Hickman (Mr. Whitlock); Richard Tucker (Mr. Dillingham); Sam McDaniel (Porter); Billy Gilbert (Barney the Cafe Owner); Frank Conroy (District Attorney Farley); Sherry Hall (Court Clerk); Stanley Andrews (Judge); Matty Roubert (Newsboy); Craufurd Kent (Guest); Ruth Warren (Miss Meade, John Prentice's Secretary); Bob Perry (Juryman); Larry Steers (Diner-Extra).

New York Premiere: Capitol Theatre—November 9, 1934
New York Television Debut: CBS—May 6, 1961

### Synopsis

While married to John Prentice, a noted criminal lawyer, Evelyn discovers that John, on one of his business trips, has had an affair with Nancy Harrison. The disillusioned Evelyn seeks sympathy from poet Lawrence Kennard, who has been trying to win her affections. She sees him a few times and even sends him some letters, but she soon comprehends the danger from these innocent meetings and breaks her friendship with him. John returns home and all is forgiven. He and Evelyn plan a European trip with their daughter Dorothy. However, Lawrence induces her to come to his apartment on an important matter and once there he threatens to show the letters to John, unless she gives him $15,000. Evelyn picks up a pistol from the table and demands the letters which Lawrence hands over to her. He then strikes her and as she hits the wall the gun goes off and Lawrence falls to the floor. She rushes out of the apartment, just as Lawrence's mistress, Judith Wilson enters. Being found with the body, Judith is arrested and charged with murder. Evelyn postpones the European trip and induces John to defend Judith. At the trial, courtroom spectator Evelyn loses control of herself and shouts out that she had committed the crime. John, by clever cross-examination, brings out in Judith's testimony the fact that the shot that killed Lawrence was actually fired by her. Evelyn and John reconcile and take their daughter on the planned-for European jaunt.

217

The advertisement for William Powell and Myrna Loy's third joint screen effort of 1934 smartly announced, "The stars of *The Thin Man* are Together Again."

W. E. Woodward's psychological novel (1933) underwent excruciating rewrites for its screen rendition, which, because of Lenore Coffee's artistry in turning the project into a very commercial and safe venture, was ranked "Agreeable rather than stimulating, it manages with the exception of a surprise climax, to be predictable at almost any given point" [Andre Sennwald (*New York Times*)].

In each of their co-starring screen ventures to date, the public was asked to accept the husband-and-wife teaming of Powell and Loy in a new light. They were idealistic in *Manhattan Melodrama*, chic yet jocular in *The Thin Man*, and now in *Evelyn Prentice* they were melo-dramatic in the grand *Madame X* tradition. Unlike their roles in the Dashiell Hammett tale, they now both took marriage and homicide very seriously in *Evelyn Prentice*.

Most viewers were perhaps most surprised by Loy's impersonation of the title character in *Evelyn Prentice*. In *Manhattan Melodrama* she had functioned as the mistress of charming gangster Clark Gable, an immoral lady by the standards of the time, but her noble goal-seeking in that same picture redeemed her questionable character. However, in *Evelyn Prentice* it is a different matter. Here Loy is a wife and mother who finds her marital security undermined by her husband's romantic peccadillos and she deliberately sets about to break the double standard situation by obtaining some extracurricular sympathy from an obvious gigolo (sup-posedly made more romantic for her and the viewer because he was labeled a would-be poet). If it is a little embarrassing to discover that always well-composed Powell can dabble so cavalierly in extramarital byplay with flirtatious Rosalind Russell, it is absolutely astonishing to find Loy—fast becoming the perfect screen wife in the public's eye—losing her grip on sensible morality, no matter what the seeming provocation. To observe Loy not jealous but hurt at her husband's outside romantic activi-ties and her attempt to rendezvous with the unappealing Harvey Stephens is bad enough. However, in the big confrontation scene, to have the irate parasite (Stephens) then slap her, is really startling! Such a scene (and change of pace for Loy) makes the subsequent gun accident bit decidedly anti-climactic.

In her long performing career to date, Loy has never been particularly convincing in heavily dramatic sequences. Her brittle quality as an actress sags into heavyhanded rhetoric and is made all the more unbelievable by a quivering quality that sends her voice into a more high-pitched tone. Thus in the key courtroom scene where the near-hysterical Loy can bear her guilt no longer, the viewer must endure the less amenable sides of Loy's histrionics. This scene becomes almost as painful for the seasoned watcher as it is supposed to be for the oncamera heroine.

Despite all its faults (MGM excised seven minutes of "extraneous" footage from the release print), *Evelyn Prentice* managed to reinforce the positive screen chemistry of the Powell-Loy pairing, even with the less adept William K. Howard directing the film. Sennwald of the *Times* was led to report of the stars, that they " . . . continue to be the most engaging of the current cinema teams" because they portray "decent, intelligent, delightful and reliably amusing people."

*Evelyn Prentice* would be rehashed by MGM as the programmer *Stronger than Desire* (1939) with Walter Pidgeon and Virginia Bruce cast in the key assignments.

## THE GREAT ZIEGFELD
### (MGM, 1936) 180M.

Producer, Hunt Stromberg; director, Robert Z. Leonard; story-screenplay, William Anthony McGuire; art director, Cedric Gibbons; costumes, Adrian; music director, Arthur Lange; orchestrator, Frank Skinner; songs, Walter Donaldson and Harold Adamson; Irving Berlin; Harriet Hoctor ballet; lyrics, Herb Magidson, ballet music, Con Conrad, choreography, Seymour Felix; sound, Douglas Shearer; camera, Oliver T. Marsh, Ray June, George Folsey, Merritt B. Gerstad; editor, William S. Gray.

William Powell (Florenz Ziegfeld); Luise Rainer (Anna Held); Myrna Loy (Billie Burke); Frank Morgan (Billings); Reginald Owen (Sampston); Nat Pendleton (Sandow); Virginia Bruce (Audrey Lane); Ernest Cossart (Sidney); Robert Greig (Joe); Raymond Walburn (Sage); Fannie Brice (Herself); Jean Chatburn (Mary Lou); Ann Pennington (Herself); Ray Bolger (Himself); Harriett Hoctor (Herself); Charles Trowbridge (Julian Mitchell); Gilda Gray (Herself); A. A. Trimble (Will Rogers); Joan Holland (Patricia Ziegfeld); Buddy Doyle (Eddie Cantor); Charles Judels (Pierre); Leon Errol (Himself); Marcelle Corday (Marie); Esther Muir (Prima Donna); Herman Bing (Customer); Paul Irving (Erlanger); William Demarest (Gene Buck); Alfred P. James (Stage Door Man); Miss Morocco (Little Egypt); Suzanne Kaaren (Miss Blair); Sarah Edwards (Wardrobe Woman); James P. Burtis (Bill); Mickey Daniel (Telegraph Boy); William Griffith (Husband); Grace Hayle (Wife); Richard Tucker, Clay Clement, Lawrence Wheat, Selmer Jackson (Customers); Alice Keating (Alice); Rosina Lawrence (Marilyn Miller); Jack Baxley (Detective); Charles Coleman (Carriage Starter); Eric Wilton (Desk Clerk); Mary Howard (Miss Carlisle); Bert Hanlon (Jim); Evelyn Dockson (Fat Woman); Franklyn Ardell (Allen); John Larkin (Sam); David Burns (Clarence); Phil Tead (Press Agent); Susan Fleming (Girl with Sage); Adrienne d'Ambricourt (Wife of French Ambassador); Charles Fallon (French Ambassador); Boothe Howard (Willie Zimmerman); Edwin Maxwell (Charles Froman); Ruth

Gillette (Lillian Russell); John Hyams (Dave Stamper); Wallis Clark (Broker); Ray Brown (Inspector Doyle); Pat Nixon (Extra).

New York Premiere: Astor Theatre—April 8, 1936
New York Television Debut: CBS—October 4, 1957

## Synopsis

Within the course of the film, the plot traces the development of the career of Florenz Ziegfeld from a barker at a side show at the Chicago Fair to the world's greatest theatrical producer. Having made a great deal of money exploiting Sandow the Strong Man, Flo departs for Europe where he squanders his earnings at the gaming tables of Monte Carlo. But he is heedless of his loss, for he has discovered the wondrousness of the great actress Anna Held and succeeds in not only maneuvering her into signing a performing contract with him instead of his arch-rival Billings, but later managing to win her hand in love. Their marriage is stormy, as his extravagances are matched by her temperamental, jealous nature. When she sees him kissing a showgirl, she considers it to be a final break, and the couple thereafter divorce. Flo continues with his meteoric career, a highlight being his meeting with the lovely actress Billie Burke whom he soon weds. With her generous, patient ways Billie is able to restrain many of Flo's greatest excesses. For a short while, she even makes him into an adoring father when she gives birth to a daughter. When his financial situation suddenly takes a turn for the worse, it is Billie who insists he use her jewels to back new productions and once again Flo is able to rise to the top of his profession. But then the stock market crash occurs and he is wiped out. Heartbroken and ill, he dies soon thereafter.

◆━━◆━━◆

Originally this gargantuan film was to be produced in 1933 by Universal Pictures, but in one of the earlier examples of a major property changing studio hands, it was abandoned by Universal as being too costly. MGM acquired the rights to the William Anthony McGuire story-screenplay at a cost of $250,000 and, during the next two years, produced its $1.5 million feature. When the musical extravaganza debuted on Broadway as a two-a-day roadshow attraction at a two-dollar ticket top, *Variety* rightly reported the proceedings as being "the last gasp in filmmusical entertainment and undeniable box office." The flamboyant movie was voted an Academy Award as the Best Picture of the year.

Anyone expecting to obtain a revealing study of the collossal showman from *The Great Ziegfeld* was bound to be disappointed. Not only did polished star William Powell not look like Ziegfeld, he acted nothing like what the showman (1867-1932) was known to be like. It should be noted that Powell had never met Ziegfeld. As *Punch* magazine observed, "The Ziegfeld character is displayed not by Mr. Powell, but by the revolving stages, the rows and rows of beautiful girls, the steps spiralling higher every time, the silk curtains, the lights. . . . " All this reflected director Robert Z. Leonard's decision to base the very lengthy film not so much on the precise events in Ziegfeld's tempestuous life, but rather on the concepts that guided the producer's resplendent stage world of "glorification, femininity, and pulchritude." Hence, the highlight of the picture was the mammoth elaboration of the Irving Berling song, "A Pretty Girl Is Like a Melody," into a $240,000 production number that might have been a miniature movie musical in itself.

Producer Hunt Stromberg did his very best to create an ambiance of Broadway lustre in this marathon screen rendition, hiring such former Ziegfeld celebrities as Fannie Brice, Ray Bolger, Harriet Hoctor, and Leon Errol to play themselves in the glittery array of scenes. The greatest of all living Ziegfeld stars, Marilyn Miller, had demanded an exorbitant salary and a starring role in the proceedings (which was vetoed), while other protégés of the legendary producer like Gilda Gray found their scenes mostly on the cutting room floor by the time of the spectacular premiere. A. A. Trimble was hired to portray the late Will Rogers while Buddy Doyle offered a passable imitation-performance as the still very much alive Eddie "Banjo Eyes" Cantor.

If filmgoers in 1936 were far less familiar with the real life actress Anna Held (1873-1918), played in the film by Luise Rainer, they were certainly very much aware of stage and screen celebrity Billie Burke (1885-1970), who was then in the height of her character movie star period. All of which made it pretty difficult for Myrna Loy to carry through her mimicry in *The Great Ziegfeld* without suffering comparison or offending the original. Therefore, she settled for being herself on-camera, while batting her eyelashes a bit in the Burke manner. "Miss Loy is a stately Billie Burke, and somewhat lacking, we fear, in Miss Burke's effervescence and gayety" [Frank S. Nugent (*New York Times*)]. Richard Watts, Jr. (*New York Herald-Tribune*) was more severe: ". . . as one of the Loy Worshippers, I must still say that I suspect Miss Burke, however would have been a bit better at it." Compounding the inherent problems to Loy's performance was the fact that her Billie Burke, within the film's context, was basically the interloper, the one upon whom errant Powell fastens his romantic attention to the detriment of Rainer's Anna Held.

Ironically, just as MGM had replaced Loy in William Powell's *Escapade* (1935) with studio newcomer Rainer, so it was Rainer who effectively diverted attention and audience sympathy from Loy's key role in *The Great Ziegfeld*. Rainer offered a most winning, if mannered, piece of work as the dedicated actress who cannot hold her husband. Audience empathy and the Academy Award were captured for Rainer by the telling telephone scene in which she broken-heartedly calls to congratulate Powell on his wedding to Loy ("Hello . . . Flo? . . . This . . . is Anna . . .").

Within *The Great Ziegfeld*, Powell and Loy share a few tender scenes together, intimate by nature and in deliberate contrast to the elephantine production numbers. Powell first meets Loy at a costume ball at the famous Sixty Club where he spies the slender, red-gold-haired Loy on the arm of his rival, Billings (Frank Morgan). Powell knows that destiny has great things in store for he and Loy, for it was the first recent occasion when her stage producer Charles Froman had allowed her to attend a public function, removing his customary tight lid of secrecy from his prize star. Powell and Loy marry, living contentedly, she giving birth to a daughter, and he continuing to produce stage hits. Then he suddenly finds himself labeled a failure. Discouraged, he returns home to Loy's side, and in a rousing speech she convinces him he is not washed up in show business.

"Flo, I'm disappointed in you. I didn't think you'd ever lose confidence in yourself. It's been your sublime superiority more than anything else that has made up for many of your faults—and you have faults, dear, you know that. Don't be afraid of yourself. In here [she produces a box] is all the jewelry you've ever given me—thousands of dollars worth; and many more thousands in bonds I bought myself. I've been saving it all for Patricia—but I'm going to give it to you on one condition—and that is you keep your promise and have four hits on Broadway." He does, astounding everyone by producing a quartet of simultaneous successes: *Rio Rita, Rosalie, The Three Musketeers,* and *Showboat.*

Schmaltz has always been an effective way to tie together a gaudy entertainment package, and *The Great Ziegfeld* was no exception. In the final reel, the elderly producer is physically and emotionally worn out, reduced to a near bankrupt status. Discouraged, dreamy, and dying, he has a tear-provoking encounter with his faithful servant Sidney (Ernest Cossart).

Powell: ". . . I can't laugh any more, Sidney, because I've been wrong. I've got nothing to leave Billie or my baby."

Cossart: "Nothing, sir? You'll leave them memories of the finest things ever done on the stage, sir."

Powell: "That was nice of you, Sidney, to say that." After whispering these words, Powell sinks back in his arm chair and soon dies.

Interestingly, Powell was not Oscar nominated for his *The Great Ziegfeld* performance but for his work on loan to Universal in *My Man Godfrey* (1936). However, he lost the Best Actor's Award to Paul Muni of *The Story of Louis Pasteur.* When MGM assembled its *Ziegfeld Follies* (1946), Powell was called upon to play a celestial Florenz Ziegfeld, who sets the heavenly scene for the revue acts to follow within the picture.

## LIBELED LADY
### (MGM, 1936) 98M.

Producer, Lawrence Weingarten; director, Jack Conway; story, Wallace

Sullivan; screenplay, Maurine Watkins, Howard Emmett Rogers, George Oppenheimer; art directors, Cedric Gibbons, William A. Horning; interior director, Edwin B. Willis; music, William Axt; wardrobe, Dolly Tree; sound, Douglas Shearer; camera, Norbert Brodine; editor, Frederick Y. Smith.

William Powell (Bill Chandler); Myrna Loy (Connie Allenbury); Jean Harlow (Gladys Benton); Spencer Tracy (Warren Haggerty); Walter Connolly (James B. Allenbury); Charley Grapewin (Hollis Bane); Cora Witherspoon (Mrs. Burns-Norvell); E. E. Clive (Evans the Fishing Instructor); Bunny Lauri Beatty (Babs Burns-Norvell); Otto Yamaoka (Ching); Charles Trowbridge (Graham); Spencer Charters (Magistrate McCall); George Chandler (Bellhop); Greta Meyer (Connie's Maid); William Benedict (Joe); Hal K. Dawson (Harvey Allen); Fred Graham (Press Man); William Stack (Editor); Selmer Jackson (Adams, Editor of Washington *Chronicle*); William Newell (Divorce Detective); Duke York (Taxi Driver); Pat West (Detective); Ed Stanley (Clerk); Wally Maher (Photographer); Tom Mahoney (Alex); Pat Somerset (Photographer); Richard Tucker (Barker); Libby Taylor (Tiny, Gladys' Maid); Jack Mulhall (Barker); Eric Lonsdale, Olaf Hytten (Reporters); Pinky Parker, Harry Lash (Photographers); Charles Irwin (Steward); Eddie Shubert (Mac, the Circulation Editor); George Davis (Waiter); Thomas Pogue (Minister); Myra Marsh (Secretary); Hattie McDaniel (Maid in Hall); Howard Hickman (Cable Editor); Charles King (Barker); James T. Mack (Pop); Nick Thompson (Hot Dog Stand Man); Ines Palange (Fortune Teller); Harry C. Bradley (Justice of Peace); Bodil Ann Rosing (Wife of Justice of Peace); Barnett Parker (Butler); Robin Adair (Palmer the English Reporter); Charles Croker King (Charles Archibald the Lawyer); Dennis O'Keefe (Barker); Sherry Hall (Denver *Courier* Editor); Alphonse Martel (Table Captain); Eric Wilton (Steward on Dock); Jay Eaton, Ralph Brooks (Dance Extras).

New York Premiere: Capital Theatre—October 30, 1936
New York Television Debut: CBS—January 11, 1959

## Synopsis

When managing editor Warren Haggerty prints a front page story that wealthy Connie Allenbury is stealing another woman's husband on the playgrounds of Europe, Connie, who knows the tale is false, announces she is suing the newspaper for five million dollars. The news reaches Warren just before he is to wed Gladys Benton, and the ceremonies have to be postponed, much to Gladys' annoyance. Warren has a brainstorm. He hires ex-worker Bill Chandler to wed Gladys in name only, so that later Bill can make Connie fall in love with him, and then Gladys can sue her for alienation of Bill's affections. In this way, Connie's libel suit against the newspaper would become pointless.

223

Bill boards the ship upon which Connie and her father, James B. Allenbury, are returning from England to America. Bill insinuates himself into their good graces, and is invited to the Allenbury country home in the Adirondacks for some fishing. Only when Bill, by accident, snares the frolicsome trout that Allenbury has been after for years does Connie become more cordial. Bill's plan soon backfires, however, for he finds that he and Connie are falling in love. Bill tries to talk Connie out of the pending libel suit, but when Warren learns that Bill is serious about Connie, he has Gladys proceed with her alienation suit. Bill is able to talk her out of the action. The showdown occurs in Bill's hotel room, where it is finally settled that Glady's first marriage was legal, but that she will now divorce Bill and marry Warren as originally planned. Connie, who has known the denouement all along, is pleased that she and Bill can now wed. Allenbury makes a delayed appearance on the scene and is baffled by the intertwined relationships.

The biggest casting surprise of the film was the deft comedy work by ex-screen gangster Spencer Tracy. Then, too, the critics and public alike were delighted that MGM had wisely returned blonde Jean Harlow to brash farce. But it was still the combination of William Powell (then very steadily dating Harlow offcamera) and Myrna Loy which gave *Libeled Lady* its enduring status as "Gay, goofy, sparkling and sly" [Bland Johaneson (*New York Daily Mirror*)]. Where else but in Hollywood movies of the mid-1930s would divorce suits and libel cases be the headlined events of the day, overshadowing the Depression and international politics. Where else but in a MGM picture of this period would Powell and Loy be teamed so advantageously for sheer audience entertainment? As the *London Times* analyzed, "In this film he [Powell] is fortunate in having with him once again Miss Myrna Loy, who is almost as dexterous as he in maneuvering through familiar situations as though they had just been recorded for the first time. Both of them bring to the screen an air of gaiety and spontaneity under which the dullest and most carefully thought-out lines freshen."

While Tracy, as the harassed managing editor of the New York *Evening Star* was certainly a game fall guy in *Libeled Lady*, he had to work harder than his illustrious co-stars to garner sufficient screen attention because his role was so functional and staid in comparison to those of the other players. As his screen vis-a-vis, Harlow was at her natural oncamera irresistible self as the tough, nagging dame with a wisecrack on her sensual lips and a look of love in her wide-open eyes, alternately playing easy and hard to get depending on the particular plot situation of the moment. But smoothest of all was Powell, whose long experience as a debonair silver-screen con artist rose to a peak in *Libeled Lady* in which he inveigles the angriest of girls (Harlow) and wins over the toughest of romantic opponents (Loy).

Powell has two particular scenes in *Libeled Lady* that stand out as highlights within the brisk film. In the wedding scene between Powell and his reluctant bride Harlow, each is anxious to get the blasted ceremony over with as quickly as possible. The minister has completed his expected wordage and Powell then politely pecks the unblushing bride on the cheek. Suddenly she throws herself into the arms of nearby best man Tracy. To assuage the very surprised clergyman, Powell drolly explains that Tracy is merely "a good friend." But the two are kissing so voraciously and with such longevity that Powell feels obligated to add (with perfect timing), "a very good friend." The other beautiful moment is the famous trout fishing scene. Powell, despite having listened to E. E. Clive's instructions on the art of fishing and scanning the how-to books on the subject, is still amuck with rod in hand and finds himself at the mercy of mother nature. He is desperate to prove to irascible Walter Connolly that he is a suitable catch for daughter Loy, but nothing is working right for Powell, who has bragged what a great fisherman he is. Only by sheer luck, wonderfully engineered for the screen, does the adept boudoir gentleman Powell snag the elusive fish named "Wall Eyes," who has been Connolly's particular target for years.

As had become standard practice with the Powell-Loy silver screen ventures, the couple interacted with discreet rambunctiousness that always verged on the madcap but had its basis set firmly in carefree whimsy. He, as always, is a man who exists by his wit and charm while she is the Doris Duke-like blue blood who is rather unspoiled considering her rarified pedigree. It was thanks to the convincing tact of Loy's screen character that the rip-roaring movie concluded without fist fights or other mundane endings. She shows herself to be as adept in handling her obstreperous father as well as the conniving Powell.

*Libeled Lady* would be remade as *Easy to Wed* (1946) with a cast headed by Van Johnson, Esther Williams, Lucille Ball, and Keenan Wynn.

## AFTER THE THIN MAN
### (MGM, 1936) 110M.

Producer, Hunt Stromberg; director, W. S. Van Dyke II; story, Dashiell Hammett; screenplay, Frances Goodrich, Albert Hackett; songs, Arthur Freed and Nacio Herb Brown; Bob Wright, Chet Forrest, and Walter Donaldson; music, Herbert Stothart; camera, Oliver T. Marsh; editor, Robert J. Kern.

Myrna Loy (Nora Charles); William Powell (Nick Charles); James Stewart (David Graham); Joseph Calleia (Dancer); Elissa Landi (Selma Landis); Jessie Ralph (Aunt Katherine Forrest); Alan Marshal (Robert Landis); Sam Levene (Lieutenant Abrams); Penny Singleton (Polly Byrnes); Dorothy Vaughn (Charlotte); Maude Turner Gordon (Helen);

Teddy Hart (Floyd Casper); William Law (Lum Kee); William Burress (General); Thomas Pogue (William); George Zucco (Dr. Adolph Kammer); Tom Ricketts (Henry the Butler); Paul Fix (Phil Byrnes); Joe Caits (Joe); Joe Phillips (Willie); Edith Kingdon (Hattie); John T. Murray (Jerry); John Kelly (Harold); Clarence Kolb (Lucius); Zeffie Tilbury (Lucy); Donald Briggs, Fredric Santly, Jack Norton (Reporters); Baldwin Cooke, Sherry Hall, Jack E. Raymond (Photographers); Ed Dearing (Bill the San Francisco Policeman); Dick Rush (San Francisco Detective); Monte Vandergrift, Eddie Allen, Jimmy Lucas (Men); Heinie Conklin (Trainman); Mary Gordon (Rose the Cook); Ben Hall (Butcher Boy); George H. Reed (Porter); John Butler (Racetrack Tout); Vince Barnett (Wrestler's Manager); Ethel Jackson (Girl with Fireman); Arthur Housman (Man Rehearsing Welcome Speech); Jack Daley (Bartender); Bert Scott (Man at Piano); George Guhl (San Francisco Police Captain); Norman Willis (Fireman); Edith Craig (Girl with Fireman); Kewpie Martin (Boy Friend of Girl Standing on Hands); Bert Lindley (Station Agent); James Blaine (San Francisco Policeman); Guy Usher (Chief of Detectives); Bob Murphy (Arresting Detective); Harry Tyler (Fingers); Bobby Watson (Leader of Late Crowd); Eric Wilton (Peter the Butler); Henry Roquemore (Actor's Agent); Constantine Romanoff (Wrestler); Sam McDaniel (Pullman Porter); Ernie Alexander (Filing Clerk in Morgue); Louis Natheaux (Racetrack Tout); Jonathan Hale (Night City Editor); Jennie Roberts (Girl Who Works with Jerry); Charlie Arnt (Drunk); Harvey Parry (Man Who Stands on Hands); Jesse Graves (Red Cap); Alice H. Smith (Emily); Richard Powell (Surprised Policeman); Cecil Elliott, Phyllis Coghlan (Servants); Frank Otto (Taxi Driver); Jack Adair (Escort of Dizzy Blonde); Irene Coleman, Claire Rochelle, Jean Barry, Jane Tallant (Chorus Girls); Sue Moore (Sexy Blonde); Edith Trivers (Hat Check Girl); George Taylor (Eddie); Lee Phelps (Flop House Proprietor); Chester Gan (Chinese Waiter); Richard Loo (Chinese Head Waiter); Lew Harvey, Jimmy Brewster (Thugs); Harlan Briggs (Burton Forrest); Billy Benedict (Newsboy); Murray Alper (Kid); Charles Trowbridge (Police Examiner); Eadie Adams (Girl).

New York Premiere: Capitol Theatre—December 25, 1936
New York Television Debut: CBS—March 29, 1960

### Synopsis

No sooner do Nick and Nora Charles return to their San Francisco home from New York than they are confronted by family problems. Selma Landis, Nora's cousin, pleads with Nick to help find her husband, Robert Landis, who has been missing for three days. Nick locates him in a Chinese cafe, and learns from the intoxicated man that he has been having an affair with cafe singer Polly Byrnes. David Graham, Polly's former sweetheart, gives Robert $25,000 in bonds to go away and leave Selma alone. Robert accepts the funds and prepares to leave town when he is shot. Selma, who had been following Robert and planning herself to shoot him, is unaware that Robert was being trailed by several others, including David and the cafe owner, Dancer, the latter having planned to black-mail Robert with the help of Polly. Robert takes Selma's gun, instructing her not to speak with anyone, and then throws the gun into the river. Selma is later held on suspicion for the murder. In the course of the in-vestigation, three other people are killed. Nick finally solves the case by proving that the now insane David had committed all the murders out of revenge. He had been so enraged when Selma rejected him to marry Robert that he determined to get even. The case concluded, Nick and Nora leave for New York, with Selma as their guest. Nick is overjoyed when Nora informs him she is going to have a baby.

◆━━◆━━◆

If the fourth estate and popcorn munchers alike were skeptical whether the sequel, *After the Thin Man*, could measure up to the original, the new entry was engineered to put all viewers at ease by creating an ambiance that made them feel they were merely watching a continuation of the original. There were the same delightful co-stars. William Powell, Myrna Loy, and Asta the dog, the same producer, director, author, and screenwriters. The result for the most part proved to be a "brisk-paced and intriguing mixture of violence and brash fooling. . . . it recaptures a great deal of its notable prototype's bright, insouciant quality" [Howard Barnes (*New York Herald-Tribune*)].

Once again the chief joy of the murder mystery was not so much the whodunit aspect of the plot (most filmgoers were thrown clearly off the track by the contra casting of wholesome, gangling James Stewart as the crazed killer), but the repartee of the elegant married couple who are back on home ground (San Francisco) and find themselves once more en-gaged in solving homicide capers which baffle the obtuse police, partic-ularly the unperceptive police lieutenant Abrams (Sam Levine).

Powell and Loy's couple are up to their own hybrid way of life, he lazing away the day and she always seeming to be the fetching picture of chicness and a wife smart enough for any man. Together they drink their way through most of the night, sleeping most of the day, and just awakening for breakfast in bed at a time when most normal people are sitting down to their evening dinner. No matter what the harried situa-tion around them, nothing much seems to penetrate their almost perfect cool. Pleasantly tart Loy is always eager to be in on her husband's sleuth-ing, while he sets about in his own lackadaisical, but endearing, manner to pinpoint the enigma with suavity and only occasional gunplay (mostly the fireworks are on the part of others). The couple's general patience and tact in dealing with their peculiar relatives (including melodramatic

Elissa Landi, scolding, irritable aunt Jessie Ralph, and playboy Alan Marshal) is exemplary, while the amateur sleuth's amusing, if insultingly polite, demeanor in coping with some of the other offbeat characters inhabiting this tale of Nob Hill and its environs is totally extraordinary. No one but Nick and Nora could deal straight forwardly with the likes of Joseph Calleia and his Oriental partner William Law or the brassy songstress Penny Singleton.

If there was any fault to *After the Thin Man*, it was the overemphasis on the canine antics of Asta, the hydrant fancier, who in this installment gains a family. Much to Asta's dismay he discovers that one of the newborn pups is black and that a coal-colored Scottie, who resides next door, has tunneled under the fence to be near Mrs. Asta. Eventually Asta drags a lawnmower to cover the tunnel hole, solving his domestic problem.

Kate Cameron in her three-and-one-half-stars *New York Daily News* review expressed the wish that this detective series "might go on indefinitely" because Powell and Loy were "the most amusing couple on the screen." The *London Times* expressed the thought that the star team ". . . play into each other's hand with the full confidence of two expert bridge players who have perfected a system of their own, and it is the gaiety, the proper but never exaggerated sophistication, the charm and the irresponsibility, within limits, they bring to their lives which more than justify this sequel." The *Newark Evening Journal* quickly summed the value of Powell and Loy to the Metro production, "If *After the Thin Man* does nothing else, it proves that the reason all the *Thin Man* imitations failed to come off was because none of the imitators were William Powell and Myrna Loy."

A perfect illustration of the Powell-Loy screen chemistry occurs appropriately at the finale of *After the Thin Man*. Aboard the San Francisco-to-New York express train, Powell comes upon Loy in their drawing room compartment knitting a baby garment of all things. He registers astonishment. She absorbs his surprise with a knowing look and then casually flips out with, "And you call yourself a detective."

Powell and Loy repeated their *After the Thin Man* roles on "Lux Radio Theatre" on June 17, 1940.

## DOUBLE WEDDING
### *(MGM, 1937) 87M.*

Producer, Joseph L. Mankiewicz; director, Richard Thorpe; based on the play *Great Love* by Ferenc Molnar; screenplay, Jo Swerling; art director, Cedric Gibbons; music, Edward Ward; camera, William Daniels; editor, Frank Sullivan.

William Powell (Charles Ledge); Myrna Loy (Margit Agnew); John Beal (Waldo Beaver); Florence Rice (Irene Agnew); Jessie Ralph (Mrs.

Kensington-Bly); Edgar Kennedy (Spike); Sidney Toler (Keough); Barnett Parker (Flint); Katharine Alexander (Claire Ledge); Priscilla Lawson (Felice); Mary Gordon (Mrs. Keough); Donald Meek (Reverend Dr. Flynn); Henry Taylor (Angelo); Bert Roach (Shrank); Irving Lipschultz (Violinist) Doodles Weaver (Fiddle Player); Charles Coleman (Mrs. Bly's Butler); Billy Dooley (Saxophonist); Roger Moore (Pianist); Oscar O'Shea (Turnkey); Josephine Whittell (Woman Customer); E. Alyn Warren (Al); Jules Cowles (Gus); Jack Baxley (Bartender); Mitchell Lewis (Orator); Gwen Lee (Woman in Crowd); John "Skins" Miller (Pickpocket); Roger Gray (Mike); George Guhl (Pete); Jack Dougherty (Chauffeur); G. Pat Collins (Mounted Policeman).

New York Premiere: Capitol Theatre—October 21, 1937
New York Television Debut: CBS—December 12, 1961

### Synopsis

Businesswoman Margit Agnew holds a stern reign over her sister Irene and Irene's fiancé, Waldo Beaver. They are too timid to even consider rebelling against her authoritarian ways. But everything changes when Charles Ledges, a roaming artist and self-proclaimed film director, takes matters into his hands. He eggs on the young couple to revolt, even suggesting that Irene fulfill her long self-suppressed desire to become an actress. At this point Margit steps into the scene and promptly denounces Charles. He is intrigued by her independent nature and because he has fallen in love with her at first sight, he sets about taming her. On her part, Margit is falling in love with him, even though she despises everything he stands for in life. Meanwhile, Irene, imagining herself to be in love with Charles, breaks her engagement to Waldo and hopefully plans to wed Charles. Charles has his own bright idea: he will get Margit to come to her sister's wedding ceremony and once there he will wed her instead. Things go amiss when Waldo, having had too much to drink, fails to show up on time to wisk Irene off the scene, and Margit begins to insist that Charles carry through with the wedding ceremony. Waldo finally makes his delayed appearance and he and Irene depart, leaving Charles and Margit to declare their love for one another, statements heard by hundreds of people who have gathered outside Charles' trailer for the ceremony.

◆ ◆ ◆

On loanout to Universal, William Powell had earned an Oscar nomination playing the iconoclastic social outcast in *My Man Godfrey* (1936) a very popular screwball picture which co-starred his ex-wife, Carole Lombard. MGM was determined to repeat the lunatic formula by casting Powell and Myrna Loy ["Those two box office dynamiters" (*Variety*)] in a goofy film based more on zany slapstick than wit, relying on the two experienced stars to bring their infectious brand of charm to the proceedings.

Just as at one point in *Double Wedding* Loy says to Powell oncamera, "You're trying awfully hard to be amusing," so Howard Barnes (*New York Herald-Tribune*) was among those aisle-sitters who detected that this film " . . . frequently forces farce beyond the point of laughter." Nevertheless, the *London Times* praised the studio for having the perspicacity at least to cast Powell and Loy in this wavering madcap comedy. "What Mr. Powell and Miss Loy can do is to make the very best of any situation which has the least subtlety in it, and any lines which have wit and imagination. . . . [however] in *Double Wedding* there is not a single situation which gives them the slightest chance of showing what a strong team they can be."

Once again, Powell, as Charles Ledge, makes it seem so easy, as he portrays life's unconventional man, a charming, cock-eyed vagabond who will accept only the joys of the world. He believes work is for workmen as the sea is for sailors. He is a self-declared Bohemian artist who has stationed his trailer in the parking lot next to Spike's (Edgar Kennedy) place. Garbed in a beret and raccoon coat Powell considers himself a match for anyone, sure that his flippant and whimsical nature can stave off any challenge life sees fit to offer. But he has not reckoned with the cool, efficient Margit Agnew (Loy), a well-bred, liberated miss who almost punctures Powell's *joi de vivre*. Although she is preoccupied in running her smart clothes shop, Loy finds time to engineer a romance between her flighty younger sister (Rice) and the girl's predetermined groom, milksop John Beal. Imagine the viewer's amusement (so MGM hoped!) when lofty, self-possessed Loy clashes fiercely with non-conformist Powell and finds that this man will not obey her every order or listen to her "logical" arguments. Therefore, aloof Loy finds herself posing for artist Powell and hoping he will keep his promise to abandon his courtship of Rice. Loy may smash a portrait over Powell's head and he may not so politely toss her out of his trailer, but any wise filmgoer knows that these two seemingly opposite types will get together before the film runs its eighty-seven minute course. Thus efficient Loy is eventually converted to Powell's custard-pie way of life, glad at least to know that Powell *could* sell any of his paintings if he chose to make an honest living.

While *Double Wedding* too often strained for its comic effects, trapping Powell into rather preposterous doings, his ingratiating manner of tomfoolery saved the cinematic day, as did Loy's unyielding miss who allows herself to fight fire with fire. This portrait was certainly a strange turn of movie events for the cinema's leading genteel screen wife!

### ANOTHER THIN MAN
### (MGM, 1939) 102M.

Producer, Hunt Stromberg; director, W. S. Van Dyke II; screenplay,

Dashiell Hammett; art director, Cedric Gibbons; music, Edward Ward; camera, Oliver T. Marsh, William Daniels; editor, Frederick Y. Smith.

William Powell (Nick Charles); Myrna Loy (Nora Charles); C. Aubrey Smith (Colonel Burr MacFay); Otto Kruger (Van Slack the Assistant District Attorney); Nat Pendleton (Lt. Guild); Virginia Grey (Lois MacFay) Tom Neal (Freddie Coleman); Muriel Hutchinson (Smitty); Ruth Hussey [Dorothy Walters (Linda Mills)]; Sheldon Leonard (Phil Church); Phyllis Gordon (Mrs. Bellam); Don Costello ("Diamond Back" Vogel); Patric Knowles (Dudley Horn); Harry Bellaver ("Creeps" Binder); Abner Biberman (Dum-Dum); Marjorie Main (Mrs. Dolley the Landlady); Asta (Himself); Horace McMahon (MacFay's Chauffeur); Nell Craig (Maid); William Anthony Poulsen (Nicky, Jr.); Milton Kibbee (Les the Deputy); Walter Fenner, Thomas Jackson (Detectives); Charles Brokaw, Frank Coletti, Edwin Parker, William Tannen (Troopers); Edward Gargan (Quinn the Detective); Joseph Dowling, Matty Fain (Thugs); Bert Roach (Cookie the Drinker); Shemp Howard (Wacky the Temporary Father); Nellie V. Nichols (Mrs. Wacky); Eddie Gribbon, Ralph Dunn (Baggage Men); George Guhl (Guard at Gate); Claire Rochelle (Telephone Operator); Winstead "Doodles" Weaver, Paul "Tiny" Newlan (Guards); Roy Barcroft (Slim the Guard); Joe Devlin (Barney the Bodyguard); Paul E. Burns (Station Agent); Milton Parsons (Medical Examiner); Dick Elliott (Investigator); Jack Gardner (Driver); Nestor Paiva (Cuban Proprietor); Anita Camargo (Hat Check Girl); Gladden James (Fingerprint Man); Charles Sherlock (Police Photographer); John Kelly (Father); Edward Hearn (Detective); Eddie Buzzard (Newsboy); Martin Garralaga (Pedro the Informant); Alexander D'Arcy (South American); Jack Clifford, Howard Mitchell, William Pagan, Lee C. Shumway (Policemen); Stanley Taylor (Taxi Driver); Frank Sully (Pete); Murray Alper (Louie); Frank Moran (Butch); James Guilfoyle (Jake); Richard Calderon (Wacky's Baby); James G. Blaine (Policeman in Charles' Suite); Rosemary Grimes, Blanca Vischer, Sandra Andreva, Tina Menard, Toni LaRue (Cafe Bits); Guy Rett, Alberto Morin, Alphonse Martel (Waiters).

New York Premiere: Capitol Theatre—November 23, 1939
New York Television Debut: CBS—March 16, 1957

### Synopsis

Upon their arrival in Manhattan, Nora Charles receives a telephone call from her guardian, Colonel Burr MacFay, who suspects that his life may be in danger. He asks Nora and Nick to come to his country home. Although they dislike the idea, the couple agree to the Long Island weekend, taking their infant son, a nurse, and Asta the dog with them. Once at the estate, many mysterious events transpire. MacFay is murdered, and

Nick's life is threatened. Before he can collect his family together and leave, yet another man is killed. At this point Nick decides to work on the case, despite the dangers involved. And, of course, Nora trails along, not wishing to miss one bit of the adventure. Their investigations bring them into contact with many odd characters, some of them rather dangerous individuals. Eventually Powell solves the case, proving the crimes were committed by MacFay's daughter Lois, who wanted her father out of the way so she could acquire her inheritance of five million dollars. She had been helped in her ploys by gangster Phil Church, but she even killed him, when she discovered he was actually in love with another woman. Both Nick and Nora claim to be relieved that their latest caper is solved and life can become "normal" again.

◆━◆━◆

It had been three years since the last oncamera detective caper with Nick and Nora Charles, and to celebrate William Powell's return to the screen after over a year's absence due to illness, MGM concocted this new adventure, relying on Dashiell Hammett to provide the screenplay. Even though W. S. Van Dyke II was again directing, and Myrna Loy again co-starring, everything was not quite the same anymore. "Some of the bloom is off the rose," argued Frank S. Nugent of the *New York Times*. As Howard Barnes (*New York Herald-Tribune*) phrased it, MGM had not been " . . . able to make a recondition job look like the original article." *Variety* was more penetrating in its evaluation, "Picture's main drawback for top bracketing is a script that lacks spontaneity, and which is inclined to several by-paths and detours that are not clearly drawn. These serve to confuse rather than develop the plot structure."

Initially it must have seemed a cute gimmick to allow the irrepressible Charles' to have their own onscreen child, but since the viewers frequently wondered how this irresponsible couple could even care for their frisky dog Asta, it was almost straining credulity to have the trouble-seeking marrieds toting along an eight-month-old baby on their sometimes dangerous adventures. As *After the Thin Man* had milked dry the over cute premise of Asta's domestic trouble, so *Another Thin Man* (the title referring erroneously to Nick, Jr.) threw human domesticity into the story whenever the plotline was running anemic, which was rather frequent. Perhaps it was his paternal overconcern, but Powell's Nick Charles seemed less perspicacious than usual. In fact, his sleuthing was on the sluggish side, making it appear he was almost as puzzled about the killer's identity as unastute police lieutenant Guild (Nat Pendleton) or the uninformed audience. Even the series' usual gimmick of having Powell round up the suspects and then pick out the culprit lacked the regular punch, as did Powell's storytelling recreation of the assorted crimes.

The picture, nevertheless, did provide some top notch diversion as Powell continued to tease "Moms" (Loy) about his flirtations, arching his eyebrows with each tall tale he tells her, or when he makes a valiant effort to curb his scotch drinking to set a good example for their baby. Loy was still relegated, too often, to the sidelines, although she functioned well as the keeper of the key to the precious liquor cabinet. She was as always the smart lady who knows how to keep her unbridled husband in his place, or the graceful miss who dances a saucy rumba with a loving Latin in a club scene, or the alert hostess who knows just when her husband is about to unravel the vital clues to the case.

Amidst the overabundance of red herrings populating *Another Thin Man*, Virginia Grey was properly colorless as the actual villainess. However, it was Sheldon Leonard as the ex-convict who dreams about murders, who proved to be very diverting in his performance, as did Marjorie Main in a brief part as an irrascible landlady of an unrespectable boarding house.

## I LOVE YOU AGAIN
### *(MGM, 1940) 99M.*

Director, W. S. Van Dyke II; based on the novel by Leon Gordon and Maurine Watkins; screenplay, Charles Lederer, George Oppenheimer, Harry Kurnitz; music director, Franz Waxman; wardrobe, Dolly Tree; art directors, Cedric Gibbons, Daniel B. Cathcart; set decorator, Edwin Willis; sound, Douglas Shearer; camera, Oliver T. Marsh; editor, Gene Ruggiero.

William Powell (Larry Wilson/George Carey); Myrna Loy (Kay Wilson); Frank McHugh (Doc Ryan); Edmund Lowe (Duke Sheldon); Donald Douglas (Herbert); Nella Walker (Kay's Mother); Pierre Watkin (Mr. Sims); Paul Stanton (Mr. Littlejohn); Morgan Wallace (Mr. Belenson); Charles Arnt (Billings); Harlan Briggs (Mayor Carver); Dix Davis (Corporal Belenson); Carl Alfalfa Switzer (Harkspur, Jr.); Bobby Blake (Littlejohn, Jr.); Winifred Harris (Mrs. Watkins); Mary Currier (Mrs. Gordon); Hazel Keener (Mrs. Lederer); Bea Nigro (Mrs. Kurnitz); Leni Lynn (Maurine); Edward Earle (Mr. Watkins); Harry Hayden (Mr. Wayne); Harry Lash (Steward); William Tannen (Clerk); Ray Teal (Watchman); Barbara Bedford (Miss Stingecombe); George Lloyd (Policeman Sergeant); Charles Wagenheim (Fingerprint Man); Jack Mulhall, Jason Robards, John Dilson, Ted Thompson, Hooper Atchley, Warren Rock, Paul Parry, Hal Cooke, Raymond Bailey (Men); Nell Craig (Maid); Arthur Hoyt (Floorwalker); Joe Bernard (Watchman); Jack Daley (Band Leader); Eric Wilton (Headwaiter); George Lollier (Police Photographer); Howard Mitchell (Ranger Leader); Sally Payne, Claire Rochelle, Gladys Blake (Salesgirls); Edward Hearn (Guard).

New York Premiere: Capitol Theatre—August 15, 1940
New York Television Debut: CBS—March 29, 1960

## Synopsis

Larry Wilson, allegedly a pompous bore, is returning from Europe. He finds such drunken fellow ship passengers as Doc Ryan an annoyance, particularly since he is earnestly trying to abstain from liquor. Soused Ryan falls overboard. When Larry tosses him a lifeline, his foot becomes entangled in the rope and he is yanked overboard. The crew quickly lower a life boat to rescue the two drowning men, but one of the sailor's oars hits Larry on the head. When he later recovers consciousness Larry recalls nothing. He questions Ryan and discovers that for the previous nine years he had been an amnesia victim. Before that time he had been a confidence man and Ryan was one of his trusty pals. Larry, who is really George Carey, decides to return to Haberville, Pennsylvania to undertake a phony oil deal. To his great surprise, Larry/George finds Kay Wilson waiting for him when the ship docks. He decides not to tell her of his sudden revelation, and is upset to learn that she is going to divorce him to wed another. Determined not to lose her, he induces her to return to their home for a few weeks. Meanwhile, he and Ryan have their hands full picking up sufficient information to keep his guise from being discovered by the townfolk or Kay. Larry is about ready to go through with his bogus deal, but decides against it, having been converted to honesty by his love for Kay. She finds out about all his past activities, but having grown to love him for himself, she says she does not mind about his prior self. They are happily united.

◆——◆——◆

Portraying man's potential dual personality was not the exclusive province of Robert Louis Stevenson's *Dr. Jekyll and Mr. Hyde* as *I Love You Again* clearly demonstrated. This joyous comedy was built on this solid premise and was executed by a gleeful cast. "Now that the *Thin Man* formula has worn palpably thin, it is nice to have Mr. Powell and Miss Loy giving fresh and delightful portrayals of a husband and wife at comic odds" [Howard Barnes *(New York Herald-Tribune)*].

*I Love You Again* offered the starring team a fitting opportunity to excel at a raucous, but polite, screen farce with George Carey's (William Powell) con-artist alter ego joining with Kay Wilson (Myrna Loy) in puncturing the pomposity of the stuffy man Larry Wilson (Powell) had become. "Miss Loy," wrote Louis Biancolli in the *New York World Telegram,* "looking her sublime self, carries on the fine team-play tradition of *The Thin Man;* of course with a saucier slant, considering the pickle her husband's amnesia leaves her in. She keeps firing embarrassing revelations at Powell, who thus gets eye-widening glimpses into the strange aseptic ways of the man he's supposed to be and is and isn't. She can tell more with a slight optical shift than most actresses with barrels of heart-pouring mugging." Powell came in for his share of critical praise in a role that thankfully returned him to his old vibrant self after the too subdued *Another Thin Man*. "There is something about William Powell, his fruity voice, his elegant manner, his nimble walk, his dashing air, that cries out for the smoothest, the best-ordered of possible worlds for him to twirl through. A dignified existence is as much a must for his peculiar personality as citro-carbonate for a hang-over" [Cecilia Ager (*PM*)].

From the first astringent screen moment when Powell meets up with Loy, things are off to a wacky, frantic start. Powell, at one point here, admits to his "spouse," "You've turned my head." Loy retorts "I've often wished I could turn your head—on a spit over a low fire." Whatever prompted Loy to become the wife of pompous, stuffed shirt Larry Wilson is never explained by the screenplay. However, if such an explanation had been forthcoming, there might not have been a story.

Suddenly within *I Love You Again*, the "new" Powell has great insight into his former self, that miserly pottery manufacturer and staid collector of stuffed trophies and lodge buttons, the civic pride of Haberville, Pennsylvania and the tightwad who carries a pinch penny coin purse. The regenerated Powell finds himself caught between two worlds, that of the slick con artist with pals like card sharp Doc Ryan (Frank McHugh) and oil deal manipulator Duke Sheldon (Edmund Lowe), and the refined atmosphere of respectability in which he is expected to lead the Boy Rangers on their annual woodland trek.

Perhaps Powell's greatest moment of delightful lunacy occurs when he lectures annoyed Loy on the range of feathered love birds, complete with appropriate sound effects. Loy, usually prone to underplaying her moments of sight gag comedy, has her chance to be totally slapstick in her reaction as she slaps a plate of scrambled eggs over Powell's head.


## LOVE CRAZY
### (MGM, 1941) 100M.

Producer, Pandro S. Berman; director, Jack Conway; story, David Hertz, William Ludwig; screenplay, Ludwig, Charles Lederer, Hertz; art director, Cedric Gibbons; music, David Snell; camera, Ray June; editor, Ben Lewis.

William Powell (Steven Ireland); Myrna Loy (Susan Ireland); Gail Patrick (Isobel Grayson); Jack Carson (Ward Willoughby); Florence Bates (Mrs. Cooper); Sidney Blackmer (George Hennie); Vladimir Sokoloff (Dr. Klugle); Kathleen Lockhart (Mrs. Bristol); Sig Rumann (Dr. Wuthering); Donald MacBride ("Pinky" Grayson); Sara Haden (Cecilia Landis); Fern Emmett (Martha); Elisha Cook, Jr. (Elevator Boy); Joseph Crehan (Judge); Jimmy Ames (Taxi Driver); George Meeker (DeWest); Aldrich Bowker (Doorman); George Guhl, Harry Fleischmann (Drivers); Barbara Bedford (Secretary); Clarence Muse (Robert); Jay Eaton, Larry Steers, James H. McNamara, Richard Kipling, Broderick O'Farrell (Guests); Ian Wolfe,

Edward Van Sloan, George Irving, Douglas Wood, Byron Shores, Roy Gordon, Emmett Vogan, Selmer Jackson (Doctors); William Tannen (Attendant); Jesse Graves (Butler); Jack Mulhall (Court Clerk); Joan Barclay (Telephone Operator); Ralph Bushman, Lee Phelps, George Magrill, Bill Lally, Ken Christy (Guards); Harry Strang (Sergeant); Wade Boteler (Captain of Detectives); Ed Peil, Sr., Dick Allen, Eddie Hart, Philo McCullough, Kai Robinson, George Lollier, James Millican, Paul Palmer, Charles McMurphy, Pat Gleason, James Pierce, Rudy Steinbock (Detectives).

New York Premiere: Capitol Theatre—June 5, 1941
New York Television Debut: CBS—February 14, 1960

## Synopsis

Just as Steven and Susan Ireland are about to celebrate their fourth wedding anniversary, the couple are annoyed at the unexpected arrival of Susan's mother, Mrs. Cooper. After staying for dinner, the matron prepares to leave, but sprains her ankle and is required to extend her stay. While Susan is out on an errand for her mother, the angered, lonesome Steven decides to step out for a few drinks with an old friend, Isobel Grayson, who lives with her husband in the same building. Mrs. Cooper, having overheard Steven's conversation with Isobel, tells Susan of the rendezvous. Assorted complications arise when Susan decides to make Steven jealous and, in doing so, becomes involved with a strange man, Ward Willoughby. When the slightly inebriated Steven returns home and tells Susan what happened, she refuses to believe him and leaves. Upon the suggestion of his attorney, George Hennie, Steven pretends to be insane, in order to prevent Susan from carrying through with her threatened divorce. However, she promptly sees through Steven's trick and has him committed to a mental institution. He finally escapes and rushes home, only to find that the police have been there looking for him. Dressed in a wig and ladies' clothing, he poses as his own sister. Susan knows full well who this "relative" is, but enjoys the posing too much to give away Steven's ploy. Eventually they are reconciled.

◆——◆——◆

"The steady progression toward insanity has been perceptible in the William Powell-Myrna Loy films [and] is climaxed by a perfect consummation in their latest" [Bosley Crowther (*New York Times*)]. Other critics were less enthusiastic about the overall quality of the vehicle. "The script lacks the superficial dignity and the smart talk that Miss Loy and Mr. Powell handle better than almost any other player on the screen, but it has enough honest humor and entertainment to carry it hilariously along its wacky way" (*Richmond News Leader*).

Whereas *The Thin Man* series had been constructed around the felicity of marriage, *Love Crazy* deals with the opposite in oversized terms. It is a daffy farce of the cockeyed school of comedy that is kept within bounds by the still dignified Loy, who makes the institution of wedded "bliss" seem both wacky and wonderful.

The premise of *Love Crazy* provided an ideal opportunity for Powell, who once again had a lion's share of screentime, to indulge in complete liberation of any and all inhibitions that may have confined his movie characters in past years. The "insane" Stevens can be as goofy as he wishes, from knocking out Loy's bothersome new-found companion (Jack Carson) who wants to wed her, to the satisfying moment when he pushes his irksome mother-in-law (Florence Bates) into the swimming pool. It is hard to erase the memory of a tipsy Powell, caught in the elevator with brunette siren Isobel Grayson (Gail Patrick), attempting to extricate himself from the stalled enclosure and ending up with his head stuck between the sliding doors and left hanging by his ears.

To later prove he is "insane," Powell jumps into the irrational guise whole-heartedly, pretending to be Abraham Lincoln and emancipating his black servants. Then there is the moment when a disrobed Powell falls from a window while trying to retrieve his wrist watch from a persnickety parrot. Once he is incarcerated at the sanitarium, it is a case of who is crazier, the patients, the psychiatrists (including doctors Sig Rumann and Vladimir Sokoloff), or "touched" Powell. The height of daffiness in *Love Crazy* occurs when Powell, predating Jack Benny, who later in 1941 would cavort onscreen in *Charley's Aunt,* uses a dress, two balls of yarn, a gray-haired wig, and a *pince nez* (and minus his moustache) poses as his own spinster sister, complete with falsetto voice.

But all good things come to an end, and this lively study of marital disharmony and reconciliation concludes on a note of debonair domesticity that must have caught the Hays' office napping, for at the fadeout there is Loy opening Powell's bedroom door and offering a deft response to her pesky mother's advice to "get a good night's sleep."

## SHADOW OF THE THIN MAN
### *(MGM, 1941) 97M.*

Producer, Hunt Stromberg; director, W. S. Van Dyke II; story, Harry Kurnitz; screenplay, Irving Brecher, Harry Kurnitz; camera, William Daniels; editor, Robert J. Kern.

William Powell (Nick Charles); Myrna Loy (Nora Charles); Barry Nelson (Paul Clarke); Donna Reed (Molly Ford); Sam Levene (Lt. Abrams); Alan Baxter (Whitey Barrow); Dickie Hall (Nick Charles, Jr.); Loring Smith

(Link Stephens); Joseph Anthony (Fred Macy); Henry O'Neill (Major Jason I. Sculley); Stella Adler (Claire Porter); Lou Lubin ("Rainbow" Benny Loomis); Louise Beavers (Stella); Will Wright (Maguire); Edgar Dearing (Motor Cop); Noel Cravat (Baku); Tito Vuolo (Luis); Oliver Blake (Fenster); John Dilson, Arthur Aylesworth (Coroners); James Flavin, Edward Hearn, Art Belasco, Bob Ireland, Robert Kellard (Cops); Cliff Danielson, J. Louis Smith, Jerry Jerome, Roger Moore, Buddy Roosevelt, Hal Le Sueur (Reporters); Cardiff Giant (Bouncing Tschekov); Richard Frankie Burke (Buddy Burns); Tor Johnson (Jack the Ripper); Johnnie Berkes (Paleface); John Kelly (Meatballs Murphy); Joe Oakie (Spider Webb); Jody Gilbert (Lana); Dan Tobey (Announcer); Tommy Mack (Soft Drink Vendor); Joe Devlin (Mugg); Bill Fisher, Aldrich Bowker (Watchmen); Charles Calvert (Referee); Joey Ray (Stephen's Clerk); Inez Cooper (Girl in Cab); Adeline deWalt Reynolds (Landlady); Duke York (Valentino); Seldon Bennett (Mario); Sidney Melton (Fingers); George Lloyd (Pipey); Patti Moore (Lefty's Wife); Jerry Mandy (Waiter); Hardboiled Haggerty, Eddie Simms, Abe Dinovitch, Wee Willie Davis, Sailor Vincent, Jack Roper, Harry Wilson (Muggs); Ray Teal (Cab Driver); Sam Bernard (Counterman); Ken Christy (Detective); David Dornack (Lefty's Kid); Lyle Latell, Matt Gilman, Fred Graham (Waiters with Steaks); Harry Burns (Greek Janitor); Fred Walburn (Kid on Merry-go-Round); Arch Hendricks (Photographer); Pat McGee (Handler).

New York Premiere: Capitol Theatre—November 20, 1941
New York Television Debut: CBS—November 26, 1958

### Synopsis

Nick and Nora Charles arrive at the race track, escorted by a motorcycle policeman who had given Nick a speeding ticket, but considered him important enough to escort. The Charleses arrive at the same time as Lieutenant Abrams and members of the police force, for, as Nick is informed, a jockey has been murdered. Despite Abrams' plea, Nick refuses to become involved in the perplexing case. However, when newspaper reporter Whitey Barrow, who is involved with gamblers, is killed, and another reporter, Paul Clarke, is held on suspicion of murder, Nora urges Nick to investigate. Once again, Nora, who thrives on excitement and suspense, insists upon accompanying Nick on his sleuthing rounds. For a while Nick is able to elude her, but she always manages to catch up with him. During the course of the investigations another man, "Rainbow" Benny Loomis, is murdered. Although Nick decides that the jockey had been killed accidentally, he lets it appear as if he thought the victim had been murdered by the same man who killed Whitey Barrow, his scheme being to bring the relaxed murderer out into the open. He then requests Lieutenant Abrams to collect all the suspects in his office, so as to listen to each one's story. The murderer, Major Jason I. Sculley, talks himself right into the trap and is caught.

◆━━◆━━◆

This entry might better have been tagged *The Thin Man in the Sports World* for the Irving Brecher-Harry Kurnitz screenplay finds those two indomitable amateur sleuths, William Powell and Myrna Loy, hobnobbing with the lowbrows of the race track and wrestling arena set as they try to unravel the clues which have baffled the police. While it was readily agreed, "It's always good fun when Myrna Loy and William Powell get together on screen to work out somebody else's problem" *(New York Post),* and that the two stars ". . . are greatly welcome, even in something very familiar" *(New York Herald-Tribune),* the movie itself did not pass muster by very much of a safe margin. "It is only a shadow of the smart and puzzling mystery melodrama that introduced Nick Charles, debonair gumshoe, and his wife, Nora, three sequels ago" *(Brooklyn Daily Eagle).*

MGM stated in its promotional copy for this fourth *Thin Man* outing, "Bless their hilarious hearts, they're better than ever." Unfortunately, this certainly was not the case at all. As if to demonstrate just how much time had elapsed since the series first began, the Charles' son (Dickie Hall) is now four years old, and Powell's Nick is conventionally insistent that marriage and parenthood are enough responsibility for any man. How times have changed! Hall's Nick, Jr. may be taught the facts of life from Powell's favorite reading matter, the racing form, but the young squirt reverses the situation by having his screen dad learn to drink a glass of milk ("Milk? Me. I'd rather face bullets.") like all good little boys. When Powell takes his son and the ever-present Asta for a walk, it is a toss-up which one of the scampering charges will yank harder at the leash or attempt to grab more screen attention.

Because of their popular forays into screen slapstick apart from the detective series, Powell and Loy were gradually allowed to include more such tomfoolery into their once chic, but relatively staid, sleuthing characterizations. No longer were the never-failing gumshoes the tart couple of the mid-1930s. Thus we have Powell and Loy at a wrestling match with her becoming overanimated in voice and gesture (when she extends good wishes to the groaning wrestlers, they take time out to thank her), while the patrons around her become engrossed in the ringside banter about her unique chapeau. Later Loy and Powell become embroiled in a night club free-for-all, which allows them to engage in some fancy athletics to show that the fist is often mightier than the word. Powell's slapstick highlight in *Shadow of the Thin Man* occurs when he escorts junior on an amusement park outing. Not content to let the spirited little boy ride on the merry-go-round alone, Powell insists upon joining him and even attempts to pull the brass ring off the pole. When Loy catches up to her two men, sonny is fine, but Powell is suffering from a very bad case of *mal de mer*.

More so than past *Thin Man* follow-up entries, *Shadow of the Thin Man* reflected a downgrading of the series. Its production values were lessened, and more importance was given to showcasing MGM stock contractees such as Barry Nelson and Donna Reed, the latter particularly effective as Alan Baxter's ex-girlfriend who is now the gal of gambler Loring Smith. In this 1941 Nick and Charles caper, the real culprit was not very difficult to spot, which did nothing to bolster the weary plot and made it pretty tough for the players to generate any real excitement. Much of the tension was left for Loy, who, with the instincts of a confused bloodhound always at Powell's heels, bravely throws herself on the gun that the murderer has picked up, only to have suave Powell calmly admit later that the pistol had not had bullets in it since the time it was used for junior's teething ring.

MGM obviously was anxious to earn its money back on *Shadow of the Thin Man* as quickly as possible, for it was released as a Thanksgiving entry and parcelled out to 360 theatres around the country for the holiday.

## THE THIN MAN GOES HOME
### (MGM, 1944) 100M.

Producer, Everett Riskin; director, Richard Thorpe; based on characters created by Dashiell Hammett; story, Robert Riskin, Harry Kurnitz; screenplay, Riskin, Dwight Taylor; art directors, Cedric Gibbons, Edward Carfagno; set decorator, Edward B. Willis; assistant director, Al Jennings; sound, James K. Burbridge; music, David Snell; camera, Karl Freund; editor, Ralph E. Winters.

William Powell (Nick Charles); Myrna Loy (Nora Charles); Lucile Watson (Mrs. Charles); Gloria DeHaven (Laura Ronson); Anne Revere (Crazy Mary); Harry Davenport (Dr. Charles); Helen Vinson (Helena Draque); Lloyd Corrigan (Bruce Clayworth); Donald Meek (Willie Crump); Edward Brophy (Brogan); Leon Ames (Edgar Draque); Paul Langton (Tom Clayworth); Donald MacBride (Chief MacGregor); Minor Watson (Sam Ronson); Anita Bolster (Hilda); Charles Halton (Tatum); Morris Ankrum (Willoughby); Nora Cecil (Miss Peavy); Wally Cassell (Bill Burns); Arthur Hohl (Charlie); Anthony Warde (Captain); Bill Smith, Lucille Brown (Skating Act); Mickey Harris (Contortionist); Rex Evans (Fat Man); Harry Hayden (Conductor); Connie Gilchrist (Woman with Baby); Robert Emmet O'Connor (Baggage Man); Dick Botiller (Big Man's Companion); John Wengraf (Big Man); Ralph Brooks (Tom Burton); Jane Green (Housekeeper); Irving Bacon (Tom the Proprietor); Virginia Sale (Tom's Wife); Garry Owen (Pool Player); Saul Gorse (Bartender); Bert May

(Sailor); Chester Clute (Drunk); Clarence Muse (Porter); Tom Fadden, Joseph Greene, Sarah Edwards, Frank Jaquet (Train Passengers); Oliver Blake (Reporter); Don Wilson (Masseur); Etta McDaniel (Ronson's Maid); Tom Dugan (Slugs); Ed Gargan (Mickey); Thomas Dillon, Bill Hunter (Officers); Marjorie Wood (Montage Mother); Catherine McLeod (Montage Daughter); Clancy Cooper (Butcher); Joe Yule (Barber); Robert Homans (Railroad Clerk); Lee Phelps (Cop); Helyn Eby Rock, Jean Acker (Tarts); Mike Mazurki, Mitchell Lewis, Ray Teal (Men).

New York Premiere: Capitol Theatre—January 1, 1945
New York Television Debut: CBS—November 30, 1957

## Synopsis

Nick and Nora Charles return to his home town of Sycamore Springs for a reunion with his parents, Dr. and Mrs. Charles. Very soon after arriving, Nick finds himself drawn into a murder case when a local boy is shot to death just as he trys to speak with him. Through an old school chum, Bruce Clayworth, Nick learns that the victim had been a landscape painter, some of whose paintings had been sold to Willie Crump the owner of a small art shop. When Nick learns that the paintings had been purchased by strangers newly arrived in town, he suspects that there may be some link between the paintings and the killing, and with possible espionage involving a local defense plant and a new war plane propeller. As a result of Nick's investigation, suspicion falls on some of the town's prominent citizens who threaten to withdraw their financial support for a hospital planned by Dr. Charles. The physician insists his son continue with the case, and Nick discovers that a local character, Crazy Mary, is actually the mother of the deceased youth. When Nick arrives at her shack, he finds Crazy Mary's corpse as she had been murdered. While on the premises, Nick unearths an important sketch, a drawing for which some of the suspects had been searching. Now positive that a few of the suspects are accomplices in a spy ring operating in the area, Nick summons all those connected with the case to a meeting at his dad's home. There he cleverly tricks Bruce into revealing himself as the head spy.

◆—◆—◆

Because of her new marriage and her charity work for the war effort, Myrna Loy was off the screen for three years before MGM was able to reunite her with William Powell in yet another *Thin Man* caper, which proved to be a real comedown from the original film made eleven years prior. This was the first of the series not to be directed by (Major) W. S. Van Dyke II who had died in 1944. As Otis L. Guernsey, Jr. (*New York Herald-Tribune*) observed, this picture " . . . doesn't rate the artistic superlatives but there is no one like Nick, Nora and Asta for a gay, dependable whodunit."

241

Despite the nostalgic presence of the very familiar Charleses, there was a lot missing from this latest addition to the screen detection canon, which tried to recast the once-droll formula into the currently fashionable spy drama. Not only was Nick, Jr. (thankfully) missing from the proceedings, but Powell's Nick was acting on his best behavior. As least, so his character reasoned, if he could not satisfy his screen parents' wish that he become a doctor, he could remain sober and respectful during the sojourn, presenting himself as a model of decorum. This forced conservatism which seems to have inhibited his deductive reasoning in this case, rubbed off on Loy's Nora, making both of them far blander than anyone could reasonably expect. In addition their low-keyed behavior allowed the secondary characters (including spoiled rich girl Gloria DeHaven, traveling salesman Edward Brophy, well-dressed crook Leon Ames, et al.) to assume too far great an importance for the tale's proper balance.

## SONG OF THE THIN MAN
### (MGM, 1947) 86M.

Producer, Nat Perrin; director, Edward Buzzell; based on characters created by Dashiell Hammett; story, Stanley Roberts; screenplay, Steve Fisher, Perrin; additional dialog, James O'Hanlon, Harry Crane; art directors, Cedric Gibbons, Randall Duell; set decorators, Edwin B. Willis, Alfred E. Spencer; music, David Snell; song, Herb Magidson and Ben Oakland; assistant director, Jerry Bergman; sound, Douglas Shearer; camera, Charles Rosher; editor, Gene Ruggiero.

William Powell (Nick Charles); Myrna Loy (Nora Charles); Keenan Wynn (Clarence "Clinker" Krause); Dean Stockwell (Nick Charles, Jr.); Phillip Reed (Tommy Drake); Patricia Morison (Phyllis Talbin); Gloria Grahame (Fran Page); Jayne Meadows (Janet Thayer); Don Taylor (Buddy Hollis); Leon Ames (Mitchell Talbin); Ralph Morgan (David I. Thayer); Warner Anderson (Dr. Monolaw); William Bishop (Al Amboy); Bruce Cowling (Phil Brant); Bess Flowers (Jessica Thayer); Connie Gilchrist (Bertha); James Burke (Callahan); Tom Trout (Lewie the Shiv); Henry Nemo (The Neem); Marie Windsor (Helen Amboy); Asta, Jr. (Asta); Tom Dugan (Davis the Cop); John Sheehan (Manager); Lennie Bremen, Lyle Latell (Mugs); Eddie Simms, Jimmy O'Gatty (Hoods); James Flavin (Reardon the Cop); Bill Harbach (Whitley); George Anderson (Dunne); Donald Kerr (News Photographer); Alan Bridge (Nagle the Policeman); Esther Howard (Counterwoman); Harry Burns (Italian); William Roberts (Pete); Clarke Hardwicke (Bert); Henry Sylvester (Butler); Matt McHugh (Taxi Driver); Clinton Sundburg (Desk Clerk); Gregg Barton (Nurse); Earl Hodgins (Baggage Man); Howard Negley (Kramer); George Sorel (Headwaiter); Charles Sullivan (Sergeant); Robert Strickland (Musician); Jeffrey

Sayre (Croupier); Morris Ankrum (Inspector); Maria San Marco (Oriental Girl); George Chan (Young Chinese); Jerry Fragnol (Young Nick—Age Five).

New York Premiere: Capitol Theatre—August 28, 1947
New York Television Debut: CBS—June 26, 1958

## Synopsis

Following their attendance at a social affair on a gambling ship, Nick and Nora Charles learn that Tommy Drake, the ship's bandleader, has been murdered. Later they are visited by Phil Brant, the ship's owner, and Janet Thayer, his bride. They are seeking Nick's professional aid. Brant had quarreled with Drake prior to the murder and the police seek him as a suspect. As they talk, a mysterious attempt is made to shoot Brant. The incident brings Nick out of retirement, and, aided by Nora and Clarence "Clinker" Krause, a member of Drake's band, they track down the killer. In the course of the investigation, several suspects are aligned: Al Amboy, a gambler to whom Drake owed $12,000; Buddy Hollis, a clarinetist who hated Drake because he had won the love of Fran Page, the band vocalist; Fran, because she was tossed aside by Drake; Mitchell Talbin, an actor's agent who refused to loan Drake any money to settle his debts; and David I. Thayer, Janet's dad, who is opposed to her marriage to Brant and might have wanted to put her in a spot. Later Fran is murdered, which forces Nick and Nora to convene a social gathering on the gambling ship at which Talbin is revealed as the killer. It seems his wife Phyllis was having an affair with Drake.

◆——◆——◆

Almost three more years had elapsed between the last *Thin Man* excursion and this new picture, which was the *thirteenth* screen teaming of William Powell and Myrna Loy. This proved to be the last of their six-entry series as the famed Charleses. As soon as the advance publicity for the feature was made available, it was clear that most every bit of inventiveness had been drained from the property.
"All New and Music too.
It's Toot-Toot Terrific.
Who Dun It, Who Sung It, Who Swung it.
Murder Makes the Hit Parade.
Nick and Nora Make Solving Mysteries Seem Like Fun.
It's a Bow Wow of a Hit."
While Powell and Loy continued to ". . . exhibit the same old zest and bantering affection they have always brought to their performances" [Thomas M. Pryor (*New York Times*)], time was definitely passing (there was even a new Asta here), and everyone concerned, including filmgoers, was ready for something else.

243

Once more retired sleuth Powell is dragged back into the detection service, but now there was such a welter of confusing details and red herrings that it seemed a miracle he had the astuteness to solve the caper. Loy functioned as the regulation inquisitive wife, but, like Powell, she seemed almost mummified by the imposed strictures of the traditional role. It was left for the now "grown up," young Nick, Jr. (Dean Stockwell) to be the focal point of the case, even to the extent of becoming the object of kidnapping mobsters. As further distraction or entertainment—depending on one's point of view—*Song of the Thin Man* was heavily laced with a jazz music ambiance, ranging from hepcat Keenan Wynn to nightclub thrush Goria Grahame, the latter chirping "You're Not So Easy To Forget."

## THE SENATOR WAS INDISCREET
### *(Universal, 1947) 88M.*

Producer, Nunnally Johnson; associate producer, Gene Fowler, Jr.; director, George S. Kaufman; story, Edwin Lanham; screenplay, Charles MacArthur; art directors, Bernard Herzbrun, Boris Levin; set decorators, Russell A. Gausman, Ken Swartz; music, Daniele Amfitheatrof; assistant director, Jack Voglin; sound, Leslie I. Carey, Richard DeWeese; special effects, David S. Horsley; camera, William Mellor; editor, Sherman A. Rose.

William Powell (Senator Melvin G. Ashton); Ella Raines (Poppy McNaughton); Peter Lind Hayes (Lew Gibson); Arleen Whelan (Valerie Shepherd); Ray Collins (Houlihan); Allen Jenkins (Farrell); Charles D. Brown (Dinty); Hans Conried (Waiter); Whit Bissell (Oakes); Norma Varden (Woman at Banquet); Milton Parsons ("You Know Who"); Francis Pierlot (Frank); Cynthia Corley (Helen); Oliver Blake, Chief Thundercloud, Chief Yowlachie, Iron Eyes Cody (Indians); Boyd B. Davis, Rodney Bell, Tom Coleman, John Alban (Politicos); Edward Clark (Eddie); William Forrest (U.S. Officer); Douglas Wood (University President); Tom Dugan (Attendant at Stand); George K. Mann (Texas); Claire Carleton (Ingred); William H. Vedder (Book Dealer); Nina Lunn (Girl in Elevator); John R. Wald (Broadcaster); Vincent Pelletier (Quiz Master); Alex Davidoff, Forrest Dickson, Howard Mitchell (Guests); Don Wilson (Commentator); Beatrice Roberts (Woman); Martin Garralaga, John Bagni (Italian Waiters); Leon Lenoir (French Waiter); Billy Newell (Elevator Operator); Billy Bletcher (Newsboy); John A. Butler, John O'Connor, Franklin Parker, Clarence Straight (Reporters); Mervin Williams (Newsreel Man); Eddie Coke (Ticket Buyer); Bruce Riley, Ethan Laidlaw, Richard Gordon, Walton DeCardo, Watson Downs, Cedric Stevens, Rex Dale (Men); Sven Hugo Borg (Swedish Waiter); John Valentine (Desk Clerk); Walter

Soderling (Hotel Clerk); Jimmy Clark, Russ Whiteman (Bellboys); Mike Stokey (Night Clerk); Laura R. Parrish (Aunt Abby); Dutch Schlickenmeyer (Man Buying Ticket); Gene Fowler, Sr. (Charlie); Myrna Loy (Mrs. Ashton).

New York Premiere: Criterion Theatre—December 26, 1947
New York Television Debut: WOR-TV—November 16, 1954

## Synopsis

Aged Senator Melvin G. Ashton, a pompous, stupid politician, has presidential aspirations after twenty years in the Senate. He proceeds to build himself up as a candidate through skillful ballyhoo. He accomplishes this feat by keeping the party leaders at bay, threatening to reveal the contents of a diary he has kept which will tell all about his thirty years to date in politics. When the valuable diary suddenly disappears, frantic party leaders alert politicians throughout the country to prepare to leave the U.S. in a hurry should the contents be made public. The telltale journal is eventually recovered by Lew Gibson, Ashton's press agent, who in a fit of moral consciousness turns it over to his newspaperwoman sweetheart Poppy McNaughton. She in turn publishes Ashton's detailed records. The crooked party leaders, including the senator and his wife, are forced to flee, seeking asylum in Hawaii.

◆━◆━◆

With all of his grade A feature work, including his Oscar-nominated performance in *Life with Father* (1947) behind him, William Powell turned to a series of minor vehicles, including the unusual Universal release, *The Senator Was Indiscreet*, which was labeled a "rather heavy-handed attempt to spoof a Congressional windbag" (*New Yorker*). Bosley Crowther of the *New York Times* commended the star who " . . . does about everything a competent actor of farce comedy could do to make him a joke."

The biggest problem with *The Senator Was Indiscreet* was that neither director George S. Kaufman nor scripter Charles MacArthur had the gumption or the studio approval to make this satire as ascerbic as it needed to be. The picture carefully avoided name calling, and only made the most susceptible faces on Capitol Hill flush a very light pink. The proceedings were a sad distillation of such forerunners as that stage warhorse *Of Thee I Sing*, or the more recent Broadway hit *State of the Union* (which became a less tidy version when transferred to the screen in 1948).

The funniest moments of *The Senator Was Indiscreet* find white-wigged Powell, offered as a more dignified but rascally offshoot of Fred Allen's Senator Claghorn, making a series of absurd platform promises to the public. He urges a three-day work week with eight days of pay, while he hints to management that labor will be made to toil for eight days for two days' wages. To ease the mailman's burden, he suggests all letters be written on tissue paper. If elected, he promises that cows will only produce malted milk, that doctors' prescriptions will be inscribed in English, and that every man, woman, and child will be able to attend Harvard College if he or she so chooses. Powell's best visual moment occurs when he dons a costume and is inducted into an Indian tribe.

Where does Myrna Loy fit into the proceedings? As a gag and as a favor to Powell she joined in the film's finale, playing none other than the Senator's wife.


## THE YEARS AFTER

By the time nearly sixty-year old William Powell returned to MGM for *It's a Big Country* (1951), the industry and the country's temperament had altered so considerably that he found himself an outmoded commodity with scarcely a film job in view. He made what proved to be his cinema swansong in *Mister Roberts* (1955) portraying the character role of the genial but cynical Doc. Thereafter he retired to Palm Springs with his third wife, ex-MGM starlet Diana Lewis.

Loy had one of the best roles in her career in Samuel Goldwyn's *The Best Years of Our Lives* (1946), as Fredric March's understanding spouse, and followed it with two prime comedies, *The Bachelor and the Bobby Soxer* (1947) and the even better-remembered *Mr. Blandings Builds His Dream House* (1948) with Cary Grant and Melvyn Douglas. There were two films with a brood of children, *Cheaper By the Dozen* (1950) and *Belles on Their Toes* (1952) the first lime-lighting Clifton Webb, the second focusing on Jeanne Crain. Loy had attended the early United Nations' meeting in 1945, and in the mid-1950s accepted a post with UNESCO as a U.S. representative in Paris. She played an alcoholic in both *Lonelyhearts* (1958) and *From the Terrace* (1960). Her final theatrical feature to date has been the comedy *The April Fools* (1969) with Jack Lemmon. She made her legitimate stage debut in the early 1960s with summer stock tours of *The Marriage-Go-Round* and *There Must Be a Pony*, and later joined the national tour of *Barefoot in the Park*. Her belated Broadway stage bow occurred in the short-lived revival of *The Women* (1973) in which she essayed Kim Hunter's wise mother. In late 1974, Loy, who continually pops up in cameo telefeature roles, went on the road again, this time in a new concert version of *Don Juan in Hell*. In *Airport '75* (1974), she again played an onscreen alcoholic, a refinement of her performance in *From the Terrace* (1960).

At her Town Hall, New York evening of tribute in 1973 as one of the legendary ladies of the cinema, Loy spoke fondly of Powell whom she admits is a tough man ever to see in person, stating that a hearing impairment has made him shy of people. But she related that she and he, the Nora and Nick Charles of old, had had a grand reunion recently at his Palm Springs home and she found him nearly as handsome as ever.

In **The Petrified Forest** (WB, 1936)

# Chapter 9

# Leslie Howard
# &
# Bette Davis

## LESLIE HOWARD

6′
149 pounds
Blond hair
Brown eyes
Aries

*Real name: Leslie Howard Stainer. Born April 3, 1893, London, England. Married Ruth Martin (1916), children: Ronald, Leslie. Died June 1, 1943.*

**FEATURE FILMS:**

*The Lackey and the Lady* (B.A.F.C., 1919)
*Outward Bound* (WB, 1930)
*Never the Twain Shall Meet* (MGM, 1931)
*A Free Soul* (MGM, 1931)
*Five and Ten* (MGM, 1931)
*Devotion* (RKO, 1931)
*Reserved for Ladies* (Par., 1932)
*Smilin' Through* (MGM, 1932)
*The Animal Kingdom* (RKO, 1932)
*Secrets* (UA, 1933)
*Captured!* (WB, 1933)
*Berkeley Square* (Fox, 1933)
*The Lady Is Willing* (Col., 1934)
*Of Human Bondage* (RKO, 1934)
*British Agent* (FN, 1934)
*The Scarlet Pimpernel* (UA, 1935)
*The Petrified Forest* (WB, 1936)
*Romeo and Juliet* (MGM 1936)
*It's Love I'm After* (FN, 1937)
*Stand-In* (UA, 1937)
*Pygmalion* (MGM, 1938)
*Gone with the Wind* (MGM, 1939)

*Intermezzo* (UA, 1939)
*The 49th Parallel (The Invaders)* (General Film Distributors, 1941)

*Pimpernel Smith (Mister V)* (Anglo, 1941)
*The First of the Few (Spitfire)* (General Film Distributors, 1942)

# BETTE DAVIS

5' 3½"
122 pounds
Dark blonde hair
Blue eyes
Aries

*Real name: Ruth Elizabeth Davis. Born April 5, 1908, Lowell, Massachusetts. Married Harmon Nelson (1932); divorced 1938. Married Arthur Farnsworth (1940); widowed 1943. Married William Grant Sherry (1945), child: Barbara; divorced 1949. Married Gary Merrill (1950), children: Margo, Michael; divorced 1960.*

**FEATURE FILMS:**

*Bad Sister* (Univ., 1931)
*Seed* (Univ., 1931)
*Waterloo Bridge* (Univ., 1931)
*Way Back Home* (RKO, 1932)
*The Menace* (Col., 1932)
*Hell's House* (Capital Films Exchange, 1932)
*The Man Who Played God* (WB, 1932)
*So Big* (WB, 1932)
*The Rich Are Always with Us* (FN, 1932)
*The Dark Horse* (FN, 1932)
*Cabin in the Cotton* (FN, 1932)
*Three on a Match* (FN, 1932)
*20,000 Years in Sing Sing* (FN, 1933)
*Parachute Jumper* (WB, 1933)
*The Working Man* (WB, 1933)
*Ex-Lady* (WB, 1933)
*Bureau of Missing Persons* (FN, 1933)
*Fashions of 1934* (FN, 1934)
*The Big Shakedown* (FN, 1934)

*Jimmy the Gent* (WB, 1934)
*Fog over Frisco* (FN, 1934)
*Of Human Bondage* (RKO, 1934)
*Housewife* (WB, 1934)
*Bordertown* (WB, 1935)
*The Girl from Tenth Avenue* (FN, 1935)
*Front Page Woman* (WB, 1935)
*Special Agent* (WB, 1935)
*Dangerous* (WB, 1935)
*The Petrified Forest* (WB, 1936)
*The Golden Arrow* (FN, 1936)
*Satan Met a Lady* (WB, 1936)
*Marked Woman* (WB, 1937)
*Kid Galahad* (WB, 1937)
*That Certain Woman* (WB, 1937)
*It's Love I'm After* (FN, 1937)
*Jezebel* (WB, 1938)
*The Sisters* (WB, 1938)
*Dark Victory* (WB, 1939)
*Juarez* (WB, 1939)

*The Old Maid* (WB, 1939)

*The Private Lives of Elizabeth and Essex* (WB, 1939)

*All This and Heaven Too* (WB, 1940)

*The Letter* (WB, 1940)

*The Great Lie* (WB, 1941)

*The Bride Came C.O.D.* (WB, 1941)

*The Little Foxes* (RKO, 1941)

*The Man Who Came to Dinner* (WB, 1941)

*In This Our Life* (WB, 1942)

*Now, Voyager* (WB, 1942)

*Watch on the Rhine* (WB, 1943)

*Thank Your Lucky Stars* (WB, 1943)

*Old Acquaintance* (WB, 1943)

*Mr. Skeffington* (WB, 1944)

*Hollywood Canteen* (WB, 1944)

*The Corn Is Green* (WB, 1945)

*A Stolen Life* (WB, 1946)

*Deception* (WB, 1946)

*Winter Meeting* (WB, 1948)

*June Bride* (WB, 1948)

*Beyond the Forest* (WB, 1949)

*All About Eve* (20th, 1950)

*Payment on Demand* (RKO, 1951)

*Another Man's Poison* (UA, 1952)

*Phone Call from a Stranger* (20th, 1952)

*The Star* (20th, 1953)

*The Virgin Queen* (20th, 1955)

*Storm Center* (Col., 1956)

*The Catered Affair* (MGM, 1956)

*John Paul Jones* (WB, 1959)

*The Scapegoat* (MGM, 1959)

*Pocketful of Miracles* (UA, 1961)

*Whatever Happened to Baby Jane?* (WB, 1962)

*Dead Ringer* (WB, 1964)

*The Empty Canvas* (Emb., 1964)

*Where Love Has Gone* (Par., 1964)

*Hush . . . Hush, Sweet Charlotte* (20th, 1964)

*The Nanny* (20th, 1965)

*The Anniversary* (20th, 1968)

*Connecting Rooms* (London Screen, 1969)

*Bunny O'Hare* (AIP, 1971)

*The Scientific Card Player* (Italian, 1973)

In **Of Human Bondage** (RKO, 1934)

In **Of Human Bondage**

In a publicity pose for **It's Love I'm After** (FN, 1937)

In **It's Love I'm After**

## OF HUMAN BONDAGE
### *(RKO, 1934) 83M.*

Producer, Pandro S. Berman; director, John Cromwell; based on the novel by W. Somerset Maugham; screenplay, Lester Cohen; music director, Max Steiner; art director, Van Nest Polglase, Carroll Clark; camera, Henry W. Gerrard; editor, William Morgan.

Leslie Howard (Philip Carey); Bette Davis (Mildred Rogers); Frances Dee (Sally Athelny); Reginald Owen (Thorpe Athelny); Reginald Denny (Harry Griffiths); Kay Johnson (Norah); Alan Hale (Emil Miller); Reginald Sheffield (Dunsford); Desmond Roberts (Dr. Jacobs); Tempe Pigott (Landlady).

New York Premiere: Radio City Music Hall—June 28, 1934
No New York Television Showing

### Synopsis

Overly sensitive, club-footed Philip Carey, an orphan boy reared in rural England by very strict relatives, has spent four years studying painting in Paris. When he realizes that he will never be more than a second-rate artist, he returns to England to study medicine. Being older and less adept than the other students, he must work and study for long hours to even remain on a scholastic par with his lesser classmates. At a nearby teashop he meets Mildred Rogers, a vain, ignorant, and mildly ugly waitress to whom he finds himself physically attracted. When she later breaks a date with him to rendezvous with a loutish German salesman named Emil Miller, Philip berates her. She casually replies that she could not possibly become romantically involved with a cripple, and, besides, Miller has promised to wed her. Later Philip, still struggling to remain in medical school, encounters an attractive older woman, Norah, who instructs him in taste and manner and loves him truly. Philip arrives home one evening to find Mildred, broke and despondent. Miller did not marry her, and she is now pregnant. Norah disappears from Philip's life when she learns he intends to wed Mildred after the tart's child is born. Again Philip is rejected by the strumpet Mildred when she runs off with his medical student friend, Harry Griffiths. Philip eventually becomes an intern and at a charity hospital he becomes acquainted with Thorpe Athelny who invites him to his home to spend a day with he and his daughter, Sally. Sally's kindness to Philip is not based on pity, which is a good foundation for a potentially strong relationship. Thereafter, Mildred returns with her child, once again apologizing for having left him. Philip allows her to stay but despises himself for not being stronger and curtailing this human bondage. When Philip rejects her indifferent offer of herself, and leaves in a pique of disgust, she becomes angered, wrecking the contents of his apartment and burning the bonds he needs in order to pay his tuition fees. Unable to continue medical school, he finds employment as a salesman, but becomes despondent and is nursed back to health by the Athelnys. Finally, he has corrective surgery on his club foot. While recuperating he inherits a sum which allows him to return to his studies. At the hospital he learns from Griffiths that Mildred is expiring in the charity ward. Before he arrives, she dies in a coma. Finally freed of his long-standing obsession, he can now ask Sally to wed him, and can finally begin to return her full love.

◆——◆——◆

When RKO acquired screen rights to W. Somerset Maugham's massive novel *Of Human Bondage* (1915) many rightly wondered how the lengthy narrative could be telescoped into proper screen length. Moreover, how could a film whose anti-Adonis hero was a club-footed introvert and its focal lady a slatternly Cockney sustain audience interest? Regarding the first point, Mordaunt Hall *(New York Times)* happily reported, "*Of Human Bondage* has come through the operation of being transferred to the screen in an unexpectedly healthy fashion. John Cromwell's film version emerges as a literal, intelligent and visually attractive translation of the novel." Maugham's native country press was more severe in its pragmatic appraisal, complaining that the picturization was ". . . more like a series of illustrations to the book than an adequate translation of it" *(London Times)*.

Some forty years after its creation, critical appraisal still is divided on whether RKO did right by the difficult casting problem in choosing Leslie Howard and Bette Davis for the vital lead assignments. Casting forty-one-year-old British star Howard as Philip Carey was certainly a commercial idea. On Broadway and in Hollywood he had gained a sterling reputation as the proficient delineator of the aesthetic, genteel, overly dignified soul—a dramatic type then very much *en courant* but regarded as a ridiculous, artificial pose by the bulk of today's generation. Thus in seeking a name performer to portray the repressed Philip Carey who rises above his mundane surroundings with the peculiar majesty of a true-born gentleman, it was natural for astute producer Pandro S. Berman and talented director Cromwell to light upon the idea of borrowing Howard from Warner Bros. for this major celluloid adaptation. But *Of Human Bondage*, which was never really popular with the mass audiences, provided an overdose showcase of Howard's entrenched, finicky screen persona,* at a time when audiences were far more intrigued with the dynamic personalities of the likes of James Cagney, Edward G. Robinson, Clark Gable, and Paul Muni. *Liberty* magazine had its pulse on the consumer taste level when it deli-

---

*Similarly *An American Tragedy* had surfeited audience response to Phillips Holmes, who like Howard was a superior exponent of the passive, cerebral type of sensitive soul.

cately reported, "Leslie Howard gives his usual restraint and charm to a part that cries for something more than restraint and charm."

Today, Davis' much-touted performance in *Of Human Bondage* is regarded with a mixture of awe, bewilderment, and amusement, for it is extremely theatrical in nature, exhibiting all the star's later established acting tricks of speech and movement. But in 1934 it was quite a different matter. She was *not* a super star then! In fact, she had to embark on a six-month-long battle of wills with her studio boss, Jack L. Warner, before he consented to loan her to RKO for this unsavory characterization which he was convinced was so unsympathetic a role that it would teach Davis a much-deserved lesson. (All the leading RKO actresses, including Katharine Hepburn, Irene Dunne, and Ann Harding, had rejected or been rejected for the assignment, which soon became touted as the undesirable screen role of the year.) Having won the role, Davis was convinced that the role of Mildred Rogers would prove to be the watershed mark of her movie career and she dug into the part with a ferocity. She even contracted a British wardrobe woman to stay with her, so she could study a proper Cockney accent.

When Davis arrived on the *Of Human Bondage* set, she discovered her real battle was just starting. *Star* Howard and his clique were vastly annoyed that twenty-six-year-old Davis had been made part of the *Of Human Bondage* loan package to RKO. He thought it entirely wrong for an American girl to be playing the very British Mildred. [The major mistake of allowing Joan Crawford to portray an aristocratic British miss in MGM's *Today We Live* (1933) was still very much on everyone's mind.] And Howard was quick to make his strong feelings known to his young co-player, both by a lack of cordiality off the set, and by indifference on the soundstages. It is reported he would often sit reading a book offcamera while feeding Davis her onscreen lines. However, when director Cromwell advised Howard that Davis was rapidly walking away with the picture, Howard pitched in, burying his annoyance very quickly.

Many may have regarded Davis as just another super-charged, not particularly beautiful, ingenue before *Of Human Bondage* but once the prestige film was released, her characterization of the tawdry tart made quite a stir. "Bette Davis, in the first part she has ever had which has required more than handsome clothes and an enigmatic expression makes Mildred almost as unpleasant to see as she was to imagine" (*Time* magazine). "No more unsympathetic character ever has been attempted by a young actress. Miss Davis bravely assumes it, performing the monstrous role with a finish and a force which merits cheers" [Bland Johaneson (*New York Daily Mirror*)]. Richard Watts, Jr. (*New York Herald-Tribune*) was one of the more level-headed critics when he observed, "Unfortunately she never permits you to forget that she is giving a performance and it is this difference between a show and a character which suggests the weakness of her work." Despite this astute comment, it was the general critical consensus that Davis should have been at least nominated for an Oscar for her role, and when the Academy of Motion Pictures Arts and Sciences failed to make the nomination, Warner Bros. began its own write-in campaign. However, Claudette Colbert of *It Happened One Night* was the 1934 idea of Best Actress. When Davis won an Oscar the following year for the lesser *Dangerous* (1935), it was considered delayed recompense.

If Howard was a bit "mature" to be portraying the tender young Philip Carey, he dug deep into his vast acting powers to convey the torments of intellectual quandary and emotional inferiority which engulfed the hero for so much of his life. Because the truncated screenplay eliminated the whole earlier portion of Maugham's novel, any audience member who had not read the book might be easily confused as to what beyond the club foot syndrome had made Philip what he was, a sensitive but ill-adapted soul wandering through life trying to find himself.

In the best of literary and screen conventions, it is three contrasting women who lead Howard's Philip into maturity and provide the crux of the plot progression. Unfortunately, two of the intriguing female assignments, Kay Johnson's Norah, a writer of romantic fiction, and Frances Dee's Sally, a very aware young lady, are so shorted in oncamera time that it is only because of each actress' agility at conveying both outward and inward beauty that these two parts take on any dimension at all and make sensible Howard's lessons in life learned at each lady's earnest direction. Just as one wishes Howard's Philip might have responded to Johnson's overt courting, one is (or should be) envious also by the climax to *Of Human Bondage*, which finds the unburdened Howard crossing a street with the radiant Dee, each confident that the future belongs to them together. To accentuate the rich warmness of Dee's Sally, the closing shot shows her head bathed in halo-like lighting.

For the uninitiated, Davis' Mildred seems the height of screen garishness as she deteriorates oncamera from being the indifferent waitress in a modest London teashop to becoming a slovenly slut as incautious of appearance as she is of talk and manner. But in reality, the Mildred of Maugham's novel was even less appetizing a sight, being a flat-chested wench with thin pale lips and a delicate skin "of a faint green colour, without a touch of red even in the cheeks," who in her last months (as she is dying of syphilis) turns even thinner with "the skin, yellow and dryish . . . drawn more tightly over her cheekbones."

Only because of the unique qualities that Howard and Davis brought to their individual characterizations do their joint scenes derive any interest, for there is very little ensemble playing between the two performers in this picture. In the teashop scenes, Howard is the cautious, meek soul, staring moon-eyed at the mundane Davis, while she is the unnecessarily haughty girl who is fearful least any of her co-workers spot her mild flirtation with a cripple. As their relationship continues, with dinners out, a night at the theatre, and Howard escorting her home, there is a perverted isolation (as in the novel) about the couple's strange courtship. She appears mostly distracted in their joint outings, mumbling, "I don't mind" to his pathetic beggings for permission to bestow considerations upon her, her eyes flitting this way and that, but never looking directly at him for fear her contempt for the man will all too clearly show itself.

Later in a scene very similar to one in *The Light That Failed* (1939), Davis seeks revenge for being physically rejected by the now disgusted Howard who is aghast that he is subject to his baser passions. She flies into a rage, admitting how much he has bored and repelled her and that every time he dared to kiss her, she just had to wipe her lips clean. (Howard effectively winces at each of these verbal slaps.) With the utmost of scorn she calls him the cruelest thing possible, a cripple. Later she slashes, breaks, and burns everything in the apartment that is meaningful or valuable to the impoverished young would-be doctor.

Davis' final encounter with Howard within *Of Human Bondage* occurs when she has reached the virtual end of her road and is now a sleezy whore stricken with a terminal disease. Her ravaged looks, guaranteed to shock filmgoers used to viewing their screen actresses with some semblance of illusory glamour, were far more impressive than her dramatics, as she rants about the cruelty of life and pitifully tries to be coy with the now inured Howard. With her subsequent death, Howard's Philip is finally released from his years of "human bondage."

In reviewing the overall tone of Davis' performance in *Of Human Bondage* this author must agree with film historian Jerry Vermilye who in his book *Bette Davis* (1973) stated, "Seen today, in the light of more subtle contemporary acting and directing styles, Davis's Mildred occasionally seems too mannered and overwrought. Her bravura performance undoubtedly grips the attention, but in her tirades against Philip Carey, Davis seems out of control and makes it very difficult to understand why so cultured a gentleman would tolerate such a guttersnipe for so long."

*Of Human Bondage* would be remade twice, with Paul Henreid and Eleanor Parker in 1946, and with Laurence Harvey and Kim Novak in 1964. Each time, Maugham's novel suffered further diminuations of its original story values. The saddest aspect of the subsequent remakes is that because of copyright problems, the Howard-Davis rendition is not currently available for general audience viewing.

## THE PETRIFIED FOREST
### *(Warner Bros., 1936) 75M.*

Associate producer, Henry Blanke; director, Archie Mayo; based on the play by Robert E. Sherwood; screenplay, Charles Kenyon, Delmer Daves; music, Bernhard Kaun; music director, Leo F. Forbstein; assistant director, Dick Mayberry; art director, John Hughes; gowns, Orry-Kelly; special effects, Warren E. Lynch, Fred Jackman, Willard Van Enger; sound, Charles Land; camera, Sol Polito; editor, Owen Marks.

Leslie Howard (Alan Squier); Bette Davis (Gabrielle Maple); Genevieve Tobin (Mrs. Chisholm); Dick Foran (Boz Hertzlinger); Humphrey Bogart (Duke Mantee); Joseph Sawyer (Jackie); Porter Hall (Jason Maple); Charley Grapewin (Gramp Maple); Paul Harvey (Mr. Chisholm); Eddie Acuff (Lineman); Adrian Morris (Ruby); Nina Campana (Paula); Slim Thompson (Slim); John Alexander (Joseph).

New York Premiere: Radio City Music Hall—February 6, 1936
New York Television Debut: CBS—June 2, 1958

## Synopsis

Alan Squier, an unsuccessful New England author, who has left his European life as the "kept" husband of a rich divorcee and is hitch-hiking to California, stops off at the Black Mesa Bar B-Q, a gasoline station and lunch room in the Arizona desert. He quickly falls in love with the equally idealistic Gabby Maple, an American-French girl with a fascination for modern art and romantic poetry, and a desperate longing to be really loved. Also at the station are her stolid mundane father, Gramps, who has large savings in Liberty Bonds which he refuses to share with his family, and gum-chewing Boze Hertzlinger, a former college football player with an unsubtle passion for Gabby. On the very day the impoverished Alan arrives at the Maple's place, the notorious Duke Mantee and his gang massacre several people in Oklahoma as they move southwest in their efforts to escape to Mexico. Meanwhile, Gabby, convinced she is in love with Alan, persuades two customers, Mr. and Mrs. Chisholm, to give Alan a lift to the next town. On the road the chauffeur-driven Chisholms are stopped by Mantee and his gang who commandeer the car and head back for the Maples' place. Alan is left to return by foot, and soon everyone is being held at bay by the rugged Mantee and his restless mob. In an attempt at completing one good thing in his life, Alan signs over his $5,000 insurance policy to Gabby and then begs Mantee to shoot him when he leaves the station. When the law enforcers surround the Bar-B-Q building, Mantee and his gang decide to make a break for liberty. Alan forces Mantee to live up to his bargain, and, after being shot, dies in Gabby's arms. He expires contentedly, knowing that she will now be able to realize her dream of going to France. Later, the Maples hear a radio broadcast detailing that Mantee and his surviving men have been killed.

◆━━◆━━◆

In the two years since they were last teamed, Bette Davis had won an Oscar and earned the respect and friendship of co-star Leslie Howard.

He was more than pleased° when she was selected to play opposite him in the filming of Robert Sherwood's 1934 drama in which he had successfully starred on Broadway. It was Howard who insisted that Warners cast another of the original stage cast members, Humphrey Bogart, in a recreation of his part of the brutish criminal, Duke Mantee. For reasons of artistry and economy it was decided to make the film version of *The Petrified Forest* a very precise adaptation of the Broadway original with sound-stage-bound sets and little background music, leading Frank S. Nugent *(New York Times)* to appraise the movie as "a faithful and letter-perfect copy" which has been "so piously contrived that we fear any revival of the play would only evoke cries of 'fraud.'" (Actually Warners had been fearful of literally following the downbeat ending of the play script and had filmed two endings for the picture, one in which Howard does not die, and the other where he does die as Sherwood had originally written. After a few test engagements the latter ending was deemed the more appropriate, if unfulfilling, climax.)

The forceful message of Sherwood's story concerns the present decadent civilization in which nature is "taking the world away from the intellectuals and giving it back to the apes" with the symbolic petrified forest as the graveyard of our dying society. Without losing the thrust of Sherwood's theme, the film version visually focuses on two other main themes: the unrequited love of Howard and Davis, and the power-crazed despair of Bogart's gangster.

There was no question that Howard was the perfect screen artist to essay the wandering fatalist in this picture. "So well did he fit the role in the play, and so well did it fit him, that Alan Squier and *The Petrified Forest* are, by nature, inseparable" [Frank S. Nugent *(New York Times)*]. Within the story, Howard arrives at the run-down Black Mesa Bar B-Q restaurant and gas station, just as Boze Hertzlinger (Dick Foran) has finished telling his would-be sweetheart (Davis), "It's easy to tell when a girl's ready for love." And so she is, but not for the clumsy Foran. She is immediately attracted to this tall, thin "tourist afoot" who claims he is "an American once removed and wants to see the Pacific—perhaps to drown in it." When Davis learns that Howard has spent time on the French Riviera she reveals that her mother had long ago left her father and returned to France, explaining that reading François Villon (whose name she constantly mispronounces) brings her closer to her mother and to the finer things of life. She confesses she wants to go to France to find "something beautiful to look at, wine and dancing in the street," admitting "there's something in me that wants something different." (Her dynamic, flashing

°Davis would later recall that in the scenes within *The Petrified Forest* calling for her and Howard to remain on the floor while being victimized by Bogart, Howard would tease her by playfully nibbling on her arms.

eyes certainly convey that point.) Howard, in his dreamy, distracted way, lets slip that he too is looking for something to believe in (and die for).

In their telescoped romance, during which time Howard orders a lunch special for which he cannot pay, Davis inquires, "Wouldn't you like someone to be in love with you?"

Howard rejoins that, "Just worshipping love makes people too old too soon." As in *Of Human Bondage*, Howard's character is not capable of any realistic passion for Davis' oncamera woman. His past disillusionments with the parasitic rich life have made him incapable of responding to her romanticism, except in a very etheral manner.

Later, like the prophet of doom, Howard returns to the Black Mesa Bar B-Q, enunciating that "Carnage is imminent and I'm due to be among the fallen." Despite the dangerous presence of criminal Duke Mantee (Bogart) and his hoodlum pals, and the annoying distraction of the spoiled rich couple (Genevieve Tobin and Paul Harvey), Davis is delighted to have Howard back again, even though she has admitted to jealous Foran that because she is just a desert rat, "He doesn't give a hoot and a hot plate about me." But she is an optimist and hopes to put some heart back into Howard's faded idealism.

Gabbing, selfish Gramp Maple (Charley Grapewin) is thrilled with the excitement of having a real killer and old-fashioned bruiser like Bogart on the premises. In contrast, Gramps finds Howard just as much a bafflement as his enigmatic, artistic granddaughter (Davis). To round out the character interaction, Howard admits his admiration for Bogart, regarding him as "the last great apostle of rugged individualism," while Bogart is nonplussed by this shopworn idealist who has so little gut interest in remaining alive.

The fast-resolving climax has Howard signing over his insurance policy, conveniently carried in his knapsack, to Davis, believing it to be his ticket to immortality. He insists that "any woman is worth anything any man has to give . . . . it's the excuse for his whole existence." As Davis' dad (Porter Hall) and the Black Mesa vigilantes surround the cafe, unruffled Howard, soon to meet his fate, quietly observes "This is an impressive spectacle." With gun in hand Bogart makes a run for it and because Howard deliberately stands in his way, the gangster is forced to live up to his bargain. When Bogart shoots him, the crumpling Howard says to the killer, "I'll be seeing you soon." Thereafter, Howard dies in the arms of the hysterical Davis. She soon regains her composure and decides that Howard must be buried within the petrified forest.

Near the end of *The Petrified Forest*, Grapewin's Gramps states of Howard, "Funny thing about that fella. I could never make him out." It is exactly this point which contains both the charm and frustration of Howard's Alan Squier, a "thin, wan vague man" about whom there is "an afterglow of elegance." He is a man with a bitter past and no future, a dreamer who finds his twisted moment of glory in the sun-parched desert.

He is the true focal point of this grim little study in futility, a far cry from the typical 1930s movie hero.

Davis, already tagged by many as of the James Cagney school of acting, was not ideally cast as the unblossomed desert flower who seeks life's beauty. "She lacks the poetic quality one would associate with a young lady who paints in the desert . . . [but she] is pert and very amusing" [Rose Pelwick (*New York American*)]. In her dark gray jumper skirt and simple blouse, Davis strives, not always successfully, to capture the elusive qualities of her unfulfilled character: a girl dissatisfied with her muscle-bound suitor (Foran) and who hopes that a more fertile setting will liberate the creativity of her soul. Although her heavily-made up eyes (big false eyelashes and all) distract from her intended well-scrubbed look, as do her occasional overindulgence in vocal and physical mannerisms, Davis demonstrates that "she does not have to be hysterical to be credited with a grand portrayal, . . ." (Nugent of the *Times*).

Particular credit in *The Petrified Forest* must go to Bogart's Duke Mantee, the unshaven hood with the brush-cut hairdo whose favorite words are "sure," "yeah", "sister," and "bub." In his own way, Bogart's Mantee has his sterling code of ethics. He may kill mercilessly but he is truly indignant when the annoyed Howard suggests that miserly Grapewin drop dead in a hurry and do something worthwhile with his hoarded money. Even Bogart is a victim to romance, having detoured from his escape plan to catch up with his two-timing moll.

*The Petrified Forest* would serve as the basis for Warners' reworked World War II drama, *Escape in the Desert* (1945). In 1955, Bogart would recreate his Duke Mantee characterization yet again, this time on a television special of *The Petrified Forest* with Henry Fonda as Alan Squier and Lauren Bacall as Gabrielle Maple. A variation of Robert Sherwood's drama appeared on Broadway in the 1973-1974 season in Mark Medoff's kinky play, *When You Comin' Back, Red Ryder?*

## IT'S LOVE I'M AFTER
### (First National-Warner Bros., 1937) 90M.

Executive producer, Hal B. Wallis; director, Archie Mayo; story, Maurice Hanline; screenplay, Casey Robinson; art director, Carl Jules Weyl; music, Heinz Roemheld; music director, Leo F. Forbstein; gowns, Orry-Kelly; camera, James Van Trees; editor, Owen Marks.

Leslie Howard (Basil Underwood); Bette Davis (Joyce Arden); Olivia de Havilland (Marcia West); Eric Blore (Digges); Patric Knowles (Henry Grant); George Barbier (William West); Spring Byington (Aunt Ella Paisley); Bonita Granville (Gracie Kane); E. E. Clive (Butler); Veda Ann Borg (Elsie); Valerie Bergere (Joyce's Maid); Georgia Caine (Mrs. Kane); Sarah Edwards (Mrs. Hinkle); Grace Field (Mrs. Babson); Harvey Clark (Mr.

Babson); Thomas Pogue (Mr. Hinkle); Ed Mortimer. (Mr. Kane); Thomas R. Mills (Butler); Lionel Belmore (Friar Lawrence); Ellen Clancy, Patricia Walthall, Rosella Towne, Helen Valkis (Autograph Hunters); Herbert Ashley (Doorman); Paul Irving (House Manager); Jack Mower (Hotel Clerk); Irving Bacon (Elevator Man); Georgie Cooper (Woman Guest).

New York Premiere: Strand Theatre—October 10, 1937
New York Television Debut: CBS—April 5, 1963

## Synopsis

Joyce Arden and Basil Underwood are world-famous as the most effective acting team on the stage. While they are professionally in accord with their romantic roles, offstage they are egotistical, jealous, and petty, causing them to postpone their announced nuptials some eleven times. When a friend of Basil's dad, Henry Grant, requests the star to quench the infatuation that his light-headed fiancée, Marcia West, has developed for Basil, the chance for grand theatrics is too much for Basil to turn down. Once more he postpones his wedding to Joyce, and while she frets and rants in her Los Angeles hotel suite, he traipses off to the West estate in Santa Barbara. His plan is to dispel Marcia's fantasy by acting boorishly to her family, insulting the servants, and worst (best) of all, sneaking into her bedroom, threatening her with a fate worse than death. However, in the boudoir the starry-eyed Marcia is so enthusiastic about Basil's leering advances that he beats a hasty retreat. When Marcia breaks her engagement to Henry, he asks Joyce to save the day. She arrives on the scene, pretending to be Basil's estranged wife, although on the sly the revenge-seeking actress encourages Marcia in her pursuit of Basil, and tells Henry that the matinee idol has really fallen for the heiress. Just when Marcia is about to announce her plan to wed Basil, Joyce comes to a timely rescue by displaying pictures of two children whom she claims are her youngsters by Basil. The shocked Marcia rushes back into the arms of the forgiving Henry. Reunited once again with Basil, Joyce plans to wed him before anything else can happen, but then with their temperaments. . . .

◆ ◆ ◆

In her autobiography (1962) Bette Davis says, "I have always adored comedy. It was my misfortune however that, when I was given a 'new facet,' I was given farce, which has never been my dish." To this day Davis still passes off *It's Love I'm After* as a minor, unworthy film. However, reviewers of the time felt differently. "It is a rippling farce, brightly written and deftly directed, and it has been played to the limit by an ingratiating cast" [Frank S. Nugent *(New York Times)*]. While certainly not in the screwball comedy leagues of *My Man Godfrey* (1936) or *Nothing Sacred* (1937), *It's Love I'm After* is a very diverting screen exercise, displaying lighter aspects of two stars more noted for their dramatic performances.

Howard had played opposite Norma Shearer in MGM's *Romeo and Juliet* (1936). As the male member of an Alfred Lunt-Lynn Fontanne Shakespearian acting team in *It's Love I'm After,* he had an engaging opportunity in the play-within-the-movie to again perform the tomb scene from *Romeo and Juliet,* subtly burlesquing the great bard as he and Davis emote to the oncamera audience while quietly bickering among themselves onstage. (He tells her "Get away from my face. The audience can't see me.") This scene quickly establishes the frivolous tenor for Howard's performance as the last of the old-type, egotistical matinèe idols, a man so entranced by the footlights that he can never forget them for one instance. He is his own greatest fan and cannot resist a command performance, even if it for the likes of an enraptured socialite [Olivia de Havilland in a role she would virtually repeat in *Four's a Crowd* (1938)]. Once at George Barbier's elaborate home, Howard enacts his role to the hilt as an insufferable hedonist, ordering whiskey for breakfast and throwing the household into a tizzy by his paraphrasing actions from the Petrucio role of *The Taming of the Shrew.*

Howard, professionally recognized as a man who knew how casually to steal the limelight from less aware players, was evenly matched by Davis in this respect, she being no slouch in the scene-stealing school of dramatics. As the attractive, quick-witted, acid-tongued foil to preening Howard, she was kept constantly on her toes, as much by the dialog of the Casey Robinson screenplay as by Archie Mayo's rapid fire direction. Her darting eyes, mobile hand gestures and distinctive gait all combined to give her Joyce Arden an oversized theatrical flavor, perfectly in keeping with the tone of the film. She can be grandly dramatic onstage in a bit of Shakespeare, effulgent to her fans, devastating in her jealousy—professional and romantic—of Howard's Basil Underwood, and play outrageously her flirtatious bogus wife in the suburban mansion scenes. Howard Barnes (*New York Herald-Tribune*) perhaps understated Davis in *It's Love I'm After* when he described her performance as having "verve and assurance."

With two such highly individualistic personalities as Davis and Howard, it is little wonder that they found themselves cast in such unusual joint movie love stories over the years. In *Of Human Bondage,* their romance is one of bruised puppy dogs hankering for a synthetic morsel; in *The Petrified Forest* their "romancing" is ethereal, taking on semi-personal proportions only in the cafe hostage sequences, where they must exchange their abortive courtship dialog to one another in full view and hearing of an assemblage. Equally unreal is the couple's romantic sparring in *It's Love I'm After,* filled with sparkling platitudinizing and oversized gesturing in which they subvert their inner needs for one another beneath their professional jealousies, which in turn causes the pair's ardor to change to temporary hate. Perhaps their grandest joint moments together in this comedy occur in the dressing room scenes where the couple are occupied with their cosmetic rituals, while being embroiled in an argument. Suddenly there is a knocking at the door, Each falls prey to his/her dramatic instinct. They both start violently, with Howard posturing, "Your husband" in a mock soap opera melodramatic fashion. Later, at the finale, as the tempestuous Davis barricades her dressing room against the advances of a recalcitrant Howard, the latter calmly slips into her fortress through an open window, once again commanding the spotlight and taking away her thunder.

## THE YEARS AFTER

*It's Love I'm After* proved to be Leslie Howard's final film on the Warner Bros. lot although he and David were almost reunited when *Gone with the Wind* (1939) was in its initial packaging stages and she was being considered for the prize role of Scarlett O'Hara. It was Vivien Leigh who eventually played that Oscar-winning assignment to Clark Gable's Rhett Butler and Howard's Ashley Wilkes (a part he did not want to play). Howard co-produced the remake of *Intermezzo* (1939) in which he co-starred with Ingrid Bergman, but plans fell through for the star to continue his *Pygmalion* (1939) collaboration with Gabriel Pascal in film projects about Lord Nelson and Lawrence of Arabia. By 1940 Howard had reestablished himself in London, planning to help revitalize the British film industry, which he did in such projects as *The First of the Few* (A.K.A. *Spitfire*) (1942), a film he directed and in which he appeared as R. J. Mitchell, the inventor of the Spitfire plane. He was on a government mission to Spain and Portugal in early 1943, when, on his return flight from Lisbon, the Germans shot down his plane, believing Winston Churchill was aboard.

Davis won her second Oscar for *Jezebel* (1938), but thereafter, despite several additional Academy Award nominations, she could never muster sufficient votes for another victory. She was the venomous Regina in Samuel Goldwyn's *The Little Foxes* (1941), the cinema's all-time repressed spinster in *Now, Voyager* (1942) and created a marathon performance as the vain society belle in *Mr. Skeffington* (1944). Her long time Warner Bros. association came to a close with the embarrassing *Beyond the Forest* (1949) and, after the classic *All about Eve* (1950), she had to wait another decade for a meaty screen role, this time in the grand guignol melodrama, *What Ever Happened to Baby Jane?* (1962). Meanwhile she had appeared on Broadway in the unpopular revue *Two's Company* (1952) and the important but secondary role in Tennessee Williams' *The Night of the Iguana* (1961). Her fourth marriage—to actor Garry Merrill—was dissolved in 1960, leading her to title her memoirs *The Lonely Life* (1962). Since then she has remained, like Joan Crawford and Gloria Swanson, one of the grandest ladies of the cinema, always in search of a good film role, or even one that meets her salary demands. Two parts that she earnestly wished to play oncamera went to others—to Elizabeth Taylor in *Who's Afraid of Virginia Woolf* (1966) and to Beryl Reid in *The Killing of Sister*

*George* (1969). One of Davis' most recent theatrical films, *Bunny O'Hare* (1971), reteamed her with Ernest Borgnine in unsympathetic roles as Geritol-set hippie bank robbers. The latter project must have been some fun for the two veteran stars to have made, but hardly impressed audiences one way or the other.

Ever the compleat show-woman, Davis never remains out of the limelight for long. In the spring of 1973, she made a stellar appearance at New York's Town Hall, with an evening of film clips and brittle discussion. She later went on the road with this program, garnering rave reviews wherever she appeared. Not to be outdone by the rash of authors (including myself) who have written about her, she provided her own coup to the publishing industry by providing a running commentary (in red ink) to Whitney Stine's biography, *Mother Goddam* (1974). Among her other activities, Davis had taken on the chore of starring in the Broadway-bound *Miss Moffat*, a musical version of *The Corn Is Green*. Thirty years before, when she starred in the film version of the Emlyn Williams drama, she had been considered too young for the part of the schoolmarm. Today . . .?

Because Davis was and still is such a dynamic screen force, it is almost as easy to pass over her trio of screen teamings with cultivated, placid Howard, as it is to recall that she made eleven joint film appearances with even more unassuming George Brent. However, *Of Human Bondage, The Petrified Forest,* and *It's Love I'm After* provide an intriguing array of emotionally contrasting performances by the two stars, demonstrating that their salt and pepper professional natures benefited greatly from the silver screen interplay.

In **The Bride Comes Home** (Par., 1935)

# Chapter 10

# Fred MacMurray
# &
# Claudette Colbert

## FRED MacMURRAY

6′ 3″
185 pounds
Black hair
Blue eyes
Virgo

*Real name: same. Born August 30, 1907, Kankakee, Illinois. Married Lillian Lamont (1936), children: Susan, Robert; widowed 1953. Married June Haver (1954), children: Kathryn, Laurie.*

FEATURE FILMS:

*Friends of Mr. Sweeney* (WB, 1934)
*Grand Old Girl* (RKO, 1935)
*The Gilded Lily* (Par., 1935)
*Car 99* (Par., 1935)
*Men Without Names* (Par., 1935)
*Alice Adams* (RKO, 1935)
*Hands Across the Table* (Par., 1935)
*The Bride Comes Home* (Par., 1935)
*The Trail of the Lonesome Pine* (Par., 1936)
*13 Hours by Air* (Par., 1936)
*The Princess Comes Across* (Par., 1936)

*The Texas Rangers* (Par., 1936)
*Maid of Salem* (Par., 1937)
*Champagne Waltz* (Par., 1937)
*Swing High—Swing Low* (Par., 1937)
*Exclusive* (Par., 1937)
*True Confession* (Par., 1937)
*Cocoanut Grove* (Par., 1938)
*Sing You Sinners* (Par., 1938)
*Men with Wings* (Par., 1938)
*Cafe Society* (Par., 1939)
*Invitation to Happiness* (Par., 1939)
*Honeymoon in Bali* (Par., 1939)
*Little Old New York* (20th, 1940)

Remember the Night (Par., 1940)
Too Many Husbands (Par., 1940)
Rangers of Fortune (Par., 1940)
Virginia (Par., 1941)
One Night in Lisbon (Par., 1941)
New York Town (Par., 1941)
Dive Bomber (WB, 1941)
The Lady Is Willing (Col., 1942)
Take a Letter, Darling (Par., 1942)
The Forest Rangers (Par., 1942)
Star Spangled Rhythm (Par., 1942)
Flight for Freedom (RKO, 1943)
Above Suspicion (MGM, 1943)
No Time for Love (Par., 1943)
Standing Room Only (Par., 1944)
And the Angels Sing (Par., 1944)
Double Indemnity (Par., 1944)
Murder, He Says (Par., 1945)
Practically Yours (Par., 1945)
Where Do We Go from Here? (20th, 1945)
Captain Eddie (20th, 1945)
Pardon My Past (Col., 1946)
Smoky (20th, 1946)
Suddenly It's Spring (Par., 1947)
The Egg and I (Univ., 1947)
Singapore (Univ., 1947)
The Miracle of the Bells (RKO, 1948)
On Our Merry Way (UA, 1948)
Don't Trust Your Husband (UA, 1948)
Family Honeymoon (Univ., 1948)
Father Was a Fullback (20th, 1949)

Borderline (Univ., 1950)
Never a Dull Moment (RKO, 1950)
A Millionaire for Christy (20th, 1951)
Callaway Went Thataway (MGM, 1951)
Fair Wind to Java (Rep., 1953)
The Moonlighter (WB, 1953)
The Caine Mutiny (Col., 1954)
Pushover (Col., 1954)
Woman's World (20th, 1954)
The Far Horizons (Par., 1955)
The Rains of Ranchipur (20th, 1955)
At Gunpoint (AA, 1955)
There's Always Tomorrow (Univ., 1956)
Gun for a Coward (Univ., 1957)
Quantez (Univ., 1957)
Day of the Bad Man (Univ., 1958)
Good Day for a Hanging (Col., 1958)
The Shaggy Dog (BV, 1959)
Face of a Fugitive (Col., 1959)
The Oregon Trail (20th, 1959)
The Apartment (UA, 1960)
The Absent-Minded Professor (BV, 1961)
Bon Voyage (BV, 1962)
Son of Flubber (BV, 1963)
Kisses for My President (WB, 1964)
Follow Me, Boys (BV, 1966)
The Happiest Millionaire (BV, 1967)
Charley and the Angel (BV, 1973)

# CLAUDETTE COLBERT

5′ 4½″
108 pounds
Reddish brown hair
Hazel eyes
Virgo

*Real name: Lily Chauchoin. Born September 13, 1905, Paris, France. Married Norman Foster (1928); divorced 1935. Married Dr. Joel Pressman (1935); widowed 1968.*

**FEATURE FILMS:**

*For the Love of Mike* (FN, 1927)
*The Hole in the Wall* (Par., 1929)
*The Lady Lies* (Par., 1929)
*The Big Pond* (Par., 1930)
*La Grande Mare* (Par., 1930)
*Young Man of Manhattan* (Par., 1930)
*L'Enigmatique Monsieur Parkes* (Par., 1930)
*Manslaughter* (Par., 1930)
*The Smiling Lieutenant* (Par., 1931)
*Le Lieutenant Souriant* (Par., 1931)
*His Woman* (Par., 1931)
*Secrets of a Secretary* (Par., 1931)
*Honor Among Lovers* (Par., 1931)
*The Wiser Sex* (Par., 1932)
*The Misleading Lady* (Par., 1932)
*The Man from Yesterday* (Par., 1932)
*Make Me a Star* (Par., 1932)
*The Phantom President* (Par., 1932)
*The Sign of the Cross* (Par., 1932)
*Tonight Is Ours* (Par., 1933)
*I Cover the Waterfront* (UA, 1933)
*Three Cornered Moon* (Par., 1933)
*Torch Singer* (Par., 1933)
*Four Frightened People* (Par., 1934)
*It Happened One Night* (Col., 1934)
*Cleopatra* (Par., 1934)
*Imitation of Life* (Univ., 1934)
*The Gilded Lily* (Par., 1935)
*Private Worlds* (Par., 1935)
*She Married Her Boss* (Col., 1935)
*The Bride Comes Home* (Par., 1935)
*Under Two Flags* (20th, 1936)
*Maid of Salem* (Par., 1937)

*I Met Him in Paris* (Par., 1937)
*Tovarich* (WB, 1937)
*Bluebeard's Eighth Wife* (Par., 1938)
*Zaza* (Par., 1939)
*Midnight* (Par., 1939)
*It's a Wonderful World* (MGM, 1939)
*Drums Along the Mohawk* (20th, 1939)
*Boom Town* (MGM, 1940)
*Arise, My Love* (Par., 1940)
*Skylark* (Par., 1941)
*Remember the Day* (20th, 1941)
*The Palm Beach Story* (Par., 1942)
*No Time for Love* (Par., 1943)
*So Proudly We Hail* (Par., 1943)
*Since You Went Away* (UA, 1944)
*Practically Yours* (Par., 1945)
*Guest Wife* (UA, 1945)
*Without Reservations* (RKO, 1946)
*Tomorrow Is Forever* (RKO, 1946)
*The Secret Heart* (MGM, 1946)
*The Egg and I* (Univ., 1947)
*Sleep, My Love* (UA, 1948)
*Family Honeymoon* (Univ., 1948)
*Bride for Sale* (RKO, 1949)
*Three Came Home* (20th, 1950)
*The Secret Fury* (RKO, 1950)
*Thunder on the Hill* (Univ., 1951)
*Let's Make It Legal* (20th, 1951)
*Outpost in Malaya* (UA, 1952)
*Daughters of Destiny* (French, 1954)
*Texas Lady* (RKO, 1955)
*Royal Affairs in Versailles* (Times, 1957)
*Parrish* (WB, 1961)

In **Maid of Salem** (Par., 1937)

In **The Gilded Lily** (Par., 1935)

In **No Time for Love** (Par., 1943)

In **Practically Yours** (Par., 1945)

Advertisement for **The Egg and I** (Univ., 1947)

Richard Long, Fred MacMurray, and Claudette Colbert in **The Egg and I**

Fred MacMurray, Claudette Colbert, Jimmy Hunt, Gigi Perreau, and Peter Miles in **Family Honeymoon** (Univ., 1948)

# THE GILDED LILY
*(Paramount, 1935) 80M.*

Producer, Albert Lewis; director, Wesley Ruggles; story, Melville Baker, Jack Kirland; screenplay, Claude Binyon; song, Sam Coslow and Arthur Johnston; costumes, Travis Banton; camera, Victor Milner; editor, Otho Lovering.

Claudette Colbert (Lillian David); Fred MacMurray (Peter Dawes); Raymond Milland [Charles Gray (Granville)]; C. Aubrey Smith (Lloyd Granville); Eddie Craven (Eddie); Luis Alberni (Nate); Donald Meek (Hankerson); Michelette Burani (Lily's Maid); Claude King (Boat Captain); Charles Irwin (Oscar); Ferdinand Munier (Otto Bushe); Rita Carlyle (Proprietor's Wife); Forrester Harvey (English Inn Proprietor); Edward Gargan (Guard); Leonid Kinskey (Vocal Teacher); Jimmy Aubrey (Purser); Charles Wilson (Pete's Editor); Walter Shumway (Assistant Editor); Rollo Lloyd (City Editor); Reginald Barlow (Managing Editor); Esther Muir (Divorcee); Grace Bradley (Daisy); Pat Somerset (Man in London Club); Eddie Dunn (Reporter); Tom Dugan (Bum); Warren Hymer (Taxi Driver); Rudy Cameron, Jack Egan, Jack Norton (Photographers); Hayden Stevenson, Perry Ivans, Cherry Campbell, Samuel E. Hines (Cameramen at New York Apartment); Mel Ruick (English Band Leader); Stanley Mann (Steward with Telegram); Ambrose Barker, David Thursby (British Reporters); William Begg, Dick French, Ronald Rondell, Rebecca Wassem, Adele Corliss, Gale Ronn (Patrons at Nate's Cafe); Albert Pollet, Cyril Ring (Head Waiters).

New York Premiere: Paramount Theatre—February 8, 1935
New York Television Debut: CBS—July 29, 1962

## Synopsis

After a chance meeting on a subway, Lillian David and Charles Gray fall deeply in love with one another. She thinks he is poor and without a job and hopes to help him.' Peter Dawes, a newspaper reporter who is Lillian's best friend, loves her and is decidedly unhappy when she informs him of her infatuation for Charles. Charles in reality is Lord Granville, a British nobleman. Wishing to be kind to Lillian, Charles tells her that he is going down South for a position. In reality he sails for England to break off his engagement to his society girl, then to return to America, tell Lillian about himself and hopefully wed her. When Lillian sees Charles' photograph in the newspapers she is heartbroken for she is convinced that he has just been toying with her affections. Peter, angry because Lillian has been duped, prints a story about Lillian's refusal to wed Charles and she becomes famous as the "no" girl, which eventually leads to a lucrative

276

nightclub job for her. She becomes quite successful, but she is unhappy because Charles has not returned. After reading the news story, Charles feels sure that Lillian never loved him and just used the relationship as a publicity stunt. When Lillian is later offered a position in England she readily accepts. In London she and Charles meet again. Peter, who had accompanied her to England, goes back to America believing that now he is only in the way. Lillian is content for a time but soon realizes that Charles does not ever intend to ask her to wed him. She bids him goodbye, returns to America, and is reunited with Peter.

◆——◆

Claudette Colbert, one of the most polished screen comediennes extant, finally was allowed her cinema forte in *Three Cornered Moon* (1933), a wacky laugh fest released during her fifth year with Paramount Pictures. It was the first good industry break she had had since Cecil B. DeMille cast her as the voluptuous, decadent Poppaea in his epic *The Sign of the Cross* (1932), and reaffirmed that her reputation as one of the most engaging ingenues on Broadway in the 1920s was not without solid merit. After surprising the industry, and herself, by winning an Oscar on loanout to Columbia for *It Happened One Night* (1934), and then delivering a sassy performance in DeMille's *Cleopatra* (1934), and a staunchly noble depiction of motherhood in *Imitation of Life* (1934), Paramount took the hint. Here was an actress who deserved better than a run of soggy melodramas. In the height of her full glory and popularity she was cast in the Wesley Ruggles-directed rendition of *The Gilded Lily*.

Among those who tested for the below-the-title co-star role was twenty-eight-year-old newcomer Fred MacMurray, a former saxophonist-vocalist-Broadway performer, who had made his feature film debut the previous year at Warner Bros. in *Friends of Mr. Sweeney,* starring director Ruggles' actor-brother, Charles. Paramount was so pleased by MacMurray's test that they signed him to a studio contract which would last for the next decade of his moviemaking career.

Above and beyond her chic presence, her mellifluous deep voice, husky laugh and impeccable timing, Colbert's best acting asset was her uncanny ability to make her roles seem very real and true. Anyone could play a gum-chewing stenographer or a status-seeking private secretary, but it remained for Colbert in such parts as Lillian David of *The Gilded Lily* to desplay a finesse in making a commonplace working girl seem both typical yet unique. Her character may rise to celebrity status within the screenplay as in *The Gilded Lily*, but nearly always her screen person remained a consistent, logical human being. Illinois-born MacMurray, on the other hand, in *The Gilded Lily*, cemented his novice-induced lumbering casualness into an acceptable screen style, gauging his newly established movie image to be somewhere between that of James Stewart and Pat O'Brien. His 6'3" manly figure in tandem with Colbert's petit 5'4½" frame made an interesting visual contrast as did their verbal sparring which, more often than not, found Colbert's intellectually superior character acceding to the plotline demands of MacMurray's masculinely stubborn man of the streets.

Of the team's seven co-starring roles over a thirteen year period, *The Gilded Lily* (for the record, one paints the flower, not gilds it), remains this writer's favorite. Its premise is simple and its execution unstrained. In addition, third fiddle Ray(mond) Milland is far easier to accept than some of the later "other" parties who would decorate the likable stars' features.

A question raised by the picture was, which is better nibbling food, peanuts or popcorn? This writer still is uncertain and so were Colbert and MacMurray's characters. They would meet on each Thursday evening on a park bench nearby the main branch of the Public Library on 42nd Street, debate the relative merits of their two favorite snacks, and converse on the progress of their lives. These scenes alone make the picture worthwhile, but one cannot ignore Colbert's subway encounter with the lordly Milland or the overall effectiveness of the star's interlude as a fledgling nightclub chanteuse who admits her nervousness to the oncamera audience and then proceeds to make a valiant stab at entertaining the assembled paying public with a rendition of "Something about Romance."

Melodrama was kept to a minimum within the story's framework, with Colbert only occasionally feeling sorry for herself at having lost Milland, or MacMurray pridefully bowing out when he believes Colbert and Milland are about to reestablish their waning romance. It might be carped that Colbert's Lillian David deserved better than to wed in the end a shipping news reporter, but then again, movie characters, just as in real life, cannot have everything.

The general consensus was that *The Gilded Lily* was "A bright-faced romantic lark, . . ." [Andre Sennwald *(New York Times)*]. As for the stars, Richard Watts, Jr. *(New York Herald-Tribune)* said it all, "Miss Colbert is humorous and sympathetic in the title role, playing with all of her customary shrewdness and charm. Mr. MacMurray, who was a member of the band called the California Collegians and impersonated Rudy Vallee on the stage in *Roberta*, is engaging and unaffected as the ship news man."

Colbert and MacMurray would repeat their *The Gilded Lily* assignments on "Lux Radio Theatre" on January 11, 1937.


## THE BRIDE COMES HOME
### *(Paramount, 1935) 83M.*

Producer-director, Wesley Ruggles; story, Elisabeth Sanxay Holding; screenplay, Claude Binyon; art director, Hans Dreier, Robert Usher; camera, Leo Tover.

Claudette Colbert (Jeannette Desmereau); Fred MacMurray (Cyrus Anderson); Robert Young (Jack Bristow); William Collier, Sr. (Alfred Desmereau); Donald Meek (The Judge); Richard Carle (Frank the Butler); Edgar Kennedy (Henry); Johnny Arthur (Otto); Kate MacKenna (Emma); James Conlin (Len Noble); William R. "Billy" Arnold (Elevator Starter); Belle Mitchell (Helene the Maid); Tom Kennedy (Husky); Edward Gargan (Cab Driver); Robert McKenzie (Painter); Ruth Warren (Girl in Elevated); Frank Mills (Conductor on Elevated); Tom Dugan, James Quinn (Conductors); Harry Depp, Maxine Elliot Hicks, Jack Raymond, Alex Woloshin, Gertrude Simpson, Mabelle Moore, Alice Keating, Howard Bruce, Phil Ryley, Art Rowland (Passengers); Jerry Mandy (Waiter); Charles West, Esther Michelson (Bystanders); Charles Sylber (Office Clerk); A. S. "Pop" Byron (Chicago Park Cop); C. L. Sherwood (Bartender); Tom Hanlon (Man in Nightclub).

New York Premiere: Paramount Theatre—December 25, 1935
New York Television Debut: CBS—February 10, 1964


### Synopsis

After Jeannette Desmereau's father loses his fortune, she decides to find a job. She applies to Jack Bristow for a position on his newly formed magazine, of which Cyrus Anderson is the editor. At first Cyrus objects to having socialite Jeannette in the office, but when he learns that she is in need of the salary, his attitude changes. They fall in love with one another and decide to wed, much against the advice of Jack who also loves Jeannette. Jack sets the time for the marriage, but arrives earlier and finds Jeannette in the midst of cleaning up his apartment. A quarrel ensues and they call off the nuptuals. Jeannette listens to Jack's plea to wed him and they set out to elope. But they are prevented from marrying by the intervention of Cyrus and her father who have rushed after them. There is a quick switch in bridegrooms and Jeanette weds Cyrus whom she wanted all along.

*The Gilded Lily* talent quartet of producer-director Wesley Ruggles, scenarist Claude Binyon, and stars Claudette Colbert and Fred MacMurray were quickly rematched for *The Bride Comes Home.* This picture did not equal the original entry or even MacMurray's similar foray into screen farce with Carole Lombard, *Hands Across the Table* (1935), but *The Bride Comes Home* was still "Flippant, gay and laugh provoking" *(New York Evening Journal).* ". . . the swift little tale is told in dialogue that balances beautifully between naturalness and brightness, it's a delight throughout" *(Liberty* magazine).
The setting for this comedy excursion was Chicago and the "other"

man was charming but bland Robert Young on loanout from MGM. In all other respects, however, the interplay between the stars was fortuitously similar to *The Gilded Lily*. Unlike their earlier picture, MacMurray had the upper edge, being cast as Colbert's on-the-job boss and a hard-working individual at that, while she was presented as somewhat unsympathetically unproletarian in her role as the blue-blooded, pampered, bad-tempered society gal who now must make a living. Once more at the crux of the film was the age-old struggle between polite masculine "might-is-right" and shaded feminine wiles, the very essence of the Colbert-MacMurray screen chemistry. The question of who wins the battle this round, Colbert's Depression-wrecked heiress or MacMurray's know-it-all gentle bully, is resolved into a tie game again, since both characters end up with whom they subconsciously wanted all along—namely, each other.

*The Bride Comes Home* was highlighted by two outstanding sequences. The first occurred when meticulous, industrious Colbert decides that if she and MacMurray are to wed, then his bachelor digs (which he shares with Young, who prefers it to his own swank abode) must receive a major cleaning overhaul. But MacMurray likes his dirt where he can find it, and before Colbert can sweep another smidgen into a dust pan, they are engaged in a battle royal, with dominance again the primary issue. The second scene of especial merit occurred almost at the finale as MacMurray is chasing after his would-be bride on his motorcycle. She has arrived at Crown Point, Indiana, to quickly wed Young at the home of justice of the peace Edgar Kennedy. But Kennedy is no ordinary civil servant, for he has developed his own special fancy marriage ritual which is an elaborate embroidery of the legal ceremony. He intends to complete the lengthy service word for word, no matter how many interruptions he suffers or how harrassed he becomes with his impatient customers.

Elegantly stylish Colbert received her usual critical accolades. "It's a made-to-measure framework for Miss Colbert, presenting her in the always attractive position of a young lady beset by two lovers, both fascinating and both collapsible at her slightest whim" *(Variety)*. The reviewers turned in a good progress report on MacMurray as the bruised male ego part of the most quarrelsome love-bird couple of the year. "Fred MacMurray, who has made remarkable strides in his brief career, continues to vault toward the top, gaining sureness before the camera with each succeeding part" [Regina Crewe *(New York American)*].


## MAID OF SALEM
### *(Paramount, 1937) 85M.*

Producer-director, Frank Lloyd; story, Bradley King; adaptation, Walter Ferris, King, Durward Grinstead; art directors, Hans Dreier, Bernard Herzbrun; set decorator, A. E. Freudeman; costumes, Travis Banton;

music, Victor Young; music director, Boris Morris; assistant director, William Tummel; sound, Gene Merritt, Louis Masenkop; camera, Leo Tover; editor, Hugh Bennett.

Claudette Colbert (Barbara Clarke); Fred MacMurray (Roger Coverman); Harvey Stephens (Dr. John Harding); Gale Sondergaard (Martha Harding); Louise Dresser (Ellen Clarke); Bennie Bartlett (Timothy Clarke); Edward Ellis (Elder Goode); Beulah Bondi (Abigail Goode); Bonita Granville (Ann Goode); Virginia Weidler (Nabby Goode); Donald Meek (Ezra Cheeves); E. E. Clive (Bilge); Halliwell Hobbes (Jeremiah); Pedro de Cordoba (Mr. Morse); Madame Sul-te-wan (Tituba); Lucy Beaumont (Rebecca); Henry Kolker (Crown Chief Justice Laughton); William Farnum (Crown Justice Sewall); Ivan F. Simpson (Reverend Parris); Brandon Hurst (Tithing Man); Sterling Holloway (Miles Corbin); Zeffie Tilbury (Goody Hodgers); Babs Nelson (Baby Mercy Cheeves); Mary Treen (Suzy Abbott); J. Farrell MacDonald (Captain of Ship); Stanley Fields (First Mate); Lionel Belmore (Tavern Keeper); Kathryn Sheldon (Mrs. Deborah Cheeves); Rosita Butler (Mary Watkins); Madge Collins (Elizabeth); Amelia Falleur (Sarah); Clarence Kolb (Town Crier); Russell Simpson (Village Marshal); Colin Tapley (Roger's Friend); Tom Ricketts (Giles Cory); Ricca K. Allen, Agnes Ayres, Wilson Benge, Sidney Bracy, Fritzi Brunette, Herbert Evans, Fryda Gagne, Edith Hallor, Frank E. Hammond, Carol Halloway, Harold Howard, Ward Lane, Stella Le Saint, Ralph Lewis, Vera Lewis, Anne O'Neal, Rita Owin, Audrey Reynolds, Allen D. Sewall, Walter Soderling, Al H. Stewart, William Wagner (Bits); Chief Big Tree (Indian); Harold Entwistle (Court Clerk); Harold Nelson (Judge); Hayden Stevenson (Deputy Marshal); Thomas L. Brower (Salem Town Marshal); James Marcus (Sea Captain); John Power (Minister); Jack Deery, Clive Morgan (Non-Commissioned Officers); Colin Kenny, Sidney D'Albrook (Hunters); J. R. Tozer (Clergyman); Grace Kern (Convict); Wally Albright (Jaspar); Jack H. Richardson (Sheriff); George Magrill (Sailor); Charles McAvoy (Father); Vangie Beilby (Mother).

New York Premiere: Paramount Theatre—March 3, 1937
New York Television Debut: CBS—August 20, 1960

## Synopsis

In 1692 Salem, Massachusetts, Barbara Clarke, who lives with her aunt and cousin, at times rebels against the enforced sobriety of her life. When she encounters Roger Coverman, a fugitive from Virginia, a new and fascinating world opens up for her, but she is compelled to meet him surreptitiously for fear that he be apprehended by the authorities. Ann Goode, daughter of the leading elder, starts a wave of hysteria in the village and it soon spreads among all the inhabitants. Ann, hating her black slave Tituba, and wanting to get even, pretends to be possessed by her. In a short time, many innocent people, including Tituba, are burned at the stake. Roger, knowing that Barbara is in danger because of her sympathy with the victims, tells her that she must go away with him. He leaves for Boston to make arrangements for their passage, but is recognized and thrown into prison. Meanwhile, Barbara is arrested for practicing witchcraft. At the trial, Martha Harding, the jealous wife of the local physician who had been trying to help Barbara, blurts out the fact that Barbara's mother had been burned in England for practicing witchcraft. Barbara is sentenced to death. Roger, however, escapes from prison and arrives just in time to establish Barbara's innocence and insure their future happiness. Ann later confesses her guilt.

◆◆◆

Scottish-born film director Frank Lloyd, who had a penchant for romanticizing history onscreen [*Cavalcade* (1933), *Mutiny on the Bounty* (1935)] and who had directed Claudette Colbert in the Twentieth Century-Fox desert actioner, *Under Two Flags* (1936), produced-directed the very odd *Maid of Salem*. It was strange that Paramount or the usually very commercial-minded Colbert should have gambled on such an unlikely subject, since witchcraft had never been a popular subject for Hollywood filmmakers. *The House of the Seven Gables* (1940) would be one of the few United States-made celluloid efforts to delve into this area of American colonial history which most people wished to forget. When Arthur Miller used this "taboo" subject as the basis of his *The Crucible*, which further upset people by drawing parallels to the 1950s McCarthy Red scare hearings, the project had to be picturized in the safer climate of France.

In all fairness, Lloyd and the Paramount production crew must be credited with creating a solid, atmospheric recreation of 1690s Salem, Massachusetts on a huge outdoor set at Santa Cruz, California. But the uneven blend of history, romantic fiction, and cliffhanger-style story progression (the uncharacteristic Victor Young score would have better served a Republic serial), all added up to unsatisfactory entertainment on every level. The *New York Post* judged the film ". . . lavish, ambitious, careful and a little dull." Compounding the picture's artistic-commercial plight was the obviously last-minute re-editing job which left the plot development even more confusing and pulsatingly choppy.

"Miss Colbert has a flair for modern comedy and the run of sob stuff and history is no help to her and her following. Mr. MacMurray, to make a pun, is made of wood, being genial but no actor" wrote the *Brooklyn Daily Eagle*. Colbert barely passed muster as the rebellious maid of old Salem, but MacMurray, a man very much of the twentieth century, looked embarrassingly awkward in his cavalier-style costumes. He was a sore reminder that, despite everyone's efforts to reassemble the flavor of a bygone time with its stocks, pillories, blue laws, and house raisings, this group of modern performers were play acting at a massive costume ball.

Nor was the dialog style much help to contemporaneous MacMurray, who was exceedingly uneasy at spouting forth such lines as "I am he you mistook for the devil." The sight of MacMurray riding onto the scene for the (literally) last minute rescue was certainly more mirth-provoking than heroics-evoking.

Within *Maid of Salem*, Colbert does have one impassioned scene as she rises in full court to defend herself and speak forth on the unbridled hysteria which has fanned the Puritans' bigotry into wholesale persecution of innocent people. [This Portia-like scene foreshadows Colbert's patriotic finale speech in *Arise, My Love* (1940).] For a rare change in a Colbert vehicle, it was the supporting cast who gave the picture whatever viability it had: Madame Sul-te-wan as the innocent victim of her West Indies heritage, Edward Ellis and Beulah Bondi as the stern but homey parents of the trouble-making Bonita Granville [paralleling her similar role in *These Three* (1936)], and the always exotic Gale Sondergaard as the overly-jealous wife of physician Harvey Stephens.

## NO TIME FOR LOVE
*(Paramount, 1943) 83M.*

Producer, Mitchell Leisen; associate producer, Fred Kohlmar; director, Leisen; story, Robert Lees, Fred Rinaldo; adaptation, Warren Duff; screenplay, Claude Binyon; music, Victor Young; art directors, Hans Dreier, Robert Usher; set decorator, Sam Comer; assistant director, Chico Alonso; costumes, Edith Head; Miss Colbert's gowns, Irene; sound, Earl Hayman, Don Johnson; process camera, Farciot Edouart; special camera effects, Gordon Jennings; camera, Charles Lang, Jr.; editor, Alma Macrorie.

Claudette Colbert (Katherine Grant); Fred MacMurray (Jim Ryan); Ilka Chase (Happy Grant); Richard Haydn (Roger); Paul McGrath (Henry Fulton); June Havoc (Darlene); Marjorie Gateson (Sophie); Bill Goodwin (Christley); Robert Herrick (Kent); Morton Lowry (Dunbar); Rhys Williams (Clancy); Murray Alper (Moran); John Kelly (Morrisey); Jerome De Nuccio (Leon Brice); Grant Withers (Pete Hanagan); Rod Cameron (Taylor); Willard Robertson (President of Construction Company); Arthur Loft (Vice-President); Fred Kohler, Jr., Tom Neal, Max Laur, Oscar G. Hendrian, Tex Harris, Ted E. Jacques, Art Potter, Sammy Stein, Jack Roper (Sand Hogs); Frank Moran (Erector Tender); Alan Hale, Jr. (Union Checker); Dave Wengren (Jack Tender); Bob Homans (Pop Murphy); Walter Soderling (Gate Man); Mickey Simpson (Doctor); Lorin Raker (Sweetzer the Stage Manager); Faith Brook (Pert Brunette); Frederic Henry (Man at Party); Paul Phillips (Office Worker); Mitchell Ingraham (City Commissioner); Ben Taggart (City General Manager); Pat McVey

(City Chief Engineer); Jack Shay (Second Engineer); Lillian Randolph (Hilda); Keith Richards (Reporter); Kenneth Christy, Jack Gardner (Photographers); Charles Irwin (O'Conner); Ronnie Rondell, George Dolenz, Jack Roberts (Captain of Waiters); Pat West (Waiter at Murphy's Place).

New York Premiere: Paramount Theatre—November 1, 1943
New York Television Debut: CBS—February 12, 1961

## Synopsis

After an argument with her managing editor because of her abiding love for arty pictures, Katherine Grant is sent to a tunnel project to photograph the sandhogs at work. There she encounters Jim Ryan, a two-fisted Irishman who regards her as a jinx. Katherine does save Jim's life when she pushes him out of the way of a falling girder. When one of the sandhogs accuses Jim of showing off, Jim knocks him unconscious. Katherine snaps the action picture. After exchanging insults with Jim, Katherine departs, leaving her tripod behind. Curious about what kind of a woman she is, Jim visits her apartment, using the return of the tripod as an excuse. Meanwhile, Katherine, who has been amused at Jim's antics, tells her pals about him and refers to him as "Superman." When Jim arrives at her apartment her male friends try to make light of his strength. Jim knocks their heads together, and stomps out. When the pictures of Jim fighting in the tunnel are published he is suspended from his job for six months. To make amends and in hope of curing her growing love for him, Katherine hires Jim as her assistant. Jim's cavalier attitude to his new job results in assorted complications, including his involvement with chorus girl Darlene. Both Katherine and Jim find themselves falling deeply in love with one another, but his male pride is hurt when he learns she had hired him originally to prove how superior she was to him. Later when Jim learns that the tunnel project will have to be abandoned because of mud oozing into the work area, he invents a freezing machine to save the excavation site. Katherine goes to the tunnel to photograph the test. The machine fails to hold back the mud, but as a result of the snapshots Katherine takes, it is proved that Jim's idea, when refined, will work. Katherine and Jim are reconciled.

◆◆◆

Conflicting working schedules had been the primary cause for six years elapsing since Claudette Colbert and Fred MacMurray last co-starred. They had almost been paired in Mitchell Leisen's *Remember the Night* (1940), and were actually set to do Leisen's *Take a Letter, Darling* (1942) but at the last minute Paramount persuaded Colbert to take over the role intended for Carole Lombard in Preston Sturges' *The Palm Beach Story* (1942). Finally, with *No Time for Love*, Leisen, who had handled

284

Colbert so beautifully in *Midnight* (1939) and *Arise, My Love* (1940), had the opportunity to match her with MacMurray once again. The project was scripted by her past cooperative scenarist, Claude Binyon. Charles Lang, Jr., who would photograph eight of Colbert's features, was behind the camera again, knowing well that the demanding star would only be lensed from face left or occasionally from front face.

"You've seen and heard the story under other titles and disguises many times. It's usually amusing and usually proper.

"If you're a Colbert fan or a MacMurray fan or both—and their cohorts are counted in the millions—you should find *No Time for Love* enough to your liking" [G. E. Blackford *(New York Journal-American)*].

*No Time for Love* was based on the age-old girl-boy premise that opposites attract, in this case the intellectual chic fashion photographer Colbert versus muscular, brawling MacMurray. With two such professional stars, who thoroughly enjoyed working with one another in front of the cameras, this rendition of brainy girl meets brawny boy worked amazingly well, being "timed so perfectly and acted so delightfully, it's a laugh all the way down the line" [Lee Mortimer *(New York Daily Mirror)*].

Colbert was in fine fettle as a Margaret Bourke-White type photographer who prefers lensing white eggs against black velvet backdrops. This New York-based celebrity with her acid-tongued sister (Ilka Chase) moves among Manhattan's intellectual and social sets, whose members include Richard Haydn and staid Paul McGrath, the latter Colbert's fiancé. Because of all the inherent slapstick within this film, this was one picture outing where lofty Colbert spared neither herself nor her sartorial elegance, but jumped into the foray with a glee that was obvious in the final product. For those detractors who had always suspected that McMurray's oncamera clumsiness was no mere act, he proved to the contrary in *No Time for Love*, building upon his characterization of a happy-go-lucky guy who has his share of brains (he turns out to be a college man!), but who prefers getting down to the basics of life on more simplistic levels.

Amid the hurly-burly of *No Time for Love*, four scenes in particular are outstanding. Colbert, having slummed with her ritzy pals by going to an Irish saloon for corned beef and cabbage, encounters MacMurray and soon finds that his rambunctiousness is bound to arouse the hot tempers of his sandhog buddies. Desperately trying to avert the brewing storm, Colbert delicately suggests that they all engage in a game of musical chairs. But the threatened donnybrook still erupts. On another occasion Colbert, finding herself deeply attached to MacMurray, dreams a la *Lady in the Dark* (a Mitchell Leisen film of 1944) that she is being pursued by a villain (McGrath) when along comes a Superman-garbed hero (MacMurray) to rescue her from a fate worse than death. This intriguing but gratuitous sequence was severely edited before the film was released. Later in the film, having discovered that sharp words do not affect mercenary chorine Darlene (June Havoc), who is her nail-clawing rival for MacMurray's attentions, the emancipated Colbert takes matters in hand and physically knocks out the opposition. Finally—and the picture was building to this scene all along—Colbert is photographing MacMurray's mud-freezing method in the Hudson River tunnel when all havoc breaks loose and the malicious mud comes oozing into the excavation site, soon engulfing the bewildered Colbert and the annoyed MacMurray in one of the thickest, dirtiest baths on film before or since *McLintock!* (1963).

## PRACTICALLY YOURS
### *(Paramount, 1945) 90M.*

Producer, Mitchell Leisen; associate producer, Harry Tugend; director, Leisen; screenplay, Norman Krasna; art directors, Hans Dreier, Robert Usher; set decorator, Stephen Seymour; assistant director, John Coonan; Miss Colbert's gowns, Howard Greer; music, Victor Young; sound, Donald McKay; process camera, Farciot Edouart; special camera effects, Gordon Jennings, J. Devereaux Jennings; camera, Charles Lang, Jr.; editor, Doane Harrison.

Claudette Colbert (Peggy Martin); Fred MacMurray [Lieutenant (S. G.) Daniel Bellamy]; Gil Lamb (Albert Beagell); Cecil Kellaway (Marvin P. Meglin); Robert Benchley (Judge Oscar Stimson); Tom Powers (Commander Harpe); Jane Frazee (Musical Comedy Star); Rosemary De Camp (Ellen Macy); Isabel Randolph (Mrs. Meglin); Mikhail Rasumny (La Crosse); Arthur Loft (Uncle Ben Bellamy); Edgar Norton (Harvey the Butler); Donald MacBride (Sam); Donald Kerr (Meglin's Chauffeur); Clara Reid (Meglin's Maid); Don Barclay (Himself); Rommie (Piggy the Dog); Charles Irwin (Patterson); Will Wright (Senator Cowling); Isabel Withers (Grace Mahoney); George Carleton (Mr. Hardy); Frederic Nay (Michael); Stan Johnson (Pilot); Byron Barr (Navigator); Allen Fox, George Turner, Reggie Simpson (Reporters); Ralph Lynn, Jerry James, William Meader (Cameramen); John Whitney (Pilot with Bellamy); Sam Ash, John Wald (Radio Announcers); Hugh Beaumont (Cutter); Warren Ashe (Cameraman in News Room); Roy Brent (Sound Man); Gary Bruce (Camera Operator); John James (Usher); Mike Lally (Assistant Cameraman); Jack Rice (Couturier); George Melford (Senate Vice-President); Ottola Nesmith (Hysterical Woman in Senate); Len Hendry (Naval Lieutenant in Senate); Nell Craig (Meglin's Secretary); Charles Hamilton (Prudential Guard); Yvonne De Carlo, Julie Gibson (Girl Employees); Allen Pinson (Stimson's Chauffeur); Edward Earle (Assistant Manager at Hadley's Store); Mimi Doyle (Red Cross Worker); Louise Currie, Dorothy Granger (Girls); Helen Dickson (Woman in Subway); Gladys Blake (Brooklyn Girl in Subway); Jack Clifford (Subway Conductor); Thomas Quinn (Photographer); Earle Hodgins (Man with Pen Knife); Stanley

Andrews (Shipyards Official); Charles A. Hughes (Radio Announcer); Kitty Kelly (Wife-Newsreel Theatre); Marjean Neville (Little girl at Newsreel Theatre); Tom Kennedy (Burly Citizen at Newsreel Theatre); Michael Miller, Hugh Binyon, Sonny Boy Williams (Boys in Park); Louise La Planche (Attractive Girl); Maxine Fife (Pretty Girl in Park); Eddie Hall, Stephen Wayne (Radio Men—PBY); Ronnie Rondell (Left Gunner—PBY); Anthony Marsh (Plane Captain—PBY); Larry Thompson (Right Gunner— PBY); Tex Taylor (Mechanic); Jan Buckingham (Nursemaid in Park).

New York Premiere: Paramount Theatre—March 28, 1945
New York Television Debut: CBS—May 10, 1964

### Synopsis

Lieutenant Dan Bellamy sinks a Japanese carrier in the South Pacific by crash diving his fighter plane into the vessel and by releasing two bombs he carriers. His last words are picked up by naval monitor and later relayed to the world. The momentous message says he would like to be home at his old desk at Meglin's Typewriter Company and to walk through Central Park with Peggy. However, Dan does not die and he did not say Peggy, but Piggy his canine terrier. Later, when it is learned that Dan is alive and he is returning to the States on furlough, Peggy Martin, the "girl" of the message, is besieged by newsreels, radio, and newspapers. Peggy meets Dan at the airport, accompanied by her boss, Marvin P. Meglin. Dan permits himself to be dragged to the Meglin household as a house guest, with Peggy accompanying him. When Peggy discovers that she is not the object of Dan's publicized dreams, she informs him that it's just as well since her love belongs to Albert Beagell, manager of Meglin's accounts receivable department. Both Peggy and Dan soon decide that they must keep up the pretense, at least while he is in New York, but Dan insists that her "boyfriend" Albert must come along on each and every one of their outings. Although Peggy has told Albert the whole story, he tries to become amorous with her nevertheless which makes Dan hit Albert on the jaw, and later ask Peggy to wed him when the war is finally over. But Peggy wants her bit of revenge for Dan's previous thoughtlessness, so, at the last minute, with the connivance of Mrs. Meglin and the latter's amiable brother, Judge Oscar Stimson, she tells Dan that their romance is off. Matters end happily, however, at the destroyer-launching ceremony, where, with the eager public listening into the radio coverage, the judge announces his intention to wed Peggy and Dan right there and then.

◆◆◆

"Is She His or Is She Ain't?" was the promotional copy for this manufactured froth produced and directed by Mitchell Leisen whose special adeptness for well-timed comedy pacing was a major factor in the film's success. If the mistaken identity gimmick seemed very familiar, it was, since scripter Norman Krasna, who had worked on past Leisen films, had employed a variation of it for his exceptionally popular Broadway comedy *Dear Ruth*.

*Practically Yours* found the two stars playing their roles "with all the hectic humor of actors experienced in light romance" [Bosley Crowther *(New York Times)*]. But with the approaching end of World War II—the film was lensed February-April 1944, but not released till the following year—times and tastes were rapidly changing and both Colbert, at age forty, and MacMurray, at age thirty-eight, knew they were too old for the lead assignments, and could not disguise their discomfort with the inopportune casting. In any case, *Practically Yours* proved to be her final studio picture, as she decided to freelance thereafter. MacMurray, with his Paramount contract nearly expired, had been allowed to go dramatic in *Double Indemnity* (1944) and surprised both employers and public by being very effective in that murder thriller. But his portrayal of the middle-to-low brow, good-natured male was his etched screen type and no one would give MacMurray much of a chance above and beyond the *Practically Yours* type of film.

Certainly *Practically Yours* pushed neither Colbert nor MacMurray to any new heights of comedy experience. They simply did what they had been doing so well previously once more, giving some viewers the uneasy feeling that the seeming spontaneity of this star team was too carefully prefabricated and precisely calculated. Nevertheless, the movie did exceedingly well at the boxoffice.

Although Gil Lamb's performance as the 4-F civilian lover verged on the grotesque, this Leisen entry benefitted greatly from the always benign Cecil Kellaway, the chipper Robert Benchley and Rosemary DeCamp as a war wife whose husband does not return from service.

## THE EGG AND I
### *(Universal, 1947) 108M.*

Producer, Chester Erskine, Fred F. Finklehoffe; associate producer, Leonard Goldstein; director, Erskine; based on the book by Betty Mac-Donald; music, Frank Skinner; assistant director, Frank Shaw; production designer, Bernard Herzbrun; sound, Charles Felstead; camera, Milton Krasner; editor, Russell Schoengarth.

Claudette Colbert (Betty MacDonald); Fred MacMurray (Bob Mac-Donald); Marjorie Main (Ma Kettle); Louise Allbritton (Harriet Putnam); Percy Kilbride (Pa Kettle); Richard Long (Tom Kettle); Billy House (Billy Reed); Ida Moore (Old Lady); Donald MacBride (Mr. Henty); Samuel S. Hinds (Sheriff); Esther Dale (Mrs. Hicks); Elisabeth Risdon (Betty's Mother); John Berkes (Geoduck); Vic Potel (Crowbar); Fuzzy Knight (Cab Driver); Isabel O'Madigan (Mrs. Hicks' Mother); Dorothy Vaughan (Maid); Sam McDaniel (Waiter); Jesse Graves (Porter); Herbert Heywood (Mailman); Joe Bernard (Pettingrew); Ralph Littlefield (Photographer); Jack

Baxley (Judge); Carl Bennett (Attendant); Howard Mitchell (Announcer); George Lloyd (Farm Hand); Robert Cherry, Joe Hiser, Joe Recht, Sammy Schultz, Joe Ploski (Goons); Hector V. Sarno (Burlaga); Lou Mason (Bergheimer); Judith Bryant, Gloria Moore, Eugene Persson, Diane Florentine, George McDonald, Colleen Alpaugh, Teddy Infuhr, Robert Winane, Diane Graeff, Kathleen Mackey, Robert Beyers (Kettle Children); Bob Perry, William Norton Bailey, Polly Van Bailey, Vangie Beilby, Earl Bennett, Nella Spaugh (People at Social); Nolan Leary (Announcer); Beatrice Roberts (Nurse).

New York Premiere: Radio City Music Hall—April 24, 1947
New York Television Debut: NBC—December 23, 1961

### Synopsis

Disgusted with the brokerage business, ex-Marine Bob MacDonald, just back from the war, informs his bride, Betty, that he has purchased a chicken farm which is to be their future home. Arriving at the farm Betty is horrified to find it to be a hopeless wreck, but she hides her disappointment in order not to spoil Bob's enthusiasm. Both of them plunge into their new rural life and attempt to restore their abode and the farm to some semblance of usability. Betty has other problems with which to contend, namely the interest shown in Bob by Harriet Putnam, a wealthy, flirtatious widow who owns a modern mechanized farm which fascinates Bob. Later Bob and Betty are heartbroken when their renovated farm is destroyed by fire, but helpful neighbors contribute enough building material to make a fresh start. At the county fair Betty discovers she is about to be a mother, but before she can tell Bob, he traipses off to visit Harriet's farm. When he fails to return home for dinner, Betty allows her fertile imagination to run wild and she runs off in a tissy to her mother's. During her absence, Bob writes her regularly but she returns his letters unopened. After her baby is born, Betty reconsiders and decides to return to Bob. She returns to the farm only to discover that he has moved into Harriet's home. Betty storms into the place determined to break with him for good. Only after her tirade against him does she learn that Bob had purchased the farm to give her and their child a decent home. She shamefacedly begs his forgiveness.

◆━━◆━━◆

Revealing that professional times had certainly changed since they teamed in *The Gilded Lily* twelve years prior, *Variety* reported, "Claudette Colbert and Fred MacMurray in starring roles are only moderate boxoffice draws currently, so the picture must pretty well stand on its own feet . . ."

The newly restructured Universal studios had acquired the screen rights to Betty MacDonald's diary-styled bestseller (one million copies had already been published by August 15, 1946) for a $100,000 downpayment plus a profit percentage. To insure that the film factory's first new big screen project would be a boxoffice dazzler, Colbert and MacMurray were corralled into the leading roles. The critics who had generally adored the book ("the tittering treatise on poultry") were not happy about the casting of the lead performers. "Against its bits of honest humor, MacMurray's portrait of a stock Hollywood goof and Miss Colbert's skilled smirking over situations which might better have been played straight, look flashy, flimsy and false" (*Time* magazine). "Miss Colbert is appealing but not entirely believable. . . . MacMurray runs through his role in his routine, superficial fashion" *(Variety)*.

However, the public felt entirely different, turning *The Egg and I* into a $5.5 million winner, and making it the best remembered starring film for the two stars. It must be recalled that this film appeared long before such derivative situation comedy television shows as "Green Acres" made this subject matter commonplace. Audiences of the 1940s found it novel and amusing to observe the misadventures of city-bred folks stumbling against mother nature and the eccentricities of country living. Under producer-director Chester Erskine's guidance the stars ignored subtlety in order to emphasize the overall broad effects. "Miss Colbert does a wheel-horse job of keeping up a long-winded jest. . . . MacMurray plays the role of the husband dead-pan, getting laughs only when he trips over things or fells a tree with prideful zeal right on top of his chicken house" [Howard Barnes *(New York Herald-Tribune)*].

Obviously, in translating *The Egg and I* to the screen, it was necessary to remove most of the authoress' racier sequences. Nevertheless, it was a pity that much of the book's earthy tang was distilled, that a phony romantic triangle was inserted for conventional audience appeal, and that technical customs of the time allowed the outdoorsy film to be filmed on obvious soundstage sets. As Bosley Crowther *(New York Times)* pointed out, ". . . a good opportunity was here lost to do a delightful satire upon the movement back to the farm."

Most of the oncamera misadventures fall, of course, to Colbert, because it is supposed to be always funnier to watch a well-bred miss run amuck in the backyard. Thus we have her tangling with a tricky kitchen stove, falling down in a muddy pigpen, dropping into the rain barrel off the roof, or coping with a weird assortment of characters who insist upon dancing with her at the community supper. Given the tenor of *The Egg and I* it is not surprising that a good deal of Colbert's screen time is devoted to coping with jealousy rather than the productivity of her egg-laying chickens. If Colbert is a bit too arch in these farce scenes, and too proficiently slick in her motherhood sequences, she certainly comes alive in her encouragement speech when she tells the disheartened MacMurray that if San Francisco and Chicago can be rebuilt, so can their destroyed little chicken farm.

When *The Egg and I* was not focusing on the half-demented shenanigans of its proponents with their sagging porches, leaking roofs, washed out vegetable gardens, and overly stubborn pigs, it offered filmgoers their first delightful peek at the oddest screwball screen family of all times, the Kettle family, who live down the road apiece from Colbert and MacMurray. With nasal-twanged Percy Kilbride as the devoutly lazy father and sand-paper-voiced, herculean Marjorie Main as the mother, they presided over a brood of thirteen unruly hillbilly children, living in a shambles of a farm that made *Tobacco Road* look magnificent. So popular were these subordinate characters in *The Egg and I* (Main would be Oscar-nominated but lose the Best Supporting Actress bid to Celeste Holm of *Gentlemen's Agreement*) that Universal would reteam the character players into the long running *Ma and Pa Kettle* feature film series.

## FAMILY HONEYMOON
*(Universal, 1948) 80M.*

Producer, John Beck, Z. Wayne Griffin; director, Claude Binyon; based on the novel by Homer Croy; screenplay, Dane Lussier; art directors, Bernard Herzbrun, Richard H. Riedel; set decorators, Russell A. Gausman, Al Fields, music, Frank Skinner; music director, Milton Schwarzwald; orchestrator, David Tamkin; assistant director, Frank Shaw; costumes, Orry-Kelly; makeup, Bud Westmore; sound, Leslie I. Carey; special effects, David S. Horsley; camera, William Daniels; editor, Milton Carruth.

Claudette Colbert (Katie Armstrong Jordan); Fred MacMurray (Grant Jordan); Rita Johnson (Minna Fenster); Gigi Perreau (Zoe); Jimmy Hunt (Charlie); Peter Miles (Abner); Lillian Bronson (Aunt Jo); Hattie McDaniel (Phyllis); Chill Wills (Fred); Catherine Doucet (Mrs. Abercrombie); Paul Harvey (Richard Fenster); Irving Bacon (Mr. Webb); Chick Chandler (Taxi Driver); Frank Jenks (Gas Station Attendant); Wally Brown (Tom Roscoe); Holmes Herbert (Reverend Miller); John Gallaudet (Professor Pickering); Wilton Graff (Dr. Wilson); Fay Baker (Fran Wilson); O. Z. Whitehead (Jess); Lorin Raker (Hotel Clerk); Sarah Edwards (Mrs. Carp); Anne Nagel (Irene Barlett); Lois Austin (Louise Pickering); Beatrice Roberts (Belle); William Norton Bailey (Todd); Frank MacGregor (Saunders); Barbara Challis, Lois Hall, Denise Kay (Girls); Frank Orth (Candy Butcher); Harry Hayden (Railroad Conductor); Almira Sessions (Maid); Constance Purdy (Helen Hockinson); Minerva Urecal (Mrs. Webb); Syd Saylor (Station Master); Joel Fluellen (Waiter); Smoki Whitfield (Porter); Jay Silverheels (Elevator Boy); Harold Goodwin (Guide); Nick Thompson (Indian Buck); Herbert Heywood (Station Agent); Edmund Cobb (Stage Driver); Richard Dumas, Carl Vernell, Bill Murphy, (Boys); Tom Chatterton (Stewart); John O'Connor (Interne); Ella Ethridge (Woman); Edward Short (Red Cap); Vangie Beilby (Woman Passenger); Snub Pollard (Man Passenger); Heinie Conklin (Man on Train).

New York Premiere: Radio City Music Hall—February 24, 1949
New York Television Debut: CBS—February 16, 1963

## Synopsis

Katie Armstrong, the widowed mother of three children (Zoe, Charlie, Abner), agrees to wed college professor Grant Jordan. On the day of the wedding, Katie's sister suffers an accident, leaving her with no one to care for the children. Thus she is forced to take the three kids along on her honeymoon trip to the Grand Canyon. The trip is marked by considerable confusion and delay when the children get off the train at a small wayside station and are left behind. After a hectic search they are eventually found at the home of farmer Webb. Since it had become necessary to spend the night at the farm, Katie is forced to sleep with the children, and Grant with the hired hand. After an arduous trip by day coach, they finally reach the Grand Canyon, where Katie is distraught to find among the resort guests, blonde Minna Fenster, her former rival for Grant's affections. Between Minna's machinations and the children's endless mischievous pranks, Katie and Grant are unable to find any time for themselves. When Grant finally loses his patience and gives the kids a much-deserved spanking, Katie becomes incensed and they quarrel. He calls off the honeymoon and they make their way home separately. Katie, arriving first, learns that Minna is already back in town and has arranged a welcome-home party just to embarrass Katie. But through clever maneuvering, Katie arranges a reconciliation with Grant, and they are able to enter their home together and be properly "surprised."

◆◆◆

With the boxoffice goldmine of *The Egg and I* as a glittering precedent, Universal promptly allowed ex-scriptwriter-now-director Claude Binyon to handle *Family Honeymoon* which it was hoped would lure the public into theatres. The film did just that but to a far lesser extent than *The Egg and I,* partly because it was a much less congenial comedy than the similarly folksy *Mr. Blandings Builds His Dream House* (1948), and partly because it duplicated most of the situations of its screen original.

If *The Egg and I* had seen Claudette Colbert and Fred MacMurray being yanked down from their seemingly unimpeachable stardom thrones, *Family Honeymoon* accelerated the process. "The most familiar thing about this picture is its stars, who may have put in too many years as models of romantic discomfiture" (*Time* magazine). "The stars bravely maintain the characteristics that have endeared them to the public, but in this case they cannot intrigue any one. Miss Colbert, mothering the holy terrors, is mostly sunny and warm, and even her jealousy at a rival [Rita Johnson] has gentle overtones. MacMurray tries valiantly and naively to be a father to the kids and a husband to his wife, and he worked the whipped-puppy look for all it is worth, when the one interferes with the other" [Otis L. Gurnsey, Jr. *(New York Herald-Tribune)*].

Buried within the faulty contrivances of this cinema exercise was a basic error in the idea of forcing the audience to laugh at the outrageous pranks of Colbert's and MacMurray's onscreen children, who would become, it was hoped, the viewer's children due to the audience's identification with the stars. By anyone's standards, it was hardly funny, and even downright humiliating, to guffaw at one's offsprings for eighty minutes.

Colbert and MacMurray would offer their *Family Honeymoon* characterizations on "Lux Radio Theatre" on April 4, 1949 and again on April 23, 1951.

## THE YEARS AFTER

Although Claudette Colbert's 1950s film work was negligible, in particular, illness forcing her out of *All about Eve* (1950), she turned in some very effective television emoting, especially on the "Best of Broadway" video series. Happily for those fortunate enough to obtain tickets, she returned to the New York stage in *The Marriage-Go-Round* (1958) with her past movie vis-a-vis, Charles Boyer, cast as her droll co-star. Her next stage effort, *Julia, Jake and Uncle Joe* (1961) closed within a night, and her last movie to date, *Parrish* (1961), was a Delmer Daves color showcase, but only for Troy Donahue's sweaters and the Connecticut tobacco fields and not Colbert as the youth's mother. *The Irregular Verb to Love* (1963) with Cyril Ritchard proved to be her last Broadway sojourn for some spell, even though at one time she was mentioned as a possible replacement of Katharine Hepburn in *Coco* (1970). In 1973-1974, Colbert abandoned her estate in St. James, Barbados, to embark on a national tour of the late Moss Hart's previously unproduced play *Landing,* now called *Community for Two.* As any playgoer who saw the production can attest, age has not dimmed her beauty, charm or comedy timing.

Like Henry Fonda, James Stewart, and John Wayne, Fred MacMurray has proven to be one of the most enduring leading men on the Hollywood scene. He was stagnating in middling screen Westerns in the late 1950s when Walt Disney cast him in *The Shaggy Dog* (1959) which brought $11.6 million in distributors' domestic rentals. It was the first of seven features he would make for Disney's Buena Vista releasing company. Meanwhile, in 1960, director Billy Wilder of *Double Indemnity* cast the star as a realistic executive heel in *The Apartment,* and MacMurray debuted in his half-hour video series, "My Three Sons," which enjoyed a run of twelve seasons and a total of 311 episodes. Today, MacMurray, his wife June Haver, and their children reside in fortified luxury, but the actor is still busy at his craft, most recently as a television spokesman for Greyhound Bus. His *The Chadwicks* (1974) telefeature pilot did not sell as a sustaining video series.

Although the settings and clothing styles of a Colbert-MacMurray film may now seem very dated, viewing one of the team's several movies is still, today, a most envigorating experience. The duo, particularly Colbert, has few peers in the world cinema when it comes to romantically sparring in the best of movie comedy traditions. It would take a sterner soul than this writer not to find delight anew in rewatching the acting pair maneuver through their dialog and action, creating a blend of expert, if artificial interaction, that finds a comfortable middle ground between the alluring exotica of a Marlene Dietrich-Gary Cooper encounter and the more roisterous intermingling of a Paulette Goddard-Ray Milland foray.

In a pose for **Sweethearts** (MGM, 1938)

# Chapter 11

# Nelson Eddy
# &
# Jeanette MacDonald

## NELSON EDDY

6′
180 pounds
Blond hair
Blue eyes
Cancer

*Real name: Same. Born June 29, 1901, Providence, Rhode Island. Married Anne Franklin (1939). Died March 6, 1967.*

FEATURE FILMS:

*Broadway to Hollywood* (MGM, 1933)
*Dancing Lady* (MGM, 1933)
*Student Tour* (MGM, 1934)
*Hollywood Party* (MGM, 1934)°†
*David Copperfield* (MGM, 1935)°†
*Naughty Marietta* (MGM, 1935)
*Rose Marie* (MGM, 1936)
*Maytime* (MGM, 1937)
*Rosalie* (MGM, 1937)
*The Girl of the Golden West* (MGM, 1938)
*Sweethearts* (MGM, 1938)

*Let Freedom Ring* (MGM, 1939)
*Balalaika* (MGM, 1939)
*New Moon* (MGM, 1940)
*Bitter Sweet* (MGM, 1940)
*The Chocolate Soldier* (MGM, 1941)
*I Married an Angel* (MGM, 1942)
*The Phantom of the Opera* (Univ., 1943)
*Knickerbocker Holiday* (UA, 1944)
*Make Mine Music* (RKO, 1946)°
*Northwest Outpost* (Rep., 1947)

°Voice only
†Positive verification has yet to be accomplished

# JEANETTE MacDONALD

**5′ 4″**
**110 pounds**
**Red gold hair**
**Blue green eyes**
**Gemini**

*Real name: Same. Born June 18, 1901, Philadelphia, Pennsylvania. Married Gene Raymond (1937). Died January 14, 1965.*

**FEATURE FILMS:**

*The Love Parade* (Par., 1929)
*The Vagabond King* (Par., 1930)
*Galas de la Paramount* (Spanish version of *Paramount on Parade*) (Par., 1930)
*Monte Carlo* (Par., 1930)
*Let's Go Native* (Par., 1930)
*The Lottery Bride* (UA, 1930)
*Oh, for a Man* (Fox, 1930)
*Don't Bet on Women* (Fox, 1931)
*Annabelle's Affairs* (Fox, 1931)
*One Hour with You* (Par., 1932)
*Love Me Tonight* (Par., 1932)
*The Cat and the Fiddle* (MGM, 1934)
*The Merry Widow* (MGM, 1934)
*Naughty Marietta* (MGM, 1935)
*Rose Marie* (MGM, 1936)

*San Francisco* (MGM, 1936)
*Maytime* (MGM, 1937)
*The Firefly* (MGM, 1937)
*The Girl of the Golden West* (MGM, 1938)
*Sweethearts* (MGM, 1938)
*Broadway Serenade* (MGM, 1939)
*New Moon* (MGM, 1940)
*Bitter Sweet* (MGM, 1940)
*Smilin' Through* (MGM, 1941)
*I Married an Angel* (MGM, 1942)
*Cairo* (MGM, 1942)
*Follow the Boys* (Univ., 1944)
*Three Daring Daughters* (MGM, 1948)
*The Sun Comes Up* (MGM, 1948)

In **New Moon** (MGM, 1940)

In **Rose Marie** (MGM, 1936)

In **Naughty Marietta** (MGM, 1935)

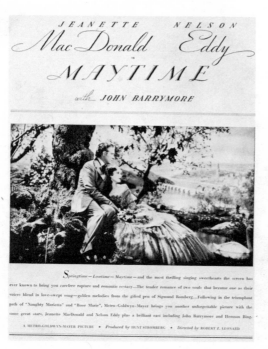

Advertisement for **Maytime** (MGM, 1937)

Paul Lucas, Jeanette MacDonald, and Nelson Eddy in the scrapped version of **Maytime**

In **Maytime**

Nelson Eddy, Frank O'Connor, Jeanette MacDonald, Ynez Seabury in **The Girl of the Golden West** (MGM, 1938)

In a publicity pose for **I Married an Angel** (MGM, 1942)

On the set of **Sweethearts** (MGM, 1938)

Advertisement for **Bitter Sweet** (MGM, 1940)

Nelson Eddy, Jeanette MacDonald, Felix Bressart, and Curt Bois in **Bitter Sweet**

# NAUGHTY MARIETTA
## *(MGM, 1935) 106M.*

Producer, Hunt Stromberg; director, W. S. Van Dyke II; based on the operetta by Rida Johnson Young and Victor Herbert; screenplay, John Lee Mahin, Frances Goodrich, Albert Hackett; music adaptor, Herbert Stothart; songs, Herbert, Young, and Gus Kahn; art director, Cedric Gibbons; assistant director, Eddie Woehler; costumes, Adrian; sound, Douglas Shearer; camera, William Daniels; editor, Blanche Sewell.

Jeanette MacDonald [Princess Marie (Marietta)]; Nelson Eddy (Captain Warrington); Frank Morgan (Governor d'Annard); Elsa Lanchester (Madame d'Annard); Douglass Dumbrille (Uncle); Joseph Cawthorn (Herr Schuman); Cecilia Parker (Julie); Walter Kingsford (Don Carlos); Greta Meyer (Frau Schuman); Akim Tamiroff (Rudolpho); Harold Huber (Abe); Edward Brophy (Zeke); Mary Doran, Jean Chatburn, Pat Farley, Jane Barnes, Kay English, Linda Parker, Jane Mercer (Casquette Girls); Walter Long (Pirate Leader); Dr. Edouard Lippe (Innkeeper); Olive Carey (Madame Renavant); William Desmond (Gendarme Chief); Cora Sue Collins (Felice); Guy Usher (Ship's Captain); Louis Mercier (Duelist); Robert McKenzie (Town Crier); Ben Hall (Mama's Boy); Harry Tenbrook (Prospective Groom); Edward Keane (Major Bonnell); Edward Norris, Ralph Brooks (Suitors); Richard Powell (Messenger); Wilfred Lucas (Announcer); Arthur Belasco, Tex Driscoll, Edward Hearn, Edmund Cobb, Charles Dunbar, Frank Hagney, Ed Brady (Scouts).

New York Premiere: Capitol Theatre—March 22, 1935
New York Television Debut: CBS—April 19, 1957

### Synopsis

Princess Marie de la Bonfain is to be wed against her will to Don Carlos de Braganza, a Spanish Grandee. This forthcoming marriage is pleasing to her uncle, the Prince de le Bonfain, and sanctioned by His Majesty, Louis XV of France. When Marie learns that the wedding is to take place the following week, she quickly decides upon changing places with her maid Marietta who is to be among the casquette girls leaving for Louisiana to become the wives of colonists. Marietta is actually in love with a young man from Marseilles but they are too poor to wed. Marie offers to give her the needed money so she can marry her sweetheart, and she takes Marietta's place. During the long voyage to America, Marie tries to complete the song started by her old singing teacher and keeps aloof from most of the girls. As they near land, the ship is seized by pirates and the brigands take the girls ashore. A band of Yankee scouts, under the leadership of Captain Richard Warrington, rescues the girls. Marie finds herself attracted to Richard, but he informs

303

her he has no intention of marrying because he enjoys his soldier's life. The girls are then escorted to New Orleans where they are expected to choose husbands from the colonists. Marie does not want to wed any of them so she tells Governor d'Annard she is a bad girl. He has her taken away from the other girls and she gets a job working with a marionette show. Richard finds her and escorts her through the city. He finds he loves her and is about to confess his love when she is apprehended by the Governor's representatives. He has learned her real identity and the Prince and Don Carlos have come to take her back to France. That night a ball is given in her honor at the Governor's palace. Her uncle informs her that unless she agrees to sail for France, Richard will be harmed. When Richard arrives at the ball she pretends she is not sailing for several days. When he learns the truth, he induces her to elope with him and they will go to the wilderness where the French government can never reach them. They leave the palace with the help of Richard's faithful soldiers.

◆◆◆

When the Victor Herbert-Rida Johnson Young operetta *Naughty Marietta* was first produced on Broadway in 1910 with Emma Trentini and Orville Harrold, it enjoyed a 136-performance run. The big question, however, was how would audiences react to the veteran property some twenty-five years later when it was refurbished for the screen?

Soprano Jeanette MacDonald thought she knew the answer. After all, she had been a musical comedy player on Broadway in the 1920s and had enjoyed two peaks (1929, 1932) of popularity at Paramount in Ernst Lubitsch musical movies, often teamed with Maurice Chevalier. When Louis B. Mayer in 1933 signed the operetta star to a MGM contract, he offered her a choice of Jerome Kern's *The Cat and the Fiddle* or *Naughty Marietta* for her cinema bow on the Metro lot. She thought *both* vehicles hopelessly outdated and detested the idea of filming *either* one, but finally settled on *The Cat and the Fiddle* (1934) with fading studio lead Ramon Novarro as her vis-a-vis. She would have much preferred starring in Richard Rodgers' and Lorenz Hart's *I Married an Angel*, but the original script was so spicy in concept that the newly restructured production code office had rejected it. (The composers retrieved their material and turned it into a Broadway show in 1938.)

Thereafter, Mayer was insistent that his pet project, *Naughty Marietta*, be filmed, but a suitable leading man could not be located, even though MGM was considering pairing MacDonald with opera and concert performer Nelson Eddy in a non-musical remake of *The Prisoner of Zenda*. Eddy had made his movie debut at MGM in 1933 in *Broadway to Hollywood*, followed by two more assignments, in each of which he had one specialty song number. Meanwhile, Chevalier and Lubitsch had come over to MGM to film a new rendition of *The Merry Widow* with Metropolitan Opera star Grace Moore,* but when she had a dispute

*When her Columbia picture *One Night of Love* (1934) emerged as a surprise hit, it not only revitalized her screen career but gave a new breath of vitality to movie operettas.

with the Frenchman over billing, she withdrew and MacDonald stepped into the casting breech. While that film was too expensively mounted to be a financial success, MGM was convinced of MacDonald's further boxoffice potential, and renegotiated her contract for a five year term.

Allan Jones, who would later have a feature role in MacDonald's *Rose Marie* (1936) and then co-star with her in *The Firefly* (1937), was Mayer's choice when the mogul decided it was time for *Naughty Marietta* to be filmed and no one else would do. However, the Shubert Brothers refused to release Jones from his stage contract, so Mayer finally agreed to give baritone Eddy his big film opportunity.

Just as a far different type of screen musical, *42nd Street* (1933), had made Depression-weary audiences forget their problems, so *Naughty Marietta* proved an excellent elixir for the problems of contemporary living. It was celluloid escapism at its best: lavishly mounted, grandly romantic, beautifully melodic. Its commercial and artistic success allowed MGM finally to accept its inability to turn Lawrence Tibbett and Grace Moore into enduring screen celebrities in the early 1930s. And, best of all, the two *Naughty Marietta* leads were greeted with hosannas by the critics and an adoring public.

Edwin Schallert *(Los Angeles Times)* happily alerted his readers, "For facility in an interpretation, Jeanette MacDonald quite surpasses herself. . . . [she] invests her portrayal with charm and humanness." Richard Watts, Jr. *(New York Herald-Tribune)* penned, "With all proper respect for Miss MacDonald, however, the triumph of the Van Dyke version is registered by Nelson Eddy, of the concert stage. . . . Mr. Eddy has a brilliant baritone voice, he seems thoroughly masculine, he is engaging and good looking and he gives the appearance of being unaffected. . . . He seems to me a far more valuable acquisition than even the celebrated Mr. [Lawrence] Tibbett."

A major ingredient in the success of *Naughty Marietta* was that both MGM and its director, W. S. Van Dyke II,* had greatly profited from Lubitsch's error in making the 1934 *The Merry Widow* such a cynical and disillusioned product. Throughout *Naughty Marietta* there is a thankfully exuberant spirit which makes the somewhat absurd melodramatics of the creaky storyline forgivable and allows viewers to concentrate on the operetta-style romancing and the gorgeous Herbert score (with new lyrics by Gus Kahn).

A prime delight of this *Naughty Marietta* is the comic talent of perky MacDonald, who lightens the potential austerity of certain parts of the film by her vivacious, tongue-in-cheek characterization. Anyone who has ever disputed MacDonald's sterling abilities as a funny lady oncamera need only study the opening shipboard scene in *Naughty Marietta* to learn differently. At this point in the story she has run away from her

---

*Van Dyke II was having equal success in guiding the destinies of another screen team at MGM. He had helmed *Manhattan Melodrama* (1934) and *The Thin Man* (1934) which launched William Powell and Myrna Loy as a perfect screen duo.

dour uncle (Douglass Dumbrille) and has secreted herself among the casquette girls heading for America. To make sure that the French soldiers passing among the girls on the loading ship do not suspect her actual identity, she launches into an Elsa Lanchester type pose, complete with frumpy attire and spectacles, chawing noisily on an end of bread and making outlandish grimaces. Could anyone suspect this bizarre creature is the pretty Princess Marie? No siree! To complete her masquerade, MacDonald even waves an energetic goodbye to a drunk tottering on the dock, pretending the soused man is her brother.

Another wonderful sequence within *Naughty Marietta* that typifies the best of the MacDonald-Eddy silver screen interplay occurs when the casquette girls have been taken ashore by the pirates, who are about to molest the frightened young women. Suddenly, there is the sound of men singing "Tramp, Tramp, Tramp" and soon Captain Richard Warrington (Eddy) and his brave woodsmen march into view, dispatch the dastardly pirates, and put the damsels at their ease. Frontiersman Eddy, in his fringed buckskin outfit, quickly spots the attractive MacDonald and compliments her by saying, "Nothing short of a wooden leg should have kept you from getting married." Eddy soon is captivated by MacDonald's jaunty air and, as they later sit at the campfire, he tells "Blue Eyes" (his pet name for her), "So you like me as a nightingale. Wasn't I magnificent. . . . I was known as the mudlark of the Mississippi. Don't tell a soul." MacDonald: "I won't. You will." Thereafter, when MacDonald begins to posture and become haughty in the evening light, Eddy chides her oncamera, "There goes that chin to the moon again." This continual teasing quality to their shared dialog makes this *Naughty Marietta* hero and heroine a very engaging couple. They are quite relaxed and human, hardly as lugubrious as the team's detractors would have us believe.

While "The Italian Street Song" sung by MacDonald would remain a perennial favorite of the actress' fans, it was "Ah, Sweet Mystery of Life" which emerged as the big hit number of the film, making the "ancient" song seem freshly new. Audience interest in this tune is kept alive throughout the picture, since, early in the story during the Parisian scenes, MacDonald is seen taking a lesson from her music teacher (Joseph Cawthorn) and he plays the tune. Nevertheless, he cannot find the right tempo or full lyrics for its completion. Aboard ship MacDonald thinks about how to finish the song, and does. Later at the Governor's (Frank Morgan) ball, she gives the tune a full scale performance. She is dressed in Louis XV style finery, including a white wig, while Eddy is garbed in accepted formal wear of the day, from his stylish shoes to his powdered hair. With more than the requisite urgency needed for the dramatic sequence of an operetta, the two lovers sing of their passion for one another, each not wanting to accept the idea that they may be parted at any moment to endure separate fates. With the resplendent visual backgrounds and the Herbert Stothart scoring-adaptation, a viewer can hardly help being overwhelmed by this emotional show piece. Truly, "Ah, Sweet Mystery of Life" is a grand moment of musical movie history.

At the opening of *Naughty Marietta*, MacDonald's princess has said, "I haven't seen a man I could love. I'd like to see him standing tall and strong in the wind and the sun." For her, Eddy's Warrington is just such a man, and near the finale, she informs him, "You're all that I want. All there is." The finale finds Eddy and MacDonald (she garbed in a fetching cloak and lace cap) riding off on horseback into the wilderness with his faithful men as guard, as the principals and chorus re-sing bits of "Tramp, Tramp, Tramp" and "Ah, Sweet Mystery of Life."

MacDonald and Eddy would recreate their *Naughty Marietta* roles on "Lux Radio Theatre" on June 12, 1944.

## ROSE MARIE
### *(MGM, 1936) 113M.*

Producer, Hunt Stromberg; director, W. S. Van Dyke II; based on the operetta by Otto A. Harbach, Oscar Hammerstein II, Rudolf Friml, Herbert Stothart; screenplay, Frances Goodrich, Albert Hackett, Alice Duer Miller; music director, Herbert Stothart; songs, Harbach, Hammerstein II, and Friml; Kahn and Herbert Stothart; Sam Lewis, Joe Young, and Harry Akst; Shelton Brooks; totem pole dance staged by Chester Hale; operatic episodes staged by William von Wymetal; art directors, Cedric Gibbons, Joseph Wright, Edwin B. Willis; gowns, Adrian; sound, Douglas Shearer; camera, William Daniels; editor, Blanche Sewell.

Jeanette MacDonald (Marie de Flor); Nelson Eddy (Sergeant Bruce); James Stewart (John Flower); Reginald Owen (Meyerson); Allan Jones (Romeo); Gilda Gray (Bella); George Regas (Boniface); Robert Greig (Cafe Manager); Una O'Connor (Anna); Lucien Littlefield (Storekeeper); Alan Mowbray (Premier); David Niven (Teddy); Herman Bing (Mr. Daniels); James Conlin (Joe); Dorothy Gray (Edith); Mary Anita Loos (Corn Queen); Aileen Carlyle (Susan); Halliwell Hobbes (Mr. Gordon); Paul Porcasi (Emil); Ed Dearing (Mounted Policeman); Pat West (Traveling Salesman); Milton Owen (Stage Manager); David Clyde (Doorman); Russell Hicks (Commandant); Rolfe Sedan, Jack Pennick (Men); David Robel, Rinaldo Alacorn (Dancers); Leonard Carey (Louis); Bert Lindley (Trapper).

New York Premiere: Capitol Theatre—January 31, 1936
New York Television Debut: CBS—September 19, 1958

### Synopsis

Opera star Marie de Flor is on Canadian tour. While in Montreal she makes a conquest of the Premier of Canada, hoping to get him to pardon her brother, John Flower, who is in prison for having participated in a hold-up. When Marie learns that her brother has escaped from jail, killing a mountie in the process, and is now hiding out in the wilderness, she decides to see her brother. Her guide, Boniface, later steals her purse, and she decides to sing in a dancehall in order to earn some obviously needed money. The habituees of the place do not appreciate her type of singing, however, and she is discouraged. But Sergeant Bruce of the Northwest Mounted Police, who has been sent to capture Flower, recognizes the diva and when she leaves he follows her. He offers to help her get back her purse and takes her to the place where the Indians are staging their dances. She manages to spot Boniface, he returns her money, and agrees to complete the trek with her. Meanwhile, Bruce, wondering what she is doing in this wild country, deduces that she must be the hunted man's sister and decides to follow her. When Boniface observes the lawman following them, he departs quickly, leaving her alone. Bruce takes care of her and they go on together. She unwittingly leads him to her brother, and even though Bruce loves her, he must be true to his duty. Flower becomes Bruce's prisoner. Marie returns to the operatic stage, but one night while singing Tosca she collapses. She suffers a complete breakdown, seemingly losing all desire to recover. Her kindly manager Myerson, knowing her love for Bruce, sends for him. They are joyfully reunited.

◆—◆—◆

Rose Marie had wowed Broadway audiences for a 557-performance run in 1924, and later was a 1928 MGM silent picture with Joan Crawford and James Murray. When Metro planned a remake for the 1936 film season and Grace Moore again proved unavailable, Jeanette MacDonald and Nelson Eddy were reteamed. MGM hoped that, like Naughty Marietta, the public would find the new Rose Marie living up to the studio's blurb, "Lovers heartbeats set to enchanting music."

To suit the particular talents of MacDonald and Eddy, the Rose Marie storyline was drastically revamped to make it a showcase tale of "A Pampered Pet of the Opera [who] Meets a Rugged Canadian Mountie." The critics were generally enchanted with the silver screen results, insisting that the operetta ". . . comes to the screen unimpaired, if not improved" [Thornton Delehanty (New York Post)], and that the stars ". . . prove to be fully as delightful a combination here as they were in the film of Victor Herbert's Naughty Marietta" [Frank S. Nugent (New York Times)].

With W. S. Van Dyke II° at the helm of Rose Marie, the movie musical proved that an operetta could leave the confines of a stage-bound setting and not lose its essential intimacy. It showed that a melding of the Western picture and musical comedy was quite feasible. Although

°Later that year Van Dyke II would guide MacDonald and co-star Clark Gable through the paces of the exceedingly popular San Francisco (1936).

the location footage was shot at Lake Tahoe, on the California-Nevada border, *Rose Marie* has the look of the great Canadian wilderness, leading Nugent of the *Times* to state the movie is ". . . rich in scenic beauty as any picture that has come from Hollywood."

Tuneful versatility proved to be the keynote of the success of *Rose Marie*. Since MacDonald is cast as an opera star (her long real-life ambition) the picture opens at the Montreal Opera House with her performance of the waltz song, "Je Veux Vivre dans Ce Rêve," from *Romeo and Juliet°* and dueting with Allan Jones the death scene from the same opera Later, when MacDonald has left civilization and finds herself forced to perform at a frontier saloon to earn her keep, it is none other than ex-shimmy dancer Gilda Gray who instructs the prima donna in the art of putting over a number in a barroom setting. In the backwoods honky tonk, MacDonald performs snatches of "Dinah" and "Some of These Days" (with Gray) in a mock pop style that is entertaining to behold. Meanwhile, Eddy, who had scored in *Naughty Marietta* with the chorus-supported "Tramp, Tramp, Tramp," has a similar entry in *Rose Marie* when he is joined by fellow policemen in a rendering of "Song of the Mounties." His clarion call to love is enunciated in "Rose Marie I Love You." If the movie team's "Ah, Sweet Mystery of Life" had been well appreciated in *Naughty Marietta*, their dueting and continual refraining of "Indian Love Call"°° (which at times seems to echo from the very mountain peaks) would surmount their former success in enthusiastic response from moviegoers. "Indian Love Call" reflects the essence of the stars' romantic interaction in *Rose Marie* which is geared not on the pristine elegance of period piece ballrooms, but of the rugged outdoors. Still later, the film returns to an operatic milieu as MacDonald and Jones appear in a scene from *Tosca*, singing "He Asked Thy Life or My Love" (from Act 3 of Puccini's opera).

It is during the well-handled outdoor sequences of *Rose Marie* that the picture and its stars come most vibrantly to life. Paddling along the lakes in canoes, riding horseback along the mountain trails, or camping out under the stars, there is an idyllic open-air ambiance that buoys the storyline towards its well-wrought conclusion. It is difficult for any viewer to dismiss the hypnotic "Totem Tom Tom" Indian dance (extravagantly staged by Chester Hale). Likewise one cannot help but enjoy the joshing interplay between stubborn MacDonald and teasing Eddy when he begins to prepare supper over the campfire and she, although starving, is at first too proud to accept his hospitality.

*Rose Marie* surpassed *Naughty Marietta* in boxoffice receipts and acclaim, leading Richard Watts, Jr. *(New York Herald-Tribune)* to label

---

°MGM, never shy about promoting its own forthcoming products, was reminding viewers in its usual unsubtle way that later in 1936 they could witness an elaborate rendering of Shakespeare's *Romeo and Juliet* starring Norma Shearer and Leslie Howard.

°°Their RCA recording of that song in 1935 sold over one million copies. A too brief excerpt from *Rose Marie* with Eddy-MacDonald singing "Indian Love Call" was spotted in the compilation feature *That's Entertainment* (1974).

MacDonald and Eddy that "efficient screen operetta team." Watts enthused, "Never does she go to extremes in revealing the tirades of the eccentric star. . . . Always he manages to seem a genuine human being, which, I suspect, is something of an achievement for a singing actor with pretensions to vocal excellence."

In 1950, on radio's "Showtime U.S.A." MacDonald and Eddy recreated their *Rose Marie* roles.

When MGM yet again remade *Rose Marie* in 1954, this time in CinemaScope and color, with Ann Blyth and Howard Keel starred, it made one appreciate all the more general excellencies of the MacDonald-Eddy version, which is now shown on television under the title *Indian Love Call*.

## MAYTIME
### *(MGM, 1937) 132M.*

Producer, Hunt Stromberg; director, Robert Z. Leonard; based on the operetta by Rida Johnson Young, Sigmund Romberg; screenplay, Noel Langley; music adaptor-director, Herbert Stothart; songs, Stothart; Romberg and Young; Stothart, Bob Wright and Chet Forrest; James A. Bland; Wright and Forrest; Young, Cyrus Wood, and Romberg; adaptor of French libretto, Gilles Guilbert; vocal arranger, Leo Arnaud; opera sequences, William von Wymetal; art directors, Cedric Gibbons, Fredric Hope, Edwin B. Willis; gowns, Adrian; choreography, Val Raset; sound, Douglas Shearer; montages, Slavko Vorkapich; camera, Oliver T. Marsh; editor, Conrad A. Nervig.

Jeanette MacDonald [Marcia Mornay (Miss Morrison)]; Nelson Eddy (Paul Allison); John Barrymore (Nicolai Nazaroff); Herman Bing (August Archipenko); Tom Brown (Kip); Lynne Carver (Barbara Roberts); Rafaela Ottiano (Ellen); Charles Judels (Cabby); Paul Porcasi (Composer Trentini); Sig Rumann (Fanchon); Walter Kingsford (Rudyard); Edgar Norton (Secretary); Guy Bates Post (Emperor Louis Napoleon); Iphigenie Castiglioni (Empress Eugenie); Anna Demetrio (Madame Fanchon); Frank Puglia (Orchestra Conductor); Adia Kuznetzoff (Czaritza's Minister/Student at Cafe); John Le Sueur (Maypole Dancer); Russell Hicks (M. Bulliet the Voice Coach); Harry Davenport, Harry Hayden, Howard Hickman, Robert C. Fischer (Opera Directors); Harlan Briggs (Bearded Director); Frank Sheridan (O'Brien, a Director); Billy Gilbert (Drunk); Ivan Lebedeff (Empress' Dinner Companion); Leonid Kinsky (Student in Bar); Clarence Wilson (Waiter); Maurice Cass (Opera House Manager); Douglas Wood (Hotel Manager); Bernard Suss (Assistant Manager); Henry Roquemore (Publicity Man); Alexander Schonberg (French Proprietor); Mariska Aldrich (Opera Singer); The Don Cossack Chorus (Singers).

New York Premiere: Capitol Theatre—March 18, 1937
New York Television Debut: CBS—May 1, 1960

### Synopsis

In a tiny American town on May Day, 1906, a celebration is in progress. Miss Morrison, an elderly woman about whom little is known by the townspeople, goes to the town square to watch the program. When she learns that Kip Stuart may lose his sweetheart because the latter wants to go to New York for a singing career, she asks the girl to come see her. Miss Morrison reveals to Barbara that she is Marcia Mornay, the once great opera star, and decides to tell the girl her story. The scene fades to 1865 in the days of Louis Napoleon's France. Under the careful training of Nicolai Nazaroff, Marcia becomes a famous opera singer, believing she owes everything to her instructor. He has always treated her with the utmost of respect for which she is grateful, and, when he proposes marriage, she feels obligated to accept. Just before her marriage she meets Paul Allison, a carefree young American singer who has been living in Paris and refuses to take his music seriously. In a short time they fall in love, but Marcia insists she cannot go back on her word to Nazaroff, and so the lovers part. She weds Nazaroff. Years later in New York Paul and Marcia meet again, for he has been chosen to sing opposite her at the opening night of the Metropolitan Opera. The stirring love duet they sing so breaks down their reserve that they resolve not to part again. Nazaroff, who is desperately in love with his wife, cannot bear the thought of losing her, and in a fit of jealousy he goes to Paul's apartment and shoots him. The scene then fades back to Miss Morrison's garden where Kip has returned. Barbara says she is going to stay with him and they both leave arm in arm. Back in the garden life goes out of Miss Morrison's frail body and the young Marcia Mornay arises to meet the spirit of Paul Allison who sings from the gate. They move off happily, singing "Sweethearts."

◆━━◆

When Victor Herbert's *Maytime* descended on Broadway in August, 1917, Peggy Wood, Charles Purcell, and Ralph J. Herbert were the stars, and the operetta went on to a successful 492-performance run. B. P. Schulberg's Preferred Pictures produced a silent photoplay of the work in 1923 with Ethel Sannon and Harrison Ford starred and Clara Bow in a support role. MGM's Irving Thalberg believed the play was a perfect vehicle for Jeanette MacDonald, who had risen to number nine position in the survey of the top ten boxoffice attractions in America (largely through her work in *San Francisco*). With Nelson Eddy assigned as her co-star and Paul Lukas and Frank Morgan heading the supporting cast, the Edmund Goulding-directed project went before the Technicolor cameras. But then on September 14, 1936, thirty-seven-year-old Thalberg died. Production on *Maytime* was halted while the studio reorganized. In the reshuffling it was decreed that Hunt Stromberg would assume producer's responsibilities on the movie, and that as such almost all of the footage° already shot would be scrapped. The script which had focused most of the action in America was revised so that in the new scenario MacDonald and Eddy do not wed, but suffer the more tragic fate of being unfulfilled lovers who via the ending can remain young eternally. John Barrymore and Herman Bing were cast to replace the departing Lukas and Morgan. Robert Z. Leonard was chosen to direct the new version.

The resultant black-and-white version of *Maytime* cost some $1.5 million (probably including the approximate $500,000 spent on the abortive color version). However, despite the expenses incurred and the production problems endured, the results were worth it. *Maytime* emerged as the best of the team's features together, a "rich melancholy tapestry of music, love and regret" [Archer Winsten (*New York Post*)]. "The screen can do no wrong while these two are singing; when, in addition, it places a splendid production behind them, the result approaches perfection" [Frank S. Nugent (*New York Times*)].

In his survey book, *Gotta Sing Gotta Dance* (1970), film historian John Kobal points out, "All the resources of the world's most powerful film studio were lavished on . . . [*Maytime*]. The Empress Eugenie dresses, designed by Adrian, almost move themselves; Cedric Gibbons' reconstruction of the last days of the third Empire, requiring ball rooms, period apartments, Parisian bohemian quarters, and then the early American small town at the turn of the century, are uniformly superlative. Sydney Guilaroff designed the magnificent hairstyles, William Daniel's photography glows, and the story, based on the Sigmund Romberg operetta, gave MacDonald a part with greater range and depth than most she played at MGM. . . . [she] exhibits a self-mocking fundamental honesty and integrity that is part of her artless charm."

Without a doubt, *Maytime* is one of the most romantic films of the sound film era. It is so imposingly mounted that most viewers easily can forgive the basic maudlin nature of the screenplay, in which music and tears are so consciously intermingled. From the opening sequence which leads to the flashback we know that the heroine has endured a tragic fate, and the purpose of the 132-minute film is to elaborate upon the crucial events as prettily and melodiously as possible. Leonard, who would direct three of the team's screen pieces, gives full reign to the acting excellence of the aging Barrymore, cast as a Svengali type, which no doubt inspired MacDonald to loftier histrionics which in turn bolster her emotional scenes with Eddy.

Each MacDonald-Eddy film has its share of mocking courtship scenes,

°Several songs, including "Farewell to Dreams" which MacDonald-Eddy recorded for RCA and was a best seller, and selections from the second act of *Tosca*, were deleted from the second *Maytime*.

and *Maytime* is no exception. In this film the jibbing tomfoolery occurs the night Nicholai Nazaroff (Barrymore) asks Marcia Mornay (MacDonald) to wed him. She later finds herself restless and impulsively takes a horse drawn cab ride at two a.m. The trip ends in front of a cellar cafe on a bohemian type of street. She hears singing from inside and enters to find Paul Allison (Eddy) leading a group in harmonizing the "Students' Drinking Song." When she is recognized by the students, he rescues her from the tumult, and soon finds himself attracted to this fellow American. As he escorts the lovely lady to her carriage, he urges her to lunch with him the next afternoon. She initially refuses, but the next day she does come to his attic rooms where his teacher Archipenko (Bing) is present. After preparing the menu of ham and eggs, the soon-to-be-sweethearts, MacDonald and Eddy, toy with "Carry Me Back to Ole Virginny." The teasing intimacy of this sequence is matched by the extravagant tenderness of the St. Cloud's May Day country fair. Within this intricately staged affair Eddy is seen gently pushing MacDonald to and fro in a majestic swing, with her 'midst the revellers, and later strolling to a quiet forest spot at sunset where they sing "Will You Remember (Sweetheart)." This duet, the only hold-over from the stage show original, would become the screen team's theme song for years to come. It is this wonderfully bittersweet, romantic, dramatic number which they repeat at the teary fantasy-finale of *Maytime*.

Operatic sequences are quite craftily maneuvered into *Maytime* and seem far more appropriate than in most films of the day seeking to give the lead songstress opportunities to perform grand opera. At the palace reception of Louis Napoleon, she sings for the French sovereign, and later at the opera house she is performing a selection onstage while in the oncamera audience, Eddy and Bing are being ejected from their illegitimately gained seats. After MacDonald and Eddy separate and she pursues her career, she is seen in a "success" montage of operatic highlights. If the passages from Bizet's *Les Filles de Cadiz* and Meyerbeer's *Les Huguenots* had seemed impressive earlier in *Maytime,* they were merely preludes to the *Czaritza** performed by MacDonald-Eddy during a ten-minute Metropolitan Opera House stage scene.

If there were any filmgoers left who had not fallen victim to the charms of *Maytime* during its leisurely unfolding, the film's finale was guaranteed to solve that. The dying Eddy lies in MacDonald's arms and he tells her, "That day [at St. Cloud] did last all of my life." We then flash forward to see the elderly Miss Morrison (MacDonald) informing Barbara (Lynne Carver), "I only told you because I wanted to help you decide about Kip. I met Paul too late but you and Kip have all the world before you if you want to take it." After the young lovers make up and go off together, MacDonald slumps back in her seat. Just as she dies, we

---

*A "shadow opera" especially created for *Maytime* by Herbert Stothart, based on Tchaikovsky's Fifth Symphony.

witness the superimposed figure of the youthful opera singer, MacDonald, rising from the spot, summoned by the lilting call of Eddy's refrain of "Will You Remember (Sweetheart)." In death, a la *Peter Ibbetson*, the couple are finally reunited and walk together blissfully down the road, dueting "their song."

MacDonald and Eddy recreated their *Maytime* roles on "Lux Radio Theatre" on September 4, 1944.

*Maytime* has remained such an enduringly favorite picture that in many cities throughout America it is a standard item for television showing each May Day.

## THE GIRL OF THE GOLDEN WEST
### *(MGM, 1938) 120M.*°

Producer, William Anthony McGuire; director, Robert Z. Leonard; based on the play by David Belasco; screenplay, Isabel Dawn, Boyce DeGraw; music director, Herbert Stothart; choreography, Albertina Rasch; songs, Sigmund Romberg and Gus Kahn; art director, Cedric Gibbons; sound, Douglas Shearer; montages, Slavko Vorkapich; camera, Oliver Marsh; editor, W. Donn Hayes.

Jeanette MacDonald (Mary Robbins); Nelson Eddy [Ramerez (Lt. Johnson)]; Walter Pidgeon (Sheriff Jack Rance); Leo Carrillo (Mosquito); Buddy Ebsen (Alabama); Leonard Penn (Pedro); Priscilla Lawson (Nina Martinez); Bob Murphy (Sonora Slim); Olin Howland (Trinidad Joe); Cliff Edwards (Minstrel Joe); Billy Bevan (Nick); Brandon Tynan (The Professor); H. B. Warner (Father Sienna); Monty Woolley (Governor); Charley Grapewin (Uncle Davy); Noah Beery, Sr. (The General); Bill Cody, Jr. (Gringo); Jeanne Ellis (The Girl Mary); Ynez Seabury (Wowkle); Victor Potel (Stage Driver); Nick Thompson (Billy Jack Rabbit); Tom Mahoney (Handsome Charlie); Phillip Armenta (Long Face); Chief Big Tree (Indian Chief); Russell Simpson (Pioneer); Armand "Curley" Wright, Pedro Regas (Renegades); Gene Coogan (Manuel); Sergei Arabeloff (Jose); Alberto Morin (Juan); Joe Dominiguez (Felipe); Frank McGlynn (Pete, a Gambler); Cy Kendall Hank, a Gambler); E. Alyn Warren, Francis Ford (Miners); Hank Bell (Deputy); Walter Bonn (Lieutenant Johnson); Richard Tucker (Colonel); Virginia Howell (Governor's Wife).

New York Premiere: Capitol Theatre—March 24, 1938
New York Television Debut: CBS—December 14, 1957

°Filmed in Sepia

## Synopsis

Mary Robbins, the owner of the Polka Saloon in Cloudy Mountain, is respected by all, and loved by Sheriff Jack Rance. While on a trip to Monterey to visit Father Sienna, whom she had known for years, she meets and falls in love with Ramerez, outlaw leader of a robber gang, whom she later encounters at the governor's ball, he being disguised as Lieutenant Johnson. She returns home, filled with thoughts of him, and so when Rance asks her to marry him, she refuses. Ramerez arrives at the settlement to steal the money Mary is holding in safekeeping for the miners; but when he sees her, he naturally does not carry out his mission. She invites him to her cabin where he proposes marriage and she accepts. Rance, who has meanwhile discovered Ramerez's identity, goes to Mary's cabin and reveals the facts to her. This makes Mary quite unhappy and when Rance leaves, she orders Ramerez, who had been hiding in the cabin, to go. Later, when he is wounded by one of the sheriff's men, he returns to her cabin and she hides him once more. Rance returns, knowing that Ramerez is there. He agrees to play a game of poker with Mary in order to settle the matter. She loses, which means that Ramerez is to go free and that she will wed Rance. On the day of the marriage, the lovers accidentally meet at the church. When Rance overhears their conversation, he realizes the power of the love that Mary and Ramerez have for each other and decides to give up Mary. The lovers marry and leave for another state to start life anew.

◆◆◆

After *Maytime*, both Jeanette MacDonald and Nelson Eddy played opposite other leads in MGM screen musicals. She had joined with Allan Jones in *The Firefly* (1937) in which both were cast as master spies during the Napoleonic Wars in Spain. Eddy, meantime, had been paired with Ilona Massey (reputedly hired by Metro as a threat to the occasionally recalcitrant MacDonald) in a Cole Porter musical, *Rosalie* (1937), which spotlighted him as a Dick Powell type, and Eleanor Powell as his Ruby Keeler. The moderate success of these two films proved to the studio that the public would accept MacDonald and Eddy in separate screen vehicles, but not to the same popular degree as when they performed oncamera together. MGM finally took the hint and thereafter geared their publicity machinery towards promoting the two players in force as the illustrious movie team they were.*

The unfortunately cumbersome project selected to reunite the musical songbirds was *The Girl of the Golden West,* based on the 1905 David Belasco play hit which had starred Blanche Bates, Robert Hilliard,

---

*It did not seem to bother fans that in 1937 MacDonald wed actor Gene Raymond or that two years later Eddy married Anne Franklin. The team's onscreen romantic chemistry remained for most viewers as credible as ever.

and Frank Keenan. There had already been three (1914, 1923, 1930) photoplays of the drama, but this was to be the first screen musical adaptation, leading Metro to proclaim, "Glory bursts from the screen in the greatest musical love story of our times."

Sadly the 120-minute° film, lavishly mounted in sepia photography, was not what the fans wanted or the critics would accept. The *New York Times'* Frank S. Nugent called it ". . . a hopelessly old-fashioned piece of operatic machinery." With its archaic, melodramatic lowjinks, and its employment of all the artificiality and forced gaiety of a staged operetta, nothing jelled in proper proportion. Because of the film's extended prologue section, it was actually some forty-five minutes into the movie tale before the love team actually appeared onscreen together!

It was perhaps demanding too much of the histrionic talents of either MacDonald or Eddy to ask them to carry across the difficult characterizations in *The Girl of the Golden West* with any degree of marked success. MacDonald as Mary Robbins had to be a swaggering cowgirl, wearing breeches, sixshooter, and sombrero, and speak slangy language in a Southern drawl. On the other hand, Eddy as Ramerez was required to be the dark-haired, dashing Mexican-accented bandit, while as Lieutenant Johnson he was to be a rakish army officer of the Errol Flynn variety. At least MacDonald tossed a little levity into her performance (some viewers might have recalled her discomfiture when forced to wear costumed, corseted finery at the governor's ball), by which her character took on more human qualities. Unfortunately, there were very little acting distractions to relieve the wooden stick figure of Eddy's portrayal.

The critics were rather kind when reporting the state of *The Girl of the Golden West* to the legion of MacDonald-Eddy fans. "Jeanette MacDonald's voice, like her acting, seems continually to be improving. This cannot be said of her pictures" [Eileen Creelman *(New York Sun)*]. "His rich and glorious baritone almost saves the situation for him. But, really, he's not the type, in spite of a workmanlike but distinctly not a colorful portrayal of the outlaw Ramerez" [Irene Thirer *(New York Post)*].

Not unsurprisingly, *The Girl of the Golden West* had a rather unmemorable score, making one wish that some of the arias from Puccini's opera on the same subject could have been included. Among the film's songs we have MacDonald performing "Liebestraum" at the Polka Saloon for the boys while at the parish church she consents to sing "Ave Maria" for the congregation. On the way to the governor's ball when Eddy is pretending to be Lieutenant Johnson, he sings "Señorita" to her (a number dueted by Eddy and MacDonald at the picture's end). Thereafter, he becomes a bit too amorous, she slaps him, and then she hastens to the party without her escort. At the reception she performs "The

°Scenes including Ray Bolger as Happy Moore and Carol Tevis as Trixie La Verne were excised from the release print of *The Girl of the Golden West*.

Mariachi," which includes "Dance with Me My Love" done with Eddy, and later both stars perform "Who Are We to Say," the latter being the film's best received number. The movie even relies on a comedy relief song, "The West Ain't Wild Anymore" (performed by Buddy Ebsen), for some needed distraction from the starched main plot.

## SWEETHEARTS
### *(MGM, 1938) C-120M.*

Producer, Hunt Stromberg; director, W. S. Van Dyke II; based on the operetta by Harry B. Smith, Fred DeGresac, Robert B. Smith, Victor Herbert; screenplay, Dorothy Parker, Alan Campbell; songs, Herbert, Chet Forrest, Bob Wright; gowns, Adrian; art director, Cedric Gibbons; sound, Douglas Shearer; camera, Oliver Marsh, Allen Davey; editor, Robert J. Kern.

Jeanette MacDonald (Gwen Marlowe); Nelson Eddy (Ernest Lane); Frank Morgan (Felix Lehman); Ray Bolger (Hans); Florence Rice (Kay Jordan); Mischa Auer (Leo Kronk); Fay Holden (Hannah); Terry Kilburn (Gwen's Brother); Betty Jaynes (Una Wilson); Douglas McPhail (Harvey Horton); Reginald Gardiner (Norman Trumpett); Herman Bing (Oscar Engel); Allyn Joslyn (Dink Rogers); Raymond Walburn (Orlando Lane); Lucile Watson (Mrs. Merrill); Philip Loeb (Samuel Silver); Kathleen Lockhart (Aunt Amelia); Gene Lockhart (Augustus); Berton Churchill (Sheridan Lane); Olin Howland (Appleby); Gerald Hamer (Harry); Marvin Jones (Boy); Dorothy Gray (Girl); Emory Parnell (Fire Inspector); Maude Turner Gordon (Dowager); Jack George (Violinist); Charles Sullivan (Tommy the Fighter); Mira McKinney, Grace Hayle, Barbara Pepper (Telephone Operators); Irving Bacon (Assistant Director); Lester Dorr (Dance Director); Dalies Frantz (Concert Pianist).

New York Premiere: Capitol Theatre—November 22, 1938
New York Television Debut: CBS—December 20, 1959

### Synopsis

Gwen Marlowe and Ernest Lane, darlings of the Broadway musical comedy stage, are celebrating both the sixth anniversary of their appearance in *Sweethearts* and their sixth wedding anniversary, for they ran away and were married shortly after the curtain went up on the opening night. Idolized as sweethearts in private life as well as in their stage roles, they have become a Broadway symbol. Only on this special anniversary night do they realize how tired they are of the show and its routines and the stunts engineered to keep it before the public. The climax comes when the "intimate little party" to which producer Felix Lehman has invited them, turns out to be a national broadcast. When they return

317

home that night and quarrel with their relatives, they decide that Hollywood and the movies, a possible career that they always had rejected, might be the needed avenue of escape. Lehman, anxious to keep the pair in New York, has a sudden bright idea. His librettist Leo Kronk has just written a play on the theme that a woman in love can always be made to believe that she has a rival. By reading the play to Gwen and leading her to believe it is based on her own husband's infidelity to her, he plants the idea that Ernest is really in love with Kay Jordan, who is secretary to Gwen and Ernest. A violent quarrel breaks out between the two stars, they separate and form separate road companies to go on tour. While they are away, Kronk's play is produced, but flops. However, both Gwen and Ernest read reviews which reveal the show's plot and they realize how they had been tricked. They get in touch with one another, rush back to New York, and confront Lehman with proof of his perfidy. By emphasizing their loyalty to the stage he persuades them to remain true to the Broadway public by reopening the show.

◆ ◆ ◆

After the archaic *The Girl of the Golden West,* MGM determined to do better by their famed love team. While the vehicle selected, *Sweethearts,* derived from a 1913 Victor Herbert operetta set in a mythical kingdom, the Dorothy Parker-Alan Campbell screenplay relegated much of the original stage material to the operetta-within-the-movie sequences, and created a new *contemporary* storyline material for the bulk of the film. To insure the success of *Sweethearts,* Metro assigned W. S. Van Dyke II as director and allotted a liberal budget which permitted the use of the newly perfected three-color Technicolor.

The multi-hued two-hour songfest lived up to the studio's publicity which grandly announced, "Your heart will pound with excitement at the wonders of this great Show of Shows." *Sweethearts,* which even included an Adrian-designed fashion show, emerged an outstanding moneymaker of 1938 (and thereafter in reissue). Archer Winsten *(New York Post)* may have coyly quipped, ". . . somewhere in the course of modernizing *Sweethearts* both the heart and the sweetness have been lost," but that critic was in the distinct minority. B. R. Crisler *(New York Times)* acclaimed, ". . . such a dream of ribbons, tinsel, Technicolor, and sweet, theatrical sentiment. . . ."

Within their previous joint entries, MacDonald and Eddy had been somewhat hampered by the confines of the operetta form. In *Sweethearts,* this stylization was de-emphasized during the course of the backstage story which allowed the stars to emote in a far more natural manner. ". . . they are the loveliest, doviest couple we have met in the last decade, even in a movie . . ." claimed Crisler of the *Times.* The reviewer might have mentioned that the scenarists had smartly contrived to allow the co-leads to lightly parody themselves as the Lunts of the operetta world. Within the picture, MacDonald and Eddy cavort in a three-ring circus of bickering, apologizing, making up, posturing, quarreling, reconciling, romancing, charming the public, and, most of all, harmonizing together almost as often as they sing separately. Interesting parallels could be made between the storyline and performances of *Sweethearts* with Warner Bros.' *It's Love I'm After* (1937), starring Leslie Howard and Bette Davis.

Ray Bolger, whose oncamera antics had been deleted from *The Girl of the Golden West*, was very much in evidence in *Sweethearts* in his role as MacDonald's dancing partner in the musical comedy-within-the-movie. He first performs the "Zuyder Zee" routine, and then joins with her in "Jeanette and Her Little Wooden Shoe" in which Mac-Donald wears a very fetching Dutch outfit. These sequences are followed by MacDonald singing the "Angelus," and dueting with Eddy in "Every Lover Must Meet His Fate" and, of course, "Sweethearts." At the subsequent St. Regis Hotel party scene, MacDonald and Eddy together perform "Pretty As a Picture," "Mademoiselle," and once again, "Sweethearts." As a novelty number, there is the at-home song, "I Bring a Breath of Springtime," done by MacDonald, Eddy, and their family members (all of whom constantly remind everyone that they used to be show business stars). Later there is another hearthside duet by MacDonald and Eddy of "Little Grey Home in the West."

For a change of musical backdrop in *Sweethearts,* Metro recreated on its soundstages the National Broadcasting Company's auditorium as a setting for MacDonald to sing "Summer Serenade" backed by Dalies Frantz at the piano and an eighty-piece orchestra. Not to be outdone, Eddy at this broadcasting studio set performs "On Parade," supported by a contingent of Marine Band members. If anything proved the effectiveness of the screen teaming of MacDonald and Eddy it was having to witness the pair being temporarily separated within the film on the road tours. She has as her new onscreen partner, lumbering Douglas MacPhail while Eddy is saddled with Betty Jaynes. (MacPhail and Jaynes, who offscreen were husband and wife, were highly touted at the time as MacDonald's own protégées.)

MacDonald and Eddy would graciously replay their *Sweethearts* roles on radio's "Screen Guild Players" in March and December, 1947.

## NEW MOON
### *(MGM, 1940) 105M.*

Producer-director, Robert Z. Leonard; based on the operetta by Oscar Hammerstein II, Frank Mandel, Laurence Schwab, Sigmund Romberg; screenplay, Jacques Deval, Robert Arthur; music director, Herbert Stothart; choreography, Val Raset; songs, Hammerstein II and Romberg; art directors, Cedric Gibbons, Eddie Imazu; set decorator, Edwin B. Willis; gowns, Adrian; men's costumes, Gile Steele; makeup, Jack Dawn; sound, Douglas Shearer; camera, William Daniels; editor, Harold F. Kress.

319

Jeanette MacDonald (Marianne de Beaumanoir); Nelson Eddy (Charles, Duc de Villiers); Mary Boland (Valerie de Rossac); George Zucco (Vicomte Bibaud); H. B. Warner (Father Michel); Grant Mitchell (Governor of New Orleans); Stanley Fields (Tambour); Richard Purcell (Alexander); John Miljan (Pierre Brugnon); Ivan Simpson (Guizot); William Tannen (Pierre); Bunty Cutler (Julie); Claude King (Monsieur du Bois); Cecil Cunningham (Governor's Wife); Joe Yule (Maurice); George Irving (Ship's Captain); Rafael Storm (Monsieur De Piron); Winifred Harris (Lady); Robert Warwick (Commissar).

New York Premiere: Capitol Theatre—July 9, 1940
New York Television Debut: CBS—June 16, 1957

### Synopsis

In 1788 Marianne de Beaumanoir is en route from Paris to New Orleans to inspect a plantation in the New World left to her by an uncle. On the same ship, concealed in the hold, is a motley collection of bondsmen, taken to the southern city to be sold into "slavery." Among these men is Charles, Duc de Villiers, a political enemy of the king who has escaped execution by posing as a bondsman. Marianne encounters Charles in the captain's cabin, and she mistakes him for one of the ship's officers. Later in New Orleans she is amazed to find that he has been purchased by her plantation manager as a new domestic. Only then does she learn the truth and when she comments on his fine manners, Charles tells her he was formerly employed by the Duc de Villiers. Charles soon becomes indispensable to the household and Marianne finds herself more than casually interested in the young man. The romance, however, is rudely disrupted when a French official arrives at the plantation and reveals the identity of her servant. Charles, who hears this conversation, loses no time in organizing the escape he has been plotting for himself and the other bondsmen. Seizing a ship in the harbor, the troupe sails away. The disillusioned Marianne decides to return to Paris. She is permitted to sail with her aunt, Valerie De Rossac, on the "New Moon" which, she is told, must first stop at Martinique to unload one hundred girls going as brides to the men in the colony. En route, the "New Moon" is set upon by a pirate ship. The pirates board and Marianne discovers their leader is Charles. A storm comes up and the conglomeration of passengers aboard the "New Moon" manage to reach shore, where Charles sets up a new republic. Many of the young girls choose husbands from among Charles' crew. Marianne remains aloof and is later annoyed to discover that Charles is a great favorite among the remaining eligible women. Half in fun, half in earnest, Charles suggests he and Marianne wed to protect one another. Marianne is angry at first but soon realizes it is the only way out of the difficulty. Their wedding is celebrated at an elaborate island feast, but the couple share no joy in their "forced" union.

When the sails of a French ship are sighted, Charles determines to give himself up to French justice rather than endanger the lives of the colonists. At this point, Marianne realizes how much she loves him. When the ship finally flies a flag of truce, and representatives land on the island, they bring news that the French Revolution has occurred and that Charles is free. Now Marianne and Charles can find happiness together.

◆◆◆

For the 1939 film season, MGM had the "bright" notion of dividing their money-making team of Jeanette MacDonald and Nelson Eddy, reasoning that separately each might make very profitable productions for the studio. The studio was proved wrong shortly. MacDonald was excellent in the contemporary backstage tale, *Broadway Serenade*, with Lew Ayres as her non-singing vis-a-vis. And Eddy overcame the historical, patriotic pastiche of *Let Freedom Ring,* with Virginia Bruce, to perform resolutely in *Balalaika,* with Hungarian-born Ilona Massey. However, the financial returns to the studio on these three pictures were nowhere near what had been anticipated. So it was decided to reteam Mac-Donald and Eddy.

*New Moon,* based on the 1928 operetta which had a 518-performance Broadway run, had already been turned into a 1930 MGM musical with Lawrence Tibbett and Grace Moore. While that picture version had switched the storyline to a Russian setting and used a different plot,* the 1940 adaptation proved to be a cheap rehash of *Naughty Marietta* in which MacDonald once again sails for New Orleans, encounters outdoorsman Eddy and his band of helpers, all of which is set at the time of Louis XVI rather than the Louis XV period of the previous picture.

The five years which separated *Naughty Marietta* and *New Moon* had seen the rebirth and the new death of the screen operetta when its rediscovered conventions became clichés once more. It amazed the less resilient filmgoers that, while the globe was being engulfed by World War II, and swing and boogie woogie were becoming the new music crazes, MacDonald and Eddy could continue as before with no perceptible change, other than their advancing ages. Reviewers hastened to note that *New Moon* is ". . . a massive and unstinting production, but one which is as often dull as it is entertaining. The action makes its way haltingly from one big musical interlude to another, when it invariably stops dead in its tracks. The stars, being more intent on their vocalizing than their acting, posture instead of giving engaging romantic portrayals and somewhere in the shuffle a story and an excellent group of supporting players are completely lost" [Howard Barnes (*New York Herald-Tribune*)]. Bosley Crowther (*New York Times*) despaired, ". . . somehow the familiar lilt of the old MacDonald-Eddy extravaganzas is missing from this *New Moon.* . . . it never quite comes alive."

Decked out in the handsome wigs and voluminous gowns of the late eighteenth century, MacDonald parades through *New Moon* as a high-

*Inexplicably this 1930 film was retitled *Parisian Belle* when sold to television.

born lady possessing a lovely voice. Aboard the ship *Joie-des-Anges* she sings "I Was a Stranger in Paris" (Eddy in the ship's hold offers a mockery of this song). In the new world she performs the rondelet "One Kiss." Eddy has the opportunity to sing "Softly as in a Morning Sunrise" while polishing shoes in the yard. He joins with the bondsmen in "Stout Hearted Men," a visually moving number, and duets two long songs with the heroine —"Wanting You," and "Lover Come Back to Me." (The latter song is first sung by MacDonald while Eddy is away on what seems to be a dangerous mission.) There is even a spiritual worked into the proceedings, with a group of black slaves doing "No More Weepin'."

As was her custom, MacDonald plays her screen role with a good deal of lighthearted comedy. Unfortunately, Eddy, grown much plumper and even more wooden, seems intent on adding his own comic touches which are more laudable for effort than execution. His attempts at witty repartee in *New Moon* more often than not fall amiss, as in the captain's cabin aboard the *Joie-des-Anges* with MacDonald in which he compliments her, "Obviously . . . all dreams do not come in sleep." The necessary swashbuckler's charm is missing from his delivery. While most of the film's redeeming comedy moments are supplied by rotund Mary Boland as MacDonald's flighty, gossipy aunt, the star team does come briefly to life when they submit to their marriage of convenience. MacDonald executes one of her famed pseudo-sarcastic screen routines as Eddy orders his new bride to "smile." He is concerned that the wedding guests might assume the union is not a happy one. With a wry look on her pretty face and fire in her sparkling eyes, she coyly informs the assemblage, "There are no words to express my real feelings." (Her eyes knowingly dart to Eddy.) "This is a day I shall not forget." Then the "blissful" couple join the group singing "Our Sincere Appreciation." Later that evening in their honeymoon cabin, MacDonald insists upon bolting the bedroom door to insure Eddy remains a gentleman and stays on the outside. She accidentally drops the wooden bar on her foot and he rushes to the rescue:

Eddy: "Don't you know I am a specialist."
MacDonald: "A doctor?"
Eddy: "No. Footman."

## BITTER SWEET
### (MGM, 1940) C-92M.

Producer, Victor Saville; director, W. S. Van Dyke II; based on the play by Noel Coward; screenplay, Lester Samuels; songs, Coward; additional lyrics, Gus Kahn; music director, Herbert Stothart; vocal-orchestral arranger, Murray Cutter, Ken Darby; choreography, Ernst Matray; art directors, Cedric Gibbons, John S. Dieterle; set decorator, Edwin B. Willis; gowns, Adrian; men's costumes, Gile Steele; makeup, Jack Dawn; sound, Douglas Shearer; camera, Oliver T. Marsh, Allan Davey; editor, Harold F. Kress.

Jeanette MacDonald (Sarah Millick); Nelson Eddy (Carl Linden); George Sanders (Baron Von Tranisch); Ian Hunter (Lord Shayne); Felix Bressart (Max); Edward Ashley (Harry Daventry); Lynne Carver (Dolly); Diana Lewis (Jane); Curt Bois (Ernst); Fay Holden (Mrs. Millick); Sig Rumann (Herr Schlick); Janet Beecher (Lady Daventry); Charles Judels (Herr Wyler); Veda Ann Borg (Manon); Herman Bing (Market Keeper); Greta Meyer (Mama Luden); Philip Winter (Edgar); Armand Kaliz (Headwaiter); Alexander Pollard (Butler); Colin Campbell (Sir Arthur Fenchurch); Art Berry, Sr. (Cabbie); Sam Savitsky (Bearded Man); Howard Lang (Pawnbroker); Lester Sharpe, Hans Joby, Jeff Corey (Boarders); Paul E. Burns (Lathered Man); Hans Conried (Rudolph); John Hendrick (Fritz); Ruth Tobey (Market Keeper's Child); Warren Rock (Wyler's Secretary); William Tannen (Secretary of Employment Agency); Davison Clark (Attendant); Jean De Briac (Croupier); Ernest Verebes (Orderly); Pamela Randall (Hansi); Muriel Goodspeed (Freda); Earl Wallace (Wine Waiter); Louis Natheaux (Officer); Margaret Bert (Woman on Stairs); Julius Tannen (Schlick's Companion); Armand Cortes (Croupier); Irene Colman, June Wilkins (Girls in Casino); Jack Chefe, Gino Corrado (Waiters); Eugene Beday (Civilian); Max Barwyn (Bartender); Major Sam Harris (Officer Seen Dining); Kay Williams (Entertainer).

New York Premiere: Radio City Music Hall—November 21, 1940
New York Television Debut: CBS—September 13, 1958

### Synopsis

On the eve of her marriage to Harry Daventry, Victorian belle Sarah Millick scandalizes her family and her friends by her unnaturally excited conduct at a London ball and then by eloping to Vienna with her singing teacher, Carl Linden. There they live in poverty, but happily, among Carl's friends, which include Max and Ernst, penniless musicians who pawn Carl's furniture when all else fails. Sarah and Carl become street singers with Max and Ernst at the resort city of Baden. Carl's hope of selling an operetta he has composed meets with no response, but fortune changes when Sarah wins the attention of Lord Shayne and his gambling opponent Baron von Tranisch of the Imperial Cavalry. Shayne believes Sarah's singing brings him luck while Tranisch has a more personal interest. He instructs Herr Schlick to hire Sarah as an entertainer in his Vienna cafe, where Carl is to play the piano. When Tranisch pays unwelcome attention to Sarah, she resists. But Daventry, appointed to the Viennese Embassy by now, and Jane, who has wed him, are witnesses to Tranisch's advances and report the matter to Carl. He takes no interest in their gossip but Sarah refuses to return to the cafe. There comes a night, however, when Herr Wyler, the impressario, is believed to be a guest at the cafe and willing to hear Carl's operetta. Max and Ernst go to bring Sarah so that she may sing it. But again Tranisch makes himself offensive. Carl finds himself forced into a duel which he has no hope of winning, and Tranisch runs him through. He dies in Sarah's arms. She finds new hope, however, when Lord Shayne persuades Wyler to produce the operetta with her as star. Carl will live on through her singing since every time she sings his music, she feels he is with her.

◆◆◆

Noel Coward's gracious 1929 musical play which had been well received in London and on Broadway had previously (1933) been filmed in England with Anna Neagle.° After the rather modestly produced *New Moon*, MGM lavished great care and budget on the new, plush Technicolor "chocolate-box rendition" of *Bitter Sweet*. Coward was not pleased with the results, nor were many of the critics. ". . . [the film] is resplendent with red plush and gilt; also plum full of pseudo hilarity, tuneful waltz airs, bustles and bonnets—and dialogue as outmoded as the story's gay nineties setting" [Irene Thirer *(New York Post)*]. As for the *Bitter Sweet* stars, both of whom were approaching forty years and showed it on the color screen, Bosley Crowther *(New York Times)* carped, "Miss MacDonald and Mr. Eddy play it all with such an embarrassing lack of ease—she with self-conscious high-spirit and he with painful pomposity." The *New York Morning Telegraph* inquired, "Isn't it about time that either Mr. Eddy or Miss MacDonald went their separate ways, looking for scripts, instead of just music?"

Perhaps if more of Coward's basic play had survived the new screen treatment, *Bitter Sweet* might have evolved as a more satisfactory cinema outing. However, much of the charm had disappeared, and instead the viewer was treated to a ponderous overstuffed tale, too often weighed down by tedium. The *New York Sun* termed the plot "as gushing as a schoolgirl's poem."

Then too, maybe producer Victor Saville should have heeded the scenarists' words of warning put in the mouth of MacDonald's stuffy fiancé (Edward Ashley), who, early in the film, advises her, "I don't disapprove of music, but I feel there should be a restraint about it." The Coward songs, some with new lyrics by Gus Kahn, were a mixed bag rather than a musical treat. "I'll See You Again" is first sung by MacDonald and Eddy at her London party. It is reprised again at a later audition, and at the finale where MacDonald, as in *Maytime*, joins with the heavenly apparition of Eddy in yet another duet of the song. Among the other numbers, there is the charming "Dear Little Cafe" dueted by the leads. MacDonald performs "Love in Any Language" ("Bonne Nuit Merci") and is particularly captivating in rendering "Ladies of the Town" with a mock Parisian accent, and singing in grand operetta style the "Zigeuner" song from Eddy's posthumously produced work. Eddy and the chorus offer "Tokay," while alone he does part of "The Call of Life" entitled "If You Could Only Come with Me."

Throughout the ninety-two minutes of *Bitter Sweet*, MacDonald

°MacDonald was originally scheduled for this British film production.

and Eddy struggled to inject some infectiousness into the tame proceedings, but their efforts did not ring true. It was hard for viewers to enter into the intended romantic spirit of the story when Eddy is offhandedly telling MacDonald that life for them in Vienna will be a mixture of "the bitter with the sweet," or when the duo inadvertently competes with a shopkeeper (Herman Bing) for the same chicken, paying for it by giving Bing's daughter music lessons. Not even the weepy segments held up as one would have liked. Thus, we have MacDonald turgidly informing the dying Eddy, "I'll love you always, do you hear me." The tugs at the heartstrings were minimal here, or even when MacDonald tells another character, "This is my home. This is the place he loved. Carl didn't die. I did a little. This will always be his place. When I sing, I hear him. When I play, I hear him."

In contrast, the supporting cast breezed through *Bitter Sweet* with ease. There was Diana Lewis as MacDonald's scatterbrained London friend who could maneuver a man to her will, but had difficulty saying her "r's," George Sanders as a stereotype of the monocled cad, Veda Ann Borg as a tough pawn of the smart set, Felix Bressart and Curt Bois as Eddy's jovial Vienna pals, Greta Meyer as the enthusiastic beer garden proprietress, and Bing as the bewildered-turned-angry shopman.

## I MARRIED AN ANGEL
### *(MGM, 1942) 84M.*

Producer, Hunt Stromberg; director, Major W. S. Van Dyke II; based on the musical adaptation by Richard Rodgers and Lorenz Hart of the play by Vaszary Janos; screenplay, Anita Loos; art directors, Cedric Gibbons, John S. Detlie, Motley; set decorator, Edwin B. Willis; songs, Rodgers and Hart; additional lyrics, Bob Wright and Chet Forrest; choreography, Ernst Matray; costumes, Motley; gowns, Kallock; makeup, Jack Dawn; sound, Douglas Shearer; special effects, Arnold Gillespie, Warren Newcombe; camera, Ray June; editor, Conrad A. Nervig.

Jeanette MacDonald (Anna/Briggitta); Nelson Eddy (Count Willi Palaffi); Edward Everett Horton (Peter); Binnie Barnes (Peggy); Reginald Owen (Whiskers); Douglas Dumbrille (Baron Szigethy); Mona Maris (Marika); Janis Carter (Sufi); Inez Cooper (Iren); Leonid Kinskey (Zinski); Anne Jeffreys (Polly); Marion Rosamond (Dolly).

New York Premiere: Capitol Theatre—July 9, 1942
New York Television Debut: CBS—December 23, 1960

### Synopsis

Anna Zador, a drab stenographer in the Budapest bank run by Count Willi Palaffi, secretly loves her boss, whose only interests in life are wine, women and song. Willi is warned by "Whiskers" that the bank's stockholders are complaining about his lavish life style, but Willi laughs it off and proceeds to plan his birthday party. At Whisker's request, Marika, Willi's beautiful secretary, invites Anna to the party and maliciously suggests that she come as an angel. Anna's costume amuses the assemblage, but Willi kindly dances with the self-conscious girl. Complaining that his feet hurt, Willi excuses himself and goes to his room. He falls asleep and dreams: Anna comes through the window as an angel wearing a beautiful robe, with wings and a halo, and calling herself Briggitta. In the fantasy the two are off on their honeymoon, and Willi discovers that an angel can be trying. His wife wants to leave him the first night to sleep on a cloud but he persuades her to remain, and the next morning she discovers that she has lost her wings. She now proceeds to ruin all his plans by behaving in a very angelic manner. She will not tell a falsehood for one thing which causes him no end of trouble, such as when at a later banquet held to appease his stockholders, she proceeds to adhere to the truth, and tells it with such alacrity that the guests depart in amazement. Briggitta halts a possible run on the bank by transferring her attentions to Baron Szigethy, the bank's wealthiest depositor. Willi later awakens from his dream, and sighs with relief that it was not all real. He returns to the party and finds Anna sitting by herself. He announced to the guests that it is Anna he is going to marry, and the bewildered but loving Anna accepts him.

◆━◆━◆

Although MGM had expressly acquired *Show Boat* and *The Vagabond King*, among other properties as future vehicles for the Jeanette MacDonald-Nelson Eddy team, 1941 found her performing in a remake of *Smilin' Through* with her real life husband, Gene Raymond. In the meantime Eddy was joined with Rise Stevens in *The Chocolate Soldier*. To reunite the two singing stars in what would prove to be their final onscreen venture, MGM reacquired the screen rights to *I Married an Angel*, the property which the film censors had rejected back in 1933 because it dealt openly with an angel who lost her virtue. In the meantime, Broadway had proven more receptive to the sophisticated venture and the Richard Rodgers-Lorenz Hart musical comedy had become a 338-performance success with Dennis King, Vera Zorina, Vivienne Segal, and Walter Slezak in the lead roles.

Almost everything about the picturized black-and-white *I Married an Angel* smacked of haste and economy, a lessening of everything distinctive about past MacDonald-Eddy features. All the captivating charm of the New York stage show seemed to be lost in its translation to this heavy-handed screen venture. "It's hardly a musical anymore!" wrote an amazed Herbert Cohn (*Brooklyn Daily Eagle*). The critics were downright frank in their disapproval of the stars' performances. "Between Eddy and MacDonald the middle European fantasy, *I Married an Angel* become a laborious dream indeed, more nightmare than anything else" [Archer

Winsten (New York Post)]. "At best Jeanette MacDonald and Nelson Eddy are not exactly a pair of sylphs and no one should willfully embarrass them by asking that they pretend that they are" [Bosley Crowther (New York Times)].

Before the film finishes its tired eighty-four-minute course, the viewer is satiated with the renditions of the title tune by Eddy alone or in unison with MacDonald. Among the other musical numbers, the couple dueted "I'll Tell Every Man in the Street" and "Spring Is Here." MacDonald soloed "Song with the Harps," and Eddy performed "May I Present the Girl." In the special montage sequence, MacDonald performed the gypsy song from *Carmen,* the trio from *Faust,* and a Hawaiian hula (with a double substituting for some of her movements) done to the tune "Aloha Oe." Ironically, the most enjoyable songs in *I Married an Angel* are rendered by the supporting cast. Edward Everett Horton exhibits perfect timing as he does a recitative of the "Birthday Song" while Eddy's oncamera girlfriends (Janis Carter, Mona Maris, Marion Rosamond, Anne Jeffreys, Inez Cooper) harmonize on the catchy "Brides Song." Finally, in a very pleasant uplifting manner Binnie Barnes revives the film's pace by instructing MacDonald on the art of "A Twinkle in Your Eye" (causing MacDonald to make an unattractive attempt at being hep as she carries out Barnes' man-catching advice).

MacDonald and Eddy offered an audio preview of their *I Married an Angel* on "Hollywood Radio Theatre" on June 1, 1942.


### THE YEARS AFTER

After *I Married an Angel,* Jeanette MacDonald made one more MGM picture, the low-budgeted spy spoof *Cairo* (1942), which terminated her studio contract. During the war years she devoted much time to U.S.O. tours, making her opera debut in *Romeo and Juliet* (1943), and giving recitals. In the late 1940s producer Joe Pasternak induced MacDonald to return° to Metro to play the mother of *Three Daring Daughters* (1948) and then to appear in the Lassie picture *The Sun Comes Up* (1949). In the 1950s, she continued with summer appearances and, in 1957, performed in the television special, *Charley's Aunt.*

Meanwhile, after *I Married an Angel,* Nelson Eddy left MGM, and the following year showed up in as a "romantic" lead in Universal's remake of *The Phantom of the Opera* (1943). Later came *Knickerbocker Holiday* (1944), an offcamera role in Walt Disney's animated feature *Make Mine Music* (1946), and his final feature film, *Northwest Outpost* (1947), which reunited him with Ilona Massey. He had a popular radio show in the 1940s, sang at Carnegie Hall in 1944, and continued to

°Ilona Massey played the role in *Holiday in Mexico* (1946) that MGM had planned for MacDonald.

appear in concerts throughout America. In the 1960s, he made a comeback on the nightclub circuit with Gale Sherwood as his singing partner.

From the time they first professionally split, MacDonald and Eddy were hounded by fans who wanted to know when they would be reunited oncamera. There was talk of Universal starring them in *East Wind*, or MGM rematching them in *Crescent Carnival* based on the Frances Parkinson Keyes book. MacDonald did guest on Eddy's radio show and he was a surprise visitor when Ralph Edwards did a "This Is Your Life" segment on Jeanette MacDonald in the November 12, 1952 installment of that television program. In December 1956 the two performers were reunited on CBS-TV's "The Big Record." In 1959 they joined together to record "Jeanette MacDonald and Nelson Eddy in Hi-Fi" which became a million-seller LP album. As late as 1963, producers contemplated pairing the former screen operetta team in new pictures, with Ross Hunter offering them the Arlene Francis-Edward Andrews' roles in Doris Day's *The Thrill of It All*. But as Eddy once explained, ". . . we decided that because we had hit the top and created an image for all time, we were not going to sit around and watch that image destroyed. As it was, we felt we could hold our heads high and if we had to go out we would go out on top."

MacDonald died of a heart ailment in 1965, and two years later, while performing in a Miami Beach hotel club, Eddy passed away. However, through their (joint) films, and the tremendously active Jeanette MacDonald-Nelson Eddy international fan club, the team's bright memory lives on for generations to come.

In **The Private Lives of Elizabeth and Essex** (WB, 1939)

# Chapter 12

# Errol Flynn
# &
# Olivia de Havilland

## ERROL FLYNN

6' 2"
180 pounds
Brown hair
Brown eyes
Gemini

*Real name: Errol Leslie Flynn. Born June 20, 1909, Hobart, Tasmania. Married Lili Damita (1935), child: Sean; divorced 1940. Married Nora Eddington (1943), children: Deidre, Rory; divorced 1949. Married Patrice Wymore (1950). Died October 14, 1959.*

FEATURE FILMS:

*In the Wake of the Bounty* (Expeditionary Films, 1933)
*Murder at Monte Carlo* (WB, 1935)
*The Case of the Curious Bride* (FN, 1935)
*Don't Bet on Blondes* (WB, 1935)
*Captain Blood* (FN, 1935)
*The Charge of the Light Brigade* (WB, 1936)
*Green Light* (FN, 1937)
*The Prince and the Pauper* (FN, 1937)

*Another Dawn* (WB, 1937)
*The Perfect Specimen* (FN, 1937)
*The Adventures of Robin Hood* (FN, 1938)
*Four's a Crowd* (WB, 1938)
*The Sisters* (WB, 1938)
*The Dawn Patrol* (WB, 1938)
*Dodge City* (WB, 1939)
*The Private Lives of Elizabeth and Essex* (WB, 1939)
*Virginia City* (WB, 1940)

The Sea Hawk (WB, 1940)
Santa Fe Trail (WB, 1940)
Footsteps in the Dark (WB, 1941)
Dive Bombers (WB, 1941)
They Died with Their Boots On (WB, 1941)
Desperate Journey (WB, 1942)
Gentleman Jim (WB, 1942)
Edge of Darkness (WB, 1943)
Thank Your Lucky Stars (WB, 1943)
Northern Pursuit (WB, 1943)
Uncertain Glory (WB, 1944)
Objective, Burma! (WB, 1945)
San Antonio (WB, 1945)
Never Say Goodbye (WB, 1946)
Cry Wolf (WB, 1947)
Escape Me Never (WB, 1947)
Silver River (WB, 1948)
Adventures of Don Juan (WB, 1948)
It's a Great Feeling (WB, 1949)

That Forsyte Woman (MGM, 1949)
Montana (WB, 1950)
Rocky Mountain (WB, 1950)
Kim (MGM, 1951)
Hello God (William Marshall, 1951)
Adventures of Captain Fabian (Rep., 1951)
Maru Maru (WB, 1952)
Against All Flags (Univ., 1952)
The Master of Ballantrae (WB, 1953)
Crossed Swords (UA, 1954)
Let's Make Up (UA, 1955)
The Warriors (AA, 1955)
King's Rhapsody (UA, 1955)
The Big Boodle (UA, 1957)
The Sun Also Rises (20th, 1957)
Too Much, Too Soon (WB, 1958)
The Roots of Heaven (20th, 1958)
Cuban Rebel Girls (Joseph Brenner, 1959)

# OLIVIA DE HAVILLAND

**5′ 3½″**
**112 pounds**
**Dark brown hair**
**Brown eyes**
**Cancer**

*Real name: same. Born, July 1, 1916, Tokyo, Japan. Married Marcus Goodrich (1946), child: Benjamin; divorced 1952. Married Pierre Paul Galante (1955), child: Giselle.*

FEATURE FILMS:

A Midsummers' Night Dream (WB, 1935)
Alibi Ike (WB, 1935)
The Irish in Us (WB, 1935)
Captain Blood (FN, 1935)
Anthony Adverse (WB, 1936)
The Charge of the Light Brigade (WB, 1936)
Call It a Day (WB, 1937)

The Great Garrick (WB, 1937)
It's Love I'm After (FN, 1937)
Gold Is Where You Find It (WB, 1938)
Hard to Get (WB, 1938)
The Adventures of Robin Hood (FN, 1938)
Four's a Crowd (WB, 1938)

*Wings of the Navy* (WB, 1939)
*Dodge City* (WB, 1939)
*The Private Lives of Elizabeth and Essex* (WB, 1939)
*Gone with the Wind* (MGM, 1939)
*Raffles* (UA, 1940)
*My Love Came Back* (WB, 1940)
*Santa Fe Trail* (WB, 1940)
*Strawberry Blonde* (WB, 1941)
*Hold Back the Dawn* (Par., 1941)
*They Died with Their Boots On* (WB, 1941)
*The Male Animal* (WB, 1942)
*In This Our Life* (WB, 1942)
*Thank Your Lucky Stars* (WB, 1943)
*Princess O'Rourke* (WB, 1943)
*Government Girl* (RKO, 1943)
*Devotion* (WB, 1946)

*The Well-Groomed Bride* (Par., 1946)
*To Each His Own* (Par., 1946)
*The Dark Mirror* (Univ., 1946)
*The Snake Pit* (20th, 1948)
*The Heiress* (Par., 1949)
*My Cousin Rachel* (20th, 1953)
*That Lady* (20th, 1955)
*Not As a Stranger* (UA, 1955)
*The Ambassador's Daughter* (UA, 1956)
*The Proud Rebel* (BV, 1958)
*Libel* (MGM, 1959)
*Light in the Piazza* (MGM, 1962)
*Hush . . . Hush, Sweet Charlotte* (20th, 1964)
*Lady in a Cage* (Par., 1964)
*The Adventurers* (Par., 1970)
*Pope Joan* (Col., 1972)

In **Captain Blood** (FN, 1935)

Walter Connolly, Olivia de Havilland, and Errol Flynn in **Four's A Crowd** (WB, 1938)

In **The Charge of the Light Brigade** (WB, 1936)

In a publicity pose for **The Adventures of Robin Hood** (FN, 1938)

Spencer Charters, Olivia de Havilland, and Errol Flynn in **Dodge City** (WB, 1939)

At a "premiere" showing of **Santa Fe Trail** (WB, 1940) in Needles, California

Olivia de Havilland, Errol Flynn, and Ronald Reagan in **Santa Fe Trail**

Director Raoul Walsh, Olivia de Havilland, and Errol Flynn on the set of **They Died with Their Boots On** (WB, 1941)

In a pose for **They Died with Their Boots On**

Advertisement for **They Died with Their Boots On**

Olivia de Havilland, George Tobias, and Ida Lupino in **Thank Your Lucky Stars** (WB, 1943)

Monte Blue and Errol Flynn in **Thank Your Lucky Stars**

# CAPTAIN BLOOD
*(First National-Warner Bros., 1935) 119M.*

Executive producer, Hal B. Wallis; associate producer, Harry Joe Brown, Gordon Hollingshead; director, Michael Curtiz; based on the novel by Rafael Sabatini; screenplay, Casey Robinson; assistant director, Sherry Shourds; fencing master, Fred Cavens; dialog director, Stanley Logan; art director, Anton Grot; gowns, Milo Anderson; music, Erich Wolfgang Korngold; orchestrator, Hugh Freidhofer, Ray Heindorf; sound, C. A. Riggs; camera, Hal Mohr; additional camera, Ernest Haller; editor, George Amy.

Errol Flynn (Peter Blood); Olivia de Havilland (Arabella Bishop); Lionel Atwill (Colonel Bishop); Basil Rathbone (Captain Levasseur); Ross Alexander (Jeremy Pitt); Guy Kibbee (Hagthorpe); Henry Stephenson (Lord Willoughby); Robert Barrat (Wolverstone); Hobart Cavanaugh (Dr. Bronson); Donald Meek (Dr. Whacker); Jessie Ralph (Mrs. Barlowe); Forrester Harvey (Honesty Nuttall); Frank McGlynn, Sr. (Reverend Ogle); Holmes Herbert (Captain Gardner); David Torrence (Andrew Baynes); J. Carroll Naish (Cahusac); Pedro de Cordoba (Don Diego); George Hassell (Governor Steed); Harry Cording (Kent); Leonard Mudie (Baron Jeffreys); Ivan Simpson (Prosecutor); Stuart Casey (Captain Hobart); Denis d'Auburn (Lord Gildoy); Mary Forbes (Mrs. Steed); E. E. Clive (Court Clerk); Colin Kenny (Lord Chester Dyke); Maude Leslie (Mrs. Baynes); Gardner James (Branded Slave); Vernon Steele (King James II); Georges Renavent (French Captain); Murray Kinnell (Clerk in Governor Steed's Court); Harry Cording (Kent); Maude Leslie (Baynes' Wife); Stymie Beard (Governor's Attendant); Ivan F. Simpson (Judge Advocate); Yola D'Avril, Tina Menard (Girls in Tavern); Sam Appel (Gunner); Chris Pin Martin (Sentry); Frank Puglia (French Officer); Artie Ortego, Gene Alsace, Kansas Moehring, Tom Steele, Blackie Whiteford, Jim Thorpe, William Yetter, Buddy Roosevelt, Jimmy Mason (Pirates).

New York Premiere: Strand Theatre—December 26, 1935
New York Television Debut: CBS—September 19, 1959

## Synopsis

Peter Blood, a physician and a native of Dublin, is caught by King James' soldiers treating a wounded rebel, and together with the insurgents is sentenced to slavery in the West Indies. When he arrives at Barbados, he is purchased by Arabella Bishop, who had been attracted by his manner and looks. He is put to work in the mines of her uncle, Colonel Bishop. Through her influence, he is taken from the mines and made personal physician to the governor. Gradually he plans his escape and that of his rebel friends. When the town is set upon by Spanish pirates, Peter and his men sneak aboard the pirate vessel while its crew is out looting the town. After taking possession of the ship, they decide to roam the seas as buccaneers. In short order they become notorious as pirates in their own right. When Colonel Bishop is made governor he vows to bring back Peter and his men. Meanwhile, Peter becomes connected with Captain Levasseur, a French pirate, and they agree to share future booty. Peter later learns that Levasseur has captured an English ship and that he holds as prisoners both Arabella, who is on her way back to the West Indies from England, and Lord Willoughby, the King's representative. Peter offers to buy Arabella from Levasseur, but the pirate declines the offer. Peter then fights a duel with him and the latter is killed. Arabella refuses to credit Peter with any noble traits, believing he had fought the duel just to possess her. On the journey back to the West Indies, Lord Willoughby informs Peter that James is no longer King and that the new King has offered Peter and his men freedom on condition that they join the King's forces. Peter and his men rejoice at this news and prove their courage by fighting a fierce battle and vanquishing the enemy ships that have attached Barbados. As a reward, Peter is made governor in place of the corrupt Colonel Bishop, who had left his administrative post in a time of war to go in search of Peter. Now Peter can claim Arabella as his wife.

◆—◆—◆

With the excellent boxoffice success of *The Count of Monte Cristo* and *Treasure Island,* both of 1934, Hollywood was convinced that a new genre cycle was in the works and that swashbuckling epics were the answer to wooing the Depression-weary public into movie theatres. Warner Bros. planned to sign Britisher Robert Donat, star of *Monte Cristo,* for their remake of the 1923 *Captain Blood,* but negotiations broke off at the last juncture. At this point, the studio was all set to roll on the new project and delay meant financial waste to company boss Jack L. Warner. Warner instructed director Michael Curtiz, who was to helm the epic, to test twenty-six-year-old contractee Errol Flynn in the part. [Curtiz had directed Flynn in his brief scenes in the earlier *The Case of the Curious Bride* (1935).] The 6'2" performer from Hobart, Tasmania, acquitted himself well and the role was his. Such are the way movie players are launched into stardom.

It was a standing Hollywood rule that the female lead in an epic movie be a beautiful cardboard figure, enchanting enough of features to launch a thousand ships, enticing of personality to both hero and villain, but docile enough of nature not to intrude upon the established storyline in which she was merely a one-dimensional mannequin. Obviously such a role is not an artistically easy or rewarding task for any young actress, but if sufficiently well handled it could supply the player with a visual showcase, hopefully leading to more meaty roles at a later date. Thus, when nineteen-year-old Olivia de Havilland, who had joined Warner Bros. for the picturization of *A Midsummers' Night's Dream* (1935) and remained thereafter, was selected over Jean Muir and Bette Davis for the role of Arabella Bishop in *Captain Blood* she felt rewarded with the part, but was even then wise enough to realize it would not provide her with the acting challenges she yearned for. It was but one of the steps up the career ladder for an ambitious starlet.

The combination of ingredients in the new *Captain Blood* proved to be ingeniously apt, ranging from Michael Curtiz' pulsating direction and imaginative ability in stretching the relatively modest budget, to the lush Erich Wolfgang Korngold score and the Anton Grot sets. *Variety* judged the picture ". . . a spectacular cinematic entry which, while not flawless, is quite compelling." The use of miniature sets (for the ships and much of Port Royal), interpolated film clips from the 1923 *Captain Blood* and *The Sea Hawk* (1924), and the location work at Laguna Beach, subtly enhanced the carefully allotted one million dollar production, giving its 119 minutes all the sweep and flow of the original Rafael Sabatini novel (1922).

Most of all what insured the overall success of *Captain Blood* was the swaggering zest of relative screen newcomer Flynn. As Richard Watts, Jr. *(New York Herald-Tribune)* pointed out, "The photoplay, to be sure, hardly comes under the head of mature, adult drama, but that is one of its great virtues. It never pretends to be anything but hearty romantic fiction, picturesquely produced." The screenplay required just the right sort of actor to carry across this particularized *joie de vie* so that audiences would believe the hero whether he was combatting the enemy or courting the heroine. Flynn was just that sort of man. He was physically very handsome, athletically fit, emotionally reckless, and, most of all, he possessed a tremendous charm which he dispensed with a flick of his eyelash or a flash of his sparkling smile. He would learn more acting tricks later, but in *Captain Blood* he displayed a combination of earnestness and devil-may-care adventurousness that made his Peter Blood a most credible gentleman corsair. Whether spouting forth the rather flowery dialog, dueling to the death with the wonderfully villainous Basil Rathbone, or elegantly flirting with the self-willed de Havilland, Flynn proved to be most everyone's personification of the latter day swashbuckling hero, perfectly in tune with the established Douglas Fairbanks, Sr. tradition.

"If you haven't heard of Errol Flynn (and don't call him Leon Errol) it won't be long now. It is our prediction that Mr. Flynn will soon be as popular as the music of *Top Hat*" [Thornton Delehanty *(New York Post)*]. Lee Mortimer *(New York Daily Mirror)* was even more far-reaching in his adulation of the new "star." "The first authentic matinee idol since Valentino finally appears upon the screen . . . whose rich voice and glamorous personality are sure to set the seminaries and the bridge-clubs all a'flutter. He is not the sleek-type either. The men will applaud him enthusiastically . . ." Such was the contemporary reaction to the arrival of Flynn on the stardom horizon.

With so much of the film devoted to pirate action on the high seas or dueling scenes on shore, there was relatively little opportunity for Oxford-accented Flynn and sweetly modulated de Havilland to romantically spar and spark, which some sources, including *Variety,* insisted was one of the "prime shortcomings of the production." Nevertheless, what there was of the give and take interaction between the two players smacked of the proper screen chemistry, convincing viewers everywhere that de Havilland was ". . . a lady of rapturous loveliness and well worth fighting for" [Andre Sennwald *(New York Times)*].

Flynn and de Havilland would recreate their *Captain Blood* roles on "Lux Radio Theatre" on February 22, 1937. The film itself would be nationally reissued by Warner Bros. in 1951. Later, Flynn's son Sean would appear in the far less engaging feature film *Son of Captain Blood* in 1963.

## THE CHARGE OF THE LIGHT BRIGADE
*(Warner Bros., 1936) 115M.*

Executive producer, Hal B. Wallis; associate producer, Samuel Bischoff; based on a story by Michel Jacoby; screenplay, Jacoby, Rowland Leigh; dialog director, Stanley Logan; music, Max Steiner; orchestrator, Hugo Friedhofer; technical adviser, Captain E. Rochfort-John; technical adviser of drills and tactics, Major Sam Harris; director of horse action, B. Reeves Eason; assistant director, Jack Sullivan; art director, John Hughes; gowns, Milo Anderson; sound, C. A. Riggs; special effects, Fred Jackman, H. F. Koenekamp; camera, Sol Polito; editor, George Amy.

Errol Flynn (Captain Geoffrey Vickers); Olivia de Havilland (Elsa Campbell); Patric Knowles (Captain Perry Vickers); Donald Crisp (Colonel Campbell); Henry Stephenson (Sir Charles Macefield); Nigel Bruce (Sir Benjamin Warrenton); David Niven (Captain James Randall); G. P. Huntley, Jr. (Major Jowett); Spring Byington (Lady Octavia Warrenton); C. Henry Gordon (Surat Khan); E. E. Clive (Sir Humphrey Harcourt); Lumsden Hare (Colonel Woodward); Robert Barrat (Count Igor Volonoff); Walter Holbrook (Cornet Barclay); Charles Sedgwick (Cornet Pearson); J. Carroll Naish (Subahdar Major Puran Singh); Scotty Beckett (Prema Singh); Princess Baigum (Prema's Mother); George Regas (Wazir); Helen Sanborn (Mrs. Jowett); George Sorel (Surwan); George David (Suristani); Carlos San Martin (Court Interpreter); Dick Botiller (Native); Herbert Evans (Major Domo); Jon Kristen (Panjari); Phillis Coghlan (Woman at Ball); Stephen Moritz, Arthur Thalasso, Jack Curtis, Lal Chand Mehra (Sepoys); R. Singh, Jimmy Aubrey, David Thursby, Denis d'Auburn (Orderlies); Martin Garralaga, Frank Lackteen, (Panjaris); Carlyle Moore, Jr. (Junior Officer); Reginald Sheffield (Bentham); Georges Renavent (General Canrobert); Charles Croker King (Lord Cardigan); Brandon Hurst (Lord Raglan); Wilfred Lucas (Captain); Frank Baker, Ben F. Hendricks, Olaf Hytten (Officers); Craufurd Kent (Captain Brown); Boyd Irwin (General Dunbar); Gordon Hart (Colonel Coventry); Holmes Herbert (General O'Neill); Yakima Canutt (Double for Erroll Flynn).

New York Premiere: Strand Theatre—November 1, 1936
New York Television Debut: CBS—March 3, 1957

## Synopsis

When Surat Khan, a leading chieftain of 1850s India, is denied his rich annuity from England, he enters into a secret alliance with Russia. Major Geoffrey Vickers of the British 27th Lancers is dispatched to Arabia to purchase troop horses for the British Army, preparatory to the conflict with Russia. En route he stops off in Calcutta to meet with his fiancée, Elsa Campbell. She feels honor bound to wed Geoffrey, but she has really fallen in love with his brother, Perry. Later, when the riled Surat Khan and his men destroy the 27th Lancers' garrison at Chukoti, Geoffrey and Elsa manage to escape. Thereafter, the 27th Lancers are transferred to the trouble-brewing Crimea. When Geoffrey learns that Surat Khan is among the Russian contingent, he manages to substitute one military order for another, so that he and his men can revenge the slaughter at Chukoti. Under the revised dispatch, Geoffrey leads more than six hundred of his men into the Valley of Death, where a goodly number are slaughtered. However, before he too dies, Geoffrey throws a lance which kills Surat Khan.

◆━━◆━━◆

Because Hungarian-born director Michael Curtiz did so well in handling *Captain Blood*, Warner Bros. assigned him to guide Errol Flynn in subsequent celluloid excursions, including *The Charge of the Light Brigade* which "provides a legitimate wallop for jaded filmgoers in search of new dramatic territory" *(New York World Telegram)*. Ironically, Flynn abhorred working with the driving perfectionist Curtiz. "I was to spend five miserable years with him," the actor once said. "In each [picture] he tried to make all scenes so realistic that my skin didn't seem to matter. Nothing delighted him more than real bloodshed." But it was Curtiz's very imaginative penchant for ultra-credible action sequences that made Flynn's vehicles so vibrantly alive and enduring, and above all so commercial. Therefore, both these temperamental personalities found themselves joined in film projects, with the moviegoer the biggest victor in the process.

Thanks to Alfred Lord Tennyson's poem, written in December, 1854, generations of people have assumed that the famous charge,

> "Half a league, half a league
> Half a league onward.
> All in the valley of death
> Rode the six hundred."

was a gallant act of military bravery. But, as one French general of the time observed of the feat, "It is magnificent, but it is not war." For in that reckless encounter, the Russian general Lirandi retained control of the decisive Balaklave Heights in the Crimea while the British lost 247 of their 675 charging troops, and 497 of the men's horses.

The Michel Jacoby-Rowland Leigh screenplay for *The Charge of the Light Brigade* ably weaves a lengthy fictional prelude to the famous charge, setting most of the preliminary action in India, with its romantic flavor of British colonialism, regimental romances, as well as a chilling recounter of the slaughter of the British garrison by the fictitious Surat Khan (C. Henry Gordon). Figuring prominently in these outpost sequences was Olivia de Havilland in a role originally scheduled for Anita Louise. (The two actresses had appeared together the previous year in the expansive screen version of *Anthony Adverse* directed by Mervyn LeRoy and starring Fredric March in the title role.) De Havilland was cast as Elsa Campbell, the young lady uncertain whether to follow duty and wed fiancé Flynn° or to accede to love and marry his brother Patric Knowles. While once again the contrived screen romantics were the leading irritants to some unromantic critics, audiences expected *and* wanted brief respites from the action in which the dashing hero displayed his chivalrous gallantry to the fair lady. The *New York American* backhandedly remarked of de Havilland that she "lives up to her high-toned name." Some compliment! *Variety* was more generous: "a fascinating, sincere daughter of the regiment. It is the only meaty femme role, and she makes the most of it."

Obviously, as the film's title implies, the highlight of this $1.2 million production was the famous charge, which by scenario twisting diverts history and transforms the foolhardy act into a feat of military gallantry rather than what it actually was—an example of wartime stupidity and insubordination. If any viewer thinks carefully about the implications of the actions of Flynn's character ("Our objective is Surat Kahn!") it becomes obvious that it is a criminal act for Flynn's Geoffrey Vickers to lead some 599 men to their death in order to free the way for de Havilland to honorably wed Knowles. But such were the conventions of the 1930s cinema! In staging this fabulous oncamera charge, filmed at Chatsworth in the San Fernando Valley with additional action shots near Sonora in northern California, director Curtiz worked closely with B. Reeves Eason, a second-unit action specialist. A good deal of this segment's emotional impact on audiences was due to the rousing film score by Max Steiner.

Flynn would later admit that of all his filmmaking in Hollywood, *The Charge of the Light Brigade* was the most arduous in view of the extensive shooting schedule and the complexities of the action sequences.

---

°At this point in his undisciplined life, Flynn was already wed to the tempestuous actress Lili Damita, but he was convinced he was in love with de Havilland, his frequent leading lady. As he later stated, his ardor for her made "acting in that hard-to-make picture . . . bearable . . . all through it I fear I bothered Miss de Havilland in my teasing ways—though I was really trying to display my affection." A typical Flynn show of affection was to place a dead snake in aloof de Havilland's dressing room wardrobe, namely her panties.

(Yakima Canutt did many of Flynn's stunts in this film.) Flynn's sincere and charming performance, very authentic in its Victorian officer manner, was well-received by the public, proving once again that he was "the perfect hero for melodrama" *(New York Sun)*. Only the more severe of critics minded that Flynn was a bit unsubtle in the dramatic sequences and somewhat coy in the romantic interludes.

In 1968, Tony Richardson directed a $5.5 million rendition of *The Charge of the Light Brigade*, starring David Hemmings and Trevor Howard, which proved to be more an anti-war sermon than the hoped-for epic. Previous to the Flynn-de Havilland production there had been three earlier screen renditions of the subject produced in 1903, 1913, and 1931.


## THE ADVENTURES OF ROBIN HOOD
*(First National-Warner Bros., 1938) C-102M.*

Executive producer, Hal B. Wallis; associate producer, Henry Blanke; directors, Michael Curtiz, William Keighley; based upon the legends of Robin Hood; contributor to screenplay treatment, Rowland Leigh; screenplay, Norman Reilly Raine, Seton I. Miller; dialog director, Irving Rapper; art director, Carl Jules Weyl; music, Erich Wolfgang Korngold; orchestrator, Hugh Friedhofer, Milan Roder; assistant directors, Lee Katz, Jack Sullivan; costumes, Milo Anderson; makeup, Perc Westmore; technical adviser, Louis Van Den Ecker; fencing master, Fred Cavens; archery supervisor, Howard Hill; jousting scenes directed by B. Reeves Eason; sound, C. A. Riggs; camera, Sol Polito, Tony Gaudio; editor, Ralph Dawson.

Errol Flynn (Robin Hood); Olivia de Havilland (Maid Marian); Claude Rains (Prince John); Basil Rathbone (Sir Guy of Gisbourne); Ian Hunter (King Richard); Eugene Pallette (Friar Tuck); Alan Hale (Little John); Melville Cooper (High Sheriff of Nottingham); Patric Knowles (Will Scarlett); Herbert Mundin (Much the Miller's Son); Montagu Love (Bishop of Black Canon); Harry Cording (Dicken Malbott); Robert Warwick (Sir Geoffrey); Robert Noble (Sir Ralfe); Kenneth Hunter (Sir Mortimer); Leonard Willey (Sir Essex); Lester Mathews (Sir Ivor); Colin Kenny (Sir Baldwin); Howard Hill (Captain of Archers); Ivan F. Simpson (Proprietor of Kent Road Tavern); Charles McNaughton (Crippen); Lionel Belmore (Humility Prin the Tavern Keeper); Janet Shaw (Humility's Daughter); Austin Fairman (Sir Nigel); Craufurd Kent (Sir Norbett); Val Stanton, Ernie Stanton, Olaf Hytten, Alec Harford, Peter Hobbes, Edward Dew, Sidney Baron (Robin's Outlaws); John Sutton, Paul Power, Ivo Henderson, Jack Deery (Richard's Knights); Marten Lamont (Sir Guy's Squire); Hal Brazeale (High Sheriff's Squire); Leonard Mudie (Town Crier); Denis d'Auburn, Cyril Thornton, Gerald Rogers, Charles Irwin (Saxon Men);

Connie Leon, Phillis Coghlan (Saxon Women); Herbert Evans (Senechal); Frank Hagney, James Baker (Men-at-Arms); Thomas R. Mills (Priest); George Bunny (Butcher); Dave Thursby (Archer); Joe North (Friar); Jack Richardson (Serf); Claude Wisberg (Blacksmith's Apprentice); Harold Entwistle (Tailor); Leyland Hodgson (Norman Officer); Harold Howard (Beggar); Bob Stevenson, Dick Rich (Soldiers); Nick de Ruiz (Executioner); Bob St. Angelo (Pierre de Caan); Wilson Benge (Monk); Frank Baker (Turnkey); Lowden Adams (Old Crusader); Holmes Herbert (Referee); Reginald Sheffield (Herald); Charles Bennett (Pedlar); James Baker (Philip of Arras); D'Arcy Corrigan (Villager).

New York Premiere: Radio City Music Hall—May 12, 1938
New York City Television Debut: CBS—October 29, 1959

## Synopsis

When news reaches Nottingham Castle that King Richard has been captured while on his way home from the Crusades, and is now being held for ransom, his scheming brother, Prince John, decides to take over the English regency. Having cruelly suppressed the Saxons during his brother's absence, Prince John imposes even more taxes on his subjects, pretending that the money is to be used to pay the ransom. He is abetted in his schemes by the traitorous Sir Guy of Gisbourne. Robin, whose estate and title had been taken from him by Prince John, and who had turned outlaw to help the oppressed, warns the Normans that he will take a Norman life for each Saxon life, and he carries out his threats. Together with his small band of followers, Robin Hood steals from the rich to aid the poor. Prince John is outraged and orders his men to kill Robin Hood, but to no avail, for each time Robin is captured, he manages to escape. Robin frequently places himself in the path of danger just to encounter Maid Marian, the King's ward, with whom he has fallen deeply in love. At first she opposes him, but after learning the truth of his activities, she attempts to help him, particularly because she in turn has fallen in love with him. King Richard and a few followers eventually return to England, disguised in clerical robes. With the help of Robin and his men, the King is successful in getting into the palace in time to prevent Prince John from declaring himself King. In a duel with Robin, Sir Guy is killed. The King banishes Prince John and the other traitors from the kingdom, bringing peace to England once again. As a reward for his bravery, Robin receives back his title and his estates, and obtains the King's consent to his marriage with Maid Marian.

◆━◆━◆

Warner Bros. was astutely varying Errol Flynn's filmmaking chores, casting him in contemporary romantic dramas, *Green Light* and *Another Dawn*, both 1937, and an occasional lark in wacky comedy, *The Perfect*

*Specimen* (1937). But the public still preferred him in historical epics like *The Prince and the Pauper* (1937), so it was back to costumes and broadswords, the new entry being *The Adventures of Robin Hood*. Meanwhile, the studio had been continuing the bridling Olivia de Havilland in period heroine assignments such as in *The Great Garrick* (1937), or sticking her with skittish heiress roles as the second female lead in *It's Love I'm After* (1937). Thus, it was a logical choice to pair de Havilland once again on-camera with the roguish Flynn who had charmed his way into being a top boxoffice attraction.

As in other Flynn-de Havilland spectacles (this was the first of their efforts to be lensed in color) action was the prime but not only ingredient of the enthusiastically-mounted production. With such imposing villains as Claude Rains, Basil Rathbone, and Melville Cooper, a saintly leader (Ian Hunter), such flamboyant accomplices as Little John (Alan Hale), Friar Tuck (Eugene Pallette), Much the Miller's son (Herbert Mundin), and the iconoclastic Una O'Connor as de Havilland's flirtatious crone of a maid servant, there was scarcely a chance for audience interest to lag in the course of the 102 minutes of film. Nearly all the old wives' legends of the famed Sherwood Forest bandit and his merry men were brought forth for the audience's enjoyment, including the archery tournament, the quarterstaves jousting bout between Flynn and Hale, and Pallette's agreeing to carry Flynn piggyback across the stream.

*The Adventures of Robin Hood* had started filming its Sherwood Forest sequences in September 1937 in Chico, California, under the direction of William Keighley who had directed Flynn in *The Prince and the Pauper*. But Jack L. Warner later replaced Keighley with the more epic-oriented Michael Curtiz who helmed all the interior scenes as well as some additional action footage lensed near Lake Sherwood, west of the San Fernando Valley. Erich Wolfgang Korngold provided another of his richly orchestrated, rousing scores which so effectively underlines the majesty of the onscreen action, witty dialog, and the impressively multi-hued settings. Korngold's score won an Oscar as did Carl Jules Weyl's (castle set) art direction, and Ralph Dawson's fluid editing. *The Adventures of Robin Hood*, which was a huge money-maker both in initial release and subsequent reissues, was nominated for Best Picture of the year, but lost the Academy Award to *You Can't Take It with You*.

Since the initial collection of English ballads about the legendary folk hero Robin Hood appeared in 1490, the public had been overwhelmingly intrigued by this capricious, colorful character who robbed from the rich to help the poor. The subject matter was a cinema natural, and in 1923 Douglas Fairbanks, Sr. produced a lavish rendition, which was thought unduplicable until Warner Bros. presented its two million-dollar, three-color, Technicolor edition in 1938. The storyline differed considerably from the silent edition, but in deeds of zesty swashbuckling and chivalrous courtship, it was a very worthy successor, labeled a classic of its kind in the sound cinema. ". . . it holds its own as entertainment in any coin of the realm" [Howard Barnes *(New York Herald-Tribune)*. "Life and the movies have their compensations, and such a film as this is payment in full for many dull hours of picture-going" [Frank S. Nugent (New York *Times*)].

Flynn may not have been as acrobatic as Fairbanks, but he created his own special brand of "swashbuckler from peeked cap to pointed toe." In a noticeable progression from the rather unsure swordplay of *Captain Blood*, Flynn evinced far more conviction in his metal clanging in *The Adventures of Robin Hood*. Under the expert guidance of fencing master Fred Cavens, Flynn and Rathbone engaged in a climatic duel at Nottingham Castle, with their broadsword battle raging down a curved staircase, across a stout table, and over a disarrayed huge candelabra. Then, too, in no other Flynn-de Havilland joint cinema epic was Flynn so gallant in his courtship of the lofty miss. Their romancing correctly blended courtly behavior with unbridled jesting as each attempted to outdo the other in his/her amorous game of oneupsmanship. Although her role was a stock costumed heroine's part, de Havilland with her growing expertise made her part affectingly regal yet at times warm, and always captivatingly beautiful. By this point in her career, viewers could never be sure where the actress left off and the role began, leading Nugent of the *Times* to suggest, "Maid Marian has the grace to suit Olivia de Havilland."

### FOUR'S A CROWD
*(Warner Bros., 1938) 91M.*

Executive producer, Hal B. Wallis; associate producer, David Lewis; director, Michael Curtiz; story, Wallace Sullivan; screenplay, Casey Robinson, Sig Herzig; music, Heinz Roemheld, Ray Heindorf; dialog director, Irving Rapper; assistant director, Sherry Shourds; art director, Max Parker; gowns, Orry-Kelly; sound, Robert B. Lee; camera, Ernest Haller; editor, Clarence Kolster.

Errol Flynn (Robert Kensington Lansford); Olivia de Havilland (Lorri Dillingwell); Rosalind Russell (Jean Christy); Patric Knowles (Patterson Buckley); Walter Connolly (John P. Dillingwell); Hugh Herbert (Silas Jenkins); Melville Cooper (Bingham); Franklin Pangborn (Preston); Herman Bing (Herman the Barber); Margaret Hamilton (Amy); Joseph Crehan (Pierce the Butler); Joe Cunningham (Young); Dennie Moore (Buckley's Secretary); Gloria Blondell, Carole Landis (Lansford's Secretaries); Renie Riano (Mrs. Jenkins); Charles Trowbridge (Dr. Ives); Spencer Charters (Charlie);

New York Premiere: Radio City Music Hall—August 11, 1938
New York Television Debut: CBS—February 5, 1960

## Synopsis

Breezy newspaper reporter Jean Christy persuades millionaire newspaper publisher Patterson Buckley to reengage Robert Kensington Lansford as managing editor. Robert, who in the meantime has become a rather well-known press agent, accepts the job only because it will give him a chance to meet John P. Dillingwell, an eccentric millionaire who had refused to become one of his clients. As a means of reaching Dillingwell, Robert plays up to Lorri, Dillingwell's pert granddaughter. This enrages Buckley, Lorri's supposed fiancé, and he discharges Robert. But Robert finally gets to meet Dillingwell and wins his admiration by some tricks that he is adept at pulling. Jean and Robert love one another, but he has to continue paying court to Lorri, which aggravates Jean. When Jean obtains some confidential data on Dillingwell that Robert does not want published, he appeals to her not to divulge it. Buckley, in an effort to obtain the information from her, suggests that they wed that night, and she agrees. When Robert learns of this, he rushes to the same Justice of the Peace with Lorri. Everything is eventually straightened out with the proper parties marrying one another.

◆◆◆

The previous year under Michael Curtiz' solid direction, Errol Flynn had proven himself somewhat adept at restrained farce in *The Perfect Specimen*, with Joan Blondell as his balmy co-star. It was decided to re-match Flynn and Curtiz in another such dizzy screwball comedy excursion, making this one more hectic, more star-loaded, and more shallow, which, with "its unblushingly superficial attitude toward romance," would be slanted in such a way that the four leading characters could as easily have been paired off one way as another. With a lengthy ninety-one-minute running time, it depended largely on supercharged Rosalind Russell, crotchety Walter Connolly, and the absurd likes of Hugh Herbert, Melville Cooper, Franklin Pangborn, Herman Bing and Margaret Hamilton to carry successfully the somewhat labored farce. As the pretty, rich ingenue, Olivia de Havilland was only required to be a paper thin representation of a daffy heiress, but, in order to prove her point that she was more than just a face and a figure, she managed to instill some telling moments as the nitwit debutante.

Flynn's character was based on the real life Ivy Ledbetter Lee, a Princeton graduate who became a resourceful, colorful publicist, numbering the Rockefellers among his clients, and cramming in a rather full life's existence before he died in 1934. For some reason the Casey Robinson-Sig Herzig screenplay avoided most of the charming excesses of the actual Lee, and instead made Flynn's Robert Kensington Lansford a shallow, base person. It is largely because of the star's charming, Cary Grant-like performance that the wild cinema concoction works at all.

No one was expected to take *Four's a Crowd* realistically, with its implausible newspaper office setup, and its eccentric millionaire (Connolly) who enjoys being the best hated man in America and only cares for his miniature electric railroad setup and his kennel of mastiffs. At times a viewer might have wondered what all the characters were shouting about, but then the loose talk would fade into a delightful Mack Sennett-like chase: adventurous Flynn probing too close to the kennel and winding up on the wrong end of a running playoff between himself and the Great Danes, an exciting derailment on the electric train layout, or the finale in which the wrongly matched lovers are racing by cab to the justice of the peace.

It could be rightly said that *Four's a Crowd* was a cinema mongrel, having borrowed successful bits from this or that previous screwball screen comedy. The Hugh Herbert justice of the peace with his own wacky marriage service was right out of Paramount's *The Bride Comes Home* (1935), and much of the leading players' interrelationships paralleled very closely the setup in MGM's *Libeled Lady* (1937). But in the 1930s golden age of movies the films kept pouring out of the movie factories in such streams of quantity that hardly anyone had time to analyze too closely the origins of a new picture. A viewer or critic would simply see it and let his gut reaction carry the day. In its limited way, *Four's a Crowd* was amusing and entertaining. Certainly, no one expected anything more from it than that.

### DODGE CITY
*(Warner Bros., 1939) C-104M.*

Executive producer, Hal B. Wallis; associate producer, Robert Lord; director, Michael Curtiz; screenplay, Robert Buckner; music, Max Steiner; orchestrator, Hugh Friedhofer; assistant director, Sherry Shourds; dialog director, Jo Graham; costumes, Milo Anderson; makeup, Perc Westmore; art director, Ted Smith; sound, Oliver S. Garretson; special effects, Byron Haskin, Rex Wimpy; camera, Sol Polito; associate Technicolor camera, Ray Rennahan; editor, George Amy.

Errol Flynn (Wade Hatton); Olivia de Havilland (Abbie Irving); Ann Sheridan (Ruby Gilman); Bruce Cabot (Jeff Surrett); Frank McHugh (Joe Clemens); Alan Hale (Rusty Hart); John Litel (Matt Cole); Victor Jory (Yancy); Henry Travers (Dr. Irving); Henry O'Neill (Colonel Dodge); Guinn "Big Boy" Williams (Tex Baird); Gloria Holden (Mrs. Cole); Douglas Fowley (Munger); William Lundigan (Lee Irving); Georgia Caine (Mrs. Irving); Charles Halton (Surrett's Lawyer); Ward Bond (Bud Taylor); Bobs Watson (Harry Cole); Nat Carr (Crocker); Russell Simpson (Orth); Clem Bevans (Charlie the Barber); Cora Witherspoon (Mrs. McCoy); Joe Crehan (Hammond); Thurston Hall (Twitchell); Chester Clute (Coggins); Monte Blue (Barlow the Indian Agent); James Burke (Cattle Auctioneer); Robert Homans (Mail Clerk); George Guhl (Jason the Marshal); Spencer

Charters (Clergyman); Bud Osborne (Stagecoach Driver/Waiter); Wilfred Lucas (Bartender); Jack Mower, Horace Carpenter, Francis Sayles, Ky Robinson, William Crowell, Earl Dwire, Bob Stevenson, Bruce Mitchell, Hal Craig, Howard Mitchell, George Chesebro, Frank Pharr, Ed Peil, Sr., Frank Mayo, Guy Wilkerson, Steve Clark, William McCormick (Men); Ralph Sanford (Brawler); Earle Hodgins (Spieler); Pat Flaherty (Cowhand); Vera Lewis (Woman); Milton Kibbee (Printer); Richard Cramer (Clerk); Henry Otho, Pat O'Malley (Conductors); Fred Graham (Al); James Farley (Engineer); Tom Chatterton (Passenger).

New York Premiere: Strand Theatre—April 7, 1939
New York Television Premiere: CBS—January 7, 1957

## Synopsis

Having completed their roundup of cattle for the railroad, Wade Hatton, an Irish soldier of fortune, and his two pals, Rusty Hart and Tex Baird, plan to move on to other pastures looking for new excitement. Wade incurs the enmity of Jeff Surrett, a villainous Dodge City character, when he provides the federal authorities with information on Surrett's theft of steers belonging to the range Indians. Sometime later, Wade returns to Dodge City as the leader of a caravan of settlers. He is upset because of a trail incident which caused the death of Lee Irving and left the latter's sister, Abbie, in a state of grief. When Wade enters Dodge City, he finds the place a hotbed of crime, for the town is now completely controlled by grasping Surrett and his tough henchmen. The decent folk of Dodge City, admiring Wade's courage, urge him to become the new sheriff. At first he refuses, but later changes his mind, and begins the task of trying to straighten things out. By this point Abbie has changed her opinion of Wade, becoming his staunch supporter. Law and order finally come to Dodge City, but not without plenty of bloodshed. Surrett and his gang are killed in a battle with Wade's forces. Wade and Abbie, who have decided to wed, now plan to move further westward.

◆◆◆

"As the reconstruction of a key town and a significant period in our national development, it is too fanciful and formularized to be considered an important historical document. There is enough rousing melodrama in the show, though, to keep most spectators from bothering about the authenticity of the characters and the incident" [Howard Barnes (*New York Herald-Tribune*)].

Warner Bros. had exploited Errol Flynn, their answer to MGM's Clark Gable, in almost every screen genre but the Western, and 1939 seemed an appropriate time to initiate the star in a stirring sagebrush tale. It was the year of the big horse opera movie revival, with an amazing array of Western pictures, including *Destry Rides Again, Jesse James,*

*Man of Conquest, Stagecoach,* and Warners' own *The Oklahoma Kid* (with James Cagney and Humphrey Bogart). In a Technicolor showcase that cost approximately $1.5 million to mount, director Michael Curtiz launched Flynn into a new screen field with the flourish that was so much a part of that director's style. Curtiz in *Dodge City* demonstrated that the star's charm and athletic prowess, with fists more than with six shooters, could carry him through a brawling horse opera in fine form. (Flynn would make seven other Westerns in the course of his film career.) To explain away Flynn's inescapable British accent, the *Dodge City* scenario carefully established that Flynn's Wade Hatton was an Irish soldier of fortune who, among other global rovings, had been a Texas cowboy after the Civil War.

The setting for this film was the rollicking Kansas town of Dodge City, known as the Bagdad of the old West, where the huge profits to be made from the new train line from Dodge City to Wichita inspired skunks like Jeff Surrett (Bruce Cabot) to grab for control of the town. Opposing Cabot and his henchmen (including Victor Jory and Douglas Fowley) was free-booter Flynn who finds his underlying sense of decency and his overt love of the lady newspaper owner (Olivia de Havilland) sufficient cause to accept the demanding and dangerous post of sheriff and become the champion of the local decent folk.

As the righteous, then forgiving, and finally loving heroine, de Havilland was as "pretty as ever" and made a plausible reward for Flynn's screen hijinks. More so than in their previous joint screen outings, de Havilland's role cast her as a reformer who set the standards to which Flynn's rapscallion character must aspire, and who holds back her acceptance of marriage until Flynn has proven himself in the field of battle. In deliberate contrast to spirited but demure de Havilland was redheaded Ann Sheridan in a cameo-length role as Ruby Gilman, songstress extraordinaire of the Gay Lady Saloon, who proved in her sexy *Dodge City* projection that her "oomph girl" tag was fully warranted. [At the wrong end of their careers, Sheridan and Flynn would co-star in the flimsier *Silver River* (1948).]

By today's socalled adult Western standards, with the obligatory interweaving of psychological under- and overtones, *Dodge City* seems outrageously basic, being geared strictly for action, with its character delineation purely in black and white terms. This simpler approach with its right is might theory is firmly flaunted in the action-packed finale, the slam-bang brawl occurring in the Gay Lady Saloon, where the good, of course, triumph over the unworthy. The expansive fight, which lasts a good ten minutes onscreen, required five days to film and a host of stunt men to carry out the choreographed display of fisticuffs which ranged all over the detailed set, as glass and furniture crash and smash, and two of the oncamera cowboys plummet through to the floor level from a balcony staircase.

Although location work for *Dodge City* was lensed at the studio ranch in Calabasas, and at Modesto, California, the world premiere for the big Western was held on April 1, 1939, at Dodge City where the picture was simultaneously screened at four local theatres. While neither Flynn nor de Havilland made the eastern trek for the gala occasion, cast members Ann Sheridan, Frank McHugh, and Alan Hale were present at the festivities as well as studio contract players Priscilla and Rosemary Lane.

## THE PRIVATE LIVES OF ELIZABETH AND ESSEX
### *(Warner Bros., 1939) C-106M.*

Executive producer, Hal B. Wallis; associate producer, Robert Lord; director, Michael Curtiz; based on the play *Elizabeth the Queen* by Maxwell Anderson; screenplay, Norman Reilly Raine, Aeneas MacKenzie; music, Erich Wolfgang Korngold; orchestrator, Hugh Friedhofer, Milan Roder; assistant director, Sherry Shourds; dialog director, Stanley Logan; art director, Anton Grot; costumes, Orry-Kelly; makeup, Perc Westmore; technical adviser, Ali Hubert; sound, C. A. Riggs; special effects, Byron Haskin, H. F. Koenekamp; camera, Sol Polito; associate Technicolor camera, W. Howard Greene; editor, Owen Marks.

Bette Davis (Queen Elizabeth); Errol Flynn (Robert Devereaux, the Earl of Essex); Olivia de Havilland (Lady Penelope Gray); Donald Crisp (Francis Bacon); Alan Hale (Earl of Tyrone); Vincent Price (Sir Walter Raleigh); Henry Stephenson (Lord Burghley); Henry Daniell (Sir Robert Cecil); James Stephenson (Sir Thomas Egerton); Nanette Fabray (Mistress Margaret Radcliffe); Ralph Forbes (Lord Knollys); Robert Warwick (Lord Mountjoy); Leo G. Carroll (Sir Edward Coke); and Forrester Harvey, Doris Lloyd, Maris Wrixon, Rosella Towne, John Sutton, Guy Bellis, Stanford I. Jolley.

New York Premiere: Strand Theatre—December 1, 1939
New York Television Debut: CBS—October 13, 1957

### Synopsis

Robert Devereaux, the Earl of Essex, returns to England in glory, the hero who conquered the Spanish fleet at Cadiz. When Robert meets with his loved one, Queen Elizabeth, at Whitehall Palace, she berates him for allowing the enemy to sink their treasure fleet, while he sought personal glory by storming Cadiz. To demonstrate her displeasure, Elizabeth raises Robert's rival, Sir Walter Raleigh, to a high government post, forcing Robert to retire to his castle at Wanstead in shame. Only when Elizabeth sends him a personal request does he return to London. Robert is appointed Master of the Ordnance on Elizabeth's order, for she is afraid to send her lover to combat the rebellious Earl of Tyrone in Ireland. However, at a subsequent council meeting the boastful Robert is duped into accepting the dangerous challenge of opposing Tyrone. Later Francis Bacon joins a conspiracy to separate Elizabeth from her Robert by having Lady Penelope Gray, the Queen's lady-in-waiting, withhold all correspondence between the regal lovers. Although Robert's sally against Tyrone is unsuccessful, he returns to London a popular hero, a man planning to take over the throne of England. He supervises the seizure of Whitehall Palace. When the contrite Elizabeth effects a reconciliation with Robert, who blames her for the Irish defeat, he disbands his troops, permitting the Queen to have him seized and jailed on charges of treason. The royal ruler offers to spare his life—even to share her throne with him—but the proud Robert insists he must have complete control or nothing. When it becomes clear that she cannot barter for his life, Elizabeth is left to her tears, as Robert is taken to the chopping block in the courtyard below.

◆━◆━◆

The King (Errol Flynn) and the Queen (Bette Davis) of the Warner Bros. lot had been feuding since 1938 when he was given top billing over her in their joint project *The Sisters* (1938). This contretemps led Davis later to claim that she had refused the packaging of herself in the lead and Warner Bros. in the financing of *Gone with the Wind*, because Flynn was supposed to be the Rhett Butler. Whatever their personal professional differences, when Warners cast her in a picturization of Maxwell Anderson's verse drama *Elizabeth the Queen* (which had run for 145 performances on Broadway in 1930 with Lynn Fontanne and Alfred Lunt starred), Flynn and not her hoped-for vis-a-vis Laurence Olivier was assigned to the role of the Earl of Essex. After Flynn's swashbuckling screen part was beefed up for the project and the film retitled *The Knight and the Lady*, Davis raised a storm of major proportions. Her anger resulted in a further reshifting of the scenario and the film's final release title, *The Private Lives of Elizabeth and Essex.*

In actuality, Queen Elizabeth (1533-1603) was sixty-eight years old when Robert Devereaux (1566-1601) went to the block. In the motion picture Davis' monarch was altered to a matronly ruler, a vain woman who loves her proud peacock of a consort more than is politically wise for a person of her esteemed stature. The vying for power between the aging, neurotic, red-wigged Queen and her vehement young soldier lover (Flynn) occupies a good deal of the screen drama, as they continually battle.

Davis: "You believe you'd rule England better because you are a man."

Flynn: "I would indeed! And that is why you fail. Because you can't act and think like a man."

Even with his vanity and his political future at stake, Flynn's flashy Earl cannot decide how best to deal with Davis' mercurial Queen. "I love her, I hate her, I adore her," thunders the baffled consort. His indecision eventually leads to his demise. On the other hand, she salvages her throne

355

but at the supreme cost of the man she loves. She realizes to the fullest extent that "to be a queen is to be less than human."

In this elegant atmosphere of major romance and intense court intrigue there is little room in the picture for the development of the subsidiary relationship between Flynn and Olivia de Havilland, she being the Queen's favorite lady-in-waiting. As Lady Penelope Gray, costume-encased de Havilland has little opportunity to display her emotional problems, torn between her unrequited love for Flynn and an ever overriding loyalty to her monarch. Later, through court pressures brought on by Francis Bacon (Donald Crisp), de Havilland finds herself participating in the chamber intrigues. That fear for her life is a major factor behind her eventual choice of loyalties is demonstrated when Sir Robert Cecil (Henry Daniell) warns her, "You have a lovely head and neck, milady. It would be a pity to separate them."

To flesh out the stage drama which on Broadway was confined to the royal palace, the screenplay opens up the film's settings, including montages of the great Cadiz battle, Flynn's triumphant entry into London, the Irish marsh battle where the Earl of Tyrone (Alan Hale) defeats Flynn, and a dungeon in the Tower of London. (After the initial first release engagements, a final scene showing the execution block in the courtyard was deleted from prints.) Bolstering the majesty of the Technicolor drama were the elaborate Orry-Kelly costumes, the stately Anton Grot sets, and the sweeping music score of Erich Wolfgang Korngold.

While *The Private Lives of Elizabeth and Essex* succeeds as courtly adventure drama, and Davis' showy performance as the ranting, storming, coquettish elder stateslady was applauded if not commended, the other major players failed to gain any critical endorsement. "Unfortunately she [Davis] has been given virtually no support by Errol Flynn in the part of Essex or by Olivia de Havilland as Lady Penelope Gray. Flynn gives so stolid a portrayal of the proud lover of Elizabeth, who quixotically preferred having his head chopped off to giving up his insatiable ambition that wooden would be a kind adjective for his acting. Miss de Havilland merely walks through a part which she clearly does not comprehend" [Howard Barnes (*New York Herald-Tribune*)]. *The Daily Worker* was even less respectful of Flynn's caperings as the costumed rebel, labeling him "an Elizabethan Frank Merriwell in tights."

In 1955, Davis would appear in *The Virgin Queen*, a CinemaScope variation of the life and times of Queen Elizabeth, focusing on her romantic relationship with Sir Walter Raleigh (Richard Todd) and the latter's courtship of a court attendant (Joan Collins).

## SANTA FE TRAIL
### (Warner Bros., 1940) 110M.

Executive producer, Hal B. Wallis; associate producer, Robert Fellows;

director, Michael Curtiz; screenplay, Robert Buckner; music, Max Steiner; orchestrator, Hugo Friedhofer; assistant director, Jack Sullivan; art director, John Hughes; costumes, Milo Anderson; makeup, Perc Westmore; dialog director, Jo Graham; sound, Robert B. Lee; special effects, Byron Haskin, H. D. Koenekamp; camera, Sol Polito; editor, George Amy.

Errol Flynn (Jeb Stuart); Olivia de Havilland (Kit Carson Halliday); Raymond Massey (John Brown); Ronald Reagan (George Custer); Alan Hale (Barfoot Brody); Guinn Williams (Tex Bell); Van Heflin (Rader); Henry O'Neill (Cyrus Halliday); William Lundigan (Bob Halliday); John Litel (Harlan); Gene Reynolds (Jason Brown); Alan Baxter (Oliver Brown); Moroni Olsen (Robert E. Lee); Erville Alderson (Jefferson Davis); Susan Peters (Charlotte Davis); Charles D. Brown (Major Sumner); David Bruce (Phil Sheridan); Frank Wilcox (James Longstreet); William Marshall (George Pickett); George Haywood (John Hood); Russell Simpson (Shoubel Morgan); Joseph Sawyer (Kitzmiller); Hobart Cavanaugh (Barber Doyle); Spencer Charters (Conductor); Ward Bond (Townley); Wilfred Lucas (Weiner); Charles Middleton (Gentry); Russell Hicks (J. Boyce Russell); Napoleon Simpson (Samson); Cliff Clark (Instructor); Harry Strang (Sergeant); Emmett Vogan (Lieutenant); Selmer Jackson, Joseph Crehan, William Hopper (Officers); Clinton Rosemond, Bernice Pilot, Libby Taylor, Mildred Gover (Blacks); Roy Barcroft, Frank Mayo (Engineers); Grace Stafford (Farmer's Wife); Louis Jean Heydt (Farmer); Lane Chandler (Adjutant); Richard Kipling (Army Doctor); Jack Mower (Surveyor); Trevor Bardette, Nestor Paiva (Agitators); Mira McKinney (Woman); Harry Cording, James Farley, Alan Bridge, Eddy Waller (Men); John Meyer (Workman); Maris Wrixon, Lucia Carroll, Mildred Coles (Girls); Georgia Caine (Officer's Wife); Arthur Aylsworth, Walter Soderling, Henry Hall (Abolitionists); Theresa Harris (Black Maid); Jess Lee Brooks (Black Doorman); Eddy Chandler, Ed Cobb, Ed Peil, Ed Hearn (Guards); Victor Kilian (Dispatch Rider); Creighton Hale (Telegraph Operator); Alec Proper (Townsman); Reverend Neal Dodd (Minister); Lafe McKee (Minister); Addison Richards (Sheriff).

New York Premiere: Strand Theatre—December 20, 1940
New York Television Debut: CBS—May 6, 1957

## Synopsis

In the U.S. Military Academy at West Point in 1854, some of the cadets form strong friendships. One of the men, the flashy Jeb Stuart, is constantly taunted by Rader, the latter a John Brown disciple. One day the argument comes to a head, and both men fight. Rader is dishonorably discharged and promptly joins Brown and his band. Upon graduation, Jeb and his friends are sent to "Bloody" Kansas, which pleases them because it means plenty of action and excitement. Both Jeb and his good companion George Custer fall in love with Bob Halliday's sister, Kit. She finally admits her love for Jeb. Later, Jeb and Custer, while acting as military convoy for a freight shipment, meet Brown, who, posing as John Smith, intercepts the shipments and asks for the delivery to him of a consignment of bibles. One of the boxes falls to the ground and breaks open, revealing that its contents are rifles not bibles. A battle ensues with Jeb and Custer the victors. Thereafter, Jeb, in civilian clothes, goes to town in an effort to uncover information as to Brown's future plans. He is accompanied by two guides, Barfoot Brody and Tex Bell. When Jeb is captured by Rader and taken to Brown's secreted headquarters, Custer and his soldiers rescue him. Later, when Brown does not pay Rader the salary he has promised him, Rader goes to Jeb to tell him that Brown is planning to seize the U.S. arsenal at Harper's Ferry. The soldiers leave for the ford on the Potomac, and a hard-fought battle ensues. Brown is taken prisoner, tried, and hanged. But the ideal for which he had been fighting begins to take root, as several of the army men show sympathy for the martyr's cause. Finally, Jeb is now free to wed Kit.

◆ ◆ ◆

"As the biggest non-sequitur of the season, from the directional, historical and titular point of view, we give you *Santa Fe Trail*. . . . Don't get us wrong, we aren't saying that it lacks what is known as mass appeal" [Bosley Crowther *(New York Times)*]. The left-wing *Daily Worker* was not, it must be admitted, so far off base when it prejudicially enunciated, "Either the script writers were desperate for some way they could make heroes out of their military graduates and turned them loose against John Brown, or there is more calculated political venom behind it all. For the heroes of this weird movie are Jefferson Davis, Jeb Stuart, General Lee. . . . The villain is John Brown."

There is little historical accuracy in this atypical Western film, which has Jeb Stuart (1833-1864) graduating from West Point the same year as such noted Civil War figures as George Custer, James Hood, James Longstreet, George Pickett, and Philip Sheridan. The film's title was decidedly a misnomer since the drama is scarcely involved with the famed Missouri to New Mexico trade route. Compounding the factual exaggerations was a script that had the lead characters, Jeb Stuart (Flynn) and George Custer (Ronald Reagan), scarcely grow in dimension as they undergo obviously shattering adventures. Instead, director Michael Curtiz bends all the elements of the film to a visual study of the United States Army vs John "Osawatomie" Brown (1800-1859) (Raymond Massey).\* The final result was a do-not-offend-anyone screenplay which has the anti-slave martyr emerging as a madman who just happened to use bad methods for a just cause. Pandering to the lowest common denominator

\*Massey would again portray the fascinating John Brown in the low-budgeted *Seven Angry Men* (1955).

of audience taste, the film has the U.S. Cavalry riding to the rescue on several occasions, creating a gratuitous patriotic atmosphere in what is essentially just an action film.

In between episodes of Army post camaraderie between dashing Flynn and preening Reagan, the strained comic relief of perennial screen sidekicks Alan Hale and Guinn Williams, and the dominating theatrics of Massey, there was the subsidiary romancing between Flynn and de Havilland. For the first time in a Flynn-de Havilland costume picture, she spends most of her screen scenes not in Milo Anderson-created finery but in the garb of a pioneer cowgirl, foreshadowing her part in *They Died with Their Boots On* and such later screen roles as her part in *The Proud Rebel* (1958).

The ending of *Santa Fe Trail* is distinctly ambiguous in tone. The "culprit" Brown is killed, the Army emerges victorious, and Flynn and de Havilland are together for a happy fadeout (a growing rarity in their joint movies), but there is the ominous foreboding of the approaching Civil War and all the chaos that it was to bring.

*Santa Fe Trail* had its world premiere at Santa Fe, New Mexico on December 15, 1940, five days before its official New York City opening.


### THEY DIED WITH THEIR BOOTS ON
*(Warner Bros., 1941) 140M.*

Executive producer, Hal B. Wallis; associate producer, Robert Fellows; director, Raoul Walsh; screenplay, Wally Kine, Aeneas MacKenzie; music, Max Steiner; art director, John Hughes; assistant director, Russell Saunders; dialog director, Edward A. Blatt; technical adviser, Lieutenant Colonel J. G. Taylor, U.S. Army, Retired; gowns, Milo Anderson; makeup, Perc Westmore; sound, Dolph Thomas; camera, Bert Glennon; editor, William Holmes.

Errol Flynn (George Armstrong Custer); Olivia de Havilland (Elizabeth Bacon Custer); Arthur Kennedy (Ned Sharp, Jr.); Charles Grapewin (California Joe); Gene Lockhart (Samuel Bacon); Anthony Quinn (Crazy Horse); Stanley Ridges (Major Romulus Taipe); John Litel (General Philip Sheridan); Walter Hampden (Senator Sharp); Sydney Greenstreet (General Winfield Scott); Regis Toomey (Fitzhugh Lee); Hattie McDaniel (Callie); G. P. Huntley, Jr. (Lieutenant Butler); Frank Wilcox (Captain Webb); Joseph Sawyer (Sergeant Doolittle); Minor Watson (Senator Smith); Gig Young (Lieutenant Roberts); John Ridgley (Second Lieutenant Davis); Joseph Crehan (President Grant); Aileen Pringle (Mrs. Sharp); Anna Q. Nilsson (Mrs. Taipe); Harry Lewis (Youth); Tod Andrews (Cadet Brown); Walter Brooke (Rosser); Selmer Jackson (Captain McCook); William Hopper (Frazier); Eddie Acuff (Corporal Smith); Sam McDaniel (Waiter);

George Reed (Charles); Pat McVey (Jones); William Forrest (Adjutant); James Seay (Lieutenant Walsh); George Eldredge (Captain Riley); John Hamilton (Colonel); Renie Riano, Edna Holland, Minerva Urecal, Virginia Sale (Nurses); Vera Lewis (Head Nurse); Spencer Charters (Station Master); Frank Orth, Ray Teal (Barflies); Hobart Bosworth (Clergyman); Dick Wessell (Staff Sergeant Brown); Weldon Heyburn (Staff Officer); Harry Strang, Max Hoffman, Jr., Frank Mayo (Orderlies); Irving Bacon (Salesman); Garland Smith, Roy Barcroft, Dick French, Marty Faust, Bob Perry, Paul Kruger, Steve Darrell (Officers); Russell Hicks (Colonel of First Michigan); Victor Zimmerman (Colonel of Fifth Michigan); Ian MacDonald (Soldier); Lane Chandler, Ed Parker (Sentries); Sol Gorss, Addison Richards (Adjutants); Jack Mower (Telegrapher); Alberta Gary (Jane the Kitchen Maid); Annabelle Jones (Maid); Hugh Sothern (Major Smith); Arthur Loft (Tillaman); Carl Harbaugh (Sergeant); G. Pat Collins (Corporal); Virginia Brissac (Woman); Walter Baldwin (Settler); Joe Devlin, Fred Kelsey, Wade Crosby (Bartenders); Herbert Heywood (Newsman); Joseph King (Chairman); Ed Keane (Congressman); Francis Ford (Veteran); Frank Ferguson (Grant's Secretary).

New York Premiere: Strand Theatre—November 20, 1941
New York Television Debut: CBS—August 27, 1960

## Synopsis

George Armstrong Custer enters West Point in 1857. Being a poor scholar, he constantly gets into trouble, but as an equestrian and a fighter he is at the top of his class. He falls in love at first sight with Libby Bacon when she visits West Point, but his sudden call to arms in the Union Army prevents his seeing her for some time. Once in Washington, George longs for battle action and finally convinces General Winfield Scott, commander-in-chief of the Army, that his place is with the famous Second Cavalry. Through an error, George is made a Brigadier General, but he shows himself to be a brilliant leader. At the end of the Civil War he returns a hero, and weds Libby. However, civilian life makes him restless. He rejects an offer by Senator William Sharp and his son Ned, a former cavalry soldier, to join them in a scheme that would make him wealthy. Through Libby's efforts George is restored to active Cavalry duty, and is assigned to Fort Lincoln in the Dakota territory as commander of the Seventh Regiment. He soon turns a regiment of drunkards into fine soldiers, but by so doing he earns the enmity of Ned Sharp who has settled there, for he had put a stop to Sharp's selling liquor to the soldiers and guns to the Indians. George ends the recurring Indian raids by promising Chief Crazy Horse that white men will not overrun the Black Hills. But the Sharps have other ideas, intending to build a railroad line through the Indians' sacred hunting grounds. By starting a false rumor of a gold strike in the Black Hills, the

Sharps bring many people into the territory. George brings charges against the Sharps, but at a Washington hearing politics block him, and he is held for court-martial for striking a government official. George is able to convince President Grant that he belongs with the regiment, since the Indian tribes have combined forces to go on the warpath. George returns to Fort Lincoln and leads his troop into battle, knowing that he and his men are going to their deaths. Nevertheless, he feels they have to be sacrificed in order to hold the redskins in check until reinforcements arrive. Ned, whom George has kidnapped, fights and dies with the others. George leaves a letter accusing the Sharps and the official he had struck. His widow Libby demands that these men abandon their schemes and the government official resign, otherwise she will make the letter public and they would be lynched. They agree, and peace is brought to the territory.

◆ ◆ ◆

*Dive Bomber* (1941) had been the final Errol Flynn picture to be directed by Michael Curtiz. The friction between star and director had grown too strong, and Curtiz' penchant for going over-budget on spectacles was increasing at too rapid a rate for Warner Bros. to tolerate. Therefore veteran helmer Raoul Walsh was assigned to *They Died with Their Boots On,* the first of seven Flynn vehicles he would handle. At 140 minutes, the black and white feature was a staggering prairie epic. "The film is a cross between two types the studio usually manages with distinction —the dignified biography and the epic, roaring Western. The chief trouble with the attempt is that it takes too long to get to the Indians" *(Newsweek* magazine).

According to the cold eye of history, George Armstrong Custer (1839-1876) was a preening glory hunter, who wrote up his colorful exploits for the pulp magazines, whooped it up on the battlefield, and was as reckless with his own life as with others. Obviously, the real man was no fit subject for a Flynn-type of heroic swashbuckling celluloid escapade. Therefore, the screenplay changed the officer into an over-enthusiastic, natural-born leader of men, who, according to the film, in the climactic encounter with the Indians on June 25, 1876, sacrificed his small force to prevent the warring Indians from descending upon General Terry's unsuspecting regiment. This fictionalized viewpoint is definitely in variance with historical accounts of the tragedy, although even Chief Sitting Bull was forced to later admit of Custer, "He stood like a sheaf of corn with all the ears fallen around him." [Even the representation of Custer in the facetious *Little Big Man* (1970) was closer to reality.]

Just as the bulk of *The Charge of the Light Brigade* was merely a diverting prelude to the climactic ride to the death, so the larger portion of *They Died with Their Boots On*—including the Civil War battle scenes— was merely a warm-up for the meticulously staged encounter between Flynn and his smartly-dressed soldiers and Chief Crazy Horse (Anthony

Quinn) and his shrieking braves. The magnificent sweep of a disastrous encounter between Army troops and redskins has rarely been so excellently presented before or since onscreen.

In what would be their final joint acting screen appearance, Flynn and Olivia de Havilland portrayed a dimension to their courtship-marriage relationship which made their previous screen encounters seem shallow. Undoubtedly a good deal of credit must go to director Walsh who instilled a personal touch to this landscape-sized picture. As the attractive daughter of persnickety Gene Lockhart, de Havilland's Libby is a self-willed but gentle creature who is as attracted to Flynn as he is to her. His wooing of her, interrupted by the Civil War, is charming, believable, and pertinent to the tale. One soon senses the dimensions of de Havilland's liberated woman who not only stands by her husband in times of glory, but urges him onward when his morale is down, or maneuvers with military political circles to insure his reinstatement to active duty. If any of their shared scenes strike a posturing, false note, it is the overly noble interlude before he sets out for the fatal Black Hills encounter.

De Havilland: "You can't go. You'll be killed. I won't let you go."

Flynn: "I must go. It's my duty! I'm an officer in the United States Army."

With tears in her expressive eyes, she falls into into a martyred pose as he jauntily walks out of their post living quarters and later gallantly rides to his certain death.

Although *They Died with Their Boots On*, was yet another example of the love team's characters not living happily ever after (for far different emotional affect than the sad finales of the Margaret Sullavan-James Stewart movie entries of the late 1930s), de Havilland is given at long last the opportunity here to show her ability as an actress. In subsequent scenes following the Little Big Horn massacre, she bravely puts her tears aside. As the widow of a national hero, she sallies forth to do battle with the corrupt forces in President Grant's administrations, making a final, impassioned plea to Congress that her husband's death, and that of his valiant men, be not in vain. For a change, de Havilland received due credit for her oncamera participation in a Flynn screen epic. "The love affair was uncomplicated and derives interest only from the ardor which Olivia de Havilland can always supply. Nor is this warm-blooded actress lacking in beauty. She wears her off-the-shoulder period decollette with bewitching effect" [John Rosenfield (*Dallas Morning News*)].

## THANK YOUR LUCKY STARS
*(Warner Bros., 1943) 127M.*

Producer, Mark Hellinger; director, David Butler; story, Everett Freeman, Arthur Schwartz; screenplay, Norman Panama, Melvin Frank,

James V. Kern; songs, Arthur Schwartz and Frank Loesser; vocal arranger, Dudley Chambers; orchestral arrangements, Ray Heindorf; musical adaptor, Heinz Roemhold; orchestrator, Maurice de Packh; dialog director, Herbert Farjean; art director, Anton Grot, Leo K. Kuter; set decorator, Walter F. Tilford; gowns, Milo Anderson; makeup, Perc Westmore; assistant director, Phil Quinn; choreography-dance stager, LeRoy Prinz; sound, Francis J. Scheid, Charles David Forrest; special effects, H. F. Koenekamp; camera, Arthur Edeson; editor, Irene Morra.

Eddie Cantor (Joe Sampson/Himself); Joan Leslie (Pat Dixon); Dennis Morgan (Tommy Randolph); Dinah Shore (Herself); S. Z. Sakall (Dr. Schlenna); Edward Everett Horton (Farnsworth); Ruth Donnelly (Nurse Hamilton); Joyce Reynolds (Girl with Book); Richard Lane (Barney Jackson); Don Wilson (Himself); Henry Armetta (Angelo); Willie Best (Soldier); Humphrey Bogart, Jack Carson, Bette Davis, Olivia de Havilland, Errol Flynn, John Garfield, Alan Hale, Ida Lupino, Ann Sheridan, Alexis Smith, George Tobias, Spike Jones and His City Slickers (Specialties); Jack Mower, Creighton Hale (Engineers); Don Barclay (Pete); Stanley Clements, James Copedge (Boys); Leah Baird, Joan Matthews, Phyllis Godfrey, Lillian West, Morgan Brown, George French (Bus Passengers); Joe DeRita (Milquetoast Type); Frank Faylen (Sailor); Eleanor Counts (Sailor's Girl Friend); Charles Soldani, J. W. Cody (Indians); Noble Johnson (Charlie the Indian); Harry Pilcer (Man in Broadcasting Station); Mike Mazurki (Olaf); Bennie Bartlett (Page Boy); Marjorie Hoshelle, Anne O'Neal (Maids); Jerry Mandy (Chef); Betty Farrington (Assistant Chef); Billy Wayne (Chauffeur); William Haade (Butler); Howard Mitchell, James Flavin (Policemen); Lou Marcelle (Commentator); Mary Treen (Fan); Ed Gargan (Doorman); Dick Rich (Fred); Ralph Dunn (Marty); James Burke (Bill the Interne Guard); Paul Harvey (Dr. Kirby); Frank Mayo (Dr. Wheaton); Bert Gordon (Patient); Angi O. Poulos (Waiter); Billy Benedict (Bus Boy); Boyd Irwin (Man); Lelah Tyler (Woman); Helen O'Hara (Whow Girl); Juanita Stark (Secretary); ICE COLD KATIE NUMBER: Hattie McDaniel (Gossip); Rita Christiani (Ice Cold Katie); Jess Lee Brooks (Justice); Ford, Harris, and Jones (Trio); Mathew Jones (Gambler); ERROL FLYNN NUMBER: Monte Blue, Art Foster, Fred Kelsey, Elmer Ballard, Buster Wiles, Howard Davies, Tudor Williams, Alan Cook, Fred McEvoy, Bobby Hale, Will Stanton, Charles Irwin, David Thursby, Henry Ibling, Earl Hunsaker, Hubert Hend, Dudley Kuzello, Ted Billings (Pub Characters); BETTE DAVIS NUMBER: Jack Norton (Drunk); Henri DeSoto (Maitre d'Hotel); Dick Elliott (Customer); Harry Adams (Doorman); Sam Adams (Bartender); Conrad Wiedell (Jitterbug); Dick Earle (Customer); Charles Francis, Harry Bailey (Bald Headed Men); Joan Winfield (Cigarette Girl); Sylvia Opert, Nancy Worth (Hat Check Girls); THE LUCKY STARS: Harriette Haddon, Harriett Olsen, Nancy Worth, Joy Barlowe, Janet Barrett, Dorothy Schoemer, Dorothy Dayton, Lucille

LaMarr, Sylvia Opert, Mary Landa; HUMPHREY BOGART SEQUENCE: Matt McHugh (Fireman); ANN SHERIDAN NUMBER: Georgia Lee Settle, Virginia Patton (Girls); GOOD NIGHT, GOOD NEIGHBOR NUMBER: Igor DeNavrotsky (Dancer); Brandon Hurst (Cab Driver); Angelita Mari (Duenna); Lynne Baggett (Miss Latin America); Mary Landa (Miss Spain).

New York Premiere: Strand Theatre—October 1, 1943
New York Television Debut: Channel 5—March 3, 1957

## Synopsis

Joe Simpson, a Hollywood tour guide, finds his dramatic ambitions stifled because of his close resemblance to that obstreperous radio star Eddie Cantor. When the producers of a charity affair seek Dinah Shore for their show, Eddie, who has Dinah under contract, agrees to her appearance, provided that he be appointed program chairman. Songwriter Pat Dixon and singer Tommy Randolph try to join the show, but Eddie vetoes the idea. With the aid of three friendly Indians, Pat and Tommy lure Eddie away from the theatre and arrange with Joe to impersonate Cantor. Unaware that they are dealing with the bogus Cantor, the producers agree to Pat and Tommy going on the show. Meanwhile Eddie escapes from the Indians, only to land in an asylum where he is mistaken for a deranged patient. He finally escapes and reaches the theatre, but too late to prevent Joe from singing a song and being acclaimed as the real Eddie Cantor.

◆━◆━◆

Of the several wartime all-star movie musical revues, *Thank Your Lucky Stars* was far more self-conscious than such competing efforts as Paramount's *Star Spangled Rhythm* (1942) or MGM's *Thousands Cheer* (1943). While *Thank Your Lucky Stars* employed the gimmick of having its celebrity cast perform routines not generally associated with their screen personae, the 127-minute showcase led reviewers such as Kate Cameron *(New York Daily News)* to complain, "They have put everything lying around loose on the lot into *Thank Your Lucky Stars*, with the exception of good taste. Of that, they couldn't find a modicum on the set."

Dinah Shore sang the film's theme song, as well as "How Sweet You Are," and "The Dreamer." Dennis Morgan and Joan Leslie dueted "I'm Riding for a Fall." Ann Sheridan vocalized "Love Isn't Born, It's Made." Bette Davis sang (!) and jitterbugged (!) to "They're Either Too Young or Too Old," and John Garfield talk-sung "Blues in the Night." Olivia de Havilland had a hotcha boogie woogie number (a swing version of "The Dreamer") with Ida Lupino and George Tobias, with the two actresses dressed in checkered skirts, blouses, and big bows in their hair. They cavorted with Tobias in the true style of children of Brooklyn. (Lynn Martin provided Olivia's singing voice.)

One of the few outstanding sequences of this marathon variety show was Errol Flynn's sketch in which he entered a London pub as a moustached Cockney sailor. In addition, as a send-up of his status as a cinema war hero, he sang "That's What You Jolly Well Get," incorporating into his rendition references to his cinema soundstage exploits in the various theatres of war. After he was carried shoulder high about the pub, with the patrons singing "Hurrah, He's Won the War," the annoyed men toss him through a window in the street. The sketch revealed that Flynn had far more potential versatility than his swashbuckling and other screen roles to that date had displayed. In the final ensemble, Flynn does a satirical operatic bit, in which a dubbed voice provides the star's aria, with Flynn oncamera admitting he wishes he had as good a voice as the real singer's.

## THE YEARS AFTER

Olivia de Havilland thought her confining Warner Bros. contract was concluded in 1943* after performing in *Princess O'Rourke* on the home lot and in *Government Girl* on loan to RKO. However, the studio claimed she owed them an additional six months for the time she had been on suspension. She filed suit and, backed by the Screen Actors Guild, engaged in a protracted legal battle. She eventually won her point, establishing the rule that seven years is the top limit for any film contract (even including suspension periods). When she could return to moviemaking she won an Oscar for Best Actress in Paramount's *To Each His Own* (1946) and another for the same studio's *The Heiress* (1949), the latter based on Henry James' *Washington Square*. In the early 1950s she fumbled on Broadway in stage renditions of *Romeo and Juliet* and *Candida*, but returned to the screen in *My Cousin Rachel* (1953). After making *Not as a Stranger* (1955) and the same year marrying Pierre Galante, the editor of Paris *Match*, she moved to France and stated she no longer cared much about moviemaking. In 1961 she was on Broadway with Henry Fonda in the tearjerker play *A Gift of Time*. In 1963 she penned her anecdotal account of Parisian life, *Every Frenchman Has One*, and in 1964 performed in two Hollywoodian exercises of grand guignol drama. Her best television performance to date has been *Noon Wine* (1967), followed in 1970 by a nude performance in the trashy *The Adventurers*. She is currently at work on her memoirs, and perhaps now will detail more fully her at-the-time unspoken crush on co-star Errol Flynn. At a London film retrospective in August, 1971, she did admit to the audience that it was a shame neither she nor Flynn had ever "let on" about their mutual attraction, then promptly added, "No it isn't, he would have ruined my life."

Errol Flynn's post de Havilland years* at Warners found the actor

---

*In *The March of Time*'s short subject entry *Show Business at War* (1943) de Havilland and Flynn were among the celebrities featured in this newsreel report.

continuing with his screen derring-dos in a rash of cinema war dramas, before returning, unsuccessfully, to his old costume drama stance in *Adventures of Don Juan* (1948) with Viveca Lindfors. Then MGM borrowed him for the stodgy period piece, *That Forsyte Woman* (1949) with Greer Garson. Flynn's personal decline (due to overdrinking) was temporarily halted when he married his third wife, Warner Bros. starlet Patrice Wymore, in 1950. He wrote the screenplay for the flimsy *The Adventures of Captain Fabian* (1951) made at Republic, and concluded his Warners' tenure with the trite adventure yarn, *Mara Maru* (1952). A trio of swashbuckling pictures followed, but the old Flynn zest was gone; an ill-fated project of *William Tell* was never completed, and then there were leaden co-starring ventures with Britain's Anna Neagle. He hosted a modestly successful video anthology series, and then was rescued from screen ignominy by Darryl F. Zanuck who cast him as a drunk in *The Sun Also Rises* (1957) and *The Roots of Heaven* (1958). In between he portrayed the champion real-life actor-drinker of them all, John Barrymore, in a torpid biography of Diana Barrymore entitled *Too Much, Too Soon* (1958). Flynn's last film was the semi-documentary *Cuban Rebel Girls* (1959) featuring his then current girlfriend, teen-aged Beverly Aadland. That same year, during which his successful autobiography *My Wicked, Wicked Ways* was published, he died on October 14th. Although he was only fifty-one at the time, his vigorous life style had worn him out years before, making him what Jack Warner termed "a living corpse" long before his actual demise.

In **Next Time We Love** (Univ., 1936)

# Chapter 13

# James Stewart
# &
# Margaret Sullavan

## JAMES STEWART

6' 2½"
165 pounds
Brown hair
Gray eyes
Taurus

*Real name: James Maitland Stewart. Born May 20, 1908, Indiana, Pennsylvania. Married Gloria McLean (1949), children: Judy, Kelly.*

FEATURE FILMS:

*Murder Man* (MGM, 1935)
*Rose Marie* (MGM, 1936)
*Next Time We Love* (Univ., 1936)
*Wife Vs. Secretary* (MGM, 1936)
*Small Town Girl* (MGM, 1936)
*Speed* (MGM, 1936)
*The Gorgeous Hussy* (MGM, 1936)
*Born to Dance* (MGM, 1936)
*After the Thin Man* (MGM, 1936)
*Seventh Heaven* (20th, 1937)
*The Last Gangster* (MGM, 1937)
*Navy Blue and Gold* (MGM, 1937)

*Of Human Hearts* (MGM, 1938)
*Vivacious Lady* (RKO, 1938)
*The Shopworn Angel* (MGM, 1938)
*You Can't Take It with You* (Col., 1938)
*Made for Each Other* (UA, 1939)
*Ice Follies of 1939* (MGM, 1939)
*It's a Wonderful World* (MGM, 1939)
*Mr. Smith Goes to Washington* (Col., 1939)
*Destry Rides Again* (Univ., 1939)

*The Shop Around the Corner* (MGM, 1940)

*The Mortal Storm* (MGM, 1940)

*No Time for Comedy* (WB, 1940)

*The Philadelphia Story* (MGM, 1940)

*Come Live With Me* (MGM, 1941)

*Pot O' Gold* (UA, 1941)

*Ziegfeld Girl* (MGM, 1941)

*It's a Wonderful Life* (RKO, 1946)

*Magic Town* (RKO, 1947)

*Call Northside 777* (20th, 1948)

*On Our Merry Way* (UA, 1948)

*Rope* (WB, 1948)

*You Gotta Stay Happy* (Univ., 1948)

*The Stratton Story* (MGM, 1949)

*Malaya* (MGM, 1949)

*Winchester '73* (Univ., 1950)

*Broken Arrow* (20th, 1950)

*The Jackpot* (20th, 1950)

*Harvey* (Univ., 1950)

*No Highway in the Sky* (20th, 1951)

*The Greatest Show on Earth* (Par., 1952)

*Bend of the River* (Univ., 1952)

*Carbine Williams* (MGM, 1952)

*The Naked Spur* (MGM, 1953)

*Thunder Bay* (Univ., 1953)

*The Glenn Miller Story* (Univ., 1954)

*Rear Window* (Par., 1954)

*The Far Country* (Univ., 1955)

*Strategic Air Command* (Par., 1955)

*The Man from Laramie* (Col., 1955)

*The Man Who Knew Too Much* (Par., 1956)

*The Spirit of St. Louis* (WB, 1957)

*Night Passage* (Univ., 1957)

*Vertigo* (Par., 1958)

*Bell, Book and Candle* (Col., 1958)

*Anatomy of a Murder* (Col., 1959)

*The FBI Story* (WB, 1959)

*The Mountain Road* (Col., 1960)

*Two Rode Together* (Col., 1961)

*X-15* (UA, 1961)°

*The Man Who Shot Liberty Valance* (Par., 1962)

*Mr. Hobbs Takes a Vacation* (20th, 1962)

*How the West Was Won* (MGM, 1963)

*Take Her, She's Mine* (20th, 1963)

*Cheyenne Autumn* (WB, 1964)

*Dear Brigitte* (20th, 1965)

*Shenandoah* (Univ., 1965)

*Flight of the Phoenix* (20th, 1966)

*The Rare Breed* (Univ., 1966)

*Firecreek* (WB-7 Arts, 1968)

*Bandolero* (20th, 1968)

*The Cheyenne Social Club* (National General, 1970)

*Fools' Parade* (Col., 1971)

*That's Entertainment* (UA, 1974)

°Narrator

# MARGARET SULLAVAN

5′ 2½″
109 pounds
Brown hair
Gray eyes
Taurus

*Real name: Margaret Brooke Sullavan. Born May 16, 1909, Norfolk, Virginia. Married Henry Fonda (1931); divorced 1932. Married William Wyler (1934); divorced 1936. Married Leland Hayward (1936), children: Brooke, Bridget, William; divorced 1947. Married Kenneth Wagg (1950). Died January 1, 1960.*

**FEATURE FILMS:**

*Only Yesterday* (Univ., 1933)
*Little Man, What Now?* (Univ., 1934)
*The Good Fairy* (Univ., 1935)
*So Red the Rose* (Par., 1935)
*Next Time We Love* (Univ., 1936)
*The Moon's Our Home* (Par., 1936)
*Three Comrades* (MGM, 1938)
*The Shopworn Angel* (MGM, 1938)
*The Shining Hour* (MGM, 1938)

*The Shop Around the Corner* (MGM, 1940)
*The Mortal Storm* (MGM, 1940)
*So Ends Our Night* (UA, 1941)
*Back Street* (Univ., 1941)
*Appointment for Love* (Univ., 1941)
*Cry Havoc* (MGM, 1943)
*No Sad Songs for Me* (Col., 1950)

In **The Shopworn Angel** (MGM, 1938)

In **The Shop Around the Corner** (MGM, 1940)

In **The Shopworn Angel**

Advertisement for **The Mortal Storm** (MGM, 1940)

James Stewart, Margaret Sullavan, and Irene Rich in **The Mortal Storm**

# NEXT TIME WE LOVE
### (*Universal, 1936*) 87M.

Producer, Paul Kohner; director, Edward H. Griffith; based on the story *Say Goodbye Again* by Ursula Parrott; screenplay, Melville Baker; camera, Joseph Valentine; editor, Ted Kent.

Margaret Sullavan (Cicily); James Stewart (Christopher); Ray Milland (Tommy); Anna Demetrio (Madame Donato); Grant Mitchell (Jennings); Robert McWade (Cartaret); Harry C. Bradley (Desk Clerk); Jack Daley, Broderick O'Farrell (Conductors); Buddy Williams (Porter); Dutch Hendrian, Philip Morris, Al Hill, Jack Cheatham (Taxi Drivers); Hattie McDaniel (Hanna); Emmett Vogan (Bartender); Harry Bowen, Jack Mower (Waiters); Donna Mae Roberts (Cigarette Girl); Albert Conti (Charles); George Davis, Ludwig Lowey (Waiters); Tyler Brooke (Author); Leonid Kinsky (Designer); Eddie Phillips (Ticket Taker); John Dilson (Stage Manager); Nat Carr (Assistant); Clark Williams, Clive Morgan (Leading Men); John King (Juvenile); Nan Grey (Ingenue); Tom Manning, King Baggott (Character Men); Daisy Bufford (Maid); Alfred P. James (Aquarium Attendant); Billy Gratton (Kit at Age Three); Jacqueline Smylle (Susan); Ronnie Cosbey (Kit at Age Eight); Charles Fallen (French Teacher); Florence Roberts (Mrs. Talbot); Arthur Aylesworth (Secretary); Julie Carter (Sob Sister); Don Roberts (City Editor); Paddy O'Flynn (Reporter); Harry Tracy (Valet); Jane Keckley (Nurse); Miki Morita (Dr. Ito); Selmer Jackson (Dr. Campbell); Teru Shimada (Steward); Otto Fries (Conductor); Christian Rub (Swiss Innkeeper); Gottleib Huber (Swiss Porter); Patsy Green (Stand-in for Sullavan); Hugh Harrison (Stand-in for Stewart); Jack Parker (Stand-in for Milland).

New York Premiere: Radio City Music Hall—January 30, 1936
New York Television Debut: CBS—July 22, 1963

## Synopsis

Cicily leaves college to wed Christopher, a struggling young newspaper reporter. Tommy, their best friend, helps them out by introducing Cicily to a theatrical manager who engages her for his new play. She makes good progress. When Christopher is offered the post of Rome foreign correspondent, she refuses to go along with him, feeling that she might be in his way. After he leaves, she confides to Tommy that she is going to have a baby. Her landlady writes to Christopher when the child is born. He deserts his post without permission and rushes back home, promising never to leave her and their son again. His editor discharges him and he is reduced to doing cub reporting for a news service bureau at very low pay. Tommy again comes to their aid by getting Cicily a theatrical engagement. Knowing that Christopher is unhappy,

Cicily goes to his former editor and pleads with him to reinstate her husband. She is even willing to let him take a foreign assignment again. He is forced to leave for Europe immediately. Meanwhile, she rises in her profession and becomes a famous actress, able to live luxuriously. She only sees Christopher infrequently, and learns to do without him, but she never really stops loving him. Tommy confesses his love for her and begs her to divorce Christopher and wed him. She leaves for Europe to talk the matter over with Christopher, and they plan a pleasant vacation together. However, he suddenly leaves. She rushes after him and joins him on the train. She suddenly realizes that he is quite ill and he admits he is dying from a disease he contracted while in China. Cicily tells him, while choking back the sobs, that she will stay with him until the end.

◆◆◆

Petite Margaret Sullavan was already noted as a top-ranking sob star of the cinema (remember the marvelous catchy choke to her voice?) when she undertook *Next Time We Love,* requesting her Massachusetts summer stock pal, James Stewart, to be loaned from MGM to play opposite her in this tearjerker. It was this picture, his third feature film, that did so much to transform lanky Stewart into a cinema star, proving that he was far more than the usual run-of-the-mill Hollywood screen juvenile.

Even by the more dreamy standards of 1936, Ursula Parrott's tear-stained, piously moral story should have made filmgoers ponder the premise more than they did. Even the scenario virtue built out of Sullavan's desertion of husband Stewart at a most critical time in his career should have been questioned, but wasn't. Given this inverted value basis, *Next Time We Love* escalates into grand soap opera with unlicensed nobility exhibited by each spouse, till only in tragedy can the couple share a few happy weeks together. In short, the film craftily maneuvers away from a shaky particular event to encompass the audience within an universal truth wish, "next time we live, maybe we'll have time for each other."

*Next Time We Love* covers almost a decade in the lives of Sullavan's and Stewart's screen characters. He rises from a twenty-five-dollar-a-week newsman to a respected foreign correspondent, while she matures from a love-struck elfin co-ed into an ultra-sophisticated stage star. Neither player ages much physically during the chronicle's unveiling, but, then again, their emotional growth is amazingly retarded, despite the cacophony of events, including parenthood, which befalls them within the picture's eighty-seven minutes. Despite these stated disparities in the continuity, and many other disturbing elements, this writer must agree with Richard Watts, Jr. *(New York Herald-Tribune)* who wrote, "But the highest tribute to the picture is that you seldom fail to believe that its people really exist. I think you must know how rare that is in the cinema."

If anyone is a bit perturbed by the grandiloquent nature of Sullavan's Cicily who becomes a condescending celebrity rather than a sympathetic wife or dedicated mother once she has attained legitimate stardom within *Next Time We Love,* that person has to be thankful that Stewart's newsman avoids all the clichés that have inhabited oncamera representations of that profession since *The Front Page* (1931), etc. created concrete stereotypes for future filmgoers to endure. Perhaps it is this very give and take of assets and deficits within their characterizations that make Sullavan and Stewart so appealingly right and creditable together. She can effectively be at once both naive and poised, egotistical and benevolent, while his range moved from the gangling hickish to the resolutely mature. Each had a captivating way of projecting decisively distinctive vocal mannerisms which were guaranteed to spellbind the least susceptible viewer. As a team they radiated a reserved warmth which made moviegoers believe that viewing into the characters' private lives was not a salacious event but a delicately shared experience, revealing not just company best manners, but honest to goodness real emotion.

*Next Time We Love* both benefited and suffered by the presence of Ray Milland as the elegantly wealthy Tommy, the best friend who serves as a passive Greek chorus until he wakes up late in the story when he requests Sullavan to divorce Stewart and wed him. It might strike some viewers as a bit odd that Milland is the person who sits with the troubled Sullavan on park benches and listens to her domestic problems (i.e., would Sullavan's Cicily really have revealed her pregnancy to Milland instead of some girl friend, or was it that Cicily was meant to have unrealized catty traits which prevented her from enduring confiding girl friends?), or that Milland is the one to coo-coo baby talk to Sullavan's infant boy. As if scripter Melville Baker realized there should be a contrasting force to Milland's prim presence, the film has on hand Italian-born character actress Ann Demetrio as the well-meaning, dialectal landlady Madame Donato, who in her ample frame and effulgent personality adds a much-needed humane touch to the domestic tale.

Only near its finale does *Next Time We Love* shake off its preeminent preoccupation with the battle of the sexes in which the question of whether one spouse should sacrifice his/her job and ambitions for the sake of the other is paramount. For a time the script threatens to conclude the argument with the standard cinematic ploy (i.e., "for the sake of the child") but that cliché is tossed aside and in its place a commercially sound but absolutely flabby and maudlin ending sidetracks the debate. The story has ranged from New York to Eastern and Western Europe, and finally ends at the Alpine village of Anton with an emotion-grabbing confrontation between Stewart and Sullavan. For once their characters' careers and personal lives are not at cross purposes, and each, as ably delineated by the co-stars, creates in the viewer's mind the belief that this couple will take their few remaining weeks on earth together to start anew, to enjoy that unselfish love which was lost somewhere along the line.

Considering the unsubstantially delineated roles with which each star had to work, the star team was surprisingly effective in making much ado about relatively nothing. They built an impressive situation out of the scripter's forced scenario. "Miss Sullavan does so well that she almost convinces us that Cicily is not as stupid as her actions imply. . . . [James Stewart] promises . . . to be a welcome addition to the roster of leading men" [Frank S. Nugent *(New York Times)*]. Watts, Jr. of the *Herald-Tribune* found Sullavan here "honest and beautiful" and Stewart's performance "admirable."

## THE SHOPWORN ANGEL
### *(MGM, 1938) 85M.*

Producer, Joseph L. Mankiewicz; director, H. C. Potter; based on the story *Private Pettigrew's Girl* by Dana Burnett; screenplay, Waldo Salt; art directors, Cedric Gibbons, Joseph C. Wright, Edwin B. Willis; music, Edward Ward; song, George Asaf and Felix Powell; sound, Douglas Shearer; gowns, Adrian; choreography, Val Raset; montages, Slavko Vorkapich; camera, Joseph Ruttenberg; editor, W. Donn Hayes.

Margaret Sullavan (Daisy Heath); James Stewart (Bill Pettigrew); Walter Pidgeon (Sam Bailey); Nat Pendleton (Dice); Alan Curtis (Guy with Thin Lips); Sam Levene (Guy with Leer); Hattie McDaniel (Martha the Maid); Charley Grapewin (Wilson the Caretaker); Charles D. Brown (Mr. Gonigle the Stage Manager); Jimmy Butler (Elevator Boy); Eleanor Lynn (Sally the Waitress); William Stack (Minister); Hudson Shotwell (Jack the Soldier); John Merton (Speaker); Wesley Giraud (Bellboy); Harry Tyler (Eddy); Mary Howard, Virginia Grey (Chorus Girls); Wade Boteler (Irish Policeman); James Flavin (Guard); George Chandler (Soldier); Grace Hayle (Mistress of Ceremonies); Jack Murphy (Sailor); Frank McGlynn, Jr. (Motorcyclist); Edward Keane (Captain); Mary Dees (First Babe); Joan Mitchell (Second Babe); Frances Millen (Third Babe); Eddy Chandler (Corporal); Paul Speigel (Stage Manager); Don Brodie (Attendant); Robert Converse (Hotel Clerk); Francesco Maran (Headwaiter); Paul Kruger (Riveter); Dorothy Granger (Dancer).

New York Premiere: Capitol Theatre—July 7, 1938
New York Television Debut: CBS—March 15, 1957

### Synopsis

In World War I days, Bill Pettigrew, a young farm lad from Texas who has enlisted in the Army and is stationed in New York, accidentally meets Daisy Heath, a young, hard-boiled actress. He falls madly in love with her even though she considers him just a silly, hickish youngster. She later helps Bill out of an embarrassing situation by pretending, in the presence of his Army buddies, to be good friends with him. Bill calls to see her thereafter. His visit annoys Sam Bailey, Daisy's producer-lover, who for the first time in their relationship shows signs of jealousy. Daisy insists that Sam is the man she loves, but he warns her that her association with Bill might put her in a different position. When Bill learns that his detachment has been ordered to sail for France that night, he rushes to Daisy and pleads with her to wed him. Realizing all that she means to him, she marries him. Sam forgives her the deception, and she tells Sam that when Bill returns it will be time enough to tell him the truth. Once at the front lines, Bill is killed in an attack. Daisy receives the news with tears in her eyes, as Sam comforts her. They both know that through Bill they have a better perspective on love.

◆ ◆ ◆

Since the last movie teaming of Margaret Sullavan and James Stewart she had wed agent Leland Hayward who had engineered a six-picture MGM pact with this film becoming her second feature under the lucrative agreement. Stewart, meanwhile, had been gaining screen experience in a variety of not always appropriate roles, including the empty remake of *Seventh Heaven* (1937) done on loan to Twentieth Century-Fox. He did demonstrate a knack for lighthearted comedy in RKO's *Vivacious Lady* (1938) with Ginger Rogers, and an ability to create sentimental drama in Americana settings, as in *Of Human Hearts* (1938). But it was with the shorter (one foot to be exact) Sullavan that tall and gangly Stewart exuded that touching warmth of soul which made their pictures together so memorable.

In choosing to remake the World War I drama, *Shopworn Angel* (1929), which had been a very well received part-talkie film with Nancy Carroll and Gary Cooper, MGM ran the risk that the original sparse literary material (a 1918 *Saturday Evening Post* story) would seem too quaint to post-Depression filmgoers or too unsettling to movie watchers who might want to forget that a new European war was brewing on the Continent. Then too, in the roaring 1920s, there had been a novelty in having heroine Daisy Heath "enjoy" a tarnished reputation for being a mistress, but a decade later mores had changed and her moral status no longer appeared so daringly different.

Scripter Waldo Salt, in dealing with these scenario problems, retained the bitter sweet quality of the original photoplay, but softened the stark, hard-bitten nature of the heroine, a girl too smart to stick out her chin for life to hit her. This alteration gave the new version a much warmer glow. On the whole, the Sullavan-Stewart edition was considered to have toed the mark reasonably well, and, having its own virtues and movement, was sufficient to make most older viewers forget the earlier film production.

Sullavan's Daisy Heath, save for her glamorous contemporary bob hairdo and the wearing of pajamas, is very much a person of 1917. She is more fortunate than most career girls, being the callous mistress of an affluent, debonair play producer-manager. She could indulge her penchant for staying up late and drinking too much, unconcerned that her daily hangovers make her perpetually late for rehearsals. Sullavan's character exists in rather luxurious surroundings in her penthouse apartment, but still she is discontent. Something is missing, and neither she nor Pidgeon can determine just why they have not yet wedded and become a conventionally married couple. Then comes that fateful day in April when the streets are jammed with people and the crowds are frenzied with excitement over the United States' entry into World War I. It is at this juncture that her chauffeur-driven car nearly runs Bill Pettigrew (Stewart) down. It proves to be the beginning of a new life for her, since her acquaintanceship with the gawky, shy, straightforward Texas youth transforms her from a cynical, hard-boiled blonde into a dewy-eyed romantic, who once again believes in love, life, and men.

Once again in this picture as in *Next Time We Love*, it is Sullavan's character who is the more sophisticated and knowing one, who indulges her companion (Stewart) in his naive excesses, whether it is a Coney Island amusement park outing or a hasty Army camp wedding so the soldier may embark for overseas with something "fine" to remember.

A perfect illustration of Sullavan's motherly attitude to inexperienced Stewart (and he was very expert at this acting guise by now) was one of their interchanges during their Coney Island trip.

Sullavan: "If I was a tall handsome soldier I'd go for some nice plump little dish like that waitress over there."

Stewart: "No . . . that's the kind of a sweetheart the rest of the guys got."

Sullavan: "Well . . . maybe I've just got a practical mind."

Stewart: "No . . . I guess it's me . . . If I can't get exactly what I want, I just . . . I guess I can explain it easier by telling you about the pie."

He goes on to relate in his inimitable folksy way with all those vocal tricks and hand gestures that have become his trademark, "You see, my mother made the best hot apple pie you ever tasted and after she died I couldn't get any. And if I couldn't get any like that, I didn't want any." (He feels the same way about a girl, either it is the one he knows is best, or none at all.)

Sullavan, who has been only half-heartedly listening to this philosophical recitation, perks back to him: "Texas, if that's a line, it's a new one on me. The difference between us is that I'd rather eat bread than wait around for hot apple pie." And it was just this difference that made the couple such an effective co-starring movie team.

As in their last joint screen effort, *The Shopworn Angel* leads only find mutual happiness in tragedy, for she marries him out of a mixture of pity and affection, and he weds her to try to fulfill his fantasy romance with her. Only later, while he is at the front lines facing danger, and

Sullavan is back at her show business career, do they have a spiritual union, caring for each other in a mystical way that has improved their lives.

In true regard for the established Sullavan picture formula, *The Shop-worn Angel* concludes on a sad note. She is just about to go "on" with her club act when she receives word that Stewart has died in action. Bravely, swallowing her tears, she launches into her rendition° of "Pack up your Troubles in Your Old Kitbag and Smile, Smile, Smile," the lyrics tearing at her (and the audience's) heart. In Stewart's death she has been re-deemed, and is no longer just a shopworn angel.

A few idealistic souls like B. R. Crisler *(New York Times)* bemoaned, ". . . there really ought to be a Margaret Sullavan act to prevent the charm-ing and gifted lady of that name from wasting her talents on such frivolously tragic productions, from having to speak such forced insincere lines, from growing finally to look almost spooky herself because of the maudlin unreality of the character she is trying to portray." There were also those critics who carped that Sullavan here was ". . . under the severe handicap of being regenerated by the Private Pettigrew of James Stewart, who interprets the role by giving an imitation of Stan Laurel" *(New York Daily Mirror)*.

But other reviewers reflected the general audience reaction and agreed with Howard Barnes *(New York Herald-Tribune)* that ". . . she invests scene after scene with eloquence and vigor. There is a quality to her voice and an authority in her every gesture which I am frank to admit I go for. In much the same manner James Stewart brings the Texan private to glowing life and keeps the characterization solid and ap-pealing even when the script gives him little aid. Unless I am mistaken, *The Shopworn Angel* boasts two of the finest actors appearing on the screen today."

## THE SHOP AROUND THE CORNER
### (MGM, 1940) 97M.

Producer-director, Ernst Lubitsch; based on a play, *Parfumerie*, by Nikolaus Laszlo; screenplay, Samson Raphaelson; music, Werner Hey-mann; art directors, Cedric Gibbons, Wade B. Rubottom; set decorator, Edwin B. Willis; camera, William Daniels; editor, Gene Ruggiero.

James Stewart (Alfred Kralik); Margaret Sullavan (Klara Novak); Frank Morgan (Matuschek); Joseph Schildkraut (Ferencz Vadas); Sara Haden (Flora); Felix Bressart (Perovitch); William Tracy (Pepi Katena); Inez Courtney (Ilona); Charles Halton (Detective); Charles Smith (Rudy); Sarah Edwards, Gertrude Simpson (Woman Customers); Grace Hayle

°Dubbed by Mary Martin

381

(Plump Woman); Charles Arnt (Policeman); William Edmunds (Waiter); Mary Carr (Grandmother); Mabel Colcord (Aunt Anna); Renie Riano, Claire DuBrey, Ruth Warren, Joan Blair, Mira McKinney (Customers).

New York Premiere: Radio City Music Hall—January 25, 1940
New York Television Debut: CBS—August 31, 1957

### Synopsis

Alfred Kralik, head clerk in Matuschek's special store in Budapest, carries on a correspondence with a young lady who had advertised in the newspaper for a pen-pal who was interested in developing mentally. They do not divulge their names to one another, merely signing their letters "Dear Friend." Matuschek engages Klara Novak as a clerk during the Christmas rush. Unknown to Alfred, she is the girl to whom he has been corresponding. Klara, likewise, is unaware of Alfred's letter-writing activities. At work Klara and Alfred do not get along well together, quarreling constantly over the most trivial matters. Having made an appointment to finally meet his unknown letter-writing friend, Alfred arrives at the appointed place only to find, to his dismay, that the girl is none other than Klara. He greets her without revealing that he is the man for whom she is waiting, but she insists that he stop pestering her, for she is expecting someone. Meantime, Matuschek discovers that his wife is conducting an affair with one of his employees. He naturally suspects Alfred, for he is the only one who was ever invited to the Matuschek home. Alfred is discharged and is heartbroken over the matter. But when Matuschek learns that the guilty man is actually Ferencz Vadas, he is ashamed and attempts to shoot himself. His messenger boy prevents him from doing so. Matuschek then goes to a hospital for a rest, meantime re-engaging Alfred and making him the general manager of the store. By now Alfred has fallen in love with Klara, and she has become very attracted to him. When he finally reveals his identity to her, she is pleased and they are happily united.

◆◆◆

As Margaret Sullavan had been Oscar-nominated in 1938 for *Three Comrades*, so James Stewart had made an Academy Award bid in 1939 with *Mr. Smith Goes to Washington*. Metro was having difficulty accommodating the professionally hard-to-please Sullavan and agreed to reteam her with full-fledged star Stewart in *The Shop Around the Corner*, to be directed by Ernst Lubitsch, who had made Greta Garbo laugh so effectively oncamera in *Ninotschka* (1939).

"The plot of the new Music Hall offering does not make much of a claim on one's photoplay memories, but the characters and the incidents have been so brilliantly treated that the film becomes disarming and beguiling comedy" [Howard Barnes *(New York Herald-Tribune)*]. More to the point: "It is gay and light and beautiful and as sparkling as the foam atop a glass of Pilsener" [Lee Mortimer *(New York Daily Mirror)*]. *The*

*Shop Around the Corner* was deliberately filmed as an antidote to the gloomy global situation, and, with its nostalgic memories of a bygone, carefree central Europe, it admirably succeeded. As *Variety* summed it up, "It's smart and clever, but still packaged with easily understandable situations and problems of middle-class folk."

Relying strictly on soundstage settings, *The Shop Around the Corner* creates its own special old world atmosphere, with the focal point, of course, in Frank Morgan's cheery luggage and novelty emporium, an efficiently neat store in which the clerks display proper deference to the employer and most of all to the almighty customer, no matter how fickle. Among the staff there is brow-beaten clerk Felix Bressart, snazzily dressed heart-breaker Joseph Schildkraut, good-natured Inez Courtney, and most of all, plodding energetic Stewart as the store's leather goods employee who considers his job a crucial one. This set-up is fine by wealthy but humane upper-class Morgan, who rules his domain with both sharp discipline and kindness.

Within *The Shop Around the Corner,* Stewart's Alfred Kralik is as idealistic as Sullavan's Klara Novak, each aspiring to intellectually motivated romance, hoping a special love will lift them out of the ordinary run of life. But while Stewart has his energy-consuming job to sustain him contentedly, Sullavan finds life a struggle, a daily task to survive both financially and emotionally. Since beginning her pen-pal correspondence, the focal point of her day is post office box 237, with its mysterious hope of future satisfaction. Whereas she is inclined to be impatient, more intelligent than practical, and demanding of life, Stewart, following his accepted screen personae is far more elastic in his demands on life and carefree in his attainment of these goals. Thus, without being initially aware of it, the two lead characters are ideally suited to one another, and it is the ploy of *The Shop Around the Corner* to expend ninety-seven minutes for the hero and heroine to learn this basic fact midst feuding, fussing, and exploring the resources of their souls.

Just as *The Shop Around the Corner* was hailed for its infectious charm, the critics heartily endorsed the co-stars, providing them with the best reviews of their screen teams. ". . . Mr. Stewart bringing all of his great gift for shy understatement. . . . Once more she shows that she has few colleagues who can match her for crowding a line or scene with emotional intensity, even when it is a minor situation . . ." [Howard Barnes (*New York Herald-Tribune*)]. Interestingly, this was the only one of the four Sullavan-Stewart screen ventures in which both parties lived happily ever after with one another.

The Shop Around the Corner was restyled into a Judy Garland-Van Johnson screen musical *In the Good Old Summertime* (1949) and in 1963 it was converted into a Broadway musical, *She Loves Me.* Plans were announced in 1970 to picturize *She Loves Me* with Julie Andrews starring and Blake Edwards directing, but the project was later dropped.

# THE MORTAL STORM
## *(MGM, 1940) 100M.*

Director, Frank Borzage; based on the novel by Phyllis Bottome; screenplay, Claudine West, Anderson Ellis, George Froeschel; assistant director, Lew Borzage; art directors, Cedric Gibbons, Wade Rubottom; music, Edward Kane; gowns, Adrian; men's wardrobe, Giles Steele; sound, Douglas Shearer; makeup, Jack Dawn; camera, William Daniels; editor, Elmo Vernon.

Margaret Sullavan (Freya Roth); James Stewart (Martin Brietner); Robert Young (Fritz Marberg); Frank Morgan (Professor Roth); Irene Rich (Mrs. Roth); Maria Ouspenskaya (Mrs. Brietner); William Orr (Erich Von Rohn); Robert Stack (Otto Von Rohn); Bonita Granville (Elsa); Gene Reynolds (Rudi); Russell Hicks (Rector); William Edmunds (Lehman); Thomas Ross (Professor Werner); Ward Bond (Franz); Esther Dale (Marta); Fritz Leiber (Oppenheim); Dan Dailey, Jr. (Holl); Robert O. Davis (Hartman); Granville Bates (Berg); Sue Moore (Theresa); Harry Depp, Julius Tannen, Gus Glassmire (Colleagues); Dick Rich, Ted Oliver (Guards); Howard Lang (Man); Bodil Rosing (Woman); Lucien Prival, Dick Elliott (Passport Officials); Henry Victor, John Stark (Gestapo Officials); William Irving (Waiter in Cafe); Bert Roach (Fat Man in Cafe); Bob Stevenson (Gestapo Guard); Max Davidson (Old Man).

New York Premiere: Capitol Theatre—June 20, 1940
New York Television Debut: CBS—August 17, 1957

### Synopsis

Professor Roth, his wife, daughter Freya, son Rudi, and his two stepsons, Erich and Otto, live contentedly in their home in southwestern Germany of 1933. Part of the family consists of Martin Brietner and Fritz Marberg who both love Freya. She chooses Fritz. On the professor's sixtieth birthday he is honored by his students, the faculty, and by his family. During the birthday dinner party, the news of Hitler's political appointment as head of the German state comes to the family. This brings joy to Otto, Erich, and Fritz, all loyal Hitler followers. They quarrel with Martin who refuses to share their "patriotic" happiness. In a short time, Freya, disgusted by Fritz's actions, breaks her engagement. She realizes she loves Martin. Otto and Erich leave home. Knowing that the professor is non-Aryan, his students question him about the theory of Aryan supremacy, and when he answers that such a rationale is ridiculous, they leave his class. He is soon ousted from the university, and is later arrested and sent to a concentration camp where he meets his death. Mrs. Roth, Freya, and Rudi leave for Austria to meet Martin who has been living there, unable to return home because he had helped a liberal professor to escape arrest. At one of the checkpoint stations, a Nazi official discovers a manuscript written by the professor in Freya's suitcase, and they force her to leave the train. She induces her mother and brother to continue the journey. The officials refuse to believe her story that she had no intention of publishing the manuscript. They destroy the papers and hold back her passport, making it impossible for her to leave the country. Martin, however, risks his life to return and help her to escape. They start out over the difficult snowy mountains for Austria. But they are waylaid by a Nazi patrol headed by Fritz. The soldiers fire at the fugitives and Freya is shot and dies in Martin's arms. Although Fritz is saddened by her death, he believes that it was all in the line of his duty.

◆—◆—◆

"*The Mortal Storm* strikes one today as grossly contrived and sentimental, and about as German as blueberry pie. In its crude way, however, it did bring home to U.S. audiences something of the torment through which many Germans went in the Thirties; the cast of top boxoffice names helped here too" [*Hollywood in the 1940s* (1968) by Charles Higham and Joel Greenberg].

Frank Borzage had directed Margaret Sullavan in the highly-regarded adaptation of Erich Maria Remarque's post-World War I study, *Three Comrades* (1938), winning accolades for all concerned. The new anti-Nazi project was based on Phyllis Bottome's 1938 novel of the Hitler movement in Germany. With the United States still uncommitted to World War II, *The Mortal Storm* was couched in the safe past of 1933 with Nazism as a historical catalyst to the screen action rather than a current threat. Once again Hollywood was several laps behind the headlines. Nevertheless, even at this critical stage in world events, *Variety* could report, "With the devastating directness of a stuka diver, *The Mortal Storm* is a film bomb which is about to explode in American theatres with such force as to dispel public equanimity (if, in fact, any exists) toward the vicious operations of Nazism and its fanatical proponents." But diatribes do not always make stimulating celluloid entertainment, leading *Life* magazine to evaluate, "What *The Mortal Storm* lacks in cinema values it makes up in power of pleading."

The theme of *The Mortal Storm* is best expressed by Frank Morgan's stoic physics professor, "I've never prized safety, either for myself or my children. I've prized courage." This philosophy is carried throughout the sombre film in rather black and white terms as the ideological opponents assemble in conflict. On one side are the dogmatic, cold Robert Young, William Orro, and Robert Stack, all members of Hitler's intolerant brown shirts who condone and participate in the suppression and destruction of anyone or anything that threatens the party movement. Equally one-dimensional in their devotion to other principles are Morgan, Sullavan, and Stewart, the latter the young farmer who speaks out against totalitarianism and helps the downtrodden of Hitler's Germany.

It was an unusually active role for a Stewart oncamera character, and one that did not always sit so well with his range of acting techniques. "He is scarcely the type for a German farmer, but he acts with such intense sincerity that the personal tragedy which is the core of the piece is the most sustaining note in the proceedings" [Howard Barnes *(New York Herald-Tribune)*].

Because *The Mortal Storm* was more of an illustrated lecture of dramatic situations than a perceptive character study, very often the Sullavan and Stewart characters became mere mouthpieces for expressions of democratic patriotism. Therefore, the little moments when the supporting players shine forth are usually remembered more vividly. Irene Rich's distraught mother trying to remain calm and herd her family to safety, the terror in the eyes of servant girl, Bonita Granville, who is beaten into revealing Sullavan's whereabouts, and the quiet dignity of Maria Ouspenskaya's Mrs. Brietner, a woman who has lived through other reigns of terrors.

Throughout *The Mortal Storm* it is Sullavan's Freya who rises to nobility, camera front and center. When the drama comes to its tragic end, she has been yanked off the freedom-heading train, bravely confronted the bullying Nazi officials, and then melted into girlishness as her loved one (Stewart) attempts to lead her on a ski-bound escape from the pursuing Germans. Her death ° is all the more ironic for occurring within the Swiss border, killed by Nazi bullets from without. Director Borzage provided Sullavan with an intentionally solemn exit, as she dies in Stewart's arms and he carries her lifeless body further on into the domains of free Switzerland.

## THE YEARS AFTER

After *The Mortal Storm*, Margaret Sullavan only made five more feature films, including the wartime drama *Cry Havoc* (1943) which completed her MGM obligations, and Columbia's *No Sad Songs for Me* (1950), a tasteful study of a woman dying of cancer who attempts to provide for her family's long-range emotional needs before her untimely demise. The actress, who never liked filmmaking, was much happier on Broadway where she starred in the ultra-successful comedy *The Voice of the Turtle* (1943) and thereafter, *The Deep Blue Sea* (1952), *Sabrina Fair* (1953), and *Janus* (1955). In the latter 1950s Sullavan was professionally inactive, but in December, 1959, returned to the stage in a tryout of a new drama. During the New Haven, Connecticut, engagement, she died of an overdose of sleeping pills on January 1, 1960. It was later learned that she had been almost totally deaf, a physical impairment she had been fighting since 1948.

James Stewart won his Best Actor Oscar for *The Philadelphia Story*

°At one point in production, MGM contemplated altering the ending so that she survived.

(1940) which proved his ability with screen comedy. After a trio of meaningless film roles in 1941, the patriotic Stewart enlisted in the U.S. Air Force where his war service was distinguished. Upon discharge, he surprised MGM by not renewing his studio contract, preferring to freelance in the new post-World War II Hollywood. It was back at Metro that he made *The Stratton Story* (1949) which teamed him with June Allyson for the first of three teary screen biographies, all financial successes, and proving that audiences still preferred Stewart as the resolute star of soap opera. He returned to comedy in *Harvey* (1950) and played the tragic circus clown in *The Greatest Show on Earth* (1952). Alfred Hitchcock employed Stewart in a trio of suspensers, *Rear Window* (1954), *The Man Who Knew Too Much* (1956), and *Vertigo* (1958), which did as much as a rash of movie Westerns to extend his lengthy and lucrative film career. By the 1960s, he, along with pals John Wayne and Henry Fonda, had come to symbolize the indomitable American spirit, and the trio played the image to the hilt in their assorted screen sorties, usually sagebrush tales which avoided the embarrassment of having the veteran stars perform oncamera love with much younger heroines. Stewart returned to Broadway in 1970 to take another crack at *Harvey* with Helen Hayes as his co-star. The following year he starred in a video domestic comedy program "The Jimmy Stewart Show," which failed to find its mark. However, undaunted, Stewart returned to nighttime television in the fall of 1973 with "Hawkins," a series about a country lawyer. Recently, Stewart has narrated one of the sections of the compilation tribute to MGM, *That's Entertainment* (1974), and has agreed that in early 1975 he will let British playgoers see first hand his interpretation of Elwood P. Dowd in a new theatre presentation of *Harvey*.

In a publicity pose for **Cafe Metropole** (20th, 1937)

# Chapter 14

# Tyrone Power
## &
# Loretta Young

## TYRONE POWER

6'
165 pounds
Dark brown hair
Brown eyes
Taurus

*Real name: Tyrone Edmund Power. Born May 5, 1913, Cincinnati, Ohio. Married Annabella (1939); divorced 1948. Married Linda Christian (1949), children: Romina, Taryn; divorced 1955. Married Deborah Minardos (1958) child: Tyrone. Died November 15, 1958.*

**FEATURE FILMS:**

*Tom Brown of Culver* (Univ., 1932)
*Flirtation Walk* (FN, 1934)
*Girls' Dormitory* (20th, 1936)
*Ladies in Love* (20th, 1936)
*Lloyds of London* (20th, 1937)
*Love Is News* (20th, 1937)
*Cafe Metropole* (20th, 1937)
*Thin Ice* (20th, 1937)
*Second Honeymoon* (20th, 1937)
*In Old Chicago* (20th, 1938)
*Alexander's Ragtime Band* (20th, 1938)

*Marie Antoinette* (MGM, 1938)
*Suez* (20th, 1938)
*Jesse James* (20th, 1939)
*Rose of Washington Square* (20th, 1939)
*Second Fiddle* (20th, 1939)
*The Rains Came* (20th, 1939)
*Daytime Wife* (20th, 1939)
*Johnny Apollo* (20th, 1940)
*Brigham Young-Frontiersman* (20th, 1940)
*The Return of Frank James* (20th, 1940)

The Mark of Zorro (20th, 1940)
Blood and Sand (20th, 1941)
A Yank in the R.A.F. (20th, 1941)
Son of Fury (20th, 1942)
This Above All (20th, 1942)
The Black Swan (20th, 1942)
Crash Dive (20th, 1943)
The Razor's Edge (20th, 1946)
Nightmare Alley (20th, 1947)
Captain from Castile (20th, 1947)
Luck of the Irish (20th, 1948)
That Wonderful Urge (20th, 1948)
Prince of Foxes (20th, 1949)
The Black Rose (20th, 1950)

An American Guerrilla in the Philippines
  (20th, 1950)
Rawhide (20th, 1951)
I'll Never Forget You (20th, 1951)
Diplomatic Courier (20th, 1952)
Pony Soldier (20th, 1952)
Mississippi Gambler (Univ., 1953)
King of the Khyber Rifles (20th, 1953)
The Long Gray Line (Col., 1955)
Untamed (20th, 1955)
The Eddy Duchin Story (Col., 1956)
Abandon Ship (Col., 1957)
The Rising of the Moon (WB, 1957)°
The Sun Also Rises (20th, 1957)
Witness for the Prosecution (UA, 1957)

°Narrator

# LORETTA YOUNG

**5′ 3″**
**109 pounds**
**Light brown hair**
**Blue eyes**
**Capricorn**

*Real name: Gretchen Michaela Young. Born January 6, 1913, Salt Lake City, Utah. Married Grant Withers (1930); annulled 1931. Daughter adopted in 1937. Married Thomas Lewis (1940), children: Christopher, Peter; divorced 1969.*

### FEATURE FILMS:

The Only Way (Par., 1917)
The Sheik (Par., 1921)
Naughty But Nice (FN, 1927)
Whip Woman (FN, 1928)
Laugh Clown Laugh (MGM, 1928)
Magnificent Flirt (Par., 1928)
The Head Man (FN, 1928)
Scarlet Seas (FN, 1928)
The Squall (FN, 1929)
The Girl in the Glass Cage (FN, 1929)

The Fast Life (FN, 1929)
The Careless Age (FN, 1929)
The Show of Shows (WB, 1929)
The Forward Pass (FN, 1929)
The Man from Blankley's (WB, 1930)
The Second Floor Mystery (FN, 1930)
Show Girl in Hollywood (FN, 1930)†
Loose Ankles (FN, 1930)
Road to Paradise (FN, 1930)
Kismet (FN, 1930)

†Unbilled Appearance

*The Truth About Youth* (FN, 1930)
*The Devil to Pay* (UA, 1930)
*Beau Ideal* (RKO, 1931)
*The Right of Way* (FN, 1931)
*Three Girls Lost* (Fox, 1931)
*Too Young to Marry* (WB, 1931)
*Big Business Girl* (FN, 1931)
*I Like Your Nerve* (FN, 1931)
*Platinum Blonde* (Col., 1931)
*The Ruling Voice* (FN, 1931)
*Taxi!* (WB, 1932)
*The Hatchet Man* (FN, 1932)
*Play Girl* (WB, 1932)
*Weekend Marriage* (WB, 1932)
*Life Begins* (WB, 1932)
*They Call It Sin* (WB, 1932)
*Employees' Entrance* (WB, 1933)
*Grand Slam* (WB, 1933)
*Zoo in Budapest* (Fox, 1933)
*The Life of Jimmy Dolan* (WB, 1933)
*Midnight Mary* (MGM, 1933)
*Heroes for Sale* (FN, 1933)
*The Devil's in Love* (Fox, 1933)
*She Had to Say Yes* (FN, 1933)
*Man's Castle* (Col., 1933)
*The House of Rothschild* (UA, 1934)
*Born to be Bad* (Fox, 1934)
*Bulldog Drummond Strikes Back* (UA, 1934)
*Caravan* (Fox, 1934)
*The White Parade* (Fox, 1934)
*Clive of India* (20th, 1935)
*Shanghai* (Par., 1935)
*Call of the Wild* (UA, 1935)
*The Crusades* (Par., 1935)
*The Unguarded Hour* (MGM, 1936)
*Private Number* (20th, 1936)
*Ramona* (20th, 1936)

*Ladies in Love* (20th, 1936)
*Love Is News* (20th, 1937)
*Cafe Metropole* (20th, 1937)
*Love Under Fire* (20th, 1937)
*Wife, Doctor and Nurse* (20th, 1937)
*Second Honeymoon* (20th, 1937)
*Four Men and a Prayer* (20th, 1938)
*Three Blind Mice* (20th, 1938)
*Suez* (20th, 1938)
*Kentucky* (20th, 1938)
*The Story of Alexander Graham Bell* (20th, 1939)
*Wife, Husband and Friend* (20th, 1939)
*Eternally Yours* (UA, 1939)
*The Doctor Takes a Wife* (Col., 1940)
*He Stayed for Breakfast* (Col., 1940)
*The Lady from Cheyenne* (Univ., 1941)
*The Men in Her Life* (Col., 1941)
*Bedtime Story* (Col., 1941)
*A Night to Remember* (Col., 1942)
*China* (Par., 1943)
*Ladies Courageous* (Univ., 1944)
*And Now Tomorrow* (Par., 1944)
*Along Came Jones* (RKO, 1945)
*The Stranger* (RKO, 1946)
*The Perfect Marriage* (Par., 1946)
*The Farmer's Daughter* (RKO, 1947)
*The Bishop's Wife* (RKO, 1947)
*Rachel and the Stranger* (RKO, 1948)
*The Accused* (Par., 1948)
*Mother Is a Freshman* (20th, 1949)
*Come to the Stable* (20th, 1949)
*Key to the City* (MGM, 1950)
*Cause for Alarm* (MGM, 1951)
*Half Angel* (20th, 1951)
*Paula* (Col., 1952)
*Because of You* (Univ., 1952)
*It Happens Every Thursday* (Univ., 1953)

In **Love is News** (20th, 1937)

Loretta Young, Tyrone Power, Wilfred Lawson, Paul Lukas, and Constance Bennett in **Ladies in Love** (20th, 1936)

George Andre Beranger, Tyrone Power, and Loretta Young in **Cafe Metropole**

In **Second Honeymoon** (20th, 1937)

In Suez (20th, 1938)

# LADIES IN LOVE
## (Twentieth Century-Fox, 1936) 97M.

Producer, B. G. DeSylva; director, Edward H. Griffith; based on the play by Ladislaus Bus-Fekete; screenplay, Melville Baker; music director, Louis Silvers; camera, Hal Mohr; editor, Ralph Dietrich.

Janet Gaynor (Martha Kerenye); Loretta Young (Susie Schmidt); Constance Bennett (Yoli Haydn); Simone Simon (Marie Armand); Don Ameche (Dr. Rudi Imre); Paul Lukas (John Barta); Tyrone Power, Jr. (Karl Lanyi); Alan Mowbray (Paul Sandor); Wilfrid Lawson (Ben Horath); J. Edward Bromberg (Brenner); Virginia Field (Countess Helena); Frank Dawson (Johann); Egon Brecher (Concierge); Vesey O'Davoren (Fritz); Jayne Regan (Mrs. Dreker); John Bleifer (Porter); Eleanor Wesselhoeft (Chairwoman); William Brisbane (Chauffeur); Monty Woolley (Man in Box Seat); Lynn Bari (Clerk); Helen Dickson (Woman); Paul Weigel (Waiter); Tony Merlo (Assistant Stage Manager); Paul McVey (Actor); Maxine Elliott Hicks (Girl in Audience); Edward Peil, Jr. (Boy in Audience); Hector Sarno (Turkish Waiter).

New York Premiere: Rivoli Theatre—October 28, 1936
New York Television Debut: CBS—February 14, 1962

### Synopsis

Three Budapest working girls, Martha Kerenye, Susie Schmidt, and Yoli Haydn, pool their earnings in order to rent a fashionable apartment. Their purpose is to impress the men they date. Model Yoli is in love with wealthy engineer John Barta. Afraid that she might be hurt if she dares admit to him that she loves him, she pretends to be only amused by his romantic protestations. She is heartbroken when he later weds Marie Armand, a naive country girl. Chorus girl Susie falls in love with Karl Lanyi, a wealthy nobleman. When she learns he may wed a woman of his own class, she attempts to poison herself. However, by error, Martha drinks the poisoned drink instead. Martha's illness from the drug brings her back into contact with Dr. Rudi Imre with whom she had quarreled because of her relationship with conceited magician Paul Sandor for whom she had worked. Martha decides to wed Rudi, while Yoli agrees to marry Ben Horvath, a wealthy gentleman who has long loved her. Susie consoles herself with the acquisition of a hat shop, which Ben had been generous enough to purchase for her.

◆◆◆

When Twentieth Century-Fox mogul Darryl F. Zanuck announced that he intended peopling his $750,000 production, *Ladies in Love*, with the likes of Janet Gaynor, Loretta Young, Constance Bennett, and Simone Simon, everyone expected fireworks. It was well known that Zanuck had no love for Gaynor (who in tandem with Charles Farrell had brought so much money into the studio's coffers before Zanuck assumed command), and would willingly sacrifice the success of a few additional features to insure that his predecessor's protégée would leave the studio. Perennial ingenue Young had long been a Zanuck favorite and under contract to him since the days of *The House of Rothschild* (1934). But now she was becoming increasingly demanding in her desire to consolidate her position as an "actress" rather than just another cinema clotheshorse. Bennett, Zanuck's friend of even longer standing, had passed her movie screen peak and was now on the downward swing, none of which had tempered her authoritarian temperamental ways. Simon, the youngest of the leading lady quartet and Zanuck's personal French import, was showing signs of stress from the pressure of demonstrating the executive's faith in her as a potential major film personality.

But surprise of surprises, the four actresses conducted themselves with (forced) decorum on the set and had little to say about one another or even the picture itself. Each of them, most likely, was too busy extolling her own virtues to the press. As Hollywood's grand lady of journalism, Louella Parsons, analyzed it, "I don't know why all the fuss. Don't people realize that each of us has responsibility in this picture that we cannot afford to muff? This picture is a business proposition, not a circus."

The oversized publicity campaign for *Ladies in Love* backfired in the reaction of the critics. "Maybe we anticipated too much. But, to our way of thinking, this comedy's sophistication doesn't jell" *(Liberty* magazine*)*. Or as Archer Winsten *(New York Post)* phrased it, "It's too bad that the movie bites off more than it has the time or wit to chew properly."

With its four-faceted story to tell, *Ladies in Love,* based on another Hungarian play by the prolific Ladislaus Bus-Fekete, had a difficult task in distributing sufficient screentime to any one avenue of plot or grouping of players. Young was cast as the talkative show girl, a frank, unsubtle peasant girl who is part of a variety hall chorus line. In her rather brash way she insists upon telling the truth no matter to whom or on what subject. She is the starry-eyed miss who spots Tyrone Power, and is smitten with fairytale love for this ultra-handsome count. He is polite to her, when he has a chance to sneak a word edgewise, but it is quickly clear that fate has not decreed that these two from such different social spheres shall wed. Young's melodramatic suicide attempt seems more of a plot contrivance than it should be, particularly in that she fails so badly at it (with poor Gaynor sipping the deadly drink instead). As if the scripters had run dry on what to do with Young's unresolved character, she is the only girl of the story to emerge unmarried, having to be content within *Ladies in Love* with her new millinery enterprise. A sad substitute, one might say, for the charming company of dashing Power or any man.

Compared to waifish, maternal Gaynor, or practical but overly proud Bennett, or smirking school girl Simon, Young came across in *Ladies in*

*Love* as the least appealing of the distaff quartet. She may play "Three Blind Mice" cutely on the ukulele, yet her conflicting set of character traits are no asset to her modest characterization. Fortunately, filmgoers had learned over the years not to expect great dramatics from Young, accepting her histrionic limitations with grace, and, instead, focused on her still fresh good looks and stylish way of wearing clothes.

On the other hand, *Ladies in Love* served as a fine dress rehearsal for star-in-the-grooming Tyrone Power, who, by the time of the later 1937 release, *Lloyds of London,* would be well on the way to movie stardom. The twenty-three-year-old descendant of a long-standing acting family, he had all the beautiful good looks that were already launching Robert Taylor at MGM towards top fame. Practical-minded *Variety* noted that in *Ladies in Love* "Tyrone Power, Jr. is on and off pretty fast and doesn't register either way . . ." However, his screen time was sufficient for the likes of Archer Winsten (*New York Post*) to observe for his reader that Power " . . . is as handsome as everyone seems to think Robert Taylor is." Even with his truncated movie assignment, Power had sufficient chance to register favorably in comparison to the film's other male players. Befitting his screen part, Power was truly noble, particularly in contrast to the Eastern European nobility of Count Paul Lukas, the latter cast as a man only interested in having some fun before settling down to a mining project in the Andes. In addition, the film sported the outrageous hamming of Alan Mowbray, a self-interested actor cum fop who archly inquires of employee Gaynor, "You do love me? Good. I was afraid I was slipping." Poor Don Ameche was cast as Hungary's answer to young Dr. Kildare, and was saddled with a sappy role as the dedicated physician (Gaynor cares for his experimental rabbits) and he played the part in a frenetic, but bland, manner.

## LOVE IS NEWS
### *(Twentieth Century-Fox, 1937) 78M.*

Producer, Darryl F. Zanuck; associate producers, Earl Carroll, Harold Wilson; director, Tay Garnett; story, William Lipman, Frederick Stephans; screenplay, Harry Tugend, Jack Yellen; song, Sidney Mitchell and Lew Pollack; camera, Ernest Palmer.

Tyrone Power (Steve Leyton); Loretta Young (Tony Gateson); Don Ameche (Marty Canavan); Slim Summerville (Judge); Dudley Digges (Cyrus Jeffrey); Walter Catlett (Johnson); Jane Darwell (Mrs. Flaherty); Stepin Fetchit (Penrod); George Sanders (Count de Guyon); Pauline Moore (Lois Westcott); Frank Conroy (Findlay); Charles Coleman (Bevins); Elisha Cook, Jr. (Eggleston); Paul McVey (Alford); Julius Tannen (Logan); Ed Dearing (Motor Cop); Frederick Burton (J. D. Jones); George Offerman,

Jr. (Copy Boy); Art Dupuis (Tony's Chauffeur); Charles Tannen, Sidney Fields, Arthur Rankin, Jack Byron, Sterling Campbell, Dick French, Paul Frawley, Ray Johnson, Al Jenson (Reporters); Richard Powell (Insurance Salesman); Jack Mulhall (Yacht Salesman); Sam Ash (Tailor); Harry Hayden, Harry Depp, Sherry Hall, Charles King, Emmett Vogan, Gladden James. Babe Green, Paddy O'Flynn, Larry Steers (Salesmen); Dorothy Christy (Girl); Charles Williams (Brady); Carol Tevis (Bessie); Eddie Anderson, Etta McDaniel (Black Folk); John Dilson (Clerk); Charles E. Griffin (Desk Man); Harry Watson, Leonard Kibrick (Newsboys); Mugsy Meyers (Gambler); Jack Baxley (Deputy); Joe Smith Marba (Carpenter); George Humbert (Mike Allegrett); Pop Byron, Wade Boteler, Fred Kelsey, Bruce Mitchell, Eddy Chandler (Cops); Maidel Turner (Dowager); Edwin Maxwell (Kenyon); Herbert Ashley (Gateman); Alan Davis (Pilot); Lillian West (Maid in Toni's Bathroom); Antonio Filauri (Head Waiter); Davison Clark (Foreman of Print Shop); Edward Cooper (Butler); Lynn Bari (Secretary); Dot Farley (Bit).

New York Premiere: Roxy Theatre—March 5, 1937
New York Television Debut: Channel 13—August 18, 1958


## Synopsis

Tony Gateson, allegedly the world's richest girl, is hounded by unthinking newspaper men wherever she goes. She is annoyed when she is tricked into an interview with Steve Leyton, a reporter whose editor, Marty Canavan, had threatened to discharge him if he did not bring in a story about her. She decides to teach Steve a lesson by showing him just how distasteful publicity can be. She announces to every newspaper, except Steve's, that she has broken her engagement to Count de Guyon in order to wed Steve instead. Marty is convinced Steve has double-crossed him and fires him. Steve finds himself besieged by newsmen and salesmen who refuse to believe his story that he had been framed into fame. Tony continues the farce because she actually has fallen in love with Steve, as he has with her. They quarrel, land in a country jail, but along the way enjoy many exciting experiences. Later, in an effort to prevent her cousin from wedding the fortune-hunting Count, Tony pretends that she again loves de Guyon and alerts the papers of her forthcoming wedding to him. Steve, not knowing that she has jilted the Count immediately after making the announcement, insults Tony at their next meeting. Thereafter, Steve is more surprised when he is offered the managing editor's post of his old paper, now knowing that Tony's uncle, Cyrus Jeffrey had acquired a controlling interest in the publication. Eventually everything is explained, and the lovers plan to marry.

The Depression was nearing its bitter end, but Hollywood still had not finished its lampooning of the peccadillos of the idle rich. On its own, *Love Is News* was considered a "furiously unimportant farce" [Frank S. Nugent *(New York Times)*], and that within the film "comic invention is at a low ebb" [Howard Barnes *(New York Herald-Tribune)*]. Artistically, what hurt the burlesquing film all the more was its unfavorable comparison to MGM's *Libeled Lady* (1936) which was a grade A rendition of a similar subject sparkled by a four star (Jean Harlow, Spencer Tracy, William Powell, Myrna Loy) cast and far greater plot plausibility. But this is not to say that *Love Is News* was unpopular with the general public. On the contrary, the attractive starring team of Loretta Young and Tyrone Power, while no great shakes in the histrionics department, was a pleasant pair on the optics, and moviegoers thrived on the mindless entertainment that was to become this team's speciality during the coming year.

Leaving the see-sawing angle to one side, *Love Is News* was at its most preposterous in dealing with the newspaper profession. The 1931 movie *The Front Page* had set genre stereotypes that were still being plied in this and other Hollywood pictures. Don Ameche is now the high-pressure managing editor (of the *New York Daily Express*) whose nose for news has not got a chance against his screaming mouth or desk-pounding fist, and Power is the lackadaisical star reporter who is apparently as un-inventive when gathering full-bodied big stories (he dictates his short-shifted assignments in split seconds) as he is trying to remain financially above water. Power represents the tired newsreporter type who is fired daily and then rehired with a big salary bonus. *Love Is News* pretended to offer the scoop on how reporters spend their spare time, why, when they are not engaging in fisticuffs among themselves, they are at the nearby bar playing checkers on the square tiled floor using whiskey glasses for game pieces. The portrait of newspapermen as grown-up children was a cliché by this time and hardly good film fare.

What does propel *Love Is News* along its seventy-eight minute path is the hot and cold interaction between Young and handsome Power. From the time he inveigles an interview from her at Newark Airport until the fade out where their joint future looks bright, they manage to spark adrenalin into the mild story by their seeming incompatibility. She is so busy being pampered, and he is so preoccupied with not earning a proper living that these two social opposites have plenty of opportunity to engage in verbal arguments and romantic sparking. Compared to grasping, parasitic Count de Guyon (George Sanders) who almost lands Young, self-indulgent Power is a gem. He is just the proletarian to tame the spoiled heiress.

The couple's finest screen scene in *Love Is News* occurs when rambunctious Young and Power are jailed by woebegone police officer-jailer-bailiff-what-have-you Slim Summerville. Each is sharing an adjoining cell, and they continue to carry on their unique courtship-hate session. In a delightful moment,* Young asks to share Power's last cigarette. After taking a decorous puff, she bites his fingers and grabs the remainder of the cigarette. However, Power has his revenge later on. Shortly after they are released from the rural jail he drops her in a mud puddle, but later when he purchases her indiscreet love letters he passes up the chance to publish them, for, after all, he loves the sappy miss very much indeed.

Because of Power's sensational public impact in *Lloyds of London* he was Fox's fastest-emerging new star, running a close second to the studio's veteran male lead, Oscar-winning Warner Baxter, and now considered proper material to team with Zanuck's other favorites, Sonja Henie and Alice Faye. Therefore, in this new entry, Power was billed over Young in the credits.

The studio had engineered a "romance" between Power and Young, but it did not take with the public who remembered that a short time before he was touted as "being that way" with skating star Sonja Henie who just happened to be making films (with Power) at Fox. (When Power was teamed with Alice Faye in 1938, the studio fabricated no offcamera infatuation, for by that time she was wed to Tony Martin, and the following year he would marry actress Annabella.)

The critics who had been critical of the film itself were equally tough with the stars of *Love Is News.* Howard Barnes *(New York Herald-Tribune)* dismissed Young's contribution to the film because she "is content to effect a stock impersonation." However, Barnes' reaction to Power was far different. "Endowed with a gift for make-believe as well as good looks, he should have little difficulty in becoming Hollywood's leading juvenile idol." Barnes further added about the male lead, "Even though he is involved in absurd proceedings, he keeps his characterization solid and appealing, and makes the romance palatable." (Who ever said Darryl F. Zanuck could not pick appropriate leading men for his movies?)

The basic premise of *Love Is News* would serve as the foundation for the studio's later musical, *Sweet Rosie O'Grady* (1943) starring Betty Grable, and in 1948 Power would star in a remake of *Love Is News* entitled *That Wonderful Urge* with Gene Tierney as his new vis-a-vis. The story did not hold up well in the post-World War II market.

### CAFE METROPOLE
#### *(Twentieth Century-Fox, 1937) 83M.*

Producer, Nunnally Johnson; director, Edward H. Griffith; story, Gregory Ratoff; screenplay, Jacques Duval; assistant director, William Forsyth; music director, Louis Silvers; camera, Lucien Andriot; editor, Irene Morra.

*A wry double entendre bit has bickering Power toss one of his shoes at Young. Somehow—as only it can happen in the movies—it zings through the bars of her cell. Later, jailer Sommerville is aghast to see a man's shoe in a woman's cell, and filled with moral indignation, he tells the couple, "I cain't figger out how you done it, but don't do it again."

Adolphe Menjou (Adolph); Loretta Young (Laura Ridgeway); Tyrone Power [Alexis Penayev (Alexander Brown)]; Charles Winninger (Ridgeway); Gregory Ratoff (Paul); Christian Rub (Leroy); Helen Westley (Margaret); Georges Renavent (Maitre d'Hotel); Ferdinand Gottschalk (Monnett); Hal K. Dawson (Thorndyke); Leonid Kinsky (Artist); Louis Mercier (Courtroom Attendant); Jules Raucourt, Albert Pollet, Gino Corrado, Eugene Borden (Waiters); Rolfe Sedan (Flower Clerk); Albert Morin, Charles De Ravenne (Page Boys); Leonid Snegoff, Octavio J. Giraud (Porters); Fred Cavens (Train Guard); Jean De Briac, Jean Perry (Gendarmes); Andre Cheron (Croupier); Jean Masset, Mario Dominici, George Herbert (Players); George Andre Beranger (Hat Clerk); Paul Porcasi (Police Official); Jacques Lory (Elevator Operator); Fredrik Vogeling (Attendant).

New York Premiere: Rivoli Theatre—April 26, 1937
New York Television Debut: CBS—October 15, 1963

### Synopsis

Adolph, the head waiter at the expensive Cafe Metropole in Paris, is in dire need of funds to replace the 900,000 francs he borrowed from the establishment's receipts. He tries his luck at the gaming tables, and while playing opposite Alexis, wins. Alexis writes a check for 450,000 francs, but later admits he has no money to cover the transaction. Adolph insists that the only way Alexis will remain out of jail is to follow his orders explicitly. According to the waiter's scheme, Alexis is to pose as a Russian prince and court wealthy American heiress Laura Ridgeway. When the two marry, Alexis can repay his debt from Laura's dowry. However, complications ensue when Alexis really falls in love with Laura and dislikes the thought of deceiving her. To add to his trouble, Paul, the real Russian prince, who has been working as a waiter in the cafe, now demands that Alexis refrain from using his royal name. Adolph silences Paul with money and then concocts a complex scheme to obtain the money he so desperately needs. Adolph informs Laura's father, Mr. Ridgeway, that Alexis is an imposter, and that he has taken a million francs from him. Ridgeway, thankful to Adolph for giving him this information, reimburses the waiter for his "loss." But Laura refuses to listen to reason and insists on marrying Alexis. Eventually everything is explained. Adolph is allowed to keep the million francs in return for the bad check Alexis had given him. Laura and Alexis look forward to a happy future.

Ever since the Soviet Revolution of 1917, Hollywood had been toying with a plot surmise that would have screen characters masquerade as dethroned Slavic nobility. Claudette Colbert's *Midnight* (1939) was an excellent example of such a film. *Cafe Metropole* was not far behind that vehicle, and it had a "pleasant quality of fooling" which Howard Barnes

(*New York Herald-Tribune*) admitted "slips in and out of fantastic situation, but achieves most of its amusement from the deft clowning of the principals." Not bad for a bon bon of a plot spawned from a casual idea by Darryl F. Zanuck's crony Gregory Ratoff, who endorsed his creative thought by accepting a role in the proceedings.

Once again Loretta Young was cast as a headstrong American heiress (from Akron, Ohio), this time the scion to U.S. automobile parts tycoon Charles Winninger. Her Babbitt-like dad and her prissy aunt (Helen Westley) are no match for the self-willed girl who is determined to enjoy her European lark as she sees fit. And Tyrone Power fills her bill. Almost from the start she is aware that this monocled, alleged Russian nobleman is not from the Eastern European steppes, and more likely hails from Eastern North America. As it develops, Power is actually a former Princeton man who, after taxes, has only $6,000 left from his million-dollar inheritance.

Within the Fox backlot settings for *Cafe Metropole*, these two eligible, healthy, handsome folk court through a chic playland Paris, ranging from the environs of the posh Cafe Metropole (shades of Maxime's) to the bustling Latin Quarter itself, and on to a boat train to Le Havre where Young arranges Power's arrest to prevent him from leaving her. It was already customary in the Young-Power cinema outings to have the story far less important than anything else. *Cafe Metropole* was no exception, being a wispy froufrou properly decorated by two engaging screen personalities.

In their third joint screen offering in less than a year, Young and Power were being touted by Fox (who conveniently ignored the film pairing of Errol Flynn and Olivia de Havilland) as Hollywood's solitary major young love team, a categorization which evidently excluded such couples as Jeanette MacDonald and Nelson Eddy, Fred Astaire and Ginger Rogers, Myrna Loy and William Powell, Clark Gable and Joan Crawford, or Leslie Howard and Bette Davis. Young and Power were considered an acting pair who "fulfills its lightly romantic duties pleasantly" [Frank S. Nugent (*New York Times*)]. Barnes of the *Herald-Tribune* analyzed their screen chemistry thusly: "He is far more convincingly debonair than most of Hollywood's matinee idols. Miss Young is adequately starry-eyed and flighty as the heiress." Robert Garland (*New York American*) phrased it another way: "And a well conditioned duo it is. While she remains her gracious, not unlovely self, he continues to improve."

## SECOND HONEYMOON
### (*Twentieth Century-Fox, 1937*) *79M.*

Producer, Darryl F. Zanuck; associate producer, Raymond Griffith; director, Walter Lang; story, Philip Wylie; screenplay, Kathryn Scola, Darrell

Ware; art directors, Bernard Herzbrun, David Hall; music director, David Buttolph; camera, Ernest Palmer; editor, Walter Thompson.

Tyrone Power (Raoul); Loretta Young (Vicki); Stuart Erwin (McTavish); Claire Trevor (Marcia); Marjorie Weaver (Joy); Lyle Talbot (Bob); J. Edward Bromberg (Herbie); Paul Hurst (Huggins); Jayne Regan (Paula); Mary Treen (Elsie); Hal K. Dawson (Andy); William Wagner (Dr. Sneed); Robert Kellard, Lon Chaney, Jr., Charles Tannen, Arthur Rankin, Robert Lowery, Fred Kelsey (Reporters); Major McBride (Croupier); Sarah Edwards (Woman in Airplane); Wade Boteler, Stanley Blystone (Policemen); Joseph King (Lieutenant); Herbert Fortier (Lawyer); Henry Roquemore, Alex Novinsky (Bondsmen); Harry Burkhardt, Thomas Pogue, Arthur Stuart Hull (Lawyers); Troy Brown (Piano Player); Phillipa Hilbere, Lillian Porter (Telephone Operators).

New York Premiere: Roxy Theatre—November 12, 1937
New York Television Debut: Channel 13—July 27, 1958

### Synopsis

Vicki is happily wed to her second husband, Bob. While on a Miami, Florida, vacation, however, she meets Raoul, her first husband, whom she had divorced because of his irresponsible ways. The chance meeting makes them both realize they are still wildly in love with one another. When Bob is called back up North to his business, Vicki remains in the sunny South, as does Raoul. He courts her and she cannot resist. Bob telephones Vicki to return, but she refuses. He rushes down there to bring her back. A quarrel ensues between Vicki and Bob, landing them both in jail, though they are finally released. In a subsequent quarrel with Bob, Vicki tells him just what she thinks of him and that she intends to obtain a divorce. She then takes off with Raoul in his chartered plane, happy in the thought of remarrying him.

◆◆◆

Just as the screen's *Private Lives* (1931) and *The Awful Truth* (1937) refused to take the subject of divorce seriously, so the slightly improper *Second Honeymoon* charged along its merry way, using as a premise the notion that a marriage unmade by law could be reassembled by belated romantic understanding. To a great extent, this Walter Lang-directed feature, given a bigger budget than it warranted by studio chief Darryl F. Zanuck, depended much on fetching clothing, lilting settings, zingy dialog, and jaunty revelations of life to carry it through its seventy-nine minutes. The stars, Tyrone Power and Loretta Young, were gracious mannequins at best, adorning the production with no sense of the reality of their characterizations. Fortunately, the film succeeded in its mild task of providing rather mindless entertainment, having what Kate Cameron in her three star *New York Daily News* review called ". . . a smooth, satiny finish like unto that well-advertised skin you love to touch."

Stuffy capitalists like Bob (Lyle Talbot) of Benton Belt Company were definitely the unfavored people of *Second Honeymoon*. Imagine a smug, self-satisfied businessman like Talbot who has captured skittish Young on the marital rebound, objecting to being pushed overboard with his clothes on, towed to sea by a harpooned sting ray, or leaving his flighty wife to the advances of carefree playboy Power, her ex-husband. Indeed! The film is more concerned with its study of the erotic problems of the rich, and quickly ditches the feckless Talbot to focus on the re-courtship of Young and Power. He is the charming, unpredictable idler who just might break out into a war whoop in a cocktail lounge (which he does do at one point).

Young had divorced Power because she wanted, or so she thought, an orderly, well-planned life, but her brief union to conventional Talbot has cured her of that notion. Now the fickle, impulsive young lady wishes to renew her unfinished romance with Power. Amidst the couple's frenetic chasing about in the southern playground, the duo enjoys one particularly charming sequence together. Seated on a dock, with their legs dangling over the side, they discuss the rapid-fire events which have so drastically changed their lives within such a short time. Besides, who could ask for more irrational but acceptable escapism than the picture's whimsical finale which has the attractive couple leaving all their cares behind and scooting off in Power's private plane, departing in their own blue bird of happiness.

Critical reaction had certainly solidified regarding the two players as a team ["Pretty Miss Young, Pretty Mr. Power. . . ." (*New York Daily Mirror*)], with Power generally receiving the better notices. "Mr. Power is again expert and handsome in the chief role, accenting what drama there is in a helter-skelter exposure, although he is none too plausible in a bibulous scene. The well dressed Miss Young sways languidly back and forth between first and second husband without giving any indication that she knows what is going on . . ." [Howard Barnes (*New York Herald-Tribune*)]. Likewise, Archer Winsten of the *New York Post* opined, "The Power charm beams brightly and Miss Young does her usual stuff in the manner that has lifted her to her present eminence."

*Second Honeymoon* was blessed with a sterling supporting cast, in particular, Stuart Erwin as Power's valet, a man who has passed more than ninety correspondence courses but flunks on personality. Bumbling Erwin is soon romantically linked with Marjorie Weaver—her bubbling character appropriately named Joy—a talkative brunette who came South to see the tropics and has remained to find a husband. Claire Trevor is oncamera as Young's best pal who listens and advises. In addition, there is Paul Hurst as a fisherman who drinks two bottles of Scotch in short order without spilling a drop, and of course, the rascally raccoon named Violet.

# SUEZ
## (Twentieth Century-Fox, 1938) 104M°

Producer, Darryl F. Zanuck; associate producer, Gene Markey; director, Allan Dwan; story, Sam Duncan; screenplay, Philip Dunne, Julien Josephson; art directors, Bernard Herzbrun, Rudolf Sternad; set decorator, Thomas Little; costumes, Royer; special effects, Fred Sersen; camera, J. Peverell Marley; editor, Barbara MacLean.

Tyrone Power (Ferdinand de Lesseps); Loretta Young (Empress Eugenie); Annabella (Toni Pellerin); J. Edward Bromberg (Said); Joseph Schildkraut (La Tour); Henry Stephenson (Count de Lesseps); Sidney Blackmer (Du Brey); Maurice Moscovich (Mohammed Ali); Sig Rumann (Sergeant Pellerin); Nigel Bruce (Sir Malcolm Cameron); Miles Mander (Benjamin Disraeli); George Zucco (Prime Minister); Leon Ames (Louis Napoleon); Rafaela Ottiano (Maria de Teba); Victor Varconi (Victor Hugo); Jacques Lory (Millet); Odette Myrtil (Duchess); Frank Reicher (General Chagarnier); Carlos J. de Valdez (Count Hatzfeld); Albert Conti (Fevier); Brandon Hurst (Liszt); Marcelle Corday (Mme. Paquineau); Egon Brecher (Doctor); Alphonse Martel (General St. Arnaud); C. Montague Shaw (Elderly Man); Leonard Mudie (Campaign Manager); Jean Perry (Umpire); Robert Graves (Official); Christina Moentt (Maid); Anita Pike (Julia); Louis LaBey (Servant); Frank Lackteen (Swami); Alberto Morin (Achmed); Michael Visaroff, Louis Vincenot, Fred Malastesta (Jewel Merchants); Denis d'Auburn, Jerome De Nuccio, Tony Urchal (Wrestlers); Jean De Briac (Engineer); George Sorel (Assistant); Jacques Vanaire (Old Engineer).

New York Premiere: Roxy Theatre—October 14, 1938
New York Television Debut: Channel 13—April 6, 1957

### Synopsis

Ferdinand de Lesseps and Eugenie de Montijo are in love, but Louis Napoleon, the president of France, has already noted her beauty. He arranges for Ferdinand to be ordered to Egypt as secretary for the consulate general. He pleads with Eugenie to wed him, but while flattered by Napoleon's attention, she requests more time to consider the matter. Ferdinand arrives in Egypt where he is greeted by his father, the French Consul, who advises him to make friends with Prince Said and in that manner win new favors for his country. Ferdinand and Toni Pellerin, the playful granddaughter of Sergeant Pellerin, become good friends. She falls madly in love with him, but he cannot and will not forget Eugenie. Later Ferdinand

°Filmed in Sepia

conceives the idea of a canal connecting the Red Sea and the Mediterranean. Encouraged by Mohammed Ali he travels to Paris to arrange financial backing for his venture. He learns that Eugenie has become Napoleon's mistress. When they meet, Eugenie requests Ferdinand to intercede with his father to adjourn the all powerful Assembly, she giving him Napoleon's written promise that he would later recall the government group. But Napoleon goes back on his word, and instead proclaims himself Emperor of France. The shock kills Ferdinand's father. Ashamed and discouraged, Ferdinand abandons his canal dream, but Toni reinspires him and Napoleon eventually signs a proclamation financing the work. The project does not progress smoothly, with work lagging far behind schedule. Eventually Ferdinand wins the support of England's Disraeli and the canal is at last completed. But his satisfaction is marred by the fact that Toni has been killed in a desert hurricane and that Eugenie has wed Napoleon.

◆━━◆━━◆

Anyone familiar with the previous cinema historical distortions [*The House of Rothschild* (1934), *Clive of India* (1935), *Lloyds of London* (1937)] of studio head Darryl F. Zanuck would not have been very much surprised by *Suez*, "the most frankly inane of all the historical films that have been put together" *(New Yorker* magazine*)*. Facts quickly fall by the wayside in this expensive picture, which weaves its own fictional romance between Ferdinand Marie de Lesseps (1805-1894) and Eugenie Marie de Montijo de Guzman (1826-1920) during the political ascendancy of Louis Napoleon (1808-1873). What emerges is a "handsomely sepia-tinted and ponderously implausible description" [Frank S. Nugent *(New York Times)*] of the glorified life and times of the French diplomat and promoter of the Suez canal who later (this is not shown) fails miserably with his attempted Panama Canal project. The true stars of the fabrication known as *Suez* are the magnificent sets, including recreations of the British Parliament, provincial assemblies, a viceroy's banquet hall, the French presidential ball, period drawing room, etc., and the impressive special effects. In particular, a tumultuous sandstorm was squarely in the tradition of the earthquake of *San Francisco* (1936), the storm in *The Hurricane* (1937), and the fire in *In Old Chicago* (1938).

While the more finicky moviegoer might have wished that *Suez* had been a Warner Bros. project for the team of director Michael Curtiz and stars Errol Flynn and Olivia de Havilland, the Fox contingent acquitted itself with pictorial distinction on all levels, even if the histrionic competency sagged badly in the major roles. Loretta Young, growing increasingly more restless under the Zanuck-Fox aegis, performed far below her standard competent emoting level in this endeavor, seemingly venting her displeasure with studio politics on this production. The *New York Times'* Frank S. Nugent did admit she ". . . is perfectly costumed, up to and including the Eugenie hat." No one could look finer in an 1850s wardrobe than

Young and for the majority of movie audiences that was sufficient. After all, she was coping with a paper-thin, muddled characterization of a woman more intent on social status and political manipulations than sincerity of feeling. However, the more demanding viewer was inclined to agree with Kate Cameron (*New York Daily News*) that ". . . the love she professed for de Lesseps never seems to glow on the screen with any real feeling of warmth or reality." Whether at a tennis match, a lofty ball, or ensconced in an intimate tête-à-tête, she only gave to the part what was actually demanded, a pretty profile, combined with a mannequin's grace. Adding to this situation was the obvious comparison to the film's other female lead player, French newcomer Annabella, as the tomboyish desert filly. Annabella's Toni easily woos the audience into sympathy for her lovesick character, particularly when the girl is swept to her death amidst a tumultuous sandstorm. All of this made Young something of a minor villainess to the more discerning moviegoer. A strange situation indeed for the film's alleged heroine!

Tyrone Power, who would continue to make a true specialty of such "historical" roles throughout his long movie career, strutted through *Suez* like an idealized dreamer (which was fine), never aged (which was typical of Hollywood), demonstrated his earnestness only by contorting his finely slanted eyebrows (at least showing some sign of animation), and wavered indecisively between his love for Young and Annabella (*de rigueur* for a sensitive celluloid hero). While Nugent of the *Times* observed, "It is not precisely the role for Mr. Power, who has the screen manners one associates with the young men from Ted Peck's Escort Bureau," the *New York Daily Mirror* did feel that he ". . . admittedly can wear courtly costumes like no hero in Hollywood . . ."

Regardless of the stick figure hero and heroine players, this film was no different than most any period epic turned out by the Hollywood film factories over the decades. However, thanks to expedient director Allan Dwan and the experienced Fox production crew, a visually tasteful outing guaranteed satisfaction for the eye if not for the mind. And after all, is that so bad an achievement for a picture?

An interesting sidelight of the *Suez* story is when the film was finally shown to representatives of the de Lesseps family, they initiated a law suit in France, claiming the fabricated romance between de Lesseps and Eugenie was damgaing to the reputations of the descendants. However, the court dropped the case, stating the film honored France too much to be disputed by testy private citizens.

Perhaps the final word on the historically distorted *Suez* was offered by an outraged British film journalist who queried in his review, "What would Americans think of a British film of Kentucky, with Lincoln as a plantation owner courting Harriet Beecher Stowe to the theme-song of 'Alexander's Ragtime Band'?"

# THE YEARS AFTER

Loretta Young tolerated the alleged professional mistreatment by Darryl F. Zanuck for less than a year after *Suez*, and left Twentieth Century-Fox in a huff, seeking greater glory elsewhere. It was a sad mistake on her part, for she soon found that her expensive cinema services were not especially in demand and that she had to chop her salary demands in half to reestablish herself in the competitive film market of the 1940s. One of her better movie co-stars of the World War II period was cold-eyed Alan Ladd, with whom she shared screen time in *China* (1943) and *And Now Tomorrow* (1944). It was to a great many people's surprise when Young won an Oscar in 1947 for her role as the Swedish farm girl from Minnesota in *The Farmer's Daughter*. Two years later she was Oscar-nominated again, this time for her radiant nun in *Come to the Stable*, but the Best Actress Academy Award went to Olivia de Havilland of *The Heiress*. Young's film career was slowly petering out in a welter of B features in the early 1950s when she swung into the competing television medium, becoming enormously successful with her "The Loretta Young Show," a half-hour anthology series which sashayed through eight seasons and 255 episodes. The star's weekly hostess entrance through the set's living-room set doors became a landmark of kitsch in American video entertainment. "The New Loretta Young Show" (1962) failed to find its audience, being just another domestic comedy series. Her as-told-to autobiography and advice book, *The Things I Had to Learn*, appeared in 1961. Today the former movie star devotes most of her free time to charity causes.

Throughout the early 1940s Tyrone Power was Twentieth Century-Fox's brightest lead player, performing best in a series of costumed dramas such as *Blood and Sand* (1941). After World War II service in the U.S. Marines he returned to the home lot and the screen in a lugubrious rendition of Somerset Maugham's inspirational *The Razor's Edge* (1946). While his mentor-boss, Zanuck, allowed him more latitude in film assignments, the mature Power bridled under the type of vapid pictures he was forced to headline, overstating his case by later claiming that his Fox tenure had produced hardly a memorable feature in nearly two decades. On the open market he provided several finely etched performances in the mid-1950s, ranging from his Irish-born West Point athletic instructor in *The Long Gray Line* (1955) to the society pianist in *The Eddy Duchin Story* (1956), to Marlene Dietrich's duplistic spouse in *Witness for the Prosecution* (1957). The three-time-wed Power was in Spain filming the Biblical epic *Solomon and Sheba* in November 1958 when he died of a heart attack. He was replaced in that tinsel tale by Yul Brynner.

In **Andy Hardy Meets Debutante** (MGM, 1940)

# Chapter 15

# Mickey Rooney
## &
# Judy Garland

## MICKEY ROONEY

5′ 3″
125 pounds
Light brown hair
Blue eyes
Libra

*Real name: Joe Yule, Jr. Born September 23, 1920, Brooklyn, New York. Married Ava Gardner (1942); divorced 1943. Married Betty Rase (1944), children: Mickey, Timothy; divorced 1947. Married Martha Vickers (1949), child: Ted; divorced 1951. Married Elaine Mahnken (1952); divorced 1959. Married Barbara Thomason (1959), children: Kelly, Kerry, Kimmy; widowed 1966. Married Margaret Lane (1966); divorced 1967. Married Carolyn Hockett (1969).*

FEATURE FILMS:

*Orchids and Ermine* (FN, 1927)
*High Speed* (Col., 1932)
*Information Kid* (Univ., 1932)
*Officer Thirteen* (Allied, 1932)
*Fast Companions* (Univ., 1932)
*My Pal the King* (Univ., 1932)
*Emma* (MGM, 1932)°
*Beast of the City* (MGM, 1932)

*Sin's Pay Day* (Mayfair, 1932)
*The Big Cage* (Univ., 1933)
*The Life of Jimmy Dolan* (WB, 1933)
*Broadway to Hollywood* (MGM, 1933)
*The Big Chance* (Eagle Pictures, 1933)
*The Chief* (MGM, 1933)
*The World Changes* (FN, 1933)
*Lost Jungle* (Mascot, 1934)†

°Unconfirmed

†Also in the Mascot serial version (1934)

411

Beloved (Univ., 1934)

I Like It That Way (Univ., 1934)

Love Birds (Univ., 1934)

Manhattan Melodrama (MGM, 1934)

Chained (MGM, 1934)

Hide-Out (MGM, 1934)

Half a Sinner (Univ., 1934)

Blind Date (Col., 1934)

Death on the Diamond (MGM, 1934)

County Chairman (Fox, 1935)

The Healer (Monogram, 1935)

A Midsummer Night's Dream (WB, 1935)

Reckless (MGM, 1935)

Ah, Wilderness (MGM, 1935)

Riffraff (MGM, 1935)

Little Lord Fauntleroy (UA, 1936)

The Devil Is a Sissy (MGM, 1936)

Down the Stretch (WB, 1936)

Captains Courageous (MGM, 1937)

A Family Affair (MGM, 1937)

The Hoosier Schoolboy (Monogram, 1937)

Slave Ship (20th, 1937)

Thoroughbreds Don't Cry (MGM, 1937)

Live, Love and Learn (MGM, 1937)

Love Is a Headache (MGM, 1938)

Judge Hardy's Children (MGM, 1938)

You're Only Young Once (MGM, 1938)

Hold That Kiss (MGM, 1938)

Lord Jeff (MGM, 1938)

Love Finds Andy Hardy (MGM, 1938)

Boys Town (MGM, 1938)

Out West with the Hardys (MGM, 1938)

Stablemates (MGM, 1938)

The Adventures of Huckleberry Finn (MGM, 1939)

The Hardys Ride High (MGM, 1939)

Andy Hardy Gets Spring Fever (MGM, 1939)

Babes in Arms (MGM, 1939)

Judge Hardy and Son (MGM, 1939)

Young Tom Edison (MGM, 1940)

Strike Up the Band (MGM, 1940)

Andy Hardy Meets Debutante (MGM, 1940)

Andy Hardy's Private Secretary (MGM, 1940)

Men of Boys Town (MGM, 1941)

Life Begins for Andy Hardy (MGM, 1941)

Babes on Broadway (MGM, 1941)

The Courtship of Andy Hardy (MGM, 1942)

A Yank at Eton (MGM, 1942)

Andy Hardy's Double Life (MGM, 1942)

The Human Comedy (MGM, 1943)

Thousands Cheer (MGM, 1943)

Girl Crazy (MGM, 1943)

Andy Hardy's Blonde Trouble (MGM, 1944)

National Velvet (MGM, 1944)

Love Laughs at Andy Hardy (MGM, 1946)

Killer McCoy (MGM, 1947)

Summer Holiday (MGM, 1948)

Words and Music (MGM, 1948)

The Big Wheel (UA, 1949)

Quicksand (UA, 1950)

The Fireball (20th, 1950)

He's a Cockeyed Wonder (Col., 1950)

My Outlaw Brother (Eagle Lion, 1951)

The Strip (MGM, 1951)

Sound Off (Col., 1952)

Off Limits (Par., 1953)

All Ashore (Col., 1953)

A Slight Case of Larceny (MGM, 1953)

Drive a Crooked Road (Col., 1954)

The Atomic Kid (Rep., 1954)

The Bridges at Toko-ri (Par., 1954)

The Twinkle in God's Eye (Rep., 1955)

The Bold and the Brave (RKO, 1956)

Francis in the Haunted House (Univ., 1956)

Magnificent Roughnecks (AA, 1956)

Operation Mad Ball (Col., 1957)

Baby Face Nelson (UA, 1957)

Andy Hardy Comes Home (MGM, 1958)

A Nice Little Bank That Should Be Robbed (20th, 1958)

The Last Mile (UA, 1959)

The Big Operator (MGM, 1959)

Platinum High School (MGM, 1960)

The Private Lives of Adam and Eve (Univ., 1960)

King of the Roaring 20's—The Story of Arnold Rothstein (AA, 1961)

Breakfast at Tiffany's (Par., 1961)

Everything's Ducky (Col., 1961)
Requiem for a Heavyweight (Col., 1962)
It's a Mad, Mad, Mad, Mad World (UA, 1963)
The Secret Invasion (UA, 1964)
How to Stuff a Wild Bikini (AIP, 1965)
24 Hours to Kill (7 Arts, 1965)
Ambush Bay (UA, 1966)
The Devil in Love (WB-7 Arts, 1968)
Skidoo (Par., 1968)
The Extraordinary Seaman (MGM, 1969)

The Comic (Col., 1969)
80 Steps to Jonah (WB, 1969)
The Cockeyed Cowboys of Calico County (Univ., 1970)
Journey Back to Oz (Filmation, 1971)°
B. J. Lang Presents (Maron Films, 1971)
Hollywood Blue (Sherpix, 1971)
Pulp (UA, 1972)
Richard (Aurora City Group, 1972)
The Godmothers (Ellman Enterprises, 1973)
That's Entertainment (UA, 1974)
Rachel's Man (1975)

°Voice only

# JUDY GARLAND

### 4' 11"
### 95 pounds
### Auburn hair
### Brown eyes
### Gemini

*Real name: Frances Gumm. Born June 10, 1922, Grand Rapids, Minnesota. Married David Rose (1941); divorced 1943. Married Vincente Minnelli (1945), child: Liza; divorced 1950. Married Sid Luft (1952), children: Lorna, Joseph; divorced 1965. Married Mark Herron (1965); divorced 1967. Married Mickey Deans (1969). Died June 22, 1969.*

**FEATURE FILMS:**

Pigskin Parade (20th, 1936)
Broadway Melody of 1938 (MGM, 1937)
Thoroughbreds Don't Cry (MGM, 1937)
Everybody Sing (MGM, 1938)
Listen Darling (MGM, 1938)
Love Finds Andy Hardy (MGM, 1938)
The Wizard of Oz (MGM, 1939)
Babes in Arms (MGM, 1939)
Strike Up the Band (MGM, 1940)
Little Nellie Kelly (MGM, 1940)

Andy Hardy Meets Debutante (MGM, 1940)
Ziegfeld Girl (MGM, 1941)
Life Begins For Andy Hardy (MGM, 1941)
Babes on Broadway (MGM, 1941)
For Me and My Gal (MGM, 1942)
Presenting Lily Mars (MGM, 1943)
Thousands Cheer (MGM, 1943)
Girl Crazy (MGM, 1943)
Meet Me in St. Louis (MGM, 1944)

°Voice only

413

*The Clock* (MGM, 1945)
*The Harvey Girls* (MGM, 1946)
*Ziegfeld Follies* (MGM, 1946)
*Till the Clouds Roll By* (MGM, 1946)
*The Pirate* (MGM, 1948)
*Easter Parade* (MGM, 1948)
*Words and Music* (MGM, 1948)
*In the Good Old Summertime* (MGM, 1949)

*Summer Stock* (MGM, 1950)
*A Star Is Born* (WB, 1954)
*Pepe* (Col., 1960)°
*Judgment at Nuremberg* (UA, 1961)
*Gay Purr-ee* (WB, 1962)°
*A Child Is Waiting* (UA, 1963)
*I Could Go on Singing* (UA, 1963)

°Voice Only

In **Words and Music** (MGM, 1948)

In **Girl Crazy** (MGM, 1943)

On "The Judy Garland Show" (CBS-TV, December 8, 1963)

In an MGM publicity pose (c. 1937)

Cecelia Parker, Lewis Stone, Fay Holden, Mickey Rooney, and Judy Garland in
**Love Finds Andy Hardy** (MGM, 1938)

In **Thoroughbreds Don't Cry** (MGM, 1937)

In **Babes in Arms** (MGM, 1939)

Sheet music to **Babes in Arms**

Advertisement for **Strike Up the Band** (MGM, 1940)

In **Strike Up the Band**

Advertisement for **Thousands Cheer** (MGM, 1943)

Judy Garland, Fay Holden, and Mickey Rooney in a publicity pose for **Life Begins for Andy Hardy** (MGM, 1941)

José Iturbi and Judy Garland in **Thousands Cheer**

Ray McDonald, Judy Garland, Mickey Rooney, and Richard Quine in **Babes on Broadway** (MGM, 1941)

# THOROUGHBREDS DON'T CRY
## *(MGM, 1937) 80M.*

Producer, Harry Rapf; director, Alfred E. Green; story, Eleanore Griffin, J. Walter Ruben; screenplay, Lawrence Hazard; songs, Nacio Herb Brown and Arthur Freed; music director, William Axt; costumes, Dolly Tree; camera, Leonard Smith; editor, Elmo Vernon.

Judy Garland (Cricket West); Mickey Rooney (Tim Donahue); Sophie Tucker (Mother Ralph); C. Aubrey Smith (Sir Peter Calverton); Ronald Sinclair (Roger Calverton); Forrester Harvey (Wilkins); Helen Troy (Hilda); Charles D. Brown (Click Donahue); Frankie Darro (Dink Reid); Henry Kolker (Doc Godfrey).

New York Premiere: Rialto Theatre—November 25, 1937
New York Television Debut: CBS—January 5, 1959

### Synopsis

Young Roger Calverton and his grandfather, Sir Peter Calverton, arrive in America to race their prize horse, "The Pookah," hoping to win the big race and thus secure their future. Sir Peter wins the friendship of Tim Donahue by giving him the riding whip once owned by a famous jockey, and Tim promises to ride "The Pookah" in the upcoming track event. Tim has no love for his no-good father, Click Donahue, a parasitic creature, but he is concerned when his dad says he needs $5,000 for special medical attention to save his life. Tim agrees to hold back "The Pookah" during the race, in order to obtain the needed money from Click's gambler friends who will bet against the horse. Tim loses the race, and the shock kills Sir Peter. Remorseful, Tim decides to aid Roger, who, except for the horse, is penniless. He begs Click to give him the required $1,000 to enter "The Pookah" in another racing event, but Click refuses. Tim steals the money from Click, and when Click discovers the theft, he informs the race track officials that Tim had pulled the other race and the officials rule Tim off the track. At the last minute, Roger rides the horse and wins. Tim is overjoyed, as is Cricket West, a girl from Mother Ralph's boarding house who has always given Tim encouragement in his times of need.

◆━━◆━━◆

"Short on the logic but long on the pep, it gallops gayly into the stretch," reported Bosley Crowther *(New York Times)* of this infectiously unpretentious MGM programmer. Not in the same league with *Saratoga*, the studio's big racetrack picture of the year, *Thoroughbreds Don't Cry* followed a familiar formula but peopled the proceedings with ingratiating young players. Best of all, "it is played as farce comedy, which saves it as entertainment" *(Variety)*.

Fourteen-year-old Ronnie Sinclair, imported from New Zealand as a successor to maturing Freddie Bartholomew, had the stale assignment in *Thoroughbreds Don't Cry* of the too-good-to-be-true noble youth whose excellent breeding is only matched by his impeccable diction. Much more to audiences' liking were two other studio hopefuls, fifteen-year-old Judy Garland who had finally made her feature film debut on loanout in *Pigskin Parade* (1936), and seventeen-year-old Mickey Rooney, who, after a long career in vaudeville, movie short subjects, and small feature film roles, was about to hit cinema paydirt. The first Andy Hardy picture, *A Family Affair* (1937), had been released a few months before and would soon launch Rooney on to breathtaking stardom.

In *Broadway Melody of 1938* (1937), Garland had played the daughter of theatrical boarding house keeper Sophie Tucker. In *Thoroughbreds Don't Cry*, she plays the niece of Tucker, the "red hot mama," this time a (non-singing) boarding house keeper for jockeys. Plump perky Garland is again a junior Miss-Fixit who has more good in her heart than any two Salvation Army workers. She is a joy to her amply proportioned Aunt Tucker, and always willing to lend a hand with the chores about the rooming house, a most commendable trait since slapstick maid Helen Troy is more inclined to laugh-provoking antics than house cleaning. No doubt about it, Garland in this film is a trouper through and through, always ready with a funny imitation, an optimistic song ("Got a New Pair of Shoes"; the recorded "Sun Showers" was deleted from the release print of the movie), and a cheery word of encouragement for bewildered Sinclair. But most of all Garland's Cricket West nurtures unrequited love for swaggering young jockey Rooney who has a clear view to his own self-importance, but is blind to Garland's love and admiration for him. This one-way romance between Garland and Rooney set a precedent for most of the duo's joint film's together, with misty-eyed Garland wondering when her miniature knight in shining armor will awaken to the beautiful girl within her ugly duckling shell. This was the perfect formula for the Garland-Rooney musical romps to come, and always within this structure, it is young Garland who instructs the older Rooney in the ways of humility and thoughtfulness, teaching him a stern lesson in humanity (and one he would usually forget by their next screen exercise).

While the critics and public alike were quick to note and to approve of the vocally mature Garland who seemed to be MGM's answer to Universal's Deanna Durbin, it was Rooney who received the lion's share of reviewers' attention. "When Mickey grows up, we shouldn't be a bit surprised if he turned out a second Spencer Tracy" *(New York Post)*. "As the kick, [Rooney] manages to streak with a brilliant performance which lends a certain quality to the whole picture. Swaggering, truculent, and tough, as only a jockey can b, he builds a knotty little character which holds together even in the sappy spots" [Crowther *(New York Times)*].

It was a characterization that Rooney would replay in the later *National Velvet* (1944) with young Elizabeth Taylor as the star of that horse story.

## LOVE FINDS ANDY HARDY
### *(MGM, 1938) 90M.*

Producer, Lou Ostrow; director, George B. Seitz; based upon characters created by Aurania Rouverol and stories by Vivien R. Bretherton; screenplay, William Ludwig; songs, Mack Gordon and Harry Revel; Roger Edens; costumes, Jeanne; music, David Snell; vocal arranger, Edens; camera, Lester White; editor, Ben Lewis.

Lewis Stone (Judge James Hardy); Mickey Rooney (Andrew Hardy); Judy Garland (Betsy Booth); Cecilia Parker (Marian Hardy); Fay Holden (Mrs. Hardy); Ann Rutherford (Polly Benedict); Betty Ross Clarke (Aunt Milly); Lana Turner (Cynthia Potter); Marie Blake (Augusta); Don Castle (Dennis Hunt); Gene Reynolds (Jimmy MacMahon); Mary Howard (Mrs. Tompkins); George Breakston (Beezy); Raymond Hatton (Peter Dugan); Frank Darien (Bill Collector); Rand Brooks (Judge); Erville Alderson (Court Attendant).

New York Premiere: Capitol Theatre—July 21, 1938
New York Television Debut: CBS—January 8, 1957

### Synopsis

Andy Hardy makes a twelve-dollar deposit on a jalopy car, promising to pay the eight-dollar balance before the end of the month. Not being able to scrape the money together, he enters into a business proposition with Beezy, the latter having to be out of town to visit relatives. For the sum of eight dollars Andy agrees to escort Beezy's girl friend Cynthia Potter everywhere, so that no other boy will have the opportunity to date her. But this situation gets Andy into difficulties with his own girl, Polly Benedict. As a result, neither flirtatious Cynthia nor jealous Polly will go to the Christmas dance with Andy. However, Betsy Booth, visiting her grandmother in Carvel, manages to maneuver her hero, Andy, into taking her to the country club dance. Andy, who had thought Betsy just a little girl, is amazed at the reception she receives at the party when she sings a song. Later, Betsy, knowing how Andy feels about Polly, brings the two of them together before she returns to New York. The Hardy family's joy is complete when Mrs. Hardy, who had been out of town caring for her sick mother, gets word to her husband that she will be home in time for the holiday celebrations.

◆◆◆

This, the fourth of the sixteen-entry *Andy Hardy* series, proved again to be a big audience winner for the series as it detailed homey events in the lives of America's favorite neighbors, Judge Hardy and family of Carvel, U.S.A. Mickey Rooney, who would be awarded a special Oscar in 1938 for his continuing Andy Hardy portrayal, added new laurels to his snowballing popularity with each new chapter of this screen saga. "Watching Mickey's Andy on the screen is practically as good as reading Mark Twain and Booth Tarkington; he's the perfect composite of everybody's kid brother" [Frank S. Nugent (*New York Times*)]. Even more enthusiastic was Howard Barnes (*New York Herald-Tribune*): "It is not often that you will see such a knowing and versatile characterization contributed by a stripling. With an unerring sense of timing and a remarkable command of expression, gesture and mood, he brings Andy to vivid and exciting life. . . ."

With such outstanding competition, it was no easy task for Judy Garland to step into an established film series and win her own spot in audiences' hearts, especially in a picture in which she had such tough distaff rivals as the physically mature and beautiful Lana Turner (in her first MGM picture) and the well-liked, sweet Ann Rutherford. But the moment Garland comes into camera view in *Love Finds Andy Hardy*, one almost forgets hot tomato Turner (whom one character labels a "red-headed vampire") and co-ed Rutherford. For a change, Garland's oncamera character is extremely well-groomed, for her Betsy Booth is the New York City-bred daughter of a successful musical comedy star visiting her grandmother who lives next door to the Hardy family.

Fairly soon in *Love Finds Andy Hardy*, Garland's Betsy makes her first appearance. Dressed in a tasteful dark suit with a silk scarf about her neck, Garland's character emerges from the chauffeur-driven limousine and immediately commands attention. Her gushy conversation with Lewis Stone immediately reveals that despite her mature outfit, she is still a pleasant young adolescent at heart, who can enthuse, "Christmas with Andy Hardy too!" But Rooney's Andy, not yet sixteen in this chapter, is going through the throes of his own romantic and financial problems, and seems totally disinterested when Stone later advises him that their neighbors "have a visitor, a new playmate for you." Already the die is cast; Garland's Betsy Booth is not to be among the roster of romantic conquests of Andy Hardy. Garland herself does not help matters much, for when she is first introduced to Rooney she blurts out in her most babyish, singsong manner, "I'm Betsy Booth."

A great deal of screen time within *Love Finds Andy Hardy* is devoted to Rooney's fledgling love life, with Garland's interludes always just a sidelight. "Oh, she's just a little kid next door," Rooney tells Turner at one point in the film, and no matter what Garland does to perk Rooney's interest, he treats her with total disregard. The poor girl is so frustrated in her puppy dog love that she sits right down at the piano and sings to herself about her big problem, bemoaning her fate that "I'll never be able to get a man, much less hold him." As the song concludes, she sighs to herself, "No glamour. No glamour at all."

Later, Rooney does condescend to escort her in her chauffeur-driven car to the local malt shop, where he shares a soda with her (he at least pays for it), and discourses egocentrically on his own state of amours and budgets. In this cozy little scene, Garland demonstrates her burgeoning ability to make her oncamera intensity work for her role, shaking her head, making gushy "oohs" and "umms" as she listens with full absorption to Rooney's minor tale of woe.

But it is not long before Rooney has been lured away by chesty Turner, and Garland is again left alone, returning to the piano where she croons "In Between," relating her plight that "I'm too old for toys" but "I'm too young for boys." (The song even works in the standard plugs for MGM studio personalities, as Garland sings that she is not allowed to see Clark Gable movies, and "Who knows, if I used lipstick and a powder puff, I might be Garbo in the rough.") With characteristic showladyship, Garland ends this ditty with a heart-tugging sob, praying for the day when she'll be sweet sixteen and not just in between.

One of the sneakier ingredients of the Rooney-Garland entries was the constant tantalizing pacifiers tossed to Garland's character by her love of life, Rooney. For example, in *Love Finds Andy Hardy* she agrees to accompany the perturbed youth to the dance and save him from eternal embarrassment. Rooney immediately registers interest in Garland the life saver, "Gee! Betsy, you're the best friend I've ever had." Garland and the audience thus have high hopes that maybe, just maybe, Rooney will get wise to himself and after all realize what a swell bet Garland is in the romance sweepstakes (granted, she is portraying a very young junior miss here). But no, having teased all concerned, Rooney's Andy is soon up to his old innocent tricks at the big country club dance. His confidence restored by having found a presentable girl to be his social partner, he is now once again the strutting big shot, filled with a most discouraging air of superiority. Just before vulnerable Garland, who has had a mature gown shipped all the way from Chicago for the occasion, is about to launch into her big song number, he deflates her enthusiasm by asking, "Honest, Betsy. A lot of my friends are here. Do you think you've practiced enough?" Has she ever! In contrast to her earlier soft beat numbers, she launches into a lively "It Never Rains But What It Pours" followed by a swing rendition of "Meet the Beat of My Heart."

With dispatch the film quickly concludes. Rooney's love life has been temporarily put back onto a somewhat even keel, a traumatic short wave radio scene has provided explication that Mother Hardy (Fay Holden) will soon be returning from Brigham, Canada, where she was tending her ailing mother, and now it is time for Garland's Betsy to return to Manhattan. She is a brave little soul, who has used her sharp intuition to get mature, predatory Turner out of Rooney's way and to alert Rooney that Rutherford's dance date was really the girl's cousin. Once again life is beautiful for the carefree Andy Hardy. Now Garland can leave Carvel and the storyline on an optimistic upbeat, which is a cute scripting trick considering how Rooney's character has mistreated her. "I'll never be able to thank you for last night," bubbles Garland. "I'm going to write Andy Hardy pages in my scrapbook and read it for five years. For one night I was grown up. So you see now I know how wonderful life will be when I'm sixteen."

Garland's Betsy Booth may have lost the romantic bout with Rooney in *Love Finds Andy Hardy,* but she won critical acclaim. "Based on her showing, they will have to find a permanent place for Miss Garland in the future Hardys" (*Variety*). "Although the high-and-mighty young man looked down his nose at such a youthful miss, Judy came close to snatching the picture away from him" [Herbert Cohn (*Brooklyn Daily Eagle*)]. Archer Winsten (*New York Post*) offered a rather unique suggestion for the MGM executives in his picture review: "And, quite surprisingly, Judy Garland is held in such check that one can see great possibilities if she's ever given a chance at a role as far removed as possible from her hot singing characterizations."

## BABES IN ARMS
### (MGM, 1939) 97M.

Producer, Arthur Freed; director, Busby Berkeley; based on the musical play by Richard Rodgers, Lorenz Hart; screenplay, Jack MacGowan, Kay Van Riper; art directors, Cedric Gibbons, Merrill Pye; wardrobe, Dolly Tree; songs, Rodgers and Hart; Freed, Gus Arnheim, and Abe Lyman; E. Y. Harburg and Harold Arlen; Freed and Nacio Herb Brown; camera, Ray June; editor, Frank Sullivan.

Mickey Rooney (Mickey Moran); Judy Garland (Patsy Barton); Charles Winninger (Joe Moran); Guy Kibbee (Judge Black); June Preisser (Rosalie Essex); Grace Hayes (Florrie Moran); Betty Jaynes (Molly Moran); Douglas McPhail (Don Brice); Rand Brooks (Jeff Steele); Leni Lynn (Dody Martini); John Sheffield (Bobs); Henry Hull (Maddox); Barnett Parker (William); Ann Shoemaker (Mrs. Barton); Margaret Hamilton (Martha Steele); Joseph Crehan (Mr. Essex); George McKay (Brice); Henry Roquemore (Shaw); Lelah Tyler (Mrs. Brice); Lon McCallister (Boy).

New York Premiere: Capitol Theatre—October 19, 1939
New York Television Debut: CBS—August 19, 1959

### Synopsis

Vaudeville has been dying, leaving such former troupers as Joe and Florrie Moran behind the times, but they insist there are still good years left for them, and they organize a touring revue featuring many other old timers. When they refuse to take their talented offsprings along with them, the latter decide to produce their own show not only to show the older generation that they shouldn't have been ignored but also to prove to the townfolk that they are healthy, normal youths who do not belong in a state school for underprivileged children. Mickey Moran, encouraged by Patsy Barton, writes the big show in which he will star as well as direct. Everyone is counting on Mickey's efforts, including Judge Black who has given the youths thirty days to prove their worth. Otherwise it is off to trade school for them as busybody Martha Stelle demands. Problems of financing the musical are solved when ex-child star Rosalie Essex agrees to back the show, if she is given the leading female role. This demand naturally is a shock to Patsy who is reduced to being an understudy, but Mickey and later her mother convince her that there is no other way and the good of the whole show comes before any one individual. At the last minute Rosalie withdraws from her role and Patsy goes on in her stead. The show seems to be a success, but a sudden storm ruins the evening. Mickey, however, receives a letter from a New York producer named Maddox, inviting the young showman to call on him in Manhattan and talk terms. Maddox agrees to put Mickey's revue on Broadway and because he is a long-standing pal of Joe Moran, he arranges for Joe to be given a consultant's job to the production.

◆◆◆

The first of the four Busby Berkeley-directed Mickey Rooney and Judy Garland MGM musicals was very loosely derived from the Richard Rodgers-Lorenz Hart Broadway musical hit of 1937. All that remained from the original stage version was the title tag, two songs ("Babes in Arms" and "Where Or When") and snatches of "The Lady Is a Tramp," which became background music in the movie. No matter! The black and white movie was a ninety-seven-minute entertainment bonanza that insured further energetic entries to come.

To quickly pass over the lesser points of *Babes in Arms,* the film is saddled with two unappealing second leads: phlegmatic Douglas Mc-Phail,° the very awkward young man touted as the new Nelson Eddy, who was joined oncamera by his unsvelte offscreen wife, Betty Jaynes, whose precocious operatic talents did not compensate for her bland cinema presence. Unfortunately it is this unengaging screen duo who sings the once charming "Where Or When," as it is baritone McPhail who leads the rousing "Babes in Arms" march and Jaynes whose contralto chirps in competition with swinging Garland in the "Opera

---

°McPhail died on December 7, 1944, at the age of thirty, from a self-administered dose of poison. He had attempted suicide in 1941 when he and Betty Jaynes, his wife of three years, had divorced; in the spring of 1944 he had been discharged from the army as being emotionally unequipped for military life.

versus Jazz" number. Finally, it is McPhail who is the lumbering inter-locutor in the minstrel show number.

In addition, it must be admitted that, despite his lofty cult position today, director Busby Berkeley did go overboard in staging two of the picture's big production numbers. In the call-to-arms title tune ensemble, he relied on a gambit used for similar march numbers in his *Roman Scandals*, *Gold Diggers of 1933*, and *Footlight Parade*, all from 1933, in which he marches his processional cast up and down an enclosed set to diminishing results. Here the "youngsters" march up and down the streets, ending up at the huge bonfire, then engaging in a demonstration of ring-around-the-rosie, and for no explicable reason (save to end the number) Garland and Rooney mount a conveniently placed ladder. Berkeley also refused to use artistic restraint in the over-indulgent Mr. Bones-Mr. Jones-interlocutor blackface routine which more often not sunk into its own maze of *déjà vu*.

But on to the joys of *Babes in Arms*! Garland might be saddled on-camera with the personae of a frumpy-haired young miss who has delight-ful notes in her throat and too many pounds around the waist, yet she displayed such unbounding talent in this film that her future screen career was insured. Never before had she been more energetic in front of the camera. How many viewers at the time could know that much of her effort to match Rooney's enormous performing vitality was not self-induced, but a result of expending nervous energy created from a regimen of diet and pep pills, as well as being a reaction to her abrasive relation-ship with the film's taskmaster-director, Berkeley. She later said, "I used to feel as if he had a big black bull whip and he was lashing me with it. Some-times I used to think I couldn't live through the day."

Throughout *Babes in Arms* both Rooney and Garland perform their wide assortment of tricks with absolutely no let up, whether it be ham-ming excitement as when Rooney faints in the publisher's office at the moment he receives a hundred-dollar payment check or the coy little love scene between the two "adolescents." In this scene Rooney and Garland return to their modest Long Island family homes and indulge in one of those marvelous little romantic bits that seemed so spontane-ous. Having decided that it must be awful to be a hasbeen (like their parents), Rooney magnanimously bestows his music class pin on a grateful Garland. She eagerly accepts, but asks him to express his love. She tries to make him say that he really cares for her, but all the embarrassed youth will admit is, "I do."

Garland: "You do what?"

Rooney: "I do very much what you want me to say, but I won't."

But it is not long before Rooney and Garland are engulfed in other problems, financing and preparing the big show, and most of all coping with June Preisser, who is cast as the temperamental ex-child star once known to millions as "Baby Rosalie." The script astutely puts

Garland in competition with Preisser for Rooney's affection, for it was already obvious that the lilting star of *The Wizard of Oz* (1939) (for which Garland won her own special Oscar miniature) had a delicious way with a tart line when put on the uncamera defensive. Thus, when cartwheeling Preisser arrives for the show-within-the-movie rehearsal, complete with maid, chauffeur, and dogs, the scene is set for the rivalry between the two contrasting girls. Imperious blonde Preisser, who has already vamped Rooney into submission, demands a glass of water and agog Garland runs to fetch it. "Isn't she a sweet little girl," Preisser condescendingly admits of Garland. Later, Rooney tells a perplexed Garland, "Don't go get jealous. We don't have time for that stuff." Poor, put-upon Garland, in a fit of depression, rushes off by night bus coach to visit her show-touring mother, crooning herself to sleep by singing "I Cried for You," in which she re-iterates that she is nothing but an ugly duckling, but someday, Mr. Rooney, just you wait and see.

From the time Garland's Patsy Barton returns to Long Island, the film picks up tempo. She announces to a harassed Rooney that she is back to work: "My family are all troupers. We don't walk out on any show." The revue goes on, Garland and Rooney romp through their minstrel show in blackface, and eventually find themselves and their co-workers on Broadway, performing for an enchanted public.

Perhaps in none of their other joint films does Garland have more opportunity to demonstrate her singing expertise and variety. At the publisher's office, she duets with Rooney to the bouncy "Good Morning," later with Rooney's sister (Betty Jaynes) she does the contrasting "Opera versus Jazz," still later solos the ballad "I Cried for You," and joins with the gang in the rousing street march rendition of "Babes in Arms." She perks through the minstrel show number (which interpolates "Oh Susanna," "Ida," "By the Light of the Silvery Moon," and "I'm Just Wild about Harry") and in the finale, she takes part in the patriotic ditty "God's Country." For her contributions to *Babes in Arms,* Garland was congratulated by one and all for her "simply swell sense of swing."

But once again it was the film's five-foot-three-er, Rooney, who ultimately stole the silver screen limelight. He was a man for all seasons in this picture. He was found prancing as a tot (interpolated old movie footage), maneuvering his parents, the judge, hot-tempered Preisser, and oversensitive Garland, with all the calm of an experienced ringmaster. He was involved in some of his favorite style capering in *Babes in Arms,* doing imitations of the professionals with whom he worked and liked, namely Clark Gable and Lionel Barrymore, singing a blackface rendition of "Ida" a la Eddie Cantor, playing "Good Morning" on the piano as he vocalized with Garland, later plucking on the cello strings, and thereafter conducting the orchestra. In short, Rooney provided "one of the most extensive performances ever given on the screen" (*Variety*). B. R. Crisler (*New York Times*) thought ". . . even in musical comedy no one of his

ostensibly tender years should be in the spotlight as Master Rooney is."
But the nineteen-year-old male wonder was so versatile, why not let
him display his abilities? He did just that, and admirably in *Babes in
Arms*. Master Rooney was Oscar nominated for his performance, but
lost out in the Best Actor category to Robert Donat of MGM's *Goodbye,
Mr. Chips.*

Strung throughout *Babes in Arms* is a wholesale amount of isolationist
American philosophy, guaranteed at the time to win the film eager
endorsement from similar thinking Americans. At one point Rooney
says to Garland, "A lot of foreign countries are borrowing money from us.
Why can't an American go in and borrow some?" Then in the flag-
waving finale, "God's Country," we have MGM taking the European
war very lightly indeed, proclaiming that in the U.S. "Everyone is a
dictator." That here "we've got no Duce, no Fuhrer," but "we've got
Garbo and Norma Shearer." After this rather flabbergasting re-evalua-
tion of the relative importance of the world situation, the picture launches
into the charmingly structured "My Day" sequence in which Rooney and
Garland portray Franklin D. Roosevelt and his wife Eleanor, each re-
counting how they spend their very constructive days. The film concludes with Rooney-cum-Roosevelt suggesting that the panacea for the
country's problems is "Let's Dance." For after all, "Drop your sabres, we
all want to be good neighbors." The entire cast then launches into a
jitterbugging number before the final fadeout.

A few weeks before the enormously successful *Babes in Arms* movie
premiered in New York at the Capitol Theatre, the studio's flagship
emporium, MGM launched the star team on a personal appearance
tour. This vaudeville stint in conjunction with the film's reception led
the critics to call Rooney and Garland a most "winning combination"
and an "irresistible team."

## ANDY HARDY MEETS DEBUTANTE
### (MGM, 1940) 89M.

Producer, J. J. Cohn; director, George B. Seitz; based upon characters
created by Aurania Rouverol; screenplay, Annalee Whitmore, Thomas
Seller; songs, Lester Santley, Benny Davis, and Milton Ager; Arthur
Freed and Nacio Herb Brown; music director, Georgie Stoll; music ar-
ranger, Roger Edens; vocal arranger-orchestrator, Arnaud, Salinger,
Van Eps, Haglin; costumes, Dolly Tree; camera, Sidney Wagner; editor,
Harold F. Kress.

Mickey Rooney (Andy Hardy); Lewis Stone (Judge Hardy); Fay
Holden (Mrs. Hardy); Cecilia Parker (Marion Hardy); Judy Garland (Betsy
Booth); Sara Haden (Aunt Milly); Ann Rutherford (Polly Benedict); Tom

431

Neal (Aldrich Brown); Diana Lewis (Daphne Fowler); George Breakston (Beezy); Cy Kendall (Mr. Carrillo); George Lessey (Underwood); Addison Richards (Mr. Benedict); Edwin Stanley (Surrogate); Harry Tyler (Jordan); Clyde Willson (Shirley); Sam McDaniel (Porter); Dutch Hendrian (Driver); John Merkyl (Prentice); Herbert Evans (Butler); Claire DuBrey (Mrs. Hackett); Lester Dorr (Photographer); Pat Flaherty (Bodyguard); Marjorie Gateson (Mrs. Fowler); Forbes Murray (Man); Charles Trowbridge (Davis the Butler); Charles Coleman (Headwaiter); Charles Wagenheim (Waiter); Sherrie Overton (Cigarette Girl); Gladys Blake (Gertrude); Emmett Vogan (Green); Otto Hoffmann (Poultaney); Buddy Messinger (Elevator Boy); Art Belasco (Doorman); Thomas Pogue (Carriage Coachman).

New York Premiere: Capitol Theatre—August 1, 1940
New York Television Debut: CBS—July 10, 1957

## Synopsis

Just from the photographs he has seen of Daphne Fowler, one of New York's leading debutantes, Andy Hardy is convinced that she is the girl of his destiny. When he is teased by Polly Benedict and Beezy that he really does not know the young blue blood, Andy boasts that if he were only in New York, Daphne would certainly pose for a picture with him. To his dismay, just such a chance comes about when Judge Stone informs his family that he has to go to New York to settle a legal matter regarding the Carvel Orphanage and that he is taking the family with him. Andy desperately wants not to go, but in vain. Polly and Beezy inform the departing Andy that the next issue of the high school paper will be devoted to his Manhattan sojourn and that they expect a picture of him and Daphne. Once in New York, Andy muffs his attempts to meet Daphne, that is, until he discovers that his lovelorn pal Betsy Booth really knows Daphne and can arrange for Andy to be at a party hostessed by the New York debutante. At this party Daphne agrees to pose with Andy, and he can return to Carvel as a victor. Andy, realizing that he had been wrong in considering Betsy just a "kid," promises to return to her someday. Meantime, the judge has solved his legal problems satisfactorily, and the other Hardy family members agree with him that there is no place like home.

◆◆◆

Offcamera, MGM's irrepressible, impish star Mickey Rooney was launching into his second big year as U.S. boxoffice champ, but oncamera he was having more than his share of woes in *Andy Hardy Meets Debutante*, the latest installment of the series. What possible hope was there for Rooney's famous cinema alter ego to satisfy his momentary life's desire to embrace the Princess of the Four Hundred, New York's most publicized debutante, namely Daphne Fowler (Diana Lewis)

432

when his standby, old-hat girlfriend Polly Benedict (Ann Rutherford) could so cruelly suggest to 5'3" Rooney, "Wouldn't you be happier with someone who could look up to you?"

Imagine Rooney's plight when, courtesy of the scenario, Judge Hardy (Lewis Stone) announces to his attentive family that they are about to embark on a combination business-pleasure trip to Manhattan. Now there is no excuse for Rooney to avoid attempting the impossible; he must either sink or swim in his efforts to meet and date the elusive Lewis. Before acceding to the inevitable, Rooney makes a valiant stand, conjuring up every possible argument at his adolescent command against making the trip. "What has New York got?" he asks Stone. "A lot of tall buildings. What do people do with tall buildings? Jump out of windows." This jaundiced but perhaps not too unfair view of Manhattan's concrete jungle does not convince Stone, and Rooney is dragged off to New York City.

Once in the metropolis, Rooney encounters Betsy Booth (Judy Garland) who has not lost her love or enthusiasm for Rooney since they last met. Garland's Betsy is now fifteen, and in her mother's absence has shown immense maturity by arranging living quarters (a spacious maisonette) for the Hardy family during their city stay. Proving that controlled slapstick is not above her, Garland engages in some captivating comedy as, in her enthusiasm to greet Rooney, Stone, *et al.*, she becomes entangled in her apron strings and almost burns the coffee on the stove.

Evidently, Rooney's Andy Hardy has forgotten his many past ego come-uppances, for in *Andy Hardy Meets Debutante,* he benignly informs Stone about Garland, "Dad, she doesn't mean anything. It's hero worship, that's all." At this point, Rooney's cocky "hero" could use a few stern lessons in manners and humility from the old-fashioned book of etiquette Mrs. Hardy (Fay Holden) has dutily brought to the big city with her.

But Garland's Betsy is a most game girl, one of the lass's most delightful characteristics. She just will not take no for an answer, and at her young age she is already angling for future nuptials with "Andy darling."

Garland: "Aren't weddings wonderful?"

Rooney: "I wouldn't know. I expect to live and die a bachelor." This remark thrusts Garland into momentary dejection, but she still graciously allows Rooney the use of her chauffeur-driven car, although she is smart enough to suggest she had better accompany her would-be beau on a (process screen) guided tour of New York. The couple visit Grant's Tomb. "Maybe the coffins will cheer you up," suggests Garland. Then she points out to troubled Rooney, "I'm a woman. Maybe I could help."

The rather ungrateful Rooney does rely on her assistance to select his wardrobe for an excursion to the Club Sirocco where he hopes to rub elbows with Lewis. In her following song number, appropriately titled "Alone," which she duets with a record on the player, Garland once again proves how far she had come since *Pigskin Parade*. Now she could skillfully blend her mixture of romantic vocals and theatrical gesturing with witty, sharp talk-song interludes, offering a fully-rounded performance. After telling Rooney "You're wonderful!" she is left alone to reprise stanzas of "Alone."

Later, after Rooney's character has undergone some expensive complications at the nightclub (running up a $37.25 tab he cannot pay, plus losing a borrowed four-hundred-dollar jewelry stud), Garland re-appears, looking considerably more chic in her leopard skin coat than she had in her previous outfit (black dress, with valentine-shaped white lace collar and white lace cuffs). As the always-helpful Garland telephones her good pal Lewis, she advises the perplexed Rooney, "Sometimes a woman's intuition is better than a man's brain." Next follows an adept little screen interlude as Garland switches into adult girl talk, discussing small matters with mature Lewis, before requesting an invitation for Rooney to Lewis' big dance. This scene clearly evokes shades of the maturing, sophisticated Garland.

Once at the debutante's ball, Garland is asked to sing (of course), and she confides to Lewis, "I've got a song that if it doesn't wake Andy Hardy up, he must be made of concrete." She swing sings "I'm Nobody's Baby" and Rooney promptly takes more notice of her. Later, when they are taking a horse buggy ride in Central Park, he confesses to her, "You know, you've changed a lot since you were last in Carvel . . . you've grown up and I've forgotton how swell." Garland is still overwhelmed by Rooney whom she calls "one of nature's noblemen" and they debate about kissing, and Rooney promises that he will surely return one day. Garland knows how fickle her love-of-life is and suggests, "Maybe you'd better kiss me even if you don't want to." But at the crucial moment, she stops him (shucks!) deciding amidst great tears (that must have endeared her to Louis B. Mayer's heart forever) that this momentous big moment could and must wait for another more appropriate time. At least, she is content to know that he has discovered she is truly glamorous.

Rooney does return to Carvel, and has the last laugh on Ann Rutherford and George Breakston, and once in the confines of his bedroom, peers at the array of framed photographs on his bureau. He wistfully admires the collection and sighs, "How one's women do mount up!"

Not all of *Andy Hardy Meets Debutante* is devoted to the youthful star player. A good deal of action involves Stone's efforts to combat the big city lawyers who are trying to break a trust fund which supports the Carvel Orphanage. The script has Stone point out the similarity between his conceit in thinking he could outmaneuver corporation lawyers, and his son's (Rooney's) own lack of humility regarding the virtues of small townfolk. Obviously love has blinded Rooney to any real sense of democracy and in this important matter Stone will not indulge the haywire Rooney. He drags his son to the New York Hall of Fame to show him "some nobodies who turned out to be somebodies," all to prove that in the great American tradition social standing and money do not automatically make a person superior to his materially less fortunate fellow men. This final point is expounded upon several times in the course of the picture, part of studio mogul Mayer's ever-increasing cinema dissertations on Americanism and civil liberties in the U.S.A.

## STRIKE UP THE BAND
### *(MGM, 1940) 120M.*

Producer, Arthur Freed; director, Busby Berkeley; screenplay, John Monks, Jr., Fred Finklehoffe; music director, Georgie Stoll; songs, Arthur Freed and Roger Edens; Ira and George Gershwin; camera, Ray June; editor, Ben Lewis.

Mickey Rooney (Jimmy Connors); Judy Garland (Mary Holden); Paul Whiteman and Orchestra (Themselves); June Preisser (Barbara Frances Morgan); William Tracy (Phillip Turner); Ann Shoemaker (Mrs. Connors); Larry Munn (Willie Brewster); George Lessey (Mr. Morgan); Francis Pierlot (Mr. Judd); Harry McCrillis (Booper Barton); Margaret Early (Annie); Sarah Edwards (Miss Hodges); Elliot Carpenter (Henry); Virginia Brissac (Mrs. May Holden); Howard Hickman (The Doctor); Virginia Sale (Music Teacher); Milton Kibbee (Mr. Holden); Mickey Martin, Charles Smith (Boys); Sherrie Overton, Margaret Marquis, Maxine Cook (Girls); Phil Silvers (Pitch Man); Billy Wayne (Clown); Joe Devlin (Attendant); Don Castle (Charlie); Enid Bennett (Mrs. Morgan); Helen Jerome Eddy (Mrs. Brewster); Harlan Briggs (Doctor); Dick Allen (Policeman); Jimmie Lucas, Jack Albertson (Barkers); Earle Hodgins (Hammer Concessionaire); Harry Harvey (Shooting Gallery Concessionaire); Jack Baxley (Ice Cream Concessionaire); Harry Lash, Jack Kenny (Hot Dog Concessionaires); Roland Got (House Boy); Lowden Adams (Butler); Margaret Seddon, Margaret McWade (Old Ladies); Louise LaBlanche, Lois James, Helen Seamon, Mary Jo Ellis, Naida Reynolds, Linda Johnson, Wallace Musselwhite, Myron Speth, Douglas Wilson, Sidney Miller, Vendell Darr (Students); Jack Mulhall, Henry Roquemore (Men); Leonard Sues (Trumpet Player).

New York Premiere: Capitol Theatre—September 29, 1940
New York Television Debut: CBS—November 10, 1958

### Synopsis

Mrs. Connors wants her son Jimmy to become a doctor, but the youth dreams only of being a drummer in a swing band. After explaining to her how much music means to him, she relents, stating that he should

435

do whatever he thinks best. Jimmy forms a band, composed of his River-wood High School friends, with Mary Holden as group vocalist. His plan calls for the band to practice extensively and then enter in the competition being sponsored by Paul Whiteman, the renowned bandleader, in which the best high school band will be determined. The band plays at a school dance and performs a skit at an Elks' affair in order to earn the $200 necessary for transportation expenses to Chicago. Just before the troupe is to leave, Jimmy learns that one of the boys, Willie Brewster, is gravely ill, and that his mother needs the $200 to take her son to Chicago for an immediate operation. Jimmy decides to give Mrs. Brewster the band's $200, thus stranding the band. But the day is saved when the wealthy father of Barbara Frances Morgan takes Jimmy and the band to Chicago on a special train. They compete in the contest and win it. Jimmy then has the honor of leading all the competing bands in one grand final number, which is broadcast to the nation.

◆━━◆━━◆

"As they say in Hollywood, this show has everything—music, laughter, tears . . . As usual, everything is a little too much" [Theodore Strauss *(New York Times)*]. Typically in the MGM-movieland tradition, hardly anything was left of the 1930 Broadway musical, either from the George Kaufman-Morrie Ryskind script or the George and Ira Gershwin score. But nevertheless, the restructured screenfare, tailor-made for the prize starring team of Mickey Rooney and Judy Garland, proved to be "one long jive jamboree from beginning to end" *(Philadelphia Record)*.

From start to finish *Strike Up the Band* was Rooney's personal show-case, as he furiously plays the drums and the xylophone, sings, romances, cries, sacrifices self for the greater good of one of his pals, and all along the way capering for all he is worth. "Master Rooney, who amply deserves the screen title of America's Sweetheart without Curls, muggs and acts his way through two hours of film cut-ups without one moment of in-decision . . ." [Howard Barnes *(New York Herald-Tribune)*]. "Call him cocky and brash, but he has the sort of exuberant talent that keeps your eyes on the screen, whether he's banging the trap-drums, prancing through a Conga, or hamming the old ham actors." [Strauss *(New York Times)*]. The general consensus seemed to be that Rooney, the half pint of T.N.T., the eighth wonder of the universe, could do no wrong for his studio or his fans.

Many fans have wondered why so much of the screen time of Rooney's celluloid outings with the equally popular Garland were devoted exclusively to him rather than to both of them. It was not all a case of letting Rooney have his head, but for very practical reasons. Rooney was a disciplined trouper and would earnestly rehearse each and every production number and bit he would perform oncamera. However, even in 1940, eighteen-year-old Garland was rebelling against her years of enforced slavery as a show business child, and refused to channel herself to the demands of working up complex routines for each new movie. Therefore, whenever her lack of preparation proved to be too obvious to the tell-tale lens, the film's director would mercifully pan away to Rooney who would step in and fill the breach. Thankfully, Rooney was always Garland's biggest booster, and did his yeoman's duty without complaint. Years later he would graciously say, "Judy has the uncanny ability to get in there and pull it off. When we made *Babes in Arms* and *Strike Up the Band*, she winged some of the numbers without a hell of a lot of rehearsals, and they worked out just fine. It's this spontaneous thing she has that makes her unique."

This off-the-cuff performing quirk of Garland's was accepted by the critics, leading *Variety* to favorably report: ". . . Miss Garland catches major attention for her all-around achievements. She's right there with Rooney in much of the story as his mentoring girlfriend, teams with him in the production numbers for both songs and dances, and rings the bell with several songs sold to the utmost."

*Strike Up the Band* casts Garland as a humble Riverwood High School co-ed who assists in the library after classes. Once again she must cope with vixenish June Preisser, the acrobatic rich blonde. Once more it is Garland who must console herself with the song notion, "I ain't got nobody," for it seems that her idolized Rooney has tumbled for the cuddly Preisser. While vulnerable and hurt, Garland is always there, nevertheless, at Rooney's moments of crisis (which are many) to encourage him and to insure that in the final analysis he does what is best for everyone. Her Mary Holden was a real sport, a resilient heroine, and best of all an attractive filly, who had slimmed down to a becoming, mature figure.

The highlights of the long, black and white musical (which does sag badly in the second half, particularly with the overblown rendition of the title tune and the patriotic finale) has a wonderful special effects sequence in which Rooney is bragging just how he intends to set up the group band for the contest. As Garland listens with becoming devotion, he places the contents of a fruit dish on the table, and the pieces of fruit dissolve into small puppet musicians playing their respective instruments. Then there is the intricate "Do the Conga" production number which finds Garland and Rooney leading their tireless classmates in an extensive gymnastic follow-the-leader. Thereafter comes the youths' overzealous performance of a penny dreadful old-fashioned melodrama, *Nell of New Rochelle*, complete with period costumes and oversized gesturing (this segment was shorn to seven to eight minutes before theatrical release).

More so than the other Rooney-Garland MGM pictures, *Strike Up the Band* contains a large dose of lachrymose sentiments, such as the long talks between widowed Ann Shoemaker and her music-loving son (Rooney), or when industrious Garland is mooning for some deserved-for attention from cocky Rooney, or, worst of all, the protracted sequence in which Rooney and his teary-eyed pals visit the injured Larry Munn who bravely lies in bed wishing them well, with the group coming to the practical realization that the boy's physical welfare must come before their all-important Chicago trip. As if the viewer had not been forced to indulge in sufficient whimpering, it remains for a guest star, the legendary Paul Whiteman, to conduct a fatherly chat with overambitious Rooney, explaining to the youth—in what must be one of the screen's most ludicrous metaphors—that life is based on rhythm from beginning to end, even to those "last eight bars" in the sky. This analogy makes it clear to Rooney that he cannot desert his pals and accept a New York offer for him to drum with a big group. No, he must remain with his school chums and launch the entire gang on the road to success.

Rooney and Garland repeated their *Strike Up the Band* roles on "Lux Radio Theatre" on October 28, 1940.


## LIFE BEGINS FOR ANDY HARDY
### *(MGM, 1941) 100M.*

Director, George B. Seitz; based on characters created by Aurania Rouverol; screenplay, Agnes Christine Johnson; music director, George Stoll; art director, Cedric Gibbons; costumes, Kalloch; camera, Lester White; editor, Elmo Vernon.

Mickey Rooney (Andy Hardy); Lewis Stone (Judge Hardy); Judy Garland (Betsy Booth); Fay Holden (Mrs. Hardy); Ann Rutherford (Polly Benedict); Sara Haden (Aunt Milly); Patricia Dane (Jennitt Hicks); Ray McDonald (Jimmy Frobisher); George Breakston (Beezy); Pierre Watkin (Dr. Waggoner); Frances Morris (Operator); Tommy Kelly (Chuck); Robert Winkler (Private); William Forrest (Commandant); Paul Newlan, Duke York (Truckmen); Byron Shores (Jackson); Hollis Jewell (Ted); Sidney Miller, Roger Daniel (Boys); Arthur Loft, James Flavin (Policemen); Charlotte Wynters (Elizabeth Norton); Bob Pittard (Delivery Boy); Lester Mathews (Mr. Maddox); Don Brodie (Clerk); John Harmon (Taxi Driver); Gladden James (Man); Frank Ferguson (Stationer); Leonard Sues (Kelly); George Carleton (Florist); George Ovey (Janitor); Robert Homans (Watchman); William J. Holmes (Dr. Griffin); Manart Kippen (Rabbi Strauss); Ralph Byrd (Fr. Gallagher); Ann Morriss (Miss Dean); Mira McKinney (Miss Gomez); Nora Lane (Miss Howard); John Eldredge (Paul McWilliams); Joseph Crehan (Peter Dugan); Mary Jo Ellis (Drugstore Cashier); Yolande Mollot (Drugstore Waitress); Estelle Etterre, Bess Flowers (Secretaries); Kent Rogers (Tough Boy); Purnell Pratt (Dr. Storfen).

New York Premiere: Capitol Theatre—August 21, 1941
New York Television Debut: CBS—September 20, 1960

## Synopsis

After high school graduation, Andy Hardy has a heart-to-heart talk with his father, the judge, concerning his future. Andy is uncertain whether he should attend college, thinking he might like to earn his own way for a time. Despite their fears, his parents allow him to go to New York to look for work. Betsy Booth, Andy's long-standing friend and admirer, promises to keep an eye on Andy, even though he still treats her like a child. Andy finds it difficult to obtain work in the big city, but just at the crucial moment he obtains a job as an office boy for $10 a week. Andy befriends a young man, Jimmy Frobisher, who has ambitions of becoming a dancer. Andy even sneaks him into his hotel room, since Jimmy has no money of his own. Andy is shocked when he returns home one evening to find that Jimmy has died from a heart attack. He obtains a loan to pay for a decent funeral. Andy is about to become involved with the wrong sort of girl, Jennitt Hicks, but his better judgment and the timely arrival of the judge help him to overcome this potential pitfall. Sobered by the series of events that have happened to him, Andy decides that further education is essential and he returns to Carvel, preparatory to entering college in the fall.

◆━━◆

In *Andy Hardy's Private Secretary* (1941), America's favorite youth had difficulty in graduating from Carvel High School, and in this latest entry he is hesitant about pursuing further education. "Today I am a man," Rooney's eighteen-year-old Andy brags as he sets out on his own for New York in his new roadster. "I feel just like a brass band." But the steam would soon evaporate for this overinflated youth hero, just as it had already begun to do with the *Andy Hardy* series. "It's a little saddening to see our favorite movie family slipping," explained Wanda Hale *(New York Daily News)* in her two and one half star review, "yet we knew the series couldn't hold up forever." More brutally precise was Robert W. Dana *(New York Herald-Tribune)*, ". . . the film's pedestrian manner of telling it [the story] almost puts the filmgoer to sleep."

Adding insult to MGM's commercial injury was the fact that this was the first of the *Andy Hardy* series to date to run afoul of the all-powerful Legion of Decency censoring board, which gave this entry a Class A-section 2 rating, making it *objectionable* as entertainment for children. The persuasive Legion rarely offered public statements on its monumental decisions, but in this instance felt obliged to, because of the enormous popularity of the family-oriented movie series. The Legion complained about portions of *Life Begins for Andy Hardy* which "contain incidents subject to criticism and is therefore a departure from that standard of general acceptability which marked earlier pictures in the series." The Legion was politely referring to the "daring" father-son oncamera talks between Lewis Stone and Rooney which dealt with delicate matters of romance and marriage and the later plot situation which permitted divorced vamp Patricia Dane to invite Rooney to her New York City apartment for some (innocent) fun.

More so than in her past two *Andy Hardy* outings, Judy Garland provided a stabilizing influence in *Life Begins for Andy Hardy*. Although her four recorded songs ("Abide with Me," "America," "Easy to Love," and "The Rosary") were not used in the picture, and man-chasing Dane (Garland calls her a "wolfess" in the story) had a good deal of screen footage, it is Garland's maturing Betsy Booth who offers a pleasing balance to the brashness of Rooney's brash Andy Hardy, who has so quickly forgotten from his past experiences (i.e. *Andy Hardy Meets Debutante*) that New York cannot be conquered overnight.

It had become second nature to Garland as the oncamera boon companion of Rooney to be the pining soul always on hand to comfort and sweet talk our hero when he becomes overly discouraged about his tumultuous problems. In this entry of the series he despairs of finding work in the city, his roommate (Ray McDonald) suddenly dies, and later he has a flash of insight, realizing that perhaps he is not such a big shot in the romantic field as he had imagined. It is the wise Garland who decides the situation is crucial enough to have Stone come to town to talk some sense into Rooney, and it is Garland who once again must bid goodbye to her beloved. This time he is off to college and law school, now planning to follow in his father's footsteps. Garland, once again, is left to dream about the absent Rooney.

## BABES ON BROADWAY
### *(MGM, 1941) 118M.*

Producer, Arthur Freed; director, Busby Berkeley; story, Fred Finklehoffe; screenplay, Finklehoffe, Elaine Ryan; songs, Ralph Freed and Burton Lane; E. Y. Harburg and Lane; Freed and Roger Edens; Harold Rome; Al Stillman and Jararaca and Vincente Paiva; musical adaptator, Edens; music director, Georgie Stoll; costumes, Kalloch; vocal arrangers, Leo Arnaud, Conrad Salinger, George Bassman; camera, Lester White; editor, Frederick Y. Smith.

Mickey Rooney (Tommy Williams); Judy Garland (Penny Morris); Fay Bainter (Miss Jones); Virginia Weidler (Barbara Jo Conway); Ray McDonald (Ray Lambert); Richard Quine (Morton "Hammy" Hammond); Donald Meek (Mr. Stone); James Gleason (Thornton Reed); Emma Dunn (Mrs. Williams); Frederick Burton (Professor Morris); Cliff Clark (Inspector Moriarity); William A. Post, Jr. (Announcer); Alexander Woollcott (Himself); Luis Alberni (Nicky); Carl Stockdale (Man); Dick Baron (Butch); Will Lee (Waiter); Donna Reed (Secretary); Joe Yule (Mason, Aide to Reed); Stop, Look and Listen Trio (Themselves); Tom

Hanlon (Radio Man); Renee Austin (Elinor); Roger Steele (Boy); Bryant Washburn (Director); Charles Wagenheim (Composer); Lester Dorr (Writer); Jack Lipson (Fat Man Customer); Arthur Hoyt (Little Man Customer); Barbara Bedford (Matron); Shimen Ruskin (Excited Russian); Anne Rooney, Dorothy Morris, Maxine Flores (Pit Astor Girls); Margaret O'Brien (Little Girl Auditioning); Sidney Miller (Pianist); King Baggot (Man in Audience); Jean Porter ("Hoe Down" Dancer); Leslie Brooks (Actress-Committee Extra).

New York Premiere: Radio City Music Hall—December 31, 1941
New York Television Debut: CBS—May 1, 1961

## Synopsis

Tommy Williams, Ray Lambert, and Morton "Hammy" Hammond, a singing-dancing trio, have faith in themselves as Broadway's new hope, even if they cannot convince any main stem producer of their talent. While eating at a Times Square drug store where many of the other young hopefuls congregated, Tommy meets Penny Morris, an equally unsuccessful actress. She is the daughter of a music teacher and spends much of her time helping out at her neighborhood settlement house. Tommy decides to package a show for the purpose of providing country vacations for the poor children, using for talent all his unemployed actor friends, as well as Penny. They obtain a city license to hold a block party so as to earn the rental fee necessary to take over a theatre for the show. Tommy, who has become acquainted with Miss Jones, the assistant to famous stage producer Thornton Reed, is overjoyed when she offers him a chance to join Reed's new show trying out in Philadelphia. But Penny expresses her disappointment that he would be letting down all his friends and the children, inducing him to give up the chance. Meanwhile, Miss Jones grants them permission to use an old theatre owned by Thornton Reed but abandoned many years before. On the opening night the fire department orders the closing of the show because of fire hazards; yet no member of the audience demands his admission price back, assuring the children of their vacation. Reed arrives after the audience has left and is persuaded to watch a special performance. He is so impressed that he engages the entire cast and proceeds to produce the revue on Broadway with great success.

◆━◆━◆

Just to clarify its point that *Babes on Broadway* was another Horatio Alger theatre yarn, the movie opens with eminent show business authority Alexander Woollcott conducting a radio braodcast of "Ye Town Tattler," in which he encourages the youth of America to aspire to Broadway success. Then the scene quickly fades into the story which for 118 minutes is a "brash and engaging entertainment for any holiday season" [Howard Barnes *(New York Herald-Tribune)*].

441

With much of the production talent on hand from *Babes in Arms*, the new cinema edition follows in the already established mold, promptly establishing Mickey Rooney as the experienced lead member of the "Three Balls of Fire" who are not doing much business at Nick's Cellar joint in Greenwich Village. Rooney's later encounter with Judy Garland at the Walgreen-type drugstore in Times Square is in a typical vein. She is sitting alone in a booth crying her heart out, worn out from trying to make a go of a show business career that just will not start anywhere. Spunky Rooney soon brightens her mood and walks her back to her brownstone flat which she shares with her music-teacher father (Frederick Burton). Their living room duet is perhaps most typical of any of the Rooney-Garland screen musical numbers. The inconsequential patter leads the couple into the Burton Lane-E. Y. Harburg song, "How about You?" in which Garland sings, "I like to window shop on Fifth Avenue, how about you . . ." with Rooney picking up the next lyric and carrying the song to its rhythmic conclusion. While Garland begins the tune on the piano in mock playing, she soon relinquishes her piano bench seat to Rooney who really hits the keyboards. Then as the two dance about the room, it is Garland who is deliberately obscured waist-down behind the piano to hide her less-rehearsed, less-nimble soft-shoeing. Instead it is the exuberant Rooney who takes camera front and center, singing, dancing, and piano playing, and concluding with a few well-timed cartwheels.

Further on in the movie, when the whole gang is rehearsing the elaborate hoe-down dance number at the settlement recreation room, it is Rooney, clad as a rube complete with blacked-out teeth and wire-rimmed glasses, who leads the intricate procession, while demure Garland relies more on her vocal talents than her terpsichorean abilities. The highlight of this infectious number is the tap dance solo by Ray McDonald. Douglas McVay in *The Musical Film* (1967) accurately describes this production number as one "Berkeley ensemble staging [which] is entirely disciplined, keyed to the square-dance comic ebullience of the routine's conception." McVay concludes his discussion by adding, "Berkeley's lapse into his old extravagance (some hectic tracking in toward and away from opening, closing and falling farm gates) is agreeable and doesn't protract things."

For many admirers the best moment of *Babes on Broadway* occurs at the old Duchess Theatre where Rooney and Garland quietly walk into a dusty stage setting and, inspired by the venerable history of the building, propel themselves into a medley of fleshed-out impersonations of past theatre greats. He performs bits of *Cyrano de Bergerac* a la Richard Mansfield and then does "I Belong to Glasgow" in the Harry Lauder manner. Not to be topped (but she is), Garland appears as Fay Temple in bustle gown and bit hat, then as a spangled-outfitted Blanche Ring performing "Rings on My Fingers," and wraps up her segment with an impassioned (but uncontrolled) rendition of "La Marseillaise" a la Sarah Bernhardt. The clincher for these mimicry bits occurs thereafter during the actual benefit show, in which Rooney suddenly pops through the curtain dressed as Carmen Miranda, complete with tropical garb, fruit covered hat, gold platform shoes, and red finger nails and lipstick. To prove that he could do more than look like the Brazilian Bombshell, he launches into the Portuguese song "Mama Yo Quiero" and through his gestures and vocals demonstrates that he had profited much from Miss Miranda's offstage coaching. This scene has justly earned its reputation as the camp highlight of the Rooney-Garland canon.

Since a minstrel show number had gone over so well in *Babes in Arms* it was decided to repeat the gambit in the closing scenes of *Babes on Broadway,* when producer Thornton Reed (James Gleason) has transferred the kids' show to the Amsterdam Theatre. Here Rooney and Garland in blackface are dressed in knickers, long sleeve white shirts, checkered vests, and straw hats. As Mr. Tambone, Garland rendered the energetically effective "T. R. Jones," and then for the finale changes to a white fluffy knee skirt and blouse outfit (with bare midriff!), topped with a white plume feather hat. After the lively "Waiting for the Robert E. Lee," she and the ensemble embark on a massive tap dance routine, concluding with a big full-view shot of a blinking, lighted silhouetted Broadway skyline, with Rooney and Garland walking hand in hand up the steps in white face to the accompaniment of a choral "Babes on Broadway." They kiss at the end, thus concluding their most serious movie romancing to that point.

True to formula *Babes on Broadway* contains its fair share of schmaltz. There is aging moppet actress Virginia Weidler as the settlement house spokesgirl who tearfully urges Rooney to provide her and the other kids with two wonderful weeks in the country away from the city streets. (Weidler has her helpers parade with posters reading, "Do you want rickets on your conscience? Get the kids to the country.") Later Weidler has a tearjerking scene in which she confronts an embarrassed Rooney and tells him he should think of his own career and forget the underprivileged kids, that somehow, someday in the future they will get to the country. Then there is a giant-sized maudlin moment at the July 4th block party (shot on a massively scaled studio set) where the neighborhood children are playing host to a group of displaced British refugee youths. Several of the British kids are paraded on the show platform, where via a transatlantic hookup they speak to the folks back home in bombed-out London. This is followed by Garland's rousing rendition of "Chin Up, Cheerio, Carry On" which goes on interminably with Garland urging the oncamera listeners "Don't Give Up the Ship Tommy Atkins" while the filmgoing audience is subjected to montage shots of traditionally scenic London.

The war-weary public flocked to *Babes on Broadway* in droves, substantiating that Rooney and Garland were at the height of their boxoffice appeal. Film critics kindly suggested, regarding Garland's imitations, that "she would do well to leave out the classics for the present" and that MGM's golden boy is "going to become even more effective when he teaches himself discipline." Foreshadowing events to come, *Variety* carefully reported, "Both Rooney and Miss Garland, the child wonders of some years back, are fast outgrowing, at least in appearance, this type of presentation, which depends entirely on the ah's and oh's that spring from watching precocious children."

## THOUSANDS CHEER
*(MGM, 1943) C-126M.*

Producer, Joseph Pasternak; director, George Sidney, based on the story *Private Miss Jones* by Paul Jarrico, Richard Collins; screenplay, Jarrico, Collins; songs, Ralph Blane and Hugh Martin; Ralph Freed and Burton Lane; Paul Francis Webster and Walter Jurmann; E. Y. Harburg and Earl Brent; Harold Adamson and Ferde Grofe; Andy Razaf and Fats Waller; Harburg, Harold Rome, and Herbert Stothart; Blane, Hugh Martin, and Roger Edens; George R. Brown and Lew Brown; Walter Ruick; music-music director, Stothart; art director, Cedric Gibbons, Daniel B. Cathcart; set decorators, Edwin B. Willis, Jacques Mesereau; assistant director, Sanford Roth; costumes, Irene; sound, A. Norwood Fenton; camera, George Folsey; editor, George Boemler.

Kathryn Grayson (Kathryn Jones); Gene Kelly (Eddie Marsh); Mary Astor (Hyllary Jones); José Iturbi (Himself); John Boles (Colonel Jones); Dick Simmons (Captain Avery); Ben Blue (Chuck); Frank Jenks (Sergeant Koslack); Frank Sully (Alan); Wally Cassell (Jack); Ben Lessy (Silent Monk); Frances Rafferty (Marie); Odette Myrtil (Mama Corbino); Will Kaufman (Papa Corbino); Lionel Barrymore (Announcer); Mickey Rooney, Judy Garland, Red Skelton, Eleanor Powell, Ann Sothern, Lucille Ball, Virginia O'Brien, Lena Horne, Marsha Hunt, Marilyn Maxwell, Donna Reed, Margaret O'Brien, June Allyson, Gloria DeHaven, Sara Haden, Frank Morgan, Kay Kyser and His Orchestra, Bob Crosby and his Orchestra, Chorus of United Nations, Benny Carter and Orchestra, Don Loper, Maxine Barrat (Guest Stars); Sig Arno (Uncle Algy); Connie Gilchrist (Taxicab Driver); Bea Nigro (Woman); Daisy Buford (Maid); Pierre Watkin (Alex); Peggy Remington, Ed Mortimer (Guests); Ray Teal (Ringmaster); Carl Saxe (Sergeant Major); Bryant Washburn, Jr. (Lt. Colonel Brand); Harry Strang (Captain Haines); James Millican (Sergeant Carrington and Major); William Tannen (Prison Sergeant); Florence Turner (Mother at Station); Linda Landi (Polish Girl at Station); Eileen Coghlan, Eve Whitney, Aileen Haley, Betty Jaynes, Natalie Draper (Girls at Station); Myron Healey, Cliff Danielson, James Warren, Don Taylor (Soldiers at

Station); Paul Speer (Specialty Dancer); Marta Linden (Skit Nurse); John Conte (Skit Doctor).

New York Premiere: Astor Theatre—October 13, 1943
New York Television Debut: CBS—November 15, 1958

## Synopsis

In order to effect a reconciliation between her parents, Colonel Jones and Hyllary, Kathryn forsakes a potential concert career to live with her father in an army camp. She takes an active part in entertaining the soldiers but her efforts to be friendly with Private Eddie Marsh are for naught. Eddie is rude to her because she represents all the authority he despises in the military way of life. Eventually he falls in love with her and takes Kathryn to meet his family who are aerial performers in a circus. Colonel Jones, concerned about Kathryn's infatuation for Eddie, wires for Hyllary to come on the scene. Hyllary at first insists that Kathryn return to New York with her, pointing out that army life had ruined her own marriage. Kathryn begs to be allowed to remain for the big U.S.O. show she has arranged for the following day. Meanwhile, Eddie, learning of Hyllary's intentions, leaves his post to protest to Colonel Jones. He is confined to the guardhouse for punishment. The following day, Eddie's family, who have a part in the show, induce Colonel Jones to allow Eddie to appear with the act. The show is a huge success and Kathryn and her mother prepare to leave. At this moment, Colonel Jones receives orders to take his men overseas. His pending departure reawakens Hyllary's love. She effects a reconciliation with her husband, while giving her blessings to the romance of Kathryn and Eddie.

◆—◆—◆

*Thousands Cheer* was no exception among Hollywood's World War II cycle of massive all-star musical revue pictures. "With its gaudy Technicolor sequences and its wealth of talent, the show should prove a rousing success with both the armed services and the stay-at-homes" [Howard Barnes *(New York Herald-Tribune)*]. The premiere night gala for this overstuffed entertainment spectacular alone garnered $534,000 in sales for the Third War Loan Drive, making the picture a patriotic success from its first public unreeling.

The first half of *Thousands Cheer* is devoted to a rather laborious romantic tale, establishing a proper (or so it was thought) ambiance for the subsequent gargantuan talent show to be held at the army camp with Mickey Rooney as the dynamic master of ceremonies and a string of MGM stars present to brighten the planned specialty acts. Clark Gable was off at war and thus was one MGM celebrity, among others, not available for this movie, but hyperactive Rooney made amends for this deficit by performing his inimitable imitation of Gable, and for good measure, repeated his mimicry of Lionel Barrymore.

Audiences had a wide assortment of production numbers from which to choose their favorite routines. There was June Allyson, Gloria De Haven, and Virginia O'Brien harmonizing to "In a Little Spanish Town," Lena Horne performing "Honeysuckle Rose," a tap dance turn by Eleanor Powell, an overabundance of Kathryn Grayson's vocalizing, Gene Kelly's hoofing, and comedy turns by Lucille Ball, Keenan Wynn, Ann Sothern, Margaret O'Brien, and others. But the catchiest number of the show was Judy Garland's novelty number, featuring her with classical pianist José Iturbi in his entertainment feature film debut. Together they performed a jazzy swing number, "The Joint Is Really Jumpin' in Carnegie Hall," which interpolated such lines as "even José Iturbi's gettin' hep."

## GIRL CRAZY
### *(MGM, 1943) 99M.*

Producer, Arthur Freed; director, Norman Taurog; based on the musical play by Guy Bolton, John McGowan, George and Ira Gershwin; screenplay, Fred F. Finklehoffe; music adaptor, Roger Edens; music director, Georgie Stoll; orchestrator, Conrad Salinger, Axel Stordahl, Sy Oliver; vocal arranger, Hugh Martin, Ralph Blane; "I Got Rhythm" number directed by Busby Berkeley; choreography, Charles Walters; art director, Cedric Gibbons; set decorator, Edwin B. Willis, Mac Alper; assistant director, Joseph Boyle; camera, William Daniels, Robert Planck; editor, Albert Akst.

Mickey Rooney (Danny Churchill, Jr.); Judy Garland (Ginger Gray); Gil Stratton (Bud Livermore); Robert E. Strickland (Henry Lathrop); Rags Ragland (Rags); June Allyson (Specialty); Nancy Walker (Polly Williams); Guy Kibbee (Dean Phineas Armour); Tommy Dorsey and His Band (Themselves); Frances Rafferty (Marjorie Tait); Howard Freeman (Governor Tait); Henry O'Neill (Mr. Churchill, Sr.); Sidney Miller (Ed); Eve Whitney (Brunette); Carol Gallagher, Kay Williams (Blondes); Jess Lee Brooks (Buckets); Roger Moore (Cameraman); Charles Coleman (Maitre d'Hotel); Harry Depp (Nervous Man); Richard Kipling (Dignified Man); Henry Roquemore (Fat Man); Alphonse Martel (Waiter); Frances MacInerney, Sally Cairns (Check Room Girls); Barbara Bedford (Churchill's Secretary); Victor Potel (Station Master); Joseph Geil, Jr., Ken Stewart (Students); William Beaudine, Jr. (Tom); Irving Bacon (Reception Clerk); George Offerman, Jr. (Messenger); Mary Elliott (Southern Girl); Katharine Booth (Girl); Georgia Carroll, Aileen Haley, Noreen Nash, Natalie Draper, Hazel Brooks, Eve Whitney, Mary Jane French, Inez Cooper, Linda Deane (Showgirls); Don Taylor, Jimmy Butler, Peter Lawford, John Estes, Bob Lowell (Boys); Sarah Edwards (Governor's Secretary); William Bishop, James Warren, Fred Beckner, Jr. (Radio Men); Blanche Rose, Helen Dickson, Melissa Ten Eyck, Vangie Beilby, Julia Griffith,

Lillian West, Sandra Morgan, Peggy Leon, Bess Flowers (Committee Women); Harry C. Bradley (Governor's Crony); Bill Hazlett (Indian Chief); Rose Higgins (Indian Squaw); Spec O'Donnell (Fiddle Player).

New York Premiere: Capitol Theatre—December 2, 1943
New York Television Debut: CBS—March 1, 1957

## Synopsis

Because of Danny Churchill, Jr.'s craze for girls, his father sends him to a Western desert college which enrolls men only. Danny shows his dislike for the rough and tough routines of the college, but remains at the school because of his new-found love, Ginger Gray, granddaughter of Dean Phineas Armour. When news comes that the college is to be closed because of a decline in the enrollment, Danny rallies the students. He suggests that they stage a rodeo, publicize it nationally, and save the school. Together with Ginger, he visits the governor of the state and talks him into giving the school a two-month reprieve in which to raise the necessary number of enrollments. At a party for Marjorie Tait, the governor's daughter, Danny informs the debutantes that a rodeo queen will be selected at the big day, hinting to each that she stands an excellent chance of winning. Each girl promises to attend. The rodeo is a spectacular success, and the vote for rodeo queen is a tie between Ginger and Marjorie. Danny is called upon to name the winner. Thinking of the publicity involved, he names Marjorie. Ginger accepts the decision in a sportsman-like manner. Because of the rodeo publicity, enrollment applications begin to pour into the college office. The dean and the governor are shocked to find that most of the applications are from girls. The college is then turned into a co-educational institution in order that it retain its right to function as a college. Danny and Ginger are free to continue their romance.

◆◆◆

Since the last actual Mickey Rooney-Judy Garland screen teaming in 1941, her career star had risen higher at MGM. Twentieth Century-Fox may have had its Betty Grable and Alice Faye, Paramount its Betty Hutton, and Universal their Deanna Durbin, but in *For Me and My Gal* (1942) and *Presenting Lily Mars* (1943), Metro's Garland proved she could carry a feature film by herself just as successfully as she did her near-solo radio and stage turns. Rooney was continuing to turn out his three films a year, varying his annual *Andy Hardy* entries with the likes of *A Yank at Eton* (1942) or *The Human Comedy* (1943) (for which he was Oscar nominated). However, he had been supplanted as the leading boxoffice favorite by such personalities as Abbott and Costello, Gary Cooper, Humphrey Bogart, Betty Grable, and Bob Hope.

Now that both Rooney and Garland were over twenty-one years of age it was tough to find any sort of reasonable vehicle that would pair them in the vein of the juvenile antics of *Babes in Arms* or *Strike Up the Band*. *Born to Sing* (1942) had been planned as a joint film for them but ended up as a minor effort featuring Virginia Weidler and Ray Mc-Donald. Nonetheless, producer Arthur Freed was determined to find a proper basis for another Rooney-Garland celluloid capering. Finally he convinced the studio that a new rendition of the 1930 Broadway musical *Girl Crazy* was just the ticket. The property had been a zany Wheeler and Woolsey RKO feature, but that was back in 1932. So now it was determined to give the stage show a new slant and mold it into that elusive structure that would present Rooney and Garland to their legion of fans in the best possible light.

Thus, when *Girl Crazy* premiered at the Capitol Theatre on December 2, 1943, Theodore Strauss (*New York Times*) could alert the public, "Hold your hats, folks! Mickey Rooney and Judy Garland are back in town. And if at this late date there are still a few die-hards who deny that they are the most incorrigibly talented pair of youngsters in movies then . . . [this film] should serve as final rebuttal. To be sure, the immortal Mickey does insist on bowling over his audience, though in an ingratiating sort of way, and at times he resembles nothing so much as a whirling dervish afflicted with St. Vitus' ailment. But if he never has been accused of underplaying a scene, neither has he been accused of being dull. For all his cocky precociousness, he is an entertainer to his fingertips. And with Judy, who sings and acts like an earthbound angel, to temper his brash-ness—well, they could do almost anything they wish, and we'll like it even in spite of ourselves."

Once again Rooney was amusing in his slapstick hijinks whether suffering misadventures on horseback amidst the cactus plants or en-gaging in keyboard bravura (to "Fascinating Rhythm") in evening dress. From the opening nightclub scene in which movie newcomer June Allyson scores with "Treat Me Rough" (dragging a confused Rooney into the act as her Apache dance partner), there is indication that everything is being done by director Norman Taurog to make this very much like old times. Callow playboy Rooney arrives at Cody College of Mining and Agriculture in Arizona, prepared to be the big shot on campus, but quickly discovering that as a tenderfoot he has a lot to learn, particularly from the pert postmistress, Ginger Gray (Garland). She immediately senses her attraction to this ego-stuffed, pint-sized youth, and willingly guides him through his maturation period, where he engenders a good deal of un-favorable reaction from fellow students who term him a snooty city dude. This time June Preisser was not on hand as competition to Garland, but there is comely Frances Rafferty as a most unobjectionable "other" girl, who is charming, sweet, and towers over Rooney's character both in height and manners. It is a tough rival for Garland, and for a spell, it seems she will lose her sweetheart. Naturally this allows Garland her standard ration of self-pity as she mourns her wandering Prince Charming, aided in commiserative sessions by Rags Ragland, an ex-New York City taxi driver who is now a handyman about campus.

While Rooney remained his frenetic usual self throughout all of *Girl Crazy*, Garland had reached the peak of her performing talents and could swing from one style to another with ease. Thus, in jeans she does the campfire rendition of "Bidin' My Time," while in her jalopy car, she and Rooney duet "Could You Use Me" (with Rooney doing handsprings all over the auto and along the dusty road). In her self-pitying episode there is Garland's rendition of "But Not for Me" and the more comical "Sam and Delilah." MGM decided *Girl Crazy* needed a slam bang finish to make it a terrific moneymaker, and sent for Busby Berkeley who whipped up the climactic "I Got Rhythm" number. Garland, dressed in a very becoming cowgirl outfit with fringed skirt, performs with Rooney and chorus, backed by Tommy Dorsey and His Orchestra. All hands maneuver through a sophisticated hoe down routine which bore little relationship to the Berkeley-Rooney-Garland one in *Babes on Broadway*.

*Girl Crazy* would be resurrected once again by MGM when they produced *When the Boys Meet the Girls* (1965) featuring Connie Francis and Harve Presnell. It was a weak and silly rehash at best.

### WORDS AND MUSIC
### *(MGM, 1948) C-100M.*

Producer, Arthur Freed; director, Norman Taurog; story, Guy Bolton, Jean Holloway; adaptation, Ben Feiner; screenplay, Fred Finklehoffe; musical numbers directed by Robert Alton; songs, Richard Rodgers and Lorenz Hart; women's costumes, Helen Rose; assistant director, Dolf Zimmer; orchestrator, Conrad Salinger; vocal arranger, Robert Tucker; music director, Lennie Hayton; art director, Cedric Gibbons, Jack Martin Smith; set decorators, Edwin B. Willis, Richard A. Pefferle; makeup, Jack Dawn; sound, Douglas Shearer, John A. Williams; special effects, Warren Newcombe; camera, Charles Rosher, Harry Stradling; editor, Albert Akst, Ferris Webster.

Mickey Rooney (Lorenz Hart); Perry Como (Eddie Lorrison Anders); Ann Sothern (Joyce Harmon); Tom Drake (Richard Rodgers); Betty Garrett (Peggy Lorgan McNeil); Janet Leigh (Dorothy Feiner); Marshall Thompson (Herbert Fields); Jeanette Nolan (Mrs. Hart); Richard Quine (Ben Feiner, Jr.); Clinton Sundberg (Shoe Clerk); Harry Antrim (Dr. Rodgers); Ilka Gruning (Mrs. Rodgers); June Allyson, the Blackburn Twins, Cyd Charisse, Vera-Ellen, Judy Garland, Lena Horne, Gene Kelly, Mel Torme (Guest Stars).

New York Premiere: Radio City Music Hall—December 9, 1948
New York Television Debut: CBS—July 1, 1960

## Synopsis

The story recounts the meeting of musical composers Lorenz Hart and Richard Rodgers in the early 1920s, at which time they formed a partnership and attained huge success after a brief struggle. Richard, the more sedate of the two, falls in love with Dorothy Feiner and weds her, while Lorenz romances Peggy Lorgan McNeil only to be rejected by her. In the ensuing years the partners enjoy one success after another, while Richard raises a family, and Lorenz continues to carry a torch because of his unrequited love for Peggy. His spells of loneliness eventually affect his health and he comes to a tragic end at a comparatively early age.

◆━━◆━━◆

Some said that the basic problem with filming a musical biography of the song team of Lorenz Hart (1895-1943) and Richard Rodgers (1902- ) was that that there were no major conflicts in the artists' lives. They had no financial struggles nor creative blocks, but merely met and in the course of their professional relationship turned out one hit after another. As oversimplified a theory as this may be, it perhaps explains why Metro struggled so hard to turn this Norman Taurog-directed feature into a workable commodity. It was star-studded, lensed in color and had the best possible cooperation of each of the studio's creative departments, but it still emerged a fizzle, "a patently juvenile specimen of musical biography . . ." [Bosley Crowther (*New York Times*)].

Certainly more traumatic was this brief celluloid reunion of two of MGM's boxoffice greats. Since his discharge from World War II military service, Mickey Rooney had been having great difficulty adjusting his self-estimation with the realities of post-war MGM and of the industry itself. *Love Laughs at Andy Hardy* (1947) proved a new generation of filmgoers was not interested in the adolescent problems of a perpetual juvenile, and although *Killer McCoy* (1947) demonstrated Rooney had a flair for controlled dramatics, the star could not contain his ego and came into direct conflict with studio chief Louis B. Mayer, who then was fighting to retain control of the studio. Tempers flared, and twice-divorced Rooney foolishly backed out of his Metro contract, with *Words and Music* his final studio chore. Twenty-six-year-old Judy Garland was undergoing her own periods of stress. Despite the success of her *Meet Me in St. Louis* (1944), *The Harvey Girls* (1946), and *Easter Parade* (1948), she had lost confidence in herself, the studio, and those around her. The twice-married star was becoming more temperamental, more emotionally unstable, and more reliant on the helping hand of drugs.

Much of the *Words and Music* storyline conflict revolved around Betty Garrett's rejection of Rooney's marriage offer, and its jarring effect on his future well being, particularly when his song writing partner (woodenly played by Tom Drake) was having such a blissful marital life with sweet Dorothy Feiner (Janet Leigh). The latter portion of the film

450

bogs down in bathos as the physically deteriorated Rooney courts disaster by abusing his system, and finally collapses in the rain and dies (of a broken heart?). Within the film, Rooney bounced about with the enthusiasm attributed to the short, cigar-smoking Larry Hart, but his performance was more obnoxious (at one point his character asks onscreen, "Am I really that repulsive?") than winning, leading Howard Barnes (*New York Herald-Tribune*) to cite, "Too frequently his efforts to give clarity to a difficult piece of portraiture are more embarrassing than sympathetic."

For some unknown reason, the production forces behind *Words and Music* seemed to believe that whenever the script really needed a strong dramatic situation to bring the picture back into orbit, a party sequence would suffice as well. It was at one of these junctures, when Rooney is in Hollywood, that Garland appears oncamera. With the jumping bean Rooney she duets "I Wish I Were in Love Again," and then in a solo spot, looking thin and jittery, she sings "Johnny One Note" (a song from the Broadway show *Babes in Arms* which had been dropped from the Rooney-Garland film version). Despite Garland's plaintive vocalizing, her segments were easily outshone by June Allyson's rendition of "Thou Swell" (with the Blackburn Twins).

## THE YEARS AFTER

A charting of the post-MGM professional and personal careers of both Judy Garland and Mickey Rooney reads like a crazy quilt of misspent talent, disastrous mismanagement, and a penchant for emotional self-destruction. When Hollywood turned its near-bankrupt back on Garland, the over-the-rainbow girl was launched onto a concert-LP album recording career that would have more highs and lows than the Wall Street stock market. In 1954 she made a sensational motion picture comeback with *A Star Is Born* for which she was Oscar-nominated, but lost out to Grace Kelly of *The Country Girl*. Garland did not appear in front of the cameras again till her Academy Award-nominated Supporting Actress performance in *Judgment at Nuremberg*. Less than two years later she made what proved to be her final feature, *I Could Go on Singing* (1963), a very unprophetic title for her movie swansong.

Meanwhile, Rooney continued to marry, to divorce, and to explore voraciously all facets of show business in order to resurrect some of the popularity and riches that had once been his. A television series floundered, movie roles became scarce, and the once boxoffice champ found himself happy to be garnering nightclub dates and less than lustrous video show assignments. A Best Supporting Actor nomination for *The Bold and the Brave* (1956) briefly resurrected Hollywood industry interest in the pint-sized wonder, but days of stardom had definitely bypassed him.

In the fall of 1963, Garland commenced her weekly Sunday evening television variety show, but CBS network unwisely booked her in competition with the very popular Western show "Bonanza" and Garland could not lick the opposition, let alone the (self-imposed) production problems which wreaked havoc with the musical revue program. Garland and Rooney were nostalgically reunited on the December 8, 1963, segment of her video show. "This is the love of my life," Rooney told the TV audience, "There isn't an adjective in the world to express my love for Judy. She's Judy and that's all there is to say." Together they sang "Where or When" and "Fascinatin' Rhythm" but forty-two-year-old Rooney, slightly paunchy and graying at the temples, and forty-one-year-old, thin, nervous Garland were a long way from their Andy Hardy and Betsy Booth days. They seemed more acutely aware of the passing time than the audience.

In September, 1965, Rooney stepped up on a stage during one of Garland's Hollywood concerts to hold the microphone for the star who had recently broken her arm. Their next major joint appearance was far more pathetic and tragic. Garland, wed for the fifth time, was vainly struggling to complete a club booking at London's Talk of the Town when on June 22, 1969, she was found dead from an overdose of barbiturates. Her body was flown back to New York by husband Mickey Deans, and together with her daughter Liza Minnelli, arrangements were made for the private memorial service to be held at Campbell's Funeral Home on Madison Avenue and 81st Street. Among the 350 friends and acquaintances who crowded into the Campbell Chapel on June 27, 1969, was Rooney. The funeral oration was delivered by Garland's *A Star Is Born* co-star, James Mason.

One of the most joyous, if teary, segments of *That's Entertainment* (1974) occurs in the section when host-narrator Mickey Rooney, 1970s style, bounces down the deserted, desolate backlot pathway where the Andy Hardy series filmed its Carvel street scenes. A still chipper, if much altered, Rooney then launches into a jocular recollection of those bygone days when he and Judy made all their show biz kid movies together, demonstrating via film clips how similar each movie was to the other. Carbon copies of one another or not, their joint celluloid interludes still have verve when viewed today.

Although the job pickings have become far less choice, Rooney continues to ply his assorted show business talents wherever and whenever he can, whether it be from his Florida-based headquarters, or his tie-in with a Pennsylvania resort hotel. His best screen role in many a year was as Dick Van Dyke's sidekick in the much underrated *The Comic* (1969), a fitting study of a silent screen slapstick star.

In a publicity pose for **Angels with Dirty Faces** (WB, 1938)

# Chapter 16

# James Cagney
# &
# Ann Sheridan

## JAMES CAGNEY

5′ 6″
150 pounds
Red hair
Brown eyes
Cancer

*Real name: James Francis Cagney, Jr. Born July 17, 1899, New York City, New York. Married Frances Vernon (1920).*

**FEATURE FILMS:**

*Sinner's Holiday* (WB, 1930)
*Doorway to Hell* (WB, 1930)
*Other Men's Women* (WB, 1931)
*The Millionaire* (WB, 1931)
*The Public Enemy* (WB, 1931)
*Smart Money* (WB, 1931)
*Blonde Crazy* (WB, 1931)
*Taxi!* (WB, 1932)
*The Crowd Roars* (WB, 1932)
*Winner Take All* (WB, 1932)
*Hard to Handle* (WB, 1933)
*Picture Snatcher* (WB, 1933)
*The Mayor of Hell* (WB, 1933)
*Footlight Parade* (WB, 1933)
*Lady Killer* (WB, 1933)

*Jimmy the Gent* (WB, 1934)
*He Was Her Man* (WB, 1934)
*Here Comes the Navy* (WB, 1934)
*The St. Louis Kid* (WB, 1934)
*Devil Dogs of the Air* (WB, 1935)
*G-Men* (WB, 1935)
*The Irish in Us* (WB, 1935)
*A Midsummer Night's Dream* (WB, 1935)
*Frisco Kid* (WB, 1935)
*Ceiling Zero* (WB, 1935)
*Great Guy* (Grand National, 1936)
*Something to Sing About* (Grand National, 1937)
*Boy Meets Girl* (WB, 1938)

Angels with Dirty Faces (WB, 1938)
The Oklahoma Kid (WB, 1939)
Each Dawn I Die (WB, 1939)
The Roaring Twenties (WB, 1939)
The Fighting 69th (WB, 1940)
Torrid Zone (WB, 1940).
City for Conquest (WB, 1940)
The Strawberry Blonde (WB, 1941)
The Bride Came C.O.D. (WB, 1941)
Captains of the Clouds (WB, 1942)
Yankee Doodle Dandy (WB, 1942)
Johnny Come Lately (UA, 1943)
Blood on the Sun (UA, 1945)
13 Rue Madeleine (20th, 1946)
The Time of Your Life (UA, 1948)
White Heat (WB, 1949)
The West Point Story (WB, 1950)
Kiss Tomorrow Goodbye (WB, 1950)
Come Fill the Cup (WB, 1951)

Starlift (WB, 1951)
What Price Glory? (20th, 1952)
A Lion Is in the Streets (WB, 1953)
Run for Cover (Par., 1955)
Love Me or Leave Me (MGM, 1955)
Mister Roberts (WB, 1955)
The Seven Little Foys (Par., 1955)
Tribute to a Bad Man (MGM, 1956)
These Wilder Years (MGM, 1956)
Man of a Thousand Faces (Univ., 1957)
Short Cut to Hell (Par., 1957)
Never Steal Anything Small (Univ., 1958)
Shake Hands with the Devil (UA, 1959)
The Gallant Hours (UA, 1960)
One, Two, Three (UA, 1961)
Arizona Bushwhackers (Narrator: Par., 1968)

# ANN SHERIDAN

5′ 5½″
118 pounds
Golden brown hair
Hazel eyes
Pisces

Real name: Clara Lou Sheridan. Born February 21, 1915, Denton, Texas. Married Edward Norris (1936); divorced 1939. Married George Brent (1942); divorced 1943. Married Scott McKay (1966). Died January 21, 1967.

FEATURE FILMS:

Search for Beauty (Par., 1934)
Bolero (Par., 1934)
Come On, Marines! (Par., 1934)
Murder at the Vanities (Par., 1934)
Kiss and Make Up (Par., 1934)
Shoot the Works (Par., 1934)
Notorious Sophie Lang (Par., 1934)
Ladies Should Listen (Par., 1934)
Wagon Wheels (Par., 1934)

Mrs. Wiggs of the Cabbage Patch (Par., 1934)
College Rhythm (Par., 1934)
You Belong to Me (Par., 1934)
Limehouse Blues (Par., 1934)
Enter Madame (Par., 1935)
Home on the Range (Par., 1935)
Rumba (Par., 1935)
Behold My Wife (Par., 1935)

Car 99 (Par., 1935)
Rocky Mountain Mystery (Par., 1935)
Mississippi (Par., 1935)
The Glass Key (Par., 1935)
The Crusades (Par., 1935)
Red Blood of Courage (Ambassador, 1935)
Fighting Youth (Univ., 1935)
Sing Me a Love Song (FN, 1936)
Black Legion (WB, 1936)
The Great O'Malley (WB, 1936)
San Quentin (FN, 1937)
Wine, Women and Horses (WB, 1937)
The Footloose Heiress (WB, 1937)
Alcatraz Island (WB, 1937)
She Loved a Fireman (WB, 1938)
The Patient in Room 18 (WB, 1938)
Mystery House (WB, 1938)
Cowboy from Brooklyn (WB, 1938)
Little Miss Thoroughbred (WB, 1938)
Letter of Introduction (Univ., 1938)
Broadway Musketeers (WB, 1938)
Angels with Dirty Faces (WB, 1938)
They Made Me a Criminal (WB, 1939)
Dodge City (WB, 1939)
Naughty But Nice (WB, 1939)
Winter Carnival (UA, 1939)
Indianapolis Speedway (WB, 1939)
Angels Wash Their Faces (WB, 1939)
Castle on the Hudson (WB, 1940)
It All Came True (WB, 1940)
Torrid Zone (WB, 1940)
They Drive by Night (WB, 1940)

City for Conquest (WB, 1940)
Honeymoon for Three (WB, 1941)
Navy Blues (WB, 1941)
Kings Row (WB, 1941)
The Man Who Came to Dinner (WB, 1941)
Juke Girl (WB, 1942)
Wings for the Eagle (WB, 1942)
George Washington Slept Here (WB, 1942)
Edge of Darkness (WB, 1943)
Thank Your Lucky Stars (WB, 1943)
Shine On, Harvest Moon (WB, 1944)
The Doughgirls (WB, 1944)
One More Tomorrow (WB, 1946)
Nora Prentiss (WB, 1947)
The Unfaithful (WB, 1947)
Treasure of the Sierra Madre (WB, 1948*
Silver River (WB, 1948)
Good Sam (RKO, 1948)
I Was a Male War Bride (20th, 1949)
Stella (20th, 1950)
Woman on the Run (Univ., 1950)
Steel Town (Univ., 1952)
Just Across the Street (Univ., 1952)
Take Me to Town (Univ., 1953)
Appointment in Honduras (RKO, 1953)
Come Next Spring (Rep., 1956)
The Opposite Sex (MGM, 1956)
Woman and the Hunter (Gross-Krasne-Phoenix, 1957)
The Far Out West (Univ., 1967)

*Unbilled Appearance

Advertisement for **Angels with Dirty Faces**

In **Angels with Dirty Faces**

In **Torrid Zone** (WB, 1940)

In **City for Conquest** (WB, 1940)

459

# ANGELS WITH DIRTY FACES
*(Warner Bros., 1938) 97M.*

Producer, Sam Bischoff; director, Michael Curtiz; based on the story by Rowland Brown; screenplay, John Wexley, Warren Duff; art director, Robert Haas; assistant director, Sherry Shourds; technical adviser, Father J. J. Devlin; music, Max Steiner; orchestrator, Hugo Friedhofer; song, Fred Fisher and Maurice Spitalny; sound, Everett A. Brown; costumes, Orry-Kelly; dialog director, Jo Graham; makeup, Perc Westmore; camera, Sol Polito; editor, Owen Marks.

James Cagney (Rocky Sullivan); Pat O'Brien (Jerry Connelly); Humphrey Bogart (James Frazier); Ann Sheridan (Laury Ferguson); George Bancroft (Mac Keefer); Billy Halop (Soapy); Bobby Jordan (Swing); Leo Gorcey (Bim); Bernard Punsley (Hunky); Gabriel Dell (Patsy); Huntz Hall (Crab); Frankie Burke (Rocky as a Boy); William Tracy (Jerry as a Boy); Marilyn Knowlden (Laury as a Girl); Joe Downing (Steve); Adrian Morris (Blackie); Oscar O'Shea (Guard Kennedy); Edward Pawley (Guard Edwards); William Pawley (Bugs the Gunman); Charles Sullivan, Theodore Rand (Gunmen); John Hamilton (Police Captain); Earl Dwire (Priest); The St. Brendan's Church Choir (Themselves); William Worthington (Warden); James Farley (Railroad Yard Watchman); Pat O'Malley, Jack C. Smith (Railroad Guards); Roger McGee, Vince Lombardi, Sonny Bupp (Boys); Chuck Stubbs (Red); Eddie Syracuse (Maggione Boy); George Sorel (Headwaiter); Robert Homans (Policeman); Harris Berger (Basketball Captain); Lottie Williams (Woman); Harry Hayden (Pharmacist); Dick Rich, Stevan Darrell, Joe A. Devlin (Gangsters); Donald Kerr, Jack Goodrich, Al Lloyd, Jeffrey Sayre, Charles Marsh, Alexander Lockwood, Earl Gunn, Carlyle Moore (Reporters); Lee Phelps, Jack Mower (Detectives); Belle Mitchell (Mrs. Maggione); William Edmunds (Italian Storekeeper); Charles Wilson (Buckley the Police Chief); Vera Lewis (Soapy's Mother); Eddie Brian (Newsboy); Billy McClain (Janitor); Claude Wisberg (Hanger-On); Frank Hagney, Dick Wessel (Sharpies in Bar); Wilbur Mack (Croupier); A. W. Sweatt (Boy); Frank Coghlan, Jr., David Durand (Boys in Poolroom); John Harron (Sharpie); Mary Gordon (Mrs. Patrick McGee); George Offerman, Jr. (Adult Boy in Poolroom); Joe Cunningham (Managing Editor); James Spottswood (Record Editor); John Dilson (Chronicle Editor); Charles Trowbridge (Norton J. White, Press Editor); Tommy Jackson (Press City Editor); Ralph Sanford, Galan Galt (Policemen at Call-Box); Wilfred Lucas, Elliott Sullivan (Police Officers); Emory Parnell (Officer); William Crowell (Whimpering Convict); Lane Chandler, Ben Hendricks (Guards); Sidney Bracy, George Taylor, Oscar G. Hendrian, Dan Wolheim, Brian Burke (Convicts); Jeffrey Sayre, Charles Marsh, Alexander Lockwood, Earl Gunn, Carlyle Moore (Reporters); John Marston (Well Dressed Man); Poppy Wilde (Girl at Gaming Table).

New York Premiere: Strand Theatre—November 25, 1938
New York Television Debut: Channel 5—September 7, 1958

## Synopsis

Rocky Sullivan and Jerry Connelly are two rugged Lower East Side punks with as little respect for the law as for the girls on the block. One day, the tough duo is caught by railroad yard watchmen while breaking into a boxcar loaded with fountain pens. The youths run for it and Jerry gets away, but Rocky is captured and sent to a reformatory. In the following years Rocky falls into a life of crime, eventually becoming a big time hood, while Jerry, who has never forgotten his pal, becomes a priest and is assigned to their childhood parish. After being released from his latest jail hitch, Rocky returns to the old neighborhood and rents a room in a boarding house in which his former childhood playmate Laury Ferguson resides. Rocky soon becomes the idol of the latest gang of slum kids, who quickly emulate his style, although at Father Jerry's pleading, Rocky does force the youth into attending the parish recreation center. Rocky contacts his lawyer-partner, James Frazier, who had been holding and investing a large sum of loot, only to find that now Frazier is in partnership with Mac Keefer in running a prosperous club and other rackets, and wants to renege on his deal with Rocky. When an attempt to have Rocky killed fails, Rocky kidnaps Frazier, takes his funds, and, for insurance, grabs a packet of incriminating papers. The three hoodlums find themselves working together but never trusting one another. Then Father Jerry initiates a media campaign to rid the community of the crime craze. When Rocky overhears his partners planning to eliminate Father Jerry, he kills them instead. Eventually Rocky is captured and sentenced to death in the electric chair. Father Jerry visits him in prison and asks Rocky to pretend cowardice at the end, so the kids who worship him will not have a martyred hero to lead them along the wrong path of life. Rocky complies and dies.

◆——◆——◆

Since MGM's zesty *Manhattan Melodrama* (1934) Hollywood had frequently copied the plot device of two boyhood friends growing up oncamera and eventually ending up on the opposite sides of the law. *San Francisco* (1936) was one such example, *Angels with Dirty Faces* was a far more hard-hitting illustration of how such a plot premise could be utilized as the basis for a social message on the effect of environment on men's lives. Warner Bros. had long expounded such themes in its rash of crime melodramas, and *Angels with Dirty Faces* was one of the best of this particular genre. It was quite successful in its day and is still a memorable motion picture because the exacting detail and pounding pace so dear to director Michael Curtiz ". . . tells an old tale well. The flourishes in the show are rarely used merely to whip up incidental excitement.

The narrative may be familiar but it is all of a piece" [Howard Barnes *(New York Herald-Tribune)*].

Portraying pugnacious racketeers a la *Public Enemy* (1931) was standard fare for tough guy James Cagney, who occasionally appeared on the side of the law as in *G-Men* (1935), delved into the classics as in *A Midsummer Night's Dream* (1935), hoofed in *Footlight Parade* (1933), and excelled in such rat-a-tat brittle comedy as *Boy Meets Girl* (1938). In *Angels with Dirty Faces*, Cagney played in tandem with rapidfire talker Pat O'Brien who would become best known in movies for his series of celluloid priest roles. The counterpuntal playing of these two stars, in conjunction with screen rough guys Humphrey Bogart and George Bancroft, gave the picture its violent tone. The presence of Billy Halop, Bobby Jordan, Leo Gorcey, Bernard Punsley, Gabriel Dell, and Huntz Hall [collectively known as the Dead End Kids and the focal points of such tenement dramas as *Dead End* (1937) and *Crime School* (1938)] provided the drama with the social welfare element. For love interest in the proceedings, there was budding Oomph Girl Ann Sheridan who had been at Warners since *Sing Me a Love Song* (1936), but had yet to find her movie mark as either a sizzling comedienne or a torchy looker. *Angels with Dirty Faces* was but one of nine (!) assignments Sheridan would undertake for 1938 release.

All of the above named players were tremendously adept at portraying slum habitués, individuals who had a creditable way of reacting (albeit differently) to their unpalatable environ with its downtrodden masses of humanity suffocating in the welter of a human jungle.

Within *Angels with Dirty Faces*, Rocky Sullivan (Cagney) and Laury Martin (Sheridan) are first encountered as tattered adolescents on the block. At this point, both Cagney, played as a youth by that strong look-(and act)-alike Frankie Burke, and Sheridan, played as a teenage by Marilyn Knowlden show the character traits they will possess as full-bodied adults. He is the tenderloin toughie. She is the chipper good girl who knows the score and intends to bat in a few runs on her own terms. Burke taunts Knowlden, and the resilient young lady promises to get even with the punk one day . . . no matter what!

When the two next meet, some fifteen years have flown by and a lot has happened since Cagney was ushered into a life of crime by his term at the Warrington Reform School. While he was becoming public hood number one, Sheridan has matured and married a cabbie but then, because, as she sadly admits, material betterment got the best of her, her husband had been led into a life of crime to earn more money. Like most everyone else from the district who tangles with the law, he had been killed in a shootout with the cops.

The viewer is prepared for the first adult meeting of Cagney and Sheridan by his previous encounter with parish priest Father Connelly (O'Brien). Just as O'Brien has some of the old neighborhood toughness left in him despite his clerical calling (he even slugs a guy in the pool room), so Cagney has by contrast retained a sense of humor about the turn of events in his life which have made him the underworld's delight:

O'Brien: "See you at Mass Sunday."

Cagney: "Yeah. I'll help ya with the collection."

Thereafter, Cagney arrives at 24 Dowd Street, a typical rundown rooming house, one of the many such nondescript abodes on the block. Sheridan, who lives on the ground floor, takes Cagney, whom she does not initially recognize, to the vacant room on the fourth floor. Garbed in white blouse and dark skirt and sporting her frizzled, shoulder-length hairdo, she is an attractive tenement blossom. In her own inimitable sauntering way, she shows Cagney the premises, picking up a light bulb lying loose, casually blowing the dust off it, and then telling the stranger, "Room is five dollars in advance." As they talk, Sheridan suddenly places the visitor. "Oh, I get it now. You're Rocky Sullivan. Remember me?" Cagney: "That little fresh girl with the pigtails?" In a flash, no-nonsense Sheridan slaps his smirking face and pulls his hat down over his head. As she playfully runs out of the room, she turns and yells back, "I've waited fifteen years to do that." Cagney is amused by the episode. Obviously here is one attractive doll who isn't cowed by his gangster's reputation nor reticent because of her supposed vulnerability as a woman. She deals with him on his own terms, which is fine by him.

Later, Cagney and Sheridan connect at the neighborhood corner store-turned-recreation center, where she delivers some smart-aleck illustrations of why she became Hollywood's best farceur in the 1940s.

Cagney (to Sheridan who is slouching around, wearing her standard poor girl floppy felt hat, watching the youths play basketball): "What are you doin'?"

Sheridan: "Same thing you are." (Touché.)

This conversation having failed him, Cagney attempts his special brand of flattery. "You turned out to be a pretty snappy dish . . . for a social worker." Then he poses a question, more a proposition than a query: "I ain't figured out why some smart guy ain't snapped you up."

Sheridan: "Some smart guy in the headlines, huh?"

Cagney (slightly put down): "You could do worse."

In the course of the film, just as Cagney is influenced by Sheridan's basic goodness, so she responds to his vibrant, flashy self, sensing that gentleness lurks beneath the combustible exterior. She is a sucker for his type of guy, and soon becomes his ally, particularly after he has gotten in dutch with the Bogart-Bancroft crowd for filching the $100,000 that rightfully belongs to him. At this point Sheridan pops into his room, and Cagney fills her in on his tenuous situation, adding, "I figure you're the kinda girl to mind her own business."

Sheridan: "Don't worry, I know all the rules." (To her credit, the viewer could believe that she had been through the emotional ringer before and accept her as a charter member of the school of bad luck.)

A few days later in the story, once again in Cagney's room, the couple share a rather tender love scene, considering the circumstances of their general characters. Cagney tells the intrigued Sheridan, "Don't be a sucker. You belong in the big shot class. See those white lights up there? (They are looking out the window at the Manhattan skyline.) That's where you belong."

Later, Sheridan has a chance to dress up onscreen when Cagney escorts her to Bogart's Club El Toro. She is encased in what she terms an old evening gown, but by 1938 standards it is still pretty chic, if rather obvious in its shimmery flashiness. The dress amply displays the famed Sheridan figure, as she sways on the dance floor with stern-chinned Cagney as her partner. By this point in the film, she is completely won over to Cagney's cause and readily accept the club hostess job which he arranges for her. Unfortunately, thereafter Sheridan almost fades from the storyline. When trouble does brew between Cagney and O'Brien she is on hand to tell the priest, "No matter what he is now, right or wrong, we both love him now." She states this so earnestly with her big teary eyes glowing and her deep quivering voice vibrating, that no viewer could doubt her sincerity. Later, after the cops have trapped Cagney in a building and his capture is imminent, Sheridan is seen rushing to the scene a la Sylvia Sidney, knowing that again she is to lose her man.

*Angels with Dirty Faces* concludes with a particularly memorable sequence, all the more interesting when contrasted to Clark Gable's cool exit in similar circumstances in *Manhattan Melodrama*. Cagney accedes to O'Brien's plea that he die like a yellow coward for the sake of the boys. Cagney provides a sterling demonstration of fascinating theatrics as he allows himself to be dragged screaming and squirming to the hot seat, whining for all he is worth. In the final moments of the picture, O'Brien visits the youth gang in their boiler room headquarters, insisting to the disbelieving boys, ". . . he died like they said." Then, as he starts up the stairs, he utters one of the cinema's better known exit lines, "Okay, boys. Let's go say a prayer for a boy who couldn't run as fast as I could."

"Jimmy Cagney is finally back where he belongs," proclaimed Kate Cameron in her three-and-one-half-star *New York Daily News* review. He ". . . achieved the sensitive, rounded and menacing characterization which is the mainspring of this fiction," wrote Howard Barnes of the *New York Herald-Tribune*, adding, "It is a performance which relies less on the melodramatic paraphernalia of guns and violence than on knowing make-believe." For his performance Cagney won the New York Film Critics prize and was nominated for an Academy Award (but lost to Spencer Tracy of *Boys Town*). Despite her excellent work in *Angels with Dirty Faces*, Sheridan was almost ignored in the reviews, lost in the shuffle by the critics in their analysis of the film's overall merits and Cagney's performance in particular. Her real day with the fourth estate and the public would come in the early 1940s.

## TORRID ZONE
*(Warner Bros., 1940) 88M.*

Producer, Mark Hellinger; director, William Keighley; screenplay, Richard Macaulay, Jerry Wald; art director, Ted Smith; set decorator, Edward Thorne; music, Adolph Deutsch; music director, Leo F. Forbstein; song, M. K. Jerome and Jack Scholl; costumes, Howard Shoup; makeup, Perc Westmore; technical adviser, John Mari; sound, Oliver S. Garretson; special effects, Byron Haskin, H. F. Koenekamp; camera, James Wong Howe; editor, Jack Killifer.

James Cagney (Nick Butler); Pat O'Brien (Steve Case); Ann Sheridan (Lee Donley); Andy Devine (Wally Davis); Helen Vinson (Gloria Anderson); George Tobias (Rosario); Jerome Cowan (Bob Anderson); George Reeves (Sancho); Victor Kilian (Carlos); Frank Puglia (Rodriguez); John Ridgely (Gardiner); Grady Sutton (Sam the Secretary); George Humbert (Hotel Manager); Paul Porcasi (Garcia the Hotel Bar Proprietor); Frank Yaconelli (Lopez); Paul Hurst (Daniels); Jack Mower (Schaeffer); Frank Mayo (McNamara); Dick Botiller (Hernandez); Elvira Sanchez (Rita); Paul Renay (Jose); Rafael Corio (Man); George Regas (Sergeant); Trevor Bardette, Ernesto Piedra (Policemen); Don Orlando (Employee); Manuel Lopez (Chico); Joe Dominguez (Manuel); Joe Molinas (Native); Tony Paton (Charley); and: Max Blum, Betty Sanko, Victor Sabuni.

New York Premiere: Strand Theatre—May 17, 1940
New York Television Debut: CBS—March 1, 1959

### Synopsis

In Honduras, where the U.S. controlled fruit companies rule both the economics and the underprivileged population, Baldwin Fruit Company district boss Steve Case orders stranded American entertainer Lee Donley to leave town because she is a bad influence on his easily corrupted workers. On the boat Lee encounters Nick Butler, Steve's ex-foreman who is heading back to the U.S. to accept a white collar job in Chicago. She is as intrigued by Steve as the roughneck is by her easy-going ways. Meanwhile, Steve, who has finally forgiven Nick for having played around with his wife (now ex-), cons Nick into returning to number seven plantation at Puerto Aquita, promising him a substantial bonus if he can bring in the banana crop and combat the marauding local bandit-revolutionist Rosario. Problems at the plantation increase when Gloria Anderson, the flirtatious wife of the man Nick has been sent to replace temporarily, rekindles a romance with Nick, much to the annoyance of Lee who has arrived in the area seeking refuge from persuing police. Rosario and his

465

men plague the plantation with raids and acts of sabotage, but in the final showdown, Rosario, who had become friends with Lee when they shared adjoining jail cells, relents. He orders Nick to wed Lee and be good to her, even giving them "his" land as a dowry. The crop is thus saved and can be shipped north.

◆◆◆

"Many people thought the teaming of James Cagney, Pat O'Brien, and Ann Sheridan was ample justification for entitling this picture *Torrid Zone*. But the title comes from the locale of the production, rather than from the fiery quality of the stars" (*Brooklyn Daily Eagle*). "Whether your fancy turns to bananas, sex or whimsy, *Torrid Zone* is pretty certain to earn your response" [Robert S. Dana (*New York Herald-Tribune*)].

Although director William Keighley filmed *Torrid Zone* on the Warner Bros.' backlot, its Central American setting seemed eminently authentic, what with the banana plantation, jungles, and lush seaport especially constructed for verisimilitude. Once the casting had been settled (Cagney replaced George Raft, Helen Vinson substituted for Astrid Allwyn), director Keighley settled down to the forty-one day shooting schedule in which producer Mark Hellinger got the best values out of cinematographer James Wong Howe and, especially, from the Richard Macaulay-Jerry Wald original screenplay.

In the annals of post-production code Hollywood films, *Torrid Zone* is a landmark of snappy risqué dialog spewn forth by a trio of stars who could slap out a tart line with faultless timing. Cagney and O'Brien had been portraying variations of the Quirt-Flagg camaraderie for several years, including *Here Comes the Navy* (1934), *Devil Dogs of the Air* (1935), *The Irish in Us* (1935), *Ceiling Zero* (1935), *Boy Meets Girl* (1938), and *The Fighting 69th* (1939). Therefore, they were in experienced top form in this zippy eighty-eight minute marathon of rough humor in which sexual innuendoes were tossed in every direction with seeming delight by all concerned. Sheridan, who, since her last joint teaming with Cagney (and O'Brien), had appeared in such diverse entries as *Dodge City* (1939), *Winter Carnival* (1939), and *Castle on the Hudson* (1940), was fast reaching top popularity with the studio and public alike. In *Torrid Zone* she enjoyed only a few wardrobe changes, but each revealed what a snappy, shapely doll she was. Her agility with a wisecrack proved to be as sensational as her curvaceous figure.

*Torrid Zone* opens in the steamy tropics at the local club where Sheridan, in a shimmering black sequined gown (seemingly cut to the navel) is providing the native patrons with a sultry rendition of "Mi Caballero." Standing at the bar, toying with a cigar, is Steve Case (O'Brien), who quickly orders the law to have Sheridan tossed out of the settlement on the next boat. Like Somerset Maugham's Sadie Thompson, Sheridan is a girl with a checkered past (just what, we are never told), but she has just arrived from the States this very morning and does not want to go back.

Sheridan begs O'Brien to reconsider, claiming she can handle "these sun-kissed Romeos" easily, but when he catches her playing fast and loose with a deck of cards at the boys' expense, his mind is made up. As she departs the club she cracks to O'Brien, "The stork that brought you must have been a vulture."

Many a cinema leading lady has spent an onscreen night in jail, but few have adapted to their surroundings so convincingly as Sheridan does in *Torrid Zone*. In the cell next to her is the country's leading bandit-revolutionist, Rosario (George Tobias). Is Sheridan nonplussed by her discomforting situation? Nope! She plays cards with Tobias, and is rather weepy-eyed when the colorful outlaw gives her a ring as a farewell remembrance. In fact, when Tobias later tricks his way out of facing a firing squad, Sheridan cheers with joy ("Hurrah for our side"). Thereafter, O'Brien personally escorts her to the tramp steamer which has just docked in port.

Once aboard the vessel, she has difficulty with a guard who keeps trying to prove that his hands are faster than her eyes, but moustached Cagney is on the spot and he knocks the culprit overboard.

Cagney: "Hello. I'm Nick Butler, chairman of the entertainment committee. Can we count on you for the shuffleboard tournament?"

Sheridan: "Going all the way?"

Cagney: "To the end of the line. I don't think the trip will seem so long now."

For these two rough and tumble souls, this conversation is the height of romantic billing and cooing.

Later after Sheridan has escaped from the boat, she takes shelter at Cagney's place, and is pleased by the warm reception he bestows. "Glad you stopped in," he says, "I was beginning to get lonesome." He still wonders what a game gal like her is doing in this godforsaken place. She replies, "I just figured redheads were a novelty down this way." He accepts her ambiguous answer and they play cards for the fun of it. Before long she has relieved Cagney of three hundred dollars and only later does he learn she has a justifiable reputation for having sticky fingers with a deck of cards.

By the time Cagney reaches plantation number seven at Puerto Aquita, things are pretty steamy all around. The bandits, headed by Tobias, are interfering with the work schedule, Gloria Anderson (Vinson) soon is putting pressure on Cagney to take her back north with him, and then Sheridan walks onto the scene. "Nice little park you got here, if you like bananas," she remarks. Then, in the film's most rugged bit of byplay, Cagney flips Sheridan upside down to shake loose the three hundred dollars she "owes" him. This bit of frivolity vastly amuses Cagney's sloppy, overweight pal, Wally Davis (Andy Devine). "Okay, Samson," concedes Sheridan, "I'll give it to you." (The money that is!)

Sheridan is soon explaining that she is just passing through the area, with Vinson drawling out, "Detours can be interesting." Sheridan grabs the import of that loose remark and quickly lets the possessive dame know that there is nothing between her and Cagney—yet. Vinson pretends mock horror at Sheridan's plea of innocence a la debutante, exclaiming, "I suppose she meant to take the Philadelphia local."

Vinson then reluctantly agrees to find Sheridan a room at the plantation house, with Sheridan sarcastically offering, "Don't strain yourself. I can always sleep in a tree."

Vinson: "Heredity."

Vinson then proceeds to point out an available room. "I'm sorry, this is the best we can do. We're very cramped."

Sheridan: "I wouldn't be surprised."

Sheridan is equally tart with Cagney who has just told bumbling foreman Bob Anderson (Jerome Cowan), "The next time you get in my way, I'm going to shoot right through you."

Sheridan: "That's one way you might hit him."

Later, on the patio Cagney lays it on the line to Vinson: "Like most girls you think the right guy is like a streetcar. You miss one and another will be along in five minutes." She silences him with kisses, meanwhile lighting her cigarette, which she then allows to drop to the terrace floor. Sheridan comes upon the cozy little scene, genteelly picks up the cigarette, saying, "I understand the Chicago fire started from something like that."

Vinson: "The Chicago fire was started by a cow."

Sheridan: "History repeating itself?"

In her best Mary Boland manner, Vinson then asks Cagney, "Does she try to be offensive?"

Cagney: "Just a gal who doesn't know any better."

The events follow each other fast and furious thereafter and soon Sheridan is being packed off to make her transportation connections. Cagney lends her one hundred dollars, but, "Even when you do anything human," she says, "you make it sound nasty." When it develops the train tracks have been torn up, and Sheridan cannot leave, she returns. ("Good to be home again. Same old scenery, same old sourpusses.") Later, she expresses her deep emotional interest in Cagney, but he is a tough guy, a rugged ladies' man who does not want to give any hint of sentimentality. "The trouble with you dames," he explains, "is you're always building castles and wanting to move in."

Sheridan and Vinson have their final encounter of *Torrid Zone* when Cagney announces he will not take Vinson back to Chicago.

Vinson: "Oh, I see you've [Cagney] stepped down to her level."

Sheridan: "That's still three floors above yours."

The closing scene of the film provides another frolic between Cagney and Sheridan. After he has tipped her off the cot onto the floor, spoiling her ruse that she was injured in the previous burst of gunfire, they lock in a clinch.

Sheridan: "Oh, Nick!"

Cagney: "You and your fourteen carat oomph."

An interesting nod to Sheridan's sustaining sex symbol reputation as the Oomph Girl.

In this joint cinema outing, it was Sheridan, the new luminary, who rated the lion's share of critical acclaim. "Miss Ann Sheridan, in her second film as a star, is in good company, which is a fine thing for a young player who is learning why some actors are good and some bad" [Robert W. Dana *(New York Herald-Tribune)*]. "No little of the picture's success can be laid at the feet of Miss Ann Sheridan, who in this production continues to show the surprising advances she has been making recently along the road to real acting . . ." [Lee Mortimer *(New York Daily Mirror)*].

## CITY FOR CONQUEST
### *(Warner Bros., 1940) 101M.*

Producer, Anatole Litvak; associate producer, William Cagney; director, Litvak; based on the novel by Aben Kandel; screenplay, John Wexley; art director, Robert Haas; music, Max Steiner; orchestrator, Hugo Friedhofer; music director, Leo F. Forbstein; choreography, Robert Vreeland; costumes, Howard Shoup; assistant director, Chuck Hansen; dialog director, Irving Rapper; makeup, Perc Westmore; sound, E. A. Brown; special effects, Byron Haskin, Rex Wimpy; camera, Sol Polito, James Wong Howe; editor, William Holmes.

James Cagney (Danny Kenny); Ann Sheridan (Peggy Nash); Frank Craven (Old Timer); Donald Crisp (Scotty McPherson); Arthur Kennedy (Eddie Kenny); Frank McHugh (Mutt); George Tobias (Pinky); Jerome Cowan (Dutch Schultz); Anthony Quinn (Murray Burns); Lee Patrick (Gladys); Blanche Yurka (Mrs. Nash); Elia Kazan (Googi); George Lloyd (Goldie); Joyce Compton (Lilly); Thurston Hall (Max Leonard); Ben Welden (Cobb); John Arledge (Salesman); Ed Keane (Gaul); Selmer Jackson, Joseph Crehan (Doctors); Bob Steele (Callahan); Billy Wayne (Henchman); Pat Flaherty (Floor Guard); Sidney Miller (M.C.); Ethelreda Leopold (Dressingroom Blonde); and Lee Phelps, Howard Hickman, Ed Gargan, Murray Alper, Ed Pawley, William Newell, Margaret Hayes, Lucia Carroll, Bernice Pilot.

New York Premiere: Strand Theatre—August 27, 1940
New York Television Debut: CBS—December 29, 1959

### Synopsis

Lower East Side truck driver Danny Kenny becomes a prize fighter largely to impress Peggy Nash, his girlfriend since childhood. However,

Peggy soon leaves on a dancing tour with oily gigolo Murray Burns and begins to change her set of values with her first tastes of success. Meanwhile, Danny quickly reaches the top of his rough sports profession, but now refuses to renew his relationship with Peggy. His idealistic brother Eddie, who daydreams about composing great symphonies, goes commercial and writes pop music. Having gained unwanted success, both Danny and Peggy lose it. Peggy slowly comes to the realization that her new way of life has no meaning, while Danny is blinded in a stadium fight. Although he is now reduced to selling newspapers on a street corner, he encourages his brother not to abandon work on his symphony. Peggy arrives at Danny's newsstand one evening, and together they listen to Eddie's symphony being broadcast over the radio.

◆—◆—◆

Warner Bros. promoted this oversized melodrama as "A symphony of its seven millions with all the color of a hundred different races, and the harmony of a thousand discords like the dizzy, mad whirl of an ambulance siren screaming across Forsythe and Delancey." However, critical reaction to this forebear to *The Naked City* (1948) was a different matter, ". . . for all its slaty flavor, bright lights, smell of resin, crisp and pungent dialogue, *City for Conquest* is only middling-fair fun. It is padded unnecessarily and it is episodic—so episodic, in fact, that none of its incidents fall neatly and properly into the whole pattern" [William Boehnel *(New York World Telegram)*]. Even in its day, *City for Conquest* was considered overladen with its heavy-handed social message. Now it seems quaint, contrived, and somewhat incredible. (Most television viewers today only see the truncated version assembled for the late 1940s reissue, with most of the Frank Craven narrative excised.)

The final starring cast of *City for Conquest,* on which James Cagney's brother William was associate producer, was again a matter more of accident than of deliberate design. Originally Ginger Rogers had been wanted for the female lead. Then Sylvia Sidney was assigned to the part, but as the shooting date approached, Ann Sheridan inherited the role. She would later remark, "It was a very good part, and of course it was Cagney again. He sold like wildfire. To be in a picture with him was just the greatest." George Raft, who had worked with Sheridan in *They Drive by Night* (1940), and Cesar Romero were among those tested for the part of dancer Murray Burns, a role which eventually went to Anthony Quinn.

The major stumbling block of *City of Conquest* was its overly zealous effort to duplicate the "message" drama so much a trade-in-stock of the 1930s Depression years Group Theatre. To carry across the script's propaganda, John Wexley's screenplay adopted the mechanical gimmick of *Our Town:* an onstage narrator. Thus Frank Craven, who had been the Greek chorus of *Our Town,* was hired to do a similar chore in *City for Conquest* as the Old Timer, the curbstone philosopher who appears throughout the film with his optimistic messages to the audience.

In true chronicle style the film opens with the lead characters, Danny Kenny (Cagney) and Peggy Nash (Sheridan), portrayed as youngsters. As Forsythe Street pals, Cagney wins the heart of spirited Sheridan, she promising to "always be his girl." Then Craven intrudes on the scene to tell the camera eye that with Cagney's wit, resourcefulness, and ever-ready fists, New York would take notice of him someday soon. By the age of seventeen Cagney has won amateur golden gloves boxing bouts and has a bright future in the sports world, but he wants a steady job to finance his brother's (Arthur Kennedy) music education.

Sheridan, so often cast in these years as a sensible tenement girl, portrays a good-hearted girl spoiled by materialistic longing. (Craven tells the audience it is not her fault, but merely a young girl's craving for rhythm and gaiety.) She pouts when Cagney becomes a mug of a truck driver at $27.50 weekly. She is tired of being a piano teacher and turns to lithe, black-haired Murray Burns (Quinn), who soon takes her on a tour of ballroom dancing contests. (Sheridan proves stylish in the dancing montages with Quinn.) She graduates from an anonymous member of Quinn's company to becoming his partner in an act called "Maurice and Margalo," and they embark on a national swing of key cities. On her trips back to Manhattan Sheridan and Cagney meet again. She insists she is still his girl, but he is not convinced. The rift between the two widens. As one character explains the break-up, "It's applause, not another man, who has come between you."

For a change in their joint screen efforts, it is Cagney who is inspired to change his life style to suit Sheridan. In *City for Conquest* he decides to return to the ring. As the "Young Sampson" of the canvas boards, he moves up in the dirty fight game, with Scotty McPherson (Donald Crisp) as his grizzly fight manager. Cagney becomes too cocky with his easily won fame and demands a crack at the title, wanting a match with the champ. This leads to some double dealing by gangsters and Cagney ends up almost totally blinded by resin thrown in his eyes. At this very crucial point, the embittered Crisp refuses to let the repentant Sheridan visit Cagney.

If it were not so ludicrously contrived, the final scene of *City for Conquest* might have been genuinely touching. Certainly the script had two of the best actors in Hollywood performing the histrionics. Cagney, dressed in ragged clothes, is at his humble little streetside newsstand. It is the night of his brother's big concert ("Symphony of a Great City," composed a la George Gershwin) which will be broadcasted, a feat arranged by wily Crisp. Cagney feels a tap on his shoulder, and there is well-wishing, loving Sheridan. Due to his eye injury, however, all he can now see is a blurred outline of her figure. He reaches out and they hold hands. Her expressive eyes are teary as they listen to the symphony being performed. They are glad that at least some of their dreams have come true.

The stars received better reviews than the film. "Any picture that has Mr. Cagney and Miss Sheridan is bound to be tough and salty, right off the city's streets. And this one is. Miss Sheridan waxes quite emotional, and Mr. Cagney as usual, gives the story the old one-two-punch" [Bosley Crowther *(New York Times)*]. Howard Barnes stated Cagney "weaves a theater of utter sincerity through a fraudulent continuity," while the *New York Post* commended Sheridan ". . . for giving her best performance to date."

## THE YEARS AFTER

After *City for Conquest,* James Cagney remained at Warner Bros. for scarcely more than another year, his last picture there being *Yankee Doodle Dandy* (1942) in which he played George M. Cohan to a T and won an Oscar in the process. During the World War II years he toured for the U.S.O. and sold defense bonds. Through his own production company, formed with brother William, he made such relatively unpopular features as *Johnny Come Lately* (1943) and *The Time of Your Life* (1948). Warners invited him back to star in *White Heat* (1949), a particularly brutal gangster yarn. He remained at the old studio for a few more years, joining Virginia Mayo and Doris Day in the musical *The West Point Story* (1950), and offering a well-shaded portrayal of an ex-alcoholic in *Come Fill the Cup* (1951). He was bombastic as the Captain in *Mister Roberts,* played a touching racketeer in Doris Day's *Love Me or Leave Me,* and a jovial George M. Cohan in Bob Hope's *The Seven Little Foys,* all 1955 releases. He played Lon Chaney in *Man of a Thousand Faces* (1957), directed the Western *Short Cut to Hell* (1957), and ended his career with the lead in a Billy Wilder comedy, *One, Two, Three* (1961). Cagney rarely appeared on television and today is contentedly retired, although now inspired by a rash of unauthorized biographies to write his own life story.

Like fellow Warner Bros. players Bette Davis and Olivia de Havilland, Ann Sheridan was a great believer in going on suspension rather than playing roles she did not care to perform oncamera. She did appear as the luminous Randy in *Kings Row* (1941), Jack Benny's vis-a-vis in the comedy *George Washington Slept Here* (1942), and buoyed up the witty farce *The Doughgirls* (1944) with her own brand of tart delivery and glamour. She rejected *Mildred Pierce* (1945) but did make *Nora Prentiss* and *The Unfaithful,* two very underrated 1947 releases. *Silver River* (1948), a lacklustre Western with Errol Flynn, ended her tenure at Warners and was the start of her rapid screen decline. A quartet of Universal B films did nothing for her, and while she was sincere in the farmland drama *Come Next Spring* (1956), too few people saw the modest Republic picture. In the MGM musical remake of *The Women* (1939), entitled *The Opposite Sex* (1956), she was lost in the shuffle, albeit looking quite lovely. She tried the stage, including a tour of *Kind Sir* with Scott McKay who became her third husband, and among other television performances, played in the daytime soap opera *Another World* as well as starring in a Western comedy spoof, *Pistols and Petticoats,* the latter still on the air when she died of cancer in January of 1967.

472

In **The Miniver Story** (MGM, 1950)

# Chapter 17

# Walter Pidgeon
# &
# Greer Garson

## WALTER PIDGEON

6′ 2″
190 pounds
Black hair
Gray eyes
Libra

*Real name: same. Born September 23, 1897, East St. John, New Brunswick, Canada. Married Edna Pickles (1922), child: Edna; widowed 1924. Married Ruth Walker (1930).*

FEATURE FILMS:

*Mannequin* (Par., 1926)
*The Outsider* (Fox, 1926)
*Miss Nobody* (FN, 1926)
*Old Loves and New* (FN, 1926)
*Marriage License* (Fox, 1926)
*The Heart of Salome* (Fox, 1927)
*The Girl from Rio* (Gotham-Lumas, 1927)
*The Gorilla* (FN, 1927)
*The Thirteenth Juror* (Univ., 1927)
*The Gateway of the Moon* (Fox, 1928)

*Woman Wise* (Fox, 1928)
*Turn Back the Hours* (Gotham, 1928)
*Clothes Make the Woman* (Tiffany, 1928)
*Melody of Love* (Univ., 1928)
*Her Private Life* (FN, 1929)
*A Most Immoral Lady* (FN, 1929)
*Bride of the Regiment* (FN, 1930)
*Viennese Nights* (FN, 1930)
*Sweet Kitty Bellairs* (FN, 1930)
*Show Girl in Hollywood* (FN, 1930)°

°Unbilled Appearance

Kiss Me Again (FN, 1931)
Going Wild (FN, 1931)
The Gorilla (FN, 1931)
Hot Heiress (FN, 1931)
Rockabye (RKO, 1932)
The Kiss Before the Mirror (Univ., 1933)
Journal of a Crime (FN, 1934)
Big Brown Eyes (Par., 1936)
Fatal Lady (Par., 1936)
Girl Overboard (Univ., 1937)
Saratoga (MGM, 1937)
My Dear Miss Aldrich (MGM, 1937)
Man-Proof (MGM, 1938)
Girl of the Golden West (MGM, 1938)
The Shopworn Angel (MGM, 1938)
Listen Darling (MGM, 1938)
Too Hot to Handle (MGM, 1938)
Society Lawyer (MGM, 1939)
6000 Enemies (MGM, 1939)
Stronger Than Desire (MGM, 1939)
Nick Carter, Master Detective (MGM, 1939)
It's a Date (Univ., 1940)
Dark Command (Rep., 1940)
The House Across the Bay (UA, 1940)
Phantom Raiders (MGM, 1940)
Sky Murder (MGM, 1940)
Flight Command (MGM, 1940)
Man Hunt (20th, 1941)
How Green Was My Valley (20th, 1941)
Blossoms in the Dust (MGM, 1941)
Design for Scandal (MGM, 1941)
Mrs. Miniver (MGM, 1942)
White Cargo (MGM, 1942)
The Youngest Profession (MGM, 1943)
Madame Curie (MGM, 1943)
Mrs. Parkington (MGM, 1944)
Weekend at the Waldorf (MGM, 1945)
Holiday in Mexico (MGM, 1946)
The Secret Heart (MGM, 1947)
Cass Timberlane (MGM, 1947)°
If Winter Comes (MGM, 1947)

Julia Misbehaves (MGM, 1948)
Command Decision (MGM, 1948)
The Red Danube (MGM, 1949)
That Forsyte Woman (MGM, 1949)
The Miniver Story (MGM, 1950)
Soldiers Three (MGM, 1951)
Calling Bulldog Drummond (MGM, 1951)
The Unknown Man (MGM, 1951)
Quo Vadis (MGM, 1951)†
The Sellout (MGM, 1952)
Million Dollar Mermaid (MGM, 1952)
The Bad and the Beautiful (MGM, 1952)
Scandal at Scourie (MGM, 1953)
Dream Wife (MGM, 1953)
Executive Suite (MGM, 1954)
Men of the Fighting Lady (MGM, 1954)
The Last Time I Saw Paris (MGM, 1954)
Deep in My Heart (MGM, 1954)
The Glass Slipper (MGM, 1955)†
Hit the Deck (MGM, 1955)
Forbidden Planet (MGM, 1956)
These Wilder Years (MGM, 1956)
The Rack (MGM, 1956)
Voyage to the Bottom of the Sea (20th, 1961)
Big Red (BV, 1962)
Advise and Consent (Col., 1962)
I Duo Colonelli (The Two Colonels) (Titanus, 1962)
The Shortest Day (Titanus, 1963)
Cosa Nostra, An Arch Enemy of the F.B.I. (WB, 1967)
Warning Shot (Par., 1967)
Funny Girl (Col., 1968)
Rascal (BV, 1969)†
A Qualsiasi Prezzo (The Vatican Affair) (20th, 1969)
Skyjacked (MGM, 1972)
The Neptune Factor (20th, 1973)
Harry in Your Pocket (UA, 1973)

°Unbilled appearance
†Offcamera narration

# GREER GARSON

**5′ 6″**
**112 pounds**
**Red hair**
**Blue green eyes**
**Libra**

*Real name: same. Born September 29, 1908, County Down, Ireland. Married Edwin Snelson (1933); divorced, 1937. Married Richard Ney (1943); divorced 1947. Married Elijah "Buddy" Fogelson (1949).*

**FEATURE FILMS:**

Goodbye, Mr. Chips (MGM, 1939)
Remember? (MGM, 1939)
Pride and Prejudice (MGM, 1940)
Blossoms in the Dust (MGM, 1941)
When Ladies Meet (MGM, 1941)
Mrs. Miniver (MGM, 1942)
Random Harvest (MGM, 1942)
The Youngest Profession (MGM, 1943)
Madame Curie (MGM, 1943)
Mrs. Parkington (MGM, 1944)
Valley of Decision (MGM, 1945)
Adventure (MGM, 1945)

Desire Me (MGM, 1947)
Julia Misbehaves (MGM, 1948)
That Forsyte Woman (MGM, 1949)
The Miniver Story (MGM, 1950)
The Law and the Lady (MGM, 1951)
Julius Caesar (MGM, 1953)
Scandal at Scourie (MGM, 1953)
Her Twelve Men (MGM, 1954)
Strange Lady in Town (WB, 1955)
Pepe (Col., 1960)
Sunrise at Campobello (WB, 1960)
The Singing Nun (MGM, 1966)
The Happiest Millionaire (BV, 1967)

In **Blossoms in the Dust** (MGM, 1941)

Advertisement for **Mrs. Miniver** (MGM, 1942)

In Mrs. Miniver

A couple of movie fans get their greatest thrill — they meet Greer Garson and Walter Pidgeon in person!

Advertisement for **The Youngest Profession** (MGM, 1943)

Dame May Whitty, Henry Travers, Greer Garson, and Walter Pidgeon in **Madame Curie** (MGM, 1943)

Greer Garson, Walter Pidgeon, and Guy Bellis in **Mrs. Parkington** (MGM, 1944)

Greer Garson, Walter Pidgeon, and Cesar Romero in **Julia Misbehaves** (MGM, 1948)

Greer Garson, Walter Pidgeon, and Errol Flynn in **That Forsyte Woman** (MGM, 1949)

Greer Garson, Donna Corcoran, and Walter Pidgeon in a publicity pose for **Scandals at Scourie** (MGM, 1953)

# BLOSSOMS IN THE DUST
## *(MGM, 1941) C-100M.*

Producer, Irving Asher; director, Mervyn LeRoy; story, Ralph Wheelwright; screenplay, Anita Loos; art directors, Cedric Gibbons, Urie McCleary; set decorator, Edwin B. Willis; gowns, Adrian; men's costumes, Giles Steele; music Herbert Stothart; makeup, Jack Dawn; sound, Douglas Shearer; special effects, Warren Newcombe; camera, Karl W. Freund, W. Howard Green; editor, George Boemler.

Greer Garson (Edna Gladney); Walter Pidgeon (Sam Gladney); Felix Bressart (Dr. Max Breslar); Marsha Hunt (Charlotte); Fay Holden (Mrs. Kahly); Samuel S. Hinds (Mr. Kahly); Kathleen Howard (Mrs. Keats); George Lessey (Mr. Keats); William Henry (Allan Keats); Henry O'Neill (Judge); John Eldredge (Damon); Clinton Rosemond (Zeke); Theresa Harris (Cleo); Charlie Arnt (G. Harrington Hedger); Cecil Cunningham (Mrs. Gilworth); Ann Morriss (Mrs. Loring); Richard Nichols (Sammy); Pat Barker (Tony); Mary Taylor (Helen); Marc Lawrence (La Verne).

New York Premiere: Radio City Music Hall—May 26, 1941
New York Television Debut: CBS—January 25, 1958

## Synopsis

Edna and Charlotte, daughter and adopted daughter respectively of Mr. and Mrs. Kahly of Wisconsin, are contented, well-bred young women and each of them is engaged to a fine, upstanding man. But a chance encounter between Edna and dashing Sam Gladney alters her plans, and she rejects her fiance to become engaged to Sam who has established a thriving flour mill business in Texas. Edna and Charlotte plan a double wedding, but, when Charlotte's prospective in-laws learn from her birth certificate that she had been an illegitimate child, they object to the marriage. The distraught Charlotte commits suicide. After her wedding to Sam, Edna leaves for Texas. They are overjoyed when their son is born, even after learning that she can never have any more children. The tragic, accidental death of their child a few years later almost ruins the marriage, but Edna finds a new purpose to life. She devotes her time to establishing a foundling home. Meanwhile, Sam meets with financial reverses and later dies. Edna continues with her work, despite her hardships. Eventually she is successful in persuading the state legislature to remove from birth certificates the word "illegitimate." Although she has grown very fond of one of her young charges, she realizes that for his future welfare she must agree to place him with a fine young couple who can afford to provide him with the benefits of their wealth.

◆◆◆

Although never in the mainstream of producing biographical feature films, MGM did enjoy great financial success with its *Boys Town* (1938), *Young Tom Edison* (1940), and *Men of Boys Town* (1941). The studio smartly reasoned that a distaff screen variation of an enlightened welfare crusade might also create nifty boxoffice grosses, little realizing that the resultant *Blossoms in the Dust* would provide Metro with an enormously popular formula that would buoy the studio and its oncamera genre progenitors, Greer Garson and Walter Pidgeon, throughout the World War II years.

To fashion the elaborate chronicle—blessed with a Technicolor budget —into cinematic shape, MGM selected the seemingly unlikely combination of Mervyn LeRoy, who had directed the rugged gangster yarn *Little Caesar* (1931) as director and Anita Loos as the screen playwright. She was the famous authoress of Broadway's *Gentlemen Prefer Blondes* as well as several Jean Harlow screenplays, including the tart *Riffraff* (1935). This technical team proved not to be another Louis B. Mayer whim, for LeRoy was equally at home in mawkish soap opera, having guided Kay Francis' *I Found Stella Parish* (1935) and later such melodramatic weepers as *Escape* and *Waterloo Bridge,* both for MGM in 1940. Miss Loos, an experienced madcap, had proven at MGM that she could fashion equally well dialog for sophisticated dribble like *Biography of a Bachelor Girl* (1935) or for nostalgic epics like *San Francisco* (1936). With these two commercial talents shaping the path of *Blossoms in the Dust,* little wonder that Bosley Crowther *(New York Times)* found himself ranking the film as ". . . a careful and compassionate account of one woman's selfless effort to make this world a better place in which to live."

In the early 1930s the average filmgoer had been induced to believe that any screen actress who portrayed the various stages of womanhood in a single feature film was indeed a polished thespian of the highest order. *Blossoms in the Dust* revived this notion for 1940s audiences, who would become very accustomed in the following years to witnessing the film's star, Greer Garson, aging onscreen with an enthusiasm that often surpassed the skills of Metro's makeup department. MGM publicity informed the public that motion pictures had in Garson the natural successor to such past first ladies of the dramatic cinema as Ann Harding and Irene Dunne. Within a brief two years' period on the American screen, thirty-three-year-old Garson had displayed a radiant charm that ranged from a tenderly handled cameo in *Goodbye, Mr. Chips* (1939) to the forthright spunkiness of the heroine of *Pride and Prejudice* (1940). It was well-known that Garson was fast becoming studio boss Louis B. Mayer's pride and joy, the heiress apparent to the throne of the first lady at MGM, now that the regal triumvirate of Norma Shearer, Greta Garbo, and Joan Crawford were preparing for one reason or another to leave the studio lot.

Not all of the acting glory that accrued to Garson as a result of *Blossoms in the Dust* (she was Oscar-nominated but lost to Joan Fontaine of *Rebecca*) belonged to her performance, for she was fortunate enough to have as her screen vis-a-vis that 6′ 2″ hunk of masculine dependability, Walter Pidgeon. Because of his mature years (he was forty-four in 1941), he would be on hand at the studio for future assignments with Garson and others in the early 1940s while most of his younger male co-workers were off to war. After a varied career as a vaudeville and stage lead and an abortive cinema turn as a singing lead in early sound movie musicals, Pidgeon faded into the background as a reliable leading man of B features. Then in 1937, he was hired by Louis B. Mayer, and began his long MGM association. He was doing relatively well as the Nick Carter character in a studio programmer series, and acquitting himself competently in loan-out assignments, when two 1941 pictures made Pidgeon a cinema star. Twentieth Century-Fox's Oscar-winning *How Green Was My Valley* cast Pidgeon as the morally firm mining town clergyman who runs afoul of the townfolk over his love for sprighty Maureen O'Hara. The actor displayed such a tweed coat and pipe-smoking solidity that his future eminence in such movie roles was sealed. This role led directly to his assignment in Metro's *Blossoms in the Dust.*

Within *Blossoms in the Dust,* the moment the well-bred but spunky Garson encounters gallant Texan Pidgeon, her performance takes on stature as she now has a solid focal point upon which she and the audience can rely. When her "sister" Marsha Hunt kills herself, Garson can rush into the comforting arms of the stable Pidgeon, who soon sweeps her off to the strange environment of Texas where hs provides her with enough financial and emotional support to become the grand lady of a well-appointed home. The steady stream of potentially saccharine motherly love scenes which soon dominates the film owes its creditability to the cagey presence of reliable Pidgeon. When their young son dies, Pidgeon, though without an heir apparent, graciously moves into the background while his wife fills her empty moments with an excess of charity work, directed at mothering a host of frail waifs. Scripter Loos provides Pidgeon with his own timely exit midway in the film, nobly allowing Garson to move up stage front and center to marshal her saintly ploys for the picture's wrap-up.

Few spectators of *Blossoms in the Dust* bothered to penetrate the rather uncharitable aspects of Garson's Edna Gladney, who glides over and above her husband's business plight and death with relative ease. These events merely close one chapter in her life, as she proceeds with her crusading work as the founder and superintendant of the Texas Children's Home and Aide Society. Thereafter events topple over one another as she copes with the finances and logistics of housing her "unwanted" orphans (publicity releases claimed the film used about 850 children, including one hundred babies under two years of age). The final reels of this movie provide Garson with two attention-grabbing scenes. The first is the moment when she addresses a somewhat hostile Texas Senate with her plea for the passage of her stigma-freeing law bill. She emerges triumphant and, with the audience, exhilarated by this clash. Later, despite her protective devotion to her rapidly expanding flock of Texas "blossoms" she finds herself becoming too close to one little charge in particular. For a time she selfishly wishes to keep the boy as her own, all the while knowing that she owes a commitment to all the youths and must let the child find deeper happiness with fitting adoptive parents. Eventually Garson's mature heroine bravely releases this little boy, who has fortuitously recovered from a siege of illness, to the young couple. Now, the film can satisfactorily conclude. Garson's character and the audience have no more tears. They are exhausted by the one-hundred-minute marathon of stoutheartedness by a most unusual American pioneer lady.

Even in 1941 there were critics who found *Blossoms in the Dust* to be overly lachrymose, filled with so much shining nobility that the late Edna Gladney would have been chagrined to witness the parading of "dramatized" events in her life being unreeled for a handkerchief-laden audience. However, the majority of America, sensing the pending engulfment of the United States in the global war, was thrilled to have a sterling example of selfless American womanhood brought to glorified life on the big screen. Crowther of the *Times* insisted that largely because of Garson's sterling performance "the spirit of the story is maintained on a level generally above its frequent insipid spots."

Garson and Pidgeon would later recreate their *Blossoms in the Dust* roles on "Lux Radio Theatre" (February 16, 1942).


## MRS. MINIVER
### (MGM, 1942) 134M.

Producer, Sidney Franklin; director, William Wyler; based on the novel by Jan Struther; screenplay, Arthur Wimperis, George Froeschel, James Hilton, Claudine West; music, Herbert Stothart; song, Gene Lockhart; art directors, Cedric Gibbons, Urie McCleary; set decorator, Edwin B. Willis; gowns, Kalloch; sound, Douglas Shearer; special effects, Arnold Gillespie, Warren Newcombe; camera, Joseph Ruttenberg; editor, Harold F. Kress.

Greer Garson (Mrs. Kay Miniver); Walter Pidgeon (Clem Miniver); Teresa Wright (Carol Beldon); Dame May Whitty (Lady Beldon); Henry Travers (Mr. Ballard); Reginald Owen (Foley); Miles Mander (German Agent's Voice); Henry Wilcoxon (Vicar); Richard Ney (Vin Miniver); Clare Sandars (Judy Miniver); Christopher Severn (Toby Miniver); Brenda Forbes (Gladys the Housemaid); Rhys Williams (Horace); Marie De Becker (Ada the Cook); Helmut Dantine (German Flyer); Mary Field (Miss Spriggins); Tom Conway (Man); St. Luke's Choristers (Choral Voices); Paul Scardon (Nobby); Ben Webster (Ginger); Aubrey Mather (George the

Innkeeper); Forrester Harvey (Huggins); John Abbott (Fred the Porter); Connie Leon (Simpson the Maid); Billy Bevan (Conductor); Florence Wix (Woman with Dog); Bobby Hale (Old Man); Alice Monk (Lady Passenger); Ottola Nesmith (Saleslady); Douglas Gordon (Porter); Gerald Oliver Smith (Car Dealer); Alec Craig (Joe); Clara Reid (Mrs. Huggins); Harry Allen (William); Leslie Vincent (Dancing Partner); John Burton (Halliday); Leonard Carey (Haldon's Butler); Eric Lonsdale (Marston); Guy Bellis (Barman); Charles Irwin (Mac); Ian Wolfe (Dentist); Dave Thursby (Farmer); Charles Bennett (Milkman); Arthur Wimperis (Sir Henry); David Clyde (Carruthers); Colin Campbell (Bickles); Herbert Clifton, Leslie Francis (Doctors); Dave Dunbar, Art Berry, Sr., Sid D'Albrook (Men in Store); Gene Byram, Virginia Bassett, Aileen Carlyle, Irene Denny, Herbert Evans, Eula Morgan, Vernon Steele, Vivie Steele, Marek Windheim, Tudor Williams (Glee Club Members); Kitty Watson, Hugh Greenwood, Sybil Bacon, Flo Benson (Contestants); Harold Howard (Judge); Billy Engle (Townsman); John Burton, Louise Bates (Miniver Guests); Edward Cooper (Waiter); Walter Byron, Ted Billings, Dan Maxwell, Frank Atkinson, Henry King, Gil Perkins, John Power (Men in Tavern); Thomas Louden (Mr. Verger); Peter Lawford (Pilot); Stanley Mann (Workman); Leslie Sketchley, Emerson Fisher-Smith, Frank Baker, Colin Kenny (Policemen).

New York Premiere: Radio City Music Hall—June 4, 1942
New York Television Debut: CBS—February 2, 1957

### Synopsis

In the summer of 1939, Mrs. Kay Miniver guiltily purchases a rather expensive hat in a London shop, and then hurries home to the country town of Belham. At the railroad station, the train supervisor, Mr. Ballard, asks her permission to name his new species of rose "Mrs. Miniver." She agrees with pleasure. Later she hesitates to inform her husband, Clem, about the costly hat, but he soon reveals that he has bought a new car. They laughingly admit their extravagances. The Minivers and their two youngest children, Toby and Judy, welcome home the oldest child, Vin, who has returned from Oxford. Vin soon meets Carol Beldon when she comes to the Miniver home to implore Kay to make Mr. Ballard remove his "Miniver" rose from the pending flower competition. Carol's grandmother, Lady Beldon, has always won the event and would be upset should she now lose. Vin and Carol are soon attracted to one another and fall in love. They become engaged on the very night that he is to be shipped out in a recently declared war. Later Clem and the other village men collect all available boats to help in the evacuation of Dunkirk. While he is gone, Kay encounters a wounded aviator in her yard, and turns him over to the police. Vin and Carol are married and return from their honeymoon in time for the flower show where Lady Beldon, who has been given the award, announces that Mr. Ballard is the real winner. A German air raid interrupts the show, and while rushing home, Carol is killed by machine gun bullets from a low-flying plane. The village is reduced to ruin, but the vicar gathers his congregation together, and in the roof-shattered church, he reaffirms their faith in England's future.

◆◆◆

No one at MGM was sure just how the public would react to *Mrs. Miniver*. Jan Struther had written her 1930s sketches of a "plain ordinary woman" for the *London Times* before the pieces were collected together in a book edition. Anglophile Louis B. Mayer had MGM acquire the screen rights to *Mrs. Miniver*, initially planning it as a project for the studio's soon-to-depart prestige star, Norma Shearer. The star reputedly rejected the role because she insisted that she would not portray onscreen the mother of a teenager. There were rumors that Ann Harding was signed to a Metro contract largely on the lure of the part, but with the boxoffice receipts in from *Blossoms in the Dust*, Mayer insisted that Greer Garson was now the correct choice. After a good deal of persuasion, she agreed to the pivotal role with Walter Pidgeon cast as her pipe-smoking tweedy English husband. Distinguished producer Sidney A. Franklin accepted the *Mrs. Miniver* project because, "I had the notion that someone should make a tribute, a salute to England which was battling for its life. Suddenly I realized I should be the someone." Because of the diffuse nature of Miss Struther's plotless essays, Franklin warned studio executives that he feared the picture would lose $100,000 or more, even with a restricted budget that did not provide for color photography.

Two years to the day after Winston Churchill delivered his famous speech "We Shall Go to the End . . . We Shall Never Surrender," *Mrs. Miniver* opened at the showcase Radio City Music Hall and made, as they say, boxoffice history. In the first twenty-five days of presentation, 558,966 people saw the film, outdistancing Metro's earlier movie champ *The Philadelphia Story* (1940) by some five-and-a-half-thousand tickets. *Mrs. Miniver* would go on to gross $5.5 million in distributors' domestic receipts.

The charm of Miss Struther's stories was largely that they were so very typically British in spirit and flavor, which put MGM and director William Wyler at a great disadvantage. Because of the raging Second World War it was out of the question to film the picture at Metro's British studios. Instead, the Anglo ambiance had to be recreated on the Culver City lot, with an Irish colleen and a Canadian actor to set the picture's tone. Before, during, and after the filming of *Mrs. Miniver* there were outcries from some British quarters that the impudent Americans had done it again—distilling an English story into storybook terms that would fit the U.S.'s stereotyped conception of Britishers. But as *PM* astutely observed, "Much of its persuasion is due to the fact the class it represents is the attractive, comfortable, enviable better-bred English middle class." So convincing a job did Franklin's scripters do in adding a saleable point of view to Struther's tales, that Leo Mishkin (*New York Morning Telegraph*) could marshal the critical and public consensus of this film with his urgent endorsement, "It must, certainly, be seen by everybody and anybody who considers the screen as an art form, who can look on beauty unafraid, who can believe in the dignity, pride and courage of man." It hardly matters whether the rose competition in *Mrs. Miniver* has almost equal importance as the Dunkirk evacuation! After all, this movie is not a war picture, but a picture about wartime in which an unpretentious town finds its homefront becoming the front lines, and the important element within the movie is the survival of man's human dignity.

*Mrs. Miniver* is resplendent with emotional catharsis for nearly everyone, both within the film and without in the audience. There is the post-adolescent romance of Richard Ney and Teresa Wright, culminating in a tragically short marriage. There is the aristocratic Dame May Whitty as a proud member of nobility who learns her own lesson in democracy through her fellow villagers. One observes the pleasantly unspoiled Miniver youths, romping through life basically unaware of the war about them. There is the myriad of colorful townspeople, including Henry Travers as the benign station master and Henry Wilcoxon as the comforting vicar. Best of all, *Mrs. Miniver* boasts Garson and Pidgeon as the middleclass, young-middle-aged marrieds. As one reviewer noted, "As a team they are tops."

Financially comfortable—not too rich, not too poor—the Minivers are a loving couple devoted to their family and to the people of Belham. This situation provides a perfect milieu in which Garson and Pidgeon could display their bags of assorted screen tricks, wooing the audience with an unbeatable combination of romanticized saintliness. They are, however, human beings. Do we not see them each indulging in a bit of extravagant whim, and fearing to tell the other spouse? Does not Garson lose her seemingly unassailable composure in the garden sequence when the wounded German pilot (Helmut Dantine) brags about the destruction and death brought about by his comrades-in-arms? But most of all what makes *Mrs. Miniver* work as super-screen entertainment and tangentially as allied propaganda is the solidarity of the Miniver family in the war crisis. Pidgeon takes great pride in the cozy air raid shelter he has constructed on their land, and both Garson and Pidgeon have ample opportunity to demonstrate sensibility and pervading calmness as they gallantly read *Alice in Wonderland* to their children in the shelter while the Battle of Britain rages overhead in the night. The Minivers are wise parents, instinctively realizing that upper-class Teresa Wright is at heart a sensible match for their rebellious son (Richard Ney). Each parent has a chance to show dignity while executing a brave feat. Pidgeon slips away in the night to assist with the Dunkirk evacuation, while Garson marshals her temper and courage to cope with the German "invader."

While *Mrs. Miniver* offered Pidgeon far more screen time than *Blos-*

*soms in the Dust,* it still remained Garson's picture. She has ample chance to exhibit variants of her love for her children, for her townsfolk, and even compassion for the enemy. In addition, to insure the tear-jerker quality of the film and of her role, there is the sequence in which Garson watches from her window, hoping to see Ney fly over with the R.A.F., or the more impressively maudlin scene in which the wounded Wright dies in Garson's arms.

If any one section of *Mrs. Miniver* earned total emotional endorsement for the picture from its audiences, it was the flag-waving finale in which the vicar addresses his stunned flock, and the audience at large, instilling in all a renewed faith in the eventual triumph of right over might:

"We in this quiet corner of England, have suffered the loss of friends very dear to us. Some—close to the church. . . .

"And our hearts go out in sympathy to the two families who share the cruel loss of a young girl who was married at this altar only two weeks ago. The homes of many of us have been destroyed, and the lives of young and old have been taken. There is scarcely a household that hasn't been struck to the heart.

"And why? Surely you must have asked yourself this question. Why, in all conscience, should these be the ones to suffer? Children, old people, a young girl at the height of her loveliness. Why these? Are these our soldiers? Are these our fighters? Why should they be sacrificed?

"I shall tell you why. Because this is not only a war of soldiers in uniform. It is a war of the people—of all the people—and it must be fought not only on the battlefield, but in the cities and in the villages, in the factories and on the farms, in the home and in the heart of every man, woman, and child who loves freedom. Well, we have buried our dead but we shall not forget them. Instead they will inspire us with an unbreakable determination to free ourselves and those who come after us from the tyranny and terror that threatens to strike us down.

"This is the people's war! It is our war! We are the fighters! Fight it then! Fight it with all that is in us! And may God defend the right!"

Winston Churchill stated that *Mrs. Miniver* and its closing speech (which was printed in leaflet form and dropped over Allied-enemy lines) was more valuable to the war effort than the combined work of six divisions.

When the Oscar sweepstakes for 1942 were held, *Mrs. Miniver* emerged as the champ. The film was named the best of the year, director William Wyler, cinematographer Joseph Ruttenberg, scripters Arthur Wimperis, George Froeschel, James Hilton, and Claudine West all won, and Teresa Wright was chosen Best Supporting Actress. If producer Franklin was too shy to attend the ceremonies (the Irving Thalberg Memorial Award was bestowed on him), Garson was on hand to collect her Oscar as Best Actress of 1942 and to make one of the longest acceptance speeches in the history of the Oscar.

Garson and Pidgeon (he was nominated for *Mrs. Miniver* but lost to James Cagney of *Yankee Doodle Dandy*) repeated their *Mrs. Miniver* roles on "Lux Radio Theatre" on December 6, 1943.

It was Louis B. Mayer who persuaded Garson to postpone marrying her co-player, twenty-seven-year-old Ney, until after *Mrs. Miniver* was well in release. In those halcyon days of the studio star systems, the company's product came first!

## THE YOUNGEST PROFESSION
### *(MGM, 1943) 82M.*

Producer, B. F. Ziedman; director, Edward Buzzell; based on the book by Lillian Day; screenplay, George Oppenheimer, Charles Lederer, Leonard Spigelgass; art directors, Cedric Gibbons, Edward Carfagno; set decorators, Edwin B. Willis, Helen Conway; music, David Snell; sound, Wilhelm W. Brockway; assistant director, Julian Silberstein; camera, Charles Lawton; editor, Ralph Winters.

Virginia Weidler (Jean Lyons); Edward Arnold (Mr. Lawrence Lyons); John Carroll (Hercules); Jean Porter (Patricia Drew); Marta Linden (Mrs. Edith Lyons); Dick Simmons (Douglas Sutton); Ann Ayars (Susan Thayer); Agnes Moorehead (Miss Featherstone); Marcia Mae Jones (Vera Bailey); Raymond Roe (Schuyler); Scotty Beckett (Junior Lyons); Jessie Grayson (Lilybud); Greer Garson, Walter Pidgeon, William Powell, Robert Taylor, Lana Turner (Guest Stars); Beverly Tyler (Thyra Winters); Patricia Roe (Polly); Marjorie Gateson (Mrs. Drew); Thurston Hall (Mr. Drew); Aileen Pringle (Miss Farwood); Nora Lane (Hilda); Dorothy Christy (Sally); Mary Vallee (Mary); Gloria Tucker (Gladys); Jane Isbell (Jane); Hazel Dawn (Hazel); Beverly Boyd (Beverly); Randa Allen (Randa); Ann MacLean (Ann); Gloria Mackey (Gloria); Bobby Stebbins (Richard); Shirley Coates, Mary McCarty (Girls); Mark Daniels (Les Peterson); William Tannen (Hotel Clerk); Ann Codee (Sandra's Maid); Eddie Buzzell (Man in Theatre); George Noisom (Delivery Boy); Leonard Carey (Valet); Harry Barris (Man); Herberta Williams (Hortense); Sara Haden (Salvation Army Lass); Leigh De Lacey, Vangie Beilby, Ruth Cherrington, Claire McDowell, Sandra Morgan, Leota Lorraine (Montage Bits); Ray Teal (Taxi Driver); Polly Bailey, Margaret Bert, Violet Seton, Hazel Dohlman, Alice Keating (Governesses); Dorothy Morris (Secretary); Roland Dupree, Robert Winkler (Mail Room Boys).

New York Premiere: Radio City Music Hall—June 24, 1943
New York Television Debut: CBS—September 7, 1958

### Synopsis

Jean Lyons, president of a teenage movie fan club, and her chum Patricia Drew manage to have tea with visiting movie stars Greer Garson and Walter Pidgeon. When Jean arrives home late, her parents, uninterested in her star-gazing hobby, reprimand her. The next morning, Jean, accompanied by her meddlesome governess, Miss Featherstone, visit Mr. Lyons' office where the governess sees her employer showing some lingerie to secretary Susan Thayer. Miss Featherstone assumes Mr. Lyons is having an affair, when in reality, he had been showing the girl an anniversary gift purchased for Mrs. Lyons. When Jean is later informed of the "situation" she quickly misconstrues subsequent events and decides to right matters. She arranges for circus strongman Hercules to attend a charity ball posing as a foreign diplomat and to have him make love to her mother in order to make her father jealous. The predicament leads to a fight between Hercules and Mr. Lyons. Thereafter a baffled Jean runs away from home to join the Salvation Army. She is finally located and brought home again, with the malicious Miss Featherstone being discharged for having caused all the trouble.

◆◆◆

The basic premise for *The Youngest Profession* offered a modest, offbeat idea for an engaging flyweight film but the script soon got lost in a hackneyed rendition of the little Miss Fix-it theme. To boost the movie above its programmer status, the studio pushed five of its hotter stars (of whom one critic said, they ". . . are long on reputation and here short on performance") into the proceedings for guest cameos. The results were negligible for obvious reasons.

Garson and Pidgeon continued their emoting as two cinema celebrities come to New York on a personal appearance tour. Garson retained her lofty lady image by serving tea in her hotel suite, adding nothing new to her established screen persona. However, Pidgeon had a wry moment within *The Youngest Profession* when over-enthusiastic Virginia Weidler asks his advice on what he would do if he were a father and had a daughter who did this and that. After a moment's contemplation, the usually paternalistic oncamera Pidgeon replied that he would probably kill the girl.

The overall gratuitous nature of the guest stars' appearances in *The Youngest Profession* led many to wonder about the irony of the film's credits which repeated the standard disclaimer, "The events, characters and people depicted are fictitious, any similarity to actual persons is purely coincidental." Did this apply to the cameo performers as well?

## MADAME CURIE
### (MGM, 1943) 124M.

Producer, Sidney Franklin; director, Mervyn LeRoy; based on the book by Eve Curie; screenplay, Paul Osborn, Paul H. Rameau; music, Herbert Stothart; art directors, Cedric Gibbons, Paul Groesse; set decorators, Edwin B. Willis, Hugh Hunt; assistant director, Al Shenberg; sound, W. N. Sparks; special effects, Warren Newcombe; camera, Joseph Ruttenberg; editor, Harold F. Kress.

Greer Garson (Mrs. Marie Curie); Walter Pidgeon (Pierre Curie); Robert Walker (David LeGros); Dame May Whitty (Mme. Eugene Curie);

Henry Travers (Eugene Curie); C. Aubrey Smith (Lord Kelvin); Albert Basserman (Professor Perot); Victor Francen (President of University); Reginald Owen (Dr. Henri Becquerel); Van Johnson (Reporter); Elsa Basserman (Mme. Perot); Lumsden Hare (Professor Reget); James Hilton (Narrator); Charles Trowbridge, Edward Fielding, James Kirkwood, Nestor Eristoff (Board Members); Moroni Olsen (President of Businessmen's Board); Miles Mander, Arthur Shields, Frederic Worlock (Businessmen); Eustace Wyatt (Doctor); Marek Windheim (Jewelry Salesman); Lisa Golm (Lucille); Alan Napier (Dr. Bladh); Linda Lee Gates, Marie Louise Cates (Perot Grandchildren); Ray Collins (Lecturer's Voice); Howard Freeman (Professor Constant's Voice); Francis Pierlot (M. Michaud); Almira Sessions (Mme. Michaud); Dickie Meyers (Master Michaud); Leo Mostovoy (Photographer); Margaret O'Brien (Irene at Age Five); Dorothy Gilmore (Nurse); William Edmunds (Cart Driver); Ilka Gruning (Seamstress); Harold de Becker, Guy D'Ennery (Professors); George Davis (Cart Driver); Michael Visaroff (Proud Papa); George Meader (Singing Professor); Wyndham Standing (King Oscar); Gigi Perreau (Eva at Age Eighteen Months); Franz Dorfler (Assistant Seamstress); Ray Teal (Driver); Noel Mills (Wedding Guest); Teddy Infuhr (Son); Mariska Aldrich (Tall Woman); Ruth Cherrington (Swedish Queen); Al Ferguson, Ben Gerien, Tony Carson, Maria Page, Isabelle Lamore, Justine Duney, Nita Pike (People at Accident).

New York Premiere: Radio City Music Hall—December 16, 1943
New York Television Debut: CBS—September 2, 1958

## Synopsis

Marie Sklowdowska, an impoverished Polish student in turn-of-the-century Paris, is befriended by Professor Perot who offers her an opportunity to earn some money by studying steel magnetism. Perot arranges with Professor Pierre Curie, a noted, but shy, scientist, to share his laboratory with Marie, so that she can carry on her experimentation. Pierre comes to admire Marie's brilliant work and soon falls in love with her. One day they are invited by Dr. Becquerel to observe a piece of pitchblende which under accidentally induced laboratory conditions has created strange effects. However, the couple are too involved in their own work to investigate the mystery. Marie passes her university examinations, and plans to return to Poland to teach, but Pierre finally proposes marriage. Following their honeymoon, Marie determines to delve into the pitchblende matter, and after almost five years of intense effort she uncovers the miracle of radium. The couple seek financial aid to carry on their work, and, despite the opposition from some quarters, they receive the use of an old, leaky, drafty shed for their testing. More years of struggle follow with extreme hardships and many disappointments. Finally, from the many tons of treated pitchblende they produce a single decogram of radium. After receiving the world's acclaim they seclude themselves in the country for a vacation with their seven children. On the very day they are to be honored by the University, Pierre is killed in a traffic accident. Brokenhearted, Marie still finds the courage to continue with her study of radium.

◆—◆—◆

The 1937 publication of Eve Curie's affectionate biography of her mother (1867-1934) stirred interest among Hollywood filmmakers, who believed the subject matter had the potential of being another *The Story of Louis Pasteur* (1935). Universal promptly acquired the screen rights and announced that Irene Dunne would play the lead; in fact, one of the ostensible reasons for the actress' trip to Europe that year was to meet with Eve Curie and discuss the pending project. However, Dunne returned to Hollywood and began a spate of successful movie comedies, resulting in Universal selling the property to MGM, who hired Aldous Huxley in the fall of 1938 to pen a screenplay suitable to star Greta Garbo. Years passed—and the film emerged as the latest screen pairing of Greer Garson and Walter Pidgeon, with a production fitted into the team's established successful mold by producer Sidney Franklin and director Mervyn LeRoy.

The fictionalized potpourri that was *Madame Curie* led Bosley Crowther *(New York Times)* to insist, "It is seldom that Hollywood makes much of intellectual adventure per se or that it dares to discover excitement in the pure exercise of the mind. . . . It has made their absorption as comprehensible as the urge to read good books, and it has pictured their collaborative union as a warm and richly rewarding love." Crowther further enthused, "Greer Garson and Walter Pidgeon are ideal in the leading roles, ideal, that is, to the necessity of creating warm characters. Miss Garson, the invariable patrician, plays with that gentle, wistful grace which makes her a glowing representation of feminine nobility and charm. And Mr. Pidgeon is magnificently modest and slyly masculine as the preoccupied professor whom she loves."

That was Crowther's involved way of saying that *Madame Curie* emerged more a love story with laboratory overtones, rather than the hoped-for reverse. This romanticized screen brew had the benefits of the ministrations of technical advisor Dr. R. M. Langer of the California Institute of Technology, but everyone involved with the film seemed to have forgotten the opening words of Eve Curie's book, "It would have been a crime to add the slightest ornament to the story, so like a myth." But because *Madame Curie* was another boxoffice winner, only the more serious-minded critics could quibble with the unequal proportions of fact and fiction. Once again, MGM, as in *Edison the Man* (1940), had blended the dingy world of science and movie glamour into one lucrative package.

Both Garson and Pidgeon played potentially interesting offshoots of their typical screen clichés: she as the devoted lady of science who still finds time for her family, he as the bearded, shy laboratory explorer who seemingly relies on her final word on matters of the household or test tubes. However, the production attempted to play safe on all points. Garson was hardly Polish in her demeanor and was rather glamorous for a laboratory grudge, while Pidgeon was not particularly Gallic in his portrayal as the absent-minded professor. In short, the performers posed as the reliable loving couple that audiences knew and, seemingly, loved so well. Their screen moments together were an amalgam of tried and true situations: the idyllic country trip to visit his parents and the resultant bicycle-riding honeymoon, the work-dominated couple who rush away from an evening's social event to return to the laboratory, and the myriad of scenes at the work table with the team struggling against adversity to prove their theories. These laboratory scenes were brought to a peak when Pidgeon kisses Garson's radium-burned hands and observes that if the new element can destroy healthy tissues, they can likewise be used to eliminate malignant tissues.

Pidgeon enjoyed two fine screen moments during the film, the first being when he begs his Garson not to give up her experiments at his side, and the second occurring during the middle-of-the-night proposal which finds him rushing into Marie's bedroom to ask her hand in marriage. For a change, it was Pidgeon rather than Garson who received the better reviews. "It would have been easy for him to have mugged up the part of Pierre Curie, even though he is hiding behind a beard. On the contrary, he has created a real and recognizable figure, who can never be confused with Pidgeon himself" [Howard Barnes (*New York Herald-Tribune*)].

As was now customary in the Garson-Pidgeon screen encounters, the emotional moments were reserved for Garson's special province. Whether benignly maneuvering the laboratory work and supervising her household, or insuring that she and Pidgeon surmount the inhuman and physical opposition to achieve their worthy goals, she was her regal cinema self. To her credit, on many occasions she subdued her own personality to that of her characterization. However, there was little restraint in her exhibition of the physical wear and tear of the character's years of toil, her coy femininity as she sends Pidgeon out for the promised pair of earrings to complete her wardrobe for the "victory" celebration, or her overindulgent and audience-pleasing reaction to the news that her beloved has been killed in a street accident. This protracted sequence finds her touching Pidgeon's few material possessions as she wistfully recalls their lives together, and then her realization that she must now carry on alone. Recalling Garson's effective legislative address in *Blossoms in the Dust*, *Madame Curie* provided her with another speechmaking session. This time the elderly female scientist, who would win two Nobel Prizes, addresses a conclave of fellow researchers at the University of Paris. Her talk is once again guaranteed to bring tears to the viewer's eyes.

"It is by these small candles in our darkness that we shall see before us little by little the dim outlines of that great plan that shapes the universe and I am

495

among those who think that for this reason science has a great beauty, and with its great spiritual strength will in time cleanse the world of its evils, its ignorance, its poverty, diseases, wars and heartache. . . .

"You, take the torch of knowledge, and behold the palace of the future."

*Madame Curie* won the public's endorsement but failed to garner its potential bevy of Oscars. The picture lost out to *Casablanca,* Garson was defeated by Jennifer Jones of *The Song of Bernadette,* and Pidgeon was beaten by Paul Lukas of *Watch on the Rhine.*

## MRS. PARKINGTON
### *(MGM, 1944) 124M.*

Producer, Leon Gordon; director, Tay Garnett; based on the novel by Louis Bromfield; screenplay, Robert Thoeren, Polly James; art directors, Cedric Gibbons, Randall Duell; set decorators, Edwin B. Willis, McLean Nisbet; music, Bronislau Kaper; assistant director, Marvin Stuart; sound, Newell Sparks; special effects, A. Arnold Gillespie, Warren Newcombe, Danny Hall; camera, Joseph Ruttenberg; editor, George Boemler.

Greer Garson (Susie Parkington); Walter Pidgeon (Major Augustus Parkington); Edward Arnold (Amory Stilham); Frances Rafferty (Jane Stilham); Agnes Moorehead (Aspasia Conti); Selena Royle (Mattie Trounsen); Gladys Cooper (Alice, Duchess De Brancourt); Lee Patrick (Madeleine); Dan Duryea (Jack Stilham); Rod Cameron (Al Swann); Tom Drake (Ned Talbot); Helen Freeman (Helen Stilham); Cecil Kellaway (Edward, Prince of Wales)°; Hugh Marlowe (John Marbey); Tala Birell (Lady Nora Ebbsworth)°; Peter Lawford (Thornley); Fortunio Bonanova (Signor Callini); Mary Servoss (Mrs. Graham); Gerald Oliver Smith (Taylor); Ruthe Brady (Bridgett); Byron Foulger (Vance); Wallis Clark (Captain McTavish); Ann Codee (Mme. Dupont); Frank Reicher (French Doctor); George Davis (French Policeman); Harry Cording (Humphrey); Celia Travers (Belle); Kay Medford (Minnie); Hans Conried (Mr. Ernst); Edward Fielding (Reverend Pilbridge); Alma Kruger (Mrs. Jacob Livingstone); Rhea Mitchell (Mrs. Humphrey); Ivo Henderson (Albert); Charles Pecora (Head Waiter); Mary Zavian, Erin O'Kelley (Can-Can Girls); Myron Tobias (Boy); Eugene Borden (Drunk); Charles Cane, Al Hill, Bert Le Baron, Al Ferguson, Richard Thorne (Miners); Lee Tung-Foo (Sam); Marek Windheim (Gastor); Johnny Berkes (Beggar); Franco Corsaro (Gypsy Fiddler); Anna Marie Stewart (Mme. De Thebes); Bertha Feducha, Symona Boniface (Fitters); Robert Greig (Mr. Orlando); Maurice Cass (Shopkeeper); Gordon Richards (James the Butler); Guy Bellis (Footman);

°In the European release print of *Mrs. Parkington,* the following cast changes were made: Hugo Haas as the King (instead of Cecil Kellaway's Prince of Wales), and Tala Birell as the Countess instead of Lady Nora Ebbsworth), a restructuring designed to avoid any embarrassment to British royalty.

Rex Evans (Fat Man); Doodles Weaver, Bobby Barber (Caterers); Chef Milani (Maitre d'Hotel); Grace Hayle (Fat Lady); Billy Bletcher, Harry Tyler, Vernon Dent, Bud Jamison (Quartette); Warren Farlan (Herbert Parkington at Age 2½); Betty Bricker, Dorothy Phillips, Jessie Arnold (Pedestrians in Mining Town); Margaret Bert, Naomi Childers (Nurses); Harry Adams, Nolan Leary, John Bohn, Leonard Mellin, John Phipps, Billy Engle, Fred Rapport, Maurice Briere (Waiters at Ball); Tiff Payne (Billiard Expert); Major Douglas Francis, Harvey Shepherd (Grooms); Wyndham Standing (Butler); Brandon Hurst (Footman).

New York Premiere: Radio City Music Hall—October 12, 1944
New York Television Debut: CBS—July 12, 1958

### Synopsis

On Christmas eve, 1938, at her old Fifth Avenue mansion, Mrs. Susie Parkington learns that Amory Stilham, her bombastic son-in-law, is implicated in fraudulent stock transactions and must receive financial help or face prosecution. She convenes her family to ask them whether they would be willing to forego their inheritance in order to keep Amory out of prison. While the gathered family bicker among themselves over their potential personal losses, Susie's thoughts and the movie drift back to 1872 when Major Augustus Parkington had first arrived in Leaping Rock, Nevada, to inspect his silver mines. While in the mining town he falls in love with the plucky Susie Graham, whom he weds after her mother's death in a mine disaster, and takes back to New York. Once in Manhattan, the Major enlists the aid of wordly Aspasia Conti, a French Baroness and his former mistress, to instruct Susie on the proper decorum for an aspiring member of the Four Hundred. The *nouveau riche* Major builds a stately mansion for Susie and is enraged when New York's leading socialites reject his invitations to a ball. To punish the offenders he sets about ruining them financially through his manipulations of the stock market. After the death of their son, Susie sends her husband to England while she remains at home. But she soon follows him abroad when she learns that an excessively chic noblewoman, Lady Nora Ebbsworth, has become his recurrent hostess. With the devious assistance of the Prince of Wales, whom she meets on a fox hunt, Susie soon breaks up the affair. Shortly thereafter the Major is killed in an auto accident. At this point in the narrative flashback her thoughts return to the present. Her family informs her that they refuse to assist Amory, but the matriarch sternly announces that she will repay the stolen money even if it takes every penny of her (and their) fortune.

◆━━◆━━◆

When screen rights to Louis Bromfield's 1942 period-piece novel about a New York grande dame and the decadent younger generation was purchased by MGM, the author announced that Greer Garson was his ideal choice to play the title role, a fact fully in accord with Metro's intention for their two-million-dollar production. In splendiferousness, if not in running time and theatricalism, *Mrs. Parkington* would outshine Warner Bros.' similar domestic chronicle, *Mr. Skeffington* (1944), which starred Bette Davis and Claude Rains.

The fifth screen teaming of "the ideal connubial couple," Garson and Walter Pidgeon, did not provide as much cinematic magic as Metro had intended. Most critics gave credit to the lavishness of the black and white production but argued that MGM's story department did not do right by its stars in the distilled script in which "the clichés of ideal romance have been piled up so richly and warmly that a point of suffocation is almost reached" [Bosley Crowther *(New York Times)*]. Jane Corby *(Brooklyn Citizen)* reasoned, "So much team-work may have blunted the edge of excitement of seeing these two fall in love, marry and go down the years together . . ." Perhaps *PM* said it all when it judged the picture "a long, rambling, dull and insincere piece of fiction. . . ."

The screen version of *Mrs. Parkington* contains all the basic Garson-Pidgeon film devices by being an expansive chronicle tale which hinges on the marital relationship of an outsized couple. But herein lay the fault, for in this outing the hero is a rather boisterous gallant, prone to saying "Okay, partner," sweeping pretty girls off their feet and into his bed, and taking rather drastic revenge on his social superiors when they refuse to acknowledge his money as a substitute for good breeding. Similarly, Garson, who runs the personal gambit from boarding house slavey to New York society's elderly matriarch, is devoted to no other noble humanitarian cause other than her self-centered drive to keep her bounder husband's wandering affection, particularly after her miscarriage. Their interaction has no majesty to it. Early in their union, Pidgeon cavalierly informs his bewildered child of the desert, "I'll always be a rascal, and I'll always love you." In fact, on their wedding night in New York, Pidgeon leaves his bride's side to socialize on the town.

In such a manner their lives pass: the couple argue, he storms out, feels pangs of regret, returns home, and he and Garson reconcile. On their third wedding anniversary he presents Garson with a grand mansion, furnished by none other than his ex-mistress, Agnes Moorehead. But Garson has learned a few social tricks in her New York years, and coyly advises Pidgeon and Moorehead, "You neglected to plan on a nursery. Too bad because I'm expecting a baby." On the night of the couple's big ball, when the blueblood guests fail to materialize, Garson rushes upstairs in tears, only to fall on the steps and suffer a miscarriage. Four years pass before she inadvertently learns of her husband's bizarre revenge plan, and even then she has difficulty in understanding his "eye for an eye" philosophy. If Garson's Susie was once too inexperienced to handle Moorehead's Aspasia Conti, she has grown in the art of feminine wiles and is well equipped to cope with Tala Birell's adventuress, even so far as engaging Cecil Kellaway's Prince of Wales in engineering her reconciliation with Pidgeon. But her victory is short-lived, for playboy Pidgeon is soon off again on his peccadillo jaunts, eventually dying at a cheap Cannes cafe in the company of a certain dancer.

Stripped of usual grandiose character motivation and development, the stars, Garson in particular, became too vulnerable to acute critical inspection. Neither star fared very well in the artistic moments of truth. Pidgeon was a little rowdier than his typical sedate screen self, but nevertheless, a solid rock of masculinity, defining within this film some of the less likeable aspects of the species. On the other hand, Garson seemed to have exhausted her screen magic early in *Mrs. Parkington* by allowing her famed red hair to be encased in a black wig (the better to show her aging for the black and white cameras). Her opening sequences first as the aged but vigorous grande dame and then in the first flashback as the feisty domestic at her mother's rough and tumble lodging establishment showed her to her best advantage as an actress. Thereafter, as the cinematic years pass, she becomes more refined, but far less intriguing. Even her recurring cute oncamera trick of blowing her loose lock from her forehead when becoming angry wore thin. And for the first time, Garson shared almost equal screen time with a supporting player, Moorehead, who had fought so hard with the studio to obtain this contra-casting role of the chic, upper-echelon woman who first regards her rival with jealousy and then with affection. (Moorehead would be Oscar-nominated as Best Supporting Actress but would lose to Ethel Barrymore of *None but the Lonely Heart,* as Garson would be defeated in the Best Actress category by Ingrid Bergman's performance in *Gaslight.*)

Even Garson's oncamera "younger" relatives in *Mrs. Parkington* were a more intriguing varied bag of characters than the lead. Besides the pompous, conniving Edward Arnold, there were Gladys Cooper as the divorced, dipsomaniac daughter, and the much-married Lee Patrick, who now had a cowboy husband. Among the three generations of Parkingtons, there was also the corrupted, sniveling Dan Duryea, and the sensibly sweet Frances Rafferty (the one decent person amidst the rotton bunch of relatives) who loves penniless architect Tom Drake, but needs Garson's reassurance to wed him.

Howard Barnes (*New York Herald-Tribune*) might evaluate Garson at the top of her form in the picture and say that Pidgeon ". . . supports her at every turn of the script as a co-star should." However, the handwriting was on the wall when Alton Cook (*New York World-Telegram*) could smartly state, "Greer Garson and her virtuoso makeup department continue on their epic path. . . ." In short, take away the special effects and. . . .

## JULIA MISBEHAVES
### (MGM, 1948) 99M.

Producer, Everett Riskin; director, Jack Conway; based on the novel

*The Nutmeg Tree* by Margery Sharp; adaptation, Gina Kaus, Monckton Hoffe; screenplay, William Ludwig, Harry Ruskin; Arthur Wimperis; art directors, Cedric Gibbons, Daniel B. Cathcart; set decorators, Edwin B. Willis, Jack D. Moore; music, Adolph Deutsch; songs, Jerry Seelen and Hal Borne; assistant director, Marvin Stuart; costumes, Irene; makeup, Jack Dawn; sound, Douglas Shearer, Charles E. Wallace; special effects, Warren Newcombe; camera, Joseph Ruttenberg; editor, John Dunning.

Greer Garson (Julia Packett); Walter Pidgeon (William Packett); Peter Lawford (Ritchie); Cesar Romero (Fred); Elizabeth Taylor (Susan Packett); Lucile Watson (Mrs. Packett); Nigel Bruce (Colonel Willowbrook); Mary Boland (Mrs. Gennochio); Reginald Owen (Bennie Hawkins); Ian Wolfe (Hobson); Phyllis Morris (Daisy); Edmond Breon (Jamie); Fritz Feld (Pepito); Marcelle Corday (Gabby); Veda Ann Borg (Louise); Aubrey Mather (Vicar); Henry Stephenson (Lord Pennystone); Winifred Harris (Lady Pennystone); Ted DeWayne, Henry Monzello, William Snyder, Ray Saunders, Michael Kent (Acrobatic Troupe); Elspeth Dudgeon (Woman in Pawn Shop); Stanley Fraser (Pawn Shop Clerk); Connie Leon, Almira Sessions (Women in Street); James Logan (Moving Man); Jimmy Fairfax, Harry Allen, Cyril Thornton, Jim Finlayson (Bill Collectors); Victor Wood (Postman); Herbert Wyndham (Piano Player in Pub); Sid D'Albrook (Pub Waiter); Jimmy Aubrey (Drunk); Roland Dupre (French Messenger); Alex Goudavich (Bellhop); Andre Charlot (Stage Doorman); Joanee Wayne (The Head); Mitchell Lewis (Train Official); Jean Del Val (Croupier); Albert Pallot (Bartender); Ottola Nesmith, Nan Boardman (Salesladies); Torben Meyer (Commissaire); George Volck (Urchin); Kay Norton, Fern Eggen, Susan Perry (Girls in Hotel Lobby); Lola Albright, Marjorie Jackson, Gail Langford, Joi Lansing, Elaine Sterling, Ruth Hall, Patricia Walker, Shirley Ballard (Mannequins); Art Foster, George Goldsmith, Dave Thursby (English Sailors); Berta Feducha (Woman in Theatre); Alphonse Martell (Frenchman in Theatre).

New York Premiere: Radio City Music Hall—October 7, 1948
New York Television Debut: CBS—September 3, 1957

### Synopsis

Julia, an attractive but always in debt English music hall entertainer, charms her pals into paying her debts. She receives an invitation to attend her daughter Susan's wedding. Julia has not seen Susan in the eighteen years since she separated from her society husband, William. Bennie Hawkins, an old friend, agrees to finance Julia's trip to France where William and Susan live with his domineering mother, Mrs. Packett. Julia's channel crossing is marked by her meeting with Mrs. Gennochio and her five sons, an acrobatic troupe, with whom she becomes quite friendly. Once in Paris, Julia is called upon to take the place of the indisposed Mrs.

500

Gennochio in the act, which leads to her singing and impromptu acrobatic turn on the stage. After a tearful farewell to Fred, her dogged admirer from the troupe, Julia heads for the Packett family chateau. She receives a frosty welcome from Mrs. Packett, but William and Susan are delighted to see her. In need of funds for gifts, Julia goes to Paris where she flirts with Colonel Willowbrook in order to finance her purchases, and then disappears. Back at the chateau, Julia learns that Susan is really in love with Ritchie and she brings them together. However, while doing so, she reawakens William's love for herself. The day before Susan's scheduled wedding to Ritchie, Fred arrives and becomes resentful of William's attention to Julia. Matters become worse when Colonel Willowbrook, a family friend, arrives. As Julia tries to explain her escapade with him, bedlam breaks loose with word that Susan and Ritchie have eloped. William and Julia chase after the newlyweds, who, in turn, leave them stranded in a mountain lodge where they become reconciled.

◆―◆―◆

Forty-year-old Greer Garson was experiencing a boxoffice slump and Metro was anxious to put her back onto the commercial road to success. In *Adventure* (1945) it was proudly announced "Gable's Back and Garson's Got Him." The impoverished romantic comedy did business despite its lackluster artistic qualities, but the production-plagued *Desire Me* (1947), featuring Garson and newcomer Richard Hart (who replaced an unhappy Robert Montgomery), had been a fiasco. The question facing the studio was what to do next. Even Garson was balking at her holier-than-thou screen image and the importation of Deborah Kerr as a threat-substitute did nothing to ameliorate Garson's passion to take a stab at a new brand of screen emoting. Thus the studio latched onto Margery Sharp's novel *The Nutmeg Tree* and performed a near-total overhaul of the book. The result was *Julia Misbehaves,* about which the studio boasted, "You've never seen Greer Garson and Walter Pidgeon like this before. . . . Greer in tights. [She had done that showgirl gambit before in *Random Harvest* (1942).] She's gay, giddy, and gorgeous. Greer takes a bubble bath while the wolves howl at the door. . . ." A viewer might well ponder on what had become of certain movie images. A decade before, moviegoers had seen glamorous Joan Crawford go madcap in *Love on the Run* (1936), but with Greer Garson changing, was there nothing sacred in post-World War II Hollywood? Bosley Crowther (*New York Times*) was quick to reassure his readers, "It promotes the lovely lady in so many frank delinquencies that one might be strongly suspicious of the studio's liberality, if it weren't that Walter Pidgeon is also in the film. But the presence of Mr. Pidgeon, as handsome and as fine as of yore, is adequate assurance that no dishonor will come to Miss Garson on the Music Hall screen."

The film's premise asked the audience indulgently to accept that the tweedy, respectable, sensible Pidgeon would have a momentary lapse of perspective when he had wed music hall performer Garson, a spunky girl more at home with barroom roustabouts than with the likes of Pidgeon's refined mama (Lucile Watson). Soon after the birth of their daughter, he sends his irrepressible wife packing, and she willingly leaves her daughter in his complete care. So much for Garson's noble screen image as an understanding wife and devoted mother! But to compound complications, when the viewers meet up with Garson again some eighteen years later, she has not lost one bit of her proletarian vivacity. In fact, if anything, the middle-aged miss is more prone to risque adventures than ever before, and it is a long and eventful trip for her before she arrives in France to attend her daughter's pending marriage. Along the way she become involved with a traveling acrobatic troupe, finding herself substituting for Mary Boland as the top person in the act's pyramid feat and singing a Beatrice Lillie-style song in the Paris music hall sequence. In the midst of this slapstick, Garson is carrying on rather flirtatiously with acrobat Cesar Romero. Fortuitously, in these rather labored interludes, there is the diverting presence of Boland as the *mal de mer*-plagued mama, a joy to behold under most any condition.

Once Garson arrives in Pidgeon's home town, the script attempts to play both ends against the middle. The frenetic pseudo-farce antics continue as the unwanted Garson digs money out of the gullible Nigel Bruce so she can buy her daughter a wedding gift. Later she trades drawing-room quips with Vicar Aubrey Mather and engages in other tomfoolery as her unbridled manners chafes the primness of Watson. However, someone at the studio must have remembered that audiences were accustomed to having Garson and Pidgeon appear as happily married screen couple. Therefore, while the two opposite types tumble in and out of situations, the scenario abruptly reaffirms the Establishment aspect of Garson's character. She may take a rather sexy bubble bath or lurch out of a rowboat into a mud puddle, but a previously unrevealed (in *Julia Misbehaves*, that is) nobility of spirit suddenly asserts itself. Garson launches herself into the role as a busybody by dragging daughter Taylor into the deserving arms of Peter Lawford, and then becomes all sweetness and goo over the girl, exhibiting an overwrought tendency towards treacle and mother love. Later, when Garson and Pidgeon are recuperating from their misadventures with the rain and mud, he glides into a rendition of the song "My Wonderful One," with a new dewy-eyed Garson his ever-listening partner. These latter scenes obviously were meant to demonstrate that the couple's romance has been rekindled in the traditional manner.

In short, *Julia Misbehaves* was a peculiar mixed bag of cinema bits and pieces, what with Garson really portraying snatches of a half dozen different character traits as she and Pidgeon are forced by the scenario to act more foolish and less mature than Taylor and Lawford. In the last analysis, however, despite Garson's "workmanlike job" *(New York Herald-Tribune)*, "She never obscures the illusion that she is a well-bred matron being gay" [Crowther *(New York Times)*].

# THAT FORSYTE WOMAN
## *(MGM, 1949) C-114M.*

Producer, Leon Gordon; director, Compton Bennett; based on *A Man of Property* from *The Forsyte Saga* by John Galsworthy; screenplay, Jan Lustig, Ivan Tors, James B. Williams; additional dialog, Arthur Wimperis; art directors, Cedric Gibbons, Daniel B. Cathcart; set decorators, Edwin B. Willis, Jack D. Moore; music, Bronislau Kaper; assistant director, Bob Barnes; makeup, Jack Dawn; costumes, Walter Plunkett, Valles; sound, Douglas Shearer, Ralph Pender; camera, Joseph Ruttenberg; editor, Frederick Y. Smith.

Errol Flynn (Soames Forsyte); Greer Garson (Irene Forsyte); Walter Pidgeon (Young Jolyon Forsyte); Robert Young (Philip Bosinney); Janet Leigh (June Forsyte); Harry Davenport (Old Jolyon Forsyte); Stanley Logan (Swithin Forsyte); Lumsden Hare (Roger Forsyte); Aubrey Mather (James Forsyte); Matt Moore (Timothy Forsyte); Florence Auer (Ann Forsyte Hayman); Marjorie Eaton (Hester Forsyte); Evelyn Beresford (Mrs. Taylor); Gerald Oliver Smith (Beveridge); Richard Lupino (Chester Forsyte); Wilson Wood (Eric Forsyte); Gabrielle Windsor (Jennie); Renee Mercer (Martha); Nina Ross (Louise); Constance Cavendish (Alice Forsyte); Charles McNaughton (Attendant); Wallis Clark (Cabby); Isabel Randolph (Mrs. Winthrop); Tim Hawkins (Freddie); Olaf Hytten (Assistant); Reginald Sheffield (Mr. McLean); Frank Baker (Lord Dunstable); Jean Ransome (Amelia); William Eddritt (Waiter); Leonard Carey (Butler); Morgan Farley (Bookseller); John Sheffield, Norman Rainey (Footmen); Herbert Evans (M.C.s' Voice); James Aubrey (Cabby); Billy Bevan (Porter); David Dunbar (Driver); Colin Kenny (Constable); Leyland Hodgson (Detective); Rolfe Sedan (Official); Andre Charlot (Director Braval); Lilian Bond (Maid); Blanche Franke, Jack Chefe, Olga Nina Borget, Albert Petit (Guests); Jimmy Hawkins (Gerald); Gloria Gordon (Girl).

New York Premiere: Radio City Music Hall—November 10, 1949
New York Television Debut: Channel 9—May 2, 1963

## Synopsis

A prominent artist, Young Jolyon Forsyte, thinks back on events which have made him a black sheep to his very proper Victorian London family. His daughter June had been raised by the family after her mother's death and she had not had been permitted to visit Young Jolyon. His cousin, Soames Forsyte, a very stuffy fellow, had wed Irene, a piano teacher, despite family objections to his marrying for love and not position. Later, a strong attachment grew between Irene and June, the latter asking Irene to aid her in getting the family to accept as her suitor Philip Bosinney, a carefree young architect. Through Irene's efforts, the family agrees to

June's engagement. However, Philip, attracted by Irene's charm and beauty, falls for her, despite the married woman's efforts to discourage him. Philip is brought into closer contact with Irene when Soames gives him a contract to design a new home. Philip continues to pursue her, secretly but ardently. Irene, unhappy with Soames, resists her desire for Philip because of his engagement to June. Later, Irene visits Philip secretly to urge him to forget about her. She is seen entering his apartment by June who thinks the worst. The furious June tells Soames all. When Irene returns home, Soames mistreats her and then sends for Philip. The two men quarrel and Philip declares his love for Irene. Meanwhile, Irene has returned to Philip's apartment where she meets young Jolyon, he having come to censure Philip for his treatment of June. Shortly thereafter, Soames comes to the apartment and informs them that in his haste to follow Irene, Philip was killed in a vehicle accident. Heartbroken, Irene refuses to return home and instead goes to Young Jolyon's studio. Five years later, she is living in Paris, happily wed to Young Jolyon.

◆━◆━◆

"There are moments of dramatic urgency in this M-G-M production, but they are too few and far between to sustain the translation of a celebrated novel" [Howard Barnes (New York Herald-Tribune)]. Metro borrowed still popular Errol Flynn from Warner Bros., in exchange for William Powell being loaned to that studio for Life with Father (1947), in order to bolster the roster of players heading this expensive adaptation of the first volume (1906) of John Galsworthy's The Forsyte Saga. The results were pretty dreary, with Greer Garson accepting secondary billing to visiting star Flynn, and vis-a-vis Walter Pidgeon reassigned to the thankless part of Young Jolyon Forsyte, after Flynn insisted upon playing the juicier role of Soames Forsyte.

Those viewers who hoped for a Garson-Pidgeon drama as before were sadly disappointed. "They have dressed her in ultra-gorgeous costumes," wrote Bosley Crowther (New York Times), "posed her in plush Victorian sets and filmed her in lavish Technicolor, probably the most lavish you have ever seen. They have marched pompous gentlemen up to her and had them profess their ardent love. And then they have gracefully retired her into the snugness of a cut-and-dried romance." As for Pidgeon's plight in this drama of 1880s London, Crowther noted he ". . . is perhaps the least depressing of the lot, mainly because he has little to do until he steps in toward the end."

That Forsyte Woman seemed to be vapid entertainment in 1949. Today it suffers even more by comparison with the recent B.B.C.'s fine television serial rendition of Galsworthy's initial book trilogy, which gives all the depth and dimension to the gallery of characters and the penetrating study of class variations in Victorian England that MGM had so blithely ignored.

After the moviegoer has contemplated for an appreciative time the film's settings and costumes, he/she must be struck less by the acting deficiencies of the male performers than by the shrill posturing of Garson in the focal role. She virtually buzzes from one man to another in her quest for emotional happiness while still satisfying the Victorian morality code. Whether in the confines of horse-drawn carriages, Parisian art galleries, or London town houses, the begowned Garson has such a sanctimonious air about her that the impecunious Irene becomes a tedious and slightly odious creature. Likewise, Flynn's loveless, money-conscious man of property emerged as a somewhat pitiable figure. Straddled somewhere between these opposing types were Pidgeon in the role of the understanding insurance man turned painter, and Robert Young in an ineptly sketched part as the architect fiancé of Pidgeon's daughter (Leigh) who moons about the sets, proclaiming his great admiration for Garson.

Garson and Pidgeon were among the cast of *That Forsyte Woman* who repeated their roles on "Lux Radio Theatre" on November 5, 1951.

## THE MINIVER STORY
### *(MGM, 1950) 104M.*

Producer, Sidney Franklin; director, H. C. Potter; based on characters created by Jan Struther; screenplay, Ronald Millar, George Froeschel; music, Herbert Stothart, Miklos Rosza; music director, Muir Mathieson; art director, Alfred Junge; costumes for Miss Garson, Walter Plunkett; costumes, Gaston Mallett; sound, A. W. W. Watkins; camera effects, Tom Howard; camera, Joseph Ruttenberg; editors, Harold F. Kress, Frank Clarke.

Greer Garson (Kay Miniver); Walter Pidgeon (Clem Miniver); John Hodiak (Spike Romway); Leo Genn (Steve Brunswick); Cathy O'Donnell (Judy Miniver); Reginald Owen (Mr. Foley); Anthony Bushell (Dr. Kanesley); Richard Gale (Tom Foley); Peter Finch (Polish Officer); William (James) Fox (Toby Miniver); Cicely Paget-Bowman (Mrs. Kanesley); Ann Wilton (Jeanette); Henry Wilcoxon (Vicar); Eliot Makeham (Mr. Farraday); Brian Roper (Richard); Paul Demel (Jose Antonio Campos); Alison Leggatt (Mrs. Foley).

New York Premiere: Radio City Music Hall—October 26, 1950
New York Television Debut: ABC—May 21, 1966

### Synopsis

On V-E day in London, pallid Kay Miniver rejoices in the victory celebration with American Colonel Spike Romway who admits his love for Kay prior to his departure for home. In due time, she welcomes home from overseas her family: husband Clem, daughter Judy, and son Toby. She does not reveal to them she has only a year at most to live. She has decided to devote the remaining months of her life to adjusting the family's problems. Architect Clem finds war-torn London depressing and wants to accept a Brazil assignment. A more important problem is Judy who spurns the courtship of Tom Foley, a wholesome local lad, because of her infatuation for married Brigadier General Steve Brunswick. Kay visits Brunswick and dissuades him from obtaining a divorce to marry Judy. She convinces Brunswick he still loves his wife. Judy is at first angered by her mother's interference, but eventually changes her mind when Kay shows her a letter from Romway in which he points out he is now happily married and that the love he felt for Kay was only engendered by the special wartime conditions. With Judy's problem solved, Kay's happiness is complete when Clem decides to remain in England. Later she tells the family of her condition. Heartbroken Clem does his utmost to make her remaining days happy. Kay lives long enough to see Judy wed.

◆—◆—◆

In its half-hearted determination to restore some lustre to the marquee allure of Greer Garson and Walter Pidgeon, MGM, now under the aegis of Dore Schary, unwisely decided to return to the once-lucrative world of the Minivers. Some things are best left to memory, and a post-World War II continuation of the admirable but outdated Minivers definitely belonged to this category. But once the brainstorm was in motion nothing could stop the momentum whose cinema results would greatly tarnish the halo surrounding the original *Mrs. Miniver*. As Howard Barnes *(New York Herald-Tribune)* noted, "It is more of a faded photograph than a reminder of the present."

Metro induced producer Sidney Franklin to handle the tightly budgeted black and white film project, and the original movie's cinematographer, Joseph Ruttenberg, was assigned to lens the sequel. For good measure the cast was sent to London for filming under the experienced but uninspired direction of H. C. Potter. Despite all efforts nothing could overcome the treacly storyline which relied on nobility-near-death as its trite and maudlin thesis.

From the outset, the film is dampened by unsubtle soap opera melodramatics. It is V-E Day, and everyone is in a jubilant mood, that is, everyone except Garson's Kay Miniver, who has learned she does not have long to live. (For some strange reason the scenario is oddly secretive about her illness—most likely cancer—while willing to pull every scripting trick possible to drag on her inevitable demise.) It was rather a disappointment for moviegoers who had loved the previous *Mrs. Miniver* to witness a now grown-up Judy Miniver (Cathy O'Donnell) and Toby Miniver [William (James) Fox] each returning to the family hearth, more conventional in character than endearing. Likewise, it was tedious enough for the viewer to have to cope vicariously with O'Donnell's misguided love interest. But for the viewer to suddenly discover that Garson, now posing herself on the brink of sainthood via an untimely death, had been involved in a (harmless) wartime romance with an American colonel (John Hodiak), must have disillusioned many a fan, convincing them that they did not want to witness any further blasphemies against *Mrs. Miniver.* To compound the unhappy screen situation, Pidgeon's Clem Miniver has lost all his spunk, thanks to the script. Some moviegoers might have fancied great feats of commercial derring-do from this levelheaded chap who did his bit during the war. But no, now he is a rather timorous, stock character, who passes up good business opportunities. While Pidgeon remains on the sidelines nonplused, muttering over and over to Garson that she looks as lovely as ever, Garson sets about her self-appointed tasks while constantly reminding everyone, "I won't be here for the spring." Sure enough, comes the new year and the new season, and Garson is gone. But only the most gullible viewer could have been caught with a lump in his throat as Pidgeon faces the future without his once better half.

*The Miniver Story* had its world premiere at the Ritz Theatre in London on August 22, 1950 where it met with a modest reaction from the press. American critics were no more impressed with the film than the English, in fact Bosley Crowther (*New York Times*) offered a mild diatribe in his review, "Miss Garson plays with such lofty nobleness that whatever emotion is in the story is drenched in great waves of obvious goo. So soft and beautific is her manner, so hushed and remote is her tone, that she seems, even before her passing, to have assumed her imminent state in another world. . . . As for Mr. Pidgeon, he looks and acts like a monument."

## SCANDAL AT SCOURIE
### *(MGM, 1953) C-89M.*

Producer, Edwin H. Knopf; director, Jean Negulesco; story, Mary McSherry; screenplay, Norman Corwin, Leonard Spigelgass; music, Daniele Amfitheatrof; art director, Cedric Gibbons, Wade B. Rubottom; camera, Robert Planck; editor, Ferris Webster.

Greer Garson (Mrs. Patrick McChesney); Walter Pidgeon (Patrick J. McChesney); Agnes Moorehead (Sister Josephine); Donna Corcoran (Patsy); Arthur Shields (Father Reilly); Philip Ober (B. G. Belney); Rhys Williams (Bill Swazey); Margalo Gillmore (Alice Hanover); John Lupton (Artemus); Philip Tonge (Mr. Gogarty); Wilton Graff (Mr. Leffington); Ian Wolfe (Councilman Hurdwell); Michael Pate (Reverend Williams); Tony Taylor (Edward); Patricia Tiernan (Nun); Victor Wood (James Motely); Perdita Chandler (Sister Dominique); Walter Baldwin (Michael Hayward); Ida Moore (Mrs. Ames); Maudie Prickett (Mrs. Holahan); Ivis Goulding (Mrs. O'Russell); Alex Frazer (Womsley); Matt Moore (Kenston); Charles Watts (Barber); Roger Moore, Al Ferguson, Jack Bonigul (Ad Libs); Eugene Borden (Old Man); Rudy Lee (Donald); Max Willenz (Vidocq); Ivan Triesault (Father Barrett); Wayne Farlow, Linda Greer, Kathleen Hartnagel, Warren Farlow (Children); Joann Arnold (Sister Maria); Peter Roman (Freddie); George Davis (Bartender); Vicki Joy Ereutzer (Edith); Claude Guy (Joseph); Gary Lee Jackson (Other Boy); Jill Martin (Isabella); Coral Hammond (Cecilia); Nolan Leary (Conductor); Owen McGiveney (Clark); Archer McDonald (Barber Apprentice); Earl Lee (Tweedy Man); Howard Negley (Duggin); Robert Ross (Dr. Parker); John Sherman (Mr. Pringle).

New York Premiere: Little Carnegie Theatre—June 15, 1953
New York Television Debut: CBS—March 25, 1966

## Synopsis

When a Quebec orphanage is destroyed by an accidental fire set by Patsy, one of the orphans, the nuns of the orphanage take a cross-country trip with the children, hoping to find homes for them in the towns en route. When the train reaches the predominantly Protestant town of Scourie, Patsy wanders off and meets Mrs. Patrick McChesney, whose husband owns the town's general store, is the Protestant leader, and is prominent in local politics. Not having any children of her own, Mrs. McChesney decides to adopt Patsy, but Patrick objects on the ground that the child is Catholic. The nuns also object, but they permit Mrs. McChesney to take the child when she states that Patsy will be raised as a Catholic. Patrick treats Patsy with kindness, but his forebodings prove correct when B. G. Belney, the local newspaper editor and Patrick's political rival, prints a scathing denunciation of the McChesney's adoption, branding it as a cheap trick to win votes in the upcoming election. Angered over the article, Mrs. McChesney seeks out Belney and hits him with a wet towel at the barber shop, while Patrick is forced to beat up several hecklers at a political meeting. But the editorial has its effect, for the townfolk shun the McChesneys and the politicians advise Patrick to give up Patsy if he wants to save his political future. But Patrick resents this pettiness and declares that he will keep Patsy. Later, when the local school is destroyed by fire, the villagers, on the basis of her past record, blame Patsy for the blaze. Patrick, furious over this example of intolerance, denounces the accusers and resigns, not only as a candidate for political office, but also as a church leader. Meanwhile, Patsy, knowing she has created problems for her adoptive parents, runs away in the rain. The McChesneys search for her and are joined by the townsfolk, who now know she did not start the fire. The girl is located by dawn, chilled but safe. Everyone now agrees that Patsy belongs with the McChesneys.

◆━◆━◆

The ninth and final Greer Garson-Walter Pidgeon joint screen venture was the first of their MGM features not to play Radio City Music Hall, and rightly so. Even with its Technicolor mounting, it was such a synthetic saccharine, minor confection that only the most easily pleased movie-goers could be entertained—let alone inspired—by its stale prefabrication of the mother-love theme. There were few viewers who could accept the obvious message on the evils of intolerance as anything but an unsubtle, juvenile tract by Metro studio head Dore Schary, who had engineered a similar but more effective human conduct lesson with his *Crossfire* (1947).

Within the scope of eighty-nine minutes, *Scandal at Scourie* asked a great deal and gave very little. Its plot theme rang of old time radio soap opera: can a respectable couple in a deeply Protestant Canadian small town find happiness when the Ulster-born wife insists that they take an illegitimate, orphaned Catholic girl into their household, a situation which disturbs the husband who fears the repercussion on his business and his chances in a political election, and worries the prejudiced townfolk who have come to believe the child is a pyromaniac?

The film's execution was pedestrian, filled with stock characterizations ranging from Agnes Moorehead's benevolent nun to Arthur Shields' folksy priest and to Ian Wolfe's militant councilman. Garson at age forty-five was still playing the clear-eyed do-gooder, this time equipped with an Irish brogue and a fighting spirit, enough to brook all obstacles in her path, save a bad script and the changing times which had left the screen prototypes in its wake.

## THE YEARS AFTER

A year after *Scandal at Scourie* Greer Garson asked for, and received, her MGM release. She realized that in the diminished film market of the 1950s she might do better as a freelance, and more importantly, would now have greater freedom to enjoy her good life as the wife of wealthy Elijah "Buddy" Fogelson. Not that she entirely forgot her once-adoring public. She made occasional forays into television, was among the Broadway replacements in *Auntie Mame,* was Oscar-nominated for her very mannered performance as Eleanor Roosevelt in *Sunrise at Campobello* (1960), and returned to MGM in 1966 to essay a cameo as a cliché-hallowed screen mother superior in *The Singing Nun.*

Meanwhile, Walter Pidgeon's career continued at an even, if slower, clip than had been its previous wont. He completed his MGM tenure in 1956 and arrived back on Broadway in the comedy *The Happiest Million-aire* (1957) and the musical *Take Me Along* (1959). Throughout the 1960s he continued to offer his usual competent performance both on television and in supporting roles in feature films. When it seemed that he and Garson might be reunited in Walt Disney's picturization of *The Happiest Million-aire* (1967), Disney upset Pidgeon and disappointed many Garson-Pidgeon fans by announcing that Fred MacMurray would play the lead male assignment. Disney apparently thought Pidgeon was too old for the part. In

1972, Pidgeon returned to MGM for a featured role in *Skyjacked*. While appearing a little older, he was as good as ever, which is more than could be said for that Charlton Heston feature or the producing studio itself.

When young people today, imbued with concepts of women's lib philosophy and new wave cinema styles, see a Garson-Pidgeon epic re-shown on television, they tend to classify the duo's elaborate screen fare as prehistoric balderdash. But their elders, who sigh, "They don't make pictures like that anymore," can recall when the promise of a new Garson-Pidgeon feature meant a leisurely, plush excursion into a world of nobility, gentility, and tear-inducing emotions, refinements long gone from the helter-skelter era of the 1970s.

Lana Turner visiting Clark Gable on the set of **Adventure** (MGM, 1945)

# Chapter 18

# Clark Gable
# &
# Lana Turner

## CLARK GABLE

*For biographical and career data, see Chapter 4, Clark Gable-Joan Crawford.*

## LANA TURNER

5′ 3½″
110 pounds
Blonde hair
Blue eyes
Aquarius

*Real Name: Julia Jean Mildred Frances Turner. Born February 8, 1920, Wallace, Idaho. Married Artie Shaw (1940); divorced 1940. Married Stephen Crane (1942), child: Cheryl; divorced 1944. Married Bob Topping (1948); divorced 1952. Married Lex Barker (1953); divorced 1957. Married Fred May (1960); divorced 1962. Married Robert Eaton (1965); divorced 1969. Married Robert Dante (1969); divorced 1972.*

## FEATURE FILMS:

A Star Is Born (UA, 1937)

They Won't Forget (WB, 1937)

The Great Garrick (WB, 1937)

The Adventures of Marco Polo (UA, 1938)

Four's a Crowd (WB, 1938)

Love Finds Andy Hardy (MGM, 1938)

The Chaser (MGM, 1938)

Rich Man, Poor Girl (MGM, 1938)

Dramatic School (MGM, 1938)

Calling Dr. Kildare (MGM, 1939)

These Glamour Girls (MGM, 1939)

Dancing Co-Ed (MGM, 1939)

Two Girls on Broadway (MGM), 1940)

We Who Are Young (MGM, 1940)

Ziegfeld Girl (MGM, 1941)

Dr. Jekyll and Mr. Hyde (MGM, 1941)

Honky Tonk (MGM, 1941)

Johnny Eager (MGM, 1941)

Somewhere I'll Find You (MGM, 1942)

The Youngest Profession (MGM, 1943)

Slightly Dangerous (MGM, 1943)

Du Barry Was a Lady (MGM, 1943)°

Marriage Is a Private Affair (MGM, 1944)

Keep Your Powder Dry (MGM, 1945)

Weekend at the Waldorf (MGM, 1945)

The Postman Always Rings Twice (MGM, 1946)

Green Dolphin Street (MGM, 1947)

Cass Timberlane (MGM, 1947)

Homecoming (MGM, 1948)

The Three Musketeers (MGM, 1948)

A Life of Her Own (MGM, 1950)

Mr. Imperium (MGM, 1951)

The Merry Widow (MGM, 1952)

The Bad and the Beautiful (MGM, 1952)

Latin Lovers (MGM, 1953)

Flame and the Flesh (MGM, 1954)

Betrayed (MGM, 1954)

The Prodigal (MGM, 1955)

The Sea Chase (WB, 1955)

The Rains of Ranchipur (20th, 1955)

Diane (MGM, 1956)

Peyton Place (20th, 1957)

The Lady Takes a Flyer (Univ., 1958)

Another Time, Another Place (Par., 1958)

Imitation of Life (Univ., 1959)

Portrait in Black (Univ., 1960)

By Love Possessed (UA, 1961)

Bachelor in Paradise (MGM, 1961)

Who's Got the Action? (Par., 1962)

Love Has Many Faces (Col., 1965)

Madame X (Univ., 1966)

The Big Cube (WB-7 Arts, 1969)

Persecution (Fanfare, 1974)

°Unbilled appearance

Advertisement for **Honky Tonk** (MGM, 1941)

In **Honky Tonk**

Caricature of Clark Gable and Lana Turner in **Honky Tonk**

In **Somewhere I'll Find You** (MGM, 1942)

Advertisement for **Homecoming** (MGM, 1948)

In Homecoming

Advertisement for **Betrayed** (MGM, 1954)

In **Betrayed** (MGM, 1954)

# HONKY TONK
## *(MGM, 1941) 105M.*

Producer, Pandro S. Berman; director, Jack Conway; screenplay, Marguerite Roberts, John Sanford; music, Franz Waxman; songs, Jack Yellen and Milton Ager; art director, Cedric Gibbons; sound, Douglas Shearer; camera, Harold Rosson; editor, Blanche Sewell.

Clark Gable (Candy Johnson); Lana Turner (Elizabeth Cotton); Frank Morgan (Judge Cotton); Claire Trevor (Gold Dust Nelson); Marjorie Main (Reverend Mrs. Varner); Albert Dekker (Brazos Hearn); Chill Wills (The Sniper); Henry O'Neill (Daniel Wells); John Maxwell (Kendall); Morgan Wallace (Adams); Douglas Wood (Governor Wilson); Betty Blythe (Mrs. Wilson); Hooper Atchley (Senator Ford); Harry Worth (Harry Gates); Veda Ann Borg (Pearl); Dorothy Granger (Saloon Girl); Sheila Darcy (Louise); Cy Kendall (Man with Tar); Erville Alderson (Man with Rail); John Farrell (Man with Feathers); Don Barclay (Man with Gun); Ray Teal (Poker Player); Esther Muir (Blonde on Train); Francis X. Bushman, Jr., Art Miles (Dealers); Demetrius Alexis (Tug); Anne O'Neal (Nurse); Russell Hicks (Dr. Otis); Henry Roquemore (Butcher); Lew Harvey (Blackie); John Carr (Brazos' Henchman); Ralph Peters, Eddie Gribbon, Syd Saylor, Harry Semels, Frank Mills, Art Belasco (Pallbearers)· Dick Rush (Dentist); Fay Holderness (Bricklayer); Lew Kelly, Charles McAvoy, Joe Devlin, Malcolm Waite, Earl Gunn, Ted Oliver, Charles Sullivan, Monte Montague, William Haade, Al Hill (Miners); Ed Brady (Waiter); Edward Cassidy, Jack Baxley, Carl Stockdale, Howard Mitchell, William Pagan, Jack C. Smith, John Sheehan, Bill Telaak, Tom Chatterton (Citizens); Gordon DeMain, Pat O'Malley (Guests); Eddy C. Waller (Train Conductor); Elliott Sullivan (Candy's Man); Horace Murphy (Butler); Will Wright, Alan Bridge, Lee Phelps (Men in Meeting House); Tiny Newlan (Gentleman); Dorothy Ates (Dance Hall Girl); Heinie Conklin (Dental Patient).

New York Premiere: Capitol Theatre—October 2, 1941
New York Television Debut: CBS—January 20, 1957

•

### Synopsis

Just as Candy Johnson and his pal, the Sniper, are about to be tarred and feathered by a mob, Candy, through the combination of smooth talk and a quick grab for an unprotected gun, engineers their escape and they board a passing train. On this train they meet Lucy Cotton, an attractive Bostonian, and her father Judge Cotton, the latter obviously a con artist like Candy and the Sniper. At first Lucy is only mildly attracted to Candy, but when they reach the new town and he donates a considerable sum of money for the building of a new church, she finds herself won over to his charms. Candy had acquired the funds by outmaneuvering Brazos Hearn, who runs the town's gambling spot. Soon the preacher's widow, Mrs. Varner, has her church built, while Candy has constructed a dance-hall-casino, and is well on his way to controlling the town. The judge is in on Candy's deals, but Lucy is unaware of this. When Candy agrees to give up his dancehall girl, Gold Dust Nelson, Lucy weds him. Meanwhile, the judge is shocked at his own moral delinquencies and seeks solace in drink while plotting his revenge. Although the judge exposes Candy's schemes, the gambler will not harm him. However, Hearn will, and shoots the old man. The murder of her father causes Lucy to suffer a miscarriage of her child. Candy later shoots Hearn and runs his mob out of town. Although Candy has grown enormously wealthy from his grafting tricks, he now plans to go straight. He and the Sniper hide out, leaving a secreted fortune behind for the still ill Lucy. When she recovers sufficiently, she follows after her beloved Candy.

◆◆◆

Since the phenomenally successful *Gone with the Wind* (1939), Clark Gable's subsequent MGM films had been a sundry bag of moderate goodies, his best being *Boom Town* (1940) with Spencer Tracy, Claudette Colbert, and Hedy Lamarr. Jack Conway, who directed that oil town chronicle, was assigned to *Honky Tonk*, a con artist tale situated in the old West. Originally the film was to have been a fictional account of the saga of Soapy Smith, a real-life, colorful frontier sharper and boom town dicta-tor, but his descendants demanded too much money, so Marguerite Roberts and John Sanford set to work to conceive their own version, basing Gable's character on a variation of Rhett Butler.

By 1941, Metro believed that forty-one-year-old Gable, trailing behind Mickey Rooney as number two boxoffice attraction in the country, was professionally in need of a new steady leading lady. Two of his most en-during screen partners, Joan Crawford and Norma Shearer, had well passed the brink of youth and were each soon to leave MGM. Jean Harlow, his other frequent 1930s movie co-star, had tragically died in 1937. Per-haps recalling how explosively Gable had been teamed with Harlow, the blonde bombshell, MGM paired him with another light-haired sexy dish, namely twenty-one-year-old Lana Turner.° Back in 1937 she had gained a certain amount of publicity mileage from her tight-sweater role in Warner Bros.' *They Won't Forget*. In her first Metro picture, *Love Finds Andy Hardy* (1938), she had been the rival of Judy Garland and Ann Ruther-ford for Micky Rooney's affection. *Ziegfeld Girl* (1941) saw her romanced by James Stewart, and in *Dr. Jekyll and Mr. Hyde* (1941) she had joined with Ingrid Bergman in portraying the women in Spencer Tracy's life. Temperamentally and histrionically she may not have been suited to play the prim Boston belle in *Honky Tonk*, but her visual appeal was considered to be a sufficient enough asset for the part.

°In 1938 Gable had performed test readings of *Red Dust* with newcomer Turner at MGM.

On its own sprawling level, *Honky Tonk* is an enjoyable film, but there is nothing special about its storyline which wanders in so many directions. One might call the saga of gambler Candy Brown (Gable) who comes to Yellow Creek, Nevada, a story of "almosts." He is almost lynched, he and Elizabeth (Turner) almost have a baby; she almost dies. Buried beneath these meandering themes of *Honky Tonk* is a basic plot question and premise, one that had been and would continue to be a prime scripting ruse in most Gable pictures at MGM, i.e., would fast-talking, rugged Gable prove to be the marrying kind? As Theodore Strauss *(New York Times)* observed, "It is distinctly in the tradition of Gable pictures—you know, the sort in which he slugs it out, toe to toe, with equally impetuous women. In the present instance, Lana Turner acts as his sparring partner, which helps matters no end because Miss Turner is not only beautiful but ruggedly constructed."

One of the big assets of *Honky Tonk* was its most sterling supporting cast. Benign Frank Morgan played the kindly but ineffectual old man who dies nobly, Claire Trevor was the saloon tart whose tough ways mask her heart of gold, gruff Marjorie Main portrayed the rough-living preacher's widow who has visions of mankind's better nature, and Albert Dekker was the inevitable bad man.

Viewers of *Honky Tonk* might well have wished that more oncamera time be devoted to the featured supporting players had not the teaming of Gable and Turner proved so chemically explosive. Today we might take the pairing of those two personalities for granted, but in 1941 it was considered fireworks. It was unimportant that Gable offered no new acting insights or that most of Turner's emoting was nonexistent. Together they had charisma. *Variety* effectively reported the situation: "The major power in *Honky Tonk* is in the love scenes between Gable and Miss Turner. These sequences should get wide word-of-mouth and women [will] make the matinees look like giveaway day in a department store. For the men, plus the flash of Miss Turner in black undies and opera length hose, there's enough action and gunplay to also make them willing customers." By the early 1940s, the screen was greatly in need of a new torrid love team to stimulate the imaginations of moviegoers, and MGM was the cooperative benefactor who supplied the missing commodity in the sizzling personae of Gable and Turner. The studio now seemed to have cornered the American market on celluloid love team types, with the noble romancing of Greer Garson and Walter Pidgeon, the rough and tumble amorous sparring of Marjorie Main and Wallace Beery, the youthful cavorting of Mickey Rooney and Judy Garland, and now the passionate clashings and clinchings of Gable and Turner.

In the course of *Honky Tonk*, Gable kisses° heroine Turner a good eleven times. More importantly, there are several incendiary bedroom scenes within the picture, each of them delicately skirting the outer

°MGM promoted the film with the ad, "Clark Gable Kisses Lana Turner and It's Screen History."

521

parameters of tasteful standards established by the industry's production code. One such sequence finds Gable nearly pounding down Turner's door, determined to overshadow her recent rebuff of his charms by bidding her a personal goodnight. Another instance has Gable awakening from a drunken stupor to find himself wed to Turner, and yet another boudoir confrontation follows the consummation of the marriage. These sizzling bedroom scenes were alone sufficient reasons to turn *Honky Tonk* into a solid boxoffice winner.

The October 13, 1941, issue of *Life* magazine devoted a cover story to Gable and Turner of *Honky Tonk*, proclaiming " . . . the birth of a new starring team, the hottest, most electric combination of movie personalities since Boyer and Lamarr." Scant mention was made during all this publicity of the Gable-Turner screen rapport in *Honky Tonk* that Gable was happily wed at the time to actress Carole Lombard, or that Turner was married to bandleader Artie Shaw, her co-star of *Dancing Co-Ed* (1939).

Gable and Turner would recreate their *Honky Tonk* roles for radio's "Screen Guild Playhouse" in 1950.

In 1974 MGM prepared a video pilot of *Honky Tonk* with Richard Crenna in the lead.

## SOMEWHERE I'LL FIND YOU
### *(MGM, 1942) 108M.*

Producer, Pandro S. Berman; director, Wesley Ruggles; story, Charles Hoffman; adaptation, Walter Reisch; screenplay, Marguerite Roberts; music, Bronislau Kaper; art director, Cedric Gibbons; music, Bronislau Kaper; sound, Douglas Shearer; camera, Harold Rosson; editor, Frank E. Hull.

Clark Gable (Jonathan Davis); Lana Turner (Paula Lane); Robert Sterling (Kirk Davis); Reginald Owen (Willie Manning); Lee Patrick (Eve Manning); Charles Dingle (George L. Stafford); Tamara Shayne (Mama Lugovska); Leonid Kinskey (Dorloff); Molly Lamont (Nurse Winifred); Patricia Dane (Crystal Jones); Sara Haden (Miss Coulter); Richard Kean (Professor Anatole); Francis Sayles (Pearcley); Tom O'Grady (Bartender); Donald Kerr (Waiter); Gayne Whitman (Penny's Companion); Grady Sutton (Boy); Dorothy Morris (Girl); Keye Luke (Thomas Chang); Miles Mander (Fred Kirsten); Eleanor Soohoo (Ming); Allen Jung (Sam Porto); Douglas Fowley (Captain); Benny Inocencio (Felipe Morel); Van Johnson (Lieutenant Hall); Angel Cruz (Manuel Ortega); Keenan Wynn (Sergeant Purdy); Frank Faylen (Slim); J. Lewis Smith (Pete Brady); Lee Tung-Foo (Chinese Doctor).

New York Premiere: Capitol Theatre—August 27, 1942
New York Television Debut: CBS—September 7, 1958

## Synopsis

In 1941, Jonny and Kirk Davis are brothers who have gained reputations as war correspondents. They are ordered home by their ultra-conservative managing editor, George L. Stafford, who refuses to believe their dispatches about a war in the works. Back in the States, Jonny encounters Paula Lane, who is boarding with some old friends. Within seconds of introducing himself he has kissed her and she has reciprocated the gesture. Only later does he learn she is a former cub reporter who has had a deep crush on him for years, but who is now almost engaged to Kirk. Ever loyal to his brother, Jonny sets about to prove to Kirk just how fickle Paula really is. The brothers' conflict over Paula becomes worse and is climaxed when Paula calls off her relationship with Kirk since she is convinced that Jonny really wants to wed her. But when she is ordered to report on the Japanese infiltration of Indo-China, Jonny does not attempt to stop her from undertaking the dangerous mission. Later, the brothers are assigned to the Far East to report on the situation there. They come upon Paula on the war frontier smuggling Chinese babies to safety. The triangular romance explodes again and is continued on the shores of Bataan, that is, until Kirk is killed in action. Jonny writes a hero's account of his dead brother. At the end, Paula, by now a Red Cross nurse, remains with Jonny.

◆―◆―◆

"Mr. Gable and Miss Turner Are Kissing Again—
And Pulses Are Popping
And Lovers Are Sighing
And Turnstiles Are Turning
And Money Is Flowing In."

This was MGM's way of reporting to motion picture exhibitors the happy situation concerning *Somewhere I'll Find You*, the follow up to *Honky Tonk* in which Clark Gable and Lana Turner were reunited for the public's vicarious delight. (A project for Gable and Turner, entitled *Witch in the Wilderness*, was dropped from the co-players' roster in September, 1940.) To celebrate the return pairing, publicity-conscious Turner provided some new news copy. A year before she had divorced Artie Shaw and now she invited the press to be on hand when she had her famed long tresses cut into a "Victory Bob" for *Somehwere I'll Find You*.

Production on *Somewhere I'll Find You* began about a month after Pearl Harbor. Gable, as chairman of the Hollywood Victory Committee, assigned his wife, Carole Lombard, to a bond selling tour in Indiana. After selling over two million dollars worth of bonds there she sent Gable a telegram, "Pappy you'd better join this man's Army." She then boarded a TWA plane which, on January 16, 1942, crashed into Table Mountain, near Las Vegas. There were no survivors of this air tragedy. Gable went into seclusion at the Encino ranch, with production on *Somewhere I'll Find You* halted. For a time it seemed the project might be shelved completely. However,

Gable eventually returned to the set and the picture was finished.* By the time the movie was released, Gable had enlisted in the Air Force and was a corporal in the service of Uncle Sam. Before 1942 was out, Turner would marry Stephen Crane, husband number two.

*Somewhere I'll Find You* derives from a 1940 *Cosmopolitan* magazine story, updated to an October, 1941 topical setting and encompassing a very patriotic finish. The Marguerite Roberts' scenario wavers between semi-comedy and serious overtones, but the essence of the Wesley Ruggles-directed picture is not human motivation in the face of world crisis, but the ardent romance between Gable and Turner. After all, as Robert W. Dana (*New York Herald-Tribune*) decided, Gable and Turner " . . . are the most popular lovemakers on the screen today." *Somewhere I'll Find You* was geared to uphold their screen reputation in that regard.

At one point in this film, Robert Sterling, saddled with the "other boy" role of Kirk Davis, sums up the plotline quite aptly for Turner: "I'm for you, you're for Jonny, and Jonny's for himself." With this as a guideline, *Somewhere I'll Find You* smartly mixes together the two more recurrent themes in Gable pictures, i.e., the hero's regeneration into an honorable soul and his battle of the sexes with a self-willed leading lady. His screen persona, and this film is no exception, ends up a much different guy at the end of the storyline.

*Newsweek* magazine felt obliged to inform its readers that it now considered Gable and Turner the "screen's most provocative lovers" and this film certainly continued the commercial oncamera fabrication. (Obviously the morbid curiosity of filmgoers in witnessing how real life tragedy had affected Gable's onscreen performance boosted the boxoffice take on this celluloid venture.) As the 108-minute story moves from New York to Indo-China to Manila to Bataan, and the American forces combat the Japanese in bloody skirmishes, the twin stars meet in the most unlikely locales and proceed to promote, or avoid, their torrid plotline romance. They always tantalize the rapt viewer with the question: How and when (but not why) will the two vital animals evolve into their next passionate kleig lights clinch?

*Photoplay* magazine was one of the few contemporary sources to politely but openly chide the lightweight basis of *Somewhere I'll Find You*: "Only criticism is the over-abundance of kissing (yes, kissing) between the principals. Fun is fun but a girl can't kiss forever, you know."


### HOMECOMING
### (MGM, 1948) 113M.

Producer, Sidney Franklin; associate producer, Gottfried Reinhardt;

---

*Gable refused to allow producer Pandro S. Berman to doctor the script, insisting that the dialog dealing with death and heroism remain intact and that his bruised feelings need not be spared.

director, Mervyn LeRoy; story, Sidney Kingsley; adaptation, Jan Lustig; screenplay, Paul Osborn; art directors, Cedric Gibbons, Randall Duell; set decorator, Edwin B. Willis, Henry W. Grace; music, Bronislau Kaper; music director, Charles Previn; assistant director, Norman Elzer; makeup, Jack Dawn; costumes, Helen Rose; sound, Douglas Shearer, Norwood A. Fenton; technical adviser, Paul Lund; special effects, Warren Newcombe, A. Arnold Gillespie; camera, Harold Rosson; editor, John Dunning.

Clark Gable (Ulysses Delby Johnson); Lana Turner (Lt. Jane "Snapshot" McCall); Anne Baxter (Penny Johnson); John Hodiak (Dr. Robert Sunday); Ray Collins (Lt. Colonel Avoy Silver); Gladys Cooper (Mrs. Kirby); Cameron Mitchell (Monkevickz); Art Baker (Williams); Lurene Tuttle (Miss Stoker); Jessie Grayson (Sarah); J. Louis Johnson (Sol); Bill Self (Junior Lieutenant); Jeff Corey (Cigarette Smoker); Thomas E. Breen (Young Man); Wheaton Chambers (Doctor); Phil Dunham (Elevator Operator); Frank Mayo, Roger Moore, Dan Quigg, Broderick O'Farrell, George Sherwood, Charles Miller, Nolan Leary (Doctors); Kay Mansfield (Mrs. Lovette); Peggy Baday (Miss Simpson); William Forrest, Dorothy Christy, Anne Nagel (Guests); James Bush (Instructor); David Clark (Sergeant); Joseph Crehan (Colonel Morgan C.O.); Bert Moorhouse, David Newell (Surgeons); Johnny Albright (Corpsman); Arthur Space (Colonel Norton); Wally Cassell (Patient); Frances Pyle (Red Cross Field Worker); Vernon Downing (British Soldier); Danielle Day (Young French Girl); James Taggart, Jerry Jerome (Lieutenants); Alphonse Martel, George Offerman, Jr. (Clerks); Gaylord Pendleton (Orderly); Hobart Manning, Jay Norris (Officers); Lisa Golm (Anna); Geraldine Wall (Head Nurse); Marshall Thompson (Mac); Frank Arnold (Maitre d'Hotel); Leslie Dennison (British Colonel); Olga Borget (Newswoman); Francine Bordeau, Queenie Leonard, Virginia Keiley, Fern Eggen, Mary Joe Ellis, Mimi Doyle, Eloise Hardt (Nurses); Michael Kirby, Lew Smith (Corpsmen); Edwin Cooper (Head Surgeon); William Tannen (Attendant); Gregg Barton (Captain); Louise Colombet (Frenchwoman); Ralph Montgomery, Robert Skelton (G.I.s); Charles Meredith (Major); Arthur O'Connell (Driver); Alan Hale, Jr. (M.P.); Albert Pollet (Waiter); Jean LaFayette (Girl); Leo Vandervelde (Page Boy).

New York Premiere: Capitol Theatre—April 29, 1948
New York Television Debut: CBS—March 1, 1957

### Synopsis

Before the United States enters World War II, Dr. Ulysses Johnson is engaged in a successful New York society practice. He and his wife Penny have filled their lives with material possessions and a busy social existence, all in order to do the proper thing expected of people in their station of life. When Dr. Bob Sunday, Ulysses' former schoolmate, requests his aid in saving a small town from a disease epidemic, Ulysses claims he is too busy to help out at all. Then comes Pearl Harbor. Ulysses becomes a major in the Medical Corps, although he retains such a condescending manner toward his new tasks that Bob thinks of his friend as a self-centered waster. On the transport ship to Africa, Ulysses meets Lt. Jane "Snapshot" McCall, the nurse who will assist him in his medical work. During the first few months they quarrel constantly, but in reality, they are falling in love. Only when Ulysses has a rude awakening to his sham of a life does he view events and people in a new light. With this changed attitude he encounters Snapshot during a Paris leave of duty. They enjoy an idyllic week together, but then return to their medical chores on the front lines. Some months later, after Snapshot has died of injuries received at the Battle of the Bulge, Ulysses comes home. He is a different man, now anxious to start a fresh life with Penny and to join with Bob in his crusading medical work.

◆◆◆

When Clark Gable was discharged from military service in 1944 it was considered likely that he and Lana Turner would be rematched for yet another cinema bout, but she was then busy on other projects, and Louis B. Mayer, at the moment, was more intrigued with the potential of confronting Greer Garson, the screen's *Mrs. Miniver*, with filmdom's Rhett Butler. What resulted was *Adventure* (1945) whose slogan "Gable's Back and Garson's Got Him," has far outlived the film. The novelty of the movie's casting was sufficient to stimulate boxoffice business, but like Hollywood, Gable had changed in the war years and it was obvious to all viewers. He now looked tired, restless, and decidedly bored oncamera. His next film, *The Hucksters* (1947), which he had initially rejected, was a very competent if glossy study of the Madison Avenue situation with Gable as an ex-army officer doing battle in the executive suite with despicable advertiser Sydney Greenstreet and romancing a genteel English widow (Deborah Kerr). The film did much to reaffirm his movie star prestige.

While Gable had been away in the service, Turner had been very active on the MGM homefront. Most of her assignments were fluff such as *Marriage Is a Private Affair* (1944), but there was *Weekend at the Waldorf* (1945), a very plush remake of *Grand Hotel* (1932), and *The Postman Always Rings Twice* (1946), the latter containing what many consider her best film performance. *Green Dolphin Street* (1947) was sweeping, but empty, romantic period fiction, while *Cass Timberlane* (1947), based on the Sinclair Lewis novel, was far more noteworthy for Spencer Tracy's sterling performance than Turner's lovely presence. However, each was a big boxoffice grosser. During these same years Turner had been much in the gossip column news. She had given birth to a daughter, Cheryl, divorced Stephen Crane in 1944, and, in 1947, had conducted a rather explosive romance with Twentieth Century-Fox star Tyrone Power.

When the time finally came for Gable and Turner to be reunited on film, it was first touted that they would appear in *Lucky Baldwin*, but that project fell through, and, instead, the team starred in *Homecoming*, based on a Sidney Kingsley-conceived story. Producer Sidney Franklin, long one of MGM's most distinguished packagers, was in charge of the production while Mervyn LeRoy, who had helmed Turner's memorable *They Won't Forget*, was assigned to direct the movie.

Regarding the dramatic impact of *Homecoming, The Commonweal* complained, "The total effect of the film is no greater than those endless radio dramas that make you feel clean and comfortable with their soft soap." *Modern Screen* magazine complained, "Perhaps the main flaw in this Gable-Turner number is its lack of timeliness. The story of the war interrupted marriage is somewhat old hat, and yet it is too recent to be good nostalgia." *Modern Screen* was correct, for in point of fact there was little guts to the bland film which seemed overly intent on reassuring middle American womanhood that philandering husbands would and did return from the war ready to pick up the threads of normalcy with their patient, waiting wives.

The chief point of storyline interest to this mediocre, exploitive film was the inevitable visual answer to the question of how Gable and Turner would perform together after their long professional separation. Alton Cook *(New York World-Telegram)* summed up the situation: "Lana and Clark have been over this ground often enough to make any further comment on their conduct superfluous. Clark stomps through the picture in his old boisterous, impetuous style and Lana once more spends a good deal of her time staring vacantly at him in open-mouthed amazement."

But the hordes of Gable-Turner fans were unheedful of the consistently bad reviews given *Homecoming* (it was branded one of the year's ten worst films by New York film critics), and flocked to the theatre to reacquaint themselves with the 1940s duo champs of sex appeal. While a good deal of footage was devoted to demonstrating the heroic work of doctors and nurses in the front lines during the war, there was enough tantalizing soon-to-explode magnetism between the two stars to please the majority of *Homecoming* viewers.

For the record, Anne Baxter, on loanout from Twentieth Century-Fox, was in real life wed to MGM's John Hodiak. She looked particularly fetching with her new slimmed-down figure, but unfortunately *Homecoming* presented her with the uninteresting assignment as the understanding wife who learns a new set of values herself while her husband is at war.

Gable and Turner repeated their *Homecoming* characterizations on "Screen Guild Playhouse" on January 6, 1949.

# BETRAYED
## *(MGM, 1954) C-107M.*

Director, Gottfried Reinhardt; screenplay, Ronald Millar, George Froeschel; music, Walter Goehr; camera, F. A. Young; editors, John Dunning, Raymond Poulton.

Clark Gable (Colonel Pieter Deventer); Lana Turner (Carla Van Oven); Victor Mature (The Scarf); Louis Calhern (General Ten Eyck); O. E. Hasse (Colonel Helmut Dietrich); Wilfrid Hyde White (General Charles Larraby); Ian Carmichael (Captain Jackie Lawson); Niall Mac-Ginnis (Blackie); Nora Swinburne (The Scarf's Mother); Roland Culver (General Warsleigh); Leslie Weston (Pop); Christopher Rhodes (Chris); Lilly Kann (Jan's Grandmother); Brian Smith (Jan); Anton Diffring (Captain Von Stranger).

New York Premiere: Loew's State Theatre—September 8, 1954
New York Television Debut: NBC—February 13, 1965

### Synopsis

Dutch intelligence officer Colonel Pieter Deventer is rescued from the Germans in 1943 and aided in reaching England by a Resistance leader known only as "The Scarf." London military officials decide to dispatch a radio operator to work with "The Scarf," and Pieter finds himself choosing, training, and romancing Carla Van Oven, who had previously collaborated with the Nazis and is now eager to redeem her besmirched reputation. Shortly after Carla's arrival in Holland, "The Scarf's" compact forces begin suffering heavy casualties, as their raiding parties are ambushed by Germans. Pieter appears on the scene to investigate, suspecting that Carla is the culprit, although she is convinced that "The Scarf" himself is the traitor. It develops that "The Scarf" is insanely devoted to his youngish mother, and when she had been falsely branded as a German collaborator, he had vowed revenge. Later, Carla is trapped in Arnhem with the English forces. Pieter, now realizing "The Scarf's" true nature, tricks him into providing data of a secret escape path. "The Scarf" is killed, and almost miraculously, Carla and the British soldiers emerge safely from Arnhem.

◆◆◆

After his vapid society doctor role in *Homecoming*, Clark Gable was handed the starring assignment in *Command Decision* (1948), based on the Broadway play that had featured Paul Kelly. If the role of the flight commander seemed a little beyond his acting depth, Gable made a valiant try, displaying a mature acting style that should have indicated to MGM the proper channeling of their boxoffice champ. There were plans to reunite Gable and Lana Turner* in *To Please a Lady* (1950), but Barbara Stanwyck took the distaff role in that race driver story, while MGM finally balked at touted plans to loan Gable and Turner to Columbia for *Born Yesterday* (1950). *Across the Wide Missouri* and *Lone Star* (1952) returned Gable to the Western genre which he had abandoned after *The Painted Desert* (1931). The trite *Never Let Me Go* (1953) tried to duplicate *Comrade X* (1940) but without the saving grace of a Hedy Lamarr or of any slapstick humor. Just when it seemed Gable's screen career was reaching a permanent low ebb, he was starred with Grace Kelly and Ava Gardner (she replaced Turner) in *Mogambo* (1953), the John Ford-directed remake of *Red Dust* (1932). It would prove such a substantial moneymaker that MGM and studio chief Dore Schary would earnestly regret having terminated Gable's contract in 1954 following *Betrayed*.

*Betrayed* was originally intended to pair Gable once again with Ava Gardner, but as the shooting schedule worked out, it was Turner who emerged as Gable's co-star in this unsubtle spy picture. Since *Homecoming* Turner had glided through the costumed froufrou of *The Three Musketeers* (1948) and *The Merry Widow* (1952), but offered a strong performance in the Hollywood-set *The Bad and the Beautiful* (1952). As usual, Turner's offcamera escapades had garnered more interesting speculation than the shape and depth of her movie career. She had wed and divorced Bob Topping and before marrying *Tarzan* actor Lex Barker in 1953, had passed through a torrid love affair with her *The Merry Widow* co-star, Fernando Lamas.

By the time *Betrayed* was released, Gable was a tired fifty-four-year-old man, and Turner was brunette and thirty-three. As one wag described the veteran love team's oncamera chemistry in their new picture, "Clark Gable kisses Lana Turner like a husband with a hangover." The screen rapport that made *Honky Tonk* and *Somewhere I'll Find You* exceedingly enjoyable audience adventures was gone, and not even the novelty of on location filming in Holland in widescreen, color photography could salvage this lacklustre caper. *Variety* unhappily reported, " . . . the picture unfolds as a confused, often dull, meller burdened with a running time of one hour and 47 minutes." Or as the *Detroit News'* Al Weitschat phrased it, "The authenticity of the scenery is not matched by what goes on in front of it." It was an unlucky thirteen years that separated *Betrayed* from *Honky Tonk*, and now in 1954, Karl Krug *(Pittsburg Sun-Telegraph)* would be obliged to admit that at the *Betrayed* opening at Loew's Penn Theatre in downtown Pittsburgh, "The customers were snickering in the wrong places. . . . "

The preposterous plot situations within *Betrayed* were certainly duplicated by the time-trodden dialog the unwilling cast was forced to speak.

---

*One MGM cartoon of the 1940s, set on a farm, depicted characters called Clark Gobble and Lana Turnip.

Gable: "Why did you come [to England]?"
Turner: "Because I wanted to get into the war."
Gable: "How much of yourself would *you* be willing to give?"

Later, when Gable and Turner meet again in Holland and he confronts her with his suspicions of her disloyalty to the Allied cause, she blurts out, "But surely . . . *you* don't think I betrayed them?" He does, and it takes the remainder of the film for Gable's suspicions to be allayed, just in time for a rousing reunion with Turner after the incredible Arnhem incident.

Ironically, Victor Mature, always more famed for his chesty physique than his emoting, far outshone Gable and Turner with his characterization of the intense, sneering underground leader, who, it develops, has an almost pathological love for his mom (Nora Swinburne).

## THE YEARS AFTER

Following the debacle of *Betrayed*, Clark Gable, much embittered by MGM's tart contract severance, turned to freelancing and in the remaining seven years of his life starred in nine features. They included the solid Western *The Tall Men* (1955) with Jane Russell, and a trio of May-December screen romances, *Teacher's Pet* (1958) with Doris Day, *But Not for Me* (1959) with Carroll Baker, and *It Started in Naples* (1960) with Sophia Loren. What proved to be his last movie was *The Misfits* (1961) a contemporary Western written by Arthur Miller as a starring vehicle for his wife, Marilyn Monroe. Before the film was released, Gable, once King of Hollywood, was dead, not even living long enough to witness the birth of his first child, John, a result of his marriage to Kay Spreckels.

Lana Turner remained at MGM for another year after *Betrayed* but neither *The Prodigal* nor *Diane*, both costume yarns released by Metro in 1955, enhanced her faltering status in the industry or with the public. Ironically it was the combination of a good screen performance and a shocking scandal which pushed her back into the top of the movie big leagues. Just at the time freelancer Turner was appearing on movie screens around the country as Constance MacKenzie, the star of Twentieth Century-Fox's *Peyton Place* (1957), headlines were carrying the news of the killing of gangster Johnny Stompanato by her daughter Cheryl. She lost the Best Actress Oscar to Joanne Woodward of *The Three Faces of Eve*, but she insured for herself another go-round as a movie leading lady. Producer Ross Hunter invited her to headline a new, gaudy rendition of the hoary tearjerker, *Imitation of Life* (1959) which proved to be a larger grosser than the original, leading Hunter to feature her in the less successful *Portrait in Black* (1960) and *Madame X* (1966). In 1970 Turner co-starred in a super-inflated television soap opera, "The Survivors," but this "adult" fare was so tepid it quickly faded from the video scene. By

1971 Turner was in the process of divorcing her seventh husband, and, being at professional and emotional liberty, she made her stage debut in a tour of *Forty Carats*, displaying more beauty, charm, and acting technique than one would have dared to hope for in the fifty-one-year-old sex goddess. More years passed, more announced screen projects evaporated, and then in 1974 she returned to the cinema in a British-made picture, *Persecution*. On the set she was still very much *the* Lana Turner of old.

Reviewing the quartet of features Gable and Turner made together at MGM, none of these pictures can be said to be anything more than adequate entertainment. While Turner remained languid, cool and beautiful in each of these exercises, Gable, in at least the first two of their joint pictures, responded to her youth and pulchritude, raising his famed masculine sexuality to the level of his early Joan Crawford and Jean Harlow pictures. For today's generation, unfamiliar with the more stringent mores of World War II days, the onscreen romancing of Gable-Turner might seem somewhat tame and unworthy of special comment, but for those with an appreciation of understated animal sensuality, the celluloid combination of Gable and Turner holds a special place of merit, in which two fine specimens collide, caress, and create a combustible charisma.

In **State of the Union** (MGM, 1948)

# Chapter 19

# Spencer Tracy
# & 
# Katharine Hepburn

## SPENCER TRACY

5' 10½"
165 pounds
Brown hair
Blue eyes
Aries

*Real name: same. Born April 5, 1900, Milwaukee, Wisconsin. Married Louise Treadwell (1928), children: John, Susan. Died June 10, 1967.*

FEATURE FILMS:

Up the River (Fox, 1930)
Quick Millions (Fox, 1931)
Six Cylinder Love (Fox, 1931)
She Wanted a Millionaire (Fox, 1932)
Sky Devils (UA, 1932)
Disorderly Conduct (Fox, 1932)
Young America (Fox, 1932)
Society Girl (Fox, 1932)
Painted Woman (Fox, 1932)
Me and My Gal (Fox, 1932)
20,000 Years in Sing Sing (WB, 1933)
Face in the Sky (Fox, 1933)
Shanghai Madness (Fox, 1933)
The Power and the Glory (Fox, 1933)
The Mad Game (Fox, 1933)
Man's Castle (Col., 1933)
Looking for Trouble (UA, 1934)
The Show-off (MGM, 1934)
Bottoms Up (Fox, 1934)
Now I'll Tell (Fox, 1934)
Marie Galante (Fox, 1934)
It's a Small World (Fox, 1935)
Murder Man (MGM, 1935)
Dante's Inferno (Fox, 1935)
Whipsaw (MGM, 1935)
Riffraff (MGM, 1935)
Fury (MGM, 1936)
San Francisco (MGM, 1936)
Libeled Lady (MGM, 1936)
They Gave Him a Gun (MGM, 1937)

Captains Courageous (MGM, 1937)
Big City (MGM, 1937)
Mannequin (MGM, 1938)
Test Pilot (MGM, 1938)
Boys Town (MGM, 1938)
Stanley and Livingstone (20th, 1939)
I Take This Woman (MGM, 1940)
Northwest Passage (MGM, 1940)
Edison, the Man (MGM, 1940)
Boom Town (MGM, 1940)
Men of Boys Town (MGM, 1941)
Dr. Jekyll and Mr. Hyde (MGM, 1941)
Woman of the Year (MGM, 1942)
Tortilla Flat (MGM, 1942)
Keeper of the Flame (MGM, 1942)
A Guy Named Joe (MGM, 1943)
The Seventh Cross (MGM, 1944)
Thirty Seconds Over Tokyo (MGM, 1944)
Without Love (MGM, 1945)
The Sea of Grass (MGM, 1947)
Cass Timberlane (MGM, 1947)
State of the Union (MGM, 1948)

Edward, My Son (MGM, 1949)
Adam's Rib (MGM, 1949)
Malaya (MGM, 1950)
Father of the Bride (MGM, 1950)
Father's Little Dividend (MGM, 1951)
The People Against O'Hara (MGM, 1951)
Pat and Mike (MGM, 1952)
Plymouth Adventure (MGM, 1952)
The Actress (MGM, 1953)
Broken Lance (20th, 1954)
Bad Day at Black Rock (MGM, 1954)
The Mountain (Par., 1956)
Desk Set (20th, 1957)
The Old Man and the Sea (WB, 1958)
The Last Hurrah (Col., 1958)
Inherit the Wind (UA, 1960)
The Devil at Four O'Clock (Col., 1961)
Judgment at Nuremberg (UA, 1961)
It's a Mad, Mad, Mad, Mad World (UA, 1963)
Guess Who's Coming to Dinner (Col., 1967)

# KATHARINE HEPBURN

**5' 7"**
**110 pounds**
**Brown hair**
**Blue eyes**
**Scorpio**

*Real name: Katharine Houghton Hepburn. Born November 9, 1907, Hartford, Connecticut. Married Ludlow Ogden Smith (1928); divorced 1934.*

FEATURE FILMS:

A Bill of Divorcement (RKO, 1932)
Christopher Strong (RKO, 1933)
Morning Glory (RKO, 1933)
Little Women (RKO, 1933)
Spitfire (RKO, 1934)
The Little Minister (RKO, 1934)

Break of Hearts (RKO, 1935)
Alice Adams (RKO, 1935)
Sylvia Scarlett (RKO, 1935)
Mary of Scotland (RKO, 1936)
A Woman Rebels (RKO, 1936)
Quality Street (RKO, 1937)

Stage Door (RKO, 1937)
Bringing Up Baby (RKO, 1938)
Holiday (Col., 1938)
The Philadelphia Story (MGM, 1940)
Woman of the Year (MGM, 1942)
Keeper of the Flame (MGM, 1942)
Stage Door Canteen (UA, 1943)
Dragon Seed (MGM, 1944)
Without Love (MGM, 1945)
Undercurrent (MGM, 1946)
The Sea of Grass (MGM, 1947)
Song of Love (MGM, 1947)
State of the Union (MGM, 1948)
Adam's Rib (MGM, 1949)
The African Queen (UA, 1951)
Pat and Mike (MGM, 1952)

Summertime (UA, 1955)
The Rainmaker (Par., 1956)
The Iron Petticoat (MGM, 1956)
Desk Set (20th, 1957)
Suddenly, Last Summer (Col., 1959)
Long Day's Journey into Night (Emb., 1962)
Guess Who's Coming to Dinner (Col., 1967)
The Lion in Winter (Emb., 1968)
The Madwoman of Chaillot (WB-7 Arts, 1968)
The Trojan Women (Cin., 1971)
A Delicate Balance (American Film Theatre, 1973)
Rooster Cogburn (Univ., 1975)

In Guess Who's Coming to Dinner (Col., 1967)

Katharine Hepburn, Spencer Tracy, and Michael Visaroff in **Woman of the Year** (MGM, 1942)

In **Keeper of the Flame** (MGM, 1942)

In **Without Love** (MGM, 1945)

In **The Sea of Grass** (MGM, 1947)

Advertisement for **Adam's Rib** (MGM, 1949)

In Adam's Rib

Barry Norton (foreground), Sammy White, Spencer Tracy, Lou Lubin, Katharine Hepburn, and Owen McGiveney in **Pat and Mike** (MGM, 1952)

In **Desk Set** (20th, 1957)

# WOMAN OF THE YEAR
## *(MGM, 1942) 112M.*

Producer, Joseph L. Mankiewicz; director, George Stevens; screenplay, Ring Lardner, Jr., Michael Kanin; art directors, Cedric Gibbons, Randall Duell; set decorator, Edwin B. Willis; music, Franz Waxman; costumes, Adrian; makeup, Jack Dawn; assistant director, Robert Golden; sound, Douglas Shearer; camera, Joseph Ruttenberg; editor, Frank Sullivan.

Spencer Tracy (Sam Craig); Katharine Hepburn (Tess Harding); Fay Bainter (Ellen Whitcomb); Reginald Owen (Clayton); Minor Watson (William Harding); William Bendix (Pinkie Peters); Gladys Blake (Flo Peters); Dan Tobin (Gerald); Roscoe Karns (Phil Whittaker); William Tannen (Ellis); Ludwig Stossel (Dr. Martin Lubbeck); Sara Haden (Matron at Refugee Home); Edith Evanson (Alma); George Kezas (Chris); Henry Roquemore (Justice of the Peace); Cyril Ring (Harding's Chauffeur); Ben Lessy (Punchy); Johnny Berkes (Pal); Duke York (Football Player); Winifred Harris (Chairlady); Joe Yule (Building Superintendent); Edward McWade (Adolph); William Holmes (Man at Banquet); Jimmy Conlin, Ray Teal (Reporters); Michael Visaroff (Guest).

New York Premiere: Capitol Theatre—February 5, 1942
New York Television Debut: CBS—September 9, 1957

### Synopsis

Sam Craig, the rugged sportswriter for a major New York newspaper, is more than annoyed when Tess Harding, a diplomat's daughter and the international affairs columnist for the same newspaper, makes a sneering remark on an "Information Please" radio broadcast. She states that the game of baseball should be abolished for the duration of the war. The two begin a feud through their columns, but when they actually meet and talk, Sam is immediately attracted to Tess. Much to the amazement of their mutual friends, they are soon married, seemingly proving that opposites attract. But their domestic life is a shambles, for each has very different ideas on the responsibilities of matrimony. Ironically, on the very day Tess begins to comprehend her failures as a wife, she is selected as the Woman of the Year. When her father, William Harding, reweds, Tess carefully listens to the wedding vows and with new understanding she intends to make a go of her marriage to Sam.

◆━━━◆

Ex-RKO cinema star Katharine Hepburn, a unique commodity in the Hollywood of the 1930s, and an Oscar winner for *Morning Glory* (1933), found herself labeled boxoffice poison in 1938, but licked the potential total collapse of her screen career by returning to Broadway in *The Philadelphia Story* (1939), a comedy specifically written for her by Philip Barry. She parlayed her stage triumph into a cinema comeback, demanding and receiving very favorable terms from MGM's Louis B. Mayer. The picturization of *The Philadelphia Story* (1940) proved even more popular than the Broadway original, earning Hepburn an Academy Award nomination. (She lost the Best Actress Award to another ex-RKO star, Ginger Rogers of *Kitty Foyle*.)

After completing *The Philadelphia Story*, Hepburn embarked on a national tour with the play, but then needed a new screen vehicle to perpetuate her cinema career. At this point, director-producer Garson Kanin had Ring Lardner, Jr. and Michael Kanin (Garson's brother) approach Hepburn with their original screenplay which they believed would be ideal for her. She was very impressed with the scenario and took it upon herself to sell the property to MGM at a tidy fee for the young authors. She demanded and received director and co-star approval. Her first choice was director George Cukor, but he was then at work on Greta Garbo's *Two-Faced Woman* (1941). So she "settled" for George Stevens who had guided her so expertly through *Alice Adams* (1935). For her screen vis-a-vis, Hepburn felt there could be no one else but Spencer Tracy, as the part of the sports columnist in the screenplay fit his movie image perfectly. (This was no accident since Garson Kanin, was a pal, separately, of both Hepburn and Tracy, and Lardner, Jr. was the son of a Tracy friend.) However, two-time Oscar winner Tracy was then on location in Florida for *The Yearling*. But production difficulties arose on that filming, the project was shelved and forty-one-year-old Tracy proved fortuitously available.

Before the two strong personalities first went onto the set of *Woman of the Year*, they carefully studied each other's past film work. Hepburn was particularly interested in observing how the ex-Fox leading player of the early 1930s had refined his screen technique since coming to Metro in the 1930s. A player like Tracy, who, in one year (1941), could essay the Father Flannagan figure in *Men of Boys Town* and then go on to star in a remake of *Dr. Jekyll and Mr. Hyde*, obviously had great versatility. The story has often been repeated of how, after the two headstrong stars first met°, Hepburn turned to producer Joseph L. Mankiewicz and said, "I'm afraid I'm a bit tall [5′ 7″] for Mr. Tracy [5′ 10½″]. Mankiewicz tersely replied, "Don't worry. He'll cut you down to size."

Actually each performer did a great deal to temper the screen (and private) personality of the other, leading the critics and public alike to reevaluate their capabilities. Mankiewicz said of the *Woman of the Year* filmmaking, "They seemed to be copying each other's style of acting. I've never seen Katharine act so spontaneous or Spencer give such a polished

°Interestingly, in 1938 Hepburn and Tracy had been characterized in a joint scene in Walt Disney's Mickey Mouse cartoon, *Mother Goose Goes Hollywood*.

performance." James Agee reported in *Time* magazine, "Actors Hepburn and Tracy have a fine old time in *Woman of the Year*. They take turns playing straight for each other, act one superbly directed love scene, succeed in turning several batches of cinematic corn into passable moonshine. As a lady columnist, she is just right; as a working reporter, he is practically perfect."

Although *Woman of the Year* moves along its 112-minute course quite leisurely, the beauty of the film is that each segment of the comedy has an almost self-contained unity unto itself, which allows the viewer repeatedly to gauge freshly the newly-revealed charms of the co-players. Thus we have the memorable baseball game scene in which Sam Craig (Tracy) breaks tradition by allowing a woman—this was pre-Women's Lib —to sit in the writers' box. He is determined to show Tess Harding (Hepburn) that baseball, contrary to her belief, is one of the basic things for which America is fighting in World War II. Soon Hepburn, in her wide brim white garden hat, is being taught the finer points of the game she had so quickly dismissed before. Tracy points out that a "good" ball must pass between the batter's knees and shoulders. "If the batter were smart," she says, "he'd stoop down and fool the pitcher." How can a guy win with that kind of logic?

Later the two columnists end their publicized feud when Hepburn sends him a bottle of brandy. Having reached a truce, the two news gatherers find themselves at Pinkie's quaint bar, an emporium run by William Bendix, where Miss Newslady soon imbibes more than she can safely handle. The liquor takes its effect, but she babbles on, discussing the philosophy of Spengler and explaining to Tracy that as a diplomat's daughter she met too many famous people in her youth, and it turned her head. The alcohol finally does its worst as Hepburn has drunk herself under the table.

Most men like to believe they are the chief honchos on their wedding day, but Tracy is easily outdistanced at his nuptials in *Woman of the Year*. They have gone south—to Macinock, South Carolina—hoping her father (Minor Watson) could attend the ceremony. After the justice of the peace performs the legally binding words, what happens to the efficient bride? She has rushed to the telephone to call New York and discuss more pressing matters, such as the status of a V.I.P. refugee Yugoslavian statesman. Once back in Manhattan, Tracy and Hepburn don't even have their wedding night to themselves. Hepburn promptly involves herself in a conference with the refugee, spouting away in German, while neglected Tracy slumps in a corner abjectly waiting to be remembered. Later, in the bridal chambers, the statesman's friends arrive to congratulate him for his escape from the Nazis. This is too much for Tracy. He quickly telephones his sports-loving pals at Pinkie's Bar and invites them to join the "party." Then Tracy and Hepburn retire to the sidelines to watch the mixture of guests interact.

Hepburn's Tess is really a combination Dorothy Thompson, Clare Boothe, and Tracy Lord (of *The Philadelphia Story*). She is so agog with her self-conception as the only person really capable of straightening out the tangled international scene that she has no place for any concrete thoughts about her floundering marriage. Meanwhile Tracy indulges himself in naive ideas about quiet nights at home and a batch of little kids. Imagine his joy when Hepburn informs him she is going to have a baby.

Tracy: "I hope it's a boy."

Hepburn: "It's a boy." Then she calls in Chris (George Kezas) a Greek refugee she has adopted (but whom she will soon ignore in her rush of productive activity). As for having children of her own, Hepburn admits, "it's impractical."

Within this picture, the Tracy-Hepburn marriage soon falls apart, making Hepburn's winning of the woman of the year award a most dubious distinction. When Ellen Whitcomb (Fay Bainter) presents the honor to the woman "who so magnificently symbolizes the full and rounded life," Hepburn realizes she has much to learn to live up to the accolade. Later, when trying to patch up the broken union, Hepburn discovers that although she may be a whiz with teletype machines and transatlantic telephones, she is all thumbs when it comes to being domestic in a terrifyingly modern kitchen. The eggs go asunder in the mixer, the coffee boils over in the pot, the bread continually launches out of the toaster, and the waffle batter has more yeast than Fleischmann's factory. It is a visual scene one would expect to be suited to the like of Lucille Ball, but Hepburn displays the same fine screen sense for slapstick she had shown in Howard Hawk's *Bringing Up Baby* (1938), and carries off the situation with éclat.

Perhaps Eileen Creelman *(New York Sun)* best summed up the essence of the screen chemistry between Tracy and Hepburn, "The cast is brilliant, with Spencer Tracy's steady, skillful, quietly humorous characterization, contrasted with Katharine Hepburn's tense, rather shrill portrait of an egotistic woman."

Hepburn was Oscar-nominated for her trend-breaking role of *Woman of the Year,* but lost to Greer Garson of MGM's *Mrs. Miniver.*

In the spring of 1943, Tracy and Hepburn performed a half-hour rendition of *Woman of the Year* on Radio's "Screen Guild Theatre." It was their sole professional sojourn together beyond their feature filmmaking and an American Cancer Society movie short in 1946.

## KEEPER OF THE FLAME
### *(MGM, 1942) 100M.*

Producer, Victor Saville; associate producer, Leon Gordon; director, George Cukor; based on the novel by I. A. R. Wylie; screenplay, Donald Ogden Stewart; art directors, Cedric Gibbons, Lyle Wheeler; set decorators, Edwin B. Willis, Jack Moore; sound, Douglas Shearer; costumes, Adrian; music, Bronislau Kaper; makeup, Jack Dawn; assistant director, Edward Woehler; special effects, Warren Newcombe; camera, William Daniels; editor, James E. Newcom.

Spencer Tracy (Steven O'Malley); Katharine Hepburn (Christine Forrest); Richard Whorf (Clive Kerndon); Margaret Wycherly (Mrs. Forrest); Donald Meek (Mr. Arbuthnot); Stephen McNally (Freddie Ridges); Audrey Christie (Jane Harding); Frank Craven (Dr. Fielding); Forrest Tucker (Geoffrey Midford); Percy Kilbride (Orion); Howard DaSilva (Jason Richards); Darryl Hickman (Jeb Richards); William Newell (Piggot); Rex Evans (John); Blanche Yurka (Anna); Mary McLeod (Janet); Clifford Brooke (William); Craufurd Kent (Ambassador); Mickey Martin (Messenger Boy); Manart Kippen, Donald Gallaher, Cliff Danielson (Reporters); Jay Ward (Pete); Rita Quigley (Susan); Major Sam Harris, Art Howard, Harold Miller (Men); Dick Elliott (Auctioneer); Edward McWade (Lawyer); Irvin Lee (Boy Reporter); Diana Douglas, Gloria Tucker (Girls); Robert Pittard (Tim); Louis Mason (Gardener); Dr. Charles Frederick Lindsley (Minister's Voice).

New York Premiere: Radio City Music Hall—March 28, 1943
New York Television Debut: CBS—April 1, 1957

### Synopsis

When Steven O'Malley, a respected war correspondent returns from Europe, his newspaper assigns him to write a feature story on the death of Robert V. Forrest, an American national hero who was killed when his car ran off an open bridge. The widow, Christine Forrest, has been cloistered from the general press, but when Steven informs her he is planning a biography that will perpetuate her husband's memory, she agrees to help on the research project. Later Steven overhears a conversation between Christine and Jeb Richards, the gateman's son, which suggests that she played a part in her husband's tragic accident. Only later, after much prodding, does Christine reveal enough to convince Steven that Forrest's alleged super patriotism was really a shield for his fascist activities, and that once she learned the horrendous truth, she had been motivated by love of country not to warn him of the bridge's condition. Although Steven has come to love Christine, he feels he must reveal the truth to America. This conviction is consolidated when he and she are trapped in a burning building and she dies. Steven publishes the facts, revealing Forrest's true nature while praising Christine for her right-mindedness.

◆■◆■◆

After the commercially and artistically exhilarating experience of *Woman of the Year*, it might be imagined that MGM would have immediately reteamed Spencer Tracy and Katharine Hepburn in another movie vehicle, insuring that the new cinema couple° were firmly im-

° Hepburn had divorced her first and only husband, Ludlow Ogden Smith in 1934. Tracy, married to Louise Treadwell since 1928, was the father of two children, John and Susan.

544

printed on the public's minds as another great celluloid romantic team in the tradition of the studio's Greer Garson and Walter Pidgeon, Mickey Rooney and Judy Garland, and Clark Gable and Lana Turner. But Hepburn was, is and always shall be a fiercely independent soul, and she was determined to return to the New York stage, this time in *Without Love*, an offbeat romantic comedy written especially for her by Philip Barry. After a two-month pre-Broadway tour in the spring of 1942, the playwright decided the show needed drastic revising and the star returned to Hollywood. Tracy, whose age would keep him from military service in World War II, meanwhile had starred with Hedy Lamarr and John Garfield in an adaptation of John Steinbeck's *Tortilla Flat* (1942) at Metro.

Tracy-Hepburn chronicler-pal Garson Kanin once asked Tracy why he insisted on first billing in his joint screen work with Hepburn, particularly since they were such close friends off the set.

"Why not," said Tracy.

Kanin: "Well, after all she's the lady. You're the man. Ladies first?"

Tracy: "This is a movie, chowderhead, not a lifeboat." It spoke a great deal about the professional rapport between the two superstars onscreen, eager to respect each other, but insistent on protecting his/her best interest. (It was a situation that would gradually modify over the years as Hepburn became increasingly devoted to smoothing out the path of Tracy's troubled professional and private life.)

For their second co-starring cinema vehicle, the studio selected I. A. R. Wylie's novel *Keeper of the Flame*, which, like their later *The Sea of Grass* (1947), would be a rare movie excursion into other areas than sophisticated give-and-take for the two luminaries. The story here dealt with a rather daring topic, especially in 1942 Hollywood, for its premise revolved around the possibility of fascism becoming a reality in America with a dictator taking over the country. Donald Ogden Stewart, who had scripted Hepburn's *Holiday* (1938) at Columbia, and *The Philadelphia Story*, was assigned to whip Wylie's novel into screen shape. Stewart later stated he did his upmost not to change the book's vital message, and, in fact, joined in the "conspiracy" to keep very Republican Louis B. Mayer from learning the actual contents of the picture. (A story has it that the first time the MGM chief saw *Keeper of the Flame* was at Radio City Music Hall and that he became so upset at the picture's blatant message that he stormed out of the theatre. Says Stewart, "I can't vouch for it [the story] but I'd be very happy if it were true.")

Perhaps if *Keeper of the Flame* had been produced a few years earlier it would have been more timely. But by late 1942, the United States had been in World War II for nearly a year, and the film's thesis in which isolationists as well as arrant traitors are taken to task, seemed peculiarly dated and hollow. As Howard Barnes (*New York Herald-Tribune*) offered, "From the standpoint of psychological melodrama, the new Music Hall offering is more successful than it is as a battle-cry of democracy." This consensus of opinion on the George Cukor-directed feature made the studio's publicity campaign seem all the more inappropriate: "Why is *Keeper of the Flame* the year's great emotional drama? Because it is timely . . . thrilling . . . different—with star performances."

If Tracy and Hepburn had seemingly adjusted to one another's unique acting styles while creating *Woman of the Year, Keeper of the Flame* proved that Hepburn still had an abiding and uncontrollable urge to be running the entire show. Constantly on the set, she would "interpret" to Cukor just how a scene should be properly played, where Tracy should stand, or how she should react at a given moment. Finally during the course of lensing the important fire scene, Cukor could stand no more of her genius and told his very good friend Hepburn, "It must be wonderful to know all about acting *and* all about fires."

Ironically, while *Keeper of the Flame* would prove to be Hepburn's final oncamera romantic young heroine part—albeit a strange girl at that —she and Tracy share no real love scenes together in this film. Everything about her appearance in the movie, including William Daniels' unflattering photography, emphasizes the fact that somehow she and character Christine Forrest have not come to grips with one another. On the other hand, Tracy, as the dogged reporter who is determined to reveal the truth about the revered late national hero, is staunchly firm in his truth-seeker's role, displaying a new variation of the newsman he had portrayed in *Woman of the Year* [or for that matter in *Libeled Lady* (1936) or *Stanley and Livingston* (1939)].

The public was definitely not prepared for the likes of *Keeper of the Flame*, with its Citizen Kane-like theme and its sombre message which threw a harsh spotlight of hatred on a rather common type of American. Kate Cameron in her 2½-star *New York Daily News* review labeled the film "propaganda drivel" and insisted the picture was a near dud for building up to such a terrific let-down. John T. McManus *(PM)* panned the production for "so many digressions, so much arty acting by Katharine Hepburn and glamour-girl direction by George Cukor, that when it finally blurts out its truths, they are too bald, too unbuilt-up, to have lasting meaning for all."

While the Tracy-Hepburn combination buoyed, if but briefly, *Keeper of the Flame* at the national boxoffice, it did nothing to enhance their silver screen careers. "Tracy, the dependable, looks so full of integrity that he could pose for an official portrait of George Washington, . . . that's good, but not exciting. Miss Hepburn, in sequences when she is supposed to have lost her joie de vive, sounds like a flat-footed imitation of her own worst self. The rest of the time she sounds better, but she hasn't much chance to get under your skin" [Archer Winsten *(New York Post)*].

For the record, *Keeper of the Flame*, was the only Tracy-Hepburn film in which the actress dies oncamera. Perhaps because she always seems so vital and resilient onscreen, the death scene smacks of the phony, particularly when Hepburn is forced to mouth a raft of trite prose as she lies dying. Having been shot by her late husband's confidential secretary (Richard Whorf), she is caught within a burning house. Tracy rushes to the dying woman's side. As the breath of life dribbles from her body, she whispers to him, "Write your story. Don't spare Robert. Don't spare me." He, of course, follows her sage advice.

## WITHOUT LOVE
### *(MGM, 1945) 111M.*

Producer, Lawrence A. Weingarten; director, Harold S. Bucquet; based on the play by Philip Barry; screenplay, Donald Ogden Stewart; art directors, Cedric Gibbons, Harry McAfee; set decorators, Edwin B. Willis, McLean Nisbet; music, Bronislau Kaper; assistant director, Earl McEvoy; makeup, Jack Dawn; montage, Peter Ballbusch; costumes, Irene, Marion Herwood Keyes; sound, Douglas Shearer; special effects, A. Arnold Gillespie, Danny Hall; camera, Karl Freund; editor, Frank Sullivan.

Spencer Tracy (Pat Jamieson); Katharine Hepburn (Jamie Rowan); Lucille Ball (Kitty Trimble); Keenan Wynn (Quentin Ladd); Carl Esmond (Paul Carrell); Patricia Morison (Edwina Collins); Felix Bressart (Professor Grinza); Emily Massey (Anna); Gloria Grahame (Flower Girl); George Davis (Caretaker); George Chandler (Elevator Boy); Clancy Cooper (Sergeant); Wallis Clark (Professor Thompson); Donald Curtis (Professor Ellis); Charles Arnt (Colonel Braden); Eddie Acuff (Driver); Clarence Muse (Porter); Franco Corsaro (Headwaiter); Ralph Brooks (Pageboy); William Forrest (Doctor); Garry Owen, Joe Devlin, William Newell (Soldiers); James Flavin (Sergeant); Hazel Brooks (Girl on Elevator).

New York Premiere: Radio City Music Hall—March 22, 1945
New York Television Debut: CBS—June 22, 1957

### Synopsis

Attractive widow Jamie Rowan owns a spacious home in overcrowded Washington, D.C. Experimental scientist Pat Jamieson, who is having great difficulties coping with the housing shortage in the capital, urgently requires a place where he can conduct his experiments on a new aeronautical oxygen helmet. Cooperative Jamie suggests a platonic marriage and the woman-hating bachelor accepts, particularly since he could use Jamie's assistance in his laboratory work. Although they have agreed to a loveless marriage, it soon becomes apparent to the couple, as well as to their circle of sophisticated friends, that their relationship is developing into one of true love.

◆━━◆━━◆

After *Keeper of the Flame*, Katharine Hepburn honored her limited-run commitment to the Broadway edition of *Without Love,* with Elliott Nugent as her co-star, and then came back to Culver City to star as Jade, the Chinese heroine of Pearl Buck's *Dragon Seed* (1944). As the slant-eyed patriot, she received many critical raps. Spencer Tracy, meanwhile, fared better with such World War II oriented projects as *A Guy Named Joe* (1943) with Irene Dunne, and a guest appearance as Lt. Colonel James H. Doolittle in *Thirty Seconds over Tokyo* (1944).

For the next Tracy-Hepburn production, it was determined to adapt her *Without Love* for the screen. Scripter Donald Ogden Stewart did a sterling job of readjusting the stage play to cinematic terms and appeasing the industry's production code office by realigning the characters' morality. No longer is the heroine a widowed lady who suggests a platonic wedding to an idealistic diplomat with whom she had been co-habitating. (He had had a bad prior affair which soured him on the institution of marriage.) But now in the film she is a magnanimous, efficient Washington, D.C., widow who provides inventor Tracy with an ideal spot to carry out his secret experiments, he using the guise of "marriage" to foster his cover. To insure that the viewer would not misinterpret their in-name-only liaison, Tracy occupies the main house and she resides on her farm.

After the misfire of *Keeper of the Flame* everyone was most eager to find virtues in *Without Love,* and that they did. "Miss Hepburn gives a mischievous performance as the girl who really wants to be chased, and Mr. Tracy is charmingly acerbic when confronted with her cool or coy wiles" [Bosley Crowther *(New York Times)*]. The *New Yorker* judged, "Miss Hepburn and Mr. Tracy succeed brilliantly in the leading parts. The somewhat metallic and stylized quality of Miss Hepburn's acting is almost perfectly suited to a role that is largely a vehicle for fashionable humor, and Mr. Tracy's homespun behavior seems just about right for a man who really prefers airplanes to dames."

Harold S. Bucquet, who had co-directed Hepburn's *Dragon Seed,* handled the directing chores on *Without Love,* giving the stars a free reign to display their particular brands of screen charisma. In a later revealing statement, Bucquet admitted, "Miss Hepburn requires direction, for she tends to act too much. Her acting is much less economical than Mr. Tracy's, but his style is rubbing off on her. The important thing is that I don't coach them on their scenes together. No one should do that, for they do a thorough job by themselves and know exactly what they want to accomplish when we begin a scene."

Given the unusual boy-girl relationship premise of *Without Love,* the suspense and comedy of the script naturally revolved about how and when idealistic Hepburn and practical-minded Tracy would tangle romantically. With Barry's play as a basis, scenarist Stewart was able to devise sundry situations in which the pair found themselves in embarrassingly intimate predicaments together. After all a guy who has a habit of walking in his sleep and a girl who has difficulty in keeping her feet warm on cold nights, are bound to join amorous forces somewhere along the line. Greatly aiding the proceedings were Keenan Wynn as Quentin Ladd, Hepburn's drink-prone cousin, and Lucille Ball as Kitty Trimble (a whitewashed version of her Broadway counterpart), a real estate agent who prefers to keep her eyes on two-legged masculine properties while running loose at the mouth with wisecracks.

There were few legitimate faults to find with the polished comedy of *Without Love*. There was an overabundance of coincidence in the glib storyline. Critics, as well, chided Hepburn for her still-strong Main Line accent, her peculiar walk, and her character's annoying habit of punctuating all her statements with "by gum," but all in all Hepburn's Jamie Rowan was a pretty swell girl. Her playing house with resolute Pat Jamieson (Tracy), reveals that beneath his preoccupied look, there burns a pleasing warmth and a fitting sense of humor. Thus as the twin stars played with the surface and interior characteristics of their roles here, they confirmed that in 1945, they fully deserved the title of being the prime examples of adult screen romance.

## THE SEA OF GRASS
### *(MGM, 1947) 131M.*

Producer, Pandro S. Berman; director, Elia Kazan; based on the novel by Conrad Richter; screenplay, Marguerite Roberts, Vincent Lawrence; art directors, Cedric Gibbons, Paul Groesse; set decorator, Edwin B. Willis; sound, Douglas Shearer; music, Herbert Stothart; costumes, Walter Plunkett; makeup, Jack Dawn; assistant director, Sid Sidman; camera, Harry Stradling; editor, Robert J. Kern.

Katharine Hepburn (Lutie Cameron); Spencer Tracy (Colonel James Brewton); Melvyn Douglas (Brice Chamberlain); Phyllis Thaxter (Sarah Beth Brewton); Robert Walker (Brock Brewton); Edgar Buchanan (Jeff); Harry Carey (Doc Reid); Ruth Nelson (Selena Hall); William "Bill" Phillips (Banty); James Bell (Sam Hall); Robert Barrat (Judge White); Charles Trowbridge (George Cameron); Russell Hicks (Major Harney); Robert Armstrong (Floyd McCurtin); Trevor Bardette (Andy Boggs); Morris Ankrum (Crane); Nora Cecil (Nurse); Glenn Strange (Bill Roach); Douglas Fowley (Joe Horton); Buddy Roosevelt, Earle Hodgins, Robert Bice (Cowboys); Vernon Dent (Conductor); John Vosper (Hotel Clerk); John Hamilton (Forrest Cochran); Joseph Crehan (Senator Graw); Whit Bissell (Ted the Clerk); Gertrude Chorre (Indian Nurse); Patty Smith (Sarah Beth at Age 4½); Ray Teal, Eddie Acuff (Cattlemen); Lee Phelps, Jack Baxley, George Magrill, Charles McAvoy, Nolan Leary (Homesteaders); Carol Nugent (Sarah Beth at Age Seven); Jimmie Hawkins (Brock at Age 5½); Dick Baron (Newsboy); William Challee (Deputy Sheriff); Stanley Andrews (Sheriff).

New York Premiere: Radio City Music Hall—February 27, 1947
New York Television Debut: CBS—April 8, 1961

## Synopsis

Colonel James Brewton, a middle-aged cattle tycoon, owns over a million acres of grazing land in the St. Augustine plains of the 1880s New Mexico Territory, the "sea of grass." He weds St. Louis belle Lutie Cameron, a cultured, sensitive young woman. She returns with Jim to his ranch at Salt Forke, and later gives birth to a daughter, Sarah Beth. Meanwhile, homesteaders have been moving into the grazing lands, and Jim loses a court decision to keep them off of the range. When he thereafter illegally keeps farm families from the land and turns more and more into a stern, unyielding man, she leaves him and stops over in Denver. There she reencounters Brice Chamberlain, a lawyer-judge who has displayed sympathy for the homesteaders and has thus won Lutie's affection. She has a regretful overnight affair with Brice, but soon thereafter returns to her husband. Months later she gives birth to a son, Brock, and during the delivery she confesses to Jim her adulterous activities. He tries to treat Brock like his own, but he and Lutie quarrel again and he orders her to leave the ranch. Years pass, and only after the children have grown up and are in difficulties does Lutie return to hopefully salvage the situation. However, reckless Brock has gotten into trouble because of slurs made on his parentage. He is shot and soon dies in Jim's arms. At the prompting of daughter Sarah Beth, Lutie is reconciled with Jim.

After filming *Without Love,* Spencer Tracy satisfied an urge to return to the Broadway stage in Robert Sherwood's *The Rugged Path,* directed by Garson Kanin. The venture proved to be a tremulous emotional ordeal for Tracy as he struggled to reach a viable characterization in the drama. The floundering show opened in New York in November, 1945, and closed after an eighty-one performance run. It was to be his last stage appearance on Broadway. A much-shaken Tracy arrived back in Hollywood, now a very gray-haired man. The studio promptly cast him and his very close companion Katharine Hepburn in an adaptation of Conrad Richter's 1937 novel, *The Sea of Grass.*

Producer Pandro S. Berman, who had supervised many of Hepburn's RKO films, was in charge of this expansive venture, while New York actor-recently-turned-film-director Elia Kazan, who had guided *A Tree Grows in Brooklyn* (1945), was signed to direct. It was bad enough that Marguerite Roberts and Vincent Lawrence had conceived a hackneyed, lifeless Western drama that more closely resembled soap opera on the open range, but Kazan and Tracy, who had diametrically opposed views on acting, clashed continually on the set. Hepburn soon found herself in the role of arbitrator throughout the entire seventy-five-day shooting schedule.

Not long ago, Kazan offered his own interpretation of what went wrong with *The Sea of Grass* production some thirty years ago:

"I went to see Pandro Berman, the producer, and the first thing he said was, 'I've got 10,000 feet of the most beautiful background footage you've ever seen in your life.' I should have got up, said, 'Thank you very much, Pandro,' and walked out. But I was too dumb to quit. I was in a mechanism called Metro-Goldwyn-Mayer, which was run not by Pandro Berman, and not, oddly enough, by L. B. Mayer, but by the head of the Art Department, Cedric Gibbons. He ran that damn studio. There was a rigid plan about how every film was going to be made, and this film was going to be made in front of a rear-projection screen. So what it ended up, to my vast humiliation, was that I never saw a blade of grass through that picture. Another thing that happened was I was very proud I got Katharine Hepburn to cry, because I thought she was a cool person. Not at all—if she wants to cry she turns it on. But I was very pleased with the rushes and I said to Pandro Berman, 'Gee Pandro, did you see the stuff? I think she gave a terrific performance.' He said, 'Well, Mr. Mayer doesn't think so.' So I went to see Mr. Mayer. I said, 'What are you talking about, Mr. Mayer? She's terrific in that scene—She cries all through it.' He said, 'The channel of tears is wrong.' I said, 'What do you mean?' He said, 'They go too near the nostrils.' I said, 'But, Mr. Mayer that's the way the girl's face is made.' He said, 'There's another thing some people cry with their voice, some with their throat, some with their nose, some with their eyes. But she cries with everything. And this is excessive.' I said, 'God, I still won't shoot that over, Mr. Mayer.' And he said, 'Listen' Then he got tough with me. He said, 'We're in the business of making beautiful pictures about beautiful people, and anybody who doesn't think so has no place in this industry.' I finally didn't reshoot it, . . ."

With a stagebound setting, miscast leading players, and hardly a gun-shot in the 131-minute story, there was little to recommend *The Sea of Grass* beyond the supporting roles played by Edgar Buchanan (as the ranch cook) and Harry Carey (as the cattle-country doctor). The picture sprawled everywhere but developed no excitement or peak, as prairie-loving Tracy and city-bred Hepburn clash on a personal level while the story vaguely reflects the friction between cattlemen and farmers. "Mr. Tracy is grim, purposeful, and, I'm afraid, occasionally ludicrous, while Miss Hepburn is as pert as a sparrow. As the lawyer responsible for Miss Hepburn's trouble, Melvyn Douglas is as gloomy as if *he* were the wronged husband, instead of being the worm in the domestic apple" [John McCarten (*New Yorker* magazine)].

MGM was so confounded by the desultory *The Sea of Grass* that it was shelved for nearly a year, during which time Hepburn co-starred with Robert Taylor in *Undercurrent,* a picture released in late 1946. The studio attempted to create a rousing publicity campaign for *The Sea of Grass:* "Rugged TRACY . . . Romantic HEPBURN . . . Reckless WALKER . . . Ruthless DOUGLAS" but the public was not fooled by this feckless feature in which "Hepburn Tames Tracy." Bad word-of-mouth did its toll on *The Sea of Grass.* After all, the public had already been tricked into viewing two other oversized Westerns, David O. Selznick's *Duel in the Sun* (1946) and Howard Hughes' *The Outlaw* (general release: 1946 and thereafter).

# STATE OF THE UNION
## *(MGM, 1948) 124M.*

Producer, Frank Capra; associate producer, Anthony Veiller; director, Capra; based on the play by Howard Lindsay, Russel Crouse; screenplay, Veiller, Myles Connolly; art directors, Cedric Gibbons, Urie McCleary; set decorator, Emile Kuri; sound, Douglas Shearer; music, Victor Young; assistant director, Arthur S. Black, Jr.; costumes, Irene; special effects, A. Arnold Gillespie; camera, George J. Folsey; editor, William Hornbeck.

Spencer Tracy (Grant Matthews); Katharine Hepburn (Mary Matthews); Van Johnson (Spike McManus); Angela Lansbury (Kay Thorndyke); Adolphe Menjou (Jim Conover); Lewis Stone (Sam Thorndyke); Howard Smith (Sam Parrish); Maidel Turner (Lulubelle Alexander); Raymond Walburn (Judge Alexander); Charles Dingle (Bill Hardy); Florence Auer (Grace Orval Draper); Pierre Watkin (Senator Lauterback); Margaret Hamilton (Norah); Irving Bacon (Buck); Patti Brady (Joyce); George Nokes (Grant, Jr.); Carl Switzer (Bellboy); Tom Pedi (Barber); Tom Fadden (Waiter); Charles Lane (Blink Moran); Art Baker (Leith); Rhea Mitchell (Jenny); Arthur O'Connell (Reporter); Marion Martin (Blonde Girl); Tor Johnson (Wrestler); Stanley Andrews (Senator); Dave Willock (Pilot); Russell Meeker (Politician); Frank I. Clarke (Joe Crandall); David Clarke (Rusty Miller); Dell Henderson (Broder); Edwin Cooper (Bradbury); Davison Clark (Crump); Francis Pierlot (Josephs); Brandon Beach (Editor); Eddie Phillips (Television Man); Roger Moore, Lew Smith, Gene Coogan, Douglas Carter, Charles Sherlock, Wilson Wood, George Barton, Harry Anderson, Charles Coleman, Stanley Price, Fred Zendar, Jack Boyle (Photographers); Maurice Cass (Little Man); Eve Whitney (Secretary); Bert Moorhouse, Thornton Edwards, Marshall Ruth (Men).

New York Premiere: Radio City Music Hall—April 22, 1948
New York Television Debut: CBS—January 30, 1959

### Synopsis

"Liberal" aircraft tycoon Grant Matthews is touted as a dark horse contender for the Republican nomination in the upcoming Presidential campaign. Mary Matthews, estranged from her husband, is asked to join Grant on his cross-country platform-thumping tour, to quell rumors about his liaison with Kay Thorndyke, the newspaper publisher backing his campaign bid. Others involved in the Matthews' contingent are old-line politico Jim Conover and Spike McManus, the latter a columnist hired to publicize Grant's nomination efforts. As the tour proceeds, Grant unknowingly finds himself sacrificing all his former ideals for the sake of cementing sufficient backing for his election. Mary, who all along has been chiding Grant for his letdown of values, finally speaks her piece against the corrupt politicians surrounding Grant. He suddenly becomes aware of the trap into which he has fallen, and on a national radio hookup, he informs listeners that he must withdraw from the race for he is not worthy of the citizens' votes.

◆━━◆━━◆

Katharine Hepburn had been announced by MGM to star in *Green Dolphin Street* (1947) and *B. F.'s Daughter* (1948) but Lana Turner and Barbara Stanwyck respectively claimed the top female roles in those pictures. On the other hand, Hepburn had not been touted° for the distaff lead in *State of the Union*, a film to be based on the 1945 Pulitzer Prize-winning play by Howard Lindsay and Russel Crouse. Producer-director Frank Capra had joined in the formation of Liberty Films, an independent company which was to release its first nine pictures through RKO. When that studio vetoed the $2.8 million budget for Capra's forthcoming *State of the Union* which hopefully would star Gary Cooper, he turned to MGM for a releasing deal, tying up the package by casting a willing Spencer Tracy in the lead part. Claudette Colbert, who had won an Oscar in Capra's *It Happened One Night* (1934) and later played with Tracy in *Boom Town* (1940) was hired as Tracy's vis-a-vis. Literally on the eve of production, Colbert walked off the picture because her five o'clock work stoppage was not part of the new contract. Capra then telephoned Tracy to advise him of the disastrous situation. Tracy suggested Hepburn for the part, saying, "The bag of bones has been helping me rehearse. Kinda stops you, Frank, the way she reads the woman's part. She's a real theater nut, you know. She might do it for the hell of it."

So Tracy and Hepburn were reunited for their fifth film together. As Capra described it, when they ". . . played a scene, cameras, lights, microphones, and written scripts ceased to exist. And the director did just what the crews and other actors did—sat, watched, and marveled."

The Anthony Veiller-Myles Connolly screenplay was not as pungent or pertinent as the Broadway original in its biting, topical digs on the state of the American democratic system. "By oversimplifying its politics, *State of the Union* misses a good chance to be an important film comment on president-making" *(Life* magazine). Nevertheless, the film was sufficiently solid to earn the endorsement of Bosley Crowther *(New York Times)* as a "slick piece of screen satire" following in the distinguished tradition of Capra's *Mr. Smith Goes to Washington* (1939).

Once again Tracy and Hepburn were cast as anything but a typical romantic couple. Here they were seasoned married folks . . . but estranged! He was conducting an affair (played down considerably in the film) with dynamic, pushy Kay Thorndyke (Angela Lansbury), the newspaper publisher who is promoting his presidential bid. Jim Conover (Adolphe Menjou), the campaign professional (who observes, "There's all the difference between the Democrats and the Republicans . . . they're in and we're

°Hepburn, along with Helen Hayes and Margaret Sullavan had turned down the stage role eventually played on Broadway by Ruth Hussey.

out") urges idealistic Hepburn to return to Tracy's side to make him appear a more attractive Republican candidate to the masses.

Before the picture develops into a see-sawing struggle between Hepburn's don't-fool-the-voters approach and Tracy's loosened campaign standards (he succumbs to White House fever and begins making shady political deals), the love team enjoy a felicitous bedroom sequence together. Assigned to the same boudoir, Hepburn makes it quite clear that she is now aware of the realities to the rumors of his liaison with Lansbury, and that while she will occupy the master bed, he, Mr. Candidate, can darn well bunk on the floor. Thus in round one of his political campaign, he has lost a tactical battle. Once settled in for the night, the floor-sprawled Tracy attempts to make Hepburn recant her icy stand in the matter, but she is resolute. They have entered a new arena of political and personal conflicting ideologies and the fight is to the finish.

Some critics have argued that the ending in which Tracy bolts the party, by announcing over a radio network broadcast that he is unworthy for the post and must withdraw, is hokey and unsatisfying screenfare, being pulled out of left field just to end the proceedings. Be that as it may, *State of the Union* holds up well as an interesting reflection of pre-New Frontier politicking. In its day it was regarded as "slick, chick, political drama" [Dorothy Manners (*New York Daily News*)]. The critical majority was more favorably inclined than not to the star team's interpretations of the tricky roles. ". . . Mr. Tracy is often persuasive, and Katharine Hepburn, as his wife, manages to say as if she meant them such lines as 'Grant likes to get up on the mountain and slap the hurricanes down.'" Not to be overlooked was the stellar efforts of the film's supporting cast, including Menjou's conniving politico, vixenish Lansbury who displayed fang-like intensity in her screen encounters with Hepburn, Van Johnson in a surprisingly sturdy impersonation of the Drew Pearson-like columnist hired as Tracy's campaign publicist, and Lewis Stone in a brief turn as Lansbury's ruthless, dying dad.

Just to prove that the White House regarded the film in the proper entertainment spirit, *State of the Union* was given a special showing at the Capitol Theatre in Washington, D.C., on May 1948. President Harry S. Truman and his daughter Margaret attended the black-tie affair, although stars Tracy and Hepburn were not among the celebrities present. They had already gone on to other projects.

## ADAM'S RIB
### *(MGM, 1949) 101M.*

Producer, Lawrence Weingarten; director, George Cukor; story-screenplay, Garson Kanin, Ruth Gordon; art directors, Cedric Gibbons, William Ferrari; set decorator, Edwin B. Willis, Henry W. Grace; music, Miklos Rozsa; song, Cole Porter; assistant director, Jack Greenwood; costumes, Walter Plunkett; makeup, Jack Dawn; special effects, A. Arnold Gilliespie; sound, Douglas Shearer; camera, George J. Folsey; editor, George Boemler.

Spencer Tracy (Adam Bonner); Katharine Hepburn (Amanda Bonner); Judy Holliday (Doris Attinger); Tom Ewell (Warren Attinger); David Wayne (Kip Lurie); Jean Hagen (Beryl Caighn); Hope Emerson (Olympia La Pere); Eve March (Grace); Clarence Kolb (Judge Reiser); Emerson Treacy (Jules Frikke); Polly Moran (Mrs. McGrath); Will Wright (Judge Marcasson); Elizabeth Flournoy (Dr. Margaret Brodeigh); Janna Da Loos (Mary the Maid); James Nolan (Dave); David Clarke (Roy); John Maxwell Sholes (Court Clerk); Marvin Kaplan (Court Stenographer); William Self (Benjamin Klausner); Gracille La Vinder (Police Matron); Ray Walker (Photographer); Tommy Noonan (Reporter); De Forrest Lawrence, John Fell (Adam's Assistants); Sid Dubin (Amanda's Assistant); Joe Bernard (Mr. Bonner); Madge Blake (Mrs. Bonner); Marjorie Wood (Mrs. Marcasson); Lester Luther (Judge Poynter); Anna Q. Nilsson (Mrs. Poynter); Roger David (Hurlock); Louis Mason (Elderly Elevator Operator); Rex Evans (Fat Man); Charles Bastin (Young District Attorney); E. Bradley Coleman (Subway Rider); Paula Raymond (Emerald); Glenn Gallagher, Gil Patric, Harry Cody (Criminal Attorneys); George Magrill, Bert Davidson (Subway Guards).

New York Premiere: Capitol Theatre—December 25, 1949
New York Television Debut: NBC—December 26, 1964

### Synopsis

When dumb blonde Doris Attinger shoots her straying husband Warren, who is conducting an affair with Beryl Caighn, attorney Amanda Bonner, a staunch believer in women's equal rights, takes the defense. It develops that Amanda's husband, Adam, a New York county assistant district attorney, is assigned as prosecutor in the case. It is tough enough for Adam to have to combat his wife in the courtroom, but she insists upon draping her pet theory of feminine equality about the household. In the course of the trial, Amanda has ample opportunity to provide wry and cogent dissertations on what-is-good-for-the-goose-is-good-for-the-gander, eventually winning an acquittal for Doris, whose bad gun aim had not done in her recalcitrant spouse.

◆◆◆

It had been planned to team Katharine Hepburn with Spencer Tracy in *Edward, My Son* (1949) but when director George Cukor shepherded the Metro cast to London for the filming, it was Deborah Kerr instead of Hepburn who played Tracy's tormented oncamera wife. Hepburn did accompany Tracy to England for the production work, and by the time they returned to Hollywood, MGM had undergone executive changes with Dore Schary installed as vice president in charge of production and Louis B. Mayer on his way out.

In January, 1949, the new MGM regime purchased for $175,000 all rights to an original screen story, *Man and Wife* by Garson Kanin and his actress wife, Ruth Gordon. Since the scripters were very close friends with Tracy and Hepburn, it was not coincidental that the roles admirably suited the talents of the two studio stars, who were promptly assigned to the comedy vehicle, which was retitled *Adam's Rib*.

"It's the Hilarious Answer to Who Wears the Pants . . . MGM's Rib Roarious Battle of the Sexes." For a change, a film admirably lived up to its publicity. In performing in their first original screenplay since *Woman of the Year,* Tracy and Hepburn were graced with a superior vehicle, further enhanced by having expert George Cukor as their director. Bosley Crowther *(New York Times)* praised the results as "delightful improvising on a nimble and fragile little tale."

As *Adam's Rib* opens, it appears that Adam Bonner (Tracy) and Amanda Bonner (Hepburn) are quite settled in their respective legal careers and supposedly well acquainted with each other's eccentricities much in the same vein as Fred Astaire's and Ginger Rogers' show business husband-and-wife team in MGM's *The Barkleys of Broadway* (1948). However, Hepburn's character is a crusader and her cause is women's equality. She tells her stubborn husband, "Lots of things a man can do and in society's eyes it's all hunky-dory. A woman does the same, mind you, and she's an outcast."

Tracy (countering): "If anything, females get advantages."

Hepburn: "We don't want advantages! And we don't want prejudices!" This argument proves the crux of the film as the spouses square off in opposite legal corners over the Doris Attinger (Judy Holliday) attempted homicide case. Amanda naturally agrees to defend Brooklyn-twanged Holliday and Tracy later is assigned to prosecute the case on behalf of the perplexed Warren Attinger (Tom Ewell).

Intertwined with the leads' professional and personal differences is the catalytic force of Kip Lurie (David Wayne), a crewcut society composer-neighbor, who has a yen for Hepburn and makes no bones about pursuing her in front of the annoyed Tracy. ("Amanda, my only love. Why do you stayed married to a legal beagle with ten thumbs?"). It is Wayne who composes the song, "Farewell, Amanda" (actually specially written for the film by Cole Porter), which is repeated to distraction throughout the movie.

In *Adam's Rib*, the scene shifts between the lawyer team's New York apartment, their country place (via home movies) called Bonner Hill, and, of course, to the Manhattan courtroom where Holliday is placed on trial for her misdeed, the alleged criminal offense inspired when she caught her husband "muzzlin' that tall job." After all, as the distraught but very casual Holliday informs the jury, "I got three children. She was breakin' up my home." Holliday explains she fired the gun only to scare black lingerie-clad Beryl Caighn (Jean Hagen).

As the well-publicized trial reaches its final stages, the fierce courtroom competition between Tracy and Hepburn is carried over to the homefront where the couple quibble whether they should share lamb curry together or whether he should give her an overly forceful rubdown. The jurisprudential tactics practiced by the duo are far from conventional. At one point in the film, Hepburn calls Olympia La Pere (Hope Emerson), an Amazonian carnival weight lifter, as a witness and urges the gargantuan lady to hoist an unsuspecting Tracy into mid-air to prove "that woman can be quite the equal of man in any and all fields—*if* given the opportunity." The judge and jury find it a little strange that opposing counsel call each other "Pinky," but it is even stranger still when each time Tracy drops his pencil the two attorneys pop down beneath the conference table for a private tête-à-tête. Thanks to Hepburn's unique legal tactics and the bizarreness of the case itself, the jury acquits Holliday. Tracy, his male ego very bruised, is quietly nonplussed. Hepburn suddenly realizes her victory has a bitter taste to it, and sweetly tells him, "I wish it could have been a tie, I really do."

But this is not the end of the *Adam's Rib* thesis. After Tracy has finally dispatched the unwanted neighbor (Wayne) with a feisty demonstration of fisticuffs, Tracy and Hepburn finally make up and depart for their country home, where he attempts to win the upper hand by using his wife's favorite tactic, tears. With a well-timed tear rolling down his cheek, she is prompted to inquire: "All right, then. What have you proved. What does *that* show?"

Tracy: "Shows the score."

Hepburn: "Shows what I say is true. No difference between the sexes. None. Men, women. The same."

Tracy: "They are, huh?"

Hepburn: "Well, maybe there *is* a difference. But it's a *little* difference."

Tracy: "Yuh. Well, as the French say."

Hepburn: "How do they say?"

Tracy: "Vive la difference!"

Hepburn: "Which means?"

Tracy: "Which means: Hurray for that little difference!"

Some twenty-four years after initial release, *Adam's Rib* turned up as the basis for an ABC-TV half hour comedy series filmed at MGM with Ken Howard and Blythe Danner in the old Tracy-Hepburn roles. It hardly needs to be said that it was not at all the same as before. The show folded after its first season.

## PAT AND MIKE
### (MGM, 1952) 95M.

Producer, Lawrence Weingarten; director, George Cukor; story-screenplay, Ruth Gordon, Garson Kanin; art directors, Cedric Gibbons, Urie McCleary; set decorators, Edwin B. Willis, Hugh Hunt; sound, Douglas Shearer; assistant director, Jack Greenwood; makeup, William Tuttle; wardrobe for Miss Hepburn, Orry-Kelly; music, David Raskin; montage, Peter Ballbusch; special effects, Warren Newcombe; camera, William Daniels; editor, George Boemler.

Spencer Tracy (Mike Conovan); Katharine Hepburn (Pat Pemberton); Aldo Ray (Davie Hucko); William Ching (Collier Weld); Sammy White (Barney Grau); George Mathews (Spec Cauley); Loring Smith (Mr. Beminger); Phyllis Povah (Mrs. Beminger); Charles Bronson (Hank Tasling); Frank Richards (Sam Garsell); Jim Backus (Charles Barry); Chuck Connors (Police Captain); Owen McGiveney (Harry MacWade); Lou Lubin (Waiter); Carl Switzer (Bus Boy); William Self (Pat's Caddy); Billy McLean, Frankie Darro, Paul Brinegar, "Tiny" Jimmie Kelly (Caddies); Mae Clarke, Elizabeth Holmes, Helen Eby-Rock (Women Golfers); Hank Weaver (Commentator); Tom Harmon (Sportscaster); Charlie Murray (Line Judge); Don Budge, Helen Dettweiler, Betty Hicks, Beverly Hanson, Babe Didrikson Zaharias, Gussie Moran, Alice Marble, Frank Parker (Themselves); Kay English, Jerry Schumacher, Sam Pierce, Bill Lewin, A. Cameron Grant (Reporters); John Close, Fred Coby, Russ Clark (Troopers); Tom Gibson, Kay Deslys (Shooting Gallery Proprietors); Barbara Kimbrell, Elinor Cushingham, Jane Stanton (Tennis Players); Tom Harmon (Sportscaster); Louis Mason (Railway Conductor); King Mojave (Linesman); Frank Sucack (Chairman); Crauford Kent (Tennis Umpire); Sam Hearn (Lawyer).

New York Premiere: Capitol Theatre—June 18, 1952
New York Television Debut: CBS—February 24, 1964

### Synopsis

Pat Pemberton, a chipper physical education instructor at a small California college, discovers that, whenever she is engaged in sports competition, the mere presence of her fiancé, Collier Weld, is sufficient to upset her and cause her to do poorly on the playing field. In a subsequent national golf tournament, fast-talking sports promoter Mike Conovan attempts to bribe Pat to lose, but she refuses. Thereafter, she does join up with Mike in a whirlwind golf and tennis tour, but just when everything is going well, the mere presence of Collier sends her into a tizzy and causes her to fare badly. When Collier eventually interrupts Pat and Mike in what appears to be a compromising situation, he is offended and walks out on her. Meantime, Pat has finally realized she can do quite nicely without Collier and that it is rascally Mike who is the right man for her.

◆━◆━◆

Following *Adam's Rib,* Katharine Hepburn ventured back to Broadway in a successful presentation of Shakespeare's *As You Like It* and then went on location to Africa to film *The African Queen* with co-star Humphrey Bogart. She was Oscar-nominated for the part, but lost to Vivien Leigh of *A Streetcar Named Desire.* Meantime, Spencer Tracy had scored in the comedy *Father of the Bride* (1950) with Elizabeth Taylor, but had been dissatisfied with the results of both the sequel, *Father's Little Dividend* (1950), and the following meandering cops and crooks melodrama, *The People against O'Hara* (1951). At this juncture it was suggested that Tracy and Hepburn star in a new property, *Pat and Mike,* created by Ruth Gordon and Garson Kanin, with George Cukor again assigned to direct.

MGM promoted the comedy with the tag, "Together again and it's no fib. Their funniest hit since *Adam's Rib!*" Otis L. Guernsey, Jr. (*New York Herald-Tribune*) agreed, ". . . it is a pretty good joke which adds in novelty wherever the humor needs thickening." Furthermore, he pointed out that, "the story's real spark comes from the meeting of tempered steel and cast iron in the two leading characters."

Perhaps *Pat and Mike* works so well because it has an unassuming air about it, what with its rash of funny crooks, and its casual, almost humorous attitude in depicting the seamier side of the sports world. Director Cukor would later judge that the success of *Pat and Mike* was due to the stars' portrayals: "Chemically they're so funny together because they should have no rapport at all." Hepburn as Pat Pemberton is a rather head-in-the-clouds type of gal, despite her proficiency on the playing field, and her first encounter with stubborn Mike Conovan (Tracy) and his Damon Runyonesque hanger-on Barney Grau (Sammy White) is not exactly congenial. She seriously considers them gangsters, but soon softens up to Tracy's undisclosed better nature, realizing that with a little judo and a sharp word here and there, she can easily handle him and his pal. On the other hand, Tracy initially appraises Hepburn as an "escaped fruit cake," but when he fully weighs her athletic talents against her surface primness he decides that she is a worthy match for him, a girl to be professionally and romantically trained to his way of thinking (or so he hopes). Thus he can later say of her, with full appreciation, ". . . there ain't much meat on her, but where there is, is choice."

A decade before, in *Woman of the Year,* Hepburn had abhorred sports, now it was her screen character's way of life, and she demonstrated throughout the movie her real life talent for tennis and golf. As had become customary in most of the Tracy-Hepburn celluloid outings, physical romance was a "no-no." In fact, the only time the couple really touch in *Pat and Mike* is when Hepburn has pulled a leg muscle and Tracy massages her injured gam. (This scene in itself is a little gem as Tracy employs an "I

559

really shouldn't be doing this" smirk on his face, and tense Hepburn is vainly attempting to hide the fact that the physical contact is having its romantic effect on her.)

Amidst the scenes of sports training with Hepburn enduring rigorous road workouts along side of Tracy's other prize athlete, heavyweight boxer Davie Hucko (Aldo Ray), there are sundry shots dealing with actual sports personalities who were hired to perform oncamera and give the picture an ambiance of authenticity. (This led *Newsweek* magazine to chide, "A full appreciation of *Pat and Mike* may require at least an armchair interest in athletics—particularly golf and tennis.")

Possibly the most humorous scene in *Pat and Mike* occurs after Hepburn has agreed to turn professional and to allow Tracy to be her manager. She has agreed to his belief that "There's a nice dollar laying around for you and I to pick up." The new partners dine at New York's Lindy's Restaurant where trainer Tracy proceeds to reveal to his latest pupil the yeas and nays that she must observe while in training. When he follows this strict list of do's and don'ts by insisting upon ordering her dinner himself—ignoring her preferences—she tosses out, "Don't forget to throw me over your shoulder and burp me after lunch."

Tracy: "I will if I have to."

When this odd couple eventually survive the rigors of their tours and each other's company, and decide to marry, there is no great traditional proposal scene, they merely shake hands. Finally after some ninety-five minutes of running time, she has discovered that her biggest handicap on and off the playing field was her peculiarly demoralizing fiance Collier Weld (William Ching).

*Pat and Mike* enjoyed a popular public reception making MGM regret that it was Hepburn's final picture under studio contract. Tracy would remain with the company for an additional three years.

## DESK SET
### (*Twentieth Century-Fox, 1957*) C-103M.

Producer, Henry Ephron; director, Walter Lang; based on the play *The Desk Set* by William Marchant; screenplay, Phoebe and Henry Ephron; art directors, Lyle Wheeler, Maurice Ransford; set decorators, Walter M. Scott, Paul S. Fox; assistant director, Hal Herman; music, Cyril J. Mockridge; music director, Lionel Newman; orchestrator, Edward B. Powell; costumes, Charles Le Maire; makeup, Ben Nye; sound, E. Clayton Ward, Harry M. Leonard; special camera effects, Ray Kellogg; camera, Leon Shamroy; editor, Robert Simpson.

Spencer Tracy (Richard Sumner); Katharine Hepburn (Bunny Watson); Gig Young (Mike Cutler); Joan Blondell (Peg Costello); Dina Merrill (Sylvia); Sue Randall (Ruthie); Neva Patterson (Miss Warringer); Harry

Ellerbe (Smithers); Nicholas Joy (Azae); Diane Jergens (Alice); Merry Anders (Cathy); Ida Moore (Old Lady); Rachel Stephens (Receptionist); Sammy Ogg (Kenny); King Mojave, Charles Heard, Harry Evans, Hal Taggart, Jack M. Lee, Bill Duray (Board Members); Dick Gardner (Fred); Renny McEvoy (Man); Jesslyn Fax (Mrs. Hewitt); Shirley Mitchell (Myra Smithers).

New York Premiere: Roxy Theatre—May, 15, 1957
New York Television Debut: ABC—October 5, 1963

### Synopsis

Bunny Watson heads the reference and research department for the Federal Broadcasting Company, she and her capable staff being able to field most any question on any subject handed to them. When Bunny and the girls discover that efficiency expert Richard Sumner is on the premises to plan the installation of his computer baby (the Electro-Magnetic Memory and Research Arithmetical Calculator) and that the distaff researchers may be ousted, there is immediate antipathy. As time lapses, Bunny and Richard conflict and consort, forcing Bunny's long-time suitor, network executive Mike Cutler, to finally propose to her. At this strategic point, however, Richard makes it clear to Bunny that his machine, nicknamed "Emmy," is not going to do Bunny and her workers out of jobs, but merely take over the routine work, leaving her more time for research and for Richard.

◆━━◆━━◆

If Katharine Hepburn had not favored a London production of George Shaw's *The Millionairess*, she might have signed on at MGM instead of Teresa Wright for *The Actress* (1953), playing the wife of Spencer Tracy in the picturization of Ruth Gordon's autobiographical play, *Years Ago*. It was nearly two years after *The Millionairess* before Hepburn reactivated her career, starring in the European-lensed *Summertime* (1955) based on Shirley Booth's Broadway hit, *The Time of the Cuckoo*. From the role of a regenerated schoolteacher, she next essayed a Russian aviatrix in *The Iron Petticoat* (1956), a Bob Hope unfunny comedy which bore too many plot resemblances, but not enough entertainment similarities, to Greta Garbo's *Ninotchka* (1939). Then came *The Rainmaker* (1956), in which she was a Kansas spinster of the 1920s pushed into overt femininity by traveling con artist Burt Lancaster. At this juncture she agreed to reteam on-camera with Spencer Tracy in a movie version of *The Desk Set*, a 1955 Broadway comedy which had starred Shirley Booth. The twin-pronged reason for the project was to keep Spencer Tracy in acting harness—since leaving MGM under unhappy circumstances, he had not fared well in Paramount's *The Mountain* (1956)—and to put herself back into a more sophisticated screen mold.

Twentieth Century-Fox's *Desk Set*, the first Tracy-Hepburn picture away from Metro, was in CinemaScope and color, two more firsts for the enduring love team, reputed to be the screen's best all-American movie couple. Once again the story premise had the stars competing on their standard battlefield; which one of them was the better fellow. Naturally this professional competition within the plotline leads inevitably to romance. The Broadway original of *Desk Set* had been a pleasant but slight vehicle. Expanding it for the screen to suit the personality requisites of the co-leads stretched the property almost to the bursting point.

With extravagant art direction by Lyle Wheeler and Maurice Ransford and set decorations by Walter M. Scott and Paul S. Fox, cinematographer Leon Shamroy had no difficulty in lensing Tracy and Hepburn against lush backdrops, even considering most of the scenes were supposed to be set in ordinary executive offices. Hepburn had not been so advantageously photographed in several years, which, thankfully, injected a good deal of glamour into what emerged as a predictable and pedestrian screen comedy.

As Tracy and Hepburn had tested each's physical mettle in *Pat and Mike*, so now they are intellectual rivals. As he soon discovers, she is one girl who cannot be stumped by any question. Although she is a whiz fielding obscure facts, she is very human in her outlook, concerned professionally that machines might make people outmoded. (Tracy wryly admits, "I wouldn't be a bit surprised if they stopped making them.") She is also very concerned about her single status in life, horrified that she has become "Bunny Watson, spare tire."

Scripters Phoebe and Henry Ephron did their best to personalize the rather sterile plot premise with several intimate scenes between Tracy and Hepburn. For example, there is the delightful scene of their sandwich break on the office building roof in which each is sizing up the opponent. Later Tracy is caught in a rainstorm and she takes him to her apartment. While his clothes are drying, she allows him to wear the bathrobe she purchased for boyfriend Mike Cutler's (Gig Young) Xmas present. Naturally Young shows up at this cozy point, and reaches a degree of jealousy almost as heated as Tracy's loafers which are baking dry in the stove. At the office Christmas party, Hepburn displays a touch of romantic fantasy when she begins tossing confetti about and pretending she is on a Mediterranean cruise. Tracy, amused and touched by her whimsy, joins in her frivolity. At the film's climax, when Young is about to leave for a West Coast promotional transfer and wants Hepburn to come along as his wife, she realizes she is quite attached to the finicky Tracy who has already installed his computer machine in the company's research offices.

Tracy, aware that he may quickly lose Hepburn whom he has come to love, informs her that his trusty machine went haywire when he asked it a simple question, "Should Bunny Watson marry Mike Cutler?" Thereafter the machine taps out a simple "y.e.s." when he punches another query, "Should Bunny Watson marry Richard Sumner?" How's that for a unique marriage proposal? To prove that Tracy really means he loves her more than "Emmy," she makes the machinery go berserk. He stands by stoically, but after slipping a hairpin-twisted ring on her finger, he uses another of her hairpins to repair Emmarac. By now Hepburn knows her life is irretrievably tied to his, and so she patiently agrees to wait right there while he makes some mechanical adjustments to the pet computer.

"Solely through their [Tracy and Hepburn] efforts a second-rate movie becomes tolerable and sometimes even amusing" [William K. Zinsser (New York Herald-Tribune)]. Bosley Crowther (New York Times) acceded, "Best of all, there are Miss Hepburn and Mr. Tracy. They can tote phone books on their heads or balance feathers on their chins and be amusing—which is about the size of what they do here." In the rather small Desk Set cast, the supporting players were particularly resourceful in boosting the story values to level of toleration. The cast included wise-cracking Joan Blondell as Hepburn's game assistant, Young in his standard guise as a glib, playboy "other man," Harry Ellerbe as the purveyor of office scuttlebut, and sweet, elderly Ida Moore as an employee of the broadcasting company for some thirty-six years.

### GUESS WHO'S COMING TO DINNER
#### (Columbia, 1967) C-108M.

Producer, Stanley Kramer; associate producer, George Glass; director, Kramer; screenplay, William Rose; production designer, Robert Clatworthy; set decorator, Frank Tuttle; assistant director, Ray Gosnell; song, Billy Hill; costume supervisor, Jean Louis; costumes, Joe King; music, Frank De Vol; special effects, Geza Gaspar; process camera, Larry Butler; camera, Sam Leavitt; editor, Robert C. Jones.

Spencer Tracy (Matt Drayton); Sidney Poitier (John Prentice); Katharine Hepburn (Christina Drayton); Katharine Houghton (Joey Drayton); Cecil Kellaway (Monsignor Ryan); Roy E. Glenn, Sr. (Mr. Prentice); Beah Richards (Mrs. Prentice); Isabell Sanford (Tillie); Virginia Christine (Hilary St. George); Alexandra Hay (Car Hop); Barbara Randolph (Dorothy); Tom Heaton (Peter); D'Urville Martin (Frankie); Grace Gaynor (Judith); Skip Martin (Delivery Boy); John Hudkins (Cab Driver).

New York Premiere: Beekman and New Embassy Theatres— December 11, 1967
New York Television Debut: CBS—September 19, 1971

#### Synopsis

Pert young Joey Drayton returns home to San Francisco from a ten-day Hawaiian vacation, with the man she has met there and now loves, in tow. He is thirty-seven-year-old John Prentice, a brilliant research doctor who must leave the next day for Switzerland on behalf of his work for the World Health Organization. He wants to wed Joey; the only problem is that he is black, and she wants her parents' consent. John secretly confides to Matt and Christina Drayton that he will not wed Joey unless they give their blessing to the union. This presents a crisis which tests their often-stated idealistic beliefs. Matt is an alleged liberal who operates a crusading newspaper in San Francisco, while Christina operates a chic, avant-garde art gallery. Neither Matt nor Christina can reach an immediate decision. Their friends and acquaintances have no such problem. Christina's business associate, Hilary St. George, quickly demonstrates her bigotry, while Monsignor Ryan, an old family friend, is convinced the young couple can overcome this seeming obstacle. The Drayton's black maid, Tillie, loudly berates John for his audacity for suggesting such a marital union. Eventually Christina decides to place her faith in Joey and John, but Matt refuses to be pushed into a hasty answer. The matter becomes more complex when John's parents arrive from Los Angeles, and are split in their reaction to the "good news." Finally both Matt and Mr. Prentice agree that the decision cannot lie with the parents, but must come from the children. Having relented, the group adjourn for the family dinner.

◆—◆—◆

Before starting production on the Technicolor *Guess Who's Coming to Dinner* at Columbia Pictures in February, 1967, Katharine Hepburn said of Spencer Tracy, "He is the best actor I've ever seen or worked with. I'm still learning things from Spence."

Since *Desk Set*, Hepburn had appeared in only two feature films, *Suddenly, Last Summer* (1959), and *Long Day's Journey into Night*, and was Oscar-nominated for each. Thereafter she was professionally inactive in order to be close at the side of Tracy who had become increasingly disabled throughout the 1960s by a heart ailment. As she succinctly weighed her vital relationship with Tracy, Hepburn admitted, "I have had twenty years [plus] of perfect companionship with a man among men."

Three of Tracy's four motion pictures since 1960 had been made under the aegis of producer-director Stanley Kramer, and it was Kramer who lured the ailing Tracy back to the cameras for what the actor announced would be his last film.

In retrospect, and in spite of the sobering real life circumstances surrounding the film, one has to agree with Penelope Mortimer (the *London Observer*) that William Rose's original screenplay (which won an Oscar!) was a "load of embarrassing rubbish." In the most obvious fashion, Rose's scenario and Kramer's direction established a terribly contrived, one-sided argument propounding the "daring" thesis of interracial marriage. It was all handled in such dreamland, rosy terms, that it hardly presented a very cogent panegyric.

Above and beyond the fact that Sidney Poitier was cast in his stock stereotype as the too-good-to-be-true great black hope, immaculate of manner, diction, speech and thought, the pivotal role of John Prentice found haloed Poitier as a super bright physician, a handsome, gentle soul, who knew how to be exceptionally kind and tolerant and even had a deep sorrow to his past (his wife and son had been killed in a Belgian train accident). Poitier has every qualification that a mother could ask for in a prospective son-in-law; the only stigma being his color and that, thanks to the loaded thesis here, proved to be no insurmountable barrier. As to preclude matters, even the trite tune "Glory of Love" sung over the opening credits points the way to a fantastic, improbable ending.

Twenty-five years had passed since Tracy and Hepburn appeared in *Woman of the Year* and in the interval they had perfected their interacting oncamera into a fine art worthy of the stage's Alfred Lunt and Lynn Fontanne. If grueling illness had made sixty-seven-year-old Tracy look terribly old and fragile to his still-adoring public, Hepburn appeared exceedingly glamorous in her Jean Louis-supervised wardrobe.

In essence *Guess Who's Coming to Dinner* is framed in terms of a drawing room comedy with only overtones of (hackneyed) social message. That the picture is so palatable is due to the attractive star cast, including Hepburn's youngish niece, Katharine Houghton, playing the daughter in question. In the course of the picture's 108 minutes, it is Hepburn who proves to be the mainstay of the gossamer tale (as she did on the soundstage sets, anticipating and catering to the ill Tracy's every little wish, even to the eventual distraction of Kramer). She emerges in the film as the real buoyant spirit, the contemporary thinking mother who, unlike her somewhat prejudiced husband, believes in letting others make their own free choice, no matter what she feels may be the dire consequences. Just as Hepburn's Christina Drayton is adept at ironing in the kitchen, so can she maneuver her crotchety husband, appease the genteel Monsignor (Cecil Kellaway) and fairly appraise Poitier's intruder. While everyone in the picture is overreacting pro or con to the news of Houghton's marriage proposal, Hepburn takes it all within her competent stride, displaying a maturity of personality that obviously came as much from within as from the scenario.

Throughout *Guess Who's Coming to Dinner*, which pulled in a walloping $25.5 million from distributors' domestic grosses, there were countless examples of fine interplay between Tracy and Hepburn as they manipulate their expert way through the unsubtle blend of comedy, romance, and social commentary. Whether Tracy is shaving in front of the bathroom mirror or stopping at a drive-in shop for a wild boysenberry ice cream cone, Hepburn is right at his oncamera side. She constantly is urging him onward, as she had in *State of the Union*, to shed his acquired misconceptions and to be the true liberal he once hoped to be. Perhaps the most touching line of dialog in the film occurs when Tracy says of Poitier and Houghton, "If what they feel for each other is even half what we felt, then that is everything."

*Guess Who's Coming to Dinner* concluded filming on May 26, 1967.

Some two weeks later (June 10th) Spencer Tracy was dead. This fact, alone, gives the picture, like Jean Harlow's *Saratoga* (1937) and Clark Gable's *The Misfits* (1961), a special aura. When this ninth and final Tracy-Hepburn picture was released in December, 1967, Richard Schickel *(Life* magazine) offered a particularly apt appraisal of the stars' work, "In the course of their long careers they have given us so much delight, so many fond memories, that the simple fact of their presence in the same film for one final curtain call is enough to bring a lump to your throat. They bicker fondly together in their patented manner, and for me, at least, their performances in this movie are beyond the bounds of criticism."

When Oscar time arrived, both Tracy and Hepburn were Academy Award-nominated for their performances in *Guess Who's Coming to Dinner*. Had Tracy lived he most likely would have won, but an Oscar has yet to be awarded to a star posthumously. However, Hepburn on her tenth bid for the Academy Award won her second Oscar. She was the first to say what a good many voters and fans felt, "I'm sure mine is for the two of us."

## THE YEARS AFTER

Many industry observers insisted that Spencer Tracy's untimely death would propel Katharine Hepburn into permanent retirement. Instead, the sixty-year-old actress launched herself into a spasm of professional activity. For *The Lion in Winter* (1968) she won her third Oscar, and, if *The Madwoman of Chaillot* (1969) was a boxoffice dud, her Broadway musical comedy debut in *Coco* (1969) was anything but that. As the French dress designer Coco Chanel, Hepburn offered an eccentric singing voice but displayed sufficient superstar charisma to keep the nearly-one-million-dollar production venture viable as long as she remained with the show in New York or on the road. *The Trojan Women* (1971) was a noble failure as a movie, while the far more modestly conceived *A Delicate Balance* offered Hepburn an opportunity to delve into the dramatics of Edward Albee. In 1974 she finally relented against video appearances by portraying the immortal Amanda in a telefeature version of Tennessee Williams' *The Glass Menagerie*. As if anxious to solidify her professional reputation with new types and generations of television-film audiences, Hepburn went to England to join Laurence Olivier in the telefeature, *Love Among The Ruins* (1975), and then returned to Hollywood (!) with John Wayne in *Rooster Cogburn* (1975), the sequel to *True Grit* (1969).

Garson Kanin devoted an entire volume, *Tracy and Hepburn* (1971), to explicating the mystique of his legendary friends. Hepburn summed it up so much better in one short sentence. When an interviewer posed the query, "If Tracy was a baked potato what was she?," Hepburn replied, simply and directly, "I'm a dessert. Ice cream with chocolate sauce."

In a publicity pose for **The Blue Dahlia** (Par., 1946)

# Chapter 20

# Alan Ladd
# &
# Veronica Lake

## ALAN LADD

5′ 4″
150 pounds
Blond hair
Blue eyes
Virgo

*Real name: same. Born September 3, 1913, Hot Springs, Arkansas. Married Marjorie Jane Harrold (193-), child: Alan; divorced 19--. Married Sue Carol (1942), children: David, Alana. Died January 3, 1964.*

### FEATURE FILMS:

No Man of Her Own (Par., 1932)*
Saturday's Millions (Univ., 1933)
Pigskin Parade (20th, 1936)
Last Train from Madrid (Par., 1937)
Souls at Sea (Par., 1937)
Hold 'em Navy (Par., 1937)
The Goldwyn Follies (UA, 1938)
Come on Leathernecks (Rep. 1938)
The Texans (Par., 1938)
The Green Hornet (Serial: Univ., 1940)

Rulers of The Sea (Par., 1939)
Beasts of Berlin (PRC, 1939)
Light of Western Stars (Par., 1940)
Gangs of Chicago (Rep., 1940)
In Old Missouri (Rep., 1940)
Her First Romance (Mon., 1940)
The Howards of Virginia (Col., 1940)
Those Were the Days (Par. 1940)
Captain Caution (UA, 1940)
Wildcat Bus (RKO, 1940)

*Possible Appearance

*Meet the Missus* (Rep., 1940)
*Great Guns* (20th, 1941)
*Citizen Kane* (RKO, 1941)
*Cadet Girl* (20th, 1941)
*Petticoat Politics* (Rep., 1941)
*The Black Cat* (Univ., 1941)
*The Reluctant Dragon* (RKO, 1941)
*Paper Bullets* (PRC, 1941)
*Joan of Paris* (RKO, 1942)
*This Gun for Hire* (Par., 1942)
*The Glass Key* (Par., 1942)
*Lucky Jordon* (Par., 1942)
*Star Spangled Rhythm* (Par., 1942)
*China* (Par., 1943)
*And Now Tomorrow* (Par., 1944)
*Salty O'Rourke* (Par., 1945)
*Duffy's Tavern* (Par., 1945)
*The Blue Dahlia* (Par., 1946)
*O.S.S.* (Par., 1946)
*Two Years Before the Mast* (Par., 1946)
*Calcutta* (Par., 1947)
*Variety Girl* (Par., 1947)
*Wild Harvest* (Par., 1947)
*My Favorite Brunette* (Par., 1947)*
*Saigon* (Par., 1948)
*Beyond Glory* (Par., 1948)
*Whispering Smith* (Par., 1948)
*The Great Gatsby* (Par., 1949)
*Chicago Deadline* (Par., 1949)
*Captain Carey, U.S.A.* (Par., 1950)

*Branded* (Par., 1951)
*Appointment with Danger* (Par., 1951)
*Red Mountain* (Par., 1952)
*The Iron Mistress* (WB, 1952)
*Thunder in the East* (Par., 1953)
*Desert Legion* (Univ., 1953)
*Shane* (Par., 1953)
*Botany Bay* (Par., 1953)
*Paratrooper* (Col., 1954)
*Saskatchewan* (Univ., 1954)
*Hell Below Zero* (Col., 1954)
*The Black Knight* (Col., 1954)
*Drum Beat* (WB, 1954)
*The McConnell Story* (WB, 1955)
*Hell on Frisco Bay* (WB, 1955)
*Santiago* (WB, 1956)
*Cry in the Night* (WB, 1956)†
*The Big Land* (WB, 1957)
*Boy on a Dolphin* (20th, 1957)
*The Deep Six* (WB, 1958)
*The Proud Rebel* (BV, 1958)
*The Badlanders* (MGM, 1958)
*The Man in the Net* (UA, 1959)
*Guns of the Timberland* (WB, 1960)
*All the Young Men* (Col., 1960)
*One Foot in Hell* (20th, 1960)
*13 West Street* (Col., 1962)
*The Duel of Champions* (Medallion, 1963)
*The Carpetbaggers* (Par., 1964)

*Unbilled Appearance
†Narrator

# VERONICA LAKE

**5′ 2″**
**92 pounds**
**Ash blonde hair**
**Blue-gray eyes**
**Scorpio**

*Real name: Constance Frances Marie Ockelman. Born November 14, 1919 Brooklyn, New York. Married John Detlie (1940), children: Anthony, Elaine; divorced 1943. Married Andre de Toth (1944), children: Michael, Diane; divorced 1952. Married Joseph McCarthy (1955); divorced 1959. Married Robert Carlton-Munroe (1972); separated 1972. Died July 7, 1973.*

**FEATURE FILMS:**

*All Women Have Secrets* (Par., 1939)
*Sorority House* (RKO, 1939)
*Young As You Feel* (20th, 1940)
*Forty Little Mothers* (MGM, 1940)
*I Wanted Wings* (Par., 1941)
*Sullivan's Travels* (Par., 1941)
*Hold Back the Dawn* (Par., 1941)°
*This Gun for Hire* (Par., 1942)
*The Glass Key* (Par., 1942)
*I Married a Witch* (UA, 1942)
*Star Spangled Rhythm* (Par., 1942)
*So Proudly We Hail* (Par., 1942)
*The Hour Before the Dawn* (Par., 1944)
*Bring on the Girls* (Par., 1945)
*Out of This World* (Par., 1945)

*Duffy's Tavern* (Par., 1945)
*Hold That Blonde* (Par., 1945)
*Miss Susie Slagle's* (Par., 1945)
*The Blue Dahlia* (Par., 1946)
*Ramrod* (UA, 1947)
*Variety Girl* (Par., 1947)
*The Sainted Sisters* (Par., 1948)
*Saigon* (Par., 1948)
*Isn't It Romantic?* (Par., 1948)
*Slattery's Hurricane* (20th, 1949)
*Stronghold* (Lip., 1952)
*Footsteps in the Snow* (Evergreen, 1966)
*Flesh Feast* (Viking International, 1970)

°Unbilled Appearance

Advertisement for **The Glass Key** (Par., 1942)

Brian Donlevy, Alan Ladd, and Veronica Lake in a publicity pose for **The Glass Key**

Advertisement for **Star Spangled Rhythm** (Par., 1942)

Alan Ladd, Veronica Lake, and Robert Preston in a publicity pose for **This Gun For Hire** (Par., 1942)

Advertisement for **Duffy's Tavern** (Par., 1945)

Advertisement for **The Blue Dahlia**

In **Duffy's Tavern**

Alan Ladd and Dorothy Lamour in **Variety Girl** (Par., 1947)

Douglas Dick, Veronica Lake, Wally Cassell, and Alan Ladd in **Saigon** (Par., 1948)

# THIS GUN FOR HIRE
*(Paramount, 1942) 80M.*

Producer, Richard M. Blumenthal; director, Frank Tuttle; based on the novel *A Gun for Sale* by Graham Greene; screenplay, Albert Maltz, W. R. Burnett; art director, Hans Dreier; songs, Frank Loesser and Jacques Press; camera, John Seitz; editor, Archie Marshek.

Veronica Lake (Ellen Graham); Robert Preston (Michael Crane); Laird Cregar (Willard Gates); Alan Ladd (Philip Raven); Tully Marshall (Alvin Brewster); Mikhail Rasumny (Slukey); Marc Lawrence (Tommy); Pamela Blake (Annie); Harry Shannon (Finnerty); Frank Ferguson (Albert Baker); Bernadene Hayes (Baker's Secretary); James Farley (Night Watchman); Virita Campbell (Cripple Girl); Roger Imhof (Senator Burnett); Victor Kilian (Brewster's Secretary); Olin Howland (Fletcher); Emmett Vogan (Charlie); Chester Clute (Mr. Stewart); Charles Arnt (Will Gates); Virginia Farmer (Woman in Shop); Clem Bevans (Old Timer); Harry Hayden (Restaurant Manager); Tim Ryan (Guard); Yvonne De Carlo (Show Girl); Ed Stanley (Police Captain); Eddy Chandler (Foreman); Phil Tead (Machinist); Charles R. Moore (Dining Car Waiter); Pat O'Malley (Conductor); Katherine Booth (Waitress); Sarah Padden (Mrs. Mason); Louise La Planche (Dancer); Richard Webb (Young Man); Frances Morris (Receptionist); Cyril Ring (Waiter); Lora Lee (Girl in Car); William Cabanne (Laundry Truck Driver).

New York Premiere: Paramount Theatre—May 13,1942
New York Television Debut: CBS—February 1, 1959

## Synopsis

A murderous criminal, Philip Raven, is hired by Willard Gates, contact man for Alvin Brewster, who is a wealthy head of a chemical concern and a fifth columnist, to murder Albert Baker in order to obtain secret documents from him. Willard pays Raven one thousand dollars in marked ten-dollar bills. He then reports a false holdup to police lieutenant Michael Crane, hoping that Raven will be caught passing a bill. Willard, who also runs a nightclub, hires Ellen Graham, an entertainer and girlfriend of Michael's, to perform her magic-singing act. Later she is taken to a U.S. senator who is investigating saboteurs in America and she agrees to work for him and watch Willard. When Raven spends a ten dollar bill, the serial number is recognized by the shopkeeper who notifies the police. Raven evades them and, rightfully angered, sets out to kill Willard. He follows him to a railroad station and boards the same train. En route he meets Ellen who is on her way to Los Angeles to assume her nightclub job. Willard spots the two of them on the train and wires ahead to the police. Forcing Ellen to help him, Raven escapes. Willard, suspicious of Ellen, invites her to his house and plans to kill her, but arranges for his chauffeur to do the killing. However, while outside the house, Raven learns of Willard's plans and rescues Ellen. He accompanies her to the nightclub, hoping to see Willard. But Willard is warned of Raven's whereabouts, and, with the help of policeman Michael, proposes to capture him. By using Ellen as a shield, Raven escapes again. Cornered in a railroad yard, Raven reveals to Ellen why he wants to catch Willard. On his promise that he will commit no violence, Ellen agrees to act as a decoy. The ruse fools the police and Raven makes his way to the office of Brewster and kills both him and Willard. But he, in turn, is killed by Michael, who had followed him.

◆◆◆

Paramount had acquired Graham Greene's 1936 novel *A Gun for Sale* shortly after publication, planning it for immediate production as a U.S. rendition of an Alfred Hitchcock-type yarn. But with one thing or another the project bogged down and by the time it was ready to roll the European-set tale of a spy ring and a girl, who gets mixed with a psychopathic murderer and helps to avert a world war, was badly out of date, for Hitler's Third Reich troops had marched into Czechoslavakia. More rescripting was necessitated, with the setting later changed to America and the plotline altered to coincide with the tense pre-Pearl Harbor American situation. Paramount and the public expected *This Gun for Hire* to be just a standard cops-and-gangsters-and-spies film, having no idea it would prove to be one of the big sleepers of the movie year, a chilly suspense tale with ironic humor.

Even in a period when gratuitous onscreen violence was being overshadowed by real life grand atrocities, *This Gun for Hire* was considered a sizzler. "It has two requirements of a good movie," reported *Life* magazine, "action and original characters." The *New York Herald-Tribune* probed further, "Behind scenes of violence and crisp dialogue, it suggests the background and past life of its characters with subtle restraint and brings them into bold relief in a boiling climax."

What really brought *This Gun for Hire* into dynamic focus was the onscreen pairing of two personalities, Veronica Lake and Alan Ladd. Lake had burst into international prominence with her vixenish role in *Men with Wings* (1941) in which her peek-a-book hairdo and cold baby-face looks made her the screen's newest sex sensation, definitely a newcomer with a different kind of erotic appeal. After Preston Sturges' *Sullivan's Travels* (1941) in which Lake emoted in ragamuffin outfits and her famed luxuriant hair mostly tucked under a cap, there was no doubt in Paramount's mind that Lake was big at the boxoffice. Therefore, *This Gun for Hire* was geared as *her* picture, even though it asked a lot that she was not equipped or willing to deliver. Her role as Ellen Graham required her to be a nightclub siren, who is a singer, dancer, and magician, none of which came within the real life province of casual, take-it-or-leave-it Lake's proficiencies. Director Frank Tuttle could have cameraman John Seitz fudge with Lake's onscreen time stepping, Martha Mears could dub her two songs ("Now You See It," "I've Got You") and professional magician Jan Grippo could teach the self-admitted clumsy celebrity to mock perform some simple sleight of hand tricks, but no one could push the self-indulgent Lake beyond her undeveloped potential. Josephine, the monkey, who was part of her celluloid magic act, kept biting the wispy blonde celebrity (which was not in the script), while director Tuttle kept prodding her to be more disciplined oncamera (which was futile). In addition, co-star Robert Preston, as her San Francisco police lieutenant boyfriend, countlessly redid his "passionate" love scenes with her, but to little avail. As *Variety* would weigh her appearance in *This Gun for Hire*, "Her career reaches a state of arrested development, . . ."

So why the tremendous fuss (there really was!) over *This Gun for Hire*? Because Lake oncamera in tandem with Ladd gave the illusion of being much more of a siren than she really was. The chemistry of Ladd with Lake made it seem that dilettante Lake was actually offering a respectable performance ("Uh-huh, I said performance," reported an astounded Leo Mishkin of the *New York Morning Telegraph*.)

Who was Ladd? A twenty-nine-year-old, 5'4" actor who had been on the fringes of moviemaking since 1932, but had only gained prominence earlier in 1942 with RKO's *Joan of Paris* in which he was the key subject of a very maudlin death scene. Paramount was rather half-hearted when as part of its advertising campaign for *This Gun for Hire* it described Ladd's role, "Murder is his business. His gun is for hire to anybody who has the price. The name of this strange man is Alan Ladd." But the public did not think him strange. Moviegoers were intrigued by his then-novel performance as a dispassionate, sleepy-eyed killer who loves children and milk. Everyone seemed fascinated by the disparity between his nice guy looks and his characterization as a cold-hearted murderer, a psychopath triggered into a rampage. Here was a man unperturbed by his seemingly distasteful tasks as a hit man. "How do ya feel when you're doin' a job like this?" candy munching Laird Cregar asks Ladd in *This Gun for Hire*. "I feel fine," replies the smooth-faced criminal, not a twitch in his ice-cold countenance. After all he once killed an aunt and never regretted it for a moment.

The critics were quick to compare Ladd to other established screen tough guys. The *Daily Worker* likened Ladd's performance to the "icy Bogart manner." *PM* ranked him as a "moody new trigger-man in the Alan Baxter mold." But Ladd really was a new breed modern outlaw, who "makes most of the screen's conventional gangster types seem as menacing as song-and-dance men" [Rose Pelswick *(New York Journal American)*]. What made Ladd's cinema emoting register so effectively was that "Everything he says and does fits wholly into character" [William Boehnel (*New York World Telegram*)]. Perhaps the *New Yorker* magazine best summed up the Ladd personae, "He seems to be a rather agreeable killer, his felt hat pulled down at a frivolous angle, his mouth only a trifle sullen. A different kind of mug, smooth and with even a parlor manner, he may start a vogue for a new species of melodrama—stories of nervous and gentle and sinister gunmen, without a trace of human kindness anywhere about them."

Throughout *This Gun for Hire* there exists an underplayed tension between Lake and Ladd, each so emotionally self-contained in their individual characterizations that only audience fantasizing could fill in the gaps which, of course, audiences happily did. Here was a calm killer " . . . who suggests by his deadpan acting the festering bitterness of a killer who hates everything" (*Liberty* magazine). He was a person who respects no man and manhandles women without the slightest compunction. Lake is merely a convenient tool for his gut needs and, strangest of all, she does not mind in the least. Her character has endured a rather purposeless existence, its highlight being a rather conventional romance with honest cop Preston. Now she is performing a patriotic turn for her country (helping to stop a plot to sell poison gas to the enemy), but at heart she is still a tough cookie who knows that life is full of many hard knocks, and one hurt more or less is not going to make such of a difference. Her manner and philosophy makes Ladd's crazed killer easily acceptable to her nonchalant nature. It is true that for most of this film she is being taunted and physically pushed into helping him actively or passively as a decoy. Nevertheless, a viewer could strongly suspect that had the script and the censors of the day permitted, she would have done much more for the guy without real regret. All of this was a far cry from Lana Turner's society gal falling for the aura of Robert Taylor's natty gangsterdom in MGM's *Johnny Eager* (1941) and the eager public appreciated the telling difference.

The climax of *This Gun for Hire* is perfectly in tune with all that has transpired before. The good guys may triumph, the spies may be killed or captured, but Ladd and Lake conclude their unstated passionate romance as it began—on a very different note. He dies in her lap, hardly mourned in a world that has no place for a conscienceless killer. But as one quipster of the time said, "By gosh. Better men have died with theirs in less pleasing places!" Was Ladd's Philip Raven a winner or loser in the crazy mixed-up world that he stalked? That was for each audience member to decide for himself.

*This Gun for Hire* came and went, but was certainly not forgotten. [It would be remade as the James Cagney Western *Short Cut to Hell* (1957) and as recently as 1972 Sammy Davis was considering a remake of the picture.] In his coverage of *This Gun for Hire*, Bosley Crowther (*New York Times*) editorialized, "One shudders to think of the career which Paramount must have in mind for Alan Ladd . . . Obviously, they have tagged him to be the toughest monkey loose on the screen." They certainly did and had decided to keep the luscious Veronica Lake at his oncamera side.

## THE GLASS KEY
*(Paramount, 1942) 85M.*

Associate Producer, Fred Kohlmar; director, Stuart Heisler; based on the novel by Dashiell Hammett; screenplay, Jonathan Latimer; art directors, Hans Dreier, Haldane Douglas; music, Victor Young; sound, Hugo Grenzbach, Don Johnson; camera, Theodor Sparkuhl; editor, Archie Marshek.

Brian Donlevy (Paul Madvig); Veronica Lake (Janet Henry); Alan Ladd (Ed Beaumont); Bonita Granville (Opal Madvig); Richard Denning (Taylor Henry); Joseph Calleia (Nick Varna); William Bendix (Jeff); Frances Gifford (Nurse); Donald MacBride (Farr); Margaret Hayes (Eloise Matthews); Moroni Olsen (Ralph Henry); Eddie Marr (Rusty); Arthur Loft (Clyde Matthews); George Meader (Claude Tuttle); Pat O'Malley, Ed Peil, Sr., James Millican (Politicians); Edmund Cobb, Frank Bruno, Jack Luden, Jack Gardner, Joe McGuinn, Frank Hagney (Reporters); John W. DeNoria (Groggins); Jack Mulhall (Lynch); Joseph King (Fisher); Al Hill (Bum); Freddie Walburn (Kid); Conrad Binyon (Stubby); Vernon Dent (Bartender); Stanley Price, Kenneth Chryst (Men in Barroom); Dane Clark (Henry Sloss); Norma Varden (Dowager); Frank Elliott (First Butler in Henry Home); George Cowl (Second Butler in Henry Home); Broderick O'Farrell, Arthur Hull, Tom O'Grady, Jack Fowler (Guests at Henry Dinner); Tom Fadden (Waiter); William Wagner (Butler); Charles Sullivan (Taxi Driver); Francis Sayles (Seedy-looking Man); George Turner (Doctor); Tom Dugan (Jeep); William Benedict (Sturdy); Lillian Randolph (Entertainer at Basement Club).

New York Premiere: Paramount Theatre—October 14, 1942
New York Television Debut: CBS—January 4, 1960

### Synopsis
Politician Paul Madvig backs Ralph Henry on a reform ticket against the advice of his henchman lieutenant, Ed Beaumont. Madvig's interest in Henry's daughter, Janet, was the actual motivating factor. Nick Varna, head of a gambling ring, opposes Madvig and seems to be implicated in the mysterious murder of Taylor Henry, the politician's dissipated son. However, the finger of guilt is thrust at Madvig, who had a motive since he resented Taylor's attention to his sister Opal. Varna compels publisher

Clyde Matthews to hint editorially at Madvig's guilt, knowing it will ruin Madvig politically. Ed begs Madvig to forget Janet and to make peace with Varna. Madvig refuses and he and Ed quarrel and part in anger. Varna offers Ed $10,000 to tell what he knows of Madvig's complicity in the murder. When Ed refuses to talk, Varna's henchmen beat him unmercifully. Ed eventually escapes and is confined to a hospital. When he recovers, Ed threatens to expose cringing Matthews as a tool of Varna, and the publisher kills himself. Madvig is arrested when a man known to have seen him and Taylor quarrelling is murdered. Ed tricks Jeff, one of Varna's henchmen, into confessing that he did the killing. When Varna berates Jeff, the latter strangles him. Learning that Janet had been sending anonymous notes to the district attorney indicating that Madvig had murdered her brother, Ed forces the district attorney to arrest Janet, charging her with murder. This causes her father to break; he admits that he had accidentally killed his son during a quarrel and that Madvig had kept quiet to shield him. Janet and Ed admit their love for each other and Madvig gives them his blessing.

◆——◆——◆

Paramount had enjoyed sufficient returns on its 1935 film rendition of Dashiell Hammett's *The Glass Key* which had promoted coin tossing screen gangster George Raft as a new kind of good bad guy. Since Ladd was being touted as a new variation on the Raft-style movie hoodlum, it was quickly decided to pair him and sultry Veronica Lake with reliable Brian Donlevy in a remake of this 1931 novel, newly scripted by Jonathan Latimer.

Studio ads pronounced the new star package as "The roughest, toughest trio that ever blasted the screen!

A battle of the sexes . . . and what a battle!

Brian Donlevy—He's rough!

Alan Ladd—He's tough!

Vs. Veronica Lake—Little Miss Dynamite!"

This new *The Glass Key* was not in the same league with Warner Bros.' recent remake of Hammett's *The Maltese Falcon* (1941) with Humphrey Bogart, and the Paramount film received its share of on-the-fence reviews. "[It] still has some of the fascination of the original, despite its unevenness." Even Lake would be ambiguous about the film in her autobiography (1969), stating, "Hammett fans hated our version of their favorite author's classic. Others never liked the original version with George Raft and felt we'd accomplished an improvement on the story."

The title of *The Glass Key* refers to the necessary entree into acceptable social spheres, a gambit highly desirable to the likes of such diamonds-in-the-rough as Brian Donlevy, who believes svelte, icy, desirable Lake is his quick ticket to the better world. She in turn regards him as necessary evil, playing up to him only in order to win his endorsement of her father's political campaign. Good-natured, stolid Donlevy melts at the mere sight of Lake (she being more aloof than aristocratic), but Donlevy's devoted henchman Ladd pierces right through her charade, and from their first encounter they embark on a love-hate relationship that builds through the film to its surprising conclusion. Not only is Donlevy cleared of his murder charges and regenerated by the events, but he can perceive that recent experiences have made new people of Ladd and Lake who now desire one another, not for a quick tumble in the hay, but for conventionally upright matrimonial lifemates. So in the final scenes when Ladd is cooly packing for a New York trip, Lake arrives and informs her would-be lover that she will not let him go without her, which, of course, he doesn't. Thus in its own way, *The Glass Key* is a very moral picture, disguised by a convoluted plot and assorted physical mayhem.

As noted, the critics reacted in various ways to *The Glass Key*. Strauss of the *New York Times* observed, "Miss Lake is still little more than a sullen voice and a head of yellow hair. . . . Alan Ladd is again the cold, mono-syllabic toughie he was in *This Gun for Hire*. His performance almost more than anything else, gives *The Glass Key* its frequent suspense." Audiences were less cagey. They cottoned very nicely to this new type of love team who was as far away from the likes of Jeanette MacDonald and Nelson Eddy or Myrna Loy and William Powell as corned beef hash is from tutti-fruiti ice cream.

Above and beyond the audience-pleasing quality of the astringent, chilly romance between Ladd and Lake, there was the well-promoted on-camera beating Ladd takes in the course of *The Glass Key*. More so than in the earlier Raft version, Ladd is pulverized oncamera to such a realistic extent that it provided viewers with more vicarious enjoyment than a live boxing match. (A good deal of the roughhouse success was due to the presence of burly William Bendix who would become just as integral an adjunct to Ladd's films as was Lake.) Bendix's dim-witted Jeff is the chief catalyst in this rugged confrontation, which finds the captured Ladd being pounded time and time again against the wall, until it seems either the plaster or Ladd's head will have to break. Actually the bed collapses, and brutish Bendix smashes a chair, picks up a fragment of the furniture and with glee is about to clobber his victim only to be quickly ordered to cool off in the corner. "Aw," complains the maniacal Bendix, "youse mean I don't get to smack baby no more?"

As Julian Fox wrote in the British *Films and Filming* of *The Glass Key*, "It is admittedly artful . . . the soft-key photography, the sharp editing, the admirable way in which 'violence is presented casually without emotional conflict.' A sort of ad man's demonstration of the-violences one-could-easily-live-with."

# STAR SPANGLED RHYTHM
## *(Paramount, 1942) 99M.*

Associate producer, Joseph Sistrom; director, George Marshall; screenplay, Harry Tugend; music, Robert Emmett Dolan; songs, Johnny Mercer and Harold Arlen; art director, Hans Dreier; camera, Leo Tover, Theodor Sparkuhl; editor, Paul Weatherwax.

Betty Hutton (Polly Judson); Eddie Bracken (Jimmy Webster); Victor Moore (Pop Webster); Anne Revere (Sarah); Walter Abel (Frisbee); Cass Daley (Mimi); Macdonald Carey (Louie the Lug); Gil Lamb (Hi-Pockets); William Haade (Duffy); Bob Hope (Master of Ceremonies); Fred Mac-Murray, Franchot Tone, Ray Milland, Lynne Overman (Men Playing Cards Skit); Dorothy Lamour, Veronica Lake, Paulette Goddard, Arthur Treacher, Walter Catlett, Sterling Holloway (Sweater, Sarong and Peekaboo Bang Number); Tom Dugan (Hitler); Paul Porcasi (Mussolini); Richard Loo (Hirohito); Alan Ladd (Scarface); Mary Martin, Dick Powell, Golden Gate Quartette (Dreamland Number); William Bendix, Jerry Colonna, Maxine Ardell, Marjorie Deanne, Lorraine Miller, Marion Martin, Chester Clute (Bob Hope Skit); Vera Zorina, Johnnie Johnston, Frank Faylen (Black Magic Number); Eddie "Rochester" Anderson, Katherine Dunham, Slim and Sam, Woodrow W. Strode (Smart as a Tack Number); Susan Hayward (Genevieve—Priorities Number); Ernest Truex (Murgatroyd—Priorities Number); Marjorie Reynolds, Betty Rhodes, Dona Drake, Louise LaPlanche, Lorraine Miller, Donivee Lee, Don Castle, Frederic Henry, Sherman Sanders (Swing Shift Number); Bing Crosby (Old Glory Number); Virginia Brissac (Lady from Iowa—Old Glory Number); Irving Bacon (New Hampshire Farmer—Old Glory Number); Matt McHugh (Man from Brooklyn—Old Glory Number); Peter Potter (Georgia Boy—Old Glory Number); Edward J. Marr (Heavy—Old Glory Number); Gary Crosby (Himself); Albert Dekker, Cecil Kellaway, Ellen Drew, Jimmy Lydon, Charles Smith, Frances Gifford, Susanna Foster, Robert Preston, Christopher King, Alice Kirby, Marcella Phillips (Finale); Walter Dare Wahl and Company (Specialty Act); Cecil B. DeMille, Preston Sturges, Ralph Murphy (Themselves); Maynard Holmes, James Millican (Sailors); Eddie Johnson (Tommy); Arthur Loft (Casey); Dorothy Granger, Barbara Pepper, Jean Phillips, Lynda Grey (Girls); Boyd Davis (Captain Kingsley); Frank Moran (Bit Man with Preston Sturges); Eddie Dew, Rod Cameron (Petty Officers); Barney Dean, Jack Hope (Themselves); John Shay (Sentry); Keith Richards (Officer); Jack Roberts (Assistant Director); Karin Booth (Kate); Gladys Blake (Liz).

New York Premiere: Paramount Theatre—December 30,1942
New York Television Debut: CBS—August 26, 1961

584

# Synopsis

Pop Webster, a former silent picture star and now a studio gateman at Paramount Pictures, is troubled when his sailor son Jimmy telephones and informs him that he is coming to the lot with some of his gob buddies. Pop has led Jimmy to believe that he was head of the studio. Polly Judson, a switchboard operator at the studio, decides to help Pop out of his predicament. When Frisbee, the studio chief, leaves the lot, Polly rushes Pop into Frisbee's swank office in time to greet Jimmy and his pals. While speaking with Jimmy, Pop answers calls from various production heads, and, posing as Frisbee, insults them. As a result, the entire studio ostracizes Frisbee, who is at a loss to understand why. After a tour of the lot, Polly accompanies Jimmy back to his ship and promises to marry him the following day, providing he is given shore leave. Jimmy manages to obtain the onshore pass by promising his captain that his father would provide a huge show for the fleet the next day. Once again Pop uses Frisbee's office, this time to order the stars to appear at the variety show. But Frisbee catches him and throws him off the lot. Determined to keep the truth from Jimmy, Polly speaks to the stars and persuades them to appear in the revue. Frisbee attempts to countermand this charitable offering, but the show goes on. It is a huge success, and Pop is promised a better studio job.

Paramount launched itself onto the all-star musical revue picture syndrome with this entry, picking up the grandiose formula used by the studio in its 1930s *Big Broadcast* series. The *New York Times* acknowledged that the film was full of "stars of considerable glitter [who] play vaudeville bits like good performing seals, . . . "

Alan Ladd and Veronica Lake did not share joint screen scenes in this celebrity-laden melee, but each had very effective skits. Lake joined with two other curvaceous studio stars, Paulette Goddard and Dorothy Lamour, in the song spoof, "A Sweater, a Sarong and a Peekaboo Bang" which teased the popular stars' screen images and character gimmicks. (Martha Mears again dubbed for Lake oncamera.) As a close follow-up to this trio's divertisement, Arthur Treacher, Walter Catlett, and Sterling Holloway, all more noted for their comedy talents than for their good looks, parodied the parody.

Even funnier was Ladd's brief scene which the *New York Herald Tribune* reported "practically had them in the aisles." Ladd is seen shooting pool with Macdonald Carey.

Ladd: "You rat. You squealed, didn't you?"

Carey: "Honest, Boss. I ain't the one . . . . Don't do it, boss!"

Whereupon Ladd takes out a bow and arrows and plunks the point shaft into the squealer.

# DUFFY'S TAVERN
*(Paramount, 1945) 97M.*

Associate producer, Danny Dare; director, Hal Walker; based on characters created by Ed Gardner; screenplay, Melvin Frank, Norman Panama; sketches, Frank, Panama, Abe S. Burrows, Barney Dean, George White, Eddie Davis, Matt Brooks; music director, Robert Emmett Dolan; music associate, Arthur Franklin; songs, Johnny Burke and Jimmy Van Heusen; Ben Raleigh and Bernie Wayne; art directors, Hans Dreier, William Flannery; set decorator, Stephen Seymour; choreography, Billy Daniel; assistant director, Eddie Salven; sound, Wallace Nogle, John Cape; process camera, Farciot Edouart; special effects, Gordon Jennings; camera, Lionel Lindon; editor, Arthur Schmidt.

Bing Crosby, Betty Hutton, Paulette Goddard, Alan Ladd, Dorothy Lamour, Eddie Bracken, Brian Donlevy, Sonny Tufts, Veronica Lake, Arturo De Cordova, Cass Daley, Diana Lynn, Gary Crosby, Philip Crosby, Dennis Crosby, Lindsay Crosby, William Bendix, Maurice Rocco, James Brown, Joan Caulfield, Gail Russell, Helen Walker, Jean Heather (Themselves); Barry Fitzgerald (Bing Crosby's Father); Victor Moore (Michael O'Malley); Marjorie Reynolds (Peggy O'Malley); Barry Sullivan (Danny Murphy); Ed Gardner (Archie); Charles Cantor (Finnegan); Eddie Green (Eddie the Waiter); Ann Thomas (Miss Duffy); Howard da Silva (Heavy); Billy De Wolfe (Doctor); Walter Abel (Director); Charles Quigley (Ronald); Olga San Juan (Gloria); Robert Watson (Masseur); Frank Fayle (Customer); Matt McHugh (Man Following Miss Duffy); Emmett Vogan (Makeup Man); Cyril Ring (Gaffer); Jimmie Dundee, Eddie Hall, Jack Lambert, Bill Murphy, Raymond Nash, Billy Jones, Frank Wayne, George Turner, Stephen Wayne, Len Hendry, John Indrisano, Fred Steele, Al Murphy (Waiters); Buck Harrington, Phil Dunham, Frank Faylen (Customers); Harry Tyler (Man in Bookie Joint); Audrey Young, Grace Albertson, Roberta Jonay (Telephone Operators); George M. Carleton (Mr. Richardson); Addison Richards (Mr. Smith, C.P.A.); Charles Cane (Cop with Smith); Charles B. Williams (Mr. Smith's Assistant); Lester Dorr, Charles Sullivan (Painters); Kernan Cripps (Regan's Assistant); Davidson Clark (Guard); Jack Perrin, James Flavin (Cops); Beverly Thompson, Noel Neill, Audrey Korn (School Kids); Crane Whitley (Plainclothesman); Betty Farrington (Woman with Baby); Ray Turner (Hotel Porter); Charles Mayon (Stork); Barney Dean (Himself); Theodore Rand (Stagehand); Tony Hughes (Manager of Green Star Shipping); George McKay (Regan); Jerry Maren (Midget); Julie Gibson, Catherine Craig (Nurses); Bill Edwards (Soda Fountain Clerk); Frances Morris (Woman who Screams); Valmere Barman (Girl at Soda Fountain); Albert Ruiz (Station Master-Soda Clerk).

New York Premiere: Paramount Theatre—September 5, 1945
New York Television Debut: CBS—December 31, 1959

## Synopsis

When Archie of Duffy's Tavern feeds fourteen ex-servicemen on credit, he has no idea of the repercussions of his charitable act. The men are awaiting the re-opening of a phonograph recording company owned by Michael O'Malley who claims he cannot recommence business because of the shellac shortage. Actually O'Malley is in financial straits and his credit is totally worthless. Archie's troubles begin when his employer finds a discrepancy in the books, a means by which Archie had used to conceal the credit he has extended to the veterans. With the district attorney on his trail, Archie undertakes to enlist groups of Hollywood stars to perform in a stage benefit to raise funds to re-open the record factory so that the ex-G.I.s can return to work. In the course of bringing the charity revue to fruition, Archie gets himself into numerous ticklish situations involving the stars and the ever-present police.

◆◆◆

As Ed Gardner's Archie of radio fame might say, "Let us face it," this was some hodgepodge of celebrity acts. However, the *New York Herald-Tribune* reported, "Even with the all-star cast that Paramount has tossed into this cinematic goulash, it is a rather tasteless dish. . . . For most of the time it meanders along as though there hasn't ever been an assistant director on the lot."

Among the "real live movie stars in their own flesh and blood" were Alan Ladd, Veronica Lake, and Howard da Silva in a funny blackout skit, in which eavesdroppers think the trio is indulging in vicious reality when they are only practicing a radio skit. In the scene-within-the-scene, Ladd calmly stands by while roughneck da Silva beats up vulnerable Lake, with Ladd taunting the angered abuser to new peaks of sadism on "poor" Lake. As a reversal of his movie image, Ladd refuses to assist Lake, but rather leaves the unpleasant scene, advising the "shaken" Lake, "Lady, you better get out of here before ya get your teeth kicked in."

## VARIETY GIRL
### *(Paramount, 1947) 83M.*

Producer, Daniel Dare; director, George Marshall; screenplay, Edmund Hartmann, Frank Tashlin, Robert Welch, Monte Brice; art directors, Hans Dreier, Robert Clatworthy; set decorators, Sam Comer, Ross Dowd; puppetoon sequence by George Pal; music director, Joseph J. Lilley; music associate, Troy Sanders; orchestrator, N. Van Cleave; music for puppetoon sequence, Edward Plumb; songs, Frank Loesser; assistant director, George Templeton; sound, Gene Merritt, John Cope; process camera, Farciot Edouart; special effects, Gordon Jennings; camera, Lionel Lindon, Stuart Thompson; editor, LeRoy Stone.

Mary Hatcher (Catherine Brown); Olga San Juan (Amber LaVonne); DeForest Kelley (Bob Kirby); William Demarest (Barker); Frank Faylen

(Stage Manager); Frank Ferguson (J. R. O'Connell); Russell Hicks, Crane Whitley, Charles Coleman, Hal K. Dawson, Eddie Featherston (Men at Steambath); Catherine Craig (Secretary); Bing Crosby, Bob Hope, Gary Cooper, Ray Milland, Alan Ladd, Barbara Stanwyck, Paulette Goddard, Dorothy Lamour, Veronica Lake, Sonny Tufts, Joan Caulfield, William Holden, Lizabeth Scott, Burt Lancaster, Gail Russell, Diana Lynn, Sterling Hayden, Robert Preston, John Lund, William Bendix, Barry Fitzgerald, Cass Daley, Howard Da Silva, Billy De Wolfe, Macdonald Carey, Arleen Whelan, Patric Knowles, Mona Freeman, Cecil Kellaway, Johnny Coy, Virginia Field, Richard Webb, Stanley Clements, Cecil B. DeMille, Mitchell Leisen, Frank Butler, George Marshall, Roger Dann, Pearl Bailey, The Mulcay's, Spike Jones and His City Slickers, Mikhail Rasumny, Rae Patterson, George Reeves, Wanda Hendrix, Sally Rawlinson, Nanettee Parks, Adra Verna, Patricia Barry, June Harris (Themselves); Ann Doran (Hairdresser); Glenn Tryon (Bill Farris); Nella Walker (Mrs. Webster); Torben Meyer (Andre the Headwaiter at the Brown Derby); Jack Norton (Brown Derby Busboy); Elaine Riley (Cashier); Charles Victor (Assistant to Mr. O'Connell); Gus Taute (Assistant to the Assistant); Harry Hayden (Grauman's Chinese Theatre Stage Manager); Janet Thomas, Roberta Jonay (Girls); Wallace Earl (Girl with Sheep Dog); Dick Keene (Dog Trainer); Jerry James (Assistant Director); Eric Alden (Makeup Man); Frank Mayo (Director); Lucille Barkley, Carolyn Butler (Secretaries); Pinto Collvig (Special Voice Impersonation); Edgar Dearing, Ralph Dunn (Cops); Jack Overman (Abdul); Paul Lees (Usher); Joey Ray, Hal Rand (Theatre Managers); Douglas Regan, Warren Joslin (Boys); Robert Williams (George Pal's Assistant); Lee Emery, Marilyn Gray, Renee Randall (Usherettes); Alma Macrorie (Proprietress); Micheal Harvey (American Officer); Duke Johnson (Juggler); Willa Pearl Curtis (Sister Jenkins); Mildred Boyd (Sister Jenkins' Daughter); Raymond Largay (Director of Variety Club).

New York Premiere: Paramount Theatre—October 15, 1947
New York Television Debut: CBS—February 26, 1961

## Synopsis

This tribute to the Variety Clubs of America opens with a brief flashback to eighteen years ago, depicting the finding of a homeless waif in a Pittsburgh movie theatre and the infant's adoption by a group of showmen who start the charitable Variety Club movement. Shifting to the present day, the ward, now grown to a young lady, Catherine Brown, heads for Hollywood in search of a screen career. There she becomes chums with brassy Amber LaVonne, another cinema hopeful, and both become involved in a complicated comedy of errors as they crash the Paramount studio gates in an effort to land movie contracts.

"There is a little of everything and not much of anything in *Variety Girl*" [Otis L. Guernsey, Jr. (*New York Herald-Tribune*)].

Within this eighty-three-minute jamboree the funniest sequence was provided by Spike Jones and his musical mayhem, although for many the surprise scene of the film was the dueting of Alan Ladd and Dorothy Lamour in the song "Tallahassee" which occurs in a passenger plane setting. (In his variant pre-stardom days, Ladd had appeared in such Soundies movie musical shorts as *Iron Menace*.) Ladd may have seemed a bit stiff and nervous in his rendering of the Frank Loesser lyrics, but the public was enthusiastic about the pint-sized tough guy turning crooner. There were trade rumors that Ladd would thereafter star with Betty Hutton in *Sometimes I'm Happy* (a project never made) or with the blonde bombshell in *Somebody Loves Me,* the Blossom Seeley musical biography eventually made in 1952 with Hutton and Ralph Meeker.

Because she was pregnant at the time of production work on *Variety Girl,* Lake was only briefly featured in the finale number to the picture. It is unlikely that had her condition been otherwise that she would have had much more to do, for the studio had lost almost as much interest in her as the average filmgoer. The advertisements for *Variety Girl* substantiate this conclusion. Among those studio stars featured with large sized photo cutouts are Bing Crosby, Bob Hope, Barbara Stanwyck, Ray Milland, Gary Cooper, Betty Hutton, Barry Fitzgerald, Paulette Goddard, Dorothy Lamour, and Alan Ladd. Lake was spotted in the ad in the secondary smaller sized photos. Such is passing fame!

## THE BLUE DAHLIA
### (Paramount, 1946) 96M.

Producer, George Marshall; associate producer, John Houseman; director, Marshall; story-screenplay, Raymond Chandler; art director, Hans Dreier, Walter Tyler; set decorators, Sam Comer, Jimmy Walters; assistant director, C. C. Coleman; music director, Victor Young; sound, Gene Merritt; process camera, Farciot Edouart; camera, Lionel Lindon; editor, Arthur Schmidt.

Alan Ladd (Johnny Morrison); Veronica Lake (Joyce Harwood); William Bendix (Buzz Wanchek); Howard da Silva (Eddie Harwood); Doris Dowling (Helen Morrison); Tom Powers (Captain Hendrickson); Hugh Beaumont (George Copeland); Howard Freeman (Corelli); Don Costello (Leo); Will Wright ("Dad" Newell); Frank Faylen (The Man); Walter Sande (Heath); Vera Marshe (Blonde); Mae Busch (Jenny the Maid); Gloria Williams (Assistant Maid); Harry Hayden (Mr. Hughes the Assistant Hotel Manager); George Barton (Cab Driver); Harry Barris (Bellhop); Paul Gustine

(Doorman); Roberta Jonay (Girl Hotel Clerk); Milton Kibbee (Night Hotel Clerk); Dick Winslow (Piano Player at Party); Anthony Caruso (Marine Corporal); Matt McHugh (Bartender); Arthur Loft (The Wolf); Stan Johnson (Naval Officer); Ernie Adams (Joe—Man in Coveralls); Henry Vroom (Master Sergeant); Harry Tyler (Clerk in Bus Station); Jack Clifford (Plainclothesman); George Sorel (Paul the Captain of Waiters); James Millican, Albert Ruiz (Photographers); Charles A. Hughes (Lieutenant Lloyd); Leon Lombardo (Mexican Bellhop); Nina Borget (Mexican Waitress); Douglas Carter (Bus Driver); Ed Randolph (Cop); Bea Allen (News Clerk); Perc Launders (Hotel Clerk); Jimmy Dundee (Driver of Gangster Car); Tom Dillon (Prowl Car Cop); Dick Elliott (Motor Court Owner); Clark Eggleston (Elevator Operator); George Carleton (Clerk at DeAnza Hotel); Jack Gargan (Cab Driver); Lawrence Young (Clerk); Franklin Parker (Police Stenographer); Noel Neill, Mavis Murray (Hat Check Girls); Brooke Evans, Carmen Clifford, Audrey Westphal, Lucy Knoch, Audrey Korn, Beverly Thompson, Jerry James, Charles Mayon, William Meader (Cocktail Party Guests).

New York Premiere: Paramount Theatre—May 8, 1946
New York Television Debut: CBS—March 10, 1962

## Synopsis

Upon his return from overseas, ex-Naval pilot Johnny Morrison leaves his wife, Helen, after learning that she had been too friendly with night-club owner Eddie Harwood. That same night Buzz Wanchek, Johnny's mentally-disturbed wartime buddy, strikes up an acquaintance with Helen at a bar, not knowing that she is Johnny's wife. He accepts her invitation to visit her apartment. Later she is visited by Eddie, who wants to break off relations with her, but dares not because she knows he is a fugitive from justice. Both men are observed entering the apartment by the house detective, Dad Newell, who finds Helen dead on the following morning, having been shot with Johnny's service revolver. Meanwhile, Johnny, having spent the night on the road and at a hotel where he made the acquaintance of Joyce Harwood, Eddie's estranged wife, hears a radio broadcast announcing Helen's murder and learns that the police suspect him of the crime. In the ensuing days, Johnny learns that Helen knew of Eddie's past and that the police have discerned that Buzz was with Helen the night of her murder, and also suspects his pal. Eddie, learning that Johnny has discovered his secret, has him kidnapped, but Johnny puts up a strenuous fight during which Eddie is killed by a stray bullet. With Eddie eliminated, the list of suspects narrows down to Johnny, Buzz, or Joyce, each of whom had a motive to commit the crime, or was at least circumstantially involved. But Johnny, through his tact in handling Buzz, uncovers evidence that forces a confession from Dad Newell, who, having had a personal grievance against Helen, murdered her and tried to direct suspicion onto the others.

◆——◆——◆

"The picture is as neatly stylized and synchronized, and as uninterested in moral excitement, as a good ballet; it knows its own weight and size perfectly and carries them gracefully and without self-importance; it is, barring occasional victories and noble accidents, about as good a movie as can be expected from the big factories" [James Agee (*The Nation*)]. As Bosley Crowther (*New York Times*) sized it up, the film was "a honey of a rough-em-up romance."

Once Alan Ladd returned to filmmaking after his medical discharge from the Air Corps in 1944, he promptly resolidified his growing reputation as a ranking boxoffice star. This fact was substantiated by his being top-billed over Veronica Lake in the delayed-release *The Blue Dahlia*. Her celebrity status had fast dimmed in post-1944 Hollywood, where there were such more substantial Lake successors and rivals as Lauren Bacall and, later, Lizabeth Scott. The script to the "tough and tensile" *The Blue Dahlia* was by Raymond Chandler, based on his unfinished novel. He turned out the screenplay in little over a month's time, finishing the last days of his scenario work, according to associate producer John Houseman, without drawing a sober breath.

*The Blue Dahlia* remains a gem of 1940s filmmaking and for this author is the best of the Ladd-Lake cinema outings, with Ladd's dead-pan ferocity in constant competition with her brazen coyness. Director George Marshall created such a resilient ambiance, in which his six players could emote, that the picture is as valid today as when initially released. The picture's main settings (the Cavendish Hotel apartments in Hollywood, complete with tacky neon signs, stucco walls, a seedy house detective and a juke box bar, the Blue Dahlia Club on Sunset Strip, and a rundown Los Angeles transient hotel) expertly capture the flavor of post-war tawdriness and leave their indelible mark on the movie's characters. Most impressive of all the film's settings is the claustrophobic car interior set used in the story on the rainy night when Lake picks up hitchhiking Ladd on the Cahuenga Pass and drives him to Malibu. Their moments together here, with the windshield wipers slashing in rhythm at the rain, the hum of the tires on the wet road, and the flashing lights of oncoming cars, set up the ideal isolated backdrop for the two blonde progenitors of icy cold romanticism to work their wiles on one another in taciturn friendliness. They exchange furtive glances of sexual interest, but are conscious of each's overriding need for introspective self-sufficiency, even though they vaguely chit chat at dinner and spend part of the next day together. (Later in the film there would be another car scene as the couple drive in the Hollywood Hills near the planetarium.) This scene personified the screen magic of Ladd and Lake.

In addition, the overall success\* of *The Blue Dahlia* owes a great deal to its supporting cast. Once again big-framed actor William Bendix was called upon to essay a key role in a Ladd-Lake outing, this time as the shell-shocked tail gunner who goes berserk when outside noises rattle his brain. Bendix's pathetic, fully realized Buzz Wanchek is many moon leagues away from his later, more famous, television characterization of Chester A. Riley. Also within *The Blue Dahlia*, Howard da Silva admirably captures the pretentious qualities of a rather minor underworld figure who thinks of himself as a flashy ladies' man, sending his loves blue dyed dahlias, but who is really a rather mundane-looking, middle-aged businessman. In moviegoing circles Martha Vickers may have been better known for her cinema vixens (one part kitten, one part minx) than Paramount's Doris Dowling [the 'natch girl of *The Lost Weekend* (1945)], but Dowling offers a fully realized portrayal of the type in this Ladd-Lake film. Expertly she etches a creature who not only plays house with others while hubby is away in the service, but so disvalues the welfare of infant son Danny that he is killed, not from illness as she informs Ladd, but an automobile accident in which she was a drunk driver.

Given this set of cinema characters, *The Blue Dahlia* rips into action, with war hero Ladd having reality thrust in his face his first night home, his wife proving to be nothing more than a tramp. James Cagney may have pushed a grapefruit in his woman's mug, but Ladd is more direct; he slaps Dowling hard across her face, then walks out of their apartment in disgust. All of which makes him very unreceptive to the next woman who floats into his life, who is none other than spouse (Lake) of his wife's recent boyfriend (da Silva). In the standard Ladd screen tradition, he undergoes another brutal going-over in *The Blue Dahlia* as da Silva's thugs work him over, a grueling beating that would have done in a lesser man. And as always Ladd takes his beating as stoically as Lake dishes out her emotional reactions to her new flame.

While Ladd's performance in *The Blue Dahlia* was acknowledged with enthusiasm by the public and reported with controlled admiration by the skeptical press, Lake, who had never endeared herself to the news media, had to search hard to find any favorable comments of her latest movie performance. Crowther of the *Times* was one of her few semi-champions, and even he was guarded in his offhanded praise: ". . . her contribution is essentially that of playing slightly starved for a good man's honest affection, to which she manifests an eagerness to respond. And it is indeed remarkable how obvious she makes this look without doing very much."

\*It grossed over $2.75 million.

## SAIGON
### (Paramount, 1948) 93M.

Producer, P. J. Wolfson; director, Leslie Fenton; story, Julian Zimet;

screenplay, Wolfson, Arthur Sheekman; art directors, Hans Dreier, Henry Bumstead; set decorators, Sam Comer, Bertram Granger; music-music director, Robert Emmett Dolan; assistant director, Francisco Day; makeup, Wally Westmore; costumes, Edith Head; sound, Wallace Nogle, Gene Garvin; process camera, Farciot Edouart; special effects, Gordon Jennings; camera, John F. Seitz; editor, William Shea.

Alan Ladd (Major Larry Briggs); Veronica Lake (Susan Cleaver); Douglas Dick (Captain Mike Perry); Wally Cassell (Sergeant Pete Rocco); Luther Adler (Lieutenant Keon); Morris Carnovsky (Alex Maris); Mikhail Rasumny (Clerk); Luis Van Rooten (Simon); Eugene Borden (Boat Captain); Griff Barnett (Surgeon); Frances Chung (Chinese Nurse); Betty Bryant (Singer at Waterfront Cafe); Dorothy Eveleigh (Portuguese Woman); Harry Wilson (Stevedore); William Yip (Cafe Proprietor); Lester Sharpe (Barman at Cafe); Allan Douglas (American Soldier/Vendor); Kenny O'Morrison (Air Corps Lieutenant); Lee Tung Foo (Chinese Farmer); Leo Abbey (Sinister Driver); Oie Chan (Farmer's Wife/Flower Vendor); Charles Stevens (Driver of Susan's Car); Thomas Quon Woo, Rito Punay, Quon Gong, Joe R. Bautista (Natives); Tommy Lee (Ox Cart Driver); Eddie Lee (Tea House Merchant); Billy Louie (Woman in Tea House); Moy Ming (Proprietor of Tea House); George Chan (Tea House Customer); Perry Ivins (Prisoner at Hotel); Kanza Omar (Russian Entertainer); Tom Lee (Farmer at Rice Paddy); Mary Chan (Farmer's Wife); Angel Cruz (Boat Pilot); Anthony Barredo (Boat Mechanic); Philip Ahn (Boss Merchant); Luke Chan, Ralph R. Sencuya (Tailors); Jean DeBriac, Jack Chefe (Hotel Clerks); Harold G. Fong (Bartender); George Sorel (Travel Agent); Andra Verne, Renee Randall, Hazel Shon (Girls); Jimmy Dundee (Stunt Man); Andre Charlot (Priest).

New York Premiere: Paramount Theatre—March 31, 1948
New York Television Debut: CBS—September 16, 1960

## Synopsis

Learning that their buddy Mike Perry is doomed to die within a few months because of a war injury, his pals, Major Larry Briggs and Sergeant Pete Rocco, agree to keep the news from Mike and to show him an action-packed time until the end. Needing funds to carry out their plans, the trio undertake to fly wealthy importer Alex Maris from Shanghai to Saigon, agreeing to ask no questions in lieu of the healthy $10,000 fee. Susan Cleaver, Maris' secretary, comes to the airport at departure time but Maris is delayed. When he approaches the field with the police in pursuit, the trio take off without him, accompanied by the protesting Susan who carries with her a briefcase containing $500,000, the money Maris had obtained as a war profiteer. Motor trouble compels Larry to make a forced landing, and they continue their journey by ox-cart and river boat.

Because of her apparent tie to Maris, Larry distrusts Susan, but he tolerates the mysterious girl because Mike has fallen in love with her. Larry compels her to pretend that she loves Mike, threatening to reveal her connections with Maris to detective Keon who has been trailing their every step. Despite the outward animosity, however, Larry and Susan find themselves falling in love. Complications set in when Maris arrives and resorts to violence in order to recover his money. He is eliminated by Pete and Mike, who are killed themselves when they come to Larry's defense. After attending his pal's burial, Larry and Susan vow to start a new life together.

◆◆◆

Not even the Paramount publicity department was very convincing in its efforts to promote this celluloid turkey. "It's the top LADD venture. He's gunning for the Orient's most dangerous man . . . using a half-million dollar blonde as bait!"

Having commercialized her peekaboo hairdoo to its fullest extent, *Saigon* found fast fading star Veronica Lake reshaping her blonde mop to a more conventional style trying to focus more attention to her tight black sweater-clad figure. After all, the programmer *Saigon* was presenting a "new" (not really) Lake whom the ads proclaimed, "The only thing cold about Veronica Lake is the gun in her hand," she now being touted as a sultry "siren" who can inform Alan Ladd "You're too much a man ever to be trusted."

Even in the pre-Vietnam War days of 1948, the least observant viewer could easily spot the phoniness of the picture's pseudo-exotic settings, which were as flat and empty as the screenplay and direction.

Critics like Bosley Crowther *(New York Times)*, never staunch fans of the Ladd brand of emoting, were eager to report the least public substantiation of the star's diminishing popularity and an outing to New York's Paramount Theatre to witness *Saigon* provided Crowther with just such an opportunity. ". . . it is something to hear that audience merrily hawhaw when Mr. Ladd gives them the old business that used to evoke rapturous squeals. And to hear the hoots of laughter when their boy glides up to a bar and snarls, 'Bourbon, straight, leave the bottle,' is like the sound of a Governor's reprieve. Maybe we're just a dreamer—but this looks like the rift in Ladd's lute. Wow! What a revolution if those bobby-soxers are wise!" Considering Ladd's still solid boxoffice record to come, Crowther's victory cries were a bit premature.


## THE YEARS AFTER

Less than a year after the release of *Saigon*, Veronica Lake was discharged from Paramount Pictures, and, after a secondary lead at Twentieth Century-Fox in a film directed by her husband, Andre de Toth, she pulled up stakes from California. As she later casually revealed in her salty autobiography, *Veronica* (1969), the following years were a fast descent into a self-made hell as she dwelt on the periphery of show business with television and (summer) stock appearances. She finally ended up as a barmaid at a rundown New York City hotel, then moved to Florida and later to England. She later returned to the United States and drifted out of the news once again. Few knew where she was when she died on July 7, 1973 at a Burlington, Vermont, hospital of what was attributed to acute hepatitis. Twenty-five years after Hollywood had "buried" her, the sultry peekaboo blonde was no more.

Alan Ladd, on the other hand, retained his motion picture popularity throughout most of the 1950s, winning plaudits for his quiet, but strong, performance in George Stevens' *Shane* (1953). But by the time of the CinemaScope *Boy on a Dolphin* (1957) in which Sophia Loren, twice his height and half his age (so went the joke), was the focal figure, forty-four-year-old Ladd was in professional decline. Ironically the best performance of his mature movie career was in the flamboyant *The Carpetbaggers* released some months after his untimely death on January 3, 1964. Like similarly tough screen figure John Garfield, Ladd never became a posthumous cult figure in the tradition of Humphrey Bogart. There are many who wonder why.

In a publicity pose from **Arabian Nights** (Univ., 1942)

# Chapter 21

# Jon Hall
# &
# Maria Montez

## JON HALL

6' 2"
196 pounds
Brown hair
Brown eyes
Pisces

*Real name: Charles Hall Locher. Born February 23, 1913, Fresno, California. Married Frances Langford (1938); divorced 1955. Married Racquel Ames (1959); divorced 196-. Remarried.*

**FEATURE FILMS:**

*Women Must Dress* (Mon., 1935)
*Charlie Chan in Shanghai* (20th, 1935)
*The Clutching Hand* (Serial: Stage and Screen, 1936)
*Winds of the Wasteland* (Rep., 1936)
*The Lion Man* (Normandy Pictures, 1936)
*The Mysterious Avenger* (Col., 1936)
*Mind Your Own Business* (Par., 1936)
*Girl From Scotland Yard* (Par., 1937)
*The Hurricane* (UA, 1937)
*Sailor's Lady* (20th, 1940)
*Kit Carson* (UA, 1940)

*Aloma of the South Seas* (Par., 1941)
*Tuttles of Tahiti* (RKO, 1942)
*Eagle Squadron* (Univ., 1942)
*Invisible Agent* (Univ., 1942)
*Arabian Nights* (Univ., 1942)
*White Savage* (Univ., 1943)
*Ali Baba and the Forty Thieves* (Univ., 1944)
*Lady in the Dark* (Par., 1944)
*Invisible Man's Revenge* (Univ., 1944)
*Cobra Woman* (Univ., 1944)
*Gypsy Wildcat* (Univ., 1944)
*San Diego, I Love You* (Univ., 1944)
*Sudan* (Univ., 1945)

Men in Her Diary (Univ., 1945)
The Michigan Kid (Univ., 1947)
Last of the Redmen (Col., 1947)
The Vigilantes Return (Univ., 1947)
The Prince of Theives (Col., 1948)
The Mutineers (Col., 1949)
Zamba (Eagle Lion, 1949)
Deputy Marshal (Screen Guild, 1949)
On the Isle of Samoa (Col., 1950)

When the Redskins Rode (Col., 1951)
China Corsair (Col., 1951)
Hurricane Island (Col., 1951)
Brave Warrior (Col., 1952)
Last Train from Bombay (Col., 1952)
Hell Ship Mutiny (Rep., 1957)
Forbidden Island (Col., 1959)
Beach Girls and the Monster (United States Films, 1965)

# MARIA MONTEZ

**5' 7"**
**120 pounds**
**Red brown hair**
**Brown eyes**
**Gemini**

Real name: Maria Africa Vidal de Santo Silas. Born June 6, 1920,*
Barahona, Dominican Republic. Married Jean Pierre Aumont
(1943), child: Maria Christina. Died September 7, 1951.
*Some sources list 1917

FEATURE FILMS:

Lucky Devils (Univ., 1940)
The Invisible Woman (Univ., 1941)
Boss of Bullion City (Univ., 1941)
That Night in Rio (20th, 1941)
Raiders of the Desert (Univ., 1941)
Moonlight in Hawaii (Univ., 1941)
South of Tahiti (Univ., 1941)
Bombay Clipper (Univ., 1942)
Mystery of Marie Roget (Univ., 1942)
Arabian Nights (Univ., 1942)
White Savage (Univ., 1943)
Ali Baba and the Forty Thieves (Univ., 1944)
Follow the Boys (Univ., 1944)
Cobra Woman (Univ., 1944)
Gypsy Wildcat (Univ., 1944)

Bowery to Broadway (Univ., 1944)
Sudan (Univ., 1945)
Tangier (Univ., 1946)
Pirates of Monterey (Univ., 1947)
The Exile (Univ., 1947)
Siren of Atlantis (UA, 1948)
Portrait d'un Assassin (Gauthier-Philbere, 1949)
Hans Le Marin (The Wicked City) (French, 1949)
Il Ladro Di Venezia (The Thief of Venice) (Italian, 1949)
Amore e Sangue (Love and Blood) (Italian, 1950)
La Vendetta del Corsaro (The Pirate's Revenge (Italian, 1950)

In **Gypsy Wildcat** (Univ., 1944)

Advertisement for **White Savage** (Univ., 1943)

Shemp Howard, Jeni Le Gon, Maria Montez, John Qualen, Jon Hall, Wee Willie Davis, Billy Gilbert, Harry Cording, and Sabu in **Arabian Nights**

Thomas Gomez, Maria Montez, Sabu, and Jon Hall in **White Savage**

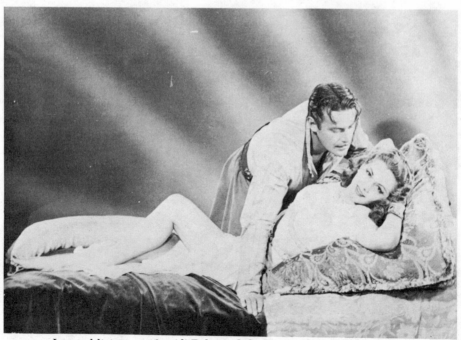

In a publicity pose for **Ali Baba and the Forty Thieves** (Univ., 1944)

In a publicity pose for **Cobra Woman** (Univ., 1944)

In **Cobra Woman**

Advertisement for **Sudan** (Univ., 1945)

Andy Devine, Jon Hall, and Maria Montez in **Sudan**

# ARABIAN NIGHTS
## (Universal, 1942) C-86M.

Producer, Walter Wanger; director, Jack Rawlins; story-screenplay, Michael Hogan; additional dialog, True Boardman;. technical adviser, Jamiel Hasson; music, Frank Skinner; assistant director, Fred Frank; production designer, Jack Orterson, Alexander Golitzen; set decorator, R. A. Gausman, Ira S. Webb; women's costumes, Vera West; music director, Charles Previn; camera, Milton Krasner; editor, Philip Cahn.

Sabu (Ali Ben Ali); Jon Hall (Haroun al Raschid); Maria Montez (Sherazad); Leif Erikson (Kamar); Billy Gilbert (Ahmad); Edgar Barrier (Hadan); Richard Lane (Corporal); Turhan Bey (Captain); John Qualen (Aladdin); Shemp Howard (Sinbad); Wee "Willie" Davis (Valda); Thomas Gomez (Hakim the Slave Trader); Jeni Le Gon (Dresser to Sherazad); Robert Greig (Eunuch-Story Teller); Charles Coleman (Eunuch); Adia Kuznetzoff (Slaver); Emory Parnell (Harem Sentry); Harry Cording (Blacksmith); Robin Raymond (Slave Girl); Carmen D'Antonio, Virginia Engels, Nedra Sanders, Mary Moore, Veronika Pataky, Jean Trent, Frances Gladwin, Rosemarie Dempsey, Patsy Mace, Pat Starling, June Ealey (Harem Girls); Andre Charlot, Frank Lackteen, Anthony Blair, Robert Barron, Art Miles, Murdock MacQuarrie (Bidders); Elyse Knox (Duenna); Burna Acquanetta (Ishya); Ernest Whitman (Nubian Slave); Eva Puig (Old Woman); Ken Christy (Provost Marshal); Johnnie Berkes (Blind Beggar); Cordell Hickman, Paul Clayton (Black Boys); Phyllis Forbes, Peggy Satterlee, Helen Pender, Eloise Hardt (Virgins); Alaine Brandes (Street Slave Girl); Jamiel Hasson, Crane Whitley, Charles Alvarado (Officers); Duke York (Archer); Mickey Simpson (Hangman); Amador Gutierrez, Ben Ayassa Wadrassi, Edward Marmolejo, Daniel Barone (Tumblers).

New York Premiere: Rivoli Theatre—December 25, 1942
New York Television Debut: CBS—October 1, 1963

## Synopsis

Because of his abiding love of Sherazad, a dancing girl who promises to marry him if he becomes caliph, Kamar seizes the throne from Caliph Haroun al Raschid, his half-brother. Kamar orders his men to kill Haroun, but he escapes and is given refuge by Ali Ben Ali, an acrobat with Ahmad's tent circus. Others in the troupe are Sinbad, Aladdin, and, of course, the star attraction, Sherazad. None know of Haroun's true identity save Ali, who agrees to keep the discovery a secret. Unknown to Kamar, his aide Hadan has Sherazad sold into slavery in order to prevent her from becoming Queen and taking away his power. In addition, the circus troupe, including Haroun, is sold. During their imprisonment, Sherazad falls in love with Haroun, although she believes him only to be a commoner. Meanwhile, Kamar furious at Sherazad's disappearance, orders Hadan to find her. Hadan goes to the slave market where he buys Sherazad from the slave trader. As he is carrying her off, Haroun and his comrades escape from the slave cell and attack their captors. Haroun frees Sherazad and, together with the troupe, they seek refuge in a small fishing village. Securing horses, they ride into the desert, where they are intercepted by Kamar and his soldiers. Taking them to his desert tent city, Kamar prepares a sumptuous feast in honor of Sherazad, and promises protection to her companions. His aide, Hadan, however, recognizes Haroun as the real Caliph, and secretly commits him to a torture chamber. Meanwhile, Ali goes to Bagdad and notifies Haroun's loyal troops of their leader's predicament. They arrive in time to set Haroun free and rout Kamar's followers. In the ensuing sword fight, Haroun kills Kamar, regaining the throne and claiming Sherazad as his bride.

◆━━◆━━◆

Allah was certainly at his most benevolent when producer Walter Wanger [a man with a penchant for the exotic East, as in *Algiers* (1938)] contracted with Universal to release his forthcoming *Arabian Nights*. This sumptuous color production brought together, for the first time onscreen, three studio contractees: Dominican Republic-born newcomer Maria Montez, Californian Jon Hall, since *The Hurricane* (1937) known as Samuel Goldwyn's gift to women, and Sabu, the boyish personality from India who had made such a hit in *Elephant Boy* (1937) and *Jungle Book* (1942). In populating the craftily lush *Arabian Nights* with its glass shots and painted backdrops, this performing trio established the studio's successful fantasy film formula and along the way created a new, exotic screen team, Montez and Hall, "they who are too beautiful."

"*Arabian Nights* is essentially for juveniles, preferably adult ones, since kiddies might find the romance 'mush' despite swashbuckling that cushions it" [Archer Winsten (*New York Post*)]. Beyond its film title and certain character names, this picture was distinctly removed from the famed 1880s collection of ancient Orient tales by British explorer Sir Richard Burton. As *PM* noted, it "is probably the gaudiest and most cynical transformation of a classic since the Ritz Brothers played *The Three Musketeers* [1939]." To insure that audiences understood that the filmmakers of *Arabian Nights* were not taking the classic stories seriously, the studio used one of the Three Stooges, Shemp Howard, as Sinbad, a dunce who always wants to relate one of his past sea adventures. However, as actor Billy Gilbert tells him, "I'd like a little less of Sinbad the Sailor and a little more of Sinbad the worker." Then there was John Qualen as a middle-aged Aladdin, an optimistic soul who hopes someday to find that elusive lamp he misplaced so he can finally make his dreams come true. To make the comic relief complete there was Gilbert exhibiting his famous wheeze and grimaces, and even donning the disguise of Sultana, the "alluring" blacksmith's woman.

So much for this film following the sacred paths of literature! Instead, *Arabian Nights* is a picture deliberately made as a plush exercise in World War II escapism with a heavy emphasis on garish multi-hued scenery ranging from a slave market to desert tent villages, and a catalog of romantic characters. These characters include a tempestuous slave girl and a knight in shining armor (in this instance he wears robes) who rides across wind-swept deserts to rescue his dark-haired love. No one was expected to judge the performers here on a charted histrionics scale, but rather to accept them as human adornments, in the midst of the bevy of diaphanous-trouser-clad harem girls. Only the more solemn reviewers bothered to offer a critical appraisal, such as Bosley Crowther *(New York Times)*, "Maria Montez plays the beauteous dancer with the hauteur of a tired night-club showgirl, and Jon Hall and Leif Erikson play the rivals with a great many tense and dirty looks."

To instill even greater picturesque remoteness to *Arabian Nights*, the main story is told within the framework of a flashback as storyteller Robert Greig allows the harem girls (straight from Hollywood Boulevard) to join with him in a recitation of times long ago when there was great rivalry between two half brothers for the Caliphate of Bagdad and the love of a sensuous dancing girl. From the film's start, the dialog is geared to astound one with its mixture of quaintness (Montez alerting Erikson, "Return to me, oh, Kamar, when you are caliph of Bagdad"), clichéd simplicity (Hall about Erikson, "He always hated me even when we were children") to delectable camp (slave girl to Montez, "Listen to them. The crowd is certainly hungry for you tonight.")

Alluringly accented Montez, who obviously relished her exotic roles as much as her audiences did, performed her Sherazad in a manner that would become standard practice for such screen successors as Yvonne De Carlo, Maureen O'Hara, Patricia Medina, and Rhonda Fleming: one part temperament ("Let them wait. Fools. Let them call."), one part bravery ("Sherazad lives in fear of no man"), one part practicality ("It is my destiny to marry a king and rule a kingdom") and a heavy dash of repressed romanticism (those smoldering looks, that sensuous walk). Montez's heroine is a self-sufficient soul who fully knows her power over men and uses her beauty and sensuality to attain her goals, which prove to be more romantic than realistic, a surprise even unto her.

With such an eye-catching heroine so distracting in her filmy silks, gaudy baubles, and turbaned headdresses, any onscreen hero in a filmed extravaganza automatically had difficulty in remaining in the audience's mind throughout the adventurous tale. Hall had made his screen reputation as the attractive, taciturn co-star of sarong-clad Dorothy Lamour in the late 1930s, and now was content to amble through film after film in a more stolid than solid manner. Still he cut a dashing figure in cinema adventures, and, more importantly, appeared to be a pleasant enough rogue-hero who, either out of complacency or ineptness, could successfully cope with the very mundane dialog and trite screen shenanigans without embarrassing himself or the audience.

Actually, in the early sections of *Arabian Nights,* it is Hall who is dependent on Montez's aid, having been wounded and needing to be hid. He relies on her nursing and kindness to keep him alive and safe from Erikson's troops. At first, bewildered by his predicament, the injured Hall can only mumble, ". . . this place. How have I come here?" But the presence of the stimulating Montez soon revives him and he tells her, "I think you are sublimely worthy. . . . You are a woman to make men dream." Once his strength has returned (it is at this point that his beard and moustache are shaved off, revealing his best oncamera feature, his handsome profile), Hall becomes a man of action, who daringly confronts Erikson ("Do you not recognize me my brother?") speaks philosophically ("Only those who wear chains know the joys of freedom") and talks in unboundingly rapturous prose of his new-found love ("the woman whose beauty shames the glory of the sunset").

Just as romantic interludes are required elements in adventure movies, so comic relief had become a staple of the genre. Universal turned to eighteen-year-old Sabu to provide child-like diversion, serving both as plot expediter (rescuing Hall, delivering messages, bringing the troops to the rescue) and more interestingly as a youthful matchmaker. As Ali Ben Ali, Sabu played the son of a son of a son of an acrobat (whom Gilbert addresses as "You ungrateful son of infamy" or "a son of a frog"). He utters such profundities as "All women like all mules are unpredictable. Only Sherazad is more unpredictable than all mules." These seemingly clever truths lead Hall to observe of Sabu, "You are very old for one so young." Actually Sabu's presence was the most charming ingredient of *Arabian Nights* as, *a la* Douglas Fairbanks, he scampers about as the top man on an acrobatic pyramid or in climbing up a tree or over a wall. He asks very little for himself in the course of the film, only wishing to faithfully serve his new-found friend (Hall).

Thus the personable trio moved through *Arabian Nights,* dispensing charm, and, like the viewer, giving more of their attention to the exotic settings about them than to the dastardly villains, Erikson and Edgar Barrier. Once the script frees the leads from their oncamera oppressors, Montez can finally query Hall about this mysterious pedigree.

Montez: "Why did you not tell me, my lord."

Hall: "I could not until I was sure of your love."

Now the couple can reside in blissful eternity, happy with one another for ever. As the film concludes, the scene shifts back to the "present." "Did that really happen?" asks one inquisitive harem girl.

"Of course it did," replies the storyteller.

# WHITE SAVAGE
## (Universal, 1943) C-75M.

Producer, George Waggner; director, Arthur Lubin; story, Peter Milne, screenplay, Richard Brooks; music, Frank Skinner; assistant director, Charles Gould; art directors, John B. Goodman, Robert Boyle; set decorators, R. A. Gausman, I. Webb; music director, Charles Previn; sound, Charles Carroll; camera, Lester White, William Snyder; editor, Russell Schoengarth.

Maria Montez (Tahia); Jon Hall (Kaloa); Sabu (Orano); Thomas Gomez (Sam Miller); Sidney Toler (Wong); Paul Guilfoyle (Erik); Turhan Bey (Tamara); Don Terry (Gris); Constance Purdy (Blossom); Al Kikume (Guard); Frederick Brunn (Sully); Pedro de Cordoba (Candlemaker); Anthony Warde (Clark); Jim Mitchell, Bella Lewitzky (Specialty Dancers); John Harmon (Williams); Minerva Urecal, Kate Lawson (Native Women).

New York Premiere: Rivoli Theatre—April 23, 1943
New York Television Debut: CBS—May 6, 1959

## Synopsis

Sam Miller, the unscrupulous operator of a trading post on Port Coral, seeks to gain possession of a gold-lined sacred pool, located on Temple Island, a small coral isle ruled over by Princess Tahia. Tahia's wayward brother Tamara is an inveterate gambler and thus an easy mark for Sam who plans to exploit this weakness. When shark fisherman Kaloa is barred from plying the waters near Temple Island, he seeks an interview with the princess, hoping to gain a concession from her. He enlists the aid of Orano, son of the princess' maid. Orano invites Kaloa to the island and arranges the meeting. Kaloa soon realizes that the ruler is none other than the girl he had met at Port Coral a short time before. The two impulsively fall in love, and she permits him to kiss her. But when he raises the subject of fishing concessions, she concludes that he only seeks to outwit her, and orders him off the island. Through a mischievous trick, Orano brings them together again and they become reconciled. Meanwhile Sam inveigles Tamara into a crooked card game, betting cash against the value of the island deed. Kaloa learns of the scheme, joins the game, and by outwitting Sam, wins the deed. Angry because of his loss, Tamara strikes Kaloa. The following day, while the natives celebrate the princess' engagement to Kaloa, Sam arrives at the island to inform all that Tamara has been murdered and that in all probability Kaloa is the culprit. Kaloa is imprisoned, but Orano helps him to escape. Eventually it is proved that Sam hired a beachcomber to do the evil work, a fact substantiated when Sam and his men seize the island in an attempt to take the gold out of the sacred pool.

But an earthquale rocks the island, toppling the temple, and they lose their lives in the ruins. Tahia and Kaloa rejoice in their love for one another.

◆——◆——◆

When *Arabian Nights* was released, Lee Mortimer in the *New York Daily Mirror* noted " . . . after her performance in this opus, Maria Montez climbs several steps in everybody's estimation." *White Savage* consolidated her starring position on the Universal lot, leading Leo Mishkin *(New York Morning Telegraph)* to report, "Montez in a sarong knows how to throw all the curves and display all the features that one could possibly ask for. . . ." Her visual salability was crassly exploited to full advantage in *White Savage,* in which Montez displayed her physical assets—as much as the censors would then allow—in a part-sarong, part-bathing suit. She posed provocatively in a succession of exciting positions and, when smiling, pouted in her most tempestuous manner (several cuts above that offered by Lupe Velez). As for Jon Hall, he was now considered an essential part of the Montez-fantasyland star package. His chief contributions to this entry were his curly hair, which was noticeably longer than usual, his bronzed makeup which was darker, and his manner, which was more relaxed in this South Seas setting than in the fairylands of make-believe Arabia. Only the more pedantic filmgoers, like Theodore Strauss *(New York Times),* could acidly carp, "If one judges by performances, Mr. Hall and Miss Montez shouldn't bore each other too quickly."

If the villain of the piece, Thomas Gomez as the German expatriate Sam Miller, is more scruffy and determined than need be ("some men would do anything for the bottom of the pool"), the romancing between Montez and Hall is far more carefree. Hall's Kaloa, fresh from fishing off Australian waters, has now set up base on Port Coral and is maneuvering along the dockside when he spots a shapely miss leaving Gomez's general store. Wolf whistles are not enough for playful Hall, who tosses out his fishing line and snares Montez's tropical dress with his hook. As he rushes to her assistance, he confides with a grin, "If you allow me, helping ladies out of difficulties is my specialty." The angered (she must be, her eyebrows are arched), impassioned (her chest *is* heaving) Montez glares at Hall. He is amused, "You're kinda cute when you're mad." From there on it is a see-saw romance, usually with intense Montez guiding the course of love, either slapping his face in playful anger, bestowing a kiss on his impassive countenance, or, in a fit of rage, ordering him from her presence and off the island. After all, she is royalty (no matter how small her domain) and pipe-smoking Hall has admitted his lowly class status, "All my life, I've been a tramp fisherman. I guess I'll end up a tramp." Later on, after Montez and Hall have become romantically tied, she is still testing him in order to see if his love is for her or for the wealth at the bottom of the fabled pool, in whose azure waters they are now splashing their feet. But he admits such material ambition is not his; he is content to carry on as he always has done. She is convinced that here is a man

609

strong enough to combat others, but weak enough to be her willing slave for life. (A running joke throughout *White Savage* concerns Hall's occupation as a shark fisherman, using his deep sea catch to obtain the commercially valuable vitamin A, extracted from fish liver. Later, a romantically satisfied Montez admits "Kaloa, no need vitamin A.")

The subordinate cast in *White Savage* was an odd mixture of Universal contractees. Besides Gomez, there was Sidney Toler, in between Charlie Chan pictures, cast as the island's Oriental doctor-lawyer-notary-detective-locksmith and general jack of all trades, who, with his look of ambiguous scrutiny, maneuvers throughout the film as a part-time observer to Gomez's chicanery and a sometime helper to Hall (loaning him the money for a new boat). Turhan Bey, in a much larger role than *Arabian Nights*, functioned as the handsome native prince, a victim of civilization which had robbed him of his dignity and corrupted his morals. Paul Guilfoyle as Gomez's seedy, tricky confederate had his moments, and, for comic relief there was hefty Constance Purdy as Montez's handmaiden and Sabu's indulgent mother. She has a coquettish scene in which she tricks Hall into thinking she is the elusive ruler of fabulous Coral Island. And of course there was Sabu, by now known as the East Indian Mickey Rooney. His part was far less athletic this time, functioning much more as a male junior duenna, frolicking in the background as he successfully pairs Montez and Hall, and clapping his hands in glee each time they clinch in a kiss. At the fadeout the two lead lovers are locked in each others' arms. What is Sabu's reward? He ends up in the company of braying goats. Poor Sabu just never got a girl!

The *New York Herald-Tribune* might carp, "Unless you are a set-up for stereotyped mumbo-jumbo dished up with whining guitars, you are likely to wonder why the picture was ever made." The answer was simple. Escapism! Within its uncomplex framework, the Technicolor *White Savage* and its South Seas setting of limpid waters, dark-stained chorines, placid visitors and lushly displayed foliage provided an admirable alternative to any serious thoughts about the horrors of World War II. If the film's main setting at Port Coral more closely resembled a combination Western mining town saloon with an adjacent swimming pool ensemble than a real tropical paradise, the viewers were more concerned that the ever vigilant censors had demanded several cuts in the footage, which made the continuity more jagged and worst of all, deleted some choicer look-sees at voluptuous Montez.

## ALI BABA AND THE FORTY THIEVES
### (*Universal, 1944*) C-87M.

Producer, Paul Malvern; director, Arthur Lubin; screenplay, Edmund L. Hartmann; art directors, John B. Goodman, Richard H. Riedel; set decorators, R. A. Gausman, Ira A. Webb; music-music director, Edward

Ward; song, J. Keirn Brennan and Ward; choreography, Paul Oscard; assistant director, Charles Gould; technical adviser, Jamiel Hasson; dialog director, Stacy Keach; sound, Bernard B. Brown, Robert Pritchard; special camera, John P. Fulton; camera, George Robinson, W. Howard Greene; editor, Russell Schoengarth.

Jon Hall (Ali Baba); Maria Montez (Amara); Turhan Bey (Jamiel); Andy Devine (Abdullah); Kurt Katch (Hulagu Khan); Frank Puglia (Prince Cassim); Fortunio Bononova (Baba); Moroni Olsen (Caliph); Ramsay Ames (Nalu); Chris Pin Martin (Fat Thief); Scotty Beckett (Ali as a Boy); Yvette Duguay (Amara as a Girl); Noel Cravat (Mongol Captain); Jimmy Conlin (Little Thief); Harry Cording (Mahmoud); Ethan Laidlaw, Hans Herbert, Dick Dickinson, Joey Ray, John Calvert, David Heywood, Pedro Regas (Thieves); Eric Braunsteiner, Jerome Andrews, Alex Goudovitch, Ed Brown, George Martin, Dick D'Arcy (Dancers); Rex Evans (Arab Major Domo); Belle Mitchell (Nursemaid); Harry Woods, Dick Alexander, Art Miles (Mongol Guards); Alphonse Berge (Tailor); Charles Wagenheim (Barber); Wee Willie Davis (Arab Giant); Norman Willis, Pierce Lyden, Don McGill (Guards); Robert Barron (Mongol Captain); James Khan (Persian Prince); Theodore Patay (Arab Priest); Angelo Rossitto (Arab Dwarf).

New York Premiere: Palace Theatre—March 15, 1944
New York Television Debut: Channel 9—April 18, 1960

## Synopsis

Aided by Prince Cassim, a traitor, Hulagu Khan, leader of the Mongols, murders the Caliph of Bagdad and seizes control of the city. Ali, the Caliph's son, escapes into the hills with the seal of Bagdad. There he comes upon a horde of thieves, led by Baba. Ali makes his identity known and offers to lead the thieves against the Khan. Admiring the boy's spunk, Baba names him "Ali Baba" and takes him into the band. Ten years later, with Bagdad despoiled by the Mongols, only the thieves, now led by the adult Ali Baba, still resist them. When a scout reports the passing of a rich caravan bearing Amara, Cassim's daughter and future bride of the Khan, Ali rushes to capture her. Instead he is corraled by the Mongols, caged and hauled back to Bagdad. Abdullah, however, escapes and alerts the thieves, who ride into the city and rescue Ali Baba from the public square. Ali, in turn, kidnaps Amara, and takes her to his secret cave. When Amara learns of Ali's identity and Ali realizes that she is Cassim's daughter, both recall that as children they had pledged themselves to each other. Ali's love for Amara overcomes his desire for revenge against Cassim and the Khan. He sends her back to Bagdad. When Jamiel, Amara's faithful servant, comes to Ali to inform him that Amara is marrying the Khan against her will, Ali determines to rescue her. He disguises himself as a wealthy merchant, and on the day of the wedding feast, hides his men in forty large jars, supposedly containing fine oils. He joins a procession of wealthy merchants and princes bearing gifts to the Khan. Within the palace gates, the thieves, at a given signal, pounce upon the Khan's guards, while Bagdad's citizens rise in revolt. The Mongols are destroyed by the surprise attack and Ali is restored to his rightful place as Caliph.

Once again lightly borrowing from Sir Richard Burton's collected tales as in *Arabian Nights*, Universal created a glorious pastel-shaded divertissement which A. H. Weiler *(New York Times)* labelled "nothing more than another in the recent line of spectacular fast-moving Westerns set in the storied Near East." But other more generous souls, and the public at large, applauded the new venture, for it contained "All the color, grandeur and excitement of a child dream" [Lee Mortimer *(New York Daily Mirror)*]. According to its press releases, Universal even managed to make this minaret-laden tale topical by drawing "a parallel with today's war activities and the Axis subjugation of peace loving people." Whew! Thus, out of respect to America's 1940s Allies, the villains of the piece were not the Chinese but Mongols. Best of all, as anyone in line to purchase a ticket to *Ali Baba and the Forty Thieves* could have told you, the film had Maria Montez and Jon Hall who ". . . keep their play-acting on the extravagant plane such a picture demands. . . ." [Dorothy Masters *(New York Daily News)*].

Of all the Maria Montez-Jon Hall celluloid escapades, *Ali Baba and the Forty Thieves* was the most resplendent, in which even the merest boulder in the background seemed transformed into a shimmering agate, sparkling in the Technicolor light, with its blue, blue skies and white clouds, and the lavish array of colorful silks, gauzes, and baubles sported everywhere to dazzle the viewers' eyes throughout the film. Universal would be so proud of the visual splendors provided in *Ali Baba and the Forty Thieves* that in 1965 money-hungry executives would concoct a remake of the film, *The Sword of Ali Baba*, just to reuse the lush footage, even going so far as to rehire some of the same performers to disguise the transition between the old and the new lensings.

*Ali Baba and the Forty Thieves* was a slickly engineered piece of entertainment geared to please all action-hungry fans. It was an amalgam of bits from the adventures of Robin Hood in Sherwood Forest, the fantastic elements of *The Thief of Bagdad* (1940), and the film owed a good deal to the mechanism of cliffhanging movie serials, what with the film's galloping horsemen (vigilantes) and that magic cave that opened to the command of the secret words ("open sesame"). There was even a smidgen of *Desert Song* to be seen, with *Ali Baba*'s comic opera villains and the heroic band (dressed in matching blue and red outfits) who have their own riding song, "Forty and One for All."

As *Ali Baba and the Forty Thieves* breezed along at breakneck speed, there was scarcely room or need for sturdy characterizations. However, for a change the storyline focused more on Hall as the fast-riding and robust hero, who, despite his royal lineage, is a man of the people leading them on against the oppressors. As usual, Hall and beauteous Montez have an on-again, off-again romance, but this time Hall is more dashing in his swashbuckling attempts to convince the self-willed maiden that he is the proper man for her. Montez, who had by now trimmed down her tidy figure even more, was at her most sensual in this picture, offering the viewer two bath scenes and a heady veiled dance, guaranteeing a sufficient dose of titillation for viewers seeking physical rather than verbal messages from the actress.

Although Sabu was absent from this installment, Turhan Bey, already billed as Hollywood's leading Turk, substituted as Montez's loyal slave who puts life and liberty aside to better serve his demanding mistress. Audiences of 1944 were used to comic relief in their adventure films, and here there was Andy Devine, that overweight bundle of optimism, complete with his cracked larynx voice, to aid the evilness of Kurt Katch's Hulagu Khan.

This was the first of four Montez-Hall color features to be photographed by George Robinson, and the picture was resplendent with the cinematographer's fluid camera work.

## COBRA WOMAN
### *(Universal, 1944) C-71M.*

Producer, George Waggner; director, Robert Siodmak; story, W. Scott Darling; screenplay, Gene Lewis, Richard Brooks; dialog director, Gene Lewis; art directors, John B. Goodman, Alexander Golitzen; assistant director, Mack Wright; music, Edward Ward; sound, Joe Pais; special effects, John Fulton; camera, George Robinson, Howard Greene; editor, Charles Maynard.

Maria Montez (Tollea/Naja); Jon Hall (Ramu); Sabu (Kado); Lon Chaney, Jr. (Hava); Edgar Barrier (Martok); Mary Nash (The Queen); Lois Collier (Veeda); Samuel S. Hinds (Father Paul); Moroni Olsen (MacDonald); Robert Barron (Chief Guard); Vivian Austin, Beth Dean, Paulita Arvizu (Handmaidens); Fritz Leiber (Venreau); Belle Mitchell (Native Woman); John Bagni (Native); Dale Van Sickel, Eddie Parker, George Magrill (Guards).

New York Premiere: Loew's Criterion Theatre—May 17, 1944
New York Television Debut: CBS—November 12, 1961

## Synopsis

On the day of her marriage to Ramu, Tollea is kidnapped and taken to Cobra Island, where she learns from the kindly Queen that she is actually the older twin sister of Naja, the island's wicked High Priestess, who exacts heavy tribute from the natives. The Queen wants Tollea to assume her rightful place as High Priestess and to bring an end to Naja's cruel reign. Meanwhile, Ramu, accompanied by Kado, his native friend, comes to Cobra Island to rescue Tollea. He is captured and imprisoned by Martok, Naja's minister of affairs. With Kado's aid, however, he manages to escape and contact Tollea. The old Queen begs Ramu to help bring about Naja's abdication. Aware that her rule is endangered, Naja orders Martok to murder the Queen. Tollea, aroused, engages Naja in a fight to the finish and comes out the victor when the evil one falls to her death. She disguises herself as Naja and, assuming the place of the High Priestess, calls a halt to the persecution of the natives. Martok, in defiance, challenges her rule, but he and his men are subdued by Ramu and Kato, who come to Tollea's aid. When Ramu sails back to Harbor Island, he is overjoyed to find that Tollea has sneaked aboard.

◆—◆—◆

If there is one film which remains a top (camp) favorite among Maria Montez fans it is *Cobra Woman*, a joyous comic strip fantasy set in the Pacific, far away from the then raging war. The critics hated the film. "A mountain of labor has gone into the production of Universal's *Cobra Woman*, but it remains a cinematic mouse" [Otis L. Guernsey, Jr. *(New York Herald-Tribune)*]. "This is a picture that could be an inspiration to the writer of a seed catalogue. It has almost every known variety of corn" [Alton Cook *(New York World-Telegram)*]. The same clique of reviewers condescended to apologize for Montez's performance, "If you were a producer with a cast of thousands, a corny tale, a stage-set volcano island, several reels of Technicolor film and Miss Montez, what would you do? Probably what Universal did. Cast her in a double role. Undress her in both, as much as the law and Will Hays allow, and let nature take its course" [Lee Mortimer *(New York Daily Mirror)*].

Watching *Cobra Woman*, any serious viewer realizes that all of Montez's previous co-starring pictures with Jon Hall had been merely tacky dress rehearsals for this major onthrust. As the kindly Tollea, Montez is at her most romantic, informing Hall, "Wherever we are, we will belong to each other . . . and make all our dreams come true." Even Montez's evil Naja is a romantic soul, although with a requisite nasty streak. Naja tells soulful Hall, "I am whomever you want to be." She adds that her "eyes of love are sharp," but later ominously informs the intruding Hall "You are not going to leave at all."

If any viewer had been only intrigued by, or had earnestly ignored, Montez's heavy accent in her past screen efforts, it was not possible here, with the star literally talking to herself on screen, mouthing such fractured English as when she tells the Queen, "I have dee-cided to marry Martok and I dee-mand your consent." Previous Montez vehicles had witnessed her regally carried in a litter (*Arabian Nights* and *Ali Baba and the Forty Thieves*) or paddled in a royal canoe (*White Savage*) with the actress taking full advantage of the oncamera charades to act out the imperious soul. But none of this nonsense was equal to the royal deportment of Montez in *Cobra Woman* in which she struts about her island domain like a little fuhrer, thriving on the processionals and ceremonies, and having the entire island at her beck and call. Her merest thought, once uttered, sets the natives trembling. "I don't like it, I don't like it at all!" says the angered Montez, and, poof, the loyal subjects turn to jellyfish, afraid of what the demanding monarch will ask of them now. "I have spoken. Go!" is enough to launch any and everyone within hearing into spasms of backward salaams as they bow out of the high priestess' presence. When for her own purposes she decides that the fire mountain "cries for more obedience" (to her laws) she advises her subordinates, "two hundred will walk the thousand steps to eternal life." What more dire but intriguing fate could await a movie extra!

Neither before nor here in *Cobra Woman* was Montez very adept at various forms of belly dancing, and in past films she either had used doubles (*Arabian Nights*) or sat on the sidelines while the handmaidens performed the rhythmic gymnastics (*White Savages*). But in *Cobra Woman* (aided by a double once again), Montez conducted the weirdest ritualistic game of eeny-meeny-miney-mo, as she writhes in contorted glee to her inspired dance to King Cobra. As the momentum builds, she strikes out one hand and then the other as she selects subjects in the throne room to have the honor of going to their fiery death. The stocky guards pick up and cart off the shrieking victims while the demonically possessed Montez sinuously cavorts about the platform in frenzied abandonment.

To provide *Cobra Woman* with entertainment balance, Sabu was back on hand, this time in a more active role as Hall's native helper, always ready with his trusty blow pipe to eliminate troublesome pests. He is again cast as a child-like young man, as foolish as his pet, Koko the chimp, and once again mouthing his own brand of English, as when he asks lovesick Hall, "You have sad sickness for Tollea?"

Among the supporting cast were guest star Lon Chaney, Jr., Universal's horror monster king, as the ruler's mute servant, Mary Nash in a most sympathetic performance as the aged monarch who meets death bravely, Edgar Barrier as the power-crazed associate of the evil Montez, and Samuel S. Hinds as the benign Father Paul who relates the legend of Cobra Island at the film's opening.

Perhaps *PM*'s reviewer, by accident, best summed up the virtues of *Cobra Woman*, ". . . [it] is not exactly an insult to the intelligence of the U.S. movie audience; it is rather like most movie advertising and lobby art, a super-colossal disregard of it."

# GYPSY WILDCAT
## (Universal, 1944) C-77M.

Producer, George Waggner; director, Roy William Neill; story, James Hogan, Ralph Stock; screenplay, Hogan, Gene Lewis, James M. Cain; additional dialog, Joseph Hoffman; art directors, John B. Goodman, Martin Obzina; music director, Edward Ward; song, Ward and Waggner; dialog director, Emory Horger; assistant director, Melville Shyer; choreography, Lester Horton; sound, Glenn E. Anderson; special effects, John Fulton; camera, George Robinson, W. Howard Greene; editor, Russell Schoengarth.

Maria Montez (Carla); Jon Hall (Michael); Leo Carrillo (Anube); Gale Sondergaard (Rhoda); Peter Coe (Tonio); Nigel Bruce (High Sheriff); Douglass Dumbrille (Baron Tovar); Curt Bois (Valdi); Harry Cording (Captain Marver).

New York Premiere: Criterion Theatre—October 5, 1944
New York Television Debut: CBS—November 12, 1961

## Synopsis

A band of gypsies, including dancer Carla and Anube their chieftain, are imprisoned by Baron Tovar and are charged with the murder of a count, whose heart had been pierced with an arrow. Michael, a soldier of fortune, is aware of the gypsies' innocence, for he had removed from the Count's body the arrow, which was marked with the Baron's coat of arms. Noticing that a pendant worn by Carla is inscribed with the crest of the dead Count's family, the Baron realizes that she is the Count's long lost daughter, and by virtue thereof, heiress to his lands and forests. Michael steals into the castle and accuses the Baron of murder. The Baron's soldiers capture and imprison him in the dungeon with the gypsies. Michael valiantly overpowers his guards and helps the gypsies to escape. Meanwhile Carla has consented to wed the Baron on his promise to free her people. Warned that the gypsies have escaped, the Baron abducts Carla and flees with her in a carriage. Michael and the gypsies pursue them, and in turn are pursued by the Baron's soldiers, who overtake them just as they halt the carriage. In the ensuing battle, the soldiers are routed and the Baron killed by one of his own arrows. Carla learns of her noble status, but does not let it interfere with her love for Michael.

◆━◆━◆

"Like other Hall-Montez scripts, *Gypsy Wildcat* is as exaggerated as a schoolboy's daydreams, minus the successful creation of the 'once upon a time' magic. It is all wall-leaning, hard riding and dungeon deliveries, a combination of a few pretty pictures and old Douglas Fairbanks tricks"

[Otis L. Guernsey, Jr. *(New York Herald-Tribune)*]. "If it weren't that *Gypsy Wildcat* is played with such deadly seriousness, you'd almost suspect its five authors were playing burlesque with the sacred deadpan of baby-faced Maria Montez and the fourth grade thespianic talents of stalwart Jon Hall. . . . The picture's so bad it's bound to make money" (*Cue* magazine).

Universal thought it would be a sensible change of film fare to take their money winning team of Maria Montez and Jon Hall out of the tropics and the Near East and thrust them into the wilds of Eastern Europe. The production was blessed with a potentially intriguing Gothic setting, with its medieval castle, dungeons, moat, and villainous baron, all of which was quite fitting for one of the studio's Transylvanian sojourns with Frankenstein. But here the emphasis was still on the romantic endeavors of the love team, as the fiery, flirtatious dancing girl is courted and rescued by a handsome soldier of fortune. For extra boxoffice insurance Leo Carrillo and Gale Sondergaard were cast as the flavorful gypsy foster parents of the alluring Montez, the latter acting the same as usual despite the change of locale and costumes.

Above and beyond the basic level of the Montez-Hall emoting, the viewer's credibility was sorely taxed in *Gypsy Wildcat,* what with the over-obvious hamming of Nigel Bruce as the blustering High Sheriff and Douglass Dumbrille as the dastardly black-hearted Baron. Nor was the ineffectual Peter Coe as Hall's lacklustre rival for Montez's affections much assistance to the general proceedings.

The two highlights of *Gypsy Wildcat* are Montez in a provocative black negligee and the excitingly staged carriage chase which creates a large momentum of excitement for the viewer that is not soon forgotten.


## SUDAN
### *(Universal, 1945) C-76M.*

Producer, Paul Malvern; director, John Rawlins; screenplay, Edmund L. Hartmann; art directors, John B. Goodman, Richard H. Riedel; set decorators, Russell A. Gausman, Leigh Smith; assistant director, William Tummel; dialog director, Stacy Keach; music, Milton Rosen; song, Rosen and Everett Carter; sound, Bernard B. Brown, William Hedgcock; camera, George Robinson; editor, Milton Carruth.

Maria Montez (Naila); Jon Hall (Merab); Turhan Bey (Herua); Andy Devine (Nebka); George Zucco (Horadef); Robert Warwick (Maatet); Phil Van Zandt (Setna); Harry Cording (Uba); George Lynn (Bata); Charles Arnt (Khafra the Horse Trader); Ray Teal (Slave Trader); Hans Herbert, Dick Dickinson (Buyers); Bob Barron (Jailer); Gene Stutenroth, Art Miles (Executioners); Charles Morton (Soldier); Tor Johnson (Slaver);

Ed Hyans (Master of Ceremonies); James Dime, George Magrill (Guards); Art Foster (Wrestler); Jimmy Lucas, Byron Ruggles, Charles McAvoy (Bettors); Dave Kashner (Crack Bull Whip); Artie Ortego (Starter); Dink Trout (Potter); Duke Johnson (Juggler); Phil Dunham, Alix Nagy, Dick Dickinson, Dan White (Men); Joe Bernard (Horse Owner); Shirley Hunter (Herita); Kay Yorke (Nephytis); Jack Chefe (Mestat); Roy Darmour (Horse Owner); Mary O'Brien (Nephytis); Ann Roberts, Maxine Leeds, Kathleen O'Malley, Rita Benjamin, Rosemarie Babbick, Vivian Mason (Girls); June Pickrell (Old Woman); Belle Mitchell (Woman); Clarke Stevens, Robert Strong (Sentries); Al Ferguson (King); Lloyd Ingraham (Elderly Man).

New York Premiere: Criterion Theatre—April 18, 1945
New York Television Debut: CBS—May 19, 1963

### Synopsis

The mysterious assassination of the King of Khemmis brings Naila, his spirited daughter, to the throne. Horadef, the scheming royal chamberlain, who had committed the murder, convinces Naila that Herua, leader of a band of escaped slaves, was responsible for the crime. Naila, bent on revenge, disguises herself and sets out to find Herua and to lead him into a trap. Meanwhile Horadaf arranges with a slave trader to kidnap Naila and "dispose" of her, so that he could take over the throne. Captured and sold into slavery, Naila makes a spectacular escape and finds her way to a desert oasis where Merab and Nebka, two vagabonds, rescue her. All three go to a nearby village only to fall into the hands of the slave trader's henchmen. Just as they are about to be executed, Herua arrives in the village, rescuing them in a rousing battle. Although attracted to Herua, Naila is still determined to avenge her father's death and lures him back to Khemmis. She seizes and jails him only to find herself in the same predicament when Horadef imprisons her and proclaims himself king. Merab and Nebka, realizing that Naila and Herua love one another, engineer Herua's escape. The enraged Horadef gathers his army and compels Naila to lead them to Herua's secret mountain stronghold. There, in a climatic battle, Horadef is killed, his army destroyed, and Naila and Herua reunited.

◆◆◆

The advertisement for this film proclaimed:
"Sudan . . Where adventure lives and romance rules!
Sudan . . Oasis of forbidden excitement!
Sudan . . Land of lawless lips and love!
Sudan . . Where boldest rogues ride for plunder!"
Universal even sent its production crew onlocation to Gallup, New Mexico, to film some of the exteriors in the famed Canyon de Chelly, and the studio employed many hundreds from the nearby Navajo reservation to portray Egyptian-style people. However, the mixture which had worked its magic

spell before, did not work this time, and the film emerged as a rather disappointing "mad melange of clichés" in which, said Bosley Crowther (*New York Times*), "Miss Montez saunters with the regality of an usherette."

By this point, Montez's boxoffice popularity was tapering off and Hall's favoritism with fans had so diminished (in inverse proportion to his growing beefiness) that although he received second billing in *Sudan*, it was the "imitation Valentino" Turhan Bey who oncamera won Montez's fair hand in love!

Perhaps because of the genre's overfamiliarity, viewers were now more aware of the technical mechanisms making up the production, from the special effect scenic splendors to the artificial foliage and rivers, and most of all, to the diminished film budget which saw fewer dancing girls parading about a lesser array of Technicolor settings. All of these points served to detract from the once alluring chemistry of this special brand of photoplay.

While Hall and fellow sidekick Andy Devine supplied plotline and comedy relief for *Sudan*, and Turhan Bey's rebels sang their paen to liberty, "Now We're Free," and Montez strode about as a veiled desert lady, it was the rousing finale which gave the picture its major redeeming quality. Captive Montez is forced to lead the sinister George Zucco and his men up a twisting mountain trail to Bey's mountain hideout. Stashed high above the perilous trail are several rock-laden containers held tight by fastened ropes. At the appropriate moment Bey's men cut them loose, allowing a torrent of stones to plummet down upon the invading army. Naturally Montez is spared from this weighty death.

## THE YEARS AFTER

Maria Montez stretched out her Universal career for a few years after *Sudan*, and then went abroad to find the type of screen role conducive to her particular brand of screen emoting. It was tough going for an exotic personality unequipped to adapt to changing cinema styles and tastes. Her untimely death in 1951, the result of a bathroom accident supposedly caused by her weakened condition from dieting, robbed the world of one of its more alluring personalities, a woman as engulfed by her legend and publicity as the legion of fans who had once rushed to her latest celluloid offering. Unfortunately, unlike her fickle public, Montez was permanently lost in her make believe world, unwilling or unable to cope with the realities of a waning career.

On the other hand, her placid co-star, Jon Hall, for whom she had little affection, has survived to readjust his living standards to a far more modest level. After leaving Universal where he had become a surplus commodity in a post-World War II market overflowing with male stars returning from military service, he signed on at Columbia. There, like another former celluloid jungle he-man (Johnny Weissmuller), the likewise hefty Hall stretched out his diminished movie career with a rash of programmers. He fared much better with a television series, "Ramar of the Jungle," and later became involved with an underwater camera equipment firm. He can now say, "I never liked acting. I don't like to be told what to do and what to say and how to say it. I'm grateful to it as it provided me with the money to do other things such as I am into now, but as a profession, it's a bore." As for his stocky frame, the elderly businessman shrugs it off: "Nowadays I don't exercise at all. It doesn't matter."

In **High Barbaree** (MGM, 1947)

# Chapter 22

# Van Johnson & June Allyson

## VAN JOHNSON

6′ 2″
185 pounds
Red blond hair
Blue eyes
Virgo

*Real name: Charles Van Johnson. Born August 25, 1916, Newport, Rhode Island. Married Eve Abbott (1947), child: Schuyler; divorced 1968.*

FEATURE FILMS:

*Too Many Girls* (RKO, 1940)
*Somewhere I'll Find You* (MGM, 1942)
*Murder in the Big House* (WB, 1942)
*The War Against Mrs. Hadley* (MGM, 1942)
*Dr. Gillespie's New Assistant* (MGM, 1942)
*The Human Comedy* (MGM, 1943)
*Pilot No. 5* (MGM, 1943)
*Madame Curie* (MGM, 1943)
*The White Cliffs of Dover* (MGM, 1944)
*Two Girls and a Sailor* (MGM, 1944)
*Thirty Seconds over Tokyo* (MGM, 1944)
*Three Men in White* (MGM, 1944)
*Between Two Women* (MGM, 1944)
*Weekend at the Waldorf* (MGM, 1945)
*Thrill of a Romance* (MGM, 1945)
*Ziegfeld Follies* (MGM, 1946)
*Till the Clouds Roll By* (MGM, 1946)
*No Leave, No Love* (MGM, 1946)
*Easy to Wed* (MGM, 1946)
*High Barbaree* (MGM, 1947)
*The Romance of Rosy Ridge* (MGM, 1947)
*State of the Union* (MGM, 1948)
*The Bride Goes Wild* (MGM, 1948)
*Command Decision* (MGM, 1948)

*Mother Is a Freshman* (20th, 1949)
*Scene of the Crime* (MGM, 1949)
*In the Good Old Summertime* (MGM, 1949)
*Battleground* (MGM, 1949)
*Grounds for Marriage* (MGM, 1950)
*The Big Hangover* (MGM, 1950)
*Duchess of Idaho* (MGM, 1950)
*Too Young to Kiss* (MGM, 1951)
*Go for Broke* (MGM, 1951)
*It's a Big Country* (MGM, 1951)
*Three Guys Named Mike* (MGM, 1951)
*Invitation* (MGM, 1952)
*When in Rome* (MGM, 1952)
*Washington Story* (MGM, 1952)
*Plymouth Adventure* (MGM, 1952)
*Confidentially Connie* (MGM, 1953)
*Remains to Be Seen* (MGM, 1953)
*Easy to Love* (MGM, 1953)
*The Caine Mutiny* (Col., 1954)
*The Siege at Red River* (20th, 1954)
*Men of the Fighting Lady* (MGM, 1954)

*The Last Time I Saw Paris* (MGM, 1954)
*Brigadoon* (MGM, 1954)
*The End of the Affair* (Col., 1955)
*Slander* (MGM, 1956)
*Miracle in the Rain* (WB, 1956)
*The Bottom of the Bottle* (20th, 1956)
*23 Paces to Baker Street* (20th, 1956)
*Kelly and Me* (Univ., 1957)
*Action of the Tiger* (MGM, 1957)
*The Last Blitzkrieg* (Col., 1958)
*Web of Evidence* (AA, 1959)
*Subway in the Sky* (UA, 1959)
*The Enemy General* (Col., 1960)
*Wives and Lovers* (Par., 1963)
*Divorce American Style* (Col., 1967)
*Yours, Mine and Ours* (UA, 1968)
*Where Angels Go. . . . Trouble Follows* (Col., 1968)
*El Largo Dia Del* (Spanish-French, 1969)
*Company of Killers* (Univ., 1970)

# JUNE ALLYSON

**5′ 1″**
**99 pounds**
**Blonde hair**
**Blue eyes**
**Libra**

*Real name: Ella Geisman. Born October 7, 1917, Bronx, New York. Married Dick Powell (1945), children: Pamela, Richard; widowed 1963. Married Alfred Glenn Maxwell (1963); divorced 1965, remarried 1966, redivorced 1970.*

### FEATURE FILMS:

*Best Foot Forward* (MGM, 1943)
*Girl Crazy* (MGM, 1943)
*Thousands Cheer* (MGM, 1943)
*Two Girls and a Sailor* (MGM, 1944)
*Meet the People* (MGM, 1944)

*Music for Millions* (MGM, 1945)
*Her Highness and the Bellboy* (MGM, 1945)
*The Sailor Takes a Wife* (MGM, 1945)
*Two Sisters from Boston* (MGM, 1946)

*Till the Clouds Roll By* (MGM, 1946)
*The Secret Heart* (MGM, 1946)
*High Barbaree* (MGM, 1947)
*Good News* (MGM, 1947)
*The Bride Goes Wild* (MGM, 1948)
*The Three Musketeers* (MGM, 1948)
*Words and Music* (MGM, 1948)
*Little Women* (MGM, 1949)
*The Stratton Story* (MGM, 1949)
*The Reformer and the Redhead* (MGM, 1950)
*Right Cross* (MGM, 1950)
*Too Young to Kiss* (MGM, 1951)
*The Girl in White* (MGM, 1952)
*Battle Circus* (MGM, 1953)
*Remains to be Seen* (MGM, 1953)
*The Glenn Miller Story* (Univ., 1954)
*Executive Suite* (MGM, 1954)
*Woman's World* (20th, 1954)
*Strategic Air Command* (Par., 1955)
*The McConnell Story* (WB, 1955)
*The Shrike* (Univ., 1955)
*The Opposite Sex* (MGM, 1956)
*You Can't Run Away from It* (Col., 1956)
*Interlude* (Univ., 1957)
*My Man Godfrey* (Univ., 1957)
*Stranger in My Arms* (Univ., 1959)
*They Only Kill Their Masters* (MGM, 1972)

June Allyson and Ray McDonald in **Till the Clouds Roll By** (MGM, 1946)

Advertisement for **Till the Clouds Roll By**

In **Two Girls and a Sailor** (MGM, 1944)

In **The Bride Goes Wild** (MGM, 1948)

In a publicity pose for **Too Young to Kiss** (MGM, 1951)

In **Too Young to Kiss**

In **Remains to Be Seen** (MGM, 1953)

# TWO GIRLS AND A SAILOR
## *(MGM, 1944) 124M.*

Producer, Joe Pasternak; director, Richard Thorpe; screenplay, Richard Connell, Gladys Lehman; music director, Georgie Stoll; vocal arranger, Kay Thompson; choreography, Sammy Lee; songs, Ralph Freed and Stoll; Freed and Sammy Fain; Freed and Jimmy McHugh; Mann Holiner and Alberta Nichols; Gus Arnheim, Jules Lemair, and Harry Tobias; Harold Adamson and Xavier Cugat; Al Feldman and Ella Fitzgerald; Jimmy Durante, Ben Ryan, and Harry Donnelly; assistant director, Earl McAvoy; sound, James K. Burbridge; camera, Robert Surtees; editor, George Boemler.

Gloria DeHaven (Jean Deyo); June Allyson (Patsy Deyo); Van Johnson (John Brown III); Tom Drake (Frank Miller); Jimmy Durante (Billy Kipp); Henry Stephenson (Mr. Brown); Henry O'Neill (Mr. Brown, II); Ben Blue (Ben); Frank Sully (Private Adams); Donald Meek (Mr. Nizby); Carlos Ramirez (Carlos); José Iturbi, Lena Horne, Albert Coates, Virginia O'Brien, Amparo Iturbi, Wilde Twins (Specialties); Harry James and His Band with Helen Forrest (Themselves), Xavier Cugat and His Band with Lina Romay (Themselves); Gracie Allen (Concerto Number); Frank Jenks (Dick Deyo); Joan Thorsen (Gladys Deyo); Doreen McCann (Patsy at Age Two); Eilene Janssen (Patsy at Age Four); Sandra Lee (Jean at Age One); Ghislaine (Gigi) Perreau (Jean at Age 2½); Ava Gardner (Rockette Girl); Billy Lechner, Allen Forienza (Call Boys); William Frambes (Boy Vaudevillian); Don Loper (Small Town Wolf); Charles Hayes (Man in Evening Clothes); Eve Whitney (Bejeweled Woman); Sheldon Jett (Fat Man); Ruth Cherrington (Stout Lady); Hazel Dohlman (Dowager); Lynn Arlen, Patricia Lenn (Debutantes); Florence Wix, Harry Adams, Ed Mortimer (Middle-aged Folk); Diane Mumby, Shelby Payne (Cigarette Girls); Fred Rapport (Captain of Waiters); Leo Mostovoy (Waiter); Eddie Kane (Headwaiter); Lee Bennett (Friend); Arthur Walsh (Lonesome Soldier); Joe Yule (Carpenter); Thomas Louden (Butler); Peggy Maley (Girl); Ralph Gardner, James Carpenter, Mickey Rentschler, Doodles Weaver (Soldiers); Fred G. Beckner (Sailor); Kathleen (Kay) Williams (Girl Flirt); Nolan Leary (Durante's Double); Sol De Garda (Man in Canteen); Buster Keaton (Durante's Son).

New York Premiere: Capitol Theatre—June 14, 1944
New York Television Debut: CBS—December 27, 1959

## Synopsis

Anxious to do their bit in the war effort, Jean and Patsy Deyo, a song-and-dance sister team, entertain servicemen at their apartment after they finish their act at a swank New York nightclub. One night the girls invite soldier Frank Miller and sailor John Brown III to their apartment. Jean, a flirtatious sort, attracts both men. Demure Patsy silently adores John. Neither girl realizes that John is a millionaire. When the girls casually mention to him that a deserted warehouse next door would make an ideal servicemen's canteen, John secretly buys the property in their name, modernizes it, but does not let on that he is the benefactor. Patsy eventually learns the truth, and, believing that John loves Jean, graciously tries to bow out of the picture. Jean, at first delighted that a millionaire is interested in her, soon comes to the realization that John loves Patsy. She brings them together, meanwhile making arrangements for her own marriage to Frank.

◆━◆━◆

If the flimsy plot to this musical seemed overly familiar, perhaps it was because MGM had used it at least twice before, in *Broadway Melody* (1929) and its remake *Two Girls on Broadway* (1940). But so what? The new picture was bursting with "melody, humor, whimsy and romance" and where else in one 124-minute cinematic bundle could one find such a wild conglomeration of guest artists, including José and Amparo Iturbi, Harry James and His Band with Helen Forrest, Xavier Cugat and His Band with Lina Romay, Lena Horne, Gracie Allen, Virginia O'Brien, Ben Blue, and Jimmy Durante in his movie comeback. Amazing as this astounding compilation of supporting performers may seem in retrospect, such talent groups were to become standard practice for producer Joe Pasternak, who had left Universal and joined Metro in 1941. Besides peppering his tuneful MGM films with appealing lead players (Gloria De-Haven, June Allyson, Van Johnson, and Tom Drake, in this one), he wanted to provide something for everyone's musical entertainment taste. "What keeps the picture from ever becoming mediocre is the producer's way of allowing his best moments to creep up on the audience" *(Christian Science Monitor)*.

This Richard Thorpe-directed feature would have tremendous importance for four of the top-featured performers. At the time, DeHaven was a more experienced screen player than Allyson, and, being first-billed, the former was considered more likely to push to the top at the studio. Nevertheless, in *Two Girls and a Sailor* she found herself directly vying with Allyson, the 5' 1", twenty-seven-year-old bundle of dynamite who had made her cinema debut only one year previous. "It's a toss-up between June Allyson and Gloria DeHaven as to which is the lovelier girl," wrote Bosley Crowther in the *New York Times*. "But," he continued, "since Miss Allyson is made the more appealing—and makes herself so—she deserved the favored nod." The handwriting was on the backdrop wall: Allyson was on her way up the career ladder at Culver City, while DeHaven would stagnate at the studio throughout the 1940s.

For 6' 2", twenty-eight-year-old Johnson, *Two Girls and a Sailor* provided him with his first screen musical assignment (although here he mostly talked and did double takes) since his film debut in RKO's *Too Many Girls* (1940). The film demonstrated yet another reason why the bobby soxers developed such a wide-spreading crush on the freckle-faced, personable performer, who was one young man available during the World War II years to make his name with the public while more physically fit actor rivals were in military service. And for the gravel-voiced Schnozole, Durante, this movie was a comeback return to MGM where he had been a comedy specialty star in the early 1930s. In *Two Girls and a Sailor* he provided several touchingly nostalgic moments as the warehouse occupant who knew the "sisters" when they were little kids.

What makes the splendiferous array of musical comedy so appealing in *Two Girls and a Sailor* is its generally unpretentious handling within the story's framework. Allyson and DeHaven are born-in-the-trunk vaudeville performers who as adults work in a plush Manhattan night spot. Between that setting and the coveted warehouse-canteen—which undergoes a magical transition that money almost could not buy—there is ample "logical" opportunity for each to perform her turn. Thus together, Allyson and DeHaven perform "A Love Like Ours," "A-Tisket A-Tasket," and bits of "Sweet and Lovely." DeHaven puts across the tune "My Mother Told Me," while Allyson sweetly rips into "The Young Man with a Horn," backed, naturally, by Harry James and His Band. When the two girls are not front and center—which is not very often—there is José and Amparo Iturbi in a piano duet of the "Ritual Fire Dance," Lena Horne in silhouette and then in full view with her rendition of "Paper Moon," the blended melody playing of James' troupe with "You, Dear," "Castles in the Air," and "Charmaine," in contrast to the Latin American rhythm of Cugat and band with "The Thrill of a New Romance," and "Babalu." O'Brien provided her deadpan singing of "Take It Easy," Durante reprised his own co-authored composition, "Inka Dinka Do," but for this author the highlight of the entertainment package was zany Allen's mock-serious rendition of "Concerto for Index Finger," in which she did just that, led in her "classic rendition" by London Symphony conductor Albert Coates! Interpolated into her "solo" piano number were fragments of "The Dance of the Hours" and "The Anvil Chorus," just in case any viewer might be taking her performance too seriously. Even Liberace could never hope to match her showmanship in this interlude.

Despite the superabundance of music, there is still sufficent time reserved in *Two Girls and a Sailor* for romantic moments, as the four leads shuffle around their amorous relationships. DeHaven, just as she would be in *Summer Stock* (1950) with Judy Garland, is the younger, flirtatious sister, pert, carefree, and somewhat mercenary, but always sidetracked into eventual conventionality by the script. Thus, when it is time for Johnson to awaken to Allyson's worth as a person, DeHaven must quickly step aside. She is supposed to prefer the Southern drawl of the blander Drake (who has a modest Texas ranch and executive ability) to the bouncier

631

appeal of Johnson, regardless of the fact that he's the scion of a sixty-million-dollar fortune. Meanwhile, Allyson, the older and wiser sister, has been pining (she even dreams that "Admiral" Johnson proposes marriage) for Johnson, almost reveling in her unrequited love, which for a time threatens to raise her to the ranks of saintliness as she nobly plans to step aside for DeHaven's desires to trap Johnson into marriage.

Could anything be more wholesome, sincere, well-scrubbed, teary-eyed than little Allyson? The answer was obviously yes, in the presence of big Johnson. Together they made a perfect film team, as unrealistically idealistic in their oncamera moments as Clark Gable and Lana Turner were fictionally torrid or Greer Garson and Walter Pidgeon were synthetically noble. More than any other studio, MGM knew what to do once two players proved to have boxoffice chemistry, and as the critics-audience tallies came in on *Two Girls and a Sailor,* it was a shoo-in that Allyson and Johnson on celluloid had that magical something. John T. McManus *(PM)* noted Allyson as a "crinkly-eyed blonde who seems to be building into another Alice Faye." Otis L. Gurnsey, Jr. *(New York Herald-Tribune)* cited that Johnson ". . . paints a most appealing, ingratiating portrait of American youth with his slow smiles and his bland personality."

## TILL THE CLOUDS ROLL BY
### *(MGM, 1946) C-137M.*

Producer, Arthur Freed; director, Richard Whorf; Judy Garland's numbers directed by Vincente Minnelli; story, Guy Bolton; adaptation, George Wells; screenplay, Myles Connolly, Jean Holloway; assistant director, Wally Worsley; art directors, Cedric Gibbons, Daniel B. Cathcart; set decorators, Edwin B. Willis, Richard Pefferle; music director, Lennie Hayton; orchestrator, Conrad Salinger; vocal arranger, Kay Thompson; songs, Jerome Kern and Oscar Hammerstein II; Kern and P. G. Wodehouse; Kern and Edward Laska; Kern and Herbert Reynolds; Kern, Otto Harbach, and Hammerstein II; Kern and Harbach; Kern and B. G. DeSylva; Kern and Ira Gershwin; Kern and Dorothy Fields; sound, Douglas Shearer; special effects, Warren Newcombe; camera, Harry Stradling, George J. Folsey; editor, Albert Akst.

Robert Walker (Jerome Kern); Judy Garland (Marilyn Miller); Lucille Bremer (Sally); Joan Wells (Sally as a Girl); Van Heflin (James I. Hessler); Paul Langton (Oscar Hammerstein); Dorothy Patrick (Mrs. Jerome Kern); Mary Nash (Mrs. Muller); Harry Hayden (Charles Frohman); Paul Maxey (Victor Herbert); Rex Evans (Cecil Keller); William "Bill" Phillips (Hennessey); Dinah Shore (Julie Sanderson); Van Johnson (Band Leader); June Allyson, Angela Lansbury, Ray McDonald (Guest Performers); Maurice Kelly, Cyd Charisse, Gower Champion (Dance Specialties); Ray Teal (Orchestra Conductor); Wilde Twins (Specialty); *Showboat* Number:

William Halligan (Captain Andy); Tony Martin (Ravenal); Kathryn Grayson (Magnolia); Virginia O'Brien (Ellie); Lena Horne (Julie); Caleb Peterson (Joe); Bruce Cowling (Steve); Frank Sinatra, Johnny Johnston (Finale); Herschel Graham, Fred Hueston, Dick Earle, Larry Steers, Reed Howes, Hazard Newsberry, Ed Elby, Lee Smith, Larry Williams, James Plato, Leonard Mellen, James Darrell, Tony Merlo, Charles Madrin, Charles Griffin (Opening Night Critics); Byron Foulger (Frohman's Secretary); Lee Phelps, Ralph Dunn (Moving Men); Lucille Casey, Mary Jane French, Beryl McCutcheon, Alice Wallace, Irene Veron, Gloria Joy Arden, Mickey Malloy, Alma Carroll, Wesley Brent (Showgirls); George Peters, Harry Denny, Bob McLean, Frank McClure, George Murray, John Alban, Lee Bennett (Stage Door Johnnies); Jean Andren (Secretary); John Albright (Call Boy); Margaret Bert (Maid); Herbert Heywood (Stagehand); Thomas Louden (Rural Postman); Ann Codee (Miss Laroche); James Finlayson (Candy Vendor); Elspeth Dudgeon, Margaret Bert (Maids); Lilyan Irene (Barmaid); Tom Stevenson (Genius); Penny Parker (Punch and Judy Operator); Robert Emmet O'Connor (Clerk); Stanley Andrews (Doctor); Russell Hicks (Motion Picture Producer); William Forrest (Motion Picture Director); Arnaut Brothers (Bird Act); Jim Grey, Douglas Wright (Bull Clown); Louis Manley (Swivel Chair Lady); Don Wayson, Howard Mitchell (Detectives); Sally Forrest, Mary Hatcher (Chorus Girls).

New York Premere: Radio City Music Hall—December 5, 1946
New York Television Debut: CBS—October 24, 1959

### Synopsis

Via flashback, the life of music composer Jerome Kern is traced. As an aspiring young song writer, Jerome visits James I. Hessler, an expert music arranger, to seek help on one of his compositions. Hessler recognizes the young man's ability and a close friendship develops. Jerome becomes convinced that Broadway producers import their musical numbers from England to guarantee hitdom. Determined to succeed he travels to England, where he sells one of his songs to an English producer who turns it into a huge success. This hit is followed by others, and Jerome soon finds himself commissioned by Charles Frohman to write the music for one of his pending Broadway shows. Meanwhile Jerome has fallen in love with an English girl. Their romance is interrupted by Jerome's trip to New York, but in time he becomes even more successful and returns to England to make her Mrs. Jerome Kern. With the passing years, Jerome's successes continue and his happiness is marred only by the ill health of his good friend Hessler. A crisis develops when Jerome, after promising Hessler's daughter, Sally, that he would put her in a show and allow her to introduce one of his songs, is compelled by the producer to give the song to star Marilyn Miller. Heartbroken, Sally runs away from home. Hessler, sick with worry over her disappearance, dies. Interested in nothing but locating

Sally, Jerome loses interest in his music. He eventually locates her in a Memphis cafe, where she convinces him of her determination to make her own way in the entertainment world. His mind eased over Sally's welfare, Jerome returns to his music and begins to write the score for *Showboat*, which will later be filmed for the movies.

❖❖❖

If Warner Bros. could re-create the life story of Cole Porter [*Night and Day* (1944)] and George Gershwin [*Rhapsody in Blue* (1945)], then MGM felt entitled to play havoc with the biography of Jerome David Kern (1885-1945) in the Technicolor *Till the Clouds Roll By*. "The story is enough of the life and not very hard times of the late Jerome Kern to make you want either not to hear any of it at all or to get the real story instead" [James Agee *(The Nation)*]. But this "mammoth and gaudily tinted variety entertainment" grossed $4.5 in distributors' domestic rentals, which proved you could fool some of the people some of the time with tidbits of fluff. Obviously producer Arthur Freed knew the acceptability threshholds of the filmgoing public.

Perhaps most incomprehensible in this mixed bag of musical offerings, is why no apparent attempt was made to reproduce the changing musical styles of presentation as the cinema highlights song numbers decade by decade. These musical numbers are produced all in the same manner, with no historical insight whatsoever. Vincente Minnelli was solely responsible for directing the episodes with his then wife, Judy Garland, who, in the guise of "being" Marilyn Miller, had two very effective numbers, "Look for the Silver Lining," and "Who Stole My Heart Away." Richard Whorf, the overall director for the picture, was most in control of the filmed excerpts from *Showboat*, with Lena Horne rendering "Can't Help Lovin' That Man" and "Why Was I Born," Virginia O'Brien playing deadpan with "Life Upon the Wicked Stage," and Frank Sinatra concertizing, in white tuxedo and all, "Ol' Man River."

June Allyson and Van Johnson did not share any screen time together in *Till the Clouds Roll By*, but they did have independent outings to please their growing coterie of fans. Allyson was at her very liveliest (admittedly there are some critics who liken her singing to a foghorn belching in the mist) performing the mock-vampish, "Cleopatterer," and only slightly less frenetic in vocalizing the bouncy "Leave It to Jane." Her one overly coy spot in the feature was her joint rendition (with Kathryn Grayson, Gower Champion, Sinatra, Lucille Bremer, Ray McDonald, Tony Martin, and Johnny Johnston) of the title tune, in which the celebrity group went splashing through soundstage puddles and performed rhythmic dramatics to the well-known lyrics.

Back in RKO's *Roberta* (1935), Fred Astaire and Ginger Rogers had liltingly performed the challenging "I Won't Dance," and to compare their rendition to the more pedestrian, unsubtle handling by Bremer and Van Johnson in *Till the Clouds Roll By*, speaks volumes about the virtues of intimate screen musicals versus overblown confectionary cinema. But post-World War II moviegoers staged no protests at the likes of this MGM song and dance "treat," nor at the hoofing of Johnson.

## HIGH BARBAREE
### (MGM, 1947) 91M.

Producer, Everett Riskin; director, Jack Conway; based on the novel by Charles Nordhoff, James Norman Hall; screenplay, Anne Morrison Chapin, Whitfield Cook, Cyril Hume; art directors, Cedric Gibbons, Gabriel Scognamilo; set decorators, Edwin B. Willis, Ralph S. Hurst; assistant director, George Rheim; music, Herbert Stothart; sound, Douglas Shearer; technical adviser, Lt. John B. Muoio, Jr., USN; special effects, A. Arnold Gillespie, Warren Newcombe; camera, Sidney Wagner; editor, Conrad A. Nervig.

Van Johnson (Alec Brooke); June Allyson (Nancy Fraser); Thomas Mitchell (Captain Thad Vail); Marilyn Maxwell (Diana Case); Henry Hull (Dr. Brooke); Claude Jarman, Jr. (Alec at Age Fourteen); Cameron Mitchell (Lt. Moore); Geraldine Wall (Mrs. Brooke); Barbara Brown (Della Parkson); Chill Wills (Lars); Paul Harvey (John Case); Charles Evans (Col. Taylor); Joan Wells (Nancy at Age Twelve); Gigi Perreau (Nancy at Age Five); James Hunt (Alec at Age Two); Stanley Andrews, Jess Cavin (Farmers); Ransom Sherman (Mr. Fraser); Ida Moore (Old Lady); Lee Phelps, Paul Kruger (Workmen); Dick Rush (Baggage Man); Robert Emmet O'Connor (Station Master); Sam McDaniel (Bertram); Steve Olsen (Barker); Paul Newlan, Robert Skelton (Truckmen); Tim Ryan (Ringmaster); Florence Stephens (Mrs. Fraser); Florence Howard (Mrs. Case); Lois Austin (Secretary); Lew Smith (Groundman); Mahlon Hamilton (Ned Flynn); Helyn Eby-Rock (Woman Helper); Ruth Brady (Young Woman Aide); George Travell (Man in Slicker); Pietro Sosso (Old Man); Paul Dunn (Boy); Linda Bieber (Girl); Howard Mitchell (Conductor); Phillip Morris (Baggage Man); Saul Martell (Bernadino); Mitchell Rhein, Phil Dunham, Drew Demorest, Mike Pat Donovan, Bob Rowe, Henry Sylvester, Phil Friedman (Vendors); Don Anderson, Frank Wilcox (Co-Pilots); Milton Kibbee (Waiter); Harry Tyler (Bartender); Larry Steers (Major); Bruce Cowling (Captain); Clarke Hardwicke (Young Man); William McKeever Riley (Office Boy); Frank Pharr, Anton Northpole, George Magrill, Harry Wilson (Vendors); William Tannen (Officer of the Deck); Bert Davidson, Robert Dardett (Naval Officers); Jeffrey Sayre (Night Officer of the Deck); Al Kikume (Tangaros); Carl Saxe, Donald S. Lewis (Marine Sergeants).

New York Premiere: Capitol Theatre—June 3, 1947
New York Television Debut: CBS—December 29, 1956

## Synopsis

When his patrol bomber is shot down by the enemy during World War II, Alec Brooke guides the drifting plane toward "High Barbaree," a mythical island, of which he had heard so much from his uncle, Captain Thad Vail. Short of food and water, Alec attempts to keep up the morale of his wounded companion, Lt. Moore, by relating the story of his life. As children, he and Nancy Fraser had been playmates and had looked forward to the infrequent visits of his scampish uncle with whom they enjoyed many unique outings. Later Nancy and her family moved West, and Alec, grown to manhood and interested in aviation, leaves medical school against the wishes of his physician father. He becomes an official of a plane factory. On the eve of his engagement to Diana Case, his employer's daughter, Nancy, now a young lady, comes East to visit with Alec's family. He falls in love with her immediately and is persuaded by Nancy to return to medicine. However, he fails to make known his deep romantic attachment to her and she returns to the West Coast. With the coming of the war, he enlists and becomes a naval pilot. Thereafter he has a reunion with Nancy just before she sets sail on a ship commanded by his uncle. As Alec finishes his lengthy tale, his buddy, feverish from thirst and hunger, dies. Alec himself passes out. Meanwhile, Nancy, driven by a premonition that Alec is injured, urges his uncle to search the seas for him. Alec is rescued in time and Nancy is able to nurse him back to health.

◆—◆—◆

Snide college newspaper surveys might list Van Johnson and June Allyson as among the worst screen performers of 1946, but the less demanding public felt differently about their Van and June. By the mid-1940s, Johnson had emerged as MGM's fair-haired wonder boy, the idol of shrieking bobby soxers, and the star of a string of movie hits, often in tandem with aquatic gold mine Esther Williams. On the other hand, Leo the Lion had not been doing as well by the ever-popular Allyson. She had been nicely served by *Music for Millions* (1945) with Margaret O'Brien as well as by *Two Sisters from Boston* (1946) with Kathryn Grayson, but had fumbled with the star entourage engulfed in the potboiler, *The Secret Heart* (1946).

Why it had taken Metro so long to rematch Allyson and Johnson is hard to fathom, but it is easily understandable why the couple was placed in the peculiar adaptation of *High Barbaree*, a 1945 novel by Charles Nordhoff and James Norman Hall. The studio was merely milking the performers' marquee allure. It didn't seem to matter that Allyson and Johnson were each far better in musical comedy than straight dramatics. The film was on the studio roster and the studio was determined that the movie was going to be made and these contract stars would grace it. Unfortunately, the critics quickly agreed that the picture was a singularly unconsumable commodity in which "Symbolism and flashback are employed with a singular lack of cinematic effect" [Howard Barnes *(New York Herald-Tribune)*].

Nearly all Americans had existed on patriotic pipedreams throughout the war years. Now in 1947, most of the public wanted a touch of credibility in their lives and entertainment. *High Barbaree* simply did not answer that need, particularly when the lead players were saddled with such bland characterizations. The only saving grace to the film was Thomas Mitchell as the strange uncle who feeds the children (Claude Jarman, Jr. as the young Johnson and Joan Wells as the child counterpart of Allyson) a healthy dose of blarney, telling them a rash of tall tales. But just as there was not enough of Mitchell's presence in the picture, or a sufficient amount of the circus interlude to spike the stale celluloid brew, so Marilyn Maxwell as Johnson's bride-to-be is short-shrifted by the screenplay, emerging hardly more than a plot tool.

The final incomprehensible element in the minor lunacy of the *High Barbaree* script, which allowed for little interplay between the adult Johnson and Allyson (they obviously love one another in the story but have little opportunity to express it), was the gimmick which allowed Allyson to locate her disabled lover in the midst of the big, wide South Pacific Ocean. This ludicrous plot device—a romantic variation of extra sensory perception—was asking a lot out of an audience, no matter how appealingly maudlin the two stars were—unshaven Johnson rambling about his life to his badly injured buddy (Cameron Mitchell), and dewy-eyed Allyson pressing onward, buoyed by her love for Naval pilot Johnson.

The critics rightly pulverized the film, but graciously spared the players' feelings, somewhat. "Mr. Johnson is fairly impressive, for all the butterscotch things he has to do, but June Allyson goes completely soggy as his boyhood sweetheart who becomes a Navy nurse" [Bosley Crowther *(New York Times)*].


## THE BRIDE GOES WILD
### *(MGM, 1948) 98M.*

Producer, William H. Wright; director, Norman Taurog; screenplay, Albert Beich; art directors, Cedric Gibbons, Harry McAfee; set decorators, Edwin B. Willis, Arthur Krams; assistant director, Sid Sidman; music, Rudolph G. Kopp; costumes, Helen Morse; makeup, Jack Dawn; sound, Douglas Shearer; camera, Ray June; editor, George Boemler.

Van Johnson (Greg Rawlings); June Allyson (Martha Terryton); Butch Jenkins (Danny); Hume Cronyn (John McGrath); Una Merkel (Miss Doberly); Richard Derr (Bruce Johnson); Lloyd Corrigan (Road House Operator); Elisabeth Risdon (Mrs. Carruthers); Clara Blandick (Aunt Pewtie); Kathleen Howard (Aunt Susan); Cecil Cunningham (Helen

Oldfield); Arlene Dahl (Tillie Smith); Clinton Sundberg (Dentist); Almira Sessions (Mrs. Williams); Napoleon Whiting (Porter); Alvin Hammer (Window Trimmer); Ferris Taylor (Floor Manager); Estelle Etterre (Mother Goose); Jean Dean (Bo Peep); Ethel Tobin (Receptionist); William Forrest (Myers); Jack Rice (Browen); Frank Ferguson (Mr. Fells); Robert Emmett Keane (Mr. Sarms); Byron Foulger (Max); Glen Arthur Berry (Lou); Eilene Janssen (Mary); Billy Jamison (Robert); Florence Stevens (Mother); Paul Power (Father); Robert Emmet O'Connor (Conductor); Celia Travers (Bess Talbot); Henry Hall (Reverend Brown); Garry Owen (Joe); Dewey Robinson (Headwaiter); Rebel Randall (Cigarette Girl); Jackie Searle, Tom Dugan (Waiters); Stanley Blystone (Bartender); John Albright (Bellhop); Phillip Bernard (Henry the Octopus); Erville Alderson (Farmer); Jack Lipson (Fat Man); Anthony Taylor, Billy Gray (Boys); Connie Gilchrist (Miss Tooker); Leo Wilson, Robert Scott (Piutes); George McDonald, Jose Alvarado (Piute Chiefs); David Bair (Mohawk); Teddy Infuhr, George Nokes (Scouts); Billy Severn (Piute Leader); Edward Earle (Stevens); Joe Whitehead (Cousin George); Rocco Lonzo (Mechanic); Robert Spencer (Best Man); Sam Ash, Roger Cole (Customers); Frank Peterson, Hank Man, Clarence Hennecke, Phil Dunham, Rhea Mitchell, George Boyce, Lou Bridge, Bess Flowers, Kay Deslys (Wedding Guests); Mickey Martin (Parking Lot Attendant); Catherine Courtney (Goose Woman).

New York Premiere: Capitol Theatre—June 3, 1948
New York Television Debut: CBS—August 7, 1959

## Synopsis

Martha Terryton, winner of a contest to illustrate a new book by "Uncle Bump," a popular children's story author, arrives in New York and discovers that the author is none other than Greg Rawlings, an irresponsible young man with an over fondness for drink. Shocked by her discovery, she declares her intention to expose Greg. In order to save the situation, publisher John McGrath informs her that Greg is a widower and that he has been driven to drink by his little son, who is a problem child. Her offer to help compels McGrath to borrow Danny from a local orphan asylum to pose as Greg's son. Danny accepts the bribe to call Greg "daddy." Martha takes them both in hand, and before long, Greg falls in love with her and proposes marriage. Quite by accident, however, Martha learns the truth about Danny and breaks off her engagement to Greg. She returns to her home town to wed a past suitor, Bruce Johnson. The split between Martha and Greg upsets Danny, because Greg had promised to adopt the boy after their marriage. Despondent, Danny runs away from the orphanage and goes to Greg. Realizing that only married persons can adopt a child, Greg takes the boy to Martha, arriving on the day of her wedding. Unable to bear the thought of her marrying another man, Greg cooks up a scheme whereby Danny disrupts the wedding and wins Martha back to their side.

MGM touted this film by telling the moviegoing public, "When a Miss from the Country Who's Prissy but Kissable Meets a Guy from the City Who's Fresh but Likeable. Watch the Screen Go Romantically Combustible."

For a change June Allyson and Van Johnson had a vehicle which allowed them to exude their screen stock-in-trade acting without the dosage becoming overly cloying. The magic elixir for this exercise was director Norman Taurog's ability to build a zany farce obstensibly around the Johnson-Allyson see-sawing romance, while focusing a goodly portion of the frenetic activities around a freckled-faced moppet named Butch Jenkins.

Some critics objected that the film leaned more in the direction of Mack Sennett than Ernst Lubitsch. "It is visually effective, but there is a considerable poverty of invention when highway close calls are substituted for the adroit manipulation of nonsense" [Howard Barnes (New York Herald-Tribune)]. Even those who acknowledged that the farcical goings-on in The Bride Goes Wild, could be diverting, warned ". . . your liking for slapstick will be the barometer of your enjoyment of the picture" (Cue magazine).

Long before Doris Day had transferred herself from screen musicals to her portrayals as the cinema's leading virgin and moral standard, appealing Allyson proved in such features as The Bride Goes Wild that she was one spunky cinema redhead who was ready to use her mitts when words failed to insure that everyone—namely Johnson—played fair. In this movie excursion, she is an energetic schoolteacher from rural Vermont, who is quite leery about visiting corrupt New York City. But how could one ignore the opportunity to illustrate the latest book by the author of The Bashful Bull and Augie the Ant? Being a children's teacher, she knows this literature's value to society, and if God gave her talent to draw, she was going to do her part to bring more such wonderful stories to the youth of the world.

So much for Allyson's personae. On the other hand, breezy Johnson by this time had mastered not only the art of the "aw shucks" smile, but could also effect a wondrous slow burn and baffled look when romance or even business was not going the right way. In past movies he might have become annoyed when the girl of his choice ignored him, but never had he revealed an oncamera character with any two such full-fledged vices as pictured in The Bride Goes Wild. Both of these personality flaws grated against the precious concepts of the masses, since his Greg Rawlings, like W. C. Fields, hated children and loved to over-imbibe.

With Johnson's Greg Rawlings and Allyson's Martha Terryton bumping heads with a certain amount of heavy-handed humor, there was bound to be some amusing situations, particularly when the catalyst who restored their on-again-off-again romance was a rambunctious young terror (Jenkins), a junior version of the stars' unrepressed alter egos. Thus we have Allyson aghast that Uncle Bump could be none other than reprobate Johnson, followed by Allyson cooing over Johnson's alleged son (Jenkins), and breathing fire that Johnson cannot cope with the mischievous tike. Finally, Allyson rushes back into the arms of her erstwhile suitor (Richard Derr) while wishing the two men in her life could be Johnson and Jenkins. In contrast, there were scenes of a lumbering, slightly stocky Johnson wincing from his latest hangover, then sweet-talking his sometimes girlfriend (Arlene Dahl), and Johnson attempting to be polite to hellion orphan Jenkins. In addition, Johnson is seen restraining himself from murdering the youth who kicks him in the shins and drops a typewriter on his foot, subconsciously wanting to kiss instead of thrash Allyson who has dumped him into a pond, and scheming with his one-time adversary (Jenkins) to win Allyson back from the land of Vermont and Derr.

Director Taurog allowed the cast to literally go wild in three slapstick situations: one a game of palefaces versus Indians in which unbridled Jenkins and his pals shoot rubbed-tipped arrows at Johnson's aching head, another when Jenkins' beloved glass-enclosed ant village breaks loose and causes havoc among Allyson's wedding guests, and the frantic highway chase with Johnson a most harassed participant.

*The Bride Goes Wild* was indeed lucky to have the services of Hume Cronyn as the pressured publisher who finds himself playing nursemaid to uncontrollable Jenkins, as well as Merkel as Cronyn's flip-tongued secretary and Dahl as a most attractive viper.

Johnson and Allyson would recreate their *The Bride Goes Wild* roles on "Lux Radio Theatre" on June 26, 1950.


## TOO YOUNG TO KISS
### *(MGM, 1951) 91M.*

Producer, Sam Zimbalist; director, Robert Z. Leonard; story, Everett Freeman; screenplay, Frances Goodrich, Albert Hackett; art directors, Cedric Gibbons, Paul Groesse; music adviser, Harold Felman; camera, Joseph Ruttenberg; editor, Conrad A. Nervig.

June Allyson (Cynthia Potter); Van Johnson (Eric Wainwright); Gig Young (John Tirsen); Paula Corday (Denise Dorcet); Kathryn Givney (Miss Benson); Larry Keating (Danny Butler); Hans Conried (Mr. Sparrow); Esther Dale (Mrs. Boykin); Jonathan Cott (Photographer); Antonio Filauri (Veloti); Jo Gilbert (Gloria); Alexander Steinert (Conductor); Bob Jellison (Sparrow's Assistant); Lisa Ferraday (Nina Marescu); Teddy Infuhr (Jeffrey); Ruthelma Stevens (Jeffrey's Mother); Albert Morin (East Indian); Ludwig Stossel (German Accompanist); Betty Farrington, Elizabeth Fournoy, Grace Hayle (Women); Josephine Whittell (Mrs. Fullerton); George McDonald (Boy in Drug Store); Erno Verebes (Headwaiter); Peter Brocco (Waiter); Everett Glass (Druggist); Jack Gargan (Paul the Chauffeur); Jimmy Ames (Cab Driver); Robert Strong, Larry Harmon, Roger Moore (Photographers); Ray Walker (Reporter); Matt Moore (Charles);

Bob Stephenson (Stagehand); John McKee (Motorcycle Officer); John Maxwell (Detective); Larry Harmon (Conductor).

New York Debut: Radio City Music Hall—November 22, 1951
New York Television Debut: ABC—August 6, 1967

## Synopsis

Unable to obtain an audition appointment with Eric Wainwright, a famous concert manager, Cynthia Potter in desperation disguises herself as a thirteen-year-old girl with braces on her teeth and enters a children's concert sponsored annually by Eric. Her brilliant piano playing wins the contest and on the following day, Eric comes to her apartment with a contract. Cynthia, pretending that she is the older sister of the girl she has impersonated, tries to persuade Eric to sign her, but he refuses and even accuses her of being jealous of her successful kid sister. Furious at his attitude, Cynthia decides to continue the hoax by signing the contract as her little sister's guardian. Dressed appropriately, she arrives at Eric's office to commence her career as a child prodigy. John Tirsen, Cynthia's newspaperman boyfriend, disapproves of the hoax and tries to make Cynthia give it up. Eric comes upon them conversing, and Cynthia is forced to introduce John as her elder sister's boyfriend. Eric, however, is shocked to later find her smoking and drinking a cocktail while with John, and decides to take her to his country home to remove her from the evil influence of John and her elder sister. Cynthia deliberately proves difficult at Eric's home, by interfering with his romance with Denise Dorcet, a temperamental singer, and by insisting that he stop drinking and smoking if he does not want her to continue these vices. After weeks of practice, however, Eric becomes very fond of his child protégée, while she has secretly been falling in love with him. Nevertheless, realizing that Eric loves Denise, Cynthia decides to wed John and forget her career after the big concert. Just before Cynthia goes on stage for her debut recital, a story exposing the hoax—written by John—appears in the evening newspaper. Eric, though embarrassed, announces the deception to the audience and Cynthia takes her place at the piano. She performs superbly, but after the concert rushes from the hall in abject humiliation. Meanwhile, Eric discovers that Cynthia was not responsible for the tell-all story. He pursues her and prevents her marriage to John by declaring his own love.

◆—◆—◆

Fannie Brice had been entrancing the public for years with her "Baby Snooks." Ginger Rogers masqueraded amusingly as a child for most of *The Major and the Minor* (1942), and *My Friend Irma* (1948) offered two adults who were children at heart and mind (Marie Wilson and Jerry Lewis). But a whole picture devoted to the perennially young cinema lady June Allyson (then thirty-four years old), portraying a thirteen-year-old

641

musical prodigy who dresses in pinafores, has teeth braces, walks pigeon-toed, looks wide-eyed, and plays with teddy bears and blocks, but when alone slugs down a hard drink or puffs on a cigarette? "Technically Miss Allyson is good in the part; but her childish quality loses its appeal when she takes on the outer characteristics of a child" [Otis L. Guernsey, Jr. (*New York Herald-Tribune*)]. Bosley Crowther (*New York Times*) was less diplomatic: "Miss Allyson had better act her age." John McCarten (*New Yorker* magazine) was even less tactful: "Miss Allyson is about as plausible in her role as Dame May Whitty would be as Cinderella."

But top-billed Allyson did make a game try in *Too Young to Kiss,* frantically alternating her pose between her young concert pianist (modeled to an extent after roles played by Diana Lynn) and a young adult version of herself. It left little opportunity for Allyson to emote with the lovable gimmickry that was so much expected from the 1940s most precious cinema girl-next-door.

Johnson as the exasperated and exasperating concert manager seemed far removed from the Sol Hurok ambiance he was supposed to personify. Instead, he oozed boyish charm that would have been more appropriate to one younger than his years. Whether reprimanding the youngster Allyson, jibing the elder Allyson, or romancing the "real" Allyson, Johnson's well-scrubbed bumbling manner won no reviewers' plaudits, and was even beginning to pale on his staunchest fans. "You have probably seen Mr. Johnson before, so I need say nothing about his inadequacies." (McCarten of the *New Yorker*) "Johnson is too slow and deliberate a stylist to be quite comfortable in what are supposed to be the frantic reactions of his part" (Guernsey, Jr. of the *Herald-Tribune*). Even having Johnson trade romantic clinches with the torchy dish known as Denise Dorcet (Paula Corday) did nothing to enhance Johnson's boxoffice standing as a he-man playboy.

## REMAINS TO BE SEEN
### *(MGM, 1953) 88M.*

Producer, Arthur Hornblow, Jr.; director, Don Weis; based on the play by Howard Lindsay, Russel Crouse; screenplay, Sidney Sheldon; art directors, Cedric Gibbons, Hans Peters; songs, Gus Kahn, Ernie Erdman, and Dan Russo; John Latouche, Ted Fetter, and Vernon Duke; Johnny Mercer and Richard A. Whiting; camera, Robert Planck; editor, Cotton Warburton.

June Allyson (Jody Revere); Van Johnson (Waldo Williams); Louis Calhern (Benjamin Goodwin); Angela Lansbury (Valeska Chauval); John Beal (Dr. Glenson); Dorothy Dandridge (Herself); Barry Kelley (Lt.

O'Flair); Sammy White (Ben); Kathryn Card (Mrs. West); Paul Harvey (Mr. Bennett); Helene Millard (Mrs. Bennett); Peter Chong (Ling Tan); Charles Lane (Examiner Delapp); Larry Blake (Detective Minetti); Morgan Farley (Kyle Manning); Howard Freeman (Clark); Frank Nelson (Fleming); Robert Foulk (Officer Miller); Dabbs Greer (Julius); Emmett Smith (Buck); Thomas P. Dillon (Frank); Dave Willock (Driver); Don Anderson (Attendant); Gregory Gay (Head Waiter); Lawrence Dobkin (Captain); Frank Scannell, Erno Verebes (Waiters); Shep Menken (Man); Veronika Pataky, Fernanda Eliscuo (Women); Dick Simmons (M.C.); Fred Welsh (Taxi Driver).

New York Premiere: Part of Multi-Theatre National Release—
May 15, 1953
New York Television Debut: ABC—July 13, 1967

## Synopsis

Waldo Williams, a New York apartment house manager, is an amateur drummer. One day he finds one of his tenants dead and notifies Benjamin Goodwin, the deceased man's attorney. Goodwin wires Jody Revere, a band vocalist and the deceased's niece, to come to New York at once. Before the body is removed, someone stabs it with a knife, and the authorities seek the culprit. When Jody arrives she learns of her uncle's death and while matters are being settled, decides to stay overnight at his place, only if Waldo agrees to stay and protect her. She wants no part of the fortune willed to her, because she despised the man when he was alive. Since Dr. Glenson now has diagnosed the man's death as heart failure, the police are more than anxious to know why the body was stabbed. Among those questioned is Valeska Chauval, an attractive brunette who had interested the dead man in financing her plan for a new, universal language. Jody takes a quick dislike to Valeska and decides to accept her uncle's fortune and give it away to charity herself. Meanwhile Waldo's awkward but sincere attentions amuse Jody, and when he shows her how adept he is with the drums she tries to get him a job with the band. When Jody retires for the night, Waldo again stands guard. He does not notice when Valeska comes through a sliding panel on the wall, puts Jody in a trance, and leads her to the edge of a balcony high above the street. The attempted murder is foiled when Waldo unwittingly turns on the radio and the blaring music breaks Jody's trance. Subsequently Waldo turns amateur sleuth and discovers that the secret entrance in the apartment leads to Valeska's apartment in the adjoining building. Thereafter he finds Valeska's body in the closet. Rushing back to the other building he is in time to save Jody from Dr. Glenson, who had hoped to acquire the deceased's fortune. All ends happily when Jody lets Waldo know that he is now officially a member of the band and that she intends to wed him.

643

Playwrights Howard Lindsay and Russel Crouse will certainly remain better known for their *Life with Father* stage comedy than for their 1951 farce-thriller *Remains to Be Seen,* which enjoyed a good Broadway run with Jackie Cooper and Janis Paige co-starring. *Remains to Be Seen* might have made a cozy feature film, but MGM studio boss Dore Schary assigned it to Don Weis, at the time a modest contract director. In addition, Schary saddled the project with a stringent budget and miscast two declining studio stars, June Allyson and Van Johnson, in the drab proceedings. It was this feature, which opened on the wrong half of double bills, that convinced Allyson that she had to leave the studio. Easy-going Johnson would hang around the Culver City lot for a few more years.

Neither Allyson nor Johnson were as effective oncamera as the stage star originals of *Remains to Be Seen.* Jody Revere was supposed to be a naive, brassy band vocalist always talking in jive lingo, but Allyson's portrayal of the girl who supposedly was very gullible did not come across as true naivete. Likewise, Johnson's Waldo Williams was established as a milquetoast apartment house manager who at heart was an irrepressible jazz drummer. However, the actor was too personable and frolicsome from the start. The team's best moments are when they are singing-hoofing in their carefree style, performing "Too Marvelous for Words," and "Toot, Toot Tootsie." Even in the musical department, Dorothy Dandridge outshone both stars with her rendering of "Taking a Chance on Love."

None of the other ingredients of this murder comedy fit together. Even the intended weird atmosphere of the dead man's apartment, stuffed with death masks and other exotic relics, seemed phony. John Beal's doctor was too mysterious from the start, Angela Lansbury too over-grasping in her exotic "other" woman role, and Louis Calhern provided one of his apparently off the cuff pseudo-droll characterizations as the rather unscrupulous attorney.

## THE YEARS AFTER

Leaving the security of MGM was a tough but realistic decision for actress June Allyson. While she had gained her own niche of immortality there as the sweetheart-next-door girl of America, she could not continue playing that form of juvenilia forever, no matter how much a portion of the public preferred that pose. Metro had teamed her twice with her real-life husband Dick Powell (in *The Reformer and The Redhead* and *Right Cross,* both 1950) but the earnest dramas did little to convince viewers that Allyson possessed a new adult resiliency to her acting. More commercial had been her teaming with lanky ex-MGMer James Stewart in *The Stratton Story* (1949), a popular matching that would later continue with *The Glenn Miller Story* (1954) and *Strategic Air Command* (1955).

These movies displayed Allyson as the more mature girl spinoff of the Van Johnson entries, now seen as a noble wife whose tremendous wholesomeness was only matched by Jane Wyatt of television's "Father Knows Best" series. Still determined to prove that there was depth to her screen abilities, Allyson went "serious" in the strident *The Shrike* (1955) and then found herself tagged as the remake queen of mid-1950s Hollywood, playing such *déjà vu* assignments as the Norma Shearer part in the musically refurbished *The Women* (1939), now trotted out as *The Opposite Sex* (1956). Between the time of her sexually starved war widow in *Stranger in My Arms* (1959) and her cameo as a lesbian in MGM's *They Only Kill Their Masters* (1972), Allyson hosted-starred in her own anthology teleseries (1960), returned to Broadway as a replacement celebrity in *Forty Carats* (1970), appeared in the national touring company of *No, No Nanette* (1972), and later worked in stock with her son.

*Easy to Love* (1953) was Johnson's final celluloid cavorting with Esther Williams; for the next year he alternated between Elizabeth Taylor in *The Last Time I Saw Paris* and pondering the mental quirks of Humphrey Bogart's Captain Queeg in *The Caine Mutiny*. Ironically, as Johnson's film career declined in his post-MGM years, he became a better performer and more controlled in exuding his freckled charm. Finally he proved in the underrated *Company of Killers* (1970) that it had been folly for him to have rejected the lead in "The Untouchables" video series. He scored a personal triumph in the London stage presentation of *The Music Man* (1961) but failed to win Broadway approval in the quick-folding *Come on Strong* (1962) with Carroll Baker. He continues to perform in dinner theatres, as a guest star on television, and waits for fate to deal him a kinder turn. He and Allyson were nostalgically rematched in the *High on a Rainbow* segment of NBC-TV's "Name of the Game" in 1968.

In **Dark Passage** (WB, 1947)

# Chapter 23

# Humphrey Bogart
# & Lauren Bacall

## HUMPHREY BOGART

5′ 10″
160 pounds
Dark brown hair
Brown eyes
Aquarius

*Real name: Humphrey DeForest Bogart. Born January 23, 1899, New York City, New York. Married Helen Mencken (1926); divorced 1928. Married Mary Phillips (1928); divorced 1938. Married Mayo Methot (1938); divorced 1945. Married Lauren Bacall (1945), children: Stephen, Leslie. Died January 14, 1957.*

FEATURE FILMS:

*A Devil with Women* (Fox, 1930)
*Up the River* (Fox, 1930)
*Body and Soul* (Fox, 1931)
*Bad Sister* (Univ., 1931)
*Women of All Nations* (Fox, 1931)
*A Holy Terror* (Fox, 1931)
*Love Affair* (Col., 1932)
*Three on a Match* (WB, 1932)
*Midnight* (Univ., 1934)
*The Petrified Forest* (WB, 1936)
*Two Against the World* (WB, 1936)

*Bullets or Ballots* (WB, 1936)
*China Clipper* (WB, 1936)
*Isle of Fury* (WB, 1936)
*The Great O'Malley* (WB, 1937)
*Black Legion* (WB, 1937)
*San Quentin* (WB, 1937)
*Marked Woman* (WB, 1937)
*Kid Galahad* (WB, 1937)
*Dead End* (UA, 1937)
*Stand-In* (UA, 1937)
*Swing Your Lady* (WB, 1938)

*Men Are Such Fools* (WB, 1938)

*The Amazing Dr. Clitterhouse* (WB, 1938)

*Racket Busters* (WB, 1938)

*Angels with Dirty Faces* (WB, 1938)

*King of the Underworld* (WB, 1939)

*The Oklahoma Kid* (WB, 1939)

*Dark Victory* (WB, 1939)

*You Can't Get Away with Murder* (WB, 1939)

*The Roaring Twenties* (WB, 1939)

*The Return of Dr. X* (WB, 1939)

*Invisible Stripes* (WB, 1939)

*Virginia City* (WB, 1940)

*It All Came True* (WB, 1940)

*Brother Orchid* (WB, 1940)

*They Drive by Night* (WB, 1940)

*High Sierra* (WB, 1941)

*The Wagons Roll at Night* (WB, 1941)

*The Maltese Falcon* (WB, 1941)

*All Through the Night* (WB, 1942)

*The Big Shot* (WB, 1942)

*In This Our Life* (WB, 1942)°

*Across the Pacific* (WB, 1942)

*Casablanca* (WB, 1942)

*Action in the North Atlantic* (WB, 1943)

*Thank Your Lucky Stars* (WB, 1943)

*Sahara* (Col., 1943)

*To Have and Have Not* (WB, 1944)

*Passage to Marseille* (WB, 1944)

*Conflict* (WB, 1945)

*The Big Sleep* (WB, 1946)

*Two Guys from Milwaukee* (WB, 1946)°

*The Two Mrs. Carrolls* (WB, 1947)

*Always Together* (WB, 1947)°

*Dead Reckoning* (Col., 1947)

*Dark Passage* (WB, 1947)

*Treasure of Sierra Madre* (WB, 1948)

*Key Largo* (WB, 1948)

*Knock on Any Door* (Col., 1949)

*Tokyo Joe* (Col., 1949)

*Chain Lightning* (WB, 1950)

*In a Lonely Place* (Col., 1950)

*The Enforcer* (WB, 1951)

*Sirocco* (Col., 1951)

*The African Queen* (UA, 1951)

*Deadline-U.S.A.* (20th, 1952)

*Battle Circus* (MGM, 1953)

*Beat the Devil* (UA, 1954)

*The Caine Mutiny* (Col., 1954)

*Sabrina* (Par., 1954)

*The Barefoot Contessa* (UA, 1954)

*Love Lottery* (Rank, 1954)°

*We're No Angels* (Par., 1955)

*The Left Hand of God* (20th, 1955)

*The Desperate Hours* (Par., 1955)

*The Harder They Fall* (Col., 1956)

°Unbilled Appearance

# LAUREN BACALL

**5′ 6½″**
**119 pounds**
**Tawny blonde hair**
**Blue green eyes**
**Virgo**

*Real name: Betty Joan Perske. Born September 16, 1924, New York City, New York. Married Humphrey Bogart (1945), children: Stephen, Leslie; widowed 1957. Married Jason Robards, Jr. (1961), child: Sam; divorced 1969.*

**FEATURE FILMS:**

*To Have and Have Not* (WB, 1944)
*Confidential Agent* (WB, 1945)
*Two Guys from Milwaukee* (WB, 1946)°
*The Big Sleep* (WB, 1946)
*Dark Passage* (WB, 1947)
*Key Largo* (WB, 1948)
*Young Man with a Horn* (WB, 1950)
*Bright Leaf* (WB, 1950)
*How to Marry a Millionaire* (20th, 1953)
*Woman's World* (20th, 1954)

*The Cobweb* (MGM, 1955)
*Blood Alley* (WB, 1955)
*Written on the Wind* (Univ., 1956)
*Designing Woman* (MGM, 1957)
*The Gift of Love* (20th, 1958)
*Flame over India* (20th, 1959)
*Shock Treatment* (20th, 1964)
*Sex and the Single Girl* (WB, 1964)
*Harper* (WB, 1966)
*Murder on the Orient Express* (Par., 1974)

°Unbilled Appearance

Advertisement for **To Have and Have Not** (WB, 1944)

**In To Have and Have Not**

Lauren Bacall and Humphrey Bogart on their wedding day (May 21, 1945)

In **The Big Sleep** (WB, 1946)

Humphrey Bogart, Lauren Bacall and their children Stephen and Leslie in 1954.

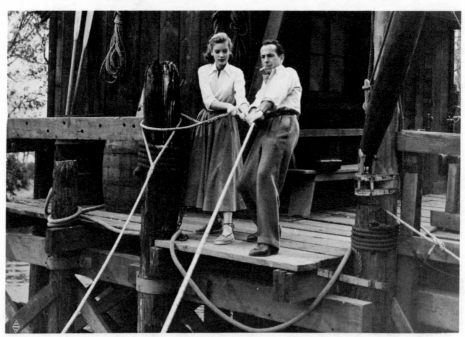

In **Key Largo** (WB, 1948)

## TO HAVE AND HAVE NOT
### *(Warner Bros., 1944) 100M.*

Producer-director, Howard Hawks; based on the novel by Ernest Hemingway; screenplay, Jules Furthman, William Faulkner; music, Franz Waxman; orchestrator, Leonid Raab; songs, Hoagy Carmichael and Johnny Mercer; Carmichael and Stanley Adams; Harry Akst and Grant Clarke; technical adviser, Louis Comien; art director, Charles Novi; set decorator, Casey Roberts; gowns, Milo Anderson; assistant director, Jack Sullivan; makeup, Perc Westmore; sound, Oliver S. Garretson; special effects, E. Roy Davidson, Rex Wimpy; camera, Sid Hickox; editor, Christian Nyby.

Humphrey Bogart (Harry Morgan); Walter Brennan (Eddie); Lauren Bacall (Marie Browning); Dolores Moran (Helene De Bursac); Hoagy Carmichael (Cricket); Walter Molnar (Paul De Bursac); Sheldon Leonard (Lt. Coyo); Marcel Dalio (Gerard); Walter Sande (Johnson); Dan Seymour (Captain M. Renard); Aldo Nadi (Bodyguard); Paul Marion (Beauclerc); Pat West (Bartender); Sir Lancelot (Horatio); Eugene Borden (Quartermaster); Elzie Emanuel, Harold Garrison (Black Urchins); Major Fred Farrell (Headwaiter); Pedro Regas (Civilian); Adrienne d'Ambricourt, Marguerita Sylva (Cashiers); Margaret Hathaway, Louise Clark, Suzette Harbin, Gussie Morris, Kanza Omar, Margaret Savage (Waitresses); Emmett Smith (Emil the Bartender); Maurice Marsac, Fred Dosch, George Suzanne, Louis Mercier, Crane Whitley (DeGaullists); Hal Kelly (Detective); Jean de Briac (Gendarme); Chef Joseph Milani (Chef); Oscar Lorraine (Bartender); Ron Rondell (Naval Ensign); Audrey Armstrong (Dancer); Marcel de la Brosse (Sailor); Edith Wilson (Black Woman); Patricia Shay (Mrs. Beauclerc); Janette Gras (Rosalie); Jack Chefe (Guide); George Sorel (French Officer); Roger Valmy, Keith Lawrence, Jack Passin (Flirtatious Frenchmen); Alphonse Dubois, James Burross, Milton Shockley, Jack Winslowe, Frank Johnson (Bits).

New York Premiere: Hollywood Theatre—October 11, 1944
New York Television Debut: CBS—May 7, 1960

### Synopsis

In the days following the fall of France, Harry Morgan, skipper of a trim cabin cruiser, and based on the island of Martinique, still hires out his boat to rich sportsmen. Returning to port with his current client, Johnson, Harry is approached by Gaullist hotelkeeper Gerard who asks him to smuggle in an important French underground leader. Morgan has no taste for politics and refuses the mission. Thereafter, an American girl, Marie Browning, arrives at the hotel, stopping en route from Trinidad to the United States. She and Harry engage in a spirited flirtation which develops into a strong romance. Later while trying to collect his fee from Johnson, Harry is caught in a Vichy police raid at the hotel's cafe. Johnson is killed and Harry finds his funds impounded by the police. Only because he wants to purchase a ticket for Marie's flight back to America does he agree to undertake the Gaullist's task. Joined by drunken derelict Eddie, Harry picks up the underground leader and his wife, Paul and Helene de Bursac. On the way back from the islet rendezvous site, Harry has a run-in with a Vichy patrol boat and Bursac is severely wounded. Harry is surprised later to walk into the hotel cafe and find Marie singing there with pianist Cricket; she obviously has decided not to use the plane ticket. After attending to Bursac's wound, Harry tells Marie to pack her bag and be prepared for a speedy exit. But just when they are ready to depart, Harry cannot locate Eddie. Captain Renard and Lieutenant Coyo of the Vichy police solve that mystery when they reveal they are holding Eddie for questioning. Harry's anger is aroused; he kills Renard's bodyguard and then forces Renard to telephone for Eddie's release. The police are turned over to the Gaullists while Harry leaves Fort de France with Eddie and Marie.

◆——◆——◆

The exceedingly popular *Casablanca* (1942) had changed forty-three-year-old Humphrey Bogart from perennial screen villain to cinema tough guy hero, and Warner Bros. was anxious to repeat the success formula. The studio acquired screen rights to Ernest Hemingway's 1937 novel and, via a William Faulkner-Jules Furthman screenplay, changed the setting from Key West, Florida to Martinique, while switching the contraband goods in question from Chinese smuggled from Cuba into the U.S.A. to ferrying Allied underground leaders under Vichy's nose. Most of Hemingway's fuzzy propaganda about collective action was ditched and, most drastically of all, the book's tough "conch," a married man with children, was altered into a bachelor (Bogart) with a burgeoning sense of patriotism and romanticism beneath his cynical exterior. In short the film script was tailor-made into a sure-fire Bogart screen role.

Otis L. Guernsey, Jr. *(New York Herald-Tribune)* found that the combination of tough-as-nails Bogart and the action scenario "adds up to a good measure of romance and adventure in the picaresque Bogart tradition." All to the good. But the big news of *To Have and Have Not* was twenty-year-old, ex-New York model Lauren Bacall. Everyone had his own special way of describing the movie newcomer: "a sort of slender version of Mae West" *(New York World-Telegram)*, "Slumbering of eye and softly reedy along the lines of Veronica Lake, she acts in the quiet way of catnip" [Bosley Crowther *(New York Times)*], "a thin face, large expressive mouth, and some highly studied mannerisms" *(New York Sun)*. As *Variety* reported it, ". . . she's an arresting personality in whom Warners has what the scouts would call a find. She can slink, brother, and no fooling!"

The oncamera chemistry and filmgoers' enthusiastic reaction proved that Bacall was the perfect screen partner for Bogart in *To Have and Have Not*. As Joan Blondell and Ann Sheridan had tamed grapefruit-pusher James Cagney in his cinema ventures, so Bacall was the ideal female to squelch rugged, iconoclastic Bogart. "They take their romance without frills, as straight as a shot of raw whiskey (Guernsey of the *Herald-Tribune*), which is what intrigued viewers in those bygone pre-women's lib days. Marlene Dietrich had vanquished men with a bat of her expressive eyes, while Mae West had proved her supremacy with her undulating hips and heaving chest, but it was lithe Bacall who called the shots with an ability to make tough men whistle at her beck and call.

Bacall first stepped into view in *To Have and Have Not* at the Hotel Martinique where she has rented the room across the hall from Bogart, he being the snarling skipper of the "Queen Conch." "Anybody got a match?" Bacall asks in her deadpan manner, with her wide expressive eyes peering directly into Bogart's craggy countenance. Always the aggressor, she lights her cigarette, flings the used match out the door and tosses the matchpack back to nonplussed Bogart. She is a liberated dame and un-embarrassed by her free wheeling status. Later on, down at the hotel bar, dressed in a gray check suit, she leans against the piano singing "Am I Blue" (dubbed by Andy Williams) with pianist Hoagy Carmichael at the keyboards. During her song, Bacall constantly turns to see if Bogart is absorbing the full impact of her "act." He is seated at the bar, hunched over with that sweaty constipated look that he would perfect for *The African Queen* (1951). After she has stolen the wallet of Bogart's erstwhile client (Walter Sande) she returns to her room. Bogart follows, locking the door behind him.

Bacall: "What do you think you're going to do?"
Bogart: "I'm going to get that wallet, slim."
Bacall: "I'm too skinny to take that kindly."

Once again, and this was Bacall's most unique contribution to films, she proves no man can best her in any given situation unless she has a mind to allow him the illusion of momentary victory.

Like all good cinema tough dames [such as Rita Hayworth in *Gilda* (1946)], Bacall's Marie Browning has a very shadowy, unconventional past. She admits she has been to Trinidad, Portugal, and Spain, and, before that, to Rio, and that she has only stopped over in Martinique to purchase a new hat. She does mention she is flat broke and that she is now traveling alone. In short, she is a movie heroine who can handle herself in most any predicament.

After she and Bogart have been released from the Vichy-Gestapo questioning, he makes clear that he has a deep thirst, so later she arrives at his room with a liquor bottle in hand. He sneeringly accepts the booze, leading the rejected gal to make an exception to her routine of life: she is forced to ask a man whether he minds if she proceeds with the satisfaction of her whim. Score one for Bogart!

When Bogart remains unresponsive to her overt sexual advances, she lets loose with, "Who's the girl, the one who left you with a high opinion of women? She must have been some girl." Still receiving no satisfactory reaction from her masculine target, she kisses the seated man. He remains ostensibly baffled, at which the monotone-purring Bacall flips out, "It's even better when you help." She starts to leave the room, but then adds, "I've been had since I met you. One look and I know what you wanted to think about me. . . . I brought that bottle up here to make you feel cheap."

This revelation breaks the ice with Bogart and a short time later she reappears in his room, asking his help in leaving the island. This business concluded, she slinks out of the room, but stops midway, turns and says, "You don't have to say anything or do anything. Maybe just whistle. [Long pause] You know how to whistle, don't you, Steve? You just put your lips together and blow." Bogart continues to sit in his chair, smoking a cigarette, and soaking in the array of recent events. After she leaves the scene, he laughs to himself and then lets loose with a low whistle. Needless to say, this interplay is one of screendom's most illustrious seduction scenes.

The next day when Bogart leaves for his undercover mission Bacall is again in the cafe, and once more she is the aggressor as she informs him, "I'll leave my address with Frenchy so you can find me." When Bogart returns, the battle of the sexes tips in his favor. While attending to wounded Walter Molnar, he takes an appreciative look at the man's wife (Dolores Moran), leading Bacall to jealously snap, "What are you trying to do, guess her weight?" Obviously it is clear to both Bogart and the viewer that Bacall's cool demeanor has its boiling point.

In one of the couple's most lighthearted screen moments, Bogart and Bacall find themselves discussing their possible futures together, particularly her role in his life.

Bogart: "I don't want you to take off my shoes, fix my breakfast or draw me a bath." Bacall reacts to this "order" by batting her eyes and saying in a mock pious southern drawl with her hands clasped, "I don't think I'll be angry again at anything you say." Thereafter, Bogart and his new prize kiss, she commenting, "I like that, except for the beard. Why don't you shave and we'll try that again."

By that evening in the story, Bacall has succumbed to Bogart's insistent superiority, admitting to him that she is tied to him. "It could be forever, or are you afraid of that. . . . I'm not hard to get Steve. All you have to do is to ask me." At this point Bacall is wearing a black taffeta dress cut almost to the navel and up the middle. (Bogart says of this dress, "You won't have to sing much in that outfit." However, she does sing "How Little We Know.")

Finally, after the last encounter with the Vichy police, Bogart and Bacall plan to scram, with boozy, limping Walter Brennan in tow. Bacall says goodbye to Carmichael, who has been playing piano, playing all this while. He asks her, "Are you still happy?" She throws back at him, "What do you think?" As Carmichael breaks into a Latin American rhythm on the keyboard, she and Bogart samba step out the door.

Although every other ingredient in *To Have and Have Not* pales in comparison to the uniqueness of the Bogart-Bacall oncamera romancing, there are other major elements in the picture: adventure and politics. As in *Casablanca* Bogart is pictured as the non-interventionist. Vichy law enforcer Captain Renard (Dan Seymour) inquires of Bogart: "By the way, what are your sympathies?"

Bogart: "Minding my own business."

But later Bogart capitulates to the war cause when he personally becomes involved in rescuing a Free French partisan. Even Bacall finds herself caught up in the patriotic movement. This change of heart is reflected when Moran cattily asks who Bacall is and she snidely replies, "Just another volunteer." However, the bulk of flag waving is left to Molnar who explains that the Germans cannot win the war because they forget "there will always be someone else" and another, and another to fight their totalitarian ways.

Even the better films have their faults, and *To Have and Have Not* is no exception. Mainly, it falls down in its persistent efforts to duplicate all the winning ingredients of *Casablanca*. If Bacall was more effective in her way than Ingrid Bergman, Carmichael and Seymour were poor substitutes for Dooley Wilson and Claude Rains of that 1942 classic. Then too, many viewers wondered in vain about the need for the obtrusive presence of folksy Brennan in *To Have and Have Not*. His gimpy-legged, drunken character soon became a repetitive bore. The only excuse of his presence seemed to be to remind viewers that Bogart does have a kind heart toward underdogs.

*To Have and Have Not* would be remade as *The Breaking Point* (1950) with John Garfield and Patricia Neal, and then as *The Gun Runners* (1958) with Audie Murphy and Patricia Owens. Both recaps were inferior to the original film. Bogart and Bacall would later appear in a syndicated radio adventure series entitled "Bold Venture" which owed its origin to *To Have and Have Not*, and in 1958, Dane Clark plied the TV series field in a video version of "Bold Venture" which was even more distantly related to the 1944 feature.

## TWO GUYS FROM MILWAUKEE
### (Warner Bros., 1946) 90M.

Producer, Alex Gottlieb; director, David Butler; screenplay, Charles Hoffman, I. A. L. Diamond; assistant director, Jesse Hibbs; art director, Leo K. Kuter; set decorator, Jack McConaghy; gowns, Leah Rhodes; music, Frederick Hollander; orchestrator, Leonid Raab; song, Charles Lawrence, Joe Greene, and Stan Kenton; sound, Stanley Jones; montages, James

Leicester; dialog director, Felix Jacoves; makeup, Perc Westmore; special effects, Harry Barndollar, Edwin B. DuPar; camera, Arthur Edeson; editor, Irene Morra.

Dennis Morgan (Prince Henry); Joan Leslie (Connie Reed); Jack Carson (Buzz Williams); Janis Paige (Polly); S. Z. Sakall (Count Oswald); Patti Brady (Peggy); Tom D'Andrea (Happy); Rosemary DeCamp (Nan); John Ridgely (Mike Collins); Pat McVey (Johnson); Franklin Pangborn (Theatre Manager); Humphrey Bogart, Lauren Bacall (Themselves); Joel Fluellen (Porter); Philo McCullough (Passenger); George Reed (Clarence the Porter); Creighton Hale (Committee Member); Marilyn Reiss, Doris Fulton (Bobby Soxers); Lottie Williams (Old Lady); Russ Clark, Jack Mower (Cops); Donald Kerr (Elevator Operator); Antonio Filauri (Italian Barber); Chester Clute (Mr. Carruthers the Customer); Tristram Coffin (Polly's Customer); Cosmo Sardo (Henry's Barber); Eddie Bruce (Bus Conductor); Jane Harker, Richard Walsh (Couple on Top of Bus); Peggy Knudsen (Juke Box Voice); Frank Marlowe (Cabby); Rory Mallinson (Ticket Taker); Jody Gilbert (Large Woman); Douglas Carter, Lex Barker (Ushers); Clifton Young (Motor Cop); Howard Mitchell (Waiter); Charles Knight (Butler); Charles Williams (Man at Microphone); George Campeau (Engineer); Bob Lowell (Announcer); Monte Blue, Ross Ford (Technicians); Charles Coleman (Valet); Charles Marsh (Proprietor); Francis Pierlot (Dr. Bauer); Patricia White (Nurse); Janet Barrett (Stewardess).

New York Premiere: Strand Theatre—July 26, 1946
New York Television Debut: CBS—March 2, 1959

### Synopsis

Prince Henry of the Balkans is making a good will tour of the United States, but once in New York he decides to disguise himself and see what the real America is like. He has two ambitions: to meet the American "common man" and to be introduced to his dream girl, Lauren Bacall. The first man of the streets he meets is Buzz Williams, a typical New York cab driver. During the two days the prince takes away from his royal duties, Buzz instructs this member of the nobility in the ways of America. Eventually the police intercept Prince Henry and escort him back for his broadcast to the people of his country, who are holding an election. Before the broadcast, the prince and Buzz are discussing the pros and cons of monarchy versus democracy, not knowing that their debate is being aired. Lo and behold, the people of his country vote for a republic and the prince is now jobless. The nonplused prince quickly finds work, as a beer salesman, and boards a plane for Milwaukee. Naturally, who should the young lady in the seat next to him be but Bacall. However, his joy is brief, for there is a tap on his shoulder and he looks up to find a tough-acting Humphrey Bogart ready to claim the prize seat.

Humphrey Bogart and Lauren "Baby" Bacall had married on May 21, 1945, and this was the first feature to reach the screen which included the newlyweds. There was nothing outstanding about the picture. The gag appearance of the Bogarts was the best element of this familiar plotline, bolstered by ". . . good direction and zestful playing" [Thomas Pryor *(New York Times)*].

## THE BIG SLEEP
*(Warner Bros., 1946) 114M.*

Producer-director, Howard Hawks; based on the novel by Raymond Chandler; screenplay, William Faulkner, Leigh Brackett, Jules Furthman; music, Max Steiner; orchestrator, Simon Bucharoff; assistant director, Robert Vreeland; art director, Carl Jules Weyl; set decorator, Fred M. MacLean; gowns, Leah Rhodes; sound, Robert B. Lee; special effects, E. Roy Davidson, Warren E. Lynch, William McGann, Robert Burks, Willard Van Enger; camera, Sid Hickox; editor, Christian Nyby.

Humphrey Bogart (Philip Marlowe); Lauren Bacall (Vivian Rutledge); John Ridgely (Eddie Mars); Martha Vickers (Carmen Sternwood); Dorothy Malone (Bookshop Proprietress); Peggy Knudsen (Mrs. Eddie Mars); Regis Toomey (Bernie Ohls); Charles Waldron (General Sternwood); Charles D. Brown (Norris); Bob Steele (Canino); Elisha Cook, Jr. (Harry Jones); Louis Jean Heydt (Joe Brody); Sonia Darrin (Agnes); James Flavin (Captain Cronjager); Thomas Jackson (District Attorney Wilde); Dan Wallace (Carol Lundgren); Theodore Von Eltz (Arthur Gwynn Geiger); Joy Barlowe (Taxicab Driver); Tom Fadden (Sidney); Ben Welden (Pete); Trevor Bardette (Art Huck); Joseph Crehan (Medical Examiner); Emmett Vogan (Ed).

New York Premier: Strand Theatre—August 23, 1946
New York Television Debut: CBS—January 24, 1959

### Synopsis

Rugged private detective Philip Marlowe is hired by wealthy General Sternwood to get rid of a troublesome blackmailer named Arthur Gwynn Geiger, who is peddling obscene photographs of Sternwood's nymphomaniac daughter, Carmen. Marlowe finds Geiger murdered, apparently killed by Sternwood's chauffeur who is known to have been attracted to Carmen. Marlowe traces Geiger's incriminating photographs to Joe Brody, the thin-skinned boyfriend of Geiger's clerk, Agnes. Later, Brody attempts to sell Carmen's revealing photographs to her older sister Vivian, but he is soon killed by Geiger's henchman, Carol Lundgren. Marlowe overtakes Lundgren and turns him over to police detective Bernie Ohls. Thereafter,

Vivian attempts to take Marlowe off the case, but the investigator is hot on the trail of Geiger's landlord, Eddie Mars, a gambler at whose casino Vivian frequently bets. When Mrs. Mars is listed as missing, allegedly having run off with a former friend of the general, Marlowe refuses to drop his investigations. He has a chance to help Vivian when he rescues her from a holdup man outside of Mars' casino. Agnes' new boy friend, Harry Jones, later offers to lead Marlowe to Mrs. Mars, but Mars' gunman, Canino, kills the squealer. Agnes baits Marlowe into going to Art Huck's garage, where he is quickly captured by Canino, who is accompanied by Mrs. Mars. Vivian is also there and during Canino's absence she unties Marlowe and he kills Canino when he returns. Joined by Vivian, Marlowe arranges to meet Mars at Geiger's house. Marlowe confronts Mars and unravels his theories on the case which hypothesize Carmen as a murderess. Mars admits the truths of Marlowe's assumptions, but assumes that his men will kill the detective. However, Marlowe forces Mars out the door and the latter is killed. Marlowe phones the police to corral the henchmen, and, with Vivian at his side, waits for the police to come.

◆◆◆

Producer-director Howard Hawks, who had such good luck with Humphrey Bogart and Lauren Bacall in *To Have and Have Not,* cast them in the picturization of Raymond Chandler's 1939 hard-boiled detective novel, which was filmed in December, 1944, but not released until mid-1946. In this interim period, Bogart had starred in an average whodunit, *Conflict* (1945), with Alexis Smith, while Bacall had suffered the embarrassment of being critically panned for her unfinished performance in *Confidential Agent* (1945) opposite Charles Boyer.

William Faulkner and Jules Furthman, who had scripted *To Have and Have Not,* were joined by Leigh Brackett in the scenario-writing of Chandler's brutal detective yarn, the final script of which many thought reached a new level in screen violence. James Agee *(The Nation)* likened the film to ". . . a smoky cocktail shaken together from most of the printable misdemeanors and some that aren't—one of those Raymond Chandler Specials which puts you, along with the cast, into a state of semi-amnesia through which tough action and reaction drum with something of the nonsensical solace of hard rain on a tin roof."

The only thing certain about *The Big Sleep* (the title refers to death) is that (above and beyond its continued popularity) the plot defies logic, leaving the viewer almost as perplexed as the characters within the film as to who did what to whom just when for what reasons. At least there is no trouble figuring out the characters' morals. General Sternwood (Charles Waldron) tells Philip Marlowe (Bogart), "Vivian is spoiled and exacting. . . . Carmen is a child who likes to pull wings off flies. . . . I presume they both had and still have all the usual vices." This statement neatly sums up the central females in *The Big Sleep.* On the other hand, Bogart's Marlowe is more devious than mysterious, a thirty-eight-year-old private eye who walks among raw-edged people and deals with everybody and everything in similar, unsubtle terms. He has a most jaundiced viewpoint, unperturbed when he is looking down the wrong end of a gun barrel or being slugged by a fisted roll of nickels. He knows full well that sometime and somewhere he will have his just revenge. He can quip wisecracks like the best of screen gumshoes, as when he informs the emotionally disturbed Martha Vickers, "I'm cute. There's no one cuter."

With all the assorted gunplay, fisticuffs, and clue chasing in *The Big Sleep* there is not much occasion for Bogart and Bacall to engage in lengthy romantics, but they do have a brief share of amorous innings in order to please the movie patrons. When the two characters first meet at her father's mansion, she languidly inquires: "What's wrong with me."

Bogart: "Nothing you can't fix."

The battle of the sexes is on, with each performer having his/her innings. And at a later point Bacall is found waiting for Bogart at his seedy office.

Bacall: "Good morning. I was beginning to think you worked in bed like Marcel Proust."

Bogart: "Who's he?"

Bacall: "You wouldn't know him. He was a French writer."

On another occasion, the sparring partners are more evenly matched.

Bacall: "You're a mess, aren't you?"

Bogart: "Next time I'll come on stilts."

Bacall: "I doubt if that will help. . . . I don't like your manner."

Bogart: "I don't like your manner either."

Later, after he has rescued her from a would-be stick-up man, she explains to her champion, "I'm not used to being scared. Give me more time." When she saddles into his coupe car, he kisses her (a distinct change from the *To Have and Have Not* syndrome) and she reacts by saying, "I like that. I'd like more." Bacall's Vivian Rutledge is no ordinary girl. Near the wrap-up of the movie Bogart takes time out from figuring his next stratagem to commend Bacall for helping him out of a past dangerous situation (during which time she had satisfied her desire in kissing the rope-bound detective). His words of praise say a mouthful: "I didn't have a chance to thank you back there. You looked good. Awfully good. I didn't know they made them that way." So once again, Bacall of the checkered tailored jacket and beret hat had won her man. With Bogart and Bacall awaiting the police's arrival, he confides to her (whom he calls "Angel"), "I don't know yet what I'm goin' to tell them . . . but it will be close to the truth."

Bogart seems to think this settles everything, but she gives him an appraising look and says, "You forgot one thing. Me."

He arches his eyebrows while she smiles. Finis.

And of course who can forget the tantalizing nightclub scene in which Bacall and Bogart engage in a mildly veiled discussion of her feelings toward men and sexual intercourse, with their conversation framed in race track terms. When she snaps that her pleasure "depends on who is in the saddle" even the more sheltered filmgoer knows that the couple are not discussing jockey handicapping.

Although *The Big Sleep* was tremendously popular with the average filmgoer, the critics were not so appreciative of the star team's emoting, particularly that of Bacall. ". . . Humphrey Bogart stalks his cold and laconic way as the resolute private detective. . . . Miss Bacall is a dangerous looking female, but she still hasn't learned to act" [Bosley Crowther *(New York Times)*]. Kate Cameron *(New York Daily News)* bit to the core of the new screen pair's vulnerability when she reported, "When Baby has Howard Hawks, who discovered her, as her director and husband Humphrey Bogart to back her up in every scene, she can do anything any other pretty Hollywood starlet can do on the screen. She has confidence and poise."

Twenty years later when Warner Bros. presented a film version of Ross Macdonald's *The Moving Target,* entitled *Harper,* the studio touted it as being very much in the Philip Marlowe-*The Big Sleep* tradition. Paul Newman in the title role was no Bogart, but Bacall was on hand to lend flavor as the wheelchair-bound Mrs. Sampson.

## DARK PASSAGE
### *(Warner Bros., 1947) 106M.*

Producer, Jerry Wald; director, Delmer Daves; based on the novel by David Goodis; assistant director, Dick Mayberry; art director, Charles H. Clarke; set decorator, William Kuehl; music, Franz Waxman; orchestrator, Leonid Raab; wardrobe, Bernard Newman; makeup, Perc Westmore; sound, Dolph Thomas; special effects, H. D. Koenekamp; camera, Sid Hickox; editor, David Weisbart.

Humphrey Bogart (Vincent Parry); Lauren Bacall (Irene Jansen); Bruce Bennett (Bob Rapf); Agnes Moorehead (Madge Rapf); Tom D'Andrea (Sam the Taxi Driver); Clifton Young (Baker); Douglas Kennedy (Detective); Rory Mallinson (George Fellsinger); Houseley Stevenson (Dr. Walter Coley); Bob Farber, Richard Walsh (Policemen); Clancy Cooper (Man on Street); Pat McVey (Taxi Driver); Dude Maschemeyer (Man on Street); Tom Fadden (Waiter in Cafe); Shimen Ruskin (Driver-Watchman); Tom Reynolds (Hotel Clerk); Lennie Bremen (Ticket Clerk); Mary Field (Mary the Lonely Woman); Michael Daves, Deborah Daves (Children); John Arledge (Lonely Man); Ross Ford (Ross, the Bus Driver); Ian MacDonald (Policeman); Ramon Ros (Waiter); Craig Lawrence (Bartender).

New York Premiere: Strand Theatre—September 5, 1947
New York Television Debut: CBS—March 12, 1960

## Synopsis

After Vincent Parry escapes from San Quentin, where he was serving a sentence for the murder of his wife, he is picked up on the outskirts of San Francisco by Irene Jansen, who agrees to sneak him past the police roadblock. Irene acknowledges that she knows his identity and, having followed the trial, that she believes him innocent. She lets him stay in her apartment. His seclusion is endangered by Bob Rapf, who is romantically interested in Irene. It develops that Rapf's wife, Madge, had been a close friend of Parry's wife and her courtroom testimony had helped convict Parry. Through the assistance of a cooperative cab driver named Sam, Parry visits a plastic surgeon who alters his countenance. When he attempts to see his pal George Fellsinger, he finds him murdered. Thereafter, Parry remains in hiding at Irene's apartment, waiting for his face to heal. After the bandages are removed, Parry insists upon tracking down the murderer of his wife and of Fellsinger. During his investigations he encounters Baker who recognizes Parry and plans to blackmail him, but in a fight, Baker is accidentally killed, having already revealed that he noted Madge's car following Parry to Fellsinger's place. Parry next visits Madge and accuses her of killing both his wife and Fellsinger. She confesses but to no avail, for, in the next minute, she accidentally tumbles to her death from the apartment window. Parry now has no hope of clearing himself. He tells Irene this, and also admits he loves her. She agrees to join him. In South America they meet again, ready to start anew.

◆—◆—◆

Although the studio advertisement read "Together Again . . . in danger as violent as their love!!!" *Dark Passage* is by far the least of the Humphrey Bogart-Lauren Bacall features, marred by a conventionally contrived storyline and composed of too much talk and too little action. The film's few sustaining virtues are insufficient to carry the picture as more than an ordinary, forgettable melodrama.

Like Robert Montgomery's Philip Marlowe screen caper, *Lady in the Lake* (1946), *Dark Passage* uses a subjective camera as the personification of the detective hero. For the opening reels of the film the viewer hears, but does not see, Bogart's Vincent Parry. Only after his plastic surgery operation does the viewer encounter Bogart front view. This gimmick, like the novelty of the San Francisco on-location filming, was soon exhausted, and only with the oncamera appearance of vixenish Madge Rapf (Agnes Moorehead) does the picture again take on intriguing dimensions. Unfortunately, Moorehead's impressive assignment as the shrewish, sensual woman was so truncated that she had to telescope her assorted powerhouse emotional reactions into a few brief scenes, all before taking that fatal step backwards and plunging to her death.

Both Bogart and Bacall were given changes of screen personae in *Dark Passage* which, unintentionally, added to the picture's overall ineffectiveness. Bogart plays a defensive and convicted murderer, very much a chastened and reserved soul, who depends on luck rather than brains to succeed. It was quite a startling change for the star and did not showcase him to good advantage. Likewise, Bacall appeared in a new characterization which subdued her established personality and transformed her into a softer, sympathetic type (some say she was still antiseptic in the role). Supposedly, because her father has been railroaded into prison, Bacall can appreciate the fugitive's plight. This facet of her character is comprehensible, but her induced interest in mealy-mouthed Bob Rapf (Bruce Bennett) is difficult to comprehend other than as a script gimmick.

Thus, Bogart in *Dark Passage* is merely a tense man on the lam and Bacall a considerate girl who grows to love the framed convict. Their romance only comes remotely alive in the brief closing moments of the film when Bogart, now forced to flee the country, is allowed by the script to reach the safety of South America. Now a permanent fugitive who has stopped running, he takes on stature as that favorite movie type, the expatriate with a very shady past. He has a peculiar sort of respectability and, like Bacall's Irene Jansen, a viewer can find new respect for him, even if it is on a modest level. By the fadeout, the duo is bantering flippancies and romantic innuendoes as of old. It almost seems too bad that the film could not have started at this belated juncture.


## KEY LARGO
### (Warner Bros., 1948) 101M.

Producer, Jerry Wald; director, John Huston; based on the play by Maxwell Anderson; screenplay, Richard Brooks, Huston; art director, Leo F. Kuter; set decorator, Fred M. MacLean; wardrobe, Leah Rhodes; makeup, Perc Westmore; song, Ralph Rainger and Howard Dietz; music, Max Steiner; orchestrator, Murray Cutter; sound, Dolph Thomas; special effects, William McGann, Robert Burks; camera, Karl Freund; editor, Rudi Fehr.

Humphrey Bogart (Frank McCloud); Edward G. Robinson [Johnny Rocco (Howard Brown)]; Lauren Bacall (Nora Temple); Lionel Barrymore (James Temple); Claire Trevor [Gaye Dawn (Maggie Mooney)]; Thomas Gomez [Curley (Richard Hoff)]; John Rodney (Deputy Clyde Sawyer); Marc Lawrence (Ziggy); Dan Seymour (Angel Garcia); Monte Blue (Sheriff Ben Wade); Jay Silverheels, Rodric Redwing (Osceola Brothers); William Haade (Ralph Freeney); Joe P. Smith (Bus Driver); Alberto Morin (Skipper); Pat Flaherty, Jerry Jerome, John Phillips, Lute Crockett (Ziggy's Henchmen); Felipa Gomez (Old Indian Woman).

New York Premiere: Strand Theatre—July 16, 1948
New York Television Debut: CBS—April 25, 1959

## Synopsis

Ex-army officer Frank McCloud arrives at a run-down hotel in lonely Key Largo, Florida. This dilapidated resort inn is run by crippled James Temple and his daughter-in-law Nora, whose deceased husband had been one of Frank's wartime pals. Frank learns that the offseason hotel guests are really once-deported gangster Johnny Rocco and his henchmen. When Frank seemingly has a good opportunity to kill the tyrannical Rocco, he passes up the chance, overly concerned about saving his own life and too disillusioned by his wartime experiences to really care about humanity. During a fierce storm which breaks over Florida, Rocco loses his control, and Frank finds new courage. He assists Gaye Dawn, Rocco's aging, drunken mistress, and, for his efforts, receives a beating from Rocco and his men. Nora is impressed by Frank's show of gallantry and Temple silently observes that Frank may be the new man both Nora and the hotel need so much. Later the sheriff comes searching for his chief deputy, only to find him murdered. Rocco pushes the blame onto a pair of local Indians who are killed by the sheriff when they attempt to escape. This sadistic act causes Frank to comprehend just how dangerous a man Rocco really is. Frank thereafter agrees to pilot a boat for Roceo, who is heading for Cuba. With the gun sneaked to him by Gaye, who is left behind by Rocco, Frank intends to destroy the gang at sea. He picks off the mob one by one, with Rocco killing the last henchman who is shivering below deck. After a chase about the small craft, Frank shoots Rocco and then heads back to Key Largo and the waiting Nora.

◆━━◆━━◆

Because of his successful ventures with director John Huston [*The Maltese Falcon* (1941), *Across the Pacific* (1942), and *The Treasure of Sierra Madre* (1948)], Humphrey Bogart was anxious to extend the working association to a new project and agreed to star with Lauren Bacall in a rendition of Maxwell Anderson's 1939 verse drama *Key Largo*. The original play starring Paul Muni as a fatalistic member of the Loyalist Army in the Spanish Civil War had enjoyed a modest, 105-performance Broadway run, but had to be considerably reworked by scripters Huston and Richard Brooks for its delayed cinema rendition. The poetry of the original play was scrapped, the "hero" became a World War II veteran of the Cassino, Italy, battles, and the theme was restructured (although diluted by pre-release editing) to have Edward G. Robinson's notorious gangster, Johnny Rocco, represent all that is evil in post-war America. Critical reaction at the time was mixed—"too full of highly crossed purposed words and implications" said Bosley Crowther of the *New York Times*—although more viewers agreed with *Newsweek* magazine's report that it was a "conventional gangster story, raised by imagination and fine craftsmanship to a high level of excitement."

In post-war Hollywood, gangster films were rare, so it was with a great deal of expectation that viewers attended the motion picture reunion of two such oncamera racketeer greats as Bogart and Robinson, the latter in his first Warners' picture since 1942. If Robinson's impersonation of America's most notorious underworld figure was bigger than life (who can forget the opening scene of the "animal" sitting naked in the bathtub, sweating violently and puffing on a cigar, his threats every five minutes to kill someone, or his sinisterly whispered obscenities to Bacall?), Bogart's Frank McCloud was far from his best remembered cinema thug or even past silver screen hero. In *Key Largo* he plays a beaten man, an ex-army major worn out by the war and all of man's inhumanity to man. "One Rocco more or less isn't worth dying for," says the seemingly cowardly jaw-twitching Bogart when he fails in his chance to plug Robinson. Only later does he realize that he must help win the peace just as he did his part in the war victory. He perceives that crippled James Temple (Lionel Barrymore) has the right slant on life, that America has "no place for the Johnny Roccos" of this world, and at this point, Bogart takes on heroic stature.

The *Times'* Crowther rated Bogart's performance as "penetrating." "The surprise of *Key Largo* is Miss Bacall, who forgets her curves to play Nora straight and comes off with a forthright, credible characterization" (*Newsweek* magazine). In what would be her final feature with Bogart, Bacall enacts a very normal, moral young woman, a war widow whose empty heart aches for some new meaning in her conventional existence. Dressed in white blouses and calf length gray skirts, she was at her unglamorous best, relying on understatement in her projection of the honest woman who, along with her wheelchair-ridden father-in-law (Barrymore), bravely confronts the likes of Robinson and his gang of punks. Once again it is Bacall's penetrating glances that reveal the soul of her characterization: such as when she first welcomes Bogart to the hotel, hoping to learn more about her late husband's last days on earth, or her minor shock when she finds that Bogart is unnerved by his confrontation with corrupt forces, or, finally, when she relies on her quiet strength as she witnesses her new-found lover's return to courage as he combats the gangs with words and, later, with deeds. Standing on the wind-swept wharf at the finale, she waits for Bogart's imminent return, effectively symbolizing the hopes of post-war America for a brave new world.

More so than in previous Bogart-Bacall screen sorties, *Key Largo* benefited from superior playing by other cast members, particularly Robinson as America's ex-crime czar who still thirsts for power, and yet in the final showdown is cowered by a rampaging hurricane and the fears of impending death. His disintegrating courage is in direct contrast to Bogart's renewed resiliency. Claire Trevor, who would win a Best Supporting Actress Oscar for *Key Largo,* offers an impressive portrayal of a pitiful soul, a fading gangster's moll, who lives for another drink in order to forget her decaying life among nature's worst element. Her pathetic strivings for self-decency and affection are much akin to the rather idyllic qualities of Bacall's Nora Temple. Rounding out the star cast is seventy-year-old Barrymore on loanout from MGM and offering one of his most controlled screen portrayals as the courageous senior citizen unafraid of brute force. He is convinced that might is right when the cause is justified, yet comprehends that idealism has its limits in the ever-continuing battle of good versus evil.

Not to be overlooked are the extremely appropriate sets of Leo K. Kuter and interiors by Fred M. MacLean which aptly recapture the wind-swept, desolate look of the Florida Keys and the despairing ambiance of a traditional resort hotel in offseason. Here is an occasion where soundstage sets probably could not be improved upon by on location filming. They admirably set the stark, lonesome tone for the battle of ideologies that fill *Key Largo's* storyline.


## THE YEARS AFTER

To demonstrate the artistic independence that Humphrey Bogart so admired, Lauren Bacall became a rebel at Warner Bros., rejecting several insipid roles in foolish pictures. Her sixth suspension in six years was caused by refusing the co-starring assignment in Errol Flynn's *Rocky Mountain* (1950). She and the studio then called it quits. On radio she and Bogart were heard in a syndicated adventure series, "Bold Venture," and, as a result of signing a Twentieth Century-Fox contract, she attempted screen comedy with Betty Grable and Marilyn Monroe in *How to Marry a Millionaire* (1953) and with June Allyson and Arlene Dahl in *Woman's World* (1954). Bacall was surprisingly good in both CinemaScope forays. Likewise, she was nifty as Richard Widmark's love interest in MGM's *The Cobweb* (1955), even if the film was not a success. However, the more meretricious *Written on the Wind* (1956) with Rock Hudson was a box-office winner. She replaced Grace Kelly in MGM's "comedy" *Designing Woman* (1957), a film completed after Bogart's death. (When he died, Bacall, known as a very devoted wife, said, "I lost a huge chunk of ir-replaceable happiness.") *Goodbye Charlie* (1959) brought her to the Broadway stage in a middling comedy which proved to be merely a warm-up for her very successful *Cactus Flower* (1967) and her personal triumph in the stage musical *Applause!* (1970). Three years later she starred in the London version of *Applause!* with outstanding results. Along the way she married and divorced Jason Robards, Jr., a union said to have been in-spired because of his temperamental similarity to Bogart.

After leaving Warner Bros., in 1949, Bogart achieved Academy Award status by his Oscar-winning performance opposite Katharine Hepburn in *The African Queen* (1951). With John Huston again directing him, Bogart turned to wry screen satire in *Beat the Devil* (1954), was again Oscar-nominated for his mentally confused captain in *The Caine Mutiny* (1954), and was pleasantly sophisticated in *Sabrina* (1954). He was a

Devil's Island escapee in the mild *We're No Angels* (1955) and posed as a clergyman in the widescreen *The Left Hand of God* (1955). *The Desperate Hours* (1955) returned him to the the the persona he knew and played best—a hunted criminal. *The Harder They Fall* (1956), his final film, found him as a sports writer turned fight promoter in a study of the corrupt boxing world. Besides his joint screen ventures with Bacall, they were together on radio in "Bold Venture" and in the 1955 television special, *The Petrified Forest*. Together they presided over the Rat Pack social group, and were the parents of two children, Stephen and Leslie. On January 14, 1957, he died of cancer.

Today, more so than any of his screen contemporaries, Bogart remains a cinema legend, a true American popular culture hero. He has always been many things to many people, but for everyone oncamera and off he was Bogie, and that was more than enough to solidify his enduring reputation as one of Hollywood's most outstanding products. Vying onscreen for supremacy with the likes of Edward G. Robinson, Bogart was very good, yet he was even better when matched with the feline grace of "Baby" Bacall who brought out the inherent tenderness within the star's tough exterior.

In **The Perfect Furlough** (Univ., 1958)

# Chapter 24

# Tony Curtis
# &
# Janet Leigh

## TONY CURTIS

**5′ 11½″**
**160 pounds**
**Black hair**
**Blue eyes**
**Gemini**

*Real name: Bernard Schwartz. Born June 3, 1925, Bronx, New York. Married Janet Leigh (1951), children: Kelly, Jamie; divorced, 1962. Married Christine Kaufmann (1963), children: Alexandria, Allegra; divorced 1967. Married Leslie Allen (1968); children: Nicholas, Benjamin.*

**FEATURE FILMS:**

*Criss Cross* (Univ., 1949)
*City Across the River* (Univ., 1949)
*The Lady Gambles* (Univ., 1949)
*Johnny Stool Pigeon* (Uni., 1949)
*Francis* (Univ., 1949)
*I Was a Shoplifter* (Univ., 1950)
*Winchester '73* (Univ., 1950)
*Kansas Raiders* (Univ., 1950)
*The Prince Who Was a Thief* (Univ., 1951)
*Flesh and Fury* (Univ., 1952)
*No Room for the Groom* (Univ., 1952)

*Son of Ali Baba* (Univ., 1952)
*Houdini* (Par., 1953)
*The All American* (Univ., 1953)
*Forbidden* (Univ., 1953)
*Beachhead* (UA, 1954)
*The Black Shield of Falworth* (Univ., 1954)
*Johnny Dark* (Univ., 1954)
*So This Is Paris* (Univ., 1954)
*The Purple Mask* (Univ., 1954)
*Six Bridges to Cross* (Univ., 1955)
*The Square Jungle* (Univ., 1955)

*Trapeze* (UA, 1956)
*The Rawhide Years* (Univ., 1956)
*Mister Cory* (Univ., 1957)
*The Midnight Story* (Univ., 1957)
*Sweet Smell of Success* (UA, 1957)
*The Vikings* (UA, 1958)
*Kings Go Forth* (UA, 1958)
*The Defiant Ones* (UA, 1958)
*The Perfect Furlough* (Univ., 1958)
*Some Like It Hot* (UA, 1959)
*Operation Petticoat* (Univ., 1959)
*Pepe* (Col., 1960)
*Who Was That Lady?* (Col., 1960)
*The Rat Race* (Par., 1960)
*Spartacus* (Univ., 1960)
*The Great Imposter* (Univ., 1960)
*The Outsider* (Univ., 1961)
*40 Pounds of Trouble* (Univ., 1962)
*Taras Bulba* (UA, 1962)
*The List of Adrian Messenger* (Univ., 1963)

*Captain Newman, M.D.* (Univ., 1963)
*Paris When It Sizzles* (Par., 1964)
*Wild and Wonderful* (Univ., 1964)
*Goodbye Charlie* (20th, 1964)
*Sex and the Single Girl* (WB, 1964)
*The Great Race* (WB, 1965)
*Boeing-Boeing* (Par., 1965)
*Not with My Wife You Don't* (WB, 1966)
*Chamber of Horrors* (WB, 1966)°
*Arrividerci, Baby* (Par., 1966)
*Don't Make Waves* (MGM, 1967)
*Rosemary's Baby* (Par., 1968)†
*The Boston Strangler* (20th, 1968)
*Those Daring Young Men in Their Jaunty Jalopies* (Par., 1969)
*On My Way to the Crusades, I Met a Girl Who . . .* (WB-7 Arts, 1969)
*Suppose They Gave a War and Nobody Came?* (Cinerama, 1970)
*You Can't Win 'em All* (Col., 1970)
*Lempke* (Par., 1974)

°Unbilled Appearance
†Voice Only

# JANET LEIGH

**5′ 6″**
**112 pounds**
**Blonde hair**
**Brown eyes**
**Cancer**

*Real name: Jeanette Helen Morrison. Born July 6, 1927, Merced, California. Married Kenneth Carlisle (1942); annulled 1942. Married Stanley Reames (1945); divorced 1948. Married Tony Curtis (1951), children: Kelly, Jamie; divorced 1962. Married Robert Brandt (1962).*

FEATURE FILMS:

*The Romance of Rosy Ridge* (MGM, 1947)
*If Winter Comes* (MGM, 1947)
*Hills of Home* (MGM, 1948)
*Words and Music* (MGM, 1948)
*Act of Violence* (MGM, 1948)
*Little Women* (MGM, 1949)
*That Forsyte Woman* (MGM, 1949)
*The Doctor and the Girl* (MGM, 1949)
*The Red Danube* (MGM, 1949)
*Holiday Affair* (RKO, 1949)
*Strictly Dishonorable* (MGM, 1951)
*Angels in the Outfield* (MGM, 1951)
*Two Tickets to Broadway* (RKO, 1951)
*It's a Big Country* (MGM, 1951)
*Just This Once* (MGM, 1952)
*Scaramouche* (MGM, 1952)
*Fearless Fagan* (MGM, 1952)
*The Naked Spur* (MGM, 1953)
*Confidentially, Connie* (MGM, 1953)
*Houdini* (Par., 1953)
*Walking My Baby Back Home* (Univ., 1953)
*Prince Valiant* (20th, 1954)

*Living It Up* (Par., 1954)
*The Black Shield of Falworth* (Univ., 1954)
*Rogue Cop* (MGM, 1954)
*Pete Kelly's Blues* (WB, 1955)
*My Sister Eileen* (Col., 1955)
*Safari* (Col., 1956)
*Jet Pilot* (Univ., 1957)
*Touch of Evil* (Univ., 1958)
*The Vikings* (UA, 1958)
*The Perfect Furlough* (Univ., 1958)
*Who Was That Lady?* (Col., 1960)
*Psycho* (Par., 1960)
*Pepe* (Col., 1960)
*The Manchurian Candidate* (UA, 1962)
*Bye Bye Birdie* (Col., 1963)
*Wives and Lovers* (Par., 1963)
*Three on a Couch* (Col., 1966)
*Harper* (WB, 1966)
*Kid Rodelo* (Par., 1966)
*An American Dream* (WB, 1966)
*Grand Slam* (Par., 1968)
*Hello Down There* (Par., 1969)
*One Is a Lonely Number* (MGM, 1972)
*Night of the Lepus* (MGM, 1972)

Tony Curtis and Janet Leigh on their wedding day (June 4, 1951)

In **Houdini** (Par., 1953)

Advertisement for **The Perfect Furlough**

Tony Curtis, Janet Leigh, Torin Thatcher, and Herbert Marshall in **The Black Shield of Falworth** (Univ., 1954)

In **The Vikings** (UA, 1958)

In **Who Was That Lady?** (Col., 1960)

676

# HOUDINI
## (Paramount, 1953) C-106M.

Producer, George Pal; associate producer, Frank Freeman, Jr.; director, George Marshall; based on the book by Harold Kellock; screenplay, Philip Yordan; music, Roy Webb; art directors, Hal Pereira, Al Nozaki; set decorators, Sam Comer, Ray Moyer; assistant director, Michael D. Moore; technical adviser, Dunninger; costumes, Edith Head; sound, Harry Mills, Gene Garvin; special camera, Gordon Jennings; camera, Ernest Laszlo; editor, George Tomasini.

Tony Curtis (Houdini); Janet Leigh (Bess); Torin Thatcher (Otto); Angela Clarke (Mrs. Weiss); Stefan Schnabel (Prosecuting Attorney); Ian Wolfe (Fante); Sig Ruman (Schultz); Michael Pate (Dooley); Connie Gilchrist (Mrs. Schultz); Mary Murphy, Joanne Gilbert (Girls); Mabel Paige (Medium); Malcolm Lee Beggs (Warden); Frank Orth (White-Haired Man); Barry Bernard (Inspector); Douglas Spencer (Sims); Peter Baldwin (Fred); Richard Shannon (Miner), Elsie Ames, Nick Arno (Entertainers); Esther Garber (Esther's Girl Friend); Norma Jean Eckart (Girl in Guillotine Act); Lewis Martin (Editor); Lawrence Ryle (German Judge); Fred Essler (Official Looking Man); Arthur Gould Porter (Alhambra Manager); Alex Harford (Assistant); Tudor Owen (Blacksmith); Harry Hines, Oliver Blake, Cliff Clark, Harold Neiman (Barkers); Erno Verebes (Professor Allegari); Anthony Warde (M.C.); Grace Hayle (Woman Who Screams); Jody Gilbert (Fat Girl); Frank Jaquet (Foreman); Billy Bletcher (Italian Basso); Lyle Latell (Calcott); Torben Meyer (Head Waiter); Tor Johnson (Strong Man); Edward Clark (Doorman).

New York Premiere: Holiday Theatre—July 2, 1953
New York Television Debut: NBC—January 30, 1965

### Synopsis

Harry Houdini, a struggling magician, is employed in a New York dime museum where he doubles as a "wild man." He becomes enamored with Bess when she visits the museum and weds her after a whirlwind courtship. She becomes a part of his magical act, but, discouraged by the rude treatment of the unruly audiences, persuades him to quit the stage. He obtains a job in a lock and safe factory but is bored by his work. One night he takes his wife to a magician's convention where he wins a round-trip ticket to Europe by freeing himself from a straight jacket. He exchanges the prize for two one-way tickets and Bess accompanies him on the transatlantic jaunt. In London, after freeing himself from an escape-proof jail, he becomes a smash stage hit. Thereafter he becomes the sensation of the Continent. Back in America he is still relatively unknown and embarks on a series of death-defying stunts to make himself into a top stage

677

attraction. With the death of his beloved mother, however, Houdini deserts the stage for over two years, turning all his attentions to his attempts to communicate with her through mediums. He eventually returns to the stage with wide acclaim. One night, to satisfy an enthusiastic audience, he attempts to escape from a sealed water tank while suspended head down and trussed in a straight jacket. He suffers an appendicitis attack in the tank, and when Bess screams, the glass tank is broken to free him. He regains consciousness, but soon dies.

◆—◆—◆

Producer George Pal, mindful of the public's abiding curiosity in the fantastic, turned from his series of successful science fiction films [*Destination Moon* (1950), *The War of the Worlds* (1953)] to the world of the inexplicably fabulous Harry Houdini (1874-1926). The famed magician, né Erich Weiss of Appleton, Wisconsin, gained a legendary reputation for his theatrical ability to extricate himself from handcuffs and locked/sealed containers of all descriptions. When the widow of the "Genius of Escape" herself died, she willed some three hundred of her husband's more famous tricks to master illusionist Dunninger, who in turn was hired by Pal and Paramount to provide technical assistance on this cinema project.

Pal had the boxoffice acumen to capitalize on the novelty of the first screen teaming of the very popular husband-and-wife cinema personalities, Tony Curtis and Janet Leigh. Fan magazines had dubbed the pair the perfect American couple, and hardly a day went by without the press somewhere printing the latest photograph of the wholesome, smiling twosome. Leigh had been discovered by Norma Shearer and put under Metro contract. The young performer had persevered vainly in a quagmire of sticky vehicles such as *The Romance of Rosy Ridge* (1947) and *Little Women* (1949). Then she was "discovered" by Howard Hughes who requested her for RKO's *Holiday Affair* (1949) and *Two Tickets to Broadway* (1951). He was a perspicacious judge of talent, for he saw screen potential in her that most of the film colony somehow overlooked. (In recent years the mature Leigh would prove that Hughes had been right, but too early.) Following her first two pictures with him the bashful billionaire starred Leigh with John Wayne in *Jet Pilot* which stood on the shelves until 1957. When it was unveiled the general critical consensus was that it might better have been shipped directly to the Smithsonian Institute. By 1953, Leigh and MGM had come near to the end of the road, a loss for no one, since that studio had no great future plans for the twenty-seven-year-old actress, and under their aegis she seemed content to amble on as before.

On the other hand, the former Bernard Schwartz of the Bronx had been a dynamo of fire since Universal placed him under contract and began spotting him in features in 1949. What he lacked in talent he more than made up for in enthusiasm, being very proficient in gymnastics if not elocution (e.g., "Yonder lies the castle of my fadder"). At this time Hollywood was overrun with the so-called milkshake set, but already Curtis was among the elite of that contingent, which included Tab Hunter, Robert Wagner. Jeffrey Hunter, John Derek, and of course Curtis' Universal rival, Rock Hudson.

Offscreen Curtis and Leigh, wed since 1951, were considered—at least by the adoring fan press and the public—as the ideal married couple; he dashing and smiling, she demure and smiling. Together oncamera, the studio felt that they might make sweet boxoffice music. A decade later a more famous, more talented, but more vulgar spouse team—Richard Burton and Elizabeth Taylor—would push the same gambit to far greater rewards and notoriety. However, this was the somnolent 1950s, when moviegoers were happy for small blessings. The congenial teaming of Curtis and Leigh was one of the dividends offered the gullible teenage segment of the film audience.

Because the Curtis-Leigh team were best noted for their amiable personalities and attractive good looks, producer Pal wisely focused his fictionalized biography of *Houdini* on the subject's professional derring-dos, rather than on the man himself. This made the rather fanciful treatment of the life and times of Harry Houdini palatable. In fact, Gordon Gow in his survey book *Hollywood in the Fifties* (1971) credits this color feature for being ". . . well above the showbiz glamour level when it gave a glimpse (however true or false) of an obsessive mentality." Interestingly, Pal and director George Marshall use the cinema medium in *Houdini* to conceal rather than reveal the mechanics behind the magician's manipulative stunts, adding a special mysticism of its own to the picture.

*Houdini* opens on a lighthearted tone as Curtis, employed as "Bruto the Wild Man" in Schultz's Dime Museum in New York, adds an extra dash of hamming to his duties for the amusement of a group of school girls, including the physically well-developed Leigh. On this corny but workable note, the two characters begin their courtship which quickly evolves into marriage. Leigh discovers to her amazement on her wedding night that Curtis is so addicted to his magician's craft that he must satisfy his professional curiosity, no matter when the whim hits him. (Here he awakens her to be the guinea pig for his sawing-in-half routine.) To provide the storyline with some needed conflict and momentum, it is Leigh who convinces Curtis to try some more normal occupation, and he, being dedicated to his art, finally convinces her that life upon the wicked stage is his primary *raison d'être*, because, as he says, "Magic is all I know."

Every time the film threatens to become merely a catalog of Houdini's most spellbinding stunts, the scenario adds a human touch to the proceedings. For example, in England, Curtis is late for his stage appearance, and the devoted Leigh whips backstage prepared to don her husband's costumes and pass herself off as the main attraction until he can make a delayed—and successful—entrance. This type of business kept *Houdini* rolling as entertainment. A rather disconcerting, but true, aspect of the movie were the sections devoted to Curtis' earnest attempts to communicate with his late mother (Angela Clarke) through mediums, a group whom he eventually exposes as fakes.

Perhaps the most exciting of Houdini's stunts reproduced in the film was the gymnast's immersion into the freezing Detroit River while enclosed in a padlocked box, and his apparent inability to emerge from his incarceration on schedule. Leigh faints and is taken away, the crowd gasps and then disperses, and only a solitary figure, Curtis' assistant (Torin Thatcher), remains to maintain guard over the ice hole, with a near frozen Curtis eventually emerging. This extended sequence fully revealed the filmmaker's intention to present Houdini as a semi-mystical figure whose super skills could not be explained by ordinary human standards.

As could have been predicted, the hardcore critics rapped *Houdini* for distorting the subject's life into pat episodes, and scolded the young stars. *The New Yorker* leveled a blast: "As the eminent escapist, Tony Curtis is a pale imitation of the man who was so incredibly dexterous at slipping out of handcuffs, cells, and straight jackets, and as his wife, Janet Leigh is decorative but little else."

However, a segment of the public, and there were a good many Curtis-Leigh fans not solely addicted to television, turned out in substantial numbers to give *Houdini* satisfactory cash returns on the relatively modest production investment. Besides, the Motion Picture Herald-Fame Poll belatedly listed both Curtis and Leigh among the 1953 crop of "Stars of Tomorrow." At that point it seemed that the show business world seemed theirs to conquer!

## THE BLACK SHIELD OF FALWORTH
### *(Universal, 1954) C-99M.*

Producer, Robert Arthur; associate producer, Melville Tucker; director, Rudolph Mate; based on the novel *Men of Iron* by Howard Pyle; screenplay, Oscar Brodney; music supervisor, Joseph Gershenson; art director, Alexander Golitzen; camera, Irving Glassberg; editor, Ted J. Kent.

Tony Curtis (Myles Falworth; Janet Leigh (Lady Anne); David Farrar (Earl of Alban); Barbara Rush (Meg Falworth); Herbert Marshall (Earl of Mackworth); Rhys Williams (Diccon Bowman); Daniel O'Herlihy (Prince Hal); Torin Thatcher (Sir James); Ian Keith (King Henry IV); Patrick O'Neal (Walter Blunt); Craig Hill (Francis Gascoyne); Doris Lloyd (Dame Ellen); Leonard Mudie (Friar Edward); Maurice Marsac (Count de Vermois); Leo Britt (Sir Robert); Charles FitzSimons (Giles); Gary Montgomery (Peter); Claud Allister (Sir George); Robin Camp (Roger Ingoldsby).

New York Premiere: Loew's State Theatre—October 6, 1954
New York Television Debut: CBS—September 24, 1966

### Synopsis

In the reign of King Henry IV of England, Myles and Meg Falworth are raised as peasants by Diccon Bowman who does not reveal to them that they are of royal lineage. When Myles thrashes a nobleman for making improper advances to Meg, Diccon has them journey to the castle of the Earl of Mackworth for safekeeping. The Earl had been a friend of Falworth's father, who, years before, had been branded a traitor and killed by the corrupt Earl of Alban. Mackworth well knew that the elder Falworth had been innocent of the charges but he always lacked sufficient power to right the wrong. Now he sees to it that Myles becomes a squire-at-arms and is trained for knighthood, while Meg is assigned as lady-in-waiting to Lady Anne, Mackworth's attractive daughter. When it becomes clear that Alban is plotting to seize the King's throne, Mackworth schemes with Prince Hal to prevent the coup. Meanwhile, Myles develops into a superior combat champion and Mackworth via a ruse tricks the King into knighting Myles so he can challenge Alban and obtain fitting revenge. When Myles and Alban face each other on the field of battle it is clear that Alban is planning on more than a friendly competition. Myles puts up a furious battle and with the aid of the squires attacks Alban and his henchmen. Mackworth then makes known Myles' royal status. The King restores his knightly rights and lands, and grants approval of his prospective marriage to the willing Lady Anne.

◆◆◆

MGM had its *Knights of the Round Table* (1953), Warner Bros. its *King Richard and the Crusaders* (1954), Twentieth Century-Fox its *Prince Valiant* (1954) and for their initial CinemaScope color spectacle, Universal produced its own gaudy tribute to bold knights and lady fairs, *The Black Shield of Falworth*, very loosely based on the 1892 novel by Howard Pyle.

To populate this unabashed recreation of comic strip-style "olde Englande" with its heroics and gallantry, Universal called to arms its athletic contract star Tony Curtis, who had previously donned costumes in *The Prince Who Was a Thief* (1951) and *Son of Ali Baba* (1952). For his leading lady who had to be fetching oncamera and little else, it was politic and commercial to select Curtis' wife, Janet Leigh, who had already aquitted herself more than adequately in a similar role in *Prince Valiant*. For additional oncamera pulchritude studio contractee Barbara Rush (a much underrated performer) was appointed Curtis' onscreen sister, with Craig Hill as her squire-suitor. To help the film over any rough spots, and certainly there were many of those in the course of its ninety-nine minutes, there were such solid professionals as Herbert Marshall as the weak but well-meaning Earl of Mackworth with David Farrar playing a road company version of a George Sanders-type villain, here the evil Earl of Alban. Buried in the cast was Maureen O'Hara's brother, Charles FitzSimons as Giles.

In no sense can *The Black Shield of Falworth* be considered an epic. It was produced under too many careless conditions, with more concern for properly filling the technical demands of the wide screen process than for displaying an adequate screenplay for any solid entertainment values. With its array of synthetic tights, tin suits, and plaster castles, one could intellectually agree with Bosley Crowther *(New York Times)* who bemoaned, "The doings of chivalrous knights and ladies here are made to look like a high school masquerade. And the cut-ups of fourteenth century playboys are pitched to the level of Martin and Lewis farce." Yet, granting all this, the film did have some moments of swashbuckling fascination, particularly in the intriguing squires' training sequences and the segments devoted to the combats on the turf.

Less satisfactory were the sections devoted to the personal problems of the characters. A viewer had to be in a very charitable mood to believe that Curtis was anything but a New York refugee capering about on the expansive Universal backlot. His colloquial phrasing and New York-accented delivery almost made one wish the film to be a silent. The combat scenes apart, *The Black Shield of Falworth* produced disconcerting images of Curtis leaping over papier-mâché castle walls to rendezvous with a cloistered Leigh, she being thankfully demure and infrequently addicted to mouthing trite lines. Likewise, the betighted Curtis swaggering about the decorated soundstage interiors trying to woo the audience with his cocky enthusiasm and dark good looks was hardly a substitute for fledgling histrionic skills. The film and its stars were a paltry descendant indeed of the Errol Flynn-Olivia de Havilland epics of late 1930s Warner Bros.

When all is said and done, however, it must be acknowledged that *The Black Shield of Falworth* was aimed at a particular market—the action/kiddie trade. Therefore, with its simpler criterion, the film met with favorable reaction as a mindless, colorful, moving picture divertissement.

## THE PERFECT FURLOUGH
*(Universal, 1958) C-93M.*

Producer, Robert Arthur; director, Blake Edwards; screenplay, Stanley Shapiro; art director, Alexander Golitzen; set decorators, Russell A. Gausman, Oliver Emert; costumes, Bill Thomas; music, Frank Skinner; music supervisor, Joseph Gershenson; song, Skinner, Diane Lampert, and Richard Loring; makeup, Bud Westmore; assistant directors, Frank Shaw, Terry Nelson; camera, Phil Lathrop; editor, Milton Carruth.

Tony Curtis (Paul Hodges); Janet Leigh (Vicki Loren); Keenan Wynn (Harvey Franklin); Linda Cristal (Sandra Roca); Elaine Stritch (Liz Baker); Marcel Dalio (Henri); Les Tremayne (Colonel Leland); Jay Novello (Rene); King Donovan (Major Collins); Troy Donahue (Sergeant Nickles); Gordon

Jones, Dick Crockett (M.P.s); Alvy Moore (Private Brewer); Lilyan Chauvin (French Nurse); Eugene Borden (French Doctor); James Lanphier (Assistant Hotel Manager); Frankie Darro (Patient).

New York Premiere: Roxy Theatre—January 21, 1959
New York Television Debut: CBS—November 12, 1964

## Synopsis

To bolster the sagging morale at an army Arctic installation, the Pentagon turns to WAC psychologist Vicki Loren, who concocts an intriguing scheme which she dubs the "perfect furlough." The scheme is to pick one of the 105 men from the base to go on a three-week Parisian fling with the girl of his choice; the other 104 men can enjoy the excursion vicariously. Corporal Paul Hodges, who has been in the Northern wastes for seven months, maneuvers himself into winning the lottery and chooses voluptuous movie queen Sandra Roca as his comely companion. The Pentagon is horrified, knowing well Paul's reputation as a military wolf. Vicki is ordered to join the couple as tour chaperone. Once in Paris, Sandra squelches Paul's amorous plans when she politely informs that she is not only married but pregnant. Naturally Paul is suspected of the deed and the military brass order him state-side. By this time, Vicki, already in love with the corporal and anxious not to lose him, announces that she too is an expectant mother. A wedding ceremony is quickly arranged with Paul happily agreeing to take Vicki as his wife.

◆◆◆

Tony Curtis, who had tried his cinematic hand at almost every genre, was relatively inexperienced in the field of bedroom farce when he blithely tackled *The Perfect Furlough*. However, he acquitted himself so agreeably in this exercise that he soon turned his full attention to becoming a latter-day Cary Grant, as in *Some Like It Hot* (1959). On the other hand, Janet Leigh, who had been increasingly neglecting her see-sawing screen career in favor of domesticity, proved that thirty was not necessarily a dangerous age for a cinema beauty. In *The Perfect Furlough* she had the best assignment of her joint screen ventures with Curtis, and, moreover, demonstrated that in the post bloom of youth she was not only exceedingly attractive but becoming rather adept with the delivery of a tart line of dialog.

With its unpretentious demeanor, *The Perfect Furlough* caught many a viewer unawares. For its kind of controlled lewd comedy, it had sparkling repartee, punchy pacing, and an enthusiastic cast. *Time* magazine congratulated writer Stanley Shapiro and director Blake Edwards for their "almost perfect formula farce" and for applying "the formula with such style that the studio has been able to guarantee the customers exactly 287 (count 'em) laughs without fear of refund."

What was most intriguing about *The Perfect Furlough* was that it accomplished its entertainment mission by utilizing to good advantage a bunch of stock characters: an overly attractive female psychologist (Leigh), a skirt-chasing, army man (Curtis), a dramatically curvaceous South American sexpot film siren (Linda Cristal), her blustery manager (Keenan Wynn), a cynical press agent (Elaine Stritch), and, to round out the proceedings, a perplexed army major (King Donovan) and a handsome army photographer (Troy Donahue).

While there was nothing novel about the predictable scrapes and double entendre situations in which the cast became involved—even the Gallic sequences were all synthetic backlot Universal lensing—the film had the saving grace of finding some refreshingly different dialog touches, just when the going was becoming too obvious. The interchange between Leigh and Stritch was a fine example of such dialogue moments:

Stritch: "I think you're going for him. Be honest now. He bugs you, doesn't he?

Leigh: "Bugs me? As far as I'm concerned, a bug is something that crawls in your bed."

Stritch: "I rest my case."

Likewise, the visual delights of the slapstick scene in which Curtis eludes his ever present bodyguard and takes the Argentine bombshell (Cristal) to the French countryside for a bit of red wine, nibbling on sandwiches and ear lobes, leads to a fast and furious mixup of intentions and actions. Throughout the scene the script never goes beyond the point of reasonably good taste. Concise controlled rhythm on the part of director Blake Edwards whipped this situation into bubbling fun.

When the virtues of *The Perfect Furlough* are contrasted to such indulgent exercises as Edwards' *The Party* (1968) or Tony Curtis' *Wild and Wonderful* (1962—with his next real-life wife, Christine Kaufmann), this earlier screen comedy becomes all the more vintage brew.


## THE VIKINGS
### *(United Artists, 1958) C-114M.*

Producer, Jerry Bresler; director, Richard Fleischer; based on the novel *The Viking* by Edison Marshall; adaption, Dale Wasserman; screenplay, Calder Willingham; assistant director, Andre Smagghe; music, Mario Nascimbene; production designer, Harper Goff; animation prologue, UPA Pictures, Inc; second unit director, Elmo Williams; makeup, John O'Gorman, Neville Smallwood; sound, Joe de Bretagne; camera, Jack Cardiff; editorial supervisor, Williams.

Kirk Douglas (Einar); Tony Curtis (Eric); Ernest Borgnine (Ragnar); Janet Leigh (Morgana); James Donald (Egbert); Alexander Knox (Father Goodwin); Frank Thring (Aella); Maxine Audley (Enid); Eileen Way

(Kitala); Edric Connor (Sandpiper); Dandy Nichols (Bridget); Per Buckhoj (Bjorm); Almut Berg (Pigtails).

New York Premiere: Victoria and Astor Theatres—June 11, 1958
New York Television Debut: ABC—September 20, 1964

## Synopsis

In the ninth century, Viking King Ragnar leads a raid on Northumberland, murdering the king and raping the queen. She bears a son, whom she sends away, and who grows up as a Viking slave known as Eric. One day he fights with Ragnar's son Einar and, in the ensuing tussle, Eric's falcon gouges out Einar's left eye. Eric is condemned to be thrown into a pool of giant rock crabs but the Norse god Odin intervenes and Eric is spared. Later, Einar captures Welsh princess Morgana and tries to make her his bride. She rejects him and escapes with Eric in a small boat bound for England with Einar and Ragnar in pursuit. Eric later captures Ragnar, who is turned over to Aella, king of Northumberland, in exchange for Morgana's hand in marriage. Ragnar is tossed into a wolf pit but Eric allows him to die honorably by giving him his sword. The angered Aella then cuts off Eric's hand and sets him adrift. Thereafter, he meets up with Einar and they agree to set aside their feud in order to rescue Morgana and to avenge Ragnar's murder. They attack Aella's castle and emerge victorious. Morgana again refuses Einar's marriage offer and tells him that Eric is really his blood brother. Einar does not believe her and charges after Eric, but as he is about to make the decisive sword thrust, he pauses, and in this brief interval Eric kills Einar. Einar's body is placed aboard a vessel which is set afire and put out to sea to make the long trip to Valhalla.

◆━◆━◆

Ever since Edison Marshall's 1951 novel hit the bestseller's list, it had been considered prime film material. In 1952 Mike Todd and Edward Small planned a joint venture in producing a film of the bloodthirsty actioner, but it remained for Kirk Douglas' Bryna production company to set the project into expensive actuality. (At the time Douglas was labeled Kirk von Stroheim for his seeming budgetary excesses on *The Vikings*.) Filmed in Technicolor and Technirama, with location work in Brittany and along the coast of Norway, and Viking ships and village replicas built at Fort La Lotte in Dinard, France, *The Vikings* cost nearly four million dollars, but grossed $6.049 million in distributors' domestic receipts.

Bosley Crowther (*New York Times*) admitted, "You haven't seen such general hell-raising on the screen since Cecil B. De Mille ditched Cleopatra and hit the sawdust trail." Hollis Alpert *(Saturday Review)*. snapped, "It seems to me that this movie is quite probably beyond the pale of criticism, and it might better be left to someone with psychological training to attempt to figure out why three grown men, all of fairly humble origins who have become enormously successful in their careers, would take roles of this kind." *Cue* magazine asserted that *The Vikings* ". . . pours out more blood per foot of film than any picture in recent memory."

*The Vikings* is a motion picture devoted to exhibiting a way of life revolving around violence and gore. There is hardly a single sensitive person in sight throughout the blood-smeared picture, which offers endless views of gougings, limb renderings, and belly slitting at nearly every specious turn. If the men of the ninth century had such unsavory demises as portrayed in this film, the women must surely have quaked at the thought that behind every shadow hunched a potential ravisher. With such barbaric life styles, there must have been little chance for subtlety in those times, which, in turn, provided scant material for any sophistication in reproducing the tumultuous period on the big screen.

At best, Calder Willingham's screenplay for *The Vikings* was serviceable. Director Richard Fleischer, who would later guide Tony Curtis through *The Boston Strangler* (1968), decided to focus not on the screenplay but on the meticulous recreation of the rugged life style of the rampaging Vikings. Jack Cardiff's stunning cinematography vividly captured the breathtaking panoramas, the authentically reproduced sets, and the overabundance of visual shocks. The directorial decisions by Fleischer left little room for more than cardboard characterizations by the players, and the actors took the occasion to oblige with zesty tributes to the god Ham, as they rollicked through this sweaty, gymnastic marathon. The male leads owed more to the makeup department for their distinguishing characterizations than to earnest acting. Douglas galloped through the film with one empty eye socket, Curtis played without the use of his fighting hand, and the beefy Ernest Borgnine countenance was buried behind bushels of whiskers. Leigh, in contrast to the Rover Boy antics of her co-stars, was amazingly restrained and dispassionate, a strange state of affairs considering she was the pivotal force behind most of the bloodshed in the yarn. *Variety* decided she "would have benefitted from some emotional charging up" in her role playing. Industry observers rumored that Leigh's oncamera indifference was a result of her growing offcamera marital problems with Curtis.

The public relished the vicarious adventures provided in *The Vikings*, but the critics had a field day outdoing one another in panning the stars, particularly stars Curtis and Leigh. *Films in Review* was the champ in this department, analyzing: "Tony Curtis was completely stymied by unlikely dialogue in incredible situations; and Janet Leigh, wearing a pair of obvious false breasts, would have been better off had her ridiculous part been wholly line-less."

For the record, *The Vikings* had one of the more exhaustive and expensive publicity campaigns of late 1950s filmmaking. To celebrate the joint Astor and Victoria Theatres' opening in New York, a 261-foot actual replica of a Norse ship was hoisted atop the adjacent marquees at a cost of some $105,000. This was just one of the gaudier gimmicks successfully used to lure the bored public back into the movies to see *The Vikings*.

## WHO WAS THAT LADY?
### *(Columbia, 1960) 115M.*

Producer, Norman Krasna; director, George Sidney; based on the play *Who Was That Lady I Saw You With?* by Krasna; screenplay, Krasna; assistant director, David Silver; music, Andre Previn; song, Sammy Cahn and James Van Heusen; gowns, Jean Louis; art director, Edward Haworth; set decorator, James M. Crowe; makeup, Ben Lane; sound, Charles J. Rich, James Flaster; camera, Harry Stradling; editor, Viola Lawrence.

Tony Curtis (David Wilson); Dean Martin (Michael Haney); Janet Leigh (Ann Wilson); James Whitmore (Harry Powell); John McIntire (Bob Doyle); Barbara Nichols (Gloria Coogle); Larry Keating (Parker); Larry Storch (Orenov); Simon Oakland (Belka); Joi Lansing (Florence Coogle); Barbara Hines (Girl); Marion Javits (Miss Melish); Michael Lane (Glinka); Kam Tong (Lee Wong); William Newell (Schultz); Mark Allen (Joe Bendix); Snub Pollard (Tattoo Artist).

New York Premiere: Criterion Theatre—April 15, 1960
New York Television Debut: ABC—December 5, 1964

### Synopsis

Ann Wilson is enraged when she catches her Columbia University chemistry professor husband David kissing an attractive student. She starts packing for Reno, but David's imaginative pal, television writer Michael Haney, comes to the timely rescue by convincing Ann that David is "really" a F.B.I. agent and that the girl in question was a possible spy. Ann swallows this yarn, and protectively follows David and Michael to a Chinese restaurant where they are dining with two blonde chorine types. Ann assumes these girls are more suspected subversives, and attempts to pass her hubby the "prop" gun he left behind at the apartment. A near riot ensues involving actual F.B.I. men with a video news unit capturing the live action. When the story of David's undercover activities hits the newspapers, real foreign agents assume David is linked to a top level university project and kidnap the trio in order to drag information from them. The three captives are later taken to the sub-basement of the Empire State Building, where, under the effect of truth serum, David admits his deception. Ann gets free and storms out of the building. When David and Michael awake they confusedly believe they are in an enemy submarine. They gallantly decide to scuttle the ship by opening all the water valves. The F.B.I. arrives in the nick of time to save the men from their watery folly, and Ann forgives her erring spouse.

◆　◆　◆

What had been a modestly successful Broadway comedy with Peter Lind Hayes, Mary Healy, and Ray Walston, proved much more viable if less engaging when transferred to the big screen. "It is a pretty lively farce even though there is a disposition to fasten the camera too long on scenes of domestic bliss, which, after all, are rather inconsequential in this milieu" [Paul V. Beckley (*New York Herald-Tribune*)].

By now, both Tony Curtis and Janet Leigh were well-seasoned screen professionals, and could focus more on their farcical characterizations than on the ambiance of a real life husband-wife team appearing oncamera. Not that the production forces behind the film overlooked the fading gimmick of their offscreen wedlock, for some of the comedy from the stage play was sacrificed to add scenes of domestic screen romancing. Such a sacrifice was proved worthwhile, for *Variety* noted, "They make a handsome couple and their marital togetherness will probably be inspiring to married spectators."

If one wondered at all how close the Curtis-Leigh oncamera antics—he as the would-be playboy spouse, she as the quick-to-anger, quick-to-forgive duped wife—paralleled reality, the absurdities of the wacky storyline made that issue totally irrelevant. As in *The Perfect Furlough*, which intelligently varied the couple's oncamera abrasive and romantic moments, *Who Was That Lady?* provided each of the leads with an even more nonsensical nature, allowing their characters to romp and romance with greater latitude. One of their best joint moments occurs in the bedroom after gullible Leigh has been taken in by the Curtis-Dean Martin fabrications. Imaginative Curtis decides to carry the ruse one step further, just to make sure that Leigh accepts the tale whole hog. Curtis embroiders his tall tale by stating to the attentive Leigh that as a sign of his secret service ranks he has four dots tatooed on his heel. (He had accomplished this feat just previously with a ball point pen.) She inspects his foot to make sure, and is properly convinced. Then he blithely adds, "J. Edgar Hoover has seven." Realizing that her husband is indeed in lofty company, she melts into his arms, gushing, "My hero."

Thanks to the carefully controlled nonchalant posing of Martin, who also sang the movie's title song, there are many easy-going respites from the frantic shenanigans of Curtis-Leigh. These highjinks, however, come fast and furious, first as she indulges in some Lucille Ball-style slapstick at the Chinese restaurant, and later at the finale as Curtis dons his junior Gary Grant guise to bring the farce to its wrap up.

*Cue* magazine judged that in this film "Tony Curtis and Janet Leigh [are] at the top of their form . . ." which given the delineated range of the couple's screen emoting abilities, was indeed a compliment.

## PEPE
### (Columbia, 1960) C-195 min.

Producer, George Sidney; associate producer, Jacques Gelman; director, Sidney; based on the play *Broadway Zauber* by Ladislas Bush-Fekete; screen story, Leonard Spigelgass, Sonya Levien; screenplay, Dorothy Kingsley, Claude Binyon; assistant director, David Silver; art director, Ted Haworth; set decorator, William Kiernan; music supervisor-background score, Johnny Green; special musical material, Sammy Cahn; Roger Eden; songs, Andre Previn, Dory Langdon; Hans Wittstatt, Langdon; Previn; Augustin Lara, Langdon; choreography, Eugene Loring, Alex Romero; makeup, Ben Lane; gowns, Edith Head; camera, Joe McDonald; editors, Viola Lawrence, Al Clark.

Cantinflas (Pepe); Dan Dailey (Ted Holt); Shirley Jones (Suzie Murphy); Carlos Montalban (Auctioneer); Vicki Trickett (Lupita); Matt Mattox (Dancer); Hank Henry (Manager); Suzanne Lloyd (Carmen); Carlos Rivas (Carlos); Stephen Bekassy (Jewelry Salesman); Carol Douglas (Waitress); Francisco Reguerra (Priest); Joe Hyams (Charro); Joey Bishop, Michael Callan, Maurice Chevalier, Charles Coburn, Richard Conte, Bing Crosby, Tony Curtis, Bobby Darin, Sammy Davis, Jr., Jimmy Durante, Zsa Zsa Gabor, the voice of Judy Garland, Greer Garson, Hedda Hopper, Ernie Kovacs, Peter Lawford, Janet Leigh, Jack Lemmon, Dean Martin, Jay North, Kim Novak, Andre Previn, Donna Reed, Debbie Reynolds, Edward G. Robinson, Cesar Romero, Frank Sinatra, Billie Burke, Ann B. Davis, William Demarest, Jack Entratter, Col. E. E. Fogelson, Jane Robinson, Bunny Waters (Guest Stars); Shirley DeBurgh (Senorita Dancer); Steve Baylor, John Burnside (Parking Lot Attendants); James Bacon (Bartender); Jimmy Cavanaugh (Dealer); Jeanne Manet (French Woman); Robert B. Williams (Immigration Officer); Stephen Bekassy (Jeweler); Bonnie Green (Dancer); Lela Bliss (Dowager); Ray Walker (Assistant Director); David Landfield (Announcer's Voice); Margie Nelson (Patron); Dorothy Abbott, Kenner C. Kemp, Steve Carruthers, Jim Waters, Billy Synder (Bits); Fred Roberto (Cashier).

New York Premiere: Criterion Theatre—December 21, 1960
New York Television Debut: CBS—February 17, 1967

### Synopsis

When his white stallion, Don Juan, is sold to a down-beat movie director named Ted Holt, Mexican ranch hand Pepe is heartbroken. He follows Ted to Hollywood and once there persuades the director to allow him to remain as the horse's groom. The south-of-the-border worker meets and becomes enamored of Suzie Murphy, a waitress who hopes for a movie career as a dancer. To help broke Ted finance a new motion picture,

Pepe takes his small savings to Las Vegas where he parlays it into a fortune. Ted makes Pepe co-producer of the new film project and gives Suzie the top role. When they run out of funds, Ted is forced to sell Don Juan to producer Edward G. Robinson. Pepe is heartbroken, but is comforted by thinking that Suzie loves him. When the picture is successfully completed, he finally understands that Suzie only feels friendship for him. Ted sells Robinson the controlling interest in the picture when he agrees to return Pepe's horse. All ends happily.

◆  ◆  ◆

One of the messier blockbuster fiascos turned out by Hollywood, *Pepe* immediately drew comparisons to *Around the World in 80 Days* because of the repeated appearance of Mexican comedy star Cantinflas, and due to a similar use of a horde of "cameo" players. The critics lashed out at the marathon bore: "In spite of the basically variety show format—the film has the shape of three Ed Sullivan shows strung end to end—it was thought fit to sew some kind of story line into its skin, and like tattoo artists the creators have relied on stock designs" [Paul V. Beckley *(New York Herald-Tribune)*].

Among the gratuitous guest entertainers—most from the Columbia roster—were Tony Curtis and Janet Leigh in what Arthur Knight *(Saturday Review)* termed a "neatly played little skit." On orders of producer Dan Dailey, Cantinflas brings flowers to Leigh. He finds her humming "My Darling Clementine" in her tub. She mistakes Cantinflas for a man whom her husband Curtis said might show *Passion* at a film festival. Cantiflas gets drunk, dances with Leigh, and switches to bemused Curtis, with the latter ending up in the indoor pool.

## THE YEARS AFTER

On the April 17, 1961, televised Oscarcast, Janet Leigh and Tony Curtis joined with Danny Kaye in a rendition of the gimmick song, "Triplets." It was among the couple's final joint professional appearances for they soon separated and divorced, claiming "we were no longer the same people we were when we first met and got married." (Indeed, his career star had risen while hers had fallen.) Their one-time legion of fans had now become middle-aged parents themselves, and were scarcely aware that their past screen heart throbs had unhitched their personal lives.

Leigh's movie career in the past decade had been a mixed bag with tart performances in such entries as *The Manchurian Candidate* (1962) and *One Is a Lonely Number* (1972), offset by overly tame appearances in the likes of *Wives and Lovers* (1963) and *Night of the Lepus* (1972). Despite the problems of reaching "that age" where she is too old to play young matrons and still too pretty to essay offbeat character roles, Leigh has displayed an increasingly more pungent acting talent and visual look. She obviously has learned a good deal about life and her craft by just weathering the years. In contrast, Curtis, who has since remarried twice, has remained the over-aged, rambunctiously boyish male lead, more effective when he is emoting in a serious manner, such as in *The Boston Strangler* (1968), than when engaged in the lumbering antics of distilled sex comedies like *Not with My Wife You Don't* (1966) or unfunny farces like *Suppose They Gave A War and Nobody Came?* (1970). While his short-lived British television series "The Persuaders" (1971) flopped, Curtis proved a game, if desperate, guy attempting to crash Broadway in Bruce J. Friedman's comedy, *One Night Stand*. The abysmal show never reached Broadway. Then, to the amazement of many—including himself—Curtis' career picked up again. He played the lead in the gangster film *Lempke* (1974), and then jaunted off to Europe to fulfill contracts for starring roles in such scheduled productions as *Bodyguard Man*, and remakes of *The Man in the Iron Mask* and *The Count of Monte Cristo*. Meantime, he dashed off a semi-autobiography, *Kid Andrew Cody*, which he hopes to have published.

Ironically, in retrospect, it was the offscreen Curtis and Leigh of the 1950s who typified that decade's young Hollywood celebrities. While fan magazine readers responded more to the activities of Curtis and Leigh than the similar team of Robert Wagner and Natalie Wood, oncamera, Curtis and Leigh were too often engaged in decorating historic mini epics, preventing them from demonstrating sufficient individuality or even conveying the particular ambivalent ambiance associated with the Korean War era and thereafter. By the time of *The Perfect Furlough* and *Who Was That Lady?*, their personal relationship was on the marital rocks and they had worn out their joint welcome with the fickle public, who by then much preferred to gawk at the histrionics, oncamera and off, of the more dynamic Paul Newman and his Oscar-winning wife, Joanne Woodward.

In a publicity pose for **Bonjour Tristesse** (Col., 1958)

# Chapter 25

# David Niven
# &
# Deborah Kerr

## DAVID NIVEN

6' 1"
187 pounds
Reddish brown hair
Blue eyes
Pisces

*Real name: James David Graham Niven. Born March 1, 1910, London, England. Married Primula Rolla (1940), children: David, Jamie; widowed 1946. Married Hjordis Tersmeden (1948), children: Kristina, Fiona.*

FEATURE FILMS:

*Mutiny on the Bounty* (MGM, 1935)
*Without Regret* (Par., 1935)
*Barbary Coast* (UA, 1935)
*A Feather in Her Hat* (Col., 1935)
*Splendour* (UA, 1935)
*Rose Marie* (MGM, 1936)
*Thank You, Jeeves* (20th, 1936)
*Palm Springs* (Par., 1936)
*The Charge of the Light Brigade* (WB, 1936)
*Dodsworth* (UA, 1936)
*Beloved Enemy* (UA, 1936)
*We Have Our Moments* (Univ., 1937)

*Dinner at the Ritz* (20th, 1937)
*The Prisoner of Zenda* (UA, 1937)
*Four Men and a Prayer* (20th, 1938)
*Bluebeard's Eighth Wife* (Par., 1938)
*Three Blind Mice* (20th, 1938)
*The Dawn Patrol* (WB, 1938)
*Wuthering Heights* (UA, 1939)
*Bachelor Mother* (RKO, 1939)
*The Real Glory* (UA, 1939)
*Eternally Yours* (UA, 1939)
*Raffles* (UA, 1940)
*The First of the Few (Spitfire)* (King, 1941)

*The Way Ahead (Immortal Battalion)* (J. Arthur Rank, 1944)

*The Perfect Marriage* (Par., 1946)

*The Magnificent Doll* (Univ., 1946)

*A Matter of Life and Death (Stairway to Heaven)* (J. Arthur Rank, 1946)

*The Other Love* (UA, 1947)

*The Bishop's Wife* (RKO, 1947)

*Bonnie Prince Charlie* (Korda, 1948)

*Enchantment* (RKO, 1948)

*The Elusive Pimpernel (The Scarlet Pimpernel)* (Caroll Pictures, 1948)

*A Kiss in the Dark* (WB, 1949)

*A Kiss for Corliss* (UA, 1949)

*The Toast of New Orleans* (MGM, 1950)

*Soldiers Three* (MGM, 1951)

*Happy Go Lovely* (MGM, 1951)

*The Lady Says No* (UA, 1951)

*Island Rescue* (Univ., 1952)

*The Moon is Blue* (UA, 1953)

*Love Lottery* (Continental Distributing, 1954)

*Tonight's the Night* (AA, 1954)

*The King's Thief* (MGM, 1955)

*Court-Martial* (Kingsley International, 1955)

*The Birds and the Bees* (Par., 1956)

*Around the World in 80 Days* (UA, 1956)

*Oh, Men! Oh, Women!* (20th, 1957)

*The Little Hut* (MGM, 1957)

*My Man Godfrey* (Univ., 1957)

*The Silken Affair* (DCA, 1957)

*Bonjour Tristesse* (Col., 1958)

*Separate Tables* (UA, 1958)

*Ask Any Girl* (MGM, 1959)

*Happy Anniversary* (UA, 1959)

*Please Don't Eat the Daisies* (MGM, 1960)

*The Guns of Navarone* (Col., 1961)

*The Captive City* (Italian, 1961)

*Guns of Darkness* (WB, 1962)

*Road to Hong Kong* (UA, 1962)°

*The Best of Enemies* (Col., 1962)

*55 Days at Peking* (AA, 1963)

*The Shortest Day* (Titanus, 1963)

*The Pink Panther* (UA, 1964)

*Bedtime Story* (Univ., 1964)

*Where the Spies Are* (MGM, 1965)

*Lady L* (MGM, 1966)

*Casino Royale* (Col., 1967)

*Eye of the Devil* (MGM, 1967)

*The Extraordinary Seaman* (MGM, 1968)

*Prudence and the Pill* (20th, 1968)

*The Impossible Years* (MGM, 1968)

*Before Winter Comes* (Col., 1969)

*The Brain* (Par., 1969)

*The Statue* (Cin., 1971)

*King, Queen, Knave* (MGM, 1972)

*Vampira* (Col., 1974)

*Paper Tiger* (1975)

°Unbilled Appearance

# DEBORAH KERR

5′ 7″
120 pounds
Reddish gold hair
Green-blue eyes
Libra

*Real name: Deborah Kerr-Trimmer. Born September 30, 1921, Helensburgh, Scotland. Married Anthony Bartley (1945), children: Francesca, Melanie; divorced 1959. Married Peter Viertel (1960).*

**FEATURE FILMS:**

*Major Barbara* (UA, 1941)
*Love on the Dole* (British National, 1941)
*The Courageous Mr. Penn* (British National, 1941)
*Hatter's Castle* (British National, 1941)
*The Avengers* (General Film Disbributors-Par., 1942)
*Life and Death of Colonel Blimp* (Archer Films-UA, 1943)
*Vacation from Marriage* (MGM-London, 1945)
*The Adventuress* (Rank-Eagle Lion, 1946)
*Black Narcissus* (Rank-Univ., 1947)
*The Hucksters* (MGM, 1947)
*If Winter Comes* (MGM, 1947)
*Edward, My Son* (MGM, 1949)
*King Solomon's Mines* (MGM, 1950)
*Please Believe Me* (MGM, 1950)
*Quo Vadis* (MGM, 1951)
*Prisoner of Zenda* (MGM, 1952)
*Thunder in the East* (Par., 1953)
*Young Bess* (MGM, 1953)
*Dream Wife* (MGM, 1953)
*Julius Caesar* (MGM, 1953)

*From Here to Eternity* (Col., 1953)
*The End of the Affair* (Col., 1955)
*The Proud and Profane* (Par., 1956)
*The King and I* (20th, 1956)
*Tea and Sympathy* (MGM, 1956)
*Heaven Knows, Mr. Allison* (20th, 1957)
*An Affair to Remember* (20th, 1957)
*Bonjour Tristesse* (Col., 1958)
*Separate Tables* (UA, 1958)
*The Journey* (MGM, 1959)
*Count Your Blessings* (MGM, 1959)
*Beloved Infidel* (20th, 1959)
*The Sundowners* (WB, 1960)
*The Grass Is Greener* (Univ., 1960)
*The Naked Edge* (UA, 1961)
*The Innocents* (20th, 1961)
*The Chalk Garden* (Univ., 1964)
*The Night of the Iguana* (MGM, 1964)
*Marriage on the Rocks* (WB, 1965)
*Casino Royale* (Col., 1967)
*Eye of the Devil* (MGM, 1967)
*Prudence and the Pill* (20th, 1968)
*The Gypsy Moths* (MGM, 1969)
*The Arrangement* (WB-7 Arts, 1969)

In **Bonjour Tristesse**

In **Separate Tables** (UA, 1958)

In **Casino Royale** (Col., 1967)

In **Eye of the Devil** (MGM, 1967)

In **Prudence and the Pill** (20th, 1968)

# BONJOUR TRISTESSE
## *(Columbia, 1958) C-93M.*

Producer, Otto Preminger; associate producer, John Palmer; director, Preminger; based on the novel by Françoise Sagan; screenplay, Arthur Laurents; art director, Raymond Simm; set director, Georges Petitot; assistant directors, Adrian Pryce-Jones, Serge Friedman; music, Georges Auric; music conductor, Lambert Williamson; song, Auric and Laurents; choreography, Tutte Lemkow; costume co-ordinator, Hope Bryce; gowns, Givenchy; jewelry, Cartiers; make-up, George Frost; titles, Saul Bass; sound, David Hildyard, Red Law; camera, Georges Perinal; editor, Helga Cranston.

Deborah Kerr (Anne Larsen); David Niven (Raymond); Jean Seberg (Cecile); Mylene Demongeot (Elsa Mackenbourg); Geoffrey Horne (Philippe); Juliette Greco (Nightclub Singer); Walter Chiari (Pablo); Martita Hunt (Philippe's Mother); Roland Culver (Mr. Lombard); Jean Kent (Mrs. Lombard); David Oxley (Jacques); Elga Anderson (Denise); Jeremy Burnham (Hubert Duclos); Eveline Eyfel (Maid); Tutte Lemkow (Pierre Schube); Roland Culver (Mr. Lombard).

New York Premiere: Capitol Theatre—January 15, 1958
New York Television Debut: ABC—November 14, 1964

## Synopsis

In flashback, Cecile recalls tragic events which have made the lives of herself and her widowed playboy father seem so futile and hollow. The last pleasant summer on the Riviera with her irresponsible father, Raymond, and his newest mistress, Elsa, was threatened by the arrival of her godmother Anne. She is a lovely but morally repressed woman who disapproves of Raymond's bad examples and of Cecile's carefree affair with Philippe. When self-indulgent Cecile learns that Raymond is considering wedding Anne, she does everything possible to reunite him with silly Elsa. Later Anne overhears Raymond dissecting her prissy nature to Elsa, and in her distraught state, Anne jumps into a car and speeds away from the villa. Confused by her emotional turmoil she either accidentally or on purpose drives off a cliff and is killed. Cecile and Raymond return to Paris, but they cannot forget Anne and the changes she has wrought in their vapid lives.

◆◆◆

Almost before she was out of her middy blouses, French schoolgirl Françoise Sagan seized the imagination of her book-reading countrymen with her first novel. The volume was slight in size, but expansive in its daring philosophy of the new generation. *Bonjour Tristesse* was on the

French bestseller list for thirty-eight weeks; in the English translation in hardback and paperback, it sold 1.3 million copies in 1956 alone. When iconoclastic producer-director Otto Preminger promptly acquired the screen rights to the book, global industry observers knew the inevitable would happen despite the planned on-location filming: a Hollywoodian rendition of a very Gallic-oriented novel. The stars cast to portray the French leads were two Britishers, David Niven and Deborah Kerr, and in the focal role of the spoiled, pampered diarist, Jean Seberg, the Iowa-born discovery of Preminger who had failed so miserably in the title role of Preminger's *Saint Joan* (1957). When the movie rendition of *Bonjour Tristesse* did appear in 1958, Bosley Crowther *(New York Times)* led the wolf pack in dissecting the film, carping that "almost everything about this picture . . . manifests bad taste, poor judgment and plain deficiency of skill." This writer disagrees with such critical appraisal and falls more in line with Preminger who said, "*Bonjour Tristesse* is a film I like . . . it was a very big success in France, and in America the critics said it wasn't French enough, which is very funny." As *Cue* magazine summed up this controversial film, ". . . a lush, sensuous, and extraordinarily amoral movie-making job."

With their prolific film careers both in Hollywood and abroad, it was strange that no one had seriously thought before of teaming forty-seven-year-old debonair David Niven with thirty-seven-year-old lady-like Deborah Kerr. Each of them was admirably adept at complementing the other's resilient screen charms: Niven the drawing room inhabitant who excelled at being prankish or slightly roguish, as in his career-boosting *Around the World in Eighty Days* (1956), and Kerr, the genteel screen successor to Greer Garson, who had displayed oncamera a suppressed craving for adventure [*King Solomon's Mines* (1950)], surfacing sensual passion [*From Here to Eternity* (1953)], or spirit and compassion [*Tea and Sympathy* (1956)]. Niven and Kerr together might well have inherited the movie mantle of Cary Grant and Irene Dunne, but until *Bonjour Tristesse* no one had had the perspicacity to sense their potential for screen teaming.

Within *Bonjour Tristesse*, Niven is a worthy exponent of the Sagan philosophy that one should hedonistically live for today despite the dangers that lurk ahead. Niven's Raymond is an affluent, handsome reprobate who, in middle age, still has the carefreeness of youth. He is almost amoral in his passion for sensual satisfaction, whether it be bedding his latest mistress, gambling at the casino, sampling a vintage wine, or sailing forth on the sunny waters. There is no one to reprimand him for his waywardness, if one, unlike Sagan, insists upon making moral judgments. Seberg's Cecile is an adolescent carbon copy of her fun-craving father. She is more restrained in her escapades only from inexperience and less evenly tempered because she has yet to weather enough of life's vagaries. Nevertheless, she is equally hedonistic in coping with the world. At her tender years she is far more intuitive than her passionate young lover (Geoffrey Horne), and certainly far more intelligent than Niven's latest girl, the empty-headed Mylene Demongeot.

Into this casual atmosphere comes chic Parisian Kerr, garbed in Givenchy outfits and Cartiers jewelry, but filled with bourgeoise conservatism. Because she refuses to become a toy in Niven's menagerie, the pampered widower finds he must promise marriage to her to satisfy his amorous goals. With Niven's playful smile and twinkling eyes, one cannot imagine his Raymond being faithful to the overly repressed Kerr for very long, should they marry. This clash of opposing spirits leads to the tragic denouement of *Bonjour Tristesse*.

Onscreen, the 1920s had their vamps, the 1930s their golddiggers, the 1940s their domestic pleasers, but the 1950s saw a reflection of the new, freer morality in which old ideals were being flaunted. In films, Kerr would become the staunchest exponent of the young matron caught between two sets of morals: starchy upright society with its code which demands righteous decorum, and the new personal standard which permits as much sexual freedom as the individual desires. Kerr's Anne Larsen could cope with a straight-laced existence in cosmopolitan Paris, but once within the influence of Niven's villa life, she is lured away from moral stance by the promise of marriage. With emotional fulfillment so close at hand, she visibly loosens her tensions, and attempts to accept some of Niven's leisurely life style. However, she is still too unsure of herself to step forth as a liberated person. In an admirably gauged scene she happens upon Niven engaging in frivolity with the light-headed Demongeot, and, worst of all, hears them poking fun at her pervading primness. Distraught beyond words, Kerr stifles her screams and sobbing hysterically drives away, soon to die in a road "accident." Not an easy scene to make successful on the screen, but Kerr was capable of that and much more. As William K. Zinsser *(New York Herald-Tribune)* observed, ". . . she gives the movie its few moments of truth and genuine anguish."

Because Niven's playboy role was so much more on the surface with its one-dimensional roué characteristics, he was far more susceptible than Kerr to critical chiding for his relaxed performance in *Bonjour Tristesse*. "David Niven is a deft actor, and in this film he tries his best, but at heart he is an English gentleman and no amount of wishing will turn him into a French rake waging a series of 'naughty' amours" [Zinsser *(New York Herald-Tribune)*].

Back in 1958, on-location photography still had a novelty for filmgoers, and in *Bonjour Tristesse* these setting did a great deal to instill an expansive ambiance to the proceedings, whether in the color flashbacks or the black and white lensing of the present scenes. Juliette Greco, who would soon flounder so badly in a misguided Hollywood-governed career, provided an authentic Gallic touch by her singing of the haunting title tune by Georges Auric and Arthur Laurents.

# SEPARATE TABLES
*(United Artists, 1958) 98M.*

Producer, Harold Hecht; director, Delbert Mann; based on the play by Terence Rattigan; screenplay, Rattigan, John Gay; music, David Raskin; songs, Harry Warren and Harold Adamson; assistant director, Thomas F. Shaw; gowns for Miss Hayworth, Edith Head; costumes, Mary Grant; production designer, Harry Horner; art director, Edward Carrere; set decorator, Edward G. Boyle; makup, Harry Maut, Frank Prehoda; camera, Charles Lang, Jr.; editor, Marjorie Fowler, Charles Ennis.

Rita Hayworth (Ann Shankland); Deborah Kerr (Sibyl Railton-Bell); David Niven (Major Pollock); Wendy Hiller (Miss Cooper); Burt Lancaster (John Malcolm); Gladys Cooper (Mrs. Railton-Bell); Cathleen Nesbitt (Lady Matheson); Felix Aylmer (Mr. Fowler); Rod Taylor (Charles); Audrey Dalton (Jean); May Hallatt (Miss Meacham); Priscilla Morgan (Doreen); Hilda Plowright (Mabel).

New York Premiere: Astor and Trans-Lux Normandie Theatres—
December 18, 1958
New York Television Debut: Channel 9—October 3, 1965

## Synopsis

Seated at separate tables in the dining room of a small private seaside hotel in Bournemouth, England, are a group of resident guests eating their dinner. They include Major Pollock, who continually reminisces about the North African campaign of World War II, the aloof and domineering Mrs. Railton-Bell, her spinsterish daughter Sybil, who secretly loves the Major but is too frightened by life to tell him, the pleasant Lady Matheson, who is controlled by her friend Mrs. Railton-Bell, lonely, elderly professor Fowler, racing buff Miss Meacham, and the unmarried young lovers, medical student Charles and his girlfriend Jean. Not present in the dining room is John Malcom, the American writer, who exists more for his drink than for his promise to wed the drab hotel proprietress Miss Cooper. The quiet hotel life is shattered when John's ex-wife Ann, an aging neurotic socialite, suddenly appears. In addition, news is circulated that the major, really just an ex-supply depot lieutenant, has been arrested for molesting women patrons in the local movie theatre. Mrs. Railton-Bell demands that the major leave at once, but the calmer Miss Cooper insists that the decision should rest with the major himself. Meantime, Ann, who has been quarreling with John, admits that she is at the time of life where she desperately needs someone to love and be loved by. At the same time John discovers new facets of himself from the self-sacrificing Miss Cooper. The following morning, preparatory to leaving, the major enters the dining rooms where the guests are breakfasting. He is acknowledged by everyone present, except Mrs. Railton-Bell. When Sybil gathers the courage to defy her mother and to speak to the major, he sends the cab away.

◆ ◆ ◆

The novelty of Terence Rattigan's efficient drama which opened on Broadway in October, 1956, with Margaret Leighton and Eric Portman repeating their London roles, was that the show was divided into two playlets with the leads playing Ann and John in the first act, and Sibyl and the Major in the second. The only storyline overlap was the British seaside resort locale. Onstage the events were separated by a month, onscreen by less than twenty hours. "The effect is just a trifle too tidy for the free-ranging film form" *(Saturday Review)*.

David Niven and Deborah Kerr, who had added such stature to *Bonjour Tristesse,* were quickly signed to join the cast of this multi-faceted, poor man's *Grand Hotel.* The filmed interaction between these two smooth players quickly overshadowed the oncamera friction and reconciliation between co-stars Burt Lancaster and Rita Hayworth, and made Kerr and Niven the true lead players of this static stage-bound drama.

Both Niven and Kerr were stringently doctored by cosmetics for their *Separate Tables* parts: he with white hair, moustache, and goatee, and she with a personality-altering mousey brown flat hairdo. Niven was never more unctuously British ("eh," "ekchully," and "quate") or prissily shabby as he peered timorously over his newspapers, biting his fingernails all the while. Kerr had never been more repressed by externals (tyrannical mother Gladys Cooper) or internals (her deep-rooted inferiority complex). Could two more pathetic souls ever be drawn together for a movie drama? How pitiable was Sibyl who, amidst finger and lip twitching, confides to the withdrawn Major that she has been studying the newspapers and has found a possible job as a telephone switchboard operator. It is this sad creature who hopes Niven—to her a splendidly dashing adventurer—will help to persuade Cooper to allow Kerr to venture out on her own in the world.

From the point in time that Kerr learns of Niven's shocking conduct (she becomes physically ill at the news), it is obvious that the scenario is building to a climactic encounter between the two, not a scene of volatile expression, but one of quiet nervous release as each unleashes unbearable burdens. Thus, within each other's company, they have the strength to admit their follies, to explain rather than apologize for the weaknesses of spirit which have brought each of them to this cul-de-sac. This scene represents one of the best examples of Niven and Kerr at their ensemble playing. The *London Times* complimented these players who by ". . . giving inarticulate accounts of their own forms of loneliness and fear in a world that is too much for them, transcend the entertainment superficialities which are the common coin of *Separate Tables* as a whole."

It is only a pity that one major weak point within the screenplay of *Separate Tables* quenched some of the possible expansion of both Niven's

703

and Kerr's characterization. Had the scenario allowed all the people at the Beauregard Hotel to interact with one another, beyond the crisis over Niven's moral behavior, one might have gained further perspective on each player's personality. For example, it is easily understandable that Kerr would have had little comprehension of the turmoil engulfing Hayworth's Ann, but there should have more interplay between Kerr and Wendy Hiller's Miss Cooper. The latter two are both plain-looking English women who have enjoyed too little of life's wonders for different, but complementary, reasons.

*Separate Tables* provided Niven with his first Best Actor Oscar, while Kerr in her fourth Oscar nomination in six years, lost to Susan Hayward who won for *I Want to Live.* Hiller won the Best Supporting Actress Academy Award for *Separate Tables,* while the film itself was nominated but lost to the musical *Gigi.*

## CASINO ROYALE
### *(Columbia, 1967) C-131M.*

Producers, Charles K. Feldman, Jerry Bresler; associate producer, John Dark; directors, John Huston, Ken Hughes, Val Guest, Robert Parrish, Joe McGrath; additional sequences, Guest; suggested by the novel by Ian Fleming; screenplay, Wolf Mankowitz, John Law; assistant directors, Roy Baird, John Stoneman, Carl Mannin; second unit directors, Richard Talmadge, Anthony Squire; production designer, Michael Stringer; art directors, John Howell, Ivor Beddoes, Lionel Couch; set decorator, Terence Morgan; music-music director, Burt Bacharach; song, Bacharach and Hal David; choreography, Tutte Lemkow; titles-montage effects, Richard Williams; sound, John W. Mitchell, Sash Fisher, Bob Jones, Dick Langford; camera, Jack Hildyard; additional camera, John Wilcox, Nicolas Roeg; editor, Bill Lenny.

David Niven (Sir James Bond); Peter Sellers (Evelyn Tremble); Ursula Andress (Vesper Lynd); Orson Welles (Le Chiffre); Joanna Pettet (Mata Bond); Daliah Lavi (The Detainer); Deborah Kerr (Agent Mimi); Woody Allen (Jimmy Bond); William Holden (Ransome); Charles Boyer (Le Grand); John Huston (M); Kurt Kasznar (Smernov); Terence Cooper (Cooper); Barbara Bouchet (Moneypenny); Angela Scoular (Buttercup); Tracey Crisp (Heather); Elaine Taylor (Peg); Gabriella Licudi (Eliza); Jacqueline Bisset (Miss Goodthighs); Alexandra Bastedo (Meg); Anna Quayle (Frau Hoffner); Derek Nimmo (Hadley); George Raft (Himself); Jean-Paul Belmondo (French Legionnaire); Peter O'Toole (Piper); Stirling Moss (Driver); Ronnie Corbett (Polo); Colin Gordon (Casino Director); Bernard Cribbins (Taxi Driver); Tracy Reed (Fang Leader); John Bluthal (Casino Doorman/M. I. 5 Man); Geoffrey Bayldon (Q); John Wells (Q's

Assistant); Duncan Macrae (Inspector Mathis); Graham Stark (Cashier); Chic Murray (Chic); Jonathan Routh (John); Richard Wattis (British Army Officer); Vladek Sheybal (Le Chiffre's Representative); Percy Herbert (First Piper); Penny Riley (Control Girl); Jeanne Roland (Captain of Guards).

New York Premiere: Loew's Capital and Cinema I Theatre—
    April 28, 1967
New York Television Debut: CBS—September 18, 1970

## Synopsis

Long after his fateful affair with Mata Hari, the one and only Sir James Bond now very middle-aged and unadventurous, is called out of retirement to combat the international crime cartel called SMERSH which is threatening to dominate the world. When Bond's superior McTarry (M) is killed, Bond heads northward to Scotland to pay his respects to the widow, Lady Fiona, unaware that she is really SMERSH agent Mimi. When Bond later rejects her passionate pleas of love, Lady Fiona renounces worldly goods and becomes a cloistered nun. Thereafter Bond snaps into action, deciding to outwit his omnipresent enemy by enlisting the aid of several agents, all to be called 007. These agents include the world's wealthiest and most alluring spy, Vesper Lynd; Evelyn Tremble, the inventor of an unbeatable baccarat system; brutishly strong Cooper, who is unassailable to women's advances; and Bond's flesh and blood, Mata Bond. Bond orders Evelyn to match SMERSH's Le Chiffre at the gaming tables of the fabled Casino Royale, outmaneuvering SMERSH's attempt to refill their depleted coffers. Later Vesper is kidnapped and Evelyn dies in an attempt to save her. Meanwhile Mata is onto a clue, but she is abducted and carried aboard a flying saucer. Sir James jumps into action, quickly discovering that the arch fiend known as Dr. Noah is really his own black sheep nephew, Jimmy Bond. Through the use of another operative, The Detainer, Jimmy is tricked into swallowing an explosive capsule, which soon explodes the Casino Royale, killing all its occupants, save Sir James who made a timely exit.

◆◆◆

Although made after *Eye of the Devil*, *Casino Royale* reached the screen first, professionally reuniting Deborah Kerr with David Niven for the first time since 1958. In the interim, Niven's career had wavered in and out of focus with such hit comedies as *Ask Any Girl* (1959) and *The Pink Panther* (1964) and such flops as *Bedtime Story* (1964) and *Lady L* (1966). While the super actioner *The Guns of Navarone* (1961) had showcased his leading man qualities to good effects, the contrived roadshow epic *55 Days at Peking* (1963) had dimmed his boxoffice worth. Since Niven had acquitted himself so adroitly in the lead of an unjustly ignored master spy spoof, *Where the Spies Are* (1965), it was unsurprising that the fifty-six-year-old luminary would be selected° as the focal figure for the twelve-million-dollar *Casino Royale*. Meanwhile, Deborah Kerr, who had divorced and married again, had won another Oscar nomination [for *The Sundowners* (1959)] and renewed her dramatic screen reputation with nicely-shaded performances of repressed damsels in *The Chalk Garden* and *The Night of the Iguana*, both made in 1964. The spirited drawing room comedy *The Grass Is Greener*, which teamed her for a third time with both Robert Mitchum and Cary Grant, substantiated the fact that elegant comedy was yet another facet of the Kerr talent. The vulgar and obvious *Marriage on the Rocks* (1965) merely confirmed that oncamera, as well as off, Kerr enjoyed running lightly with Frank Sinatra and his rat pack.

*Casino Royale*°° has been justifiably termed a "conglomerization of frenzied situations, 'in' gags and special effects, lacking discipline and cohesion" (*Variety*). Most of the intelligentsia rightly scoffed at Charles K. Feldman's overly ambitious attempt to outBond James Bond by creating a super sendup to the 007-Sean Connery-United Artists movie series. Using the same slapstick satirical approach that had worked for his hit *What's New Pussycat?* (1965), producer Feldman required the services of five directors, three scripters (plus the unbilled contributions of Val Guest, Ben Hecht, Joseph Heller, Terry Southern, and Billy Wilder) and the participation of twenty name performers to pummel the 131-minute feature into releasable shape. Unfortunately for Columbia Pictures and its backers, *Casino Royale* was "the sort of reckless, disconnected nonsense that could be telescoped or stopped at any point" [Bosley Crowther *(New York Times)*]. Too many wearied viewers wished it had concluded before it started. The film only grossed a pale $10.2 million in distributors' domestic rentals.

Niven would later claim that after he had first met with Feldman in his plush offices to read a handsome leather-bound folio copy of the *Casino Royale* script, and had agreed to star in the venture, the scenario had been thrust back into a combination safe and that was the last time he ever saw it. *Time* magazine observed of Niven's performance in the burlesque antic called *Casino Royale*, ". . . [he] comes off best because his stylish acting floats far above the script's witless, single-entendre standard: 'Beauty is only skin deep. How about some skin-diving?'"

Each critic seemed to have his least favorite moments in *Casino Royale* and the Scottish sequence came in for its share of written abuses. The

°Niven and James Bond creator Ian Fleming had been friends for years, and Fleming at first balked at anyone else but Niven playing the character onscreen, but he had little power of choice in the matter.

°°Author Fleming had allowed CBS's "Climax" series to produce a version of *Casino Royale* on television in October, 1954, with Barry Nelson starred; thereafter the screen rights were sold in 1955 and eventually were assigned to producer Charles K. Feldman. Thus, *Casino Royale* was not part of the deal made with producers Harry Saltzman and R. Broccoli in 1961 for their projected United Artists series.

bonnie northland episode found Kerr's outrageously broad burr only matched by her frenetic wisping about the castle a la Lady Macbeth, doing a highland fling, blowing a hunting horn, or vamping a perplexed Niven with her voluptuous daughters providing back-up support. "I don't like *Casino Royale*," argued Andrew Sarris of *The Village Voice*, "particularly when John Huston is flaunting the hardened arteries of David Niven and Deborah Kerr in a Scottish castle." There is no doubt that both stars were hamming their nonsensical interlude to the point of high camp, but these two performers were hardly ready for the Geritol set with their display of post-adolescent prankishness. Judith Crist *(New York World Journal Tribune)* went on record as stating, "Let us here take note that Miss Kerr in a sweeping black lace negligee makes all those mini-bikini types on hand look pretty darn Twiggy in the sexpot department." In short, at age forty-six, Kerr still had her own brand of "oomph" and was well complemented by Niven's dapper roguishness.

When all was said and done, *Casino Royale,* save for its distinctively Tijuana Brass-played theme song, came and went, with Bondian adherents relieved to return to the more nubile cinema world of the "real" 007, namely Sean Connery (later supplanted, first by George Lazenby and then more recently by Roger Moore). Anyone caring to recall the overpuffed *Casino Royale* usually gives credit to David Niven ". . . unruffled as ever playing the impeccable Edwardian-suited Sir James Bond" [Kathleen Carroll *(New York Daily News)*].

### EYE OF THE DEVIL
#### *(MGM, 1967) 90M.*

Producer, Martin Ransohoff, John Calley; director, J. Lee Thompson; based on the novel *Day of the Arrow* by Philip Loraine; screenplay, Robin Estridge, Dennis Murphy; art director, Elliot Scott; music, Gary McFarland; costumes, Julie Harris, John Furness; titles, Maurice Binder; assistant director, Basil Rayburn; sound, A. W. Watkins; camera, Erwin Hillier; editor, Ernest Walter.

Deborah Kerr (Catherine de Montfaucon); David Niven (Philippe de Montfaucon); Donald Pleasence (Pere Dominic); Edward Mulhare (Jean-Claude Ibert); Flora Robson (Countess Estelle); Emlyn Williams (Alain de Montfaucon); Sharon Tate (Odile); David Hemmings (Christian de Caray); John Le Mesurier (Dr. Monnet); Suky Appleby (Antoinette); Donald Bisset (Rennard); Robert Duncan (Jacques); Michael Miller (Grandee).

New York Premiere: Showcase—December 6, 1967
New York Television Debut: CBS—May 10, 1972

## Synopsis

When the Marquis de Bellac, Philippe de Montfaucon, is told that for the third year running his Bordeaux vineyards have failed to produce a worthy harvest, he tells his wife Catherine to remain in Paris while he goes to the ancestral chateau. But Catherine follows a few days later, accompanied by their two children, Antoinette and Jacques. She finds a strange welcome from the local dignitaries, including the priest, Pere Dominic. More peculiar is the cold behavior of Philippe's aunt Countess Estelle, and the unexplainable sulkiness of Christian de Caray and his sister Odile. While her husband is away in town, Catherine wanders through the chateau and comes upon the supposedly absent Philippe and twelve other unknown men involved in a ceremonial rite. Later she learns that Philippe's father, supposedly dead, is really alive and living in a turret of the chateau. When he informs her of the horrible fate awaiting Philippe (the head of the Montfaucon must offer himself as a blood sacrifice to restore the fertility of the crops), Catherine races to find help. However, she is brought back by Pere Dominic. Later she does manage to escape, but it is too late, for Philippe has undergone the death ritual with Christian shooting the arrow into the landowner's heart. Catherine and her two children leave the chateau the next day, she being unaware that Pere Dominic has already alerted young Jacques to his obligation as the new Marquis of Bellac.

◆—◆—◆

The most intriguing aspect of this picture is its checkered production history. Filming began in Paris on September 13, 1965, with on-location work in the Bordeaux wine country of France. On November 25th, lensing of the film, then known as *13*, was suspended in London due to the "back" injury of David Niven's co-star, Kim Novak. After a two week waiting period, filming resumed on December 13, 1965, with none other than Niven's pal, Deborah Kerr, now in the lead female role, and all of Novak's previously shot footage to be refilmed with Kerr. In the course of the lengthy production, Terry Southern worked on the screenplay, and such directorial talent as Michael Anderson, Sidney J. Furie, and Arthur Hiller came and went. The film, finally released by MGM on a weak double-bill (with another flop, *The Girl and the General*), failed miserably at the boxoffice. ". . . this picture wins the award as the biggest nothing of the week" [Archer Winsten *(New York Post)*].

Presenting aspects of witchcraft on the screen is a tricky business. Recent years have seen the grand guignol approach of *The Devil's Bride* (1968), the ritualistic reality of the highly commercial *Rosemary's Baby* (1968), or the faltering cerebral approach of the inconclusive *The Possession of Joel Delaney* (1972). *Eye of the Devil* is a little bit of everything and not much of anything, as it uses an impressive chateau setting for its gothic horror tale but loses credibility in the mock charades of the performers who amble through a very confused account. *Variety* sassed,

"The film is enough to put the Devil out of business" because "some flashy editing bits and overly-mobile camera work fail in attempts to substitute physical motion for plot action."

One feels embarrassed for two such seemingly intelligent adults as Niven and Kerr having been trapped in this tripe. Niven floats stoically through the film, occasionally furrowing his brow in mock concern at the bizarre occurrences transpiring, while Kerr, with oversized torment in her eyes, lags several hysterical paces behind the scenario in accentuating the dreaded portents awaiting her oncamera. It was a far cry from Kerr's halcyon days when she emoted in a true gothic tale, *The Innocents* (1961), a refined rendition of Henry James' *The Turn of the Screw.*

*Eye of the Devil* was so antiquated by the time of its delayed release that David Hemmings, who had had but a brief role as the silver arrow shooting youth, had already become a movie celebrity with *Blow-Up* (1967).

## PRUDENCE AND THE PILL
### *(Twentieth Century-Fox, 1968) C-92M.*

Producers, Kenneth Harper, Ronald Kahn; director, Fielder Cook; based on the novel by Hugh Mills; screenplay, Mills; assistant director, Ted Sturgis; production designer, Wilfrid Shingleton; art director, Fred Carter; set decorator, John Jarvis; music-music director, Bernard Ebbinghouse; titles, Richard Williams; animator, Errol Le Cain; sound, Albert Ross; camera, Ted Moore; editor, Norman Savage.

Deborah Kerr (Prudence Hardcastle); David Niven (Gerald Hardcastle); Robert Coote (Henry Hardcastle); Irina Demick (Elizabeth); Joyce Redman (Grace Hardcastle); Judy Geeson (Geraldine Hardcastle); Keith Michell (Dr. Alan Hewitt); Dame Edith Evans (Lady Roberta Bates); David Dundas (Tony Bates); Vickery Turner (Rose); Hugh Armstrong (Ted); Peter Butterworth (Chemist); Moyra Fraser (Woman in Tea Shop); Annette Kerr (Gerald's Secretary); Harry Towb (Race Track Official); Jonathan Lynn (Chemist's Assistant).

New York Premiere: Victoria and Murray Hill Theatres—May 23, 1968
New York Television Debut: ABC—December 2, 1973

### Synopsis

Although respectably wed, Gerald and Prudence Hardcastle hardly operate within the same spheres of life. Gerald is having an affair with Elizabeth, while Prudence is making the best of a dreary domestic situation by rendezvousing with her doctor, Allan Hewitt. Gerald's brother and sister-in-law, Henry and Grace Hardcastle are contentedly married, but find their cozy world ruffled when Grace becomes pregnant, all because their spirited daughter Geraldine has substituted aspirin for her mother's birth control pills. This crisis gives Gerald the idea of doing the same with Prudence's pills, hoping that she might become pregnant by her physician lover and thus file for a divorce, allowing Gerald to wed Elizabeth. But Gerald's plan is thwarted by the family maid Rose who borrows Prudence's pills and substitutes what she thinks are vitamins, but which are really birth control pills given her by her boyfriend Ted. After Rose becomes pregnant, Gerald realizes the problem and again substitutes aspirins for Prudence's pills. In the meantime, Geraldine, having exhausted her supply of pills, becomes pregnant by her lover, Tony Bates. The only one pleased by this turn of events is Tony's elderly guardian, Lady Roberta Bates. Eventually Prudence does become pregnant by Hewitt, as does Elizabeth by Gerald, so Gerald gives Prudence her divorce, and the couples rematch to everyone's satisfaction.

◆◆◆

With the advent of the mass-produced birth control pill in the later 1960s, it might have been thought that this revolutionary means to social change would have inspired several rollicking screen comedies, but to date, *Prudence and the Pill* is the one major motion picture to utilize the oral contraceptive as a point of departure for comedy. Despite the elegance of its cast and its color-lensed appointments, the picture raced in and out of theatres with little boxoffice results. Even the usual booster of the National Catholic Office rating the film "morally objectionable in part for all" did not prompt a rash of customers. "An arch, old-fashioned bedroom farce decked out in elegant interior decorations and photography and a couple of new-fangled twists in traditional movie morality" [Joseph Gelmis *(Newsday)*].

*Prudence and the Pill* was plagued by its own share of production problems which certainly did not lead to a spontaneous flow of onscreen action. MGM at one point withdrew its financing of the project, and Twentieth Century-Fox pinch hit in the production. Three-fifths of the way through filming, director Fiedler Cook left the project because of "differences of opinion" and the uncredited Ronald Neame completed the picture, "using Cook's style."

As *Newsweek* magazine carefully pointed out, ". . . stripped of pharmaceutical overtones, this overdressed exercise in insemination turns out to be just another British comedy of manners." It seems hardly a coincidence that the surname of most of the characters in *Prudence and the Pill* is Hardcastle, which conjurs up memories of the lusty Hardcastle family in Oliver Goldsmith's Restoration comedy *She Stoops to Conquer* (1773). Within the confines of the latest David Niven-Deborah Kerr film, there is an assortment of wildly self-indulgent souls, playing cat and mouse with each other in a lame effort to retain a semblance of propriety about his/her extracurricular love making. Even the servants flirt with the same indifference as the privileged upper class, while, likewise, relegating worldly problems to the television and spending most of their time popping in and out of bed, with one eye fastened on the door for fear of an intrusion by a rightfully indignant lovemate. Not that *Prudence and the Pill* in the final analysis actually condoned the utilization of Thenol as an inducement for immorality, for within the picture several of the women do become pregnant, demonstrating in its own inverted way that the pill is meant only for proper moral use.

With Kerr soon about to succumb to the rage of nudity onscreen in *The Gypsy Moths* and *The Arrangement*, both of 1969, it was a discreet relief to find her fully clothed in Julie Harris-designed costumes in *Prudence and the Pill*. The actress was particularly fetching in her array of alluring peignoirs. After so many years as the totally repressed perfect lady or cinema spinster, it was diverting to observe Kerr in the guise of a lusty adulteress, even if one might have wished she had picked someone more adventurous than the rather staid Harley Street doctor of Keith Michell. After all, debonair Niven, her estranged but polite spouse, did have delectable Irina Demick stashed away in a comfortable mews house. It only seems fair. . . .

Among the supporting cast of this picture which was rated "as stylishly British as high tea at the Dorchester" [Wanda Hale *(New York Daily News)*] were Judy Geeson as an overly-coy ingenue, mercifully brief in her onscreen presence. On the other hand there was too little of Dame Edith Evans as the contemporary-thinking, chic aunt. Evans dominated the film's most delicious moment as she imperturbably walks across a much-trafficked race course track, oblivious to the whirring vehicles zipping past her.

Hollis Alpert *(Saturday Review),* among others, had kinder words for the Niven-Kerr teamsmanship than for the movie: "Two impeccable professionals who know exactly when and how to raise an elegant eyebrow, to deliver a poisonous sally. Because of this they impart an aura of propriety and taste to what could otherwise have become a leering, tasteless mess."

## THE YEARS AFTER

In the seemingly vanishing world of style and grace, it was indeed a swell bonus to movie viewers that financial, artistic, and social circumstances permitted the several screen teamings of David Niven and Deborah Kerr. Their mature cinema characterizations did much to offset the trivia of the youth-oriented post-1940s movies, proving that middle age on-camera does not necessarily end emotional and sensual experimentation. In fact, as the better of the urbane stars' joint pictures aptly demonstrated, the seasoning (weathering?) of a person's soul can make life's adventures more pertinent and zestier.

Obviously, the increasingly slender feature film market has diminished the commercial feasibility of the two stars working together in future films, let alone individually. But both have reasserted their prominence in other areas of the lively arts. Kerr has returned to the London and the American stage in *The Day after the Fair*, an adaptation of a Thomas Hardy work, again putting her radiant good looks and sensitively honed skills to fine use. Niven, meanwhile, has emerged as a refreshingly modest but witty autobiographer in his best-selling *The Moon's a Balloon* (1972) and is presently at work on a novel, in addition to narrating a series of television specials entitled "Around the World."

Paul Newman and Joanne Woodward (circa 1961)

# Chapter 26

# Paul Newman
# &
# Joanne Woodward

## PAUL NEWMAN

**5′ 11″**
**165 pounds**
**Light brown hair**
**Blue eyes**
**Aquarius**

*Real name: Same. Born January 26, 1925, Shaker Heights, Ohio. Married Jacqueline Witte (1947), children: Scott, Susan, Stephanie; divorced, 1956. Married Joanne Woodward (1958), children: Eleanor, Tessa, Cleo.*

FEATURE FILMS:

*The Silver Chalice* (WB, 1954)
*Somebody Up There Likes Me* (MGM, 1956)
*The Rack* (MGM, 1956)
*Until They Sail* (MGM, 1957)
*The Helen Morgan Story* (WB, 1957)
*The Long, Hot Summer* (20th, 1958)
*The Left-Handed Gun* (WB, 1958)
*Rally 'Round the Flag, Boys!* (20th, 1958)
*Cat on a Hot Tin Roof* (MGM, 1958)
*The Young Philadelphians* (WB, 1959)
*From the Terrace* (20th, 1960)

*Exodus* (UA, 1960)
*The Hustler* (20th, 1961)
*Paris Blues* (UA, 1961)
*Sweet Bird of Youth* (MGM, 1962)
*Hemingway's Adventures of a Young Man* (20th, 1962)
*Hud* (Par., 1963)
*A New Kind of Love* (Par., 1963)
*The Prize* (MGM, 1963)
*What a Way To Go!* (20th, 1964)
*The Outrage* (MGM, 1964)
*Lady L* (MGM, 1965)

Torn Curtain (Univ., 1966)
Harper (WB, 1966)
Hombre (20th, 1967)
Cool Hand Luke (WB, 1967)
The Private War of Harry Frigg (Univ., 1968)
Winning (Univ., 1969)
Butch Cassidy and the Sundance Kid (20th, 1969)

WUSA (Par., 1970)
Sometimes a Great Notion (Univ., 1971)
Pocket Money (National General, 1972)
The Life and Times of Judge Roy Bean (National General, 1972)
The Mackintosh Man (WB, 1973)
The Sting (Univ., 1973)
The Towering Inferno (20th, 1974)
Ryan's the Name (WB, 1975)


# JOANNE WOODWARD

**5′ 4″**
**108 pounds**
**Blonde hair**
**Green eyes**
**Pisces**

*Real name: Joanne Gignilliat Woodward. Born February 27, 1930, Thomasville, Georgia. Married Paul Newman (1958), children: Eleanor, Tessa, Cleo.*

FEATURE FILMS:

Count Three and Pray (Col., 1955)
A Kiss Before Dying (UA, 1956)
The Three Faces of Eve (20th, 1957)
No Down Payment (20th, 1957)
The Long, Hot Summer (20th, 1958)
Rally 'Round the Flag, Boys! (20th, 1958)
The Sound and the Fury (20th, 1959)
The Fugitive Kind (UA, 1959)
From the Terrace (20th, 1960)
Paris Blues (UA, 1961)
The Stripper (20th, 1963)
A New Kind of Love (Par., 1963)
Signpost to Murder (MGM, 1964)

A Big Hand for the Little Lady (WB, 1966)
A Fine Madness (WB, 1966)
Rachel, Rachel (WB-7 Arts, 1968)
Winning (Univ., 1969)
WUSA (Par., 1970)
They Might Be Giants (Univ., 1971)
The Effect of Gamma Rays on Man-in-the-Moon Marigolds (20th, 1972)
Summer Wishes, Winter Dreams (Col., 1973)
Ryan's the Name (WB, 1975)

Advertisement for **The Long, Hot Summer** (20th, 1958)

In **The Long, Hot Summer**

Percy Helton, Paul Newman, and Joanne Woodward in **Rally 'Round the Flag, Boys!** (20th, 1958)

In **From the Terrace** (20th, 1960)

In **Paris Blues** (UA, 1961)

At Grauman's Chinese Theatre cement ceremony (June, 1963)

In **A New Kind of Love** (Par., 1963)

In **Winning** (Univ., 1969)

In **WUSA** (Par., 1970)

# THE LONG, HOT SUMMER
*(Twentieth Century-Fox, 1958) C-115M.*

Producer, Jerry Wald; director, Martin Ritt; based on the stories, *Barn Burning* and *The Spotted Horses*, and part of the novel *The Hamlet* by William Faulkner; screenplay, Irving Ravetch, Harriet Frank; art directors, Lyle R. Wheeler, Maurice Ransford; music, Alex North; song, Sammy Cahn and North; music director, Lionel Newman; assistant director, Eli Dunn; makeup, Ben Nye; costumes, Adele Palmer; camera, Joseph La Shelle; editor, Louis R. Loeffler.

Paul Newman (Ben Quick); Joanne Woodward (Clara Varner); Anthony Franciosa (Jody Varner); Orson Welles (Will Varner); Lee Remick (Eula Varner); Angela Lansbury (Minnie Littlejohn); Richard Anderson (Alan Stewart); Sarah Marshall (Agnes Stewart); Mabel Albertson (Mrs. Stewart); J. Pat O'Malley (Ratliff); William Walker (Lucius); George Dunn (Peabody); Jess Kirkpatrick (Armistead); Val Avery (Wilk); I. Stanford Jolley (Houstin); Nicholas King (John Fisher); Lee Erickson (Tom Shortly); Ralph Reed (J. V. Bookright); Terry Rangno (Pete Armistead); Steve Widders (Buddy Peabody); Jim Brandt (Linus Olds); Helen Wallace (Mrs. Houstin); Brian Corcoran (Harry Peabody); Byron Foulger (Harris); Victor Rodman (Justice of the Peace); Eugene Jackson (Waiter).

New York Premiere: Fine Arts and Mayfair Theatres—April 3, 1958
New York Television Debut: NBC—February 16, 1963

## Synopsis

Mississippian Ben Quick, like his late father, is reputed to be a quick-tempered man who settles his scores by barn-burning. As such, young Quick must constantly be one step ahead of his unsavory reputation. He arrives in Frenchman's Creek, a sleepy small town ruled over with an iron hand by bulbous Will Varner, a man who has easily cowed his weak-willed son Jody, but not his frustrated, spinsterish daughter Clara. Quick hires on as a sharecropper to Varner, the latter discovering after assorted clashes of will with the virile farmer that Quick might just well be the best man to wed Clara and inherit the vast Varner holdings. Meanwhile, Clara, long since tired of coping with her mother-dominated fiancé, Alan Stewart, finds herself attracted to Quick, but refuses to allow her father to railroad her into a hasty marriage with the brash upstart. She has her pride. However, when Quick saves Varner from a fiery death in a barn—a situation engineered by jealous Jody—Clara realizes her man has a great many good qualities. A double wedding is imminent, for Varner's long-standing mistress Minnie Littlejohn has finally cajoled Varner into doing right by her.

Under free-wheeling producer Jerry Wald, Twentieth Century-Fox had enjoyed tremendous commercial success with its *Peyton Place* (1957) and the next year the prolific packager and his studio strove to repeat the formula with a Southern-flavored soap opera counterpart. The results were not nearly as astounding at the boxoffice, but the film itself remains a startling representation of 1950s filmmaking, from its characterization clichés to the lush CinemaScope photography and the equally lush Alex North score. *Paul V. Beckley (New York Herald-Tribune)* recognized in this color feature "a seriousness that is not tasteless but has almost the dry lightness of the French style."

For source material, producer Wald turned the husband-and-wife scripting team of Irving Ravetch and Harriet Frank to the respected canon of William Faulkner, and from assorted stories and part of a novel they extracted a plot continuity that would function as a unified drama—no easy task with Faulkner prose. To populate the film, Wald and studio boss Buddy Adler relied on their omnibus casting theory—cram the production with a variety of studio young contractees and a smattering of seasoned veterans—a practice utilized to good results in Wald's *No Down Payment* (1957), *Mardi Gras* (1958), and *In Love and War* (1958). Fox had Joanne Woodward under contract, and she was already proving to be more resiliently versatile than the likes of her studio contemporaries which ranged from Joan Collins to Christine Carere to Patricia Owens to Sheree North. Woodward was tested for the role of Eula in *The Long, Hot Summer*, the flighty, flirtatious Dixie belle wife of Jody. However, Woodward recalls, "I begged to do Clara. I told the studio that if I had to play one more 'cukey' Southern girl [i.e., *Count Three and Pray* (1955), *The Three Faces of Eve* (1957)], I'd be tagged as the Una Merkel of our day." Wald heeded her request when the part of Clara could not be cast with a bigger name, and new studio contractee Lee Remick was substituted as the fetching Eula. Studio player Anthony Franciosa, who has "always" portrayed weak-willed men-children, was sandwiched into the production as the ineffectual Jody, and youngish character lead Angela Lansbury was hired as the good-natured plump middle-aged inn keeper Minnie Little-john. Wald and Fox considered it rather a coup to put Hollywood's errant genius, Orson Welles, then aged forty-two, into this movie, to portray a sixty-year-old variation of the fleshy Big Daddy of Tennessee Williams' *Cat on a Hot Tin Roof*. (Hollywood observers wondered how the itinerant actor-director would fare in the submissive position of being merely a player to another man's director, but he and helmer Martin Ritt worked amazingly well together.) For the focal role of Ben Quick, Fox borrowed thirty-three-year-old Paul Newman from Warner Bros., he having spent most of his slightly rebellious post-Broadway years on loan-out to MGM for various screen projects. At this point in his escalating screen career, Newman was still enduring the stigma of critical barbs which labeled him an imitation Marlon Brando both in looks and Actors' Studio method emoting.

Despite its embroidered side plots and heavy doses of extraordinarily vivid local color, *The Long, Hot Summer* is still at heart a boy-meets-girl and boy-eventually-gets-girl situation. What boosts the film to its remarkable sense of authenticity is the dry-lightning courting and conflicting of the two lead characters. As the young Mississippian redneck Newman possesses all the conceit and essential authoritarian nature that Woodward's Clara has endured for so long from Welles. If she has not succumbed to the elder's blustering techniques, she is not about to capitulate to the overt sexual advances of muscular stud Newman. That is, until the level of her sexual frustration rises higher than the temperature suffocating Frenchman's Bend. Five years of platonic engagement to the aesthete, Richard Anderson, have nearly done her in, not to mention the example of behind-twitching Remick, a girl ever anxious for a tumble in bed with Franciosa, particularly if the results might provide that heir her father-in-law so strongly demands.

Woodward and Newman engage in their strongest screen encounters more than midway through the film. During the course of a picnic outing, the two wander off by themselves, and sparked by Newman's cocksure boast that he could make her wake up in the morning with a smile on her face, Woodward launches into a sturdy essay on just what marriage and sex (in that order) mean to her, and exactly what she has to bring to such a union, and what she expects in return from her legal mate. A nonplused Newman tacitly admits defeat for the time being; but later one evening, while he is closing up Welles' general store, she stops by and they chat. He sweet-talks her and the love-hungry miss submits to his embrace, even responding passionately, before running off and calling him nothing but a lowdown barnburner. As expected, the denouement finds Woodward admitting, "I like you a whole lot, Ben Quick," and proud Welles confides to Lansbury, "Look at those two tomcats. Do I know human nature? Do I understand the workings of the human heart? I do."

By the time of the national release of *The Long, Hot Summer,* Paul Newman and Joanne Woodward, whose offcamera romancing during the making of this feature had given their screen performances an extra punch of vitality and public interest, had wed (January 29, 1958) and Woodward had won the Best Actress Oscar for her performance in *The Three Faces of Eve.* The combination of the screen's increasingly popular male sex symbol and a prestigious Academy Award-winning actress, did much to elevate the boxoffice take of *The Long, Hot Summer* and to establish the Newmans as several cuts above such other contemporary married screen teams as Tony Curtis and Janet Leigh or Natalie Wood and Robert Wagner.

Newman and Woodward earned the best critical reviews of their joint filmmaking to date for this 1958 entry. *Time* magazine rated Newman's performance "keen as a cradle-edged scythe" while Bosley Crowther (*New York Times*) opined, "He could, if the script would let him, develop a classic character." *Films in Review* heaped praise on

Woodward: "[She] is not merely a star; she is an actress . . . one of the best of our time."

Twentieth Century-Fox was invited to show *The Long, Hot Summer* in competition at the Cannes Film Festival where Newman was selected the Best Actor of 1958. Seven years later the feature would be used as the basis for a one season Twentieth Century-Fox and ABC network video series starring Roy Thinnes, Nancy Malone, Edmond O'Brien, and Ruth Roman. The drawn-out television outing was a watery concoction in no way resembling the much worthier original.

## RALLY 'ROUND THE FLAG, BOYS!
### *(Twentieth Century-Fox, 1958) C-106M.*

Producer-director, Leo McCarey; based on the novel by Max Shulman; screenplay, Claude Binyon, McCarey; assistant director, Jack Gertsman; music, Cyril J. Mockridge; music director, Lionel Newman; wardrobe, Charle LeMaire; art directors, Lyle R. Wheeler, Leland Fuller; set decorators, Walter M. Scott, Stuart A. Reiss; makeup, Ben Nye; sound, Eugene Grossman, Harry M. Leonard; special camera effects, L. B. Abbott; camera, Leon Shamroy; editor, Louis R. Loeffler.

Paul Newman (Harry Bannerman); Joanne Woodward (Grace Bannerman); Joan Collins (Angela Hoffa); Jack Carson (Captain Hoxie); Dwayne Hickman (Grady Metcalf); Tuesday Weld (Comfort Goodpasture); Gale Gordon (Colonel Thorwald); Tom Gilson (Opie); O. Z. Whitehead (Isaac Goodpasture); Ralph Osborn III (Danny Bannerman); Stanley Livingston (Peter); Jon Lormer (George Melvin); Joseph Holland (Manning Thaw); Burt Mustin (Milton Evans); Percy Helton (Waldo Pike); Nora O'Mahony (Betty O'Shiel); Richard Collier (Zack Crummitt); Murvyn Vye (Oscar Hoffa).

New York Premiere: Palace Theatre—December 23, 1958
New York Television Debut: NBC—March 7, 1964

### Synopsis

Harry Bannerman of Putnam's Landing, Connecticut, is the average suburban commuter, with a satisfactory New York City job, a pert wife, two normal sons, and a mortgaged ranch-style home. Bannerman's sole problem is his wife Grace, a woman so overwhelmingly civic-minded she has no time to offer her spouse a fair share of conjugal attention. As a result he is an easy mark for the community's femme fatale, Angela Hoffa, who is attracted to all men, except her own television executive husband. When the army initiates a top secret project at Putnam's Landing, Grace heads the opposition, sending Harry to Washington, D.C., as

725

spokesman. Grace follows to the capital planning to surprise her husband, which she does when she finds the innocent Harry fending off the advances of a pursuing Angela. With his marriage near collapse, Harry is ordered by the Army to serve as a liaison between the military and the irate townfolk of Putnam's Landing. His particular chore is to keep boorish Captain Hoxie from creating too many problems. After several chaotic skirmishes between the armed forces and the civilians, the townfolk are won over upon learning the secret project is a needed missile base. As Harry and Grace kiss and make up, they accidentally press the launching lever at the space station which sends a missile into space with the bewildered Captain Hoxie aboard.

◆◆◆

Leo McCarey had demonstrated a flair for handling a wide variety of screen comedy, ranging from Eddie Cantor's *The Kid from Spain* (1932), to the Marx Brothers' *Duck Soup* (1933) to Mae West's *Belle of the Nineties* (1934) and Irene Dunne's *The Awful Truth* (1937). Along the way he had helmed the well-regarded *Ruggles of Red Gap* (1935) and the offbeat tearjerker of old age *Make Way for Tomorrow* (1937). If the critics and public remembered the producer-director fondly for *Going My Way* (1944) and its follow-up, *The Bells of St. Mary's* (1945), there were cries of indignation at *My Son John* (1952) his heavy-handed pro-McCarthy paean to the Communist witch hunt. It was another five years before McCarey returned to filmmaking, then it was at Twentieth Century-Fox for *An Affair to Remember* (1957), a semi-musicalized remake of his prior *Love Affair* (1939).

For his next Fox film, McCarey replaced Frank Tashlin as director of Max Shulman's popular satirical novel, *Rally 'Round the Flag Boys!* In the new project, the producer-director-coscripter retained the Connecticut community setting and ribald high spirits of the book original, but deleted the story's Italian-American aspect. As part of the packaged deal, the studio handed McCarey a selection of its contract players, including Joanne Woodward and the once-again borrowed Paul Newman. Since both stars were complete newcomers to the genre of screen comedy, it was a touchy artistic situation for all concerned. As if to compensate for the leads' inexperience in the mirth-provoking field, McCarey doctored the film with a heavy lacing of lowbrow pandering, ranging from a fatuous and facetious offscreen commentary used throughout the picture to the overly broad performances of veteran funnymen Jack Carson and Gale Gordon, each as exaggerated, bombastic military types. Catapulted midway into the episodic story were the variant styles of budding funster, Tuesday Weld, as the teenage tease Comfort Goodpasture, her goofy moonstruck suitor Dwayne Hickman, and, most disconcerting of all, British import-contractee Joan Collins as a suburban femme fatale who proved more adroit in creating laughs from a swinging chandelier than from an oncamera barstool or living room sofa.

It might have been considered ideal type casting to have Newman and Woodward as an onscreen typical suburban couple with two children. However, there was something totally unbelievable about the premise which found him nearly subservient to her every whim. If the usually practical-minded Woodward seemed out of place as a whirlwind house-wife too wrapped up in a myriad of civic duties, it was asking almost too much of audiences to believe that virile, self-assured (lip-smacking with conceit) Newman could be such a hamstrung husband as to pas-sively accept the sexually slim situation at home. It was difficult indeed for anyone to accept that real-life newlywed Woodward onscreen would actually prefer campaigning for "Keep the Army Out" to keeping New-man at home. Newman, himself, would later admit that he was greatly ill at ease in the making of the first half of the film. And no wonder, what with Collins gauchely emoting as a rural siren leading sex-hungry harried commuter Newman into one unsubtle situation after another, including an overextended drunk scene. Woodward herself was a bit shrill as the young matron horrified when she pays a surprise visit to her husband in Washington and finds him in his hotel suite with his pants off and Collins frolicking about with only a sheet to cover her. Not much better was another scene in which Woodward crudely sniffs at Newman's shirt and goes into a tantrum because she smells telltale whiffs of some-one else's perfume. In this film Woodward was much better at directing her children's activities, making impassioned speeches to the townfolk, or leading the picket parades.

By the second half of *Rally 'Round the Flag Boys!*, all pretense at lighthearted comedy gives way to incredible farce; ranging from the local historical Fourth of July pageant in which Newman sinks in the bay on the miniature Mayflower ship, to the finale where the physically ram-bunctious couple have a rapprochement and begin kissing in the military space control center, thereby accidentally launching oafish Carson into space with a jabbering chimpanzee as his missile companion.

While the public accepted the overall shenanigans of *Rally 'Round the Flag Boys!* as upper crust television-style fare—decked out in Cinema-Scope and color—more than one critic carped, ". . . neither Paul Newman or Joanne Woodward seem particularly comfortable in their farcical roles" *(New York Herald-Tribune)*. *Cue* magazine observed that the screen couple ". . . tend to overact (and archly, at that). . . ." The most astute observation on the Newman-Woodward in tandem performance came from the *Toronto Globe and Mail:* "Newman and Miss Woodward try hard and this probably is the reason they don't make it."

### FROM THE TERRACE
*(Twentieth Century-Fox, 1960) C-144M.*

Producer-director, Mark Robson; based on the novel by John O'Hara;

screenplay, Ernest Lehman; assistant director, Hal Herman; art directors, Lyle R. Wheeler, Maurice Ransford, Howard Richman; set decorators, Walter M. Scott, Paul S. Fox; music, Elmer Bernstein; orchestrator, Edward B. Powell; gowns, Travilla; makeup, Ben Nye; sound, Harry M. Leonard, Alfred Bruzlin; special camera effects, L. B. Abbott, James B. Gordon; camera, Leo Tover; editor, Dorothy Spencer.

Paul Newman (Alfred Eaton); Joanne Woodward (Mary St. John); Myrna Loy (Martha Eaton); Ina Balin (Natalie); Leon Ames (Samuel Eaton); Elizabeth Allen (Sage Rimmington); Barbara Eden (Clemmie); George Grizzard (Lex Porter); Patrick O'Neal (Dr. Jim Roper); Felix Aylmer (MacHardie); Raymond Greenleaf (Fritz Thornton); Malcolm Atterbury (George Fry); Raymond Bailey (Mr. St. John); Ted de Corsia (Mr. Benziger); Howard Caine (Duffy); Mae Marsh (Governess); Kathryn Givney (Mrs. St. John); Dorothy Adams (Mrs. Benziger); Lauren Gilbert (Frolick); Blossom Rock (Nellie); Cecil Elliott (Josephine); Rory Harrity (Steve Rimmington); Ottola Nesmith (Lady Sevringham); Clive L. Halliday (Lord Sevringham); Gordon B. Clarke (Weinkoop); Ralph Dunn (Jones); Felippa Rock (Jean Duffy); Jimmy Martin (Sandy); William Quinn (Von Elm); Stuart Randall (Kelly); John Harding (Newton Orchid); Sally Winn (Mrs. Pearson); Elektra Rozanska (Mrs. Ripley).

New York Premiere: Paramount and Murray Hill Theatres—
  July 16, 1960
New York Television Debut: ABC—January 9, 1966

### Synopsis

Following World War II, Navy aviation lieutenant Alfred Eaton returns to his Pennsylvania home and his wealthy steel mill owner father and his alcoholic, adulterous mother. Determined to succeed on his own, Alfred relocates to New York and becomes a partner with his friend Lex Porter in a fledgling aeronautical enterprise. At Southampton, Alfred meets, romances, and eventually weds the socially prominent Mary St. John. When he saves the life of James Duncan Hardie's grandson, he is rewarded with a lucrative position in the gentleman's prestigious Wall Street investment firm. Alfred becomes extremely successful in his career, but at the expense of ignoring his demanding wife. She, in turn, resumes a past liaison with a sadistic psychiatrist named James Roper. After several contretemps with Mary, Alfred is dispatched to Mountain City, Pennsylvania, on business negotiations. There he promptly falls in love with Natalie Benzinger, the understanding daughter of a rural manufacturer. The lovers try to remain apart, but eventually Natalie comes to Manhattan and meets Alfred in a hotel room. A dishonest firm member learns of Alfred's affair and attempts to blackmail him into backing and completing an unstable investment project. But Alfred has reached his moment of truth and at the company board meeting, he states his case fully, quits his job, disavows Mary, and leaves to seek a happier existence with the waiting Natalie.

◆—◆—◆

Neither Paul Newman nor Joanne Woodward had ever been previously cast in to-the-manor-born screen roles, a factor which may have led them misguidedly into playing such roles in the cinema rendering of John O'Hara's bestselling but unwieldy novel. But just as each of them had fumbled in their initial motion picture comedy, so they both proved decidedly awkward at essaying a Hollywoodian conception of the East Coast social elite. Both performers had gained their cinema reputations playing anti-Establishment non-conformists always at loggerheads with society and themselves. But here the pair were adrift in a rarefied ambiance that required the likes of professionally confident Cary Grant and Irene Dunne. Woodward had the assistance of a white blonde wig and gowns by Travilla to bolster her new screen persona, but Newman had only his bag of acting tricks for support and too often he relied on his standard ploys: pouting, posturing, and lip-smacking bits of conceit. (Only when he is being rejected by his prospective Dupont family in-laws does the Newman of old come alive oncamera.) As John McCarten of *The New Yorker* magazine noted, Newman is ". . . encumbered with rhetoric, and in great, static closeups, he and Miss Balin schmooze so much that the spectator is inclined to wonder whether they are lovers or delegates to a political convention." Woodward came in for her share of critical raps. "For this role she has been chromium-plated and super-ficialized and does not seem to believe fully in the role she is portraying" [Paul V. Beckley (*New York Herald Tribune*)].

Not all the blame for *From the Terrace* lay with the Newmans. The thousand-page O'Hara novel was "shortened, manicured and deloused for movie consumption" (*New York Post*) and director Mark Robson was misled into assuming the truncated scenario could be guided along the same paths as his previous financial winner, *Peyton Place*. As a result, the overblown film emerged as "a long peep into a wealth of nothing" (*New York Times*). By telescoping the book's action which had spanned two World Wars, and eliminating the novel's juicier sex episodes, all that remained was the shell of a character study of Alfred Eaton, a man consumed by the great American dream of business success and money.

If anything detracted from the hollow bulk of *From the Terrace*, it was the picture's opening, well-publicized sequences which found the screen's former "perfect wife," actress Myrna Loy, cast as Newman's drunken mother, a woman seeking affection elsewhere because her industrialist husband (Leon Ames) has no time or love for her. Loy has never been adept at cinema melodramatics. Therefore, the combination of her uneasy presence with the jarring notion of the movie's past *Thin Man* series co-lead engaging onscreen in sordid liaisons and being verbally and physically assaulted, made anything that followed mostly anti-climactic.

Only less discriminating viewers, and evidently there were myriads of them, could or would accept Newman's sulking Alfred Eaton as a believable character. The script drenched him in bathos as he embarks on a career in the adult world, and equipped him only with the emotional maturity of a high school freshman. Woodward had an even more impossible role to play. On one hand she is the selfish, snappish executive's wife finding her pleasures as she will, but on the other hand, and far more realistically, she plays the wronged spouse, a woman almost totally ignored by her business-consumed husband. At least, unlike Loy's movie character, Woodward's Mary St. John has the grace not to get drunk in public or to be too blatant about her marital indiscretions.

To compound their faulty *From the Terrace* roles, Newman and Woodward were burdened with inappropriate co-performers. At best Ina Balin's Natalie was a sappy, starry-eyed miss. Her performance gave little indication that she understood the supposedly complex, pitiable character of Alfred Eaton. Mooning in bed with him or, at the film's finale, waiting with open arms for her lover across the picturesque brook, she was a half-dimensional mannequin defeated as much by her own anemic character interpretation as by the film's convention that the secondary leads should be nondescript people. Patrick O'Neal had little to do as the waspish psychiatrist lover of Woodward. He had to mouth catty lines, such as saying to Woodward on her wedding day, "You don't have to marry him to get what you want of him." If Balin was an unappealing soul mate for Newman, O'Neal seemed to be merely an enervating catalyst for the worst qualities of Woodward. Besides, unlike such past screen skunks as Dan Duryea or Richard Widmark, O'Neal offered few redeeming onscreen characteristics to amuse the jaded viewer.

Newman and Woodward did "share" one good scene in *From the Terrace*. During his stay in Mountain City, Pennsylvania, fuming, righteous Newman calls Woodward back in New York and again informs her, "I don't want this guy [O'Neal] in our apartment anymore." Newman hangs up, and the camera then focuses on Woodward in her bedroom. She turns away from the phone and states in a very wry way to none other than O'Neal, "You're not to come here anymore."


## PARIS BLUES
### (United Artists, 1961) 98M.

Executive producer, George Glass, Walter Seltzer; producer, Sam Shaw; director, Martin Ritt; based on the novel by Harold Flender; adaptation, Lulla Adler; screenplay, Jack Sher, Irene Kamp, Walter Bernstein; assistant director, Bernard Farrel; music adviser, William Byers; music, Duke Ellington; art director, Alexander Trauner; second unit director, Andre Smagghe; sound, Jo De Bretagne; camera, Christian Mattros; editor, Roger Dwyre.

Paul Newman (Ram Bowen); Joanne Woodward (Lillian Corning); Sidney Poitier (Eddie Cook); Louis Armstrong (Wild Man Moore); Diahann Carroll (Connie Lampson); Serge Reggiani (Michel Duvigne); Barbara Laage (Marie Seoul); Andre Luguet (Rene Bernard); Marie Versini (Nicole); Moustache (Drummer); Aaron Bridgers (Pianist); Guy Pederson (Bass Player); Maria Velasco (Pianist); Roger Blin (Gypsy Guitarist); Helene Dieudonne (The Pusher); Niko (Ricardo).

New York Premiere: Astor and Fine Arts Theatre—November 7, 1961
New York Television Debut: ABC—March 28, 1965

### Synopsis

American expatriated jazzmen Ram Bowen and Eddie Cook find Paris essential to their way of lives. Ram believes that only there can he express his musical abilities and Eddie insists the city provides a safe retreat from the racial problems of being a black man in the United States. Among their Parisian pals are Marie Seoul who operates the jazz club where they work and with whom Ram is having a casual affair, dope-addicted gypsy guitarist Michael Duvigne, and Wild Man Moore, the latter a famed trumpeter assisting Ram with his embryonic jazz concerto. Then one day the musician duo encounters two American tourists, Lillian Corning and Connie Lampson, who are on a two week Parisian holiday. The couples soon pair off, with Eddie deciding to return to America and face up to the discrimination issues. Ram loves Lillian and when his precious concerto is rejected by an impressario, he decides to give up his independence and compromise with life in the States. But eventually he realizes that he must push himself to his artistic limits in Paris. He sadly bids goodbye to the departing Lillian.

◆━━◆━━◆

The collapse of the Hollywood star system left few guidelines to control the assorted whims of freelance screen stars who were "hot properties" and could obtain needed financial backing for their latest creative brainstorms. Very often the luminaries' yen for cinematic experimentation led to costly commercial failures, which did not even have the redeeming virtue of being artistic successes. Such was the case of Paul Newman's flop (by now he was *the* superstar and Woodward *the* talented adjunct to packaged productions) *Paris Blues*. This film was doubly disappointing since it came close on the heels of his well-received *The Hustler* (1961). *Time* magazine diagnosed, "Director Martin Ritt . . . has obviously sought for artistic truth in this film, but the only general truth that *Blues* propounds is one that might have prevented this production; expatriates are a pretty dull bunch."

In its sociological aim, *Paris Blues* falls loosely somewhere between the film *The Defiant Ones* (1958) and the Broadway musical *No Strings* (1962). Like those two contrasting properties, which were financial win-

731

ners, *Paris Blues* attempted to treat the racial problem with mature direct-ness. Yet in its storyline delineation it constantly subjugated the black performers to the white players. Thus, whether in Barbara Laage's Left Bank cellar cafe or on the scenic streets of Paris, the personality and prob-lems of Newman's character always remain in strong focus while the par-allel emotional plights of co-star Sidney Poitier's piano player fade into the background. This structural deficiency is made all the more obvious by the more engaging characterizations of the black performers than their Caucasian counterparts, especially Diahann Carroll's Connie Lampson. She is an attractive chic lass, who not only knows the full score back home in America but on her Parisian lark also has enough sense to realize Poitier is a better romantic bet than Newman. (In the story Carroll firmly rejects Newman's crude amorous passes at her. Smart girl!)

What annoyed most critics and filmgoers was the seemingly extem-poraneous nature of *Paris Blues,* a picture which willfully meandered along the byways of the French capital with apparent indifference to a coherent, concise plot. It required several viewings of the picture to realize that director Ritt was striving for—and at times subtly capturing—a delicate mood effect rather than a coherent film story. The viewer knows almost as little about the superficial characters at the end of the picture as at the start. Is Woodward's wavering tourist a widow or a divorcee? Does she really accept her twelve-day love affair with Newman as just her present to him, as her character is made to say in the finale in the Gare St. Lazare sequence? Just why does blasé Newman, who can be so annoyingly in-different to most everything transpiring about him, become so enraged at the heroin addiction problems of his sideman Serge Reggiani? On the other hand, since Carroll and Poitier are mostly personifications of mouthed racial attitudes, their parts can be taken as no more than animated robots.

Being a film ostensibly about jazz men, *Paris Blues* obviously had to provide the viewer with some jam sessions, and that it did with some good improvisations by Louis Armstrong on the trumpet and a lot of old and new Duke Ellington music. But the two lead players—Newman and Poitier—were not accomplished musicians and even though Newman learned to "play" the trombone, he could not pass muster in such elegant musically creative company. Audiences might have allowed the cover-up and dub-in of Newman's trombone playing to pass by (as with Poitier at the piano), but Newman's Ram Bowen was offered as such a conceited stud filled with such high-sounding idealism about music and life that sensitive viewers were overeager to pounce on any flaws in his cinema character. The fact that Newman's instrument playing oncamera was just hot air was good enough reason to dismiss the movie character, and in turn the film, as a phoney.

### A NEW KIND OF LOVE
*(Paramount, 1963) C-110M.*

Producer-director-screenplay, Melville Shavelson; art directors, Hal

Pereira, Arthur Lonergan; set decorators, Sam Comer, James Payne; music, Leith Stevens; additional themes, Erroll Garner; assistant director, Arthur Jacobson; costumes, Edith Head; Paris Originals by Christian Dior, Pierre Cardin, Lanvin-Castille; makeup, Wally Westmore; sound, John Cartier; camera, Daniel Fapp; editor, Frank Bracht.

Paul Newman (Steve Sherman); Joanne Woodward (Samantha Blake); Thelma Ritter (Lena O'Connor); Eva Gabor (Felicienne Courbeau); George Tobias (Joseph Bergner); Marvin Kaplan (Harry Gorman); Robert Clary (Albert Sardou); Jan Moriarty (Suzanne); Valerie Varda (Mrs. Chalmers); Robert Simon (Bertram Chalmers); Joan Staley (Stewardess); Maurice Chevalier (Himself).

New York Premiere: DeMille and Coronet Theatres—October 30, 1963
New York Television Debut: ABC—September 27, 1967

### Synopsis

On the New York to Paris flight, roving newspaperman Steve Sherman encounters Samantha (Sam) Blake. She is a bachelor career girl heading to France with her employer Joseph Bergner and store buyer Lena O'Connor, where she is to pirate high fashions for Bergner's ladies' ready-wear department store. Samantha finds Steve an alcoholic boor and he regards her a snooty, defeminized miss with a boyish hair style and garb. Once in Paris, Samantha finds herself participating in the annual St. Catherine's Day celebration during which all young unmarried girls pray for a spouse. In her intoxicated state, she is inspired to have a cosmetic overhaul and rushes off to a beauty saloon. The new Samantha, complete with blonde wig and all the trimmings, is later picked up by Steve who does not recognize her. She goes along with his misconception that she is a high-priced street walker. Steve makes capital of Samantha by transcribing her imaginary tales of bedroom escapades for international newspaper success. By the time Steve learns whom Samantha really is, they are truly in love, pairing off just like Lena and her long-standing love interest, Bergner.

◆—◆—◆

Paris has been known to inspire a wide variety of pleasant insanity in visitors, but it fell far short of expectations with the creative crew involved in *A New Kind of Love*. Melville Shavelson, who produced, directed and wrote this color production, hopefully intended to emulate the bubbly froth of such Gallic-set comedies as Garbo's *Ninotchka* (1939) or Claudette Colbert's *I Met Him in Paris* (1937) and *Midnight* (1939), or even the lesser but still serviceable Tony Curtis-Janet Leigh exercise *The Perfect Furlough* (1958). Instead Shavelson failed badly in his film exercise in Continental love, filling it with excessive coyness and raw dialog instead of wit and charm. "About the best that can be said of this farce is that it has been engineered with a certain amount of cinematic slickness and ingenuity" *(Variety)*. A. H. Weiler *(New York Times)* further expli-

733

cated, ". . . sight gags and bits do not make a satisfying or original examination of the grand passion."

The few virtues to be found in *A New Kind of Love* are the on-location photography (jazzed up with an overabundance of cinematic tricks), the snatches of songs sung by Maurice Chevalier, who seemed rather bored and uneasy, and the bits of wry repartee tossed about by a generally wasted Thelma Ritter. The cast labored to little avail to liven the proceedings, but the show is loaded to the brim with vulgar clichés, extended dull scenes, a dragged-in fashion show, and the disconcerting presence of Eva Gabor as a stereotyped femme fatale. The cinema has produced its fair share of lamebrained oncamera newsmen, but Newman's Steve Sherman is an oaf par excellence. He is the type of lazy creep who says, "I ain't interested in a lousy little $200 raise," and who thinks transcribing for his readers' edification the fantasized pecadillos of a Parisian tart entitles him to a Pulitzer Prize. With this boob for a hero and a man-hating tomboy with pencils in her hair for a heroine, there is little to be done to make the stars' belated discovery of a great romance work for the disinterested visitor. (At one point flatulent Newman blurts out, "It must be a new kind of love. They ought to bottle it and label it 'instant stupid.'")

If the by-now middle-aged Newman fumbled with their realistic "fun" scenes (Woodward is certainly not apt as a comic drunk), they struck out with the recurring fantasy sequences. At the St. Catherine Day celebration an inebriated Woodward suddenly finds singing performer Chevalier fading into the image of a posturing Newman who ends up kissing a horse. In addition to the extended fantasy of Woodward imagining that she and Newman are engaged in a harried cross country bike race is dull, and the denouement is downright tasteless. There, in slow motion photography so that no one could miss its crudeness, is smirking Newman in football uniform carrying a euphoric Woodward (in a bridal gown) down the playing field into the end zone and placing her on a canopied bed while thousands in the stands cheer.

There were few filmgoers who found this mindless divertissement at all entertaining, and even fewer among the fourth estate who had good words to say about the stars. Arthur Knight *(Saturday Review)* may have insisted that Woodward "has also become one of our ablest, most endearing light comediennes, with much of the tang and sparkle of the well-remembered Carole Lombard," but more to the point was Judith Crist *(New York Herald-Tribune)* who said of the Newmans, "These two usually distinguished performers are entitled to a fling—but Doris Day and Rock Hudson they're not—and shouldn't aspire to be." Richard L. Coe *(Washington Post)* was more biting: "Even were the material witty, I have the sad feeling the Newmans wouldn't be at home in it."

*A New Kind of Love* proved conclusively that screen comedy (their second joint attempt) and Paris (their return visit after *Paris Blues*) were not the proper genre and ambiance for the screen's preferably proletarian husband-wife acting team.

# WINNING
## (Universal, 1969) C-123M.

Producer, John Foreman; associate producer, George Santore; director, James Goldstone; screenplay, Howard Rodman; art directors, Alexander Golitzen, John J. Lloyd, Joe Alves; set decorators, John McCarthy, George Milo; assistant director, Earl Bellamy, Jr.; music, Dave Grusin; makeup, Bud Westmore; sound, Waldon O. Watson, James T. Porter; camera, Richard Moore; editors, Edward A. Biery, Richard C. Meyer.

Paul Newman (Frank Capua); Joanne Woodward (Elora); Richard Thomas, Jr. (Charley); Robert Wagner (Luther Erding); David Sheiner (Leo Crawford); Clu Gulager (Larry Morchek); Barry Ford (Les Bottineau); Bob Quarry (Sam Jagin); Eileen Wesson (Miss Redburn 200); Toni Clayton (The Girl); Maxine Stuart (Miss Redburne's Mother); Karen Arthur (Miss Dairy Queen); Paulene Myers (Cleaning Woman); Ray Ballard (Trombone Player); Charles Seel (Eshovo); Alma Platt (Mrs. Eshovo); Harry Basch (The Stranger); Allen Emerson (Desk Clerk); Marianna Case (Motorcycle Girl); Carolyn McNichol (Party Girl); Bobby Unser, Tony Hulman (Themselves); George Mason (Indianapolis Policeman); Mimi Littlejohn (Indianapolis Queen); Pat Vidan (Starter); Bruce Walkup, Timothy Galbraith (Drivers); Lou Palmer, Jay Reynolds (Indianapolis Interviewers).

New York Premiere: Radio City Music Hall—May 22, 1969
No New York Television Showing

### Synopsis

Slightly drunk Frank Capua, who has just won the Redburne 200 auto race, persuades car rental worker Elora to take him for a drive. Their encounter leads to a romance and, after a trip to California where Frank lives, they wed, with the racer adopting the divorcee's thirteen-year-old-son Charley. Professionally, Frank runs into a streak of bad luck, continually losing out to his chief track rival, Luther Erding. At the Riverside stock car race, Frank's car flips over and at Minneapolis Frank loses again. At San Francisco his car motor conks out, and at Trenton he loses due to a broken lock nut. Spurred on to change his luck, Frank becomes even more absorbed in his work, ignoring Elora to such a degree that she embarks on a terse, meaningless affair with Luther. Frank discovers them in bed together, but accepts the situation stoically, moving out of the motel. Because Leo Crawford, for whom both Frank and Luther are driving special cars, has noticed a slackening in Frank's track performance, he announces that Luther will handle the preferred racer at the approaching Indianapolis 500. The arrival of Charley to see his new father in professional action encourages Frank to overhaul the car that Luther had damaged during the first qualification round. During the big race, Luther is forced out when his engine fails, and Frank emerges victorious in the meet. Frank then travels to Redburne to talk with Elora, and the couple agree to give their marriage another chance.

◆◆◆

Since the wild early twentieth-century exploits of Barney Oldfield, automobile car racing has been a recurring subject for such motion pictures as Wallace Reid's *Too Much Speed* (1921), Reginald Denny's *Sporting Youth* (1924), James Cagney's *The Crowd Roars* (1932), Pat O'Brien's *Indianapolis Speedway* (1939), Mickey Rooney's *The Big Wheel* (1949), Clark Gable's *To Please a Lady* (1950), Kirk Douglas' *The Racers* (1955), James Garner's *Grand Prix* (1966), Jean Louis Trintignant's *A Man and a Woman* (1966), and Steve McQueen's *Le Mans* (1970). None of these entires, with the exception of *A Man and a Woman*, managed to weave a memorable plot into the hectic activities on the speedway. Most of the films left the viewer with a headache from the screeching wheels and a sense of ennui, rather than amazement, from the inevitable occupational clichés surrounding the hazardous track meets. A few recent ones like *Grand Prix* and *Le Mans* did prove to be big grossers.

*Winning* was another one of those little movies that just grew. Initially it was conceived as a modestly budgeted "World Premiere" NBC telefeature, but eventually developed into a seven-million-dollar theatrical feature that its producing company, Universal, at one point, intended to roadshow. Producer John Foreman, a partner in Paul Newman's film ventures, and director James Goldstone gathered together some spectacular Panavision color racing footage, including a seventeen-car pileup at the Indianapolis 500. Super star Newman even insisted upon doing his own track driving and not using a double for the dangerous action sequences. Nevertheless, *Winning*, which grossed $6,555,000 in distributors' domestic rentals, fell victim to the artistic errors of its genre predecessors, insecurely shifting its focus back and forth from the speedway to the miniature personal drama with neither aspect emerging as strongly as intended. In the final result, the critics credited the feature with few merits, labeling it "super-efficiency assembled out of best-by-test parts" [Archer Winsten *(New York Post)*] As Kathleen Carroll *(New York Daily News)* summed it up in her three-star review, "No one would believe any of this schmaltz if it were not for the fact that Joanne Woodward plays the rent-a-car girl and Paul Newman the driver." In the long run, *Winning* gives the viewer no real sense of a racer's life with the fear of death or the pressure to win. Even with the presence of such real life racers as Bobby Unser, Tony Hulman, Dan Gurney, Roger McCluskey and Bobby Grim, most viewers seemed not to care about the track competition or even the ghastly crackups.

Not since *The Long, Hot Summer* had Newman and Woodward worked so well together onscreen, leading William Wolf (*Cue* magazine) to report, "The driver and his woman come vividly alive, thanks to the Newmans' ability to create flesh and blood people." It was obvious to moviegoers who saw *Winning* that the Newmans, unlike their gilt-edged counterparts Richard Burton and Elizabeth Taylor, were constantly striving to enhance their ensemble emoting and *Winning* was an excellent illustration of an occasion when their acting homework paid dividends. While each of these players was still prone to mannerisms (he with physical gesturing and posturing, she with flat-toned delivery and facial grimaces), the reality of Frank Capua and his Elora was self-evident. He was a depersonalized slave ("I'm doin' good, but my life is crap") to his automobiles and she was a slightly over-sexed, drab divorcee seeking a meaningful human response. Unlike *Paris Blues,* where Newman gauchely pretended to be a jazz hepcat, his nonchalant, cocky attitude worked well as a race driver. As for Woodward, she was born to be the screen persona of a sensuous ugly duckling.

In *Winning* the Newmans shared some solid film scenes together, as when on the swing Newman explains his career ambitions to his new wife. Some critics complained that the sections devoted to the two long distance phone calls and the finale confrontation between the estranged newlyweds, made the viewer feel like an eavesdropper, but what could be more of a compliment to the performers' natural emoting?

Some viewers wondered why Universal, with such a large financial stake in *Winning,* allowed the briefly shown adultery sequence to remain in the release print, causing the film to be saddled with a M (Mature) motion picture code rating. The "risqué" footage added little honesty to the drama, and by 1969 standards there was little shock or titillation value to the sight of an awkward Woodward and Robert Wagner fumbling in bed together. (Universal advertised the feature with the tasteless slogan, "Their love, like the world, is ruthless, amoral and fascinating.") On the other hand, the moment when a slightly inebriated Newman has a man-to-man talk with his gawky but very sensitive stepson revealed that a deeper probing of the leads' domestic relationship might have enhanced the film a great deal. It takes a sturdy performer to blend with the congenial acting ambiance of the experienced Newmans. While Wagner, stuck with an enigmatic character to portray, failed to break the barrier, young Richard Thomas grooved into the star team's special cinema world with apparent ease, adding a great deal of honesty to the overall production.

## WUSA
### *(Paramount, 1970) C-117M.*

Producer, Paul Newman, John Foreman; associate producer, Hank

Moonjean; director, Stuart Rosenberg; based on the novel *A Hall of Mirrors* by Robert Stone; screenplay, Stone; assistant directors, Moonjean, Howard Koch, Jr., Les Gorall, Clancy Herne, Nat Holt, Jr.; art director, Philip Jefferies; set decorator, William Kiernan; music director, Lalo Schifrin; music supervisor, Al Mack; song, Neil Diamond; sound, Jerry Jost, Richard Portman; costumes, Travilla; makeup, Lynn Reynolds, Jack Wilson; camera, Richard Moore; editor, Bob Wyman.

Paul Newman (Rheinhardt); Joanne Woodward (Geraldine); Anthony Perkins (Rainey); Laurence Harvey (Farley); Pat Hingle (Bingamon); Cloris Leachman (Philomene); Don Gordon (Bogdanovich); Michael Anderson, Jr. (Marvin); Leigh French (Girl); Moses Gunn (Clotho); Bruce Cabot (King Wolyoe); B. J. Mason (Roosevelt Berry); Robert Quarry (Noonan); Wayne Rogers (Calvin Minter); Hal Baylor (Shorty); Jim Boles (Hot Dog Vendor); Diane Ladd (Barmaid at Railroad Station); Sahdji (Hollywood); Skip Young (Jimmy Snipe); Geoff Edwards (Irving); Clifton James (Speed); Tol Avery (Senator); Paul Hampton (Rusty Fargo); Jerry Catron (Sidewinder Bates); Geraldine B. West, Lucille Benson (Matrons); Susan Batson (Teenage Girl); Zara Cully (White Haired Woman); The Preservation Hall Jazz Band of New Orleans (Themselves); David Huddleston (Heavy Man).

New York Premiere: Penthouse and Plaza Theatres—
November 1, 1970
No New York Television Showing

## Synopsis

A nearly penniless Rheinhardt arrives in New Orleans, where, after recouping part of an old debt from con man Farley, he now poses as a revivalist minister. He picks up down-and-out Geraldine and spends the night with her at her rooming house. The next day Rheinhardt bluffs his way into a post as a disc jockey-announcer at Bingamon's ultra right wing radio station, WUSA, where he must mouth super-patriotic messages to the listening public. Rheinhardt and Geraldine move into an apartment in the French quarter. Their initial contentment is soon shattered by their oversensitive, emotionally disturbed neighbor Rainey, who is aghast to discover that the survey of welfare abuse he has been conducting among the town's blacks is secretly sponsored by WUSA to create a reaction against any form of welfare. This revelation forces the constantly drunk Rheinhardt to realize that he too is only Bingamon's pawn, and in his anger he lambasts the unsettled Rainey and walks out on the baffled Geraldine. A few days later at a tremendous WUSA rally, Rainey fails in his attempt to shoot Bingamon, but instead wounds one of his colleagues. In the ensuing pandemonium, Rainey is crushed to death by the mob, while Geraldine, wandering about in a state of shock, is picked up by the police on a narcotics charge, for she has in her possession a package belonging to her hippie neighbors. She later hangs herself in her cell. Rheinhardt, who along with Farley, escaped from the melee unharmed, learns of her death. After visiting her grave, he packs his bags and leaves town.

◆━━◆━━◆

Robert Stone's first novel *A Hall of Mirrors* had received praise in many quarters, but his faulty screenplay won no plaudits. No matter how many subsequent editing cuts and reassemblings of the plotline the film would suffer, it was still a hackneyed, absurd screenplay that only inspired more blatant artistic misjudgments on the part of the other talent involved in the project. For one thing, the casting was all wrong. There seemed little point in having a dissipated Laurence Harvey portraying a dispassionate human trickster in WUSA other than to reinforce in the viewer's mind that Harvey had once starred as the brainwashed killer in *The Manchurian Candidate* (1962). An aging Anthony Perkins, in a modified recapitulation of his *Psycho* (1959) screen role, was himself playing a more intellectualized version of *The Manchurian Candidate*-style murderer. As for the overbearing performance of Pat Hingle, his typical one-cadence acting tone encumbered with a syrupy Southern drawl made the film's major character menace more a cardboard cartoon than a megalomaniacal threat to America's democratic way of life. Nor was Moses Gunn's black power leader, in the pay of the whites, any revelatory addition to the story.

Most damaging of all to *WUSA* were the problems with the film's lead parts. Newman had previously excelled onscreen in loner-loser roles [*The Hustler* (1961), *Hud* (1963), *Cool Hand Luke* (1968)], but they were each built on solid foundations. His "communicator" in *WUSA*, however, was contrived as a weak-willed dropout who rather proudly announces, "No one's more self-destructive than I am." Furthermore, he states, "You chase me to water. I'll grow gills." By the downbeat ending of the film, he enunciates, "I'm a survivor. Ain't that great." (The built-in cynicism of this statement did not enhance its corniness.) Thus, Newman is saddled with a screen character who has no pride and no redeeming qualities, at least nothing that would be acceptable in these more "realistic" days. It could be safely assumed that Newman's Rheinhardt has profited as little as the viewer from the 117 minutes of ridiculous interplay and that his inert character will go off to a new city and make the same life errors again. For all these reasons, Rheinhardt, as played by a surly Newman in a deadpan style, had little to recommend himself as a character for whom the audience could empathize or to whom to listen as the propounder of the film's viewpoint. Compounding the lackadaisical ambiance of *WUSA* was Joanne Woodward as Geraldine. Woodward was an experienced hand at portraying drab ladies, particularly of the neurotic variety such as in *The Three Faces of Eve* (1957), and even had dabbled at playing a traveling tart in *The Stripper* (1963). But her scarred-face Geraldine was quite another matter. Here was the typical screen whore with a fourteen-carat gold heart, but, unlike Shirley MacLaine's admirable loose lady in *Some Came Running* (1958), Woodward's character was a scared rabbit. She was a misused girl who always ran out on a situation when it promised any difficulty, and, on the one occasion when she had literally turned the other cheek to a nasty mess, she had been carved up by some mean guys. As with Newman's role, there was nothing intrinsically wrong with the delineation of the empty-spirited loser. However, Woodward's character had no aspect to which a viewer might cling. As a decided contrast to Woodward's lethargic, whining rendition in *WUSA*, there was Cloris Leachman's crippled girl of questionable character. In her few brief bedroom scenes, and, later, when she drags herself to Newman's pad to inform the louse of Woodward's death, Leachman makes some viewers wish that the scripter and director had provided her with more opportunity to explicate her gutsy portrayal as a woman unbeaten by life or by an ambiguous screen role.

The discomforted viewing public who was subjected to *WUSA* might have been amazed to later learn that Newman, the film's co-producer and star, himself a devoted political activist, considers this motion picture to be one of his most important films. He called the film "an emotional experience—a humanity exercise" and said that it was deliberately geared "to get people to ask themselves a lot of questions." The film's releasing company, Paramount, obviously was asking itself why it had participated in such an entertainment farrago, for it shelved *WUSA* for nearly a year, and then dumped it onto the release market knowing full well the results. The movie flopped badly. The critics generally blasted the film. "This is the kind of mess that results when moviemakers haven't got the courage of their intentions, let alone their convictions, and lack the guts to tackle a subject head-on or the faith in their public's intelligence." So argued Judith Crist in *New York* magazine, angered by the tawdry nonsense that composed *WUSA*. Crist rightly suggested that the new film was a poor successor to such superior earlier studies of American neo-fascism as *Black Legion* (1936), *All the King's Men* (1949), or even *A Face in the Crowd* (1957).

## THE YEARS AFTER

Andrew Sarris *(Village Voice)* has noted, "Paul Newman and Joanne Woodward have been working their rapport routines so long that they can shift back and forth between the myths of movie stars and the truths of complex characters without missing a beat." Besides their joint screen acting ventures, the couple have performed on such television anthology series as "Playhouse 90" (*The 80 Yard Run*, CBS-1958) and in the 1964 Actors' Studio Broadway production of *Baby Wants a Kiss*, which revealed that the Newmans had more of a flair for comedy than their screen misadventures in the genre previously demonstrated.

Newman was among the ranks of the top ten boxoffice stars throughout the mid-1960s, a feat not duplicated by Woodward who, when not acting in less commercial arty features, had either devoted herself to being a wife and mother or to joining with Newman in his lesser screen outings. In 1968, Newman turned to a new aspect of filmmaking. He directed Woodward in the well-received *Rachel, Rachel* which earned the actress an Oscar bid. Newman's production company was responsible for Woodward's co-starring venture with George C. Scott, *They Might Be Giants* (1971), and in 1973 Woodward was named Best Actress at the Cannes Film Festival for a Newman-directed screen performance, this time *The Effects of Gamma Rays on Man-in-the-Moon Marigolds* (1972), a picture which also featured one of the Newman daughters.

Today, fast approaching the age of fifty, Newman continues to churn out feature films, accepting roles to earn the fast, lucrative buck, rather than seeking the more artistically challenging parts he should be striving for at this point in his lengthy acting career. On the other hand, Woodward is apparently content to appear only in an occasional soulful feature, such as *Summer Wishes, Winter Dreams* (1973) to join oncamera with her spouse in a video special such as Wild Places (1974), a study of American wilderness areas. The couple appeared on screen together again in *Ryan's The Name* (1975), scripted by Ross Macdonald, and directed by Stuart Rosenberg, who had done the same for the team's *WUSA*. Each in his/her individual professional quarter and style, the Newmans continue to function well in major entertainment projects, a tribute to their entrenched image with the public.

In **Pillow Talk** (Univ., 1959)

# Chapter 27

# Rock Hudson
# &
# Doris Day

## ROCK HUDSON

6′ 4″
200 pounds
Black hair
Brown eyes
Scorpio

*Real name: Roy Fitzgerald, Jr. Born November 17, 1927, Winnetka, Illinois. Married Phyllis Gates (1955); divorced 1958.*

### FEATURE FILMS:

*Fighter Squadron* (WB, 1948)
*Undertow* (Univ., 1949)
*I Was a Shoplifter* (Univ., 1950)
*One Way Street* (Univ., 1950)
*Winchester '73* (Univ., 1950)
*Peggy* (Univ., 1950)
*The Desert Hawk* (Univ., 1950)
*The Fat Man* (Univ., 1951)
*Air Cadet* (Univ., 1951)
*Tomahawk* (Univ., 1951)
*Iron Man* (Univ., 1951)
*Bright Victory* (Univ., 1951)
*Bend of the River* (Univ., 1952)
*Here Comes the Nelsons* (Univ., 1952)
*Scarlet Angel* (Univ., 1952)

*Has Anybody Seen My Gal* (Univ., 1952)
*Horizons West* (Univ., 1952)
*The Lawless Breed* (Univ., 1952)
*Seminole* (Univ., 1953)
*Sea Devils* (RKO, 1953)
*The Golden Blade* (Univ., 1953)
*Back to God's Country* (Univ., 1953)
*Taza, Son of Cochise* (Univ., 1954)
*Magnificent Obsession* (Univ., 1954)
*Bengal Brigade* (Univ., 1954)
*Captain Lightfoot* (Univ., 1955)
*One Desire* (Univ., 1955)
*All That Heaven Allows* (Univ., 1955)
*Never Say Goodbye* (Univ., 1956)

Giant (WB, 1956)
Battle Hymn (Univ., 1956)
Written on the Wind (Univ., 1956)
Four Girls in Town (Univ., 1956)
Something of Value (MGM, 1957)
The Tarnished Angels (Univ., 1957)
A Farewell to Arms (20th, 1957)
Twilight for the Gods (Univ., 1958)
This Earth Is Mine (Univ., 1959)
Pillow Talk (Univ., 1959)
The Last Sunset (Univ., 1961)
Come September (Univ., 1961)
Lover Come Back (Univ., 1961)
The Spiral Road (Univ., 1962)
A Gathering of Eagles (Univ., 1963)

Man's Favorite Sport? (Univ., 1964)
Send Me No Flowers (Univ., 1964)
Strange Bedfellows (Univ., 1964)
A Very Special Favor (Univ., 1965)
Blindfold (Univ., 1966)
Seconds (Par., 1966)
Tobruk (Univ., 1967)
Ice Station Zebra (MGM, 1968)
A Fine Pair (National General, 1969)
The Undefeated (20th, 1969)
Darling Lili (Par., 1970)
Hornets' Nest (UA, 1970)
Pretty Maids All in a Row (MGM, 1971)
Showdown (Univ., 1973)

# DORIS DAY

5' 5½"
120 pounds
Blonde hair
Blue eyes
Aries

Real name: Doris von Kappelhoff. Born April 3, 1924, Cincinnati, Ohio. Married Al Jorden (1941), child: Terry; divorced 1943. Married George Weidler (1946); divorced 1949. Married Martin Melcher (1951); widowed 1968.

FEATURE FILMS:

Romance on the High Seas (WB, 1948)
My Dream Is Yours (WB, 1949)
It's a Great Feeling (WB, 1949)
Young Man with a Horn (WB, 1950)
Tea for Two (WB, 1950)
The West Point Story (WB, 1950)
Storm Warning (WB, 1950)
The Lullaby of Broadway (WB, 1951)
On Moonlight Bay (WB, 1951)
Starlift (WB, 1951)
I'll See You in My Dreams (WB, 1951)
April in Paris (WB, 1952)
The Winning Team (WB, 1952)

By the Light of the Silvery Moon (WB, 1953)
Calamity Jane (WB, 1953)
Lucky Me (WB, 1954)
Young at Heart (WB, 1954)
Love Me or Leave Me (MGM, 1955)
The Man Who Knew Too Much (Par., 1956)
Julie (MGM, 1956)
The Pajama Game (WB, 1957)
Teacher's Pet (Par., 1958)
The Tunnel of Love (MGM, 1958)
It Happened to Jane (Col., 1959)

744

*Pillow Talk* (Univ., 1959)

*Please Don't Eat the Daisies* (MGM, 1960)

*Midnight Lace* (Univ., 1960)

*Lover Come Back* (Univ., 1961)

*That Touch of Mink* (Univ., 1962)

*Billy Rose's Jumbo* (MGM, 1962)

*The Thrill of It All* (Univ., 1963)

*Move Over, Darling* (20th, 1963)

*Send Me No Flowers* (Univ., 1964)

*Do Not Disturb* (20th, 1965)

*The Glass-Bottom Boat* (MGM, 1966)

*Caprice* (20th, 1967)

*The Ballad of Josie* (Univ., 1968)

*Where Were You When the Lights Went Out?* (MGM, 1968)

*With Six You Get Eggroll* (National General, 1968)

Doris Day and Rock Hudson with their Exhibitor
(Boxoffice Star) Laurel Awards for 1959

Advertisement for **Pillow Talk**

In **Lover Come Back** (Univ., 1961)

In **Send Me No Flowers** (Univ., 1964)

## PILLOW TALK
### *(Universal, 1959) C-110M.*

Producers, Ross Hunter, Martin Melcher; director, Michael Gordon; story, Russell Rouse, Clarence Greene; screenplay, Stanley Shapiro; assistant directors, Phil Bowles, Carl Beringer; music, Frank DeVol; songs, Buddy Pepper and Inez James; Joe Lubin and I. J. Roth; Elsa Doran and Sol Lake; music director, Joseph Gershenson; art directors, Alexander Golitzen, Richard H. Riedel; set decorators, Russell A. Gausman, Ruby Levitt; makeup, Bud Westmore; gowns, Jean Louis; sound, Leslie I. Carey, Bob Pritchard; special camera, Clifford Stine, Roswell Hoffman; camera, Arthur E. Arling; editor, Milton Carruth.

Rock Hudson (Brad Allen); Doris Day (Jan Morrow); Tony Randall (Jonathan Forbes); Thelma Ritter (Alma); Nick Adams (Tony Walters); Julia Meade (Marie); Allen Jenkins (Harry); Marcel Dalio (Pierot); Lee Patrick (Mrs. Walters); Mary McCarty (Nurse Resnick); Alex Gerry (Dr. Maxwell); Hayden Rorke (Mr. Conrad); Valerie Allen (Eileen); Jacqueline Beer (Yvette); Arlen Stuart (Tilda); Perry Blackwell (Singer); Don Beddoe (Mr. Walters); Robert B. Williams (Mr. Graham); Muriel Landers (Fat Girl); William Schallert (Hotel Clerk); Karen Norris (Miss Dickenson); Lois Rayman (Jonathan's Secretary); Harry Tyler (Hansom Cabby); Joe Mell (Dry Goods Man); Boyd Red Morgan (Trucker); Dorothy Abbott (Singer).

New York Premiere: Palace and Murray Hill Theatres—October 6, 1959
New York Television Debut: ABC—October 8, 1966

### Synopsis

Song writer Brad Allen and interior decorator Jan Morrow become enemies without even meeting because they are forced to share a party line during a Manhattan telephone shortage. Every time Jan tries to use the phone, Brad is on it talking to a girl. She suggests that they use it on an alternate half-hour basis. It develops that Brad's pal, Jonathan Forbes, who is backing the Broadway show for which Brad is writing the songs, is in love with Jan. When Brad finally gets a gander at the "frustrated old maid" he has been feuding with, he quickly adopts the pose of a bashful Texan and starts wooing his neighbor, cleverly and methodically. Eventually Jan discovers the deception, which promptly halts Brad's romantic endeavors. By now in love with Jan, Brad seeks advice from Jan's continually drunk maid, Alma, who advises him to hire Jan to decorate his apartment. Jan willingly accepts Brad's invitation and has her subtle revenge by turning the residence into a horror palace. However, when Brad con-

748

fesses he had hoped the apartment might be their wedding abode, Jan relents and finally agrees to wed her "party line."

◆ ◆ ◆

In 1959, blonde, thirty-five-year-old Doris Day, long past her big vocalist and Warner Bros. musical movie stages, found her boxoffice career reaching an impasse. All of her pictures, even such inept comedies as *The Tunnel of Love* (1958) and *It Happened to Jane* (1959), were still earning tidy grosses but it was becoming increasingly more difficult to find vehicles that suited the cotton candy image of Day, whose persona as the screen innocent was reaching the point of tedium and absurdity.

Thirty-two-year-old Rock Hudson had been under contract to Universal since 1950, and in the years since *Written on the Wind* (1956) and *Something of Value* (1957) had enjoyed little in the way of artistic success. Nevertheless, in 1959, he was still number-one money-making star at the U.S. boxoffice. The question was how long he could remain so, in particular by ambling through such celluloid trivia as *Twilight of the Gods* (1958) and *This Earth Is Mine* (1959).

It was a fortuitous occasion when Day's perspicacious husband Martin Melcher partnered with Universal's Ross Hunter, the ultra-successful producer of glossy women's pictures, to produce *Pillow Talk*. These men were luckier still to obtain the services of fast-rising scenarist Stanley Shapiro and a supporting cast which included Tony Randall and Thelma Ritter. Best of all there were two stars (Day, Hudson) who were willing to wet their toes in uncharted acting areas (ribald comedy), for the sake of expanding their screen careers in new directions. It was an artistic challenge they met and conquered admirably.

The premise of *Pillow Talk* is the old-fashioned theatre device of the party line (surely an anachronism in late 1950s New York City) bringing the lead characters together. In the course of confused events, they find their mutual antipathy changing to love. This storyline fit neatly into the confines of Day's prior screen image, but now allowed the actress to tease her sacred standing as the cinema's most enduring virgin figure, who, at the slightest hint of sexual hanky panky, is known to panic and run in the opposite direction. What would women's lib do with her? In a similar vein of scenario twisting, Hudson had previously essayed the personable he-man suitor on many movie occasions. However, in *Pillow Talk* he is an out and out wolf, a male chauvinist of the highest order. Thus the film offered 110 CinemaScope color minutes of sleek, aggressive Hudson pursuing jaunty Day with the major goal being bed and the method being marriage, *only* if absolutely necessary. To sparkle the already bright proceedings there are assorted variations of the split screen device, particularly effective when Day and Hudson, each taking his/her own bath, talk to one another on the party line, while finding themselves rubbing the other's toes, which causes Day to recoil in mock horror. The actors employ

749

the spoken thought technique to bare their crafty souls. To bedazzle the women viewers, Day abandoned her casual, sporty dress look for a more chic and stunning Jean Louis wardrobe, complete with fourteen costume changes and capped by $500,000 worth of (borrowed) jewelry.

Hudson oncamera had often been described as handsome and charming, but he had never been known for Cary Grant-style drollery. *Pillow Talk*, his first real movie comedy, changed his stance. The film revealed that even with modest direction (Michael Anderson), but very good dialog, he could not only display an ambiguously wry twinkle in his eye, but he also could depict an engaging modern day Romeo, more prone to wooing than poetry-spinning. Just to balance Hudson's slightly risque characterization, comedian Randall is presented as the lovesick, good-natured pal, who may be rich and amusing, but is always losing his girl, no matter what he does. In essence he is Hudson's competition for Day's affection, but in reality he provides a very droll straight man who serves as Hudson's confident and cynical jokester.

Well-scrubbed, freckle-faced Day was an experienced master at impersonating the movie's girl next door, although, on occasion, films like *Teacher's Pet* (1958) offered her as a sensible career girl, attractive but leery of the opposite sex, especially when they have other things besides a marriage license on their mind. Before *Pillow Talk* she had flirted with the ramifications of pre-marital intercourse, but in this film and thereafter, her young matron heroines would confront the subject point blank. She still registered those famous double-takes with the open-eyed, gaping-mouthed moment of shock in rediscovering that men could be such beasts, but now she was willing to be as devious as the untrustworthy male in maneuvering her way around a delicate situation, i.e. how to convince the man in question to wed her before bedding her. One would hardly think flip, wise-cracking, gravelly-voiced Ritter would make a congenial listener-adviser to Day's daily Pollyanna dilemmas in *Pillow Talk*, but Ritter's tipsy maid somehow in contrast gave Day's character more sophistication. After all, anyone who would hire and retain such a zany domestic was surely a wordly creature herself.

From *Pillow Talk* onward, no self-respecting Day film would be complete without the attempted seduction scene(s), and this film has three such glorious occasions. The first finds Day as the unwilling escort of Nick Adams, the Harvard senior son of her client (Lee Patrick). He may be young, but his motor is racing faster than his sports car and he does his best to put the obvious make on mature Day. When they stop at a club for a drink, he soon passes out, much to her relief, and it is at this point she makes her first in-person encounter with Hudson who quickly poses as repressed Texan Rex Stetson. As Hudson's courtship of Day progresses, he lures her to Randall's Connecticut home. The soft music, the glowing fireplace, and the liquor soon take effect. However, when Hudson lets the cat out of the bag, the almost seduced Day turns into an indignant feline who hastily retreats to the sanctuary of her Manhattan apartment. The final and most surprising encounter between Hudson and Day occurs at the finale. For revenge she has decorated his apartment in the gaudiest and worst possible taste. The angered Hudson views his newly restyled abode, charges over to Day's apartment, and, when she refuses to leave her bed and get dressed, he wraps a blanket about her and carries her back to his place. He dumps her on a sofa and says she decorated the monstrosity and now can keep it. Then he storms toward the door, but crafty Day, who has her own sense of humor, reaches for a trick switch which snaps the door lock shut. As he turns toward her, she smiles, turns out the light and says that all apartments look alike in the dark. Obviously this is not the Doris Day that moviegoers once knew.

While post-Warner Bros. Day screen vehicles had soft pedaled the vocalist side of the star, save for her usually performing the title tune over the credits, *Pillow Talk* had six numbers integrated into the screenplay. Day and Hudson did stanzas of the title song. She sang "Possess Me," Hudson put forth "Inspiration," and in the nightclub scene the two stars joined vocalist Perry Blackwell in "Roly Poly." Blackwell proved to be the musical delight of the film with his renditions of "I Need No Atmosphere" and "You Lied."

*Pillow Talk* swept into national release with glowing reviews. Arthur Knight *(Saturday Review)* called it "The year's most sophisticated light comedy. . . . It's one occasion where everyone concerned seems to know exactly what he is doing, and does it well." "It has a smart, glossy texture and that part of the population likely to be entranced at the sight of a well groomed Rock Hudson being irresistible to a silver-haired Doris Day will probably enjoy it" [Paul V. Beckley *(New York Herald-Tribune)*]. Leave it to *Time* magazine to carp while offering back-handed praise to the production, ". . . the picture also offers something beyond discussion and almost beyond belief: a romantic comedy team composed of Rock Hudson and Doris Day, the boxoffice champions of the 1958-59 season. The idea was obviously to present a sort of world series of sex, but what happened to the sex? When these two magnificent objects go into a clinch, aglow from the sun lamp, a-gleam with hair lacquer, they look less like creatures of flesh and blood than a couple of 1960 Cadillacs that just happen to be parked in a suggestive position."

As proof of the rejuvenation of Day's career she was nominated for her first Academy Award, but lost the Best Actress award to Simone Signoret of *Room at the Top*. Ritter was nominated as Best Supporting Actress but was defeated by Shelley Winters of *The Diary of Anne Frank*. However, the original story of Russell Rouse-Clarence Greene and Shapiro's screenplay did win an Oscar, adding laurels to a slick production which grossed $7.5 million in distributors' domestic rentals.

And now Day was number one at the boxoffice with Hudson number two. Who could ask for anything more? Certainly not these two stars.

# LOVER COME BACK
### (*Universal, 1961*) C-107M.

Executive producer, Robert Arthur; producers, Stanley Shapiro, Martin Melcher; director, Delbert Mann; screenplay, Shapiro, Paul Henning; assistant directors, Ray Gosnell, Douglas Green; art directors, Alexander Golitzen, Robert Clatworthy; set decorator, Oliver Emert; music, Frank DeVol; songs, Alan Spilton and DeVol; William Landan and Adam Ross; sound, Joe Lapis; gowns, Irene; makeup, Bud Westmore; music supervisor, Joseph Gershenson; camera, Arthur E. Arling; editor, Marjorie Fowler.

Rock Hudson (Jerry Webster); Doris Day (Carol Templeton); Tony Randall (Peter Ramsey); Edie Adams (Rebel Davis); Jack Oakie (J. Paxton Miller); Jack Kruschen (Dr. Linus Tyler); Ann B. Davis (Millie); Joe Flynn (Hadley); Karen Norris (Kelly); Howard St. John (Brackett); Jack Albertson (Fred); Charles Watt (Charlie); Donna Douglas (Deborah); Ward Ramsey (Hodges); John Litel (Board Member).

New York Premiere: Radio City Music Hall—February 8, 1962
New York Television Debut: NBC—October 4, 1966

### Synopsis

Even though they have never met, Madison Avenue advertising account executives Jerry Webster and Carol Templeton are declared enemies. Conscientious Carol is more than annoyed at Jerry, who works for a rival agency and manages to land clients via liquor and chorus girls. When she tattles on him to the City Advertising Council, he merely induces seductive club performer Rebel Davis to testify in his behalf. As a bonus for helping him to win an acquittal, Jerry selects Rebel as a "VIP" girl, filming a series of commercials with her for a non-existent product. However, Jerry's neurotic employer Peter Ramsey has the lively commercials televised and VIP as a product is launched. To maneuver himself out of his bind, Jerry hires aardvark scientist Dr. Linus Tyler to invent any product that could be sold as VIP. All these doings lead unsuspecting Carol to visit Tyler in the hopes of stealing away the product and the account. When she appears at his laboratories she mistakes Jerry for Linus and insists she will do most anything to win the account. Jerry takes advantage of the situation and allows the innocent Carol to wine and dine him. Just at the moment when he is about to seduce Carol she discovers the truth. Once again she reports him to the Advertising Council, this time for advertising a non-existent product. But Jerry saves his neck by appearing at the hearing with a new mint-flavored candy, called VIP. The goodie, which everyone including Carol tries, has the same effect as several triple Martinis. The next morning she awakes in a motel room to find Jerry in the bed with her, a marriage license dangling on the mirror. Shocked Carol has the marriage annulled, while Jerry has himself transferred to the firm's California office. But nine months later obvious circumstances reunite them and they are rewed in a hospital maternity ward.

◆—◆—◆

For those who were pleasantly surprised (or happily shocked) to view wholesome Doris Day and Rock Hudson gamboling in *Pillow Talk, Lover Come Back* took "today's most successful romantic-comedy team" one step further into the world of saucy farce. With a script by Stanley Shapiro and Paul Henning, the film was a lighthearted, improbable spoof on sex and business rivalry in the Madison Avenue advertising world. The *New York Times'* Bosley Crowther rated it as "the funniest picture of the year" and the *Washington Post* insisted, "Blond Doris has never been more attractive or spirited and Hudson has become an adept farceur." To make the *Pillow Talk* reunion complete, Tony Randall was back on the star lineup, this time as Hudson's psychiatrist-dependent agency boss who dreads coming to his own office because it depresses his staff so much. Providing back-up support for the film were Jack Oakie as a rambunctious Dixiecrat client of Hudson, Edie Adams as the loose-living, gold-digging chorine, and Jack Kruschen as the 1960s' most absent-minded scientist. Is it any wonder the film grossed $8.5 million in distributors domestic rentals?

The crux of the lithe *Lover Come Back,* beyond its blatant spoofing, is once again the question of whether Day and Hudson will join in either bedside conferences or matrimony, or both. Day says of Hudson, "He's like a cold and there are only two things you can do with a cold. . . . You can fight it or you can go to bed with it. . . . I'm going to fight it." For 107 gorgeously appointed minutes she does just that, gliding through the plotline in her Irene wardrobe. She has her task cut out for her, what with charming, unscrupulous lecher Hudson being the unprincipled soul who has "sown so many wild oats he can qualify for a farm loan." Once more Hudson nearly succeeds in tricking the once-aboveboard Day (here she is fighting fire with fire by trying to steal away Hudson's advertising clients) by posing as the timid Nobel Prize-winning scientist with a Greenwich Village laboratory. Day is so moved by this seemingly lost soul that she promises him and the audience, "I'm going to give you confidence." Her promises lead Hudson to "beg" the fooled Day to go to bed with him. When she is about to instruct him in the fine art of love-making (where did she learn it?) the novice teacher of l'amour says, "Be gentle." But then. . . .

In *Lover Come Back* Day sings the title song in fine, typically bouncy manner, but it is her rendition of "Should I Surrender" that provides one of the picture's biggest sustained laughs. This song is performed as a stream-of-consciousness bit when she is considering taking that big jump over the chasm into the world of a non-virgin. But, of course, at the last moment she is spared this terrible fate by a sudden change of circumstances. This plot switch is all part of the scenario's gambit to tease the audience, back off, and then retantalize the viewer on the primary subject: will she or won't she? Even when Day does succumb to a combination of Hudson courting tactics and an overdose of VIP liquor mints, she is legally married before sharing that bed of love. After all, even in 1961, the movie industry and La Day had a strict moral code of ethics.

In the 1930s, Myrna Loy or Katharine Hepburn would have played Day's part and certainly Cary Grant would have performed the male lead, but no viewer could claim that he or she was shortchanged by the rapid-fire interchanges of romance and sarcasm that sparked the Day-Hudson team through this successful rematching. "Mr. Hudson and Miss Day are delicious, he in his big, sprawling way, and she in her wide-eyed, pert, pugnacious and eventually melting vein" [Bosley Crowther (*New York Times*)].

## SEND ME NO FLOWERS
### *(Universal, 1964) C-100M.*

Executive producer, Martin Melcher; producer, Harry Keller; director, Norman Jewison; based on the play by Norman Barasch, Carroll Moore; screenplay, Julius Epstein; music, Frank DeVol; song, Hal David and Burt Bacharach; choreography, David Winters; assistant director, Douglas Green; gowns, Jean Louis; makeup, Bud Westmore; art director, Alexander Golitzen, Robert Clatworthy; set decorators, John McCarthy, Oliver Emert, John Austin; camera, Daniel Fapp; editor, J. Terry Williams.

Rock Hudson (George Kimball); Doris Day (Judy Kimball); Tony Randall (Arnold Nash); Clint Walker (Bert Power); Paul Lynde (Mr. Akins); Hal March (Winston Burr); Edward Andrews (Dr. Morrissey); Patricia Barry (Linda); Clive Clerk (Vito); Dave Willock (Milkman); Aline Towne (Cora); Helene Winston (Woman Commuter); Christine Nelson (Nurse).

New York Premiere: Radio City Music Hall—November 12, 1964
New York Television Debut: NBC—September 19, 1967

### Synopsis

Despite George Kimball's abiding hypochondria, he and his wife Judy have been fairly happily married for eight years. However, one day George visits his doctor concerning a "real" chest pain, and assumes a discussion about another patient is really about him. He wrongly concludes he has but a few weeks to live. George gallantly tells his neighbor and best friend Arnold Nash, and then puts a down payment on three cemetery plots, one for himself, his wife, and her next husband. He feels very noble setting out to find Judy a new spouse, and settling on Bert Power, her college pal, who is now a rich oil tycoon. But George's efforts to bring Judy and Bert together only convince her that he must be covering up an affair of his own. Judy's suspicions are seemingly confirmed when she finds George in a compromising situation with Linda Bullard, not knowing that George is merely protecting the recently separated woman from lecherous Winston Burr. George now finds he must tell Judy all. Her initial shock changes to intense anger when George's doctor insists that her husband is in perfect health. Alcoholic Arnold gives Judy advice but it only makes matters worse, and she begins to arrange for a hasty divorce. However, when she learns of George's cemetery lot purchases, she cannot quibble with his sincerity. The repentant George promises to overcome his hypochondria, and after she has thrown away all his myriad of medicines and he has knocked out the still pesky Winston Burr, they celebrate their reconciliation.

◆ ◆ ◆

Since *Lover Come Back,* Doris Day had successfully continued in her new found sophisticated comedy genre with the equally glossy *That Touch of Mink* (1962) with Cary Grant and *The Thrill of It All* (1963) with James Garner. Rock Hudson, however, had faltered with a few middling screen dramas and above all, in the labored Howard Hawks' comedy, *Man's Favorite Sport?* (1964) with Paula Prentiss. Thus it made good box-office sense for the still popular screen stars to reunite in yet another movie vehicle. Unlike the old days of the Hollywood studio system, this re-teaming was a complex financial arrangement concluded between the assorted corporations which represented studio, stars, and production talent.

Unfortunately, the base property selected for this new cinema venture was a one-joke comedy, *Send Me No Flowers,* which had died a rather quick Broadway death in late 1960 before being relegated to the summer stock circuit. Despite his own general excellence on past occasions, scripter Julius Esptein was not a Stanley Shapiro, and the resultant scenario was full of such obvious jokes as:

Hudson (to doctor): "It hurts like the devil when I press it."

Doctor: "Then don't press it."

. . . or the cemetery salesman informing Hudson, "When you're ready, we're ready."

. . . or Hudson's good neighbor and pal, Tony Randall, commiserating with his "dying" pal, "I remember how she [Day] was when the dog died."

When *Send Me No Flowers* went into production, executive producer Martin Melcher, still Day's husband, stated that the venture would be worked into a "clean sex comedy, enticing but legal—a good formula." But things were not as they were before, even with Randall back on the home team to field spare jokes as the well-meaning but perpetually soused and maudlin attorney-neighbor. Here Day and Hudson are cast as a respectably *married* suburban Connecticut couple. Thus there is no room for bedside chases between the two too-well established stars and certainly no reason for Day to be overly protective of her high-priced virginity. Her only oncamera problem is Hudson's overconcern with the state of his physical well being. But the 6' 4" actor looked so gosh darn healthy that viewers could scarcely believe the movie's premise, certainly not for one hundred minutes. The only thing that stands Hudson in good stead in the particular characterization—and this is not too much of a help—is his "frozen stoical mien" and his "low pitched monotonous delivery" making a viewer wonder if perhaps Hudson knows something that his looks do not reveal.

As the glamorous housewife, undisturbed by ambition or sex, Day has little opportunity to do what she did best oncamera: register moral indignation or express determined career goals. She is merely a "typical" (does every Ms. Suburbia wear Jean Louis tailored gowns?) married matron who cannot balance a checkbook and very much needs a man around the house to keep her life in order. These are the reasons why thoughtful Hudson thinks that her former college chum (Clint Walker—in physical look and mien too much like Hudson) and not neighborhood wolf (Hal March) would be the logical next spouse for lovely Day. With so little in the plot to react to, no wonder the *Christian Science Monitor* thought Day in *Send Me No Flowers* performed "like a firm-willed, wind-up toy, [who] does her reliable bit."

*Time* magazine passed the film off as a "puppet show" and added, "Actor Hudson, who is sensitively cast as a half dead hero, has seldom performed so inoffensively. And actress Day, who at 40 should maybe stop trying to play Goldilocks, comes off as a cheery, energetic and wildly overdressed Mama Bear."

*Send Me No Flowers* grossed $4.5 million in distributors' domestic receipts, a healthy return, but one that indicated that the Day-Hudson gambit had played out its effectiveness.


## THE YEARS AFTER

Interestingly, soon after Doris Day and Rock Hudson went their separate cinema paths, their screen popularity sharply dipped. If *Do Not Disturb* (1965) and *The Glass-Bottom Boat* (1966), both of which paired Day with Rod Taylor, were a lessening of the star's formularized screen outing, the would-be spy spoof *Caprice* (1967) and the dismal mock Western *The Ballad of Josie* (1968) almost polished off her movie career. Since her last two features were bland enough to become nondescript television fare, her husband Martin Melcher decided that it was high time for Day to tackle a video series while her name still had a semblance of allure. When he died before "The Doris Day Show" got underway, many thought it would signal the end for Day's Trilby. However, she went ahead with the series—her son Terry by a previous marriage became the show's producer—and it evolved into a five-season winner. A recent television commercial deal insures Day of plenty of video exposure and even more cash.

While day remained in the top ten at the boxoffice in both 1965 and 1966, Hudson quickly dropped down in the national marquee ratings with such insipid adult romantic comedies as *A Very Special Favor* (1965) and *Blindfold* (1966) with Claudia Cardinale. Along the way was the underrated John Frankenheimer fantasy-suspense, *Seconds* (1966), and *Tobruk* (1967) a World War II actioner that ended his Universal association. *The Undefeated* found a mustached, forty-two-year-old Hudson playing second fiddle to veteran star John Wayne, while in the Roger Vadim-directed *Pretty Maids All in a Row* (1971) Hudson was a psychopathic-homicidal school instructor. Fortunately at this juncture, *Once upon a Dead Man,* a two hour NBC telefeature with Hudson as a married police investigator, sold, spawning a mini-series, "McMillan and Wife" in which he is co-starred with Susan Saint James. The lumbering Universal Western, *Showdown* (1973) enhanced neither Hudson's nor Dean Martin's reputations.

Interestingly, just as the teenie bopper screen team of Annette Funicello and Frankie Avalon have become an integral part of 1960s nostalgia camp, so the merest reference to the once oncamera tandem of Hudson and Day brings immediate smirks of recognition to the faces of audiences who in years past experienced the "joys" of sharing Day's celluloid vicissitudes as she engaged in battles royale with sex-hungry Hudson, in a never-ending competition for supremacy on and off of the love couch. One can only wonder what compassion Europeans have for such United States-oriented cult following, when taken in contrast to the movie antics of Sophia Loren and Marcello Mastroianni, the more earthy Continental equivalents of Hudson and Day.

In **Cleopatra** (20th, 1963)

# Chapter 28

# Richard Burton
## &
# Elizabeth Taylor

## RICHARD BURTON

**5′ 11″**
**185 pounds**
**Brown hair**
**Blue-green eyes**
**Scorpio**

*Real name: Richard Walter Jenkins, Jr. Born November 10, 1925, Pontrhydyfen, South Wales. Married Sybil Williams (1949), children: Jessica, Kate; divorced 1963. Married Elizabeth Taylor (1964); divorced 1974.*

**FEATURE FILMS:**

*The Last Days of Dolwyn* (London Films, 1948)
*Now Barabbas Was a Robber* (WB, 1949)
*Waterfront* (GFD, 1950)
*The Woman with No Name* (Rank, 1952)
*My Cousin Rachel* (20th, 1952)
*The Desert Rats* (20th, 1953)
*The Robe* (20th, 1953)
*Prince of Players* (20th, 1955)
*The Rains of Ranchipur* (20th, 1955)

*Alexander the Great* (UA, 1956)
*Sea Wife* (20th, 1957)
*Bitter Victory* (Col., 1958)
*Look Back in Anger* (WB, 1959)
*Bramble Bush* (WB, 1960)
*Ice Palace* (WB, 1960)
*A Midsummer Night's Dream* (Czeck-British, 1961)°
*The Longest Day* (20th, 1962)
*Cleopatra* (20th, 1963)
*The V.I.P.s* (MGM, 1963)
*Becket* (Par., 1964)

°Narrator

Zulu (Emb., 1964)*
The Night of the Iguana (MGM, 1964)
Hamlet (WB, 1964)
The Sandpiper (MGM, 1965)
What's New, Pussycat? (UA, 1965)†
The Spy Who Came in from the Cold
(Par., 1966)
Who's Afraid of Virginia Woolf? (WB,
1966)
The Taming of the Shrew (Col., 1967)
The Comedians (MGM, 1967)
Doctor Faustus (Col., 1968)
Boom! (Univ., 1968)
Candy (Cin., 1968)
Where Eagles Dare (MGM, 1969)

Staircase (20th, 1969)
Anne of the Thousand Days (Univ.,
1969)
Raid on Rommel (Univ., 1971)
Villain (MGM, 1971)
Hammersmith Is Out (Cin., 1972)
Bluebird (Cin., 1972)
The Assassination of Trotsky (Cin., 1972)
Under Milk Wood (Altura Films,
1973)
Massacre in Rome (National General,
1973)
The Voyage (UA, 1974)
Sutjeska (1974)
The Fifth Offense (1974)
The Klansman (Par., 1975)

*Unbilled appearance
†Narrator

# ELIZABETH TAYLOR

**5′ 4″**
**115 pounds**
**Black hair**
**Violet eyes**
**Pisces**

Real name: Elizabeth Rosemond Taylor. Born February 27, 1932, Hampstead Heath, England. Married Nicky Hilton (1949); divorced 1951. Married Michael Wilding (1952), children: Michael, Christopher; divorced 1957. Married Michael Todd (1957), child: Elizabeth; widowed 1958. Married Eddie Fisher (1959), child: Maria; divorced 1964. Married Richard Burton (1964); divorced 1974.

**FEATURE FILMS:**

There's One Born Every Minute (Univ.,
1942)
Lassie Come Home (MGM, 1943)
Jane Eyre (20th, 1944)
The White Cliffs of Dover (MGM, 1944)
National Velvet (MGM, 1944)
Courage of Lassie (MGM, 1946)

Cynthia (MGM, 1947)
Life with Father (WB, 1947)
A Date with Judy (MGM, 1948)
Julia Misbehaves (MGM, 1948)
Little Women (MGM, 1949)
Conspirator (MGM, 1950)
The Big Hangover (MGM, 1950)

*Father of the Bride* (MGM, 1950)
*Father's Little Dividend* (MGM, 1951)
*A Place in the Sun* (Par., 1951)
*Quo Vadis* (MGM, 1951)°
*Ivanhoe* (MGM, 1952)
*Love Is Better Than Ever* (MGM, 1952)
*The Girl Who Had Everything* (MGM, 1953)
*Rhapsody* (MGM, 1954)
*Elephant Walk* (Par., 1954)
*Beau Brummel* (MGM, 1954)
*The Last Time I Saw Paris* (MGM, 1954)
*Giant* (WB, 1956)
*Raintree County* (MGM, 1957)
*Cat on a Hot Tin Roof* (MGM, 1958)
*Suddenly, Last Summer* (Col., 1959)
*Scent of Mystery* (Michael Todd, Jr., 1960)
*Butterfield 8* (MGM, 1960)
*Cleopatra* (20th, 1963)
*The V.I.P.s* (MGM, 1963)

*The Sandpiper* (MGM, 1965)
*Who's Afraid of Virginia Woolf?* (WB, 1966)
*The Taming of the Shrew* (Col., 1967)
*Reflections in a Golden Eye* (WB-7 Arts, 1967)
*The Comedians* (MGM, 1967)
*Doctor Faustus* (Col., 1968)
*Boom!* (Univ., 1969)
*Secret Ceremony* (Univ., 1969)
*Anne of the Thousand Days* (Univ., 1969)°
*The Only Game in Town* (20th, 1970)
*X Y and Zee* (Col., 1972)
*Hammersmith Is Out* (Cin., 1972)
*Under Milk Wood* (Altura Films, 1972)
*Night Watch* (Avco Emb., 1973)
*Ash Wednesday* (Par., 1973)
*That's Entertainment* (MGM, 1974)
*The Driver's Sauce* (1974)
*The Blue Bird* (1975)

°Unbilled appearance

Elizabeth Taylor, director Joseph Mankiewicz, and Richard Burton on the set of **Cleopatra**

In a publicity pose for **The V.I.P.s** (MGM, 1963)

In **The Sandpiper** (MGM, 1965)

In **Who's Afraid of Virginia Woolf?** (WB, 1966)

In **The Taming of the Shrew** (Col., 1967)

In **The Comedians** (MGM, 1967)

In **Doctor Faustus** (Col., 1967)

Advertisement for **Hammersmith Is Out** (Cin., 1972)

In **Hammersmith Is Out**

Peter O'Toole, Elizabeth Taylor, and Richard Burton in **Under Milk Wood** (Altura, 1973)

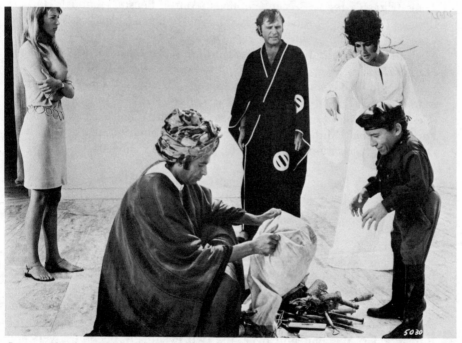

Joanna Shimkus, Fernando Piazza, Richard Burton, Elizabeth Taylor, and Michael Dunn in **Boom!** (Univ., 1968)

# CLEOPATRA
## *(Twentieth Century-Fox, 1963) C-243M.*

Producer, Walter Wanger; director, Joseph L. Mankiewicz; based on histories by Plutarch, Suetonius, Appian, and other ancient sources, and *The Life and Times of Cleopatra* by C. M. Franzero; screenplay, Mankiewicz, Ranald MacDougall, Sidney Buchman; assistant director, Fred R. Simpson; production designer, John De Cuir; art directors, Jack Martin Smith, Hilyard Brown, Herman Blumenthal, Elven Webb, Maurice Pelling, Boris Juraga; set decorators, Walter M. Scott, Paul S. Fox, Ray Moyer; costumes for Miss Taylor by Irene Sharaff; costumes, Vittorio Nino Novarese, Renie; music, Alex North; associate music director, Lionel Newman; choreography, Hermes Pan; sound, Fred Hynes, James Corcoran; camera effects, L. B. Abbott, Emil Kosa, Jr.; camera, Leon Shamroy; second unit camera, Claude Renoir, Piero Portalupi; editor, Dorothy Spencer.

Elizabeth Taylor (Cleopatra); Richard Burton (Mark Antony); Rex Harrison (Julius Caesar); Pamela Brown (High Priestess); George Cole (Flavius); Hume Cronyn (Sosigenes); Cesare Danova (Apollodorus); Kenneth Haigh (Brutus); Andrew Keir (Agrippa); Martin Landau (Rufio); Roddy McDowall (Octavian); Robert Stephens (Germanicus); Francesca Annis (Eiras); Gregoire Aslan (Pothinos); Martin Benson (Ramos); Herbert Berghof (Theodotos); John Cairney (Phoebus); Jacqui Chan (Lotos); Isabelle Cooley (Charmian); John Doucette (Achillas); Andrew Faulds (Canidius); Michael Gwynn (Cimber); Michael Hordern (Cicero); John Hoyt (Cassius); Marne Maitland (Euphranor); Carroll O'Connor (Casca); Richard O'Sullivan (Ptolemy); Gwen Watford (Calpurnia); Douglas Wilmer (Decimus); Marina Berti (Queen at Tarsus); John Karlsen (High Priest); Loris Loddi (Cesarion at age Four); Jean Marsh (Octavia); Gin Mart (Marcellus); Furio Meniconi (Mithridates); Kenneth Nash (Caesarion at Age Twelve); Del Russell (Caesarion at Age Seven); John Valva (Valvus).

New York Premiere: Rivoli Theatre—June 12, 1963
New York Television Debut: CBS—February 13 and 14, 1972

### Synopsis

Having defeated Pompey at the battle of Pharsalia, Julius Caesar, now the undisputed Consul of Rome, arrives in the Egypt of 48 B.C. Twenty-year-old Cleopatra is expelled from the throne she shares with her younger brother, Ptolemy, but intends to right matters by meeting with Caesar. She is smuggled into her palace in Alexandria where she encounters the Roman ruler. Winning him over, the two eventually become lovers and she gives him a son, a fair exchange for his having restored her kingdom to her. After Caesar has returned to Rome, he sends for Cleopatra, who enters the city in a triumphant procession. But her victory is short-circuited when Caesar is assassinated in the Curia of the Senate. Before the grief-stricken woman returns to Egypt she does capture Mark Antony's eye, but it is some three years before they again meet, this time on her royal barge at Tarsus. Now twenty-eight years old, she employs her mature charm and wit to captivate Caesar's ostensible successor. He becomes her lover, and together they return to Egypt. To maintain his political position in Rome, he is later forced to wed Octavia, the sister of his rival triumvir, Octavian, but Antony soon returns to Cleopatra. Meanwhile, the Egyptian Queen, angered by his neglect, uses her wiles to obtain from Antony the greater part of the Roman Empire's eastern provinces. This fact, plus Cleopatra's public marriage to the already wed Antony, moves Octavian to join in battle with Antony at Actium. When Cleopatra believes that Antony has been killed, she retreats with her fleet, thus quickening Octavian's victory. She retreats to a mausoleum, where her jealous major-domo Apollodorus informs Antony that the Queen is dead. Antony stabs himself and is taken to the mausoleum where he dies in Cleopatra's arms. Certain that Octavian will lead her as a humbled captive to Rome, Cleopatra kills herself with the bite of an asp.

◆ ◆ ◆

From the little one-million-dollar Joan Collins picture that producer Walter Wanger and Twentieth Century-Fox president Spyros P. Skouras envisioned in 1958, *Cleopatra* grew to an eventual cost reputed to be close to forty million dollars. Why? That's Hollywood. The "how" follows.

In the spring of 1959 with the *Cleopatra* project definitely firmed on the Fox shooting schedule, Wanger convinced the studio to increase the budget to three million dollars. Since the picture was gaining in stature, it was decided that a bigger name actress might be more logical for the key role. Elizabeth Taylor was asked to portray the title role, and instead of just saying no (her inclination) she asked for an unlikely one-million-dollar salary. Wanger was intrigued, but vetoed the star's price, with Skouras "suggesting" that the less expensive Susan Hayward should be signed to play the Egyptian queen. Wanger and his clique were now insistent that Taylor was *the* person for the movie and when she agreed to reduce her salary demand to $750,000 plus a profit participation (ten percent of the gross receipts), expenses, and a stringent overtime payroll clause, Wanger was amenable, even though it now meant the picture must be shot in Europe because of Taylor's tax situation.

Fox agreed to the Taylor terms, but now had to readjust the start of lensing until she completed a final film *(Butterfield 8)* under her MGM contract, a project itself long delayed due to an industry strike. Therefore, shooting on *Cleopatra* did not actually commence at London's Pinewood Studios until September 28, 1960. Rouben Mamoulian directed a cast that included Peter Finch as Julius Caesar (Laurence Olivier rejected the role), and Stephen Boyd as Marc Antony. On November 18, 1960, with very little filming accomplished, production was halted because star Taylor claimed to be suffering from a recurrent cold—some say she went into retreat because she was rather overweight and was on a mammoth crash diet. By January 2, 1961, the star was back on the set but now insisted that her love scenes with Finch were unplayable and had to be rewritten. On January 18th of that year, Mamoulian resigned, with only some ten-and-a-half minutes of usable film in the can. The budget was now close to six million dollars. Thereafter, Taylor's illness became complicated and she later had to undergo a tracheotomy which saved her life. Her personal physicians then stated she could not possibly return to work until September. Meanwhile, she was awarded an Oscar for *Butterfield 8*, which even she admits was a sympathy vote for her highly publicized life and death battle.

When word reached the Egyptian authorities that the new Oscar winner was quoted as saying, "It will be fun to be the first Jewish Queen of Egypt," permission for Fox to lens key scenes in that country was immediately revoked. More expensive shifting of plans and schedules. On September 13, 1961, when production on *Cleopatra* began once again, the soundstages used were in Rome, Italy, and the director was now Joseph L. Mankiewicz, who had guided Taylor through *Suddenly, Last Summer* (1959). Mankiewicz rewrote much of the existing script and Taylor had new co-stars—Richard Burton as Antony and Rex Harrison as Caesar. (Previous film commitments precluded Finch and Boyd from further work on the film.) By now the budget had been rejuggled to a fourteen-million-dollar ceiling.

The romantic entanglements on and off the *Cleopatra* set between twenty-nine-year-old Taylor (twice divorced, once widowed, and at that time wed to singer Eddie Fisher, and the mother of several children) and thirty-seven-year-old Welsh actor Burton (then wed to Sybil Williams, and the father of two children) was well documented in purple prose by the global press. As time passed, production costs escalated, Taylor suffered recurrent leg trouble, and then all pretense of calm domesticity evaporated, when both Fisher and Sybil Burton left the Rome battlefront. Thereafter, co-star Harrison, who had been given short shrift in the production, added to the moral spectacle by romancing, and later wedding, actress Rachel Roberts in March, 1962. Three months later, with a Fox studio deficit of thirty-nine-million dollars, Skouras was forced to resign, and Darryl F. Zanuck reassumed control of the company, leading to further re-editing and retakes on the seemingly unending shooting on *Cleopatra*.

When the gargantuan production effort on *Cleopatra* was finally terminated, Taylor had received her $750,000 guaranteed salary, $1,115,000 in overtime pay, plus $275,000 in expenses (which included fully staffing her luxurious villa outside of Rome). Burton, in contrast, had

770

received the "insignificant" salary of $15,000 weekly for his professional services on the epic. Fox claimed that in toto Taylor had delayed the lensing of the picture, one way or another, by some 140 days.

When the studio began editing *Cleopatra* it proposed to release the footage as two separate full length films. That idea was soon scrapped and the six hours of usable celluloid was reduced to 243 minutes for the one hundred-dollar-a-ticket premiere at the Rivoli Theatre on June 12, 1963. Shortly thereafter the film was chopped down to 222 minutes, and by the time the roadshow attraction—which had a theatre ticket price high of three dollars—reached the neighborhood spots at a $1.25 admission, it had been shorn to a miniscule 180-minute running time.

Because of the tremendous production publicity, it was almost impossible for *Cleopatra* to live up to the tremendous expectations. As Judith Crist *(New York Herald-Tribune)* phrased the general reaction to the film, " . . . at best a major disappointment, at worst an extravagant exercise in tedium." Beyond the scenes showing the queen's majestical entry into Rome, the sea battle at Actium, and a few land skirmishes, there was surprisingly little spectacle in the widescreen (Todd-AO) extravaganza. Although the Catholic Church cited the movie as "inadvisable viewing," most moviegoers could find little salacious or tantalizing material within the confines of *Cleopatra*. Not even Taylor's nude (by 1963 standards) bathing scene buoyed audience interest. Patrons were obviously disappointed that *Cleopatra* had failed to 1) reveal in explicit terms large expanses of Taylor's anatomy, 2) provide demonstrations of the Taylor-Burton style lovemaking that was the talk of Rome. In short, this picture of pictures was merely a marathon session of endless jabbering. To quote the Bard, the film was "full of sound and fury, signifying nothing."

It was to be expected that Taylor would receive very close critical scrutiny from reviewers, a group anxious to confirm the public's suspicion that no actress could be worth the rhubarb she had caused on both a professional and personal level. " . . . neither her costumes nor her performance leaves anything to the imagination," wrote Crist of the *Herald-Tribune*, " . . . her accents and acting style jarring first with those of Harrison and later with those of Burton. She is an entirely physical creature, no depth of emotion apparent in her kohl-laden eyes, no modulation in her voice that too often rises to fishwife levels." Archer Winsten *(New York Post)* was even less gallant. "*Cleopatra*, in the person of Elizabeth Taylor, falls flat, disastrously so . . . she sounds like something dragged in from a minor league. . . . It pains one to reflect that the Liz Taylor, so brutally overmatched here . . . is over the edge." In case any moviegoer might forget to make the inevitable comparisons, Taylor's Egyptian queen was contrasted—and unfavorably—to the range of previous twentieth century Cleopatras, including moviedom's Claudette Colbert and Vivien Leigh, and Helen Hayes and Talullah Bankhead onstage.

Burton, noted for his lofty stage performances rather than his abortive

771

Hollywood career of a decade before, did not emerge unscathed from the *Cleopatra* farrago. "Burton staggers around looking ghastly and spouting irrelevance, like a man who suddenly realizes that he has lost his script and is really reading some old sides from *King of Kings*. And in the big love scenes 'the ne'er-lust-wearied Antony' seems strangely bored—as if he had rehearsed too much" (*Time* magazine).

Ironically, the publicity-forgotten Harrison received the best critical notices, a surprise to Fox officials who, a short time before, had been court-ordered to hastily paint in a face of Harrison onto the huge Times Square billboard advertising *Cleopatra*. (This was the same outdoor sign which displayed a full-length painting of Taylor and Burton, in costume, reclining on a royal couch, with the body of the Queen, so it was later revealed, belonging to twenty-year-old model Lois Bennett.)

As feared, the grossly expensive *Cleopatra* did not fare very well at Oscar time. Nominated for Best Picture, it lost to *Tom Jones*; and Rex Harrison was defeated in the Best Actor's category by Sidney Poitier of *Lilies of the Fields*. Adding insult to mounting injury, Roddy McDowall, who as Octavian was a likely candidate for a Best Supporting Actor bid for his fitting performance, was inadvertently omitted from the nomination ballots, and despite a write-in campaign, he was not among the five nominees for that category. The picture did win four minor Oscars, but nothing that would revive public confidence in the film once unfavorable word-of-mouth had spread to the hinterlands.

The *Cleopatra* legend continued long thereafter. In 1964 Fox inaugurated a fifty-million-dollar law suit against Taylor, claiming her "scandalous conduct" during production had depreciated the value of the released picture. Taylor counter-sued, and the case is still not settled. In 1966, television rights to the feature were leased to ABC-TV network on a two-showing five-million-dollar deal, which still left the film some ten million dollars shy of its overall cost to that date. Several diary-style books on the epic to end all epics appeared over the years adding fact and confusion to the history of the little picture that was to be, but never was.

What was Taylor's reaction to her monumental screen role in the movie of the century? "I found it vulgar. Yes, I suppose I should still be grateful about having made the picture, for obvious reasons."

### THE V.I.P.s
#### (MGM, 1963) C-119M.

Producer, Anatole de Grunwald; associate producer, Roy Parkinson; director, Anthony Asquith; screenplay, Terence Rattigan; art director, William Kellner; set decorator, Pamela Cornell; assistant director, Kip Gowans; gowns, Hubert de Givenchy, Pierre Cardin; music, Miklos Rozsa; production adviser, Margaret Booth; Miss Taylor's makeup, Dave Aylott;

Miss Taylor's hairstyles, Vivienne Walker Zavitz; sound, Cyril Swern; camera, Jack Hildyard; editor, Frank Clarke.

Elizabeth Taylor (Frances Andros); Richard Burton (Paul Andros); Louis Jourdan (Marc Champselle); Elsa Martinelli (Gloria Gritti); Margaret Rutherford (Duchess of Brighton); Maggie Smith (Miss Mead); Rod Taylor (Les Mangam); Orson Welles (Max Buda); Linda Christian (Miriam Marshall); Dennis Price (Commander Millbank); Richard Wattis (Sanders); Ronald Fraser (Joslin); David Frost (Reporter); Robert Coote (John Coburn); Joan Benham (Miss Potter); Michael Hordern (Airport Director); Lance Percival (BOAC Official); Martin Miller (Dr. Schwutzbacher); Peter Sallis (Doctor); Stringer Davis (Hotel Waiter); Clifton Jones (Jamaican Passenger); Moyra Fraser (Air Hostess); Joyce Carey (Mrs. Damer); Griffiths Davis (Porter); Maggie McGrath (Waitress); Frank Williams (Assistant to Airport Director); Rosemary Dorken, Pamela Buckley (Airport Announcers); Ray Austin (Rolls Chauffeur); Angus Lennis (Meteorological Man); Duncan Lewis (Hotel Receptionist); Richard Briers (Met. Official); Jill Carson (Air Hostess); Terence Alexander (Captain); Richard Caldicot (Hotel Representative); Ann Castle (Lady Reporter); Clifford Mollison (Mr. River the Hotel Manager); Gordon Sterne (Official); Reginald Beckwith (Head Waiter); John Blythe (Barman); Virginia Bedard, Cal McCord (Visitors).

New York Premiere: Radio City Music Hall—September 19, 1963
New York Television Debut: ABC—January 15, 1967

### Synopsis

After a heavy fog delays the takeoff of planes from London Airport, a group of passengers en route to New York are forced to assemble in the V.I.P. lounge. Each of them has special reasons for wishing to depart England as quickly as possible. Frances Andros is leaving her millionaire husband to caper with Marc Champselle, an international gigolo. Max Buda, an eccentric film magnate, is traveling with his protégé Gloria Gritti, and he must be out of the country by midnight to avoid a financially ruinous income tax levy. The scatterbrained Duchess of Brighton has taken a social hostess post in Miami in order to raise the money to maintain her ancestral estate. Les Mangam, a self-made business tycoon, must be in New York the next day to insure a loan to prevent a giant combine from grabbing his tractor firm. When the transatlantic flight is cancelled until morning, the passengers are forced to stay at the airport hotel. Frances' husband Paul arrives after finding her farewell note. After convincing her of his deep love and need of her, she decides to remain with him. Mangam's company is saved when his loyal and adoring secretary, Miss Mead, persuades Paul to loan Mangam the necessary funds. Buda's accountant-factotum saves his client by arranging for his employer to sign over all his assets to the Italian-born Gloria, and then wedding her. Finally, the Duchess is able to return home when Buda decides to rent her estate for the location lensing of his newest picture.

◆——◆

British producer-scripter Anatole de Grunwald took smart and prompt advantage of the *Cleopatra* situation by quickly hiring Elizabeth Taylor and Richard Burton to grace *The V.I.P.s*, his modern day rendition of the Grand Hotel theme. He started shooting in London on December 19, 1962, and the film reached most theatres in the fall of 1963 before *Cleopatra* had departed its special roadshow playdates. *The V.I.P.s* was widely damned as commercially specious [' . . . like the icing on a store bought cake, it is designed to conceal the flat, unpalatable dough inside" *(Saturday Review)*.], but the less discriminating general public bought the glittery package and the film grossed $7.5 million in distributors' domestic rentals.

Because of the film's far more modest nature, the critics were obviously less savage in their dissection of the star team's emoting. "The contrast with Burton is no longer damning, for he comes down to modern speech, which is a medium she [Taylor] too can work in" [Archer Winsten *(New York Post)*]. "Mr. Burton's performance is graceful and unremittingly gloomy and Miss Taylor's—is remitting; both, of course, are beautiful to look at" [Judith Crist *(New York Herald-Tribune)*].

One may carp at the script deficiencies of *The V.I.P.s* which allow such contrasting types as Burton's level tycoon and Louis Jourdan's jellyfish playboy both to be adored by Taylor's egocentric character, or to offer such stereotype characters as the movie producer played by gargantuan Orson Welles. Nevertheless, *The V.I.P.s* emerges as a glossy soap opera in the best style, and a film so slick in its superficial entertainment qualities that it is fun to watch it again and again. With money being the prime motive driving each of the film's characters onward, everything appropriately is luxurious, from the swank London airport sets and the thumping lushness of Miklos Rozsa's music score [heavily borrowed from his previous *Ben-Hur* (1959)], to the richly lit camerawork of Jack Hildyard. Director Anthony Asquith wisely maintained a fast pace in most scenes, quickly shifting audience interest from one set of trouble-plagued individuals to another, while always an undertone of naughty keyhole peeking guaranteed to whet filmgoers' vicarious appetites.

Since her golden years at MGM in the 1950s, Taylor had never looked more beguiling than in *The V.I.P.s*, which carefully masked her overly svelte figure in well-styled outfits, in particular her hooded white fur coat ensemble. The remarkable thing about her performance is that the viewer finds himself beginning to care about her disintegrating marriage to Burton's Paul Andros. This is all the more amazing when one considers the triteness of Terence Rattigan's dialog, which has Taylor admitting of her spouse, "For most of the thirteen years I've loved him, but I don't know him." With the exception of the later *Who's Afraid of Virginia Woolf?* rarely has Burton given such a supercharged performance, first as the passionate husband who always bestows an expensive gift on his adored wife when she goes away, then as the distraught husband who explodes when he hears Taylor confirm, "It's not a joke, Paul. I'm leaving you for Mark." With nerve-jangling intensity, he fires back at her a threat, heard by every passerby at the airport, "I'm not going to let you go through that gate. I'd kill you first." As the experienced soap opera addict could well predict, it would not be long in *The V.I.P.s* before weak-willed Jourdan bows out of the story, and the Taylor-Burton marriage relationship reasserts itself.

While Taylor and Burton assume the most glamorous roles in the picture, the most charming performance in *The V.I.P.s*, is provided by Margaret Rutherford (who won a Best Supporting Actress Oscar for the film). She is the matronly Duchess of Brighton, who is about to embark on her first plane trip, horror-stricken at the travel ordeal as well as by the thought of leaving her beloved home at Brighton with its daffodil gardens. But she is determined to earn sufficient funds to pay the back taxes due on her ancestral estate by accepting a post as social hostess in a Miami Beach hotel. Hers is as theatrical a performance as that of Welles as the bulbous Hungarian filmmaker, but she is far more humane in her delineation, as is Maggie Smith's interpretation of the faithful secretary to Rod Taylor, a woman who will do most anything for her financially-troubled boss. In fact, it is Smith who provides one of the more penetrating dramatic moments in the film. Burton, engulfed by his own domestic woes, is so taken with Smith's outburst of loyalty and devotion to Rod Taylor, that he not only writes out a check to aid the man, but through her example he now realizes that love had far greater dimension than he has yet explored with delectable Elizabeth Taylor.

## THE SANDPIPER
### *(MGM, 1965) C-117M.*

Producer, Martin Ransohoff; associate producer, John Calley; director, Vincente Minnelli; story, Ransohoff; adaptation, Irene Kamp, Louis Kamp; screenplay, Dalton Trumbo, Michael Wilson; art directors, George W. Davis, Urie McCleary; set decorators, Henry Grace, Keogh Gleason; music, Johnny Mandel; song, Paul Francis Webster and Mandel; assistant director, William McGarry; titles, Herb Rosenthal; Laura's paintings by Elizabeth Duquette; Redwood sculpture by Edmund Kara; co-ordinator of Big Sur scene, Eduardo Tirella; sound, Franklin Milton; camera, Milton Krasner; wildlife camera, Richard Borden; editor, David Bretherton.

Elizabeth Taylor (Laura Reynolds); Richard Burton (Dr. Edward Hewitt); Eva Marie Saint (Claire Hewitt); Charles Bronson (Cos Erickson); Robert Webber (Ward Hendricks); James Edwards (Larry Brant); Torin Thatcher (Judge Thompson); Tom Drake (Walter Robinson); Doug Henderson (Phil Sutcliff); Morgan Mason (Danny Reynolds).

New York Premiere: Radio City Music Hall—July 15, 1965
New York Television Debut: CBS—October 2, 1969

### Synopsis

Painter Laura Reynolds and her nine-year-old illegitimate son, Danny, live together in a plush beach-side cabin in Monterey, California. She has refused to send the child to school, deciding to teach him herself. Because she so imbues him with her own unconventional ideas, the boy is constantly in difficulties with the authorities. Judge Thompson later rules that Danny must either be sent to school or removed entirely from his mother's care. Laura is forced to yield, and Danny is sent to San Simeon, a private school run by Episcopalian minister Dr. Edward Hewitt. Edward and his wife Claire are amazed to discover how advanced Danny is in literature and the other arts, as Laura is astonished at the relative ease with which the child has settled into school routine. Soon Edward and Laura, who initially disliked each other, find themselves passionately in love. Although he detests her bohemian friends, he gives in to his desire for her, bitterly ashamed and humiliated though by his actions. When the scandal comes to a head, he reviles the self-serving politicians who have been using him and the school for their own ends. He tells them the truth about himself, and sets off, leaving both Laura and Claire. He hopes once again to find the ideals which inspired his youth.

◆—◆—◆

Even though recently divorced Elizabeth Taylor and Richard Burton married in the spring of 1964 during his pre-Broadway tour of *Hamlet* in Canada, *le scandale* still raged. He later claimed that *The Sandpiper* was the only feasible (one that would pay her a one-million-dollar salary and he $750,000) joint property offered the couple. Although Taylor had remained offscreen since *The V.I.P.s*, Burton filmed *Becket, The Night of the Iguana*, and a stage version of *Hamlet*, all released in 1964. Without a doubt *The Sandpiper*, filmed largely in Paris, was "the most perfectly awful movie of the past several seasons" [Judith Crist (*New York Herald-Tribune*)]. However, it grossed seven million dollars in distributors' domestic rentals, confirming the sound economics of the domestically convenient screen teaming of Taylor and Burton regardless of the cost or trouble. In the vastly diminished feature film market of the 1960s, it was an amazing situation for (super) stars to find film work, let alone with the partner of her/his choice and at a salary that maintained the player's ego and status.

One of *The Sandpiper's* greatest sins was using "That shabby old Holly-

776

wood custom of pretending to a great piety while flirting around with material that is actually suggestive and cheap" [Bosley Crowther *(New York Times)*]. Garbed in stretch pants and plunging neckline blouses, Taylor romped through the meritorious feature as a free loving beatnik (remember those?), surrounded by bohemian friends, and mouthing such rubbish as "all my life men have stared at me and rubbed up against me." To provide dramatic structure, Taylor's hedonistic nature clashes with the religious conformity of Burton's Dr. Edward Hewitt, a repressed sinner. (Some wits said this film should have been listed as a prelude to the earlier *The Night of the Iguana*, in which he had played a defrocked clergyman.) Burton's character in *The Sandpiper* is always speaking in declamations. "Oh, God, grant me some small remembrance of honor!" begs Burton once he has been aroused by the sight of the (discreetly) nude Taylor at her beach "shack." After several furtive rounds of lovemaking, Taylor admits, "I never knew what love was before," but Burton tops her puerile statement with a gem of his own. He confesses his affair to his ever patient wife (Eva Marie Saint), "We made love—even in motels. God help me!"

While *The Sandpiper* was the first feature film to indulge the love team's reputed ability for passionate romancing, the specious finale finds the repentant Burton falling prey to his pangs of Victorian conscience and leaving everything and everyone behind. Certainly a far cry from the reality of his offcamera life.

It is acknowledged that nearly anything is possible in cinema terms, but art directors George W. Davis and Urie McCleary outdid themselves by providing Taylor with an overly plush abode to represent her simple beach home. After all, Taylor's Laura Reynolds is a long-standing unemployed aardvark who admits, "I turn out watercolors when I need groceries." (Taylor's canvas creations were actually the work of Elizabeth Duquette.)

For the record, the film's title refers to an injured wild beach bird which Taylor cares for and then watches fly away, with the viewer and Taylor left with the obvious parallel to her own life. Like her feathered charge, Taylor merely wants to "fly free." This specious theory, considering her nonsensical life style, meets approbation from the sanctimonious Burton who admits that she may have a real point regarding proper life styles and values.

Just to prove that miracles still happened in Hollywood, *The Sandpiper* did win an Oscar. So what if it was for Best Song of the Year, "The Shadow of Your Smile," composed by Paul Francis Webster and Johnny Mandel? The tune has become a well-regarded standard, insuring that years hence *The Sandpiper*, at least by association, will be still remembered.

## WHO'S AFRAID OF VIRGINIA WOOLF?
### *(Warner Bros., 1966) 132M.*

Producer, Ernest Lehman; director, Mike Nichols; based on the play by Edward Albee; screenplay, Lehman; assistant director, Bud Grace; production designer, Richard Sylbert; set decorator, George James Hopkins; music-music director, Alex North; costumes, Irene Sharaff; sound, M. A. Merrick; production adviser, Doane Harrison; camera, Haskell Wexler; editor, Sam O'Steen.

Elizabeth Taylor (Martha); Richard Burton (George); George Segal (Nick); Sandy Dennis (Honey).

New York Premiere: Criterion and Loew's Tower East Theatres—
    June 23, 1966
New York Television Debut: CBS—February 22, 1973

## Synopsis

At two A.M. on the campus of New Carthage College in New England, a forty-six-year-old associate professor of history and his older wife, the daughter of the school's president, return home from a party. Married for twenty years, their joint life has been an unending series of self-destructive, violent arguments, tempered only intermittently by intervals of subconscious tenderness. George is an ineffectual soul, a victim to misspent idealism, constantly harried by shrewish Martha, who continually contrasts him to her high-powered, successful father. Although feminine vulnerability lurks beneath her surface, she has hid it with a shield of high voltage vulgarity. For self-protection, a scapegoat, and a common meeting ground, the couple have created an imaginary "son." On this particular evening she has invited a faculty couple, newcomer Nick and his wilting wife Honey to stop by for a nightcap. No sooner do they arrive than Martha makes lewd advances toward the younger man. Honey, upset by Martha's crude behavior and dizzy from inebriation, becomes ill. Later, in the early morning, Martha drags Nick to her bedroom, while George watches their lovemaking-in-shadow from the yard below. Upon learning that Martha has divulged their secret by telling Honey of their "son," George viciously retaliates by killing the "child." Martha is driven to near hysteria by George's mock funeral service conducted in Latin. Dawn comes and the younger couple leave. Both George and Martha are physically and emotionally exhausted. As they prepare to go to bed, it seems they have found a new meeting ground for mutual compassion in each other's needs.

◆ ◆ ◆

When it was announced that Edward Albee's award-winning Broadway play (1962) *Who's Afraid of Virginia Woolf?* had been purchased for the screen at a cost of $500,000 to Warner Bros., there was a great deal of speculation as to who would star in the coveted vehicle. The industry and the public were indeed shocked and/or amazed when it was announced that Elizabeth Taylor and Richard Burton would be the lead players and that ex-nightclub comedian and Broadway director Mike Nichols would make his film directing debut with this project.

Despite most everyone's fears the results proved amazingly felicitous. Not only did the black and white picture gross a very healthy $14.5 million in distributors' domestic rentals, but both Taylor and supporting player Sandy Dennis won Oscars as did the film's cinematography and the art-set direction. Burton, who had had an Oscar bid the year before for *The Spy Who Came in from the Cold,* but lost to Lee Marvin of *Cat Balou,* was nominated for an Academy Award for this film, but was defeated by Paul Scofield who won for *The Man for All Seasons.* Both Taylor and Burton did win the British Oscars for *Who's Afraid of Virginia Woolf?*

Even with the dilution of the salty dialog and the softening of the central character relationships, *Who's Afraid of Virginia Woolf?* still emerged as "One of the most scathingly honest films ever made" [Stanley Kauffmann *(New York Times)*]. As to the film's top stars, they received heady accolades that would have to sustain them through the bathos of their subsequent minor film work. "Miss Taylor, who has proven she can act in response to sensitive direction, earned every penny of her reported million plus. Her characterization is at once sensual, spiteful, cynical, pitiable, loathsome, lustful and tender. Shrews—both male and female— always attract initial attention, but the projection of three-dimensional reality requires talent which substains the interest; the talent is here. Burton delivers a smash portrayal. He evokes sympathy during the public degradations to which his wife subjects him, and his outrage, as well as his deliberate vengeance, are totally believable. . . ." *(Variety).*

The cinema version of *Who's Afraid of Virginia Woolf?* spins its own brand of expert entertainment, heightened by penetrating direction, although diminished by somewhat obtrusive, distracting camera angles, and a most inappropriately mawkish Alex North music score. Garbed in a gray fright wig and heavy wrinkle liner makeup, deliberately blowsy Taylor takes command from the opening credits onward as she and Burton weave their drunken way home after a faculty party at her father's stately home. Entering the sloppy kitchen, puffing on a cigarette and soon munching on a fried chicken leg, Taylor, with her special whiskey-en-crusted voice, launches into the famous sequence in which, parodying the mannerisms of Bette Davis, she berates her husband for not remem-bering the god damn Warner Bros. film in which Davis had said "What a dump!" The bespectacled Burton almost caps the scene when he quietly inquires, "Do you want me to go around braying at everyone like you do?"

Soon thereafter, Nick (George Segal), a biology instructor and a self-labeled stud, arrives with his wishy-washy wife Honey (Dennis), ostensibly invited for a late nightcap, but actually for a little fun game of "Get the Guests" which soon evolves into "Humiliate the Host." Burton starts the ball rolling by informing Taylor, who has now changed into slacks and a tawdry, tight-fitting blouse, "Just don't open your mouth about you know." (He is referring to their imaginary son who will be sixteen years old the next day.) But at the moment, Taylor, with drink in hand, has other things on her lascivious mind. She taunts Segal, "Have you kept your body?" wondering aloud if he is more athletic than her "paunchy" husband. To amuse her guests, Taylor recounts a public boxing match she had enjoyed with the repressed Burton, while he in turn now emerges from the study with shotgun in hand, which, when he pulls the trigger, unleashes a little pop-open umbrella.

Soon Taylor and Burton are arguing over their non-existent son, she insisting the boy has green eyes, he claiming the child has blue orbs. By now Taylor is thoroughly drunk and her increasingly gross behavior is punctuated by a Phyllis Diller-type laugh and cackle. But she is yet sober enough to further degrade meek but seething Burton, summing him up as "sort of a great big flop," a toy man who could never stand up to her father and establish proper discipline over Taylor.

When the couples later adjourn to a roadside cafe, Taylor announces to angered Burton, "I'm goin' to finish you before I'm through with you."

Burton: "I warned you not to go too far."

Taylor: "I'm just beginning."

But it soon becomes evident that Taylor is not as ferocious as she appears, for she soon tells her spouse, "There was a second back there when we could have cut through the crap."

But they are soon at each other's throat, with Burton telling her, "Be careful, Martha. I'll rip you to pieces." Taylor, who has pathetically screamed, "I'm not a monster," has revived her vicious self again, ranting, "You're not man enough."

Another segment of the drama gets underway when Taylor and Segal who had participated in a bout of erotic dancing at the cafe, return home and engage in "Hump the Hostess," while the morose, pathetic Burton sits in the yard hearing Dennis' tale of marital woe. Taylor concludes her sexual adventure and returns to the kitchen where she replenishes her ice-clinking glass. She announces, "I'm the earth mother and you are all flops."

As a prelude to the final dramatics, Segal, baffled by the peculiar evening and his equally unfathomable hosts, admits, "Hell, I don't know when you people are lying or what."

Taylor: "Truth and illusion, George. You don't know the difference."

Burton: "But we must carry on as if we did."

Herein lies the crux to Albee's drama.

Then the final round begins, with "Bringing up Baby" the game in point. Burton advises Taylor, "We play this one to the death." She is driven to somber recollections of their imaginary child, Jim, who "was born on a September night not unlike tonight." But Burton now has his innings at bat. Just as earlier in his character's life he had killed a parent in a car accident, so now Burton's George eliminates the "son" in a similar fatality. Taylor, with her mascara running down her puffy, tear-streaked face, implores, "I won't let you decide these things." But it is too late. Burton is already conducting a conclusive mock funeral ceremony.

As the final moment approaches, Burton announces, "It's dawn. The party's over." Segal and Dennis depart, leaving the weary hosts to their own devices. Illusion is gone, and they have a dreary Sunday to live through, and then. . . . turning out the lights as the sun comes up, Burton pats his wife's shoulder, saying, "Who's afraid of Virginia Woolf?"

Taylor: "I am, George. I am."

With hands clasped, the couple heads upstairs.

Beyond the stringent dramatics, which set a new level of maturity to the tone of 1960s movies, *Who's Afraid of Virginia Woolf?* established a new milestone for a major motion picture in its rough language. (Because no one under eighteen years of age was permitted to see it unless accompanied by a parent, the film won its Motion Picture Production Code seal.) When it came time to screen the film for American television audiences in 1972 (some thirty million viewers saw it), a few "god damns" were clipped from the film, but the rest of the soundtrack remained intact.

### THE TAMING OF THE SHREW
*(Columbia, 1967) C-122M.*

Executive producer, Richard McWhorter; producers, Richard Burton, Elizabeth Taylor, Franco Zeffirelli; director, Zeffirelli; based on the play by William Shakespeare; adaptation, Paul Dehn, Suso Cecchi D'Amico, Zeffirelli; production designer, John De Cuir; art directors, Giuseppe Mariani, Elven Webb; set decorators, Dario Simoni, Carlo Gervasi; music, Nino Rota; music director, Carlo Savina; costumes for Miss Taylor by Irene Sharaff; costumes, Danilo Donati; assistant directors, Carlo Lastricati, Rinaldo Ricci, Albino Cocco; sound, David Hildyard, Aldo De Martino; special effects, Augie Lohman; camera, Oswald Morris, Luciano Trasatti; editor, Peter Taylor.

Elizabeth Taylor (Katharina); Richard Burton (Petruchio); Cyril Cusack (Grumio); Michael Hordern (Baptista); Alfred Lynch (Tranio); Alan Webb (Gremio); Victor Spinetti (Hortensio); Roy Holder (Biondello); Mark Dignam (Vincentio); Bice Valori (The Widow); Natasha Pyne (Bianca); Michael York (Lucentio); Giancarlo Cobelli (The Priest); Vernon Dobtcheff (Pedant); Ken Parry (Tailor); Anthony Gardner (Haberdasher); Alberto Bonucci (Nathaniel); Gianni Magni (Curtis); Lino Capolicchio (Gregory); Roberto Antonelli (Philip); and: Tina Perna, Milena Vucotich, Alfredo Bianchini, Valentino Bacchi.

New York Premiere: Coronet Theatre—March 8, 1967
New York Television Debut: ABC—July 8, 1973

## Synopsis

In sixteenth-century Padua, Italy, wealthy merchant Baptista has two comely daughters, the unruly and bad-tempered Katharina, and the sweet and docile Bianca. Baptista announces, to the dismay of Bianca's many suitors, that she may not wed until the elder daughter has found a husband. But Lucentio, a student from Pisa, is so besmitten by Bianca's beauty that he poses as a language teacher, obtaining a post in Baptista's home. While Lucentio is conducting his wooing, a poor scoundrel named Petruchio arrives in Padua, vainly seeking a wealthy wife. In short order, he falls prey to Katharina's verbal scorn and physical abuse, with the two exhausted participants eventually falling wearily into a heaping mound of sheep wool. He then proceeds calmly to praise her assorted charms and insists they will wed the following Sunday. On the nuptial day, he arrives late, quite drunk, and wearing slovenly clothes. But the marriage takes place, and Petruchio leads her off to his dilapidated country home. There, under the guise of proclaiming his true love for her, Petruchio rejects all manner of comfortable luxury, insisting they are unworthy of her. When Lucentio is later revealed to be the worthy son of the Vincentio of Padua and is given permission to wed Bianca, Katharina and Petruchio are invited to the wedding. At the feast, Petruchio brags that Katharina is the most obedient of all wives. To everyone's amazement, Katharina delivers a lecture on the virtues of wifely obedience.

◆—◆

Since William Shakespeare's comedy was first produced in 1593-4 it has remained a great stage favorite, and later served as the basis for a 1908 D. W. Griffith one-reel film, a forty-five-minute Norwegian version (1914) and the much more famous 1929 sound feature starring Mary Pickford and Douglas Fairbanks. Thereafter the bard's robust work became the basis of the 1948 Cole Porter Broadway musical, *Kiss Me, Kate*, which was itself put on film in 1953. Italian director Franco Zeffirelli, already well established as a leading Shakespearean authority with his several sumptuously mounted European productions, decided to film *The Taming of the Shrew* in the early 1960s, at first planning to utilize the services of Marcello Mastroianni and Sophia Loren. When nothing came of this project, time passed until Zeffirelli saw a performance of Burton's *Hamlet* in New York, and realized that the star's witty overtones to his portrayal of the Dane made him a most likely candidate to essay Petruchio. This decision led quite obviously to Elizabeth Taylor for the zesty role of Katharina.

The Burtons invested $1.4 million of their own money into this color film venture, filmed at the Dino de Laurentiis Studios some dozen miles south of Rome, where the production designers had transformed soundstages and outdoor sets into the colorful Renaissance city of Padua, Italy, as it must have appeared some four centuries ago. The production

782

of *The Taming of the Shrew* got underway on March 21, 1966. Burton began shooting his role on April 4th and Taylor went before the camera on May 3rd. Burton would spend ninety-one days playing his role of the robust Petruchio while Taylor was oncamera seventy-five days portraying the tempestuous Katharina. Shooting was completed in August, 1966.

The resultant film, which was the star team's first venture into screen comedy, was more a voluptuous pictorial delight than a histrionic feast. There was a magnificent tapesty of scenic delights devised by production designer John De Cuir. This picture was a vast artistic improvement over most of the couple's earlier screen ventures and did adhere in spirit to the zesty nature of the play, if not to the text. However, it was the consensus that both Burton and Taylor were a bit too old and heavy of body for such youthful horseplay. In addition, the emphasis here seemed to be more on overzealous Mack Sennett-style visual comedy than recapturing the majesty of Shakespeare's poetry. At least the two stars, with their still strong proletarian film public following, drew into theatres many people who had never seen a Shakespearean production before.

Bosomy Taylor, who played another type of shrew in *Who's Afraid of Virginia Woolf?*, fared much better than her bearded spouse in this production, in which she "makes Kate seem the ideal bawd of Avon—a creature of beauty with a voice shrieking howls and imprecations" (*Time* magazine). The couple careened through the 122 minutes with seeming total relish as they heaved abuses and conveniently placed stage props at one another, their first battle occurring in a storeroom filled with hanging hams. In the course of the seven minute encounter, the couple land on a woolstack where they engage in a wrestling match. (Said Taylor, "There I was with six inches of my spine fused and they expected me to toss Richard over my shoulder.") Later when Burton leads his reluctant bride homeward bound, she is forced to sit astride a recalcitrant donkey who revels in dumping its passenger load into mud puddles.

*The Taming of the Shrew* was selected for the annual British Royal Film Performance held at the Odeon Theatre in London.

## THE COMEDIANS
### (MGM, 1967) C-156M.

Producer-director, Peter Glenville; based on the novel by Graham Greene; screenplay, Greene; art director, François de Lamothe; set decorator, Robert Christides; music-music director, Laurence Rosenthal; sound, Jonathan Bates; assistant director, Jean-Michel Lacor; camera, Henri Decae; editor, Françoise Javet.

Richard Burton (Brown); Alec Guinness (Major Jones); Elizabeth Taylor (Martha Pineda); Peter Ustinov (Ambassador Pineda); Paul Ford

(Mr. Smith); Lillian Gish (Mrs. Smith); Georg Stanford Brown (Henri Philipot); Roscoe Lee Browne (Petit Pierre); Gloria Foster (Madame Philipot); James Earl Jones (Dr. Magiot); Zakes Mokae (Michel); Raymond St. Jacques (Captain Concasseur); Douta Seck (Joseph); Cicely Tyson (Marie Therese).

New York Premiere: DeMille and Coronet Theatres—October 31, 1967
New York Television Debut: CBS—October 28, 1971

### Synopsis

Mr. Brown returns to Haiti after an unsuccessful attempt to find a purchaser for his hotel, since tourists are a rare commodity in Haiti under the dictatorship of "Papa Doc" Duvalier and his secret police, the Tontons Macoute. Arriving at the same time are an elderly American couple, Mr. and Mrs. Smith, who plan to set up a vegetarian center, and the offbeat Englishman who calls himself Major Jones and is promptly jailed by the Tontons Macoute. Brown intends to mind his own business, but the Smiths shame him into joining with them to free Jones. In short order, the Smiths comprehend the depth of official corruption and brutality and leave in despair. Meanwhile, Brown is involved in an overwrought love affair with Martha, wife of South American ambassador Pineda. Jones regains official favor by maneuvering a shady armament deal, but then when the arrangement falls through, he is forced to turn to Brown for help. Brown obtains sanctuary for him in Pineda's embassy, where he becomes friendly with Martha. Aroused to jealousy, Brown leads the unsuspecting Jones into boasting that he could overthrow the present regime with a mere few rebels. Brown arranges for Jones to assume leadership over just such a group. Just before he is murdered in a surprise attack by the Tontons Macoute, Jones admits that he was never in the army, but has no thought now of backing out. Brown is persuaded to assume the identity of Major Jones and is acknowledged by the poorly equipped, untrained rebel band.

◆◆◆

*The Taming of the Shrew* had demonstrated that the boxoffice lustre of teaming Elizabeth Taylor and Richard Burton was fast on the wane. The unpopular *The Comedians* cinched the point. As this film's co-star Peter Ustinov saw the situation, "I think producers were, and are, wrong in assuming that the public will remain interested in a married couple loving each other on the screen when they know they go home together afterwards."

Obviously, Graham Greene's novel *The Comedians* could not be filmed on location in Haiti, but instead was lensed mostly in Dahomey, Africa. The book had stressed that any hope for Haiti is at the mercurial whim of its rulers, while the movie subverted the political theme to stress the dour romantic entanglements of the two stars, Burton and Taylor (she taking subordinate billing beneath Alec Guinness). The overblown, 156-minute feature was judged a "plodding, low-keyed, and eventually tedious melodrama" *(Variety)*, leading *Time* magazine to observe, *"The Comedians* has everything but economy, and Director Peter Glenville has tarried with a story that might have been twice as good at half the length."

The screen love team received mixed notices. "As a fading beauty with a German accent, Elizabeth Taylor is reasonably effective, but Richard Burton, playing an exhausted anti-hero in the same style as his memorable *The Spy Who Came in from the Cold,* seems to have stepped from the pages of the novel" *(Time* magazine). Judith Crist on the NBC-TV "Today Show" enunciated, ". . . the Burton's cinematic amours and maulings . . . are becoming not only boring but slightly less esthetic (the years are taking their toll, as they do on all sex symbols, especially from the chin-line down). . . ."

As it turned out, the most sympathetic character in the film was the romantic "villain" of the piece, Ustinov's kindly South American diplomat. Likewise, the most powerful scenes in the picture were not the depressing love interludes between Burton and Taylor (usually in the back seat of a car), but the encounters between Burton and Guinness. Near the finale, the two actors have a four minute expostulation in which, while waiting to join the Haitian guerrillas, they reexamine the diverse factors that brought them to their present "graveyard."

In comparison to the present day standards of explicitness and the rash of pro-black, anti-white celluloid action entries, *The Comedians* seems very tame in its political/racial message. But back in 1967, upon the release of the MGM film, the Haitian ambassador issued a formal protest, labeling the movie as an "inflammatory libel against Haiti" which was geared "to mislead the American people." Author Greene countered, "The rule of Haiti responsible for the murder and exile of thousands of his countrymen is really protesting against his own image in the looking glass. Like the Ugly Queen in *Snow White,* he will have to destroy all the mirrors."

### DOCTOR FAUSTUS
*(Columbia, 1968) C-93M.*

Producers, Richard Burton, Richard McWhorter; directors, Burton, Nevill Coghill; based on the play *The Tragical History of Doctor Faustus* by Christopher Marlowe; adaptation, Coghill; assistant director, Gus Agosti; production designer, John De Cuir; art director, Boris Juraga; set decorator, Dario Simoni; music director, Mario Nascimbene; costumes, Peter Hall; choreography, Jacqueline Harvey; titles, National Screen

Services; sound, David Hildyard, John Aldred; camera, Gabor Pogany; editor, John Shirley.

Richard Burton (Doctor Faustus); Andreas Teuber (Mephistopheles); Elizabeth Taylor (Helen of Troy); Ian Marten (Emperor); Elizabeth O'Donovan (Empress); David McIntosh (Lucifer); Jeremy Eccles (Belzebub); Ram Chopra (Valdes); Richard Carwardine (Cornelius); Richard Heffer, Hugh Williams (Scholars); Gwydion Thomas (Scholar/Lechery); Nicholas Loukes (Cardinal/Pride); Richard Durden-Smith (Knight); Patrick Barwise (Wagner); Adrian Benjamin (Pope); Jeremy Chandler (Attendant at Emperor's Court); Angus McIntosh (Rector Magnificus); Ambrose Coghill (Professor/Avarice); Anthony Kaufmann (Professor/Envy); Julian Wontner, Richard Harrison, Nevill Coghill (Professors); Michael Menaugh (Good Angel); John Sandbach (Boy-turned-into-Hind); Sebastian Walker (Idiot); R. Peverello (Wrath); Maria Aitken (Sloth); Valerie James (Idleness); Bridget Coghill, Petronella Pulsford, Susan Watson (Gluttony); Jacqueline Harvey, Sheila Dawson, Carolyn Bennitt (Dancers); Jane Wilford (Nun/Court Lady).

New York Premiere: Cinema Rendezvous Theatre—February 6, 1968
New York Television Debut: CBS—June 25, 1971

### Synopsis

In sixteenth-century Germany, the University of Wittenberg awards its highest academic honors to the elderly Dr. Faustus, a renowned scholar of alchemy, astrology, and philosophy. In his insatiable quest for more knowledge and power, Faustus turns to necromancy to summon Mephistopheles, a spirit from hell. Faustus sells his soul to the devil for twenty-four years of living "in all voluptuousness," signing the pact with his own blood. Mephistopheles carries through his part of the bargain by revealing to Faustus the seven deadly sins, allowing him to become invisible to harass the Pope and his cardinals, and even escorting the pupil through time to the court of Alexander the Great and his queen. Later to impress a trio of his students, Faustus summons up Helen of Troy and, becoming besmitten by her beauty, he pleads with Mephistopheles to allow him to become her love. His wish is granted, but Faustus realizes he is fast heading on the road to eternal damnation. When the appointed time comes, he follows the beckoning Helen and they descend into hell.

◆━◆━◆

There was no doubt, even to the man on the street, that Elizabeth Taylor and Richard Burton had commercially and artistically floundered in *The Comedians*. Added to the fact that *The Taming of the Shrew* had only been a qualified winner, and that she had sunk in the mire with co-star Marlon Brando in *Reflections in a Golden Eye* (1967), one would have thought that the famous cinema team would have professionally split apart in order to salvage their careers. In the halcyon days of the studio system, such a move would have already been a *fait accompli* brought about by the company's boss, but in the new era of the free-lancing superstars, it was a decision that had to come from the autonomous celebrities themselves. And Burton and Taylor, both enormously wealthy by this time, determined to remain together oncamera as well as off, a feat more commendable for disciplining their conflicting, over-indulgent natures than for providing their thinning audiences with viable filmfare.

In February, 1966, Burton had returned to his alma mater, Oxford University, where he participated in a stage performance of Christopher Marlowe's *Doctor Faustus,* directed by his former tutor, Professor Neville Coghill. Apart from Burton and Taylor (in the non-speaking role of Helen of Troy), the cast of this later-filmed production was composed entirely of Oxford students and teachers. Like the previous stage presentation, the proceeds, if any, from the film, co-produced and co-directed by Burton, were to be donated to the Oxford University Dramatic Society.

As Penelope Mortimer *(London Observer)* wrote, "When fairy god-parents like the Burtons descend on the Oxford University Dramatic Society, transport them to Rome and make what must have been a highly expensive picture for the fun of it, criticism falters." However, *Variety* was not afraid to speak its mind, judging that *Doctor Faustus* was "Probably one of the most desperately non-commercial enterprises in motion picture history."

The Faustus legend had cropped up many times in twentieth-century art forms, including the poem-play-movie *The Devil and Daniel Webster* and the Broadway musical-movie, *Damn Yankees,* but here the basic story, despite cuts and alterations from the original, was unraveled in such unremitting starkness that it provided little distraction for the unscholarly filmgoer. Burton's non-stop sententious reading of the Marlowe-Coghill dialog proceeded at a dreary audio level, while the mod visual techniques oncamera continually threatened to blend into a semblance of high camp. Particularly distracting from the ambiance intended was the recurring appearance of a non-talking Taylor, a vision of gaudy loveliness in assorted mono-hued outfits. *Women's Wear Daily* complained that she looked like a creature "with mascara and a pair of plastic breasts more apt on the nose of a Flying Fortress."

### BOOM!
*(Universal, 1968) C-113M.*

Producers, John Heyman, Norman Priggen; associate producer, Lester Persky; director, Joseph Losey; based on the story *Man, Bring This Up Road* and the play *The Milk Train Doesn't Stop Here Anymore* by Tennessee Williams; screenplay, Williams; assistant director, Carlo Lastricati; production designer, Richard MacDonald; music, John Barry; Indian music, Nazirali Jairazbnoy, Viram Jasani; song, John Dankworth, Don Black; costumes, Tiziani; sound, Leslie Hammond, Gerry Humphreys; camera, Douglas Slocombe; editor, Reginald Beck.

Elizabeth Taylor (Mrs. Flora Goforth); Richard Burton (Chris Flanders); Noel Coward (Witch of Capri); Joanna Shimkus (Blackie); Michael Dunn (Rudy); Romolo Valli (Dr. Lullo); Veronica Wells (Simonetta); Fernando Piazza (Giulio); Howard Taylor (Journalist); Gens Bloch (Photographer); Franco Pesce (Villager).

New York Premiere: Sutton and Trans-Lux West Theatres—
May 26, 1968
New York Television Debut: NBC—September 21, 1970

### Synopsis

Six times a widow, millionairess Flora Goforth spends each summer on her privately-owned Mediterranean island. She knows this year she is going to die from an incurable ailment, and has begun dictating her savage memoirs to her harassed secretary, Blackie. When aging poet Chris Flanders arrives on the island he is promptly attacked by Mrs. Goforth's dwarf bodyguard Rudy and his snarling pack of vicious dogs. Although Mrs. Goforth is warned by her effete bachelor friend, known as the Witch of Capri, that Chris has appropriately earned the name "Angel of Death" because of his constant association with expiring rich women, she allows the visitor to remain in one of the guest houses nearby to her lavishly equipped villa. As her health deteriorates, she grows more and more dependent on this stranger. As she is close to death, she invites Chris to her bedroom, who watches her die. He has already removed most of her jewels, and, once she is dead, he meanders out onto the terrace. There he pours himself a large snifter of brandy, drops a large diamond into it and allows the glass to drop into the sea below.

◆◆◆

Elizabeth Taylor had already appeared in two Tennessee Williams-derived films [*Cat on a Hot Tin Roof* (1958) and *Suddenly, Last Summer* (1959)], and Richard Burton had been in one of Williams' works, *The Night of the Iguana* (1964), when they signed for this venture directed by cultist favorite Joseph Losey. *Boom!* proved to be the lowest ebb in the career of the Taylor-Burton screen team, demeaning their once engaging screen image to new lows. ". . . there is a tired, slack quality in most of their work that is, by now, a form of insult. They do not so much act as deign to appear before us and there is neither discipline nor dignity in what they do. She is fat and will do nothing about her most glaring defect, an unpleasant voice which she cannot adequately control. He, conversely, acts with nothing but his voice, rolling out his lines with much elegance but with no feeling at all" [Richard Schickel (*Life* magazine)].

Williams' bewildering drama of disillusionment had been given three abortive stage renderings prior to the picturization: once in San Francisco, then in January, 1963, on Broadway under the title *The Milk Train Doesn't Stop Here Anymore* (with Hermione Baddeley, Paul Robeling, and Mildred Dunnock) and a year later in another Broadway outing (with Tallulah Bankhead, Tab Hunter, and Ruth Ford). At no time was the drama ever comercially or artistically sound. The film version did not change the dismal track record, even with the on location filming in Sardinia near Porto Conte, with interiors lensed at the Dino de Laurentiis studios outside of Rome. Nor was the incohesive, fuzzy script aided by "transforming" the lead role from an older woman into an oversized part handled by too young Taylor, or conversely "altering" the youthful Angel of Death into a role for too old Burton, or allowing Noel Coward to archly slide through a brief part as the Witch of Capri. These basic miscasting boners spoiled whatever semblance of coherent mood director Joseph Losey managed to create.

As the Taylor and Burton demi-characters preyed on each other's vulnerability within the scenario, it was hard to decide who was more enigmatic for less cause, he as the one-time poet now a besmirched, mellifluous visionary of death, or she, a raging shrew dying of tuberculosis who clings to life with less conviction than she displays her Camille-like fatal ailment. The star duo continued to engage in such extended, pointless verbal meanderings of, and about, worthlessness, that the viewer was soon reduced to studying the settings just to stay awake.

Deliberately adding to the film's bizarreness (or decadence) was the managerie of living creatures occupying Taylor's palatial villa. Besides a pet monkey and myna bird, there were wandering sitar-strumming Indians, dwarf actor Michael Dunn as Taylor's mean-minded bodyguard who stands watch over the estate with a pack of ferocious dogs, and Joanna Shimkus as the too young and too beautiful secretary who succumbs to Burton's "physical" charms.

Unlike Taylor's later *Secret Ceremony* (1969) co-starring Mia Farrow and Robert Mitchum, and also directed by Losey, it is difficult to find any redeeming aspects to the indulgent, mystifying production known as *Boom!*, a picture which really should have been called *Thud!* or *Dud!*

## ANNE OF THE THOUSAND DAYS
### *(Universal, 1969) C-145M.*

Producer, Hal B. Wallis; associate producer, Richard McWhorter; director, Charles Jarrott; based on the play by Maxwell Anderson; adaptation, Richard Sokolove; screenplay, John Hale, Bridget Boland; production designer, Maurice Carter; art director, Lionel Couch; set decorator, Peter Howitt; music, Georges Delerue; costumes, Margaret Furse; choreography, Mary Skeaping; assistant director, Simon Relph; technical adviser, Patrick McLoughlin; sound, John Aldred; horse master, Jeremy Taylor; camera, Arthur Ibbetson; editor, Richard Marden.

Richard Burton (King Henry VIII); Genevieve Bujold (Anne Boleyn); Irene Papas (Queen Katherine of Aragon); Anthony Quayle (Cardinal Wolsey); John Colicos (Thomas Cromwell); Michael Hordern (Thomas Boleyn); Katharine Blake (Elizabeth Boleyn); Peter Jeffrey (Norfolk); Joseph O'Connor (Fisher); William Squire (Thomas More); Esmond Knight (Kingston); Nora Swinburne (Lady Kingston); Vernon Dobtcheff (Mendoza); Brook Williams (Brereton); Gary Bond (Smeaton); T. P. McKenna (Norris); Denis Quilley (Weston); Terry Wilton (Harry Percy); Lesly Pateson (Jane Seymour); Nicola Pagett (Princess Mary); June Ellis (Bess); Kynaston Reeves (Willoughby); Marne Maitland (Compeggio); Cyril Luckham (Prior Houghton); Amanda Walter, Charlotte Selwyn, Elizabeth Counsell (Anne's Ladies-in-Waiting); Juliet Kempson, Fiona Hartford, Lilian Hutchins, Ann Tirard (Katherine's Ladies-in-Waiting); Amanda Jane Smythe (Child Elizabeth); Elizabeth Taylor (Courtesan); Kate Burton (Serving Maid); Liza Todd Burton (Beggar Maid).

New York Premiere: January 20, 1970
No New York Television Showing

## Synopsis

In 1526, King Henry VIII, weary of his plain, aging queen, Katherine of Aragon, falls in love with young Anne Boleyn. But she is no easy conquest, already engaged to marry Harry Percy and fully intending to defy the King. Percy is sent away from court and the King begins his siege. She is ordered to court as lady-in-waiting, but, once there, refuses to be his mistress and demands that any children that she will bear must be legitimate. When Cardinal Wolsey fails to arrange with the Pope to have Henry's marriage to Katherine annulled, he is disgraced. The King's secretary, Cromwell, now takes up the matter and organizes the all-important divorce, which requires a break with the Roman Church, allowing the King to become head of the Church in England and permitting him to seize the treasures of the monasteries. Thereafter the King weds Anne, who disappoints him by giving birth not to a son, but a daughter named Elizabeth. The King becomes interested in comely Jane Seymour and Anne is banished from court, only to be later recalled on her condition that Elizabeth be declared heir to the throne of England. After Anne's next child, a boy, is stillborn, the King is determined to be finished with her. He has Cromwell frame false evidence of adultery and Anne is tried and condemned. As Anne goes to her death, the King rides off to visit Jane Seymour, leaving the little Elizabeth to practice her queenly posturing.

◆——◆——◆

Producer Hal B. Wallis had struck paydirt in 1964 with *Becket* which co-starred Richard Burton and Peter O'Toole. He now turned to another historical pageant formula in the British-filmed *Anne of the Thousand Days* based on Maxwell Anderson's 1948 Broadway play. Although the film garnered an amazing $6.9 million in distributors' domestic rentals, it remained a "tawdry little soap opera . . . [that] has been treated as if it were distinguished and serious drama . . ." This film made one appreciate all the more *A Man for All Seasons* (1966) which dealt with the same period as *Anne of the Thousand Days*.

Fortunately for the well-being of *Anne of the Thousand Days*, actor Burton was in fine mettle as one of the most extravagant male chauvinists of all times, almost eclipsing the memory of Charles Laughton in *The Private Life of Henry VIII* (1933). Vincent Canby *(New York Times)* rated Burton to be "in excellent form and voice—funny, loutish and sometimes wise." Burton was nominated for an Academy Award but lost the Best Actor Oscar to indestructible John Wayne who emerged the victor with his *True Grit* performance.

In an unobtrusive way, *Anne of the Thousand Days* proved to be a family affair. In order to amuse the ever-present Elizabeth Taylor on the set, she was given a brief cameo role as the masked courtesan at the elaborate costume ball; while twelve-year-old Liza Todd Burton played a beggar maid and eleven-year-old Kate Burton was cast as a serving maid.

## HAMMERSMITH IS OUT
*(Cinerama, 1972) C-114M.*

Executive producer, Frank Beetson; producer, Alex Lucas; director, Peter Ustinov; screenplay, Stanford Whitmore; set decorator, Robert Benton; music, Dominic Frontiere; titles, Pacific Titles; assistant director, Newton Arnold; camera, Richard H. Kline; editor, David Blewitt.

Elizabeth Taylor (Jimmie Jean Jackson); Richard Burton (Hammersmith); Peter Ustinov (Doctor); Beau Bridges (Billy Breedlove); Leon Ames (General Sam Pembroke); Leon Askin (Dr. Krodt); John Schuck (Henry Joe); George Raft (Guido Scartucci); Marjorie Eaton (Princess); Lisa Jak (Kiddo); Linda Gaye Scott (Miss Quim); Mel Berger (Fat Man); Anthony Holland (Oldham); Brook Williams (Peter Rutter); Carl Donn (Cleopatra); Jose Espinosa (Duke); Stan Ross (Inmate).

New York Premiere: Trans-Lux West, Trans-Lux East, and Trans-Lux 85th Street Theatres—May 24, 1972
No New York Television Showing

## Synopsis

Criminally insane Hammersmith persuades gullible, vulgar hospital intern Billy Breedlove to help him escape from the Doctor's insane asylum. Promising to make Billy rich and famous, Hammersmith first provides a car and money for the nose-picking youth and for a dumb hash house waitress, Jimmie Jean Jackson, Billy's flame of life. Homicidal Hammersmith acquires Guido Scartucci's topless nightclub by killing its owner. He then makes Billy the head of a prosperous pill company, selling out that organization to invest in more lucrative Texas oil. Because Henry Joe is about to elope with the petulant Jimmie Jean, Hammersmith kills him and his money-heavy associates. After supporting a Presidential candidate successfully, Billy becomes a national delegate-at-large with a fine castle in Spain. He now tells Hammersmith to dispose of the annoying Jimmie Jean, but instead, the madman impregnates her. After transforming Billy into a hopeless cripple, Hammersmith drives him to suicide. At this point the Doctor catches up with Hammersmith who is returned to the asylum. Peter Rutter, the new intern, hears Hammersmith's siren song, "Get Me out of Here. I'll make you rich and strong, strong and rich."

◆——◆——◆

"*Hammersmith Is Out* may prove to be the celluloid cornerstone for those moviegoers who believe that Elizabeth Taylor and Richard Burton, at least when they are working together, cannot really be taken seriously anymore. Their antics in their latest "happening" provide their followers with a self-indulgent occasion when actors and friends get together for a few laughs and dirty words while the cameras are running" *(Independent Film Journal)*.

It had been five years since both Taylor and Burton appeared on the list of top ten boxoffice stars in the United States, a situation which did not hinder the Burtons from escalating their private and public lives on a high, wide, and handsomely extravagant style. The fan magazines still recorded their every outrageous move, but the public was fast tiring of the mindless antics of the overaged juveniles. Because Taylor had recurrently appeared in junk features during and after her Metro tenure, no one was too surprised when she continued to debase herself in later screen trash. However, it still shocked drama purists to observe the sharp artistic decline of Burton which seemed to be outdistancing even his physical decay. Salary was an important factor in his filmmaking decisions, but it could only be a strong masochistic drive that led him to saunter through the likes of *Candy* (1968), *Raid on Rommel* (1971), and *Villain* (1971), all of which seemed to be mild claptrap when compared to his later and far more horrendous *Bluebeard* and *The Assassination of Trotsky*, both 1972 releases.

Director-co-star Peter Ustinov who had appeared with the Burtons in *The Comedians* was at the creative helm of *Hammersmith Is Out*, a $1.8 million independent production filmed in Mexico. It was quickly dismissed in the United States as a pseudo version of the Faust theme (in no sane way parallel to the Burtons' *Doctor Faustus*), complete with a twisted Horatio Alger theme.

Within its lazily unfolded 114 minutes, *Hammersmith Is Out* ". . . is both too elaborate and not quite witty enough to be especially convincing as contemporary morality comedy" [Vincent Canby *(New York Times)*]. The perverse funmaking hits the viewer at all angles and level, never once sure of its mark. For example, the first view of Ustinov, as the insane asylum director, is in his crummy office where he is seen chortling over a medical text entitled *Studies in Anal Retention*. When Taylor and Beau Bridges first make love it is in the kitchen of the diner where she works. Their bed is a pile of tomatoes and during their (simulated) orgasm the audience is shown not the standard waves crashing onto rocks, but a flashing Coca Cola sign. Later Taylor-Bridges make love in the Mustang Drive-In Theatre, while the movie viewer hears the dialog to an epic movie being shown to the oncamera audience. The film-within-the-film is obvious a parody of *Cleopatra*. Burton is at his best or worst when he mouths such deliberately pretentious dialog as, "Yes, one of the first things I remember is a lady with a snake." When Taylor is feeding her snake, Burton announces, "She is suckling her young." When Taylor, unaware that Burton is about to kill her (he does not), asks what time it is, he replies, "You might say it is midnight." What nonsense!

Taylor has perhaps the most (un)intentionally funny moments in the film. As Burton is about to seduce the Southern-accented whore, she politely asks, "Could you try closing your eyes." At another point when she is making love with Henry Joe (John Schuck), the man asks her to say something dirty. Taylor thinks a brief moment and then pops out with "Pee pee."

## UNDER MILK WOOD
### *(Altura Films International, 1973) C-88M.*

Producers, Hugh French, Jules Buck; associate producer, John Comfort; director, Andrew Sinclair; based on the radio play by Dylan Thomas; screenplay, Sinclair; assistant director, Dominic Fulford; art director, Geoffrey Tozer; music, Brian Gascoigne; sound, Cyril Collick; camera, Bob Huke; editor, Willy Kemplen.

Richard Burton (First Voice); Elizabeth Taylor (Rosie Probert); Peter O'Toole (Captain Cat); Glynis Johns (Myfanwy Price); Vivien

Merchant (Mrs. Pugh); Sian Phillips (Mrs. Ogmore-Pritchard); Victor Spinetti (Mog Edwards); Ryan Davies (Second Voice); Angharad Rees (Gossamer Beynon); Ray Smith (Mr. Waldo); Michael Forrest (Sinbad Sailors); Ann Beach (Polly Garter); Glynn Edwards (Mr. Cherry Owen); Bridget Turner (Mrs. Cherry Owen); Talfryn Thomas (Mr. Pugh); Wim Wylton (Mr. Willy Nilly); Bronwen Williams (Mrs. Willy Nilly); Meg Wynn Owen (Lily Smalls); Hubert Rees (Butcher Beynon); Mary Jones (Mrs. Beynon); Aubrey Richards (Reverend Eli Jenkins); Mark Jones (Evans the Death); Dillwyn Owen (Mr. Ogmore); Richard Davies (Mr. Pritchard); David Jason (Nogood Boyo); Davydd Havard (Lord Cut Glass); David Davies (Utah Watkins); Maudie Edwards (Mrs. Utah Watkins); Griffith Davies (Ocky Milkman); Peggyann Clifford (Mrs. Utah Watkins); Dudley Jones (Dai Bread); Dorothea Phillips (Mrs. Dai Bread One); Ruth Madoc (Mrs. Dai Bread Two); David Harries (P. C. Attila Rees); Rachael Thomas (Mary Ann Sailors); Andree Gaydon (Waldo Wife One); Eira Griffiths (Second Woman/Waldo Wife Two); Margaret Courtenay (First Neighbor/Waldo Wife Three); Rhoda Lewis (First Woman/Waldo Wife Four); Pamela Miles (Waldo Wife Five); John Rees (Jack Black); Jill Britton (Mrs. Rose Cottage); Susan Penhaligon (Mae Rose Cottage); Edmond Thomas (Inspector); Richard Parry (Organ Morgan); Dilys Price (Mrs. Organ Morgan); Olwen Rees (Gwennie); Iris Jones (Mother); Gordon Styles, Brian Osbourne (Fishermen); Shane Shelton, Paul Grist, Bryn Jones, John Rainer, Bryn William (Drowned Sailors); Aldwyn Francis, Ifor Owen, Dudley Owen, Gladys Wykeham-Edwards (Villagers in "Sailors Arms"); Ieuan Rhys Williams (Gomer Owen); T. H. Evans (Old Man); Gwyneth Owen, Lucy Griffiths, Angela Brinkworth (Neighbors).

New York Premiere: East Side Cinema—January 21, 1973
No New York Television Showing

## Synopsis

On a spring night in the little fishing village of Llareggub, two shabby strangers walk the black-enveloped streets, while the townfolk are wrestling with their dreams. Old blind sea captain Cat recalls his drowned shipmates and delectable Rosie Probert, the great love of his long-lost youth. Myfanwy Price and Mog Edwards, village shopkeepers, dream of one another and of their unconsummated love, while Mrs. Ogmore-Pritchard talks in her sleep of two deceased husbands, prompting them to fulfill their household tasks. With the approach of morning, Reverend Eli Jenkins recites a poem of praise, Dai Bread rushes to the bakery, the town whore feeds her newest baby, Sinbad reopens the Sailors Arm for business, and postman Willy Nilly begins his daily rounds. In the course of the day, meek Mr. Pugh thinks of poisoning his nagging wife, Mr. Beynon the butcher taunts his gullible spouse, Organ Morgan performs Bach, and although Captain Cat cannot see, he catches all the cadences of the town's life. Sinbad desires pretty Goassamer Beynon, and the two strangers finally meet the girl they have been seeking and bed down with her. Widower Waldo obliterates his woes with drink, and in the dim of the day Eli Jenkins composes the hymn for evening. Mrs. Ogmore-Pritchard again conjures up her dead husband, Myfanwy and Mog prepare their nightly love notes, and Waldo enjoys the favors of Polly Garter while she is dwelling on her own lost love, the deceased Willy Wee.

◆━◆━◆

In 1953, Dylan Thomas' ornate verse play "for voices" was first presented on radio, and since that time has been a great favorite* of Thomas' Welsh countryman, Richard Burton. Even though a modest off-Broadway production in 1961 attempted to prove otherwise, by its very nature *Under Milk Wood* should be a rich listening experience, and not transformed into the confines of a very visual medium which could (and did) only distort the abundance of images. Even the kindest of critics admitted that the film (released in 1971 in England and two years later in the United States) was at best an artistic failure, too bogged down in its pedantic ways. "The language that comes cascading off the sound track is bottled into florid captions for an illustrated travel guide to Wales" (*Time* magazine).

As the First Voice, narrator Burton was more heard than seen, causing many a viewer just to shut his eyes and listen with appreciation to the volley of words. (But could this not be more comfortably done within the confines of one's home listening to radio or to a recording?) Peter O'Toole as the blind old captain (courtesy of heavy makeup and special contact lenses) seemed to have stepped out of his previous *Man of La Mancha* screen role, while Elizabeth Taylor in the guise of free-loving Rosie, had a brief "lie-in" role as the whore from O'Toole's youth now mouldering in the Llareggub graveyard. It is Taylor's Rosie who utters "I've forgotten that I was ever born."

The movie of *Under Milk Wood*, came, went, and seems destined for its own special oblivion, not aristocratic enough to eventually become an integral part of the repertory of elite screen drama used for college literature courses.

*Burton has made a recording of *Under Milk Wood*, issued first in England and then in the United States by Westminster Records. He told director-scriptor Andrew Sinclair before filming began, "*Under Milk Wood* was all about religion, sex and death, . . ."

## THE YEARS AFTER

While oversaturating their joint presence in theatrical filmmaking, the Burtons did battle in another entertainment arena. They appeared on late night television talk shows, a February 1968 charity show video special, and as guest stars on a September, 1970, episode of Lucille Ball's

"Here's Lucy." Then on February 6 and 7, 1973, in a two-part 180 minute color ABC network television movie, entitled *Divorce His/Divorce Hers* they made what was euphemistically called their dramatic medium debut. The show was an artistic disaster all the way around, although the performer pair gleefully collected astronomical salaries for their Rome-filmed adventure. In this bathos-tinged soap opera, Taylor mouthed such unbearable lines as, "You'll never be able to give as much of your sheer presence as I find necessary." (What does that all mean?) *Variety* came to the conclusion that "This two-part soupbone made it official: Liz and Dick Burton are the corniest act in show business since the Cherry sisters. . . . Miss Taylor wallowed in suds to a point where the many closeups between her ample bazooms failed even in distracting from the nonsense. Burton was wooden-legged and wooden-lipped, and seemed to grow stiffer as the two-night fiasco crept on its petty pace."

Just when even the most faithful of the Burton-philes had to admit that there did not seem any new fanciful whim perpetrated by the famous couple that the press could now dissect for public consumption, the movie star team proved differently. On Tuesday, July 3, 1973, Taylor announced her own special independence day and revealed through her press agent to an astonished gathering of newspapermen that she and Burton were separating. Her statement, written on Regency Hotel stationery, explained, "Maybe we have loved each other too much—not that I ever believed such a thing was possible—but we have been in each other's pockets constantly, never being apart except for matters of life or death, and I believe with all my heart that this separation will ultimately bring us back to where we should be—and that is: together!"

This turn of events caused gossip columnists, well-meaning acquaintances, and harpies the world around to suddenly become clairvoyant and proclaim with great authority exactly what Taylor's statement and her subsequent solo trip to Hollywood implied. Burton went on to a Moscow film festival, and then it was announced he and Taylor were to reconnoiter in Rome to discuss their situation. When the seemingly inevitable occurred—the couple announced they would divorce—the most cynical press members jabbered that it was a miracle this domestic and professional union had lasted as long as it did. But leave it to the illustrious couple to confound everyone (and themselves) once again, for in late 1973, when she returned to California for a series of hospital tests and assorted surgery, she and Burton reconciled. An amazed Henry Wynberg (her recent beau) and the public were left to ponder the future of the mercurial Burtons.

The pondering ceased on June 26, 1974, when the world-famous couple were granted a divorce in Gstadd, Switzerland. One of the trickier parts of the final (the couple have recently become "friends" again) separation was the twelve million dollars worth of community property—stocks, real estate, jewelry, yachts, etc.—the V.I.P. duo acquired during their hectic years together. One of Miss Taylor's lawyers commented, "Not since Jehosaphat took three days to pick up the goodies after the massacre of the Moabites, will there have been such a dividing of the spoils." [No doubt, remainder bookshops would acquire the caseloads of *Meeting Mrs. Jenkins* (1966), the book reprint of Richard Burton's article on his wife which had appeared in *Vogue* magazine under the title *Burton Writes of Taylor*.]

One good aspect of this domestic chaos was the effect it had on both players' emoting. Each returned to filmmaking with a vengeance, going from project to project nonstop. He showed in his controlled performance in *Massacre in Rome* that restrained playing was still within his power, and that perhaps it would be a shame for him to carry out his threat to retire from the medium and become a teaching don at Oxford. Taylor, having offered an extremely viable if shrill performance in the mock thriller *Night Watch* (1973) astounded even her most loyal fans by her trim figure and luscious looks in *Ash Wednesday* (1973), a quasi-tribute to the wonders of plastic surgery. Her recent film appearances indicate she is quite anxious to improve her acting status as well as to redefine her social position in the free-wheeling 1970s. She was stunning as one of the hosts for the compilation film *That's Entertainment* (1974), and one can only wait with enthusiasm to view her dual performances (as the Fairy and Light) in the projected George Cukor-directed remake of Maurice Maeterlinck's *The Blue Bird* (1975), to be the first American and Soviet co-production.

About the Author and Researchers

JAMES ROBERT PARISH, New York-based free lance writer and novelist, was born near Boston on April 21, 1944. He attended the University of Pennsylvania and graduated as a Phi Beta Kappa with a degree in English. A graduate of the University of Pennsylvania Law School, he is a member of the New York Bar. As president of Entertainment Copyright Research Co., Inc., he headed a major researching facility for the film and television industries. Later he was a film interviewer-reviewer for *Motion Picture Daily* and *Variety*. He has been responsible for such reference volumes as *The American Movies Reference Book: The Sound Era*, and *The Emmy Awards: A Pictorial History*. He is the author of *The Fox Girls, The Paramount Pretties, The RKO Gals, The Great Movie Series, The Slapstick Queens, Good Dames, The George Raft File*, and *Actors' Television Credits*, and co-author of *The Cinema of Edward G. Robinson, The Great Spy Pictures, The MGM Stock Company: The Golden Era*, and *Film Directors' Guide: The U.S.A.* Mr. Parish is an active member of the Kate Smith U.S.A. Friends Club. He is a film reviewer for several national magazines.

✿　✿　✿　✿

T. ALLAN TAYLOR, godson of the late Margaret Mitchell, has long been active in book publishing and is presently production manager of one of the largest abstracting and technical indexing services in the United States. He was editor on *The Fox Girls, The Paramount Pretties, The RKO Gals, The Slapstick Queens, The Great Spy Pictures*, and other volumes.

✿　✿　✿　✿

Since the age of five, thirty-four-year-old Brooklynite JOHN ROBERT COCCHI has been viewing and collating data on motion pictures and is now regarded as one of America's most energetic film researchers. He is the New York editor of *Boxoffice* magazine. He was research associate on *The American Movies Reference Book, The Fox Girls, Good Dames, The MGM Stock Company: The Golden Era*, and many other books. He has written cinema history articles for such journals as *Film Fan Monthly* and *Screen Facts*.

✿　✿　✿　✿

New York-born FLORENCE SOLOMON attended Hunter College and then joined Ligon Johnson's copyright research office. Later she was appointed director for research at Entertainment Copyright Research Co., Inc. and is presently a reference supervisor at A.S.C.A.P.'s Index

Division in New York City. Miss Solomon has collaborated on such works as *The American Movies Reference Book, TV Movies, The Great Movie Series, The George Raft File,* and others. She is the niece of the noted sculptor, the late Sir Jacob Epstein.

# Index

Italicized numbers refer to picture pages.

Aadland, Beverly, 366
Abbott and Costello, 447
*Abdication, The*, 58
"Abide with Me," 440
*Abie's Irish Rose*, 15, 82
*Above Suspicion*, 120
Academy of Motion Picture Arts and Sciences, 257
*Across the Pacific*, 665
*Across the Wide Missouri*, 529
*Actress, The*, 561
Adams, Edie, 753
Adams, Nick, 750
*Adam's Rib*, 538, 554-57, 559
Adler, Buddy, 723
Adrian, Gilbert, 62, 94, 111, 114, 116, 137, 312, 318
*Adventure*, 501, 512, 526
*Adventurers, The*, 365
*Adventures of Captain Fabian, The*, 366
*Adventures of Don Juan*, 366
*Adventures of Robin Hood, The*, 335, 346-49
*Affair in Trinidad*, 18
*Affair to Remember, An*, 726
*African Queen, The*, 559, 655, 667

*After the Thin Man*, 206, 225-28, 232
Agee, James, 542, 591, 634, 660
Ager, Cecilia, 235
"Ah, Sweet Mystery of Life," 306, 307, 309
"Ah, the Moon Is Here," 162
*Ah, Wilderness*, 17
Albee, Edward, 712, 778, 780
Alexander, Ross, 150, 169
*Algiers*, 605
*Ali Baba and the Forty Thieves*, 601, 610-13, 615
*Alice Adams*, 90, 541
*All About Eve*, 265, 293
*All the King's Men*, 740
Allen, Fred, 245
Allen, Gracie, 630, 631
Allison, May, 14
Allwyn, Astrid, 466
Allyson, June, 18, 19, 20, 147, 173, 387, 446, 448, 451, 622, 624-25, 625, 626, 627, 628, 630, 631, 632, 634, 636, 637, 639-40, 641-42, 644-45, 667
"Aloha Oe," 327
"Alone," 433-34
Alpert, Hollis, 685, 711

*Always in My Heart*, 196
*Always Together*, 18
"Am I Blue," 655
Ameche, Don, 397, 399
"America," 440
American International Pictures, 18
Ames, Leon, 242, 729 '
Ames, Racquel, 597
*And Now Tomorrow*, 408
Anderson, Marian, 159
Anderson, Maxwell, 355, 665, 791
Anderson, Michael, 708, 750
Anderson, Milo, 359
Anderson, Richard, 724
Andrews, Edward, 328
Andrews, Julie, 383
*Andy Hardy*, 16, 17, 129, 423, 424, 439, 447, 452
*Andy Hardy Meets Debutante*, 410, 431-35, 440
*Andy Hardy's Private Secretary*, 439
*Angel on the Amazon*, 196
*Angels with Dirty Faces*, 17, 454, 458, 460-64
"Angelus," 319
*Animal Kingdom, The*, 211
*Anna Christie*, 55
*Anna Karenina*: (book) 50; (movie) 51
Annabella, 389, 400, 407
*Anne of the Thousand Days*, 789-91
*Another Dawn*, 347
*Another Thin Man*, 198, 230-33, 234
*Anthony Adverse*, 345
*Apartment, The*, 293
*Applause!*, 667
*April Fools, The*, 246
*Arabian Nights*, 596, 600, 604-07, 609, 610, 612, 615
Ardin, Edwin, 86
*Arise, My Love*, 283, 285
Arledge, John, 169
Arlen, Michael, 52, 53
Arliss, George, 38
Armstrong, Louis, 732
Arnaz, Desi, 19
Arnold, Edward, 499
*Around the World in 80 Days*, 690, 700
*Arrangement, The*, 711
*As You Desire Me*, 55
*As You Like It*, 559
*Ash Wednesday*, 797
Ashley, Edward, 324
*Ask Any Girl*, 705
Asquith, Anthony, 774
*Assassination of Trotsky, The*, 793
Asta, 203, 208, 209, 216, 227, 228, 232, 239, 241, 243
Astaire, Fred, 16, 19-20, 111, 112, 164, 172, 173, 402, 556, 634

Asther, Nils, 56
Astor, Mary, 132
"A-Tisket A-Tasket," 631
*Auntie Mame*, 509
Auric, Georges, 701
*Autumn Leaves*, 121
Avalon, Frankie, 18, 757
"Ave Maria," 316
*Awakening, The*, 38
*Awful Truth, The*, 17, 403, 726
Ayres, Lew, 16, 321

B.B.C., 504
*B.F.'s Daughter*, 553
"Babalu," 631
*Babes in Arms*: (movie) 417, 418, 427-31, 437, 441, 443, 448, 451; (song) 428, 430
*Babes on Broadway*: (movie) 421, 440-44, 449, (song) 443
*Baby Wants a Kiss*, 740
Bacall, Lauren, 18, 262, 591, 646, 647, 649, 650, 651, 652, 654-57, 658-59, 660, 661-62, 663-64, 665, 666, 667, 668
*Bachelor and the Bobby Soxer, The*, 246
*Bad and the Beautiful, The*, 173, 529
*Bad Girl*, 15
Baddeley, Hermione, 789
Bainter, Fay, 543
Baker, Carroll, 143, 530, 645
Baker, Diane, 92
Baker, Melville, 377
Bakewell, William, 105
*Balalaika*, 321
Baldwin, Faith, 140
Balin, Ina, 729, 730
Ball, Lucille, 19, 225, 446, 543, 549, 688, 795-96
*Ballad of Josie, The*, 756
Bancroft, George, 462, 463
Bankhead, Tallulah, 115, 771, 789
Banky, Vilma, 14, 22, 24-25, 26, 27, 28-30, 31-32, 33, 34, 35, 36-38, 39, 74
Bara, Theda, 48
Barbier, George, 264
Barclay, Joan, 152
*Barefoot in the Park*, 246
Barker, Lex, 513, 529
*Barkleys of Broadway, The*, 556
Barnes, Binnie, 327
Barnes, George, 28, 32
Barnes, Howard, 118, 120, 193, 227, 230, 232, 234, 264, 290, 321, 349, 352, 356, 381, 382, 383, 386, 399, 400, 401, 402, 404, 425, 436, 441, 445, 451, 462, 464, 472, 495, 499, 504, 506, 545, 637, 639
Barrier, Edgar, 607, 615
Barry, Philip, 541, 545, 548
Barrymore, Diana, 366

802

Barrymore, Ethel, 499
Barrymore, John, 14, 312, 313, 366
Barrymore, Lionel, 50, 93, *124*, 143, 430, 445, 666, 667
Barthelmess, Richard, 14
Bartholomew, Freddie, 423
Bartley, Anthony, 695
Barty, Billy, 162
Bates, Blanche, 315
Bates, Florence, 237
Baxter, Alan, 240, 579
Baxter, Anne, 527
Baxter, Warner, 88, 111, *149*, 154, 155, 400
Bayne, Beverly, 14
Beal, John, *206*, 230, 644
*Beat the Devil*, 667
*Beau Geste*, 31
*Becket*, 776, 791
Beckley, Paul V., 688, 690, 723, 729, 751
*Bedtime Story*, 705
Beebe, Lucius, 158
Beery, Noah, 37
Beery, Wallance, 16, *126*, 129, 130, 137, 138, 521
Belasco, David, 315
*Bell, Book and Candle*, 173
Bellamy, Ralph, 94, 129, 195
*Belle of the Nineties*, 726
*Belles on Their Toes*, 246
Bellis, Guy, *481*
*Bells of St. Mary's, The*, 726
Benchley, Robert, 111, 137, 288
Bendix, William, 542, 583, 592
*Ben-Hur*, 774
Bennett, Bruce, 664
Bennett, Constance, 53, 196, *392*, 395, 396
Bennett, Leila, 90
Bennett, Lois, 772
Benny, Jack, 237, 472
Beranger, George Andre, *393*
Bergman, Ingrid, 265, 499, 520, 657
Berkeley, Busby, 79, 154, 156, 158, 160, 161, 164, 166, 168, 170, 173, 428, 429, 432, 449
Berlin, Irving, 221
Berman, Pandro S., 255, 550, 551
Bern, Paul, 123, 132
*Bernardine*, 95
Bernhardt, Sarah, 443
*Best Things in Life Are Free, The*, 78
*Best Years of Our Lives, The*, 246
*Betrayed*, *518*, 528-30
*Bette Davis*, 258
Bey, Turhan, 610, 613, 619
*Beyond the Forest*, 265
Biancolli, Louis, 234
"Bidin' My Time," 449
*Big House, The*, 129
*Big Parade, The*, 46

*Big Shakedown, The*, 93
*Big Sleep, The*, *651*, 659-62
*Big Wheel, The*, 736
Bing, Herman, 312, 313, 325, 350
Binyon, Claude, 279, 285, 292
Biograph Girl, 13
*Biography of a Bachelor Girl*, 484
Birell, Tala, 498
"Birthday Song," 327
*Bitter Sweet*, *302*, 322-25
Bizet, Georges, 313
"Bla-Bla-Bla," 88
*Black Legion*, 740
*Black Shield of Falworth, The*, 675, 680-82
Blackburn Twins, 451
Blackford, G. E., 285
Blackwell, Perry, 751
*Blessed Event*, 155
*Blindfold*, 757
Blondell, Joan, 17, 147, *150*, 158, 159, 161, 164, 172, 173, 350, 563, 655
*Blondie*, 16
*Blood and Sand*, 408
*Blossoms in the Dust*, 478, 483-86, 489, 495
*Blow-Up*, 709
Blue, Ben, 630
Blue, Monte, *339*
*Blue Bird, The*, 797
*Blue Dahlia, The*, 568, 574, 589-92
*Bluebeard*, 793
"Blues in the Night," 364
Blystone, John G., 93
Blyth, Ann, 310
*Bodyguard Man*, 691
Boehnel, William, 211, 470, 579-80
Bogart, Humphrey, 18, 260, 261, 262, 353, 447, 462, 463, 464, 559, 579, 582, 595, 645, *646*, 647-48, 649, *650*, *651*, 652, 654, 655-57, 658-59, 660-62, 663-64, 665, 666, 667-68
Bois, Curt, *302*, 325
Boland, Mary, 16, 322, 468, 502
*Bold and the Brave, The*, 451
Bolger, Ray, 221, 319
Bolton, Guy, 88
Bondi, Beulah, 283
*Bonjour Tristesse*: (movie) 692, *696*, 699-701, 703; (book) 699-700; (song) 701
*Boom!*, 767, 787-89
*Boom Town*, 520, 553
Boone, Pat, 95
Booth, Shirley, 561
Boothe, Claire, 542
Borg, Carl Oscar, 33
Borg, Veda Ann, 325
Borgnine, Ernest, 266, 686
*Born to Sing*, 448
*Born Yesterday*, 529

Borzage, Frank, 70, 73, 74, 75, 79, 120, 166, 169, 385, 386
*Boston Strangler, The,* 686, 691
Bottome, Phyllis, 385
"Boulevardier from the Bronx, A," 172
Bourke-White, Margaret, 285
Bow, Clara, 311
*Boy Meets Girl,* 462, 466
*Boy on a Dolphin,* 595
Boyd, Stephen, 770
Boyer, Charles, 173, 293, 522, 660
*Boys Town,* 464, 484
Brackett, Leigh, 660
Brando, Marlon, 723, 786
*Breaking Point, The,* 657
Breakston, George, 434
Brecher, Irving, 239
Bremer, Lucille, 634
Brendel, El, *65,* 78, 88
Brennan, Walter, 656, 657
Brent, George, 17, 154, 155, *174,* 175-76, *178, 179, 180, 181,* 183, 184, 185, 186-87, 188, 189, 190-91, 193, 194-95, 196, 266, 456
Bressart, Felix, *302,* 325, 383
Brice, Fannie, 221, 641
*Bride Comes Home, The, 268,* 278-80, 351
*Bride Goes Wild, The, 627,* 637-40
"Brides Song," 327
Bridges, Beau, 793
*Bringing Up Baby,* 543
*Broadway Melody, The,* 154, 630
*Broadway Melody of 1938,* 423
*Broadway Serenade,* 321
*Broadway to Hollywood,* 304
Brockman, James, 81
Brockwell, Gladys, 71
*Broken Blossoms,* 72
Bromfield, Louis, 497
Bronson, Charles, 19
Brooke, Hillary, 196
*Brooklyn Citizen,* 498
*Brooklyn Daily Eagle,* 132, 140, 239, 282, 326, 427, 466
Brooks, Richard, 665
Brophy, Edward, 216, 242
Brown, Clarence, 47, 48, 52
Brown, John Mack, 53, 106, *125,* 129-30
Brown, Lew, 78
Bruce, Nigel, 502, 617
Bruce, Virginia, 41, 56, 219, 321
Bryna (production company), 685
Brynner, Yul, 408
Buchanan, Edgar, 551
Buchowetsky, Dmitri, 50
Buck, Pearl, 548
Bucquet, Harold S., 548
*Bulldog Drummond,* 38
Bunny, John, 14

*Bunny O'Hare,* 266
Burke, Billie, 115, 221
Burke, Frankie, 462
Burton, Elizabeth (Liza) Todd, 760, 791
Burton, Frederick, 442
Burton, Kate, 759, 791
Burton, Richard, 19, 679, 737, *758,* 759-60, *762, 763, 764, 765, 766,* 770-72, 774-75, 776, 777, 778, 779-81, 782, 783, 784, 785, 786-87, 788-89, 791, 792-93, 795-97
Burton, Sir Richard, 605, 612
*Burton Writes of Taylor,* 797
Bus-Fekete, Ladislaus, 396
Bushman, Francis X., 14
"But Not for Me," 449, 530
Butler, David, 79, 82
Butler, Ivan, 120
*Butterfield 8,* 769, 770
Butterworth, Charles, 115
"By a Waterfall," 162
"By the Light of the Silvery Moon," 430
Byron, Walter, 38

Cabot, Bruce, 56, 353
*Cactus Flower,* 667
*Cafe Metropole, 388, 393,* 400-02
Cagney, James, 17, *150,* 160, 161, 162, 255, 262, 353, *454,* 455-56, *458,* 462-64, 466, 467-69, 470, 471-72, 490, 580, 592, 655, 736
Cagney, William, 470, 472
*Caine Mutiny, The,* 645, 667
*Cairo,* 327
Calhern, Louis, 644
California Collegians, 278
"Call of Life, The," 324
*Call of the Wild,* 138
Calleia, Joseph, 228
*Calling Dr. Kildare,* 16
Cameron, Kate, 228, 364, 403, 407, 464, 546, 662
*Camille,* 58
Campbell, Alan, 318
Canby, Vincent, 791, 793
*Candida,* 365
*Candy,* 792
"Can't Help Lovin' That Man," 634
Cantinflas, 690
Cantor, Eddie, 221, 430, 726
Canutt, Yakima, 346
Capone, Al, 129
Capra, Frank, 38, 117, 553
*Caprice,* 756
*Captain Blood,* 17, *334,* 340-43, 344, 349
*Captain Hates the Sea, The,* 58
Cardiff, Jack, 686
Cardinale, Claudia, 757
Carere, Christine, 723
Carey, Harry, 551

804

Carey, Joyce, 192
Carey, Macdonald, 585
*Carmen*, 327
Carmichael, Hoagy, 655, 656-57
Carol, Sue, 569
*Carolina*, 93
*Carpetbaggers, The*, 595
Carrillo, Leo, 617
Carroll, Diahann, 732
Carroll, Kathleen, 707, 736
Carroll, Nancy, 15, 19-20, 379
"Carry Me Back to Ole Virginny," 313
Carson, Jack, 237, 726, 727
Carter, Janis, 327
Carver, Lynne, 313
*Casablanca*, 496, 654, 657
*Case of the Curious Bride, The*, 341
*Casino Royale*, 697, 704-07
*Cass Timberlane*, 526
Cassell, Wally, 576
*Castle on the Hudson*, 466
"Castles in the Air," 631
*Cat and the Fiddle, The*, 304
*Cat Balou*, 779
*Cat on a Hot Tin Roof*, 723, 788
Catlett, Walter, 585
*Cavalcade*, 282
Cavens, Fred, 349
Cawthorn, Joseph, 306
CBS, 452
*Ceiling Zero*, 466
*Chained, 101*, 112-14
*Chalk Garden, The*, 706
Champion, Gower, 19, 634
Champion, Marge, 19
Chandler, Eddy, *180*
Chandler, Raymond, 173, 591, 660
Chanel, Coco, 566
Chaney, Lon, 472
Chaney, Lon, Jr., 615
*Change of Heart, 69*, 92-94
Chaplin, Charlie, 14, 94
*Charge of the Light Brigade, The, 335*,
    343-46, 361
*Charley's Aunt*, 237, 327
*Charlie Chan*, 610
"Charmaine," 631
Charters, Spencer, 191, *336*
Chase, Ilka, 285
Chatterton, Ruth, 175, 183, 193
*Cheaper By the Dozen*, 246
*Cheat, The*, 71
*Cherries Are Ripe*, 38
Cherrill, Virginia, 88, 89
Chevalier, Maurice, 79, 304, 734
"Chin Up, Cheerio, Carry On," 443
*China*, 408
*China Seas, 126*, 135-38
Ching, William, 560

*Chocolate Soldier, The*, 326
Christian, Linda, 389
Christian Science Monitor, 630, 756
*Christina of Sweden*, 55-56
*Christmas in July*, 173
Churchill, Winston, 488, 490
*Cinema* (magazine), 79
*Citizen Kane*, 546
*City for Conquest, 459*, 469-72
Clair, Rene, 117
Claire, Ina, 41, 54, 56
Clark, Dane, 196, 657
Clark, Davison, *180*
*Clark Gable*, 129
Clarke, Angela, 680
*Classics of the Silent Screen*, 72
*Cleopatra*, 19, 277, 758, 762, 768-72, 774,
    793
"Cleopatterer," 634
Clive, E. E., 225
*Clive of India*, 38, 406
Clooney, Rosemary, 19
Coates, Albert, 631
*Cobra Woman, 602*, 613-15
*Cobweb, The*, 667
*Coco*, 293, 566
*Cocoanuts, The*, 195
Coe, Peter, 617
Coe, Richard L., 734
Coffee, Lenore, 109, 218
Coghill, Prof. Neville, 787
Cohan, George M., 472
Cohen, John S., Jr., 91
Cohn, Herbert, 326, 427
Colbert, Claudette, 17, 117, 257, *268*, 271,
    272, 273, 274, 275, 277-78, 279, 280, 282,
    283, 284, 285-86, 288, 289-90, 291, 292-
    93, 401, 520, 553, 733, 771
*Colleen, 152*, 171-72
Collier, William, Sr., 82
Collins, Cora Sue, 56, *204*
Collins, Joan, 356, 723, 726, 727, 769
Collison, Wilson, 131
Colman, Ronald, 14, 22, 23-24, *25*, 26, 27,
    28, 29-30, 31-32, 33, 34, 35, 36-39, 74
Columbia Pictures, 18, 58, 120, 121, 173,
    211, 277, 386, 529, 545, 564, 620, 706
*Come Fill the Cup*, 472
*Come Next Spring*, 472
*Come On Strong*, 645
*Come to the Stable*, 408
*Comedians, The*, 765, 783-85, 786, 793
*Comedy of Errors, The*, 190
*Comic, The*, 452
*Command Decision*, 528
*Commonweal, The*, 527
*Company of Killers*, 645
Compton, Joyce, 83
*Comrade X*, 529

"Concerto for Index Finger," 631
*Confidential Agent*, 660
*Conflict*, 660
*Congo Maisie*, 133
Connery, Sean, 706, 707
Connolly, Bobby, 166, 168
Connolly, Myles, 553
Connolly, Walter, 225, *334*, 350
Conway Jack, 520
Cook, Alton, 499, 527, 614
Cook, Fiedler, 710
*Cool Hand Luke*, 739
Cooper, Gary, 20, 32, 293, 379, 447, 553, 589
Cooper, Gladys, 499, 703
Cooper, Inez, 327
Cooper, Jackie, 644
Cooper, Melville, 348, 350
Corbett, James J., 81
Corby, Jane, 498
Corcoran, Donna, *482*
Corday, Paula, 642
*Corn Is Green, The*, 266
Cortez Ricardo, 46, 50
*Cosmopolitan* (magazine), 524
Cosmopolitan Productions, 169
Cossart, Ernest, 222
Costello, Dolores, 14
"Could You Use Me," 449
*Count of Monte Cristo, The*, 341, 691
*Count Three and Pray*, 723
*Country Girl, The*, 451
Courtney, Inez, 383
Cowan, Jerome, 468
Coward, Noel, 324, 789
Crain, Jeanne, 246
Crane, Cheryl, 513, 526, 530
Crane, Stephen, 513, 524, 526
Craven, Frank, 90, 470, 471
Crawford, Joan, 15, 90, *96*, 98-99, *100*, *101*, *102*, *103*, 104-05, 106-07, 108-09, 111-12, 113-14, 115, 116, 117, 118, 119, 120-21, 129, 144, 216, 256, 265, 308, 402, 484, 501, 520, 531
Creelman, Eileen, 116, 316, 543
Cregar, Laird, 579
Crenna, Richard, 522
*Crescent Carnival*, 328
Crewe, Regina, 168, 280
*Crime School*, 462
Crisler, B. R., 318, 381, 430-31
Crisp, Donald, 356, 471
Crist, Judith, 707, 734, 740, 771, 774, 776, 785
Cristal, Linda, 684
*Cristilinda*, 74
Croce, Arlene, 20
Cromwell, John, 255, 256
Cronin, Hume, 640

Crosby, Bing, 20, 155, 589
*Crossfire*, 509
Crouse, Russel, 553, 644, 751
*Crowd Roars, The*, 736
Crowther, Bosley, 236, 245, 288, 290, 321, 324, 327, 358, 422, 423, 450, 472, 484, 486, 494, 498, 501, 502, 504, 507, 548, 553, 556, 563, 580, 591, 592, 594, 606, 619, 630, 637, 642, 654, 662, 665, 666, 682, 685, 700, 706, 724, 753, 754, 777
*Crucible, The*, 282
*Cry Havoc*, 386
*Cuban Rebel Girls*, 366
*Cue* (magazine), 617, 639, 685, 688, 700, 727, 737
Cugat, Xavier, and His Band, 630, 631
Cukor, George, 120, 541, 546, 555, 556, 559, 797
Cummings, Irving, 70
Cunard, Grace, 14
Curie, Eve, 494
Curtis, Tony, 18, *670*, 671-72, 673, *674*, *675*, *676*, 678-80, 681, 682, 683, 684, 686, 688, 690, 691, 724, 733
Curtiz, Michael, 86, 120, 183, 341, 342, 344, 345, 348, 350, 353, 358, 361, 406, 461
*Cynara*, 183
*Cyrano de Bergerac*, 442
*Czaritza*, 313

da Silva, Howard, 587, 592
*Daddy Long Legs*, 88
Dahl, Arlene, 640, 667
Dailey, Dan, 16, 690
*Daily Worker, The*, 356, 358, 579
*Dallas Morning News*, 362
*Dames*, *146*, 162-65
*Dames at Sea*, 154
Damita, Lili, 38, 331
*Damn Yankees*, 787
*Damned Don't Cry, The*, 120
Dana, Robert W., 439, 466, 469, 524
*Dance, Fools, Dance*, 15, *100*, 104-05, 106, 129
"Dance with Me My Love," 317
*Dancing Co-Ed*, 522
*Dancing Lady*, *96*, 109-12, 113
Dandridge, Dorothy, 644
Dane, Patricia, 440
*Dangerous*, 257
Daniell, Henry, 356
Daniels, Bebe, 14, *149*, 154, 155
Daniels, William, 52, 312, 546
Danner, Blythe, 557
Dantine, Helmut, 489
*Dark Angel, The*, 14, *26*, 28-30, 34
*Dark Passage*, *646*, 662-64
*Dark Victory*, 196
Daves, Delmer, 164, 166, 169, 188, 293

Davies, Marion, 78, 88, 169
Davis, Bette, 17, 19, 93, 120, 121, 193, 196, *248*, 250-51, *252*, *253*, 255, 256-58, 259-61, 262, 263, 264-66, 319, 341, 355-56, 364, 402, 472, 498, 779
Davis, George W., 777
Davis, Sammy, 580
Davis, Wee Willie, *600*
Dawson, Ralph, 348
Day, Doris, 16, 18, 195, 328, 472, 530, 639, 734, *742*, 744-45, *746*, 747, 749-51, 753-54, 755, 756-57
Day, Laraine, 16
*Day After the Fair, The*, 712
De Carlo, Yvonne, 606
De Cuir, John, 783
de Grunwald, Anatole, 774
de Havilland, Olivia, 17, 37, 39, 264, *330*, 332-33, *334*, *335*, *336*, *337*, *338*, *339*, 341-43, 345, 346, 348, 349, 350, 353, 354, 356, 359, 362, 364, 365, 402, 406, 408, 472, 682
De Laurentiis, Dino, 19, 782, 789
De Mille, Cecil B., 32, 277, 685
de Toth, Andre, 594
*Dead End*, 462
Dead End Kids, 462
*Deadly Game, The*, 94
Deans, Mickey, 413, 452
"Dear Little Cafe," 324
*Dear Ruth*, 288
Dearing, Edgar, *206*
*Death of a Scoundrel*, 196
DeCamp, Rosemary, 288
Dee, Frances, 257
*Deep Blue Sea, The*, 386
Dees, Mary, 142, 143
*Defiant Ones, The*, 731
DeHaven, Gloria, 242, 446, 630, 631-32
Dekker, Albert, 521
Del Rio, Dolores, 16
Delehanty, Thornton, 58, 93, 113, 129, 140, 213, 308, 342
*Delicate Balance, A*, 566
*Delicious*, *66*, 87-89
"Delishious," 88
Dell, Gabriel, 462
Demetrio, Ann, 377
Demick, Irina, 711
Demongeot, Mylene, 701
Dennis, Sandy, 779, 780, 781
Denny, Reginald, 736
Derek, John, 679
Derr, Richard, 640
*Desert Song*, 612
*Designing Woman*, 667
*Desire Me*, 501
*Desk Set*, *539*, 560-63, 564
*Desperate Hours, The*, 668

*Destination Moon*, 678
*Destry Rides Again*, 352
DeSylva, Buddy, 78
*Detective in Film, The*, 215
*Detroit News*, 529
*Devil and Daniel Webster, The*, 787
*Devil Dogs of the Air*, 466
*Devil's Bride, The*, 708
Devine, Andy, 467, *603*, 613, 619
*Diane*, 530
*Diary of Anne Frank, The*, 751
Dick, Douglas, *576*
Dickson, Gloria, *181*, 195
Dicksten, Martin, 132
*Die Sehnsucht Jeder Frau*, 38
Dietrich, Marlene, 20, 137, 293, 408, 655
Digges, Dudley, 90, 92
Diller, Phyllis, 780
Dillon, Josephine, 97, 105
"Dinah," 309
Disney, Walt, 293, 327, 509
*Disraeli*, 38
*Dive Bomber*, 361
*Divine Woman, The*, 52
*Divorce His/Divorce Hers*, 796
Dixon, Lee, 172
*Do Not Disturb*, 756
"Do the Conga," 437
*Doctor Faustus*, 765, 785-87, 793
*Dr. Jekyll and Mr. Hyde*, 234, 520, 541
Dodd, Claire, 161, 190
*Dodge City*, *336*, 351-54, 466
*Don Juan in Hell*, 246
Donahue, Troy, 18, 293, 684
Donat, Robert, 341, 431
Donlevy, Brian, *572*, 582-83
Donovan, King, 684
"Don't Give Up the Ship Tommy Atkins," 443
Doolittle, Lt. Col. James H., 548
Dorsey, Tommy, and His Orchestra, 449
*Double Indemnity*, 288, 293
*Double Life, A*, 39
*Double Wedding*, *206*, 228-30
*Doughgirls, The*, 472
Douglas, Kirk, 685, 686, 736
Douglas, Melvyn, 246, 551
*Dover Road, The*, 190
Dowling, Doris, 592
*Downstairs*, 56
Doyle, Buddy, 221
*Dragon Seed*, 466
Drake, Tom, 450, 499, 630, 631
Draper, Paul, *152*, 172
"Dreamer, The," 364
Dressler, Marie, 16
Drew, Mr. and Mrs. Sidney, 14
Dubin, Al, 158
*Duck Soup*, 726

*Duel in the Sun*, 551
*Duffy's Tavern*, 574, 575, 586-87
Dumbrille, Douglas, 306, 617
Dunn, James, 15, *69*, 88, 93
Dunn, Josephine, 54
Dunn, Michael, *767*, 789
Dunne, Irene, 17, 20, 172, 256, 484, 494, 548, 700, 726, 729
Dunninger, 678
Dunnock, Mildred, 789
Duquette, Elizabeth, 777
Durante, Jimmy, 630, 631
Durbin, Deanna, 423
Duryea, Dan, 499, 730
Dwan, Allan, 407
*Dynamite Man*, 19

Eagels, Jeanne, 132
*Eagle, The*, 31
Eason, B. Reeves, 345
*East Wind*, 328
*Easter Parade*, 450
*Easy to Love:* (movie) 645; (song) 440
*Easy to Wed*, 225
Ebsen, Buddy, 317
Eburne, Maude, 90
Eddington, Nora, 331
Eddy, Nelson, 16, 111, 112, 216, *294*, 295, *297*, *298*, *299*, *300*, 301, *302*, 304, 305, 306, 307, 308, 309-10, 311, 312-13, 314, 315, 316-17, 318-19, 321-22, 324-25, 326-28, 402, 428, 583
*Eddy Duchin Story, The*, 408
Edelman, Lou, 166
*Edison the Man*, 494
*Edward, My Son*, 555
Edwards, Blake, 383, 683, 684
Edwards, Ralph, 328
*Effects of Gamma Rays on Man-in-the-Moon Marigolds, The*, 741
*Egg and I, The*, 16, *274*, 288-91, 292
*80 Yard Run, The*, 740
Eilers, Sally, 15
Eldredge, John, 168
*Elephant Boy*, 605
*Elizabeth the Queen*, 355
Ellerbe, Harry, 563
Ellington, Duke, 732
Ellis, Edward, 215, 283
Ellis, Patricia, 189
Emerson, Hope, 557
Ephron, Henry and Phoebe, 562
Epstein, Julius, 755
Erikson, Leif, 606, 607
Errol, Leon, 221, 342
Erskine, Chester, 290
Erwin, Stuart, 114, 404
*Es War (The Undying Past)*, 47

*Escapade*, 221
*Escape*, 484
*Escape in the Desert*, 262
Essanay, 14
Evans, Dale, 18
Evans, Dame Edith, 711
*Evelyn Prentice*, *204*, 216-19
Everson, William K., 72, 215
*Every Frenchman Has One*, 365
"Every Lover Must Meet His Fate," 319
Ewell, Tom, 556
*Excess Baggage*, 54
*Eye of the Devil*, *698*, 705, 707-09

*Face in the Crowd, A*, 740
Fairbanks, Douglas, 15, 37, 342, 348, 607, 616, 782
Fairbanks, Douglas, Jr., 98, 105
*Family Affair, A*, 423
*Family Honeymoon*, 275, 291-93
"Farewell, Amanda," 556
*Farmer's Daughter, The*, 408
Farnsworth, Arthur, 250
Farrar, David, 681
Farrell, Charles, 15, 37, 39, *60*, 61-62, *63*, *64*, *65*, *66*, *67*, *68*, *69*, 71-73, 74, 75-77, 78-79, 81, 82-83, 84-85, 86, 88-92, 93-95, 166, 396
Farrell, Glenda, 184
Farrow, Mia, 789
"Fascinatin' Rhythm" 448, 452
*Father of the Bride*, 559
*Father's Little Dividend*, 559
Faulkner, William, 654, 660, 723
*Faust*, 327
Fawcett, George, 47, 50
Faye, Alice, 400, 447, 632
Fazenda, Louise, 82, 157, 172
Feldman, Charles K., 706
Felix, Seymour, 79
Ferrer, Jose, 19
Ferrer, Mel, 19
Fields, W. C., 639
*55 Days at Peking*, 705
*Fighting 69th, The*, 466
Filauri, Antonio, *152*
*Films and Filming*, 583
*Films in Review*, 686, 724-25
*Films of Nancy Carroll, The*, 20
Finch, Flora, 14
Finch, Peter, 58, 769, 770
*Firefly, The*, 305, 315
First National Pictures, 28
First National-Warner Bros., 166, 169
*First of the Few, The*, 265
*First Year, The*, *60*, 89-91
Fisher, Eddie, 760, 770
Fitzgerald, Barry, 589
Fitzmaurice, George, 29, 34

FitzSimons, Charles, 681
*Flamingo Road*, 120
Fleischer, Richard, 686
Fleming, Rhonda, 606
*Flesh and the Devil*, 15, 37, *44*, 46-49, 52
Flint, Helen, *179*, 193
*Flirtation Walk:* (movie) *150*, 165-68, 169, 170; (song) 168
*Floradora Girl, The*, 88
*Flying Down to Rio*, 16
Flynn, Errol, 17, 37, 39, 316, *330*, 331-32, *334*, *335*, *336*, 337, *338*, *339*, 341, 342-43, 344, 345-46, 347-48, 349, 350, 351, 352, 353, 354, 355-56, 358, 359, 361-62, 365-66, 402, 406, 472, 482, 504, 505, 667, 682
Flynn, Sean, 331, 343
Fogelson, Elijah "Buddy," 477, 509
Fonda, Henry, 262, 293, 365, 371, 387
Fontaine, Joan, 484
Fontanne, Lynn, 15, 196, 264, 318, 355, 565
*Footlight Parade*, *150*, 159-62, 429, 462
*For Me and My Gal*, 447
Foran, Dick, 260, 262
Forbes, Ralph, 191
Ford, Francis, 14
Ford, Glenn, 18, 20
Ford, Harrison, 311
Ford, John, 70, 529
Ford, Ruth, 789
Foreman, John, 736
Forrest, Helen, 630
*Forsaking All Others*, *102*, 114-16
*Forsyte Saga, The*, 504
"Forty and One for All," 612
*Forty Carats*, 531, 645
*42nd Street*, 16, 110, *149*, 153-56, 157, 158, 160, 163, 305
Foster, Norman, 271
*Four's a Crowd*, 264, *334*, 349-51
Fowley, Douglas, 353
Fox, Julian, 583
Fox, Paul S., 562
Fox, William, 70
Fox, William (James), 506
Fox Films, 15, 37, 48, 70, 74, 78, 79, 81, 82, 84, 86, 88, 90, 91, 93, 166
*Fox Movietone Follies of 1929*, 81
*Fox Movietone Follies of 1930*, 81
Foxe, Earle, *100*
Franciosa, Anthony, 723, 724
Francis, Arlene, 328
Francis, Connie, 449
Francis, Kay, 17, *174*, 176-77, *178*, *179*, *180*, 181, 183-84, 185, 186-87, 188-89, 190-91, 192-93, 194, 195-96, 211, 484
Francis the Talking Mule, 19
Frank, Harriet, 723

Frankenheimer, John, 757
Franklin, Joe, 72
Franklin, Sidney A., 488, 489, 490, 494, 506, 527
Frantz, Dalies, 319
Frazee, Jane, 16
*Fred Astaire and Ginger Rogers Book, The*, 20
*Free Soul, A*, 15, 105
Freed, Arthur, 448, 634
Friedman, Bruce J., 691
*Friends of Mr. Sweeney*, 277
Froeschel, George, 490
*From Here to Eternity*, 700
*From the Terrace*, 246, *718*, 727-30
Froman, Charles, 222
*Front Page, The*, 377, 399
Funicello, Annette, 18, 757
Furie, Sidney J., 708
Furthman, Jules, 137, 654, 660


Gable, Clark, 15, 90, *96*, 97-98, *100*, *101*, *102*, *103*, 105, 106, 107, 108-09, 111, 112, 113-14, 115, 116, 117, 118, 120, 121, *122*, *124*, *125*, *126*, *127*, 129-30, 131-33, 134-35, 136, 137-38, 140-41, 143, 144, *203*, 211-12, 214, 216, 218, 255, 265, 352, 402, 426, 430, 445, 464, 501, *512*, *515*, *516*, *517*, *518*, 520, 521-22, 523-24, 526, 527, 528-30, 531, 545, 566, 632, 736
Gabor, Eva, 734
Galsworthy, John, 504
Garbo, Greta, 14-15, 37, 39, *40*, 43, *44*, *45*, 46-49, 50-51, 52, 53, 54, 55-59, 74, 382, 426, 431, 484, 494, 541, 561, 733
Gardner, Ava, 133, 411, 529
Gardner, Ed, 587
Garfield, John, 20, 364, 545, 595, 657
Garland, Judy, 16, 216, 383, 410, 413-14, *414*, *415*, *416*, *417*, *418*, *419*, *420*, *421*, 423, 425-26, 427, 428, 429-30, 431, 433-434, 436-37, 438, 440, 442-44, 446, 447-49, 450, 451-52, 520, 521, 545, 631, 634
Garland, Robert, 402
Garner, James, 736, 755
Garnett, Tay, 137
Garrett, Betty, 450
Garson, Greer, 18, 38, 216, 366, *474*, 477, *478*, *479*, *480*, *481*, *482*, 484-86, 488, 489-91, 492, 494-96, 497, 498-99, 501-02, 504, 505, 506, 507, 508, 509, 510, 521, 526, 543, 545, 632, 700
Garstin, Crosbie, 136
*Gaslight*, 499
Gates, Phyllis, 743
Gaul, George, 70
Gaye, Gregory, 83

Gaynor, Janet, 15, 37, 39, *60*, 62, *63*, *64*, *65*, *66*, *67*, *68*, *69*, 70-73, 74, 75-77, 78-79, 81, 82-83, 84, 85, 86, 88-92, 93-95, 166, 395, 396, 397
Geeson, Judy, 711
Gelmis, Joseph, 710
*Gentlemen of the Press*, 196
*Gentlemen Prefer Blondes*, 484
*Gentlemen's Agreement*, 291
*George Washington Slept Here*, 472
Gershwin, George, 88, 436, 634
Gershwin, Ira, 436
Gibbons, Cedric, 140, 312, 551
*Gift of Time, A*, 365
*Gigi*, 704
Gilbert, Billy, *600*, 605, 606, 607
Gilbert, John, 14-15, 37, 39, *40*, 41-42, *44*, *45*, 46, 47-49, 50, 51, 52, 53, 54, 56, 57-58, 74
Gilbert, Leatrice Joy, 41, 58
*Gilda*, 18, 655
*Gilded Lily, The*, 17, 272, 276-78, 279, 280, 289,
Gillingwater, Claude, 92
*Girl and the General, The*, 708
"Girl at the Ironing Board, The," 164
*Girl Crazy, 415*, 446-49
*Girl Loves Boy*, 17
*Girl of the Golden West, The, 300*, 314-17, 318, 319
Gish, Dorothy, 14
Gish, Lillian, 28, 71
*Give Me Your Heart, 179*, 180, 191-93
*Glass Key, The, 572*, 581-83
*Glass Menagerie, The*, 566
*Glass-Bottom Boat, The*, 756
Glazer, Benjamin, 73
Gleason, James, 443
*Glenn Miller Story, The*, 644
Glenville, Peter, 785
"Glory of Love," 565
*G-Men*, 462
*Go into Your Dance*, 169
Goddard, Paulette, 585, 589
"God's Country," 430, 431
*Going My Way*, 726
*Gold Diggers, The*, 157
*Gold Diggers of Broadway*, 157-58
*Gold Diggers of 1933, 149*, 156-59, 429
Goldblatt, Burt, 20
Golden, John, 70
Goldsmith, Margaret, 55
Goldsmith, Oliver, 710
Goldstone, James, 736
Goldwyn, Samuel, 14, 15, 28-29, 30, 31, 32, 33, 37, 38, 246, 265, 605
Gombell, Minna, 90, 216
Gomez, Thomas, *601*, 609, 610

*Gone with the Wind*, 58, 120, 144, 265, 355, 520
*Good Earth, The*, 58, 94
"Good Morning," 430
*Goodbye, Charlie*, 667
*Goodbye, Mr. Chips*, 431, 484
*Goodbye, My Fancy*, 120-21
Goodman, Jules Eckhert, 84
Goodrich, Frances, 215
Goodrich, Marcus, 332
*Goose and the Gander, The*, 180, 189-91
Gorcey, Leo, 462
Gordon, C. Henry, 345
Gordon, Gale, 726
Gordon, Ruth, 556, 559, 561
*Gorgeous Hussy, The*, 118
"Got a New Pair of Shoes," 423
*Gotta Sing Gotta Dance*, 312
Goulding, Edmund, 50, 311
*Government Girl*, 365
Gow, Gordon, 679
Grable, Betty, 16, 400, 447, 667
Grahame, Gloria, 244
*Grand Hotel*, 55, 111, 137, 526, 703
Grand National, 17
*Grand Prix*, 736
Granger, Farley, 15
Grant, Cary, 17, 20, 246, 350, 683, 688, 700, 706, 729, 750, 754, 755
Granville, Bonita, 283, 386
Grapewin, Charley, 261, 262
*Grass Is Greener, The*, 706
Gray, Gilda, 221, 309
Grayson, Kathryn, 446, 634, 636
*Great Garrick, The*, 348
*Great Lie, The*, 196
*Great Ziegfeld, The, 204*, 219-22
*Greatest Show on Earth, The*, 387
Greco, Juliette, 701
Green, Alfred E., 190
Green, Paul, 93
Green, Stanley, 20
*Green Dolphin Street, 526*, 553
*Green Hat, The*, 52, 53
*Green Light*, 347
Greenberg, Joel, 385
Greene, Clarence, 751
Greene, Graham, 578, 784, 785
Greenstreet, Sydney, 526
Gregory, Paul, 62, 95
Greig, Robert, 606
Grey, Virginia, 233
Griffith, D. W., 782
Griffith, Richard, 38
Grim, Bobby, 736
Grippo, Jan, 579
Grot, Anton, 342, 356
Group Theatre, 470

*Guardsman, The*, 15
Guernsey, Otis, L., Jr., 241, 292, 559, 589, 614, 617, 632, 642, 654, 655
*Guess Who's Coming to Dinner*, 143, 535, 563-66
Guest, Val, 706
Guilaroff, Sydney, 312
Guilfoyle, Paul, 610
Guiness, Alec, 785
*Gun for Sale, A*, 578
*Gun Runners, The*, 657
Gunn, Moses, 739
*Guns of Navarone, The*, 705
Gurney, Dan, 736
*Guy Named Joe, A*, 548
*Gypsy Moths, The*, 711
*Gypsy Wildcat*, 599, 616-17

Hackett, Albert, 215
Hagen, Jean, 557
Haines, William, 54
Hale, Alan, 348, 354, 356, 359
Hale, Chester, 309
Hale, Wanda, 439, 711
Hall, Dickie, 239
Hall, Huntz, 462
Hall, James, 38
Hall, James Norman, 636
Hall, Jon, 18, *596*, 597-98, *599, 600, 601, 602, 603*, 605, 606-07, 609-10, 612, 613, 614, 615, 616-17, 619-20
Hall, Mordaunt, 30, 32, 33, 37, 51, 54, 58, 72, 74, 76, 79, 81, 82, 86, 89, 90, 93, 130, 183, 216, 255
Hall, Porter, 261
*Hall of Mirrors, A*, 739
Halop, Billy, 462
Hamilton, Margaret, 350
Hamilton, Neil, 107
*Hamlet*, 776, 782
*Hammersmith Is Out*, 766, 791-93
Hammett, Dashiell, 214, 218, 232, 582
Hampton, Hope, 157
*Hands Across the Table*, 279
Hanley, James, 81
Hanshue, ——, *26*
Hanson, Lars, 47, 48
*Happiest Millionaire, The*, 509
*Happy Days*, 66, 79-81
Harburg, E.Y., 442
*Harder They Fall, The*, 668
Harding, Ann, 140, 256, 484, 488
Hardy, Thomas, 712
Harlow, Jean, 15, 114, *122*, 123-24, *124, 125, 126, 127*, 129, 130, 131-33, 134-35, 136, 137-38, 140-41, 142-44, *205*, 216, 224-25, 399, 484, 520, 531, 566

Harper, 662
*Harriet Craig*, 120
Harris, Julie, 711
Harrison, Rex, 19, 770, 772
Harrold, Orville, 304
Hart, Lorenz, 304, 326, 428, 450, 451
Hart, Moss, 293
Hart, Richard, 501
Harvey: (movie) 387; (play) 387
Harvey, Laurence, 258, 739
Harvey, Paul, 261
*Harvey Girls, The*, 450
Haver, June, 269, 293
Havoc, June, 285
Hawks, Howard, 543, 662, 755
Haydn, Richard, 285
Hayes, Helen, 387, 771
Hayes, Peter Lind, 688
Hays, Will, 237, 614
Hayward, Leland, 371, 379
Hayward, Susan, 704, 769
Hayworth, Rita, 18, 20, 655, 703, 704
"He Asked Thy Life or My Love," 309
Healy, Mary, 688
Healy, Ted, 111
Heflin, Van, 120
*Heiress, The*, 365, 408
Held, Anna, 221
Heller, Joseph, 706
Hellinger, Mark, 466
*Hell's Angels*, 129
Helton, Percy, *718*
Hemingway, Ernest, 105, 654
Hemmings, David, 346, 709
Henderson, Ray, 78
Henie, Sonja, 400
Henning, Paul, 753
Henreid, Paul, 258
Henry, William, 216
Hepburn, Audrey, 19
Hepburn, Katharine, 18, 173, 256, 293, *532*, 534-35, *535, 536, 537, 538, 539*, 540-3, 544-45, 546-47, 548-49, 550-51, 553-54, 555-56, 557, 559-60, 561-63, 564, 565-66, 667, 754
Herbert, Hugh, 161, 164, 165, 172, 350, 351
Herbert, Ralph J., 311
Herbert, Victor, 304, 305, 308, 311, 318
*Here Comes the Navy*, 466
Herron, Mark, 413
Hertz, John, Jr., 201
Herzig, Sig, 350
Heston, Charlton, 33, 510
"Hey, Young Fella," 111
"Hey Ho, The Gang's All Here," 112
Hickman, Dwayne, 726
*Hidden Children, The*, 14
*High Barbaree*, 622, 635-37

*High Society Blues,* 81-83, 84, 88
Higham, Charles, 385
Hildyard, Jack, 774
Hill, Craig, 681
Hill, George, 129
Hiller, Arthur, 708
Hiller, Wendy, 704
Hilliard, Robert, 315
Hilton, James, 38, 490
Hinds, Samuel S., 615
Hingle, Pat, 739
*His Glorious Night,* 56, 58
Hitchcock, Alfred, 387, 578
Hobart, Rose, 83
Hoctor, Harriet, 221
Hodiak, John, 507, 527
Hoffe, Monckton, 74
*Hold Your Man,* 122, 126, 133-35
Holden, Fay, *416, 420, 426,* 433
Holden, William, 39
*Holiday,* 545
*Holiday Affair,* 678
Holliday, Judy, 556-57
Holloway, Sterling, 585
*Hollywood Canteen,* 120
*Hollywood in the Fifties,* 679
*Hollywood in the 1940s,* 385
Holm, Celeste, 291
*Homecoming, 517,* 524-27, 528, 529
*Honeymoon for Three,* 196
"Honeymoon Hotel," 162
"Honeysuckle Rose," 446
*Honky Tonk,* 144, *515,* 516, 519-22, 523, 529
Hope, Bob, 20, 135, 447, 472, 561, 589
Hopper, Hedda, 82
Hopwood, Avery, 157
Hornblow, Arthur, Jr., 201
Horne, Geoffrey, 701
Horne, Lena, 446, 630, 631, 634
Horton, Edward Everett, 191, 327
*Hotel Paradiso,* 190
*Houdini,* 18, *674,* 677-80
Houdini, Harry, 677-78, 679, 680
Houghton, Katharine, 565
*House of Connelly, The,* 93
*House of Rothschild, The,* 396, 406
*House of the Seven Gables, The,* 282
*House on 56th Street,* 192
"How About You?," 442
*How Green Was My Valley,* 485
"How Little We Know," 656
"How Long Can It Last," 109
"How Sweet You Are," 364
*How to Marry a Millionaire,* 667
Howard, Ken, 557
Howard, Leslie, 17, 56, *248, 249-50, 252, 253,* 255-56, *257-58,* 259-62, 264-65, 266, 319, 402

Howard, Shemp, *600,* 605
Howard, Sidney, 38
Howard, Trevor, 346
Howard, William K., 90, 219
Howe, James Wong, 466
Hoyt, John, 196
*Hucksters, The,* 526
*Hud,* 739
Hudson, Rock, 18, 667, 679, 734, *742,* 743-44, *746, 747,* 749-51, 753-54, 755, 756, 757
Hughes, Howard, 129, 551, 678
Hughes, Lloyd, 91
Hull, Henry, 84
Hulman, Tony, 736
*Human Comedy, The,* 447
Hume, Benita, 23, 39
*Humoresque,* 120
"Hungarian Rhapsody, The." *See* Banky, Vilma
Hunt, Jimmy, *275*
Hunt, Marsha, 485
Hunter, Ian, 120, *181,* 195, 348
Hunter, Jeffrey, 679
Hunter, Kim, 246
Hunter, Ross, 30, 328, 530, 749
Hunter, Tab, 679, 789
Hurok, Sol, 642
"Hurrah, He's Won the War," 365
*Hurricane, The,* 406
Hurst, Brandon, 50, 51
Hurst, Paul, 404
Hussey, Ruth, 196
*Hustler, The,* 731, 739
Huston, John, 665, 667, 707
Huston, Walter, 196
Hutton, Betty, 447, 589
Hutton, Robert, 18
Huxley, Aldous, 494

"I Aint Got Nobody," 437
"I Belong to Glasgow," 442
"I Bring a Breath of Springtime," 319
*I Could Go on Singing,* 451
"I Cried for You," 430
"I Don't Have to Dream Again" 172
*I Found Stella Parish,* 192, 484
"I Got Rhythm," 449
*I Love a Woman,* 192
*I Love You Again,* 233-35
*I Married an Angel,* 301, 304, 325-27
*I Met Him in Paris,* 733
"I Need No Atmosphere," 751
"I Only Have Eyes for You," 164, 165
*I Want a Divorce,* 173
"I Want to be Happy," 173
*I Want to Live,* 704
"I Was a Stranger in Paris," 322
"I Wish I Were in Love Again," 451

"I Won't Dance," 634
"I'd Rather Listen to Your Eyes," 170
"I'd Rather Take Orders from You," 170
"Ida," 111, 430
"If I Had a Talking Picture of You," 78
"If You Could Only Come with Me," 324
"I'll See You Again," 324
"I'll Tell Every Man in the Street," 327
"I'm a Dreamer, Aren't We All," 78
"I'm in the Market for You," 83
"I'm Just Wild About Harry," 430
*Im Letzten Augenblick*, 28
"I'm Nobody's Baby," 434
"I'm Riding for a Fall," 364
*Imitation of Life*, 277, 530
"In a Little Spanish Town," 446
"In Between," 426
*In His Steps*, 17
*In Love and War*, 723
*In Name Only*, 196
*In Old Chicago*, 406
*In the Good Old Summertime*, 383
*In This Our Life*, 196
*Independent Film Journal*, 792
"Indian Love Call," 309
*Indianapolis Speedway*, 736
Inescourt, Frieda, *179*, 193
Ingraham, Mitchell, *179*
"Inka Dinka Do," 631
*Innocents, The*, 709
*Inspiration:* (movie) 55; (song) 751
*Intermezzo*, 265
Ireland, Jill, 19
*Irene*, 753
*Irish in Us, The*, 466
*Iron Menace*, 589
*Iron Petticoat, The*, 561
*Irregular Verb to Love, The*, 293
*It Happened One Night*, 115, 117, 138, 211, 214, 257, 277, 553
*It Happened to Jane*, 749
"It Must Be June," 155
"It Never Rains But What it Pours," 426
*It Started in Naples*, 530
"Italian Street Song," 306
*It's a Big Country*, 246
*It's Love I'm After*, 17, *253*, 262-65, 266, 319, 348
Iturbi, Amparo, 630, 631
*Iturbi, José*, *421*, 446, 630, 631
"I've Got You," 579

Jackson, Thomas, 212
Jacoby, Michel, 345
James, Harry, and His Band, 630, 631
James, Henry, 365
*Janie*, 18
*Janus*, 386

Jarman, Claude, Jr., 637
Jaynes, Betty, 319, 428, 430
"Je Veux Vivre dans Ce Rêve," 309
"Jeanette and Her Little Wooden Shoe," 319
Jeans, Isabel, *181*, 195
Jeffreys, Anne, 327
Jenkins, Allen, 184
Jenkins, Butch, 639-40
*Jesse James*, 352
Jessel, George, 81
*Jet Pilot*, 678
*Jewel Robbery*, 183
*Jezebel*, 196, 265
*Joan of Paris*, 579
Johaneson, Bland, 130, 224, 256
*Johnny Come Lately*, 472
*Johnny Eager*, 580
*Johnny Guitar*, 121
"Johnny One Note," 451
Johnson, Kay, 257
Johnson, Rita, 142, 292
Johnson, Van, 18, 225, 383, 554, *622*, 623-24, *626*, 627, 628, 630-32, 634-35, 636, 637, 639-40, 642, 644, 645
Johnston, Johnny, 634
"Joint Is Really Jumpin' in Carnegie Hall, The," 446
Jolson, Al, 148, 155, 156, 169, 172, 173
Jones, Allan, 305, 309, 315
Jones, Jennifer, 496
Jones, Spike, 589
Jordan, Bobby, 462
Jordan, René, 109, 129
Jorden, Terry, 744, 757
Jory, Victor, 353
Jourdan, Louis, 774, 775
Joy, Leatrice, 41
*Judgment at Nuremberg*, 451
*Julia, Jake and Uncle Joe*, 293
*Julia Misbehaves*, *481*, 499-502
June, Ray, 135, 136, 140
*Jungle Book*, 605
"Just Like in a Storybook," 83

Kahn, Gus, 305, 324
Kanin, Garson, 541, 545, 550, 556, 559, 566
Kanin, Michael, 541
Katch, Kurt, 613
"Katinkitschka," 88
Kauffmann, Stanley, 779
Kaufman, George F., 245, 436
Kaufmann, Christine, 671
Kaye, Danny, 690
Kazan, Elia, 550
Keel, Howard, 310
Keeler, Gertrude and Helen, 156

Keeler, Ruby, 16, *146*, 148, *149, 150, 151, 152*, 154-56, 158, 159, 161, 162, 164, 165-66, 167-68, 169-70, 172-73, 315
Keenan, Frank, 316
*Keeper of the Flame, 536*, 543-47, 548
Keighley, William, 348, 466
Kellaway, Cecil, 288, 498, 565
Kelly, Gene, 446
Kelly, Grace, 133, 451, 529, 667
Kelly, Joe, *26*
Kelly, Patsy, 173
Kelly, Paul, 528
Kennedy, Arthur, 471
Kennedy, Edgar, 230, 280
Kern, Jerome, 304, 634
Kerr, Deborah, 18, 501, 526, 555, *692*, 695, *696, 697, 698*, 700, 701, 703-04, 705, 706, 707, 708, 709, 710, 711, 712
Kerrigan, J.M., 86-87
*Key Largo, 652*, 664-67
Keys, Frances Parkinson, 328
*Keyhole, The, 174*, 182-84
Kezas, George, 543
Kibbee, Guy, 107, 154, 158, 164
*Kid Andrew Cody*, 691
*Kid from Spain, The*, 726
*Kiki*, 31
Kilbride, Percy, 16, 291
*Killer McCoy*, 450
*Killing of Sister George, The*, 265-66
*Kind Sir*, 472
King, Dennis, 326
King, Henry, 31, 35
*King of Kings*, 772
*King Richard and the Crusaders*, 681
*King Solomon's Mines*, 700
*Kings Row*, 472
Kingsley, Sidney, 527
Kirk, Phyllis, 216
*Kiss Me, Kate*, 782
*Kitty Foyle*, 541
*Knickerbocker Holiday*, 327
Knight, Arthur, 690, 734, 751
*Knight and the Lady, The*, 355
*Knights of the Round Table*, 681
Knowlden, Marilyn, 462
Knowles, Patric, *180*, 193, 345
Kobal, John, 312
Kolker, Henry, 90, 184
Korngold, Erich Wolfgang, 342, 348, 356
Kramer, Stanley, 564, 565
Krasna, Norman, 288
Krug, Karl, 529
Kruger, Otto, 114
Kruschen, Jack, 753
Kurnitz, Harry, 239
Kuter, Leo K., 667
Kuttner, Alfred B., 72

*La Boheme*, 46
"La Marseillaise," 443
La Rocque, Rod, 24, 37, 38, 39
Laage, Barbara, 732
Ladd, Alan, 18, 408, *568*, 569-70, 572, *573, 574, 575, 576*, 578, 579-81, 582, 583, 585, 587, 589, 591, 592, 594
*Ladies in Love*, 94, 392, 395-97
"Ladies of the Town", 324
*Lady in Question, The*, 18
*Lady in the Dark*, 285
*Lady in the Lake*, 663
"Lady is a Tramp, The," 428
*Lady Is Willing, The*, 196
*Lady L*, 705
*Lady to Love, A*, 38
Lake, Arthur, 16
Lake, Veronica, 18, *568*, 571, 572, *573, 574, 575, 576*, 578-79, 580, 581, 582-83, 585, 587, 589, 591, 592, 594-95
Lamarr, Hedy, 520, 522, 529, 545
Lamas, Fernando, 529
Lamb, Gil, 288
Lamont, Lillian, 269
Lamour, Dorothy, 20, 173, *576*, 585, 589, 606
Lancaster, Burt, 561, 703
Lanchester, Elsa, 306
Landi, Elissa, *206*, 228
Lane, Burton, 442
Lane, Margaret, 411
Lane, Priscilla, 20, 354
Lane, Rosemary, 354
Lang, Charles, Jr., 285
Lang, Hope, 19
Lang, Walter, 403
Langer, Dr. R.M., 494
Langford, Frances, 597
Langham, Rhea, 97, 105
Lansbury, Angela, 553, 554, 644, 723, 724
Lardner, Ring, Jr., 541
Lassie, 327
*Last Time I Saw Paris, The*, 645
Latimer, Jonathan, 582
Lauder, Harry, 442
*Laughing Sinners, 100*, 106-07
Laughton, Charles, 791
Laurel, Stan, 381
Laurents, Arthur, 701
Law, William, 228
Lawford, Peter, 216, 502
Lawrence, Florence, 13
Lawrence, Vincent, 550
Lawson, Wilfred, *392*
Laye, Evelyn, 192
Lazenby, George, 707
Le Gon, Jeni, *600*
Le Mans, 736

Leachman, Cloris, 740
*Leatherface: A Tale of Old Flanders*, 37
"Leave It to Jane," 634
Lebedeff, Ivan, 117, 138
Lee, Ivy Ledbetter, 350
Lee, Sammy, 111
*Left Hand of God, The*, 668
Legion of Decency, 119, 439
Leigh, Janet, 18, 450, 505, *670*, 671, 673, *674*, *675*, *676*, 678, 679, 680, 681, 682, 683, 684, 686, 688, 690-91, 724, 733
Leigh, Rowland, 345
Leigh, Vivien, 58, 265, 559, 771
Leighton, Margaret, 703
Leisen, Mitchell, 284, 285, 287, 288
Lejeune, C.A., 57
Lemmon, Jack, 246
*Lempke*, 691
Leonard, Robert Z., 221, 312
Leonard, Sheldon, 233
LeRoy, Mervyn, 345, 484, 494, 527
*Les Filles de Cadiz*, 313
*Les Huguenots*, 313
Leslie, Joan, 364
*Let Freedom Ring*, 321
"Let's Dance," 431
"Let's Go Bavarian," 112
Levene, Sam, *206*, 227
Levien, Sonya, 88
Levine, Margaret P., 56
Lewis, Diana, 199, 246, 325, 432, 434
Lewis, Jerry, 641
Lewis, Sinclair, 526
*Libeled Lady*, 205, 222-25, 351, 399, 546
Liberace, 631
*Liberty* (magazine), 255-56, 279, 396, 580
Liberty Films, 553
"Liebestraum," 316
*Life* (magazine), 385, 522, 553, 566, 578, 789
*Life Begins for Andy Hardy*, 420, 438-40
"Life upon the Wicked Stage," 634
*Life with Father*, 245, 504, 644
*Light That Failed, The*, 258
Lightner, Winnie, 111, 158
*Lilies of the Fields*, 772
*Liliom*, 83
Lillie, Beatrice, 502
Linden, Eric, 17
Lindfors, Viveca, 366
Lindsay, Howard, 553, 644
Lingle, Jake, 105
*Lion in Winter, The*, 566
*Little Big Man*, 361
*Little Caesar*, 129, 484
*Little Foxes, The*, 265
"Little Grey Home in the West," 319
*Little Women*, 678
Littlefield, Lucien, 82

*Living On Velvet*, *178*, 184-87
Lloyd, Frank, 282
Lloyd, Harold, 14
*Lloyds of London*, 397, 400, 406
Lockhart, Gene, 362
Lockwood, Harold, 14
Loesser, Frank, 589
Lombard, Carole, 97, 120, 144, 196, 199, 229, 279, 284, 522, 523, 734
*London Observer*, 143, 564, 787
*London Times*, 88, 89, 109, 183, 190, 224, 228, 230, 488, 703
*Lone Star*, 529
*Lonely Life, The*, 265
*Lonelyhearts*, 246
*Long, Hot Summer, The*, 18, *717*, 722-25, 737
Long, Richard, 274
*Long Day's Journey into Night*, 564
*Long Gray Line, The*, 408
"Look for the Silver Lining," 634
Loos, Anita, 484, 485
Loren, Sophia, 530, 595, 757, 782
*Los Angeles Herald*, 75
*Los Angeles Times*, 305
Losey, Joseph, 788, 789
*Lost Horizon*, 38
*Lost Weekend, The*, 592
Lothar, Rudolph, 35
Louis, Jean, 565, 750, 756
Louise, Anita, 345
*Love*, *45*, 49-51
Love, Montagu, 33-34
*Love Affair*, 726
*Love Among the Ruins*, 566
*Love Crazy*, 207, 235-37
*Love Finds Andy Hardy*, *416*, 424-27, 520
"Love in Any Language" ("Bonne Nuit Merci"), 324
*Love Is News*, 392, 397-400
"Love Isn't Born, It's Made," 364
*Love Laughs at Andy Hardy*, 450
"Love Like Ours, A," 631
*Love Me or Leave Me*, 472
*Love on the Run*, *102*, 116-18, 501
*Love Parade, The*, 79
*Lover Come Back*: (movie) 747, 752-54, 755; (song) 753
"Lover Come Back to Me," 322
"Love's First Kiss," 53
Lowe, Edmund, 81, 235
Lowell, Helen, 191
Loy, Myrna, 16, *127*, 140, 141, 196, *198*, 201-02, *203*, *204*, *205*, *206*, 207, *208*, *209*, 211-13, 214, 215-16, 218-19, 221, 222, 224, 225, 227-28, 229-30, 232-33, 234-35, 236, 237, 239-40, 241-42, 243-44, 246, 399, 402, 583, 729, 730, 754

Lubitsch, Ernst, 304, 305, 382, 639
*Lucille Love, Girl of Mystery*, 14
*Lucky Baldwin*, 527
*Lucky Star*, 65, 75-77
Lucy, Arnold, 87
Luft, Sid, 413
Lukas, Paul, 299, 311, 312, *392*, 397, 496
Lunt, Alfred, 15, 196, 264, 318, 355, 565
Lupino, Ida, *339*, 364
Lyle, Edith, 31
Lynley, Carol, 143
Lynn, Diana, 642
Lynn, Sharon, *65*

*Ma and Pa Kettle*, 16, 291
MacArthur, Charles, 245
Macaulay, Richard, 466
McCallum, David, 19
McCambridge, Mercedes, 196
McCarey, Leo, 726
McCarten, John, 551, 642, 729
McCleary, Urie, 777
McCluskey, Roger, 736
MacDonald, Betty, 289
MacDonald, Jeanette, 16, 79, 216, *294*, 296, *297, 298, 299, 300, 301, 302*, 304, 305-07, 308, 309-10, 311, 312-14, 315, 316-17, 318-19, 321-22, 324-25, 326-27, 328, 402, 583
McDonald, Ray, *421*, 440, 442, 448, *625*, 634
Macdonald, Ross, 662
McDowall, Roddy, 772
MacFarlane, George, 81
McGrath, Paul, 285
McGuire, William Anthony, 220
McHugh, Frank, *150*, 161-62, 235, 354
Mackaill, Dorothy, 84
McKay, Scott, 456, 472
MacKenna, Kenneth, 85, 177
MacKenzie, Faith Compton, 56
McLaglen, Victor, 81
MacLaine, Shirley, 740
MacLane, Barton, 189
MacLean, Fred M., 667
*McLintock*, 286
MacMahon, Aline, 158
McManus, John T., 117, 143, 546, 632
MacMurray, Fred, 17, *268*, 269-70, 272, *273, 274*, 275, 277-78, 279, 280, 282-83, 284, 285-86, 288, 289-90, 291, 292-93, 509
MacPhail, Douglas, 319, 428-29
McQueen, Steve, 736
MacRae, Gordon, 16
McVay, Douglas, 442
McWade, Edward, *180*
*Madame Curie, 480*, 492-96
*Madame X*, 193, 218, 530
"Mademoiselle," 319
*Madwoman of Chaillot, The*, 566
Maeterlinck, Maurice, 797

*Magic Flame, The*, 22, 34-36
Mahin, John Lee, 114
*Maid of Salem*, 272, 280-83
Main, Marjorie, 16, 233, 291, 521
*Major and the Minor, The*, 641
*Make Mine Music*, 327
*Make Way for Tomorrow*, 726
Mallory, Jay, 192
Malone, Nancy, 725
*Maltese Falcon, The*, 214, 582, 665
"Mama Yo Quiero," 443
Mamoulian, Rouben, 769, 770
*Man and Wife*, 556
*Man for All Seasons, A*, 779, 791
*Man in the Iron Mask, The*, 691
*Man of a Thousand Faces*, 472
*Man of Conquest*, 353
*Man of La Mancha*, 795
*Man Who Came Back, The*, 67, 83-85, 88
*Man Who Knew Too Much, The*, 387
*Manchurian Candidate, The*, 690, 739
Mandel, Johnny, 777
*Manhattan Melodrama*, 203, 210-13, 214, 218, 461, 464
Mankiewicz, Joseph L., 115, 541, *762*, 770
Manners, Dorothy, 554
*Manpower*, 77
*Man's Favorite Sport?*, 755
*Man's Man, A*, 53-54
Mansfield, Richard, 442
*Mara Maru*, 366
March, Fredric, 30, 51, 246, 345
March, Hal, 756
*Mardi Gras*, 723
"Mariachi, The," 316-17
*Marianne*, 88
Marion, Frances, 29, 31, 50, 129
Maris, Mona, 117, 327
Markey, Gene, 201
Marlowe, Christopher, 787
*Marriage Is a Private Affair*, 526
*Marriage on the Rocks*, 706
*Marriage-Go-Round, The*, 246, 293
Marshal, Alan, 228
Marshall, Edison, 685
Marshall, George, 591, 679
Marshall, Herbert, 30, 53, 191, *675*, 681
Martin, Dean, 688, 757
Martin, Lynn, 364
Martin, Tony, 400, 634
Martin and Lewis, 682
Marvin, Lee, 779
Marx Brothers, 195, 726
Mason, James, 452
*Masquerader, The*, 28
*Massacre in Rome*, 797
Massey, Ilona, 315, 321, 327
Massey, Raymond, 120, 358, 359
Masters, Dorothy, 612

Mastroianni, Marcello, 757, 782
*Mata Hari*, 55
*Match* (Paris), 365
Mather, Aubrey, 502
Mature, Victor, 530
Maugham, W. Somerset, 255, 257, 258, 408, 466
Maxwell, Marilyn, 637
"May I Present the Girl," 327
Mayer, Louis B., 49, 214, 304, 305, 434, 435, 450, 484, 485, 488, 491, 526, 541, 545, 551, 556
Mayo, Archie, 264
Mayo, Virginia, 472
*Maytime*, 299, 300, 310-14, 315, 324
Mears, Martha, 579, 585
*Mechanic, The*, 19
Medina, Patricia, 606
Medoff, Mark, 262
Meek, Donald, 117
Meeker, George, 91
Meeker, Ralph, 589
*Meet Me in St. Louis*, 450
"Meet the Beat of My Heart," 426
*Meeting Mrs. Jenkins*, 797
Melcher, Martin, 744, 749, 755, 756-57
*Men of Boys Town*, 484, 541
*Men with Wings*, 578
Menjou, Adolphe, 553, 554
Menken, Helen, 70, 647
Mercer, Beryl, 87, 93
*Merely Mary Ann*, 68, 85-87
Merkel, Una, 154, 155, 640, 723
Merrill, Gary, 19, 250, 265
*Merry Widow, The*, 304, 305, 529
*Merton of the Movies*, 54
Methot, Mayo, 647
Metro-Goldwyn-Mayer, 14, 15, 16, 17, 18, 37, 38, 46, 47, 48, 49, 50, 52, 53, 54, 56, 58, 90, 104, 105, 107, 110, 111, 113, 117, 118, 120, 121, 129, 132, 134, 135, 136, 138, 140, 142, 144, 167, 169, 173, 196, 211, 214, 216, 219, 220, 221, 222, 224, 228, 229, 230, 232, 239, 240, 241, 246, 256, 264, 280, 304, 305, 308, 310, 311, 312, 315, 316, 318, 319, 321, 324, 326, 327, 328, 351, 352, 364, 366, 376, 379, 382, 386, 397, 399, 422, 423, 425, 426, 427, 428, 431, 432, 436, 437, 439, 444, 445, 447, 449, 450, 461, 472, 484, 485, 488, 494, 497, 501, 504, 506, 508, 509, 510, 520, 521, 522, 523, 526, 527, 528, 529, 530, 531, 541, 543, 544, 545, 551, 553, 555, 556, 557, 559, 560, 561, 562, 580, 630, 632, 634, 635, 636, 639, 644, 645, 667, 678, 681, 708, 710, 723, 769, 774, 785, 792
*Mexican Manhunt*, 196
Meyer, Greta, 325
Meyerbeer, Jacob, 313
"Mi Caballero," 466

Michell, Keith, 711
*Midnight*, 285, 401, 733
*Midnight Sun, The*, 95
*Midsummer Night's Dream, A*, 341, 462
*Mildred Pierce*, 120, 472
Miles, Peter, 275
*Milk Train Doesn't Stop Here Anymore, The*, 789
Milland, Ray, 278, 377, 589
Miller, Arthur, 282, 530
Miller, Marilyn, 221, 634
*Millionairess, The*, 561
*Miniver Story, The*, 474, 505-07
Minnelli, Liza, 413, 452
Minnelli, Vincente, 413, 634
Miranda, Carmen, 443
*Misfits, The*, 144, 530, 566
Mishkin, Leo, 489, 579, 609
*Miss Moffat*, 266
*Mrs. Miniver*, 478, 479, 486-91, 506, 507, 543
*Mrs. Parkington*, 481, 496-99
"Mr. and Mrs. Is the Name," 168
*Mr. Blandings Builds His Dream House*, 246, 292
*Mr. Majestyk*, 19
*Mister Roberts*, 246, 472
*Mr. Skeffington*, 265, 498
*Mr. Smith Goes to Washington*, 382, 553
Mitchell, Cameron, 637
Mitchell, Thomas, 637
Mitchum, Robert, 706, 789
*Model Wife*, 173
*Modern Screen* (magazine), 58, 527
*Mogambo*, 133, 529
Molnar, Walter, 656, 657
Monogram Pictures, 94, 196
Monroe, Marilyn, 530, 667
Montez, Maria, 18, 596, 598, 599, 600, 601, 602, 603, 605, 606, 607, 609-10, 612, 613, 614-15, 616-17, 619
Montgomery, Robert, 115, 196, 501, 663
Monti, Milli, 94
*Moon's a Balloon, The*, 712
Moore, Grace, 304, 305, 308, 321
Moore, Ida, 563
Moore, Matt, 90
Moore, Roger, 707
Moorehead, Agnes, 498, 499, 509, 663
Moorhead, Natalie, 105, 216
Moran, Dolores, 656, 657
Moran, Lois, 71
Moreno, Antonio, 33, 46
Morgan, Dennis, 364
Morgan, Frank, 222, 306, 311, 312, 383, 385, 521
Morgan, Helen, 154
*Morning Glory*, 540
*Mortal Storm, The*, 374, 384-86

Mortimer, Lee, 119, 285, 342, 382, 469, 609, 612, 614
Mortimer, Penelope, 564, 787
*Mother Carey's Chickens*, 173
*Mother Goddam*, 266
*Mother Wore Tights*, 16
*Motion Picture* (magazine), 51
*Mountain, The*, 561
*Moving Target, The*, 662
Mowbray, Alan, 397
Muir, Jean, 341
Mundin, Herbert, 348
Muni, Paul, 222, 255, 655
Munn, Larry, 437-38
*Murder, My Sweet*, 173
Murnau, Friedrich W., 70
Murphy, Audie, 657
Murray, Don, 19
Murray, James, 308
*Music for Millions*, 636
*Music Man, The*, 645
*Musical Film, The*, 442
*Mutiny on the Bounty*, 138, 282
*My Cousin Rachel*, 365
"My Dancing Lady," 112
"My Day," 431
*My Friend Irma*, 641
*My Man Godfrey*, 222, 229, 263
"My Mother Told Me," 631
*My Son John*, 726
*My Way of Life*, 121
*My Wicked, Wicked Ways*, 366
"My Wonderful One," 502
*Mysterious Lady, The*, 52

*Naked City, The*, 470
Nash, Mary, 84, 615
*Nation, The*, 591, 634, 660
*National Board of Review* (magazine), 72
National Catholic Office, 710
*National Velvet*, 424
*Naughty But Nice*, 173
*Naughty Marietta*, 16, 298, 303-07, 308, 309, 321
Neagle, Anna, 324, 366
Neal, Patricia, 657
Neame, Ronald, 710
Nelson, Barry, 240, 712
Nelson, Harmon, 250
Nelson, Ozzie, 173
Nemcek, Paul L., 20
*Never Let Me Go*, 529
*New Kind of Love, A*, 720, 732-34
*New Moon*, 297, 319-22, 324
*New York* (magazine), 740
*New York American*, 75, 168, 170, 262, 280, 345, 402
*New York Daily Mirror*, 119, 130, 224, 256, 285, 342, 381, 382, 404, 407, 469, 609, 612, 614

*New York Daily News*, 154, 228, 364, 404, 407, 439, 464, 546, 554, 612, 662, 707, 711, 736
*New York Evening Journal*, 279
New York Film Critics prize, 464
*New York Herald-Tribune*, 32, 48, 94, 113, 118, 120, 132, 135, 138, 140, 143, 156, 158, 160, 163, 170, 172, 184, 193, 214, 221, 227, 230, 232, 234, 239, 241, 256, 264, 278, 290, 305, 309, 321, 342, 349, 352, 356, 376, 378, 381, 382, 383, 386, 399, 400, 402, 404, 425, 436, 439, 441, 445, 451, 462, 464, 466, 469, 495, 499, 502, 504, 506, 524, 545, 559, 578, 585, 589, 610, 614, 617, 632, 637, 639, 642, 654, 655, 688, 690, 701, 723, 727, 729, 734, 751, 771, 774, 776
*New York Journal-American*, 285, 579
*New York Morning Telegraph*, 324, 489, 579, 609
*New York Post*, 58, 93, 113, 120, 129, 137, 140, 213, 239, 282, 308, 312, 316, 318, 324, 327, 342, 396, 397, 404, 423, 427, 472, 546, 605, 708, 729, 736, 771, 774
*New York Sun*, 91, 116, 168, 316, 324, 346, 543, 654
*New York Times*, 30, 32, 33, 37, 51, 54, 58, 72, 74, 76, 79, 81, 82, 86, 89, 90, 93, 105, 107, 115, 117, 130, 134, 143, 166, 172, 183, 187, 188, 193, 213, 216, 218, 219, 221, 232, 236, 243, 245, 255, 260, 262, 263, 278, 288, 290, 308, 309, 312, 316, 318, 321, 324, 327, 343, 349, 358, 378, 381, 399, 402, 406, 407, 422, 423, 425, 430-31, 436, 448, 450, 472, 484, 486, 494, 498, 501, 502, 504, 507, 521, 548, 553, 556, 563, 580, 583, 585, 591, 592, 594, 606, 609, 612, 619, 630, 637, 642, 654, 659, 662, 665, 666, 682, 685, 700, 706, 724, 729, 733-34, 753, 754, 777, 779, 791, 793
*New York World Journal Tribune*, 707
*New York World Telegram*, 195, 211, 234, 344, 470, 499, 527, 580, 614, 654
*New Yorker* (magazine), 245, 406, 548, 551, 580, 642, 680, 729
*Newark Evening Journal*, 228
Newman, Paul, 18-19, 662, 691, *714*, 715-16, 717, *718*, *719*, 720, 721, 723, 724, 726, 727, 729, 730, 731, 732, 734, 736, 737, 739, 740-41
*Newsday*, 710
*Newsweek* (magazine), 361, 524, 560, 665, 666, 710
*Next Time We Love*, 368, 375-78
Ney, Richard, 477, 489, 490, 491
Nichols, Mike, 779
*Night and Day*, 634
*Night Nurse*, 105
*Night of Love, The*, 27, 32-34
*Night of the Iguana, The*, 265, 706, 776, 777, 788
*Night of the Lepus*, 690

*Night Watch*, 797
*Ninotchka*, 58, 382, 561, 733
Niven, David, 18, 173, *692*, 693-94, *696*, *697*, *698*, 700, 701, 703-04, 705-06, 707, 708, 709, 710, 711, 712
*No, No, Nanette*, 173, 645
*No Down Payment*, 723
"No More Weepin'," 322
*No Sad Songs for Me*, 386
*No Strings*, 731
*No Time for Love*, 273, 283-86
*None but the Lonely Heart*, 499
*Noon Wine*, 365
*Nora Prentiss*, 472
Nordhoff, Charles, 636
Nordstrom, Clarence, 156
"Norma Shearer of Sweden, The." *See* Garbo, Greta
Norris, Kathleen, 93
North, Alex, 723, 779
North, Sheree, 723
*Northwest Outpost*, 327
*Not as a Stranger*, 365
*Not with My Wife You Don't*, 691
*Nothing Sacred*, 263
Novak, Kim, 258, 708
Novarro, Ramon, 304
*Now, Voyager*, 265
"Now We're Free," 619
"Now You See It," 579
Nugent, Elliott, 548
Nugent, Frank S., 134, 172, 187, 188, 193, 221, 232, 260, 262, 263, 308, 309, 312, 316, 349, 378, 399, 402, 406, 407, 425
*Nutmeg Tree, The*, 501

Oakie, Jack, 172, 753
Oberon, Merle, 30
O'Brien, Edmond, 725
O'Brien, George, 84
O'Brien, Margaret, 446, 636
O'Brien, Pat, 166-67, 168, 277, 462-63, 464, 466-67, 736
O'Brien, Virginia, 446, 630, 631, 634
O'Connor, Donald, 16, 19
O'Connor, Frank, *300*
O'Connor, Una, 348
O'Donnell, Cathy, 15, 506
*Of Human Bondage:* (movie) 17, *252*, 254-58, 261, 264, 266; (book) 255
*Of Human Hearts*, 379
*Of Thee I Sing*, 245
"Oh Susanna," 430
O'Hara, John, 729
O'Hara, Maureen, 485, 606, 681
*Oklahoma Kid, The*, 353
"Ol' Man River," 634
*Old Hutch*, 17
*Old Ironsides*, 71
*Old Maid, The*, 196

Oldfield, Barney, 736
Olivier, Laurence, 56, 355, 566, 769
"On Parade," 319
*Once upon a Dead Man*, 757
*One, Two, Three*, 472
*One Is a Lonely Number*, 690
"One Kiss," 322
*One Night Stand*, 691
*One Way Passage*, 183, 192
O'Neal, Patrick, 730
O'Neill, Eugene, 55
"Opera versus Jazz," 428-29, 430
*Opposite Sex, The*, 472, 645
Orczy, Baroness, 37
Orr, William, 385
Orry-Kelly, 183, 356
O'Sullivan, Maureen, 16, 83, 216
O'Toole, Peter, 767, 791, 795
*Our Modern Maidens*, 104
"Our Sincere Appreciation," 322
*Our Town*, 470
Ouspenskaya, Maria, 386
*Outcast Lady*, 53
*Outlaw, The*, 551
Owen, Reginald, 117
Owens, Patricia, 657, 723
Owsley, Monroe, 184
Oxford University Dramatic Society, 787

"Pack Up Your Troubles . . . ," 381
*Page Miss Glory*, 169
*Paid*, 104, 120
Paige, Janis, 644
Paige, Robert, 16
*Painted Desert, The*, 529
Pal, George, 678, 679
Pallette, Eugene, 348
*Palm Beach Story, The*, 284
Palmer, Ernest, 74
Palmer, Lilli, 19
Pangborn, Franklin, 350
"Paper Moon," 631
*Paper Tiger*, 712
Paramount Pictures, 15, 17, 18, 71, 90, 173, 183, 277, 282, 284, 288, 304, 351, 364, 365, 447, 578, 579, 580, 582, 585, 592, 594, 678, 740
*Paris Blues*, 719, 730-32, 734, 737
Parker, Cecilia, 17, *416*
Parker, Dorothy, 318
Parker, Eleanor, 258
*Parnell*, 143
*Parrish*, 293
Parrott, Ursula, 376
Parsons, Louella, 32, 396
*Party, The*, 684
Pascal, Gabriel, 265
Pasternak, Joe, 327, 630
*Pat and Mike*, *539*, 558-60, 562
Patrick, Gail, 237

Patrick, Lee, 499, 750
Pearson, Drew, 554
Peck, Lydell, 62, 86
Pelswick, Rose, 262, 579
Pendleton, Nat, 216, 232
Pennington, Ann, 81, 158
*People Against O'Hara, The*, 559
*Pepe*, 689-90
*Perfect Furlough, The*, 670, 675, 682-84, 688, 691, 733
*Perfect Specimen, The*, 347-48, 350
Perkins, Anthony, 739
Perreau, Gigi, 275
Perry, Kathryn, 90
*Persecution*, 531
*Peter Ibbetson*, 314
*Petrified Forest, The*, 17, 248, 258-62, 264, 266, 668
"Pettin' in the Park," 159
*Peyton Place*, 530, 723, 729
*Phantom of the Opera, The*, 327
*Philadelphia Record*, 436
*Philadelphia Story, The*: (movie) 386-87, 488, 541, 542, 545; (play) 541
Phillips, Mary, 647
*Philo Vance*, 211
*Photoplay* (magazine), 32, 33, 35, 53, 72, 75, 78, 84, 524
Piazza, Fernando, 767
Pickford, Mary, 15, 91, 782
Pidgeon, Walter, 18, 143, 216, 219, 380, *474*, *475-76*, *478*, *479*, *480*, *481*, *482*, 484, 485, 486, 488, 489-90, 491, 492, 494-95, 498-99, 501-02, 504, 505, 506-07, 508, 509-10, 521, 545, 632
*Pigskin Parade*, 423
*Pillow Talk*: (movie) 742, 746, 748-51, 753; (song) 751
*Pink Panther, The*, 705
Pitts, ZaSu, 16, 164
*Pittsburgh Sun-Telegraph*, 529
*PM*, 235, 488, 498, 546, 579, 605, 615, 632
Poitier, Sidney, 564-65, 732, 772
Porter, Cole, 315, 556, 634, 782
Portman, Eric, 703
*Portrait in Black*, 530
"Possess Me," 751
*Possessed*: (MGM) *101*, 107-09; (WB) 120
*Possession of Joel Delaney, The*, 708
*Postman Always Rings Twice, The*, 526
Potter, H. C., 506
Powell, Dick, 16, 19, *146*, 147-48, *149*, *150*, *151*, *152*, 154-55, 156, 158, 159, 161-62, 164, 165, 166-68, 169-70, 172, 173, 315, 624, 644
Powell, Eleanor, 315, 446
Powell, William, 16, 183, 196, *198*, 199-200, *203*, *204*, *205*, *206*, *207*, *208*, *209*, 211, 212-13, 214, 215-16, 218, 219, 220, 221, 222,

224-25, 227-28, 229-30, 232-33, 234-35, 236, 237, 239-40, 241-42, 243-44, 245-46, 399, 402, 504, 583
Power, Tyrone, 17-18, *388*, 389-90, *392*, *393*, *394*, 396, 397, 399-400, 402, 403, 404, 407, 408, 527
*Practically Yours*, *273*, 286-88
Preferred Pictures, 311
Preisser, June, 16, 429-30, 437, 448
Preminger, Otto, 700
Prentiss, Paula, 755
*Presenting Lily Mars*, 447
Presnell, Harve, 449
Preston, Robert, *573*, 579, 580
"Pretty As a Picture," 319
"Pretty Girl Is Like a Melody, A," 221
*Pretty Ladies*, 211
*Pretty Maids All in a Row*, 757
*Pride and Prejudice*, 484
*Prince and the Pauper, The*, 348
*Prince Valiant*, 681
*Prince Who Was a Thief, The*, 681
*Princess and the Plumber, The*, 83
*Princess O'Rourke*, 365
*Prisoner of Zenda, The*, 35, 304
*Private Life of Henry VIII, The*, 791
*Private Lives*, 403
*Private Lives of Elizabeth and Essex, The*, *330*, 354-56
*Prodigal, The*, 530
*Proud Rebels, The*, 359
Proust, Marcel, 661
*Prudence and the Pill*, 698, 709-11
Pryor, Thomas M., 243, 659
*Psycho*, 739
*Public Enemy*, 129, 462
*Punch* (magazine), 220
Punsley, Bernard, 462
Purcell, Charles, 311
Purdy, Constance, 610
Purviance, Edna, 14
*Pygmalion*, 265

Qualen, John, *600*, 605
*Queen Christina*, 44, 54-58
*Quick Millions*, 129
Quigley, Charles, 18
Quigley Publication Poll, 90
Quine, Richard, *421*
Quinn, Anthony, 361-62, 470, 471

*Racers, The*, 736
*Rachel, Rachel*, 19, 741
Rafferty, Frances, 448, 499
Raft, George, 77, 466, 470, 582, 583
Ragland, Rags, 449
*Raid on Rommel*, 792
*Rain*, 106, 111

820

Rainer, Luise, 58, 94, 221
*Rainmaker, The*, 561
Rains, Claude, 348, 498, 657
*Rally 'Round the Flag, Boys!*, *718*, 725-27
Ralph, Jessie, 228
Ralston, Vera, 196
Rambeau, Marjorie, 129
Ramsey, Walter, 58
Randall, Tony, 749, 750, 753, 755
*Random Harvest*, 38, 501
Ransford, Maurice, 562
Rat Pack, 668
Rathbone, Basil, 342, 348, 349
Ratoff, Gregory, 402
Rattigan, Terence, 703, 774
Ravetch, Irving, 723
Ray, Aldo, 560
Ray, Nicholas, 121
Raymond, Gene, 16, 132, 296, 326
*Razor's Edge, The*, 408
*Ready, Willing and Able*, 172
Reagan, Ronald, *337*, 358, 359
*Rear Window*, 387
*Rebecca*, 484
*Red Dust*, 114, *125*, 130-33, 134, 529
Reddington, John, 170
Reed, Donna, 240
*Reflections in a Golden Eye*, 786
*Reformer and the Redhead, The*, 644
Reggiani, Serge, 732
Reicher, Hedwiga, 76-77
Reid, Beryl, 265
Reid, Wallace, 736
*Religion in the Cinema*, 120
*Remains to Be Seen*, *628*, 642-44
Remarque, Erich Maria, 385
"Remember My Forgotten Man," 159, 162
*Remember the Night*, 284
Remick, Lee, 723, 724
Republic Pictures, 121, 282, 366, 472
*Rescue, The*, 38
*Reunion in France*, 120
Reynolds, Joyce, 18
*Rhapsody in Blue*, 634
Rice, Florence, *206*, 230
Rich, Irene, *374*, 386
Richardson, Frank, *65*, 78
Richardson, Tony, 346
*Richmond News Leader*, 236
Richter, Conrad, 550
*Rider on the Rain*, 19
*Riding High*, 173
*Riffraff*, 484
*Right Cross*, 644
Ring, Blanche, 442
"Rings on My Fingers," 442
*Rio Rita*, 222
Ritchard, Cyril, 293

Ritt, Martin, 723, 731, 732
Ritter, Thelma, 734, 749, 750, 751
"Ritual Fire Dance," 631
Ritz Brothers, 605
RKO Radio Pictures, 16, 164, 172, 173, 196, 211, 255, 256, 365, 379, 448, 540, 541, 550, 553, 579, 631, 634, 678
Roach, Hal, 129
Robards, Jason, Jr., 649, 667
Robeling, Paul, 789
*Roberta*, 172, 278, 634
Roberts, Marguerite, 520, 524, 550
Roberts, Rachel, 770
Robinson, Casey, 193, 264, 350
Robinson, Edward G., 38, 77, 255, 665, 666, 668, 690
Robinson, George, 613
Robson, Eleanor, 86
Robson, Mark, 729
Robson, May, 140
*Rocky Mountain*, 667
Rodgers, Richard, 304, 326, 428, 450
Rogers, Charles "Buddy," 15, 19-20
Rogers, Ginger, 16, 19-20, 93, 111, 154, 158, 164, 172, 173, 379, 402, 470, 541, 556, 634, 641
Rogers, Roy, 18
Rogers, Will, 81, 93, 221
"Roly Poly," 751
Roman, Ruth, 725
*Roman Scandals*, 429
*Romance of Rosy Ridge, The*, 678
Romay, Lina, 630
Romberg, Sigmund, 312
*Romeo and Juliet*: (movie) 82, 264; (opera) 309, 327; (play) 365
Romero, Cesar, 470, *481*, 502
*Romola*, 28
*Room at the Top*, 751
Rooney, Mickey, 16, 216, *410*, 411-13, *414*, *415*, *416*, *417*, *418,* *419*, *420*, *421*, 423-24, 425-27, 428, 429-31, 432-35, 436-38, 439-40, 442-44, 445, 447-49, 450-51, 452, 520, 521, 545, 610, 736
Roosevelt, Eleanor, 431, 509
Roosevelt, Franklin D., 189, 431
*Rooster Cogburn*, 566
*Roots of Heaven, The*, 366
*Rosalie*, 222, 315
Rosamond, Marion, 327
"Rosary, The," 440
Rose, David, 413
Rose, William, 564
*Rose Marie*, 167, 298, 305, 307-10
"Rose Marie I Love You," 309
*Rosemary's Baby*, 708
Rosenfield, John, 362
*Rosita*, 71

Rosson, Harold G. (Hal), 123, 135
Roulien, Raul, 88
Royle, Edwin, 31
Rozsa, Miklos, 774
*Rugged Path, The*, 550
Ruggles, Charles, 16, 277
Ruggles, Wesley, 277, 279, 524
*Ruggles of Red Gap*, 726
Rumann, Sig, 237
Runyon, Damon, 216, 559
Rush, Barbara, 681
Rush, Dick, *206*
Russell, Jane, 135, 530
Russell, Rosalind, 115, 137, 138, 218, 350
Rutherford, Ann, 16, 425, 426, 433, 434, 520
Rutherford, Margaret, 775
Ruttenberg, Joseph, 490, 506
Ryan, Peggy, 16
Ryskind, Morrie, 436

Sabatini, Rafael, 342
*Sabrina*, 667
*Sabrina Fair*, 386
Sabu, *600, 601*, 605, 607, 610, 613, 615
Sagan, Françoise, 699
*Saigon, 576*, 592-94
Saint, Eva Marie, 777
Saint James, Susan, 757
*Saint Joan*, 700
Salt, Waldo, 379
"Sam and Delilah," 449
*San Francisco*, 311, 406, 461, 484
Sande, Walter, 655
Sanders, George, 325, 399, 681
*Sandpiper, The, 763*, 775-77
Sanford, John, 520
Sannon, Ethel, 311
*Santa Fe Trail*, 336, 337, 356-59
*Saratoga, 124*, 141-43, 144, 422, 566
Sargeant, Howland, 201
Sarris, Andrew, 707, 740
*Saturday Evening Post*, 76, 82, 379
*Saturday Review*, 685, 690, 703, 711, 734, 751, 774
Saville, Victor, 324
*Scandal at Scourie*, 482, 507-09
*Scarlet Pimpernel, The*, 37
Schallert, Edwin, 305
Schary, Dore, 121, 506, 509, 529, 556, 644
Schickel, Richard, 566, 789
Schildkraut, Joseph, 383
Schuck, John, 793
Schulberg, B. P., 311
Scofield, Paul, 779
Scott, George C., 741
Scott, Lizabeth, 591
Scott, Walter M., 562
Screen Actors Guild, 365
*Sea Beast, The*, 14

*Sea Hawk, The*, 342
*Sea of Grass, The, 537*, 545, 549-51
Seabury, Ynez, *300*
*Seascape*, 712
Seberg, Jean, 700
*Second Honeymoon*, 393, 402-04
*Seconds*, 757
*Secret Ceremony*, 789
*Secret Heart, The*, 636
*Secret Six, The*, 15, *125*, 128-30, 136
*Secretary of Frivolous Affairs, The*, 14
*Secrets of an Actress, 181*, 194-95
Seeley, Blossom, 589
Segal, George, 779, 780, 781
Segal, Vivienne, 326
Seitz, John, 579
Selznick, David O., 94, 110, 551
Selznick, Myron, 183
*Senator Was Indiscreet, The*, 244-46
*Send Me No Flowers*, 747, 754-56
Sennett, Mack, 115, 351, 639, 783
Sennwald, Andre, 105, 107, 115, 166, 218, 219, 278, 343
"Señorita," 316
*Separate Tables, 696*, 702-04
*Seven Little Foys, The*, 472
*Seventh Heaven*: (movie) 15, 37, *64*, 70-73, 74, 75, 76, 79, 84, 85, 94, 95, 379; (play) 70, 94
Seymour, Dan, 657
*Shadow of the Thin Man, 207*, 237-40
"Shadow of Your Smile, The," 777
"Shadow Waltz," 159
*Shaggy Dog, The*, 293
Shakespeare, William, 82, 264, 559, 771, 782, 783
Shamroy, Leon, 562
*Shane*, 595
*Shanghai Express*, 137
"Shanghai Lil," 162
Shapiro, Stanley, 683, 749, 751, 753, 755
Sharp, Margery, 501
Shavelson, Melville, 733
Shaw, Artie, 513, 522, 523
Shaw, George Bernard, 561
*She Loves Me*, 383
*She Stoops to Conquer*, 710
Shearer, Norma, 15, 105, 144, 196, 216, 264, 431, 484, 488, 520, 645, 678
Sheehan, Winfield R., 70
Sheridan, Ann, 17, 173, 175, 196, 353, 354, 364, *454*, 456-57, *458*, 462, 463-64, 466-69, 470, 471-72, 655
Sherry, William Grant, 250
Sherwood, Gale, 328
Sherwood, Robert, 260, 262, 550
Shields, Arthur, 509
Shimkus, Joanna, 767, 789
*Shipmates Forever*, 151, *152*, 168-70

Shoemaker, Ann, 437
*Shop Around the Corner, The*, 372, 381-83
*Shopworn Angel, The*, 372, 373, 378-81
Shore, Dinah, 364
Short, Gertrude, 157
*Short Cut to Hell*, 472, 580
"Should I Surrender," 753
*Show Boat*, 222, 326, 634
*Show People*, 54
*Showdown*, 757
*Shrike, The*, 645
Shubert Brothers, 305
"Shuffle Off to Buffalo," 156
Shulman, Max, 726
Sidney, Sylvia, 134, 464, 470
*Sign of the Cross, The*, 277
Signoret, Simone, 751
*Silver River*, 353, 472
Simon, Simone, 73, 395, 396
Sinatra, Frank, 634, 706
Sinclair, Ronnie, 423
*Sing Me a Love Song*, 462
*Singing Nun, The*, 509
Singleton, Penny, 16, 228
*Sinners' Holiday*, 17
*Sisters, The*, 355
"Sittin' on a Backyard Fence," 162
Skouras, Spyros P., 769, 770
*Skyjacked*, 510
Slate Brothers, 81
Slezak, Walter, 326
Small, Edward, 685
*Smilin' Through*, 326
Smith, Alexis, 660
Smith, C. Aubrey, 56, 137
Smith, Loring, 240
Smith, Maggie, 775
Smith, Soapy, 520
Smith, Stanley, 161
*Snow White*, 785
"Softly as in a Morning Sunrise," 322
Sokoloff, Vladimir, 237
*Solomon and Sheba*, 408
*Some Came Running*, 740
*Some Like It Hot*, 683
"Some of These Days," 309
*Somebody Loves Me*, 589
*Someone Behind the Door*, 19
"Someone from Somewhere," 88
"Something About Romance," 278
*Something of Value*, 749
*Sometimes I'm Happy*, 589
*Somewhere I'll Find You*, 516, 522-24, 529
*Son of Ali Baba*, 681
*Son of Captain Blood*, 343
*Son of Paleface*, 135
*Son of the Sheik, The*, 31
Sondergaard, Gale, 283, 617
*Song of Bernadette, The*, 496

"Song of the Mounties," 309
*Song of the Thin Man*, 209, 242-44
"Song with the Harps," 327
Sothern, Ann, 133, 446
Soundies, 589
Southern, Terry, 706, 708
Sparks, Ned, 158
*Spitfire*. See *First of the Few, The*
*Split Second*, 173
*Sporting Youth*, 736
Spreckels, Kay, 97, 530
"Spring Is Here," 327
*Spy Who Came in from the Cold, The*, 779, 785
Stack, Robert, 385
*Stagecoach*, 353
Standing, Wyndham, 29
*Stanley and Livingston*, 546
Stanwyck, Barbara, 105, 134, 529, 553, 589
*Star Is Born, A*, 94, 451, 452
*Star Spangled Rhythm*, 364, 573, 584-85
*Starring Fred Astaire*, 20
*State Fair*, 93
*State of the Union*, 196, 245, 532, 552-54, 565
Steinbeck, John, 545
Steiner, Max, 345
*Stella Dallas*, 31
Stephens, Harvey, 218, 283
Sterling, Robert, 524
Stevens, Connie, 18
Stevens, George, 90, 541, 595
Stevens, Rise, 326
Stevenson, Robert Louis, 234
Stewart, Donald Ogden, 545, 548
Stewart, Freddy, 16
Stewart, James, 17, 20, 73, 227, 277, 293, 362, *368*, 369-70, 372, 373, 374, 376-78, 379, 380-81, 382, 383, 385-87, 520, 644
Stiller, Mauritz, 47
Stine, Whitney, 266
Stockwell, Dean, *209*, 244
Stompanato, Johnny, 530
Stone, George E., 155
Stone, Lewis, 137, 138, 170, *416*, 425, 433, 434, 439, 440, 554
Stone, Robert, 739
Storm, Gale, 94
*Story of Esther Costello, The*, 121
*Story of Louis Pasteur, The*, 222, 494
Stothart, Herbert, 306
"Stout Hearted Men," 322
*Stranded*, 179, 187-89
*Strange Cargo*, *103*, 118-20, 121
*Stranger in My Arms*, 645
*Strategic Air Command*, 644
*Stratton Story, The*, 387, 644
Strauss, Theodore, 436, 448, 521, 583, 609
*Street Angel*, 64, 73-75, 85

Streetcar Named Desire, A, 559
Strike Up the Band, 418, 419, 435-38, 448
Stripper, The, 739
Stritch, Elaine, 684
Stromberg, Hunt, 140, 221, 312
Strong, Austin, 70
Stronger Than Desire, 219
Struther, Jan, 488, 489
"Students' Drinking Song," 313
Sturges, Preston, 173, 284, 578
Sudan, 603, 617-79
Suddenly, Last Summer, 564, 770, 788
Sudermann, Hermann, 47
Suez, 394, 405-07, 408
Sullavan, Margaret, 17, 362, 368, 371, 372,
    373, 374, 376-78, 379-81, 382, 383, 385, 386
Sullivan, Ed, 690
Sullivan's Travels, 578
Sul-te-wan, Madame, 283
"Summer Serenade," 319
Summer Stock, 631
Summer Wishes, Winter Dreams, 741
Summertime, 561
Summerville, Slim, 16, 399
Sun Also Rises, The, 366
Sun Comes Up, The, 327
"Sun Showers," 423
Sundberg, Clinton, 209
Sundowners, The, 706
Sunny Side Up: (movie) 65, 77-79; (song) 78
Sunrise, 70, 73
Sunrise at Campobello, 509
Sunset Boulevard, 39
Suppose They Gave a War and Nobody
    Came?, 691
Susan Lenox: Her Fall and Rise, 55
Swanson, Gloria, 39, 265
"Sweater, a Sarong and a Peekaboo Bang,
    A," 585
"Swedish Sphinx, The." See Garbo, Greta
Sweet Aloes, 192
"Sweet and Lovely," 631
Sweet Rosie O'Grady, 400
Sweetheart of the Campus, 173
Sweetheart of the Navy, 17
Sweethearts: (movie) 294, 301, 317-19;
    (song) 319
Swinburne, Nora, 530
Sword of Ali Baba, The, 612
Sybil of the North, The, 56

"T. R. Jones," 443
Take a Letter, Darling, 284
"Take a Little One Step," 173
"Take It Easy," 631
Take Me Along, 509
"Taking a Chance on Love," 644
Talbot, Lyle, 404
Tall Men, The, 530

"Tallahassee," 589
Taming of the Shrew, The, 15, 264, 764, 781-
    83, 784, 786
Tarkington, Booth, 425
Tarnish, 28
Tarzan, The Ape Man, 16
Tarzan and His Mate, 16
Tashlin, Frank, 726
Tashman, Lilyan, 158
Taurog, Norman, 448, 450, 639, 640
Taylor, Elizabeth, 19, 265, 424, 502, 559, 645,
    679, 737, 758, 759, 760-61, 762, 763, 764,
    765, 766, 769-71, 772, 774-75, 776, 777,
    778, 779-81, 782, 783, 784, 785, 786-87,
    788-89, 791, 792, 793, 795-97
Taylor, Robert, 397, 551, 580
Taylor, Rod, 756, 775
Tazelaar, Marguerite, 94, 135, 143, 163, 170
Tea and Sympathy, 700
Tea for Two, 16
Teacher's Pet, 530, 750
Templeton, Fay, 442
Temptress, The, 46
Ten Commandments, The, 32
Tennyson, Alfred Lord, 344
Ten-Second Jailbreak, 19
Terry, Alice, 51
Tess of the Storm Country, 69, 91-92, 93
Thalberg, Irving, 129, 136, 137, 311, 490
Thank Your Lucky Stars, 339, 362-65
That Forsyte Woman, 366, 482, 503-05
That Touch of Mink, 755
That Wonderful Urge, 400
Thatcher, Torin, 675, 680
That's Entertainment, 452, 797
"That's the Rhythm of the Day," 112
"That's What You Jolly Well Get," 365
Theatre, 196
There Must Be a Pony, 246
These Three, 283
They All Kissed the Bride, 120
They Died with Their Boots On, 337, 338,
    359-62
They Drive By Night, 470
They Knew What They Wanted, 38
They Live By Night, 15
They Might Be Giants, 741
They Only Kill Their Masters, 645
They Won't Forget, 520, 527
"They're Either Too Young or Too Old," 364
Thief of Bagdad, The, 612
Thin Man, The, 16, 203, 205, 213-16, 218,
    228, 234
Thin Man Goes Home, The, 208, 240-42
Things I Had to Learn, The, 408
Thinnes, Roy, 725
Thirer, Irene, 154, 316, 324
Thirty Seconds Over Tokyo, 548
This Earth Is Mine, 749

*This Gun for Hire*, 573, 577-81, 583
*This Is Heaven*, 38
*This Woman Is Dangerous*, 120
Thomas, Dylan, 795
Thomas, Richard, 737
Thompson, Dorothy, 542
*Thoroughbreds Don't Cry*, 417, 422-24
Thorpe, Richard, 630
"Thou Swell," 451
*Thousands Cheer*, 364, 420, *421*, 444-46
*Three Comrades*, 382, 385
*Three Cornered Moon*, 277
*Three Daring Daughters*, 327
*Three Faces of Eve, The*, 530, 723, 724, 739
*Three Musketeers, The*, 222, 529, 605
Three Stooges, The, 19, 111, 605
"Thrill of a New Romance, The," 631
*Thrill of It All, The*, 328, 755
Tibbett, Lawrence, 305, 321
Tierney, Gene, 400
*Till the Clouds Roll By:* (movie) *625*, 626, 632-35; (song) 634
*Time* (magazine), 160, 256, 290, 292, 542, 683, 706, 724, 731, 751, 756, 772, 783, 785, 795
*Time of the Cuckoo, The*, 561
*Time of Your Life, The*, 472
*To Each His Own*, 365
*To Have and Have Not*, 650, 653-57, 660, 661
*To Please a Lady*, 529, 736
*Tobacco Road*, 291
Tobias, George, 339, 364, 467
Tobin, Genevieve, *180*, 190, 191, 261
*Tobruk*, 757
*Today We Live*, 111, 256
Todd, Mike, 685, 760
Todd, Richard, 356
"Tokay," 324
Toland, Gregg, 32
Toler, Sidney, 610
Tolstoy, Leo, 50, 51
*Tom Jones*, 772
Tone, Franchot, 56, 98, 111, 112, 117
*Too Many Girls*, 631
"Too Marvelous for Words," 644
*Too Much, Too Soon*, 366
*Too Much Speed*, 736
*Too Young to Kiss*, 627, *628*, 640-42
"Toot, Toot, Tootsie," 644
*Top Hat*, 342
*Topaze*, 211
Topping, Bob, 513, 529
*Torch Song*, 121
*Toronto Globe and Mail*, 727
*Torrent, The*, 46
*Torrid Zone*, *459*, 465-69
*Tortilla Flat*, 545
*Tosca*, 309
Toshiro Mifune, 712

"Totem Tom Tom," 167, 309
*Tovarich*, 194
Tracy, Lee, 111
Tracy, Spencer, 18, 143, *205*, 224, 225, 399, 423, 464, 520, 526, *532*, 533-34, *535*, *536*, *537*, *538*, *539*, 541-43, 544-45, 546-47, 548-49, 550-51, 553-54, 555-56, 557, 559-60, 561-63, 564, 565-66
*Tracy and Hepburn*, 566
"Tramp, Tramp, Tramp," 306, 307, 309
Travers, Henry, *480*, 489
Travilla, 729
Treacher, Arthur, 585
*Treasure Island*, 341
*Treasure of Sierra Madre, The*, 665
"Treat Me Rough," 448
*Tree Grows in Brooklyn, A*, 550
Trentini, Emma, 304
Trevelyan, H. B., 28, 29
Trevor, Claire, 404, 521, 666
Trimble, A. A., 221
Trintignant, Jean Louis, 736
"Triplets," 690
*Trog*, 121
*Trojan Women, The*, 566
*Trouble in Paradise*, 183
Troy, Helen, 423
*True Grit*, 566, 791
Truman, Harry S., 554
Truman, Margaret, 554
Tucker, Sophie, 423
*Tunnel of Love, The*, 749
*Turn of the Screw, The*, 709
"Turn on the Heat," 79
Turner, Lana, 30, 121, 144, 425, 426, *512*, 513-14, *515*, *516*, *517*, *518*, 520, 521-22, 523, 524, 526-27, 529-31, 545, 553, 580, 632
Tuttle, Frank, 579
Twain, Mark, 425
Twentieth Century Productions, 38
Twentieth Century-Fox, 16, 92, 94, 95, 282, 379, 395, 400, 402, 406, 407, 408, 447, 485, 527, 530, 561, 594, 667, 681, 710, 723, 725, 726, 769, 770, 771, 772
*Twilight of the Gods*, 749
"Twinkle in Your Eye, A," 327
*Two Girls and a Sailor*, *626*, 629-32
*Two Girls on Broadway*, 630
*Two Guys from Milwaukee*, 657-59
*Two Lovers*, 25, 36-38
*Two Sisters from Boston*, 636
*Two Tickets to Broadway*, 678
*Two-Faced Woman*, 58, 541
*Two's Company*, 265

Ullmann, Liv, 58
*Undefeated, The*, 757
*Under Milk Wood*, 767, 793-95
*Under Royal Patronage*, 14

*Under Two Flags*, 282
*Undercurrent*, 551
*Unfaithful, The*, 472
United Artists, 15, 31, 111, 706
Universal Pictures, 14, 16, 173, 220, 222, 229, 245, 289, 291, 292, 327, 328, 447, 472, 494, 605, 610, 612, 614, 615, 617, 618, 619, 630, 679, 681, 682, 684, 736, 737, 749, 757
Unser, Bobby, 736
*Up Pops the Devil*, 90
Usher, Guy, *180*
Ustinov, Peter, 784, 785, 793

*V.I.P.s, The*, 19, 762, 772-75, 776
Vadim, Roger, 757
*Vagabond King, The*, 326
Vail, Lester, 105
*Valachi Papers, The*, 19
Valentino, Rudolph, 31, 33, 47, 342
Vallee, Rudy, 167, 278
Valli, Virginia, 61, 86
Van Dyke, Dick, 452
Van Dyke, W. S., II, 115, 117, *205*, 214, 232, 241, 305, 308, 318
*Variety*, 30, 34, 35, 36, 48, 51, 53, 71, 82, 105, 111, 170, 184, 189, 191, 195, 220, 229, 232, 280, 290, 342, 343, 345, 383, 385, 397, 422, 427, 430, 437, 444, 521, 529, 579, 654, 686, 688, 706, 708-09, 733, 779, 785, 787, 796
Variety Clubs of America, 588
*Variety Girl*, 576, 587-89
Veiller, Anthony, 553
Velez, Lupe, 609
Vermilye, Jerry, 258
*Veronica*, 595
*Vertigo*, 387
*Very Special Favor, A*, 757
Vickers, Martha, 411, 592, 661
Viertel, Peter, 695
Viertel, Salka, 55, 56
*Vikings, The*, *676*, 684-87
*Village Voice, The*, 707, 740
*Villain*, 792
Vinson, Helen, 466, 467, 468
*Virgin Queen, The*, 356
Visaroff, Michael, *536*
Vitagraph Company, 14
*Vivacious Lady*, 379
*Vogue* (magazine), 797
*Voice of the Turtle, The*, 386

Wagner, Robert, 19, 216, 679, 691, 724, 737
"Waiting for the Robert E. Lee," 443
Wald, Jerry, 185, 466, 723
Waldron, Charles, 660
Walker, Clint, 756
Walker, Robert, 551
Wallis, Hal B., 791

Walsh, Raoul, 84, 337, 361, 362
Walston, Ray, 688
Wanger, Walter, 605, 769
"Wanting You," 322
*War Lord, The*, 33
*War of the Worlds, The*, 678
Warner, Jack L., 256, 341, 348, 366
Warner Bros., 14, 16, 17, 18, 58, 110, 120, 142, 156, 157, 160, 169, 172, 173, 183, 184, 190, 192, 193, 194, 195, 196, 211, 214, 255, 257, 260, 262, 265, 277, 319, 341, 343, 344, 347, 348, 352, 353, 355, 361, 365, 366, 406, 461, 462, 466, 470, 472, 498, 504, 520, 582, 634, 654, 662, 667, 681, 682, 723, 749, 751, 778, 779
Warren, Harry, 158
*Washington Post*, 734, 753
*Washington Square*, 365
*Watch on the Rhine*, 496
*Waterloo Bridge*, 484
Watson, Lucille, 502
Watson, Minor, 542
Watts, Richard, Jr., 113, 132, 138, 140, 156, 160, 172, 184, 215, 221, 256, 278, 305, 309-10, 342, 376, 378
*Way for a Sailor*, 58
Wayne, David, 556, 557
Wayne, John, 293, 387, 566, 678, 757, 791
Weaver, Marjorie, 404
Webb, Clifton, 246
Webster, Paul Francis, 777
*Weekend at the Waldorf*, 526
Weidler, Virginia, 443, 448, 492
Weiler, A. H., 612, 733-34
Weis, Don, 644
Weissmuller, Johnny, 16, 620
Weitschat, Al, 529
Weld, Tuesday, 726
Welford, Nancy, 158
"We'll Build a Little World of Our Own," 81
Welles, Orson, 723, 724, 774, 775
Wells, Joan, 637
"We're in the Money," 158-59
*We're No Angels*, 668
West, Claudine, 490
West, Mae, 132, 135, 654, 655, 726
"West Ain't Wild Any More, The," 317
*West Point Story, The*, 472
Westley, Helen, 402
Wexley, John, 470
Weyl, Carl Jules, 348
"What Can I Do—I Love That Man," 106
*What Ever Happened to Baby Jane?*, 121, 265
*What Price Glory*, 81
*What's New Pussycat?*, 706
Wheeler, Lyle, 562
Wheeler and Woolsey, 448

*When Ladies Meet*, 120
*When the Boys Meet the Girls*, 449
*When You Comin' Back, Red Ryder?*, 262
"Where or When," 428, 452
*Where the Spies Are*, 705
White, Grace Miller, 91
White, Marjorie, *65*, 78, 81
White, Sammy, 559
*White Angel, The*, 192
*White Heat*, 472
*White Savage*, 600, *601*, 608-10, 615
*White Shadows of the South Seas*, 54
*White Sisters, The*, 28
Whitely, Tom, 86
Whiteman, Paul, 438
Whitney, Renee, 161
Whitty, Dame May, *480*, 489, 642
"Who Are We to Say," 317
"Who Stole My Heart Away," 634
*Who Was That Lady?*, *676*, 687-88, 691
Whorf, Richard, 547, 634
*Who's Afraid of Virginia Woolf?*, 19, 265,
   763, 775, 777-81, 783
"Why Was I Born," 634
Widmark, Richard, 667, 730
*Wife Versus Secretary*, *127*, 138-41
Wilcoxon, Henry, 489
*Wild and Wonderful*, 684
*Wild Places*, 741
Wilder, Billy, 293, 472, 706
Wilding, Michael, 760
"Will You Remember (Sweetheart)," 313,
   314
William, Warren, 158, 185
*William Tell*, 366
Williams, Andy, 655
Williams, Emlyn, 266
Williams, Esther, 225, 636, 645
Williams, Guinn, 76, 77, 359
Williams, Sybil, 759, 770
Williams, Tennessee, 265, 566, 723, 788,
   789
Willingham, Calder, 686
Wilson, Dooley, 657
Wilson, John Fleming, 84
Wilson, Marie, 641
Wimperis, Arthur, 490
Wing, Toby, 156
*Wings*, 73
*Winning*, *721*, 735-37
*Winning of Barbara Worth, The*, 26, 27, 30-
   32, 33, 35
Winninger, Charles, 402
Winslow, Paula, 142
Winsten, Archer, 120, 312, 318, 326-27, 396,
   397, 404, 427, 546, 605, 708, 736, 771, 774
*Winter Carnival*, 466
Winters, Shelley, 751

*Witch in the Wilderness*, 523
Withers, Grant, 390
*Without Love*: (movie) 537, 547-49, 550;
   (play) 545, 548
*Witness for the Prosecution*, 408
*Wives and Lovers*, 690
*Wizard of Oz, The*, 430
Wolf, William, 737
Wolfe, Ian, 509
*Woman of Affairs, A*, *40*, 51-53
*Woman of the Year*, 536, 540-43, 544, 546,
   556, 559
*Woman's Face, A*, 120
*Woman's World*, 667
*Women, The*, 246, 472, 645
*Women's Wear Daily*, 787
Wood, Natalie, 19, 691, 724
Wood, Peggy, 311
Woodward, Joanne, 18-19, 530, 691, *714*,
   715, 716, *717*, *718*, *719*, *720*, *721*, 723, 724,
   726, 727, 729, 730, 731, 732, 734, 736, 737,
   739-41
Woodward, W. E., 218
Woollcott, Alexander, 441
*Words and Music*, *414*, 449-51
Worth, Constance, 175
Wray, John, 189
Wright, Harold Bell, 31
Wright, Teresa, 489, 490, 561
*Written on the Wind*, 667, 749
*WUSA*, *721*, 737-40
Wyatt, Jane, 645
Wyler, William, 371, 488, 490
Wylie, I. A. R., 545
Wymore, Patrice, 331, *366*
Wynberg, Henry, 796
Wynyard, Diana, 192
Wynn, Keenan, *209*, 225, 244, 446, 549, 684

*Yank at Eton, A*, 447
*Yankee Doodle Dandy*, 472, 490
*Yearling, The*, 541
*Years Ago*, 561
"You, Dear," 631
*You Can't Take It with You*, 348
"You Lied," 751
Young, Gig, 562, 563
Young, Loretta, 18, *388*, 390-91, *392*, *393*,
   *394*, 395, 396-97, 399-400, 402, 403, 404,
   406-07, 408
Young, Rida Johnson, 304
Young, Robert, 93, 195, 280, 385, 505
Young, Roland, *179*, 193
Young, Victor, 282
"Young and Healthy," 155
*Young in Heart, The*, 94
"Young Man with a Horn, The," 631
*Young Tom Edison*, 484

827

*Youngest Profession, The*, 480, 491-92
"You're Getting to Be a Habit with Me," 155
"You're Not So Easy to Forget," 244
"You've Gotta Know How to Dance," 172

Zangwill, Israel, 86
Zanuck, Darryl F., 38, 94, 95, 156, 157, 366, 395-96, 400, 402, 403, 406, 408, 770
Zeffirelli, Franco, 782

Ziegfeld, Florenz, 220-22
*Ziegfeld Follies*, 222
*Ziegfeld Girl*, 520
"Zigeuner," 324
Zinsser, William K., 563, 701
Zorina, Vera, 326
Zucco, George, 619
"Zuyder Zee," 319